THE OFFICIAL®

1990 PRICE GUIDE TO

BASEBALL CARDS

BY DR. JAMES BECKETT

NINTH EDITION

THE HOUSE OF COLLECTIBLES
NEW YORK, NEW YORK 10022

Errata

There are thousands of names, more than 100,000 prices, and untold other words in this book. There are going to be a few typographical errors, a few misspellings, and possibly, a number or two out of place. If you catch a blooper, drop me a note directly or in care of the publisher, and we will fix it up in the next year's edition.

Published by: The House of Collectibles
201 East 50th Street
New York, New York 10022

Distributed by Ballantine Books, a division of Random House, Inc., New York, and simultaneously in Canada by Random House of Canada Limited, Toronto.

Manufactured in the United States of America

Library of Congress Catalog Card Number: 84-645496

ISBN: 0-876-37780-0

10 9 8 7 6 5 4 3 2 1

TABLE OF CONTENTS

ABOUT THE AUTHOR

Jim Beckett, the leading authority on sport card values in the United States, maintains a wide range of activities in the world of sports. He possesses one of the finest collections of sports cards and autographs in the world, has made numerous appearances on radio and television, and has been frequently cited in many national publications. He was awarded the first "Special Achievement Award" for Contributions to the Hobby by the National Sports Collectors Convention in 1980 and the "Jock-Jasperson Award" for Hobby Dedication in 1983.

Dr. Beckett is the author of *The Sport Americana Football, Hockey, Basketball and Boxing Price Guide*, *The Official Price Guide to Football Cards*, *The Sport Americana Baseball Card Price Guide*, *The Official Price Guide to Baseball Cards*, *The Sport Americana Price Guide to Baseball Collectibles*, *The Sport Americana Baseball Memorabilia and Autograph Price Guide*, and *The Sport Americana Alphabetical Baseball Card Checklist*. In addition, he is the founder, author, and editor of *Beckett Baseball Card Monthly*, a magazine dedicated to advancing the card collecting hobby.

Jim Beckett received his Ph.D. in Statistics from Southern Methodist University in 1975. He resides in Dallas with his wife Patti and their daughters, Christina, Rebecca, and Melissa, while actively pursuing his writing and consultancy careers.

PREFACE

Isn't it great? Every year this book gets bigger and bigger with all the new sets coming out. But even more exciting is that every year there are more collectors, more shows, more stores, and ... more interest in the cards we love so much. This edition has been enhanced and expanded from the previous edition. The cards you collect — who they are, what they look like, where they are from, and (most important to many of you) what their current values are — are enumerated within. Many of the features contained in the other *Beckett Price Guides* have been incorporated into this volume, since condition grading, nomenclature, and many other aspects of collecting are common to the card hobby in general. We hope you find the book both interesting and useful in your collecting pursuits.

The *Beckett Guide* has been successful where other attempts have failed because it is complete, current, and valid. This price guide contains not just one, but three, prices by condition for all the baseball cards in the issues listed. These account for almost all the baseball cards in existence. The prices were added to the card lists just prior to printing and reflect not the author's opinions or desires but the going retail prices for each card, based on the marketplace (sports memorabilia conventions and shows, hobby papers, current mail order catalogs, local club meetings, auction results, and other firsthand reportings of actually realized prices).

What is the BEST price guide available (on the market) today? Of course, card sellers will prefer the price guide with the highest prices as the best — while card buyers will naturally prefer the one with the lowest prices. Accuracy, however, is the true test. Use the price guide used by more collectors and dealers than all the others combined. Look for the Beckett name. I won't put my name on anything I won't stake my reputation on. Not the lowest and not the highest — but the most accurate, with integrity.

To facilitate your use of this book, read the complete introductory section in the pages following before going to the pricing pages. Every collectible field has its own terminology; we've tried to capture most of these terms and definitions in our glossary. Please read carefully the section on grading and the condition of your cards, as you will not be able to determine which price column is appropriate for a given card without first knowing its condition.

Welcome to the world of baseball cards.

Sincerely, Dr. James Beckett

ACKNOWLEDGMENTS

A great deal of hard work went into this volume, and it could not have been done without help from many people. Our thanks are extended to each and every one of you.

Those who have worked closely with us on this and many other books, have again proven themselves invaluable — Frank and Vivian Barning (*Baseball Hobby News*), Chris Benjamin, Sy Berger (Topps), Card Collectors Co., Cartophilium (Andrew Pywowarczuk), Ira Cetron, Mike Cramer (Pacific Trading Cards), Bill and Diane Dodge, Richard Duglin (Baseball Cards-n-More), Gervise Ford, Larry and Jeff Fritsch, Tony Galovich (American Card Exchange), Georgia Music and Sports (Dick DeCourcy and Floyd Parr), Bill Goodwin (St. Louis Baseball Cards), Mike and Howard Gordon, John Greenwald, Wayne Grove, Bill Haber, Bill Henderson, Danny Hitt, Tom Imboden, Allan Kaye (*Baseball Card News*), Rick Keplinger, David Kohler (SportsCards Plus), Paul Lewicki, Neil Lewis (Leaf), Lew Lipset, Norman Liss (Topps), Major League Marketing (Dan Shedrick, Tom Day, Jack Kling), Mid-Atlantic Coin Exchange (Bill Bossert), David "Otis" Miller, Dick Millerd, Brian Morris, Vincent Murray (Fleer), B.A. Murry, Ralph Nozaki, Jack Pollard, Gavin Riley, Alan Rosen (Mr. Mint), John Rumierz, San Diego Sport Collectibles (Bill Goepner and Nacho Arredondo), Mike Schechter, Barry Sloate, John Spalding, Sports Collectors Store, Frank Steele, Murvin Sterling, Lee Temanson, Ed Twombly (New England Bullpen), Gary Walter, and Kit Young. Finally we owe a special acknowledgment to Dennis W. Eckes, "Mr. Sport Americana." The success of the *Beckett Price Guides* has always been the result of a team effort.

Special mention goes to two people this year. These two long-time collectors are recognized for repeated contributions to the hobby as well as to this price guide. In fact, if you look closely through some very old hobby publications from the early 1960s, you may see their names occasionally on articles and ads. Looking back, after eleven years, I just wanted to thank them for their part in the growth of the hobby and of this price guide. They are both friends and outstanding collectors. Thank you, Wayne Grove and B.A. Murry. Over the years I have gotten most of Wayne's input over the phone or in person. Wayne and I agree on most things, but when we do disagree, I pay special attention to his opinion. B.A. did a fine job marking up revised prices in last year's edition as well as last month's *Beckett Monthly*. B.A. also should be recognized for his early pioneering work on Topps series breakdowns. Discussions with him (as well as with others) over the years have been most helpful in establishing the proper series breakdowns and scarcity for early Topps cards. You both have my thanks as well as a lifetime subscription to *Beckett Monthly*.

Many other people have provided price input, illustrative material, checklist verifications, errata, and/or background information. We should like to individually thank Abco Card Galleries, Ab D Cards (Dale Wesolewski), Michael Abromavage, Jerry Adamic, Lee Adams, Ron Adelson, Tony Adkins, A.J.'s Sport Stop, Bob Alexander, All Star Sports Collectibles, Tom Allen, Bob Almeida, Read Andersen, Dennis Anderson, Bob Andrus, Rick Anthony, Rick Apter, Mark Argo (Olde South Cards), Mike Armstrong, Neil Armstrong (World Series Cards), David Aubry, B and C Collectable Cards, Ball Four Cards, Seth Banks, Joe Barney, Ed Barry (Ed's Collectibles), Jim Bartlett, Bob Bartosz (Baseball Card Shop), Bay State Cards (Lenny DeAngelico), Tom Beers, Carl Berg, Darrell Berger, Bernie's Bullpen, Beulah Sports, Joseph Binkowski, Levi Bleam, Bob Blount, Bob Boffa, Tim Bond (Tim's Cards & Comics), Sam Boxberger, Peter Brennan, John Brigandi, Charles A. Brooks, Jake Bubelis, Mike Buckley, Mike Bundschuh, Frank Burns, Jay Burton, Chris Cadwallader, California Card Co., David Call (9th Inning Baseball Card Shop), Christopher Campbell, Eric Cann, Michael Carey, Chris Caruso, Frank Caruso, Anthony Caton, Sandy Chan, Dwight Chapin, Shannon Chavez, Ray Cherry, Dick Cianciotto, Ronn Citrenbaum, CJ's Cubbie Hole, Richard Clement, Tim Cline (Home Plate Cards), Dennis Cobb, Gary Coburn, Jeff Cockrum, Andrew Cohen, Brian Cohen, G. Colatosti, Rob Cole, Jason Coleman, Barry Colla, Collectibles Unlimited (John Alward and Deb Ingram), Collection de Sport AZ (Ronald Villaneuve), Ryan Collins, Comics Plus, Alvin Conner, Curt Cooter, Kevin Corcoran, David Costantino, Wade Council, Don Covello, Nathan Crabbe, Taylor Crane, James Critzer, Brian Cummings, John Curtis, Allen Custer, Dave Dame, Dale Dannhaus, Donna R. Davis, Jason DeBrower, Joe Denning, Albert DeSantis, Mike Diacin, Gilbert Dickason, James Dickson, Greg Diehl, Ken Diemer, Ken Dinerman (California Cruizers), George Doherty, George Dolence, Richard Dolloff (Dolloff Coin Center), John Dorsey, George C. Dougherty, Kevin and Ryan Eagan, David Ebner, Ed's Card Shop, Josh Egli, Jacob Ellerbrock, Bob Elliot, Jason Ehrlich, Mike Epstein, Doak Ewing, Damon Fain, Bryan Falatovich, David and Mark Federman, Chuck Ferrero, David Festberg, Eli Fillmore, Jay Finglass, Howard Fleischman, Michael Folk, Perry Fong, Frank Fox (The Card Shop), Justin Fox, Robert Foye, Steve Freeburne, Steve Freedman, Brian French, Jeff Freyer, Brian Frost, Tom Galik (Fielders Choice), Scott Gallagher, Mike Gallela, David Garrett, Billy Gauthier, Jeffrey Gentes, Scotty Gennusa, Willie George, Bob Gilbert (Brewer Sports Collectibles), Dick Goddard, Steve Gold (AU Sports), Greg Goldstein (Dragon's Den), Jeff Goldstein, Brett Goodman, Jim Goodman, Jim Goodreid, Jan Gould, Scott Grady, Gary Graham, Stephen Grauf, Grauer's Collectables, Victor Guzman, Charlie Hall, Hall's Nostalgia, Michael Hamel, Hershell Hanks, Bill Hannan, Eric Hatch, Herbert Hatchel, Don Hartman, Mark Hausner, Brian Heathman, Leonard Hellicher, Joel Hellman, James Hilgert, P.J.

Hill, Ron Hill, David Hilshorst, Joseph John and Becky Hilton, Lee Hintze, John Hodson, Cliff Holmes, Home Plate of Utah (Ken Edick), Darcy Howe, Michael and Roger Huang, Robert Huber, Donald Hughes, Wayne Hurley, Doug Ingram, JJ's Budget Baseball Cards, J.R. Sports Collectibles, Karl Jacob, Paul Jastrzembski, Matt Jenks, Jay Johnson, Matthew Jones, Stewart W. Jones, Dave Jurgensmeier, Richard Kaiman, Jason Kaiser, Jason Karam, Brian Karimead, Jay and Mary Kasper, Frank Katen, Dr. Neil Katz, Kevin Kearns, Donald Kerstetter, Leroy King, John Kish, Russell Kitrick, Richard Klein, Ernie Kohlstruk, Aaron Kramer, Kipp Krukowski, John Kubat, Thomas Kunnecke, John Kyranos, Jason Lassic, Charles Laurent, Dan Lavin, Leasures Treasures, Phil Lee, Morley Leeking, Charles Leinberry, Irv Lerner, Tony Light, Steve Limbert, Michael Livreri, Chris Lockwood, Dale Loebs, Mike London, Casey Lowe, Jeff Lupke, Scott Lyons, Jim Macie, Mark Macrae, Adam Magary, Steve Mamanella, Dave Marabella, Paul Marchant, Pete Marcia, Nicholas Marino, Bill Mastro, Kyle Matschke, Dr. William McAvoy, Michael McDonald (The Sports Page), Gail McEldowney, Brian McEvoy, Tony McLaughlin, Steve McLemore, Mendal Mearkle (Chariots, Inc.), Ken Melanson, Kelly Melone, Wayne Menicucci, Blake Meyer (Lone Star Sportscards), Toby Meyer, Joe Michalowicz, Cary Miller, George J. Miller, John Miller, Lee Miller, Wayne Miller, Mitchell's Baseball Cards, Ida Montgomery, Mark Moore, John Moseley, Mark Muir, Bradley Nathan, Edward Nazzaro (The Collector), Tim Nepjuk, Dustin Newhouse, Tony Niemann, Ninth Inning Baseball Card Shop, Nostalgia World, Mike O'Brien, Keith Olbermann, Oldies and Goodies, Ron Oser, Michael Palazzo, Andy Paloukas, Bruce Parker (All-American Cards & Comics), Eric Passetti, Clay Pasternack, Mickey Payne, Bill Pekarik (Pastime Hobbies), Lucy Pelletier, Thomas Perozini, Michael Perrotta, Gerald Perry, Tom Pfirrmann, Jeffrey Phillips, Aaron Pierce, Bob Poet, Allen Powell, J.P. Plunkett (P.S.N. Sportscards), Paul Pollard, Michael Poynter, Mahes Prasad, Jeff Prillaman (Southern Cards), Carson Ralston, Rick Rapa and Barry Sanders (Atlanta Sports Cards), Rick Rateike (Extra Innings, Inc.), Eric Ratliff, R.W. Ray, Tom Reale, Tom Reid, Dr. Joseph Revella, Derek Reynolds, James Ricci, Dave Ring, Rich Rinker, Chad Roberts, Gene Roberts, Jeff Rockholt, Harold Rogers, Donald Rooks, Clifton Rouse, George Rusnak, Henry M. Rutland, Rick Ryan, Greg Ryer, Terry Sack, Joe Sak, Jennifer Salems, Sam's Baseball Cards (Sam Jackson), San Francisco Card Exchange, Keith Saroka, Gary Sawatzki, Robert Scagnelli, Matthew Schlesinger, Kenneth Schmitt, Shawn Schuetz, Brad Schurter, Scott and Craig's Sportsworld, David Seidman, Tom Shaughnessy, Tom Shanyfelt, Ricky Sharma, Bill Shaw, Marty Shaw, Gerry Shebib, Val Shikman, Bob Singer, Joel Slaughter, Michael Small, Robert Smathers, Art Smith, Barry Smith, Daren Smith, Shawn Smith, Michael Soroky, Phil Spector (Scoreboard, Inc.), Bill Spetrino, James Stahl, Jim Starbuck, Rick Stineman, Tim Strandberg, Richard Strobino, Richard Stroud, Ron Stumpf,

Barrie Sullivan, Superior Sport Card, Bill Susoev, Brian Swanson, Ian Taylor, Lyle Telfer, Kevin Terplak, Richard Thurman, Joshua Tjiong, Bud Tompkins, Ronald Tousignant, Kevin Trexler, Dr. Ralph Triplette, Matthew Turner, Howard Unger, James Vargas, Joe Verhaeghe, Ralph Villagomez, Dimitry Vladimirov, Jonathan Waler, Robert Wardell, Chris Waters, George Weaver, Mark Weber, Stephen Weber, Philip Wegeng, Lewis Weinerman, Larry Weinstein, Bill Wesslund, Richard West, Rick Wilcoxon, Casey Willett, Jeff Williams, Mark Willis, Eric Wilson, Todd Wilson, Opry Winston, Bill Wise, Jay Wolt (Cavalcade of Sports), Allan Wong, Stephen Wood, Pete Wooten, Kevin Wynn, Craig Wyzik, Steve Yanowsky, Sandy Yelnick, Yesterday's Heroes, Henry Yu, Ted Zanidakis, Robert Zanze, William Zeller, and Karl Zinke.

Every year we make active solicitations for input to that year's edition, and we are particularly appreciative of help (large and small) provided for this volume. While we receive many inquiries, comments, and questions regarding material within this book — and, in fact, each and every one is read and digested — time constraints prevent us from personally replying. We hope that the letters will continue, and that even though no reply is received, you will feel that you are making significant contributions to the hobby through your interest and comments.

Special thanks go the staff of *Beckett Publications* for their help. Editorial Director Fred Reed was very helpful with the editing of the introductory section, the production of the advertising pages, and the supervision of the extensive production support team. He was ably assisted by Jeff Amano, Therese Bellar, Lou Cather, Theo Chen, Pepper Hastings, Sara Jenks, Jay Johnson, Tricia Jones, and Rudy Klancnick. The overall operations of *Beckett Monthly* were skillfully directed by Claire Backus. Working with her were Jan Dickerson, Joe Galindo, Mary Gregory, Julie Grove, Beth Hartke, Debbie Kingsbury, Ruth Price, Cindy Struble, and Jay Yarid. James and Sandi Beane performed several major system programming jobs for us this year in order to help us accomplish our work faster and more accurately. The whole *Beckett Publications* team has my thanks for jobs well done. Thank you, everyone.

I also thank my family, especially my wife, Patti, and daughters, Christina, Rebecca, and Melissa, for putting up with me again.

INTRODUCTION

Welcome to the exciting world of baseball card collecting, America's fastest-growing avocation. You have made a good choice in buying this book, since it will open up to you the entire panorama of this field in the simplest, most concise way.

It is estimated that nearly a quarter of a million different baseball cards have been issued during the past century. And the number of total cards put out by all manufacturers last year has been estimated at several billion with a retail value of more than $150 million. Sales of older cards by dealers may account for a like amount. With all that cardboard available in the marketplace, it should be no surprise that several million sports fans like you collect baseball cards today, and that number is growing by hundreds of thousands each year.

The growth of *Beckett Baseball Card Monthly* is another indication of this rising crescendo of popularity for baseball cards. Founded less than four years ago by Dr. James Beckett, the author of this price guide, *Beckett Monthly* has grown to the pinnacle of the baseball card hobby with nearly a half million readers anxiously awaiting each enjoyable issue.

So collecting baseball cards — while still pursued as a hobby with youthful exuberance by kids in the neighborhood — has also taken on the trappings of an industry, with thousands of full- and part-time card dealers, as well as vendors of supplies, clubs, and conventions. In fact, each year since 1980, thousands of hobbyists have assembled for a National Sports Collectors Convention, at which hundreds of dealers have displayed their wares, seminars have been conducted, autographs penned by sports notables, and millions of cards changed hands. These colossal affairs have been staged in Los Angeles, Detroit, St. Louis, Chicago, New York, Anaheim, Arlington (TX), San Francisco, Atlantic City, and this year, back in Chicago at the Hyatt Regency downtown. So baseball card collecting is really national in scope!

This increasing interest has been reflected in card values. As more collectors compete for available supplies, card prices (especially for premium-grade cards) rise. A national publication indicated a "very strong advance" in baseball card prices during the past decade, and a quick perusal of prices in this book compared to the figures in earlier editions of this price guide will quickly confirm this. Which brings us back around again to the book you have in your hands. Many prices have literally doubled! It is the best annual guide available to this exciting world of baseball cards. Read it and use it. May your enjoyment and your card collection increase in the coming months and years.

HOW TO COLLECT

Each collection is personal and reflects the individuality of its owner. There are no set rules on how to collect cards. Since card collecting is a hobby or leisure pastime, what you collect, how much you collect, and how much time and money you spend collecting are entirely up to you. The funds you have available for collecting and your own personal taste should determine how you collect. Information and ideas presented here are intended to help you get the most enjoyment from this hobby.

It is impossible to collect every card ever produced. Therefore, beginners as well as intermediate and advanced collectors usually specialize in some way. One of the reasons this hobby is popular is that individual collectors can define and tailor their collecting methods to match their own tastes. To give you some ideas of the various approaches to collecting, we will list some of the more popular areas of specialization.

Many collectors select complete sets from particular years. For example, they may concentrate on assembling complete sets from all the years since their birth or since they became avid sports fans. They may try to collect a card for every player during that specified period of time.

Many others wish to acquire only certain players. Usually such players are the superstars of the sport, but occasionally collectors will specialize in all the cards of players who attended certain colleges or came from certain towns. Some collectors are only interested in the first cards or rookie cards of certain players. A handy guide for collectors interested in pursuing the hobby this way is the recently updated *Sport Americana Alphabetical Checklist No. 3*.

Another fun way to collect cards is by team. Most fans have a favorite team, and it is natural for that loyalty to be translated into a desire for cards of the players on that favorite team. For most of the recent years, team sets (all the cards from a given team for that year) are readily available at a reasonable price. *The Sport Americana Team Baseball Card Checklist* will open up this field to the collector.

OBTAINING CARDS

Several avenues are open to card collectors. Cards can be purchased in the traditional way at the local candy, grocery, or drug stores, with the bubble gum or other products included. In recent years, it has also become possible to purchase complete sets of baseball cards through mail order advertisers found in traditional sports media publications, such as *The Sporting News*, *Baseball Digest*, *Street & Smith* yearbooks, and others. These sets are also advertised in the card collecting periodicals. Many collectors will begin by subscribing to at least one of the monthly hobby publications, all with good up-to-date information. In fact, subscription offers can be found in the advertising section of this book.

Most serious card collectors obtain old (and new) cards from one or more of several main sources: (1) trading or buying from other collectors or dealers; (2) responding to sale or auction ads in the monthly hobby publications; and/or (3) attending sports collectibles shows or conventions. We advise that you try all three methods since each has its own distinct advantages: (1) trading is a great way to make new friends; (2) monthly hobby periodicals help you keep up with what's going on in the hobby (including when and where the conventions are happening); and (3) shows provide enjoyment and the opportunity to view millions of collectibles under one roof, in addition to meeting some of the hundreds or even thousands of other collectors with similar interests who also attend the shows.

PRESERVING YOUR CARDS

Cards are fragile. They must be handled properly in order to retain their value. Careless handling can easily result in creased or bent cards. It is, however, not recommended that tweezers or tongs be used to pick up your cards since such utensils might mar or indent card surfaces and thus reduce those cards' conditions and values. In general, your cards should be handled directly as little as possible. This is sometimes easier to say than to do. Although there are still many who use custom boxes, storage trays, or even shoe boxes, plastic sheets are the preferred method of storing cards. A collection stored in plastic pages in a three-ring album allows you to view your collection at any time without the need to touch the card itself. For a large collection, some collectors may use a combination of the above methods.

When purchasing plastic sheets for your cards, be sure that you find the pocket size that fits the cards snugly. Don't put your 1951 Bowmans in a sheet designed to fit 1981 Topps. Most hobby and collectibles shops and virtually all collectors' conventions will have these plastic pages available in quantity for the various sizes offered or you can purchase them directly from the advertisers in this book.

Damp, sunny, and/or hot conditions — no, this is not a weather forecast — are three elements to avoid in extremes if you are interested in preserving your collection. Too much (or too little) humidity can cause gradual deterioration of a card. Direct, bright sun (or fluorescent light) over time will bleach out the color of a card. Extreme heat accelerates the decomposition of the card. On the other hand, many cards have lasted more than 50 years without much scientific intervention. So be cautious, even if the above factors typically present a problem only when present in the extreme. It never hurts to be prudent.

COLLECTING/INVESTING

Collecting individual players and collecting complete sets are both popular vehicles for investment and speculation. Most investors and speculators stock up on complete sets or on quantities of players they think have good investment potential. There is obviously no guarantee in this book, or anywhere else for that matter, that cards will outperform the stock market or other investment alternatives in the future. After all, baseball cards do not pay quarterly dividends. Nevertheless, investors have noticed a favorable trend in the past performance of baseball and other sports collectibles, and certain cards and sets have outperformed just about any other investment in some years.

Some of the obvious questions are: Which cards? When to buy? When to sell? The best investment you can make is in your own education. The more you know about your collection and the hobby, the more informed the decisions you will be able to make. We're not selling investment tips. We're selling information about the current value of baseball cards. It's up to you to use that information to your best advantage.

NOMENCLATURE

Each hobby has its own language to describe its area of interest. The nomenclature traditionally used for trading cards is derived from the *American Card Catalog*, published in 1960 by Nostalgia Press. That catalog, written by Jefferson Burdick (who is called the "Father of Card Collecting" for his pioneering work), uses letter and number designations for each separate set of cards.

The letter used in the *ACC* designation refers to the generic type of card. While both sport and non-sport issues are classified in the *ACC*, we shall confine ourselves to the sport issues. The following list defines the letters and their meanings as used by the *American Card Catalog*.

(none) or	N — 19th Century U.S. Tobacco	PC — Postcards
	B — Blankets	R — Candy and Gum Cards,
	D — Bakery Inserts	1930 to Present
	Including Bread	T — 20th Century U.S. Tobacco
	E — Early Candy and Gum	UO — Gas and Oil Inserts
	F — Food Inserts	V — Canadian Candy
	H — Advertising	W — Exhibits, Strip Cards,
	M — Periodicals	Team Issues

Following the letter prefix and an optional hyphen are one-, two-, or three-digit numbers, 1-999. These typically represent the company or entity issuing the cards. In several cases, the *ACC* number is extended by an additional hyphen and another one- or two-digit numerical suffix. For example, the 1957 Topps regular series baseball card issue carries an *ACC* designation of R414-11. The "R" indicates a Candy or Gum card produced since 1930. The "414" is the *ACC* designation for Topps Chewing Gum baseball card issues, and the "11" is the *ACC* designation for the 1957 regular issue (Topps' eleventh baseball set).

Like other traditional methods of identification, this system provides order to the process of cataloging cards; however, most serious collectors learn the *ACC* designation of the popular sets by repetition and familiarity, rather than by attempting to "figure out" what they might or should be.

From 1948 forward, collectors and dealers commonly refer to all sets by their year, maker, type of issue, and any other distinguishing characteristic. For example, such a characteristic could be an unusual issue or one of several regular issues put out by a specific maker in a single year. Regional issues are usually referred to by year, maker, and sometimes by title or theme of the set.

GLOSSARY/LEGEND

Our glossary defines terms frequently used in the card collecting hobby. Many of these terms are also common to other types of sports memorabilia collecting. Some terms may have several meanings depending on use.

AAS - Action All Stars, a postcard-size set issued by the Donruss Company.

ACC - Acronym for *American Card Catalog*.

ALL STAR CARD - A card portraying an All Star Player of the previous year that says "All Star" on its face.

ALPH - Alphabetical.

AS - Abbreviation for All Star (card).

ATG - All Time Great card.

BLANKET - A felt square (normally 5" to 6") portraying a baseball player.

BOX - Card issued on a box or a card depicting a Boxer.

BRICK - A group of cards, usually 50 or more having common characteristics, that is intended to be bought, sold, or traded as a unit.

CABINETS - Popular and highly valuable photographs on thick card stock produced in the 19th and early 20th century.

CHECKLIST - A list of the cards contained in a particular set. The list is always in numerical order if the cards are numbered. Some unnumbered sets are artificially numbered in alphabetical order, or by team and alphabetically within the team for convenience.

CHECKLIST CARD - A card that lists in order the cards and players in the set or series. Older checklist cards in mint condition that have not been checked off are very desirable.

CL - Abbreviation for Checklist.

COA - Abbreviation for Coach.

COIN - A small disc of metal or plastic portraying a player in its center.

COLLECTOR - A person who engages in the hobby of collecting cards primarily for his own enjoyment, with any profit motive being secondary.

COLLECTOR ISSUE - A set produced for the sake of the card itself with no product or service sponsor. It derives its name from the fact that most of these sets are produced for sale directly to the hobby market.

COMBINATION CARD - A single card depicting two or more players (but not a team card).

COMMON CARD - The typical card of any set; it has no premium value accruing from subject matter, numerical scarcity, popular demand, or anomaly.

COM - Card issued by the Post Cereal Company through their mail-in offer.

CONVENTION - A large weekend gathering of dealers and collectors at a single location for the purpose of buying, selling, and sometimes trading sports memorabilia items. Conventions are open to the public and sometimes feature celebrities, door prizes, films, contests, etc.

CONVENTION ISSUE - A set produced in conjunction with a sports collectibles convention to commemorate or promote the show.

COR - Correct or corrected card.

COUPON - See Tab.

CREASE - A wrinkle on the card, usually caused by bending the card. Creases are a common defect from careless handling.

CY - Cy Young Award.

DEALER - A person who engages in buying, selling, and trading sports collectibles or supplies. A dealer may also be a collector, but as a dealer, he anticipates a profit.

DIE-CUT - A card with part of its stock partially cut, allowing one or more parts to be folded or removed. After removal or appropriate folding, the remaining part of the card can frequently be made to stand up.

DISC - A circular-shaped card.

DISPLAY CARD - A sheet, usually containing three to nine cards, that is printed and used by the manufacturer to advertise and/or display the packages containing his products and cards. The backs of display cards are blank or contain advertisements.

DK - Diamond King (artwork produced by Perez-Steele for Donruss).

DP - Double Print (a card that was printed in double the quantity compared to the other cards in the same series).

ERA - Earned Run Average.

ERR - Error card (see also COR).

ERROR CARD - A card with erroneous information, spelling, or depiction on either side of the card. Not all errors are corrected by the producing card company.

EXHIBIT - The generic name given to thick-stock, postcard-size cards with single color obverse pictures. The name is derived from the Exhibit Supply Co. of Chicago, the principal manufacturer of this type of card. These are also known as Arcade cards since they were found in many arcades.

FDP - First Draft Pick (see 1985 Topps Baseball).

FULL SHEET - A complete sheet of cards that has not been cut up into individual cards by the manufacturer. Also called an uncut sheet.

HALL OF FAMER - (HOF'er) A card that portrays a player who has been inducted into the Hall of Fame.

HIGH NUMBER - The cards in the last series of numbers in a year in which such higher-numbered cards were printed or distributed in significantly lesser amounts than the lower-numbered cards. The high-number designation refers to a scarcity of the high-numbered cards. Not all years have high numbers in terms of this definition.

HOC - House of Collectibles.

HOF - Acronym for Hall of Fame.

HOR - Horizontal pose on card as opposed to the standard vertical orientation found on most cards.

HR - Abbreviation for Home Run.

IA - In Action (type of card).

INSERT - A card of a different type, e.g., a poster, or any other sports collectible contained and sold in the same package along with a card or cards of a major set.

ISSUE - Synonymous with set, but usually used in conjunction with a manufacturer, e.g., a Topps issue.

KP - Kid Picture (a sub-series issued in the Topps Baseball sets of 1972 and 1973).

LAYERING - The separation or peeling of one or more layers of the card stock, usually at the corner of the card.

LEGITIMATE ISSUE - A set produced to promote or boost sales of a product or service, e.g., bubble gum, cereal, cigarettes, etc. Most collector issues are not legitimate issues in this sense.

LHP - Left Handed Pitcher.

LID - A circular-shaped card (possibly with tab) that forms the top of the container for the product being promoted.

LL - Living Legends (Donruss 1984) or large letters.

MAJOR SET - A set produced by a national manufacturer of cards containing a large number of cards. Usually 100 or more different cards comprise the set.

MG - Abbreviation for Manager.

MINI - A small card; specifically, a Topps baseball card of identical design but smaller dimensions than the regular Topps issue of 1975.

ML - Major League.

MVP - Most Valuable Player.

NNOF - No Name on Front (see 1949 Bowman).

NOF - Name on Front (see 1949 Bowman).

NON-SPORT CARD - A card from a set whose major theme is a subject other than a sports subject. A card of a sports figure or event that is part of a non-sport set is still a non-sport card, e.g., while the "Look 'N' See" non-sport card set contains a card of Babe Ruth, a sports figure, that card is a non-sport card.

NOTCHING - The grooving of the card, usually caused by fingernails, rubber bands, or bumping card edges against other objects.

NY - New York.

OBVERSE - The front, face, or pictured side of the card.

OLY - Olympics (see 1985 Topps Baseball; the members of the 1984 U.S. Olympic Baseball team were a featured sub-series).

OPT - Option.

P - Pitcher or Pitching pose.

P1 - First Printing.

P2 - Second Printing.

P3 - Third Printing.

PANEL - An extended card that is composed of two or more individual cards. Often the panel forms the back part of the container for the product being promoted, e.g., a Hostess panel, a Bazooka panel, an Esskay Meat panel.

PCL - Pacific Coast League.

PG - Price Guide.

PLASTIC SHEET - A clear, plastic page that is punched for insertion into a binder (with standard three-ring spacing) containing pockets for displaying cards. Many different styles of sheets exist with pockets of varying sizes to hold the many differing card formats.

PREMIUM - A card, sometimes on photographic stock, that is purchased or obtained in conjunction with/or redemption for another card or product. The premium is not packaged in the same unit as the primary item.

PUZZLE CARD - A card whose back contains a part of a picture which, when joined correctly with other puzzle cards, forms the completed picture.

PUZZLE PIECE - A die-cut piece designed to interlock with similar pieces.

RARE - A card or series of cards of very limited availability. Unfortunately, "rare" is a subjective term sometimes used indiscriminately. Rare cards are harder to obtain than scarce cards.

RB - Record Breaker card.

REGIONAL - A card issued and distributed only in a limited geographical area of the country. The producer is not a major, national producer of trading cards.

REVERSE - The back or narrative side of the card.

RHP - Right-Handed Pitcher.

ROY - Acronym for Rookie of the Year.

RR - Rated Rookies (a subset featured in the Donruss Baseball sets).

SA - Super Action or Sport Americana.

SASE - Self-Addressed, Stamped Envelope.

SB - Stolen Bases.

SCARCE - A card or series of cards of limited availability. This subjective term is sometimes used indiscriminately to promote or hype value. Scarce cards are not as difficult to obtain as rare cards.

SCR - Script name on back (see 1949 Bowman Baseball).

SEMI-HIGH - A card from the next to last series of a sequentially issued set. It has more value than an average card and generally less value than a high number. A card is not called a semi-high unless the next to last series in which it exists has an additional premium attached to it.

SERIES - The entire set of cards issued by a particular producer in a particular year, e.g., the 1971 Topps series. Also, within a particular set, series can refer to a group of (consecutively numbered) cards printed at the same time, e.g., the first series of the 1957 Topps issue (numbers 1 through 88).

SET - One each of the entire run of cards of the same type produced by a particular manufacturer during a single year. In other words, if you have a (complete) set of 1976 Topps then you have every card from number 1 up through and including number 660, i.e., all the different cards that were produced.

SKIP-NUMBERED - A set that has many unissued card numbers between the lowest number in the set and the highest number in the set, e.g., the 1948 Leaf baseball set contains 98 cards skip-numbered from number 1 to number 168. A major set in which a few numbers were not printed is not considered to be skip-numbered.

SO - Strikeouts.

SP - Single or Short Print (a card which was printed in lesser quantity compared to the other cards in the same series; see also DP and TP).

SPECIAL CARD - A card that portrays something other than a single player or team, for example, a card that portrays the previous year's statistical leaders or the results from the previous year's post-season action.

SS - Abbreviation for Shortstop.

STAMP - Adhesive-backed papers depicting a player. The stamp may be individual or in a sheet of many stamps. Moisture must be applied to the adhesive in order for the stamp to be attached to another surface.

STAR CARD - A card that portrays a player of some repute, usually determined by his ability; however, sometimes referring to sheer popularity.

STICKER - A card with a removable layer that can be affixed to (stuck onto) another surface.

STOCK - The cardboard or paper on which the card is printed.

STRIP CARDS - A sheet or strip of cards, particularly popular in the 1920s and 1930s, with the individual cards usually separated by broken or dotted lines.

SUPERSTAR CARD - A card that portrays a superstar, e.g., a Hall of Fame member or a Hall of Fame prospect.

SV - Super Veteran.

TAB - A card portion set off from the rest of the card, usually with perforations, that may be removed without damaging the central character or event depicted by the card.

TBC - Turn Back the Clock cards.

TEAM CARD - A card that depicts an entire team.

TEST SET - A set, usually containing a small number of cards, issued by a national card producer and distributed in a limited section or sections of the country. Presumably, the purpose of a test set is to test market appeal for a particular type of card.

TL - Team Leader card.

TP - Triple Print (a card that was printed in triple the quantity compared to the other cards in the same series).

TR - Trade or Traded.

TRIMMED - A card cut down from its original size. Trimmed cards are undesirable to most collectors.

VARIATION - One of two or more cards from the same series with the same number (or player with identical pose if the series is unnumbered) differing from one another by some aspect, the different feature stemming from the printing or stock of the card. This can be caused when the manufacturer of the cards notices an error in one (or more) of the cards, makes the changes, and then resumes the print run. In this case there will be two versions or variations of the same card. Sometimes one of the variations is relatively scarce.

VERT - Vertical pose on card.

WAS - Washington.

WS - World Series card.

HISTORY OF BASEBALL CARDS

Today's version of the baseball card, with its colorful front and statistical back, is a far cry from its earliest predecessors. The issue remains cloudy as to which was the very first baseball card ever produced, but the institution of baseball cards dates from the latter half of the 19th century, more than 100 years ago. Early issues, generally printed on heavy cardboard, were of poor quality, with photographs, drawings and printing far short of today's standards.

Goodwin & Co., of New York, makers of Gypsy Queen, Old Judge, and other cigarette brands, is considered by many to be the first issuer of baseball and other sports cards. Their issues, predominantly in the 1 1/2" by 2 1/2" size, generally consisted of photographs of baseball players, boxers, wrestlers, and other subjects mounted on stiff cardboard. More than 2,000 different photos of baseball players alone have been identified. These "Old Judges," a collective name commonly used for the Goodwin & Co. cards, were issued from 1886 to 1890 and are treasured parts of many collections today.

Among the other cigarette companies which issued baseball cards that still attract attention today are Allen & Ginter, D. Buchner & Co. (Gold Coin Chewing Tobacco), and P.H. Mayo & Brother. Cards from the first two companies bore colored line drawings, while the Mayos are sepia photographs on black cardboard.

In addition to the small-size cards from this era, several tobacco companies issued cabinet-size baseball cards. These "cabinets" were considerably larger than the small cards, usually about 4 1/4" by 6 1/2", and were printed on heavy stock. Goodwin & Co.'s Old Judge cabinets and the National Tobacco Works' "Newsboy" baseball photos are two that remain popular today.

By 1895 the American Tobacco Company began to dominate its competition. They discontinued baseball card inserts in their cigarette packages (actually slide boxes in those days). The lack of competition in the cigarette market had made these inserts unnecessary. This marked the end of the first era of the baseball card.

At the dawn of the 20th century, few baseball cards were being issued. But once again it was the cigarette companies — particularly, the American Tobacco Company — followed to a lesser extent by the candy and gum makers that revived the practice of including baseball cards with their products. The bulk of these cards, identified in the *American Card Catalog* (designated hereafter as *ACC*) as T or E cards for 20th century "Tobacco" or "Early Candy and Gum" issues respectively, were released from 1909 to 1915.

This romantic and popular era of baseball card collecting produced many desirable items. The most outstanding is the fabled T-206 Honus Wagner card. Other perennial favorites among collectors are the T-206 Eddie Plank card, and the T-206 Magee error card. The former was once the second most valuable card and only recently relinquished that position to a more distinctive and aesthetically pleasing Napoleon Lajoie card from the 1933/34 Goudey Gum series. The latter misspells the player's name as "Magie," the most famous and valuable blooper card.

The ingenuity and distinctiveness of this era has yet to be surpassed. Highlights include the T-202 Hassan triple-folders, one of the best looking and the most distinctive cards ever issued; the durable T-201 Mecca double-folders, one of the first sets with players' records on the reverse; the T-3 Turkey Reds, the hobby's most popular cabinet card; the E-145 Cracker Jacks, the only major set containing Federal League player cards; and the T-204 Ramlys, with their distinctive black and white oval photos and ornate gold borders. These are but a few of the varieties issued during this period.

While the American Tobacco Company dominated the field, several other tobacco companies, as well as clothing manufacturers, newspapers and periodicals, game makers, and companies whose identities remain anonymous, also issued cards during this period. In fact, the Collins-McCarthy Candy Company, makers of Zeenuts Pacific Coast League baseball cards, issued cards yearly from 1911 to 1938. Their record for continuous annual card production has been exceeded only by the Topps Chewing Gum Company. The era of the tobacco card issues closed with the onset of World War I, with the exception of the Red Man chewing tobacco sets produced from 1952 to 1955.

The next flurry of card issues broke out in the roaring and prosperous 1920s, the era of the E card. The caramel companies (National Caramel, American Caramel, York Caramel) were the leading distributors of these E cards. In addition, the strip card, a continous strip with several cards divided by dotted lines or other sectioning features, flourished during this time. While the E cards and the strip cards are generally considered less imaginative than the T cards or the recent candy and gum issues, they are still sought after by many advanced collectors.

Another significant event of the 1920s was the introduction of the arcade card. Taking its designation from its issuer, the Exhibit Supply Company of Chicago, it is usually known as the "Exhibit" card. Once a trademark of the penny arcades, amusement parks, and county fairs across the country, Exhibit machines dispensed nearly postcard-size photos on thick stock for one penny. These picture cards bore likenesses of a favorite cowboy, actor, actress, or baseball player. Exhibit Supply and its associated companies produced baseball cards during a longer time span, although discontinuous, than any other manufacturer. Its first cards appeared in 1921, while its last issue was in 1966. In 1979, the Exhibit Supply Company was bought and somewhat revived by a collector/dealer who has since reprinted Exhibit photos of the past.

If the T card period, from 1909 to 1915, can be said to be the "Golden Age" of baseball card collecting, then perhaps the "Silver Age" commenced with the introduction of the Big League Gum series of 239 cards in 1933 (a 240th card was added in 1934). These are the forerunners of today's baseball gum cards, and the Goudey Gum Company of Boston is responsible for their success. This era spanned the period from the Depression days of 1933 to America's formal involvement in World War II in 1941.

Goudey's attractive designs, with full-color line drawings on thick card stock, influenced greatly other cards being issued at that time. As a result, the most attractive and popular cards in collecting history were produced in this "Silver Age." The 1933 Goudey Big League Gum series also owes its popularity to the more than 40 Hall of Fame players in the set. These include four cards of Babe Ruth and two of Lou Gehrig. Goudey's reign continued in 1934 when it issued a 96-card set in color, together with the single remaining card from the 1933 series, #106, the Napoleon Lajoie card.

In addition to Goudey, several other bubble gum manufacturers issued baseball cards during this era. DeLong Gum Company issued an extremely attractive set in 1933. National Chicle Company's 192-card "Batter-Up" series of 1934-1936 became the largest die-cut set in card history. In addition, that company offered the popular "Diamond Stars" series during the same period. Other popular sets included the "Tattoo Orbit" set of 60 color cards issued in 1933 and Gum Products' 75-card "Double Play" set, featuring sepia depictions of two players per card.

In 1939 Gum Inc., which later became Bowman Gum, replaced Goudey Gum as the leading baseball card producer. In 1939 and the following year, it issued two important sets of black and white cards. In 1939 its "Play Ball America" set consisted of 162 cards. The larger, 240-card "Play Ball" set of 1940 is still considered by many to be the most attractive black and white cards ever produced. That firm introduced its only color set in 1941, consisting of 72 cards entitled "Play Ball Sports Hall of Fame." Many of these were colored repeats of poses from the black and white 1940 series.

In addition to regular gum cards, many manufacturers distributed premium issues during the 1930s. These premiums were printed on paper or photographic stock, rather than card stock. They were much larger than the regular cards and were sold for a penny across the counter with gum (which was packaged separately from the premium). They were often redeemed at the store or through the mail in exchange for the wrappers of previously purchased gum cards, a la proof-of-purchase box-top premiums today. The gum premiums are scarcer than the card issues of the 1930s and in most cases no manufacturer's name is present.

World War II brought an end to this popular era of card collecting when paper and rubber shortages curtailed the production of bubble gum baseball cards. They were resurrected again in 1948 by the Bowman Gum Company (the direct descendant of Gum, Inc.). This marked the beginning of the modern era of card collecting.

In 1948, Bowman Gum issued a 48-card set in black and white, consisting of one card and one slab of gum in every one-cent pack. That same year, the Leaf Gum Company also issued a set of cards. Although rather poor in quality, these cards were issued in color. A squabble over the rights to use players' pictures developed between Bowman and Leaf. Eventually Leaf dropped out of the card market, but not before it had left a lasting heritage to the hobby by issuing some of the rarest cards now in existence. Leaf's baseball card series of 1948-49 contained 98 cards, skip numbered to #168 (not all numbers were printed). Of these 98 cards, 49 are relatively plentiful; however, the other 49 are rare and quite valuable.

Bowman continued its production of cards in 1949 with a color series of 240 cards. Because there are many scarce "high numbers" this series remains the most difficult Bowman regular issue to complete. Although the set was printed in color and commands great interest due to its scarcity, it is considered aesthetically inferior to the Goudey and National Chicle issues of the 1930s. In addition to the regular issue of 1949, Bowman also produced a set of 36 Pacific Coast League players. While this was not a regular issue, it is still prized by collectors. In fact, it has become the most valuable Bowman series.

In 1950 (Bowman's one-year monopoly of the baseball card market), the company began a string of top quality cards which continued until its demise in 1955. The 1950 series was itself something of an oddity because the "low" numbers, rather than the traditional high numbers, were the more difficult cards to obtain.

The year 1951 marked the beginning of the most competitive and perhaps the highest quality period of baseball card production. In that year Topps Chewing Gum Company of Brooklyn entered the market. Topps' 1951 series consisted of two sets of 52 cards each, one set with red backs and the other with blue backs. In addition, Topps also issued 31 insert cards, three of which remain the rarest Topps cards ("Current All-Stars" Konstanty, Roberts, and Stanky). The 1951 Topps cards were unattractive and paled in comparison to the 1951 Bowman issues. However, they were successful, and Topps has continued to produce cards ever since.

Topps issued a larger and much more attractive card in 1952. This larger size became standard for the next five years. (Bowman followed with larger-size baseball cards in 1953.) This 1952 Topps set has become, like the 1933 Goudey series and the T-206 white border series, the classic set of its era. The 407-card set is a collector's dream of scarcities, rarities, errors, and variations. It also contains the first Topps issues of Mickey Mantle and Willie Mays.

As with Bowman and Leaf in the late 1940s, competition over player rights arose. Ensuing court battles occurred between Topps and Bowman. The market split due to stiff competition, and in January, 1956, Topps bought out Bowman. Topps remained relatively unchallenged as the primary producer of baseball cards through 1980. So, the story of major baseball card sets from 1956 through 1980 is by and large the story of Topps' issues with few exceptions. Fleer Gum produced small sets in 1959, 1960, 1961, and 1963, and several cartoon sets in the 1970s, and more recently Kellogg's Cereal and Hostess Cakes issued baseball cards to promote their products.

A court decision in 1980 paved the way for two other large gum companies to enter, or reenter, the baseball card arena. The Fleer Corporation, which had last made photo cards in 1963, and the Donruss Company (a division of General Mills) secured rights to produce baseball cards of current players, breaking Topps' monopoly. Each company issued major card sets in 1981 with bubble gum products. Then a higher court decision in that year overturned the lower court ruling against Topps. It appeared that Topps had regained its sole position as a producer of baseball cards. Undaunted by the revocation ruling, Fleer and Donruss continued to issue cards in 1982 but without bubble gum or any other edible product. Fleer issued its current player baseball cards with "team logo stickers," while Donruss issued its cards with a piece of a baseball jigsaw puzzle.

Since 1981, these three major baseball card producers have all thrived, sharing relatively equal recognition. Each has steadily increased its involvement in terms of numbers of issues per year. To the delight of collectors, their competition has generated novel, and in some cases exceptional, issues of current major league baseball players. These major producers have become increasingly aware of the organized collecting market. While the corner candy store remains the major marketplace for card sales, an increasing number of issues have been directed to this organized hobby marketplace. In fact, many of these issues have been distributed exclusively through hobby channels. Although no one can ever say what the future will bring, one can only surmise that the hobby market will play a significant role in future plans of all the major baseball card producers.

The above has been a thumbnail sketch of card collecting from its inception in the 1880s to the present. It is difficult to tell the whole story in just a few pages — there are several other good sources of information. Serious collectors should subscribe to at least one of the excellent hobby periodicals. We also suggest that collectors attend a sports collectibles convention in their area. Card collecting is still a young and informal hobby. Chances are good that you will run into one or more of the "experts" at such a show. They are usually more than happy to share their knowledge with you.

BUSINESS OF BASEBALL CARD COLLECTING

DETERMINING VALUE

Why are some cards more valuable than others? Obviously, the economic law of supply and demand is applicable to card collecting, just as it is to any other field where a commodity is bought, sold, or traded.

Supply (the number of cards available on the market) is less than the total number of cards originally produced since attrition diminishes that original quantity. Each year a percentage of cards are typically thrown away, destroyed, or otherwise lost to collectors. This percentage is smaller today than it was in the past because more and more people have become increasingly aware of the value of their cards. For those who collect only "Mint" condition cards, the supply of older cards can be quite small indeed. Until recently, collectors were not so conscious of the need to preserve the condition of their cards. For this reason, it is difficult to know exactly how many 1953 Topps are currently available, Mint or otherwise. It is generally accepted that there are fewer 1953 Topps available than 1963, 1973, or 1983 Topps cards. If demand were equal for each of these sets, the law of supply and demand would increase the price for the least available sets. Demand, however, is not equal for all sets, so price correlations can be complicated.

The demand for a card is influenced by many factors. These include: (1) the age of the card; (2) the number of cards printed; (3) the player(s) portrayed on the card; (4) the attractiveness and popularity of the set; and perhaps most important, (5) the physical condition of the card.

In general, (1) the older the card, (2) the fewer the number of the cards printed, (3) the more famous the player, (4) the more attractive and popular the set, or (5) the better the condition of the card, the higher the value of the card will be. There are exceptions to all but one of these factors: the condition of the card. Given two cards similar in all respects except condition, the one in the best condition will always be valued higher.

While there are certain guidelines that help to establish the value of a card, the exceptions and peculiarities make any simple, direct mathematical formula to determine card values impossible.

REGIONAL VARIATION

Two types of price variations exist among the sections of the country where a card is bought or sold. The first is the general price variation on all cards bought and sold in one geographical area as compared to another. Card prices are slightly higher on the East and West coasts, and slightly lower in the middle of the country. Although prices may vary from the East to the West, or from the Southwest to the Midwest, the prices listed in this guide are nonetheless presented as a consensus of all sections of this large and diverse country.

Still, prices for a particular player's cards may well be higher in his home team's area than in other regions. This exhibits the second type of regional price variation in which local players are favored over those from distant areas. For example, an

Al Kaline card would be valued higher in Detroit than in Cincinnati because Kaline played in Detroit; therefore, the demand there for Al Kaline cards is higher than it is in Cincinnati. On the other hand, a Johnny Bench card would be priced higher in Cincinnati where he played than in Detroit for similar reasons. Sometimes even common player cards command such a premium from hometown collectors.

SET PRICES

A somewhat paradoxical situation exists in the price of a complete set versus the combined cost of the individual cards in the set. In nearly every case, the sum of the prices for the individual cards is higher than the cost for the complete set. This is especially prevalent in the cards of the past few years. The reasons for this apparent anomaly stem from the habits of collectors and from the carrying costs to dealers. Today each card in a set is normally produced in the same quantity as all others in its set. However, many collectors pick up only stars, superstars, and particular teams. As a result, the dealer is left with a shortage of certain player cards and an abundance of others. He therefore incurs an expense in simply "carrying" these less desirable cards in stock. On the other hand, if he sells a complete set, he gets rid of large numbers of cards at one time. For this reason, he is often willing to receive less money for a complete set. By doing this, he recovers all of his costs and also receives some profit.

The disparity between the price of the complete set and that for the sum of the individual cards has also been influenced by the fact that the major manufacturers are now pre-collating card sets. Since "pulling" individual cards from the sets of all three manufacturers involves a specific type of labor (and cost), the singles or star card market is not affected significantly by pre-collation.

Set prices also do not include rare card varieties, unless specifically stated. Of course, the prices for sets do include one example of each type for the given set, but this is the least expensive variety.

SCARCE SERIES

Scarce series occur because cards issued before 1974 were made available to the public each year in several series of finite numbers of cards, rather than all cards of the set being available for purchase at one time. At some point during the year, usually toward the end of the baseball season, interest in current year baseball cards waned. Consequently, the manufacturers produced smaller numbers of these later series of cards. Nearly all nationwide issues from post-World

War II manufacturers (1948 to 1973) exhibit these series variations. In the past Topps, for example, has issued series consisting of many different numbers of cards, including 55, 66, 80, 88, and others. Recently Topps has settled on what is now their standard sheet size of 132 cards.

While the number of cards within a given series is usually the same as the number of cards on one printed sheet, this is not always the case. For example, Bowman used 36 cards on its standard printed sheets, but in 1948 substituted 12 cards during later print runs of that year's baseball cards. Twelve of the cards from the initial sheet of 36 cards were removed and replaced by 12 different cards giving, in effect, a first series of 36 cards and a second series of 12 new cards. This replacement produced a scarcity of 24 cards — the 12 cards removed from the original sheet and the 12 new cards added to the sheet. A full sheet of 1948 Bowman cards (second printing) shows that card numbers 37 through 48 have replaced 12 of the cards on the first printing sheet.

The Topps Gum Company has also created scarcities and/or excesses of certain cards in many of their sets. Topps, however, has most frequently gone the other direction by double printing some of the cards. Double printing causes an abundance of cards of the players who are on the same sheet more than one time. During the years from 1978 to 1981, Topps double printed 66 cards out of their large 726-card set. The Topps' practice of double printing cards in earlier years is the most logical explanation for the known scarcities of particular cards in some of these Topps sets.

GRADING YOUR CARDS

Each hobby has its own grading terminology — stamps, coins, comic books, beer cans, right down the line. Collectors of sports cards are no exception. The one invariable criterion for determining the value of a card is its condition: the better the condition of the card, the more valuable it is. However, condition grading is very subjective. Individual card dealers and collectors differ in the strictness of their grading, but the stated condition of a card should be determined without regard to whether it is being bought or sold.

The physical defects which lower the condition of a card are usually quite apparent, but each individual places his own estimation (negative value in this case) on these defects. We present the condition guide for use in determining values listed in this price guide in the hopes that excess subjectivity can be minimized.

The defects listed in the condition guide below are those either placed in the card at the time of printing — uneven borders, focus — or those defects that can occur to a card under normal handling — corner sharpness, gloss, edge wear, light creases — and finally, environmental conditions — browning. Other defects to cards are caused by human carelessness, and in all cases should be noted separately and in addition to the condition grade. Among the more common alterations are heavy creases, tape, tape stains, rubber band marks, water damage, smoke damage, trimming, paste, tears, writing, pin or tack holes, any back damage, and missing parts (tabs, tops, coupons, backgrounds).

CENTERING

It is important to define in words and pictures what is meant by certain frequently used hobby terms relating to grading cards. The adjacent pictures portray various stages of centering. Centering can range from well-centered to slightly off-centered to off-centered to badly off-centered to miscut.

Slightly Off-Centered: A slightly off-center card is one which upon close inspection is found to have one border bigger than the opposite border. This degree is only offensive to a purist.

Off-Centered: An off-center card has one border which is noticeably more than twice as wide as the opposite border.

Badly Off-Centered: A badly off-center card has virtually no border on one side of the card.

Miscut: A miscut card actually shows part of the adjacent card in its larger border and consequently a corresponding amount of its card is cut off.

CORNER WEAR

Degrees of corner wear generate several common terms used and useful to accurate grading. The wear on card corners can be expressed as fuzzy corners, corner wear or slightly rounded corners, rounded corners, badly rounded corners.

Fuzzy Corners: Fuzzy corners still come to a right angle (to a point) but the point has begun to fray slightly.

Corner Wear or Slightly Rounded Corners: The slight fraying of the corners has increased to where there is no longer a point to the corner. Nevertheless the corner is still reasonably sharp. There may be evidence of some slight loss of color in the corner also.

CENTERING

WELL-CENTERED

SLIGHTLY OFF-CENTERED

OFF-CENTERED

BADLY OFF-CENTERED

MISCUT

Rounded Corners: The corner is definitely no longer sharp but is not badly rounded.

Badly Rounded Corners: The corner is rounded to an objectionable degree. Excessive wear and rough handling are evident.

CREASES

The third, and perhaps most frequent, common defect is the crease; the degree of creasing in a card is very difficult to show in a drawing or picture. On giving the specific condition of an expensive card for sale, the seller should note any creases additionally. Creases can be categorized as to severity according to the following scale.

Light Crease: A light crease is a crease which is barely noticeable on close inspection. In fact when cards are in plastic sheets or holders, a light crease may not be seen (until the card is taken out of the holder). A light crease on the front is much more serious than a light crease on the card back only.

Medium Crease: A medium crease is noticeable when held and studied at arm's length by the naked eye, but does not overly detract from the appearance of the card. It is an obvious crease, but not one that breaks the picture surface of the card.

Heavy Crease: A heavy crease is one which has torn or broken through the card's picture surface, e.g., puts a tear in the photo surface.

ALTERATIONS

Deceptive Trimming: Deceptive trimming occurs when someone alters the card in order (1) to shave off edge wear, (2) to improve the sharpness of the corners, or (3) to improve centering — obviously their objective is to falsely increase the perceived value of the card to an unsuspecting buyer. The shrinkage is usually only evident if the trimmed card is compared to an adjacent full-sized card or if the trimmed card is itself measured.

Obvious Trimming: Obvious trimming is noticeable and unfortunate. It is usually performed by non-collectors who give no thought to the present or future value of their cards.

Deceptively Retouched Borders: This occurs when the borders (especially on those cards with dark borders) are touched up on the edges and corners with magic marker of appropriate color in order to make the card appear to be mint.

CATEGORIZATION OF DEFECTS

A "Micro Defect" would be fuzzy corners, slight off-centering, printer's lines, printer's spots, slightly out of focus, or slight loss of original gloss. A NrMT card may have one micro defect. An Ex-MT card may have two or more micro defects.

A "Minor Defect" would be corner wear or slight rounding, off-centering, light crease on back, wax or gum stains on reverse, loss of original gloss, writing or tape marks on back, or rubber band marks. An Excellent card may have minor defects.

A "Major Defect" would be rounded corner(s), badly off-centering, crease(s), deceptive trimming, deceptively retouched borders, pin hole, staple hole, incidental writing or tape marks on front, warping, water stains, or sun fading. A VG card may have one major defect. A Good card may have two or more major defects.

A "Catastrophic Defect" is the worst kind of defect and would include such defects as badly rounded corner(s), miscutting, heavy crease(s), obvious trimming, punch hole, tack hole, tear(s), corner missing or clipped, destructive writing on front. A Fair card may have one catastrophic defect. A Poor card has two or more catastrophic defects.

CONDITION GUIDE

MINT (M OR MT) - A card with no defects. The card has sharp corners, even borders, original gloss or shine on the surface, sharp focus of the picture, smooth edges, no signs of wear, and white borders. A Mint card (that is, a card that is worth a "Mint" price) does NOT have printers' lines or other printing defects or other serious quality control problems that should have been discovered by the producing card company before distribution. Note also that there is no allowance made for the age of the card.

NEAR MINT (NrMT) - A card with a micro defect. Any of the following would be sufficient to lower the grade of a card from Mint to the Near Mint category: layering at some of the corners (fuzzy corners), a very small amount of the original gloss lost, very minor wear on the edges, slightly off-center borders, slight wear visible only on close inspection, slight off-whiteness of the borders.

EXCELLENT-MINT (EX-MT) - A card with micro defects, but no minor defects. Two or three of the following would be sufficient to lower the grade of a card from Mint to the Excellent-Mint category: layering at some of the corners (fuzzy corners), a very small amount of the original gloss lost, minor wear on the edges, slightly off-center borders, slight wear visible only on close inspection, slight off-whiteness of the borders.

EXCELLENT (EX OR E) - A card with minor defects. Any of the following would be sufficient to lower the grade of a card from Mint to the Excellent category: slight rounding at some of the corners, a small amount of the original gloss lost, minor wear on the edges, off-center borders, wear visible only on close inspection; off-whiteness of the borders.

VERY GOOD (VG) - A card that has been handled but not abused: Some rounding at all corners, slight layering or scuffing at one or two corners, slight notching on edges, gloss lost from the surface but not scuffed, borders might be somewhat uneven but some white is visible on all borders, noticeable yellowing or browning of borders, pictures may be slightly off focus.

GOOD (G) - A well-handled card, rounding and some layering at the corners, scuffing at the corners and minor scuffing on the face, borders noticeably uneven and browning, loss of gloss on the face, notching on the edges.

FAIR (F) - Round and layering corners, brown and dirty borders, frayed edges, noticeable scuffing on the face, white not visible on one or more borders, cloudy focus.

POOR (P) - An abused card: The lowest grade of card, frequently some major physical alteration has been performed on the card, collectible only as a filler until a better-condition replacement can be obtained.

Categories between these major condition grades are frequently used, such as Very Good to Excellent (VG-E), Fair to Good (F-G), etc. Such grades indicate a card with all qualities at least in the lower of the two categories, but with several qualities in the higher of the two categories. In the case of EX-MT, it essentially refers to a card which is halfway between Excellent and Mint.

Unopened "Mint" cards and factory-collated sets are considered Mint in their unknown (and presumed perfect) state. However, once opened or broken out, each of these cards is graded (and valued) in its own right by taking into account any quality control defects (such as off-centering, printer's lines, machine creases, or gum stains) that may be present in spite of the fact that the card has never been handled.

Cards before 1980 which are priced in the price guide in a top condition of NrMT are obviously worth an additional premium when offered in strict Mint condition. This additional premium increases relative to the age and scarcity of the card. For example, Mint cards from the late '70s may bring only a 10% premium for Mint (above NrMT), whereas high demand cards from pre-World War II vintage sets can be sold for as much as double the NrMT price when offered in strict Mint condition.

SELLING YOUR CARDS

Just about every collector sells cards or will sell cards eventually. Someday you may be interested in selling your duplicates or maybe even your whole collection. You may sell to other collectors, friends, or dealers. You may even sell cards you purchased from a certain dealer back to that same dealer. In any event, it helps to know some of the mechanics of the typical transaction between buyer and seller.

Dealers will buy cards in order to resell them to other collectors who are interested in the cards. Dealers will always pay a higher percentage for items which (in their opinion) can be resold quickly, and a much lower percentage for those items which are perceived as having low demand and hence are slow moving. In either case, dealers must buy at a price that allows for the expense of doing business and a fair margin for profit.

If you have cards for sale, the best advice we can give is that you get three offers for your cards and take the best offer, all things considered. Note, the "best" offer may not be the one for the highest amount. And remember, if a dealer really wants your cards, he won't let you get away without making his best competitive offer. Another alternative is to take your cards to a nearby convention and either auction them off in the show auction or offer them for sale to some of the dealers present.

Many people think nothing of going into a department store and paying $15 for an item of clothing for which the store paid $5. But, if you were selling your $15 card to a dealer and he offered you only $5 for it, you might think his mark-up unreasonable. To complete the analogy: most department stores (and card dealers) that pay $10 for $15 items eventually go out of business. An exception to this is when the dealer knows that a willing buyer for the merchandise you are attempting to sell is only a phone call away. Then an offer of 2/3 or maybe 70% of the book value will still allow him to make a reasonable profit due to the short time he will need to hold the merchandise. Nevertheless, most cards and collections will bring offers in the range of 25% to 50% of retail price. Material from the past five to ten years or so is very plentiful. Don't be surprised if your best offer is only 20% of the book value for these recent years.

INTERESTING NOTES

The numerically first card of an issue is the single card most likely to obtain excessive wear. Consequently, you will typically find the price on the number one card (in Mint condition) somewhat higher than might otherwise be the case. Similarly, but to a lesser extent (because normally the less important, reverse side of the card is the one exposed), the numerically last card in an issue is also prone to abnormal wear. This extra wear and tear occurs because the first and last cards are exposed to the elements (human element included) more than any other cards. They are generally end cards in any brick formations, rubber bandings, stackings on wet surfaces, and like activities.

Sports cards have no intrinsic value. The value of a card, like the value of other collectibles, can only be determined by you and your enjoyment in viewing and possessing these cardboard swatches.

Remember, the buyer ultimately determines the price of each baseball card. You are the determining price factor because you have the ability to say "No" to the price of any card by not exchanging your hard-earned money for a given card. When the cost of a trading card exceeds the enjoyment you will receive from it, your answer should be "No." We assess and report the prices. You set them!

We are always interested in receiving the price input of collectors and dealers from around the country. We happily credit major contributors. We welcome your opinions, since your contributions assist us in ensuring a better guide each year. If you would like to join our survey list for the next editions of this book and others authored by Dr. Beckett, please send your name and address to Dr. James Beckett, 3410 MidCourt, Suite 110, Carrollton, Texas 75006.

ADVERTISING

Within this price guide you will find advertisements for sports memorabilia material, mail order, and retail sports collectibles establishments. All advertisements were accepted in good faith based on the reputation of the advertiser; however, neither the author, the publisher, the distributors, nor the other advertisers in the price guide accept any responsibility for any particular advertiser not complying with the terms of his or her ad.

Readers should also be aware that prices in advertisements are subject to change over the annual period before a new edition of this volume is issued each spring. When replying to an advertisement late in the baseball year, the reader should take this into account, and contact the dealer by phone or in writing for up-to-date price information. Should you come into contact with any of the advertisers in this guide as a result of their advertisement herein, please mention to them this source as your contact.

ADDITIONAL READING

With the increase in popularity of the hobby in recent years, there has been a corresponding increase in available literature. Below is a list of the books and periodicals which receive our highest recommendation and which we hope will further advance your knowledge and enjoyment of our great hobby.

The Sport Americana Price Guide to Baseball Collectibles by Dr. James Beckett (Second Edition, $12.95, released 1988, published by Edgewater Book Company) — the complete guide/checklist with up to date values for box cards, coins, labels, Canadian cards, stamps, stickers, pins, etc.

The Sport Americana Football, Hockey, Basketball and Boxing Card Price Guide by Dr. James Beckett (Fifth Edition, $12.95, released 1987, published by Edgewater Book Company) — the most comprehensive price guide/checklist ever issued on football and other non-baseball sports cards. No serious hobbyist should be without it.

The Official Price Guide to Football Cards by Dr. James Beckett (Eighth Edition, $4.95, released 1988, published by The House of Collectibles) — an abridgement of the *Sport Americana Price Guide* listed above in a convenient and economical pocket-size format providing Dr. Beckett's pricing of the major football sets since 1948.

The Sport Americana Baseball Memorabilia and Autograph Price Guide by Dr. James Beckett and Dennis W. Eckes (First Edition, $8.95, released 1982, co-published by Den's Collectors Den and Edgewater Book Company) — the most complete book ever produced on baseball memorabilia other than baseball cards.

This book presents in an illustrated, logical fashion information on baseball memorabilia and autographs which had been heretofore unavailable to the collector.

The Sport Americana Alphabetical Baseball Card Checklist by Dr. James Beckett (Third Edition, $9.95, released 1988, co-published by Den's Collectors Den and Edgewater Book Company) — an illustrated, alphabetical listing, by the last name of the player portrayed on the card, of virtually all baseball cards (Major League and Minor League) produced up through 1988.

The Sport Americana Price Guide to the Non-Sports Cards by Christopher Benjamin and Dennis W. Eckes (Third Edition (Part Two), $12.95, released 1988, published by Edgewater Book Company) — the definitive guide to all popular non-sports American tobacco and bubble gum cards. In addition to cards, illustrations and prices for wrappers are also included. Part Two covers non-sports cards from 1961 through 1987.

The Sport Americana Baseball Address List by Jack Smalling and Dennis W. Eckes (Fifth Edition, $10.95, released 1988, published by Edgewater Book Company) — the definitive guide for autograph hunters giving addresses and deceased information for virtually all major league baseball players past and present.

The Sport Americana Baseball Card Team Checklist by Jeff Fritsch and Dennis W. Eckes (Third Edition, $9.95, released 1987, co-published by Den's Collectors Den and Edgewater Book Company) — includes all Topps, Bowman, Fleer, Play Ball, Goudey, and Donruss cards, with the players portrayed on the cards listed with the teams for whom they played. The book is invaluable to the collector who specializes in an individual team because it is the most complete baseball card team checklist available.

Hockey Card Checklist and Price Guide by Andrew Pywowarczuk (Ninth Edition, publisher: Cartophilium) — contains the most complete list of hockey card checklists ever assembled including a listing of Bee Hive photos.

The Encyclopedia of Baseball Cards, Volume I: 19th Century Cards by Lew Lipset ($11.95, released 1983, published by the author) — everything you ever wanted to know about 19th-century cards.

The Encyclopedia of Baseball Cards, Volume II: Early Gum and Candy Cards by Lew Lipset ($10.95, released 1984, published by the author) — everything you ever wanted to know about Early Candy and Gum cards.

The Encyclopedia of Baseball Cards, Volume III: 20th Century Tobacco Cards, 1909-1932 by Lew Lipset ($12.95, released 1986, published by the author) — everything you ever wanted to know about old tobacco cards.

Beckett Baseball Card Monthly authored and edited by Dr. James Beckett — contains the most extensive and accepted monthly price guide, feature articles, "who's hot and who's not" section, convention calendar, and numerous letters to and responses from the editor. Now published 12 times annually, it is the hobby's largest paid circulation periodical.

PRICES IN THIS GUIDE

Prices found in this guide reflect current retail rates just prior to the printing of this book. They do not reflect the FOR SALE prices of the author, the publisher, the distributors, the advertisers, or any card dealers associated with this guide. No one is obligated in any way to buy, sell, or trade his or her cards based on these prices. The price listings were compiled by the author from actual buy/sell transactions at sports conventions, buy/sell advertisements in the hobby papers, for sale prices from dealer catalogs and price lists, and discussions with leading hobbyists in the U.S. and Canada. All prices are in U.S. dollars.

1952 Topps

The cards in this 407-card set measure 2 ⅝ " by 3 ¾ ". The 1952 Topps set is Topps' first truly major set. Card numbers 1 to 80 were issued with red or black backs, both of which are less plentiful than card numbers 81 to 250. In fact the first series is considered the most difficult with respect to finding Mint condition cards. Card number 48 (Joe Page) and number 49 (Johnny Sain) can be found with each other's write-up on their back. Card numbers 251 to 310 are somewhat scarce and numbers 311 to 407 are quite scarce. Cards 281-300 were single printed compared to the other cards in the next to last series. Cards 311-313 were double printed on the last high number printing sheet. The key card in the set is obviously Mickey Mantle #311, Mickey's first of many Topps cards.

		NRMT	VG-E	GOOD
	Complete Set (407)	37500.	14000.	5000.
	Common Player (1-80)	50.00	20.00	5.00
	Common Player (81-250)	20.00	8.00	2.00
	Common Player (251-280)	40.00	16.00	4.00
	Common Player (281-300)	50.00	20.00	5.00
	Common Player (301-310)	40.00	16.00	4.00
	Common Player (311-407)	150.00	60.00	15.00
☐	1 Andy Pafko	900.00	40.00	8.00
☐	2 Pete Runnels	55.00	22.00	5.50
☐	3 Hank Thompson	55.00	22.00	5.50
☐	4 Don Lenhardt	50.00	20.00	5.00
☐	5 Larry Jansen	50.00	20.00	5.00

		NRMT	VG-E	GOOD
☐	6 Grady Hatton	50.00	20.00	5.00
☐	7 Wayne Terwilliger	50.00	20.00	5.00
☐	8 Fred Marsh	50.00	20.00	5.00
☐	9 Robert Hogue	50.00	20.00	5.00
☐	10 Al Rosen	70.00	28.00	7.00
☐	11 Phil Rizzuto	135.00	54.00	13.50
☐	12 Romanus Basgall	50.00	20.00	5.00
☐	13 Johnny Wyrostek	50.00	20.00	5.00
☐	14 Bob Elliott	55.00	22.00	5.50
☐	15 Johnny Pesky	55.00	22.00	5.50
☐	16 Gene Hermanski	50.00	20.00	5.00
☐	17 Jim Hegan	55.00	22.00	5.50
☐	18 Merrill Combs	50.00	20.00	5.00
☐	19 Johnny Bucha	50.00	20.00	5.00
☐	20 Billy Loes	80.00	32.00	8.00
☐	21 Ferris Fain	55.00	22.00	5.50
☐	22 Dom DiMaggio	75.00	30.00	7.50
☐	23 Billy Goodman	55.00	22.00	5.50
☐	24 Luke Easter	55.00	22.00	5.50
☐	25 Johnny Groth	50.00	20.00	5.00
☐	26 Monte Irvin	90.00	36.00	9.00
☐	27 Sam Jethroe	50.00	20.00	5.00
☐	28 Jerry Priddy	50.00	20.00	5.00
☐	29 Ted Kluszewski	70.00	28.00	7.00
☐	30 Mel Parnell	55.00	22.00	5.50
☐	31 Gus Zernial	60.00	24.00	6.00
☐	32 Eddie Robinson	50.00	20.00	5.00
☐	33 Warren Spahn	150.00	60.00	15.00
☐	34 Elmer Valo	50.00	20.00	5.00
☐	35 Hank Sauer	60.00	24.00	6.00
☐	36 Gil Hodges	125.00	50.00	11.00
☐	37 Duke Snider	250.00	100.00	22.00
☐	38 Wally Westlake	50.00	20.00	5.00
☐	39 Dizzy Trout	55.00	22.00	5.50
☐	40 Irv Noren	50.00	20.00	5.00
☐	41 Bob Wellman	50.00	20.00	5.00
☐	42 Lou Kretlow	50.00	20.00	5.00
☐	43 Ray Scarborough	50.00	20.00	5.00
☐	44 Con Dempsey	50.00	20.00	5.00
☐	45 Eddie Joost	50.00	20.00	5.00
☐	46 Gordon Goldsberry	50.00	20.00	5.00
☐	47 Willie Jones	50.00	20.00	5.00
☐	48A Joe Page COR	65.00	26.00	6.50
☐	48B Joe Page ERR	275.00	110.00	27.00
	(bio for Sain)			
☐	49A Johnny Sain COR	80.00	32.00	8.00
☐	49B Johnny Sain ERR	275.00	110.00	27.00
	(bio for Page)			
☐	50 Marv Rickert	50.00	20.00	5.00

			NRMT	VG-E	GOOD				NRMT	VG-E	GOOD
☐	51	Jim Russell	50.00	20.00	5.00	☐	100	Del Rice	20.00	8.00	2.00
☐	52	Don Mueller	60.00	24.00	6.00	☐	101	Max Lanier	20.00	8.00	2.00
☐	53	Chris Van Cuyk	50.00	20.00	5.00	☐	102	Bill Kennedy	20.00	8.00	2.00
☐	54	Leo Kiely	50.00	20.00	5.00	☐	103	Cliff Mapes	20.00	8.00	2.00
☐	55	Ray Boone	55.00	22.00	5.50	☐	104	Don Kolloway	20.00	8.00	2.00
☐	56	Tommy Glaviano	50.00	20.00	5.00	☐	105	Johnny Pramesa	20.00	8.00	2.00
☐	57	Ed Lopat	85.00	34.00	8.50	☐	106	Mickey Vernon	22.00	9.00	2.20
☐	58	Bob Mahoney	50.00	20.00	5.00	☐	107	Connie Ryan	20.00	8.00	2.00
☐	59	Robin Roberts	110.00	45.00	11.00	☐	108	Jim Konstanty	24.00	10.00	2.40
☐	60	Sid Hudson	50.00	20.00	5.00	☐	109	Ted Wilks	20.00	8.00	2.00
☐	61	Tookie Gilbert	50.00	20.00	5.00	☐	110	Dutch Leonard	20.00	8.00	2.00
☐	62	Chuck Stobbs	50.00	20.00	5.00	☐	111	Peanuts Lowrey	20.00	8.00	2.00
☐	63	Howie Pollet	50.00	20.00	5.00	☐	112	Hank Majeski	20.00	8.00	2.00
☐	64	Roy Sievers	55.00	22.00	5.50	☐	113	Dick Sisler	20.00	8.00	2.00
☐	65	Enos Slaughter	110.00	45.00	11.00	☐	114	Willard Ramsdell	20.00	8.00	2.00
☐	66	Preacher Roe	85.00	34.00	8.50	☐	115	Red Munger	20.00	8.00	2.00
☐	67	Allie Reynolds	90.00	36.00	9.00	☐	116	Carl Scheib	20.00	8.00	2.00
☐	68	Cliff Chambers	50.00	20.00	5.00	☐	117	Sherm Lollar	22.00	9.00	2.20
☐	69	Virgil Stallcup	50.00	20.00	5.00	☐	118	Ken Raffensberger	20.00	8.00	2.00
☐	70	Al Zarilla	50.00	20.00	5.00	☐	119	Mickey McDermott	20.00	8.00	2.00
☐	71	Tom Upton	50.00	20.00	5.00	☐	120	Bob Chakales	20.00	8.00	2.00
☐	72	Karl Olson	50.00	20.00	5.00	☐	121	Gus Niarhos	20.00	8.00	2.00
☐	73	Bill Werle	50.00	20.00	5.00	☐	122	Jackie Jensen	60.00	24.00	6.00
☐	74	Andy Hansen	50.00	20.00	5.00	☐	123	Eddie Yost	20.00	8.00	2.00
☐	75	Wes Westrum	55.00	22.00	5.50	☐	124	Monte Kennedy	20.00	8.00	2.00
☐	76	Eddie Stanky	50.00	20.00	5.00	☐	125	Bill Rigney	20.00	8.00	2.00
☐	77	Bob Kennedy	50.00	20.00	5.00	☐	126	Fred Hutchinson	25.00	10.00	2.50
☐	78	Ellis Kinder	50.00	20.00	5.00	☐	127	Paul Minner	20.00	8.00	2.00
☐	79	Jerald Staley	50.00	20.00	5.00	☐	128	Don Bollweg	20.00	8.00	2.00
☐	80	Herman Wehmeier	50.00	20.00	5.00	☐	129	Johnny Mize	70.00	28.00	7.00
☐	81	Vernon Law	27.00	11.00	2.70	☐	130	Sheldon Jones	20.00	8.00	2.00
☐	82	Duane Pillette	20.00	8.00	2.00	☐	131	Morrie Martin	20.00	8.00	2.00
☐	83	Billy Johnson	20.00	8.00	2.00	☐	132	Clyde Klutz	20.00	8.00	2.00
☐	84	Vern Stephens	22.00	9.00	2.20	☐	133	Al Widmar	20.00	8.00	2.00
☐	85	Bob Kuzava	20.00	8.00	2.00	☐	134	Joe Tipton	20.00	8.00	2.00
☐	86	Ted Gray	20.00	8.00	2.00	☐	135	Dixie Howell	20.00	8.00	2.00
☐	87	Dale Coogan	20.00	8.00	2.00	☐	136	Johnny Schmitz	20.00	8.00	2.00
☐	88	Bob Feller	110.00	45.00	11.00	☐	137	Roy McMillan	20.00	8.00	2.00
☐	89	Johnny Lipon	20.00	8.00	2.00	☐	138	Bill MacDonald	20.00	8.00	2.00
☐	90	Mickey Grasso	20.00	8.00	2.00	☐	139	Ken Wood	20.00	8.00	2.00
☐	91	Red Schoendienst	32.00	13.00	3.20	☐	140	Johnny Antonelli	22.00	9.00	2.20
☐	92	Dale Mitchell	28.00	11.50	2.80	☐	141	Clint Hartung	20.00	8.00	2.00
☐	93	Al Sima	20.00	8.00	2.00	☐	142	Harry Perkowski	20.00	8.00	2.00
☐	94	Sam Mele	20.00	8.00	2.00	☐	143	Les Moss	20.00	8.00	2.00
☐	95	Ken Holcombe	20.00	8.00	2.00	☐	144	Ed Blake	20.00	8.00	2.00
☐	96	Willard Marshall	20.00	8.00	2.00	☐	145	Joe Haynes	20.00	8.00	2.00
☐	97	Earl Torgeson	20.00	8.00	2.00	☐	146	Frank House	20.00	8.00	2.00
☐	98	Billy Pierce	25.00	10.00	2.50	☐	147	Bob Young	20.00	8.00	2.00
☐	99	Gene Woodling	45.00	18.00	4.50	☐	148	Johnny Klippstein	20.00	8.00	2.00

	NRMT	VG-E	GOOD		NRMT	VG-E	GOOD
☐ 149 Dick Kryhoski	20.00	8.00	2.00	☐ 198 Phil Haugstad	20.00	8.00	2.00
☐ 150 Ted Beard	20.00	8.00	2.00	☐ 199 George Zuverink	20.00	8.00	2.00
☐ 151 Wally Post	22.00	9.00	2.20	☐ 200 Ralph Houk	60.00	24.00	6.00
☐ 152 Al Evans	20.00	8.00	2.00	☐ 201 Alex Kellner	20.00	8.00	2.00
☐ 153 Bob Rush	20.00	8.00	2.00	☐ 202 Joe Collins	25.00	10.00	2.50
☐ 154 Joe Muir	20.00	8.00	2.00	☐ 203 Curt Simmons	25.00	10.00	2.50
☐ 155 Frank Overmire	20.00	8.00	2.00	☐ 204 Ron Northey	20.00	8.00	2.00
☐ 156 Frank Hiller	20.00	8.00	2.00	☐ 205 Clyde King	22.00	9.00	2.20
☐ 157 Bob Usher	20.00	8.00	2.00	☐ 206 Joe Ostrowski	20.00	8.00	2.00
☐ 158 Eddie Waitkus	20.00	8.00	2.00	☐ 207 Mickey Harris	20.00	8.00	2.00
☐ 159 Saul Rogovin	20.00	8.00	2.00	☐ 208 Marlin Stuart	20.00	8.00	2.00
☐ 160 Owen Friend	20.00	8.00	2.00	☐ 209 Howie Fox	20.00	8.00	2.00
☐ 161 Bud Byerly	20.00	8.00	2.00	☐ 210 Dick Fowler	20.00	8.00	2.00
☐ 162 Del Crandall	22.00	9.00	2.20	☐ 211 Ray Coleman	20.00	8.00	2.00
☐ 163 Stan Rojek	20.00	8.00	2.00	☐ 212 Ned Garver	20.00	8.00	2.00
☐ 164 Walt Dubiel	20.00	8.00	2.00	☐ 213 Nippy Jones	20.00	8.00	2.00
☐ 165 Eddie Kazak	20.00	8.00	2.00	☐ 214 Johnny Hopp	22.00	9.00	2.20
☐ 166 Paul LaPalme	20.00	8.00	2.00	☐ 215 Hank Bauer	40.00	16.00	4.00
☐ 167 Bill Howerton	20.00	8.00	2.00	☐ 216 Richie Ashburn	45.00	18.00	4.50
☐ 168 Charlie Silvera	22.00	9.00	2.20	☐ 217 Snuffy Stirnweiss	22.00	9.00	2.20
☐ 169 Howie Judson	20.00	8.00	2.00	☐ 218 Clyde McCullough	20.00	8.00	2.00
☐ 170 Gus Bell	22.00	9.00	2.20	☐ 219 Bobby Shantz	27.00	11.00	2.70
☐ 171 Ed Erautt	20.00	8.00	2.00	☐ 220 Joe Presko	20.00	8.00	2.00
☐ 172 Eddie Miksis	20.00	8.00	2.00	☐ 221 Granny Hamner	20.00	8.00	2.00
☐ 173 Roy Smalley	20.00	8.00	2.00	☐ 222 Hoot Evers	20.00	8.00	2.00
☐ 174 Clarence Marshall	20.00	8.00	2.00	☐ 223 Del Ennis	22.00	9.00	2.20
☐ 175 Billy Martin	200.00	80.00	20.00	☐ 224 Bruce Edwards	20.00	8.00	2.00
☐ 176 Hank Edwards	20.00	8.00	2.00	☐ 225 Frank Baumholtz	20.00	8.00	2.00
☐ 177 Bill Wight	20.00	8.00	2.00	☐ 226 Dave Philley	20.00	8.00	2.00
☐ 178 Cass Michaels	20.00	8.00	2.00	☐ 227 Joe Garagiola	60.00	24.00	6.00
☐ 179 Frank Smith	20.00	8.00	2.00	☐ 228 Al Brazle	20.00	8.00	2.00
☐ 180 Charley Maxwell	20.00	8.00	2.00	☐ 229 Gene Bearden	20.00	8.00	2.00
☐ 181 Bob Swift	20.00	8.00	2.00	☐ 230 Matt Batts	20.00	8.00	2.00
☐ 182 Billy Hitchcock	20.00	8.00	2.00	☐ 231 Sam Zoldak	20.00	8.00	2.00
☐ 183 Erv Dusak	20.00	8.00	2.00	☐ 232 Billy Cox	24.00	10.00	2.40
☐ 184 Bob Ramazotti	20.00	8.00	2.00	☐ 233 Bob Friend	25.00	10.00	2.50
☐ 185 Bill Nicholson	20.00	8.00	2.00	☐ 234 Steve Souchock	20.00	8.00	2.00
☐ 186 Walt Masterson	20.00	8.00	2.00	☐ 235 Walt Dropo	22.00	9.00	2.20
☐ 187 Bob Miller	20.00	8.00	2.00	☐ 236 Ed Fitzgerald	20.00	8.00	2.00
☐ 188 Clarence Podbielan	20.00	8.00	2.00	☐ 237 Jerry Coleman	25.00	10.00	2.50
☐ 189 Pete Reiser	25.00	10.00	2.50	☐ 238 Art Houtteman	20.00	8.00	2.00
☐ 190 Don Johnson	20.00	8.00	2.00	☐ 239 Rocky Bridges	20.00	8.00	2.00
☐ 191 Yogi Berra	250.00	100.00	22.00	☐ 240 Jack Phillips	20.00	8.00	2.00
☐ 192 Myron Ginsberg	20.00	8.00	2.00	☐ 241 Tommy Byrne	22.00	9.00	2.20
☐ 193 Harry Simpson	20.00	8.00	2.00	☐ 242 Tom Poholsky	20.00	8.00	2.00
☐ 194 Joe Hatton	20.00	8.00	2.00	☐ 243 Larry Doby	30.00	12.00	3.00
☐ 195 Minnie Minoso	50.00	20.00	5.00	☐ 244 Vic Wertz	22.00	9.00	2.20
☐ 196 Solly Hemus	20.00	8.00	2.00	☐ 245 Sherry Robertson	20.00	8.00	2.00
☐ 197 George Strickland	20.00	8.00	2.00	☐ 246 George Kell	60.00	24.00	6.00

		NRMT	VG-E	GOOD
☐ 247	Randy Gumpert ...	20.00	8.00	2.00
☐ 248	Frank Shea	20.00	8.00	2.00
☐ 249	Bobby Adams	20.00	8.00	2.00
☐ 250	Carl Erskine	50.00	20.00	5.00
☐ 251	Chico Carrasquel ..	40.00	16.00	4.00
☐ 252	Vern Bickford	40.00	16.00	4.00
☐ 253	Johnny Berardino ..	50.00	20.00	5.00
☐ 254	Joe Dobson	40.00	16.00	4.00
☐ 255	Clyde Vollmer	40.00	16.00	4.00
☐ 256	Pete Suder	40.00	16.00	4.00
☐ 257	Bobby Avila	45.00	18.00	4.50
☐ 258	Steve Gromek	40.00	16.00	4.00
☐ 259	Bob Addis	40.00	16.00	4.00
☐ 260	Pete Castiglione ..	40.00	16.00	4.00
☐ 261	Willie Mays 1000.00	400.00	100.00	
☐ 262	Virgil Trucks	45.00	18.00	4.50
☐ 263	Harry Brecheen ...	40.00	16.00	4.00
☐ 264	Roy Hartsfield	40.00	16.00	4.00
☐ 265	Chuck Diering	40.00	16.00	4.00
☐ 266	Murry Dickson	40.00	16.00	4.00
☐ 267	Sid Gordon	40.00	16.00	4.00
☐ 268	Bob Lemon	150.00	60.00	15.00
☐ 269	Willard Nixon	40.00	16.00	4.00
☐ 270	Lou Brissie	40.00	16.00	4.00
☐ 271	Jim Delsing	40.00	16.00	4.00
☐ 272	Mike Garcia	50.00	20.00	5.00
☐ 273	Erv Palica	40.00	16.00	4.00
☐ 274	Ralph Branca	75.00	30.00	7.50
☐ 275	Pat Mullin	40.00	16.00	4.00
☐ 276	Jim Wilson	40.00	16.00	4.00
☐ 277	Early Wynn	150.00	60.00	15.00
☐ 278	Allie Clark	40.00	16.00	4.00
☐ 279	Eddie Stewart	40.00	16.00	4.00
☐ 280	Cloyd Boyer	45.00	18.00	4.50
☐ 281	Tommy Brown SP ..	50.00	20.00	5.00
☐ 282	Birdie Tebbetts SP .	55.00	22.00	5.50
☐ 283	Phil Masi SP	50.00	20.00	5.00
☐ 284	Hank Arft SP	50.00	20.00	5.00
☐ 285	Cliff Fannin SP ...	50.00	20.00	5.00
☐ 286	Joe DeMaestri SP .	50.00	20.00	5.00
☐ 287	Steve Bilko SP	50.00	20.00	5.00
☐ 288	Chet Nichols SP ...	50.00	20.00	5.00
☐ 289	Tommy Holmes SP .	55.00	22.00	5.50
☐ 290	Joe Astroth SP ...	50.00	20.00	5.00
☐ 291	Gil Coan SP	50.00	20.00	5.00
☐ 292	Floyd Baker SP ...	50.00	20.00	5.00
☐ 293	Sibby Sisti SP	50.00	20.00	5.00
☐ 294	Walker Cooper SP .	50.00	20.00	5.00
☐ 295	Phil Cavarretta SP .	60.00	24.00	6.00
☐ 296	Red Rolfe SP	60.00	24.00	6.00
☐ 297	Andy Seminick SP .	50.00	20.00	5.00
☐ 298	Bob Ross SP	50.00	20.00	5.00
☐ 299	Ray Murray SP ...	50.00	20.00	5.00
☐ 300	Barney McCosky SP	50.00	20.00	5.00
☐ 301	Bob Porterfield ...	40.00	16.00	4.00
☐ 302	Max Surkont	40.00	16.00	4.00
☐ 303	Harry Dorish	40.00	16.00	4.00
☐ 304	Sam Dente	40.00	16.00	4.00
☐ 305	Paul Richards	50.00	20.00	5.00
☐ 306	Lou Sleater	40.00	16.00	4.00
☐ 307	Frank Campos	40.00	16.00	4.00
☐ 308	Luis Aloma	40.00	16.00	4.00
☐ 309	Jim Busby	40.00	16.00	4.00
☐ 310	George Metkovich .	60.00	24.00	6.00
☐ 311	Mickey Mantle DP .	6500.00	2000.00	500.00
☐ 312	Jackie Robinson DP	800.00	320.00	80.00
☐ 313	Bobby Thomson DP	175.00	70.00	18.00
☐ 314	Roy Campanella ..	1250.00	500.00	100.00
☐ 315	Leo Durocher	250.00	100.00	25.00
☐ 316	Dave Williams	175.00	70.00	18.00
☐ 317	Conrado Marrero ..	150.00	60.00	15.00
☐ 318	Harold Gregg	150.00	60.00	15.00
☐ 319	Al Walker	150.00	60.00	15.00
☐ 320	John Rutherford ...	150.00	60.00	15.00
☐ 321	Joe Black	200.00	80.00	20.00
☐ 322	Randy Jackson	150.00	60.00	15.00
☐ 323	Bubba Church	150.00	60.00	15.00
☐ 324	Warren Hacker	150.00	60.00	15.00
☐ 325	Bill Serena	150.00	60.00	15.00
☐ 326	George Shuba	175.00	70.00	18.00
☐ 327	Al Wilson	150.00	60.00	15.00
☐ 328	Bob Borkowski	150.00	60.00	15.00
☐ 329	Ike Delock	150.00	60.00	15.00
☐ 330	Turk Lown	150.00	60.00	15.00
☐ 331	Tom Morgan	150.00	60.00	15.00
☐ 332	Anthony Bartirome .	150.00	60.00	15.00
☐ 333	Pee Wee Reese ..	600.00	240.00	60.00
☐ 334	Wilmer Mizell	150.00	60.00	15.00
☐ 335	Ted Lepcio	150.00	60.00	15.00
☐ 336	Dave Koslo	150.00	60.00	15.00
☐ 337	Jim Hearn	150.00	60.00	15.00
☐ 338	Sal Yvars	150.00	60.00	15.00
☐ 339	Russ Meyer	150.00	60.00	15.00
☐ 340	Bob Hooper	150.00	60.00	15.00
☐ 341	Hal Jeffcoat	150.00	60.00	15.00
☐ 342	Clem Labine	175.00	70.00	18.00
☐ 343	Dick Gernert	150.00	60.00	15.00
☐ 344	Ewell Blackwell ...	175.00	70.00	18.00

		NRMT	VG-E	GOOD
☐ 345	Sammy White	150.00	60.00	15.00
☐ 346	George Spencer	150.00	60.00	15.00
☐ 347	Joe Adcock	200.00	80.00	20.00
☐ 348	Robert Kelly	150.00	60.00	15.00
☐ 349	Bob Cain	150.00	60.00	15.00
☐ 350	Cal Abrams	150.00	60.00	15.00
☐ 351	Alvin Dark	200.00	80.00	20.00
☐ 352	Karl Drews	150.00	60.00	15.00
☐ 353	Bobby Del Greco	150.00	60.00	15.00
☐ 354	Fred Hatfield	150.00	60.00	15.00
☐ 355	Bobby Morgan	150.00	60.00	15.00
☐ 356	Toby Atwell	150.00	60.00	15.00
☐ 357	Smoky Burgess	175.00	70.00	18.00
☐ 358	John Kucab	150.00	60.00	15.00
☐ 359	Dee Fondy	150.00	60.00	15.00
☐ 360	George Crowe	150.00	60.00	15.00
☐ 361	William Posedel	150.00	60.00	15.00
☐ 362	Ken Heintzelman	150.00	60.00	15.00
☐ 363	Dick Rozek	150.00	60.00	15.00
☐ 364	Clyde Sukeforth	150.00	60.00	15.00
☐ 365	Cookie Lavagetto	150.00	60.00	15.00
☐ 366	Dave Madison	150.00	60.00	15.00
☐ 367	Ben Thorpe	150.00	60.00	15.00
☐ 368	Ed Wright	150.00	60.00	15.00
☐ 369	Dick Groat	250.00	100.00	25.00
☐ 370	Billy Hoeft	150.00	60.00	15.00
☐ 371	Bobby Hofman	150.00	60.00	15.00
☐ 372	Gil McDougald	275.00	110.00	27.00
☐ 373	Jim Turner CO	175.00	70.00	18.00
☐ 374	John Benton	150.00	60.00	15.00
☐ 375	John Merson	150.00	60.00	15.00
☐ 376	Faye Throneberry	150.00	60.00	15.00
☐ 377	Chuck Dressen MG	175.00	70.00	18.00
☐ 378	Leroy Fusselman	150.00	60.00	15.00
☐ 379	Joe Rossi	150.00	60.00	15.00
☐ 380	Clem Koshorek	150.00	60.00	15.00
☐ 381	Milton Stock	150.00	60.00	15.00
☐ 382	Sam Jones	175.00	70.00	18.00
☐ 383	Del Wilber	150.00	60.00	15.00
☐ 384	Frank Crosetti CO	250.00	100.00	25.00
☐ 385	Herman Franks	175.00	70.00	18.00
☐ 386	John Yuhas	150.00	60.00	15.00
☐ 387	Billy Meyer	150.00	60.00	15.00
☐ 388	Bob Chipman	150.00	60.00	15.00
☐ 389	Ben Wade	150.00	60.00	15.00
☐ 390	Glenn Nelson	150.00	60.00	15.00
☐ 391	Ben Chapman	150.00	60.00	15.00
	(photo actually Sam Chapman)			
☐ 392	Hoyt Wilhelm	425.00	170.00	42.00

		NRMT	VG-E	GOOD
☐ 393	Ebba St.Claire	150.00	60.00	15.00
☐ 394	Billy Herman CO	225.00	90.00	22.00
☐ 395	Jake Pitler CO	150.00	60.00	15.00
☐ 396	Dick Williams	200.00	80.00	20.00
☐ 397	Forrest Main	150.00	60.00	15.00
☐ 398	Hal Rice	150.00	60.00	15.00
☐ 399	Jim Fridley	150.00	60.00	15.00
☐ 400	Bill Dickey CO	500.00	200.00	50.00
☐ 401	Bob Schultz	150.00	60.00	15.00
☐ 402	Earl Harrist	150.00	60.00	15.00
☐ 403	Bill Miller	150.00	60.00	15.00
☐ 404	Dick Brodowski	150.00	60.00	15.00
☐ 405	Eddie Pellagrini	150.00	60.00	15.00
☐ 406	Joe Nuxhall	200.00	80.00	20.00
☐ 407	Eddie Mathews	1500.00	400.00	80.00

1953 Topps

*The cards in this 274-card set measure 2⅝"
by 3¾". Although the last card is numbered
280, there are only 274 cards in the set since
numbers 253, 261, 267, 268, 271, and 275
were not issued. The 1953 Topps series
contains line drawings of players in full color.
The name and team panel at the card base
is easily damaged, making it very difficult to
complete a mint set. The high number
series, 221 to 280, was produced in shorter
supply late in the year and hence is more
difficult to complete than the lower numbers.
The key cards in the set are Mickey Mantle
#82 and Willie Mays #244. There are a num-
ber of double-printed cards (actually not*

double but 50% more of each of these numbers were printed compared to the other cards in the series) indicated by DP in the checklist below. In addition there are five numbers which were printed in with the more plentiful series 166-220; these cards (94, 107, 131, 145, and 156) are also indicated by DP in the checklist below. There were some three-card advertising panels produced by Topps; the players include Johnny Mize, Clem Koshorek, and Toby Atwell and Mickey Mantle, Johnny Wyrostek, and Sal Yvars. When cut apart, these advertising cards are distinguished by the nonstandard card back, i.e., part of an advertisement for the 1953 Topps set instead of the typical statistics and biographical information about the player pictured.

	NRMT	VG-E	GOOD
Complete Set (274)	10500.00	4500.00	1500.00
Common Player (1-165)	20.00	8.00	2.00
Common DP (1-165)	12.00	5.00	1.20
Common Player (166-220)	12.00	5.00	1.20
Common Player (221-280)	60.00	24.00	6.00
Common DP (221-280)	30.00	12.00	3.00

		NRMT	VG-E	GOOD
☐	1 Jackie Robinson DP	400.00	100.00	20.00
☐	2 Luke Easter DP	12.00	5.00	1.20
☐	3 George Crowe DP	12.00	5.00	1.20
☐	4 Ben Wade	20.00	8.00	2.00
☐	5 Joe Dobson	20.00	8.00	2.00
☐	6 Sam Jones	20.00	8.00	2.00
☐	7 Bob Borkowski DP	12.00	5.00	1.20
☐	8 Clem Koshorek DP	12.00	5.00	1.20
☐	9 Joe Collins	27.00	11.00	2.70
☐	10 Smoky Burgess	22.00	9.00	2.20
☐	11 Sal Yvars	20.00	8.00	2.00
☐	12 Howie Judson DP	12.00	5.00	1.20
☐	13 Conrado Marrero DP	12.00	5.00	1.20
☐	14 Clem Labine	27.00	11.00	2.70
☐	15 Bobo Newsom	22.00	9.00	2.20
☐	16 Peanuts Lowrey	20.00	8.00	2.00
☐	17 Billy Hitchcock	20.00	8.00	2.00
☐	18 Ted Lepcio DP	12.00	5.00	1.20
☐	19 Mel Parnell DP	14.00	5.75	1.40
☐	20 Hank Thompson	22.00	9.00	2.20
☐	21 Billy Johnson	20.00	8.00	2.00
☐	22 Howie Fox	20.00	8.00	2.00
☐	23 Toby Atwell DP	12.00	5.00	1.20
☐	24 Ferris Fain	22.00	9.00	2.20
☐	25 Ray Boone	22.00	9.00	2.20
☐	26 Dale Mitchell DP	14.00	5.75	1.40
☐	27 Roy Campanella DP	135.00	54.00	13.50
☐	28 Eddie Pellagrini	20.00	8.00	2.00
☐	29 Hal Jeffcoat	20.00	8.00	2.00
☐	30 Willard Nixon	20.00	8.00	2.00
☐	31 Ewell Blackwell	27.00	11.00	2.70
☐	32 Clyde Vollmer	20.00	8.00	2.00
☐	33 Bob Kennedy DP	12.00	5.00	1.20
☐	34 George Shuba	22.00	9.00	2.20
☐	35 Irv Noren DP	12.00	5.00	1.20
☐	36 Johnny Groth DP	12.00	5.00	1.20
☐	37 Eddie Mathews DP	70.00	28.00	7.00
☐	38 Jim Hearn DP	12.00	5.00	1.20
☐	39 Eddie Miksis	20.00	8.00	2.00
☐	40 John Lipon	20.00	8.00	2.00
☐	41 Enos Slaughter	55.00	22.00	5.50
☐	42 Gus Zernial DP	10.00	4.00	1.00
☐	43 Gil McDougald	30.00	12.00	3.00
☐	44 Ellis Kinder	20.00	8.00	2.00
☐	45 Grady Hatton DP	12.00	5.00	1.20
☐	46 Johnny Klippstein DP	12.00	5.00	1.20
☐	47 Bubba Church DP	12.00	5.00	1.20
☐	48 Bob Del Greco DP	12.00	5.00	1.20
☐	49 Faye Throneberry DP	12.00	5.00	1.20
☐	50 Chuck Dressen MG DP	14.00	5.75	1.40
☐	51 Frank Campos DP	12.00	5.00	1.20
☐	52 Ted Gray DP	12.00	5.00	1.20
☐	53 Sherm Lollar DP	14.00	5.75	1.40
☐	54 Bob Feller	80.00	32.00	8.00
☐	55 Maurice McDermott DP	12.00	5.00	1.20
☐	56 Jerry Staley DP	12.00	5.00	1.20
☐	57 Carl Scheib DP	12.00	5.00	1.20
☐	58 George Metkovich	20.00	8.00	2.00
☐	59 Karl Drews DP	12.00	5.00	1.20
☐	60 Cloyd Boyer DP	12.00	5.00	1.20
☐	61 Early Wynn	55.00	22.00	5.50
☐	62 Monte Irvin DP	27.00	11.00	2.70
☐	63 Gus Niarhos DP	12.00	5.00	1.20
☐	64 Dave Philley	20.00	8.00	2.00
☐	65 Earl Harrist	20.00	8.00	2.00
☐	66 Minnie Minoso	27.00	11.00	2.70
☐	67 Roy Sievers DP	14.00	5.75	1.40
☐	68 Del Rice	20.00	8.00	2.00
☐	69 Dick Brodowski DP	12.00	5.00	1.20
☐	70 Ed Yuhas	20.00	8.00	2.00
☐	71 Tony Bartirome	20.00	8.00	2.00
☐	72 Fred Hutchinson	22.00	9.00	2.20
☐	73 Eddie Robinson	20.00	8.00	2.00

		NRMT	VG-E	GOOD			NRMT	VG-E	GOOD
☐	74 Joe Rossi	20.00	8.00	2.00	☐ 123	Tommy Byrne DP	14.00	5.75	1.40
☐	75 Mike Garcia	22.00	9.00	2.20	☐ 124	Sibby Sisti DP	12.00	5.00	1.20
☐	76 Pee Wee Reese	90.00	36.00	9.00	☐ 125	Dick Williams DP	15.00	6.00	1.50
☐	77 Johnny Mize DP	45.00	18.00	4.50	☐ 126	Bill Connelly DP	12.00	5.00	1.20
☐	78 Al (Red) Schoendienst	30.00	12.00	3.00	☐ 127	Clint Courtney DP	12.00	5.00	1.20
☐	79 Johnny Wyrostek DP	12.00	5.00	1.20	☐ 128	Wilmer Mizell DP	12.00	5.00	1.20
☐	80 Jim Hegan	22.00	9.00	2.20	☐ 129	Keith Thomas	20.00	8.00	2.00
☐	81 Joe Black	30.00	12.00	3.00	☐ 130	Turk Lown DP	12.00	5.00	1.20
☐	82 Mickey Mantle	1750.00	650.00	150.00	☐ 131	Harry Byrd DP	12.00	5.00	1.20
☐	83 Howie Pollet	20.00	8.00	2.00	☐ 132	Tom Morgan	20.00	8.00	2.00
☐	84 Bob Hooper DP	12.00	5.00	1.20	☐ 133	Gil Coan	20.00	8.00	2.00
☐	85 Bobby Morgan DP	12.00	5.00	1.20	☐ 134	Rube Walker	22.00	9.00	2.20
☐	86 Billy Martin	65.00	26.00	6.50	☐ 135	Al Rosen DP	25.00	10.00	2.50
☐	87 Ed Lopat	32.00	13.00	3.20	☐ 136	Ken Heintzelman DP	12.00	5.00	1.20
☐	88 Willie Jones DP	12.00	5.00	1.20	☐ 137	John Rutherford DP	12.00	5.00	1.20
☐	89 Chuck Stobbs DP	12.00	5.00	1.20	☐ 138	George Kell	45.00	18.00	4.50
☐	90 Hank Edwards DP	12.00	5.00	1.20	☐ 139	Sammy White	20.00	8.00	2.00
☐	91 Ebba St.Claire DP	12.00	5.00	1.20	☐ 140	Tommy Glaviano	20.00	8.00	2.00
☐	92 Paul Minner DP	12.00	5.00	1.20	☐ 141	Allie Reynolds DP	25.00	10.00	2.50
☐	93 Hal Rice DP	12.00	5.00	1.20	☐ 142	Vic Wertz	22.00	9.00	2.20
☐	94 Bill Kennedy DP	12.00	5.00	1.20	☐ 143	Billy Pierce	27.00	11.00	2.70
☐	95 Willard Marshall DP	12.00	5.00	1.20	☐ 144	Bob Schultz DP	12.00	5.00	1.20
☐	96 Virgil Trucks	22.00	9.00	2.20	☐ 145	Harry Dorish DP	12.00	5.00	1.20
☐	97 Don Kolloway DP	12.00	5.00	1.20	☐ 146	Granny Hamner	20.00	8.00	2.00
☐	98 Cal Abrams DP	12.00	5.00	1.20	☐ 147	Warren Spahn	80.00	32.00	8.00
☐	99 Dave Madison	20.00	8.00	2.00	☐ 148	Mickey Grasso	20.00	8.00	2.00
☐	100 Bill Miller	20.00	8.00	2.00	☐ 149	Dom DiMaggio DP	25.00	10.00	2.50
☐	101 Ted Wilks	20.00	8.00	2.00	☐ 150	Harry Simpson DP	12.00	5.00	1.20
☐	102 Connie Ryan DP	12.00	5.00	1.20	☐ 151	Hoyt Wilhelm	50.00	20.00	5.00
☐	103 Joe Astroth DP	12.00	5.00	1.20	☐ 152	Bob Adams DP	12.00	5.00	1.20
☐	104 Yogi Berra	135.00	54.00	13.50	☐ 153	Andy Seminick DP	12.00	5.00	1.20
☐	105 Joe Nuxhall DP	14.00	5.75	1.40	☐ 154	Dick Groat	27.00	11.00	2.70
☐	106 Johnny Antonelli	22.00	9.00	2.20	☐ 155	Dutch Leonard	20.00	8.00	2.00
☐	107 Danny O'Connell DP	12.00	5.00	1.20	☐ 156	Jim Rivera DP	12.00	5.00	1.20
☐	108 Bob Porterfield DP	12.00	5.00	1.20	☐ 157	Bob Addis DP	12.00	5.00	1.20
☐	109 Alvin Dark	25.00	10.00	2.50	☐ 158	Johnny Logan	22.00	9.00	2.20
☐	110 Herman Wehmeier DP	12.00	5.00	1.20	☐ 159	Wayne Terwilliger DP	12.00	5.00	1.20
☐	111 Hank Sauer DP	14.00	5.75	1.40	☐ 160	Bob Young	20.00	8.00	2.00
☐	112 Ned Garver DP	12.00	5.00	1.20	☐ 161	Vern Bickford DP	12.00	5.00	1.20
☐	113 Jerry Priddy	20.00	8.00	2.00	☐ 162	Ted Kluszewski	32.00	13.00	3.20
☐	114 Phil Rizzuto	65.00	26.00	6.50	☐ 163	Fred Hatfield DP	12.00	5.00	1.20
☐	115 George Spencer	20.00	8.00	2.00	☐ 164	Frank Shea DP	12.00	5.00	1.20
☐	116 Frank Smith DP	12.00	5.00	1.20	☐ 165	Billy Hoeft	20.00	8.00	2.00
☐	117 Sid Gordon DP	12.00	5.00	1.20	☐ 166	Billy Hunter	12.00	5.00	1.20
☐	118 Gus Bell DP	14.00	5.75	1.40	☐ 167	Art Schult	12.00	5.00	1.20
☐	119 Johnny Sain	32.00	13.00	3.20	☐ 168	Willard Schmidt	12.00	5.00	1.20
☐	120 Davey Williams	25.00	10.00	2.50	☐ 169	Dizzy Trout	12.00	5.00	1.20
☐	121 Walt Dropo	22.00	9.00	2.20	☐ 170	Bill Werle	12.00	5.00	1.20
☐	122 Elmer Valo	20.00	8.00	2.00	☐ 171	Bill Glynn	12.00	5.00	1.20

	NRMT	VG-E	GOOD
☐ 172 Rip Repulski	12.00	5.00	1.20
☐ 173 Preston Ward	12.00	5.00	1.20
☐ 174 Billy Loes	14.00	5.75	1.40
☐ 175 Ron Kline	12.00	5.00	1.20
☐ 176 Don Hoak	14.00	5.75	1.40
☐ 177 Jim Dyck	12.00	5.00	1.20
☐ 178 Jim Waugh	12.00	5.00	1.20
☐ 179 Gene Hermanski	12.00	5.00	1.20
☐ 180 Virgil Stallcup	12.00	5.00	1.20
☐ 181 Al Zarilla	12.00	5.00	1.20
☐ 182 Bobby Hofman	12.00	5.00	1.20
☐ 183 Stu Miller	12.00	5.00	1.20
☐ 184 Hal Brown	12.00	5.00	1.20
☐ 185 Jim Pendleton	12.00	5.00	1.20
☐ 186 Charlie Bishop	12.00	5.00	1.20
☐ 187 Jim Fridley	12.00	5.00	1.20
☐ 188 Andy Carey	14.00	5.75	1.40
☐ 189 Ray Jablonski	12.00	5.00	1.20
☐ 190 Dixie Walker	12.00	5.00	1.20
☐ 191 Ralph Kiner	40.00	16.00	4.00
☐ 192 Wally Westlake	12.00	5.00	1.20
☐ 193 Mike Clark	12.00	5.00	1.20
☐ 194 Eddie Kazak	12.00	5.00	1.20
☐ 195 Ed McGhee	12.00	5.00	1.20
☐ 196 Bob Keegan	12.00	5.00	1.20
☐ 197 Del Crandall	14.00	5.75	1.40
☐ 198 Forrest Main	12.00	5.00	1.20
☐ 199 Marion Fricano	12.00	5.00	1.20
☐ 200 Gordon Goldsberry	12.00	5.00	1.20
☐ 201 Paul LaPalme	12.00	5.00	1.20
☐ 202 Carl Sawatski	12.00	5.00	1.20
☐ 203 Cliff Fannin	12.00	5.00	1.20
☐ 204 Dick Bokelman	12.00	5.00	1.20
☐ 205 Vern Benson	12.00	5.00	1.20
☐ 206 Ed Bailey	14.00	5.75	1.40
☐ 207 Whitey Ford	70.00	28.00	7.00
☐ 208 Jim Wilson	12.00	5.00	1.20
☐ 209 Jim Greengrass	12.00	5.00	1.20
☐ 210 Bob Cerv	14.00	5.75	1.40
☐ 211 J.W. Porter	12.00	5.00	1.20
☐ 212 Jack Dittmer	12.00	5.00	1.20
☐ 213 Ray Scarborough	12.00	5.00	1.20
☐ 214 Bill Bruton	14.00	5.75	1.40
☐ 215 Gene Conley	14.00	5.75	1.40
☐ 216 Jim Hughes	12.00	5.00	1.20
☐ 217 Murray Wall	12.00	5.00	1.20
☐ 218 Les Fusselman	12.00	5.00	1.20
☐ 219 Pete Runnels	12.00	5.00	1.20
(photo actually Don Johnson)			

	NRMT	VG-E	GOOD
☐ 220 Satchel Paige UER	275.00	110.00	27.00
(misspelled Satchell on card front)			
☐ 221 Bob Milliken	60.00	24.00	6.00
☐ 222 Vic Janowicz DP	30.00	12.00	3.00
☐ 223 Johnny O'Brien DP	30.00	12.00	3.00
☐ 224 Lou Sleater DP	30.00	12.00	3.00
☐ 225 Bobby Shantz	75.00	30.00	7.50
☐ 226 Ed Erautt	60.00	24.00	6.00
☐ 227 Morrie Martin	60.00	24.00	6.00
☐ 228 Hal Newhouser	90.00	36.00	9.00
☐ 229 Rocky Krsnich	60.00	24.00	6.00
☐ 230 Johnny Lindell DP	30.00	12.00	3.00
☐ 231 Solly Hemus DP	30.00	12.00	3.00
☐ 232 Dick Kokos	60.00	24.00	6.00
☐ 233 Al Aber	60.00	24.00	6.00
☐ 234 Ray Murray DP	30.00	12.00	3.00
☐ 235 John Hetki DP	30.00	12.00	3.00
☐ 236 Harry Perkowski DP	30.00	12.00	3.00
☐ 237 Bud Podbielan DP	30.00	12.00	3.00
☐ 238 Cal Hogue DP	30.00	12.00	3.00
☐ 239 Jim Delsing	60.00	24.00	6.00
☐ 240 Fred Marsh	60.00	24.00	6.00
☐ 241 Al Sima DP	30.00	12.00	3.00
☐ 242 Charlie Silvera	60.00	24.00	6.00
☐ 243 Carlos Bernier DP	30.00	12.00	3.00
☐ 244 Willie Mays	1400.00	500.00	125.00
☐ 245 Bill Norman	60.00	24.00	6.00
☐ 246 Roy Face DP	60.00	24.00	6.00
☐ 247 Mike Sandlock DP	30.00	12.00	3.00
☐ 248 Gene Stephens DP	30.00	12.00	3.00
☐ 249 Eddie O'Brien	60.00	24.00	6.00
☐ 250 Bob Wilson	60.00	24.00	6.00
☐ 251 Sid Hudson	60.00	24.00	6.00
☐ 252 Hank Foiles	60.00	24.00	6.00
☐ 253 Does not exist	0.00	.00	.00
☐ 254 Preacher Roe DP	60.00	24.00	6.00
☐ 255 Dixie Howell	60.00	24.00	6.00
☐ 256 Les Peden	60.00	24.00	6.00
☐ 257 Bob Boyd	60.00	24.00	6.00
☐ 258 Jim Gilliam	275.00	110.00	27.00
☐ 259 Roy McMillan DP	30.00	12.00	3.00
☐ 260 Sam Calderone	75.00	30.00	7.50
☐ 261 Does not exist	0.00	.00	.00
☐ 262 Bob Oldis	60.00	24.00	6.00
☐ 263 Johnny Podres	250.00	100.00	25.00
☐ 264 Gene Woodling DP	60.00	24.00	6.00
☐ 265 Jackie Jensen	100.00	40.00	10.00
☐ 266 Bob Cain	60.00	24.00	6.00
☐ 267 Does not exist	0.00	.00	.00

		NRMT	VG-E	GOOD
☐ 268	Does not exist	0.00	.00	.00
☐ 269	Duane Pillette	60.00	24.00	6.00
☐ 270	Vern Stephens	75.00	30.00	7.50
☐ 271	Does not exist	0.00	.00	.00
☐ 272	Bill Antonello	60.00	24.00	6.00
☐ 273	Harvey Haddix	90.00	36.00	9.00
☐ 274	John Riddle	60.00	24.00	6.00
☐ 275	Does not exist	0.00	.00	.00
☐ 276	Ken Raffensberger	60.00	24.00	6.00
☐ 277	Don Lund	60.00	24.00	6.00
☐ 278	Willie Miranda	75.00	30.00	7.50
☐ 279	Joe Coleman DP	30.00	12.00	3.00
☐ 280	Milt Bolling	225.00	35.00	7.00

1954 Topps

The cards in this 250-card set measure 2 ⅝"
by 3 ¾". Each of the cards in the 1954 Topps
set contains a large "head" shot of the player
in color plus a smaller full-length photo in
black and white set against a color background. This series contains the rookie
cards of Hank Aaron, Ernie Banks, and Al
Kaline and two separate cards of Ted Williams (number 1 and number 250). Con-
spicuous by his absence is Mickey Mantle
who apparently was the exclusive property
of Bowman during 1954 (and 1955).

	NRMT	VG-E	GOOD
Complete Set (250)	.6000.00	2500.00	900.00
Common Player (1-50)	7.00	2.80	.70
Common Player (51-75)	18.00	7.25	1.80

		NRMT	VG-E	GOOD
Common Player (76-125)		8.00	3.25	.80
Common Player (126-250)		10.00	4.00	1.00
☐ 1	Ted Williams	500.00	125.00	25.00
☐ 2	Gus Zernial	8.00	3.25	.80
☐ 3	Monte Irvin	21.00	8.50	2.10
☐ 4	Hank Sauer	8.00	3.25	.80
☐ 5	Ed Lopat	14.00	5.75	1.40
☐ 6	Pete Runnels	8.00	3.25	.80
☐ 7	Ted Kluszewski	13.00	5.25	1.30
☐ 8	Bob Young	7.00	2.80	.70
☐ 9	Harvey Haddix	8.00	3.25	.80
☐ 10	Jackie Robinson	175.00	70.00	18.00
☐ 11	Paul Leslie Smith	7.00	2.80	.70
☐ 12	Del Crandall	8.00	3.25	.80
☐ 13	Billy Martin	45.00	18.00	4.50
☐ 14	Preacher Roe	13.00	5.25	1.30
☐ 15	Al Rosen	12.00	5.00	1.20
☐ 16	Vic Janowicz	8.00	3.25	.80
☐ 17	Phil Rizzuto	45.00	18.00	4.50
☐ 18	Walt Dropo	7.00	2.80	.70
☐ 19	Johnny Lipon	7.00	2.80	.70
☐ 20	Warren Spahn	55.00	22.00	5.50
☐ 21	Bobby Shantz	9.00	3.75	.90
☐ 22	Jim Greengrass	7.00	2.80	.70
☐ 23	Luke Easter	8.00	3.25	.80
☐ 24	Granny Hamner	7.00	2.80	.70
☐ 25	Harvey Kuenn	20.00	8.00	2.00
☐ 26	Ray Jablonski	7.00	2.80	.70
☐ 27	Ferris Fain	8.00	3.25	.80
☐ 28	Paul Minner	7.00	2.80	.70
☐ 29	Jim Hegan	8.00	3.25	.80
☐ 30	Eddie Mathews	45.00	18.00	4.50
☐ 31	Johnny Klippstein	7.00	2.80	.70
☐ 32	Duke Snider	100.00	40.00	10.00
☐ 33	Johnny Schmitz	7.00	2.80	.70
☐ 34	Jim Rivera	7.00	2.80	.70
☐ 35	Jim Gilliam	13.00	5.25	1.30
☐ 36	Hoyt Wilhelm	24.00	10.00	2.40
☐ 37	Whitey Ford	55.00	22.00	5.50
☐ 38	Eddie Stanky	8.00	3.25	.80
☐ 39	Sherm Lollar	8.00	3.25	.80
☐ 40	Mel Parnell	8.00	3.25	.80
☐ 41	Willie Jones	7.00	2.80	.70
☐ 42	Don Mueller	8.00	3.25	.80
☐ 43	Dick Groat	9.00	3.75	.90
☐ 44	Ned Garver	7.00	2.80	.70
☐ 45	Richie Ashburn	16.00	6.50	1.60
☐ 46	Ken Raffensberger	7.00	2.80	.70

			NRMT	VG-E	GOOD
☐	47	Ellis Kinder	7.00	2.80	.70
☐	48	Billy Hunter	7.00	2.80	.70
☐	49	Ray Murray	7.00	2.80	.70
☐	50	Yogi Berra	150.00	60.00	15.00
☐	51	Johnny Lindell	18.00	7.25	1.80
☐	52	Vic Power	20.00	8.00	2.00
☐	53	Jack Dittmer	18.00	7.25	1.80
☐	54	Vern Stephens	22.00	9.00	2.20
☐	55	Phil Cavarretta	22.00	9.00	2.20
☐	56	Willie Miranda	18.00	7.25	1.80
☐	57	Luis Aloma	18.00	7.25	1.80
☐	58	Bob Wilson	18.00	7.25	1.80
☐	59	Gene Conley	20.00	8.00	2.00
☐	60	Frank Baumholtz	18.00	7.25	1.80
☐	61	Bob Cain	18.00	7.25	1.80
☐	62	Eddie Robinson	20.00	8.00	2.00
☐	63	Johnny Pesky	20.00	8.00	2.00
☐	64	Hank Thompson	22.00	9.00	2.20
☐	65	Bob Swift	18.00	7.25	1.80
☐	66	Ted Lepcio	18.00	7.25	1.80
☐	67	Jim Willis	18.00	7.25	1.80
☐	68	Sam Calderone	18.00	7.25	1.80
☐	69	Bud Podbielan	18.00	7.25	1.80
☐	70	Larry Doby	30.00	12.00	3.00
☐	71	Frank Smith	18.00	7.25	1.80
☐	72	Preston Ward	18.00	7.25	1.80
☐	73	Wayne Terwilliger	18.00	7.25	1.80
☐	74	Bill Taylor	18.00	7.25	1.80
☐	75	Fred Haney	18.00	7.25	1.80
☐	76	Bob Scheffing	8.00	3.25	.80
☐	77	Ray Boone	9.00	3.75	.90
☐	78	Ted Kazanski	8.00	3.25	.80
☐	79	Andy Pafko	9.00	3.75	.90
☐	80	Jackie Jensen	12.00	5.00	1.20
☐	81	Dave Hoskins	8.00	3.25	.80
☐	82	Milt Bolling	8.00	3.25	.80
☐	83	Joe Collins	10.00	4.00	1.00
☐	84	Dick Cole	8.00	3.25	.80
☐	85	Bob Turley	15.00	6.00	1.50
☐	86	Billy Herman	15.00	6.00	1.50
☐	87	Roy Face	12.00	5.00	1.20
☐	88	Matt Batts	8.00	3.25	.80
☐	89	Howie Pollet	8.00	3.25	.80
☐	90	Willie Mays	250.00	100.00	25.00
☐	91	Bob Oldis	8.00	3.25	.80
☐	92	Wally Westlake	8.00	3.25	.80
☐	93	Sid Hudson	8.00	3.25	.80
☐	94	Ernie Banks	500.00	200.00	50.00
☐	95	Hal Rice	8.00	3.25	.80
☐	96	Charlie Silvera	8.00	3.25	.80
☐	97	Jerald Hal Lane	8.00	3.25	.80
☐	98	Joe Black	11.00	4.50	1.10
☐	99	Bobby Hofman	8.00	3.25	.80
☐	100	Bob Keegan	8.00	3.25	.80
☐	101	Gene Woodling	11.00	4.50	1.10
☐	102	Gil Hodges	45.00	18.00	4.50
☐	103	Jim Lemon	9.00	3.75	.90
☐	104	Mike Sandlock	8.00	3.25	.80
☐	105	Andy Carey	10.00	4.00	1.00
☐	106	Dick Kokos	8.00	3.25	.80
☐	107	Duane Pillette	8.00	3.25	.80
☐	108	Thornton Kipper	8.00	3.25	.80
☐	109	Bill Bruton	9.00	3.75	.90
☐	110	Harry Dorish	8.00	3.25	.80
☐	111	Jim Delsing	8.00	3.25	.80
☐	112	Bill Renna	8.00	3.25	.80
☐	113	Bob Boyd	8.00	3.25	.80
☐	114	Dean Stone	8.00	3.25	.80
☐	115	Rip Repulski	8.00	3.25	.80
☐	116	Steve Bilko	8.00	3.25	.80
☐	117	Solly Hemus	8.00	3.25	.80
☐	118	Carl Scheib	8.00	3.25	.80
☐	119	Johnny Antonelli	10.00	4.00	1.00
☐	120	Roy McMillan	8.00	3.25	.80
☐	121	Clem Labine	10.00	4.00	1.00
☐	122	Johnny Logan	9.00	3.75	.90
☐	123	Bobby Adams	8.00	3.25	.80
☐	124	Marion Fricano	8.00	3.25	.80
☐	125	Harry Perkowski	8.00	3.25	.80
☐	126	Ben Wade	10.00	4.00	1.00
☐	127	Steve O'Neill	10.00	4.00	1.00
☐	128	Hank Aaron	800.00	320.00	80.00
☐	129	Forrest Jacobs	10.00	4.00	1.00
☐	130	Hank Bauer	16.50	7.00	1.50
☐	131	Reno Bertoia	10.00	4.00	1.00
☐	132	Tom Lasorda	125.00	50.00	12.50
☐	133	Dave Baker	10.00	4.00	1.00
☐	134	Cal Hogue	10.00	4.00	1.00
☐	135	Joe Presko	10.00	4.00	1.00
☐	136	Connie Ryan	10.00	4.00	1.00
☐	137	Wally Moon	15.00	6.00	1.50
☐	138	Bob Borkowski	10.00	4.00	1.00
☐	139	The O'Briens	15.00	6.00	1.50
		Johnny O'Brien			
		Eddie O'Brien			
☐	140	Tom Wright	10.00	4.00	1.00
☐	141	Joey Jay	11.00	4.50	1.10
☐	142	Tom Poholsky	10.00	4.00	1.00

		NRMT	VG-E	GOOD			NRMT	VG-E	GOOD
☐ 143	Ralston Hemsley ...	10.00	4.00	1.00	☐ 192	Ellis Deal	10.00	4.00	1.00
☐ 144	Bill Werle	10.00	4.00	1.00	☐ 193	Johnny Hopp	12.00	5.00	1.20
☐ 145	Elmer Valo	10.00	4.00	1.00	☐ 194	Bill Sarni	10.00	4.00	1.00
☐ 146	Don Johnson	10.00	4.00	1.00	☐ 195	Billy Consolo	10.00	4.00	1.00
☐ 147	Johnny Riddle	10.00	4.00	1.00	☐ 196	Stan Jok	10.00	4.00	1.00
☐ 148	Bob Trice	10.00	4.00	1.00	☐ 197	Lynwood Rowe	12.00	5.00	1.20
☐ 149	Al Robertson	10.00	4.00	1.00	☐ 198	Carl Sawatski	10.00	4.00	1.00
☐ 150	Dick Kryhoski	10.00	4.00	1.00	☐ 199	Glenn (Rocky) Nelson	10.00	4.00	1.00
☐ 151	Alex Grammas	10.00	4.00	1.00	☐ 200	Larry Jansen	11.00	4.50	1.10
☐ 152	Michael Blyzka	10.00	4.00	1.00	☐ 201	Al Kaline	500.00	200.00	50.00
☐ 153	Al Walker	11.00	4.50	1.10	☐ 202	Bob Purkey	10.00	4.00	1.00
☐ 154	Mike Fornieles	10.00	4.00	1.00	☐ 203	Harry Brecheen ...	11.00	4.50	1.10
☐ 155	Bob Kennedy	10.00	4.00	1.00	☐ 204	Angel Scull	10.00	4.00	1.00
☐ 156	Joe Coleman	10.00	4.00	1.00	☐ 205	Johnny Sain	20.00	8.00	2.00
☐ 157	Don Lenhardt	10.00	4.00	1.00	☐ 206	Ray Crone	10.00	4.00	1.00
☐ 158	Peanuts Lowrey ...	10.00	4.00	1.00	☐ 207	Tom Oliver	10.00	4.00	1.00
☐ 159	Dave Philley	10.00	4.00	1.00	☐ 208	Grady Hatton	10.00	4.00	1.00
☐ 160	Ralph Kress	10.00	4.00	1.00	☐ 209	Chuck Thompson ..	10.00	4.00	1.00
☐ 161	John Hetki	10.00	4.00	1.00	☐ 210	Bob Buhl	12.00	5.00	1.20
☐ 162	Herman Wehmeier .	10.00	4.00	1.00	☐ 211	Don Hoak	11.00	4.50	1.10
☐ 163	Frank House	10.00	4.00	1.00	☐ 212	Bob Micelotta	10.00	4.00	1.00
☐ 164	Stu Miller	10.00	4.00	1.00	☐ 213	Johnny Fitzpatrick .	10.00	4.00	1.00
☐ 165	Jim Pendleton	10.00	4.00	1.00	☐ 214	Arnie Portocarrero .	10.00	4.00	1.00
☐ 166	Johnny Podres	20.00	8.00	2.00	☐ 215	Warren McGhee ...	10.00	4.00	1.00
☐ 167	Don Lund	10.00	4.00	1.00	☐ 216	Al Sima	10.00	4.00	1.00
☐ 168	Morrie Martin	10.00	4.00	1.00	☐ 217	Paul Schreiber ...	10.00	4.00	1.00
☐ 169	Jim Hughes	10.00	4.00	1.00	☐ 218	Fred Marsh	10.00	4.00	1.00
☐ 170	James (Dusty) Rhodes	12.00	5.00	1.20	☐ 219	Chuck Kress	10.00	4.00	1.00
☐ 171	Leo Kiely	10.00	4.00	1.00	☐ 220	Ruben Gomez	10.00	4.00	1.00
☐ 172	Harold Brown	10.00	4.00	1.00	☐ 221	Dick Brodowski ...	10.00	4.00	1.00
☐ 173	Jack Harshman	10.00	4.00	1.00	☐ 222	Bill Wilson	10.00	4.00	1.00
☐ 174	Tom Qualters	10.00	4.00	1.00	☐ 223	Joe Haynes	10.00	4.00	1.00
☐ 175	Frank Leja	11.00	4.50	1.10	☐ 224	Dick Weik	10.00	4.00	1.00
☐ 176	Robert Keeley	10.00	4.00	1.00	☐ 225	Don Liddle	10.00	4.00	1.00
☐ 177	Bob Milliken	10.00	4.00	1.00	☐ 226	Jehosie Heard	10.00	4.00	1.00
☐ 178	Bill Glynn	10.00	4.00	1.00	☐ 227	Colonel Mills	10.00	4.00	1.00
☐ 179	Gair Allie	10.00	4.00	1.00	☐ 228	Gene Hermanski ..	10.00	4.00	1.00
☐ 180	Wes Westrum	11.00	4.50	1.10	☐ 229	Bob Talbot	10.00	4.00	1.00
☐ 181	Mel Roach	10.00	4.00	1.00	☐ 230	Bob Kuzava	12.00	5.00	1.20
☐ 182	Chuck Harmon	10.00	4.00	1.00	☐ 231	Roy Smalley	11.00	4.50	1.10
☐ 183	Earle Combs	15.00	6.00	1.50	☐ 232	Lou Limmer	10.00	4.00	1.00
☐ 184	Ed Bailey	10.00	4.00	1.00	☐ 233	Augie Galan	10.00	4.00	1.00
☐ 185	Chuck Stobbs	10.00	4.00	1.00	☐ 234	Jerry Lynch	12.00	5.00	1.20
☐ 186	Karl Olson	10.00	4.00	1.00	☐ 235	Vernon Law	14.00	5.75	1.40
☐ 187	Henry Manush	15.00	6.00	1.50	☐ 236	Paul Penson	10.00	4.00	1.00
☐ 188	Dave Jolly	10.00	4.00	1.00	☐ 237	Dominic Ryba	10.00	4.00	1.00
☐ 189	Floyd Ross	10.00	4.00	1.00	☐ 238	Al Aber	10.00	4.00	1.00
☐ 190	Ray Herbert	10.00	4.00	1.00	☐ 239	Bill Skowron	40.00	16.00	4.00
☐ 191	John (Dick) Schofield	11.00	4.50	1.10	☐ 240	Sam Mele	10.00	4.00	1.00

		NRMT	VG-E	GOOD
☐ 241	Robert Miller	10.00	4.00	1.00
☐ 242	Curt Roberts	10.00	4.00	1.00
☐ 243	Ray Blades	10.00	4.00	1.00
☐ 244	Leroy Wheat	10.00	4.00	1.00
☐ 245	Roy Sievers	12.00	5.00	1.20
☐ 246	Howie Fox	10.00	4.00	1.00
☐ 247	Ed Mayo	10.00	4.00	1.00
☐ 248	Al Smith	12.00	5.00	1.20
☐ 249	Wilmer Mizell	12.00	5.00	1.20
☐ 250	Ted Williams	500.00	150.00	30.00

1955 Topps

*The cards in this 206-card set measure 2⅝"
by 3¾". Both the large "head" shot and the
smaller full-length photos used on each card
of the 1955 Topps set are in color. The card
fronts were designed horizontally for the first
time in Topps' history. The first card features
Dusty Rhodes, hitting star for the Giants'
1954 World Series sweep over the Indians.
A "high" series, 161 to 210, is more difficult
to find than cards 1 to 160. Numbers 175,
186, 203, and 209 were never issued. To fill
in for the four cards not issued in the high
number series, Topps double printed four
players, those appearing on cards 170, 172,
184, and 188.*

	NRMT	VG-E	GOOD
Complete Set (206) ...	4250.00	1900.00	650.00
Common Player (1-150) ...	5.00	2.00	.50
Common Player (151-160) ...	10.00	4.00	1.00
Common Player (161-210) ...	12.50	5.00	1.25

		NRMT	VG-E	GOOD
☐ 1	Dusty Rhodes	25.00	5.00	1.00
☐ 2	Ted Williams	200.00	80.00	20.00
☐ 3	Art Fowler	5.00	2.00	.50
☐ 4	Al Kaline	80.00	32.00	8.00
☐ 5	Jim Gilliam	9.00	3.75	.90
☐ 6	Stan Hack	5.50	2.20	.55
☐ 7	Jim Hegan	5.50	2.20	.55
☐ 8	Harold Smith	5.00	2.00	.50
☐ 9	Robert Miller	5.00	2.00	.50
☐ 10	Bob Keegan	5.00	2.00	.50
☐ 11	Ferris Fain	5.50	2.20	.55
☐ 12	Vernon Thies	5.00	2.00	.50
☐ 13	Fred Marsh	5.00	2.00	.50
☐ 14	Jim Finigan	5.00	2.00	.50
☐ 15	Jim Pendleton	5.00	2.00	.50
☐ 16	Roy Sievers	5.50	2.20	.55
☐ 17	Bobby Hofman	5.00	2.00	.50
☐ 18	Russ Kemmerer ..	5.00	2.00	.50
☐ 19	Billy Herman	9.00	3.75	.90
☐ 20	Andy Carey	7.00	2.80	.70
☐ 21	Alex Grammas	5.00	2.00	.50
☐ 22	Bill Skowron	10.00	4.00	1.00
☐ 23	Jack Parks	5.00	2.00	.50
☐ 24	Hal Newhouser	8.00	3.25	.80
☐ 25	Johnny Podres	10.00	4.00	1.00
☐ 26	Dick Groat	7.50	3.00	.75
☐ 27	Billy Gardner	5.50	2.20	.55
☐ 28	Ernie Banks	65.00	26.00	6.50
☐ 29	Herman Wehmeier ..	5.00	2.00	.50
☐ 30	Vic Power	5.50	2.20	.55
☐ 31	Warren Spahn	36.00	15.00	3.60
☐ 32	Warren McGhee ..	5.00	2.00	.50
☐ 33	Tom Qualters	5.00	2.00	.50
☐ 34	Wayne Terwilliger .	5.00	2.00	.50
☐ 35	Dave Jolly	5.00	2.00	.50
☐ 36	Leo Kiely	5.00	2.00	.50
☐ 37	Joe Cunningham ..	5.50	2.20	.55
☐ 38	Bob Turley	9.00	3.75	.90
☐ 39	Bill Glynn	5.00	2.00	.50
☐ 40	Don Hoak	5.50	2.20	.55
☐ 41	Chuck Stobbs	5.00	2.00	.50
☐ 42	John (Windy) McCall	5.00	2.00	.50
☐ 43	Harvey Haddix	5.50	2.20	.55
☐ 44	Harold Valentine ..	5.00	2.00	.50
☐ 45	Hank Sauer	5.50	2.20	.55
☐ 46	Ted Kazanski	5.00	2.00	.50
☐ 47	Hank Aaron	200.00	80.00	20.00
☐ 48	Bob Kennedy	5.00	2.00	.50
☐ 49	J.W. Porter	5.00	2.00	.50
☐ 50	Jackie Robinson ..	135.00	54.00	13.50

		NRMT	VG-E	GOOD			NRMT	VG-E	GOOD
☐ 51	Jim Hughes	5.00	2.00	.50	☐ 100	Monte Irvin	17.00	7.00	1.70
☐ 52	Bill Tremel	5.00	2.00	.50	☐ 101	Johnny Gray	5.00	2.00	.50
☐ 53	Bill Taylor	5.00	2.00	.50	☐ 102	Wally Westlake	5.00	2.00	.50
☐ 54	Lou Limmer	5.00	2.00	.50	☐ 103	Chuck White	5.00	2.00	.50
☐ 55	Rip Repulski	5.00	2.00	.50	☐ 104	Jack Harshman	5.00	2.00	.50
☐ 56	Ray Jablonski	5.00	2.00	.50	☐ 105	Chuck Diering	5.00	2.00	.50
☐ 57	Billy O'Dell	5.00	2.00	.50	☐ 106	Frank Sullivan	5.00	2.00	.50
☐ 58	Jim Rivera	5.00	2.00	.50	☐ 107	Curt Roberts	5.00	2.00	.50
☐ 59	Gair Allie	5.00	2.00	.50	☐ 108	Al Walker	5.00	2.00	.50
☐ 60	Dean Stone	5.00	2.00	.50	☐ 109	Ed Lopat	11.00	4.50	1.10
☐ 61	Forrest Jacobs	5.00	2.00	.50	☐ 110	Gus Zernial	5.50	2.20	.55
☐ 62	Thornton Kipper	5.00	2.00	.50	☐ 111	Bob Milliken	5.00	2.00	.50
☐ 63	Joe Collins	6.00	2.40	.60	☐ 112	Nelson King	5.00	2.00	.50
☐ 64	Gus Triandos	6.00	2.40	.60	☐ 113	Harry Brecheen	5.00	2.00	.50
☐ 65	Ray Boone	5.50	2.20	.55	☐ 114	Louis Ortiz	5.00	2.00	.50
☐ 66	Ron Jackson	5.00	2.00	.50	☐ 115	Ellis Kinder	5.00	2.00	.50
☐ 67	Wally Moon	6.00	2.40	.60	☐ 116	Tom Hurd	5.00	2.00	.50
☐ 68	Jim Davis	5.00	2.00	.50	☐ 117	Mel Roach	5.00	2.00	.50
☐ 69	Ed Bailey	5.50	2.20	.55	☐ 118	Bob Purkey	5.00	2.00	.50
☐ 70	Al Rosen	8.00	3.25	.80	☐ 119	Bob Lennon	5.00	2.00	.50
☐ 71	Ruben Gomez	5.00	2.00	.50	☐ 120	Ted Kluszewski	10.00	4.00	1.00
☐ 72	Karl Olson	5.00	2.00	.50	☐ 121	Bill Renna	5.00	2.00	.50
☐ 73	Jack Shepard	5.00	2.00	.50	☐ 122	Carl Sawatski	5.00	2.00	.50
☐ 74	Bob Borkowski	5.00	2.00	.50	☐ 123	Sandy Koufax	450.00	180.00	45.00
☐ 75	Sandy Amoros	8.00	3.25	.80	☐ 124	Harmon Killebrew	225.00	90.00	22.00
☐ 76	Howie Pollet	5.00	2.00	.50	☐ 125	Ken Boyer	30.00	12.00	3.00
☐ 77	Arnie Portocarrero	5.00	2.00	.50	☐ 126	Dick Hall	5.00	2.00	.50
☐ 78	Gordon Jones	5.00	2.00	.50	☐ 127	Dale Long	5.50	2.20	.55
☐ 79	Clyde Schell	5.00	2.00	.50	☐ 128	Ted Lepcio	5.00	2.00	.50
☐ 80	Bob Grim	8.00	3.25	.80	☐ 129	Elvin Tappe	5.00	2.00	.50
☐ 81	Gene Conley	5.50	2.20	.55	☐ 130	Mayo Smith MG	5.00	2.00	.50
☐ 82	Chuck Harmon	5.00	2.00	.50	☐ 131	Grady Hatton	5.00	2.00	.50
☐ 83	Tom Brewer	5.00	2.00	.50	☐ 132	Bob Trice	5.00	2.00	.50
☐ 84	Camilo Pascual	7.00	2.80	.70	☐ 133	Dave Hoskins	5.00	2.00	.50
☐ 85	Don Mossi	7.00	2.80	.70	☐ 134	Joey Jay	5.00	2.00	.50
☐ 86	Bill Wilson	5.00	2.00	.50	☐ 135	Johnny O'Brien	5.00	2.00	.50
☐ 87	Frank House	5.00	2.00	.50	☐ 136	Vernon Stewart	5.00	2.00	.50
☐ 88	Bob Skinner	6.00	2.40	.60	☐ 137	Harry Elliott	5.00	2.00	.50
☐ 89	Joe Frazier	5.00	2.00	.50	☐ 138	Ray Herbert	5.00	2.00	.50
☐ 90	Karl Spooner	5.00	2.00	.50	☐ 139	Steve Kraly	5.00	2.00	.50
☐ 91	Milt Bolling	5.00	2.00	.50	☐ 140	Mel Parnell	7.00	3.00	.55
☐ 92	Don Zimmer	11.00	4.50	1.10	☐ 141	Tom Wright	5.00	2.00	.50
☐ 93	Steve Bilko	5.00	2.00	.50	☐ 142	Jerry Lynch	5.50	2.20	.55
☐ 94	Reno Bertoia	5.00	2.00	.50	☐ 143	John (Dick) Schofield	5.50	2.20	.55
☐ 95	Preston Ward	5.00	2.00	.50	☐ 144	John (Joe) Amalfitano	5.00	2.00	.50
☐ 96	Chuck Bishop	5.00	2.00	.50	☐ 145	Elmer Valo	5.00	2.00	.50
☐ 97	Carlos Paula	5.00	2.00	.50	☐ 146	Dick Donovan	5.00	2.00	.50
☐ 98	John Riddle	5.00	2.00	.50	☐ 147	Hugh Pepper	5.00	2.00	.50
☐ 99	Frank Leja	5.00	2.00	.50	☐ 148	Hector Brown	5.00	2.00	.50

		NRMT	VG-E	GOOD
☐ 149	Ray Crone	5.00	2.00	.50
☐ 150	Mike Higgins	5.00	2.00	.50
☐ 151	Ralph Kress	10.00	4.00	1.00
☐ 152	Harry Agganis	50.00	20.00	5.00
☐ 153	Bud Podbielan	10.00	4.00	1.00
☐ 154	Willie Miranda	10.00	4.00	1.00
☐ 155	Eddie Mathews	70.00	28.00	7.00
☐ 156	Joe Black	15.00	6.00	1.50
☐ 157	Robert Miller	10.00	4.00	1.00
☐ 158	Tommy Carroll	12.00	5.00	1.20
☐ 159	Johnny Schmitz . . .	10.00	4.00	1.00
☐ 160	Ray Narleski	12.00	5.00	1.20
☐ 161	Chuck Tanner	16.00	6.50	1.60
☐ 162	Joe Coleman	12.50	5.00	1.25
☐ 163	Faye Throneberry . .	12.50	5.00	1.25
☐ 164	Roberto Clemente . .	750.00	300.00	75.00
☐ 165	Don Johnson	12.50	5.00	1.25
☐ 166	Hank Bauer	21.00	8.50	2.10
☐ 167	Thomas Casagrande	12.50	5.00	1.25
☐ 168	Duane Pillette	12.50	5.00	1.25
☐ 169	Bob Oldis	12.50	5.00	1.25
☐ 170	Jim Pearce DP	7.50	3.00	.75
☐ 171	Dick Brodowski . . .	12.50	5.00	1.25
☐ 172	Frank Baumholtz DP	7.50	3.00	.75
☐ 173	Johnny Kline	12.50	5.00	1.25
☐ 174	Rudy Minarcin	12.50	5.00	1.25
☐ 175	Does not exist	0.00	.00	.00
☐ 176	Norm Zauchin	12.50	5.00	1.25
☐ 177	Al Robertson	12.50	5.00	1.25
☐ 178	Bobby Adams	12.50	5.00	1.25
☐ 179	Jim Bolger	12.50	5.00	1.25
☐ 180	Clem Labine	16.00	6.50	1.60
☐ 181	Roy McMillan	12.50	5.00	1.25
☐ 182	Humberto Robinson	12.50	5.00	1.25
☐ 183	Anthony Jacobs . . .	12.50	5.00	1.25
☐ 184	Harry Perkowski DP	7.50	3.00	.75
☐ 185	Don Ferrarese	12.50	5.00	1.25
☐ 186	Does not exist	0.00	.00	.00
☐ 187	Gil Hodges	100.00	40.00	10.00
☐ 188	Charlie Silvera DP . .	7.50	3.00	.75
☐ 189	Phil Rizzuto	100.00	40.00	10.00
☐ 190	Gene Woodling	16.00	6.50	1.60
☐ 191	Eddie Stanky	16.00	6.50	1.60
☐ 192	Jim Delsing	12.50	5.00	1.25
☐ 193	Johnny Sain	21.00	8.50	2.10
☐ 194	Willie Mays	350.00	140.00	35.00
☐ 195	Ed Roebuck	16.00	6.50	1.60
☐ 196	Gale Wade	12.50	5.00	1.25
☐ 197	Al Smith	14.00	5.75	1.40

		NRMT	VG-E	GOOD
☐ 198	Yogi Berra	160.00	65.00	16.00
☐ 199	Odbert Hamric	12.50	5.00	1.25
☐ 200	Jackie Jensen	30.00	12.00	3.00
☐ 201	Sherm Lollar	14.00	5.75	1.40
☐ 202	Jim Owens	12.50	5.00	1.25
☐ 203	Does not exist	0.00	.00	.00
☐ 204	Frank Smith	12.50	5.00	1.25
☐ 205	Gene Freese	12.50	5.00	1.25
☐ 206	Pete Daley	12.50	5.00	1.25
☐ 207	Billy Consolo	12.50	5.00	1.25
☐ 208	Ray Moore	12.50	5.00	1.25
☐ 209	Does not exist	0.00	.00	.00
☐ 210	Duke Snider	375.00	100.00	20.00

1956 Topps

The cards in this 340-card set measure 2 ⅝" by 3 ¾". Following up with another horizontally oriented card in 1956, Topps improved the format by layering the color "head" shot onto an actual action sequence involving the player. Cards 1 to 180 come with either white or gray backs: in the 1 to 100 sequence, gray backs are less common (worth about 10% more) and in the 101 to 180 sequence, white backs are less common (worth 30% more). The team cards, used for the first time in a regular set by Topps, are found dated 1955, or undated, with the team name appearing on either side. The two unnumbered checklist cards are highly prized (must be unmarked to qualify as excellent or mint). The complete set price below does not include

the unnumbered checklist cards or any of
the variations.

			NRMT	VG-E	GOOD
	Complete Set (340)		4250.00	1900.00	650.00
	Common Player (1-100)		4.00	1.60	.40
	Common Player (101-180)		5.00	2.00	.50
	Common Player (181-260)		9.00	3.75	.90
	Common Player (261-340)		6.00	2.40	.60
☐	1	William Harridge (AL President)	75.00	7.50	1.50
☐	2	Warren Giles DP (NL President)	10.00	4.00	1.00
☐	3	Elmer Valo	4.00	1.60	.40
☐	4	Carlos Paula	4.00	1.60	.40
☐	5	Ted Williams	175.00	70.00	18.00
☐	6	Ray Boone	4.00	1.60	.40
☐	7	Ron Negray	4.00	1.60	.40
☐	8	Walter Alston MG	18.00	7.25	1.80
☐	9	Ruben Gomez	4.00	1.60	.40
☐	10	Warren Spahn DP	27.00	11.00	2.70
☐	11A	Chicago Cubs (centered)	8.00	3.25	.80
☐	11B	Cubs Team (dated 1955)	30.00	12.00	3.00
☐	11C	Cubs Team (name at far left)	10.00	4.00	1.00
☐	12	Andy Carey	5.00	2.00	.50
☐	13	Roy Face	6.00	2.40	.60
☐	14	Ken Boyer	9.00	3.75	.90
☐	15	Ernie Banks DP	40.00	16.00	4.00
☐	16	Hector Lopez	4.00	1.60	.40
☐	17	Gene Conley	4.00	1.60	.40
☐	18	Dick Donovan	4.00	1.60	.40
☐	19	Chuck Diering	4.00	1.60	.40
☐	20	Al Kaline	50.00	20.00	5.00
☐	21	Joe Collins	5.00	2.00	.50
☐	22	Jim Finigan	4.00	1.60	.40
☐	23	Fred Marsh	4.00	1.60	.40
☐	24	Dick Groat	6.00	2.40	.60
☐	25	Ted Kluszewski	9.00	3.75	.90
☐	26	Grady Hatton	4.00	1.60	.40
☐	27	Nelson Burbrink	4.00	1.60	.40
☐	28	Bobby Hofman	4.00	1.60	.40
☐	29	Jack Harshman	4.00	1.60	.40
☐	30	Jackie Robinson DP	100.00	40.00	10.00
☐	31	Hank Aaron DP (small photo actually W.Mays)	135.00	54.00	13.50
☐	32	Frank House	4.00	1.60	.40
☐	33	Roberto Clemente	175.00	70.00	18.00
☐	34	Tom Brewer	4.00	1.60	.40
☐	35	Al Rosen DP	7.00	2.80	.70
☐	36	Rudy Minarcin	4.00	1.60	.40
☐	37	Alex Grammas	4.00	1.60	.40
☐	38	Bob Kennedy	4.00	1.60	.40
☐	39	Don Mossi	5.00	2.00	.50
☐	40	Bob Turley	7.00	2.80	.70
☐	41	Hank Sauer	5.00	2.00	.50
☐	42	Sandy Amoros	5.00	2.00	.50
☐	43	Ray Moore	4.00	1.60	.40
☐	44	Windy McCall	4.00	1.60	.40
☐	45	Gus Zernial	4.00	1.60	.40
☐	46	Gene Freese	4.00	1.60	.40
☐	47	Art Fowler	4.00	1.60	.40
☐	48	Jim Hegan	4.00	1.60	.40
☐	49	Pedro Ramos	4.00	1.60	.40
☐	50	Dusty Rhodes	5.00	2.00	.50
☐	51	Ernie Oravetz	4.00	1.60	.40
☐	52	Bob Grim	5.00	2.00	.50
☐	53	Arnie Portocarrero	4.00	1.60	.40
☐	54	Bob Keegan	4.00	1.60	.40
☐	55	Wally Moon	6.00	2.40	.60
☐	56	Dale Long	5.00	2.00	.50
☐	57	Duke Maas	4.00	1.60	.40
☐	58	Ed Roebuck	5.00	2.00	.50
☐	59	Jose Santiago	4.00	1.60	.40
☐	60	Mayo Smith MG	4.00	1.60	.40
☐	61	Bill Skowron	8.00	3.25	.80
☐	62	Hal Smith	4.00	1.60	.40
☐	63	Roger Craig	12.00	5.00	1.20
☐	64	Luis Arroyo	5.00	2.00	.50
☐	65	Johnny O'Brien	4.00	1.60	.40
☐	66	Bob Speake	4.00	1.60	.40
☐	67	Vic Power	4.00	1.60	.40
☐	68	Chuck Stobbs	4.00	1.60	.40
☐	69	Chuck Tanner	6.00	2.40	.60
☐	70	Jim Rivera	4.00	1.60	.40
☐	71	Frank Sullivan	4.00	1.60	.40
☐	72A	Phillies Team DP (centered)	6.00	2.40	.60
☐	72B	Phillies Team (dated 1955)	30.00	12.00	3.00
☐	72C	Phillies Team (name at far left)	10.00	4.00	1.00
☐	73	Wayne Terwilliger	4.00	1.60	.40
☐	74	Jim King	4.00	1.60	.40
☐	75	Roy Sievers	5.00	2.00	.50
☐	76	Ray Crone	4.00	1.60	.40
☐	77	Harvey Haddix	5.00	2.00	.50

		NRMT	VG-E	GOOD
☐ 78	Herman Wehmeier	4.00	1.60	.40
☐ 79	Sandy Koufax	175.00	70.00	18.00
☐ 80	Gus Triandos	5.00	2.00	.50
☐ 81	Wally Westlake	4.00	1.60	.40
☐ 82	Bill Renna	4.00	1.60	.40
☐ 83	Karl Spooner	5.00	2.00	.50
☐ 84	Babe Birrer	4.00	1.60	.40
☐ 85A	Cleveland Indians (centered)	8.00	3.25	.80
☐ 85B	Indians Team (dated 1955)	30.00	12.00	3.00
☐ 85C	Indians Team (name at far left)	10.00	4.00	1.00
☐ 86	Ray Jablonski	4.00	1.60	.40
☐ 87	Dean Stone	4.00	1.60	.40
☐ 88	Johnny Kucks	5.00	2.00	.50
☐ 89	Norm Zauchin	4.00	1.60	.40
☐ 90A	Cincinnati Redlegs Team (centered)	8.00	3.25	.80
☐ 90B	Reds Team (dated 1955)	30.00	12.00	3.00
☐ 90C	Reds Team (name at far left)	10.00	4.00	1.00
☐ 91	Gail Harris	4.00	1.60	.40
☐ 92	Bob (Red) Wilson	4.00	1.60	.40
☐ 93	George Susce	4.00	1.60	.40
☐ 94	Ron Kline	4.00	1.60	.40
☐ 95A	Milwaukee Braves Team (centered)	8.00	3.25	.80
☐ 95B	Braves Team (dated 1955)	30.00	12.00	3.00
☐ 95C	Braves Team (name at far left)	10.00	4.00	1.00
☐ 96	Bill Tremel	4.00	1.60	.40
☐ 97	Jerry Lynch	4.00	1.60	.40
☐ 98	Camilo Pascual	5.00	2.00	.50
☐ 99	Don Zimmer	7.00	2.80	.70
☐ 100A	Baltimore Orioles Team (centered)	8.00	3.25	.80
☐ 100B	Orioles Team (dated 1955)	30.00	12.00	3.00
☐ 100C	Orioles Team (name at far left)	10.00	4.00	1.00
☐ 101	Roy Campanella	90.00	36.00	9.00
☐ 102	Jim Davis	5.00	2.00	.50
☐ 103	Willie Miranda	5.00	2.00	.50
☐ 104	Bob Lennon	5.00	2.00	.50
☐ 105	Al Smith	5.00	2.00	.50
☐ 106	Joe Astroth	5.00	2.00	.50

		NRMT	VG-E	GOOD
☐ 107	Eddie Mathews	32.00	13.00	3.20
☐ 108	Laurin Pepper	5.00	2.00	.50
☐ 109	Enos Slaughter	21.00	8.50	2.10
☐ 110	Yogi Berra	90.00	36.00	9.00
☐ 111	Boston Red Sox Team Card	12.50	5.00	1.25
☐ 112	Dee Fondy	5.00	2.00	.50
☐ 113	Phil Rizzuto	30.00	12.00	3.00
☐ 114	Jim Owens	5.00	2.00	.50
☐ 115	Jackie Jensen	9.00	3.75	.90
☐ 116	Eddie O'Brien	5.00	2.00	.50
☐ 117	Virgil Trucks	6.00	2.40	.60
☐ 118	Nellie Fox	12.00	5.00	1.20
☐ 119	Larry Jackson	5.00	2.00	.50
☐ 120	Richie Ashburn	13.00	5.25	1.30
☐ 121	Pittsburgh Pirates Team Card	10.00	4.00	1.00
☐ 122	Willard Nixon	5.00	2.00	.50
☐ 123	Roy McMillan	5.00	2.00	.50
☐ 124	Don Kaiser	5.00	2.00	.50
☐ 125	Minnie Minoso	9.00	3.75	.90
☐ 126	Jim Brady	5.00	2.00	.50
☐ 127	Willie Jones	5.00	2.00	.50
☐ 128	Eddie Yost	5.00	2.00	.50
☐ 129	Jake Martin	5.00	2.00	.50
☐ 130	Willie Mays	200.00	80.00	20.00
☐ 131	Bob Roselli	5.00	2.00	.50
☐ 132	Bobby Avila	6.00	2.40	.60
☐ 133	Ray Narleski	5.00	2.00	.50
☐ 134	St. Louis Cardinals Team Card	10.00	4.00	1.00
☐ 135	Mickey Mantle	700.00	280.00	70.00
☐ 136	Johnny Logan	6.00	2.40	.60
☐ 137	Al Silvera	5.00	2.00	.50
☐ 138	Johnny Antonelli	7.00	2.80	.70
☐ 139	Tommy Carroll	6.00	2.40	.60
☐ 140	Herb Score	11.00	4.50	1.10
☐ 141	Joe Frazier	5.00	2.00	.50
☐ 142	Gene Baker	5.00	2.00	.50
☐ 143	Jim Piersall	8.00	3.25	.80
☐ 144	Leroy Powell	5.00	2.00	.50
☐ 145	Gil Hodges	28.00	11.50	2.80
☐ 146	Washington Nationals Team Card	9.00	3.75	.90
☐ 147	Earl Torgeson	5.00	2.00	.50
☐ 148	Alvin Dark	8.00	3.25	.80
☐ 149	Dixie Howell	5.00	2.00	.50
☐ 150	Duke Snider	80.00	32.00	8.00
☐ 151	Spook Jacobs	5.00	2.00	.50

		NRMT	VG-E	GOOD			NRMT	VG-E	GOOD
☐ 152	Billy Hoeft	5.00	2.00	.50	☐ 199	Hank Thompson	11.00	4.50	1.10
☐ 153	Frank Thomas	6.00	2.40	.60	☐ 200	Bob Feller	75.00	30.00	7.50
☐ 154	Dave Pope	5.00	2.00	.50	☐ 201	Rip Repulski	9.00	3.75	.90
☐ 155	Harvey Kuenn	8.00	3.25	.80	☐ 202	Jim Hearn	9.00	3.75	.90
☐ 156	Wes Westrum	6.00	2.40	.60	☐ 203	Bill Tuttle	9.00	3.75	.90
☐ 157	Dick Brodowski	5.00	2.00	.50	☐ 204	Art Swanson	9.00	3.75	.90
☐ 158	Wally Post	6.00	2.40	.60	☐ 205	Whitey Lockman	10.00	4.00	1.00
☐ 159	Clint Courtney	5.00	2.00	.50	☐ 206	Erv Palica	9.00	3.75	.90
☐ 160	Billy Pierce	7.00	2.80	.70	☐ 207	Jim Small	9.00	3.75	.90
☐ 161	Joe DeMaestri	5.00	2.00	.50	☐ 208	Elston Howard	25.00	10.00	2.50
☐ 162	Dave (Gus) Bell	6.00	2.40	.60	☐ 209	Max Surkont	9.00	3.75	.90
☐ 163	Gene Woodling	7.00	2.80	.70	☐ 210	Mike Garcia	11.00	4.50	1.10
☐ 164	Harmon Killebrew	50.00	20.00	5.00	☐ 211	Murry Dickson	9.00	3.75	.90
☐ 165	Red Schoendienst	9.00	3.75	.90	☐ 212	Johnny Temple	11.00	4.50	1.10
☐ 166	Brooklyn Dodgers Team Card	110.00	45.00	11.00	☐ 213	Detroit Tigers Team Card	25.00	10.00	2.50
☐ 167	Harry Dorish	5.00	2.00	.50	☐ 214	Bob Rush	9.00	3.75	.90
☐ 168	Sammy White	5.00	2.00	.50	☐ 215	Tommy Byrne	11.00	4.50	1.10
☐ 169	Bob Nelson	5.00	2.00	.50	☐ 216	Jerry Schoonmaker	9.00	3.75	.90
☐ 170	Bill Virdon	8.00	3.25	.80	☐ 217	Billy Klaus	9.00	3.75	.90
☐ 171	Jim Wilson	5.00	2.00	.50	☐ 218	Joe Nuxall (sic, Nuxhall)	11.00	4.50	1.10
☐ 172	Frank Torre	5.00	2.00	.50					
☐ 173	Johnny Podres	11.00	4.50	1.10	☐ 219	Lew Burdette	15.00	6.00	1.50
☐ 174	Glen Gorbous	5.00	2.00	.50	☐ 220	Del Ennis	11.00	4.50	1.10
☐ 175	Del Crandall	6.00	2.40	.60	☐ 221	Bob Friend	11.00	4.50	1.10
☐ 176	Alex Kellner	5.00	2.00	.50	☐ 222	Dave Philley	9.00	3.75	.90
☐ 177	Hank Bauer	10.00	4.00	1.00	☐ 223	Randy Jackson	9.00	3.75	.90
☐ 178	Joe Black	7.00	2.80	.70	☐ 224	Bud Podbielan	9.00	3.75	.90
☐ 179	Harry Chiti	5.00	2.00	.50	☐ 225	Gil McDougald	18.00	7.25	1.80
☐ 180	Robin Roberts	21.00	8.50	2.10	☐ 226	New York Giants Team Card	40.00	16.00	4.00
☐ 181	Billy Martin	45.00	18.00	4.50					
☐ 182	Paul Minner	9.00	3.75	.90	☐ 227	Russ Meyer	9.00	3.75	.90
☐ 183	Stan Lopata	9.00	3.75	.90	☐ 228	Mickey Vernon	12.00	5.00	1.20
☐ 184	Don Bessent	9.00	3.75	.90	☐ 229	Harry Brecheen	10.00	4.00	1.00
☐ 185	Bill Bruton	9.00	3.75	.90	☐ 230	Chico Carrasquel	9.00	3.75	.90
☐ 186	Ron Jackson	9.00	3.75	.90	☐ 231	Bob Hale	9.00	3.75	.90
☐ 187	Early Wynn	25.00	10.00	2.50	☐ 232	Toby Atwell	9.00	3.75	.90
☐ 188	Chicago White Sox Team Card	18.00	7.25	1.80	☐ 233	Carl Erskine	16.00	6.50	1.60
					☐ 234	Pete Runnels	11.00	4.50	1.10
☐ 189	Ned Garver	9.00	3.75	.90	☐ 235	Don Newcombe	25.00	10.00	2.50
☐ 190	Carl Furillo	18.00	7.25	1.80	☐ 236	Kansas City Athletics Team Card	15.00	6.00	1.50
☐ 191	Frank Lary	12.00	5.00	1.20					
☐ 192	Smoky Burgess	12.00	5.00	1.20	☐ 237	Jose Valdivielso	9.00	3.75	.90
☐ 193	Wilmer Mizell	9.00	3.75	.90	☐ 238	Walt Dropo	11.00	4.50	1.10
☐ 194	Monte Irvin	22.00	9.00	2.20	☐ 239	Harry Simpson	9.00	3.75	.90
☐ 195	George Kell	25.00	10.00	2.50	☐ 240	Whitey Ford	75.00	30.00	7.50
☐ 196	Tom Poholsky	9.00	3.75	.90	☐ 241	Don Mueller	11.00	4.50	1.10
☐ 197	Granny Hamner	9.00	3.75	.90	☐ 242	Hershell Freeman	9.00	3.75	.90
☐ 198	Ed Fitzgerald	9.00	3.75	.90	☐ 243	Sherm Lollar	11.00	4.50	1.10

		NRMT	VG-E	GOOD			NRMT	VG-E	GOOD
☐ 244	Bob Buhl	9.00	3.75	.90	☐ 292	Luis Aparicio	80.00	32.00	8.00
☐ 245	Billy Goodman	11.00	4.50	1.10	☐ 293	Stu Miller	6.00	2.40	.60
☐ 246	Tom Gorman	9.00	3.75	.90	☐ 294	Ernie Johnson	6.00	2.40	.60
☐ 247	Bill Sarni	9.00	3.75	.90	☐ 295	Clem Labine	8.00	3.25	.80
☐ 248	Bob Porterfield	9.00	3.75	.90	☐ 296	Andy Seminick	6.00	2.40	.60
☐ 249	Johnny Klippstein	9.00	3.75	.90	☐ 297	Bob Skinner	7.00	2.80	.70
☐ 250	Larry Doby	15.00	6.00	1.50	☐ 298	Johnny Schmitz	6.00	2.40	.60
☐ 251	New York Yankees	120.00	50.00	12.00	☐ 299	Charlie Neal	12.00	5.00	1.20
	Team Card				☐ 300	Vic Wertz	7.00	2.80	.70
☐ 252	Vern Law	11.00	4.50	1.10	☐ 301	Marv Grissom	6.00	2.40	.60
☐ 253	Irv Noren	11.00	4.50	1.10	☐ 302	Eddie Robinson	6.00	2.40	.60
☐ 254	George Crowe	9.00	3.75	.90	☐ 303	Jim Dyck	6.00	2.40	.60
☐ 255	Bob Lemon	25.00	10.00	2.50	☐ 304	Frank Malzone	12.00	5.00	1.20
☐ 256	Tom Hurd	9.00	3.75	.90	☐ 305	Brooks Lawrence	6.00	2.40	.60
☐ 257	Bobby Thomson	14.00	5.75	1.40	☐ 306	Curt Roberts	6.00	2.40	.60
☐ 258	Art Ditmar	11.00	4.50	1.10	☐ 307	Hoyt Wilhelm	25.00	10.00	2.50
☐ 259	Sam Jones	11.00	4.50	1.10	☐ 308	Chuck Harmon	6.00	2.40	.60
☐ 260	Pee Wee Reese	85.00	34.00	8.50	☐ 309	Don Blasingame	6.00	2.40	.60
☐ 261	Bobby Shantz	10.00	4.00	1.00	☐ 310	Steve Gromek	6.00	2.40	.60
☐ 262	Howie Pollet	6.00	2.40	.60	☐ 311	Hal Naragon	6.00	2.40	.60
☐ 263	Bob Miller	6.00	2.40	.60	☐ 312	Andy Pafko	7.00	2.80	.70
☐ 264	Ray Monzant	6.00	2.40	.60	☐ 313	Gene Stephens	6.00	2.40	.60
☐ 265	Sandy Consuegra	6.00	2.40	.60	☐ 314	Hobie Landrith	6.00	2.40	.60
☐ 266	Don Ferrarese	6.00	2.40	.60	☐ 315	Milt Bolling	6.00	2.40	.60
☐ 267	Bob Nieman	6.00	2.40	.60	☐ 316	Jerry Coleman	8.00	3.25	.80
☐ 268	Dale Mitchell	7.00	2.80	.70	☐ 317	Al Aber	6.00	2.40	.60
☐ 269	Jack Meyer	6.00	2.40	.60	☐ 318	Fred Hatfield	6.00	2.40	.60
☐ 270	Billy Loes	7.00	2.80	.70	☐ 319	Jack Crimian	6.00	2.40	.60
☐ 271	Foster Castleman	6.00	2.40	.60	☐ 320	Joe Adcock	8.00	3.25	.80
☐ 272	Danny O'Connell	6.00	2.40	.60	☐ 321	Jim Konstanty	7.00	2.80	.70
☐ 273	Walker Cooper	6.00	2.40	.60	☐ 322	Karl Olson	6.00	2.40	.60
☐ 274	Frank Baumholtz	6.00	2.40	.60	☐ 323	Willard Schmidt	6.00	2.40	.60
☐ 275	Jim Greengrass	6.00	2.40	.60	☐ 324	Rocky Bridges	6.00	2.40	.60
☐ 276	George Zuverink	6.00	2.40	.60	☐ 325	Don Liddle	6.00	2.40	.60
☐ 277	Daryl Spencer	6.00	2.40	.60	☐ 326	Connie Johnson	6.00	2.40	.60
☐ 278	Chet Nichols	6.00	2.40	.60	☐ 327	Bob Wiesler	6.00	2.40	.60
☐ 279	Johnny Groth	6.00	2.40	.60	☐ 328	Preston Ward	6.00	2.40	.60
☐ 280	Jim Gilliam	10.00	4.00	1.00	☐ 329	Lou Berberet	6.00	2.40	.60
☐ 281	Art Houtteman	6.00	2.40	.60	☐ 330	Jim Busby	6.00	2.40	.60
☐ 282	Warren Hacker	6.00	2.40	.60	☐ 331	Dick Hall	6.00	2.40	.60
☐ 283	Hal Smith	6.00	2.40	.60	☐ 332	Don Larsen	15.00	6.00	1.50
☐ 284	Ike Delock	6.00	2.40	.60	☐ 333	Rube Walker	7.00	2.80	.70
☐ 285	Eddie Miksis	6.00	2.40	.60	☐ 334	Bob Miller	6.00	2.40	.60
☐ 286	Bill Wight	6.00	2.40	.60	☐ 335	Don Hoak	7.00	2.80	.70
☐ 287	Bobby Adams	6.00	2.40	.60	☐ 336	Ellis Kinder	6.00	2.40	.60
☐ 288	Bob Cerv	9.00	3.75	.90	☐ 337	Bobby Morgan	6.00	2.40	.60
☐ 289	Hal Jeffcoat	6.00	2.40	.60	☐ 338	Jim Delsing	6.00	2.40	.60
☐ 290	Curt Simmons	8.00	3.25	.80	☐ 339	Rance Pless	6.00	2.40	.60
☐ 291	Frank Kellert	6.00	2.40	.60	☐ 340	Mickey McDermott	15.00	4.00	.80

	NRMT	VG-E	GOOD
☐ 341 Checklist 1/3 ...... (unnumbered)	175.00	35.00	5.00
☐ 342 Checklist 2/4 ...... (unnumbered)	175.00	35.00	5.00

1957 Topps

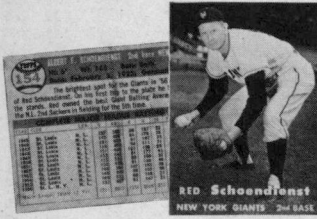

RED Schoendienst
NEW YORK GIANTS 2nd BASE

*The cards in this 407-card set measure 2 ½"
by 3 ½". In 1957, Topps returned to the vertical obverse, adopted what we now call the
standard card size, and used a large, unclut-
tered color photo for the first time since
1952. Cards in the series 265 to 352 and the
unnumbered checklist cards are scarcer
than other cards in the set. The first star
combination cards, #400 and #407, are quite
popular with collectors. They feature the big
stars of the previous season's World Series
teams, the Dodgers (Furillo, Hodges, Campanella, and Snider) and Yankees (Berra
and Mantle). The complete set price below
does not include the unnumbered checklist
cards.*

	NRMT	VG-E	GOOD
Complete Set (407)	5250.00	2400.00	800.00
Common Player (1-88)	4.00	1.60	.40
Common Player (89-264) .	3.00	1.20	.30
Common Player (265-352) .	12.50	5.00	1.25
Common Player (353-407) .	3.50	1.40	.35

		NRMT	VG-E	GOOD
☐	1 Ted Williams	350.00	80.00	20.00
☐	2 Yogi Berra	80.00	32.00	8.00

		NRMT	VG-E	GOOD
☐	3 Dale Long	5.00	2.00	.50
☐	4 Johnny Logan	5.00	2.00	.50
☐	5 Sal Maglie	6.00	2.40	.60
☐	6 Hector Lopez	4.00	1.60	.40
☐	7 Luis Aparicio	20.00	8.00	2.00
☐	8 Don Mossi	5.00	2.00	.50
☐	9 Johnny Temple ...	5.00	2.00	.50
☐	10 Willie Mays	150.00	60.00	15.00
☐	11 George Zuverink ..	4.00	1.60	.40
☐	12 Dick Groat	6.00	2.40	.60
☐	13 Wally Burnette	4.00	1.60	.40
☐	14 Bob Nieman	4.00	1.60	.40
☐	15 Robin Roberts	16.00	6.50	1.60
☐	16 Walt Moryn	4.00	1.60	.40
☐	17 Billy Gardner	5.00	2.00	.50
☐	18 Don Drysdale	125.00	50.00	12.50
☐	19 Bob Wilson	4.00	1.60	.40
☐	20 Hank Aaron	175.00	70.00	18.00
	(reverse negative photo on front)			
☐	21 Frank Sullivan	4.00	1.60	.40
☐	22 Jerry Snyder	4.00	1.60	.40
	(photo actually Ed Fitzgerald)			
☐	23 Sherm Lollar	5.00	2.00	.50
☐	24 Bill Mazeroski ...	21.00	8.50	2.10
☐	25 Whitey Ford	36.00	15.00	3.60
☐	26 Bob Boyd	4.00	1.60	.40
☐	27 Ted Kazanski	4.00	1.60	.40
☐	28 Gene Conley	4.00	1.60	.40
☐	29 Whitey Herzog ...	16.00	6.50	1.60
☐	30 Pee Wee Reese ..	36.00	15.00	3.60
☐	31 Ron Northey	4.00	1.60	.40
☐	32 Hershell Freeman .	4.00	1.60	.40
☐	33 Jim Small	4.00	1.60	.40
☐	34 Tom Sturdivant ...	4.00	1.60	.40
☐	35 Frank Robinson ...	135.00	54.00	13.50
☐	36 Bob Grim	5.00	2.00	.50
☐	37 Frank Torre	4.00	1.60	.40
☐	38 Nellie Fox	10.00	4.00	1.00
☐	39 Al Worthington ...	4.00	1.60	.40
☐	40 Early Wynn	14.00	5.75	1.40
☐	41 Hal W. Smith	4.00	1.60	.40
☐	42 Dee Fondy	4.00	1.60	.40
☐	43 Connie Johnson ..	4.00	1.60	.40
☐	44 Joe DeMaestri ...	4.00	1.60	.40
☐	45 Carl Furillo	9.00	3.75	.90
☐	46 Robert J. Miller ..	4.00	1.60	.40
☐	47 Don Blasingame ..	4.00	1.60	.40
☐	48 Bill Bruton	5.00	2.00	.50
☐	49 Daryl Spencer	4.00	1.60	.40

			NRMT	VG-E	GOOD
☐	50	Herb Score	6.00	2.40	.60
☐	51	Clint Courtney	4.00	1.60	.40
☐	52	Lee Walls	4.00	1.60	.40
☐	53	Clem Labine	5.00	2.00	.50
☐	54	Elmer Valo	4.00	1.60	.40
☐	55	Ernie Banks	40.00	16.00	4.00
☐	56	Dave Sisler	4.00	1.60	.40
☐	57	Jim Lemon	4.00	1.60	.40
☐	58	Ruben Gomez	4.00	1.60	.40
☐	59	Dick Williams	5.00	2.00	.50
☐	60	Billy Hoeft	4.00	1.60	.40
☐	61	James "Dusty" Rhodes	5.00	2.00	.50
☐	62	Billy Martin	28.00	11.50	2.80
☐	63	Ike Delock	4.00	1.60	.40
☐	64	Pete Runnels	5.00	2.00	.50
☐	65	Wally Moon	5.00	2.00	.50
☐	66	Brooks Lawrence	4.00	1.60	.40
☐	67	Chico Carrasquel	4.00	1.60	.40
☐	68	Ray Crone	4.00	1.60	.40
☐	69	Roy McMillan	4.00	1.60	.40
☐	70	Richie Ashburn	10.00	4.00	1.00
☐	71	Murry Dickson	4.00	1.60	.40
☐	72	Bill Tuttle	4.00	1.60	.40
☐	73	George Crowe	4.00	1.60	.40
☐	74	Vito Valentinetti	4.00	1.60	.40
☐	75	Jim Piersall	6.00	2.40	.60
☐	76	Roberto Clemente	100.00	40.00	10.00
☐	77	Paul Foytack	4.00	1.60	.40
☐	78	Vic Wertz	5.00	2.00	.50
☐	79	Lindy McDaniel	5.00	2.00	.50
☐	80	Gil Hodges	25.00	10.00	2.50
☐	81	Herman Wehmeier	4.00	1.60	.40
☐	82	Elston Howard	9.00	3.75	.90
☐	83	Lou Skizas	4.00	1.60	.40
☐	84	Moe Drabowsky	4.00	1.60	.40
☐	85	Larry Doby	6.00	2.40	.60
☐	86	Bill Sarni	4.00	1.60	.40
☐	87	Tom Gorman	4.00	1.60	.40
☐	88	Harvey Kuenn	7.00	2.80	.70
☐	89	Roy Sievers	4.00	1.60	.40
☐	90	Warren Spahn	35.00	14.00	3.50
☐	91	Mack Burk	3.00	1.20	.30
☐	92	Mickey Vernon	4.00	1.60	.40
☐	93	Hal Jeffcoat	3.00	1.20	.30
☐	94	Bobby Del Greco	3.00	1.20	.30
☐	95	Mickey Mantle	700.00	280.00	70.00
☐	96	Hank Aguirre	3.00	1.20	.30
☐	97	New York Yankees Team Card	25.00	10.00	2.50
☐	98	Alvin Dark	5.00	2.00	.50
☐	99	Bob Keegan	3.00	1.20	.30
☐	100	Giles and Harridge League Presidents	5.00	2.00	.50
☐	101	Chuck Stobbs	3.00	1.20	.30
☐	102	Ray Boone	4.00	1.60	.40
☐	103	Joe Nuxhall	4.00	1.60	.40
☐	104	Hank Foiles	3.00	1.20	.30
☐	105	Johnny Antonelli	4.00	1.60	.40
☐	106	Ray Moore	3.00	1.20	.30
☐	107	Jim Rivera	3.00	1.20	.30
☐	108	Tommy Byrne	4.00	1.60	.40
☐	109	Hank Thompson	4.00	1.60	.40
☐	110	Bill Virdon	5.00	2.00	.50
☐	111	Hal R. Smith	3.00	1.20	.30
☐	112	Tom Brewer	3.00	1.20	.30
☐	113	Wilmer Mizell	3.00	1.20	.30
☐	114	Milwaukee Braves Team Card	7.00	2.80	.70
☐	115	Jim Gilliam	7.50	3.00	.75
☐	116	Mike Fornieles	3.00	1.20	.30
☐	117	Joe Adcock	4.00	1.60	.40
☐	118	Bob Porterfield	3.00	1.20	.30
☐	119	Stan Lopata	3.00	1.20	.30
☐	120	Bob Lemon	14.00	5.75	1.40
☐	121	Clete Boyer	8.00	3.25	.80
☐	122	Ken Boyer	6.50	2.60	.65
☐	123	Steve Ridzik	3.00	1.20	.30
☐	124	Dave Philley	3.00	1.20	.30
☐	125	Al Kaline	40.00	16.00	4.00
☐	126	Bob Wiesler	3.00	1.20	.30
☐	127	Bob Buhl	3.00	1.20	.30
☐	128	Ed Bailey	3.00	1.20	.30
☐	129	Saul Rogovin	3.00	1.20	.30
☐	130	Don Newcombe	7.00	2.80	.70
☐	131	Milt Bolling	3.00	1.20	.30
☐	132	Art Ditmar	3.00	1.20	.30
☐	133	Del Crandall	4.00	1.60	.40
☐	134	Don Kaiser	3.00	1.20	.30
☐	135	Bill Skowron	9.00	3.75	.90
☐	136	Jim Hegan	4.00	1.60	.40
☐	137	Bob Rush	3.00	1.20	.30
☐	138	Minnie Minoso	6.50	2.60	.65
☐	139	Lou Kretlow	3.00	1.20	.30
☐	140	Frank Thomas	4.00	1.60	.40
☐	141	Al Aber	3.00	1.20	.30
☐	142	Charley Thompson	3.00	1.20	.30
☐	143	Andy Pafko	3.00	1.20	.30
☐	144	Ray Narleski	3.00	1.20	.30

		NRMT	VG-E	GOOD
☐ 145	Al Smith	3.00	1.20	.30
☐ 146	Don Ferrarese	3.00	1.20	.30
☐ 147	Al Walker	3.00	1.20	.30
☐ 148	Don Mueller	4.00	1.60	.40
☐ 149	Bob Kennedy	3.00	1.20	.30
☐ 150	Bob Friend	4.00	1.60	.40
☐ 151	Willie Miranda	3.00	1.20	.30
☐ 152	Jack Harshman	3.00	1.20	.30
☐ 153	Karl Olson	3.00	1.20	.30
☐ 154	Red Schoendienst	6.50	2.60	.65
☐ 155	Jim Brosnan	4.00	1.60	.40
☐ 156	Gus Triandos	4.00	1.60	.40
☐ 157	Wally Post	4.00	1.60	.40
☐ 158	Curt Simmons	4.00	1.60	.40
☐ 159	Solly Drake	3.00	1.20	.30
☐ 160	Billy Pierce	4.00	1.60	.40
☐ 161	Pittsburgh Pirates Team Card	5.00	2.00	.50
☐ 162	Jack Meyer	3.00	1.20	.30
☐ 163	Sammy White	3.00	1.20	.30
☐ 164	Tommy Carroll	3.00	1.20	.30
☐ 165	Ted Kluszewski	9.00	3.75	.90
☐ 166	Roy Face	5.00	2.00	.50
☐ 167	Vic Power	4.00	1.60	.40
☐ 168	Frank Lary	4.00	1.60	.40
☐ 169	Herb Plews	3.00	1.20	.30
☐ 170	Duke Snider	70.00	28.00	7.00
☐ 171	Boston Red Sox Team Card	6.50	2.60	.65
☐ 172	Gene Woodling	5.00	2.00	.50
☐ 173	Roger Craig	8.00	3.00	.75
☐ 174	Willie Jones	3.00	1.20	.30
☐ 175	Don Larsen	7.00	2.80	.70
☐ 176	Gene Baker	3.00	1.20	.30
☐ 177	Eddie Yost	3.00	1.20	.30
☐ 178	Don Bessent	3.00	1.20	.30
☐ 179	Ernie Oravetz	3.00	1.20	.30
☐ 180	Dave (Gus) Bell	4.00	1.60	.40
☐ 181	Dick Donovan	3.00	1.20	.30
☐ 182	Hobie Landrith	3.00	1.20	.30
☐ 183	Chicago Cubs Team Card	6.00	2.40	.60
☐ 184	Tito Francona	4.00	1.60	.40
☐ 185	Johnny Kucks	4.00	1.60	.40
☐ 186	Jim King	3.00	1.20	.30
☐ 187	Virgil Trucks	4.00	1.60	.40
☐ 188	Felix Mantilla	3.00	1.20	.30
☐ 189	Willard Nixon	3.00	1.20	.30
☐ 190	Randy Jackson	3.00	1.20	.30
☐ 191	Joe Margoneri	3.00	1.20	.30
☐ 192	Jerry Coleman	4.00	1.60	.40
☐ 193	Del Rice	3.00	1.20	.30
☐ 194	Hal Brown	3.00	1.20	.30
☐ 195	Bobby Avila	3.00	1.20	.30
☐ 196	Larry Jackson	3.00	1.20	.30
☐ 197	Hank Sauer	4.00	1.60	.40
☐ 198	Detroit Tigers Team Card	7.50	3.00	.75
☐ 199	Vern Law	4.00	1.60	.40
☐ 200	Gil McDougald	7.50	3.00	.75
☐ 201	Sandy Amoros	4.00	1.60	.40
☐ 202	Dick Gernert	3.00	1.20	.30
☐ 203	Hoyt Wilhelm	13.00	5.25	1.30
☐ 204	Kansas City Athletics Team Card	5.00	2.00	.50
☐ 205	Charlie Maxwell	3.00	1.20	.30
☐ 206	Willard Schmidt	3.00	1.20	.30
☐ 207	Gordon (Billy) Hunter	3.00	1.20	.30
☐ 208	Lou Burdette	5.00	2.00	.50
☐ 209	Bob Skinner	4.00	1.60	.40
☐ 210	Roy Campanella	65.00	26.00	6.50
☐ 211	Camilo Pascual	4.00	1.60	.40
☐ 212	Rocco Colavito	30.00	12.00	3.00
☐ 213	Les Moss	3.00	1.20	.30
☐ 214	Philadelphia Phillies Team Card	5.00	2.00	.50
☐ 215	Enos Slaughter	14.00	5.75	1.40
☐ 216	Marv Grissom	3.00	1.20	.30
☐ 217	Gene Stephens	3.00	1.20	.30
☐ 218	Ray Jablonski	3.00	1.20	.30
☐ 219	Tom Acker	3.00	1.20	.30
☐ 220	Jackie Jensen	5.50	2.20	.55
☐ 221	Dixie Howell	3.00	1.20	.30
☐ 222	Alex Grammas	3.00	1.20	.30
☐ 223	Frank House	3.00	1.20	.30
☐ 224	Marv Blaylock	3.00	1.20	.30
☐ 225	Harry Simpson	3.00	1.20	.30
☐ 226	Preston Ward	3.00	1.20	.30
☐ 227	Jerry Staley	3.00	1.20	.30
☐ 228	Smoky Burgess	4.00	1.60	.40
☐ 229	George Susce	3.00	1.20	.30
☐ 230	George Kell	13.00	5.25	1.30
☐ 231	Solly Hemus	3.00	1.20	.30
☐ 232	Whitey Lockman	4.00	1.60	.40
☐ 233	Art Fowler	3.00	1.20	.30
☐ 234	Dick Cole	3.00	1.20	.30
☐ 235	Tom Poholsky	3.00	1.20	.30
☐ 236	Joe Ginsberg	3.00	1.20	.30

		NRMT	VG-E	GOOD
☐ 237	Foster Castleman ..	3.00	1.20	.30
☐ 238	Eddie Robinson ...	3.00	1.20	.30
☐ 239	Tom Morgan	3.00	1.20	.30
☐ 240	Hank Bauer	7.50	3.00	.75
☐ 241	Joe Lonnett	3.00	1.20	.30
☐ 242	Charlie Neal	4.00	1.60	.40
☐ 243	St. Louis Cardinals .	7.00	2.80	.70
	Team Card			
☐ 244	Billy Loes	4.00	1.60	.40
☐ 245	Rip Repulski	3.00	1.20	.30
☐ 246	Jose Valdivielso ...	3.00	1.20	.30
☐ 247	Turk Lown	3.00	1.20	.30
☐ 248	Jim Finigan	3.00	1.20	.30
☐ 249	Dave Pope	3.00	1.20	.30
☐ 250	Eddie Mathews	22.00	8.50	2.10
☐ 251	Baltimore Orioles ..	6.00	2.40	.60
	Team Card			
☐ 252	Carl Erskine	6.50	2.60	.65
☐ 253	Gus Zernial	4.00	1.60	.40
☐ 254	Ron Negray	3.00	1.20	.30
☐ 255	Charlie Silvera	3.00	1.20	.30
☐ 256	Ron Kline	3.00	1.20	.30
☐ 257	Walt Dropo	3.00	1.20	.30
☐ 258	Steve Gromek	3.00	1.20	.30
☐ 259	Eddie O'Brien	3.00	1.20	.30
☐ 260	Del Ennis	4.00	1.60	.40
☐ 261	Bob Chakales	3.00	1.20	.30
☐ 262	Bobby Thomson	5.00	2.00	.50
☐ 263	George Strickland ..	3.00	1.20	.30
☐ 264	Bob Turley	6.50	2.60	.65
☐ 265	Harvey Haddix	16.00	6.50	1.60
☐ 266	Ken Kuhn	12.50	5.00	1.25
☐ 267	Danny Kravitz	12.50	5.00	1.25
☐ 268	Jack Collum	12.50	5.00	1.25
☐ 269	Bob Cerv	14.00	5.75	1.40
☐ 270	Washington Senators	20.00	8.00	2.00
	Team Card			
☐ 271	Danny O'Connell ...	12.50	5.00	1.25
☐ 272	Bobby Shantz	20.00	8.00	2.00
☐ 273	Jim Davis	12.50	5.00	1.25
☐ 274	Don Hoak	14.00	5.75	1.40
☐ 275	Cleveland Indians ..	20.00	8.00	2.00
	Team Card			
☐ 276	Jim Pyburn	12.50	5.00	1.25
☐ 277	Johnny Podres	50.00	20.00	5.00
☐ 278	Fred Hatfield	12.50	5.00	1.25
☐ 279	Bob Thurman	12.50	5.00	1.25
☐ 280	Alex Kellner	12.50	5.00	1.25
☐ 281	Gail Harris	12.50	5.00	1.25

		NRMT	VG-E	GOOD
☐ 282	Jack Dittmer	12.50	5.00	1.25
☐ 283	Wes Covington	14.00	5.75	1.40
☐ 284	Don Zimmer	16.00	6.50	1.60
☐ 285	Ned Garver	12.50	5.00	1.25
☐ 286	Bobby Richardson .	80.00	32.00	8.00
☐ 287	Sam Jones	14.00	5.75	1.40
☐ 288	Ted Lepcio	12.50	5.00	1.25
☐ 289	Jim Bolger	12.50	5.00	1.25
☐ 290	Andy Carey	14.00	5.75	1.40
☐ 291	Windy McCall	12.50	5.00	1.25
☐ 292	Billy Klaus	12.50	5.00	1.25
☐ 293	Ted Abernathy	12.50	5.00	1.25
☐ 294	Rocky Bridges	12.50	5.00	1.25
☐ 295	Joe Collins	14.00	5.75	1.40
☐ 296	Johnny Klippstein .	12.50	5.00	1.25
☐ 297	Jack Crimian	12.50	5.00	1.25
☐ 298	Irv Noren	12.50	5.00	1.25
☐ 299	Chuck Harmon	12.50	5.00	1.25
☐ 300	Mike Garcia	14.00	5.75	1.40
☐ 301	Sammy Esposito ..	12.50	5.00	1.25
☐ 302	Sandy Koufax	300.00	120.00	30.00
☐ 303	Billy Goodman	14.00	5.75	1.40
☐ 304	Joe Cunningham ..	14.00	5.75	1.40
☐ 305	Chico Fernandez ..	12.50	5.00	1.25
☐ 306	Darrell Johnson ...	14.00	5.75	1.40
☐ 307	Jack D. Phillips ...	12.50	5.00	1.25
☐ 308	Dick Hall	12.50	5.00	1.25
☐ 309	Jim Busby	12.50	5.00	1.25
☐ 310	Max Surkont	12.50	5.00	1.25
☐ 311	Al Pilarcik	12.50	5.00	1.25
☐ 312	Tony Kubek	90.00	36.00	9.00
☐ 313	Mel Parnell	14.00	5.75	1.40
☐ 314	Ed Bouchee	12.50	5.00	1.25
☐ 315	Lou Berberet	12.50	5.00	1.25
☐ 316	Billy O'Dell	12.50	5.00	1.25
☐ 317	New York Giants ..	40.00	16.00	4.00
	Team Card			
☐ 318	Mickey McDermott .	12.50	5.00	1.25
☐ 319	Gino Cimoli	14.00	5.75	1.40
☐ 320	Neil Chrisley	12.50	5.00	1.25
☐ 321	John (Red) Murff ..	12.50	5.00	1.25
☐ 322	Cincinnati Reds ...	40.00	16.00	4.00
	Team Card			
☐ 323	Wes Westrum	14.00	5.75	1.40
☐ 324	Brooklyn Dodgers .	80.00	32.00	8.00
	Team Card			
☐ 325	Frank Bolling	12.50	5.00	1.25
☐ 326	Pedro Ramos	12.50	5.00	1.25
☐ 327	Jim Pendleton	12.50	5.00	1.25

		NRMT	VG-E	GOOD
☐ 328	Brooks Robinson	300.00	120.00	30.00
☐ 329	Chicago White Sox Team Card	20.00	8.00	2.00
☐ 330	Jim Wilson	12.50	5.00	1.25
☐ 331	Ray Katt	12.50	5.00	1.25
☐ 332	Bob Bowman	12.50	5.00	1.25
☐ 333	Ernie Johnson	12.50	5.00	1.25
☐ 334	Jerry Schoonmaker	12.50	5.00	1.25
☐ 335	Granny Hamner	12.50	5.00	1.25
☐ 336	Haywood Sullivan	14.00	5.75	1.40
☐ 337	Rene Valdes	12.50	5.00	1.25
☐ 338	Jim Bunning	100.00	40.00	10.00
☐ 339	Bob Speake	12.50	5.00	1.25
☐ 340	Bill Wight	12.50	5.00	1.25
☐ 341	Don Gross	12.50	5.00	1.25
☐ 342	Gene Mauch	16.00	6.50	1.60
☐ 343	Taylor Phillips	12.50	5.00	1.25
☐ 344	Paul LaPalme	12.50	5.00	1.25
☐ 345	Paul Smith	12.50	5.00	1.25
☐ 346	Dick Littlefield	12.50	5.00	1.25
☐ 347	Hal Naragon	12.50	5.00	1.25
☐ 348	Jim Hearn	12.50	5.00	1.25
☐ 349	Nellie King	12.50	5.00	1.25
☐ 350	Eddie Miksis	12.50	5.00	1.25
☐ 351	Dave Hillman	12.50	5.00	1.25
☐ 352	Ellis Kinder	12.50	5.00	1.25
☐ 353	Cal Neeman	3.50	1.40	.35
☐ 354	W. (Rip) Coleman	3.50	1.40	.35
☐ 355	Frank Malzone	4.50	1.80	.45
☐ 356	Faye Throneberry	3.50	1.40	.35
☐ 357	Earl Torgeson	3.50	1.40	.35
☐ 358	Jerry Lynch	4.50	1.80	.45
☐ 359	Tom Cheney	3.50	1.40	.35
☐ 360	Johnny Groth	3.50	1.40	.35
☐ 361	Curt Barclay	3.50	1.40	.35
☐ 362	Roman Mejias	3.50	1.40	.35
☐ 363	Eddie Kasko	3.50	1.40	.35
☐ 364	Cal McLish	3.50	1.40	.35
☐ 365	Ozzie Virgil	3.50	1.40	.35
☐ 366	Ken Lehman	3.50	1.40	.35
☐ 367	Ed Fitzgerald	3.50	1.40	.35
☐ 368	Bob Purkey	3.50	1.40	.35
☐ 369	Milt Graff	3.50	1.40	.35
☐ 370	Warren Hacker	3.50	1.40	.35
☐ 371	Bob Lennon	3.50	1.40	.35
☐ 372	Norm Zauchin	3.50	1.40	.35
☐ 373	Pete Whisenant	3.50	1.40	.35
☐ 374	Don Cardwell	3.50	1.40	.35
☐ 375	Jim Landis	3.50	1.40	.35

		NRMT	VG-E	GOOD
☐ 376	Don Elston	3.50	1.40	.35
☐ 377	Andre Rodgers	3.50	1.40	.35
☐ 378	Elmer Singleton	3.50	1.40	.35
☐ 379	Don Lee	3.50	1.40	.35
☐ 380	Walker Cooper	3.50	1.40	.35
☐ 381	Dean Stone	3.50	1.40	.35
☐ 382	Jim Brideweser	3.50	1.40	.35
☐ 383	Juan Pizarro	3.50	1.40	.35
☐ 384	Bobby G. Smith	3.50	1.40	.35
☐ 385	Art Houtteman	3.50	1.40	.35
☐ 386	Lyle Luttrell	3.50	1.40	.35
☐ 387	Jack Sanford	6.00	2.40	.60
☐ 388	Pete Daley	3.50	1.40	.35
☐ 389	Dave Jolly	3.50	1.40	.35
☐ 390	Reno Bertoia	3.50	1.40	.35
☐ 391	Ralph Terry	8.00	3.25	.80
☐ 392	Chuck Tanner	5.00	2.00	.50
☐ 393	Raul Sanchez	3.50	1.40	.35
☐ 394	Luis Arroyo	4.50	1.80	.45
☐ 395	J.M. (Bubba) Phillips	3.50	1.40	.35
☐ 396	K. (Casey) Wise	3.50	1.40	.35
☐ 397	Roy Smalley	3.50	1.40	.35
☐ 398	Al Cicotte	4.50	1.80	.45
☐ 399	Billy Consolo	3.50	1.40	.35
☐ 400	Dodgers' Sluggers Carl Furillo Gil Hodges Roy Campanella Duke Snider	150.00	60.00	15.00
☐ 401	Earl Battey	4.50	1.80	.45
☐ 402	Jim Pisoni	3.50	1.40	.35
☐ 403	Dick Hyde	3.50	1.40	.35
☐ 404	Harry Anderson	3.50	1.40	.35
☐ 405	Duke Maas	3.50	1.40	.35
☐ 406	Bob Hale	3.50	1.40	.35
☐ 407	Yankee Power Hitters Mickey Mantle Yogi Berra	250.00	100.00	25.00
☐ 408	Checklist 1/2 (unnumbered)	80.00	10.00	2.00
☐ 409	Checklist 2/3 (unnumbered)	125.00	15.00	3.00
☐ 410	Checklist 3/4 (unnumbered)	250.00	35.00	5.00
☐ 411	Checklist 4/5 (unnumbered)	400.00	50.00	8.00

1958 Topps

The cards in this 494-card set measure 2 ½"
by 3 ½". Although the last card is numbered
495, number 145 was not issued, bringing
the set total to 494 cards. The 1958 Topps
set contains the first Sport Magazine All-Star
Selection series (475-495) and expanded
use of combination cards. The team cards
carried series checklists on back (Milwaukee, Detroit, Baltimore, and Cincinnati
are also found with players listed alphabetically). Cards with the scarce yellow name
(YL) or team (YT) lettering, as opposed to
the common white lettering, are noted in the
checklist. In the last series cards of Stan
Musial and Mickey Mantle were triple
printed; the cards they replaced (443, 446,
450, and 462) on the printing sheet were
hence printed in shorter supply than other
cards in the last series and are marked with
an SP in the list below.

		NRMT	VG-E	GOOD
	Complete Set (494)	3250.00	1400.00	500.00
	Common Player (1-110)	3.00	1.20	.30
	Common Player (111-198)	2.25	.90	.22
	Common Player (199-352)	2.00	.80	.20
	Common Player (353-440)	2.00	.80	.20
	Common Player (441-474)	1.75	.70	.17
	Common Player (475-495)	2.00	.80	.20
☐	1 Ted Williams	300.00	75.00	15.00
☐	2A Bob Lemon	13.00	5.25	1.30
☐	2B Bob Lemon YT	30.00	12.00	3.00
☐	3 Alex Kellner	3.00	1.20	.30

		NRMT	VG-E	GOOD
☐	4 Hank Foiles	3.00	1.20	.30
☐	5 Willie Mays	125.00	50.00	12.50
☐	6 George Zuverink	3.00	1.20	.30
☐	7 Dale Long	4.00	1.60	.40
☐	8A Eddie Kasko	3.00	1.20	.30
☐	8B Eddie Kasko YL	20.00	8.00	2.00
☐	9 Hank Bauer	6.00	2.40	.60
☐	10 Lou Burdette	5.00	2.00	.50
☐	11A Jim Rivera	3.00	1.20	.30
☐	11B Jim Rivera YT	15.00	6.00	1.50
☐	12 George Crowe	3.00	1.20	.30
☐	13A Billy Hoeft	3.00	1.20	.30
☐	13B Billy Hoeft YL	20.00	8.00	2.00
☐	14 Rip Repulski	3.00	1.20	.30
☐	15 Jim Lemon	4.00	1.60	.40
☐	16 Charlie Neal	4.00	1.60	.40
☐	17 Felix Mantilla	3.00	1.20	.30
☐	18 Frank Sullivan	3.00	1.20	.30
☐	19 New York Giants Team Card (checklist on back)	12.00	3.00	.60
☐	20A Gil McDougald	7.00	2.80	.70
☐	20B Gil McDougald YL	25.00	10.00	2.50
☐	21 Curt Barclay	3.00	1.20	.30
☐	22 Hal Naragon	3.00	1.20	.30
☐	23A Bill Tuttle	3.00	1.20	.30
☐	23B Bill Tuttle YL	20.00	8.00	2.00
☐	24A Hobie Landrith	3.00	1.20	.30
☐	24B Hobie Landrith YL	20.00	8.00	2.00
☐	25 Don Drysdale	25.00	10.00	2.50
☐	26 Ron Jackson	3.00	1.20	.30
☐	27 Bud Freeman	3.00	1.20	.30
☐	28 Jim Busby	3.00	1.20	.30
☐	29 Ted Lepcio	3.00	1.20	.30
☐	30A Hank Aaron	125.00	50.00	12.50
☐	30B Hank Aaron YL	200.00	80.00	20.00
☐	31 Tex Clevenger	3.00	1.20	.30
☐	32A J.W. Porter	3.00	1.20	.30
☐	32B J.W. Porter YL	20.00	8.00	2.00
☐	33A Cal Neeman	3.00	1.20	.30
☐	33B Cal Neeman YT	15.00	6.00	1.50
☐	34 Bob Thurman	3.00	1.20	.30
☐	35A Don Mossi	4.00	1.60	.40
☐	35B Don Mossi YT	15.00	6.00	1.50
☐	36 Ted Kazanski	3.00	1.20	.30
☐	37 Mike McCormick (photo actually Ray Monzant)	4.00	1.60	.40
☐	38 Dick Gernert	3.00	1.20	.30
☐	39 Bob Martyn	3.00	1.20	.30

		NRMT	VG-E	GOOD
☐ 40	George Kell	12.00	5.00	1.20
☐ 41	Dave Hillman	3.00	1.20	.30
☐ 42	John Roseboro	5.00	2.00	.50
☐ 43	Sal Maglie	5.00	2.00	.50
☐ 44	Washington Senators Team Card (checklist on back)	5.00	1.50	.30
☐ 45	Dick Groat	5.00	2.00	.50
☐ 46A	Lou Sleater	3.00	1.20	.30
☐ 46B	Lou Sleater YL	20.00	8.00	2.00
☐ 47	Roger Maris	300.00	120.00	30.00
☐ 48	Chuck Harmon	3.00	1.20	.30
☐ 49	Smoky Burgess	4.00	1.60	.40
☐ 50A	Billy Pierce	5.00	2.00	.50
☐ 50B	Billy Pierce YT	20.00	8.00	2.00
☐ 51	Del Rice	3.00	1.20	.30
☐ 52A	Bob Clemente	65.00	26.00	6.50
☐ 52B	Bob Clemente YT	125.00	50.00	12.50
☐ 53A	Morrie Martin	3.00	1.20	.30
☐ 53B	Morrie Martin YL	20.00	8.00	2.00
☐ 54	Norm Siebern	3.00	1.20	.30
☐ 55	Chico Carrasquel	3.00	1.20	.30
☐ 56	Bill Fischer	3.00	1.20	.30
☐ 57A	Tim Thompson	3.00	1.20	.30
☐ 57B	Tim Thompson YL	20.00	8.00	2.00
☐ 58A	Art Schult	3.00	1.20	.30
☐ 58B	Art Schult YT	15.00	6.00	1.50
☐ 59	Dave Sisler	3.00	1.20	.30
☐ 60A	Del Ennis	4.00	1.60	.40
☐ 60B	Del Ennis YL	20.00	8.00	2.00
☐ 61A	Darrell Johnson	4.00	1.60	.40
☐ 61B	Darrell Johnson YL	20.00	8.00	2.00
☐ 62	Joe DeMaestri	3.00	1.20	.30
☐ 63	Joe Nuxhall	4.00	1.60	.40
☐ 64	Joe Lonnett	3.00	1.20	.30
☐ 65A	Von McDaniel	3.00	1.20	.30
☐ 65B	Von McDaniel YL	20.00	8.00	2.00
☐ 66	Lee Walls	3.00	1.20	.30
☐ 67	Joe Ginsberg	3.00	1.20	.30
☐ 68	Daryl Spencer	3.00	1.20	.30
☐ 69	Wally Burnette	3.00	1.20	.30
☐ 70A	Al Kaline	35.00	14.00	3.50
☐ 70B	Al Kaline YL	70.00	28.00	7.00
☐ 71	Dodgers Team (checklist on back)	15.00	3.50	.75
☐ 72	Bud Byerly	3.00	1.20	.30
☐ 73	Pete Daley	3.00	1.20	.30
☐ 74	Roy Face	5.00	2.00	.50
☐ 75	Gus Bell	4.00	1.60	.40

		NRMT	VG-E	GOOD
☐ 76A	Dick Farrell	4.00	1.60	.40
☐ 76B	Dick Farrell YT	20.00	8.00	2.00
☐ 77A	Don Zimmer	5.00	2.00	.50
☐ 77B	Don Zimmer YT	20.00	8.00	2.00
☐ 78A	Ernie Johnson	3.00	1.20	.30
☐ 78B	Ernie Johnson YL	20.00	8.00	2.00
☐ 79A	Dick Williams	4.00	1.60	.40
☐ 79B	Dick Williams YT	20.00	8.00	2.00
☐ 80	Dick Drott	3.00	1.20	.30
☐ 81A	Steve Boros	4.00	1.60	.40
☐ 81B	Steve Boros YT	20.00	8.00	2.00
☐ 82	Ron Kline	3.00	1.20	.30
☐ 83	Bob Hazle	4.00	1.60	.40
☐ 84	Billy O'Dell	3.00	1.20	.30
☐ 85A	Luis Aparicio	14.00	5.75	1.40
☐ 85B	Luis Aparicio YT	30.00	12.00	3.00
☐ 86	Valmy Thomas	3.00	1.20	.30
☐ 87	Johnny Kucks	3.00	1.20	.30
☐ 88	Duke Snider	45.00	18.00	4.00
☐ 89	Billy Klaus	3.00	1.20	.30
☐ 90	Robin Roberts	12.00	5.00	1.20
☐ 91	Chuck Tanner	4.00	1.60	.40
☐ 92A	Clint Courtney	3.00	1.20	.30
☐ 92B	Clint Courtney YL	20.00	8.00	2.00
☐ 93	Sandy Amoros	4.00	1.60	.40
☐ 94	Bob Skinner	3.00	1.20	.30
☐ 95	Frank Bolling	3.00	1.20	.30
☐ 96	Joe Durham	3.00	1.20	.30
☐ 97A	Larry Jackson	3.00	1.20	.30
☐ 97B	Larry Jackson YL	20.00	8.00	2.00
☐ 98A	Billy Hunter	3.00	1.20	.30
☐ 98B	Billy Hunter YL	20.00	8.00	2.00
☐ 99	Bobby Adams	3.00	1.20	.30
☐ 100A	Early Wynn	12.00	5.00	1.20
☐ 100B	Early Wynn YT	30.00	12.00	3.00
☐ 101A	Bobby Richardson	10.00	4.00	1.00
☐ 101B	Bobby Richardson YT	30.00	12.00	3.00
☐ 102	George Strickland	3.00	1.20	.30
☐ 103	Jerry Lynch	3.00	1.20	.30
☐ 104	Jim Pendleton	3.00	1.20	.30
☐ 105	Billy Gardner	4.00	1.60	.40
☐ 106	Dick Schofield	3.00	1.20	.30
☐ 107	Ossie Virgil	3.00	1.20	.30
☐ 108A	Jim Landis	3.00	1.20	.30
☐ 108B	Jim Landis YT	15.00	6.00	1.50
☐ 109	Herb Plews	3.00	1.20	.30
☐ 110	Johnny Logan	4.00	1.60	.40
☐ 111	Stu Miller	2.25	.90	.22
☐ 112	Gus Zernial	3.00	1.20	.30

		NRMT	VG-E	GOOD
☐ 113	Jerry Walker	2.25	.90	.22
☐ 114	Irv Noren	2.25	.90	.22
☐ 115	Jim Bunning	10.00	4.00	1.00
☐ 116	Dave Philley	2.25	.90	.22
☐ 117	Frank Torre	2.25	.90	.22
☐ 118	Harvey Haddix	3.50	1.40	.35
☐ 119	Harry Chiti	2.25	.90	.22
☐ 120	Johnny Podres	6.00	2.40	.60
☐ 121	Eddie Miksis	2.25	.90	.22
☐ 122	Walt Moryn	2.25	.90	.22
☐ 123	Dick Tomanek	2.25	.90	.22
☐ 124	Bobby Usher	2.25	.90	.22
☐ 125	Alvin Dark	3.50	1.40	.35
☐ 126	Stan Palys	2.25	.90	.22
☐ 127	Tom Sturdivant	3.00	1.20	.30
☐ 128	Willie Kirkland	3.00	1.20	.30
☐ 129	Jim Derrington	2.25	.90	.22
☐ 130	Jackie Jensen	6.00	2.40	.60
☐ 131	Bob Henrich	2.25	.90	.22
☐ 132	Vern Law	3.00	1.20	.30
☐ 133	Russ Nixon	4.00	1.60	.40
☐ 134	Philadelphia Phillies Team Card (checklist on back)	5.00	1.50	.30
☐ 135	Mike (Moe) Drabowsky	3.00	1.20	.30
☐ 136	Jim Finigan	2.25	.90	.22
☐ 137	Russ Kemmerer	2.25	.90	.22
☐ 138	Earl Torgeson	2.25	.90	.22
☐ 139	George Brunet	2.25	.90	.22
☐ 140	Wes Covington	3.00	1.20	.30
☐ 141	Ken Lehman	2.25	.90	.22
☐ 142	Enos Slaughter	13.00	5.25	1.30
☐ 143	Billy Muffett	2.25	.90	.22
☐ 144	Bobby Morgan	2.25	.90	.22
☐ 145	Never issued	0.00	.00	.00
☐ 146	Dick Gray	2.25	.90	.22
☐ 147	Don McMahon	3.00	1.20	.30
☐ 148	Billy Consolo	2.25	.90	.22
☐ 149	Tom Acker	2.25	.90	.22
☐ 150	Mickey Mantle	450.00	180.00	45.00
☐ 151	Buddy Pritchard	2.25	.90	.22
☐ 152	Johnny Antonelli	3.00	1.20	.30
☐ 153	Les Moss	2.25	.90	.22
☐ 154	Harry Byrd	2.25	.90	.22
☐ 155	Hector Lopez	2.25	.90	.22
☐ 156	Dick Hyde	2.25	.90	.22
☐ 157	Dee Fondy	2.25	.90	.22

		NRMT	VG-E	GOOD
☐ 158	Cleveland Indians Team Card (checklist on back)	5.00	1.50	.30
☐ 159	Taylor Phillips	2.25	.90	.22
☐ 160	Don Hoak	3.00	1.20	.30
☐ 161	Don Larsen	5.00	2.00	.50
☐ 162	Gil Hodges	16.00	6.50	1.60
☐ 163	Jim Wilson	2.25	.90	.22
☐ 164	Bob Taylor	2.25	.90	.22
☐ 165	Bob Nieman	2.25	.90	.22
☐ 166	Danny O'Connell	2.25	.90	.22
☐ 167	Frank Baumann	2.25	.90	.22
☐ 168	Joe Cunningham	3.00	1.20	.30
☐ 169	Ralph Terry	4.00	1.60	.40
☐ 170	Vic Wertz	3.00	1.20	.30
☐ 171	Harry Anderson	2.25	.90	.22
☐ 172	Don Gross	2.25	.90	.22
☐ 173	Eddie Yost	2.25	.90	.22
☐ 174	Athletics Team (checklist on back)	5.00	1.50	.30
☐ 175	Marv Throneberry	6.00	2.40	.60
☐ 176	Bob Buhl	2.25	.90	.22
☐ 177	Al Smith	2.25	.90	.22
☐ 178	Ted Kluszewski	6.50	2.60	.65
☐ 179	Willie Miranda	2.25	.90	.22
☐ 180	Lindy McDaniel	3.00	1.20	.30
☐ 181	Willie Jones	2.25	.90	.22
☐ 182	Joe Caffie	2.25	.90	.22
☐ 183	Dave Jolly	2.25	.90	.22
☐ 184	Elvin Tappe	2.25	.90	.22
☐ 185	Ray Boone	3.00	1.20	.30
☐ 186	Jack Meyer	2.25	.90	.22
☐ 187	Sandy Koufax	75.00	30.00	7.50
☐ 188	Milt Bolling (photo actually Lou Berberet)	2.25	.90	.22
☐ 189	George Susce	2.25	.90	.22
☐ 190	Red Schoendienst	4.50	1.80	.45
☐ 191	Art Ceccarelli	2.25	.90	.22
☐ 192	Milt Graff	2.25	.90	.22
☐ 193	Jerry Lumpe	2.25	.90	.22
☐ 194	Roger Craig	6.00	2.20	.55
☐ 195	Whitey Lockman	3.00	1.20	.30
☐ 196	Mike Garcia	3.00	1.20	.30
☐ 197	Haywood Sullivan	3.00	1.20	.30
☐ 198	Bill Virdon	3.50	1.40	.35
☐ 199	Don Blasingame	2.00	.80	.20
☐ 200	Bob Keegan	2.00	.80	.20
☐ 201	Jim Bolger	2.00	.80	.20
☐ 202	Woody Held	2.00	.80	.20

		NRMT	VG-E	GOOD
☐ 203	Al Walker	2.00	.80	.20
☐ 204	Leo Kiely	2.00	.80	.20
☐ 205	Johnny Temple	2.50	1.00	.25
☐ 206	Bob Shaw	2.00	.80	.20
☐ 207	Solly Hemus	2.00	.80	.20
☐ 208	Cal McLish	2.00	.80	.20
☐ 209	Bob Anderson	2.00	.80	.20
☐ 210	Wally Moon	3.00	1.20	.30
☐ 211	Pete Burnside	2.00	.80	.20
☐ 212	Bubba Phillips	2.00	.80	.20
☐ 213	Red Wilson	2.00	.80	.20
☐ 214	Willard Schmidt	2.00	.80	.20
☐ 215	Jim Gilliam	6.00	2.40	.60
☐ 216	St. Louis Cardinals Team Card (checklist on back)	5.00	1.50	.30
☐ 217	Jack Harshman	2.00	.80	.20
☐ 218	Dick Rand	2.00	.80	.20
☐ 219	Camilo Pascual	2.50	1.00	.25
☐ 220	Tom Brewer	2.00	.80	.20
☐ 221	Jerry Kindall	2.50	1.00	.25
☐ 222	Bud Daley	2.00	.80	.20
☐ 223	Andy Pafko	2.50	1.00	.25
☐ 224	Bob Grim	2.50	1.00	.25
☐ 225	Billy Goodman	2.50	1.00	.25
☐ 226	Bob Smith	2.00	.80	.20
☐ 227	Gene Stephens	2.00	.80	.20
☐ 228	Duke Maas	2.00	.80	.20
☐ 229	Frank Zupo	2.00	.80	.20
☐ 230	Richie Ashburn	8.00	3.25	.80
☐ 231	Lloyd Merritt	2.00	.80	.20
☐ 232	Reno Bertoia	2.00	.80	.20
☐ 233	Mickey Vernon	2.50	1.00	.25
☐ 234	Carl Sawatski	2.00	.80	.20
☐ 235	Tom Gorman	2.00	.80	.20
☐ 236	Ed Fitzgerald	2.00	.80	.20
☐ 237	Bill Wight	2.00	.80	.20
☐ 238	Bill Mazeroski	7.00	2.80	.70
☐ 239	Chuck Stobbs	2.00	.80	.20
☐ 240	Bill Skowron	7.50	3.00	.75
☐ 241	Dick Littlefield	2.00	.80	.20
☐ 242	Johnny Klippstein	2.00	.80	.20
☐ 243	Larry Raines	2.00	.80	.20
☐ 244	Don Demeter	2.00	.80	.20
☐ 245	Frank Lary	2.50	1.00	.25
☐ 246	New York Yankees Team Card (checklist on back)	25.00	6.00	1.00
☐ 247	Casey Wise	2.00	.80	.20
☐ 248	Herman Wehmeier	2.00	.80	.20
☐ 249	Ray Moore	2.00	.80	.20
☐ 250	Roy Sievers	3.00	1.20	.30
☐ 251	Warren Hacker	2.00	.80	.20
☐ 252	Bob Trowbridge	2.00	.80	.20
☐ 253	Don Mueller	2.50	1.00	.25
☐ 254	Alex Grammas	2.00	.80	.20
☐ 255	Bob Turley	6.00	2.40	.60
☐ 256	Chicago White Sox Team Card (checklist on back)	5.00	1.50	.30
☐ 257	Hal Smith	2.00	.80	.20
☐ 258	Carl Erskine	5.00	2.00	.50
☐ 259	Al Pilarcik	2.00	.80	.20
☐ 260	Frank Malzone	3.00	1.20	.30
☐ 261	Turk Lown	2.00	.80	.20
☐ 262	Johnny Groth	2.00	.80	.20
☐ 263	Eddie Bressoud	2.00	.80	.20
☐ 264	Jack Sanford	2.50	1.00	.25
☐ 265	Pete Runnels	2.50	1.00	.25
☐ 266	Connie Johnson	2.00	.80	.20
☐ 267	Sherm Lollar	2.50	1.00	.25
☐ 268	Granny Hamner	2.00	.80	.20
☐ 269	Bob Boyd	2.00	.80	.20
☐ 270	Warren Spahn	22.00	9.00	2.20
☐ 271	Billy Martin	7.00	2.80	.70
☐ 272	Ray Crone	2.00	.80	.20
☐ 273	Hal Smith	2.00	.80	.20
☐ 274	Rocky Bridges	2.00	.80	.20
☐ 275	Elston Howard	6.50	2.60	.65
☐ 276	Bobby Avila	2.50	1.00	.25
☐ 277	Virgil Trucks	2.50	1.00	.25
☐ 278	Mack Burk	2.00	.80	.20
☐ 279	Bob Boyd	2.00	.80	.20
☐ 280	Jim Piersall	4.50	1.80	.45
☐ 281	Sammy Taylor	2.00	.80	.20
☐ 282	Paul Foytack	2.00	.80	.20
☐ 283	Ray Shearer	2.00	.80	.20
☐ 284	Ray Katt	2.00	.80	.20
☐ 285	Frank Robinson	40.00	16.00	4.00
☐ 286	Gino Cimoli	2.50	1.00	.25
☐ 287	Sam Jones	2.50	1.00	.25
☐ 288	Harmon Killebrew	25.00	10.00	2.50
☐ 289	Series Hurling Rivals Lou Burdette Bobby Shantz	3.50	1.40	.35
☐ 290	Dick Donovan	2.00	.80	.20
☐ 291	Don Landrum	2.00	.80	.20
☐ 292	Ned Garver	2.00	.80	.20

		NRMT	VG-E	GOOD
☐ 293	Gene Freese	2.00	.80	.20
☐ 294	Hal Jeffcoat	2.00	.80	.20
☐ 295	Minnie Minoso	5.00	2.00	.45
☐ 296	Ryne Duren	6.50	2.60	.65
☐ 297	Don Buddin	2.00	.80	.20
☐ 298	Jim Hearn	2.00	.80	.20
☐ 299	Harry Simpson	2.00	.00	.20
☐ 300	Harridge and Giles	4.00	1.60	.40
	League Presidents			
☐ 301	Randy Jackson	2.00	.80	.20
☐ 302	Mike Baxes	2.00	.80	.20
☐ 303	Neil Chrisley	2.00	.80	.20
☐ 304	Tigers' Big Bats	6.50	2.60	.65
	Harvey Kuenn			
	Al Kaline			
☐ 305	Clem Labine	3.00	1.20	.30
☐ 306	Whammy Douglas	2.00	.80	.20
☐ 307	Brooks Robinson	45.00	18.00	4.50
☐ 308	Paul Giel	2.00	.80	.20
☐ 309	Gail Harris	2.00	.80	.20
☐ 310	Ernie Banks	35.00	14.00	3.50
☐ 311	Bob Purkey	2.00	.80	.20
☐ 312	Boston Red Sox	7.00	2.00	.40
	Team Card			
	(checklist on back)			
☐ 313	Bob Rush	2.00	.80	.20
☐ 314	Dodgers' Boss and	12.50	5.00	1.25
	Power: Duke Snider			
	Walt Alston			
☐ 315	Bob Friend	3.00	1.20	.30
☐ 316	Tito Francona	2.00	.80	.20
☐ 317	Albie Pearson	3.00	1.20	.30
☐ 318	Frank House	2.00	.80	.20
☐ 319	Lou Skizas	2.00	.80	.20
☐ 320	Whitey Ford	27.00	11.00	2.70
☐ 321	Sluggers Supreme	18.00	7.25	1.80
	Ted Kluszewski			
	Ted Williams			
☐ 322	Harding Peterson	2.00	.80	.20
☐ 323	Elmer Valo	2.00	.80	.20
☐ 324	Hoyt Wilhelm	12.00	5.00	1.20
☐ 325	Joe Adcock	3.00	1.20	.30
☐ 326	Bob Miller	2.00	.80	.20
☐ 327	Chicago Cubs	5.00	1.50	.30
	Team Card			
	(checklist on back)			
☐ 328	Ike Delock	2.00	.80	.20
☐ 329	Bob Cerv	2.50	1.00	.25
☐ 330	Ed Bailey	2.50	1.00	.25

		NRMT	VG-E	GOOD
☐ 331	Pedro Ramos	2.00	.80	.20
☐ 332	Jim King	2.00	.80	.20
☐ 333	Andy Carey	3.00	1.20	.30
☐ 334	Mound Aces	3.00	1.20	.30
	Bob Friend			
	Billy Pierce			
☐ 335	Ruben Gomez	2.00	.80	.20
☐ 336	Bert Hamric	2.00	.80	.20
☐ 337	Hank Aguirre	2.00	.80	.20
☐ 338	Walt Dropo	2.00	.80	.20
☐ 339	Fred Hatfield	2.00	.80	.20
☐ 340	Don Newcombe	5.00	2.00	.50
☐ 341	Pittsburgh Pirates	5.00	1.50	.30
	Team Card			
	(checklist on back)			
☐ 342	Jim Brosnan	2.50	1.00	.25
☐ 343	Orlando Cepeda	30.00	12.00	3.00
☐ 344	Bob Porterfield	2.00	.80	.20
☐ 345	Jim Hegan	2.50	1.00	.25
☐ 346	Steve Bilko	2.00	.80	.20
☐ 347	Don Rudolph	2.00	.80	.20
☐ 348	Chico Fernandez	2.00	.80	.20
☐ 349	Murry Dickson	2.00	.80	.20
☐ 350	Ken Boyer	4.50	1.80	.45
☐ 351	Braves Fence Busters	16.00	6.50	1.60
	Del Crandall			
	Eddie Mathews			
	Hank Aaron			
	Joe Adcock			
☐ 352	Herb Score	4.00	1.75	.35
☐ 353	Stan Lopata	2.00	.80	.20
☐ 354	Art Ditmar	2.50	1.00	.25
☐ 355	Bill Bruton	2.50	1.00	.25
☐ 356	Bob Malkmus	2.00	.80	.20
☐ 357	Danny McDevitt	2.00	.80	.20
☐ 358	Gene Baker	2.00	.80	.20
☐ 359	Billy Loes	2.00	.80	.20
☐ 360	Roy McMillan	2.00	.80	.20
☐ 361	Mike Fornieles	2.00	.80	.20
☐ 362	Ray Jablonski	2.00	.80	.20
☐ 363	Don Elston	2.00	.80	.20
☐ 364	Earl Battey	2.50	1.00	.25
☐ 365	Tom Morgan	2.00	.80	.20
☐ 366	Gene Green	2.00	.80	.20
☐ 367	Jack Urban	2.00	.80	.20
☐ 368	Rocky Colavito	7.50	3.00	.75
☐ 369	Ralph Lumenti	2.00	.80	.20
☐ 370	Yogi Berra	50.00	20.00	5.00
☐ 371	Marty Keough	2.00	.80	.20

		NRMT	VG-E	GOOD
☐ 372	Don Cardwell	2.00	.80	.20
☐ 373	Joe Pignatano	2.00	.80	.20
☐ 374	Brooks Lawrence	2.00	.80	.20
☐ 375	Pee Wee Reese	28.00	11.50	2.80
☐ 376	Charley Rabe	2.00	.80	.20
☐ 377A	Milwaukee Braves Team Card (alphabetical)	6.00	2.40	.60
☐ 377B	Milwaukee Team numerical checklist	45.00	5.00	1.00
☐ 378	Hank Sauer	2.50	1.00	.25
☐ 379	Ray Herbert	2.00	.80	.20
☐ 380	Charley Maxwell	2.00	.80	.20
☐ 381	Hal Brown	2.00	.80	.20
☐ 382	Al Cicotte	2.50	1.00	.25
☐ 383	Lou Berberet	2.00	.80	.20
☐ 384	John Goryl	2.00	.80	.20
☐ 385	Wilmer Mizell	2.00	.80	.20
☐ 386	Birdie's Sluggers Ed Bailey Birdie Tebbetts Frank Robinson	6.00	2.40	.60
☐ 387	Wally Post	2.50	1.00	.25
☐ 388	Billy Moran	2.00	.80	.20
☐ 389	Bill Taylor	2.00	.80	.20
☐ 390	Del Crandall	2.50	1.00	.25
☐ 391	Dave Melton	2.00	.80	.20
☐ 392	Bennie Daniels	2.00	.80	.20
☐ 393	Tony Kubek	11.00	4.50	1.10
☐ 394	Jim Grant	2.50	1.00	.25
☐ 395	Willard Nixon	2.00	.80	.20
☐ 396	Dutch Dotterer	2.00	.80	.20
☐ 397A	Detroit Tigers Team Card (alphabetical)	6.00	2.40	.60
☐ 397B	Detroit Team numerical checklist	45.00	5.00	1.00
☐ 398	Gene Woodling	3.00	1.20	.30
☐ 399	Marv Grissom	2.00	.80	.20
☐ 400	Nellie Fox	7.50	3.00	.75
☐ 401	Don Bessent	2.50	1.00	.25
☐ 402	Bobby Gene Smith	2.00	.80	.20
☐ 403	Steve Korcheck	2.00	.80	.20
☐ 404	Curt Simmons	2.50	1.00	.25
☐ 405	Ken Aspromonte	2.00	.80	.20
☐ 406	Vic Power	2.50	1.00	.25
☐ 407	Carlton Willey	2.00	.80	.20

		NRMT	VG-E	GOOD
☐ 408A	Baltimore Orioles Team Card (alphabetical)	6.00	2.40	.60
☐ 408B	Baltimore Team numerical checklist	45.00	5.00	1.00
☐ 409	Frank Thomas	2.50	1.00	.25
☐ 410	Murray Wall	2.00	.80	.20
☐ 411	Tony Taylor	2.00	.80	.20
☐ 412	Jerry Staley	2.00	.80	.20
☐ 413	Jim Davenport	2.50	1.00	.25
☐ 414	Sammy White	2.00	.80	.20
☐ 415	Bob Bowman	2.00	.80	.20
☐ 416	Foster Castleman	2.00	.80	.20
☐ 417	Carl Furillo	6.00	2.40	.60
☐ 418	World Series Batting Foes: Mickey Mantle Hank Aaron	100.00	40.00	10.00
☐ 419	Bobby Shantz	4.00	1.60	.40
☐ 420	Vada Pinson	12.00	5.00	1.20
☐ 421	Dixie Howell	2.00	.80	.20
☐ 422	Norm Zauchin	2.00	.80	.20
☐ 423	Phil Clark	2.00	.80	.20
☐ 424	Larry Doby	4.00	1.60	.40
☐ 425	Sammy Esposito	2.00	.80	.20
☐ 426	Johnny O'Brien	2.00	.80	.20
☐ 427	Al Worthington	2.00	.80	.20
☐ 428A	Cincinnati Reds Team Card (alphabetical)	6.00	2.40	.60
☐ 428B	Cincinnati Team numerical checklist	45.00	5.00	1.00
☐ 429	Gus Triandos	2.50	1.00	.25
☐ 430	Bobby Thomson	3.50	1.40	.35
☐ 431	Gene Conley	2.00	.80	.20
☐ 432	John Powers	2.00	.80	.20
☐ 433A	Pancho Herrer ERR	400.00	160.00	40.00
☐ 433B	Pancho Herrera COR	2.50	1.00	.25
☐ 434	Harvey Kuenn	4.50	1.80	.45
☐ 435	Ed Roebuck	2.50	1.00	.25
☐ 436	Rival Fence Busters Willie Mays Duke Snider	40.00	16.00	4.00
☐ 437	Bob Speake	2.00	.80	.20
☐ 438	Whitey Herzog	4.00	1.60	.40
☐ 439	Ray Narleski	2.00	.80	.20
☐ 440	Eddie Mathews	20.00	8.00	2.00
☐ 441	Jim Marshall	1.75	.70	.17
☐ 442	Phil Paine	1.75	.70	.17
☐ 443	Billy Harrell SP	7.50	3.00	.75

	NRMT	VG-E	GOOD
☐ 444 Danny Kravitz	1.75	.70	.17
☐ 445 Bob Smith	1.75	.70	.17
☐ 446 Carroll Hardy SP ...	7.50	3.00	.75
☐ 447 Ray Monzant	1.75	.70	.17
☐ 448 Charlie Lau	4.00	1.60	.40
☐ 449 Gene Fodge	1.75	.70	.17
☐ 450 Preston Ward SP ..	7.50	3.00	.75
☐ 451 Joe Taylor	1.75	.70	.17
☐ 452 Roman Mejias	1.75	.70	.17
☐ 453 Tom Qualters	1.75	.70	.17
☐ 454 Harry Hanebrink ...	1.75	.70	.17
☐ 455 Hal Griggs	1.75	.70	.17
☐ 456 Dick Brown	1.75	.70	.17
☐ 457 Milt Pappas	3.50	1.40	.35
☐ 458 Julio Becquer	1.75	.70	.17
☐ 459 Ron Blackburn	1.75	.70	.17
☐ 460 Chuck Essegian ...	1.75	.70	.17
☐ 461 Ed Mayer	1.75	.70	.17
☐ 462 Gary Geiger SP ...	7.50	3.00	.75
☐ 463 Vito Valentinetti	1.75	.70	.17
☐ 464 Curt Flood	10.00	4.00	1.00
☐ 465 Arnie Portocarrero .	1.75	.70	.17
☐ 466 Pete Whisenant ...	1.75	.70	.17
☐ 467 Glen Hobbie	1.75	.70	.17
☐ 468 Bob Schmidt	1.75	.70	.17
☐ 469 Don Ferrarese	1.75	.70	.17
☐ 470 R.C. Stevens	1.75	.70	.17
☐ 471 Lenny Green	1.75	.70	.17
☐ 472 Joey Jay	2.50	1.00	.25
☐ 473 Bill Renna	1.75	.70	.17
☐ 474 Roman Semproch ..	1.75	.70	.17
☐ 475 Haney/Stengel AS . (checklist back)	12.50	4.00	.80
☐ 476 Stan Musial AS TP .	21.00	8.50	2.10
☐ 477 Bill Skowron AS ...	3.50	1.40	.35
☐ 478 Johnny Temple AS .	2.00	.80	.20
☐ 479 Nellie Fox AS	4.50	1.80	.45
☐ 480 Eddie Mathews AS .	9.00	3.75	.90
☐ 481 Frank Malzone AS .	2.00	.80	.20
☐ 482 Ernie Banks AS	11.00	4.50	1.10
☐ 483 Luis Aparicio AS ..	7.00	2.80	.70
☐ 484 Frank Robinson AS	10.00	4.00	1.00
☐ 485 Ted Williams AS ..	40.00	16.00	4.00
☐ 486 Willie Mays AS	25.00	10.00	2.50
☐ 487 Mickey Mantle AS TP	50.00	20.00	5.00
☐ 488 Hank Aaron AS ...	25.00	10.00	2.50
☐ 489 Jackie Jensen AS ..	3.00	1.20	.30
☐ 490 Ed Bailey AS	2.00	.80	.20
☐ 491 Sherm Lollar AS ..	2.00	.80	.20

	NRMT	VG-E	GOOD
☐ 492 Bob Friend AS	2.00	.80	.20
☐ 493 Bob Turley AS	2.50	1.00	.25
☐ 494 Warren Spahn AS .	10.00	4.00	1.00
☐ 495 Herb Score AS ...	4.00	1.60	.40

1959 Topps

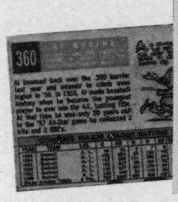

The cards in this 572-card set measure 2 ½ " by 3 ½ ". The 1959 Topps set contains bust pictures of the players in a colored circle. Card numbers 551 to 572 are Sporting News All-Star Selections. High numbers 507 to 572 have the card number in a black background on the reverse rather than a green background as in the lower numbers. The high numbers are more difficult to obtain. Several cards in the 300's exist with or without an extra traded or option line on the back of the card. Cards 199 to 286 exist with either white or gray backs. Cards 461 to 470 contain "Highlights" while cards 116 to 146 give an alphabetically ordered listing of "Rookie Prospects." These Rookie Prospects (RP) were Topps' first organized inclusion of untested "Rookie" cards. Card 440 features Lew Burdette erroneously posing as a left-handed pitcher. There were some three-card advertising panels produced by Topps; the players included are from the first series; one panel shows Don McMahon, Red Wilson, and Bob Boyd on the front with Ted Kluszewski's reverse on one of the backs. When cut apart, these *advertising cards are distinguished by the non-standard card back, i.e., part of an advertisement for the 1959 Topps set instead of the typical statistics and biographical information about the player pictured.*

		NRMT	VG-E	GOOD
Complete Set (572)		3250.00	1400.00	500.00
Common Player (1-110)		2.25	.90	.22
Common Player (111-506)		1.75	.70	.17
Common Player (507-550)		7.50	3.00	.75
Common Player (551-572)		9.00	3.75	.90
☐ 1	Ford Frick	35.00	3.50	.70
☐ 2	Eddie Yost	2.25	.90	.22
☐ 3	Don McMahon	2.25	.90	.22
☐ 4	Albie Pearson	2.25	.90	.22
☐ 5	Dick Donovan	2.25	.90	.22
☐ 6	Alex Grammas	2.25	.90	.22
☐ 7	Al Pilarcik	2.25	.90	.22
☐ 8	Phillies Team	6.50	1.50	.25
	(checklist on back)			
☐ 9	Paul Giel	2.25	.90	.22
☐ 10	Mickey Mantle	300.00	120.00	30.00
☐ 11	Billy Hunter	2.25	.90	.22
☐ 12	Vern Law	3.00	1.20	.30
☐ 13	Dick Gernert	2.25	.90	.22
☐ 14	Pete Whisenant	2.25	.90	.22
☐ 15	Dick Drott	2.25	.90	.22
☐ 16	Joe Pignatano	2.25	.90	.22
☐ 17	Danny's Stars	3.50	1.40	.35
	Frank Thomas			
	Danny Murtaugh			
	Ted Kluszewski			
☐ 18	Jack Urban	2.25	.90	.22
☐ 19	Eddie Bressoud	2.25	.90	.22
☐ 20	Duke Snider	40.00	16.00	4.00
☐ 21	Connie Johnson	2.25	.90	.22
☐ 22	Al Smith	2.25	.90	.22
☐ 23	Murry Dickson	2.25	.90	.22
☐ 24	Red Wilson	2.25	.90	.22
☐ 25	Don Hoak	3.00	1.20	.30
☐ 26	Chuck Stobbs	2.25	.90	.22
☐ 27	Andy Pafko	3.00	1.20	.30
☐ 28	Al Worthington	2.25	.90	.22
☐ 29	Jim Bolger	2.25	.90	.22
☐ 30	Nellie Fox	7.00	2.80	.70
☐ 31	Ken Lehman	2.25	.90	.22
☐ 32	Don Buddin	2.25	.90	.22
☐ 33	Ed Fitzgerald	2.25	.90	.22

		NRMT	VG-E	GOOD
☐ 34	Pitchers Beware	6.00	2.40	.60
	Al Kaline			
	Charley Maxwell			
☐ 35	Ted Kluszewski	5.00	2.00	.50
☐ 36	Hank Aguirre	2.25	.90	.22
☐ 37	Gene Green	2.25	.90	.22
☐ 38	Morrie Martin	2.25	.90	.22
☐ 39	Ed Bouchee	2.25	.90	.22
☐ 40	Warren Spahn	25.00	10.00	2.50
☐ 41	Bob Martyn	2.25	.90	.22
☐ 42	Murray Wall	2.25	.90	.22
☐ 43	Steve Bilko	2.25	.90	.22
☐ 44	Vito Valentinetti	2.25	.90	.22
☐ 45	Andy Carey	3.50	1.40	.35
☐ 46	Bill R. Henry	2.25	.90	.22
☐ 47	Jim Finigan	2.25	.90	.22
☐ 48	Orioles Team	6.50	1.50	.25
	(checklist on back)			
☐ 49	Bill Hall	2.25	.90	.22
☐ 50	Willie Mays	90.00	36.00	9.00
☐ 51	Rip Coleman	2.25	.90	.22
☐ 52	Coot Veal	2.25	.90	.22
☐ 53	Stan Williams	2.25	.90	.22
☐ 54	Mel Roach	2.25	.90	.22
☐ 55	Tom Brewer	2.25	.90	.22
☐ 56	Carl Sawatski	2.25	.90	.22
☐ 57	Al Cicotte	2.25	.90	.22
☐ 58	Eddie Miksis	2.25	.90	.22
☐ 59	Irv Noren	2.25	.90	.22
☐ 60	Bob Turley	4.50	1.80	.45
☐ 61	Dick Brown	2.25	.90	.22
☐ 62	Tony Taylor	2.25	.90	.22
☐ 63	Jim Hearn	2.25	.90	.22
☐ 64	Joe DeMaestri	2.25	.90	.22
☐ 65	Frank Torre	2.25	.90	.22
☐ 66	Joe Ginsberg	2.25	.90	.22
☐ 67	Brooks Lawrence	2.25	.90	.22
☐ 68	Dick Schofield	2.25	.90	.22
☐ 69	Giants Team	6.50	1.50	.25
	(checklist on back)			
☐ 70	Harvey Kuenn	4.00	1.60	.40
☐ 71	Don Bessent	2.25	.90	.22
☐ 72	Bill Renna	2.25	.90	.22
☐ 73	Ron Jackson	2.25	.90	.22
☐ 74	Directing Power	3.00	1.20	.30
	Jim Lemon			
	Cookie Lavagetto			
	Roy Sievers			
☐ 75	Sam Jones	3.00	1.20	.30

		NRMT	VG-E	GOOD
☐ 76	Bobby Richardson	7.00	2.80	.70
☐ 77	John Goryl	2.25	.90	.22
☐ 78	Pedro Ramos	2.25	.90	.22
☐ 79	Harry Chiti	2.25	.90	.22
☐ 80	Minnie Minoso	4.50	1.80	.45
☐ 81	Hal Jeffcoat	2.25	.90	.22
☐ 82	Bob Boyd	2.25	.90	.22
☐ 83	Bob Smith	2.25	.90	.22
☐ 84	Reno Bertoia	2.25	.90	.22
☐ 85	Harry Anderson	2.25	.90	.22
☐ 86	Bob Keegan	2.25	.90	.22
☐ 87	Danny O'Connell	2.25	.90	.22
☐ 88	Herb Score	3.50	1.40	.35
☐ 89	Billy Gardner	3.00	1.20	.30
☐ 90	Bill Skowron	7.00	2.80	.70
☐ 91	Herb Moford	2.25	.90	.22
☐ 92	Dave Philley	2.25	.90	.22
☐ 93	Julio Becquer	2.25	.90	.22
☐ 94	White Sox Team (checklist on back)	6.50	1.50	.25
☐ 95	Carl Willey	2.25	.90	.22
☐ 96	Lou Berberet	2.25	.90	.22
☐ 97	Jerry Lynch	2.25	.90	.22
☐ 98	Arnie Portocarrero	2.25	.90	.22
☐ 99	Ted Kazanski	2.25	.90	.22
☐ 100	Bob Cerv	3.00	1.20	.30
☐ 101	Alex Kellner	2.25	.90	.22
☐ 102	Felipe Alou	6.00	2.40	.60
☐ 103	Billy Goodman	3.00	1.20	.30
☐ 104	Del Rice	2.25	.90	.22
☐ 105	Lee Walls	2.25	.90	.22
☐ 106	Hal Woodeshick	2.25	.90	.22
☐ 107	Norm Larker	3.00	1.20	.30
☐ 108	Zack Monroe	2.25	.90	.22
☐ 109	Bob Schmidt	2.25	.90	.22
☐ 110	George Witt	2.25	.90	.22
☐ 111	Redlegs Team (checklist on back)	6.00	1.50	.25
☐ 112	Billy Consolo	1.75	.70	.17
☐ 113	Taylor Phillips	1.75	.70	.17
☐ 114	Earl Battey	1.75	.70	.17
☐ 115	Mickey Vernon	2.50	1.00	.25
☐ 116	Bob Allison RP	4.50	1.80	.45
☐ 117	John Blanchard RP	2.50	1.00	.25
☐ 118	John Buzhardt RP	1.75	.70	.17
☐ 119	John Callison RP	3.50	1.40	.35
☐ 120	Chuck Coles RP	1.75	.70	.17
☐ 121	Bob Conley RP	1.75	.70	.17
☐ 122	Bennie Daniels RP	1.75	.70	.17
☐ 123	Don Dillard RP	1.75	.70	.17
☐ 124	Dan Dobbek RP	1.75	.70	.17
☐ 125	Ron Fairly RP	3.50	1.40	.35
☐ 126	Ed Haas RP	2.50	1.00	.25
☐ 127	Kent Hadley RP	1.75	.70	.17
☐ 128	Bob Hartman RP	1.75	.70	.17
☐ 129	Frank Herrera RP	1.75	.70	.17
☐ 130	Lou Jackson RP	1.75	.70	.17
☐ 131	Deron Johnson RP	2.50	1.00	.25
☐ 132	Don Lee RP	1.75	.70	.17
☐ 133	Bob Lillis RP	2.50	1.00	.25
☐ 134	Jim McDaniel RP	1.75	.70	.17
☐ 135	Gene Oliver RP	1.75	.70	.17
☐ 136	Jim O'Toole RP	2.50	1.00	.25
☐ 137	Dick Ricketts RP	1.75	.70	.17
☐ 138	John Romano RP	2.50	1.00	.25
☐ 139	Ed Sadowski RP	1.75	.70	.17
☐ 140	Charlie Secrest RP	1.75	.70	.17
☐ 141	Joe Shipley RP	1.75	.70	.17
☐ 142	Dick Stigman RP	1.75	.70	.17
☐ 143	Willie Tasby RP	1.75	.70	.17
☐ 144	Jerry Walker RP	1.75	.70	.17
☐ 145	Dom Zanni RP	1.75	.70	.17
☐ 146	Jerry Zimmerman RP	1.75	.70	.17
☐ 147	Cubs Clubbers Dale Long Ernie Banks Walt Moryn	6.50	2.60	.65
☐ 148	Mike McCormick	2.50	1.00	.25
☐ 149	Jim Bunning	8.00	3.25	.80
☐ 150	Stan Musial	85.00	34.00	8.50
☐ 151	Bob Malkmus	1.75	.70	.17
☐ 152	Johnny Klippstein	1.75	.70	.17
☐ 153	Jim Marshall	1.75	.70	.17
☐ 154	Ray Herbert	1.75	.70	.17
☐ 155	Enos Slaughter	12.00	5.00	1.20
☐ 156	Ace Hurlers Billy Pierce Robin Roberts	3.50	1.40	.35
☐ 157	Felix Mantilla	1.75	.70	.17
☐ 158	Walt Dropo	1.75	.70	.17
☐ 159	Bob Shaw	1.75	.70	.17
☐ 160	Dick Groat	3.50	1.40	.35
☐ 161	Frank Baumann	1.75	.70	.17
☐ 162	Bobby G. Smith	1.75	.70	.17
☐ 163	Sandy Koufax	70.00	28.00	7.00
☐ 164	Johnny Groth	1.75	.70	.17
☐ 165	Bill Bruton	1.75	.70	.17

		NRMT	VG-E	GOOD
☐ 166	Destruction Crew ..	3.00	1.20	.30
	Minnie Minoso			
	Rocky Colavito			
	(misspelled Colovito on card back)			
	Larry Doby			
☐ 167	Duke Maas	1.75	.70	.17
☐ 168	Carroll Hardy	1.75	.70	.17
☐ 169	Ted Abernathy	1.75	.70	.17
☐ 170	Gene Woodling	2.50	1.00	.25
☐ 171	Willard Schmidt	1.75	.70	.17
☐ 172	Athletics Team	6.00	1.50	.25
	(checklist on back)			
☐ 173	Bill Monbouquette ..	1.75	.70	.17
☐ 174	Jim Pendleton	1.75	.70	.17
☐ 175	Dick Farrell	1.75	.70	.17
☐ 176	Preston Ward	1.75	.70	.17
☐ 177	John Briggs	1.75	.70	.17
☐ 178	Ruben Amaro	1.75	.70	.17
☐ 179	Don Rudolph	1.75	.70	.17
☐ 180	Yogi Berra	40.00	16.00	4.00
☐ 181	Bob Porterfield	1.75	.70	.17
☐ 182	Milt Graff	1.75	.70	.17
☐ 183	Stu Miller	1.75	.70	.17
☐ 184	Harvey Haddix	2.50	1.00	.25
☐ 185	Jim Busby	1.75	.70	.17
☐ 186	Mudcat Grant	1.75	.70	.17
☐ 187	Bubba Phillips	1.75	.70	.17
☐ 188	Juan Pizarro	1.75	.70	.17
☐ 189	Neil Chrisley	1.75	.70	.17
☐ 190	Bill Virdon	3.00	1.20	.30
☐ 191	Russ Kemmerer	1.75	.70	.17
☐ 192	Charlie Beamon	1.75	.70	.17
☐ 193	Sammy Taylor	1.75	.70	.17
☐ 194	Jim Brosnan	1.75	.70	.17
☐ 195	Rip Repulski	1.75	.70	.17
☐ 196	Billy Moran	1.75	.70	.17
☐ 197	Ray Semproch	1.75	.70	.17
☐ 198	Jim Davenport	2.50	1.00	.25
☐ 199	Leo Kiely	1.75	.70	.17
☐ 200	Warren Giles	4.00	1.60	.40
	(NL President)			
☐ 201	Tom Acker	1.75	.70	.17
☐ 202	Roger Maris	85.00	34.00	8.50
☐ 203	Ossie Virgil	1.75	.70	.17
☐ 204	Casey Wise	1.75	.70	.17
☐ 205	Don Larsen	4.00	1.60	.40
☐ 206	Carl Furillo	4.50	1.80	.45
☐ 207	George Strickland ..	1.75	.70	.17
☐ 208	Willie Jones	1.75	.70	.17

		NRMT	VG-E	GOOD
☐ 209	Lenny Green	1.75	.70	.17
☐ 210	Ed Bailey	1.75	.70	.17
☐ 211	Bob Blaylock	1.75	.70	.17
☐ 212	Fence Busters	16.00	6.50	1.60
	Hank Aaron			
	Eddie Mathews			
☐ 213	Jim Rivera	1.75	.70	.17
☐ 214	Marcelino Solis	1.75	.70	.17
☐ 215	Jim Lemon	1.75	.70	.17
☐ 216	Andre Rodgers	1.75	.70	.17
☐ 217	Carl Erskine	3.50	1.40	.35
☐ 218	Roman Mejias	1.75	.70	.17
☐ 219	George Zuverink	1.75	.70	.17
☐ 220	Frank Malzone	2.50	1.00	.25
☐ 221	Bob Bowman	1.75	.70	.17
☐ 222	Bobby Shantz	3.00	1.20	.30
☐ 223	Cardinals Team	6.00	1.50	.25
	(checklist on back)			
☐ 224	Claude Osteen	3.00	1.20	.30
☐ 225	Johnny Logan	2.50	1.00	.25
☐ 226	Art Ceccarelli	1.75	.70	.17
☐ 227	Hal W. Smith	1.75	.70	.17
☐ 228	Don Gross	1.75	.70	.17
☐ 229	Vic Power	1.75	.70	.17
☐ 230	Bill Fischer	1.75	.70	.17
☐ 231	Ellis Burton	1.75	.70	.17
☐ 232	Eddie Kasko	1.75	.70	.17
☐ 233	Paul Foytack	1.75	.70	.17
☐ 234	Chuck Tanner	2.50	1.00	.25
☐ 235	Valmy Thomas	1.75	.70	.17
☐ 236	Ted Bowsfield	1.75	.70	.17
☐ 237	Run Preventers	4.50	1.80	.45
	Gil McDougald			
	Bob Turley			
	Bobby Richardson			
☐ 238	Gene Baker	1.75	.70	.17
☐ 239	Bob Trowbridge	1.75	.70	.17
☐ 240	Hank Bauer	4.50	1.80	.45
☐ 241	Billy Muffett	1.75	.70	.17
☐ 242	Ron Samford	1.75	.70	.17
☐ 243	Marv Grissom	1.75	.70	.17
☐ 244	Ted Gray	1.75	.70	.17
☐ 245	Ned Garver	1.75	.70	.17
☐ 246	J.W. Porter	1.75	.70	.17
☐ 247	Don Ferrarese	1.75	.70	.17
☐ 248	Red Sox Team	6.50	1.50	.25
	(checklist on back)			
☐ 249	Bobby Adams	1.75	.70	.17
☐ 250	Billy O'Dell	1.75	.70	.17

		NRMT	VG-E	GOOD
☐ 251	Clete Boyer	3.50	1.40	.35
☐ 252	Ray Boone	2.50	1.00	.25
☐ 253	Seth Morehead	1.75	.70	.17
☐ 254	Zeke Bella	1.75	.70	.17
☐ 255	Del Ennis	2.50	1.00	.25
☐ 256	Jerry Davie	1.75	.70	.17
☐ 257	Leon Wagner	1.75	.70	.17
☐ 258	Fred Kipp	1.75	.70	.17
☐ 259	Jim Pisoni	1.75	.70	.17
☐ 260	Early Wynn	12.00	5.00	1.20
☐ 261	Gene Stephens	1.75	.70	.17
☐ 262	Hitters' Foes	4.50	1.80	.45
	Johnny Podres			
	Clem Labine			
	Don Drysdale			
☐ 263	Bud Daley	1.75	.70	.17
☐ 264	Chico Carrasquel	1.75	.70	.17
☐ 265	Ron Kline	1.75	.70	.17
☐ 266	Woody Held	1.75	.70	.17
☐ 267	John Romonosky	1.75	.70	.17
☐ 268	Tito Francona	2.50	1.00	.25
☐ 269	Jack Meyer	1.75	.70	.17
☐ 270	Gil Hodges	12.50	5.00	1.25
☐ 271	Orlando Pena	1.75	.70	.17
☐ 272	Jerry Lumpe	1.75	.70	.17
☐ 273	Joey Jay	1.75	.70	.17
☐ 274	Jerry Kindall	2.50	1.00	.25
☐ 275	Jack Sanford	2.50	1.00	.25
☐ 276	Pete Daley	1.75	.70	.17
☐ 277	Turk Lown	1.75	.70	.17
☐ 278	Chuck Essegian	2.50	1.00	.25
☐ 279	Ernie Johnson	1.75	.70	.17
☐ 280	Frank Bolling	1.75	.70	.17
☐ 281	Walt Craddock	1.75	.70	.17
☐ 282	R.C. Stevens	1.75	.70	.17
☐ 283	Russ Heman	1.75	.70	.17
☐ 284	Steve Korcheck	1.75	.70	.17
☐ 285	Joe Cunningham	2.50	1.00	.25
☐ 286	Dean Stone	1.75	.70	.17
☐ 287	Don Zimmer	3.50	1.40	.35
☐ 288	Dutch Dotterer	1.75	.70	.17
☐ 289	Johnny Kucks	2.50	1.00	.25
☐ 290	Wes Covington	2.50	1.00	.25
☐ 291	Pitching Partners	2.50	1.00	.25
	Pedro Ramos			
	Camilo Pascual			
☐ 292	Dick Williams	2.50	1.00	.25
☐ 293	Ray Moore	1.75	.70	.17
☐ 294	Hank Foiles	1.75	.70	.17
☐ 295	Billy Martin	6.50	2.60	.65
☐ 296	Ernie Broglio	2.50	1.00	.25
☐ 297	Jackie Brandt	1.75	.70	.17
☐ 298	Tex Clevenger	1.75	.70	.17
☐ 299	Billy Klaus	1.75	.70	.17
☐ 300	Richie Ashburn	7.00	2.80	.70
☐ 301	Earl Averill	1.75	.70	.17
☐ 302	Don Mossi	2.50	1.00	.25
☐ 303	Marty Keough	1.75	.70	.17
☐ 304	Cubs Team	6.00	1.50	.25
	(checklist on back)			
☐ 305	Curt Raydon	1.75	.70	.17
☐ 306	Jim Gilliam	4.50	1.80	.45
☐ 307	Curt Barclay	1.75	.70	.17
☐ 308	Norm Siebern	1.75	.70	.17
☐ 309	Sal Maglie	3.50	1.40	.35
☐ 310	Luis Aparicio	11.00	4.50	1.10
☐ 311	Norm Zauchin	1.75	.70	.17
☐ 312	Don Newcombe	3.00	1.20	.30
☐ 313	Frank House	1.75	.70	.17
☐ 314	Don Cardwell	1.75	.70	.17
☐ 315	Joe Adcock	3.00	1.20	.30
☐ 316A	Ralph Lumenti	1.75	.70	.17
	(option)			
	(photo actually Camilo Pascual)			
☐ 316B	Ralph Lumenti	75.00	30.00	7.50
	(no option)			
	(photo actually Camilo Pascual)			
☐ 317	Hitting Kings	12.50	5.00	1.25
	Willie Mays			
	Richie Ashburn			
☐ 318	Rocky Bridges	1.75	.70	.17
☐ 319	Dave Hillman	1.75	.70	.17
☐ 320	Bob Skinner	2.50	1.00	.25
☐ 321A	Bob Giallombardo	1.75	.70	.17
	(option)			
☐ 321B	Bob Giallombardo	75.00	30.00	7.50
	(no option)			
☐ 322A	Harry Hanebrink	1.75	.70	.17
	(traded)			
☐ 322B	Harry Hanebrink	75.00	30.00	7.50
	(no trade)			
☐ 323	Frank Sullivan	1.75	.70	.17
☐ 324	Don Demeter	1.75	.70	.17
☐ 325	Ken Boyer	4.00	1.60	.40
☐ 326	Marv Throneberry	3.00	1.20	.30
☐ 327	Gary Bell	1.75	.70	.17
☐ 328	Lou Skizas	1.75	.70	.17

		NRMT	VG-E	GOOD				NRMT	VG-E	GOOD
☐ 329	Tigers Team (checklist on back)	6.50	1.50	.25	☐ 369	Dick Tomanek	· 1.75	.70	.17
☐ 330	Gus Triandos	2.50	1.00	.25	☐ 370	Pete Runnels	2.50	1.00	.25
☐ 331	Steve Boros	2.50	1.00	.25	☐ 371	Dick Brodowski	1.75	.70	.17
☐ 332	Ray Monzant	1.75	.70	.17	☐ 372	Jim Hegan	2.50	1.00	.25
☐ 333	Harry Simpson	1.75	.70	.17	☐ 373	Herb Plews	1.75	.70	.17
☐ 334	Glen Hobbie	1.75	.70	.17	☐ 374	Art Ditmar	1.75	.70	.17
☐ 335	Johnny Temple	2.50	1.00	.25	☐ 375	Bob Nieman	1.75	.70	.17
☐ 336A	Billy Loes (with traded line)	1.75	.70	.17	☐ 376	Hal Naragon	1.75	.70	.17
					☐ 377	John Antonelli	2.50	1.00	.25
☐ 336B	Billy Loes (no trade)	75.00	30.00	7.50	☐ 378	Gail Harris	1.75	.70	.17
					☐ 379	Bob Miller	1.75	.70	.17
☐ 337	George Crowe	1.75	.70	.17	☐ 380	Hank Aaron	70.00	28.00	7.00
☐ 338	Sparky Anderson	11.00	4.50	1.10	☐ 381	Mike Baxes	1.75	.70	.17
☐ 339	Roy Face	3.50	1.40	.35	☐ 382	Curt Simmons	2.50	1.00	.25
☐ 340	Roy Sievers	2.50	1.00	.25	☐ 383	Words of Wisdom Don Larsen Casey Stengel	6.00	2.40	.60
☐ 341	Tom Qualters	1.75	.70	.17					
☐ 342	Ray Jablonski	1.75	.70	.17					
☐ 343	Billy Hoeft	1.75	.70	.17	☐ 384	Dave Sisler	1.75	.70	.17
☐ 344	Russ Nixon	2.50	1.00	.25	☐ 385	Sherm Lollar	2.50	1.00	.25
☐ 345	Gil McDougald	4.50	1.80	.45	☐ 386	Jim Delsing	1.75	.70	.17
☐ 346	Batter Bafflers Dave Sisler Tom Brewer	2.50	1.00	.25	☐ 387	Don Drysdale	16.00	6.50	1.60
					☐ 388	Bob Will	1.75	.70	.17
					☐ 389	Joe Nuxhall	2.50	1.00	.25
☐ 347	Bob Buhl	1.75	.70	.17	☐ 390	Orlando Cepeda	7.00	2.80	.70
☐ 348	Ted Lepcio	1.75	.70	.17	☐ 391	Milt Pappas	2.50	1.00	.25
☐ 349	Hoyt Wilhelm	11.00	4.50	1.10	☐ 392	Whitey Herzog	3.50	1.40	.35
☐ 350	Ernie Banks	30.00	12.00	3.00	☐ 393	Frank Lary	2.50	1.00	.25
☐ 351	Earl Torgeson	1.75	.70	.17	☐ 394	Randy Jackson	1.75	.70	.17
☐ 352	Robin Roberts	12.00	5.00	1.20	☐ 395	Elston Howard	4.50	1.80	.45
☐ 353	Curt Flood	3.50	1.40	.35	☐ 396	Bob Rush	1.75	.70	.17
☐ 354	Pete Burnside	1.75	.70	.17	☐ 397	Senators Team (checklist on back)	6.00	1.50	.25
☐ 355	Jim Piersall	3.00	1.20	.30					
☐ 356	Bob Mabe	1.75	.70	.17	☐ 398	Wally Post	2.50	1.00	.25
☐ 357	Dick Stuart	2.50	1.00	.25	☐ 399	Larry Jackson	1.75	.70	.17
☐ 358	Ralph Terry	2.50	1.00	.25	☐ 400	Jackie Jensen	3.50	1.40	.35
☐ 359	Bill White	6.00	2.40	.60	☐ 401	Ron Blackburn	1.75	.70	.17
☐ 360	Al Kaline	30.00	12.00	3.00	☐ 402	Hector Lopez	1.75	.70	.17
☐ 361	Willard Nixon	1.75	.70	.17	☐ 403	Clem Labine	2.50	1.00	.25
☐ 362A	Dolan Nichols (with option line)	1.75	.70	.17	☐ 404	Hank Sauer	2.50	1.00	.25
					☐ 405	Roy McMillan	1.75	.70	.17
☐ 362B	Dolan Nichols (no option)	75.00	30.00	7.50	☐ 406	Solly Drake	1.75	.70	.17
					☐ 407	Moe Drabowsky	1.75	.70	.17
☐ 363	Bobby Avila	1.75	.70	.17	☐ 408	Keystone Combo Nellie Fox Luis Aparicio	5.50	2.20	.55
☐ 364	Danny McDevitt	1.75	.70	.17					
☐ 365	Gus Bell	2.50	1.00	.25					
☐ 366	Humberto Robinson	1.75	.70	.17	☐ 409	Gus Zernial	2.50	1.00	.25
☐ 367	Cal Neeman	1.75	.70	.17	☐ 410	Billy Pierce	3.00	1.20	.30
☐ 368	Don Mueller	2.50	1.00	.25	☐ 411	Whitey Lockman	2.50	1.00	.25
					☐ 412	Stan Lopata	1.75	.70	.17

		NRMT	VG-E	GOOD
☐ 413	Camilo Pascual	2.50	1.00	.25
	(listed as Camillo on front)			
☐ 414	Dale Long	2.50	1.00	.25
☐ 415	Bill Mazeroski	4.50	1.80	.45
☐ 416	Haywood Sullivan ..	2.50	1.00	.25
☐ 417	Virgil Trucks	2.50	1.00	.25
☐ 418	Gino Cimoli	1.75	.70	.17
☐ 419	Braves Team	6.50	1.50	.25
	(checklist on back)			
☐ 420	Rocky Colavito	4.50	1.80	.45
☐ 421	Herman Wehmeier .	1.75	.70	.17
☐ 422	Hobie Landrith	1.75	.70	.17
☐ 423	Bob Grim	2.50	1.00	.25
☐ 424	Ken Aspromonte ...	1.75	.70	.17
☐ 425	Del Crandall	2.50	1.00	.25
☐ 426	Jerry Staley	1.75	.70	.17
☐ 427	Charlie Neal	2.50	1.00	.25
☐ 428	Buc Hill Aces	3.00	1.20	.30
	Ron Kline			
	Bob Friend			
	Vernon Law			
	Roy Face			
☐ 429	Bobby Thomson ...	3.00	1.20	.30
☐ 430	Whitey Ford	24.00	10.00	2.40
☐ 431	Whammy Douglas ..	1.75	.70	.17
☐ 432	Smoky Burgess	2.50	1.00	.25
☐ 433	Billy Harrell	1.75	.70	.17
☐ 434	Hal Griggs	1.75	.70	.17
☐ 435	Frank Robinson ...	25.00	10.00	2.50
☐ 436	Granny Hamner ...	1.75	.70	.17
☐ 437	Ike Delock	1.75	.70	.17
☐ 438	Sammy Esposito ...	1.75	.70	.17
☐ 439	Brooks Robinson ..	30.00	12.00	3.00
☐ 440	Lou Burdette	4.50	1.80	.45
	(posing as if lefthanded)			
☐ 441	John Roseboro	2.50	1.00	.25
☐ 442	Ray Narleski	1.75	.70	.17
☐ 443	Daryl Spencer	1.75	.70	.17
☐ 444	Ron Hansen	2.50	1.00	.25
☐ 445	Cal McLish	1.75	.70	.17
☐ 446	Rocky Nelson	1.75	.70	.17
☐ 447	Bob Anderson	1.75	.70	.17
☐ 448	Vada Pinson	3.50	1.40	.35
☐ 449	Tom Gorman	1.75	.70	.17
☐ 450	Eddie Mathews	18.00	7.25	1.80
☐ 451	Jimmy Constable ..	1.75	.70	.17
☐ 452	Chico Fernandez ..	1.75	.70	.17
☐ 453	Les Moss	1.75	.70	.17
☐ 454	Phil Clark	1.75	.70	.17
☐ 455	Larry Doby	3.00	1.20	.30
☐ 456	Jerry Casale	1.75	.70	.17
☐ 457	Dodgers Team	12.00	3.00	.50
	(checklist on back)			
☐ 458	Gordon Jones	1.75	.70	.17
☐ 459	Bill Tuttle	1.75	.70	.17
☐ 460	Bob Friend	2.50	1.00	.25
☐ 461	Mantle Hits Homer	25.00	10.00	2.50
☐ 462	Colavito's Catch ..	3.00	1.20	.30
☐ 463	Kaline Batting Champ	6.50	2.60	.65
☐ 464	Mays' Series Catch	14.00	5.75	1.40
☐ 465	Sievers Sets Mark .	2.50	1.00	.25
☐ 466	Pierce All-Star ...	2.50	1.00	.25
☐ 467	Aaron Clubs Homer	14.00	5.75	1.40
☐ 468	Snider's Play	8.00	3.25	.80
☐ 469	Hustler Banks	7.00	2.80	.70
☐ 470	Musial's 3000 Hit .	10.00	4.00	1.00
☐ 471	Tom Sturdivant ...	1.75	.70	.17
☐ 472	Gene Freese	1.75	.70	.17
☐ 473	Mike Fornieles ...	1.75	.70	.17
☐ 474	Moe Thacker	1.75	.70	.17
☐ 475	Jack Harshman ...	1.75	.70	.17
☐ 476	Indians Team	6.00	1.50	.25
	(checklist on back)			
☐ 477	Barry Latman	1.75	.70	.17
☐ 478	Bob Clemente	50.00	20.00	5.00
☐ 479	Lindy McDaniel ...	2.50	1.00	.25
☐ 480	Red Schoendienst .	3.50	1.40	.35
☐ 481	Charlie Maxwell ...	1.75	.70	.17
☐ 482	Russ Meyer	1.75	.70	.17
☐ 483	Clint Courtney	1.75	.70	.17
☐ 484	Willie Kirkland ...	1.75	.70	.17
☐ 485	Ryne Duren	3.00	1.20	.30
☐ 486	Sammy White	1.75	.70	.17
☐ 487	Hal Brown	1.75	.70	.17
☐ 488	Walt Moryn	1.75	.70	.17
☐ 489	John Powers	1.75	.70	.17
☐ 490	Frank Thomas	2.50	1.00	.25
☐ 491	Don Blasingame ..	1.75	.70	.17
☐ 492	Gene Conley	1.75	.70	.17
☐ 493	Jim Landis	1.75	.70	.17
☐ 494	Don Pavletich	1.75	.70	.17
☐ 495	Johnny Podres ...	3.50	1.40	.35
☐ 496	Wayne Terwilliger .	1.75	.70	.17
☐ 497	Hal R. Smith	1.75	.70	.17
☐ 498	Dick Hyde	1.75	.70	.17
☐ 499	Johnny O'Brien ...	1.75	.70	.17
☐ 500	Vic Wertz	2.50	1.00	.25
☐ 501	Bob Tiefenauer ...	1.75	.70	.17

		NRMT	VG-E	GOOD
☐ 502	Alvin Dark	3.00	1.20	.30
☐ 503	Jim Owens	1.75	.70	.17
☐ 504	Ossie Alvarez	1.75	.70	.17
☐ 505	Tony Kubek	7.50	3.00	.75
☐ 506	Bob Purkey	1.75	.70	.17
☐ 507	Bob Hale	7.50	3.00	.75
☐ 508	Art Fowler	7.50	3.00	.75
☐ 509	Norm Cash	20.00	8.00	2.00
☐ 510	Yankees Team	36.00	6.50	1.25
	(checklist on back)			
☐ 511	George Susce	7.50	3.00	.75
☐ 512	George Altman	7.50	3.00	.75
☐ 513	Tommy Carroll	7.50	3.00	.75
☐ 514	Bob Gibson	225.00	90.00	22.00
☐ 515	Harmon Killebrew	50.00	20.00	5.00
☐ 516	Mike Garcia	9.00	3.75	.90
☐ 517	Joe Koppe	7.50	3.00	.75
☐ 518	Mike Cueller	12.00	5.00	1.20
	(sic, Cuellar)			
☐ 519	Infield Power	10.00	4.00	1.00
	Pete Runnels			
	Dick Gernert			
	Frank Malzone			
☐ 520	Don Elston	7.50	3.00	.75
☐ 521	Gary Geiger	7.50	3.00	.75
☐ 522	Gene Snyder	7.50	3.00	.75
☐ 523	Harry Bright	7.50	3.00	.75
☐ 524	Larry Osborne	7.50	3.00	.75
☐ 525	Jim Coates	7.50	3.00	.75
☐ 526	Bob Speake	7.50	3.00	.75
☐ 527	Solly Hemus	7.50	3.00	.75
☐ 528	Pirates Team	21.00	2.50	.50
	(checklist on back)			
☐ 529	George Bamberger	12.00	5.00	1.20
☐ 530	Wally Moon	10.00	4.00	1.00
☐ 531	Ray Webster	7.50	3.00	.75
☐ 532	Mark Freeman	7.50	3.00	.75
☐ 533	Darrell Johnson	9.00	3.75	.90
☐ 534	Faye Throneberry	7.50	3.00	.75
☐ 535	Ruben Gomez	7.50	3.00	.75
☐ 536	Danny Kravitz	7.50	3.00	.75
☐ 537	Rudolph Arias	7.50	3.00	.75
☐ 538	Chick King	7.50	3.00	.75
☐ 539	Gary Blaylock	7.50	3.00	.75
☐ 540	Willie Miranda	7.50	3.00	.75
☐ 541	Bob Thurman	7.50	3.00	.75
☐ 542	Jim Perry	12.00	5.00	1.20

		NRMT	VG-E	GOOD
☐ 543	Corsair Trio	30.00	12.00	3.00
	Bob Skinner			
	Bill Virdon			
	Roberto Clemente			
☐ 544	Lee Tate	7.50	3.00	.75
☐ 545	Tom Morgan	7.50	3.00	.75
☐ 546	Al Schroll	7.50	3.00	.75
☐ 547	Jim Baxes	7.50	3.00	.75
☐ 548	Elmer Singleton	7.50	3.00	.75
☐ 549	Howie Nunn	7.50	3.00	.75
☐ 550	Roy Campanella	80.00	32.00	8.00
	(Symbol of Courage!)			
☐ 551	Fred Haney MG AS	9.00	3.75	.90
☐ 552	Casey Stengel MG AS	18.00	7.25	1.80
☐ 553	Orlando Cepeda AS	12.00	5.00	1.20
☐ 554	Bill Skowron AS	10.00	4.00	1.00
☐ 555	Bill Mazeroski AS	10.00	4.00	1.00
☐ 556	Nellie Fox AS	12.00	5.00	1.20
☐ 557	Ken Boyer AS	10.00	4.00	1.00
☐ 558	Frank Malzone AS	9.00	3.75	.90
☐ 559	Ernie Banks AS	25.00	10.00	2.50
☐ 560	Luis Aparicio AS	15.00	6.00	1.50
☐ 561	Hank Aaron AS	60.00	24.00	6.00
☐ 562	Al Kaline AS	28.00	11.50	2.80
☐ 563	Willie Mays AS	60.00	24.00	6.00
☐ 564	Mickey Mantle AS	150.00	60.00	15.00
☐ 565	Wes Covington AS	9.00	3.75	.90
☐ 566	Roy Sievers AS	9.00	3.75	.90
☐ 567	Del Crandall AS	9.00	3.75	.90
☐ 568	Gus Triandos AS	9.00	3.75	.90
☐ 569	Bob Friend AS	9.00	3.75	.90
☐ 570	Bob Turley AS	10.00	4.00	1.00
☐ 571	Warren Spahn AS	25.00	10.00	2.50
☐ 572	Billy Pierce AS	10.00	4.00	1.00

1960 Topps

The cards in this 572-card set measure 2 ½"
by 3 ½". The 1960 Topps set is the only
Topps standard size issue to use a horizontally oriented front. World Series cards appeared for the first time (385 to 391), and
there is a Rookie Prospect (RP) series (117-
148), the most famous of which is Carl
Yastrzemski, and a Sport Magazine All-Star
Selection (AS) series (553-572). There are
16 manager cards listed alphabetically from
212 through 227. The coaching staff of each
team was also afforded their own card in a
16-card subset (455-470). Cards 375 to 440
come with either gray or white backs, and
the high series (507-572) were printed on a
more limited basis than the rest of the set.
The team cards have series checklists on
the reverse.

	NRMT	VG-E	GOOD
Complete Set (572)	.3000.00	1350.00	450.00
Common Player (1-286) . . .	1.25	.50	.12
Common Player (287-440) . .	1.50	.60	.15
Common Player (441-506) . .	2.50	1.00	.25
Common Player (507-552) .	7.00	2.80	.70
Common Player (553-572) .	8.00	3.25	.80

			NRMT	VG-E	GOOD
☐	1	Early Wynn	25.00	5.00	1.00
☐	2	Roman Mejías	1.25	.50	.12
☐	3	Joe Adcock	1.75	.70	.17
☐	4	Bob Purkey	1.25	.50	.12
☐	5	Wally Moon	1.75	.70	.17
☐	6	Lou Berberet	1.25	.50	.12

			NRMT	VG-E	GOOD
☐	7	Master and Mentor	8.00	3.25	.80
		Willie Mays			
		Bill Rigney			
☐	8	Bud Daley	1.25	.50	.12
☐	9	Faye Throneberry ·	1.25	.50	.12
☐	10	Ernie Banks	21.00	8.50	2.10
☐	11	Norm Siebern	1.25	.50	.12
☐	12	Milt Pappas	1.75	.70	.17
☐	13	Wally Post	1.25	.50	.12
☐	14	Jim Grant	1.25	.50	.12
☐	15	Pete Runnels	1.75	.70	.17
☐	16	Ernie Broglio	1.75	.70	.17
☐	17	Johnny Callison . . .	1.75	.70	.17
☐	18	Dodgers Team	9.00	2.50	.50
		(checklist on back)			
☐	19	Felix Mantilla	1.25	.50	.12
☐	20	Roy Face	2.50	1.00	.25
☐	21	Dutch Dotterer	1.25	.50	.12
☐	22	Rocky Bridges	1.25	.50	.12
☐	23	Eddie Fisher	1.25	.50	.12
☐	24	Dick Gray	1.25	.50	.12
☐	25	Roy Sievers	1.75	.70	.17
☐	26	Wayne Terwilliger . .	1.25	.50	.12
☐	27	Dick Drott	1.25	.50	.12
☐	28	Brooks Robinson . . .	24.00	10.00	2.40
☐	29	Clem Labine	1.75	.70	.17
☐	30	Tito Francona	1.75	.70	.17
☐	31	Sammy Esposito . .	1.25	.50	.12
☐	32	Sophomore Stalwarts	1.75	.70	.17
		Jim O'Toole			
		Vada Pinson			
☐	33	Tom Morgan	1.25	.50	.12
☐	34	George Anderson .	3.50	1.40	.35
☐	35	Whitey Ford	21.00	8.50	2.10
☐	36	Russ Nixon	1.75	.70	.17
☐	37	Bill Bruton	1.25	.50	.12
☐	38	Jerry Casale	1.25	.50	.12
☐	39	Earl Averill	1.25	.50	.12
☐	40	Joe Cunningham . . .	1.75	.70	.17
☐	41	Barry Latman	1.25	.50	.12
☐	42	Hobie Landrith	1.25	.50	.12
☐	43	Senators Team	4.00	1.00	.20
		(checklist on back)			
☐	44	Bobby Locke	1.25	.50	.12
☐	45	Roy McMillan	1.25	.50	.12
☐	46	Jerry Fisher	1.25	.50	.12
☐	47	Don Zimmer	2.50	1.00	.25
☐	48	Hal W. Smith	1.25	.50	.12
☐	49	Curt Raydon	1.25	.50	.12

		NRMT	VG-E	GOOD
☐ 50	Al Kaline	21.00	8.50	2.10
☐ 51	Jim Coates	1.25	.50	.12
☐ 52	Dave Philley	1.25	.50	.12
☐ 53	Jackie Brandt	1.25	.50	.12
☐ 54	Mike Fornieles	1.25	.50	.12
☐ 55	Bill Mazeroski	3.00	1.20	.30
☐ 56	Steve Korcheck	1.25	.50	.12
☐ 57	Win Savers	1.75	.70	.17
	Turk Lown			
	Jerry Staley			
☐ 58	Gino Cimoli	1.25	.50	.12
☐ 59	Juan Pizarro	1.25	.50	.12
☐ 60	Gus Triandos	1.75	.70	.17
☐ 61	Eddie Kasko	1.25	.50	.12
☐ 62	Roger Craig	3.50	1.40	.35
☐ 63	George Strickland	1.25	.50	.12
☐ 64	Jack Meyer	1.25	.50	.12
☐ 65	Elston Howard	4.00	1.60	.40
☐ 66	Bob Trowbridge	1.25	.50	.12
☐ 67	Jose Pagan	1.25	.50	.12
☐ 68	Dave Hillman	1.25	.50	.12
☐ 69	Billy Goodman	1.75	.70	.17
☐ 70	Lew Burdette	2.50	1.00	.25
☐ 71	Marty Keough	1.25	.50	.12
☐ 72	Tigers Team	6.50	1.50	.25
	(checklist on back)			
☐ 73	Bob Gibson	25.00	10.00	2.50
☐ 74	Walt Moryn	1.25	.50	.12
☐ 75	Vic Power	1.25	.50	.12
☐ 76	Bill Fischer	1.25	.50	.12
☐ 77	Hank Foiles	1.25	.50	.12
☐ 78	Bob Grim	1.25	.50	.12
☐ 79	Walt Dropo	1.25	.50	.12
☐ 80	Johnny Antonelli	1.75	.70	.17
☐ 81	Russ Snyder	1.25	.50	.12
☐ 82	Ruben Gomez	1.25	.50	.12
☐ 83	Tony Kubek	4.00	1.60	.40
☐ 84	Hal R. Smith	1.25	.50	.12
☐ 85	Frank Lary	1.75	.70	.17
☐ 86	Dick Gernert	1.25	.50	.12
☐ 87	John Romonosky	1.25	.50	.12
☐ 88	John Roseboro	1.75	.70	.17
☐ 89	Hal Brown	1.25	.50	.12
☐ 90	Bobby Avila	1.25	.50	.12
☐ 91	Bennie Daniels	1.25	.50	.12
☐ 92	Whitey Herzog	3.50	1.40	.35
☐ 93	Art Schult	1.25	.50	.12
☐ 94	Leo Kiely	1.25	.50	.12
☐ 95	Frank Thomas	1.75	.70	.17

		NRMT	VG-E	GOOD
☐ 96	Ralph Terry	2.50	1.00	.25
☐ 97	Ted Lepcio	1.25	.50	.12
☐ 91	Gordon Jones	1.25	.50	.12
☐ 99	Lenny Green	1.25	.50	.12
☐ 100	Nellie Fox	4.50	1.80	.45
☐ 101	Bob Miller	1.25	.50	.12
☐ 102	Kent Hadley	1.25	.50	.12
☐ 103	Dick Farrell	1.25	.50	.12
☐ 104	Dick Schofield	1.25	.50	.12
☐ 105	Larry Sherry	2.50	1.00	.25
☐ 106	Billy Gardner	1.25	.50	.12
☐ 107	Carlton Willey	1.25	.50	.12
☐ 108	Pete Daley	1.25	.50	.12
☐ 109	Clete Boyer	2.50	1.00	.25
☐ 110	Cal McLish	1.25	.50	.12
☐ 111	Vic Wertz	1.75	.70	.17
☐ 112	Jack Harshman	1.25	.50	.12
☐ 113	Bob Skinner	1.75	.70	.17
☐ 114	Ken Aspromonte	1.25	.50	.12
☐ 115	Fork and Knuckler	3.50	1.40	.35
	Roy Face			
	Hoyt Wilhelm			
☐ 116	Jim Rivera	1.25	.50	.12
☐ 117	Tom Borland RP	1.25	.50	.12
☐ 118	Bob Bruce RP	1.25	.50	.12
☐ 119	Chico Cardenas RP	1.75	.70	.17
☐ 120	Duke Carmel RP	1.25	.50	.12
☐ 121	Camilo Carreon RP	1.75	.70	.17
☐ 122	Don Dillard RP	1.25	.50	.12
☐ 123	Dan Dobbek RP	1.25	.50	.12
☐ 124	Jim Donohue RP	1.25	.50	.12
☐ 125	Dick Ellsworth RP	1.75	.70	.17
☐ 126	Chuck Estrada RP	1.75	.70	.17
☐ 127	Ron Hansen RP	1.75	.70	.17
☐ 128	Bill Harris RP	1.25	.50	.12
☐ 129	Bob Hartman RP	1.25	.50	.12
☐ 130	Frank Herrera RP	1.25	.50	.12
☐ 131	Ed Hobaugh RP	1.25	.50	.12
☐ 132	Frank Howard RP	8.00	3.25	.80
☐ 133	Manuel Javier RP	1.75	.70	.17
	(sic, Julian)			
☐ 134	Deron Johnson RP	1.75	.70	.17
☐ 135	Ken Johnson RP	1.25	.50	.12
☐ 136	Jim Kaat RP	20.00	8.00	2.00
☐ 137	Lou Klimchock RP	1.25	.50	.12
☐ 138	Art Mahaffey RP	1.75	.70	.17
☐ 139	Carl Mathias RP	1.25	.50	.12
☐ 140	Julio Navarro RP	1.75	.70	.17
☐ 141	Jim Proctor RP	1.25	.50	.12

		NRMT	VG-E	GOOD
☐ 142	Bill Short RP	1.75	.70	.17
☐ 143	Al Spangler RP	1.25	.50	.12
☐ 144	Al Stieglitz RP	1.25	.50	.12
☐ 145	Jim Umbricht RP	1.25	.50	.12
☐ 146	Ted Wieand RP	1.25	.50	.12
☐ 147	Bob Will RP	1.25	.50	.12
☐ 148	Carl Yastrzemski RP	250.00	100.00	25.00
☐ 149	Bob Nieman	1.25	.50	.12
☐ 150	Billy Pierce	2.50	1.00	.25
☐ 151	Giants Team	5.00	1.00	.20
	(checklist on back)			
☐ 152	Gail Harris	1.25	.50	.12
☐ 153	Bobby Thomson	2.50	1.00	.25
☐ 154	Jim Davenport	1.75	.70	.17
☐ 155	Charlie Neal	1.75	.70	.17
☐ 156	Art Ceccarelli	1.25	.50	.12
☐ 157	Rocky Nelson	1.25	.50	.12
☐ 158	Wes Covington	1.75	.70	.17
☐ 159	Jim Piersall	2.50	1.00	.25
☐ 160	Rival All-Stars	25.00	10.00	2.50
	Mickey Mantle			
	Ken Boyer			
☐ 161	Ray Narleski	1.25	.50	.12
☐ 162	Sammy Taylor	1.25	.50	.12
☐ 163	Hector Lopez	1.25	.50	.12
☐ 164	Reds Team	5.00	1.00	.20
	(checklist on back)			
☐ 165	Jack Sanford	1.75	.70	.17
☐ 166	Chuck Essegian	1.25	.50	.12
☐ 167	Valmy Thomas	1.25	.50	.12
☐ 168	Alex Grammas	1.25	.50	.12
☐ 169	Jake Striker	1.25	.50	.12
☐ 170	Del Crandall	1.75	.70	.17
☐ 171	Johnny Groth	1.25	.50	.12
☐ 172	Willie Kirkland	1.25	.50	.12
☐ 173	Billy Martin	5.50	2.20	.55
☐ 174	Indians Team	4.00	1.00	.20
	(checklist on back)			
☐ 175	Pedro Ramos	1.25	.50	.12
☐ 176	Vada Pinson	3.00	1.20	.30
☐ 177	Johnny Kucks	1.25	.50	.12
☐ 178	Woody Held	1.25	.50	.12
☐ 179	Rip Coleman	1.25	.50	.12
☐ 180	Harry Simpson	1.25	.50	.12
☐ 181	Billy Loes	1.25	.50	.12
☐ 182	Glen Hobbie	1.25	.50	.12
☐ 183	Eli Grba	1.25	.50	.12
☐ 184	Gary Geiger	1.25	.50	.12
☐ 185	Jim Owens	1.25	.50	.12

		NRMT	VG-E	GOOD
☐ 186	Dave Sisler	1.25	.50	.12
☐ 187	Jay Hook	1.25	.50	.12
☐ 188	Dick Williams	1.75	.70	.17
☐ 189	Don McMahon	1.25	.50	.12
☐ 190	Gene Woodling	1.75	.70	.17
☐ 191	Johnny Klippstein	1.25	.50	.12
☐ 192	Danny O'Connell	1.25	.50	.12
☐ 193	Dick Hyde	1.25	.50	.12
☐ 194	Bobby Gene Smith	1.25	.50	.12
☐ 195	Lindy McDaniel	1.75	.70	.17
☐ 196	Andy Carey	1.75	.70	.17
☐ 197	Ron Kline	1.25	.50	.12
☐ 198	Jerry Lynch	1.25	.50	.12
☐ 199	Dick Donovan	1.25	.50	.12
☐ 200	Willie Mays	70.00	28.00	7.00
☐ 201	Larry Osborne	1.25	.50	.12
☐ 202	Fred Kipp	1.25	.50	.12
☐ 203	Sammy White	1.25	.50	.12
☐ 204	Ryne Duren	2.50	1.00	.25
☐ 205	Johnny Logan	1.75	.70	.17
☐ 206	Claude Osteen	1.75	.70	.17
☐ 207	Bob Boyd	1.25	.50	.12
☐ 208	White Sox Team	4.00	1.00	.20
	(checklist on back)			
☐ 209	Ron Blackburn	1.25	.50	.12
☐ 210	Harmon Killebrew	16.00	6.50	1.60
☐ 211	Taylor Phillips	1.25	.50	.12
☐ 212	Walt Alston MG	6.00	2.40	.60
☐ 213	Chuck Dressen MG	1.75	.70	.17
☐ 214	Jimmy Dykes MG	1.75	.70	.17
☐ 215	Bob Elliott MG	1.25	.50	.12
☐ 216	Joe Gordon MG	1.75	.70	.17
☐ 217	Charlie Grimm MG	1.75	.70	.17
☐ 218	Solly Hemus MG	1.25	.50	.12
☐ 219	Fred Hutchinson MG	1.75	.70	.17
☐ 220	Billy Jurges MG	1.25	.50	.12
☐ 221	Cookie Lavagetto MG	1.25	.50	.12
☐ 222	Al Lopez MG	5.00	2.00	.50
☐ 223	Danny Murtaugh MG	1.75	.70	.17
☐ 224	Paul Richards MG	1.75	.70	.17
☐ 225	Bill Rigney MG	1.75	.70	.17
☐ 226	Eddie Sawyer MG	1.75	.70	.17
☐ 227	Casey Stengel MG	12.00	5.00	1.20
☐ 228	Ernie Johnson	1.25	.50	.12
☐ 229	Joe M. Morgan	4.50	1.80	.45
☐ 230	Mound Magicians	5.00	2.00	.50
	Lou Burdette			
	Warren Spahn			
	Bob Buhl			

		NRMT	VG-E	GOOD			NRMT	VG-E	GOOD
☐ 231	Hal Naragon	1.25	.50	.12	☐ 277	Harry Bright	1.25	.50	.12
☐ 232	Jim Busby	1.25	.50	.12	☐ 278	Stan Williams	1.25	.50	.12
☐ 233	Don Elston	1.25	.50	.12	☐ 279	Chuck Tanner	1.75	.70	.17
☐ 234	Don Demeter	1.25	.50	.12	☐ 280	Frank Sullivan	1.25	.50	.12
☐ 235	Gus Bell	1.75	.70	.17	☐ 281	Ray Boone	1.75	.70	.17
☐ 236	Dick Ricketts	1.25	.50	.12	☐ 282	Joe Nuxhall	1.75	.70	.17
☐ 237	Elmer Valo	1.25	.50	.12	☐ 283	John Blanchard	1.75	.70	.17
☐ 238	Danny Kravitz	1.25	.50	.12	☐ 284	Don Gross	1.25	.50	.12
☐ 239	Joe Shipley	1.25	.50	.12	☐ 285	Harry Anderson	1.25	.50	.12
☐ 240	Luis Aparicio	10.00	4.00	1.00	☐ 286	Ray Semproch	1.25	.50	.12
☐ 241	Albie Pearson	1.25	.50	.12	☐ 287	Felipe Alou	2.50	1.00	.25
☐ 242	Cardinals Team	4.50	1.00	.20	☐ 288	Bob Mabe	1.50	.60	.15
	(checklist on back)				☐ 289	Willie Jones	1.50	.60	.15
☐ 243	Bubba Phillips	1.25	.50	.12	☐ 290	Jerry Lumpe	1.50	.60	.15
☐ 244	Hal Griggs	1.25	.50	.12	☐ 291	Bob Keegan	1.50	.60	.15
☐ 245	Eddie Yost	1.25	.50	.12	☐ 292	Dodger Backstops	2.00	.80	.20
☐ 246	Lee Maye	1.25	.50	.12		Joe Pignatano			
☐ 247	Gil McDougald	3.50	1.40	.35		John Roseboro			
☐ 248	Del Rice	1.25	.50	.12	☐ 293	Gene Conley	1.50	.60	.15
☐ 249	Earl Wilson	1.75	.70	.17	☐ 294	Tony Taylor	1.50	.60	.15
☐ 250	Stan Musial	65.00	26.00	6.50	☐ 295	Gil Hodges	11.00	4.50	1.10
☐ 251	Bob Malkmus	1.25	.50	.12	☐ 296	Nelson Chittum	1.50	.60	.15
☐ 252	Ray Herbert	1.25	.50	.12	☐ 297	Reno Bertoia	1.50	.60	.15
☐ 253	Eddie Bressoud	1.25	.50	.12	☐ 298	George Witt	1.50	.60	.15
☐ 254	Arnie Portocarrero	1.25	.50	.12	☐ 299	Earl Torgeson	1.50	.60	.15
☐ 255	Jim Gilliam	3.50	1.40	.35	☐ 300	Hank Aaron	75.00	30.00	7.50
☐ 256	Dick Brown	1.25	.50	.12	☐ 301	Jerry Davie	1.50	.60	.15
☐ 257	Gordy Coleman	1.75	.70	.17	☐ 302	Phillies Team	4.50	1.25	.20
☐ 258	Dick Groat	3.00	1.20	.30		(checklist on back)			
☐ 259	George Altman	1.25	.50	.12	☐ 303	Billy O'Dell	1.50	.60	.15
☐ 260	Power Plus	1.75	.70	.17	☐ 304	Joe Ginsberg	1.50	.60	.15
	Rocky Colavito				☐ 305	Richie Ashburn	5.50	2.20	.55
	Tito Francona				☐ 306	Frank Baumann	1.50	.60	.15
☐ 261	Pete Burnside	1.25	.50	.12	☐ 307	Gene Oliver	1.50	.60	.15
☐ 262	Hank Bauer	2.50	1.00	.25	☐ 308	Dick Hall	1.50	.60	.15
☐ 263	Darrell Johnson	1.75	.70	.17	☐ 309	Bob Hale	1.50	.60	.15
☐ 264	Robin Roberts	11.00	4.50	1.10	☐ 310	Frank Malzone	2.00	.80	.20
☐ 265	Rip Repulski	1.25	.50	.12	☐ 311	Raul Sanchez	1.50	.60	.15
☐ 266	Joey Jay	1.25	.50	.12	☐ 312	Charley Lau	2.00	.80	.20
☐ 267	Jim Marshall	1.25	.50	.12	☐ 313	Turk Lown	1.50	.60	.15
☐ 268	Al Worthington	1.25	.50	.12	☐ 314	Chico Fernandez	1.50	.60	.15
☐ 269	Gene Green	1.25	.50	.12	☐ 315	Bobby Shantz	2.50	1.00	.25
☐ 270	Bob Turley	2.50	1.00	.25	☐ 316	Willie McCovey	90.00	36.00	9.00
☐ 271	Julio Becquer	1.25	.50	.12	☐ 317	Pumpsie Green	1.50	.60	.15
☐ 272	Fred Green	1.25	.50	.12	☐ 318	Jim Baxes	1.50	.60	.15
☐ 273	Neil Chrisley	1.25	.50	.12	☐ 319	Joe Koppe	1.50	.60	.15
☐ 274	Tom Acker	1.25	.50	.12	☐ 320	Bob Allison	2.00	.80	.20
☐ 275	Curt Flood	2.50	1.00	.25	☐ 321	Ron Fairly	2.00	.80	.20
☐ 276	Ken McBride	1.25	.50	.12	☐ 322	Willie Tasby	1.50	.60	.15

		NRMT	VG-E	GOOD
☐ 323	John Romano	1.50	.60	.15
☐ 324	Jim Perry	2.50	1.00	.25
☐ 325	Jim O'Toole	2.00	.80	.20
☐ 326	Bob Clemente	60.00	24.00	6.00
☐ 327	Ray Sadecki	1.50	.60	.15
☐ 328	Earl Battey	1.50	.60	.15
☐ 329	Zack Monroe	1.50	.60	.15
☐ 330	Harvey Kuenn	2.50	1.00	.25
☐ 331	Henry Mason	1.50	.60	.15
☐ 332	Yankees Team	16.00	4.00	1.00
	(checklist on back)			
☐ 333	Danny McDevitt	1.50	.60	.15
☐ 334	Ted Abernathy	1.50	.60	.15
☐ 335	Red Schoendienst	3.00	1.20	.30
☐ 336	Ike Delock	1.50	.60	.15
☐ 337	Cal Neeman	1.50	.60	.15
☐ 338	Ray Monzant	1.50	.60	.15
☐ 339	Harry Chiti	1.50	.60	.15
☐ 340	Harvey Haddix	2.00	.80	.20
☐ 341	Carroll Hardy	1.50	.60	.15
☐ 342	Casey Wise	1.50	.60	.15
☐ 343	Sandy Koufax	60.00	24.00	6.00
☐ 344	Clint Courtney	1.50	.60	.15
☐ 345	Don Newcombe	2.50	1.00	.25
☐ 346	J.C. Martin	1.50	.60	.15
	(face actually Gary Peters)			
☐ 347	Ed Bouchee	1.50	.60	.15
☐ 348	Barry Shetrone	1.50	.60	.15
☐ 349	Moe Drabowsky	1.50	.60	.15
☐ 350	Mickey Mantle	300.00	120.00	30.00
☐ 351	Don Nottebart	1.50	.60	.15
☐ 352	Cincy Clouters	3.50	1.40	.35
	Gus Bell			
	Frank Robinson			
	Jerry Lynch			
☐ 353	Don Larsen	2.50	1.00	.25
☐ 354	Bob Lillis	2.00	.80	.20
☐ 355	Bill White	2.50	1.00	.25
☐ 356	Joe Amalfitano	1.50	.60	.15
☐ 357	Al Schroll	1.50	.60	.15
☐ 358	Joe DeMaestri	1.50	.60	.15
☐ 359	Buddy Gilbert	1.50	.60	.15
☐ 360	Herb Score	2.00	.80	.20
☐ 361	Bob Oldis	1.50	.60	.15
☐ 362	Russ Kemmerer	1.50	.60	.15
☐ 363	Gene Stephens	1.50	.60	.15
☐ 364	Paul Foytack	1.50	.60	.15
☐ 365	Minnie Minoso	3.50	1.40	.35
☐ 366	Dallas Green	6.50	2.60	.65

		NRMT	VG-E	GOOD
☐ 367	Bill Tuttle	1.50	.60	.15
☐ 368	Daryl Spencer	1.50	.60	.15
☐ 369	Billy Hoeft	1.50	.60	.15
☐ 370	Bill Skowron	4.50	1.80	.45
☐ 371	Bud Byerly	1.50	.60	.15
☐ 372	Frank House	1.50	.60	.15
☐ 373	Don Hoak	1.50	.60	.15
☐ 374	Bob Buhl	1.50	.60	.15
☐ 375	Dale Long	2.00	.80	.20
☐ 376	John Briggs	1.50	.60	.15
☐ 377	Roger Maris	75.00	30.00	7.50
☐ 378	Stu Miller	1.50	.60	.15
☐ 379	Red Wilson	1.50	.60	.15
☐ 380	Bob Shaw	1.50	.60	.15
☐ 381	Braves Team	4.50	1.25	.20
	(checklist on back)			
☐ 382	Ted Bowsfield	1.50	.60	.15
☐ 383	Leon Wagner	1.50	.60	.15
☐ 384	Don Cardwell	1.50	.60	.15
☐ 385	World Series Game 1	2.50	1.00	.25
	Neal Steals Second			
☐ 386	World Series Game 2	2.50	1.00	.25
	Neal Belts 2nd Homer			
☐ 387	World Series Game 3	3.00	1.20	.30
	Furillo Breaks Game			
☐ 388	World Series Game 4	4.00	1.60	.40
	Hodges' Homer			
☐ 389	World Series Game 5	4.00	1.60	.40
	Luis Swipes Base			
☐ 390	World Series Game 6	2.50	1.00	.25
	Scrambling After Ball			
☐ 391	World Series Summary	2.50	1.00	.25
	The Champs Celebrate			
☐ 392	Tex Clevenger	1.50	.60	.15
☐ 393	Smoky Burgess	2.00	.80	.20
☐ 394	Norm Larker	1.50	.60	.15
☐ 395	Hoyt Wilhelm	11.00	4.50	1.10
☐ 396	Steve Bilko	1.50	.60	.15
☐ 397	Don Blasingame	1.50	.60	.15
☐ 398	Mike Cuellar	2.00	.80	.20
☐ 399	Young Hill Stars	2.00	.80	.20
	Milt Pappas			
	Jack Fisher			
	Jerry Walker			
☐ 400	Rocky Colavito	3.50	1.40	.35
☐ 401	Bob Duliba	1.50	.60	.15
☐ 402	Dick Stuart	2.00	.80	.20
☐ 403	Ed Sadowski	1.50	.60	.15
☐ 404	Bob Rush	1.50	.60	.15

		NRMT	VG-E	GOOD
☐ 405	Bobby Richardson	4.50	1.80	.45
☐ 406	Billy Klaus	1.50	.60	.15
☐ 407	Gary Peters	2.00	.80	.20
	(face actually J.C. Martin)			
☐ 408	Carl Furillo	3.50	1.40	.35
☐ 409	Ron Samford	1.50	.60	.15
☐ 410	Sam Jones	2.00	.80	.20
☐ 411	Ed Bailey	1.50	.60	.15
☐ 412	Bob Anderson	1.50	.60	.15
☐ 413	Athletics Team	4.00	1.00	.20
	(checklist on back)			
☐ 414	Don Williams	1.50	.60	.15
☐ 415	Bob Cerv	2.00	.80	.20
☐ 416	Humberto Robinson	1.50	.60	.15
☐ 417	Chuck Cottier	2.00	.80	.20
☐ 418	Don Mossi	2.00	.80	.20
☐ 419	George Crowe	1.50	.60	.15
☐ 420	Eddie Mathews	18.00	7.25	1.80
☐ 421	Duke Maas	1.50	.60	.15
☐ 422	John Powers	1.50	.60	.15
☐ 423	Ed Fitzgerald	1.50	.60	.15
☐ 424	Pete Whisenant	1.50	.60	.15
☐ 425	Johnny Podres	3.00	1.20	.30
☐ 426	Ron Jackson	1.50	.60	.15
☐ 427	Al Grunwald	1.50	.60	.15
☐ 428	Al Smith	1.50	.60	.15
☐ 429	AL Kings	3.00	1.20	.30
	Nellie Fox			
	Harvey Kuenn			
☐ 430	Art Ditmar	1.50	.60	.15
☐ 431	Andre Rodgers	1.50	.60	.15
☐ 432	Chuck Stobbs	1.50	.60	.15
☐ 433	Irv Noren	1.50	.60	.15
☐ 434	Brooks Lawrence	1.50	.60	.15
☐ 435	Gene Freese	1.50	.60	.15
☐ 436	Marv Throneberry	2.50	1.00	.25
☐ 437	Bob Friend	2.00	.80	.20
☐ 438	Jim Coker	1.50	.60	.15
☐ 439	Tom Brewer	1.50	.60	.15
☐ 440	Jim Lemon	1.50	.60	.15
☐ 441	Gary Bell	2.50	1.00	.25
☐ 442	Joe Pignatano	2.50	1.00	.25
☐ 443	Charley Maxwell	2.50	1.00	.25
☐ 444	Jerry Kindall	2.50	1.00	.25
☐ 445	Warren Spahn	21.00	8.50	2.10
☐ 446	Ellis Burton	2.50	1.00	.25
☐ 447	Ray Moore	2.50	1.00	.25
☐ 448	Jim Gentile	3.50	1.40	.35
☐ 449	Jim Brosnan	2.50	1.00	.25

		NRMT	VG-E	GOOD
☐ 450	Orlando Cepeda	6.50	2.60	.65
☐ 451	Curt Simmons	3.00	1.20	.30
☐ 452	Ray Webster	2.50	1.00	.25
☐ 453	Vern Law	3.50	1.40	.35
☐ 454	Hal Woodeshick	2.50	1.00	.25
☐ 455	Baltimore Coaches	3.50	1.40	.35
	Eddie Robinson			
	Harry Brecheen			
	Luman Harris			
☐ 456	Red Sox Coaches	4.00	1.60	.40
	Rudy York			
	Billy Herman			
	Sal Maglie			
	Del Baker			
☐ 457	Cubs Coaches	3.50	1.40	.35
	Charlie Root			
	Lou Klein			
	Elvin Tappe			
☐ 458	White Sox Coaches	3.50	1.40	.35
	Johnny Cooney			
	Don Gutteridge			
	Tony Cuccinello			
	Ray Berres			
☐ 459	Reds Coaches	3.50	1.40	.35
	Reggie Otero			
	Cot Deal			
	Wally Moses			
☐ 460	Indians Coaches	4.00	1.60	.40
	Mel Harder			
	Jo-Jo White			
	Bob Lemon			
	Ralph (Red) Kress			
☐ 461	Tigers Coaches	4.00	1.60	.40
	Tom Ferrick			
	Luke Appling			
	Billy Hitchcock			
☐ 462	Athletics Coaches	3.50	1.40	.35
	Fred Fitzsimmons			
	Don Heffner			
	Walker Cooper			
☐ 463	Dodgers Coaches	4.00	1.60	.40
	Bobby Bragan			
	Pete Reiser			
	Joe Becker			
	Greg Mulleavy			

		NRMT	VG-E	GOOD
☐ 464	Braves Coaches ...	3.50	1.40	.35
	Bob Scheffing			
	Whitlow Wyatt			
	Andy Pafko			
	George Myatt			
☐ 465	Yankees Coaches ..	7.00	2.80	.70
	Bill Dickey			
	Ralph Houk			
	Frank Crosetti			
	Ed Lopat			
☐ 466	Phillies Coaches ...	3.50	1.40	.35
	Ken Silvestri			
	Dick Carter			
	Andy Cohen			
☐ 467	Pirates Coaches ...	3.50	1.40	.35
	Mickey Vernon			
	Frank Oceak			
	Sam Narron			
	Bill Burwell			
☐ 468	Cardinals Coaches .	3.50	1.40	.35
	Johnny Keane			
	Howie Pollet			
	Ray Katt			
	Harry Walker			
☐ 469	Giants Coaches ...	3.50	1.40	.35
	Wes Westrum			
	Salty Parker			
	Bill Posedel			
☐ 470	Senators Coaches .	3.50	1.40	.35
	Bob Swift			
	Ellis Clary			
	Sam Mele			
☐ 471	Ned Garver	2.50	1.00	.25
☐ 472	Alvin Dark	3.50	1.40	.35
☐ 473	Al Cicotte	2.50	1.00	.25
☐ 474	Haywood Sullivan .	3.00	1.20	.30
☐ 475	Don Drysdale ...	18.00	7.25	1.80
☐ 476	Lou Johnson	2.50	1.00	.25
☐ 477	Don Ferrarese	2.50	1.00	.25
☐ 478	Frank Torre	2.50	1.00	.25
☐ 479	Georges Maranda ..	2.50	1.00	.25
☐ 480	Yogi Berra	40.00	16.00	4.00
☐ 481	Wes Stock	2.50	1.00	.25
☐ 482	Frank Bolling	2.50	1.00	.25
☐ 483	Camilo Pascual ...	3.00	1.20	.30
☐ 484	Pirates Team	12.50	4.00	1.00
	(checklist on back)			
☐ 485	Ken Boyer	5.00	2.00	.50
☐ 486	Bobby Del Greco ..	2.50	1.00	.25

		NRMT	VG-E	GOOD
☐ 487	Tom Sturdivant ...	2.50	1.00	.25
☐ 488	Norm Cash	4.00	1.60	.40
☐ 489	Steve Ridzik	2.50	1.00	.25
☐ 490	Frank Robinson ...	25.00	10.00	2.50
☐ 491	Mel Roach	2.50	1.00	.25
☐ 492	Larry Jackson	2.50	1.00	.25
☐ 493	Duke Snider	33.00	13.00	3.00
☐ 494	Orioles Team	7.50	2.00	.40
	(checklist on back)			
☐ 495	Sherm Lollar	3.00	1.20	.30
☐ 496	Bill Virdon	3.50	1.40	.35
☐ 497	John Tsitouris	2.50	1.00	.25
☐ 498	Al Pilarcik	2.50	1.00	.25
☐ 499	Johnny James	2.50	1.00	.25
☐ 500	Johnny Temple	3.00	1.20	.30
☐ 501	Bob Schmidt	2.50	1.00	.25
☐ 502	Jim Bunning	7.50	3.00	.75
☐ 503	Don Lee	2.50	1.00	.25
☐ 504	Seth Morehead	2.50	1.00	.25
☐ 505	Ted Kluszewski ...	4.50	1.80	.45
☐ 506	Lee Walls	2.50	1.00	.25
☐ 507	Dick Stigman	7.00	2.80	.70
☐ 508	Billy Consolo	7.00	2.80	.70
☐ 509	Tommy Davis	12.00	5.00	1.20
☐ 510	Jerry Staley	7.00	2.80	.70
☐ 511	Ken Walters	7.00	2.80	.70
☐ 512	Joe Gibbon	7.00	2.80	.70
☐ 513	Chicago Cubs ...	17.00	5.00	1.00
	Team Card			
	(checklist on back)			
☐ 514	Steve Barber	7.00	2.80	.70
☐ 515	Stan Lopata	7.00	2.80	.70
☐ 516	Marty Kutyna	7.00	2.80	.70
☐ 517	Charlie James	7.00	2.80	.70
☐ 518	Tony Gonzalez	7.00	2.80	.70
☐ 519	Ed Roebuck	7.00	2.80	.70
☐ 520	Don Buddin	7.00	2.80	.70
☐ 521	Mike Lee	7.00	2.80	.70
☐ 522	Ken Hunt	7.00	2.80	.70
☐ 523	Clay Dalrymple	7.00	2.80	.70
☐ 524	Bill Henry	7.00	2.80	.70
☐ 525	Marv Breeding	7.00	2.80	.70
☐ 526	Paul Giel	7.00	2.80	.70
☐ 527	Jose Valdivielso ..	7.00	2.80	.70
☐ 528	Ben Johnson	7.00	2.80	.70
☐ 529	Norm Sherry	8.00	3.25	.80
☐ 530	Mike McCormick ..	8.00	3.25	.80
☐ 531	Sandy Amoros	8.00	3.25	.80
☐ 532	Mike Garcia	10.00	4.00	1.00

	NRMT	VG-E	GOOD
☐ 533 Lu Clinton	7.00	2.80	.70
☐ 534 Ken MacKenzie	7.00	2.80	.70
☐ 535 Whitey Lockman	8.00	3.25	.80
☐ 536 Wynn Hawkins	7.00	2.80	.70
☐ 537 Boston Red Sox Team Card (checklist on back)	17.00	5.00	1.00
☐ 538 Frank Barnes	7.00	2.80	.70
☐ 539 Gene Baker	7.00	2.80	.70
☐ 540 Jerry Walker	7.00	2.80	.70
☐ 541 Tony Curry	7.00	2.80	.70
☐ 542 Ken Hamlin	7.00	2.80	.70
☐ 543 Elio Chacon	7.00	2.80	.70
☐ 544 Bill Monbouquette	8.00	3.25	.80
☐ 545 Carl Sawatski	7.00	2.80	.70
☐ 546 Hank Aguirre	7.00	2.80	.70
☐ 547 Bob Aspromonte	7.00	2.80	.70
☐ 548 Don Mincher	8.00	3.25	.80
☐ 549 John Buzhardt	7.00	2.80	.70
☐ 550 Jim Landis	7.00	2.80	.70
☐ 551 Ed Rakow	7.00	2.80	.70
☐ 552 Walt Bond	7.00	2.80	.70
☐ 553 Bill Skowron AS	9.00	3.75	.90
☐ 554 Willie McCovey AS	32.00	13.00	3.20
☐ 555 Nellie Fox AS	12.00	5.00	1.20
☐ 556 Charlie Neal AS	8.00	3.25	.80
☐ 557 Frank Malzone AS	8.00	3.25	.80
☐ 558 Eddie Mathews AS	21.00	8.50	2.10
☐ 559 Luis Aparicio AS	16.00	6.50	1.60
☐ 560 Ernie Banks AS	28.00	11.50	2.80
☐ 561 Al Kaline AS	28.00	11.50	2.80
☐ 562 Joe Cunningham AS	8.00	3.25	.80
☐ 563 Mickey Mantle AS	150.00	60.00	15.00
☐ 564 Willie Mays AS	65.00	26.00	6.50
☐ 565 Roger Maris AS	55.00	22.00	5.50
☐ 566 Hank Aaron AS	65.00	26.00	6.50
☐ 567 Sherm Lollar AS	8.00	3.25	.80
☐ 568 Del Crandall AS	8.00	3.25	.80
☐ 569 Camilo Pascual AS	8.00	3.25	.80
☐ 570 Don Drysdale AS	20.00	8.00	2.00
☐ 571 Billy Pierce AS	8.00	3.25	.80
☐ 572 Johnny Antonelli AS	10.00	4.00	1.00

1961 Topps

The cards in this 587-card set measure 2 ½" by 3 ½". In 1961, Topps returned to the vertical obverse format. Introduced for the first time were "League Leaders" (41 to 50) and separate, numbered checklist cards. Two number 463's exist: the Braves team card carrying that number was meant to be number 426. There are three versions of the second series checklist card #98; the variations are distinguished by the color of the "CHECKLIST" headline on the front of the card, the color of the printing of the card number on the bottom of the reverse, and the presence of the copyright notice running vertically on the card back. There are two groups of managers (131-139 and 219-226) as well as separate series of World Series cards (306-313), Baseball Thrills (401 to 410), previous MVP's (AL 471-478 and NL 479-486) and Sporting News All-Stars (566 to 589). The usual last series scarcity (523 to 589) exists. The set actually totals 587 cards since numbers 587 and 588 were never issued.

	NRMT	VG-E	GOOD
Complete Set (587)	4000.00	1800.00	800.00
Common Player (1-110)	.85	.34	.08
Common Player (111-370)	1.00	.40	.10
Common Player (371-446)	1.25	.50	.12
Common Player (447-522)	1.75	.70	.17
Common Player (523-565)	16.00	6.50	1.60
Common Player (566-589)	18.00	7.25	1.80

		NRMT	VG-E	GOOD
☐	1 Dick Groat	10.00	1.00	.20
☐	2 Roger Maris	75.00	30.00	7.00
☐	3 John Buzhardt	.85	.34	.08
☐	4 Lenny Green	.85	.34	.08
☐	5 John Romano	.85	.34	.08
☐	6 Ed Roebuck	.85	.34	.08
☐	7 White Sox Team ...	2.00	.00	.20
☐	8 Dick Williams	1.50	.60	.15
☐	9 Bob Purkey	.85	.34	.08
☐	10 Brooks Robinson ..	20.00	8.00	2.00
☐	11 Curt Simmons	1.25	.50	.12
☐	12 Moe Thacker	.85	.34	.08
☐	13 Chuck Cottier	.85	.34	.08
☐	14 Don Mossi	1.25	.50	.12
☐	15 Willie Kirkland	.85	.34	.08
☐	16 Billy Muffett	.85	.34	.08
☐	17 Checklist 1	4.50	.50	.10
☐	18 Jim Grant	.85	.34	.08
☐	19 Clete Boyer	1.50	.60	.15
☐	20 Robin Roberts	10.00	4.00	1.00
☐	21 Zorro Versalles	1.25	.50	.12
☐	22 Clem Labine	1.50	.60	.15
☐	23 Don Demeter	.85	.34	.08
☐	24 Ken Johnson	.85	.34	.08
☐	25 Reds' Heavy Artillery	3.50	1.40	.35
	Vada Pinson			
	Gus Bell			
	Frank Robinson			
☐	26 Wes Stock	1.25	.50	.12
☐	27 Jerry Kindall	.85	.34	.08
☐	28 Hector Lopez	.85	.34	.08
☐	29 Don Nottebart	.85	.34	.08
☐	30 Nellie Fox	4.00	1.60	.40
☐	31 Bob Schmidt	.85	.34	.08
☐	32 Ray Sadecki	.85	.34	.08
☐	33 Gary Geiger	.85	.34	.08
☐	34 Wynn Hawkins	.85	.34	.08
☐	35 Ron Santo	8.00	3.25	.80
☐	36 Jack Kralick	.85	.34	.08
☐	37 Charley Maxwell ...	.85	.34	.08
☐	38 Bob Lillis	1.25	.50	.12
☐	39 Leo Posada	.85	.34	.08
☐	40 Bob Turley	2.00	.80	.20
☐	41 NL Batting Leaders .	2.50	1.00	.25
	Dick Groat			
	Norm Larker			
	Willie Mays			
	Roberto Clemente			

		NRMT	VG-E	GOOD
☐	42 AL Batting Leaders	1.50	.60	.15
	Pete Runnels			
	Al Smith			
	Minnie Minoso			
	Bill Skowron			
☐	43 NL Home Run Leaders	5.00	2.00	.50
	Ernie Banks			
	Hank Aaron			
	Ed Mathews			
	Ken Boyer			
☐	44 AL Home Run Leaders	12.00	5.00	1.20
	Mickey Mantle			
	Roger Maris			
	Jim Lemon			
	Rocky Colavito			
☐	45 NL ERA Leaders ..	1.50	.60	.15
	Mike McCormick			
	Ernie Broglio			
	Don Drysdale			
	Bob Friend			
	Stan Williams			
☐	46 AL ERA Leaders ..	1.50	.60	.15
	Frank Baumann			
	Jim Bunning			
	Art Ditmar			
	H. Brown			
☐	47 NL Pitching Leaders	1.50	.60	.15
	Ernie Broglio			
	Warren Spahn			
	Vern Law			
	Lou Burdette			
☐	48 AL Pitching Leaders	1.50	.60	.15
	Chuck Estrada			
	Jim Perry			
	Bud Daley			
	Art Ditmar			
	Frank Lary			
	Milt Pappas			
☐	49 NL Strikeout Leaders	2.50	1.00	.25
	Don Drysdale			
	Sandy Koufax			
	Sam Jones			
	Ernie Broglio			
☐	50 AL Strikeout Leaders	1.50	.60	.15
	Jim Bunning			
	Pedro Ramos			
	Early Wynn			
	Frank Lary			

		NRMT	VG-E	GOOD
☐ 51	Detroit Tigers Team Card	2.00	.80	.20
☐ 52	George Crowe	.85	.34	.08
☐ 53	Russ Nixon	1.50	.50	.12
☐ 54	Earl Francis	.85	.34	.08
☐ 55	Jim Davenport	1.25	.50	.12
☐ 56	Russ Kemmerer	.85	.34	.08
☐ 57	Marv Throneberry	1.50	.60	.15
☐ 58	Joe Schaffernoth	.85	.34	.08
☐ 59	Jim Woods	.85	.34	.08
☐ 60	Woody Held	.85	.34	.08
☐ 61	Ron Piche	.85	.34	.08
☐ 62	Al Pilarcik	.85	.34	.08
☐ 63	Jim Kaat	6.00	2.40	.60
☐ 64	Alex Grammas	.85	.34	.08
☐ 65	Ted Kluszewski	3.50	1.40	.35
☐ 66	Billy Henry	.85	.34	.08
☐ 67	Ossie Virgil	.85	.34	.08
☐ 68	Deron Johnson	1.25	.50	.12
☐ 69	Earl Wilson	.85	.34	.08
☐ 70	Bill Virdon	1.50	.60	.15
☐ 71	Jerry Adair	.85	.34	.08
☐ 72	Stu Miller	.85	.34	.08
☐ 73	Al Spangler	.85	.34	.08
☐ 74	Joe Pignatano	.85	.34	.08
☐ 75	Lindy Shows Larry Lindy McDaniel Larry Jackson	1.25	.50	.12
☐ 76	Harry Anderson	.85	.34	.08
☐ 77	Dick Stigman	.85	.34	.08
☐ 78	Lee Walls	.85	.34	.08
☐ 79	Joe Ginsberg	.85	.34	.08
☐ 80	Harmon Killebrew	14.00	5.75	1.40
☐ 81	Tracy Stallard	.85	.34	.08
☐ 82	Joe Christopher	.85	.34	.08
☐ 83	Bob Bruce	.85	.34	.08
☐ 84	Lee Maye	.85	.34	.08
☐ 85	Jerry Walker	.85	.34	.08
☐ 86	Los Angeles Dodgers Team Card	3.00	1.20	.30
☐ 87	Joe Amalfitano	.85	.34	.08
☐ 88	Richie Ashburn	4.00	1.60	.40
☐ 89	Billy Martin	4.50	1.80	.45
☐ 90	Jerry Staley	.85	.34	.08
☐ 91	Walt Moryn	.85	.34	.08
☐ 92	Hal Naragon	.85	.34	.08
☐ 93	Tony Gonzalez	.85	.34	.08
☐ 94	Johnny Kucks	.85	.34	.08
☐ 95	Norm Cash	2.50	1.00	.25

		NRMT	VG-E	GOOD
☐ 96	Billy O'Dell	.85	.34	.08
☐ 97	Jerry Lynch	.85	.34	.08
☐ 98A	Checklist 2 (red "Checklist," 98 black on white)	4.50	.50	.10
☐ 98B	Checklist 2 (yellow "Checklist," 98 black on white)	4.50	.50	.10
☐ 98C	Checklist 2 (yellow "Checklist," 98 white on black, no copyright)	4.50	.50	.10
☐ 99	Don Buddin	.85	.34	.08
☐ 100	Harvey Haddix	1.50	.60	.15
☐ 101	Bubba Phillips	.85	.34	.08
☐ 102	Gene Stephens	.85	.34	.08
☐ 103	Ruben Amaro	.85	.34	.08
☐ 104	John Blanchard	1.25	.50	.12
☐ 105	Carl Willey	.85	.34	.08
☐ 106	Whitey Herzog	3.00	1.00	.25
☐ 107	Seth Morehead	.85	.34	.08
☐ 108	Dan Dobbek	.85	.34	.08
☐ 109	Johnny Podres	2.50	1.00	.25
☐ 110	Vada Pinson	2.50	1.00	.25
☐ 111	Jack Meyer	1.00	.40	.10
☐ 112	Chico Fernandez	1.00	.40	.10
☐ 113	Mike Fornieles	1.00	.40	.10
☐ 114	Hobie Landrith	1.00	.40	.10
☐ 115	Johnny Antonelli	1.50	.60	.15
☐ 116	Joe DeMaestri	1.00	.40	.10
☐ 117	Dale Long	1.25	.50	.12
☐ 118	Chris Cannizzaro	1.00	.40	.10
☐ 119	A's Big Armor Norm Siebern Hank Bauer Jerry Lumpe	1.25	.50	.12
☐ 120	Eddie Mathews	14.00	5.75	1.40
☐ 121	Eli Grba	1.00	.40	.10
☐ 122	Chicago Cubs Team Card	2.25	.90	.22
☐ 123	Billy Gardner	1.25	.50	.12
☐ 124	J.C. Martin	1.00	.40	.10
☐ 125	Steve Barber	1.00	.40	.10
☐ 126	Dick Stuart	1.50	.60	.15
☐ 127	Ron Kline	1.00	.40	.10
☐ 128	Rip Repulski	1.00	.40	.10
☐ 129	Ed Hobaugh	1.00	.40	.10
☐ 130	Norm Larker	1.25	.50	.12
☐ 131	Paul Richards MG	1.25	.50	.12
☐ 132	Al Lopez MG	3.50	1.40	.35
☐ 133	Ralph Houk MG	2.50	1.00	.25
☐ 134	Mickey Vernon MG	1.25	.50	.12

		NRMT	VG-E	GOOD
☐ 135	Fred Hutchinson MG	1.25	.50	.12
☐ 136	Walt Alston MG	4.00	1.60	.40
☐ 137	Chuck Dressen MG	1.25	.50	.12
☐ 138	Danny Murtaugh MG	1.25	.50	.12
☐ 139	Solly Hemus MG	1.25	.50	.12
☐ 140	Gus Triandos	1.25	.50	.12
☐ 141	Billy Williams	50.00	20.00	5.00
☐ 142	Luis Arroyo	1.25	.50	.12
☐ 143	Russ Snyder	1.00	.40	.10
☐ 144	Jim Coker	1.00	.40	.10
☐ 145	Bob Buhl	1.00	.40	.10
☐ 146	Marty Keough	1.00	.40	.10
☐ 147	Ed Rakow	1.00	.40	.10
☐ 148	Julian Javier	1.25	.50	.12
☐ 149	Bob Oldis	1.00	.40	.10
☐ 150	Willie Mays	70.00	28.00	7.00
☐ 151	Jim Donohue	1.00	.40	.10
☐ 152	Earl Torgeson	1.00	.40	.10
☐ 153	Don Lee	1.00	.40	.10
☐ 154	Bobby Del Greco	1.00	.40	.10
☐ 155	Johnny Temple	1.25	.50	.12
☐ 156	Ken Hunt	1.00	.40	.10
☐ 157	Cal McLish	1.00	.40	.10
☐ 158	Pete Daley	1.00	.40	.10
☐ 159	Orioles Team	2.25	.90	.22
☐ 160	Whitey Ford	21.00	8.50	2.10
☐ 161	Sherman Jones	1.00	.40	.10
	(photo actually Eddie Fisher)			
☐ 162	Jay Hook	1.00	.40	.10
☐ 163	Ed Sadowski	1.00	.40	.10
☐ 164	Felix Mantilla	1.00	.40	.10
☐ 165	Gino Cimoli	1.00	.40	.10
☐ 166	Danny Kravitz	1.00	.40	.10
☐ 167	San Francisco Giants Team Card	2.25	.90	.22
☐ 168	Tommy Davis	2.50	1.00	.25
☐ 169	Don Elston	1.00	.40	.10
☐ 170	Al Smith	1.00	.40	.10
☐ 171	Paul Foytack	1.00	.40	.10
☐ 172	Don Dillard	1.00	.40	.10
☐ 173	Beantown Bombers Frank Malzone Vic Wertz Jackie Jensen	1.50	.60	.15
☐ 174	Ray Semproch	1.00	.40	.10
☐ 175	Gene Freese	1.00	.40	.10
☐ 176	Ken Aspromonte	1.00	.40	.10
☐ 177	Don Larsen	1.75	.70	.17
☐ 178	Bob Nieman	1.00	.40	.10
☐ 179	Joe Koppe	1.00	.40	.10
☐ 180	Bobby Richardson	4.00	1.60	.40
☐ 181	Fred Green	1.00	.40	.10
☐ 182	Dave Nicholson	1.00	.40	.10
☐ 183	Andre Rodgers	1.00	.40	.10
☐ 184	Steve Bilko	1.00	.40	.10
☐ 185	Herb Score	1.75	.70	.17
☐ 186	Elmer Valo	1.00	.40	.10
☐ 187	Billy Klaus	1.00	.40	.10
☐ 188	Jim Marshall	1.00	.40	.10
☐ 189	Checklist 3	5.00	.50	.10
☐ 190	Stan Williams	1.00	.40	.10
☐ 191	Mike De La Hoz	1.00	.40	.10
☐ 192	Dick Brown	1.00	.40	.10
☐ 193	Gene Conley	1.00	.40	.10
☐ 194	Gordy Coleman	1.25	.50	.12
☐ 195	Jerry Casale	1.00	.40	.10
☐ 196	Ed Bouchee	1.00	.40	.10
☐ 197	Dick Hall	1.00	.40	.10
☐ 198	Carl Sawatski	1.00	.40	.10
☐ 199	Bob Boyd	1.00	.40	.10
☐ 200	Warren Spahn	15.00	6.00	1.50
☐ 201	Pete Whisenant	1.00	.40	.10
☐ 202	Al Neiger	1.00	.40	.10
☐ 203	Eddie Bressoud	1.00	.40	.10
☐ 204	Bob Skinner	1.25	.50	.12
☐ 205	Billy Pierce	1.50	.60	.15
☐ 206	Gene Green	1.00	.40	.10
☐ 207	Dodger Southpaws Sandy Koufax Johnny Podres	9.00	3.75	.90
☐ 208	Larry Osborne	1.00	.40	.10
☐ 209	Ken McBride	1.00	.40	.10
☐ 210	Pete Runnels	1.25	.50	.12
☐ 211	Bob Gibson	16.00	6.50	1.60
☐ 212	Haywood Sullivan	1.25	.50	.12
☐ 213	Bill Stafford	1.25	.50	.12
☐ 214	Danny Murphy	1.00	.40	.10
☐ 215	Gus Bell	1.25	.50	.12
☐ 216	Ted Bowsfield	1.00	.40	.10
☐ 217	Mel Roach	1.00	.40	.10
☐ 218	Hal Brown	1.00	.40	.10
☐ 219	Gene Mauch MG	1.50	.60	.15
☐ 220	Alvin Dark MG	1.50	.60	.15
☐ 221	Mike Higgins MG	1.25	.50	.12
☐ 222	Jimmy Dykes MG	1.25	.50	.12
☐ 223	Bob Scheffing MG	1.00	.40	.10
☐ 224	Joe Gordon MG	1.25	.50	.12
☐ 225	Bill Rigney MG	1.00	.40	.10

		NRMT	VG-E	GOOD
☐ 226	Harry Lavagetto MG	1.25	.50	.12
☐ 227	Juan Pizarro	1.00	.40	.10
☐ 228	New York Yankees Team Card	12.00	5.00	1.20
☐ 229	Rudy Hernandez	1.00	.40	.10
☐ 230	Don Hoak	1.25	.50	.12
☐ 231	Dick Drott	1.00	.40	.10
☐ 232	Bill White	1.50	.60	.15
☐ 233	Joey Jay	1.00	.40	.10
☐ 234	Ted Lepcio	1.00	.40	.10
☐ 235	Camilo Pascual	1.25	.50	.12
☐ 236	Don Gile	1.00	.40	.10
☐ 237	Billy Loes	1.00	.40	.10
☐ 238	Jim Gilliam	2.50	1.00	.25
☐ 239	Dave Sisler	1.00	.40	.10
☐ 240	Ron Hansen	1.00	.40	.10
☐ 241	Al Cicotte	1.00	.40	.10
☐ 242	Hal Smith	1.00	.40	.10
☐ 243	Frank Lary	1.25	.50	.12
☐ 244	Chico Cardenas	1.00	.40	.10
☐ 245	Joe Adcock	1.50	.60	.15
☐ 246	Bob Davis	1.00	.40	.10
☐ 247	Billy Goodman	1.25	.50	.12
☐ 248	Ed Keegan	1.00	.40	.10
☐ 249	Cincinnati Reds Team Card	2.75	1.10	.27
☐ 250	Buc Hill Aces Vern Law Roy Face	1.50	.60	.15
☐ 251	Bill Bruton	1.25	.50	.12
☐ 252	Bill Short	1.00	.40	.10
☐ 253	Sammy Taylor	1.00	.40	.10
☐ 254	Ted Sadowski	1.00	.40	.10
☐ 255	Vic Power	1.00	.40	.10
☐ 256	Billy Hoeft	1.00	.40	.10
☐ 257	Carroll Hardy	1.00	.40	.10
☐ 258	Jack Sanford	1.50	.60	.15
☐ 259	John Schaive	1.00	.40	.10
☐ 260	Don Drysdale	13.00	5.25	1.30
☐ 261	Charlie Lau	1.50	.60	.15
☐ 262	Tony Curry	1.00	.40	.10
☐ 263	Ken Hamlin	1.00	.40	.10
☐ 264	Glen Hobbie	1.00	.40	.10
☐ 265	Tony Kubek	4.50	1.80	.45
☐ 266	Lindy McDaniel	1.25	.50	.12
☐ 267	Norm Siebern	1.00	.40	.10
☐ 268	Ike Delock	1.00	.40	.10
☐ 269	Harry Chiti	1.00	.40	.10
☐ 270	Bob Friend	1.25	.50	.12

		NRMT	VG-E	GOOD
☐ 271	Jim Landis	1.00	.40	.10
☐ 272	Tom Morgan	1.00	.40	.10
☐ 273	Checklist 4	5.00	.50	.10
☐ 274	Gary Bell	1.00	.40	.10
☐ 275	Gene Woodling	1.50	.60	.15
☐ 276	Ray Rippelmeyer	1.00	.40	.10
☐ 277	Hank Foiles	1.00	.40	.10
☐ 278	Don McMahon	1.25	.50	.12
☐ 279	Jose Pagan	1.00	.40	.10
☐ 280	Frank Howard	2.50	1.00	.25
☐ 281	Frank Sullivan	1.00	.40	.10
☐ 282	Faye Throneberry	1.00	.40	.10
☐ 283	Bob Anderson	1.00	.40	.10
☐ 284	Dick Gernert	1.00	.40	.10
☐ 285	Sherm Lollar	1.25	.50	.12
☐ 286	George Witt	1.00	.40	.10
☐ 287	Carl Yastrzemski	125.00	50.00	12.50
☐ 288	Albie Pearson	1.00	.40	.10
☐ 289	Ray Moore	1.00	.40	.10
☐ 290	Stan Musial	60.00	24.00	6.00
☐ 291	Tex Clevenger	1.00	.40	.10
☐ 292	Jim Baumer	1.00	.40	.10
☐ 293	Tom Sturdivant	1.00	.40	.10
☐ 294	Don Blasingame	1.00	.40	.10
☐ 295	Milt Pappas	1.25	.50	.12
☐ 296	Wes Covington	1.25	.50	.12
☐ 297	Athletics Team	2.00	.80	.20
☐ 298	Jim Golden	1.00	.40	.10
☐ 299	Clay Dalrymple	1.00	.40	.10
☐ 300	Mickey Mantle	300.00	120.00	30.00
☐ 301	Chet Nichols	1.00	.40	.10
☐ 302	Al Heist	1.00	.40	.10
☐ 303	Gary Peters	1.25	.50	.12
☐ 304	Rocky Nelson	1.00	.40	.10
☐ 305	Mike McCormick	1.25	.50	.12
☐ 306	World Series Game 1 Virdon Saves Game	2.50	1.00	.25
☐ 307	World Series Game 2 Mantle 2 Homers	20.00	8.00	2.00
☐ 308	World Series Game 3 Richardson is Hero	3.50	1.40	.35
☐ 309	World Series Game 4 Cimoli Safe	2.50	1.00	.25
☐ 310	World Series Game 5 Face Saves the Day	3.00	1.20	.30
☐ 311	World Series Game 6 Ford Second Shutout	5.00	2.00	.50
☐ 312	World Series Game 7 Mazeroski's Homer	4.00	1.60	.40

		NRMT	VG-E	GOOD
☐ 313	World Series Summary	2.50	1.00	.25
	Pirates Celebrate			
☐ 314	Bob Miller	1.00	.40	.10
☐ 315	Earl Battey	1.00	.40	.10
☐ 316	Bobby Gene Smith ..	1.00	.40	.10
☐ 317	Jim Brewer	1.00	.40	.10
☐ 318	Danny O'Connell ...	1.00	.40	.10
☐ 319	Valmy Thomas	1.00	.40	.10
☐ 320	Lou Burdette	2.00	.80	.20
☐ 321	Marv Breeding	1.00	.40	.10
☐ 322	Bill Kunkel	1.50	.60	.15
☐ 323	Sammy Esposito ...	1.00	.40	.10
☐ 324	Hank Aguirre	1.00	.40	.10
☐ 325	Wally Moon	1.50	.60	.15
☐ 326	Dave Hillman	1.00	.40	.10
☐ 327	Matty Alou	2.50	1.00	.25
☐ 328	Jim O'Toole	1.25	.50	.12
☐ 329	Julio Becquer	1.00	.40	.10
☐ 330	Rocky Colavito	3.00	1.20	.30
☐ 331	Ned Garver	1.00	.40	.10
☐ 332	Dutch Dotterer	1.25	.50	.12
	(photo actually Tommy Dotterer, Dutch's brother)			
☐ 333	Fritz Brickell	1.00	.40	.10
☐ 334	Walt Bond	1.00	.40	.10
☐ 335	Frank Bolling	1.00	.40	.10
☐ 336	Don Mincher	1.25	.50	.12
☐ 337	Al's Aces	3.50	1.40	.35
	Early Wynn			
	Al Lopez			
	Herb Score			
☐ 338	Don Landrum	1.00	.40	.10
☐ 339	Gene Baker	1.00	.40	.10
☐ 340	Vic Wertz	1.25	.50	.12
☐ 341	Jim Owens	1.00	.40	.10
☐ 342	Clint Courtney	1.00	.40	.10
☐ 343	Earl Robinson	1.00	.40	.10
☐ 344	Sandy Koufax	55.00	22.00	5.50
☐ 345	Jim Piersall	2.00	.80	.20
☐ 346	Howie Nunn	1.00	.40	.10
☐ 347	St. Louis Cardinals .	2.25	.90	.22
	Team Card			
☐ 348	Steve Boros	1.25	.50	.12
☐ 349	Danny McDevitt	1.00	.40	.10
☐ 350	Ernie Banks	18.00	7.25	1.80
☐ 351	Jim King	1.00	.40	.10
☐ 352	Bob Shaw	1.00	.40	.10
☐ 353	Howie Bedell	1.00	.40	.10
☐ 354	Billy Harrell	1.00	.40	.10

		NRMT	VG-E	GOOD
☐ 355	Bob Allison	1.25	.50	.12
☐ 356	Ryne Duren	1.50	.60	.15
☐ 357	Daryl Spencer	1.00	.40	.10
☐ 358	Earl Averill	1.00	.40	.10
☐ 359	Dallas Green	3.00	1.20	.30
☐ 360	Frank Robinson ...	20.00	8.00	2.00
☐ 361A	Checklist 5	5.00	1.00	.20
	(no ad on back)			
☐ 361B	Checklist 5	10.00	2.00	.40
	(Special Feature ad on back)			
☐ 362	Frank Funk	1.00	.40	.10
☐ 363	John Roseboro ...	1.25	.50	.12
☐ 364	Moe Drabowsky ...	1.00	.40	.10
☐ 365	Jerry Lumpe	1.00	.40	.10
☐ 366	Eddie Fisher	1.00	.40	.10
☐ 367	Jim Rivera	1.00	.40	.10
☐ 368	Bennie Daniels ...	1.00	.40	.10
☐ 369	Dave Philley	1.00	.40	.10
☐ 370	Roy Face	2.25	.90	.22
☐ 371	Bill Skowron SP ..	6.50	2.60	.65
☐ 372	Bob Hendley	1.25	.50	.12
☐ 373	Boston Red Sox ..	2.50	1.00	.25
	Team Card			
☐ 374	Paul Giel	1.25	.50	.12
☐ 375	Ken Boyer	4.00	1.60	.40
☐ 376	Mike Roarke	1.25	.50	.12
☐ 377	Ruben Gomez	1.25	.50	.12
☐ 378	Wally Post	1.25	.50	.12
☐ 379	Bobby Shantz ...	2.50	1.00	.25
☐ 380	Minnie Minoso ...	3.00	1.20	.30
☐ 381	Dave Wickersham .	1.25	.50	.12
☐ 382	Frank Thomas	1.75	.70	.17
☐ 383	Frisco First Liners .	1.75	.70	.17
	Mike McCormick			
	Jack Sanford			
	Billy O'Dell			
☐ 384	Chuck Essegian ..	1.75	.70	.17
☐ 385	Jim Perry	2.50	1.00	.20
☐ 386	Joe Hicks	1.25	.50	.12
☐ 387	Duke Maas	1.25	.50	.12
☐ 388	Bob Clemente	50.00	20.00	5.00
☐ 389	Ralph Terry	2.50	1.00	.20
☐ 390	Del Crandall	1.75	.70	.17
☐ 391	Winston Brown ...	1.25	.50	.12
☐ 392	Reno Bertoia	1.25	.50	.12
☐ 393	Batter Bafflers ...	1.75	.70	.17
	Don Cardwell			
	Glen Hobbie			
☐ 394	Ken Walters	1.25	.50	.12

		NRMT	VG-E	GOOD
☐ 395	Chuck Estrada	1.75	.70	.17
☐ 396	Bob Aspromonte	1.25	.50	.12
☐ 397	Hal Woodeshick	1.25	.50	.12
☐ 398	Hank Bauer	2.00	.80	.20
☐ 399	Cliff Cook	1.25	.50	.12
☐ 400	Vern Law	2.00	.80	.20
☐ 401	Ruth 60th Homer	12.00	5.00	1.20
☐ 402	Perfect Game	5.00	2.00	.50
	(Don Larsen)			
☐ 403	26 Inning Tie	2.00	.80	.20
☐ 404	Hornsby .424 Average	3.00	1.20	.30
☐ 405	Gehrig's Streak	7.00	2.80	.70
☐ 406	Mantle 565 Ft. Homer	21.00	8.50	2.10
☐ 407	Chesbro Wins 41	2.00	.80	.20
☐ 408	Mathewson Fans 267	3.00	1.20	.30
☐ 409	Johnson Shutouts	3.00	1.20	.30
☐ 410	Haddix 12 Perfect Innings	2.00	.80	.20
☐ 411	Tony Taylor	1.25	.50	.12
☐ 412	Larry Sherry	1.75	.70	.17
☐ 413	Eddie Yost	1.25	.50	.12
☐ 414	Dick Donovan	1.25	.50	.12
☐ 415	Hank Aaron	75.00	30.00	7.50
☐ 416	Dick Howser	7.00	2.80	.70
☐ 417	Juan Marichal	75.00	30.00	7.50
☐ 418	Ed Bailey	1.25	.50	.12
☐ 419	Tom Borland	1.25	.50	.12
☐ 420	Ernie Broglio	1.75	.70	.17
☐ 421	Ty Cline	1.25	.50	.12
☐ 422	Bud Daley	1.25	.50	.12
☐ 423	Charlie Neal SP	3.50	1.40	.35
☐ 424	Turk Lown	1.25	.50	.12
☐ 425	Yogi Berra	40.00	16.00	4.00
☐ 426	Milwaukee Braves Team Card (back numbered 463)	6.00	2.40	.60
☐ 427	Dick Ellsworth	2.00	.80	.20
☐ 428	Ray Barker SP	3.00	1.20	.30
☐ 429	Al Kaline	25.00	10.00	2.50
☐ 430	Bill Mazeroski SP	6.50	2.60	.65
☐ 431	Chuck Stobbs	1.25	.50	.12
☐ 432	Coot Veal	1.25	.50	.12
☐ 433	Art Mahaffey	1.25	.50	.12
☐ 434	Tom Brewer	1.25	.50	.12
☐ 435	Orlando Cepeda	4.50	1.80	.45
☐ 436	Jim Maloney	4.50	1.80	.45
☐ 437A	Checklist 6 440 Louis Aparicio	6.00	.60	.10

		NRMT	VG-E	GOOD
☐ 437B	Checklist 6 440 Luis Aparicio	6.00	.60	.10
☐ 438	Curt Flood	2.50	1.00	.25
☐ 439	Phil Regan	1.75	.70	.17
☐ 440	Luis Aparicio	10.00	4.00	1.00
☐ 441	Dick Bertell	1.25	.50	.12
☐ 442	Gordon Jones	1.25	.50	.12
☐ 443	Duke Snider	25.00	10.00	2.50
☐ 444	Joe Nuxhall	1.75	.70	.17
☐ 445	Frank Malzone	2.00	.80	.20
☐ 446	Bob Taylor	1.25	.50	.12
☐ 447	Harry Bright	1.75	.70	.17
☐ 448	Del Rice	1.75	.70	.17
☐ 449	Bob Bolin	1.75	.70	.17
☐ 450	Jim Lemon	2.50	1.00	.25
☐ 451	Power for Ernie Daryl Spencer Bill White Ernie Broglio	2.50	1.00	.25
☐ 452	Bob Allen	1.75	.70	.17
☐ 453	Dick Schofield	1.75	.70	.17
☐ 454	Pumpsie Green	1.75	.70	.17
☐ 455	Early Wynn	10.00	4.00	1.00
☐ 456	Hal Bevan	1.75	.70	.17
☐ 457	John James	1.75	.70	.17
☐ 458	Willie Tasby	1.75	.70	.17
☐ 459	Terry Fox	1.75	.70	.17
☐ 460	Gil Hodges	10.00	4.00	1.00
☐ 461	Smoky Burgess	2.50	1.00	.25
☐ 462	Lou Klimchock	1.75	.70	.17
☐ 463	Jack Fisher (See also 426)	2.50	1.00	.25
☐ 464	Lee Thomas	3.50	1.50	.30
☐ 465	Roy McMillan	1.75	.70	.17
☐ 466	Ron Moeller	1.75	.70	.17
☐ 467	Cleveland Indians Team Card	3.50	1.40	.35
☐ 468	John Callison	2.50	1.00	.25
☐ 469	Ralph Lumenti	1.75	.70	.17
☐ 470	Roy Sievers	2.50	1.00	.25
☐ 471	Phil Rizzuto MVP	10.00	4.00	.90
☐ 472	Yogi Berra MVP	27.00	11.00	2.50
☐ 473	Bob Shantz MVP	2.50	1.00	.25
☐ 474	Al Rosen MVP	3.00	1.20	.25
☐ 475	Mickey Mantle MVP	75.00	30.00	7.50
☐ 476	Jackie Jensen MVP	3.00	1.20	.25
☐ 477	Nellie Fox MVP	3.50	1.50	.30
☐ 478	Roger Maris MVP	27.00	11.00	2.50
☐ 479	Jim Konstanty MVP	2.50	1.00	.25

		NRMT	VG-E	GOOD			NRMT	VG-E	GOOD
☐ 480	Roy Campanella MVP	21.00	8.00	2.00	☐ 526	R.C. Stevens	16.00	6.50	1.60
☐ 481	Hank Sauer MVP	2.50	1.00	.25	☐ 527	Gene Leek	16.00	6.50	1.60
☐ 482	Willie Mays MVP	30.00	12.00	2.70	☐ 528	Pedro Ramos	16.00	6.50	1.60
☐ 483	Don Newcombe MVP	3.00	1.20	.25	☐ 529	Bob Roselli	16.00	6.50	1.60
☐ 484	Hank Aaron MVP	30.00	12.00	2.70	☐ 530	Bob Malkmus	16.00	6.50	1.60
☐ 485	Ernie Banks MVP	11.00	4.50	1.00	☐ 531	Jim Coates	16.00	6.50	1.60
☐ 486	Dick Groat MVP	2.50	1.00	.25	☐ 532	Bob Hale	16.00	6.50	1.60
☐ 487	Gene Oliver	1.75	.70	.17	☐ 533	Jack Curtis	16.00	6.50	1.60
☐ 488	Joe McClain	1.75	.70	.17	☐ 534	Eddie Kasko	16.00	6.50	1.60
☐ 489	Walt Dropo	1.75	.70	.17	☐ 535	Larry Jackson	16.00	6.50	1.60
☐ 490	Jim Bunning	7.00	2.80	.70	☐ 536	Bill Tuttle	16.00	6.50	1.60
☐ 491	Philadelphia Phillies	3.50	1.40	.35	☐ 537	Bobby Locke	16.00	6.50	1.60
	Team Card				☐ 538	Chuck Hiller	16.00	6.50	1.60
☐ 492	Ron Fairly	2.50	1.00	.25	☐ 539	Johnny Klippstein	16.00	6.50	1.60
☐ 493	Don Zimmer	3.00	1.20	.30	☐ 540	Jackie Jensen	24.00	10.00	2.40
☐ 494	Tom Cheney	1.75	.70	.17	☐ 541	Roland Sheldon	16.00	6.50	1.60
☐ 495	Elston Howard	4.00	1.60	.40	☐ 542	Minnesota Twins	35.00	14.00	3.50
☐ 496	Ken MacKenzie	1.75	.70	.17		Team Card			
☐ 497	Willie Jones	1.75	.70	.17	☐ 543	Roger Craig	24.00	10.00	2.40
☐ 498	Ray Herbert	1.75	.70	.17	☐ 544	George Thomas	16.00	6.50	1.60
☐ 499	Chuck Schilling	1.75	.70	.17	☐ 545	Hoyt Wilhelm	50.00	20.00	5.00
☐ 500	Harvey Kuenn	3.00	1.20	.30	☐ 546	Marty Kutyna	16.00	6.50	1.60
☐ 501	John DeMerit	1.75	.70	.17	☐ 547	Leon Wagner	16.00	6.50	1.60
☐ 502	Clarence Coleman	1.75	.70	.17	☐ 548	Ted Wills	16.00	6.50	1.60
☐ 503	Tito Francona	2.50	1.00	.25	☐ 549	Hal R. Smith	16.00	6.50	1.60
☐ 504	Billy Consolo	1.75	.70	.17	☐ 550	Frank Baumann	16.00	6.50	1.60
☐ 505	Red Schoendienst	3.00	1.20	.30	☐ 551	George Altman	16.00	6.50	1.60
☐ 506	Willie Davis	5.00	2.00	.50	☐ 552	Jim Archer	16.00	6.50	1.60
☐ 507	Pete Burnside	1.75	.70	.17	☐ 553	Bill Fischer	16.00	6.50	1.60
☐ 508	Rocky Bridges	1.75	.70	.17	☐ 554	Pittsburgh Pirates	30.00	12.00	3.00
☐ 509	Camilo Carreon	1.75	.70	.17		Team Card			
☐ 510	Art Ditmar	1.75	.70	.17	☐ 555	Sam Jones	18.00	7.25	1.80
☐ 511	Joe M. Morgan	3.50	1.40	.35	☐ 556	Ken R. Hunt	16.00	6.50	1.60
☐ 512	Bob Will	1.75	.70	.17	☐ 557	Jose Valdivielso	16.00	6.50	1.60
☐ 513	Jim Brosnan	2.50	1.00	.25	☐ 558	Don Ferrarese	16.00	6.50	1.60
☐ 514	Jake Wood	1.75	.70	.17	☐ 559	Jim Gentile	18.00	7.25	1.80
☐ 515	Jackie Brandt	1.75	.70	.17	☐ 560	Barry Latman	16.00	6.50	1.60
☐ 516	Checklist 7	7.00	.75	.15	☐ 561	Charley James	16.00	6.50	1.60
☐ 517	Willie McCovey	35.00	14.00	3.50	☐ 562	Bill Monbouquette	16.00	6.50	1.60
☐ 518	Andy Carey	2.50	1.00	.25	☐ 563	Bob Cerv	18.00	7.25	1.80
☐ 519	Jim Pagliaroni	1.75	.70	.17	☐ 564	Don Cardwell	16.00	6.50	1.60
☐ 520	Joe Cunningham	2.50	1.00	.25	☐ 565	Felipe Alou	18.00	7.25	1.80
☐ 521	Brother Battery	2.50	1.00	.25	☐ 566	Paul Richards MG AS	18.00	7.25	1.80
	Norm Sherry				☐ 567	Danny Murtaugh			
	Larry Sherry					MG AS	18.00	7.25	1.80
☐ 522	Dick Farrell	2.50	1.00	.25	☐ 568	Bill Skowron AS	20.00	8.00	2.00
☐ 523	Joe Gibbon	16.00	6.50	1.60	☐ 569	Frank Herrera AS	18.00	7.25	1.80
☐ 524	Johnny Logan	18.00	7.25	1.80	☐ 570	Nellie Fox AS	25.00	10.00	2.50
☐ 525	Ron Perranoski	18.00	7.25	1.80	☐ 571	Bill Mazeroski AS	20.00	8.00	2.00

		NRMT	VG-E	GOOD
☐ 572	Brooks Robinson AS	60.00	24.00	6.00
☐ 573	Ken Boyer AS	20.00	8.00	2.00
☐ 574	Luis Aparicio AS	35.00	14.00	3.50
☐ 575	Ernie Banks AS	60.00	24.00	6.00
☐ 576	Roger Maris AS	70.00	28.00	7.00
☐ 577	Hank Aaron AS	125.00	50.00	12.50
☐ 578	Mickey Mantle AS	300.00	120.00	30.00
☐ 579	Willie Mays AS	125.00	50.00	12.50
☐ 580	Al Kaline AS	65.00	26.00	6.50
☐ 581	Frank Robinson AS	60.00	24.00	6.00
☐ 582	Earl Battey AS	18.00	7.25	1.80
☐ 583	Del Crandall AS	18.00	7.25	1.80
☐ 584	Jim Perry AS	18.00	7.25	1.80
☐ 585	Bob Friend AS	18.00	7.25	1.80
☐ 586	Whitey Ford AS	60.00	24.00	6.00
☐ 587	Does not exist	0.00	.00	.00
☐ 588	Does not exist	0.00	.00	.00
☐ 589	Warren Spahn AS	100.00	30.00	6.00

1962 Topps

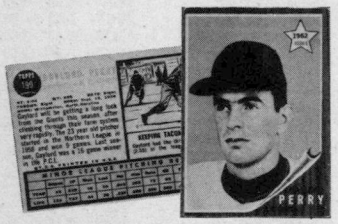

The cards in this 598-card set measure 2 ½" by 3 ½". The 1962 Topps set contains a mini-series spotlighting Babe Ruth (135 to 144). Other subsets in the set include League Leaders (51-60), World Series cards (232-237), In Action cards (311-319), NL All Stars (390-399), AL All Stars (466-475), and Rookie Prospects (591-598). The second series had two distinct printings which are distinguishable by numerous color and pose variations. Card number 139 exists as A: Babe Ruth Special card, B: Hal Reniff with arms over head, or C: Hal Reniff in the same pose as card number 159. In addition, two poses exist for players depicted on card numbers 129, 132, 134, 147, 174, 176, and 190. The high number series, 523 to 598, is somewhat more difficult to obtain than other cards in the set. The set price listed does not include the pose variations (see checklist below for individual values).

	NRMT	VG-E	GOOD
Complete Set	3600.00	1600.00	575.00
Common Player (1-109)	.85	.34	.08
Common Player (110-196)	.85	.34	.08
Common Player (197-283)	1.00	.40	.10
Common Player (284-370)	1.25	.50	.12
Common Player (371-446)	1.75	.70	.17
Common Player (447-522)	2.25	.90	.22
Common Player (523-590)	8.00	3.25	.80
Common Player (591-598)	12.00	5.00	1.20

			NRMT	VG-E	GOOD
☐	1	Roger Maris	150.00	30.00	6.00
☐	2	Jim Brosnan	1.00	.40	.10
☐	3	Pete Runnels	1.00	.40	.10
☐	4	John DeMerit	.85	.34	.08
☐	5	Sandy Koufax	50.00	20.00	5.00
☐	6	Marv Breeding	.85	.34	.08
☐	7	Frank Thomas	1.00	.40	.10
☐	8	Ray Herbert	.85	.34	.08
☐	9	Jim Davenport	1.00	.40	.10
☐	10	Bob Clemente	50.00	20.00	5.00
☐	11	Tom Morgan	.85	.34	.08
☐	12	Harry Craft MG	.85	.34	.08
☐	13	Dick Howser	2.00	.80	.20
☐	14	Bill White	1.50	.60	.15
☐	15	Dick Donovan	.85	.34	.08
☐	16	Darrell Johnson	1.00	.40	.10
☐	17	John Callison	1.00	.40	.10
☐	18	Managers' Dream	80.00	32.00	8.00
		Mickey Mantle			
		Willie Mays			
☐	19	Ray Washburn	.85	.34	.08
☐	20	Rocky Colavito	3.00	1.00	.25
☐	21	Jim Kaat	3.50	1.40	.35
☐	22A	Checklist 1 COR	4.00	.40	.08
☐	22B	Checklist 1 ERR	5.00	.50	.10
		(121-176 on back)			
☐	23	Norm Larker	1.00	.40	.10
☐	24	Tigers Team	2.00	.80	.20
☐	25	Ernie Banks	14.00	5.75	1.40
☐	26	Chris Cannizzaro	.85	.34	.08

			NRMT	VG-E	GOOD
☐	27	Chuck Cottier	1.00	.40	.10
☐	28	Minnie Minoso	2.00	.80	.20
☐	29	Casey Stengel MG .	12.00	5.00	1.20
☐	30	Eddie Mathews	12.00	5.00	1.20
☐	31	Tom Tresh	6.00	2.40	.60
☐	32	John Roseboro	1.00	.40	.10
☐	33	Don Larsen	1.50	.60	.15
☐	34	Johnny Temple	1.00	.40	.10
☐	35	Don Schwall	1.00	.40	.10
☐	36	Don Leppert	.85	.34	.08
☐	37	Tribe Hill Trio	1.00	.40	.10
		Barry Latman			
		Dick Stigman			
		Jim Perry			
☐	38	Gene Stephens	.85	.34	.08
☐	39	Joe Koppe	.85	.34	.08
☐	40	Orlando Cepeda ...	4.00	1.60	.40
☐	41	Cliff Cook	.85	.34	.08
☐	42	Jim King	.85	.34	.08
☐	43	Los Angeles Dodgers	3.00	1.20	.30
		Team Card			
☐	44	Don Taussig	.85	.34	.08
☐	45	Brooks Robinson ..	15.00	5.75	1.40
☐	46	Jack Baldschun	.85	.34	.08
☐	47	Bob Will	.85	.34	.08
☐	48	Ralph Terry	1.50	.60	.15
☐	49	Hal Jones	.85	.34	.08
☐	50	Stan Musial	45.00	18.00	4.50
☐	51	AL Batting Leaders .	1.50	.60	.15
		Norm Cash			
		Jim Piersall			
		Al Kaline			
		Elston Howard			
☐	52	NL Batting Leaders .	2.00	.80	.20
		Bob Clemente			
		Vada Pinson			
		Ken Boyer			
		Wally Moon			
☐	53	AL Home Run Leaders	12.00	5.00	1.20
		Roger Maris			
		Mickey Mantle			
		Jim Gentile			
		Harmon Killebrew			
☐	54	NL Home Run Leaders	3.00	1.20	.30
		Orlando Cepeda			
		Willie Mays			
		Frank Robinson			

			NRMT	VG-E	GOOD
☐	55	AL ERA Leaders ..	1.50	.60	.15
		Dick Donovan			
		Bill Stafford			
		Don Mossi			
		Milt Pappas			
☐	56	NL ERA Leaders ..	1.50	.60	.15
		Warren Spahn			
		Jim O'Toole			
		Curt Simmons			
		Mike McCormick			
☐	57	AL Wins Leaders ..	1.50	.60	.15
		Whitey Ford			
		Frank Lary			
		Steve Barber			
		Jim Bunning			
☐	58	NL Wins Leaders ..	1.50	.60	.15
		Warren Spahn			
		Joe Jay			
		Jim O'Toole			
☐	59	AL Strikeout Leaders	1.50	.60	.15
		Camilo Pascual			
		Whitey Ford			
		Jim Bunning			
		Juan Pizzaro			
☐	60	NL Strikeout Leaders	2.50	1.00	.25
		Sandy Koufax			
		Stan Williams			
		Don Drysdale			
		Jim O'Toole			
☐	61	Cardinals Team ...	2.00	.80	.20
☐	62	Steve Boros	1.00	.40	.10
☐	63	Tony Cloninger ...	.85	.34	.08
☐	64	Russ Snyder	.85	.34	.08
☐	65	Bobby Richardson .	3.50	1.40	.35
☐	66	Cuno Barragon ...	.85	.34	.08
☐	67	Harvey Haddix ...	1.50	.60	.15
☐	68	Ken Hunt	.85	.34	.08
☐	69	Phil Ortega	.85	.34	.08
☐	70	Harmon Killebrew .	12.00	5.00	1.20
☐	71	Dick LeMay	.85	.34	.08
☐	72	Bob's Pupils	1.00	.40	.10
		Steve Boros			
		Bob Scheffing			
		Jake Wood			
☐	73	Nellie Fox	3.50	1.40	.35
☐	74	Bob Lillis	1.00	.40	.10
☐	75	Milt Pappas	1.00	.40	.10
☐	76	Howie Bedell	.85	.34	.08
☐	77	Tony Taylor	.85	.34	.08

		NRMT	VG-E	GOOD
☐ 78	Gene Green	.85	.34	.08
☐ 79	Ed Hobaugh	.85	.34	.08
☐ 80	Vada Pinson	2.00	.80	.20
☐ 81	Jim Pagliaroni	.85	.34	.08
☐ 82	Deron Johnson	1.00	.40	.10
☐ 83	Larry Jackson	.85	.34	.08
☐ 84	Lenny Green	.85	.34	.08
☐ 85	Gil Hodges	9.00	3.75	.90
☐ 86	Donn Clendenon	1.50	.60	.15
☐ 87	Mike Roarke	1.00	.40	.10
☐ 88	Ralph Houk MG	2.00	.75	.15
☐ 89	Barney Schultz	.85	.34	.08
☐ 90	Jim Piersall	1.50	.60	.15
☐ 91	J.C. Martin	.85	.34	.08
☐ 92	Sam Jones	1.00	.40	.10
☐ 93	John Blanchard	1.50	.60	.15
☐ 94	Jay Hook	.85	.34	.08
☐ 95	Don Hoak	1.00	.40	.10
☐ 96	Eli Grba	.85	.34	.08
☐ 97	Tito Francona	1.00	.40	.10
☐ 98	Checklist 2	4.00	.40	.08
☐ 99	John (Boog) Powell	9.00	3.75	.90
☐ 100	Warren Spahn	12.00	5.00	1.20
☐ 101	Carroll Hardy	.85	.34	.08
☐ 102	Al Schroll	.85	.34	.08
☐ 103	Don Blasingame	.85	.34	.08
☐ 104	Ted Savage	.85	.34	.08
☐ 105	Don Mossi	1.00	.40	.10
☐ 106	Carl Sawatski	.85	.34	.08
☐ 107	Mike McCormick	1.00	.40	.10
☐ 108	Willie Davis	1.50	.60	.15
☐ 109	Bob Shaw	.85	.34	.08
☐ 110	Bill Skowron	3.50	1.40	.35
☐ 111	Dallas Green	2.00	.80	.20
☐ 112	Hank Foiles	.85	.34	.08
☐ 113	Chicago White Sox Team Card	2.00	.80	.20
☐ 114	Howie Koplitz	.85	.34	.08
☐ 115	Bob Skinner	1.00	.40	.10
☐ 116	Herb Score	1.50	.60	.15
☐ 117	Gary Geiger	.85	.34	.08
☐ 118	Julian Javier	1.00	.40	.10
☐ 119	Danny Murphy	.85	.34	.08
☐ 120	Bob Purkey	.85	.34	.08
☐ 121	Billy Hitchcock MG	.85	.34	.08
☐ 122	Norm Bass	.85	.34	.08
☐ 123	Mike De La Hoz	.85	.34	.08
☐ 124	Bill Pleis	.85	.34	.08
☐ 125	Gene Woodling	1.25	.50	.12
☐ 126	Al Cicotte	.85	.34	.08
☐ 127	Pride of A's Norm Siebern Hank Bauer Jerry Lumpe	1.25	.50	.12
☐ 128	Art Fowler	.85	.34	.08
☐ 129A	Lee Walls (facing right)	.85	.34	.08
☐ 129B	Lee Walls (face left)	10.00	4.00	1.00
☐ 130	Frank Bolling	.85	.34	.08
☐ 131	Pete Richert	.85	.34	.08
☐ 132A	Angels Team (without photo)	2.00	.80	.20
☐ 132B	Angels Team (with photo)	10.00	4.00	1.00
☐ 133	Felipe Alou	1.50	.60	.15
☐ 134A	Billy Hoeft (facing right)	.85	.34	.08
☐ 134B	Billy Hoeft (facing straight)	10.00	4.00	1.00
☐ 135	Babe Ruth Special 1 Babe as a Boy	6.00	2.40	.60
☐ 136	Babe Ruth Special 2 Babe Joins Yanks	6.00	2.40	.60
☐ 137	Babe Ruth Special 3 Babe with Huggins	6.00	2.40	.60
☐ 138	Babe Ruth Special 4 Famous Slugger	6.00	2.40	.60
☐ 139A	Babe Ruth Special 5	9.00	3.75	.90
☐ 139B	Hal Reniff PORT	10.00	4.00	1.00
☐ 139C	Hal Reniff (pitching)	40.00	16.00	4.00
☐ 140	Babe Ruth Special 6 Gehrig and Ruth	8.00	3.25	.80
☐ 141	Babe Ruth Special 7 Twilight Years	6.00	2.40	.60
☐ 142	Babe Ruth Special 8 Coaching Dodgers	6.00	2.40	.60
☐ 143	Babe Ruth Special 9 Greatest Sports Hero	6.00	2.40	.60
☐ 144	Babe Ruth Special 10 Farewell Speech	6.00	2.40	.60
☐ 145	Barry Latman	.85	.34	.08
☐ 146	Don Demeter	.85	.34	.08
☐ 147A	Bill Kunkel PORT	.85	.34	.08
☐ 147B	Bill Kunkel (pitching pose)	10.00	4.00	1.00
☐ 148	Wally Post	1.00	.40	.10

		NRMT	VG-E	GOOD
☐ 149	Bob Duliba	.85	.34	.08
☐ 150	Al Kaline	15.00	6.00	1.50
☐ 151	Johnny Klippstein	.85	.34	.08
☐ 152	Mickey Vernon	1.25	.50	.12
☐ 153	Pumpsie Green	.85	.34	.08
☐ 154	Lee Thomas	2.00	.75	.15
☐ 155	Stu Miller	.85	.34	.08
☐ 156	Merritt Ranew	.85	.34	.08
☐ 157	Wes Covington	1.00	.40	.10
☐ 158	Braves Team	2.00	.80	.20
☐ 159	Hal Reniff	1.50	.60	.15
☐ 160	Dick Stuart	1.50	.50	.12
☐ 161	Frank Baumann	.85	.34	.08
☐ 162	Sammy Drake	.85	.34	.08
☐ 163	Hot Corner Guard	1.25	.50	.12
	Billy Gardner			
	Cletis Boyer			
☐ 164	Hal Naragon	.85	.34	.08
☐ 165	Jackie Brandt	.85	.34	.08
☐ 166	Don Lee	.85	.34	.08
☐ 167	Tim McCarver	12.00	5.00	1.20
☐ 168	Leo Posada	.85	.34	.08
☐ 169	Bob Cerv	1.00	.40	.10
☐ 170	Ron Santo	2.50	1.00	.25
☐ 171	Dave Sisler	.85	.34	.08
☐ 172	Fred Hutchinson MG	1.25	.50	.12
☐ 173	Chico Fernandez	.85	.34	.08
☐ 174A	Carl Willey	.85	.34	.08
	(capless)			
☐ 174B	Carl Willey	10.00	4.00	1.00
	(with cap)			
☐ 175	Frank Howard	2.00	.80	.20
☐ 176A	Eddie Yost PORT	.85	.34	.08
☐ 176B	Eddie Yost BATTING	10.00	4.00	1.00
☐ 177	Bobby Shantz	1.50	.60	.15
☐ 178	Camilo Carreon	.85	.34	.08
☐ 179	Tom Sturdivant	.85	.34	.08
☐ 180	Bob Allison	1.25	.50	.12
☐ 181	Paul Brown	.85	.34	.08
☐ 182	Bob Nieman	.85	.34	.08
☐ 183	Roger Craig	2.00	.80	.20
☐ 184	Haywood Sullivan	1.00	.40	.10
☐ 185	Roland Sheldon	.85	.34	.08
☐ 186	Mack Jones	.85	.34	.08
☐ 187	Gene Conley	.85	.34	.08
☐ 188	Chuck Hiller	.85	.34	.08
☐ 189	Dick Hall	.85	.34	.08
☐ 190A	Wally Moon PORT	1.00	.40	.10
☐ 190B	Wally Moon BATTING	10.00	4.00	1.00

		NRMT	VG-E	GOOD
☐ 191	Jim Brewer	.85	.34	.08
☐ 192A	Checklist 3	4.00	.40	.08
	(without comma)			
☐ 192B	Checklist 3	6.00	.60	.12
	(comma after Checklist)			
☐ 193	Eddie Kasko	.85	.34	.08
☐ 194	Dean Chance	1.50	.60	.15
☐ 195	Joe Cunningham	1.00	.40	.10
☐ 196	Terry Fox	.85	.34	.08
☐ 197	Daryl Spencer	1.00	.40	.10
☐ 198	Johnny Keane MG	1.00	.60	.15
☐ 199	Gaylord Perry	75.00	30.00	7.50
☐ 200	Mickey Mantle	350.00	140.00	35.00
☐ 201	Ike Delock	1.00	.40	.10
☐ 202	Carl Warwick	1.00	.40	.10
☐ 203	Jack Fisher	1.00	.40	.10
☐ 204	Johnny Weekly	1.00	.40	.10
☐ 205	Gene Freese	1.00	.40	.10
☐ 206	Senators Team	2.00	.80	.20
☐ 207	Pete Burnside	1.00	.40	.10
☐ 208	Billy Martin	5.00	2.00	.50
☐ 209	Jim Fregosi	5.00	2.00	.50
☐ 210	Roy Face	2.00	.80	.20
☐ 211	Midway Masters	1.25	.50	.12
	Frank Bolling			
	Roy McMillan			
☐ 212	Jim Owens	1.00	.40	.10
☐ 213	Richie Ashburn	4.00	1.60	.40
☐ 214	Dom Zanni	1.00	.40	.10
☐ 215	Woody Held	1.00	.40	.10
☐ 216	Ron Kline	1.00	.40	.10
☐ 217	Walt Alston MG	4.00	1.60	.40
☐ 218	Joe Torre	10.00	4.00	1.00
☐ 219	Al Downing	3.00	1.20	.30
☐ 220	Roy Sievers	1.25	.50	.12
☐ 221	Bill Short	1.00	.40	.10
☐ 222	Jerry Zimmerman	1.00	.40	.10
☐ 223	Alex Grammas	1.00	.40	.10
☐ 224	Don Rudolph	1.00	.40	.10
☐ 225	Frank Malzone	1.25	.50	.12
☐ 226	San Francisco Giants	2.00	.80	.20
	Team Card			
☐ 227	Bob Tiefenauer	1.00	.40	.10
☐ 228	Dale Long	1.25	.50	.12
☐ 229	Jesus McFarlane	1.00	.40	.10
☐ 230	Camilo Pascual	1.25	.50	.12
☐ 231	Ernie Bowman	1.00	.40	.10
☐ 232	World Series Game 1	2.25	.90	.22
	Yanks win opener			

		NRMT	VG-E	GOOD
☐ 233	World Series Game 2 Jay ties it up	2.25	.90	.22
☐ 234	World Series Game 3 Maris wins in 9th	7.50	3.00	.75
☐ 235	World Series Game 4 Ford sets new mark	5.00	2.00	.50
☐ 236	World Series Game 5 Yanks crush Reds	2.25	.90	.22
☐ 237	World Series Summary Yanks celebrate	2.25	.90	.22
☐ 238	Norm Sherry	1.25	.50	.12
☐ 239	Cecil Butler	1.00	.40	.10
☐ 240	George Altman	1.00	.40	.10
☐ 241	Johnny Kucks	1.00	.40	.10
☐ 242	Mel McGaha	1.00	.40	.10
☐ 243	Robin Roberts	10.00	4.00	1.00
☐ 244	Don Gile	1.00	.40	.10
☐ 245	Ron Hansen	1.00	.40	.10
☐ 246	Art Ditmar	1.00	.40	.10
☐ 247	Joe Pignatano	1.00	.40	.10
☐ 248	Bob Aspromonte	1.00	.40	.10
☐ 249	Ed Keegan	1.00	.40	.10
☐ 250	Norm Cash	2.50	1.00	.25
☐ 251	New York Yankees Team Card	10.00	4.00	1.00
☐ 252	Earl Francis	1.00	.40	.10
☐ 253	Harry Chiti	1.00	.40	.10
☐ 254	Gordon Windhorn	1.00	.40	.10
☐ 255	Juan Pizarro	1.00	.40	.10
☐ 256	Elio Chacon	1.00	.40	.10
☐ 257	Jack Spring	1.00	.40	.10
☐ 258	Marty Keough	1.00	.40	.10
☐ 259	Lou Klimchock	1.00	.40	.10
☐ 260	Billy Pierce	1.50	.60	.15
☐ 261	George Alusik	1.00	.40	.10
☐ 262	Bob Schmidt	1.00	.40	.10
☐ 263	The Right Pitch Bob Purkey Jim Turner Joe Jay	1.25	.50	.12
☐ 264	Dick Ellsworth	1.25	.50	.12
☐ 265	Joe Adcock	1.50	.60	.15
☐ 266	John Anderson	1.00	.40	.10
☐ 267	Dan Dobbek	1.00	.40	.10
☐ 268	Ken McBride	1.00	.40	.10
☐ 269	Bob Oldis	1.00	.40	.10
☐ 270	Dick Groat	2.00	.80	.20
☐ 271	Ray Rippelmeyer	1.00	.40	.10
☐ 272	Earl Robinson	1.00	.40	.10

		NRMT	VG-E	GOOD
☐ 273	Gary Bell	1.00	.40	.10
☐ 274	Sammy Taylor	1.00	.40	.10
☐ 275	Norm Siebern	1.00	.40	.10
☐ 276	Hal Kolstad	1.00	.40	.10
☐ 277	Checklist 4	4.50	.50	.10
☐ 278	Ken Johnson	1.00	.40	.10
☐ 279	Hobie Landrith	1.00	.40	.10
☐ 280	Johnny Podres	2.50	1.00	.25
☐ 281	Jake Gibbs	1.25	.50	.12
☐ 282	Dave Hillman	1.00	.40	.10
☐ 283	Charlie Smith	1.00	.40	.10
☐ 284	Ruben Amaro	1.25	.50	.12
☐ 285	Curt Simmons	1.75	.70	.17
☐ 286	Al Lopez MG	3.00	1.20	.30
☐ 287	George Witt	1.25	.50	.12
☐ 288	Billy Williams	16.00	6.50	1.60
☐ 289	Mike Krsnich	1.25	.50	.12
☐ 290	Jim Gentile	1.75	.70	.17
☐ 291	Hal Stowe	1.25	.50	.12
☐ 292	Jerry Kindall	1.25	.50	.12
☐ 293	Bob Miller	1.25	.50	.12
☐ 294	Phillies Team	2.50	1.00	.25
☐ 295	Vern Law	1.75	.70	.17
☐ 296	Ken Hamlin	1.25	.50	.12
☐ 297	Ron Perranoski	1.75	.70	.17
☐ 298	Bill Tuttle	1.25	.50	.12
☐ 299	Don Wert	1.25	.50	.12
☐ 300	Willie Mays	80.00	32.00	8.00
☐ 301	Galen Cisco	1.25	.50	.12
☐ 302	Johnny Edwards	1.25	.50	.12
☐ 303	Frank Torre	1.25	.50	.12
☐ 304	Dick Farrell	1.25	.50	.12
☐ 305	Jerry Lumpe	1.25	.50	.12
☐ 306	Redbird Rippers Lindy McDaniel Larry Jackson	1.75	.70	.17
☐ 307	Jim Grant	1.25	.50	.12
☐ 308	Neil Chrisley	1.25	.50	.12
☐ 309	Moe Morhardt	1.25	.50	.12
☐ 310	Whitey Ford	20.00	8.00	2.00
☐ 311	Tony Kubek IA	2.50	1.00	.25
☐ 312	Warren Spahn IA	6.00	2.40	.60
☐ 313	Roger Maris IA	12.50	5.00	1.25
☐ 314	Rocky Colavito IA	2.50	1.00	.25
☐ 315	Whitey Ford IA	6.00	2.40	.60
☐ 316	Harmon Killebrew IA	5.00	2.00	.50
☐ 317	Stan Musial IA	10.00	4.00	1.00
☐ 318	Mickey Mantle IA	35.00	14.00	3.50
☐ 319	Mike McCormick IA	1.75	.70	.17

		NRMT	VG-E	GOOD
☐ 320	Hank Aaron	80.00	32.00	8.00
☐ 321	Lee Stange	1.25	.50	.12
☐ 322	Alvin Dark	1.75	.70	.17
☐ 323	Don Landrum	1.25	.50	.12
☐ 324	Joe McClain	1.25	.50	.12
☐ 325	Luis Aparicio	10.00	4.00	1.00
☐ 326	Tom Parsons	1.25	.50	.12
☐ 327	Ozzie Virgil	1.25	.50	.12
☐ 328	Ken Walters	1.25	.50	.12
☐ 329	Bob Bolin	1.25	.50	.12
☐ 330	John Romano	1.25	.50	.12
☐ 331	Moe Drabowsky	1.25	.50	.12
☐ 332	Don Buddin	1.25	.50	.12
☐ 333	Frank Cipriani	1.25	.50	.12
☐ 334	Boston Red Sox Team Card	2.50	1.00	.25
☐ 335	Bill Bruton	1.75	.70	.17
☐ 336	Billy Muffett	1.25	.50	.12
☐ 337	Jim Marshall	1.25	.50	.12
☐ 338	Billy Gardner	1.75	.70	.17
☐ 339	Jose Valdivielso	1.25	.50	.12
☐ 340	Don Drysdale	18.00	7.25	1.80
☐ 341	Mike Hershberger	1.25	.50	.12
☐ 342	Ed Rakow	1.25	.50	.12
☐ 343	Albie Pearson	1.25	.50	.12
☐ 344	Ed Bauta	1.25	.50	.12
☐ 345	Chuck Schilling	1.25	.50	.12
☐ 346	Jack Kralick	1.25	.50	.12
☐ 347	Chuck Hinton	1.25	.50	.12
☐ 348	Larry Burright	1.25	.50	.12
☐ 349	Paul Foytack	1.25	.50	.12
☐ 350	Frank Robinson	18.00	7.25	1.80
☐ 351	Braves' Backstops Joe Torre Del Crandall	1.75	.70	.17
☐ 352	Frank Sullivan	1.25	.50	.12
☐ 353	Bill Mazeroski	3.00	1.20	.30
☐ 354	Roman Mejias	1.25	.50	.12
☐ 355	Steve Barber	1.25	.50	.12
☐ 356	Tom Haller	1.75	.70	.17
☐ 357	Jerry Walker	1.25	.50	.12
☐ 358	Tommy Davis	2.50	1.00	.25
☐ 359	Bobby Locke	1.25	.50	.12
☐ 360	Yogi Berra	40.00	16.00	4.00
☐ 361	Bob Hendley	1.25	.50	.12
☐ 362	Ty Cline	1.25	.50	.12
☐ 363	Bob Roselli	1.25	.50	.12
☐ 364	Ken Hunt	1.25	.50	.12
☐ 365	Charlie Neal	1.75	.70	.17

		NRMT	VG-E	GOOD
☐ 366	Phil Regan	1.75	.70	.17
☐ 367	Checklist 5	4.50	.50	.10
☐ 368	Bob Tillman	1.25	.50	.12
☐ 369	Ted Bowsfield	1.25	.50	.12
☐ 370	Ken Boyer	3.50	1.40	.35
☐ 371	Earl Battey	1.75	.70	.17
☐ 372	Jack Curtis	1.75	.70	.17
☐ 373	Al Heist	1.75	.70	.17
☐ 374	Gene Mauch	2.50	1.00	.25
☐ 375	Ron Fairly	1.75	.70	.17
☐ 376	Bud Daley	1.75	.70	.17
☐ 377	John Orsino	1.75	.70	.17
☐ 378	Bennie Daniels	1.75	.70	.17
☐ 379	Chuck Essegian	1.75	.70	.17
☐ 380	Lou Burdette	3.00	1.20	.30
☐ 381	Chico Cardenas	1.75	.70	.17
☐ 382	Dick Williams	2.50	1.00	.25
☐ 383	Ray Sadecki	1.75	.70	.17
☐ 384	K.C. Athletics Team Card	3.50	1.40	.35
☐ 385	Early Wynn	10.00	4.00	1.00
☐ 386	Don Mincher	2.50	1.00	.25
☐ 387	Lou Brock	80.00	32.00	8.00
☐ 388	Ryne Duren	2.50	1.00	.25
☐ 389	Smoky Burgess	2.50	1.00	.25
☐ 390	Orlando Cepeda AS	3.50	1.40	.35
☐ 391	Bill Mazeroski AS	3.00	1.20	.30
☐ 392	Ken Boyer AS	3.00	1.20	.30
☐ 393	Roy McMillan AS	2.50	1.00	.25
☐ 394	Hank Aaron AS	22.00	9.00	2.20
☐ 395	Willie Mays AS	22.00	9.00	2.20
☐ 396	Frank Robinson AS	8.50	3.50	.85
☐ 397	John Roseboro AS	2.50	1.00	.25
☐ 398	Don Drysdale AS	7.00	2.80	.70
☐ 399	Warren Spahn AS	8.00	3.25	.80
☐ 400	Elston Howard	5.00	2.00	.50
☐ 401	AL/NL Homer Kings Roger Maris Orlando Cepeda	18.00	7.25	1.80
☐ 402	Gino Cimoli	1.75	.70	.17
☐ 403	Chet Nichols	1.75	.70	.17
☐ 404	Tim Harkness	1.75	.70	.17
☐ 405	Jim Perry	2.50	1.00	.25
☐ 406	Bob Taylor	1.75	.70	.17
☐ 407	Hank Aguirre	1.75	.70	.17
☐ 408	Gus Bell	1.75	.70	.17
☐ 409	Pittsburgh Pirates Team Card	3.50	1.40	.35
☐ 410	Al Smith	1.75	.70	.17

		NRMT	VG-E	GOOD
☐ 411	Danny O'Connell	1.75	.70	.17
☐ 412	Charlie James	1.75	.70	.17
☐ 413	Matty Alou	2.50	1.00	.25
☐ 414	Joe Gaines	1.75	.70	.17
☐ 415	Bill Virdon	3.00	1.20	.30
☐ 416	Bob Scheffing MG	1.75	.70	.17
☐ 417	Joe Azcue	1.75	.70	.17
☐ 418	Andy Carey	1.75	.70	.17
☐ 419	Bob Bruce	1.75	.70	.17
☐ 420	Gus Triandos	2.50	1.00	.25
☐ 421	Ken MacKenzie	1.75	.70	.17
☐ 422	Steve Bilko	1.75	.70	.17
☐ 423	Rival League	4.00	1.60	.40
	Relief Aces:			
	Roy Face			
	Hoyt Wilhelm			
☐ 424	Al McBean	1.75	.70	.17
☐ 425	Carl Yastrzemski	135.00	54.00	13.50
☐ 426	Bob Farley	1.75	.70	.17
☐ 427	Jake Wood	1.75	.70	.17
☐ 428	Joe Hicks	1.75	.70	.17
☐ 429	Billy O'Dell	1.75	.70	.17
☐ 430	Tony Kubek	7.00	2.80	.70
☐ 431	Bob Rodgers	3.50	1.40	.35
☐ 432	Jim Pendleton	1.75	.70	.17
☐ 433	Jim Archer	1.75	.70	.17
☐ 434	Clay Dalrymple	1.75	.70	.17
☐ 435	Larry Sherry	2.50	1.00	.25
☐ 436	Felix Mantilla	1.75	.70	.17
☐ 437	Ray Moore	1.75	.70	.17
☐ 438	Dick Brown	1.75	.70	.17
☐ 439	Jerry Buchek	1.75	.70	.17
☐ 440	Joey Jay	1.75	.70	.17
☐ 441	Checklist 6	5.00	.50	.10
☐ 442	Wes Stock	2.50	1.00	.25
☐ 443	Del Crandall	2.50	1.00	.25
☐ 444	Ted Wills	1.75	.70	.17
☐ 445	Vic Power	1.75	.70	.17
☐ 446	Don Elston	1.75	.70	.17
☐ 447	Willie Kirkland	2.25	.90	.22
☐ 448	Joe Gibbon	2.25	.90	.22
☐ 449	Jerry Adair	2.25	.90	.22
☐ 450	Jim O'Toole	3.00	1.20	.30
☐ 451	Jose Tartabull	2.25	.90	.22
☐ 452	Earl Averill	2.25	.90	.22
☐ 453	Cal McLish	2.25	.90	.22
☐ 454	Floyd Robinson	2.25	.90	.22
☐ 455	Luis Arroyo	3.00	1.20	.30
☐ 456	Joe Amalfitano	2.25	.90	.22

		NRMT	VG-E	GOOD
☐ 457	Lou Clinton	2.25	.90	.22
☐ 458A	Bob Buhl	2.25	.90	.22
	(Braves cap emblem)			
☐ 458B	Bob Buhl	35.00	14.00	3.50
	(no emblem on cap)			
☐ 459	Ed Bailey	2.25	.90	.22
☐ 460	Jim Bunning	7.00	2.80	.70
☐ 461	Ken Hubbs	6.50	2.60	.65
☐ 462A	Willie Tasby	2.25	.90	.22
	(Senators cap emblem)			
☐ 462B	Willie Tasby	35.00	14.00	3.50
	(no emblem on cap)			
☐ 463	Hank Bauer	3.00	1.20	.30
☐ 464	Al Jackson	2.25	.90	.22
☐ 465	Reds Team	4.50	1.80	.45
☐ 466	Norm Cash AS	3.50	1.40	.35
☐ 467	Chuck Schilling AS	3.00	1.20	.30
☐ 468	Brooks Robinson AS	10.00	4.00	1.00
☐ 469	Luis Aparicio AS	6.00	2.40	.60
☐ 470	Al Kaline AS	10.00	4.00	1.00
☐ 471	Mickey Mantle AS	75.00	30.00	7.50
☐ 472	Rocky Colavito AS	3.50	1.40	.35
☐ 473	Elston Howard AS	3.50	1.40	.35
☐ 474	Frank Lary AS	3.00	1.20	.30
☐ 475	Whitey Ford AS	9.00	3.75	.90
☐ 476	Orioles Team	4.50	1.80	.45
☐ 477	Andre Rodgers	2.25	.90	.22
☐ 478	Don Zimmer	4.00	1.60	.40
☐ 479	Joel Horlen	3.00	1.20	.30
☐ 480	Harvey Kuenn	3.50	1.40	.35
☐ 481	Vic Wertz	3.00	1.20	.30
☐ 482	Sam Mele MG	2.25	.90	.22
☐ 483	Don McMahon	2.25	.90	.22
☐ 484	Dick Schofield	2.25	.90	.22
☐ 485	Pedro Ramos	2.25	.90	.22
☐ 486	Jim Gilliam	5.00	2.00	.50
☐ 487	Jerry Lynch	2.25	.90	.22
☐ 488	Hal Brown	2.25	.90	.22
☐ 489	Julio Gotay	2.25	.90	.22
☐ 490	Clete Boyer	3.50	1.40	.35
☐ 491	Leon Wagner	2.25	.90	.22
☐ 492	Hal W. Smith	2.25	.90	.22
☐ 493	Danny McDevitt	2.25	.90	.22
☐ 494	Sammy White	2.25	.90	.22
☐ 495	Don Cardwell	2.25	.90	.22
☐ 496	Wayne Causey	2.25	.90	.22
☐ 497	Ed Bouchee	2.25	.90	.22
☐ 498	Jim Donohue	2.25	.90	.22
☐ 499	Zoilo Versalles	2.25	.90	.22

		NRMT	VG-E	GOOD
☐ 500	Duke Snider	30.00	12.00	3.00
☐ 501	Claude Osteen	3.00	1.20	.30
☐ 502	Hector Lopez	2.25	.90	.22
☐ 503	Danny Murtaugh MG	2.25	.90	.22
☐ 504	Eddie Bressoud	2.25	.90	.22
☐ 505	Juan Marichal	21.00	8.50	2.10
☐ 506	Charlie Maxwell	2.25	.90	.22
☐ 507	Ernie Broglio	2.25	.90	.22
☐ 508	Gordy Coleman	3.00	1.20	.30
☐ 509	Dave Giusti	3.00	1.20	.30
☐ 510	Jim Lemon	3.00	1.20	.30
☐ 511	Bubba Phillips	2.25	.90	.22
☐ 512	Mike Fornieles	2.25	.90	.22
☐ 513	Whitey Herzog	4.00	1.60	.40
☐ 514	Sherm Lollar	3.00	1.20	.30
☐ 515	Stan Williams	2.25	.90	.22
☐ 516	Checklist 7	8.00	.80	.10
☐ 517	Dave Wickersham	2.25	.90	.22
☐ 518	Lee Maye	2.25	.90	.22
☐ 519	Bob Johnson	2.25	.90	.22
☐ 520	Bob Friend	3.00	1.20	.30
☐ 521	Jacke Davis	2.25	.90	.22
☐ 522	Lindy McDaniel	3.00	1.20	.30
☐ 523	Russ Nixon	10.00	4.00	1.00
☐ 524	Howie Nunn	8.00	3.25	.80
☐ 525	George Thomas	8.00	3.25	.80
☐ 526	Hal Woodeshick	8.00	3.25	.80
☐ 527	Dick McAuliffe	10.00	4.00	1.00
☐ 528	Turk Lown	8.00	3.25	.80
☐ 529	John Schaive	8.00	3.25	.80
☐ 530	Bob Gibson	85.00	34.00	8.50
☐ 531	Bobby G. Smith	8.00	3.25	.80
☐ 532	Dick Stigman	8.00	3.25	.80
☐ 533	Charley Lau	10.00	4.00	1.00
☐ 534	Tony Gonzalez	8.00	3.25	.80
☐ 535	Ed Roebuck	8.00	3.25	.80
☐ 536	Dick Gernert	8.00	3.25	.80
☐ 537	Cleveland Indians Team Card	15.00	6.00	1.50
☐ 538	Jack Sanford	10.00	4.00	1.00
☐ 539	Billy Moran	8.00	3.25	.80
☐ 540	Jim Landis	8.00	3.25	.80
☐ 541	Don Nottebart	8.00	3.25	.80
☐ 542	Dave Philley	8.00	3.25	.80
☐ 543	Bob Allen	8.00	3.25	.80
☐ 544	Willie McCovey	85.00	34.00	8.50
☐ 545	Hoyt Wilhelm	40.00	16.00	4.00
☐ 546	Moe Thacker	8.00	3.25	.80
☐ 547	Don Ferrarese	8.00	3.25	.80
☐ 548	Bobby Del Greco	8.00	3.25	.80
☐ 549	Bill Rigney MG	8.00	3.25	.80
☐ 550	Art Mahaffey	8.00	3.25	.80
☐ 551	Harry Bright	8.00	3.25	.80
☐ 552	Chicago Cubs Team Card	15.00	6.00	1.50
☐ 553	Jim Coates	8.00	3.25	.80
☐ 554	Bubba Morton	8.00	3.25	.80
☐ 555	John Buzhardt	8.00	3.25	.80
☐ 556	Al Spangler	8.00	3.25	.80
☐ 557	Bob Anderson	8.00	3.25	.80
☐ 558	John Goryl	8.00	3.25	.80
☐ 559	Mike Higgins MG	8.00	3.25	.80
☐ 560	Chuck Estrada	10.00	4.00	1.00
☐ 561	Gene Oliver	8.00	3.25	.80
☐ 562	Bill Henry	8.00	3.25	.80
☐ 563	Ken Aspromonte	8.00	3.25	.80
☐ 564	Bob Grim	8.00	3.25	.80
☐ 565	Jose Pagan	8.00	3.25	.80
☐ 566	Marty Kutyna	8.00	3.25	.80
☐ 567	Tracy Stallard	8.00	3.25	.80
☐ 568	Jim Golden	8.00	3.25	.80
☐ 569	Ed Sadowski	8.00	3.25	.80
☐ 570	Bill Stafford	8.00	3.25	.80
☐ 571	Billy Klaus	8.00	3.25	.80
☐ 572	Bob G. Miller	8.00	3.25	.80
☐ 573	Johnny Logan	10.00	4.00	1.00
☐ 574	Dean Stone	8.00	3.25	.80
☐ 575	Red Schoendienst	12.00	5.00	1.20
☐ 576	Russ Kemmerer	8.00	3.25	.80
☐ 577	Dave Nicholson	8.00	3.25	.80
☐ 578	Jim Duffalo	8.00	3.25	.80
☐ 579	Jim Schaffer	8.00	3.25	.80
☐ 580	Bill Monbouquette	8.00	3.25	.80
☐ 581	Mel Roach	8.00	3.25	.80
☐ 582	Ron Piche	8.00	3.25	.80
☐ 583	Larry Osborne	8.00	3.25	.80
☐ 584	Minnesota Twins Team Card	15.00	6.00	1.50
☐ 585	Glen Hobbie	8.00	3.25	.80
☐ 586	Sammy Esposito	8.00	3.25	.80
☐ 587	Frank Funk	8.00	3.25	.80
☐ 588	Birdie Tebbetts MG	8.00	3.25	.80
☐ 589	Bob Turley	12.00	5.00	1.20
☐ 590	Curt Flood	12.00	5.00	1.20

1963 Topps

		NRMT	VG-E	GOOD
☐ 591	Rookie Pitchers	25.00	10.00	2.50
	Sam McDowell			
	Ron Taylor			
	Ron Nischwitz			
	Art Quirk			
	Dick Radatz			
☐ 592	Rookie Pitchers	40.00	16.00	4.00
	Dan Pfister			
	Bo Belinsky			
	Dave Stenhouse			
	Jim Bouton			
	Joe Bonikowski			
☐ 593	Rookie Pitchers	20.00	8.00	2.00
	Jack Lamabe			
	Craig Anderson			
	Jack Hamilton			
	Bob Moorhead			
	Bob Veale			
☐ 594	Rookie Catchers ...	110.00	45.00	11.00
	Doc Edwards			
	Ken Retzer			
	Bob Uecker			
	Doug Camilli			
	Don Pavletich			
☐ 595	Rookie Infielders ...	12.00	5.00	1.20
	Bob Sadowski			
	Felix Torres			
	Marlan Coughtry			
	Ed Charles			
☐ 596	Rookie Infielders ...	25.00	10.00	2.50
	Bernie Allen			
	Joe Pepitone			
	Phil Linz			
	Rich Rollins			
☐ 597	Rookie Infielders ...	12.00	5.00	1.20
	Jim McKnight			
	Rod Kanehl			
	Amado Samuel			
	Denis Menke			
☐ 598	Rookie Outfielders .	20.00	6.00	1.25
	Al Luplow			
	Manny Jimenez			
	Howie Goss			
	Jim Hickman			
	Ed Olivares			

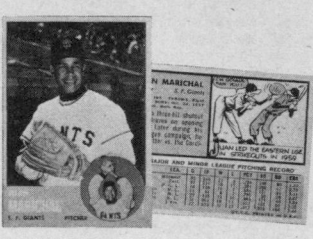

The cards in this 576-card set measure 2 ½ " by 3 ½ ". The sharp color photographs of the 1963 set are a vivid contrast to the drab pictures of 1962. In addition to the "League Leaders" series (1-10) and World Series cards (142-148), the seventh and last series of cards (507-576) contains seven rookie cards (each depicting four players). This set has gained special prominence in recent years since it contains the rookie card of Pete Rose, #537.

		NRMT	VG-E	GOOD
Complete Set (576)		3400.00	1500.00	500.00
Common Player (1-109) ..		.50	.20	.05
Common Player (110-196)		.60	.24	.06
Common Player (197-283)		.75	.30	.07
Common Player (284-446)		1.00	.40	.10
Common Player (447-506)		6.00	2.40	.60
Common Player (507-576)		4.00	1.60	.40
☐ 1	NL Batting Leaders	16.00	2.50	.50
	Tommy Davis			
	Frank Robinson			
	Stan Musial			
	Hank Aaron			
	Bill White			
☐ 2	AL Batting Leaders	7.50	3.00	.60
	Pete Runnels			
	Mickey Mantle			
	Floyd Robinson			
	Norm Siebern			
	Chuck Hinton			

			NRMT	VG-E	GOOD
☐	3	NL Home Run Leaders	7.50	3.00	.60
		Willie Mays			
		Hank Aaron			
		Frank Robinson			
		Orlando Cepeda			
		Ernie Banks			
☐	4	AL Home Run Leaders	2.50	1.00	.20
		Harmon Killebrew			
		Norm Cash			
		Rocky Colavito			
		Roger Maris			
		Jim Gentile			
		Leon Wagner			
☐	5	NL ERA Leaders	2.50	1.00	.20
		Sandy Koufax			
		Bob Shaw			
		Bob Purkey			
		Bob Gibson			
		Don Drysdale			
☐	6	AL ERA Leaders	2.00	.90	.15
		Hank Aguirre			
		Robin Roberts			
		Whitey Ford			
		Eddie Fisher			
		Dean Chance			
☐	7	AL Pitching Leaders	1.50	.60	.15
		Don Drysdale			
		Jack Sanford			
		Bob Purkey			
		Billy O'Dell			
		Art Mahaffey			
		Joe Jay			
☐	8	AL Pitching Leaders	1.50	.60	.15
		Ralph Terry			
		Dick Donovan			
		Ray Herbert			
		Jim Bunning			
		Camilo Pascual			
☐	9	NL Strikeout Leaders	3.00	1.20	.30
		Don Drysdale			
		Sandy Koufax			
		Bob Gibson			
		Billy O'Dell			
		Dick Farrell			

			NRMT	VG-E	GOOD
☐	10	AL Strikeout Leaders	1.50	.60	.15
		Camilo Pascual			
		Jim Bunning			
		Ralph Terry			
		Juan Pizarro			
		Jim Kaat			
☐	11	Lee Walls	.50	.20	.05
☐	12	Steve Barber	.50	.20	.05
☐	13	Philadelphia Phillies	1.00	.40	.10
		Team Card			
☐	14	Pedro Ramos	.50	.20	.05
☐	15	Ken Hubbs	1.50	.60	.15
☐	16	Al Smith	.50	.20	.05
☐	17	Ryne Duren	1.00	.40	.10
☐	18	Buc Blasters	6.50	2.60	.65
		Smoky Burgess			
		Dick Stuart			
		Bob Clemente			
		Bob Skinner			
☐	19	Pete Burnside	.50	.20	.05
☐	20	Tony Kubek	3.00	1.20	.30
☐	21	Marty Keough	.50	.20	.05
☐	22	Curt Simmons	.75	.30	.07
☐	23	Ed Lopat MG	1.00	.40	.10
☐	24	Bob Bruce	.50	.20	.05
☐	25	Al Kaline	14.00	5.75	1.40
☐	26	Ray Moore	.50	.20	.05
☐	27	Choo Choo Coleman	.50	.20	.05
☐	28	Mike Fornieles	.50	.20	.05
☐	29A	1963 Rookie Stars	1.25	.50	.12
		Sammy Ellis			
		Ray Culp			
		John Boozer			
		Jesse Gonder			
☐	29B	1962 Rookie Stars	4.00	1.60	.40
		Sammy Ellis			
		Ray Culp			
		John Boozer			
		Jesse Gonder			
☐	30	Harvey Kuenn	1.00	.40	.10
☐	31	Cal Koonce	.50	.20	.05
☐	32	Tony Gonzalez	.50	.20	.05
☐	33	Bo Belinsky	.75	.30	.07
☐	34	Dick Schofield	.50	.20	.05
☐	35	John Buzhardt	.50	.20	.05
☐	36	Jerry Kindall	.50	.20	.05
☐	37	Jerry Lynch	.50	.20	.05
☐	38	Bud Daley	.50	.20	.05
☐	39	Angels Team	1.00	.40	.10

			NRMT	VG-E	GOOD
☐	40	Vic Power	.50	.20	.05
☐	41	Charley Lau	1.00	.40	.10
☐	42	Stan Williams	.50	.20	.05
☐	43	Veteran Masters	3.00	1.20	.30
		Casey Stengel			
		Gene Woodling			
☐	44	Terry Fox	.50	.20	.05
☐	45	Bob Aspromonte	.50	.20	.05
☐	46	Tommy Aaron	.75	.30	.07
☐	47	Don Lock	.50	.20	.05
☐	48	Birdie Tebbetts MG	.50	.20	.05
☐	49	Dal Maxvill	.75	.30	.07
☐	50	Billy Pierce	1.00	.40	.10
☐	51	George Alusik	.50	.20	.05
☐	52	Chuck Schilling	.50	.20	.05
☐	53	Joe Moeller	.50	.20	.05
☐	54A	1963 Rookie Stars	3.50	1.40	.35
		Nelson Mathews			
		Harry Fanok			
		Jack Cullen			
		Dave DeBusschere			
☐	54B	1962 Rookie Stars	7.00	2.80	.70
		Nelson Mathews			
		Harry Fanok			
		Jack Cullen			
		Dave DeBusschere			
☐	55	Bill Virdon	1.00	.40	.10
☐	56	Dennis Bennett	.50	.20	.05
☐	57	Billy Moran	.50	.20	.05
☐	58	Bob Will	.50	.20	.05
☐	59	Craig Anderson	.50	.20	.05
☐	60	Elston Howard	3.50	1.40	.35
☐	61	Ernie Bowman	.50	.20	.05
☐	62	Bob Hendley	.50	.20	.05
☐	63	Reds Team	1.00	.40	.10
☐	64	Dick McAuliffe	.75	.30	.07
☐	65	Jackie Brandt	.50	.20	.05
☐	66	Mike Joyce	.50	.20	.05
☐	67	Ed Charles	.50	.20	.05
☐	68	Friendly Foes	6.50	2.60	.65
		Duke Snider			
		Gil Hodges			
☐	69	Bud Zipfel	.50	.20	.05
☐	70	Jim O'Toole	.75	.30	.07
☐	71	Bobby Wine	.75	.30	.07
☐	72	Johnny Romano	.50	.20	.05
☐	73	Bobby Bragan MG	.50	.20	.05
☐	74	Denny Lemaster	.50	.20	.05
☐	75	Bob Allison	.75	.30	.07

			NRMT	VG-E	GOOD
☐	76	Earl Wilson	.50	.20	.05
☐	77	Al Spangler	.50	.20	.05
☐	78	Marv Throneberry	1.00	.40	.10
☐	79	Checklist 1	3.50	.35	.07
☐	80	Jim Gilliam	2.00	.80	.20
☐	81	Jim Schaffer	.50	.20	.05
☐	82	Ed Rakow	.50	.20	.05
☐	83	Charley James	.50	.20	.05
☐	84	Ron Kline	.50	.20	.05
☐	85	Tom Haller	.75	.30	.07
☐	86	Charley Maxwell	.50	.20	.05
☐	87	Bob Veale	.75	.30	.07
☐	88	Ron Hansen	.50	.20	.05
☐	89	Dick Stigman	.50	.20	.05
☐	90	Gordy Coleman	.75	.30	.07
☐	91	Dallas Green	1.50	.60	.15
☐	92	Hector Lopez	.50	.20	.05
☐	93	Galen Cisco	.50	.20	.05
☐	94	Bob Schmidt	.50	.20	.05
☐	95	Larry Jackson	.50	.20	.05
☐	96	Lou Clinton	.50	.20	.05
☐	97	Bob Duliba	.50	.20	.05
☐	98	George Thomas	.50	.20	.05
☐	99	Jim Umbricht	.50	.20	.05
☐	100	Joe Cunningham	.75	.30	.07
☐	101	Joe Gibbon	.50	.20	.05
☐	102A	Checklist 2	4.00	.40	.08
		(red on yellow)			
☐	102B	Checklist 2	6.00	.60	.10
		(white on red)			
☐	103	Chuck Essegian	.50	.20	.05
☐	104	Lew Krausse	.50	.20	.05
☐	105	Ron Fairly	.75	.30	.07
☐	106	Bobby Bolin	.50	.20	.05
☐	107	Jim Hickman	.50	.20	.05
☐	108	Hoyt Wilhelm	7.00	2.80	.70
☐	109	Lee Maye	.50	.20	.05
☐	110	Rich Rollins	.60	.24	.06
☐	111	Al Jackson	.60	.24	.06
☐	112	Dick Brown	.60	.24	.06
☐	113	Don Landrum	1.00	.40	.10
		(photo actually Ron Santo)			
☐	114	Dan Osinski	.60	.24	.06
☐	115	Carl Yastrzemski	60.00	24.00	6.00
☐	116	Jim Brosnan	.75	.30	.07
☐	117	Jacke Davis	.60	.24	.06
☐	118	Sherm Lollar	.75	.30	.07
☐	119	Bob Lillis	.75	.30	.07
☐	120	Roger Maris	35.00	14.00	3.50

		NRMT	VG-E	GOOD
☐ 121	Jim Hannan	.60	.24	.06
☐ 122	Julio Gotay	.60	.24	.06
☐ 123	Frank Howard	1.75	.70	.17
☐ 124	Dick Howser	1.25	.50	.12
☐ 125	Robin Roberts	8.00	3.25	.80
☐ 126	Bob Uecker	25.00	10.00	2.50
☐ 127	Bill Tuttle	.60	.24	.06
☐ 128	Matty Alou	.75	.30	.07
☐ 129	Gary Bell	.60	.24	.06
☐ 130	Dick Groat	1.00	.40	.10
☐ 131	Washington Senators Team Card	1.25	.50	.12
☐ 132	Jack Hamilton	.60	.24	.06
☐ 133	Gene Freese	.60	.24	.06
☐ 134	Bob Scheffing MG	.60	.24	.06
☐ 135	Richie Ashburn	3.50	1.40	.35
☐ 136	Ike Delock	.60	.24	.06
☐ 137	Mack Jones	.60	.24	.06
☐ 138	Pride of NL Willie Mays Stan Musial	20.00	8.00	2.00
☐ 139	Earl Averill	.60	.24	.06
☐ 140	Frank Lary	.75	.30	.07
☐ 141	Manny Mota	3.50	1.40	.35
☐ 142	World Series Game 1 Ford wins series opener	3.50	1.40	.35
☐ 143	World Series Game 2 Sanford flashes shutout magic	2.00	.80	.20
☐ 144	World Series Game 3 Maris sparks Yankee rally	6.00	2.40	.60
☐ 145	World Series Game 4 Hiller blasts grand slammer	2.00	.80	.20
☐ 146	World Series Game 5 Tresh's homer defeats Giants	2.00	.80	.20
☐ 147	World Series Game 6 Pierce stars in 3 hit victory	2.00	.80	.20
☐ 148	World Series Game 7 Yanks celebrate as Terry wins	2.00	.80	.20
☐ 149	Marv Breeding	.60	.24	.06
☐ 150	Johnny Podres	1.75	.70	.17
☐ 151	Pirates Team	1.25	.50	.12
☐ 152	Ron Nischwitz	.60	.24	.06
☐ 153	Hal Smith	.60	.24	.06
☐ 154	Walt Alston MG	3.00	1.20	.30
☐ 155	Bill Stafford	.60	.24	.06
☐ 156	Roy McMillan	.60	.24	.06
☐ 157	Diego Segui	.60	.24	.06
☐ 158	Rookie Stars Rogelio Alvares Dave Roberts Tommy Harper Bob Saverine	1.00	.40	.10
☐ 159	Jim Pagliaroni	.60	.24	.06
☐ 160	Juan Pizarro	.60	.24	.06
☐ 161	Frank Torre	.60	.24	.06
☐ 162	Twins Team	1.25	.50	.12
☐ 163	Don Larsen	1.25	.50	.12
☐ 164	Bubba Morton	.60	.24	.06
☐ 165	Jim Kaat	3.00	1.20	.30
☐ 166	Johnny Keane MG	1.00	.40	.10
☐ 167	Jim Fregosi	1.50	.60	.15
☐ 168	Russ Nixon	1.00	.40	.10
☐ 169	Rookie Stars Dick Egan Julio Navarro Tommie Sisk Gaylord Perry	16.00	6.50	1.60
☐ 170	Joe Adcock	.75	.30	.07
☐ 171	Steve Hamilton	.60	.24	.06
☐ 172	Gene Oliver	.60	.24	.06
☐ 173	Bombers' Best Tom Tresh Mickey Mantle Bobby Richardson	30.00	12.00	3.00
☐ 174	Larry Burright	.60	.24	.06
☐ 175	Bob Buhl	.60	.24	.06
☐ 176	Jim King	.60	.24	.06
☐ 177	Bubba Phillips	.60	.24	.06
☐ 178	Johnny Edwards	.60	.24	.06
☐ 179	Ron Piche	.60	.24	.06
☐ 180	Bill Skowron	1.50	.60	.15
☐ 181	Sammy Esposito	.60	.24	.06
☐ 182	Albie Pearson	.60	.24	.06
☐ 183	Joe Pepitone	2.50	1.00	.25
☐ 184	Vern Law	.75	.30	.07
☐ 185	Chuck Hiller	.60	.24	.06
☐ 186	Jerry Zimmerman	.60	.24	.06
☐ 187	Willie Kirkland	.60	.24	.06
☐ 188	Eddie Bressoud	.60	.24	.06
☐ 189	Dave Giusti	.75	.30	.07
☐ 190	Minnie Minoso	1.75	.70	.17

		NRMT	VG-E	GOOD
☐ 191	Checklist 3	4.00	.40	.08
☐ 192	Clay Dalrymple	.60	.24	.06
☐ 193	Andre Rodgers	.60	.24	.06
☐ 194	Joe Nuxhall	.75	.30	.07
☐ 195	Manny Jimenez	.60	.24	.06
☐ 196	Doug Camilli	.60	.24	.06
☐ 197	Roger Craig	1.75	.70	.17
☐ 198	Lenny Green	.75	.30	.07
☐ 199	Joe Amalfitano	.75	.30	.07
☐ 200	Mickey Mantle	300.00	120.00	30.00
☐ 201	Cecil Butler	.75	.30	.07
☐ 202	Boston Red Sox ...	1.75	.70	.17
	Team Card			
☐ 203	Chico Cardenas	.75	.30	.07
☐ 204	Don Nottebart	.75	.30	.07
☐ 205	Luis Aparicio	8.00	3.25	.80
☐ 206	Ray Washburn	.75	.30	.07
☐ 207	Ken Hunt	.75	.30	.07
☐ 208	Rookie Stars	.75	.30	.07
	Ron Herbel			
	John Miller			
	Wally Wolf			
	Ron Taylor			
☐ 209	Hobie Landrith	.75	.30	.07
☐ 210	Sandy Koufax	70.00	28.00	7.00
☐ 211	Fred Whitfield	.75	.30	.07
☐ 212	Glen Hobbie	.75	.30	.07
☐ 213	Billy Hitchcock MG .	.75	.30	.07
☐ 214	Orlando Pena	.75	.30	.07
☐ 215	Bob Skinner	.75	.30	.07
☐ 216	Gene Conley	.75	.30	.07
☐ 217	Joe Christopher ...	.75	.30	.07
☐ 218	Tiger Twirlers	1.50	.60	.15
	Frank Lary			
	Don Mossi			
	Jim Bunning			
☐ 219	Chuck Cottier	.75	.30	.07
☐ 220	Camilo Pascual	1.00	.40	.10
☐ 221	Cookie Rojas	2.00	.80	.20
☐ 222	Cubs Team	1.75	.70	.17
☐ 223	Eddie Fisher	.75	.30	.07
☐ 224	Mike Roarke	.75	.30	.07
☐ 225	Joey Jay	.75	.30	.07
☐ 226	Julian Javier	1.00	.40	.10
☐ 227	Jim Grant	.75	.30	.07

		NRMT	VG-E	GOOD
☐ 228	Rookie Stars	21.00	8.50	2.10
	Max Alvis			
	Bob Bailey			
	Pedro Oliva			
	Ed Kranepool			
☐ 229	Willie Davis	1.50	.60	.15
☐ 230	Pete Runnels	1.00	.40	.10
☐ 231	Eli Grba	1.00	.40	.10
	(large photo is Ryne Duren)			
☐ 232	Frank Malzone	1.00	.40	.10
☐ 233	Casey Stengel MG	10.00	4.00	1.00
☐ 234	Dave Nicholson ...	.75	.30	.07
☐ 235	Billy O'Dell	.75	.30	.07
☐ 236	Bill Bryan	.75	.30	.07
☐ 237	Jim Coates	.75	.30	.07
☐ 238	Lou Johnson	.75	.30	.07
☐ 239	Harvey Haddix	1.25	.50	.12
☐ 240	Rocky Colavito ...	2.50	1.00	.25
☐ 241	Bob Smith	.75	.30	.07
☐ 242	Power Plus	11.00	4.50	1.10
	Ernie Banks			
	Hank Aaron			
☐ 243	Don Leppert	.75	.30	.07
☐ 244	John Tsitouris	.75	.30	.07
☐ 245	Gil Hodges	8.00	3.25	.80
☐ 246	Lee Stange	.75	.30	.07
☐ 247	Yankees Team	8.00	3.25	.80
☐ 248	Tito Francona	1.00	.40	.10
☐ 249	Leo Burke	.75	.30	.07
☐ 250	Stan Musial	60.00	24.00	6.00
☐ 251	Jack Lamabe	.75	.30	.07
☐ 252	Ron Santo	2.00	.80	.20
☐ 253	Rookie Stars	.75	.30	.07
	Len Gabrielson			
	Pete Jernigan			
	John Wojcik			
	Deacon Jones			
☐ 254	Mike Hershberger .	.75	.30	.07
☐ 255	Bob Shaw	.75	.30	.07
☐ 256	Jerry Lumpe	.75	.30	.07
☐ 257	Hank Aguirre	.75	.30	.07
☐ 258	Alvin Dark MG ...	1.25	.50	.12
☐ 259	Johnny Logan	1.00	.50	.10
☐ 260	Jim Gentile	1.25	.50	.12
☐ 261	Bob Miller	.75	.30	.07
☐ 262	Ellis Burton	.75	.30	.07
☐ 263	Dave Stenhouse ..	.75	.30	.07
☐ 264	Phil Linz	1.25	.50	.12
☐ 265	Vada Pinson	2.00	.80	.20

		NRMT	VG-E	GOOD
☐ 266	Bob Allen	.75	.30	.07
☐ 267	Carl Sawatski	.75	.30	.07
☐ 268	Don Demeter	.75	.30	.07
☐ 269	Don Mincher	1.00	.40	.10
☐ 270	Felipe Alou	1.50	.60	.15
☐ 271	Dean Stone	.75	.30	.07
☐ 272	Danny Murphy	.75	.30	.07
☐ 273	Sammy Taylor	.75	.30	.07
☐ 274	Checklist 4	4.00	.40	.08
☐ 275	Eddie Mathews	11.00	4.50	1.10
☐ 276	Barry Shetrone	.75	.30	.07
☐ 277	Dick Farrell	.75	.30	.07
☐ 278	Chico Fernandez . .	.75	.30	.07
☐ 279	Wally Moon	1.00	.40	.10
☐ 280	Bob Rodgers	1.75	.70	.17
☐ 281	Tom Sturdivant	.75	.30	.07
☐ 282	Bobby Del Greco . .	.75	.30	.07
☐ 283	Roy Sievers	1.50	.60	.15
☐ 284	Dave Sisler	1.00	.40	.10
☐ 285	Dick Stuart	1.50	.60	.15
☐ 286	Stu Miller	1.00	.40	.10
☐ 287	Dick Bertell	1.00	.40	.10
☐ 288	Chicago White Sox .	2.00	.80	.20
	Team Card			
☐ 289	Hal Brown	1.00	.40	.10
☐ 290	Bill White	2.00	.80	.20
☐ 291	Don Rudolph	1.00	.40	.10
☐ 292	Pumpsie Green	1.00	.40	.10
☐ 293	Bill Pleis	1.00	.40	.10
☐ 294	Bill Rigney MG	1.00	.40	.10
☐ 295	Ed Roebuck	1.00	.40	.10
☐ 296	Doc Edwards	1.50	.50	.10
☐ 297	Jim Golden	1.00	.40	.10
☐ 298	Don Dillard	1.00	.40	.10
☐ 299	Rookie Stars	1.00	.40	.10
	Dave Morehead			
	Bob Dustal			
	Tom Butters			
	Dan Schneider			
☐ 300	Willie Mays	80.00	32.00	8.00
☐ 301	Bill Fischer	1.00	.40	.10
☐ 302	Whitey Herzog	2.50	1.00	.25
☐ 303	Earl Francis	1.00	.40	.10
☐ 304	Harry Bright	1.00	.40	.10
☐ 305	Don Hoak	1.50	.60	.15
☐ 306	Star Receivers	2.00	.80	.20
	Earl Battey			
	Elston Howard			
☐ 307	Chet Nichols	1.00	.40	.10
☐ 308	Camilo Carreon . . .	1.00	.40	.10
☐ 309	Jim Brewer	1.00	.40	.10
☐ 310	Tommy Davis	2.00	.80	.20
☐ 311	Joe McClain	1.00	.40	.10
☐ 312	Houston Colts	6.00	2.40	.60
	Team Card			
☐ 313	Ernie Broglio	1.00	.40	.10
☐ 314	John Goryl	1.00	.40	.10
☐ 315	Ralph Terry	1.50	.60	.15
☐ 316	Norm Sherry	1.00	.40	.10
☐ 317	Sam McDowell	2.00	.80	.20
☐ 318	Gene Mauch MG . . .	1.50	.60	.15
☐ 319	Joe Gaines	1.00	.40	.10
☐ 320	Warren Spahn	15.00	6.00	1.50
☐ 321	Gino Cimoli	1.00	.40	.10
☐ 322	Bob Turley	2.00	.80	.20
☐ 323	Bill Mazeroski	2.50	1.00	.25
☐ 324	Rookie Stars	2.00	.80	.20
	George Williams			
	Pete Ward			
	Phil Ward			
	Vic Davalillo			
☐ 325	Jack Sanford	1.50	.60	.15
☐ 326	Hank Folles	1.00	.40	.10
☐ 327	Paul Foytack	1.00	.40	.10
☐ 328	Dick Williams	1.50	.60	.15
☐ 329	Lindy McDaniel	1.50	.60	.15
☐ 330	Chuck Hinton	1.00	.40	.10
☐ 331	Series Foes	1.50	.60	.15
	Bill Stafford			
	Bill Pierce			
☐ 332	Joel Horlen	1.00	.40	.10
☐ 333	Carl Warwick	1.00	.40	.10
☐ 334	Wynn Hawkins	1.00	.40	.10
☐ 335	Leon Wagner	1.00	.40	.10
☐ 336	Ed Bauta	1.00	.40	.10
☐ 337	Dodgers Team	6.00	2.40	.60
☐ 338	Russ Kemmerer . . .	1.00	.40	.10
☐ 339	Ted Bowsfield	1.00	.40	.10
☐ 340	Yogi Berra	35.00	14.00	3.50
☐ 341	Jack Baldschun . . .	1.00	.40	.10
☐ 342	Gene Woodling . . .	1.50	.60	.15
☐ 343	Johnny Pesky MG . .	1.50	.60	.15
☐ 344	Don Schwall	1.50	.60	.15
☐ 345	Brooks Robinson . .	27.00	11.00	2.70
☐ 346	Billy Hoeft	1.00	.40	.10
☐ 347	Joe Torre	3.50	1.40	.35
☐ 348	Vic Wertz	1.50	.60	.15
☐ 349	Zoilo Versalles	1.00	.40	.10

		NRMT	VG-E	GOOD
□ 350	Bob Purkey	1.00	.40	.10
□ 351	Al Luplow	1.00	.40	.10
□ 352	Ken Johnson	1.00	.40	.10
□ 353	Billy Williams	11.00	4.50	1.10
□ 354	Dom Zanni	1.00	.40	.10
□ 355	Dean Chance	1.50	.60	.15
□ 356	John Schaive	1.00	.40	.10
□ 357	George Altman	1.00	.40	.10
□ 358	Milt Pappas	1.50	.60	.15
□ 359	Haywood Sullivan	1.50	.60	.15
□ 360	Don Drysdale	12.00	5.00	1.20
□ 361	Clete Boyer	2.00	.80	.20
□ 362	Checklist 5	4.00	.40	.08
□ 363	Dick Radatz	2.00	.80	.20
□ 364	Howie Goss	1.00	.40	.10
□ 365	Jim Bunning	5.00	2.00	.50
□ 366	Tony Taylor	1.00	.40	.10
□ 367	Tony Cloninger	1.00	.40	.10
□ 368	Ed Bailey	1.00	.40	.10
□ 369	Jim Lemon MG	1.50	.60	.15
□ 370	Dick Donovan	1.00	.40	.10
□ 371	Rod Kanehl	1.00	.40	.10
□ 372	Don Lee	1.00	.40	.10
□ 373	Jim Campbell	1.00	.40	.10
□ 374	Claude Osteen	1.50	.60	.15
□ 375	Ken Boyer	2.50	1.00	.25
□ 376	John Wyatt	1.00	.40	.10
□ 377	Baltimore Orioles Team Card	2.00	.80	.20
□ 378	Bill Henry	1.00	.40	.10
□ 379	Bob Anderson	1.00	.40	.10
□ 380	Ernie Banks	25.00	10.00	2.50
□ 381	Frank Baumann	1.00	.40	.10
□ 382	Ralph Houk MG	2.00	.60	.15
□ 383	Pete Richert	1.00	.40	.10
□ 384	Bob Tillman	1.00	.40	.10
□ 385	Art Mahaffey	1.00	.40	.10
□ 386	Rookie Stars Ed Kirkpatrick John Bateman Larry Bearnarth Garry Roggenburk	1.50	.60	.15
□ 387	Al McBean	1.00	.40	.10
□ 388	Jim Davenport	1.50	.60	.15
□ 389	Frank Sullivan	1.00	.40	.10
□ 390	Hank Aaron	80.00	32.00	8.00
□ 391	Bill Dailey	1.00	.40	.10

		NRMT	VG-E	GOOD
□ 392	Tribe Thumpers Johnny Romano Tito Francona	1.50	.60	.15
□ 393	Ken MacKenzie	1.00	.40	.10
□ 394	Tim McCarver	4.00	1.60	.40
□ 395	Don McMahon	1.50	.60	.15
□ 396	Joe Koppe	1.00	.40	.10
□ 397	Kansas City Athletics Team Card	2.00	.80	.20
□ 398	Boog Powell	4.00	1.60	.40
□ 399	Dick Ellsworth	1.50	.60	.15
□ 400	Frank Robinson	25.00	10.00	2.50
□ 401	Jim Bouton	3.50	1.40	.35
□ 402	Mickey Vernon	1.50	.60	.15
□ 403	Ron Perranoski	1.50	.60	.15
□ 404	Bob Oldis	1.00	.40	.10
□ 405	Floyd Robinson	1.00	.40	.10
□ 406	Howie Koplitz	1.00	.40	.10
□ 407	Rookie Stars Frank Kostro Chico Ruiz Larry Elliot Dick Simpson	1.00	.40	.10
□ 408	Billy Gardner	1.00	.40	.10
□ 409	Roy Face	2.00	.80	.20
□ 410	Earl Battey	1.50	.60	.15
□ 411	Jim Constable	1.00	.40	.10
□ 412	Dodger Big Three Johnny Podres Don Drysdale Sandy Koufax	20.00	8.00	2.00
□ 413	Jerry Walker	1.00	.40	.10
□ 414	Ty Cline	1.00	.40	.10
□ 415	Bob Gibson	20.00	8.00	2.00
□ 416	Alex Grammas	1.00	.40	.10
□ 417	Giants Team	2.00	.80	.20
□ 418	John Orsino	1.00	.40	.10
□ 419	Tracy Stallard	1.00	.40	.10
□ 420	Bobby Richardson	4.00	1.60	.40
□ 421	Tom Morgan	1.00	.40	.10
□ 422	Fred Hutchinson MG	1.50	.60	.15
□ 423	Ed Hobaugh	1.00	.40	.10
□ 424	Charlie Smith	1.00	.40	.10
□ 425	Smoky Burgess	1.50	.60	.15
□ 426	Barry Latman	1.00	.40	.10
□ 427	Bernie Allen	1.00	.40	.10
□ 428	Carl Boles	1.00	.40	.10
□ 429	Lou Burdette	2.00	.80	.20
□ 430	Norm Siebern	1.00	.40	.10

	NRMT	VG-E	GOOD
☐ 431A Checklist 6	4.00	.40	.08
(white on red)			
☐ 431B Checklist 6	8.00	.80	.15
(black on orange)			
☐ 432 Roman Mejias	1.00	.40	.10
☐ 433 Denis Menke	1.00	.40	.10
☐ 434 John Callison	1.50	.60	.15
☐ 435 Woody Held	1.00	.40	.10
☐ 436 Tim Harkness	1.00	.40	.10
☐ 437 Bill Bruton	1.00	.40	.10
☐ 438 Wes Stock	1.00	.40	.10
☐ 439 Don Zimmer	2.00	.80	.20
☐ 440 Juan Marichal	16.00	6.50	1.60
☐ 441 Lee Thomas	2.00	.80	.20
☐ 442 J.C. Hartman	1.00	.40	.10
☐ 443 Jim Piersall	2.00	.80	.20
☐ 444 Jim Maloney	2.00	.80	.20
☐ 445 Norm Cash	2.50	1.00	.25
☐ 446 Whitey Ford	25.00	10.00	2.50
☐ 447 Felix Mantilla	6.00	2.40	.60
☐ 448 Jack Kralick	6.00	2.40	.60
☐ 449 Jose Tartabull	6.00	2.40	.60
☐ 450 Bob Friend	7.00	2.80	.70
☐ 451 Indians Team	11.00	4.50	1.10
☐ 452 Buddy Schultz	6.00	2.40	.60
☐ 453 Jake Wood	6.00	2.40	.60
☐ 454A Art Fowler	6.00	2.40	.60
(card number on white background)			
☐ 454B Art Fowler	10.00	4.00	1.00
(card number on orange background)			
☐ 455 Ruben Amaro	6.00	2.40	.60
☐ 456 Jim Coker	6.00	2.40	.60
☐ 457 Tex Clevenger	6.00	2.40	.60
☐ 458 Al Lopez MG	11.00	4.50	1.10
☐ 459 Dick LeMay	6.00	2.40	.60
☐ 460 Del Crandall	7.00	2.80	.70
☐ 461 Norm Bass	6.00	2.40	.60
☐ 462 Wally Post	6.00	2.40	.60
☐ 463 Joe Schaffernoth ...	6.00	2.40	.60
☐ 464 Ken Aspromonte ...	6.00	2.40	.60
☐ 465 Chuck Estrada	7.00	2.80	.70
☐ 466 Rookie Stars SP ...	20.00	8.00	2.00
Nate Oliver			
Tony Martinez			
Bill Freehan			
Jerry Robinson			
☐ 467 Phil Ortega	6.00	2.40	.60
☐ 468 Carroll Hardy	6.00	2.40	.60
☐ 469 Jay Hook	6.00	2.40	.60
☐ 470 Tom Tresh SP	20.00	8.00	2.00
☐ 471 Ken Retzer	6.00	2.40	.60
☐ 472 Lou Brock	75.00	30.00	7.50
☐ 473 New York Mets	20.00	8.00	2.00
Team Card			
☐ 474 Jack Fisher	6.00	2.40	.60
☐ 475 Gus Triandos	7.00	2.80	.70
☐ 476 Frank Funk	6.00	2.40	.60
☐ 477 Donn Clendenon ...	7.00	2.80	.70
☐ 478 Paul Brown	6.00	2.40	.60
☐ 479 Ed Brinkman	6.00	2.40	.60
☐ 480 Bill Monbouquette ..	6.00	2.40	.60
☐ 481 Bill Taylor	6.00	2.40	.60
☐ 482 Felix Torres	6.00	2.40	.60
☐ 483 Jim Owens	6.00	2.40	.60
☐ 484 Dale Long	7.00	2.80	.70
☐ 485 Jim Landis	6.00	2.40	.60
☐ 486 Ray Sadecki	6.00	2.40	.60
☐ 487 John Roseboro	7.00	2.80	.70
☐ 488 Jerry Adair	6.00	2.40	.60
☐ 489 Paul Toth	6.00	2.40	.60
☐ 490 Willie McCovey	60.00	24.00	6.00
☐ 491 Harry Craft MG	6.00	2.40	.60
☐ 492 Dave Wickersham .	6.00	2.40	.60
☐ 493 Walt Bond	6.00	2.40	.60
☐ 494 Phil Regan	7.00	2.80	.70
☐ 495 Frank Thomas	7.00	2.80	.70
☐ 496 Rookie Stars	7.00	2.80	.70
Steve Dalkowski			
Fred Newman			
Jack Smith			
Carl Bouldin			
☐ 497 Bennie Daniels	6.00	2.40	.60
☐ 498 Eddie Kasko	6.00	2.40	.60
☐ 499 J.C. Martin	6.00	2.40	.60
☐ 500 Harmon Killebrew .	40.00	16.00	4.00
☐ 501 Joe Azcue	6.00	2.40	.60
☐ 502 Daryl Spencer	6.00	2.40	.60
☐ 503 Braves Team	11.00	4.50	1.10
☐ 504 Bob Johnson	6.00	2.40	.60
☐ 505 Curt Flood	11.00	4.50	1.10
☐ 506 Gene Green	6.00	2.40	.60
☐ 507 Roland Sheldon ...	4.00	1.60	.40
☐ 508 Ted Savage	4.00	1.60	.40
☐ 509A Checklist 7	12.00	1.50	.15
(copyright centered)			
☐ 509B Checklist 7	12.00	1.50	.15
(copyright to right)			
☐ 510 Ken McBride	4.00	1.60	.40

		NRMT	VG-E	GOOD
☐ 511	Charlie Neal	5.00	2.00	.50
☐ 512	Cal McLish	4.00	1.60	.40
☐ 513	Gary Geiger	4.00	1.60	.40
☐ 514	Larry Osborne	4.00	1.60	.40
☐ 515	Don Elston	4.00	1.60	.40
☐ 516	Purnell Goldy	4.00	1.60	.40
☐ 517	Hal Woodeshick	4.00	1.60	.40
☐ 518	Don Blasingame	4.00	1.60	.40
☐ 519	Claude Raymond	4.00	1.60	.40
☐ 520	Orlando Cepeda	11.00	4.50	1.10
☐ 521	Dan Pfister	4.00	1.60	.40
☐ 522	Rookie Stars	6.00	2.40	.60
	Mel Nelson			
	Gary Peters			
	Jim Roland			
	Art Quirk			
☐ 523	Bill Kunkel	5.00	2.00	.50
☐ 524	Cardinals Team	9.00	3.75	.90
☐ 525	Nellie Fox	8.50	3.50	.85
☐ 526	Dick Hall	4.00	1.60	.40
☐ 527	Ed Sadowski	4.00	1.60	.40
☐ 528	Carl Willey	4.00	1.60	.40
☐ 529	Wes Covington	5.00	2.00	.50
☐ 530	Don Mossi	5.00	2.00	.50
☐ 531	Sam Mele MG	4.00	1.60	.40
☐ 532	Steve Boros	5.00	2.00	.50
☐ 533	Bobby Shantz	6.00	2.40	.60
☐ 534	Ken Walters	4.00	1.60	.40
☐ 535	Jim Perry	6.00	2.40	.60
☐ 536	Norm Larker	5.00	2.00	.50
☐ 537	Rookie Stars	600.00	240.00	60.00
	Pedro Gonzales			
	Ken McMullen			
	Al Weis			
	Pete Rose			
☐ 538	George Brunet	4.00	1.60	.40
☐ 539	Wayne Causey	4.00	1.60	.40
☐ 540	Bob Clemente	110.00	45.00	11.00
☐ 541	Ron Moeller	4.00	1.60	.40
☐ 542	Lou Klimchock	4.00	1.60	.40
☐ 543	Russ Snyder	4.00	1.60	.40
☐ 544	Rookie Stars	25.00	10.00	2.50
	Duke Carmel			
	Bill Haas			
	Rusty Staub			
	Dick Phillips			
☐ 545	Jose Pagan	4.00	1.60	.40
☐ 546	Hal Reniff	4.00	1.60	.40
☐ 547	Gus Bell	5.00	2.00	.50

		NRMT	VG-E	GOOD
☐ 548	Tom Satriano	4.00	1.60	.40
☐ 549	Rookie Stars	4.00	1.60	.40
	Marcelino Lopez			
	Pete Lovrich			
	Paul Ratliff			
	Elmo Plaskett			
☐ 550	Duke Snider	50.00	20.00	5.00
☐ 551	Billy Klaus	4.00	1.60	.40
☐ 552	Detroit Tigers	16.00	6.50	1.60
	Team Card			
☐ 553	Rookie Stars	150.00	60.00	15.00
	Brock Davis			
	Jim Gosger			
	Willie Stargell			
	John Herrnstein			
☐ 554	Hank Fischer	4.00	1.60	.40
☐ 555	John Blanchard	5.00	2.00	.50
☐ 556	Al Worthington	4.00	1.60	.40
☐ 557	Cuno Barragan	4.00	1.60	.40
☐ 558	Rookie Stars	4.00	1.60	.40
	Bill Faul			
	Ron Hunt			
	Al Moran			
	Bob Lipski			
☐ 559	Danny Murtaugh MG	4.00	1.60	.40
☐ 560	Ray Herbert	4.00	1.60	.40
☐ 561	Mike De La Hoz	4.00	1.60	.40
☐ 562	Rookie Stars	8.00	3.25	.80
	Randy Cardinal			
	Dave McNally			
	Ken Rowe			
	Don Rowe			
☐ 563	Mike McCormick	5.00	2.00	.50
☐ 564	George Banks	4.00	1.60	.40
☐ 565	Larry Sherry	5.00	2.00	.50
☐ 566	Cliff Cook	4.00	1.60	.40
☐ 567	Jim Duffalo	4.00	1.60	.40
☐ 568	Bob Sadowski	4.00	1.60	.40
☐ 569	Luis Arroyo	5.00	2.00	.50
☐ 570	Frank Bolling	4.00	1.60	.40
☐ 571	Johnny Klippstein	4.00	1.60	.40
☐ 572	Jack Spring	4.00	1.60	.40
☐ 573	Coot Veal	4.00	1.60	.40
☐ 574	Hal Kolstad	4.00	1.60	.40
☐ 575	Don Cardwell	4.00	1.60	.40
☐ 576	Johnny Temple	6.50	2.00	.40

1964 Topps

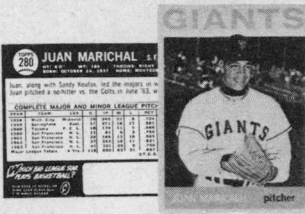

The cards in this 587-card set measure 2 ½"
by 3 ½". Players in the 1964 Topps baseball
series were easy to sort by team due to the
giant block lettering found at the top of each
card. The name and position of the player
are found underneath the picture, and the
card is numbered in a ball design on the
orange-colored back. The usual last series
scarcity holds for this set (523 to 587). Subsets within this set include League Leaders
(1-12) and World Series cards (136-140).

	NRMT	VG-E	GOOD
Complete Set (587)	2000.00	900.00	300.00
Common Player (1-370) . . .	.60	.24	.06
Common Player (371-522) .	1.00	.40	.10
Common Player (523-587) .	3.50	1.40	.35

			NRMT	VG-E	GOOD
☐	1	NL ERA Leaders . . .	9.00	1.50	.30
		Sandy Koufax			
		Dick Ellsworth			
		Bob Friend			
☐	2	AL ERA Leaders . . .	1.50	.60	.15
		Gary Peters			
		Juan Pizarro			
		Camilo Pascual			
☐	3	NL Pitching Leaders	5.00	2.00	.40
		Sandy Koufax			
		Juan Marichal			
		Warren Spahn			
		Jim Maloney			
☐	4	AL Pitching Leaders	1.50	.60	.15
		Whitey Ford			
		Camilo Pascual			
		Jim Bouton			
☐	5	NL Strikeout Leaders	4.00	1.60	.35
		Sandy Koufax			
		Jim Maloney			
		Don Drysdale			
☐	6	AL Strikeout Leaders	1.50	.60	.15
		Camilo Pascual			
		Jim Bunning			
		Dick Stigman			
☐	7	NL Batting Leaders	3.00	1.20	.25
		Tommy Davis			
		Bob Clemente			
		Dick Groat			
		Hank Aaron			
☐	8	AL Batting Leaders	4.00	1.60	.35
		Carl Yastrzemski			
		Al Kaline			
		Rich Rollins			
☐	9	NL Home Run Leaders	7.50	3.00	.60
		Hank Aaron			
		Willie McCovey			
		Willie Mays			
		Orlando Cepeda			
☐	10	AL Home Run Leaders	1.50	.60	.15
		Harmon Killebrew			
		Dick Stuart			
		Bob Allison			
☐	11	NL RBI Leaders . . .	2.50	1.00	.20
		Hank Aaron			
		Ken Boyer			
		Bill White			
☐	12	AL RBI Leaders . . .	2.00	.80	.20
		Dick Stuart			
		Al Kaline			
		Harmon Killebrew			
☐	13	Hoyt Wilhelm	6.50	2.60	.65
☐	14	Dodgers Rookies . .	.60	.24	.06
		Dick Nen			
		Nick Willhite			
☐	15	Zoilo Versalles	.60	.24	.06
☐	16	John Boozer	.60	.24	.06
☐	17	Willie Kirkland	.60	.24	.06
☐	18	Billy O'Dell	.60	.24	.06
☐	19	Don Wert	.60	.24	.06
☐	20	Bob Friend	.75	.30	.07
☐	21	Yogi Berra	25.00	10.00	2.50

		NRMT	VG-E	GOOD
☐ 22	Jerry Adair	.60	.24	.06
☐ 23	Chris Zachary	.60	.24	.06
☐ 24	Carl Sawatski	.60	.24	.06
☐ 25	Bill Monbouquette	.60	.24	.06
☐ 26	Gino Cimoli	.60	.24	.06
☐ 27	New York Mets	2.00	.80	.20
	Team Card			
☐ 28	Claude Osteen	.75	.30	.07
☐ 29	Lou Brock	21.00	8.50	2.10
☐ 30	Ron Perranoski	.75	.30	.07
☐ 31	Dave Nicholson	.60	.24	.06
☐ 32	Dean Chance	1.00	.40	.10
☐ 33	Reds Rookies	.75	.30	.07
	Sammy Ellis			
	Mel Queen			
☐ 34	Jim Perry	1.00	.40	.10
☐ 35	Eddie Mathews	9.00	3.75	.90
☐ 36	Hal Reniff	.60	.24	.06
☐ 37	Smoky Burgess	.75	.30	.07
☐ 38	Jim Wynn	1.50	.60	.15
☐ 39	Hank Aguirre	.60	.24	.06
☐ 40	Dick Groat	1.00	.40	.10
☐ 41	Friendly Foes	3.00	1.20	.30
	Willie McCovey			
	Leon Wagner			
☐ 42	Moe Drabowsky	.60	.24	.06
☐ 43	Roy Sievers	.75	.30	.07
☐ 44	Duke Carmel	.60	.24	.06
☐ 45	Milt Pappas	.75	.30	.07
☐ 46	Ed Brinkman	.60	.24	.06
☐ 47	Giants Rookies	1.00	.40	.10
	Jesus Alou			
	Ron Herbel			
☐ 48	Bob Perry	.60	.24	.06
☐ 49	Bill Henry	.60	.24	.06
☐ 50	Mickey Mantle	200.00	80.00	20.00
☐ 51	Pete Richert	.60	.24	.06
☐ 52	Chuck Hinton	.60	.24	.06
☐ 53	Denis Menke	.60	.24	.06
☐ 54	Sam Mele MG	.60	.24	.06
☐ 55	Ernie Banks	12.00	5.00	1.20
☐ 56	Hal Brown	.60	.24	.06
☐ 57	Tim Harkness	.60	.24	.06
☐ 58	Don Demeter	.60	.24	.06
☐ 59	Ernie Broglio	.60	.24	.06
☐ 60	Frank Malzone	.75	.30	.07
☐ 61	Angel Backstops	1.00	.40	.10
	Bob Rodgers			
	Ed Sadowski			

		NRMT	VG-E	GOOD
☐ 62	Ted Savage	.60	.24	.06
☐ 63	John Orsino	.60	.24	.06
☐ 64	Ted Abernathy	.60	.24	.06
☐ 65	Felipe Alou	1.00	.40	.10
☐ 66	Eddie Fisher	.60	.24	.06
☐ 67	Tigers Team	1.50	.60	.15
☐ 68	Willie Davis	1.00	.40	.10
☐ 69	Clete Boyer	1.00	.40	.10
☐ 70	Joe Torre	1.75	.70	.17
☐ 71	Jack Spring	.60	.24	.06
☐ 72	Chico Cardenas	.60	.24	.06
☐ 73	Jimmie Hall	1.00	.40	.10
☐ 74	Pirates Rookies	.60	.24	.06
	Bob Priddy			
	Tom Butters			
☐ 75	Wayne Causey	.60	.24	.06
☐ 76	Checklist 1	3.00	.30	.06
☐ 77	Jerry Walker	.60	.24	.06
☐ 78	Merritt Ranew	.60	.24	.06
☐ 79	Bob Heffner	.60	.24	.06
☐ 80	Vada Pinson	1.50	.60	.15
☐ 81	All-Star Vets	4.00	1.60	.40
	Nellie Fox			
	Harmon Killebrew			
☐ 82	Jim Davenport	.75	.30	.07
☐ 83	Gus Triandos	.75	.30	.07
☐ 84	Carl Willey	.60	.24	.06
☐ 85	Pete Ward	.60	.24	.06
☐ 86	Al Downing	.75	.30	.07
☐ 87	St. Louis Cardinals	1.50	.60	.15
	Team Card			
☐ 88	John Roseboro	.75	.30	.07
☐ 89	Boog Powell	2.00	.80	.20
☐ 90	Earl Battey	.75	.30	.07
☐ 91	Bob Bailey	.60	.24	.06
☐ 92	Steve Ridzik	.60	.24	.06
☐ 93	Gary Geiger	.60	.24	.06
☐ 94	Braves Rookies	.60	.24	.06
	Jim Britton			
	Larry Maxie			
☐ 95	George Altman	.60	.24	.06
☐ 96	Bob Buhl	.60	.24	.06
☐ 97	Jim Fregosi	1.00	.40	.10
☐ 98	Bill Bruton	.60	.24	.06
☐ 99	Al Stanek	.60	.24	.06
☐ 100	Elston Howard	2.50	1.00	.25
☐ 101	Walt Alston MG	2.50	1.00	.25
☐ 102	Checklist 2	3.00	.30	.06
☐ 103	Curt Flood	1.50	.60	.15

		NRMT	VG-E	GOOD
☐ 104	Art Mahaffey	.60	.24	.06
☐ 105	Woody Held	.60	.24	.06
☐ 106	Joe Nuxhall	.75	.30	.07
☐ 107	White Sox Rookies	.60	.24	.06
	Bruce Howard			
	Frank Kreutzer			
☐ 108	John Wyatt	.60	.24	.06
☐ 109	Rusty Staub	4.50	1.80	.45
☐ 110	Albie Pearson	.60	.24	.06
☐ 111	Don Elston	.60	.24	.06
☐ 112	Bob Tillman	.60	.24	.06
☐ 113	Grover Powell	.60	.24	.06
☐ 114	Don Lock	.60	.24	.06
☐ 115	Frank Bolling	.60	.24	.06
☐ 116	Twins Rookies	7.00	2.80	.70
	Jay Ward			
	Tony Oliva			
☐ 117	Earl Francis	.60	.24	.06
☐ 118	John Blanchard	.75	.30	.07
☐ 119	Gary Kolb	.60	.24	.06
☐ 120	Don Drysdale	8.50	3.50	.85
☐ 121	Pete Runnels	.75	.30	.07
☐ 122	Don McMahon	.75	.30	.07
☐ 123	Jose Pagan	.60	.24	.06
☐ 124	Orlando Pena	.60	.24	.06
☐ 125	Pete Rose	165.00	65.00	15.00
☐ 126	Russ Snyder	.60	.24	.06
☐ 127	Angels Rookies	.60	.24	.06
	Aubrey Gatewood			
	Dick Simpson			
☐ 128	Mickey Lolich	7.50	3.00	.75
☐ 129	Amado Samuel	.60	.24	.06
☐ 130	Gary Peters	.75	.30	.07
☐ 131	Steve Boros	.75	.30	.07
☐ 132	Braves Team	1.50	.60	.15
☐ 133	Jim Grant	.60	.24	.06
☐ 134	Don Zimmer	1.00	.40	.10
☐ 135	Johnny Callison	.75	.30	.07
☐ 136	World Series Game 1	6.50	2.60	.65
	Koufax strikes out 15			
☐ 137	World Series Game 2	2.00	.80	.20
	Davis sparks rally			
☐ 138	World Series Game 3	2.00	.80	.20
	LA 3 straight			
☐ 139	World Series Game 4	2.00	.80	.20
	Sealing Yanks doom			
☐ 140	World Series Summary	2.00	.80	.20
	Dodgers celebrate			
☐ 141	Danny Murtaugh MG	.60	.24	.06

		NRMT	VG-E	GOOD
☐ 142	John Bateman	.60	.24	.06
☐ 143	Bubba Phillips	.60	.24	.06
☐ 144	Al Worthington	.60	.24	.06
☐ 145	Norm Siebern	.60	.24	.06
☐ 146	Indians Rookies	30.00	12.00	3.00
	Tommy John			
	Bob Chance			
☐ 147	Ray Sadecki	.60	.24	.06
☐ 148	J.C. Martin	.60	.24	.06
☐ 149	Paul Foytack	.60	.24	.06
☐ 150	Willie Mays	50.00	20.00	5.00
☐ 151	Athletics Team	1.25	.50	.12
☐ 152	Denny Lemaster	.60	.24	.06
☐ 153	Dick Williams	.75	.30	.07
☐ 154	Dick Tracewski	.60	.24	.06
☐ 155	Duke Snider	16.00	6.50	1.60
☐ 156	Bill Dailey	.60	.24	.06
☐ 157	Gene Mauch MG	.75	.30	.07
☐ 158	Ken Johnson	.60	.24	.06
☐ 159	Charlie Dees	.60	.24	.06
☐ 160	Ken Boyer	3.50	1.40	.35
☐ 161	Dave McNally	1.50	.60	.15
☐ 162	Hitting Area	1.00	.40	.10
	Dick Sisler			
	Vada Pinson			
☐ 163	Donn Clendenon	.75	.30	.07
☐ 164	Bud Daley	.60	.24	.06
☐ 165	Jerry Lumpe	.60	.24	.06
☐ 166	Marty Keough	.60	.24	.06
☐ 167	Senators Rookies	18.00	7.25	1.80
	Mike Brumley			
	Lou Piniella			
☐ 168	Al Weis	.60	.24	.06
☐ 169	Del Crandall	.75	.30	.07
☐ 170	Dick Radatz	1.00	.40	.10
☐ 171	Ty Cline	.60	.24	.06
☐ 172	Indians Team	1.25	.50	.12
☐ 173	Ryne Duren	1.00	.40	.10
☐ 174	Doc Edwards	1.50	.60	.15
☐ 175	Billy Williams	9.00	3.75	.90
☐ 176	Tracy Stallard	.60	.24	.06
☐ 177	Harmon Killebrew	9.00	3.75	.90
☐ 178	Hank Bauer MG	1.00	.40	.10
☐ 179	Carl Warwick	.60	.24	.06
☐ 180	Tommy Davis	1.00	.40	.10
☐ 181	Dave Wickersham	.60	.24	.06
☐ 182	Sox Sockers	7.50	3.00	.75
	Carl Yastrzemski			
	Chuck Schilling			

	NRMT	VG-E	GOOD			NRMT	VG-E	GOOD
☐ 183 Ron Taylor	.60	.24	.06	☐ 226 Colts Rookies	.75	.30	.07
☐ 184 Al Luplow	.60	.24	.06	Gerald Grote			
☐ 185 Jim O'Toole	.75	.30	.07	Larry Yellen			
☐ 186 Roman Mejias	.60	.24	.06	☐ 227 Barry Latman	.60	.24	.06
☐ 187 Ed Roebuck	.60	.24	.06	☐ 228 Felix Mantilla	.60	.24	.06
☐ 188 Checklist 3	3.00	.30	.06	☐ 229 Charley Lau	1.00	.40	.10
☐ 189 Bob Hendley	.60	.24	.06	☐ 230 Brooks Robinson	20.00	8.00	2.00
☐ 190 Bobby Richardson	3.50	1.40	.35	☐ 231 Dick Calmus	.60	.24	.06
☐ 191 Clay Dalrymple	.60	.24	.06	☐ 232 Al Lopez MG	2.00	.80	.20
☐ 192 Cubs Rookies	.60	.24	.06	☐ 233 Hal Smith	.60	.24	.06
John Boccabella				☐ 234 Gary Bell	.60	.24	.06
Billy Cowan				☐ 235 Ron Hunt	.60	.24	.06
☐ 193 Jerry Lynch	.60	.24	.06	☐ 236 Bill Faul	.60	.24	.06
☐ 194 John Goryl	.60	.24	.06	☐ 237 Cubs Team	1.25	.50	.12
☐ 195 Floyd Robinson	.60	.24	.06	☐ 238 Roy McMillan	.60	.24	.06
☐ 196 Jim Gentile	.75	.30	.07	☐ 239 Herm Starrette	.60	.24	.06
☐ 197 Frank Lary	.75	.30	.07	☐ 240 Bill White	1.00	.40	.10
☐ 198 Len Gabrielson	.60	.24	.06	☐ 241 Jim Owens	.60	.24	.06
☐ 199 Joe Azcue	.60	.24	.06	☐ 242 Harvey Kuenn	1.25	.50	.12
☐ 200 Sandy Koufax	50.00	20.00	5.00	☐ 243 Phillies Rookies	10.00	4.00	1.00
☐ 201 Orioles Rookies	.75	.30	.07	Richie Allen			
Sam Bowens				John Herrnstein			
Wally Bunker				☐ 244 Tony LaRussa	6.00	2.40	.60
☐ 202 Galen Cisco	.60	.24	.06	☐ 245 Dick Stigman	.60	.24	.06
☐ 203 John Kennedy	.60	.24	.06	☐ 246 Manny Mota	1.00	.40	.10
☐ 204 Matty Alou	.75	.30	.07	☐ 247 Dave DeBusschere	2.50	1.00	.25
☐ 205 Nellie Fox	3.00	1.20	.30	☐ 248 Johnny Pesky MG	.75	.30	.07
☐ 206 Steve Hamilton	.60	.24	.06	☐ 249 Doug Camilli	.60	.24	.06
☐ 207 Fred Hutchinson MG	.75	.30	.07	☐ 250 Al Kaline	14.00	5.75	1.40
☐ 208 Wes Covington	.75	.30	.07	☐ 251 Choo Choo Coleman	.60	.24	.06
☐ 209 Bob Allen	.60	.24	.06	☐ 252 Ken Aspromonte	.60	.24	.06
☐ 210 Carl Yastrzemski	60.00	24.00	6.00	☐ 253 Wally Post	.60	.24	.06
☐ 211 Jim Coker	.60	.24	.06	☐ 254 Don Hoak	.60	.24	.06
☐ 212 Pete Lovrich	.60	.24	.06	☐ 255 Lee Thomas	1.00	.40	.10
☐ 213 Angels Team	1.25	.50	.12	☐ 256 Johnny Weekly	.60	.24	.06
☐ 214 Ken McMullen	.75	.30	.07	☐ 257 San Francisco Giants	1.50	.60	.15
☐ 215 Ray Herbert	.60	.24	.06	Team Card			
☐ 216 Mike De La Hoz	.60	.24	.06	☐ 258 Garry Roggenburk	.60	.24	.06
☐ 217 Jim King	.60	.24	.06	☐ 259 Harry Bright	.60	.24	.06
☐ 218 Hank Fischer	.60	.24	.06	☐ 260 Frank Robinson	12.00	5.00	1.20
☐ 219 Young Aces	1.50	.60	.15	☐ 261 Jim Hannan	.60	.24	.06
Al Downing				☐ 262 Cards Rookies	2.50	1.00	.25
Jim Bouton				Mike Shannon			
☐ 220 Dick Ellsworth	.75	.30	.07	Harry Fanok			
☐ 221 Bob Saverine	.60	.24	.06	☐ 263 Chuck Estrada	.75	.30	.07
☐ 222 Billy Pierce	1.00	.40	.10	☐ 264 Jim Landis	.60	.24	.06
☐ 223 George Banks	.60	.24	.06	☐ 265 Jim Bunning	3.50	1.40	.35
☐ 224 Tommie Sisk	.60	.24	.06	☐ 266 Gene Freese	.60	.24	.06
☐ 225 Roger Maris	35.00	14.00	3.50	☐ 267 Wilbur Wood	1.25	.50	.12

		NRMT	VG-E	GOOD				NRMT	VG-E	GOOD
☐ 268	Bill's Got It	.75	.30	.07	☐ 308	Gene Stephens		.60	.24	.06
	Danny Murtaugh				☐ 309	Paul Toth		.60	.24	.06
	Bill Virdon				☐ 310	Jim Gilliam		2.00	.80	.20
☐ 269	Ellis Burton	.60	.24	.06	☐ 311	Tom Brown		.60	.24	.06
☐ 270	Rich Rollins	.75	.30	.07	☐ 312	Tigers Rookies		.60	.24	.06
☐ 271	Bob Sadowski	.60	.24	.06		Fritz Fisher				
☐ 272	Jake Wood	.60	.24	.06		Fred Gladding				
☐ 273	Mel Nelson	.60	.24	.06	☐ 313	Chuck Hiller		.60	.24	.06
☐ 274	Checklist 4	3.00	.30	.06	☐ 314	Jerry Buchek		.60	.24	.06
☐ 275	John Tsitouris	.60	.24	.06	☐ 315	Bo Belinsky		.75	.30	.07
☐ 276	Jose Tartabull	.60	.24	.06	☐ 316	Gene Oliver		.60	.24	.06
☐ 277	Ken Retzer	.60	.24	.06	☐ 317	Al Smith		.60	.24	.06
☐ 278	Bobby Shantz	1.00	.40	.10	☐ 318	Minnesota Twins		1.25	.50	.12
☐ 279	Joe Koppe (glove	.75	.30	.07		Team Card				
	on wrong hand)				☐ 319	Paul Brown		.60	.24	.06
☐ 280	Juan Marichal	8.00	3.25	.80	☐ 320	Rocky Colavito		2.00	.80	.20
☐ 281	Yankees Rookies	.75	.30	.07	☐ 321	Bob Lillis		.75	.30	.07
	Jake Gibbs				☐ 322	George Brunet		.60	.24	.06
	Tom Metcalf				☐ 323	John Buzhardt		.60	.24	.06
☐ 282	Bob Bruce	.60	.24	.06	☐ 324	Casey Stengel MG		9.00	3.75	.90
☐ 283	Tom McCraw	.75	.30	.07	☐ 325	Hector Lopez		.60	.24	.06
☐ 284	Dick Schofield	.60	.24	.06	☐ 326	Ron Brand		.60	.24	.06
☐ 285	Robin Roberts	7.50	3.00	.75	☐ 327	Don Blasingame		.60	.24	.06
☐ 286	Don Landrum	.60	.24	.06	☐ 328	Bob Shaw		.60	.24	.06
☐ 287	Red Sox Rookies	7.50	3.00	.75	☐ 329	Russ Nixon		1.00	.40	.10
	Tony Conigliaro				☐ 330	Tommy Harper		.75	.30	.07
	Bill Spanswick				☐ 331	AL Bombers		50.00	20.00	5.00
☐ 288	Al Moran	.60	.24	.06		Roger Maris				
☐ 289	Frank Funk	.60	.24	.06		Norm Cash				
☐ 290	Bob Allison	.75	.30	.07		Mickey Mantle				
☐ 291	Phil Ortega	.60	.24	.06		Al Kaline				
☐ 292	Mike Roarke	.60	.24	.06	☐ 332	Ray Washburn		.60	.24	.06
☐ 293	Phillies Team	1.25	.50	.12	☐ 333	Billy Moran		.60	.24	.06
☐ 294	Ken L. Hunt	.60	.24	.06	☐ 334	Lew Krausse		.60	.24	.06
☐ 295	Roger Craig	1.50	.60	.15	☐ 335	Don Mossi		.75	.30	.07
☐ 296	Ed Kirkpatrick	.60	.24	.06	☐ 336	Andre Rodgers		.60	.24	.06
☐ 297	Ken MacKenzie	.60	.24	.06	☐ 337	Dodgers Rookies		2.00	.80	.20
☐ 298	Harry Craft MG	.60	.24	.06		Al Ferrara				
☐ 299	Bill Stafford	.60	.24	.06		Jeff Torborg				
☐ 300	Hank Aaron	50.00	20.00	5.00	☐ 338	Jack Kralick		.60	.24	.06
☐ 301	Larry Brown	.60	.24	.06	☐ 339	Walt Bond		.60	.24	.06
☐ 302	Dan Pfister	.60	.24	.06	☐ 340	Joe Cunningham		.75	.30	.07
☐ 303	Jim Campbell	.60	.24	.06	☐ 341	Jim Roland		.60	.24	.06
☐ 304	Bob Johnson	.60	.24	.06	☐ 342	Willie Stargell		30.00	12.00	3.00
☐ 305	Jack Lamabe	.60	.24	.06	☐ 343	Senators Team		1.25	.50	.12
☐ 306	Giant Gunners	11.00	4.50	1.10	☐ 344	Phil Linz		.75	.30	.07
	Willie Mays				☐ 345	Frank Thomas		.75	.30	.07
	Orlando Cepeda				☐ 346	Joey Jay		.60	.24	.06
☐ 307	Joe Gibbon	.60	.24	.06	☐ 347	Bobby Wine		.60	.24	.06

		NRMT	VG-E	GOOD
☐ 348	Ed Lopat MG	1.00	.40	.10
☐ 349	Art Fowler	.60	.24	.06
☐ 350	Willie McCovey	12.50	5.00	1.25
☐ 351	Dan Schneider	.60	.24	.06
☐ 352	Eddie Bressoud	.60	.24	.06
☐ 353	Wally Moon	1.00	.40	.10
☐ 354	Dave Giusti	.75	.30	.07
☐ 355	Vic Power	.60	.24	.06
☐ 356	Reds Rookies	.75	.30	.07
	Bill McCool			
	Chico Ruiz			
☐ 357	Charley James	.60	.24	.06
☐ 358	Ron Kline	.60	.24	.06
☐ 359	Jim Schaffer	.60	.24	.06
☐ 360	Joe Pepitone	1.50	.60	.15
☐ 361	Jay Hook	.60	.24	.06
☐ 362	Checklist 5	3.00	.30	.06
☐ 363	Dick McAuliffe	.75	.30	.07
☐ 364	Joe Gaines	.60	.24	.06
☐ 365	Cal McLish	.60	.24	.06
☐ 366	Nelson Mathews	.60	.24	.06
☐ 367	Fred Whitfield	.60	.24	.06
☐ 368	White Sox Rookies	1.00	.40	.10
	Fritz Ackley			
	Don Buford			
☐ 369	Jerry Zimmerman	.60	.24	.06
☐ 370	Hal Woodeshick	.60	.24	.06
☐ 371	Frank Howard	2.00	.80	.20
☐ 372	Howie Koplitz	1.00	.40	.10
☐ 373	Pirates Team	2.00	.80	.20
☐ 374	Bobby Bolin	1.00	.40	.10
☐ 375	Ron Santo	2.00	.80	.20
☐ 376	Dave Morehead	1.00	.40	.10
☐ 377	Bob Skinner	1.00	.40	.10
☐ 378	Braves Rookies	2.00	.80	.20
	Woody Woodward			
	Jack Smith			
☐ 379	Tony Gonzalez	1.00	.40	.10
☐ 380	Whitey Ford	14.00	5.75	1.40
☐ 381	Bob Taylor	1.00	.40	.10
☐ 382	Wes Stock	1.00	.40	.10
☐ 383	Bill Rigney MG	1.00	.40	.10
☐ 384	Ron Hansen	1.00	.40	.10
☐ 385	Curt Simmons	1.50	.60	.15
☐ 386	Lenny Green	1.00	.40	.10
☐ 387	Terry Fox	1.00	.40	.10
☐ 388	A's Rookies	1.00	.40	.10
	John O'Donoghue			
	George Williams			

		NRMT	VG-E	GOOD
☐ 389	Jim Umbricht	1.00	.40	.10
☐ 390	Orlando Cepeda	4.50	1.80	.45
☐ 391	Sam McDowell	2.00	.80	.20
☐ 392	Jim Pagliaroni	1.00	.40	.10
☐ 393	Casey Teaches	3.50	1.40	.35
	Casey Stengel			
	Ed Kranepool			
☐ 394	Bob Miller	1.00	.40	.10
☐ 395	Tom Tresh	2.00	.80	.20
☐ 396	Dennis Bennett	1.00	.40	.10
☐ 397	Chuck Cottier	1.00	.40	.10
☐ 398	Mets Rookies	1.00	.40	.10
	Bill Haas			
	Dick Smith			
☐ 399	Jackie Brandt	1.00	.40	.10
☐ 400	Warren Spahn	13.00	5.25	1.30
☐ 401	Charlie Maxwell	1.00	.40	.10
☐ 402	Tom Sturdivant	1.00	.40	.10
☐ 403	Reds Team	2.00	.80	.20
☐ 404	Tony Martinez	1.00	.40	.10
☐ 405	Ken McBride	1.00	.40	.10
☐ 406	Al Spangler	1.00	.40	.10
☐ 407	Bill Freehan	3.00	1.20	.30
☐ 408	Cubs Rookies	1.00	.40	.10
	Jim Stewart			
	Fred Burdette			
☐ 409	Bill Fischer	1.00	.40	.10
☐ 410	Dick Stuart	1.50	.60	.15
☐ 411	Lee Walls	1.00	.40	.10
☐ 412	Ray Culp	1.00	.40	.10
☐ 413	Johnny Keane MG	1.50	.60	.15
☐ 414	Jack Sanford	1.50	.60	.15
☐ 415	Tony Kubek	5.00	2.00	.50
☐ 416	Lee Maye	1.00	.40	.10
☐ 417	Don Cardwell	1.00	.40	.10
☐ 418	Orioles Rookies	1.50	.60	.15
	Darold Knowles			
	Les Narum			
☐ 419	Ken Harrelson	4.50	1.80	.45
☐ 420	Jim Maloney	2.00	.80	.20
☐ 421	Camilo Carreon	1.00	.40	.10
☐ 422	Jack Fisher	1.00	.40	.10
☐ 423	Tops in NL	36.00	15.00	3.60
	Hank Aaron			
	Willie Mays			
☐ 424	Dick Bertell	1.00	.40	.10
☐ 425	Norm Cash	2.00	.80	.20
☐ 426	Bob Rodgers	2.00	.80	.20
☐ 427	Don Rudolph	1.00	.40	.10

		NRMT	VG-E	GOOD
☐ 428	Red Sox Rookies ..	1.00	.40	.10
	Archie Skeen			
	Pete Smith			
☐ 429	Tim McCarver	3.50	1.40	.35
☐ 430	Juan Pizarro	1.00	.40	.10
☐ 431	George Alusik	1.00	.40	.10
☐ 432	Ruben Amaro	1.00	.40	.10
☐ 433	Yankees Team	8.00	3.25	.80
☐ 434	Don Nottebart	1.00	.40	.10
☐ 435	Vic Davalillo	1.50	.60	.15
☐ 436	Charlie Neal	1.50	.60	.15
☐ 437	Ed Bailey	1.00	.40	.10
☐ 438	Checklist 6	4.00	.40	.08
☐ 439	Harvey Haddix	1.50	.60	.15
☐ 440	Bob Clemente	45.00	18.00	4.50
☐ 441	Bob Duliba	1.00	.40	.10
☐ 442	Pumpsie Green	1.00	.40	.10
☐ 443	Chuck Dressen MG .	1.00	.40	.10
☐ 444	Larry Jackson	1.00	.40	.10
☐ 445	Bill Skowron	2.00	.80	.20
☐ 446	Julian Javier	1.50	.60	.15
☐ 447	Ted Bowsfield	1.00	.40	.10
☐ 448	Cookie Rojas	1.50	.60	.15
☐ 449	Deron Johnson	1.00	.40	.10
☐ 450	Steve Barber	1.00	.40	.10
☐ 451	Joe Amalfitano	1.00	.40	.10
☐ 452	Giants Rookies	2.00	.80	.20
	Gil Garrido			
	Jim Ray Hart			
☐ 453	Frank Baumann	1.00	.40	.10
☐ 454	Tommie Aaron	1.50	.60	.15
☐ 455	Bernie Allen	1.00	.40	.10
☐ 456	Dodgers Rookies ..	2.50	1.00	.25
	Wes Parker			
	John Werhas			
☐ 457	Jesse Gonder	1.00	.40	.10
☐ 458	Ralph Terry	1.50	.60	.15
☐ 459	Red Sox Rookies ..	1.00	.40	.10
	Pete Charton			
	Dalton Jones			
☐ 460	Bob Gibson	17.00	7.00	1.70
☐ 461	George Thomas	1.00	.40	.10
☐ 462	Birdie Tebbetts MG .	1.00	.40	.10
☐ 463	Don Leppert	1.00	.40	.10
☐ 464	Dallas Green	2.50	1.00	.25
☐ 465	Mike Hershberger ..	1.00	.40	.10
☐ 466	A's Rookies	1.50	.60	.15
	Dick Green			
	Aurelio Monteagudo			
☐ 467	Bob Aspromonte ..	1.00	.40	.10
☐ 468	Gaylord Perry	17.00	7.00	1.70
☐ 469	Cubs Rookies	1.50	.60	.15
	Fred Norman			
	Sterling Slaughter			
☐ 470	Jim Bouton	3.00	1.20	.30
☐ 471	Gates Brown	2.00	.80	.20
☐ 472	Vern Law	1.50	.60	.15
☐ 473	Baltimore Orioles ..	2.00	.80	.20
	Team Card			
☐ 474	Larry Sherry	1.50	.60	.15
☐ 475	Ed Charles	1.00	.40	.10
☐ 476	Braves Rookies ...	5.00	2.00	.50
	Rico Carty			
	Dick Kelley			
☐ 477	Mike Joyce	1.00	.40	.10
☐ 478	Dick Howser	2.00	.80	.20
☐ 479	Cardinals Rookies .	1.00	.40	.10
	Dave Bakenhaster			
	Johnny Lewis			
☐ 480	Bob Purkey	1.00	.40	.10
☐ 481	Chuck Schilling ...	1.00	.40	.10
☐ 482	Phillies Rookies ...	2.00	.80	.20
	John Briggs			
	Danny Cater			
☐ 483	Fred Valentine	1.00	.40	.10
☐ 484	Bill Pleis	1.00	.40	.10
☐ 485	Tom Haller	1.50	.60	.15
☐ 486	Bob Kennedy MG .	1.00	.40	.10
☐ 487	Mike McCormick ..	1.50	.60	.15
☐ 488	Yankees Rookies ..	1.00	.40	.10
	Pete Mikkelsen			
	Bob Meyer			
☐ 489	Julio Navarro	1.00	.40	.10
☐ 490	Ron Fairly	1.50	.60	.15
☐ 491	Ed Rakow	1.00	.40	.10
☐ 492	Colts Rookies	1.00	.40	.10
	Jim Beauchamp			
	Mike White			
☐ 493	Don Lee	1.00	.40	.10
☐ 494	Al Jackson	1.00	.40	.10
☐ 495	Bill Virdon	2.00	.80	.20
☐ 496	White Sox Team ..	2.00	.80	.20
☐ 497	Jeoff Long	1.00	.40	.10
☐ 498	Dave Stenhouse ..	1.00	.40	.10
☐ 499	Indians Rookies ...	1.00	.40	.10
	Chico Salmon			
	Gordon Seyfried			
☐ 500	Camilo Pascual ...	1.50	.60	.15

		NRMT	VG-E	GOOD
☐ 501	Bob Veale	1.50	.60	.15
☐ 502	Angels Rookies	1.50	.60	.15
	Bobby Knoop			
	Bob Lee			
☐ 503	Earl Wilson	1.00	.40	.10
☐ 504	Claude Raymond	1.00	.40	.10
☐ 505	Stan Williams	1.00	.40	.10
☐ 506	Bobby Bragan MG	1.00	.40	.10
☐ 507	Johnny Edwards	1.00	.40	.10
☐ 508	Diego Segui	1.00	.40	.10
☐ 509	Pirates Rookies	2.00	.80	.20
	Gene Alley			
	Orlando McFarlane			
☐ 510	Lindy McDaniel	1.50	.60	.15
☐ 511	Lou Jackson	1.00	.40	.10
☐ 512	Tigers Rookies	5.00	2.00	.50
	Willie Horton			
	Joe Sparma			
☐ 513	Don Larsen	2.00	.80	.20
☐ 514	Jim Hickman	1.00	.40	.10
☐ 515	Johnny Romano	1.00	.40	.10
☐ 516	Twins Rookies	1.00	.40	.10
	Jerry Arrigo			
	Dwight Siebler			
☐ 517A	Checklist 7 COR	5.00	.50	.10
	(correct numbering on back)			
☐ 517B	Checklist 7 ERR	8.00	.80	.20
	(incorrect numbering sequence on back)			
☐ 518	Carl Bouldin	1.00	.40	.10
☐ 519	Charlie Smith	1.00	.40	.10
☐ 520	Jack Baldschun	1.00	.40	.10
☐ 521	Tom Satriano	1.00	.40	.10
☐ 522	Bob Tiefenauer	1.00	.40	.10
☐ 523	Lou Burdette	6.00	2.40	.60
	(pitching lefty)			
☐ 524	Reds Rookies	3.50	1.40	.35
	Jim Dickson			
	Bobby Klaus			
☐ 525	Al McBean	3.50	1.40	.35
☐ 526	Lou Clinton	3.50	1.40	.35
☐ 527	Larry Bearnarth	3.50	1.40	.35
☐ 528	A's Rookies	4.50	1.80	.45
	Dave Duncan			
	Tommie Reynolds			
☐ 529	Alvin Dark MG	4.50	1.80	.45
☐ 530	Leon Wagner	3.50	1.40	.35
☐ 531	Los Angeles Dodgers Team Card	8.00	3.25	.80

		NRMT	VG-E	GOOD
☐ 532	Twins Rookies	3.50	1.40	.35
	Bud Bloomfield			
	(Bloomfield photo actually Jay Ward)			
	Joe Nossek			
☐ 533	Johnny Klippstein	3.50	1.40	.35
☐ 534	Gus Bell	4.50	1.80	.45
☐ 535	Phil Regan	4.50	1.80	.45
☐ 536	Mets Rookies	3.50	1.40	.35
	Larry Elliot			
	John Stephenson			
☐ 537	Dan Osinski	3.50	1.40	.35
☐ 538	Minnie Minoso	6.00	2.40	.60
☐ 539	Roy Face	4.50	1.80	.45
☐ 540	Luis Aparicio	12.50	5.00	1.25
☐ 541	Braves Rookies	80.00	32.00	8.00
	Phil Roof			
	Phil Niekro			
☐ 542	Don Mincher	4.50	1.80	.45
☐ 543	Bob Uecker	45.00	18.00	4.50
☐ 544	Colts Rookies	4.50	1.80	.45
	Steve Hertz			
	Joe Hoerner			
☐ 545	Max Alvis	3.50	1.40	.35
☐ 546	Joe Christopher	3.50	1.40	.35
☐ 547	Gil Hodges	9.00	3.75	.90
☐ 548	NL Rookies	3.50	1.40	.35
	Wayne Schurr			
	Paul Speckenbach			
☐ 549	Joe Moeller	3.50	1.40	.35
☐ 550	Ken Hubbs	8.00	3.25	.80
	(in memoriam)			
☐ 551	Billy Hoeft	3.50	1.40	.35
☐ 552	Indians Rookies	4.50	1.80	.45
	Tom Kelley			
	Sonny Siebert			
☐ 553	Jim Brewer	3.50	1.40	.35
☐ 554	Hank Foiles	3.50	1.40	.35
☐ 555	Lee Stange	3.50	1.40	.35
☐ 556	Mets Rookies	3.50	1.40	.35
	Steve Dillon			
	Ron Locke			
☐ 557	Leo Burke	3.50	1.40	.35
☐ 558	Don Schwall	3.50	1.40	.35
☐ 559	Dick Phillips	3.50	1.40	.35
☐ 560	Dick Farrell	3.50	1.40	.35
☐ 561	Phillies Rookies	4.50	1.80	.45
	Dave Bennett			
	(19 ... is 18)			
	Rick Wise			

1965 Topps

		NRMT	VG-E	GOOD
☐ 562	Pedro Ramos	3.50	1.40	.35
☐ 563	Dal Maxvill	3.50	1.40	.35
☐ 564	AL Rookies	3.50	1.40	.35
	Joe McCabe			
	Jerry McNertney			
☐ 565	Stu Miller	3.50	1.40	.35
☐ 566	Ed Kranepool	4.50	1.80	.45
☐ 567	Jim Kaat	8.00	3.25	.80
☐ 568	NL Rookies	3.50	1.40	.35
	Phil Gagliano			
	Cap Peterson			
☐ 569	Fred Newman	3.50	1.40	.35
☐ 570	Bill Mazeroski	6.00	2.40	.60
☐ 571	Gene Conley	3.50	1.40	.35
☐ 572	AL Rookies	3.50	1.40	.35
	Dave Gray			
	Dick Egan			
☐ 573	Jim Duffalo	3.50	1.40	.35
☐ 574	Manny Jimenez	3.50	1.40	.35
☐ 575	Tony Cloninger	3.50	1.40	.35
☐ 576	Mets Rookies	3.50	1.40	.35
	Jerry Hinsley			
	Bill Wakefield			
☐ 577	Gordy Coleman	3.50	1.40	.35
☐ 578	Glen Hobbie	3.50	1.40	.35
☐ 579	Red Sox Team	8.00	3.25	.80
☐ 580	Johnny Podres	5.50	2.20	.55
☐ 581	Yankees Rookies ..	3.50	1.40	.35
	Pedro Gonzalez			
	Archie Moore			
☐ 582	Rod Kanehl	3.50	1.40	.35
☐ 583	Tito Francona	4.50	1.80	.45
☐ 584	Joel Horlen	4.50	1.80	.45
☐ 585	Tony Taylor	3.50	1.40	.35
☐ 586	Jim Piersall	5.50	2.20	.55
☐ 587	Bennie Daniels	4.50	1.80	.45

*The cards in this 598-card set measure 2 ½"
by 3 ½". The cards comprising the 1965
Topps set have team names located within a
distinctive pennant design below the picture.
The cards have blue borders on the reverse
and were issued by series. Cards 523 to 598
are more difficult to obtain than all other
series. In addition, the sixth series (447-522)
is more difficult to obtain than series one
through five. Featured subsets within this set
include League Leaders (1-12) and World
Series cards (132-139). Key cards in this set
include Steve Carlton's rookie and Pete
Rose.*

		NRMT	VG-E	GOOD
	Complete Set (598)	2200.00	950.00	325.00
	Common Player (1-196) ..	.45	.18	.04
	Common Player (197-283)	.75	.30	.07
	Common Player (284-370)	.75	.30	.07
	Common Player (371-446)	.85	.34	.08
	Common Player (447-522)	1.50	.60	.15
	Common Player (523-598)	3.00	1.20	.30
☐ 1	AL Batting Leaders	7.50	1.00	.20
	Tony Oliva			
	Elston Howard			
	Brooks Robinson			
☐ 2	NL Batting Leaders	4.50	1.80	.45
	Bob Clemente			
	Hank Aaron			
	Rico Carty			

			NRMT	VG-E	GOOD
☐	3	AL Home Run Leaders	7.50	3.00	.75
		Harmon Killebrew			
		Mickey Mantle			
		Boog Powell			
☐	4	NL Home Run Leaders	4.00	1.60	.40
		Willie Mays			
		Billy Williams			
		Jim Ray Hart			
		Orlando Cepeda			
		Johnny Callison			
☐	5	AL RBI Leaders	7.50	3.00	.75
		Brooks Robinson			
		Harmon Killebrew			
		Mickey Mantle			
		Dick Stuart			
☐	6	NL RBI Leaders	2.00	.80	.20
		Ken Boyer			
		Willie Mays			
		Ron Santo			
☐	7	AL ERA Leaders	1.25	.50	.12
		Dean Chance			
		Joel Horlen			
☐	8	NL ERA Leaders	5.00	2.00	.50
		Sandy Koufax			
		Don Drysdale			
☐	9	AL Pitching Leaders	1.25	.50	.12
		Dean Chance			
		Gary Peters			
		Dave Wickersham			
		Juan Pizarro			
		Wally Bunker			
☐	10	NL Pitching Leaders	1.25	.50	.12
		Larry Jackson			
		Ray Sadecki			
		Juan Marichal			
☐	11	AL Strikeout Leaders	1.25	.50	.12
		Al Downing			
		Dean Chance			
		Camilo Pascual			
☐	12	NL Strikeout Leaders	2.00	.80	.20
		Bob Veale			
		Don Drysdale			
		Bob Gibson			
☐	13	Pedro Ramos	.45	.18	.04
☐	14	Len Gabrielson	.45	.18	.04
☐	15	Robin Roberts	6.50	2.60	.65
☐	16	Houston Rookies	40.00	16.00	4.00
		Joe Morgan			
		Sonny Jackson			
☐	17	Johnny Romano	.45	.18	.04
☐	18	Bill McCool	.45	.18	.04
☐	19	Gates Brown	.75	.30	.07
☐	20	Jim Bunning	3.50	1.40	.35
☐	21	Don Blasingame	.45	.18	.04
☐	22	Charlie Smith	.45	.18	.04
☐	23	Bob Tiefenauer	.45	.18	.04
☐	24	Minnesota Twins Team Card	2.00	.80	.20
☐	25	Al McBean	.45	.18	.04
☐	26	Bobby Knoop	.45	.18	.04
☐	27	Dick Bertell	.45	.18	.04
☐	28	Barney Schultz	.45	.18	.04
☐	29	Felix Mantilla	.45	.18	.04
☐	30	Jim Bouton	1.50	.60	.15
☐	31	Mike White	.45	.18	.04
☐	32	Herman Franks MG	.45	.18	.04
☐	33	Jackie Brandt	.45	.18	.04
☐	34	Cal Koonce	.45	.18	.04
☐	35	Ed Charles	.45	.18	.04
☐	36	Bobby Wine	.45	.18	.04
☐	37	Fred Gladding	.45	.18	.04
☐	38	Jim King	.45	.18	.04
☐	39	Gerry Arrigo	.45	.18	.04
☐	40	Frank Howard	1.25	.50	.12
☐	41	White Sox Rookies	.45	.18	.04
		Bruce Howard			
		Marv Staehle			
☐	42	Earl Wilson	.45	.18	.04
☐	43	Mike Shannon	1.00	.40	.10
☐	44	Wade Blasingame	.45	.18	.04
☐	45	Roy McMillan	.45	.18	.04
☐	46	Bob Lee	.45	.18	.04
☐	47	Tommy Harper	.75	.30	.07
☐	48	Claude Raymond	.45	.18	.04
☐	49	Orioles Rookies	1.00	.40	.10
		Curt Blefary			
		John Miller			
☐	50	Juan Marichal	7.50	3.00	.75
☐	51	Bill Bryan	.45	.18	.04
☐	52	Ed Roebuck	.45	.18	.04
☐	53	Dick McAuliffe	.75	.30	.07
☐	54	Joe Gibbon	.45	.18	.04
☐	55	Tony Conigliaro	3.00	1.20	.30
☐	56	Ron Kline	.45	.18	.04
☐	57	Cardinals Team	1.25	.50	.12
☐	58	Fred Talbot	.45	.18	.04
☐	59	Nate Oliver	.45	.18	.04
☐	60	Jim O'Toole	.45	.18	.04

			NRMT	VG-E	GOOD
☐	61	Chris Cannizzaro ..	.45	.18	.04
☐	62	Jim Katt (sic, Kaat) .	4.00	1.60	.40
☐	63	Ty Cline	.45	.18	.04
☐	64	Lou Burdette	1.00	.40	.10
☐	65	Tony Kubek	3.00	1.20	.30
☐	66	Bill Rigney MG	.45	.18	.04
☐	67	Harvey Haddix	.75	.30	.07
☐	68	Del Crandall	.75	.30	.07
☐	69	Bill Virdon	1.00	.40	.10
☐	70	Bill Skowron	1.25	.50	.12
☐	71	John O'Donoghue ..	.45	.18	.04
☐	72	Tony Gonzalez	.45	.18	.04
☐	73	Dennis Ribant	.45	.18	.04
☐	74	Red Sox Rookies ..	3.00	1.20	.30
		Rico Petrocelli			
		Jerry Stephenson			
☐	75	Deron Johnson	.75	.30	.07
☐	76	Sam McDowell	.75	.30	.07
☐	77	Doug Camilli	.45	.18	.04
☐	78	Dal Maxvill	.75	.30	.07
☐	79	Checklist 1	3.00	.30	.06
☐	80	Turk Farrell	.45	.18	.04
☐	81	Don Buford	.75	.30	.07
☐	82	Braves Rookies	1.00	.40	.10
		Santos Alomar			
		John Braun			
☐	83	George Thomas ...	.45	.18	.04
☐	84	Ron Herbel	.45	.18	.04
☐	85	Willie Smith	.45	.18	.04
☐	86	Les Narum	.45	.18	.04
☐	87	Nelson Mathews ...	.45	.18	.04
☐	88	Jack Lamabe	.45	.18	.04
☐	89	Mike Hershberger ..	.45	.18	.04
☐	90	Rich Rollins	.75	.30	.07
☐	91	Cubs Team	1.25	.50	.12
☐	92	Dick Howser	1.25	.50	.12
☐	93	Jack Fisher	.45	.18	.04
☐	94	Charlie Lau	.75	.30	.07
☐	95	Bill Mazeroski	1.50	.60	.15
☐	96	Sonny Siebert	.75	.30	.07
☐	97	Pedro Gonzalez ...	.45	.18	.04
☐	98	Bob Miller	.45	.18	.04
☐	99	Gil Hodges MG	5.00	2.00	.50
☐	100	Ken Boyer	2.00	.80	.20
☐	101	Fred Newman	.45	.18	.04
☐	102	Steve Boros	.75	.30	.07
☐	103	Harvey Kuenn	1.00	.40	.10
☐	104	Checklist 2	3.00	.30	.06
☐	105	Chico Salmon	.45	.18	.04

			NRMT	VG-E	GOOD
☐	106	Gene Oliver	.45	.18	.04
☐	107	Phillies Rookies ...	1.75	.70	.17
		Pat Corrales			
		Costen Shockley			
☐	108	Don Mincher	.75	.30	.07
☐	109	Walt Bond	.45	.18	.04
☐	110	Ron Santo	1.25	.50	.12
☐	111	Lee Thomas	1.00	.40	.10
☐	112	Derrell Griffith	.45	.18	.04
☐	113	Steve Barber	.45	.18	.04
☐	114	Jim Hickman	.45	.18	.04
☐	115	Bobby Richardson .	2.50	1.00	.25
☐	116	Cardinals Rookies .	1.00	.40	.10
		Dave Dowling			
		Bob Tolan			
☐	117	Wes Stock	.45	.18	.04
☐	118	Hal Lanier	1.50	.60	.15
☐	119	John Kennedy	.45	.18	.04
☐	120	Frank Robinson ...	10.00	4.00	1.00
☐	121	Gene Alley	.75	.30	.07
☐	122	Bill Pleis	.45	.18	.04
☐	123	Frank Thomas	.75	.30	.07
☐	124	Tom Satriano	.45	.18	.04
☐	125	Juan Pizarro	.45	.18	.04
☐	126	Dodgers Team	3.50	1.40	.35
☐	127	Frank Lary	.75	.30	.07
☐	128	Vic Davalillo	.75	.30	.07
☐	129	Bennie Daniels ...	.45	.18	.04
☐	130	Al Kaline	13.00	5.25	1.30
☐	131	Johnny Keane MG .	.75	.30	.07
☐	132	World Series Game 1	1.75	.70	.17
		Cards take opener			
☐	133	World Series Game 2	1.75	.70	.17
		Stottlemyre wins			
☐	134	World Series Game 3	20.00	8.00	2.00
		Mantle's homer			
☐	135	World Series Game 4	2.50	1.00	.25
		Boyer's grand-slam			
☐	136	World Series Game 5	1.75	.70	.17
		10th inning triumph			
☐	137	World Series Game 6	2.50	1.00	.25
		Bouton wins again			
☐	138	World Series Game 7	3.50	1.40	.35
		Gibson wins finale			
☐	139	World Series Summary	1.75	.70	.17
		Cards celebrate			
☐	140	Dean Chance	.75	.30	.07
☐	141	Charlie James ...	.45	.18	.04
☐	142	Bill Monbouquette .	.45	.18	.04

		NRMT	VG-E	GOOD
☐ 143	Pirates Rookies	.45	.18	.04
	John Gelnar			
	Jerry May			
☐ 144	Ed Kranepool	1.00	.40	.10
☐ 145	Luis Tiant	7.50	3.00	.75
☐ 146	Ron Hansen	.45	.18	.04
☐ 147	Dennis Bennett ...	.45	.18	.04
☐ 148	Willie Kirkland	.45	.18	.04
☐ 149	Wayne Schurr	.45	.18	.04
☐ 150	Brooks Robinson ..	14.00	5.75	1.40
☐ 151	Athletics Team	1.00	.40	.10
☐ 152	Phil Ortega	.45	.18	.04
☐ 153	Norm Cash	1.50	.60	.15
☐ 154	Bob Humphreys ...	.45	.18	.04
☐ 155	Roger Maris	32.00	13.00	3.20
☐ 156	Bob Sadowski	.45	.18	.04
☐ 157	Zoilo Versalles	.75	.30	.07
☐ 158	Dick Sisler	.45	.18	.04
☐ 159	Jim Duffalo	.45	.18	.04
☐ 160	Bob Clemente	30.00	12.00	3.00
☐ 161	Frank Baumann ...	.45	.18	.04
☐ 162	Russ Nixon	1.00	.40	.10
☐ 163	Johnny Briggs	.45	.18	.04
☐ 164	Al Spangler	.45	.18	.04
☐ 165	Dick Ellsworth	.75	.30	.07
☐ 166	Indians Rookies ...	1.00	.40	.10
	George Culver			
	Tommie Agee			
☐ 167	Bill Wakefield	.45	.18	.04
☐ 168	Dick Green	.45	.18	.04
☐ 169	Dave Vineyard	.45	.18	.04
☐ 170	Hank Aaron	42.00	18.00	4.00
☐ 171	Jim Roland	.45	.18	.04
☐ 172	Jim Piersall	1.00	.40	.10
☐ 173	Detroit Tigers	1.50	.60	.15
	Team Card			
☐ 174	Joey Jay	.45	.18	.04
☐ 175	Bob Aspromonte ...	.45	.18	.04
☐ 176	Willie McCovey	9.00	3.75	.90
☐ 177	Pete Mikkelsen ...	.45	.18	.04
☐ 178	Dalton Jones	.45	.18	.04
☐ 179	Hal Woodeshick ...	.45	.18	.04
☐ 180	Bob Allison	.75	.30	.07
☐ 181	Senators Rookies ..	.45	.18	.04
	Don Loun			
	Joe McCabe			
☐ 182	Mike De La Hoz ...	.45	.18	.04
☐ 183	Dave Nicholson	.45	.18	.04
☐ 184	John Boozer	.45	.18	.04

		NRMT	VG-E	GOOD
☐ 185	Max Alvis	.45	.18	.04
☐ 186	Billy Cowan	.45	.18	.04
☐ 187	Casey Stengel MG	8.00	3.25	.80
☐ 188	Sam Bowens	.45	.18	.04
☐ 189	Checklist 3	3.00	.30	.06
☐ 190	Bill White	1.00	.40	.10
☐ 191	Phil Regan	.75	.30	.07
☐ 192	Jim Coker	.45	.18	.04
☐ 193	Gaylord Perry	8.00	3.25	.80
☐ 194	Rookie Stars	.75	.30	.07
	Bill Kelso			
	Rick Reichardt			
☐ 195	Bob Veale	.75	.30	.07
☐ 196	Ron Fairly	.75	.30	.07
☐ 197	Diego Segui	.75	.30	.07
☐ 198	Smoky Burgess ...	1.00	.40	.10
☐ 199	Bob Heffner	.75	.30	.07
☐ 200	Joe Torre	1.75	.70	.17
☐ 201	Twins Rookies	1.00	.40	.10
	Sandy Valdespino			
	Cesar Tovar			
☐ 202	Leo Burke	.75	.30	.07
☐ 203	Dallas Green	2.00	.80	.20
☐ 204	Russ Snyder	.75	.30	.07
☐ 205	Warren Spahn	10.00	4.00	1.00
☐ 206	Willie Horton	1.50	.60	.15
☐ 207	Pete Rose	150.00	60.00	15.00
☐ 208	Tommy John	7.50	3.00	.75
☐ 209	Pirates Team	1.50	.60	.15
☐ 210	Jim Fregosi	1.50	.60	.15
☐ 211	Steve Ridzik	.75	.30	.07
☐ 212	Ron Brand	.75	.30	.07
☐ 213	Jim Davenport	1.00	.40	.10
☐ 214	Bob Purkey	.75	.30	.07
☐ 215	Pete Ward	.75	.30	.07
☐ 216	Al Worthington ...	.75	.30	.07
☐ 217	Walt Alston MG ...	2.50	1.00	.25
☐ 218	Dick Schofield ...	.75	.30	.07
☐ 219	Bob Meyer	.75	.30	.07
☐ 220	Billy Williams	7.50	3.00	.75
☐ 221	John Tsitouris	.75	.30	.07
☐ 222	Bob Tillman	.75	.30	.07
☐ 223	Dan Osinski	.75	.30	.07
☐ 224	Bob Chance	.75	.30	.07
☐ 225	Bo Belinsky	1.00	.40	.10
☐ 226	Yankees Rookies ..	1.00	.40	.10
	Elvio Jimenez			
	Jake Gibbs			
☐ 227	Bobby Klaus	.75	.30	.07

		NRMT	VG-E	GOOD			NRMT	VG-E	GOOD
☐ 228	Jack Sanford	1.00	.40	.10	☐ 273	Checklist 4	3.00	.30	.06
☐ 229	Lou Clinton	.75	.30	.07	☐ 274	Lum Harris MG	.75	.30	.07
☐ 230	Ray Sadecki	.75	.30	.07	☐ 275	Dick Groat	1.50	.60	.15
☐ 231	Jerry Adair	.75	.30	.07	☐ 276	Hoyt Wilhelm	6.50	2.60	.65
☐ 232	Steve Blass	1.50	.60	.15	☐ 277	Johnny Lewis	.75	.30	.07
☐ 233	Don Zimmer	1.50	.60	.15	☐ 278	Ken Retzer	.75	.30	.07
☐ 234	White Sox Team	1.50	.60	.15	☐ 279	Dick Tracewski	.75	.30	.07
☐ 235	Chuck Hinton	.75	.30	.07	☐ 280	Dick Stuart	1.00	.40	.10
☐ 236	Denny McLain	9.00	3.75	.90	☐ 281	Bill Stafford	.75	.30	.07
☐ 237	Bernie Allen	.75	.30	.07	☐ 282	Giants Rookies	1.00	.40	.10
☐ 238	Joe Moeller	.75	.30	.07		Dick Estelle			
☐ 239	Doc Edwards	1.50	.60	.15		Masanori Murakami			
☐ 240	Bob Bruce	.75	.30	.07	☐ 283	Fred Whitfield	.75	.30	.07
☐ 241	Mack Jones	.75	.30	.07	☐ 284	Nick Willhite	.75	.30	.07
☐ 242	George Brunet	.75	.30	.07	☐ 285	Ron Hunt	.75	.30	.07
☐ 243	Reds Rookies	1.50	.60	.15	☐ 286	Athletics Rookies	.75	.30	.07
	Ted Davidson					Jim Dickson			
	Tommy Helms					Aurelio Monteagudo			
☐ 244	Lindy McDaniel	1.00	.40	.10	☐ 287	Gary Kolb	.75	.30	.07
☐ 245	Joe Pepitone	1.50	.60	.15	☐ 288	Jack Hamilton	.75	.30	.07
☐ 246	Tom Butters	.75	.30	.07	☐ 289	Gordy Coleman	1.00	.40	.10
☐ 247	Wally Moon	1.00	.40	.10	☐ 290	Wally Bunker	1.00	.40	.10
☐ 248	Gus Triandos	1.00	.40	.10	☐ 291	Jerry Lynch	.75	.30	.07
☐ 249	Dave McNally	1.50	.60	.15	☐ 292	Larry Yellen	.75	.30	.07
☐ 250	Willie Mays	60.00	24.00	6.00	☐ 293	Angels Team	1.50	.60	.15
☐ 251	Billy Herman MG	2.00	.80	.20	☐ 294	Tim McCarver	2.50	1.00	.25
☐ 252	Pete Richert	.75	.30	.07	☐ 295	Dick Radatz	1.00	.40	.10
☐ 253	Danny Cater	1.00	.40	.10	☐ 296	Tony Taylor	.75	.30	.07
☐ 254	Roland Sheldon	.75	.30	.07	☐ 297	Dave Debusschere	2.50	1.00	.25
☐ 255	Camilo Pascual	1.00	.40	.10	☐ 298	Jim Stewart	.75	.30	.07
☐ 256	Tito Francona	1.00	.40	.10	☐ 299	Jerry Zimmerman	.75	.30	.07
☐ 257	Jim Wynn	1.50	.60	.15	☐ 300	Sandy Koufax	50.00	20.00	5.00
☐ 258	Larry Bearnarth	.75	.30	.07	☐ 301	Birdie Tebbetts MG	.75	.30	.07
☐ 259	Tigers Rookies	1.50	.60	.15	☐ 302	Al Stanek	.75	.30	.07
	Jim Northrup				☐ 303	John Orsino	.75	.30	.07
	Ray Oyler				☐ 304	Dave Stenhouse	.75	.30	.07
☐ 260	Don Drysdale	8.50	3.50	.85	☐ 305	Rico Carty	1.25	.50	.12
☐ 261	Duke Carmel	.75	.30	.07	☐ 306	Bubba Phillips	.75	.30	.07
☐ 262	Bud Daley	.75	.30	.07	☐ 307	Barry Latman	.75	.30	.07
☐ 263	Marty Keough	.75	.30	.07	☐ 308	Mets Rookies	1.00	.40	.10
☐ 264	Bob Buhl	.75	.30	.07		Cleon Jones			
☐ 265	Jim Pagliaroni	.75	.30	.07		Tom Parsons			
☐ 266	Bert Campaneris	3.00	1.20	.30	☐ 309	Steve Hamilton	.75	.30	.07
☐ 267	Senators Team	1.50	.60	.15	☐ 310	Johnny Callison	1.00	.40	.10
☐ 268	Ken McBride	.75	.30	.07	☐ 311	Orlando Pena	.75	.30	.07
☐ 269	Frank Bolling	.75	.30	.07	☐ 312	Joe Nuxhall	1.00	.40	.10
☐ 270	Milt Pappas	1.00	.40	.10	☐ 313	Jim Schaffer	.75	.30	.07
☐ 271	Don Wert	.75	.30	.07	☐ 314	Sterling Slaughter	.75	.30	.07
☐ 272	Chuck Schilling	.75	.30	.07	☐ 315	Frank Malzone	1.00	.40	.10

		NRMT	VG-E	GOOD
☐ 316	Reds Team	1.50	.60	.15
☐ 317	Don McMahon	.75	.30	.07
☐ 318	Matty Alou	1.25	.50	.12
☐ 319	Ken McMullen	.75	.30	.07
☐ 320	Bob Gibson	12.00	5.00	1.20
☐ 321	Rusty Staub	3.00	1.20	.30
☐ 322	Rick Wise	1.00	.40	.10
☐ 323	Hank Bauer MG	1.00	.40	.10
☐ 324	Bobby Locke	.75	.30	.07
☐ 325	Donn Clendenon	1.00	.40	.10
☐ 326	Dwight Siebler	.75	.30	.07
☐ 327	Denis Menke	.75	.30	.07
☐ 328	Eddie Fisher	.75	.30	.07
☐ 329	Hawk Taylor	.75	.30	.07
☐ 330	Whitey Ford	12.00	5.00	1.20
☐ 331	Dodgers Rookies	1.00	.40	.10
	Al Ferrara			
	John Purdin			
☐ 332	Ted Abernathy	.75	.30	.07
☐ 333	Tom Reynolds	.75	.30	.07
☐ 334	Vic Roznovsky	.75	.30	.07
☐ 335	Mickey Lolich	2.50	1.00	.25
☐ 336	Woody Held	.75	.30	.07
☐ 337	Mike Cuellar	1.50	.60	.15
☐ 338	Philadelphia Phillies	1.50	.60	.15
	Team Card			
☐ 339	Ryne Duren	1.00	.40	.10
☐ 340	Tony Oliva	4.00	1.60	.40
☐ 341	Bob Bolin	.75	.30	.07
☐ 342	Bob Rodgers	1.50	.60	.15
☐ 343	Mike McCormick	1.00	.40	.10
☐ 344	Wes Parker	1.25	.50	.12
☐ 345	Floyd Robinson	.75	.30	.07
☐ 346	Bobby Bragan MG	.75	.30	.07
☐ 347	Roy Face	1.50	.60	.15
☐ 348	George Banks	.75	.30	.07
☐ 349	Larry Miller	.75	.30	.07
☐ 350	Mickey Mantle	375.00	150.00	37.00
☐ 351	Jim Perry	1.00	.40	.10
☐ 352	Alex Johnson	1.00	.40	.10
☐ 353	Jerry Lumpe	.75	.30	.07
☐ 354	Cubs Rookies	.75	.30	.07
	Billy Ott			
	Jack Warner			
☐ 355	Vada Pinson	1.50	.60	.15
☐ 356	Bill Spanswick	.75	.30	.07
☐ 357	Carl Warwick	.75	.30	.07
☐ 358	Albie Pearson	.75	.30	.07
☐ 359	Ken Johnson	.75	.30	.07
☐ 360	Orlando Cepeda	4.00	1.60	.40
☐ 361	Checklist 5	3.00	.30	.06
☐ 362	Don Schwall	.75	.30	.07
☐ 363	Bob Johnson	.75	.30	.07
☐ 364	Galen Cisco	.75	.30	.07
☐ 365	Jim Gentile	1.00	.40	.10
☐ 366	Dan Schneider	.75	.30	.07
☐ 367	Leon Wagner	.75	.30	.07
☐ 368	White Sox Rookies	1.00	.40	.10
	Ken Berry			
	Joel Gibson			
☐ 369	Phil Linz	1.00	.40	.10
☐ 370	Tommy Davis	1.50	.60	.15
☐ 371	Frank Kreutzer	.85	.34	.08
☐ 372	Clay Dalrymple	.85	.34	.08
☐ 373	Curt Simmons	1.00	.40	.10
☐ 374	Angels Rookies	1.00	.40	.10
	Jose Cardenal			
	Dick Simpson			
☐ 375	Dave Wickersham	.85	.34	.08
☐ 376	Jim Landis	.85	.34	.08
☐ 377	Willie Stargell	20.00	8.00	2.00
☐ 378	Chuck Estrada	1.00	.40	.10
☐ 379	Giants Team	1.75	.70	.17
☐ 380	Rocky Colavito	2.00	.80	.20
☐ 381	Al Jackson	.85	.34	.08
☐ 382	J.C. Martin	.85	.34	.08
☐ 383	Felipe Alou	1.00	.40	.10
☐ 384	Johnny Klippstein	.85	.34	.08
☐ 385	Carl Yastrzemski	55.00	22.00	5.50
☐ 386	Cubs Rookies	1.00	.40	.10
	Paul Jaeckel			
	Fred Norman			
☐ 387	Johnny Podres	1.50	.60	.15
☐ 388	John Blanchard	1.00	.40	.10
☐ 389	Don Larsen	1.50	.60	.15
☐ 390	Bill Freehan	2.25	.90	.22
☐ 391	Mel McGaha MG	.85	.34	.08
☐ 392	Bob Friend	1.00	.40	.10
☐ 393	Ed Kirkpatrick	.85	.34	.08
☐ 394	Jim Hannan	.85	.34	.08
☐ 395	Jim Ray Hart	1.00	.40	.10
☐ 396	Frank Bertaina	.85	.34	.08
☐ 397	Jerry Buchek	.85	.34	.08
☐ 398	Reds Rookies	1.00	.40	.10
	Dan Neville			
	Art Shamsky			
☐ 399	Ray Herbert	.85	.34	.08
☐ 400	Harmon Killebrew	10.00	4.00	1.00

		NRMT	VG-E	GOOD
☐ 401	Carl Willey	.85	.34	.08
☐ 402	Joe Amalfitano	.85	.34	.08
☐ 403	Boston Red Sox Team Card	1.75	.70	.17
☐ 404	Stan Williams	1.00	.40	.10
☐ 405	John Roseboro	1.00	.40	.10
☐ 406	Ralph Terry	1.25	.50	.12
☐ 407	Lee Maye	.85	.34	.08
☐ 408	Larry Sherry	1.00	.40	.10
☐ 409	Astros Rookies Jim Beauchamp Larry Dierker	1.25	.50	.12
☐ 410	Luis Aparicio	7.00	2.80	.70
☐ 411	Roger Craig	2.00	.80	.20
☐ 412	Bob Bailey	.85	.34	.08
☐ 413	Hal Reniff	.85	.34	.08
☐ 414	Al Lopez MG	2.50	1.00	.25
☐ 415	Curt Flood	1.75	.70	.17
☐ 416	Jim Brewer	.85	.34	.08
☐ 417	Ed Brinkman	.85	.34	.08
☐ 418	Johnny Edwards	.85	.34	.08
☐ 419	Ruben Amaro	.85	.34	.08
☐ 420	Larry Jackson	.85	.34	.08
☐ 421	Twins Rookies Gary Dotter Jay Ward	.85	.34	.08
☐ 422	Aubrey Gatewood	.85	.34	.08
☐ 423	Jesse Gonder	.85	.34	.08
☐ 424	Gary Bell	.85	.34	.08
☐ 425	Wayne Causey	.85	.34	.08
☐ 426	Braves Team	1.75	.70	.17
☐ 427	Bob Saverine	.85	.34	.08
☐ 428	Bob Shaw	.85	.34	.08
☐ 429	Don Demeter	.85	.34	.08
☐ 430	Gary Peters	1.00	.40	.10
☐ 431	Cards Rookies Nelson Briles Wayne Spiezio	1.50	.60	.15
☐ 432	Jim Grant	.85	.34	.08
☐ 433	John Bateman	.85	.34	.08
☐ 434	Dave Morehead	.85	.34	.08
☐ 435	Willie Davis	1.25	.50	.12
☐ 436	Don Elston	.85	.34	.08
☐ 437	Chico Cardenas	.85	.34	.08
☐ 438	Harry Walker MG	1.00	.40	.10
☐ 439	Moe Drabowsky	.85	.34	.08
☐ 440	Tom Tresh	1.50	.60	.15
☐ 441	Denny Lemaster	.85	.34	.08
☐ 442	Vic Power	.85	.34	.08
☐ 443	Checklist 6	3.50	.40	.07
☐ 444	Bob Hendley	.85	.34	.08
☐ 445	Don Lock	.85	.34	.08
☐ 446	Art Mahaffey	.85	.34	.08
☐ 447	Julian Javier	2.00	.80	.20
☐ 448	Lee Stange	1.50	.60	.15
☐ 449	Mets Rookies Jerry Hinsley Gary Kroll	1.50	.60	.15
☐ 450	Elston Howard	3.50	1.40	.35
☐ 451	Jim Owens	1.50	.60	.15
☐ 452	Gary Geiger	1.50	.60	.15
☐ 453	Dodgers Rookies Willie Crawford John Werhas	2.00	.80	.20
☐ 454	Ed Rakow	1.50	.60	.15
☐ 455	Norm Siebern	1.50	.60	.15
☐ 456	Bill Henry	1.50	.60	.15
☐ 457	Bob Kennedy MG	1.50	.60	.15
☐ 458	John Buzhardt	1.50	.60	.15
☐ 459	Frank Kostro	1.50	.60	.15
☐ 460	Richie Allen	4.00	1.60	.40
☐ 461	Braves Rookies Clay Carroll Phil Niekro	25.00	10.00	2.50
☐ 462	Lew Krausse (photo actually Pete Lovrich)	1.50	.60	.15
☐ 463	Manny Mota	2.00	.80	.20
☐ 464	Ron Piche	1.50	.60	.15
☐ 465	Tom Haller	2.00	.80	.20
☐ 466	Senators Rookies Pete Craig Dick Nen	1.50	.60	.15
☐ 467	Ray Washburn	1.50	.60	.15
☐ 468	Larry Brown	1.50	.60	.15
☐ 469	Don Nottebart	1.50	.60	.15
☐ 470	Yogi Berra MG	30.00	12.00	3.00
☐ 471	Billy Hoeft	1.50	.60	.15
☐ 472	Don Pavletich	1.50	.60	.15
☐ 473	Orioles Rookies Paul Blair Dave Johnson	8.00	3.25	.80
☐ 474	Cookie Rojas	2.00	.80	.20
☐ 475	Clete Boyer	2.50	1.00	.25
☐ 476	Billy O'Dell	1.50	.60	.15
☐ 477	Cards Rookies Fritz Ackley Steve Carlton	150.00	60.00	15.00
☐ 478	Wilbur Wood	2.00	.80	.20

		NRMT	VG-E	GOOD
☐ 479	Ken Harrelson	3.00	1.20	.30
☐ 480	Joel Horlen	1.50	.60	.15
☐ 481	Cleveland Indians Team Card	3.00	1.20	.30
☐ 482	Bob Priddy	1.50	.60	.15
☐ 483	George Smith	1.50	.60	.15
☐ 484	Ron Perranoski	2.00	.80	.20
☐ 485	Nellie Fox	4.00	1.60	.40
☐ 486	Angels Rookies Tom Egan Pat Rogan	1.50	.60	.15
☐ 487	Woody Woodward	2.00	.80	.20
☐ 488	Ted Wills	1.50	.60	.15
☐ 489	Gene Mauch MG	2.00	.80	.20
☐ 490	Earl Battey	1.50	.60	.15
☐ 491	Tracy Stallard	1.50	.60	.15
☐ 492	Gene Freese	1.50	.60	.15
☐ 493	Tigers Rookies Bill Roman Bruce Brubaker	1.50	.60	.15
☐ 494	Jay Ritchie	1.50	.60	.15
☐ 495	Joe Christopher	1.50	.60	.15
☐ 496	Joe Cunningham	2.00	.80	.20
☐ 497	Giants Rookies Ken Henderson Jack Hiatt	2.00	.80	.20
☐ 498	Gene Stephens	1.50	.60	.15
☐ 499	Stu Miller	1.50	.60	.15
☐ 500	Eddie Mathews	16.00	6.50	1.60
☐ 501	Indians Rookies Ralph Gagliano Jim Rittwage	1.50	.60	.15
☐ 502	Don Cardwell	1.50	.60	.15
☐ 503	Phil Gagliano	1.50	.60	.15
☐ 504	Jerry Grote	1.50	.60	.15
☐ 505	Ray Culp	1.50	.60	.15
☐ 506	Sam Mele MG	1.50	.60	.15
☐ 507	Sammy Ellis	1.50	.60	.15
☐ 508	Checklist 7	5.00	.50	.10
☐ 509	Red Sox Rookies Bob Guindon Gerry Vezendy	1.50	.60	.15
☐ 510	Ernie Banks	27.00	11.00	2.70
☐ 511	Ron Locke	1.50	.60	.15
☐ 512	Cap Peterson	1.50	.60	.15
☐ 513	New York Yankees Team Card	7.50	3.00	.75
☐ 514	Joe Azcue	1.50	.60	.15
☐ 515	Vern Law	2.00	.80	.20

		NRMT	VG-E	GOOD
☐ 516	Al Weis	1.50	.60	.15
☐ 517	Angels Rookies Paul Schaal Jack Warner	1.50	.60	.15
☐ 518	Ken Rowe	1.50	.60	.15
☐ 519	Bob Uecker	40.00	16.00	4.00
☐ 520	Tony Cloninger	1.50	.60	.15
☐ 521	Phillies Rookies Dave Bennett Morrie Stevens	1.50	.60	.15
☐ 522	Hank Aguirre	1.50	.60	.15
☐ 523	Mike Brumley	3.00	1.20	.30
☐ 524	Dave Giusti	3.00	1.20	.30
☐ 525	Eddie Bressoud	3.00	1.20	.30
☐ 526	Athletics Rookies Rene Lachemann Johnny Odom Jim Hunter ERR ("Tim" on back) Skip Lockwood	60.00	24.00	6.00
☐ 527	Jeff Torborg	4.00	1.60	.40
☐ 528	George Altman	3.00	1.20	.30
☐ 529	Jerry Fosnow	3.00	1.20	.30
☐ 530	Jim Maloney	4.00	1.60	.40
☐ 531	Chuck Hiller	3.00	1.20	.30
☐ 532	Hector Lopez	3.00	1.20	.30
☐ 533	Mets Rookies Dan Napoleon Ron Swoboda Tug McGraw Jim Bethke	13.50	6.00	1.25
☐ 534	John Herrnstein	3.00	1.20	.30
☐ 535	Jack Kralick	3.00	1.20	.30
☐ 536	Andre Rodgers	3.00	1.20	.30
☐ 537	Angels Rookies Marcelino Lopes Phil Roof Rudy May	4.00	1.60	.40
☐ 538	Chuck Dressen MG	3.00	1.20	.30
☐ 539	Herm Starrette	3.00	1.20	.30
☐ 540	Lou Brock	30.00	12.00	3.00
☐ 541	White Sox Rookies Greg Bollo Bob Locker	3.00	1.20	.30
☐ 542	Lou Klimchock	3.00	1.20	.30
☐ 543	Ed Connolly	3.00	1.20	.30
☐ 544	Howie Reed	3.00	1.20	.30
☐ 545	Jesus Alou	3.00	1.20	.30

	NRMT	VG-E	GOOD
☐ 546 Indians Rookies ...	3.00	1.20	.30
Bill Davis			
Mike Hedlund			
Ray Barker			
Floyd Weaver			
☐ 547 Jake Wood	3.00	1.20	.30
☐ 548 Dick Stigman	3.00	1.20	.30
☐ 549 Cubs Rookies	5.00	2.00	.50
Roberto Pena			
Glenn Beckert			
☐ 550 Mel Stottlemyre	12.00	5.00	1.20
☐ 551 New York Mets	8.00	3.25	.80
Team Card			
☐ 552 Julio Gotay	3.00	1.20	.30
☐ 553 Astros Rookies	3.00	1.20	.30
Dan Coombs			
Gene Ratliff			
Jack McClure			
☐ 554 Chico Ruiz	3.00	1.20	.30
☐ 555 Jack Baldschun	3.00	1.20	.30
☐ 556 Red Schoendienst MG	5.00	2.00	.50
☐ 557 Jose Santiago	3.00	1.20	.30
☐ 558 Tommie Sisk	3.00	1.20	.30
☐ 559 Ed Bailey	3.00	1.20	.30
☐ 560 Boog Powell	5.00	2.00	.50
☐ 561 Dodgers Rookies ..	6.50	2.60	.65
Dennis Daboll			
Mike Kekich			
Hector Valle			
Jim Lefebvre			
☐ 562 Billy Moran	3.00	1.20	.30
☐ 563 Julio Navarro	3.00	1.20	.30
☐ 564 Mel Nelson	3.00	1.20	.30
☐ 565 Ernie Broglio	3.00	1.20	.30
☐ 566 Yankees Rookies ..	3.00	1.20	.30
Gil Blanco			
Ross Moschitto			
Art Lopez			
☐ 567 Tommie Aaron	4.00	1.60	.40
☐ 568 Ron Taylor	3.00	1.20	.30
☐ 569 Gino Cimoli	3.00	1.20	.30
☐ 570 Claude Osteen	4.00	1.60	.40
☐ 571 Ossie Virgil	3.00	1.20	.30
☐ 572 Baltimore Orioles ..	6.00	2.40	.60
Team Card			
☐ 573 Red Sox Rookies .	6.00	2.40	.60
Jim Lonborg			
Gerry Moses			
Bill Schlesinger			
Mike Ryan			
☐ 574 Roy Sievers	4.00	1.60	.40
☐ 575 Jose Pagan	3.00	1.20	.30
☐ 576 Terry Fox	3.00	1.20	.30
☐ 577 AL Rookie Stars ..	3.00	1.20	.30
Darold Knowles			
Don Buschhorn			
Richie Scheinblum			
☐ 578 Camilo Carreon ...	3.00	1.20	.30
☐ 579 Dick Smith	3.00	1.20	.30
☐ 580 Jimmie Hall	4.00	1.60	.40
☐ 581 NL Rookie Stars ..	45.00	18.00	4.50
Tony Perez			
Dave Ricketts			
Kevin Collins			
☐ 582 Bob Schmidt	3.00	1.20	.30
☐ 583 Wes Covington ...	3.00	1.20	.30
☐ 584 Harry Bright	3.00	1.20	.30
☐ 585 Hank Fischer	3.00	1.20	.30
☐ 586 Tom McCraw	3.00	1.20	.30
☐ 587 Joe Sparma	3.00	1.20	.30
☐ 588 Lenny Green	3.00	1.20	.30
☐ 589 Giants Rookies ...	3.00	1.20	.30
Frank Linzy			
Bob Schroder			
☐ 590 John Wyatt	3.00	1.20	.30
☐ 591 Bob Skinner	3.00	1.20	.30
☐ 592 Frank Bork	3.00	1.20	.30
☐ 593 Tigers Rookies ...	3.00	1.20	.30
Jackie Moore			
John Sullivan			
☐ 594 Joe Gaines	3.00	1.20	.30
☐ 595 Don Lee	3.00	1.20	.30
☐ 596 Don Landrum	3.00	1.20	.30
☐ 597 Twins Rookies ...	3.00	1.20	.30
Joe Nossek			
John Sevcik			
Dick Reese			
☐ 598 Al Downing	4.50	1.50	.30

1966 Topps

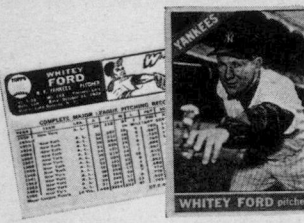

*The cards in this 598-card set measure 2 ½"
by 3 ½". There are the same number of
cards as in the 1965 set. Once again, the
seventh series cards (523 to 598) are considered more difficult to obtain than any
other series cards in the set. The only featured subset within this set is League
Leaders (215-226). Noteworthy rookie cards
in the set include Jim Palmer (126) and Don
Sutton (288). Palmer is described in the bio
(on his card back) as a lefthander.*

	NRMT	VG-E	GOOD
Complete Set (598)	2900.00	1250.00	400.00
Common Player (1-110)	.40	.16	.04
Common Player (111-370)	.60	.24	.06
Common Player (371-446)	.85	.34	.08
Common Player (447-522)	2.50	1.00	.25
Common Player (523-598)	12.00	5.00	1.20

			NRMT	VG-E	GOOD
☐	1	Willie Mays	100.00	25.00	5.00
☐	2	Ted Abernathy	.40	.16	.04
☐	3	Sam Mele MG	.40	.16	.04
☐	4	Ray Culp	.40	.16	.04
☐	5	Jim Fregosi	1.00	.40	.10
☐	6	Chuck Schilling	.40	.16	.04
☐	7	Tracy Stallard	.40	.16	.04
☐	8	Floyd Robinson	.40	.16	.04
☐	9	Clete Boyer	.75	.30	.07
☐	10	Tony Cloninger	.40	.16	.04
☐	11	Senators Rookies	.40	.16	.04
		Brant Alyea			
		Pete Craig			
☐	12	John Tsitouris	.40	.16	.04
☐	13	Lou Johnson	.40	.16	.04
☐	14	Norm Siebern	.40	.16	.04
☐	15	Vern Law	.75	.30	.07
☐	16	Larry Brown	.40	.16	.04
☐	17	John Stephenson	.40	.16	.04
☐	18	Roland Sheldon	.40	.16	.04
☐	19	San Francisco Giants	1.00	.40	.10
		Team Card			
☐	20	Willie Horton	1.00	.40	.10
☐	21	Don Nottebart	.40	.16	.04
☐	22	Joe Nossek	.40	.16	.04
☐	23	Jack Sanford	.40	.16	.04
☐	24	Don Kessinger	1.25	.50	.12
☐	25	Pete Ward	.40	.16	.04
☐	26	Ray Sadecki	.40	.16	.04
☐	27	Orioles Rookies	.75	.30	.07
		Darold Knowles			
		Andy Etchebarren			
☐	28	Phil Niekro	12.00	5.00	1.20
☐	29	Mike Brumley	.40	.16	.04
☐	30	Pete Rose	60.00	24.00	6.00
☐	31	Jack Cullen	.40	.16	.04
☐	32	Adolfo Phillips	.40	.16	.04
☐	33	Jim Pagliaroni	.40	.16	.04
☐	34	Checklist 1	3.00	.30	.06
☐	35	Ron Swoboda	.75	.30	.07
☐	36	Jim Hunter	14.00	5.75	1.40
☐	37	Billy Herman MG	1.25	.50	.12
☐	38	Ron Nischwitz	.40	.16	.04
☐	39	Ken Henderson	.40	.16	.04
☐	40	Jim Grant	.40	.16	.04
☐	41	Don LeJohn	.40	.16	.04
☐	42	Aubrey Gatewood	.40	.16	.04
☐	43	Don Landrum	.40	.16	.04
☐	44	Indians Rookies	.40	.16	.04
		Bill Davis			
		Tom Kelley			
☐	45	Jim Gentile	.75	.30	.07
☐	46	Howie Koplitz	.40	.16	.04
☐	47	J.C. Martin	.40	.16	.04
☐	48	Paul Blair	.75	.30	.07
☐	49	Woody Woodward	.40	.16	.04
☐	50	Mickey Mantle	175.00	70.00	18.00
☐	51	Gordon Richardson	.40	.16	.04
☐	52	Power Plus	.75	.30	.07
		Wes Covington			
		Johnny Callison			
☐	53	Bob Duliba	.40	.16	.04
☐	54	Jose Pagan	.40	.16	.04

			NRMT	VG-E	GOOD
☐	55	Ken Harrelson	1.25	.50	.10
☐	56	Sandy Valdespino	.40	.16	.04
☐	57	Jim Lefebvre	1.00	.40	.10
☐	58	Dave Wickersham	.40	.16	.04
☐	59	Reds Team	1.00	.40	.10
☐	60	Curt Flood	1.00	.40	.10
☐	61	Bob Bolin	.40	.16	.04
☐	62A	Merritt Ranew (with sold line)	.40	.16	.04
☐	62B	Merritt Ranew (without sold line)	25.00	10.00	2.50
☐	63	Jim Stewart	.40	.16	.04
☐	64	Bob Bruce	.40	.16	.04
☐	65	Leon Wagner	.40	.16	.04
☐	66	Al Weis	.40	.16	.04
☐	67	Mets Rookies Cleon Jones Dick Selma	.75	.30	.07
☐	68	Hal Reniff	.40	.16	.04
☐	69	Ken Hamlin	.40	.16	.04
☐	70	Carl Yastrzemski	45.00	18.00	4.50
☐	71	Frank Carpin	.40	.16	.04
☐	72	Tony Perez	8.00	3.25	.80
☐	73	Jerry Zimmerman	.40	.16	.04
☐	74	Don Mossi	.75	.30	.07
☐	75	Tommy Davis	1.00	.40	.10
☐	76	Red Schoendienst MG	1.00	.40	.10
☐	77	John Orsino	.40	.16	.04
☐	78	Frank Linzy	.40	.16	.04
☐	79	Joe Pepitone	1.25	.50	.10
☐	80	Richie Allen	1.50	.60	.15
☐	81	Ray Oyler	.40	.16	.04
☐	82	Bob Hendley	.40	.16	.04
☐	83	Albie Pearson	.40	.16	.04
☐	84	Braves Rookies Jim Beauchamp Dick Kelley	.40	.16	.04
☐	85	Eddie Fisher	.40	.16	.04
☐	86	John Bateman	.40	.16	.04
☐	87	Dan Napoleon	.40	.16	.04
☐	88	Fred Whitfield	.40	.16	.04
☐	89	Ted Davidson	.40	.16	.04
☐	90	Luis Aparicio	6.50	2.60	.65
☐	91A	Bob Uecker (with traded line)	15.00	6.00	1.25
☐	91B	Bob Uecker (no traded line)	60.00	24.00	6.00
☐	92	Yankees Team	3.00	1.20	.30
☐	93	Jim Lonborg	1.00	.40	.07

			NRMT	VG-E	GOOD
☐	94	Matty Alou	.75	.30	.07
☐	95	Pete Richert	.40	.16	.04
☐	96	Felipe Alou	.75	.30	.07
☐	97	Jim Merritt	.40	.16	.04
☐	98	Don Demeter	.40	.16	.04
☐	99	Buc Belters Willie Stargell Donn Clendenon	3.00	1.20	.30
☐	100	Sandy Koufax	40.00	16.00	4.00
☐	101A	Checklist 2 (115 Bill Henry)	4.00	.40	.08
☐	101B	Checklist 2 (115 W. Spahn)	8.00	.80	.15
☐	102	Ed Kirkpatrick	.40	.16	.04
☐	103A	Dick Groat (with traded line)	1.00	.40	.10
☐	103B	Dick Groat (no traded line)	25.00	10.00	2.50
☐	104A	Alex Johnson (with traded line)	.75	.30	.07
☐	104B	Alex Johnson (no traded line)	25.00	10.00	2.50
☐	105	Milt Pappas	.75	.30	.07
☐	106	Rusty Staub	1.75	.75	.15
☐	107	A's Rookies Larry Stahl Ron Tompkins	.40	.16	.04
☐	108	Bobby Klaus	.40	.16	.04
☐	109	Ralph Terry	.75	.30	.07
☐	110	Ernie Banks	11.00	4.50	1.10
☐	111	Gary Peters	.75	.30	.07
☐	112	Manny Mota	.75	.30	.07
☐	113	Hank Aguirre	.60	.24	.06
☐	114	Jim Gosger	.60	.24	.06
☐	115	Bill Henry	.60	.24	.06
☐	116	Walt Alston MG	2.50	1.00	.25
☐	117	Jake Gibbs	.75	.30	.07
☐	118	Mike McCormick	.75	.30	.07
☐	119	Art Shamsky	.60	.24	.06
☐	120	Harmon Killebrew	10.00	4.00	1.00
☐	121	Ray Herbert	.60	.24	.06
☐	122	Joe Gaines	.60	.24	.06
☐	123	Pirates Rookies Frank Bork Jerry May	.60	.24	.06
☐	124	Tug McGraw	2.50	1.00	.25
☐	125	Lou Brock	11.00	4.50	1.10
☐	126	Jim Palmer	75.00	30.00	7.50
☐	127	Ken Berry	.60	.24	.06

		NRMT	VG-E	GOOD
☐ 128	Jim Landis	.60	.24	.06
☐ 129	Jack Kralick	.60	.24	.06
☐ 130	Joe Torre	1.25	.50	.12
☐ 131	Angels Team	1.25	.50	.12
☐ 132	Orlando Cepeda	3.00	1.20	.30
☐ 133	Don McMahon	.60	.24	.06
☐ 134	Wes Parker	.75	.30	.07
☐ 135	Dave Morehead	.60	.24	.06
☐ 136	Woody Held	.60	.24	.06
☐ 137	Pat Corrales	.75	.30	.07
☐ 138	Roger Repoz	.60	.24	.06
☐ 139	Cubs Rookies	.60	.24	.06
	Byron Browne			
	Don Young			
☐ 140	Jim Maloney	1.00	.40	.10
☐ 141	Tom McCraw	.60	.24	.06
☐ 142	Don Dennis	.60	.24	.06
☐ 143	Jose Tartabull	.60	.24	.06
☐ 144	Don Schwall	.60	.24	.06
☐ 145	Bill Freehan	1.25	.50	.12
☐ 146	George Altman	.60	.24	.06
☐ 147	Lum Harris MG	.60	.24	.06
☐ 148	Bob Johnson	.60	.24	.06
☐ 149	Dick Nen	.60	.24	.06
☐ 150	Rocky Colavito	1.50	.60	.15
☐ 151	Gary Wagner	.60	.24	.06
☐ 152	Frank Malzone	.75	.30	.07
☐ 153	Rico Carty	1.00	.40	.10
☐ 154	Chuck Hiller	.60	.24	.06
☐ 155	Marcelino Lopez	.60	.24	.06
☐ 156	Double Play Combo	.75	.30	.07
	Dick Schofield			
	Hal Lanier			
☐ 157	Rene Lachemann	1.00	.40	.10
☐ 158	Jim Brewer	.60	.24	.06
☐ 159	Chico Ruiz	.60	.24	.06
☐ 160	Whitey Ford	11.00	4.50	1.10
☐ 161	Jerry Lumpe	.60	.24	.06
☐ 162	Lee Maye	.60	.24	.06
☐ 163	Tito Francona	.75	.30	.07
☐ 164	White Sox Rookies	.75	.30	.07
	Tommie Agee			
	Marv Staehle			
☐ 165	Don Lock	.60	.24	.06
☐ 166	Chris Krug	.60	.24	.06
☐ 167	Boog Powell	1.75	.70	.17
☐ 168	Dan Osinski	.60	.24	.06
☐ 169	Duke Sims	.60	.24	.06
☐ 170	Cookie Rojas	.75	.30	.07

		NRMT	VG-E	GOOD
☐ 171	Nick Willhite	.60	.24	.06
☐ 172	Mets Team	1.50	.60	.15
☐ 173	Al Spangler	.60	.24	.06
☐ 174	Ron Taylor	.60	.24	.06
☐ 175	Bert Campaneris	.75	.30	.07
☐ 176	Jim Davenport	.75	.30	.07
☐ 177	Hector Lopez	.60	.24	.06
☐ 178	Bob Tillman	.60	.24	.06
☐ 179	Cards Rookies	.75	.30	.07
	Dennis Aust			
	Bob Tolan			
☐ 180	Vada Pinson	1.25	.50	.12
☐ 181	Al Worthington	.60	.24	.06
☐ 182	Jerry Lynch	.60	.24	.06
☐ 183	Checklist 3	3.00	.30	.06
☐ 184	Denis Menke	.60	.24	.06
☐ 185	Bob Buhl	.60	.24	.06
☐ 186	Ruben Amaro	.60	.24	.06
☐ 187	Chuck Dressen MG	.75	.30	.07
☐ 188	Al Luplow	.60	.24	.06
☐ 189	John Roseboro	.75	.30	.07
☐ 190	Jimmie Hall	.75	.30	.07
☐ 191	Darrell Sutherland	.60	.24	.06
☐ 192	Vic Power	.60	.24	.06
☐ 193	Dave McNally	1.00	.40	.10
☐ 194	Senators Team	1.25	.50	.12
☐ 195	Joe Morgan	12.50	5.00	1.25
☐ 196	Don Pavletich	.60	.24	.06
☐ 197	Sonny Siebert	.75	.30	.07
☐ 198	Mickey Stanley	1.00	.40	.10
☐ 199	Chisox Clubbers	.75	.30	.07
	Bill Skowron			
	Johnny Romano			
	Floyd Robinson			
☐ 200	Eddie Mathews	9.00	3.75	.90
☐ 201	Jim Dickson	.60	.24	.06
☐ 202	Clay Dalrymple	.60	.24	.06
☐ 203	Jose Santiago	.60	.24	.06
☐ 204	Cubs Team	1.25	.50	.12
☐ 205	Tom Tresh	1.25	.50	.12
☐ 206	Al Jackson	.60	.24	.06
☐ 207	Frank Quilici	.60	.24	.06
☐ 208	Bob Miller	.60	.24	.06
☐ 209	Tigers Rookies	1.25	.50	.12
	Fritz Fisher			
	John Hiller			
☐ 210	Bill Mazeroski	1.50	.60	.15
☐ 211	Frank Kreutzer	.60	.24	.06
☐ 212	Ed Kranepool	.75	.30	.07

		NRMT	VG-E	GOOD
☐ 213	Fred Newman	.60	.24	.06
☐ 214	Tommy Harper	.75	.30	.07
☐ 215	NL Batting Leaders .	10.00	4.00	1.00
	Bob Clemente			
	Hank Aaron			
	Willie Mays			
☐ 216	AL Batting Leaders .	2.50	1.00	.25
	Tony Oliva			
	Carl Yastrzemski			
	Vic Davalillo			
☐ 217	NL Home Run Leaders	7.50	3.00	.75
	Willie Mays			
	Willie McCovey			
	Billy Williams			
☐ 218	AL Home Run Leaders	1.50	.60	.15
	Tony Conigliaro			
	Norm Cash			
	Willie Horton			
☐ 219	NL RBI Leaders ...	2.50	1.00	.25
	Deron Johnson			
	Frank Robinson			
	Willie Mays			
☐ 220	AL RBI Leaders ...	1.50	.60	.15
	Rocky Colavito			
	Willie Horton			
	Tony Oliva			
☐ 221	NL ERA Leaders ...	2.50	1.00	.25
	Sandy Koufax			
	Juan Marichal			
	Vern Law			
☐ 222	AL ERA Leaders ...	1.50	.60	.15
	Sam McDowell			
	Eddie Fisher			
	Sonny Siebert			
☐ 223	NL Pitching Leaders	2.50	1.00	.25
	Sandy Koufax			
	Tony Cloninger			
	Don Drysdale			
☐ 224	AL Pitching Leaders	1.50	.60	.15
	Jim Grant			
	Mel Stottlemyre			
	Jim Kaat			
☐ 225	NL Strikeout Leaders	3.00	1.20	.30
	Sandy Koufax			
	Bob Veale			
	Bob Gibson			

		NRMT	VG-E	GOOD
☐ 226	AL Strikeout Leaders	1.50	.60	.15
	Sam McDowell			
	Mickey Lolich			
	Dennis McLain			
	Sonny Siebert			
☐ 227	Russ Nixon	1.00	.40	.10
☐ 228	Larry Dierker	.75	.30	.07
☐ 229	Hank Bauer MG ...	1.00	.40	.10
☐ 230	Johnny Callison ...	.75	.30	.07
☐ 231	Floyd Weaver	.60	.24	.06
☐ 232	Glenn Beckert	.75	.30	.07
☐ 233	Dom Zanni	.60	.24	.06
☐ 234	Yankees Rookies .	3.50	1.40	.35
	Rich Beck			
	Roy White			
☐ 235	Don Cardwell	.60	.24	.06
☐ 236	Mike Hershberger .	.60	.24	.06
☐ 237	Billy O'Dell	.60	.24	.06
☐ 238	Dodgers Team	2.00	.80	.20
☐ 239	Orlando Pena	.60	.24	.06
☐ 240	Earl Battey	.75	.30	.07
☐ 241	Dennis Ribant	.60	.24	.06
☐ 242	Jesus Alou	.60	.24	.06
☐ 243	Nelson Briles	.75	.30	.07
☐ 244	Astros Rookies ...	.60	.24	.06
	Chuck Harrison			
	Sonny Jackson			
☐ 245	John Buzhardt	.60	.24	.06
☐ 246	Ed Bailey	.60	.24	.06
☐ 247	Carl Warwick	.60	.24	.06
☐ 248	Pete Mikkelsen ..	.60	.24	.06
☐ 249	Bill Rigney MG ...	.60	.24	.06
☐ 250	Sammy Ellis	.60	.24	.06
☐ 251	Ed Brinkman	.60	.24	.06
☐ 252	Denny Lemaster ..	.60	.24	.06
☐ 253	Don Wert	.60	.24	.06
☐ 254	Phillies Rookies ..	20.00	8.00	2.00
	Ferguson Jenkins			
	Bill Sorrell			
☐ 255	Willie Stargell	12.50	5.00	1.25
☐ 256	Lew Krausse	.60	.24	.06
☐ 257	Jeff Torborg	1.25	.50	.12
☐ 258	Dave Giusti	.75	.30	.07
☐ 259	Boston Red Sox ..	1.25	.50	.12
	Team Card			
☐ 260	Bob Shaw	.60	.24	.06
☐ 261	Ron Hansen	.60	.24	.06
☐ 262	Jack Hamilton ...	.60	.24	.06
☐ 263	Tom Egan	.60	.24	.06

		NRMT	VG-E	GOOD
☐ 264	Twins Rookies .... Andy Kosco Ted Uhlaender	.60	.24	.06
☐ 265	Stu Miller	.60	.24	.06
☐ 266	Pedro Gonzalez ... (misspelled Gonzales on card back)	.60	.24	.06
☐ 267	Joe Sparma	.60	.24	.06
☐ 268	John Blanchard	.75	.30	.07
☐ 269	Don Heffner MG	.60	.24	.06
☐ 270	Claude Osteen	.75	.30	.07
☐ 271	Hal Lanier	.75	.30	.07
☐ 272	Jack Baldschun	.60	.24	.06
☐ 273	Astro Aces .... Bob Aspromonte Rusty Staub	1.00	.40	.10
☐ 274	Buster Narum	.60	.24	.06
☐ 275	Tim McCarver	1.75	.70	.17
☐ 276	Jim Bouton	1.50	.60	.15
☐ 277	George Thomas	.60	.24	.06
☐ 278	Cal Koonce	.60	.24	.06
☐ 279	Checklist 4	3.00	.30	.06
☐ 280	Bobby Knoop	.60	.24	.06
☐ 281	Bruce Howard	.60	.24	.06
☐ 282	Johnny Lewis	.60	.24	.06
☐ 283	Jim Perry	.75	.30	.07
☐ 284	Bobby Wine	.60	.24	.06
☐ 285	Luis Tiant	1.75	.70	.17
☐ 286	Gary Geiger	.60	.24	.06
☐ 287	Jack Aker	.60	.24	.06
☐ 288	Dodgers Rookies .. Bill Singer Don Sutton	60.00	24.00	6.00
☐ 289	Larry Sherry	.75	.30	.07
☐ 290	Ron Santo	1.25	.50	.12
☐ 291	Moe Drabowsky ...	.60	.24	.06
☐ 292	Jim Coker	.60	.24	.06
☐ 293	Mike Shannon	1.00	.40	.10
☐ 294	Steve Ridzik	.60	.24	.06
☐ 295	Jim Ray Hart	.75	.30	.07
☐ 296	Johnny Keane MG ..	.75	.30	.07
☐ 297	Jim Owens	.60	.24	.06
☐ 298	Rico Petrocelli ...	1.00	.40	.10
☐ 299	Lou Burdette	1.25	.50	.12
☐ 300	Bob Clemente	50.00	20.00	5.00
☐ 301	Greg Bollo	.60	.24	.06
☐ 302	Ernie Bowman	.60	.24	.06
☐ 303	Cleveland Indians .. Team Card	1.25	.50	.12
☐ 304	John Herrnstein ...	.60	.24	.06

		NRMT	VG-E	GOOD
☐ 305	Camilo Pascual ...	.75	.30	.07
☐ 306	Ty Cline	.60	.24	.06
☐ 307	Clay Carroll	.60	.24	.06
☐ 308	Tom Haller	.75	.30	.07
☐ 309	Diego Segui	.60	.24	.06
☐ 310	Frank Robinson ...	18.00	7.25	1.80
☐ 311	Reds Rookies .... Tommy Helms Dick Simpson	.75	.30	.07
☐ 312	Bob Saverine	.60	.24	.06
☐ 313	Chris Zachary	.60	.24	.06
☐ 314	Hector Valle	.60	.24	.06
☐ 315	Norm Cash	1.50	.60	.15
☐ 316	Jack Fisher	.60	.24	.06
☐ 317	Dalton Jones	.60	.24	.06
☐ 318	Harry Walker MG ..	.60	.24	.06
☐ 319	Gene Freese	.60	.24	.06
☐ 320	Bob Gibson	12.00	5.00	1.20
☐ 321	Rick Reichardt	.60	.24	.06
☐ 322	Bill Faul	.60	.24	.06
☐ 323	Ray Barker	.60	.24	.06
☐ 324	John Boozer	.60	.24	.06
☐ 325	Vic Davalillo	.75	.30	.07
☐ 326	Braves Team	1.25	.50	.12
☐ 327	Bernie Allen	.60	.24	.06
☐ 328	Jerry Grote	.60	.24	.06
☐ 329	Pete Charton	.60	.24	.06
☐ 330	Ron Fairly	.75	.30	.07
☐ 331	Ron Herbel	.60	.24	.06
☐ 332	Bill Bryan	.60	.24	.06
☐ 333	Senators Rookies . Joe Coleman Jim French	.60	.24	.06
☐ 334	Marty Keough	.60	.24	.06
☐ 335	Juan Pizarro	.60	.24	.06
☐ 336	Gene Alley	.75	.30	.07
☐ 337	Fred Gladding	.60	.24	.06
☐ 338	Dal Maxvill	.60	.24	.06
☐ 339	Del Crandall	.75	.30	.07
☐ 340	Dean Chance	.75	.30	.07
☐ 341	Wes Westrum MG ..	.60	.24	.06
☐ 342	Bob Humphreys ...	.60	.24	.06
☐ 343	Joe Christopher ...	.60	.24	.06
☐ 344	Steve Blass	.75	.30	.07
☐ 345	Bob Allison	.75	.30	.07
☐ 346	Mike De La Hoz ..	.60	.24	.06
☐ 347	Phil Regan	.75	.30	.07
☐ 348	Orioles Team	1.25	.50	.12
☐ 349	Cap Peterson	.60	.24	.06

		NRMT	VG-E	GOOD
☐ 350	Mel Stottlemyre	2.50	1.00	.25
☐ 351	Fred Valentine	.60	.24	.06
☐ 352	Bob Aspromonte ...	.60	.24	.06
☐ 353	Al McBean	.60	.24	.06
☐ 354	Smoky Burgess	.75	.30	.07
☐ 355	Wade Blasingame ..	.60	.24	.06
☐ 356	Red Sox Rookies ..	.60	.24	.06
	Owen Johnson			
	Ken Sanders			
☐ 357	Gerry Arrigo	.60	.24	.06
☐ 358	Charlie Smith	.60	.24	.06
☐ 359	Johnny Briggs	.60	.24	.06
☐ 360	Ron Hunt	.60	.24	.06
☐ 361	Tom Satriano	.60	.24	.06
☐ 362	Gates Brown	.75	.30	.07
☐ 363	Checklist 5	3.00	.30	.06
☐ 364	Nate Oliver	.60	.24	.06
☐ 365	Roger Maris	35.00	14.00	3.50
☐ 366	Wayne Causey	.60	.24	.06
☐ 367	Mel Nelson	.60	.24	.06
☐ 368	Charlie Lau	.75	.30	.07
☐ 369	Jim King	.60	.24	.06
☐ 370	Chico Cardenas ...	.60	.24	.06
☐ 371	Lee Stange	.85	.34	.08
☐ 372	Harvey Kuenn	1.50	.60	.15
☐ 373	Giants Rookies	.85	.34	.08
	Jack Hiatt			
	Dick Estelle			
☐ 374	Bob Locker	.85	.34	.08
☐ 375	Donn Clendenon ...	1.00	.40	.10
☐ 376	Paul Schaal	.85	.34	.08
☐ 377	Turk Farrell	1.00	.40	.10
☐ 378	Dick Tracewski	.85	.34	.08
☐ 379	Cardinal Team	1.75	.70	.17
☐ 380	Tony Conigliaro ...	3.50	1.40	.35
☐ 381	Hank Fischer	.85	.34	.08
☐ 382	Phil Roof	.85	.34	.08
☐ 383	Jackie Brandt	.85	.34	.08
☐ 384	Al Downing	1.00	.40	.10
☐ 385	Ken Boyer	2.00	.80	.20
☐ 386	Gil Hodges MG	4.50	1.80	.45
☐ 387	Howie Reed	.85	.34	.08
☐ 388	Don Mincher	1.00	.40	.10
☐ 389	Jim O'Toole	.85	.34	.08
☐ 390	Brooks Robinson ..	12.00	5.00	1.20
☐ 391	Chuck Hinton	.85	.34	.08
☐ 392	Cubs Rookies	1.25	.50	.12
	Bill Hands			
	Randy Hundley			
☐ 393	George Brunet	.85	.34	.08
☐ 394	Ron Brand	.85	.34	.08
☐ 395	Len Gabrielson ...	.85	.34	.08
☐ 396	Jerry Stephenson .	.85	.34	.08
☐ 397	Bill White	1.25	.50	.12
☐ 398	Danny Cater	1.00	.40	.10
☐ 399	Ray Washburn	.85	.34	.08
☐ 400	Zoilo Versalles	.85	.34	.08
☐ 401	Ken McMullen	.85	.34	.08
☐ 402	Jim Hickman	.85	.34	.08
☐ 403	Fred Talbot	.85	.34	.08
☐ 404	Pittsburgh Pirates	1.75	.70	.17
	Team Card			
☐ 405	Elston Howard	2.50	1.00	.25
☐ 406	Joey Jay	.85	.34	.08
☐ 407	John Kennedy	.85	.34	.08
☐ 408	Lee Thomas	1.25	.50	.12
☐ 409	Billy Hoeft	.85	.34	.08
☐ 410	Al Kaline	13.00	5.25	1.30
☐ 411	Gene Mauch MG ..	1.00	.40	.10
☐ 412	Sam Bowens	.85	.34	.08
☐ 413	Johnny Romano ...	.85	.34	.08
☐ 414	Dan Coombs	.85	.34	.08
☐ 415	Max Alvis	.85	.34	.08
☐ 416	Phil Ortega	.85	.34	.08
☐ 417	Angels Rookies ...	.85	.34	.08
	Jim McGlothlin			
	Ed Sukla			
☐ 418	Phil Gagliano	.85	.34	.08
☐ 419	Mike Ryan	.85	.34	.08
☐ 420	Juan Marichal	7.50	3.00	.75
☐ 421	Roy McMillan	.85	.34	.08
☐ 422	Ed Charles	.85	.34	.08
☐ 423	Ernie Broglio	.85	.34	.08
☐ 424	Reds Rookies	2.00	.80	.20
	Lee May			
	Darrell Osteen			
☐ 425	Bob Veale	1.00	.40	.10
☐ 426	White Sox Team ..	1.75	.70	.17
☐ 427	John Miller	.85	.34	.08
☐ 428	Sandy Alomar	1.00	.40	.10
☐ 429	Bill Monbouquette .	.85	.34	.08
☐ 430	Don Drysdale	8.00	3.25	.80
☐ 431	Walt Bond	.85	.34	.08
☐ 432	Bob Heffner	.85	.34	.08
☐ 433	Alvin Dark MG ...	1.25	.50	.12
☐ 434	Willie Kirkland ...	.85	.34	.08
☐ 435	Jim Bunning	4.50	1.80	.45
☐ 436	Julian Javier	1.00	.40	.10

		NRMT	VG-E	GOOD
☐ 437	Al Stanek	.85	.34	.08
☐ 438	Willie Smith	.85	.34	.08
☐ 439	Pedro Ramos	.85	.34	.08
☐ 440	Deron Johnson	1.00	.40	.10
☐ 441	Tommie Sisk	.85	.34	.08
☐ 442	Orioles Rookies	.85	.34	.08
	Ed Barnowski			
	Eddie Watt			
☐ 443	Bill Wakefield	.85	.34	.08
☐ 444	Checklist 6	4.00	.40	.08
☐ 445	Jim Kaat	4.00	1.60	.40
☐ 446	Mack Jones	.85	.34	.08
☐ 447	Dick Ellsworth	3.50	1.40	.35
	(photo actually Ken Hubbs)			
☐ 448	Eddie Stanky MG	3.50	1.40	.35
☐ 449	Joe Moeller	2.50	1.00	.25
☐ 450	Tony Oliva	5.00	2.00	.50
☐ 451	Barry Latman	2.50	1.00	.25
☐ 452	Joe Azcue	2.50	1.00	.25
☐ 453	Ron Kline	2.50	1.00	.25
☐ 454	Jerry Buchek	2.50	1.00	.25
☐ 455	Mickey Lolich	4.00	1.60	.40
☐ 456	Red Sox Rookies	2.50	1.00	.25
	Darrell Brandon			
	Joe Foy			
☐ 457	Joe Gibbon	2.50	1.00	.25
☐ 458	Manny Jiminez	2.50	1.00	.25
☐ 459	Bill McCool	2.50	1.00	.25
☐ 460	Curt Blefary	2.50	1.00	.25
☐ 461	Roy Face	3.50	1.40	.35
☐ 462	Bob Rodgers	3.50	1.40	.35
☐ 463	Philadelphia Phillies	5.00	2.00	.50
	Team Card			
☐ 464	Larry Bearnarth	2.50	1.00	.25
☐ 465	Don Buford	2.50	1.00	.25
☐ 466	Ken Johnson	2.50	1.00	.25
☐ 467	Vic Roznovsky	2.50	1.00	.25
☐ 468	Johnny Podres	4.00	1.60	.40
☐ 469	Yankees Rookies	9.00	3.75	.90
	Bobby Murcer			
	Dooley Womack			
☐ 470	Sam McDowell	3.50	1.40	.35
☐ 471	Bob Skinner	2.50	1.00	.25
☐ 472	Terry Fox	2.50	1.00	.25
☐ 473	Rich Rollins	2.50	1.00	.25
☐ 474	Dick Schofield	2.50	1.00	.25
☐ 475	Dick Radatz	2.50	1.00	.25
☐ 476	Bobby Bragan MG	2.50	1.00	.25
☐ 477	Steve Barber	2.50	1.00	.25
☐ 478	Tony Gonzalez	2.50	1.00	.25
☐ 479	Jim Hannan	2.50	1.00	.25
☐ 480	Dick Stuart	2.50	1.00	.25
☐ 481	Bob Lee	2.50	1.00	.25
☐ 482	Cubs Rookies	2.50	1.00	.25
	John Boccabella			
	Dave Dowling			
☐ 483	Joe Nuxhall	3.50	1.40	.35
☐ 484	Wes Covington	2.50	1.00	.25
☐ 485	Bob Bailey	2.50	1.00	.25
☐ 486	Tommy John	7.50	3.00	.75
☐ 487	Al Ferrara	2.50	1.00	.25
☐ 488	George Banks	2.50	1.00	.25
☐ 489	Curt Simmons	3.50	1.40	.35
☐ 490	Bobby Richardson	7.50	3.00	.75
☐ 491	Dennis Bennett	2.50	1.00	.25
☐ 492	Athletics Team	5.00	2.00	.50
☐ 493	Johnny Klippstein	2.50	1.00	.25
☐ 494	Gordy Coleman	2.50	1.00	.25
☐ 495	Dick McAuliffe	3.50	1.40	.35
☐ 496	Lindy McDaniel	3.50	1.40	.35
☐ 497	Chris Cannizzaro	2.50	1.00	.25
☐ 498	Pirates Rookies	3.50	1.40	.35
	Luke Walker			
	Woody Fryman			
☐ 499	Wally Bunker	2.50	1.00	.25
☐ 500	Hank Aaron	65.00	26.00	6.50
☐ 501	John O'Donoghue	2.50	1.00	.25
☐ 502	Lenny Green	2.50	1.00	.25
☐ 503	Steve Hamilton	2.50	1.00	.25
☐ 504	Grady Hatton MG	2.50	1.00	.25
☐ 505	Jose Cardenal	2.50	1.00	.25
☐ 506	Bo Belinsky	3.50	1.40	.35
☐ 507	Johnny Edwards	2.50	1.00	.25
☐ 508	Steve Hargan	2.50	1.00	.25
☐ 509	Jake Wood	2.50	1.00	.25
☐ 510	Hoyt Wilhelm	11.00	4.50	1.10
☐ 511	Giants Rookies	2.50	1.00	.25
	Bob Barton			
	Tito Fuentes			
☐ 512	Dick Stigman	2.50	1.00	.25
☐ 513	Camilo Carreon	2.50	1.00	.25
☐ 514	Hal Woodeshick	2.50	1.00	.25
☐ 515	Frank Howard	3.50	1.40	.35
☐ 516	Eddie Bressoud	2.50	1.00	.25
☐ 517A	Checklist 7	8.00	.75	.15
	529 White Sox Rookies			
	544 Cardinals Rookies			

		NRMT	VG-E	GOOD
☐ 517B	Checklist 7 .... 529 W. Sox Rookies 544 Cards Rookies	8.00	.75	.15
☐ 518	Braves Rookies .... Herb Hippauf Arnie Umbach	2.50	1.00	.25
☐ 519	Bob Friend	3.50	1.40	.35
☐ 520	Jim Wynn	3.50	1.40	.35
☐ 521	John Wyatt	2.50	1.00	.25
☐ 522	Phil Linz	3.50	1.40	.35
☐ 523	Bob Sadowski	12.00	5.00	1.20
☐ 524	Giants Rookies SP . Ollie Brown Don Mason	20.00	8.00	2.00
☐ 525	Gary Bell SP	20.00	8.00	2.00
☐ 526	Twins Team SP ...	40.00	16.00	4.00
☐ 527	Julio Navarro	12.00	5.00	1.20
☐ 528	Jesse Gonder SP ..	20.00	8.00	2.00
☐ 529	White Sox Rookies . Lee Elia Dennis Higgins Bill Voss	15.00	6.00	1.50
☐ 530	Robin Roberts	35.00	14.00	3.50
☐ 531	Joe Cunningham SP	20.00	8.00	2.00
☐ 532	Aurelio Monteagudo SP	20.00	8.00	2.00
☐ 533	Jerry Adair SP ...	20.00	8.00	2.00
☐ 534	Mets Rookies ..... Dave Eilers Rob Gardner	12.00	5.00	1.20
☐ 535	Willie Davis	18.00	7.25	1.80
☐ 536	Dick Egan	12.00	5.00	1.20
☐ 537	Herman Franks MG	12.00	5.00	1.20
☐ 538	Bob Allen	12.00	5.00	1.20
☐ 539	Astros Rookies .... Bill Heath Carroll Sembera	12.00	5.00	1.20
☐ 540	Denny McLain SP ..	40.00	16.00	4.00
☐ 541	Gene Oliver	12.00	5.00	1.20
☐ 542	George Smith	12.00	5.00	1.20
☐ 543	Roger Craig SP ...	25.00	10.00	2.50
☐ 544	Cardinals Rookies SP Joe Hoerner George Kernek Jimmy Williams	20.00	8.00	2.00
☐ 545	Dick Green SP	20.00	8.00	2.00
☐ 546	Dwight Siebler	12.00	5.00	1.20
☐ 547	Horace Clarke SP ..	30.00	12.00	3.00
☐ 548	Gary Kroll SP	20.00	8.00	2.00

		NRMT	VG-E	GOOD
☐ 549	Senators Rookies . Al Closter Casey Cox	12.00	5.00	1.20
☐ 550	Willie McCovey ...	90.00	36.00	9.00
☐ 551	Bob Purkey SP ...	20.00	8.00	2.00
☐ 552	Birdie Tebbetts MG	12.00	5.00	1.20
☐ 553	Rookie Stars ..... Pat Garrett Jackie Warner	12.00	5.00	1.20
☐ 554	Jim Northrup	14.00	5.75	1.40
☐ 555	Ron Perranoski SP	20.00	8.00	2.00
☐ 556	Mel Queen SP ...	20.00	8.00	2.00
☐ 557	Felix Mantilla	12.00	5.00	1.20
☐ 558	Red Sox Rookies . Guido Grilli Pete Magrini George Scott	16.00	6.50	1.60
☐ 559	Roberto Pena	12.00	5.00	1.20
☐ 560	Joel Horlen	12.00	5.00	1.20
☐ 561	Choo Choo Coleman SP	30.00	12.00	3.00
☐ 562	Russ Snyder	12.00	5.00	1.20
☐ 563	Twins Rookies .... Pete Cimino Cesar Tovar	12.00	5.00	1.20
☐ 564	Bob Chance SP ...	20.00	8.00	2.00
☐ 565	Jim Piersall SP ...	25.00	10.00	2.50
☐ 566	Mike Cuellar SP ..	25.00	10.00	2.50
☐ 567	Dick Howser SP ..	25.00	10.00	2.50
☐ 568	Athletics Rookies .. Paul Lindblad Rod Stone	12.00	5.00	1.20
☐ 569	Orlando McFarlane SP	20.00	8.00	2.00
☐ 570	Art Mahaffey SP ..	20.00	8.00	2.00
☐ 571	Dave Roberts SP .	20.00	8.00	2.00
☐ 572	Bob Priddy	12.00	5.00	1.20
☐ 573	Derrell Griffith ...	12.00	5.00	1.20
☐ 574	Mets Rookies ..... Bill Hepler Bill Murphy	12.00	5.00	1.20
☐ 575	Earl Wilson	12.00	5.00	1.20
☐ 576	Dave Nicholson ...	12.00	5.00	1.20
☐ 577	Jack Lamabe SP ..	20.00	8.00	2.00
☐ 578	Chi Chi Olivo SP ..	20.00	8.00	2.00
☐ 579	Orioles Rookies ... Frank Bertaina Gene Brabender Dave Johnson	16.00	6.50	1.60
☐ 580	Billy Williams	50.00	20.00	5.00

		NRMT	VG-E	GOOD
☐ 581	Tony Martinez	12.00	5.00	1.20
☐ 582	Garry Roggenburk .	12.00	5.00	1.20
☐ 583	Tigers Team SP ..	75.00	30.00	7.50
☐ 584	Yankees Rookies ..	12.00	5.00	1.20
	Frank Fernandez			
	Fritz Peterson			
☐ 585	Tony Taylor	12.00	5.00	1.20
☐ 586	Claude Raymond ..	12.00	5.00	1.20
☐ 587	Dick Bertell	12.00	5.00	1.20
☐ 588	Athletics Rookies ..	12.00	5.00	1.20
	Chuck Dobson			
	Ken Suarez			
☐ 589	Lou Klimchock	12.00	5.00	1.20
☐ 590	Bill Skowron SP ..	35.00	14.00	3.50
☐ 591	NL Rookies SP	20.00	8.00	2.00
	Bart Shirley			
	Grant Jackson			
☐ 592	Andre Rodgers	12.00	5.00	1.20
☐ 593	Doug Camilli SP ..	20.00	8.00	2.00
☐ 594	Chico Salmon	12.00	5.00	1.20
☐ 595	Larry Jackson	12.00	5.00	1.20
☐ 596	Astros Rookies SP .	20.00	8.00	2.00
	Nate Colbert			
	Greg Sims			
☐ 597	John Sullivan	12.00	5.00	1.20
☐ 598	Gaylord Perry SP ..	200.00	50.00	10.00

1967 Topps

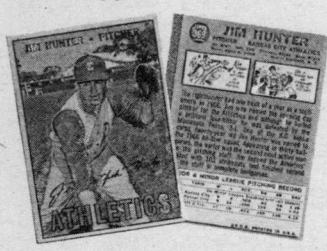

The cards in this 609-card set measure 2 ½ " by 3 ½". The 1967 Topps series is considered by some collectors to be one of the company's finest accomplishments in baseball card production. Excellent color photographs are combined with easy-to-read backs. Cards 458 to 533 are slightly harder to find than numbers 1 to 457, and the inevitable (difficult to find) high series (534 to 609) exists. Each checklist card features a small circular picture of a popular player included in that series. Printing discrepancies resulted in some high series cards being in short supply. Featured subsets within this set include World Series cards (151-155) and League Leaders (233-244). Although there are several relatively expensive cards in this popular set, the key cards in the set are undoubtedly the Tom Seaver rookie card (581) and the Rod Carew rookie card (569).

		NRMT	VG-E	GOOD
Complete Set (609)		2800.00	1250.00	400.00
Common Player (1-110) ..		.45	.18	.04
Common Player (111-370).		.60	.24	.06
Common Player (371-457)		.85	.34	.08
Common Player (458-533).		2.50	1.00	.25
Common Player (534-609).		6.00	2.40	.60
☐ 1	The Champs	8.00	2.00	.40
	Frank Robinson			
	Hank Bauer			
	Brooks Robinson			
☐ 2	Jack Hamilton	.45	.18	.04
☐ 3	Duke Sims	.45	.18	.04
☐ 4	Hal Lanier	.75	.30	.07
☐ 5	Whitey Ford UER .	10.00	4.00	1.00
	(1953 listed as 1933 in stats on back)			
☐ 6	Dick Simpson	.45	.18	.04
☐ 7	Don McMahon	.45	.18	.04
☐ 8	Chuck Harrison ...	.45	.18	.04
☐ 9	Ron Hansen	.45	.18	.04
☐ 10	Matty Alou	.75	.30	.07
☐ 11	Barry Moore	.45	.18	.04
☐ 12	Dodgers Rookies ..	.75	.30	.07
	Jim Campanis			
	Bill Singer			
☐ 13	Joe Sparma	.45	.18	.04
☐ 14	Phil Linz	.75	.30	.07
☐ 15	Earl Battey	.45	.18	.04
☐ 16	Bill Hands	.45	.18	.04
☐ 17	Jim Gosger	.45	.18	.04
☐ 18	Gene Oliver	.45	.18	.04
☐ 19	Jim McGlothlin ...	.45	.18	.04
☐ 20	Orlando Cepeda ..	4.00	1.60	.40

			NRMT	VG-E	GOOD
☐	21	Dave Bristol MG ...	.45	.18	.04
☐	22	Gene Brabender ...	.45	.18	.04
☐	23	Larry Elliot	.45	.18	.04
☐	24	Bob Allen	.45	.18	.04
☐	25	Elston Howard	2.25	.90	.20
☐	26A	Bob Priddy	.45	.18	.04
		(with traded line)			
☐	26B	Bob Priddy	25.00	10.00	2.50
		(no traded line)			
☐	27	Bob Saverine	.45	.18	.04
☐	28	Barry Latman	.45	.18	.04
☐	29	Tom McCraw	.45	.18	.04
☐	30	Al Kaline	10.00	4.00	1.00
☐	31	Jim Brewer	.45	.18	.04
☐	32	Bob Bailey	.45	.18	.04
☐	33	Athletic Rookies ...	1.50	.60	.15
		Sal Bando			
		Randy Schwartz			
☐	34	Pete Cimino	.45	.18	.04
☐	35	Rico Carty	.75	.30	.07
☐	36	Bob Tillman	.45	.18	.04
☐	37	Rick Wise	.75	.30	.07
☐	38	Bob Johnson	.45	.18	.04
☐	39	Curt Simmons	.75	.30	.07
☐	40	Rick Reichardt	.45	.18	.04
☐	41	Joe Hoerner	.45	.18	.04
☐	42	Mets Team	1.50	.60	.15
☐	43	Chico Salmon	.45	.18	.04
☐	44	Joe Nuxhall	.75	.30	.07
☐	45	Roger Maris	22.00	9.00	2.20
☐	46	Lindy McDaniel	.75	.30	.07
☐	47	Ken McMullen	.45	.18	.04
☐	48	Bill Freehan	1.00	.40	.10
☐	49	Roy Face	.75	.30	.07
☐	50	Tony Oliva	2.50	1.00	.25
☐	51	Astros Rookies	.45	.18	.04
		Dave Adlesh			
		Wes Bales			
☐	52	Dennis Higgins	.45	.18	.04
☐	53	Clay Dalrymple	.45	.18	.04
☐	54	Dick Green	.45	.18	.04
☐	55	Don Drysdale	7.50	3.00	.75
☐	56	Jose Tartabull	.45	.18	.04
☐	57	Pat Jarvis	.45	.18	.04
☐	58	Paul Schaal	.45	.18	.04
☐	59	Ralph Terry	.75	.30	.07
☐	60	Luis Aparicio	5.50	2.20	.55
☐	61	Gordy Coleman	.45	.18	.04
☐	62	Checklist 1	2.50	.25	.05
		Frank Robinson			
☐	63	Cards' Clubbers ...	4.50	1.80	.45
		Lou Brock			
		Curt Flood			
☐	64	Fred Valentine	.45	.18	.04
☐	65	Tom Haller	.75	.30	.07
☐	66	Manny Mota	.75	.30	.07
☐	67	Ken Berry	.45	.18	.04
☐	68	Bob Buhl	.45	.18	.04
☐	69	Vic Davalilo	.45	.18	.04
☐	70	Ron Santo	1.00	.40	.10
☐	71	Camilo Pascual ...	.75	.30	.07
☐	72	Tigers Rookies ...	.75	.30	.07
		George Korince			
		(Photo actually James Murray Brown)			
		John (Tom) Matchick			
☐	73	Rusty Staub	1.50	.60	.15
☐	74	Wes Stock	.45	.18	.04
☐	75	George Scott	1.00	.40	.10
☐	76	Jim Barbieri	.45	.18	.04
☐	77	Dooley Womack	.45	.18	.04
☐	78	Pat Corrales	.75	.30	.07
☐	79	Bubba Morton	.45	.18	.04
☐	80	Jim Maloney	.75	.30	.07
☐	81	Eddie Stanky MG ...	.75	.30	.07
☐	82	Steve Barber	.45	.18	.04
☐	83	Ollie Brown	.45	.18	.04
☐	84	Tommie Sisk	.45	.18	.04
☐	85	Johnny Callison ...	.75	.30	.07
☐	86A	Mike McCormick ..	.75	.30	.07
		(with traded line)			
☐	86B	Mike McCormick ..	25.00	10.00	2.50
		(no traded line)			
☐	87	George Altman	.45	.18	.04
☐	88	Mickey Lolich	1.50	.60	.15
☐	89	Felix Millan	.45	.18	.04
☐	90	Jim Nash	.45	.18	.04
☐	91	Johnny Lewis	.45	.18	.04
☐	92	Ray Washburn	.45	.18	.04
☐	93	Yankees Rookies .	2.50	1.00	.25
		Stan Bahnsen			
		Bobby Murcer			
☐	94	Ron Fairly	.75	.30	.07
☐	95	Sonny Siebert	.75	.30	.07
☐	96	Art Shamsky	.45	.18	.04
☐	97	Mike Cuellar	.75	.30	.07
☐	98	Rich Rollins	.75	.30	.07
☐	99	Lee Stange	.45	.18	.04

		NRMT	VG-E	GOOD
☐ 100	Frank Robinson ...	9.00	3.75	.90
☐ 101	Ken Johnson	.45	.18	.04
☐ 102	Philadelphia Phillies Team Card	1.00	.40	.10
☐ 103	Checklist 2 .... Mickey Mantle	5.00	1.00	.20
☐ 104	Minnie Rojas	.45	.18	.04
☐ 105	Ken Boyer	1.50	.60	.15
☐ 106	Randy Hundley	.75	.30	.07
☐ 107	Joel Horlen	.45	.18	.04
☐ 108	Alex Johnson	.75	.30	.07
☐ 109	Tribe Thumpers ... Rocky Colavito Leon Wagner	1.00	.40	.10
☐ 110	Jack Aker	.45	.18	.04
☐ 111	John Kennedy	.60	.24	.06
☐ 112	Dave Wickersham ..	.60	.24	.06
☐ 113	Dave Nicholson	.60	.24	.06
☐ 114	Jack Baldschun	.60	.24	.06
☐ 115	Paul Casanova	.60	.24	.06
☐ 116	Herman Franks MG	.60	.24	.06
☐ 117	Darrell Brandon ...	.60	.24	.06
☐ 118	Bernie Allen	.60	.24	.06
☐ 119	Wade Blasingame ..	.60	.24	.06
☐ 120	Floyd Robinson	.60	.24	.06
☐ 121	Eddie Bressoud	.60	.24	.06
☐ 122	George Brunet	.60	.24	.06
☐ 123	Pirates Rookies .... Jim Price Luke Walker	.75	.30	.07
☐ 124	Jim Stewart	.60	.24	.06
☐ 125	Moe Drabowsky	.60	.24	.06
☐ 126	Tony Taylor	.60	.24	.06
☐ 127	John O'Donoghue ..	.60	.24	.06
☐ 128	Ed Spiezio	.60	.24	.06
☐ 129	Phil Roof	.60	.24	.06
☐ 130	Phil Regan	.75	.30	.07
☐ 131	Yankees Team	3.00	1.20	.30
☐ 132	Ozzie Virgil	.60	.24	.06
☐ 133	Ron Kline	.60	.24	.06
☐ 134	Gates Brown	.75	.30	.07
☐ 135	Deron Johnson	.75	.30	.07
☐ 136	Carroll Sembera ...	.60	.24	.06
☐ 137	Twins Rookies ..... Ron Clark Jim Ollum	.60	.24	.06
☐ 138	Dick Kelley	.60	.24	.06
☐ 139	Dalton Jones	.60	.24	.06
☐ 140	Willie Stargell	11.00	4.50	1.10

		NRMT	VG-E	GOOD
☐ 141	John Miller	.60	.24	.06
☐ 142	Jackie Brandt	.60	.24	.06
☐ 143	Sox Sockers ...... Pete Ward Don Buford	.75	.30	.07
☐ 144	Bill Hepler	.60	.24	.06
☐ 145	Larry Brown	.60	.24	.06
☐ 146	Steve Carlton	50.00	20.00	5.00
☐ 147	Tom Egan	.60	.24	.06
☐ 148	Adolfo Phillips	.60	.24	.06
☐ 149	Joe Moeller	.60	.24	.06
☐ 150	Mickey Mantle	200.00	80.00	20.00
☐ 151	World Series Game 1 Moe mows down 11	1.75	.70	.17
☐ 152	World Series Game 2 Palmer blanks Dodgers	3.50	1.40	.35
☐ 153	World Series Game 3 Blair's homer defeats L.A.	1.75	.70	.17
☐ 154	World Series Game 4 Orioles 4 straight	1.75	.70	.17
☐ 155	World Series Summary Winners celebrate	1.75	.70	.17
☐ 156	Ron Herbel	.60	.24	.06
☐ 157	Danny Cater	.60	.24	.06
☐ 158	Jimmie Coker	.60	.24	.06
☐ 159	Bruce Howard	.60	.24	.06
☐ 160	Willie Davis	1.00	.40	.10
☐ 161	Dick Williams MG ..	.75	.30	.07
☐ 162	Billy O'Dell	.60	.24	.06
☐ 163	Vic Roznovsky	.60	.24	.06
☐ 164	Dwight Siebler	.60	.24	.06
☐ 165	Cleon Jones	.60	.24	.06
☐ 166	Eddie Mathews	8.00	3.25	.80
☐ 167	Senators Rookies . Joe Coleman Tim Cullen	.60	.24	.06
☐ 168	Ray Culp	.60	.24	.06
☐ 169	Horace Clarke	.75	.30	.07
☐ 170	Dick McAuliffe	.75	.30	.07
☐ 171	Cal Koonce	.60	.24	.06
☐ 172	Bill Heath	.60	.24	.06
☐ 173	St. Louis Cardinals Team Card	1.25	.50	.12
☐ 174	Dick Radatz	.75	.30	.07
☐ 175	Bobby Knoop	.60	.24	.06
☐ 176	Sammy Ellis	.60	.24	.06
☐ 177	Tito Fuentes	.60	.24	.06
☐ 178	John Buzhardt	.60	.24	.06

		NRMT	VG-E	GOOD
☐ 179	Braves Rookies .... Charles Vaughan Cecil Upshaw	.60	.24	.06
☐ 180	Curt Blefary	.75	.30	.07
☐ 181	Terry Fox	.60	.24	.06
☐ 182	Ed Charles	.60	.24	.06
☐ 183	Jim Pagliaroni	.60	.24	.06
☐ 184	George Thomas ...	.60	.24	.06
☐ 185	Ken Holtzman	1.50	.60	.15
☐ 186	Mets Maulers ..... Ed Kranepool Ron Swoboda	1.00	.40	.10
☐ 187	Pedro Ramos	.60	.24	.06
☐ 188	Ken Harrelson	1.25	.50	.12
☐ 189	Chuck Hinton	.60	.24	.06
☐ 190	Turk Farrell	.60	.24	.06
☐ 191A	Checklist 3 .... (214 Tom Kelley) (Willie Mays)	3.00	.30	.06
☐ 191B	Checklist 3 .... (214 Dick Kelley) (Willie Mays)	6.00	.60	.12
☐ 192	Fred Gladding	.60	.24	.06
☐ 193	Jose Cardenal	.60	.24	.06
☐ 194	Bob Allison	.75	.30	.07
☐ 195	Al Jackson	.60	.24	.06
☐ 196	Johnny Romano	.60	.24	.06
☐ 197	Ron Perranoski	.75	.30	.07
☐ 198	Chuck Hiller	.60	.24	.06
☐ 199	Billy Hitchcock MG .	.60	.24	.06
☐ 200	Willie Mays	45.00	18.00	4.50
☐ 201	Hal Reniff	.60	.24	.06
☐ 202	Johnny Edwards ...	.60	.24	.06
☐ 203	Al McBean	.60	.24	.06
☐ 204	Orioles Rookies ... Mike Epstein Tom Phoebus	.75	.30	.07
☐ 205	Dick Groat	1.00	.40	.10
☐ 206	Dennis Bennett	.60	.24	.06
☐ 207	John Orsino	.60	.24	.06
☐ 208	Jack Lamabe	.60	.24	.06
☐ 209	Joe Nossek	.60	.24	.06
☐ 210	Bob Gibson	9.00	3.75	.90
☐ 211	Twins Team	1.25	.50	.12
☐ 212	Chris Zachary	.60	.24	.06
☐ 213	Jay Johnstone	1.00	.40	.10
☐ 214	Dick Kelley	.60	.24	.06
☐ 215	Ernie Banks	9.00	3.75	.90

		NRMT	VG-E	GOOD
☐ 216	Bengal Belters .... Norm Cash Al Kaline	3.50	1.40	.35
☐ 217	Rob Gardner	.60	.24	.06
☐ 218	Wes Parker	.75	.30	.07
☐ 219	Clay Carroll	.60	.24	.06
☐ 220	Jim Ray Hart	.75	.30	.07
☐ 221	Woodie Fryman ...	.75	.30	.07
☐ 222	Reds Rookies .... Darrell Osteen Lee May	1.00	.40	.10
☐ 223	Mike Ryan	.60	.24	.06
☐ 224	Walt Bond	.60	.24	.06
☐ 225	Mel Stottlemyre ...	1.50	.60	.15
☐ 226	Julian Javier	.75	.30	.07
☐ 227	Paul Lindblad	.60	.24	.06
☐ 228	Gil Hodges MG ...	4.00	1.60	.40
☐ 229	Larry Jackson	.60	.24	.06
☐ 230	Boog Powell	1.75	.70	.17
☐ 231	John Bateman	.60	.24	.06
☐ 232	Don Buford	.75	.30	.07
☐ 233	AL ERA Leaders .. Gary Peters Joel Horlen Steve Hargan	1.50	.60	.15
☐ 234	NL ERA Leaders .. Sandy Koufax Mike Cuellar Juan Marichal	4.00	1.60	.40
☐ 235	AL Pitching Leaders Jim Kaat Denny McLain Earl Wilson	1.50	.60	.15
☐ 236	NL Pitching Leaders Sandy Koufax Juan Marichal Bob Gibson Gaylord Perry	8.00	3.25	.80
☐ 237	AL Strikeout Leaders Sam McDowell Jim Kaat Earl Wilson	1.50	.60	.15
☐ 238	NL Strikeout Leaders Sandy Koufax Jim Bunning Bob Veale	2.50	1.00	.25

		NRMT	VG-E	GOOD
☐ 239	AL Batting Leaders .	3.50	1.40	.35
	Frank Robinson			
	Tony Oliva			
	Al Kaline			
☐ 240	NL Batting Leaders .	1.50	.60	.15
	Matty Alou			
	Felipe Alou			
	Rico Carty			
☐ 241	AL RBI Leaders ...	2.50	1.00	.25
	Frank Robinson			
	Harmon Killebrew			
	Boog Powell			
☐ 242	NL RBI Leaders ...	4.00	1.60	.40
	Hank Aaron			
	Bob Clemente			
	Richie Allen			
☐ 243	AL Home Run Leaders	2.50	1.00	.25
	Frank Robinson			
	Harmon Killebrew			
	Boog Powell			
☐ 244	NL Home Run Leaders	4.00	1.60	.40
	Hank Aaron			
	Richie Allen			
	Willie Mays			
☐ 245	Curt Flood	1.25	.50	.12
☐ 246	Jim Perry	.75	.30	.07
☐ 247	Jerry Lumpe	.60	.24	.06
☐ 248	Gene Mauch MG ..	.75	.30	.07
☐ 249	Nick Willhite	.60	.24	.06
☐ 250	Hank Aaron	45.00	18.00	4.50
☐ 251	Woody Held	.60	.24	.06
☐ 252	Bob Bolin	.60	.24	.06
☐ 253	Indians Rookies ...	.60	.24	.06
	Bill Davis			
	Gus Gil			
☐ 254	Milt Pappas	.75	.30	.07
☐ 255	Frank Howard	1.25	.50	.12
☐ 256	Bob Hendley	.60	.24	.06
☐ 257	Charlie Smith	.60	.24	.06
☐ 258	Lee Maye	.60	.24	.06
☐ 259	Don Dennis	.60	.24	.06
☐ 260	Jim Lefebvre	1.00	.40	.10
☐ 261	John Wyatt	.60	.24	.06
☐ 262	Athletics Team	1.25	.50	.12
☐ 263	Hank Aguirre	.60	.24	.06
☐ 264	Ron Swoboda	.75	.30	.07
☐ 265	Lou Burdette	1.25	.50	.12

		NRMT	VG-E	GOOD
☐ 266	Pitt Power	3.50	1.40	.35
	Willie Stargell			
	Donn Clendenon			
☐ 267	Don Schwall	.60	.24	.06
☐ 268	Johnny Briggs	.60	.24	.06
☐ 269	Don Nottebart	.60	.24	.06
☐ 270	Zoilo Versalles ...	.60	.24	.06
☐ 271	Eddie Watt	.60	.24	.06
☐ 272	Cubs Rookies	.60	.24	.06
	Bill Connors			
	Dave Dowling			
☐ 273	Dick Lines	.60	.24	.06
☐ 274	Bob Aspromonte ..	.60	.24	.06
☐ 275	Fred Whitfield	.60	.24	.06
☐ 276	Bruce Brubaker ...	.60	.24	.06
☐ 277	Steve Whitaker ...	.60	.24	.06
☐ 278	Checklist 4	2.50	.25	.05
	Jim Kaat			
☐ 279	Frank Linzy	.60	.24	.06
☐ 280	Tony Conigliaro ...	2.50	1.00	.25
☐ 281	Bob Rodgers	1.00	.40	.10
☐ 282	John Odom	.60	.24	.06
☐ 283	Gene Alley	.75	.30	.07
☐ 284	Johnny Podres ...	1.25	.50	.12
☐ 285	Lou Brock	11.00	4.50	1.10
☐ 286	Wayne Causey	.60	.24	.06
☐ 287	Mets Rookies	.60	.24	.06
	Greg Goossen			
	Bart Shirley			
☐ 288	Denny Lemaster ..	.60	.24	.06
☐ 289	Tom Tresh	1.25	.50	.12
☐ 290	Bill White	1.00	.40	.10
☐ 291	Jim Hannan	.60	.24	.06
☐ 292	Don Pavletich	.60	.24	.06
☐ 293	Ed Kirkpatrick	.60	.24	.06
☐ 294	Walt Alston MG ...	2.50	1.00	.25
☐ 295	Sam McDowell	1.00	.40	.10
☐ 296	Glenn Beckert	.75	.30	.07
☐ 297	Dave Morehead ...	.60	.24	.06
☐ 298	Ron Davis	.60	.24	.06
☐ 299	Norm Siebern	.60	.24	.06
☐ 300	Jim Kaat	3.00	1.20	.30
☐ 301	Jesse Gonder	.60	.24	.06
☐ 302	Orioles Team	1.25	.50	.12
☐ 303	Gil Blanco	.60	.24	.06
☐ 304	Phil Gagliano	.60	.24	.06
☐ 305	Earl Wilson	.60	.24	.06
☐ 306	Bud Harrelson	.75	.30	.07
☐ 307	Jim Beauchamp ..	.60	.24	.06

		NRMT	VG-E	GOOD
☐ 308	Al Downing	.75	.30	.07
☐ 309	Hurlers Beware	1.00	.40	.10
	Johnny Callison			
	Richie Allen			
☐ 310	Gary Peters	.75	.30	.07
☐ 311	Ed Brinkman	.60	.24	.06
☐ 312	Don Mincher	.75	.30	.07
☐ 313	Bob Lee	.60	.24	.06
☐ 314	Red Sox Rookies	3.00	1.20	.30
	Mike Andrews			
	Reggie Smith			
☐ 315	Billy Williams	6.00	2.40	.60
☐ 316	Jack Kralick	.60	.24	.06
☐ 317	Cesar Tovar	.60	.24	.06
☐ 318	Dave Giusti	.60	.24	.06
☐ 319	Paul Blair	.75	.30	.07
☐ 320	Gaylord Perry	6.00	2.40	.60
☐ 321	Mayo Smith MG	.60	.24	.06
☐ 322	Jose Pagan	.60	.24	.06
☐ 323	Mike Hershberger	.60	.24	.06
☐ 324	Hal Woodeshick	.60	.24	.06
☐ 325	Chico Cardenas	.60	.24	.06
☐ 326	Bob Uecker	15.00	6.00	1.50
☐ 327	California Angels	1.25	.50	.12
	Team Card			
☐ 328	Clete Boyer	1.00	.40	.10
☐ 329	Charlie Lau	.75	.30	.07
☐ 330	Claude Osteen	.75	.30	.07
☐ 331	Joe Foy	.60	.24	.06
☐ 332	Jesus Alou	.60	.24	.06
☐ 333	Fergie Jenkins	5.00	2.00	.50
☐ 334	Twin Terrors	3.00	1.20	.30
	Bob Allison			
	Harmon Killebrew			
☐ 335	Bob Veale	.75	.30	.07
☐ 336	Joe Azcue	.60	.24	.06
☐ 337	Joe Morgan	6.50	2.60	.65
☐ 338	Bob Locker	.60	.24	.06
☐ 339	Chico Ruiz	.60	.24	.06
☐ 340	Joe Pepitone	1.25	.50	.12
☐ 341	Giants Rookies	.60	.24	.06
	Dick Dietz			
	Bill Sorrell			
☐ 342	Hank Fischer	.60	.24	.06
☐ 343	Tom Satriano	.60	.24	.06
☐ 344	Ossie Chavarria	.60	.24	.06
☐ 345	Stu Miller	.60	.24	.06
☐ 346	Jim Hickman	.60	.24	.06
☐ 347	Grady Hatton MG	.60	.24	.06
☐ 348	Tug McGraw	1.25	.50	.12
☐ 349	Bob Chance	.60	.24	.06
☐ 350	Joe Torre	1.50	.60	.15
☐ 351	Vern Law	.75	.30	.07
☐ 352	Ray Oyler	.60	.24	.06
☐ 353	Bill McCool	.60	.24	.06
☐ 354	Cubs Team	1.25	.50	.12
☐ 355	Carl Yastrzemski	80.00	32.00	8.00
☐ 356	Larry Jaster	.60	.24	.06
☐ 357	Bill Skowron	1.00	.40	.10
☐ 358	Ruben Amaro	.60	.24	.06
☐ 359	Dick Ellsworth	.75	.30	.07
☐ 360	Leon Wagner	.60	.24	.06
☐ 361	Checklist 5	3.00	.30	.06
	Roberto Clemente			
☐ 362	Darold Knowles	.60	.24	.06
☐ 363	Dave Johnson	1.75	.70	.17
☐ 364	Claude Raymond	.60	.24	.06
☐ 365	John Roseboro	.75	.30	.07
☐ 366	Andy Kosco	.60	.24	.06
☐ 367	Angels Rookies	.60	.24	.06
	Bill Kelso			
	Don Wallace			
☐ 368	Jack Hiatt	.60	.24	.06
☐ 369	Jim Hunter	8.00	3.25	.80
☐ 370	Tommy Davis	1.00	.40	.10
☐ 371	Jim Lonborg	1.75	.70	.17
☐ 372	Mike De La Hoz	.85	.34	.08
☐ 373	White Sox Rookies	.85	.34	.08
	Duane Josephson			
	Fred Klages			
☐ 374	Mel Queen	.85	.34	.08
☐ 375	Jake Gibbs	1.00	.40	.10
☐ 376	Don Lock	.85	.34	.08
☐ 377	Luis Tiant	2.00	.80	.20
☐ 378	Detroit Tigers	1.75	.70	.17
	Team Card			
☐ 379	Jerry May	.85	.34	.08
☐ 380	Dean Chance	1.00	.40	.10
☐ 381	Dick Schofield	.85	.34	.08
☐ 382	Dave McNally	1.25	.50	.12
☐ 383	Ken Henderson	.85	.34	.08
☐ 384	Cardinals Rookies	.85	.34	.08
	Jim Cosman			
	Dick Hughes			
☐ 385	Jim Fregosi	1.50	.60	.15
	(batting wrong)			
☐ 386	Dick Selma	.85	.34	.08
☐ 387	Cap Peterson	.85	.34	.08

		NRMT	VG-E	GOOD
☐ 388	Arnold Earley	.85	.34	.08
☐ 389	Alvin Dark MG	1.25	.50	.12
☐ 390	Jim Wynn	1.25	.50	.12
☐ 391	Wilbur Wood	1.00	.40	.10
☐ 392	Tommy Harper	1.00	.40	.10
☐ 393	Jim Bouton	1.75	.70	.17
☐ 394	Jake Wood	.85	.34	.08
☐ 395	Chris Short	.85	.34	.08
☐ 396	Atlanta Aces	1.00	.40	.10
	Denis Menke			
	Tony Cloninger			
☐ 397	Willie Smith	.85	.34	.08
☐ 398	Jeff Torborg	1.25	.50	.12
☐ 399	Al Worthington	.85	.34	.08
☐ 400	Bob Clemente	35.00	14.00	3.50
☐ 401	Jim Coates	.85	.34	.08
☐ 402	Phillies Rookies	1.00	.40	.10
	Grant Jackson			
	Billy Wilson			
☐ 403	Dick Nen	.85	.34	.08
☐ 404	Nelson Briles	1.00	.40	.10
☐ 405	Russ Snyder	.85	.34	.08
☐ 406	Lee Elia	1.50	.60	.15
☐ 407	Reds Team	1.75	.70	.17
☐ 408	Jim Northrup	1.00	.40	.10
☐ 409	Ray Sadecki	.85	.34	.08
☐ 410	Lou Johnson	.85	.34	.08
☐ 411	Dick Howser	1.50	.60	.15
☐ 412	Astros Rookies	1.75	.70	.17
	Norm Miller			
	Doug Rader			
☐ 413	Jerry Grote	.85	.34	.08
☐ 414	Casey Cox	.85	.34	.08
☐ 415	Sonny Jackson	.85	.34	.08
☐ 416	Roger Repoz	.85	.34	.08
☐ 417	Bob Bruce	.85	.34	.08
☐ 418	Sam Mele MG	.85	.34	.08
☐ 419	Don Kessinger	1.25	.50	.12
☐ 420	Denny McLain	3.00	1.00	.25
☐ 421	Dal Maxvill	1.00	.40	.10
☐ 422	Hoyt Wilhelm	6.50	2.60	.65
☐ 423	Fence Busters	10.00	4.00	1.00
	Willie Mays			
	Willie McCovey			
☐ 424	Pedro Gonzalez	.85	.34	.08
☐ 425	Pete Mikkelsen	.85	.34	.08
☐ 426	Lou Clinton	.85	.34	.08
☐ 427	Ruben Gomez	.85	.34	.08

		NRMT	VG-E	GOOD
☐ 428	Dodgers Rookies	1.25	.50	.12
	Tom Hutton			
	Gene Michael			
☐ 429	Garry Roggenburk	.85	.34	.08
☐ 430	Pete Rose	75.00	30.00	7.50
☐ 431	Ted Uhlaender	.85	.34	.08
☐ 432	Jimmie Hall	1.00	.40	.10
☐ 433	Al Luplow	.85	.34	.08
☐ 434	Eddie Fisher	.85	.34	.08
☐ 435	Mack Jones	.85	.34	.08
☐ 436	Pete Ward	.85	.34	.08
☐ 437	Senators Team	1.75	.70	.17
☐ 438	Chuck Dobson	.85	.34	.08
☐ 439	Byron Browne	.85	.34	.08
☐ 440	Steve Hargan	.85	.34	.08
☐ 441	Jim Davenport	1.00	.40	.10
☐ 442	Yankees Rookies	1.50	.60	.15
	Bill Robinson			
	Joe Verbanic			
☐ 443	Tito Francona	1.00	.40	.10
☐ 444	George Smith	.85	.34	.08
☐ 445	Don Sutton	15.00	6.00	1.50
☐ 446	Russ Nixon	1.25	.50	.12
☐ 447	Bo Belinsky	1.25	.50	.12
☐ 448	Harry Walker MG	.85	.34	.08
☐ 449	Orlando Pena	.85	.34	.08
☐ 450	Richie Allen	2.50	1.00	.25
☐ 451	Fred Newman	.85	.34	.08
☐ 452	Ed Kranepool	1.25	.50	.12
☐ 453	Aurelio Monteagudo	.85	.34	.08
☐ 454A	Checklist 6	3.50	.40	.10
	Juan Marichal			
	(missing left ear)			
☐ 454B	Checklist 6	6.00	.60	.15
	Juan Marichal			
	(left ear showing)			
☐ 455	Tommy Agee	1.00	.40	.10
☐ 456	Phil Niekro	7.50	3.00	.75
☐ 457	Andy Etchebarren	.85	.34	.08
☐ 458	Lee Thomas	3.50	1.40	.35
☐ 459	Senators Rookies	2.50	1.00	.25
	Dick Bosman			
	Pete Craig			
☐ 460	Harmon Killebrew	20.00	8.00	2.00
☐ 461	Bob Miller	2.50	1.00	.25
☐ 462	Bob Barton	2.50	1.00	.25
☐ 463	Hill Aces	3.50	1.40	.35
	Sam McDowell			
	Sonny Siebert			

		NRMT	VG-E	GOOD			NRMT	VG-E	GOOD
☐ 464	Dan Coombs	2.50	1.00	.25	☐ 505	Tommy Helms	3.50	1.40	.35
☐ 465	Willie Horton	3.50	1.40	.35	☐ 506	Smoky Burgess	3.50	1.40	.35
☐ 466	Bobby Wine	2.50	1.00	.25	☐ 507	Orioles Rookies	2.50	1.00	.25
☐ 467	Jim O'Toole	2.50	1.00	.25		Ed Barnowski			
☐ 468	Ralph Houk MG	3.50	1.40	.35		Larry Haney			
☐ 469	Len Gabrielson	2.50	1.00	.25	☐ 508	Dick Hall	2.50	1.00	.25
☐ 470	Bob Shaw	2.50	1.00	.25	☐ 509	Jim King	2.50	1.00	.25
☐ 471	Rene Lachemann	3.50	1.40	.35	☐ 510	Bill Mazeroski	5.00	2.00	.50
☐ 472	Rookies Pirates	2.50	1.00	.25	☐ 511	Don Wert	2.50	1.00	.25
	John Gelnar				☐ 512	Red Schoendienst MG	5.00	2.00	.50
	George Spriggs				☐ 513	Marcelino Lopez	2.50	1.00	.25
☐ 473	Jose Santiago	2.50	1.00	.25	☐ 514	John Werhas	2.50	1.00	.25
☐ 474	Bob Tolan	2.50	1.00	.25	☐ 515	Bert Campaneris	3.50	1.40	.35
☐ 475	Jim Palmer	35.00	14.00	3.50	☐ 516	Giants Team	5.00	2.00	.50
☐ 476	Tony Perez SP	35.00	14.00	3.50	☐ 517	Fred Talbot	2.50	1.00	.25
☐ 477	Braves Team	5.00	2.00	.50	☐ 518	Denis Menke	2.50	1.00	.25
☐ 478	Bob Humphreys	2.50	1.00	.25	☐ 519	Ted Davidson	2.50	1.00	.25
☐ 479	Gary Bell	2.50	1.00	.25	☐ 520	Max Alvis	2.50	1.00	.25
☐ 480	Willie McCovey	20.00	8.00	2.00	☐ 521	Bird Bombers	3.50	1.40	.35
☐ 481	Leo Durocher MG	5.00	2.00	.50		Boog Powell			
☐ 482	Bill Monbouquette	2.50	1.00	.25		Curt Blefary			
☐ 483	Jim Landis	2.50	1.00	.25	☐ 522	John Stephenson	2.50	1.00	.25
☐ 484	Jerry Adair	2.50	1.00	.25	☐ 523	Jim Merritt	2.50	1.00	.25
☐ 485	Tim McCarver	6.50	2.60	.65	☐ 524	Felix Mantilla	2.50	1.00	.25
☐ 486	Twins Rookies	3.50	1.40	.35	☐ 525	Ron Hunt	2.50	1.00	.25
	Rich Reese				☐ 526	Tigers Rookies	3.50	1.40	.35
	Bill Whitby					Pat Dobson			
☐ 487	Tommie Reynolds	2.50	1.00	.25		George Korince			
☐ 488	Gerry Arrigo	2.50	1.00	.25		(See 67T-72)			
☐ 489	Doug Clemens	2.50	1.00	.25	☐ 527	Dennis Ribant	2.50	1.00	.25
☐ 490	Tony Cloninger	2.50	1.00	.25	☐ 528	Rico Petrocelli	3.50	1.40	.35
☐ 491	Sam Bowens	2.50	1.00	.25	☐ 529	Gary Wagner	2.50	1.00	.25
☐ 492	Pittsburgh Pirates	5.00	2.00	.50	☐ 530	Felipe Alou	3.50	1.40	.35
	Team Card				☐ 531	Checklist 7	6.00	.60	.10
☐ 493	Phil Ortega	2.50	1.00	.25		Brooks Robinson			
☐ 494	Bill Rigney MG	2.50	1.00	.25	☐ 532	Jim Hicks	2.50	1.00	.25
☐ 495	Fritz Peterson	2.50	1.00	.25	☐ 533	Jack Fisher	2.50	1.00	.25
☐ 496	Orlando McFarlane	2.50	1.00	.25	☐ 534	Hank Bauer MG	10.00	4.00	1.00
☐ 497	Ron Campbell	2.50	1.00	.25	☐ 535	Donn Clendenon SP	15.00	6.00	1.50
☐ 498	Larry Dierker	2.50	1.00	.25	☐ 536	Cubs Rookies	18.00	7.25	1.80
☐ 499	Indians Rookies	2.50	1.00	.25		Joe Niekro			
	George Culver					Paul Popovich			
	Jose Vidal				☐ 537	Chuck Estrada	6.00	2.40	.60
☐ 500	Juan Marichal	12.50	5.00	1.25	☐ 538	J.C. Martin	6.00	2.40	.60
☐ 501	Jerry Zimmerman	2.50	1.00	.25	☐ 539	Dick Egan	6.00	2.40	.60
☐ 502	Derrell Griffith	2.50	1.00	.25	☐ 540	Norm Cash SP	20.00	8.00	2.00
☐ 503	Los Angeles Dodgers	7.50	3.00	.75	☐ 541	Joe Gibbon	6.00	2.40	.60
	Team Card								
☐ 504	Orlando Martinez	2.50	1.00	.25					

		NRMT	VG-E	GOOD
☐ 542	Athletics Rookies ..	10.00	4.00	1.00
	Rick Monday			
	Tony Pierce			
☐ 543	Dan Schneider	6.00	2.40	.60
☐ 544	Cleveland Indians ..	15.00	6.00	1.50
	Team Card			
☐ 545	Jim Grant	6.00	2.40	.60
☐ 546	Woody Woodward .	6.00	2.40	.60
☐ 547	Red Sox Rookies ..	6.00	2.40	.60
	Russ Gibson			
	Bill Rohr			
☐ 548	Tony Gonzalez	6.00	2.40	.60
☐ 549	Jack Sanford	6.00	2.40	.60
☐ 550	Vada Pinson	10.00	4.00	1.00
☐ 551	Doug Camilli	6.00	2.40	.60
☐ 552	Ted Savage	6.00	2.40	.60
☐ 553	Yankees Rookies SP	15.00	6.00	1.50
	Mike Hegan			
	Thad Tillotson			
☐ 554	Andre Rodgers	6.00	2.40	.60
☐ 555	Don Cardwell	6.00	2.40	.60
☐ 556	Al Weis	6.00	2.40	.60
☐ 557	Al Ferrara SP	15.00	6.00	1.50
☐ 558	Orioles Rookies SP .	20.00	8.00	2.00
	Mark Belanger			
	Bill Dillman			
☐ 559	Dick Tracewski	6.00	2.40	.60
☐ 560	Jim Bunning SP ...	35.00	14.00	3.50
☐ 561	Sandy Alomar SP ..	15.00	6.00	1.50
☐ 562	Steve Blass	6.00	2.40	.60
☐ 563	Joe Adcock SP	15.00	6.00	1.50
☐ 564	Astros Rookies	6.00	2.40	.60
	Alonzo Harris			
	Aaron Pointer			
☐ 565	Lew Krausse	6.00	2.40	.60
☐ 566	Gary Geiger	6.00	2.40	.60
☐ 567	Steve Hamilton SP .	15.00	6.00	1.50
☐ 568	John Sullivan	6.00	2.40	.60
☐ 569	AL Rookies	175.00	70.00	18.00
	Rod Carew			
	Hank Allen			
☐ 570	Maury Wills SP ...	75.00	30.00	7.50
☐ 571	Larry Sherry	6.00	2.40	.60
☐ 572	Don Demeter SP ..	15.00	6.00	1.50
☐ 573	Chicago White Sox .	15.00	6.00	1.50
	Team Card			
☐ 574	Jerry Buchek SP ...	15.00	6.00	1.50
☐ 575	Dave Boswell	6.00	2.40	.60

		NRMT	VG-E	GOOD
☐ 576	NL Rookies SP	15.00	6.00	1.50
	Ramon Hernandez			
	Norm Gigon			
☐ 577	Bill Short	6.00	2.40	.60
☐ 578	John Boccabella ..	6.00	2.40	.60
☐ 579	Bill Henry	6.00	2.40	.60
☐ 580	Rocky Colavito ...	25.00	10.00	2.50
☐ 581	Mets Rookies SP ..	550.00	220.00	55.00
	Bill Denehy			
	Tom Seaver			
☐ 582	Jim Owens........	6.00	2.40	.60
☐ 583	Ray Barker SP	15.00	6.00	1.50
☐ 584	Jim Piersall SP ...	20.00	8.00	2.00
☐ 585	Wally Bunker	6.00	2.40	.60
☐ 586	Manny Jimenez ...	15.00	6.00	1.50
☐ 587	NL Rookies SP ...	20.00	8.00	2.00
	Don Shaw			
	Gary Sutherland			
☐ 588	Johnny Klippstein .	6.00	2.40	.60
☐ 589	Dave Ricketts	6.00	2.40	.60
☐ 590	Pete Richert......	6.00	2.40	.60
☐ 591	Ty Cline	6.00	2.40	.60
☐ 592	NL Rookies SP ...	15.00	6.00	1.50
	Jim Shellenback			
	Ron Willis			
☐ 593	Wes Westrum MG .	6.00	2.40	.60
☐ 594	Dan Osinski	6.00	2.40	.60
☐ 595	Cookie Rojas SP ..	15.00	6.00	1.50
☐ 596	Galen Cisco	6.00	2.40	.60
☐ 597	Ted Abernathy	6.00	2.40	.60
☐ 598	White Sox Rookies SP	15.00	6.00	1.50
	Walt Williams			
	Ed Stroud			
☐ 599	Bob Duliba	6.00	2.40	.60
☐ 600	Brooks Robinson SP	180.00	75.00	18.00
☐ 601	Bill Bryan	6.00	2.40	.60
☐ 602	Juan Pizarro	6.00	2.40	.60
☐ 603	Athletics Rookies ..	6.00	2.40	.60
	Tim Talton			
	Ramon Webster			
☐ 604	Red Sox Team SP ..	50.00	20.00	5.00
☐ 605	Mike Shannon SP .	20.00	8.00	2.00
☐ 606	Ron Taylor	6.00	2.40	.60
☐ 607	Mickey Stanley SP	20.00	8.00	2.00
☐ 608	Cubs Rookies	6.00	2.40	.60
	Rich Nye			
	John Upham			
☐ 609	Tommy John SP ..	80.00	32.00	8.00

1968 Topps

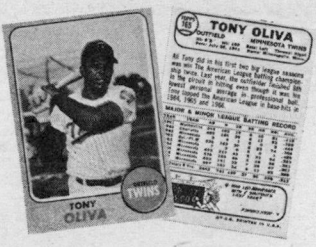

The cards in this 598-card set measure 2 ½"
by 3 ½". The 1968 Topps set includes Sporting News All-Star Selections as card numbers 361 to 380. Other subsets in the set
include League Leaders (1-12) and World
Series cards (151-158). The front of each
checklist card features a picture of a popular
player inside a circle. High numbers 534 to
598 are slightly more difficult to obtain. The
first series looks different from the other
series, as it has a lighter, wider mesh background on the card front. The later series all
had a much darker, finer mesh pattern. Key
cards in the set are the rookie cards of
Johnny Bench (247) and Nolan Ryan (177).

	NRMT	VG-E	GOOD
Complete Set (598)	1350.00	550.00	175.00
Common Player (1-110) ...	.50	.20	.05
Common Player (111-457) .	.40	.16	.04
Common Player (458-533) .	.65	.26	.06
Common Player (534-598) .	.70	.28	.07

			NRMT	VG-E	GOOD
☐	1	NL Batting Leaders . Bob Clemente Tony Gonzales Matty Alou	6.00	1.00	.20
☐	2	AL Batting Leaders . Carl Yastrzemski Frank Robinson Al Kaline	5.00	2.00	.45
☐	3	NL RBI Leaders ... Orlando Cepeda Bob Clemente Hank Aaron	3.50	1.50	.30
☐	4	AL RBI Leaders ... Carl Yastrzemski Harmon Killebrew Frank Robinson	5.00	2.00	.45
☐	5	NL Home Run Leaders Hank Aaron Jim Wynn Ron Santo Willie McCovey	2.50	1.00	.25
☐	6	NL Home Run Leaders Carl Yastrzemski Harmon Killebrew Frank Howard	3.50	1.40	.35
☐	7	NL ERA Leaders .. Phil Niekro Jim Bunning Chris Short	1.25	.50	.12
☐	8	AL ERA Leaders .. Joel Horlen Gary Peters Sonny Siebert	1.00	.40	.10
☐	9	NL Pitching Leaders Mike McCormick Ferguson Jenkins Jim Bunning Claude Osteen	1.25	.50	.12
☐	10	AL Pitching Leaders Jim Lonborg Earl Wilson Dean Chance	1.00	.40	.10
☐	11	NL Strikeout Leaders Jim Bunning Ferguson Jenkins Gaylord Perry	1.50	.60	.15
☐	12	AL Strikeout Leaders Jim Lonborg Sam McDowell Dean Chance	1.00	.40	.10
☐	13	Chuck Hartenstein .	.50	.20	.05
☐	14	Jerry McNertney ..	.50	.20	.05
☐	15	Ron Hunt	.50	.20	.05
☐	16	Indians Rookies ... Lou Piniella Richie Scheinblum	2.00	.80	.20
☐	17	Dick Hall	.50	.20	.05

		NRMT	VG-E	GOOD
☐ 18	Mike Hershberger ..	.50	.20	.05
☐ 19	Juan Pizarro	.50	.20	.05
☐ 20	Brooks Robinson ..	9.00	3.75	.90
☐ 21	Ron Davis	.50	.20	.05
☐ 22	Pat Dobson	.60	.24	.06
☐ 23	Chico Cardenas ...	.50	.20	.05
☐ 24	Bobby Locke	.50	.20	.05
☐ 25	Julian Javier	.60	.24	.06
☐ 26	Darrell Brandon ...	.50	.20	.05
☐ 27	Gil Hodges MG	3.50	1.40	.35
☐ 28	Ted Uhlaender	.50	.20	.05
☐ 29	Joe Verbanic	.50	.20	.05
☐ 30	Joe Torre	1.00	.40	.10
☐ 31	Ed Stroud	.50	.20	.05
☐ 32	Joe Gibbon	.50	.20	.05
☐ 33	Pete Ward	.50	.20	.05
☐ 34	Al Ferrara	.50	.20	.05
☐ 35	Steve Hargan	.50	.20	.05
☐ 36	Pirates Rookies	.75	.30	.07
	Bob Moose			
	Bob Robertson			
☐ 37	Billy Williams	5.50	2.20	.55
☐ 38	Tony Pierce	.50	.20	.05
☐ 39	Cookie Rojas	.60	.24	.06
☐ 40	Denny McLain	3.00	1.20	.30
☐ 41	Julio Gotay	.50	.20	.05
☐ 42	Larry Haney	.50	.20	.05
☐ 43	Gary Bell	.50	.20	.05
☐ 44	Frank Kostro	.50	.20	.05
☐ 45	Tom Seaver	75.00	30.00	7.50
☐ 46	Dave Ricketts	.50	.20	.05
☐ 47	Ralph Houk MG ...	.75	.30	.07
☐ 48	Ted Davidson	.50	.20	.05
☐ 49A	Eddie Brinkman ...	.50	.20	.05
	(white team name)			
☐ 49B	Eddie Brinkman ...	40.00	16.00	4.00
	(yellow team name)			
☐ 50	Willie Mays	36.00	15.00	3.60
☐ 51	Bob Locker	.50	.20	.05
☐ 52	Hawk Taylor	.50	.20	.05
☐ 53	Gene Alley	.60	.24	.06
☐ 54	Stan Williams	.50	.20	.05
☐ 55	Felipe Alou	.60	.24	.06
☐ 56	Orioles Rookies ...	.60	.24	.06
	Dave Leonhard			
	Dave May			
☐ 57	Dan Schneider	.50	.20	.05
☐ 58	Eddie Mathews	7.00	2.80	.70
☐ 59	Don Lock	.50	.20	.05

		NRMT	VG-E	GOOD
☐ 60	Ken Holtzman	.75	.30	.07
☐ 61	Reggie Smith	1.00	.40	.10
☐ 62	Chuck Dobson	.50	.20	.05
☐ 63	Dick Kenworthy ...	.50	.20	.05
☐ 64	Jim Merritt	.50	.20	.05
☐ 65	John Roseboro	.60	.24	.06
☐ 66A	Casey Cox	.50	.20	.05
	(white team name)			
☐ 66B	Casey Cox	40.00	16.00	4.00
	(yellow team name)			
☐ 67	Checklist 1	2.50	.25	.05
	Jim Kaat			
☐ 68	Ron Willis	.50	.20	.05
☐ 69	Tom Tresh	.75	.30	.07
☐ 70	Bob Veale	.60	.24	.06
☐ 71	Vern Fuller	.50	.20	.05
☐ 72	Tommy John	3.50	1.40	.35
☐ 73	Jim Ray Hart	.60	.24	.06
☐ 74	Milt Pappas	.60	.24	.06
☐ 75	Don Mincher	.60	.24	.06
☐ 76	Braves Rookies ...	.60	.24	.06
	Jim Britton			
	Ron Reed			
☐ 77	Don Wilson	.50	.20	.05
☐ 78	Jim Northrup	.75	.30	.07
☐ 79	Ted Kubiak	.50	.20	.05
☐ 80	Rod Carew	40.00	16.00	4.00
☐ 81	Larry Jackson	.50	.20	.05
☐ 82	Sam Bowens	.50	.20	.05
☐ 83	John Stephenson ..	.50	.20	.05
☐ 84	Bob Tolan	.60	.24	.06
☐ 85	Gaylord Perry	5.00	2.00	.50
☐ 86	Willie Stargell	8.00	3.25	.80
☐ 87	Dick Williams MG ..	.60	.24	.06
☐ 88	Phil Regan	.60	.24	.06
☐ 89	Jake Gibbs	.50	.20	.05
☐ 90	Vada Pinson	1.00	.40	.10
☐ 91	Jim Ollom	.50	.20	.05
☐ 92	Ed Kranepool	.60	.24	.06
☐ 93	Tony Cloninger ...	.50	.20	.05
☐ 94	Lee Maye	.50	.20	.05
☐ 95	Bob Aspromonte ..	.50	.20	.05
☐ 96	Senator Rookies ..	.50	.20	.05
	Frank Coggins			
	Dick Nold			
☐ 97	Tom Phoebus	.50	.20	.05
☐ 98	Gary Sutherland ..	.50	.20	.05
☐ 99	Rocky Colavito ...	1.25	.50	.12
☐ 100	Bob Gibson	10.00	4.00	1.00

		NRMT	VG-E	GOOD
☐ 101	Glenn Beckert	.60	.24	.06
☐ 102	Jose Cardenal	.50	.20	.05
☐ 103	Don Sutton	5.00	2.00	.50
☐ 104	Dick Dietz	.50	.20	.05
☐ 105	Al Downing	.60	.24	.06
☐ 106	Dalton Jones	.50	.20	.05
☐ 107A	Checklist 2	2.50	.25	.05
	Juan Marichal			
	(tan wide mesh)			
☐ 107B	Checklist 2	2.50	.25	.05
	Juan Marichal			
	(brown fine mesh)			
☐ 108	Don Pavletich	.50	.20	.05
☐ 109	Bert Campaneris	.75	.30	.07
☐ 110	Hank Aaron	36.00	15.00	3.60
☐ 111	Rich Reese	.60	.24	.06
☐ 112	Woodie Fryman	.40	.16	.04
☐ 113	Tigers Rookies	.40	.16	.04
	Tom Matchick			
	Daryl Patterson			
☐ 114	Ron Swoboda	.60	.24	.06
☐ 115	Sam McDowell	.75	.30	.07
☐ 116	Ken McMullen	.40	.16	.04
☐ 117	Larry Jaster	.40	.16	.04
☐ 118	Mark Belanger	1.00	.40	.10
☐ 119	Ted Savage	.40	.16	.04
☐ 120	Mel Stottlemyre	1.25	.50	.10
☐ 121	Jimmie Hall	.60	.24	.06
☐ 122	Gene Mauch MG	.60	.24	.06
☐ 123	Jose Santiago	.40	.16	.04
☐ 124	Nate Oliver	.40	.16	.04
☐ 125	Joel Horlen	.40	.16	.04
☐ 126	Bobby Etheridge	.40	.16	.04
☐ 127	Paul Lindblad	.40	.16	.04
☐ 128	Astros Rookies	.40	.16	.04
	Tom Dukes			
	Alonzo Harris			
☐ 129	Mickey Stanley	.75	.30	.07
☐ 130	Tony Perez	4.00	1.60	.40
☐ 131	Frank Bertaina	.40	.16	.04
☐ 132	Bud Harrelson	.60	.24	.06
☐ 133	Fred Whitfield	.40	.16	.04
☐ 134	Pat Jarvis	.40	.16	.04
☐ 135	Paul Blair	.60	.24	.06
☐ 136	Randy Hundley	.60	.24	.06
☐ 137	Twins Team	1.00	.40	.10
☐ 138	Ruben Amaro	.40	.16	.04
☐ 139	Chris Short	.40	.16	.04
☐ 140	Tony Conigliaro	1.50	.60	.15

		NRMT	VG-E	GOOD
☐ 141	Dal Maxvill	.60	.24	.06
☐ 142	White Sox Rookies	.40	.16	.04
	Buddy Bradford			
	Bill Voss			
☐ 143	Pete Cimino	.40	.16	.04
☐ 144	Joe Morgan	4.50	1.80	.45
☐ 145	Don Drysdale	6.50	2.60	.65
☐ 146	Sal Bando	.75	.30	.07
☐ 147	Frank Linzy	.40	.16	.04
☐ 148	Dave Bristol MG	.40	.16	.04
☐ 149	Bob Saverine	.40	.16	.04
☐ 150	Bob Clemente	24.00	10.00	2.40
☐ 151	World Series Game 1	3.00	1.20	.30
	Brock socks 4 hits			
	in opener			
☐ 152	World Series Game 2	5.00	2.00	.50
	Yaz smashes 2 homers			
☐ 153	World Series Game 3	1.75	.70	.17
	Briles cools Boston			
☐ 154	World Series Game 4	3.00	1.20	.30
	Gibson hurls shutout			
☐ 155	World Series Game 5	1.75	.70	.17
	Lonborg wins again			
☐ 156	World Series Game 6	1.75	.70	.17
	Petrocelli 2 homers			
☐ 157	World Series Game 7	1.75	.70	.17
	St. Louis wins it			
☐ 158	World Series Summary	1.75	.70	.17
	Cardinals celebrate			
☐ 159	Don Kessinger	.60	.24	.06
☐ 160	Earl Wilson	.40	.16	.04
☐ 161	Norm Miller	.40	.16	.04
☐ 162	Cards Rookies	.75	.30	.07
	Hal Gilson			
	Mike Torrez			
☐ 163	Gene Brabender	.40	.16	.04
☐ 164	Ramon Webster	.40	.16	.04
☐ 165	Tony Oliva	2.25	.90	.22
☐ 166	Claude Raymond	.40	.16	.04
☐ 167	Elston Howard	2.25	.90	.22
☐ 168	Dodgers Team	1.50	.60	.15
☐ 169	Bob Bolin	.40	.16	.04
☐ 170	Jim Fregosi	.75	.30	.07
☐ 171	Don Nottebart	.40	.16	.04
☐ 172	Walt Williams	.40	.16	.04
☐ 173	John Boozer	.40	.16	.04
☐ 174	Bob Tillman	.40	.16	.04
☐ 175	Maury Wills	3.50	1.40	.35
☐ 176	Bob Allen	.40	.16	.04

		NRMT	VG-E	GOOD
☐ 177	Mets Rookies	200.00	80.00	20.00
	Jerry Koosman			
	Nolan Ryan			
☐ 178	Don Wert	.40	.16	.04
☐ 179	Bill Stoneman	.40	.16	.04
☐ 180	Curt Flood	1.00	.40	.10
☐ 181	Jerry Zimmerman	.40	.16	.04
☐ 182	Dave Giusti	.60	.24	.06
☐ 183	Bob Kennedy MG	.40	.16	.04
☐ 184	Lou Johnson	.40	.16	.04
☐ 185	Tom Haller	.60	.24	.06
☐ 186	Eddie Watt	.40	.16	.04
☐ 187	Sonny Jackson	.40	.16	.04
☐ 188	Cap Peterson	.40	.16	.04
☐ 189	Bill Landis	.40	.16	.04
☐ 190	Bill White	.75	.30	.07
☐ 191	Dan Frisella	.40	.16	.04
☐ 192	Checklist 3	3.00	.50	.10
	Carl Yastrzemski			
☐ 193	Jack Hamilton	.40	.16	.04
☐ 194	Don Buford	.60	.24	.06
☐ 195	Joe Pepitone	1.00	.40	.10
☐ 196	Gary Nolan	.40	.16	.04
☐ 197	Larry Brown	.40	.16	.04
☐ 198	Roy Face	.75	.30	.07
☐ 199	A's Rookies	.40	.16	.04
	Roberto Rodriquez			
	Darrell Osteen			
☐ 200	Orlando Cepeda	3.00	1.20	.30
☐ 201	Mike Marshall	1.25	.50	.12
☐ 202	Adolfo Phillips	.40	.16	.04
☐ 203	Dick Kelley	.40	.16	.04
☐ 204	Andy Etchebarren	.40	.16	.04
☐ 205	Juan Marichal	5.00	2.00	.50
☐ 206	Cal Ermer MG	.40	.16	.04
☐ 207	Carroll Sembera	.40	.16	.04
☐ 208	Willie Davis	.75	.30	.07
☐ 209	Tim Cullen	.40	.16	.04
☐ 210	Gary Peters	.60	.24	.06
☐ 211	J.C. Martin	.40	.16	.04
☐ 212	Dave Morehead	.40	.16	.04
☐ 213	Chico Ruiz	.40	.16	.04
☐ 214	Yankees Rookies	.75	.30	.07
	Stan Bahnsen			
	Frank Fernandez			
☐ 215	Jim Bunning	3.00	1.20	.30
☐ 216	Bubba Morton	.40	.16	.04
☐ 217	Turk Farrell	.40	.16	.04
☐ 218	Ken Suarez	.40	.16	.04

		NRMT	VG-E	GOOD
☐ 219	Rob Gardner	.40	.16	.04
☐ 220	Harmon Killebrew	7.50	3.00	.75
☐ 221	Braves Team	1.00	.40	.10
☐ 222	Jim Hardin	.40	.16	.04
☐ 223	Ollie Brown	.40	.16	.04
☐ 224	Jack Aker	.40	.16	.04
☐ 225	Richie Allen	1.50	.60	.15
☐ 226	Jimmie Price	.40	.16	.04
☐ 227	Joe Hoerner	.40	.16	.04
☐ 228	Dodgers Rookies	.60	.24	.06
	Jack Billingham			
	Jim Fairey			
☐ 229	Fred Klages	.40	.16	.04
☐ 230	Pete Rose	45.00	18.00	4.50
☐ 231	Dave Baldwin	.40	.16	.04
☐ 232	Denis Menke	.40	.16	.04
☐ 233	George Scott	.60	.24	.06
☐ 234	Bill Monbouquette	.40	.16	.04
☐ 235	Ron Santo	1.00	.40	.10
☐ 236	Tug McGraw	1.00	.40	.10
☐ 237	Alvin Dark MG	.60	.24	.06
☐ 238	Tom Satriano	.40	.16	.04
☐ 239	Bill Henry	.40	.16	.04
☐ 240	Al Kaline	10.00	4.00	1.00
☐ 241	Felix Millan	.40	.16	.04
☐ 242	Moe Drabowsky	.40	.16	.04
☐ 243	Rich Rollins	.60	.24	.06
☐ 244	John Donaldson	.40	.16	.04
☐ 245	Tony Gonzalez	.40	.16	.04
☐ 246	Fritz Peterson	.40	.16	.04
☐ 247	Reds Rookies	200.00	80.00	20.00
	Johnny Bench			
	Ron Tompkins			
☐ 248	Fred Valentine	.40	.16	.04
☐ 249	Bill Singer	.40	.16	.04
☐ 250	Carl Yastrzemski	30.00	12.00	3.00
☐ 251	Manny Sanguillen	2.00	.80	.20
☐ 252	Angels Team	1.00	.40	.10
☐ 253	Dick Hughes	.40	.16	.04
☐ 254	Cleon Jones	.40	.16	.04
☐ 255	Dean Chance	.75	.30	.07
☐ 256	Norm Cash	1.50	.60	.15
☐ 257	Phil Niekro	4.50	1.80	.45
☐ 258	Cubs Rookies	.40	.16	.04
	Jose Arcia			
	Bill Schlesinger			
☐ 259	Ken Boyer	1.25	.50	.12
☐ 260	Jim Wynn	.75	.30	.07
☐ 261	Dave Duncan	.40	.16	.04

		NRMT	VG-E	GOOD
☐ 262	Rick Wise	.60	.24	.06
☐ 263	Horace Clarke	.60	.24	.06
☐ 264	Ted Abernathy	.40	.16	.04
☐ 265	Tommy Davis	.75	.30	.07
☐ 266	Paul Popovich	.40	.16	.04
☐ 267	Herman Franks MG	.40	.16	.04
☐ 268	Bob Humphreys	.40	.16	.04
☐ 269	Bob Tiefenauer	.40	.16	.04
☐ 270	Matty Alou	.60	.24	.06
☐ 271	Bobby Knoop	.40	.16	.04
☐ 272	Ray Culp	.40	.16	.04
☐ 273	Dave Johnson	1.00	.40	.10
☐ 274	Mike Cuellar	.75	.30	.07
☐ 275	Tim McCarver	1.50	.60	.15
☐ 276	Jim Roland	.40	.16	.04
☐ 277	Jerry Buchek	.40	.16	.04
☐ 278	Checklist 4	2.50	.50	.10
	Orlando Cepeda			
☐ 279	Bill Hands	.40	.16	.04
☐ 280	Mickey Mantle	175.00	70.00	18.00
☐ 281	Jim Campanis	.40	.16	.04
☐ 282	Rick Monday	.75	.30	.07
☐ 283	Mel Queen	.40	.16	.04
☐ 284	Johnny Briggs	.40	.16	.04
☐ 285	Dick McAuliffe	.60	.24	.06
☐ 286	Cecil Upshaw	.40	.16	.04
☐ 287	White Sox Rookies	.40	.16	.04
	Mickey Abarbanel			
	Cisco Carlos			
☐ 288	Dave Wickersham	.40	.16	.04
☐ 289	Woody Held	.40	.16	.04
☐ 290	Willie McCovey	7.00	2.80	.70
☐ 291	Dick Lines	.40	.16	.04
☐ 292	Art Shamsky	.40	.16	.04
☐ 293	Bruce Howard	.40	.16	.04
☐ 294	Red Schoendienst MG	1.00	.40	.10
☐ 295	Sonny Siebert	.60	.24	.06
☐ 296	Byron Browne	.40	.16	.04
☐ 297	Russ Gibson	.40	.16	.04
☐ 298	Jim Brewer	.40	.16	.04
☐ 299	Gene Michael	.60	.24	.06
☐ 300	Rusty Staub	1.25	.50	.12
☐ 301	Twins Rookies	.40	.16	.04
	George Mitterwald			
	Rick Renick			
☐ 302	Gerry Arrigo	.40	.16	.04
☐ 303	Dick Green	.40	.16	.04
☐ 304	Sandy Valdespino	.40	.16	.04
☐ 305	Minnie Rojas	.40	.16	.04

		NRMT	VG-E	GOOD
☐ 306	Mike Ryan	.40	.16	.04
☐ 307	John Hiller	.75	.30	.07
☐ 308	Pirates Team	1.00	.40	.10
☐ 309	Ken Henderson	.40	.16	.04
☐ 310	Luis Aparicio	5.00	2.00	.50
☐ 311	Jack Lamabe	.40	.16	.04
☐ 312	Curt Blefary	.40	.16	.04
☐ 313	Al Weis	.40	.16	.04
☐ 314	Red Sox Rookies	.40	.16	.04
	Bill Rohr			
	George Spriggs			
☐ 315	Zoilo Versalles	.40	.16	.04
☐ 316	Steve Barber	.40	.16	.04
☐ 317	Ron Brand	.40	.16	.04
☐ 318	Chico Salmon	.40	.16	.04
☐ 319	George Culver	.40	.16	.04
☐ 320	Frank Howard	1.00	.40	.10
☐ 321	Leo Durocher MG	1.50	.60	.15
☐ 322	Dave Boswell	.40	.16	.04
☐ 323	Deron Johnson	.60	.24	.06
☐ 324	Jim Nash	.40	.16	.04
☐ 325	Manny Mota	.60	.24	.06
☐ 326	Dennis Ribant	.40	.16	.04
☐ 327	Tony Taylor	.40	.16	.04
☐ 328	Angels Rookies	.40	.16	.04
	Chuck Vinson			
	Jim Weaver			
☐ 329	Duane Josephson	.40	.16	.04
☐ 330	Roger Maris	18.00	7.25	1.80
☐ 331	Dan Osinski	.40	.16	.04
☐ 332	Doug Rader	.75	.30	.07
☐ 333	Ron Herbel	.40	.16	.04
☐ 334	Orioles Team	1.00	.40	.10
☐ 335	Bob Allison	.75	.30	.07
☐ 336	John Purdin	.40	.16	.04
☐ 337	Bill Robinson	.75	.30	.07
☐ 338	Bob Johnson	.40	.16	.04
☐ 339	Rich Nye	.40	.16	.04
☐ 340	Max Alvis	.40	.16	.04
☐ 341	Jim Lemon MG	.60	.24	.06
☐ 342	Ken Johnson	.40	.16	.04
☐ 343	Jim Gosger	.40	.16	.04
☐ 344	Donn Clendenon	.60	.24	.06
☐ 345	Bob Hendley	.40	.16	.04
☐ 346	Jerry Adair	.40	.16	.04
☐ 347	George Brunet	.40	.16	.04
☐ 348	Phillies Rookies	.40	.16	.04
	Larry Colton			
	Dick Thoenen			

		NRMT	VG-E	GOOD
☐ 349	Ed Spiezio	.40	.16	.04
☐ 350	Hoyt Wilhelm	5.00	2.00	.50
☐ 351	Bob Barton	.40	.16	.04
☐ 352	Jackie Hernandez	.40	.16	.04
☐ 353	Mack Jones	.40	.16	.04
☐ 354	Pete Richert	.40	.16	.04
☐ 355	Ernie Banks	8.00	3.25	.80
☐ 356A	Checklist 5	2.50	.50	.10
	Ken Holtzman			
	(head centered within circle)			
☐ 356B	Checklist 5	2.50	.50	.10
	Ken Holtzman			
	(head shifted right within circle)			
☐ 357	Len Gabrielson	.40	.16	.04
☐ 358	Mike Epstein	.40	.16	.04
☐ 359	Joe Moeller	.40	.16	.04
☐ 360	Willie Horton	1.00	.40	.07
☐ 361	Harmon Killebrew AS	4.00	1.60	.40
☐ 362	Orlando Cepeda AS	1.25	.50	.12
☐ 363	Rod Carew AS	7.00	2.80	.70
☐ 364	Joe Morgan AS	2.50	1.00	.25
☐ 365	Brooks Robinson AS	4.50	1.80	.45
☐ 366	Ron Santo AS	.75	.30	.07
☐ 367	Jim Fregosi AS	.60	.24	.06
☐ 368	Gene Alley AS	.60	.24	.06
☐ 369	Carl Yastrzemski AS	8.50	3.50	.85
☐ 370	Hank Aaron AS	8.50	3.50	.85
☐ 371	Tony Oliva AS	1.00	.40	.10
☐ 372	Lou Brock AS	4.00	1.60	.40
☐ 373	Frank Robinson AS	4.00	1.60	.40
☐ 374	Bob Clemente AS	7.50	3.00	.75
☐ 375	Bill Freehan AS	.75	.30	.07
☐ 376	Tim McCarver AS	1.00	.40	.10
☐ 377	Joel Horlen AS	.60	.24	.06
☐ 378	Bob Gibson AS	4.00	1.60	.40
☐ 379	Gary Peters AS	.60	.24	.06
☐ 380	Ken Holtzman AS	.60	.24	.06
☐ 381	Boog Powell	1.50	.60	.15
☐ 382	Ramon Hernandez	.40	.16	.04
☐ 383	Steve Whitaker	.40	.16	.04
☐ 384	Reds Rookies	3.50	1.40	.35
	Bill Henry			
	Hal McRae			
☐ 385	Jim Hunter	6.00	2.40	.60
☐ 386	Greg Goossen	.40	.16	.04
☐ 387	Joe Foy	.40	.16	.04
☐ 388	Ray Washburn	.40	.16	.04
☐ 389	Jay Johnstone	.75	.30	.07
☐ 390	Bill Mazeroski	1.00	.40	.10

		NRMT	VG-E	GOOD
☐ 391	Bob Priddy	.40	.16	.04
☐ 392	Grady Hatton MG	.40	.16	.04
☐ 393	Jim Perry	.75	.30	.07
☐ 394	Tommie Aaron	.60	.24	.06
☐ 395	Camilo Pascual	.60	.24	.06
☐ 396	Bobby Wine	.40	.16	.04
☐ 397	Vic Davalillo	.60	.24	.06
☐ 398	Jim Grant	.40	.16	.04
☐ 399	Ray Oyler	.40	.16	.04
☐ 400A	Mike McCormick	.60	.24	.06
	(yellow letters)			
☐ 400B	Mike McCormick	20.00	8.00	2.00
	(team name in white letters)			
☐ 401	Mets Team	1.25	.50	.12
☐ 402	Mike Hegan	.40	.16	.04
☐ 403	John Buzhardt	.40	.16	.04
☐ 404	Floyd Robinson	.40	.16	.04
☐ 405	Tommy Helms	.60	.24	.06
☐ 406	Dick Ellsworth	.60	.24	.06
☐ 407	Gary Kolb	.40	.16	.04
☐ 408	Steve Carlton	30.00	12.00	3.00
☐ 409	Orioles Rookies	.40	.16	.04
	Frank Peters			
	Don Stone			
☐ 410	Fergie Jenkins	3.00	1.20	.30
☐ 411	Ron Hansen	.40	.16	.04
☐ 412	Clay Carroll	.40	.16	.04
☐ 413	Tom McCraw	.40	.16	.04
☐ 414	Mickey Lolich	1.75	.70	.17
☐ 415	Johnny Callison	.60	.24	.06
☐ 416	Bill Rigney MG	.40	.16	.04
☐ 417	Willie Crawford	.40	.16	.04
☐ 418	Eddie Fisher	.40	.16	.04
☐ 419	Jack Hiatt	.40	.16	.04
☐ 420	Cesar Tovar	.40	.16	.04
☐ 421	Ron Taylor	.40	.16	.04
☐ 422	Rene Lachemann	.75	.30	.07
☐ 423	Fred Gladding	.40	.16	.04
☐ 424	Chicago White Sox	1.00	.40	.10
	Team Card			
☐ 425	Jim Maloney	.60	.24	.06
☐ 426	Hank Allen	.40	.16	.04
☐ 427	Dick Calmus	.40	.16	.04
☐ 428	Vic Roznovsky	.40	.16	.04
☐ 429	Tommie Sisk	.40	.16	.04
☐ 430	Rico Petrocelli	.60	.24	.06
☐ 431	Dooley Womack	.40	.16	.04

		NRMT	VG-E	GOOD
☐ 432	Indians Rookies ...	.40	.16	.04
	Bill Davis			
	Jose Vidal			
☐ 433	Bob Rodgers	.75	.30	.07
☐ 434	Ricardo Joseph	.40	.16	.04
☐ 435	Ron Perranoski	.60	.24	.06
☐ 436	Hal Lanier	.60	.24	.06
☐ 437	Don Cardwell	.40	.16	.04
☐ 438	Lee Thomas	.75	.30	.07
☐ 439	Lum Harris MG ...	.40	.16	.04
☐ 440	Claude Osteen	.60	.24	.06
☐ 441	Alex Johnson	.60	.24	.06
☐ 442	Dick Bosman	.40	.16	.04
☐ 443	Joe Azcue	.40	.16	.04
☐ 444	Jack Fisher	.40	.16	.04
☐ 445	Mike Shannon	.75	.30	.07
☐ 446	Ron Kline	.40	.16	.04
☐ 447	Tigers Rookies	.40	.16	.04
	George Korince			
	Fred Lasher			
☐ 448	Gary Wagner	.40	.16	.04
☐ 449	Gene Oliver	.40	.16	.04
☐ 450	Jim Kaat	3.00	1.20	.30
☐ 451	Al Spangler	.40	.16	.04
☐ 452	Jesus Alou	.40	.16	.04
☐ 453	Sammy Ellis	.40	.16	.04
☐ 454A	Checklist 6	2.50	.50	.10
	Frank Robinson			
	(cap complete within circle)			
☐ 454B	Checklist 6	2.50	.50	.10
	Frank Robinson			
	(cap partially within circle)			
☐ 455	Rico Carty	.75	.30	.07
☐ 456	John O'Donoghue ..	.40	.16	.04
☐ 457	Jim Lefebvre	.75	.30	.07
☐ 458	Lew Krausse	.65	.26	.06
☐ 459	Dick Simpson	.65	.26	.06
☐ 460	Jim Lonborg	1.00	.40	.10
☐ 461	Chuck Hiller	.65	.26	.06
☐ 462	Barry Moore	.65	.26	.06
☐ 463	Jim Schaffer	.65	.26	.06
☐ 464	Don McMahon	.65	.26	.06
☐ 465	Tommie Agee	.65	.26	.06
☐ 466	Bill Dillman	.65	.26	.06
☐ 467	Dick Howser	1.00	.40	.10
☐ 468	Larry Sherry	.65	.26	.06
☐ 469	Ty Cline	.65	.26	.06
☐ 470	Bill Freehan	1.50	.60	.15
☐ 471	Orlando Pena	.65	.26	.06
☐ 472	Walt Alston MG	2.00	.80	.20
☐ 473	Al Worthington	.65	.26	.06
☐ 474	Paul Schaal	.65	.26	.06
☐ 475	Joe Niekro	1.50	.60	.15
☐ 476	Woody Woodward ..	.65	.26	.06
☐ 477	Philadelphia Phillies	1.50	.60	.15
	Team Card			
☐ 478	Dave McNally	1.00	.40	.10
☐ 479	Phil Gagliano	.65	.26	.06
☐ 480	Manager's Dream .	8.00	3.25	.80
	Tony Oliva			
	Chico Cardenas			
	Bob Clemente			
☐ 481	John Wyatt	.65	.26	.06
☐ 482	Jose Pagan	.65	.26	.06
☐ 483	Darold Knowles ...	.65	.26	.06
☐ 484	Phil Roof	.65	.26	.06
☐ 485	Ken Berry	.65	.26	.06
☐ 486	Cal Koonce	.65	.26	.06
☐ 487	Lee May	1.00	.40	.10
☐ 488	Dick Tracewski ...	.65	.26	.06
☐ 489	Wally Bunker	.65	.26	.06
☐ 490	Super Stars	35.00	14.00	3.50
	Harmon Killebrew			
	Willie Mays			
	Mickey Mantle			
☐ 491	Denny Lemaster .	.65	.26	.06
☐ 492	Jeff Torborg	1.00	.40	.10
☐ 493	Jim McGlothlin	.65	.26	.06
☐ 494	Ray Sadecki	.65	.26	.06
☐ 495	Leon Wagner	.65	.26	.06
☐ 496	Steve Hamilton	.65	.26	.06
☐ 497	Cards Team	1.50	.60	.15
☐ 498	Bill Bryan	.65	.26	.06
☐ 499	Steve Blass	1.00	.40	.10
☐ 500	Frank Robinson ...	10.00	4.00	1.00
☐ 501	John Odom	.65	.26	.06
☐ 502	Mike Andrews	.65	.26	.06
☐ 503	Al Jackson	.65	.26	.06
☐ 504	Russ Snyder	.65	.26	.06
☐ 505	Joe Sparma	.65	.26	.06
☐ 506	Clarence Jones	.65	.26	.06
☐ 507	Wade Blasingame	.65	.26	.06
☐ 508	Duke Sims	.65	.26	.06
☐ 509	Dennis Higgins	.65	.26	.06
☐ 510	Ron Fairly	1.00	.40	.10
☐ 511	Bill Kelso	.65	.26	.06
☐ 512	Grant Jackson	.65	.26	.06
☐ 513	Hank Bauer MG ...	1.00	.40	.10

	NRMT	VG-E	GOOD
☐ 514 Al McBean	.65	.26	.06
☐ 515 Russ Nixon	1.00	.40	.10
☐ 516 Pete Mikkelsen	.65	.26	.06
☐ 517 Diego Segui	.65	.26	.06
☐ 518A Checklist 7	3.00	.50	.10
(539 ML Rookies)			
(Clete Boyer)			
☐ 518B Checklist 7	6.00	1.00	.20
(539 AL Rookies)			
(Clete Boyer)			
☐ 519 Jerry Stephenson	.65	.26	.06
☐ 520 Lou Brock	10.00	4.00	1.00
☐ 521 Don Shaw	.65	.26	.06
☐ 522 Wayne Causey	.65	.26	.06
☐ 523 John Tsitouris	.65	.26	.06
☐ 524 Andy Kosco	.65	.26	.06
☐ 525 Jim Davenport	1.00	.40	.10
☐ 526 Bill Denehy	.65	.26	.06
☐ 527 Tito Francona	1.00	.40	.10
☐ 528 Tigers Team	7.00	2.80	.70
☐ 529 Bruce Von Hoff	.65	.26	.06
☐ 530 Bird Belters	5.00	2.00	.50
Brooks Robinson			
Frank Robinson			
☐ 531 Chuck Hinton	.65	.26	.06
☐ 532 Luis Tiant	1.50	.60	.15
☐ 533 Wes Parker	1.00	.40	.10
☐ 534 Bob Miller	.70	.28	.07
☐ 535 Danny Cater	.70	.28	.07
☐ 536 Bill Short	.70	.28	.07
☐ 537 Norm Siebern	.70	.28	.07
☐ 538 Manny Jimenez	.70	.28	.07
☐ 539 Major League Rookies	1.00	.40	.10
Jim Ray			
Mike Ferraro			
☐ 540 Nelson Briles	1.00	.40	.10
☐ 541 Sandy Alomar	.70	.28	.07
☐ 542 John Boccabella	.70	.28	.07
☐ 543 Bob Lee	.70	.28	.07
☐ 544 Mayo Smith MG	.70	.28	.07
☐ 545 Lindy McDaniel	1.00	.40	.10
☐ 546 Roy White	1.25	.50	.12
☐ 547 Dan Coombs	.70	.28	.07
☐ 548 Bernie Allen	.70	.28	.07
☐ 549 Orioles Rookies	.70	.28	.07
Curt Motton			
Roger Nelson			
☐ 550 Clete Boyer	1.25	.50	.12
☐ 551 Darrell Sutherland	.70	.28	.07

	NRMT	VG-E	GOOD
☐ 552 Ed Kirkpatrick	.70	.28	.07
☐ 553 Hank Aguirre	.70	.28	.07
☐ 554 A's Team	1.50	.60	.15
☐ 555 Jose Tartabull	.70	.28	.07
☐ 556 Dick Selma	.70	.28	.07
☐ 557 Frank Quilici	.70	.28	.07
☐ 558 Johnny Edwards	.70	.28	.07
☐ 559 Pirates Rookies	1.00	.40	.10
Carl Taylor			
Luke Walker			
☐ 560 Paul Casanova	.70	.28	.07
☐ 561 Lee Elia	1.00	.40	.10
☐ 562 Jim Bouton	1.50	.60	.15
☐ 563 Ed Charles	.70	.28	.07
☐ 564 Eddie Stanky MG	1.00	.40	.10
☐ 565 Larry Dierker	1.00	.40	.10
☐ 566 Ken Harrelson	1.50	.60	.15
☐ 567 Clay Dalrymple	.70	.28	.07
☐ 568 Willie Smith	.70	.28	.07
☐ 569 NL Rookies	.70	.28	.07
Ivan Murrell			
Les Rohr			
☐ 570 Rick Reichardt	.70	.28	.07
☐ 571 Tony LaRussa	1.50	.60	.15
☐ 572 Don Bosch	.70	.28	.07
☐ 573 Joe Coleman	.70	.28	.07
☐ 574 Cincinnati Reds	1.50	.60	.15
Team Card			
☐ 575 Jim Palmer	15.00	6.00	1.50
☐ 576 Dave Adlesh	.70	.28	.07
☐ 577 Fred Talbot	.70	.28	.07
☐ 578 Orlando Martinez	.70	.28	.07
☐ 579 NL Rookies	1.00	.40	.10
Larry Hisle			
Mike Lum			
☐ 580 Bob Bailey	.70	.28	.07
☐ 581 Garry Roggenburk	.70	.28	.07
☐ 582 Jerry Grote	.70	.28	.07
☐ 583 Gates Brown	1.00	.40	.10
☐ 584 Larry Shepard MG	.70	.28	.07
☐ 585 Wilbur Wood	1.00	.40	.10
☐ 586 Jim Pagliaroni	.70	.28	.07
☐ 587 Roger Repoz	.70	.28	.07
☐ 588 Dick Schofield	.70	.28	.07
☐ 589 Twins Rookies	.70	.28	.07
Ron Clark			
Moe Ogier			
☐ 590 Tommy Harper	1.00	.40	.10
☐ 591 Dick Nen	.70	.28	.07

		NRMT	VG-E	GOOD
☐ 592	John Bateman	.70	.28	.07
☐ 593	Lee Stange	.70	.28	.07
☐ 594	Phil Linz	1.00	.40	.10
☐ 595	Phil Ortega	.70	.28	.07
☐ 596	Charlie Smith	.70	.28	.07
☐ 597	Bill McCool	.70	.28	.07
☐ 598	Jerry May	1.50	.40	.08

1969 Topps

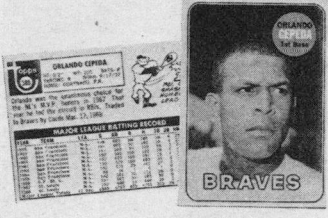

The cards in this 664-card set measure 2 ½ " by 3 ½ ". The 1969 Topps set includes Sporting News All-Star Selections as card numbers 416 to 435. Other popular subsets within this set include League Leaders (1-12) and World Series cards (162-169). The fifth series contains several variations; the more difficult variety consists of cards with the player's first name, last name, and/or position in white letters instead of lettering in some other color. These are designated in the checklist below by WL (white letters). Each checklist card features a different popular player's picture inside a circle on the front of the checklist card. Two different poses of Clay Dalrymple and Donn Clendenon exist as indicated in the checklist.

	NRMT	VG-E	GOOD
Complete Set (664)	1300.00	600.00	175.00
Common Player (1-218)	.40	.16	.04
Common Player (219-327)	.75	.30	.07
Common Player (328-512)	.40	.16	.04

			NRMT	VG-E	GOOD
	Common Player (513-588)		.50	.20	.05
	Common Player (589-664)		.65	.26	.06
☐ 1	AL Batting Leaders		5.00	1.00	.20
	Carl Yastrzemski				
	Danny Cater				
	Tony Oliva				
☐ 2	NL Batting Leaders		3.00	1.20	.30
	Pete Rose				
	Matty Alou				
	Felipe Alou				
☐ 3	AL RBI Leaders		1.25	.50	.12
	Ken Harrelson				
	Frank Howard				
	Jim Northrup				
☐ 4	NL RBI Leaders		2.00	.80	.20
	Willie McCovey				
	Ron Santo				
	Billy Williams				
☐ 5	AL Home Run Leaders		1.25	.50	.12
	Frank Howard				
	Willie Horton				
	Ken Harrelson				
☐ 6	NL Home Run Leaders		2.00	.80	.20
	Willie McCovey				
	Richie Allen				
	Ernie Banks				
☐ 7	AL ERA Leaders		1.25	.50	.12
	Luis Tiant				
	Sam McDowell				
	Dave McNally				
☐ 8	NL ERA Leaders		1.25	.50	.12
	Bob Gibson				
	Bobby Bolin				
	Bob Veale				
☐ 9	AL Pitching Leaders		1.25	.50	.12
	Denny McLain				
	Dave McNally				
	Luis Tiant				
	Mel Stottlemyre				
☐ 10	NL Pitching Leaders		2.00	.80	.20
	Juan Marichal				
	Bob Gibson				
	Fergie Jenkins				
☐ 11	AL Strikeout Leaders		1.25	.50	.12
	Sam McDowell				
	Denny McLain				
	Luis Tiant				

		NRMT	VG-E	GOOD
☐ 12	NL Strikeout Leaders	1.25	.50	.12
	Bob Gibson			
	Fergie Jenkins			
	Bill Singer			
☐ 13	Mickey Stanley	.60	.24	.06
☐ 14	Al McBean	.40	.16	.04
☐ 15	Boog Powell	1.50	.60	.15
☐ 16	Giants Rookies	.40	.16	.04
	Cesar Gutierrez			
	Rich Robertson			
☐ 17	Mike Marshall	.75	.30	.07
☐ 18	Dick Schofield	.40	.16	.04
☐ 19	Ken Suarez	.40	.16	.04
☐ 20	Ernie Banks	7.50	3.00	.75
☐ 21	Jose Santiago	.40	.16	.04
☐ 22	Jesus Alou	.40	.16	.04
☐ 23	Lew Krausse	.40	.16	.04
☐ 24	Walt Alston MG	1.50	.60	.15
☐ 25	Roy White	.75	.30	.07
☐ 26	Clay Carroll	.40	.16	.04
☐ 27	Bernie Allen	.40	.16	.04
☐ 28	Mike Ryan	.40	.16	.04
☐ 29	Dave Morehead	.40	.16	.04
☐ 30	Bob Allison	.60	.24	.06
☐ 31	Mets Rookies	1.25	.50	.12
	Gary Gentry			
	Amos Otis			
☐ 32	Sammy Ellis	.40	.16	.04
☐ 33	Wayne Causey	.40	.16	.04
☐ 34	Gary Peters	.60	.24	.06
☐ 35	Joe Morgan	4.50	1.80	.45
☐ 36	Luke Walker	.40	.16	.04
☐ 37	Curt Motton	.40	.16	.04
☐ 38	Zoilo Versalles	.40	.16	.04
☐ 39	Dick Hughes	.40	.16	.04
☐ 40	Mayo Smith MG	.40	.16	.04
☐ 41	Bob Barton	.40	.16	.04
☐ 42	Tommy Harper	.60	.24	.06
☐ 43	Joe Niekro	1.00	.40	.10
☐ 44	Danny Cater	.40	.16	.04
☐ 45	Maury Wills	2.00	.80	.20
☐ 46	Fritz Peterson	.40	.16	.04
☐ 47A	Paul Popovich	.40	.16	.04
	(no helmet emblem)			
☐ 47B	Paul Popovich	12.00	5.00	1.20
	(C emblem on helmet)			
☐ 48	Brant Alyea	.40	.16	.04

		NRMT	VG-E	GOOD
☐ 49A	Royals Rookies	.40	.16	.04
	Steve Jones			
	E. Rodriguez "g"			
☐ 49B	Royals Rookies	12.00	5.00	1.20
	Steve Jones			
	E. Rodriguez "q"			
☐ 50	Bob Clemente	22.00	9.00	2.20
☐ 51	Woodie Fryman	.40	.16	.04
☐ 52	Mike Andrews	.40	.16	.04
☐ 53	Sonny Jackson	.40	.16	.04
☐ 54	Cisco Carlos	.40	.16	.04
☐ 55	Jerry Grote	.40	.16	.04
☐ 56	Rich Reese	.40	.16	.04
☐ 57	Checklist 1	2.00	.30	.06
	Denny McLain			
☐ 58	Fred Gladding	.40	.16	.04
☐ 59	Jay Johnstone	.75	.30	.07
☐ 60	Nelson Briles	.60	.24	.06
☐ 61	Jimmie Hall	.60	.24	.06
☐ 62	Chico Salmon	.40	.16	.04
☐ 63	Jim Hickman	.40	.16	.04
☐ 64	Bill Monbouquette	.40	.16	.04
☐ 65	Willie Davis	.75	.30	.07
☐ 66	Orioles Rookies	.60	.24	.06
	Mike Adamson			
	Merv Rettenmund			
☐ 67	Bill Stoneman	.40	.16	.04
☐ 68	Dave Duncan	.40	.16	.04
☐ 69	Steve Hamilton	.40	.16	.04
☐ 70	Tommy Helms	.60	.24	.06
☐ 71	Steve Whitaker	.40	.16	.04
☐ 72	Ron Taylor	.40	.16	.04
☐ 73	Johnny Briggs	.40	.16	.04
☐ 74	Preston Gomez MG	.40	.16	.04
☐ 75	Luis Aparicio	5.00	2.00	.50
☐ 76	Norm Miller	.40	.16	.04
☐ 77A	Ron Perranoski	.60	.24	.06
	(no emblem on cap)			
☐ 77B	Ron Perranoski	12.00	5.00	1.20
	(LA on cap)			
☐ 78	Tom Satriano	.40	.16	.04
☐ 79	Milt Pappas	.60	.24	.06
☐ 80	Norm Cash	1.00	.40	.10
☐ 81	Mel Queen	.40	.16	.04
☐ 82	Pirates Rookies	8.00	3.25	.80
	Rich Hebner			
	Al Oliver			
☐ 83	Mike Ferraro	.60	.24	.06
☐ 84	Bob Humphreys	.40	.16	.04

		NRMT	VG-E	GOOD
☐ 85	Lou Brock	7.50	3.00	.75
☐ 86	Pete Richert	.40	.16	.04
☐ 87	Horace Clarke	.40	.16	.04
☐ 88	Rich Nye	.40	.16	.04
☐ 89	Russ Gibson	.40	.16	.04
☐ 90	Jerry Koosman	1.50	.60	.15
☐ 91	Alvin Dark MC	.60	.24	.06
☐ 92	Jack Billingham	.40	.16	.04
☐ 93	Joe Foy	.40	.16	.04
☐ 94	Hank Aguirre	.40	.16	.04
☐ 95	Johnny Bench	70.00	28.00	7.00
☐ 96	Denny Lemaster	.40	.16	.04
☐ 97	Buddy Bradford	.40	.16	.04
☐ 98	Dave Giusti	.60	.24	.06
☐ 99A	Twins Rookies	15.00	6.00	1.50
	Danny Morris			
	Graig Nettles			
	(no loop)			
☐ 99B	Twins Rookies	30.00	12.00	3.00
	(errant loop in upper left corner			
	of obverse)			
☐ 100	Hank Aaron	30.00	12.00	3.00
☐ 101	Daryl Patterson	.40	.16	.04
☐ 102	Jim Davenport	.60	.24	.06
☐ 103	Roger Repoz	.40	.16	.04
☐ 104	Steve Blass	.60	.24	.06
☐ 105	Rick Monday	.60	.24	.06
☐ 106	Jim Hannan	.40	.16	.04
☐ 107A	Checklist 2	2.00	.25	.05
	(161 Jim Purdin)			
	(Bob Gibson)			
☐ 107B	Checklist 2	5.00	.50	.10
	(161 John Purdin)			
	(Bob Gibson)			
☐ 108	Tony Taylor	.40	.16	.04
☐ 109	Jim Lonborg	.75	.30	.07
☐ 110	Mike Shannon	.75	.30	.07
☐ 111	Johnny Morris	.40	.16	.04
☐ 112	J.C. Martin	.40	.16	.04
☐ 113	Dave May	.40	.16	.04
☐ 114	Yankees Rookies ..	.40	.16	.04
	Alan Closter			
	John Cumberland			
☐ 115	Bill Hands	.40	.16	.04
☐ 116	Chuck Harrison	.40	.16	.04
☐ 117	Jim Fairey	.40	.16	.04
☐ 118	Stan Williams	.40	.16	.04
☐ 119	Doug Rader	.60	.24	.06
☐ 120	Pete Rose	30.00	12.00	3.00

		NRMT	VG-E	GOOD
☐ 121	Joe Grzenda	.40	.16	.04
☐ 122	Ron Fairly	.60	.24	.06
☐ 123	Wilbur Wood	.60	.24	.06
☐ 124	Hank Bauer MG	.60	.24	.06
☐ 125	Ray Sadecki	.40	.16	.04
☐ 126	Dick Tracewski	.40	.16	.04
☐ 127	Kevin Collins	.40	.16	.04
☐ 128	Tommie Aaron	.60	.24	.06
☐ 129	Bill McCool	.40	.16	.04
☐ 130	Carl Yastrzemski ..	25.00	10.00	2.50
☐ 131	Chris Cannizzaro ...	.40	.16	.04
☐ 132	Dave Baldwin	.40	.16	.04
☐ 133	Johnny Callison	.60	.24	.06
☐ 134	Jim Weaver	.40	.16	.04
☐ 135	Tommy Davis	.75	.30	.07
☐ 136	Cards Rookies	.60	.24	.06
	Steve Huntz			
	Mike Torrez			
☐ 137	Wally Bunker	.40	.16	.04
☐ 138	John Bateman	.40	.16	.04
☐ 139	Andy Kosco	.40	.16	.04
☐ 140	Jim Lefebvre	.75	.30	.07
☐ 141	Bill Dillman	.40	.16	.04
☐ 142	Woody Woodward ..	.60	.24	.06
☐ 143	Joe Nossek	.40	.16	.04
☐ 144	Bob Hendley	.40	.16	.04
☐ 145	Max Alvis	.40	.16	.04
☐ 146	Jim Perry	.75	.30	.07
☐ 147	Leo Durocher MG ..	1.25	.50	.12
☐ 148	Lee Stange	.40	.16	.04
☐ 149	Ollie Brown	.40	.16	.04
☐ 150	Denny McLain	2.00	.80	.20
☐ 151A	Clay Dalrymple	.40	.16	.04
	(Portrait, Orioles)			
☐ 151B	Clay Dalrymple	12.00	5.00	1.20
	(Catching, Phillies)			
☐ 152	Tommie Sisk	.40	.16	.04
☐ 153	Ed Brinkman	.40	.16	.04
☐ 154	Jim Britton	.40	.16	.04
☐ 155	Pete Ward	.40	.16	.04
☐ 156	Houston Rookies ..	.40	.16	.04
	Hal Gilson			
	Leon McFadden			
☐ 157	Bob Rodgers	.75	.30	.07
☐ 158	Joe Gibbon	.40	.16	.04
☐ 159	Jerry Adair	.40	.16	.04
☐ 160	Vada Pinson	1.00	.40	.10
☐ 161	John Purdin	.40	.16	.04

		NRMT	VG-E	GOOD
☐ 162	World Series Game 1 Gibson fans 17	3.00	1.20	.30
☐ 163	World Series Game 2 Tiger homers deck the Cards	1.75	.70	.17
☐ 164	World Series Game 3 McCarver's homer	2.00	.80	.20
☐ 165	World Series Game 4 Brock lead-off homer	3.00	1.20	.30
☐ 166	World Series Game 5 Kaline's key hit	4.00	1.60	.40
☐ 167	World Series Game 6 Northrup grandslam	1.75	.70	.17
☐ 168	World Series Game 7 Lolich outduels Bob Gibson	3.00	1.20	.30
☐ 169	World Series Summary Tigers celebrate	1.75	.70	.17
☐ 170	Frank Howard	1.00	.40	.10
☐ 171	Glenn Beckert	.60	.24	.06
☐ 172	Jerry Stephenson	.40	.16	.04
☐ 173	White Sox Rookies Bob Christian Gerry Nyman	.40	.16	.04
☐ 174	Grant Jackson	.40	.16	.04
☐ 175	Jim Bunning	2.50	1.00	.25
☐ 176	Joe Azcue	.40	.16	.04
☐ 177	Ron Reed	.40	.16	.04
☐ 178	Ray Oyler	.40	.16	.04
☐ 179	Don Pavletich	.40	.16	.04
☐ 180	Willie Horton	.75	.30	.06
☐ 181	Mel Nelson	.40	.16	.04
☐ 182	Bill Rigney MG	.40	.16	.04
☐ 183	Don Shaw	.40	.16	.04
☐ 184	Roberto Pena	.40	.16	.04
☐ 185	Tom Phoebus	.40	.16	.04
☐ 186	Johnny Edwards	.40	.16	.04
☐ 187	Leon Wagner	.40	.16	.04
☐ 188	Rick Wise	.60	.24	.06
☐ 189	Red Sox Rookies Joe Lahoud John Thibodeau	.40	.16	.04
☐ 190	Willie Mays	30.00	12.00	3.00
☐ 191	Lindy McDaniel	.60	.24	.06
☐ 192	Jose Pagan	.40	.16	.04
☐ 193	Don Cardwell	.40	.16	.04
☐ 194	Ted Uhlaender	.40	.16	.04
☐ 195	John Odom	.40	.16	.04
☐ 196	Lum Harris MG	.40	.16	.04

		NRMT	VG-E	GOOD
☐ 197	Dick Selma	.40	.16	.04
☐ 198	Willie Smith	.40	.16	.04
☐ 199	Jim French	.40	.16	.04
☐ 200	Bob Gibson	7.00	2.80	.70
☐ 201	Russ Snyder	.40	.16	.04
☐ 202	Don Wilson	.40	.16	.04
☐ 203	Dave Johnson	1.00	.40	.10
☐ 204	Jack Hiatt	.40	.16	.04
☐ 205	Rick Reichardt	.40	.16	.04
☐ 206	Phillies Rookies Larry Hisle Barry Lersch	.60	.24	.06
☐ 207	Roy Face	.75	.30	.07
☐ 208A	Donn Clendenon (Houston)	.60	.24	.06
☐ 208B	Donn Clendenon (Expos)	12.00	5.00	1.20
☐ 209	Larry Haney (reverse negative)	.40	.16	.04
☐ 210	Felix Millan	.40	.16	.04
☐ 211	Galen Cisco	.40	.16	.04
☐ 212	Tom Tresh	.60	.24	.06
☐ 213	Gerry Arrigo	.40	.16	.04
☐ 214	Checklist 3 With 69T deckle CL on back (no player)	2.00	.25	.05
☐ 215	Rico Petrocelli	.60	.24	.06
☐ 216	Don Sutton	4.00	1.60	.40
☐ 217	John Donaldson	.40	.16	.04
☐ 218	John Roseboro	.60	.24	.05
☐ 219	Freddie Patek	1.00	.40	.10
☐ 220	Sam McDowell	1.25	.50	.12
☐ 221	Art Shamsky	.75	.30	.07
☐ 222	Duane Josephson	.75	.30	.07
☐ 223	Tom Dukes	.75	.30	.07
☐ 224	Angels Rookies Bill Harrelson Steve Kealey	.75	.30	.07
☐ 225	Don Kessinger	1.00	.40	.10
☐ 226	Bruce Howard	.75	.30	.07
☐ 227	Frank Johnson	.75	.30	.07
☐ 228	Dave Leonhard	.75	.30	.07
☐ 229	Don Lock	.75	.30	.07
☐ 230	Rusty Staub	1.50	.60	.15
☐ 231	Pat Dobson	1.00	.40	.10
☐ 232	Dave Ricketts	.75	.30	.07
☐ 233	Steve Barber	.75	.30	.07
☐ 234	Dave Bristol MG	.75	.30	.07
☐ 235	Jim Hunter	7.50	3.00	.75

		NRMT	VG-E	GOOD
☐ 236	Manny Mota	1.00	.40	.10
☐ 237	Bobby Cox	1.00	.40	.10
☐ 238	Ken Johnson	.75	.30	.07
☐ 239	Bob Taylor	.75	.30	.07
☐ 240	Ken Harrelson	1.25	.50	.12
☐ 241	Jim Brewer	.75	.30	.07
☐ 242	Frank Kostro	.75	.30	.07
☐ 243	Ron Kline	.75	.30	.07
☐ 244	Indians Rookies	1.00	.40	.10
	Ray Fosse			
	George Woodson			
☐ 245	Ed Charles	.75	.30	.07
☐ 246	Joe Coleman	.75	.30	.07
☐ 247	Gene Oliver	.75	.30	.07
☐ 248	Bob Priddy	.75	.30	.07
☐ 249	Ed Spiezio	.75	.30	.07
☐ 250	Frank Robinson	11.00	4.50	1.10
☐ 251	Ron Herbel	.75	.30	.07
☐ 252	Chuck Cottier	.75	.30	.07
☐ 253	Jerry Johnson	.75	.30	.07
☐ 254	Joe Schultz	.75	.30	.07
☐ 255	Steve Carlton	25.00	10.00	2.50
☐ 256	Gates Brown	1.00	.40	.10
☐ 257	Jim Ray	.75	.30	.07
☐ 258	Jackie Hernandez	.75	.30	.07
☐ 259	Bill Short	.75	.30	.07
☐ 260	Reggie Jackson	250.00	100.00	25.00
☐ 261	Bob Johnson	.75	.30	.07
☐ 262	Mike Kekich	.75	.30	.07
☐ 263	Jerry May	.75	.30	.07
☐ 264	Bill Landis	.75	.30	.07
☐ 265	Chico Cardenas	.75	.30	.07
☐ 266	Dodger Rookies	.75	.30	.07
	Tom Hutton			
	Alan Foster			
☐ 267	Vicente Romo	.75	.30	.07
☐ 268	Al Spangler	.75	.30	.07
☐ 269	Al Weis	.75	.30	.07
☐ 270	Mickey Lolich	1.75	.70	.17
☐ 271	Larry Stahl	.75	.30	.07
☐ 272	Ed Stroud	.75	.30	.07
☐ 273	Ron Willis	.75	.30	.07
☐ 274	Clyde King MG	.75	.30	.07
☐ 275	Vic Davalillo	1.00	.40	.10
☐ 276	Gary Wagner	.75	.30	.07
☐ 277	Elrod Hendricks	.75	.30	.07
☐ 278	Gary Geiger	1.00	.40	.10
	(Batting wrong)			
☐ 279	Roger Nelson	.75	.30	.07
☐ 280	Alex Johnson	1.00	.40	.10
☐ 281	Ted Kubiak	.75	.30	.07
☐ 282	Pat Jarvis	.75	.30	.07
☐ 283	Sandy Alomar	.75	.30	.07
☐ 284	Expos Rookies	.75	.30	.07
	Jerry Robertson			
	Mike Wegener			
☐ 285	Don Mincher	1.00	.40	.10
☐ 286	Dock Ellis	1.00	.40	.10
☐ 287	Jose Tartabull	.75	.30	.07
☐ 288	Ken Holtzman	1.00	.40	.10
☐ 289	Bart Shirley	.75	.30	.07
☐ 290	Jim Kaat	3.50	1.40	.35
☐ 291	Vern Fuller	.75	.30	.07
☐ 292	Al Downing	1.00	.40	.10
☐ 293	Dick Dietz	.75	.30	.07
☐ 294	Jim Lemon MG	.75	.30	.07
☐ 295	Tony Perez	4.00	1.60	.40
☐ 296	Andy Messersmith	1.50	.60	.15
☐ 297	Deron Johnson	1.00	.40	.10
☐ 298	Dave Nicholson	.75	.30	.07
☐ 299	Mark Belanger	1.00	.40	.10
☐ 300	Felipe Alou	1.00	.40	.10
☐ 301	Darrell Brandon	.75	.30	.07
☐ 302	Jim Pagliaroni	.75	.30	.07
☐ 303	Cal Koonce	.75	.30	.07
☐ 304	Padres Rookies	1.00	.40	.10
	Bill Davis			
	Clarence Gaston			
☐ 305	Dick McAuliffe	1.00	.40	.10
☐ 306	Jim Grant	.75	.30	.07
☐ 307	Gary Kolb	.75	.30	.07
☐ 308	Wade Blasingame	.75	.30	.07
☐ 309	Walt Williams	.75	.30	.07
☐ 310	Tom Haller	1.00	.40	.10
☐ 311	Sparky Lyle	3.50	1.40	.35
☐ 312	Lee Elia	1.00	.40	.10
☐ 313	Bill Robinson	1.00	.40	.10
☐ 314	Checklist 4	2.50	.25	.05
	Don Drysdale			
☐ 315	Eddie Fisher	.75	.30	.07
☐ 316	Hal Lanier	1.00	.40	.10
☐ 317	Bruce Look	.75	.30	.07
☐ 318	Jack Fisher	.75	.30	.07
☐ 319	Ken McMullen	.75	.30	.07
☐ 320	Dal Maxvill	.75	.30	.07
☐ 321	Jim McAndrew	.75	.30	.07
☐ 322	Jose Vidal	.75	.30	.07
☐ 323	Larry Miller	.75	.30	.07

		NRMT	VG-E	GOOD
☐ 324	Tiger Rookies	.75	.30	.07
	Les Cain			
	Dave Campbell			
☐ 325	Jose Cardenal	.75	.30	.07
☐ 326	Gary Sutherland ...	.75	.30	.07
☐ 327	Willie Crawford	.75	.30	.07
☐ 328	Joel Horlen	.40	.16	.04
☐ 329	Rick Joseph	.40	.16	.04
☐ 330	Tony Conigliaro	1.25	.50	.12
☐ 331	Braves Rookies	.60	.24	.06
	Gil Garrido			
	Tom House			
☐ 332	Fred Talbot	.40	.16	.04
☐ 333	Ivan Murrell	.40	.16	.04
☐ 334	Phil Roof	.40	.16	.04
☐ 335	Bill Mazeroski	1.00	.40	.10
☐ 336	Jim Roland	.40	.16	.04
☐ 337	Marty Martinez	.40	.16	.04
☐ 338	Del Unser	.40	.16	.04
☐ 339	Reds Rookies	.40	.16	.04
	Steve Mingori			
	Jose Pena			
☐ 340	Dave McNally	.75	.30	.07
☐ 341	Dave Adlesh	.40	.16	.04
☐ 342	Bubba Morton	.40	.16	.04
☐ 343	Dan Frisella	.40	.16	.04
☐ 344	Tom Matchick	.40	.16	.04
☐ 345	Frank Linzy	.40	.16	.04
☐ 346	Wayne Comer	.40	.16	.04
☐ 347	Randy Hundley	.60	.24	.06
☐ 348	Steve Hargan	.40	.16	.04
☐ 349	Dick Williams MG ..	.60	.24	.06
☐ 350	Richie Allen	1.00	.40	.10
☐ 351	Carroll Sembera ...	.40	.16	.04
☐ 352	Paul Schaal	.40	.16	.04
☐ 353	Jeff Torborg	.60	.24	.06
☐ 354	Nate Oliver	.40	.16	.04
☐ 355	Phil Niekro	4.00	1.60	.40
☐ 356	Frank Quilici MG ...	.40	.16	.04
☐ 357	Carl Taylor	.40	.16	.04
☐ 358	Athletics Rookies ..	.40	.16	.04
	George Lauzerique			
	Roberto Rodriquez			
☐ 359	Dick Kelley	.40	.16	.04
☐ 360	Jim Wynn	.60	.24	.06
☐ 361	Gary Holman	.40	.16	.04
☐ 362	Jim Maloney	.60	.24	.06
☐ 363	Russ Nixon	.75	.30	.06
☐ 364	Tommie Agee	.60	.24	.06

		NRMT	VG-E	GOOD
☐ 365	Jim Fregosi	.75	.30	.07
☐ 366	Bo Belinsky	.60	.24	.06
☐ 367	Lou Johnson	.40	.16	.04
☐ 368	Vic Roznovsky	.40	.16	.04
☐ 369	Bob Skinner	.40	.16	.04
☐ 370	Juan Marichal	4.50	1.80	.45
☐ 371	Sal Bando	.75	.30	.07
☐ 372	Adolfo Phillips	.40	.16	.04
☐ 373	Fred Lasher	.40	.16	.04
☐ 374	Bob Tillman	.40	.16	.04
☐ 375	Harmon Killebrew .	10.00	4.00	1.00
☐ 376	Royals Rookies	.40	.16	.04
	Mike Fiore			
	Jim Rooker			
☐ 377	Gary Bell	.40	.16	.04
☐ 378	Jose Herrera	.40	.16	.04
☐ 379	Ken Boyer	1.00	.40	.10
☐ 380	Stan Bahnsen	.40	.16	.04
☐ 381	Ed Kranepool	.60	.24	.06
☐ 382	Pat Corrales	.60	.24	.06
☐ 383	Casey Cox	.40	.16	.04
☐ 384	Larry Shepard MG .	.40	.16	.04
☐ 385	Orlando Cepeda ...	2.50	1.00	.25
☐ 386	Jim McGlothlin	.40	.16	.04
☐ 387	Bobby Klaus	.40	.16	.04
☐ 388	Tom McCraw	.40	.16	.04
☐ 389	Dan Coombs	.40	.16	.04
☐ 390	Bill Freehan	1.00	.40	.10
☐ 391	Ray Culp	.40	.16	.04
☐ 392	Bob Burda	.40	.16	.04
☐ 393	Gene Brabender ...	.40	.16	.04
☐ 394	Pilots Rookies	2.25	.90	.22
	Lou Piniella			
	Marv Staehle			
☐ 395	Chris Short	.40	.16	.04
☐ 396	Jim Campanis	.40	.16	.04
☐ 397	Chuck Dobson	.40	.16	.04
☐ 398	Tito Francona	.60	.24	.06
☐ 399	Bob Bailey	.40	.16	.04
☐ 400	Don Drysdale	6.50	2.60	.65
☐ 401	Jake Gibbs	.40	.16	.04
☐ 402	Ken Boswell	.40	.16	.04
☐ 403	Bob Miller	.40	.16	.04
☐ 404	Cubs Rookies	.40	.16	.04
	Vic LaRose			
	Gary Ross			
☐ 405	Lee May	.60	.24	.06
☐ 406	Phil Ortega	.40	.16	.04
☐ 407	Tom Egan	.40	.16	.04

		NRMT	VG-E	GOOD
☐ 408	Nate Colbert	.40	.16	.04
☐ 409	Bob Moose	.40	.16	.04
☐ 410	Al Kaline	8.00	3.25	.80
☐ 411	Larry Dierker	.60	.24	.06
☐ 412	Checklist 5	5.00	1.00	.20
	Mickey Mantle			
☐ 413	Roland Sheldon	.40	.16	.04
☐ 414	Duke Sims	.40	.16	.04
☐ 415	Ray Washburn	.40	.16	.04
☐ 416	Willie McCovey AS .	4.00	1.60	.40
☐ 417	Ken Harrelson AS .	.60	.24	.06
☐ 418	Tommy Helms AS ..	.60	.24	.06
☐ 419	Rod Carew AS	5.00	2.00	.50
☐ 420	Ron Santo AS	.75	.30	.07
☐ 421	Brooks Robinson AS	4.00	1.60	.40
☐ 422	Don Kessinger AS .	.60	.24	.06
☐ 423	Bert Campaneris AS	.60	.24	.06
☐ 424	Pete Rose AS	10.00	4.00	1.00
☐ 425	Carl Yastrzemski AS	8.00	3.25	.80
☐ 426	Curt Flood AS	.75	.30	.07
☐ 427	Tony Oliva AS	1.00	.40	.10
☐ 428	Lou Brock AS	4.00	1.60	.40
☐ 429	Willie Horton AS ...	.60	.24	.06
☐ 430	Johnny Bench AS ..	10.00	4.00	1.00
☐ 431	Bill Freehan AS ...	.75	.30	.07
☐ 432	Bob Gibson AS	3.50	1.40	.35
☐ 433	Denny McLain AS ..	.75	.30	.07
☐ 434	Jerry Koosman AS .	.60	.24	.06
☐ 435	Sam McDowell AS .	.60	.24	.06
☐ 436	Gene Alley	.60	.24	.06
☐ 437	Luis Alcaraz	.40	.16	.04
☐ 438	Gary Waslewski ...	.40	.16	.04
☐ 439	White Sox Rookies .	.40	.16	.04
	Ed Herrmann			
	Dan Lazar			
☐ 440A	Willie McCovey	11.00	4.50	1.10
☐ 440B	Willie McCovey WL .	75.00	30.00	7.50
	(McCovey white)			
☐ 441A	Dennis Higgins	.40	.16	.04
☐ 441B	Dennis Higgins WL	12.00	5.00	1.20
	(Higgins white)			
☐ 442	Ty Cline	.40	.16	.04
☐ 443	Don Wert	.40	.16	.04
☐ 444A	Joe Moeller	.40	.16	.04
☐ 444B	Joe Moeller WL	12.00	5.00	1.20
	(Moeller white)			
☐ 445	Bobby Knoop	.40	.16	.04
☐ 446	Claude Raymond ..	.40	.16	.04
☐ 447A	Ralph Houk MG	.75	.30	.07

		NRMT	VG-E	GOOD
☐ 447B	Ralph Houk WL MG	12.00	5.00	1.20
	(Houk white)			
☐ 448	Bob Tolan	.60	.24	.06
☐ 449	Paul Lindblad	.40	.16	.04
☐ 450	Billy Williams	4.50	1.80	.45
☐ 451A	Rich Rollins	.60	.24	:06
☐ 451B	Rich Rollins WL ...	12.00	5.00	1.20
	(Rich and 3B white)			
☐ 452A	Al Ferrara	.40	.16	.04
☐ 452B	Al Ferrara WL	12.00	5.00	1.20
	(Al and OF white)			
☐ 453	Mike Cuellar	1.00	.40	.10
☐ 454A	Phillies Rookies ...	.60	.24	.06
	Larry Colton			
	Don Money			
☐ 454B	Phillies Rookies WL	12.00	5.00	1.20
	Larry Colton			
	Don Money			
	(names in white)			
☐ 455	Sonny Siebert	.60	.24	.06
☐ 456	Bud Harrelson	.60	.24	.06
☐ 457	Dalton Jones	.40	.16	.04
☐ 458	Curt Blefary	.40	.16	.04
☐ 459	Dave Boswell	.40	.16	.04
☐ 460	Joe Torre	1.00	.40	.10
☐ 461A	Mike Epstein	.40	.16	.04
☐ 461B	Mike Epstein WL ...	12.00	5.00	1.20
	(Epstein white)			
☐ 462	Red Schoendienst MG	1.00	.40	.10
☐ 463	Dennis Ribant	.40	.16	.04
☐ 464A	Dave Marshall	.40	.16	.04
☐ 464B	Dave Marshall WL .	12.00	5.00	1.20
	(Marshall white)			
☐ 465	Tommy John	3.50	1.40	.35
☐ 466	John Boccabella ..	.40	.16	.04
☐ 467	Tommie Reynolds .	.40	.16	.04
☐ 468A	Pirates Rookies ...	.40	.16	.04
	Bruce Dal Canton			
	Bob Robertson			
☐ 468B	Pirates Rookies WL	12.00	5.00	1.20
	Bruce Dal Canton			
	Bob Robertson			
	(names in white)			
☐ 469	Chico Ruiz	.40	.16	.04
☐ 470A	Mel Stottlemyre ...	1.00	.40	.10
☐ 470B	Mel Stottlemyre WL	15.00	6.00	1.50
	(Stottlemyre white)			
☐ 471A	Ted Savage	.40	.16	.04

	NRMT	VG-E	GOOD
☐ 471B Ted Savage WL ...	12.00	5.00	1.20
(Savage white)			
☐ 472 Jim Price	.40	.16	.04
☐ 473A Jose Arcia	.40	.16	.04
☐ 473B Jose Arcia WL	12.00	5.00	1.20
(Jose and 2B white)			
☐ 474 Tom Murphy	.40	.16	.04
☐ 475 Tim McCarver	1.25	.50	.12
☐ 476A Boston Rookies	.60	.24	.06
Ken Brett			
Gerry Moses			
☐ 476B Boston Rookies WL	12.00	5.00	1.20
Ken Brett			
Gerry Moses			
(names in white)			
☐ 477 Jeff James	.40	.16	.04
☐ 478 Don Buford	.60	.24	.06
☐ 479 Richie Scheinblum .	.40	.16	.04
☐ 480 Tom Seaver	50.00	20.00	5.00
☐ 481 Bill Melton	.40	.16	.04
☐ 482A Jim Gosger	.40	.16	.04
☐ 482B Jim Gosger WL	12.00	5.00	1.20
(Jim and OF white)			
☐ 483 Ted Abernathy	.40	.16	.04
☐ 484 Joe Gordon MG	.60	.24	.06
☐ 485A Gaylord Perry	5.50	2.20	.55
☐ 485B Gaylord Perry WL ..	45.00	18.00	4.50
(Perry white)			
☐ 486A Paul Casanova	.40	.16	.04
☐ 486B Paul Casanova WL .	12.00	5.00	1.20
(Casanova white)			
☐ 487 Denis Menke	.40	.16	.04
☐ 488 Joe Sparma	.40	.16	.04
☐ 489 Clete Boyer	.60	.24	.06
☐ 490 Matty Alou	.60	.24	.06
☐ 491A Twins Rookies	.40	.16	.04
Jerry Crider			
George Mitterwald			
☐ 491B Twins Rookies WL .	12.00	5.00	1.20
Jerry Crider			
George Mitterwald			
(names in white)			
☐ 492 Tony Cloninger	.40	.16	.04
☐ 493A Wes Parker	.60	.24	.06
☐ 493B Wes Parker WL	12.00	5.00	1.20
(Parker white)			
☐ 494 Ken Berry	.40	.16	.04
☐ 495 Bert Campaneris ...	.75	.30	.07
☐ 496 Larry Jaster	.40	.16	.04

	NRMT	VG-E	GOOD
☐ 497 Julian Javier	.60	.24	.06
☐ 498 Juan Pizarro	.40	.16	.04
☐ 499 Astro Rookies	.40	.16	.04
Don Bryant			
Steve Shea			
☐ 500A Mickey Mantle	150.00	60.00	15.00
☐ 500B Mickey Mantle WL .	500.00	200.00	50.00
(Mantle white)			
☐ 501A Tony Gonzalez	.40	.16	.04
☐ 501B Tony Gonzalez WL .	12.00	5.00	1.20
(Tony and OF white)			
☐ 502 Minnie Rojas	.40	.16	.04
☐ 503 Larry Brown	.40	.16	.04
☐ 504 Checklist 6	2.50	.30	.05
Brooks Robinson			
☐ 505A Bobby Bolin	.40	.16	.04
☐ 505B Bobby Bolin WL ...	12.00	5.00	1.20
(Bolin white)			
☐ 506 Paul Blair	.60	.24	.06
☐ 507 Cookie Rojas	.60	.24	.06
☐ 508 Moe Drabowsky ...	.40	.16	.04
☐ 509 Manny Sanguillen .	.75	.30	.07
☐ 510 Rod Carew	25.00	10.00	2.50
☐ 511A Diego Segui	.40	.16	.04
☐ 511B Diego Segui WL ...	12.00	5.00	1.20
(Diego and P white)			
☐ 512 Cleon Jones	.40	.16	.04
☐ 513 Camilo Pascual ...	.75	.30	.07
☐ 514 Mike Lum	.50	.20	.05
☐ 515 Dick Green	.50	.20	.05
☐ 516 Earl Weaver MG ...	4.00	1.60	.40
☐ 517 Mike McCormick ...	.75	.30	.07
☐ 518 Fred Whitfield	.50	.20	.05
☐ 519 Yankees Rookies ..	.50	.20	.05
Gerry Kenney			
Len Boehmer			
☐ 520 Bob Veale	.75	.30	.07
☐ 521 George Thomas ...	.50	.20	.05
☐ 522 Joe Hoerner	.50	.20	.05
☐ 523 Bob Chance	.50	.20	.05
☐ 524 Expos Rookies ...	.50	.20	.05
Jose Laboy			
Floyd Wicker			
☐ 525 Earl Wilson	.50	.20	.05
☐ 526 Hector Torres	.50	.20	.05
☐ 527 Al Lopez MG	2.00	.80	.20
☐ 528 Claude Osteen	.75	.30	.07
☐ 529 Ed Kirkpatrick	.50	.20	.05
☐ 530 Cesar Tovar	.50	.20	.05

		NRMT	VG-E	GOOD
☐ 531	Dick Farrell	.50	.20	.05
☐ 532	Bird Hill Aces	.75	.30	.07
	Tom Phoebus			
	Jim Hardin			
	Dave McNally			
	Mike Cuellar			
☐ 533	Nolan Ryan	70.00	28.00	7.00
☐ 534	Jerry McNertney	.50	.20	.05
☐ 535	Phil Regan	.75	.30	.07
☐ 536	Padres Rookies	.50	.20	.05
	Danny Breeden			
	Dave Roberts			
☐ 537	Mike Paul	.50	.20	.05
☐ 538	Charlie Smith	.50	.20	.05
☐ 539	Ted Shows How	3.50	1.40	.35
	Mike Epstein			
	Ted Williams			
☐ 540	Curt Flood	1.00	.40	.10
☐ 541	Joe Verbanic	.50	.20	.05
☐ 542	Bob Aspromonte	.50	.20	.05
☐ 543	Fred Newman	.50	.20	.05
☐ 544	Tigers Rookies	.50	.20	.05
	Mike Kilkenny			
	Ron Woods			
☐ 545	Willie Stargell	10.00	4.00	1.00
☐ 546	Jim Nash	.50	.20	.05
☐ 547	Billy Martin MG	2.50	1.00	.25
☐ 548	Bob Locker	.50	.20	.05
☐ 549	Ron Brand	.50	.20	.05
☐ 550	Brooks Robinson	10.00	4.00	1.00
☐ 551	Wayne Granger	.50	.20	.05
☐ 552	Dodgers Rookies	.75	.30	.07
	Ted Sizemore			
	Bill Sudakis			
☐ 553	Ron Davis	.50	.20	.05
☐ 554	Frank Bertaina	.50	.20	.05
☐ 555	Jim Ray Hart	.75	.30	.07
☐ 556	A's Stars	.75	.30	.07
	Sal Bando			
	Bert Campaneris			
	Danny Cater			
☐ 557	Frank Fernandez	.50	.20	.05
☐ 558	Tom Burgmeier	.75	.30	.07
☐ 559	Cardinals Rookies	.50	.20	.05
	Joe Hague			
	Jim Hicks			
☐ 560	Luis Tiant	1.25	.50	.12
☐ 561	Ron Clark	.50	.20	.05
☐ 562	Bob Watson	2.50	1.00	.25
☐ 563	Marty Pattin	.50	.20	.05
☐ 564	Gil Hodges MG	6.00	2.40	.60
☐ 565	Hoyt Wilhelm	5.50	2.20	.55
☐ 566	Ron Hansen	.50	.20	.05
☐ 567	Pirates Rookies	.50	.20	.05
	Elvio Jimenez			
	Jim Shellenback			
☐ 568	Cecil Upshaw	.50	.20	.05
☐ 569	Billy Harris	.50	.20	.05
☐ 570	Ron Santo	1.00	.40	.10
☐ 571	Cap Peterson	.50	.20	.05
☐ 572	Giants Heroes	6.50	2.60	.65
	Willie McCovey			
	Juan Marichal			
☐ 573	Jim Palmer	12.00	5.00	1.20
☐ 574	George Scott	.75	.30	.07
☐ 575	Bill Singer	.75	.30	.07
☐ 576	Phillies Rookies	.50	.20	.05
	Ron Stone			
	Bill Wilson			
☐ 577	Mike Hegan	.50	.20	.05
☐ 578	Don Bosch	.50	.20	.05
☐ 579	Dave Nelson	.50	.20	.05
☐ 580	Jim Northrup	.75	.30	.07
☐ 581	Gary Nolan	.50	.20	.05
☐ 582A	Checklist 7	2.50	.30	.05
	(white circle on back)			
	(Tony Oliva)			
☐ 582B	Checklist 7	4.00	.40	.07
	(red circle on back)			
	(Tony Oliva)			
☐ 583	Clyde Wright	.50	.20	.05
☐ 584	Don Mason	.50	.20	.05
☐ 585	Ron Swoboda	.75	.30	.07
☐ 586	Tim Cullen	.50	.20	.05
☐ 587	Joe Rudi	1.50	.60	.15
☐ 588	Bill White	1.00	.40	.10
☐ 589	Joe Pepitone	1.00	.40	.10
☐ 590	Rico Carty	1.00	.40	.10
☐ 591	Mike Hedlund	.65	.26	.06
☐ 592	Padres Rookies	.65	.26	.06
	Rafael Robles			
	Al Santorini			
☐ 593	Don Nottebart	.65	.26	.06
☐ 594	Dooley Womack	.65	.26	.06
☐ 595	Lee Maye	.65	.26	.06
☐ 596	Chuck Hartenstein	.65	.26	.06

		NRMT	VG-E	GOOD
☐ 597	A.L. Rookies	20.00	8.00	2.00
	Bob Floyd			
	Larry Burchart			
	Rollie Fingers			
☐ 598	Ruben Amaro	.65	.26	.06
☐ 599	John Boozer	.65	.26	.06
☐ 600	Tony Oliva	2.25	.90	.22
☐ 601	Tug McGraw	1.50	.60	.15
☐ 602	Cubs Rookies	.65	.26	.06
	Alec Distaso			
	Don Young			
	Jim Qualls			
☐ 603	Joe Keough	.65	.26	.06
☐ 604	Bobby Etheridge ...	.65	.26	.06
☐ 605	Dick Ellsworth	.65	.26	.06
☐ 606	Gene Mauch MG ...	1.00	.40	.10
☐ 607	Dick Bosman	.65	.26	.06
☐ 608	Dick Simpson	.65	.26	.06
☐ 609	Phil Gagliano	.65	.26	.06
☐ 610	Jim Hardin	.65	.26	.06
☐ 611	Braves Rookies	1.00	.40	.10
	Bob Didier			
	Walt Hriniak			
	Gary Neibauer			
☐ 612	Jack Aker	.65	.26	.06
☐ 613	Jim Beauchamp ...	.65	.26	.06
☐ 614	Houston Rookies ..	.65	.26	.06
	Tom Griffin			
	Skip Guinn			
☐ 615	Len Gabrielson	.65	.26	.06
☐ 616	Don McMahon	.65	.26	.06
☐ 617	Jesse Gonder	.65	.26	.06
☐ 618	Ramon Webster ...	.65	.26	.06
☐ 619	Royals Rookies	1.00	.40	.10
	Bill Butler			
	Pat Kelly			
	Juan Rios			
☐ 620	Dean Chance	1.00	.40	.10
☐ 621	Bill Voss	.65	.26	.06
☐ 622	Dan Osinski	.65	.26	.06
☐ 623	Hank Allen	.65	.26	.06
☐ 624	NL Rookies	.65	.26	.06
	Darrel Chaney			
	Duffy Dyer			
	Terry Harmon			
☐ 625	Mack Jones	.65	.26	.06
	(Batting wrong)			
☐ 626	Gene Michael	1.00	.40	.10
☐ 627	George Stone	.65	.26	.06

		NRMT	VG-E	GOOD
☐ 628	Red Sox Rookies .	1.00	.40	.10
	Bill Conigliaro			
	Syd O'Brien			
	Fred Wenz			
☐ 629	Jack Hamilton	.65	.26	.06
☐ 630	Bobby Bonds	8.00	3.25	.80
☐ 631	John Kennedy	.65	.26	.06
☐ 632	Jon Warden	.65	.26	.06
☐ 633	Harry Walker MG .	.65	.26	.06
☐ 634	Andy Etchebarren .	.65	.26	.06
☐ 635	George Culver	.65	.26	.06
☐ 636	Woody Held	.65	.26	.06
☐ 637	Padres Rookies ...	.65	.26	.06
	Jerry DaVanon			
	Frank Reberger			
	Clay Kirby			
☐ 638	Ed Sprague	.65	.26	.06
☐ 639	Barry Moore	.65	.26	.06
☐ 640	Fergie Jenkins ...	3.00	1.20	.30
☐ 641	NL Rookies	.65	.26	.06
	Bobby Darwin			
	John Miller			
	Tommy Dean			
☐ 642	John Hiller	1.00	.40	.10
☐ 643	Billy Cowan	.65	.26	.06
☐ 644	Chuck Hinton	.65	.26	.06
☐ 645	George Brunet	.65	.26	.06
☐ 646	Expos Rookies ...	.65	.26	.06
	Dan McGinn			
	Carl Morton			
☐ 647	Dave Wickersham .	.65	.26	.06
☐ 648	Bobby Wine	.65	.26	.06
☐ 649	Al Jackson	.65	.26	.06
☐ 650	Ted Williams MG .	6.00	2.40	.60
☐ 651	Gus Gil	.65	.26	.06
☐ 652	Eddie Watt	.65	.26	.06
☐ 653	Aurelio Rodriguez .	1.50	.60	.15
	(photo actually Angels' batboy)			
☐ 654	White Sox Rookies .	1.00	.40	.10
	Carlos May			
	Don Secrist			
	Rich Morales			
☐ 655	Mike Hershberger .	.65	.26	.06
☐ 656	Dan Schneider	.65	.26	.06
☐ 657	Bobby Murcer	1.25	.50	.12
☐ 658	AL Rookies	.65	.26	.06
	Tom Hall			
	Bill Burbach			
	Jim Miles			

		NRMT	VG-E	GOOD
☐ 659	Johnny Podres	1.25	.50	.12
☐ 660	Reggie Smith	1.50	.60	.15
☐ 661	Jim Merritt	.65	.26	.06
☐ 662	Royals Rookies	1.00	.40	.10
	Dick Drago			
	George Spriggs			
	Bob Oliver			
☐ 663	Dick Radatz	1.00	.40	.10
☐ 664	Ron Hunt	1.00	.40	.10

1970 Topps

*The cards in this 720-card set measure 2 ½"
by 3 ½". The Topps set for 1970 has color
photos surrounded by white frame lines and
gray borders. The backs have a blue
biographical section and a yellow record
section. All-Star selections are featured on
cards 450 to 469. Other topical subsets
within this set include League Leaders (61-
72), Playoffs cards (195-202), and World
Series cards (305-310). There are gradua-
tions of scarcity, terminating in the high
series (634-720), which are outlined in the
value summary.*

	NRMT	VG-E	GOOD
Complete Set (720) 1250.00	500.00	175.00
Common Player (1-132) ...	.25	.10	.02
Common Player (133-263) .	.30	.12	.03
Common Player (264-459) .	.35	.14	.03
Common Player (460-546) .	.50	.20	.05
Common Player (547-633) .	.85	.34	.08
Common Player (634-720) .	2.00	.80	.20

		NRMT	VG-E	GOOD
☐ 1	New York Mets ...	6.00	1.00	.20
	Team Card			
☐ 2	Diego Segui	.25	.10	.02
☐ 3	Darrel Chaney	.25	.10	.02
☐ 4	Tom Egan	.25	.10	.02
☐ 5	Wes Parker	.40	.16	.04
☐ 6	Grant Jackson	.25	.10	.02
☐ 7	Indians Rookies ...	.25	.10	.02
	Gary Boyd			
	Russ Nagelson			
☐ 8	Jose Martinez	.25	.10	.02
☐ 9	Checklist 1	1.50	.20	.04
☐ 10	Carl Yastrzemski .	24.00	10.00	2.40
☐ 11	Nate Colbert	.25	.10	.02
☐ 12	John Hiller	.40	.16	.04
☐ 13	Jack Hiatt	.25	.10	.02
☐ 14	Hank Allen	.25	.10	.02
☐ 15	Larry Dierker	.40	.16	.04
☐ 16	Charlie Metro MG .	.25	.10	.02
☐ 17	Hoyt Wilhelm	3.50	1.40	.35
☐ 18	Carlos May	.25	.10	.02
☐ 19	John Boccabella ..	.25	.10	.02
☐ 20	Dave McNally	.40	.16	.04
☐ 21	A's Rookies	2.00	.80	.20
	Vida Blue			
	Gene Tenace			
☐ 22	Ray Washburn	.25	.10	.02
☐ 23	Bill Robinson	.40	.16	.04
☐ 24	Dick Selma	.25	.10	.02
☐ 25	Cesar Tovar	.25	.10	.02
☐ 26	Tug McGraw	.75	.30	.07
☐ 27	Chuck Hinton	.25	.10	.02
☐ 28	Billy Wilson	.25	.10	.02
☐ 29	Sandy Alomar	.25	.10	.02
☐ 30	Matty Alou	.40	.16	.04
☐ 31	Marty Pattin	.25	.10	.02
☐ 32	Harry Walker MG ..	.25	.10	.02
☐ 33	Don Wert	.25	.10	.02
☐ 34	Willie Crawford ...	.25	.10	.02
☐ 35	Joel Horlen	.25	.10	.02
☐ 36	Red Rookies	.40	.16	.04
	Danny Breeden			
	Bernie Carbo			
☐ 37	Dick Drago	.25	.10	.02
☐ 38	Mack Jones	.25	.10	.02
☐ 39	Mike Nagy	.25	.10	.02
☐ 40	Rich Allen	.75	.30	.07
☐ 41	George Lauzerique	.25	.10	.02
☐ 42	Tito Fuentes	.25	.10	.02
☐ 43	Jack Aker	.25	.10	.02

		NRMT	VG-E	GOOD
☐ 44	Roberto Pena	.25	.10	.02
☐ 45	Dave Johnson	.75	.30	.06
☐ 46	Ken Rudolph	.25	.10	.02
☐ 47	Bob Miller	.25	.10	.02
☐ 48	Gil Garrido	.25	.10	.02
☐ 49	Tim Cullen	.25	.10	.02
☐ 50	Tommie Agee	.25	.10	.02
☐ 51	Bob Christian	.25	.10	.02
☐ 52	Bruce Dal Canton	.25	.10	.02
☐ 53	John Kennedy	.25	.10	.02
☐ 54	Jeff Torborg	.40	.16	.04
☐ 55	John Odom	.25	.10	.02
☐ 56	Phillies Rookies	.25	.10	.02
	Joe Lis			
	Scott Reid			
☐ 57	Pat Kelly	.25	.10	.02
☐ 58	Dave Marshall	.25	.10	.02
☐ 59	Dick Ellsworth	.40	.16	.04
☐ 60	Jim Wynn	.40	.16	.04
☐ 61	NL Batting Leaders	3.00	1.20	.30
	Pete Rose			
	Bob Clemente			
	Cleon Jones			
☐ 62	AL Batting Leaders	1.25	.50	.12
	Rod Carew			
	Reggie Smith			
	Tony Oliva			
☐ 63	NL RBI Leaders	1.25	.50	.12
	Willie McCovey			
	Ron Santo			
	Tony Perez			
☐ 64	AL RBI Leaders	1.75	.70	.17
	Harmon Killebrew			
	Beog Powell			
	Reggie Jackson			
☐ 65	NL Home Run Leaders	2.00	.80	.20
	Willie McCovey			
	Hank Aaron			
	Lee May			
☐ 66	AL Home Run Leaders	2.00	.80	.20
	Harmon Killebrew			
	Frank Howard			
	Reggie Jackson			
☐ 67	NL ERA Leaders	3.50	1.40	.35
	Juan Marichal			
	Steve Carlton			
	Bob Gibson			

		NRMT	VG-E	GOOD
☐ 68	AL ERA Leaders	1.25	.50	.12
	Dick Bosman			
	Jim Palmer			
	Mike Cuellar			
☐ 69	NL Pitching Leaders	2.50	1.00	.25
	Tom Seaver			
	Phil Niekro			
	Fergie Jenkins			
	Juan Marichal			
☐ 70	AL Pitching Leaders	1.25	.50	.12
	Dennis McLain			
	Mike Cuellar			
	Dave Boswell			
	Dave McNally			
	Jim Perry			
	Mel Stottlemyre			
☐ 71	NL Strikeout Leaders	1.25	.50	.12
	Fergie Jenkins			
	Bob Gibson			
	Bill Singer			
☐ 72	AL Strikeout Leaders	1.25	.50	.12
	Sam McDowell			
	Mickey Lolich			
	Andy Messersmith			
☐ 73	Wayne Granger	.25	.10	.02
☐ 74	Angels Rookies	.25	.10	.02
	Greg Washburn			
	Wally Wolf			
☐ 75	Jim Kaat	2.00	.80	.20
☐ 76	Carl Taylor	.25	.10	.02
☐ 77	Frank Linzy	.25	.10	.02
☐ 78	Joe Lahoud	.25	.10	.02
☐ 79	Clay Kirby	.25	.10	.02
☐ 80	Don Kessinger	.40	.16	.04
☐ 81	Dave May	.25	.10	.02
☐ 82	Frank Fernandez	.25	.10	.02
☐ 83	Don Cardwell	.25	.10	.02
☐ 84	Paul Casanova	.25	.10	.02
☐ 85	Max Alvis	.25	.10	.02
☐ 86	Lum Harris MG	.25	.10	.02
☐ 87	Steve Renko	.25	.10	.02
☐ 88	Pilots Rookies	.25	.10	.02
	Miguel Fuentes			
	Dick Baney			
☐ 89	Juan Rios	.25	.10	.02
☐ 90	Tim McCarver	.75	.30	.07
☐ 91	Rich Morales	.25	.10	.02
☐ 92	George Culver	.25	.10	.02
☐ 93	Rick Renick	.25	.10	.02

		NRMT	VG-E	GOOD
☐ 94	Freddie Patek	.40	.16	.04
☐ 95	Earl Wilson	.25	.10	.02
☐ 96	Cardinals Rookies	2.25	.90	.22
	Leron Lee			
	Jerry Reuss			
☐ 97	Joe Moeller	.25	.10	.02
☐ 98	Gates Brown	.40	.16	.04
☐ 99	Bobby Pfeil	.25	.10	.02
☐ 100	Mel Stottlemyre	.75	.30	.06
☐ 101	Bobby Floyd	.25	.10	.02
☐ 102	Joe Rudi	.50	.20	.04
☐ 103	Frank Reberger	.25	.10	.02
☐ 104	Gerry Moses	.25	.10	.02
☐ 105	Tony Gonzalez	.25	.10	.02
☐ 106	Darold Knowles	.25	.10	.02
☐ 107	Bobby Etheridge	.25	.10	.02
☐ 108	Tom Burgmeier	.25	.10	.02
☐ 109	Expos Rookies	.40	.16	.04
	Garry Jestadt			
	Carl Morton			
☐ 110	Bob Moose	.25	.10	.02
☐ 111	Mike Hegan	.25	.10	.02
☐ 112	Dave Nelson	.25	.10	.02
☐ 113	Jim Ray	.25	.10	.02
☐ 114	Gene Michael	.40	.16	.04
☐ 115	Alex Johnson	.40	.16	.04
☐ 116	Sparky Lyle	1.00	.40	.07
☐ 117	Don Young	.25	.10	.02
☐ 118	George Mitterwald	.25	.10	.02
☐ 119	Chuck Taylor	.25	.10	.02
☐ 120	Sal Bando	.60	.24	.06
☐ 121	Orioles Rookies	.40	.16	.04
	Fred Beene			
	Terry Crowley			
☐ 122	George Stone	.25	.10	.02
☐ 123	Don Gutteridge	.25	.10	.02
☐ 124	Larry Jaster	.25	.10	.02
☐ 125	Deron Johnson	.25	.10	.02
☐ 126	Marty Martinez	.25	.10	.02
☐ 127	Joe Coleman	.25	.10	.02
☐ 128	Checklist 2	1.50	.20	.04
☐ 129	Jimmie Price	.25	.10	.02
☐ 130	Ollie Brown	.25	.10	.02
☐ 131	Dodgers Rookies	.25	.10	.02
	Ray Lamb			
	Bob Stinson			
☐ 132	Jim McGlothlin	.25	.10	.02
☐ 133	Clay Carroll	.30	.12	.03
☐ 134	Danny Walton	.30	.12	.03
☐ 135	Dick Dietz	.30	.12	.03
☐ 136	Steve Hargan	.30	.12	.03
☐ 137	Art Shamsky	.30	.12	.03
☐ 138	Joe Foy	.30	.12	.03
☐ 139	Rich Nye	.30	.12	.03
☐ 140	Reggie Jackson	50.00	20.00	5.00
☐ 141	Pirates Rookies	.50	.20	.05
	Dave Cash			
	Johnny Jeter			
☐ 142	Fritz Peterson	.30	.12	.03
☐ 143	Phil Gagliano	.30	.12	.03
☐ 144	Ray Culp	.30	.12	.03
☐ 145	Rico Carty	.50	.20	.05
☐ 146	Danny Murphy	.30	.12	.03
☐ 147	Angel Hermoso	.30	.12	.03
☐ 148	Earl Weaver MG	1.00	.40	.10
☐ 149	Billy Champion	.30	.12	.03
☐ 150	Harmon Killebrew	5.00	2.00	.50
☐ 151	Dave Roberts	.30	.12	.03
☐ 152	Ike Brown	.30	.12	.03
☐ 153	Gary Gentry	.30	.12	.03
☐ 154	Senators Rookies	.30	.12	.03
	Jim Miles			
	Jan Dukes			
☐ 155	Denis Menke	.30	.12	.03
☐ 156	Eddie Fisher	.30	.12	.03
☐ 157	Manny Mota	.50	.20	.05
☐ 158	Jerry McNertney	.30	.12	.03
☐ 159	Tommy Helms	.50	.20	.05
☐ 160	Phil Niekro	3.50	1.40	.35
☐ 161	Richie Scheinblum	.30	.12	.03
☐ 162	Jerry Johnson	.30	.12	.03
☐ 163	Syd O'Brien	.30	.12	.03
☐ 164	Ty Cline	.30	.12	.03
☐ 165	Ed Kirkpatrick	.30	.12	.03
☐ 166	Al Oliver	2.00	.80	.20
☐ 167	Bill Burbach	.30	.12	.03
☐ 168	Dave Watkins	.30	.12	.03
☐ 169	Tom Hall	.30	.12	.03
☐ 170	Billy Williams	4.00	1.60	.40
☐ 171	Jim Nash	.30	.12	.03
☐ 172	Braves Rookies	1.00	.40	.10
	Garry Hill			
	Ralph Garr			
☐ 173	Jim Hicks	.30	.12	.03
☐ 174	Ted Sizemore	.50	.20	.05
☐ 175	Dick Bosman	.30	.12	.03
☐ 176	Jim Ray Hart	.50	.20	.05
☐ 177	Jim Northrup	.50	.20	.05

		NRMT	VG-E	GOOD
☐ 178	Denny Lemaster ...	.30	.12	.03
☐ 179	Ivan Murrell	.30	.12	.03
☐ 180	Tommy John	2.25	.90	.22
☐ 181	Sparky Anderson MG	1.00	.40	.10
☐ 182	Dick Hall	.30	.12	.03
☐ 183	Jerry Grote	.30	.12	.03
☐ 184	Ray Fosse	.30	.12	.03
☐ 185	Don Mincher	.50	.20	.05
☐ 186	Rick Joseph	.30	.12	.03
☐ 187	Mike Hedlund	.30	.12	.03
☐ 188	Manny Sanguillen ..	.50	.20	.05
☐ 189	Yankees Rookies ..	35.00	14.00	3.50
	Thurman Munson			
	Dave McDonald			
☐ 190	Joe Torre	1.00	.40	.10
☐ 191	Vicente Romo	.30	.12	.03
☐ 192	Jim Qualls	.30	.12	.03
☐ 193	Mike Wegener	.30	.12	.03
☐ 194	Chuck Manuel	.30	.12	.03
☐ 195	NL Playoff Game 1 .	3.00	1.20	.30
	Seaver wins opener			
☐ 196	NL Playoff Game 2 .	1.25	.50	.12
	Mets show muscle			
☐ 197	NL Playoff Game 3 .	3.00	1.20	.30
	Ryan saves the day			
☐ 198	NL Playoff Summary	1.25	.50	.12
	Mets celebrate			
☐ 199	AL Playoff Game 1 .	1.25	.50	.12
	Orioles win			
	squeaker (Cuellar)			
☐ 200	AL Playoff Game 2 .	1.25	.50	.12
	Powell scores			
	winning run			
☐ 201	AL Playoff Game 3 .	1.25	.50	.12
	Birds wrap it up			
☐ 202	AL Playoff Summary	1.25	.50	.12
	Orioles celebrate			
☐ 203	Rudy May	.30	.12	.03
☐ 204	Len Gabrielson	.30	.12	.03
☐ 205	Bert Campaneris ...	.50	.20	.05
☐ 206	Clete Boyer	.50	.20	.05
☐ 207	Tigers Rookies	.30	.12	.03
	Norman McRae			
	Bob Reed			
☐ 208	Fred Gladding	.30	.12	.03
☐ 209	Ken Suarez	.30	.12	.03
☐ 210	Juan Marichal	4.00	1.60	.40
☐ 211	Ted Williams MG ...	5.00	2.00	.50
☐ 212	Al Santorini	.30	.12	.03

		NRMT	VG-E	GOOD
☐ 213	Andy Etchebarren .	.30	.12	.03
☐ 214	Ken Boswell	.30	.12	.03
☐ 215	Reggie Smith	.75	.30	.07
☐ 216	Chuck Hartenstein .	.30	.12	.03
☐ 217	Ron Hansen	.30	.12	.03
☐ 218	Ron Stone	.30	.12	.03
☐ 219	Jerry Kenney	.30	.12	.03
☐ 220	Steve Carlton	12.00	5.00	1.20
☐ 221	Ron Brand	.30	.12	.03
☐ 222	Jim Rooker	.30	.12	.03
☐ 223	Nate Oliver	.30	.12	.03
☐ 224	Steve Barber	.30	.12	.03
☐ 225	Lee May	.50	.20	.05
☐ 226	Ron Perranoski ...	.50	.20	.05
☐ 227	Astros Rookies ...	1.00	.40	.10
	John Mayberry			
	Bob Watkins			
☐ 228	Aurelio Rodriguez .	.30	.12	.03
☐ 229	Rich Robertson ...	.30	.12	.03
☐ 230	Brooks Robinson ..	7.50	3.25	.70
☐ 231	Luis Tiant	1.00	.40	.10
☐ 232	Bob Didier	.30	.12	.03
☐ 233	Lew Krausse	.30	.12	.03
☐ 234	Tommy Dean	.30	.12	.03
☐ 235	Mike Epstein	.30	.12	.03
☐ 236	Bob Veale	.50	.20	.05
☐ 237	Russ Gibson	.30	.12	.03
☐ 238	Jose Laboy	.30	.12	.03
☐ 239	Ken Berry	.30	.12	.03
☐ 240	Fergie Jenkins	2.25	.90	.22
☐ 241	Royals Rookies ...	.30	.12	.03
	Al Fitzmorris			
	Scott Northey			
☐ 242	Walter Alston MG .	1.50	.60	.15
☐ 243	Joe Sparma	.30	.12	.03
☐ 244A	Checklist 3	2.00	.30	.05
	(red bat on front)			
☐ 244B	Checklist 3	2.50	.30	.05
	(brown bat on front)			
☐ 245	Leo Cardenas	.30	.12	.03
☐ 246	Jim McAndrew	.30	.12	.03
☐ 247	Lou Klimchock	.30	.12	.03
☐ 248	Jesus Alou	.30	.12	.03
☐ 249	Bob Locker	.30	.12	.03
☐ 250	Willie McCovey ...	6.00	2.40	.60
☐ 251	Dick Schofield	.30	.12	.03
☐ 252	Lowell Palmer	.30	.12	.03
☐ 253	Ron Woods	.30	.12	.03
☐ 254	Camilo Pascual ...	.50	.20	.05

		NRMT	VG-E	GOOD
☐ 255	Jim Spencer	.30	.12	.03
☐ 256	Vic Davalillo	.30	.12	.03
☐ 257	Dennis Higgins	.30	.12	.03
☐ 258	Paul Popovich	.30	.12	.03
☐ 259	Tommie Reynolds	.30	.12	.03
☐ 260	Claude Osteen	.50	.20	.05
☐ 261	Curt Motton	.30	.12	.03
☐ 262	Padres Rookies	.50	.20	.05
	Jerry Morales			
	Jim Williams			
☐ 263	Duane Josephson	.30	.12	.03
☐ 264	Rich Hebner	.75	.30	.07
☐ 265	Randy Hundley	.50	.20	.05
☐ 266	Wally Bunker	.35	.14	.03
☐ 267	Twins Rookies	.35	.14	.03
	Herman Hill			
	Paul Ratliff			
☐ 268	Claude Raymond	.35	.14	.03
☐ 269	Cesar Gutierrez	.35	.14	.03
☐ 270	Chris Short	.35	.14	.03
☐ 271	Greg Goossen	.35	.14	.03
☐ 272	Hector Torres	.35	.14	.03
☐ 273	Ralph Houk MG	.50	.20	.05
☐ 274	Gerry Arrigo	.35	.14	.03
☐ 275	Duke Sims	.35	.14	.03
☐ 276	Ron Hunt	.35	.14	.03
☐ 277	Paul Doyle	.35	.14	.03
☐ 278	Tommie Aaron	.50	.20	.05
☐ 279	Bill Lee	.75	.30	.07
☐ 280	Donn Clendenon	.50	.20	.05
☐ 281	Casey Cox	.35	.14	.03
☐ 282	Steve Huntz	.35	.14	.03
☐ 283	Angel Bravo	.35	.14	.03
☐ 284	Jack Baldschun	.35	.14	.03
☐ 285	Paul Blair	.50	.20	.05
☐ 286	Dodgers Rookies	5.00	2.00	.50
	Jack Jenkins			
	Bill Buckner			
☐ 287	Fred Talbot	.35	.14	.03
☐ 288	Larry Hisle	.50	.20	.05
☐ 289	Gene Brabender	.35	.14	.03
☐ 290	Rod Carew	15.00	5.75	1.40
☐ 291	Leo Durocher MG	1.25	.50	.12
☐ 292	Eddie Leon	.35	.14	.03
☐ 293	Bob Bailey	.35	.14	.03
☐ 294	Jose Azcue	.35	.14	.03
☐ 295	Cecil Upshaw	.35	.14	.03
☐ 296	Woody Woodward	.50	.20	.05
☐ 297	Curt Blefary	.35	.14	.03
☐ 298	Ken Henderson	.35	.14	.03
☐ 299	Buddy Bradford	.35	.14	.03
☐ 300	Tom Seaver	30.00	12.00	3.00
☐ 301	Chico Salmon	.35	.14	.03
☐ 302	Jeff James	.35	.14	.03
☐ 303	Brant Alyea	.35	.14	.03
☐ 304	Bill Russell	1.50	.60	.15
☐ 305	World Series Game 1	1.25	.50	.12
	Buford leadoff homer			
☐ 306	World Series Game 2	1.25	.50	.12
	Clendenon's homer			
	breaks ice			
☐ 307	World Series Game 3	1.25	.50	.12
	Agee's catch			
	saves the day			
☐ 308	World Series Game 4	1.25	.50	.12
	Martin's bunt			
	ends deadlock			
☐ 309	World Series Game 5	1.25	.50	.12
	Koosman shuts door			
☐ 310	World Series Summary	1.25	.50	.12
	Mets whoop it up			
☐ 311	Dick Green	.35	.14	.03
☐ 312	Mike Torrez	.50	.20	.05
☐ 313	Mayo Smith MG	.35	.14	.03
☐ 314	Bill McCool	.35	.14	.03
☐ 315	Luis Aparicio	3.50	1.40	.35
☐ 316	Skip Guinn	.35	.14	.03
☐ 317	Red Sox Rookies	.50	.20	.05
	Billy Conigliaro			
	Luis Alvarado			
☐ 318	Willie Smith	.35	.14	.03
☐ 319	Clay Dalrymple	.35	.14	.03
☐ 320	Jim Maloney	.50	.20	.05
☐ 321	Lou Piniella	1.00	.40	.10
☐ 322	Luke Walker	.35	.14	.03
☐ 323	Wayne Comer	.35	.14	.03
☐ 324	Tony Taylor	.35	.14	.03
☐ 325	Dave Boswell	.35	.14	.03
☐ 326	Bill Voss	.35	.14	.03
☐ 327	Hal King	.35	.14	.03
☐ 328	George Brunet	.35	.14	.03
☐ 329	Chris Cannizzaro	.35	.14	.03
☐ 330	Lou Brock	5.00	2.00	.50
☐ 331	Chuck Dobson	.35	.14	.03
☐ 332	Bobby Wine	.35	.14	.03
☐ 333	Bobby Murcer	1.00	.40	.10
☐ 334	Phil Regan	.50	.20	.05
☐ 335	Bill Freehan	.75	.30	.07

		NRMT	VG-E	GOOD
☐ 336	Del Unser	.35	.14	.03
☐ 337	Mike McCormick	.50	.20	.05
☐ 338	Paul Schaal	.35	.14	.03
☐ 339	Johnny Edwards	.35	.14	.03
☐ 340	Tony Conigliaro	1.00	.40	.10
☐ 341	Bill Sudakis	.35	.14	.03
☐ 342	Wilbur Wood	.50	.20	.05
☐ 343A	Checklist 4 (red bat on front)	2.00	.30	.05
☐ 343B	Checklist 4 (brown bat on front)	2.50	.30	.05
☐ 344	Marcelino Lopez	.35	.14	.03
☐ 345	Al Ferrara	.35	.14	.03
☐ 346	Red Schoendienst MG	.75	.30	.07
☐ 347	Russ Snyder	.35	.14	.03
☐ 348	Mets Rookies Mike Jorgensen Jesse Hudson	.35	.14	.03
☐ 349	Steve Hamilton	.35	.14	.03
☐ 350	Roberto Clemente	22.00	9.00	2.20
☐ 351	Tom Murphy	.35	.14	.03
☐ 352	Bob Barton	.35	.14	.03
☐ 353	Stan Williams	.35	.14	.03
☐ 354	Amos Otis	.75	.30	.07
☐ 355	Doug Rader	.50	.20	.05
☐ 356	Fred Lasher	.35	.14	.03
☐ 357	Bob Burda	.35	.14	.03
☐ 358	Pedro Borbon	.35	.14	.03
☐ 359	Phil Roof	.35	.14	.03
☐ 360	Curt Flood	.75	.30	.07
☐ 361	Ray Jarvis	.35	.14	.03
☐ 362	Joe Hague	.35	.14	.03
☐ 363	Tom Shopay	.35	.14	.03
☐ 364	Dan McGinn	.35	.14	.03
☐ 365	Zoilo Versalles	.35	.14	.03
☐ 366	Barry Moore	.35	.14	.03
☐ 367	Mike Lum	.35	.14	.03
☐ 368	Ed Herrmann	.35	.14	.03
☐ 369	Alan Foster	.35	.14	.03
☐ 370	Tommy Harper	.50	.20	.05
☐ 371	Rod Gaspar	.35	.14	.03
☐ 372	Dave Giusti	.50	.20	.05
☐ 373	Roy White	.75	.30	.07
☐ 374	Tommie Sisk	.35	.14	.03
☐ 375	Johnny Callison	.50	.20	.05
☐ 376	Lefty Phillips MG	.35	.14	.03
☐ 377	Bill Butler	.35	.14	.03
☐ 378	Jim Davenport	.50	.20	.05
☐ 379	Tom Tischinski	.35	.14	.03

		NRMT	VG-E	GOOD
☐ 380	Tony Perez	3.00	1.20	.30
☐ 381	Athletics Rookies Bobby Brooks Mike Olivo	.35	.14	.03
☐ 382	Jack DiLauro	.35	.14	.03
☐ 383	Mickey Stanley	.50	.20	.05
☐ 384	Gary Neibauer	.35	.14	.03
☐ 385	George Scott	.50	.20	.05
☐ 386	Bill Dillman	.35	.14	.03
☐ 387	Baltimore Orioles Team Card	1.00	.40	.10
☐ 388	Byron Browne	.35	.14	.03
☐ 389	Jim Shellenback	.35	.14	.03
☐ 390	Willie Davis	.75	.30	.07
☐ 391	Larry Brown	.35	.14	.03
☐ 392	Walt Hriniak	.50	.20	.05
☐ 393	John Gelnar	.35	.14	.03
☐ 394	Gil Hodges MG	3.50	1.40	.35
☐ 395	Walt Williams	.35	.14	.03
☐ 396	Steve Blass	.50	.20	.05
☐ 397	Roger Repoz	.35	.14	.03
☐ 398	Bill Stoneman	.35	.14	.03
☐ 399	New York Yankees Team Card	1.50	.60	.15
☐ 400	Denny McLain	1.00	.40	.10
☐ 401	Giants Rookies John Harrell Bernie Williams	.35	.14	.03
☐ 402	Ellie Rodriguez	.35	.14	.03
☐ 403	Jim Bunning	2.50	1.00	.25
☐ 404	Rich Reese	.35	.14	.03
☐ 405	Bill Hands	.35	.14	.03
☐ 406	Mike Andrews	.35	.14	.03
☐ 407	Bob Watson	.75	.30	.07
☐ 408	Paul Lindblad	.35	.14	.03
☐ 409	Bob Tolan	.50	.20	.05
☐ 410	Boog Powell	2.00	.80	.20
☐ 411	Los Angeles Dodgers Team Card	1.25	.50	.12
☐ 412	Larry Burchart	.35	.14	.03
☐ 413	Sonny Jackson	.35	.14	.03
☐ 414	Paul Edmondson	.35	.14	.03
☐ 415	Julian Javier	.50	.20	.05
☐ 416	Joe Verbanic	.35	.14	.03
☐ 417	John Bateman	.35	.14	.03
☐ 418	John Donaldson	.35	.14	.03
☐ 419	Ron Taylor	.35	.14	.03
☐ 420	Ken McMullen	.35	.14	.03
☐ 421	Pat Dobson	.50	.20	.05

		NRMT	VG-E	GOOD			NRMT	VG-E	GOOD
☐ 422	Royals Team	1.00	.40	.10	☐ 460	Matty Alou AS	.75	.30	.07
☐ 423	Jerry May	.35	.14	.03	☐ 461	Carl Yastrzemski AS	6.00	2.40	.60
☐ 424	Mike Kilkenny	.35	.14	.03	☐ 462	Hank Aaron AS	6.00	2.40	.60
	(inconsistent design,				☐ 463	Frank Robinson AS	3.50	1.40	.35
	card # in white circle)				☐ 464	Johnny Bench AS	6.00	2.40	.60
☐ 425	Bobby Bonds	2.00	.80	.20	☐ 465	Bill Freehan AS	.75	.30	.07
☐ 426	Bill Rigney MG	.35	.14	.03	☐ 466	Juan Marichal AS	3.00	1.20	.30
☐ 427	Fred Norman	.35	.14	.03	☐ 467	Denny McLain AS	.75	.30	.07
☐ 428	Don Buford	.50	.20	.05	☐ 468	Jerry Koosman AS	.75	.30	.07
☐ 429	Cubs Rookies	.35	.14	.03	☐ 469	Sam McDowell AS	.75	.30	.07
	Randy Bobb				☐ 470	Willie Stargell AS	6.00	2.40	.60
	Jim Cosman				☐ 471	Chris Zachary	.50	.20	.05
☐ 430	Andy Messersmith	.50	.20	.05	☐ 472	Braves Team	1.00	.40	.10
☐ 431	Ron Swoboda	.50	.20	.05	☐ 473	Don Bryant	.50	.20	.05
☐ 432A	Checklist 5	2.00	.80	.30	☐ 474	Dick Kelley	.50	.20	.05
	("Baseball" in yellow letters)				☐ 475	Dick McAuliffe	.75	.30	.07
☐ 432B	Checklist 5	2.50	.30	.03	☐ 476	Don Shaw	.50	.20	.05
	("Baseball" in white letters)				☐ 477	Orioles Rookies	.50	.20	.05
☐ 433	Ron Bryant	.35	.14	.03		Al Severinsen			
☐ 434	Felipe Alou	.50	.20	.05		Roger Freed			
☐ 435	Nelson Briles	.50	.20	.05	☐ 478	Bobby Heise	.50	.20	.05
☐ 436	Philadelphia Phillies	1.00	.40	.10	☐ 479	Dick Woodson	.50	.20	.05
	Team Card				☐ 480	Glenn Beckert	.75	.30	.07
☐ 437	Danny Cater	.35	.14	.03	☐ 481	Jose Tartabull	.50	.20	.05
☐ 438	Pat Jarvis	.35	.14	.03	☐ 482	Tom Hilgendorf	.50	.20	.05
☐ 439	Lee Maye	.35	.14	.03	☐ 483	Gail Hopkins	.50	.20	.05
☐ 440	Bill Mazeroski	1.00	.40	.10	☐ 484	Gary Nolan	.50	.20	.05
☐ 441	John O'Donoghue	.35	.14	.03	☐ 485	Jay Johnstone	.75	.30	.07
☐ 442	Gene Mauch MG	.50	.20	.05	☐ 486	Terry Harmon	.50	.20	.05
☐ 443	Al Jackson	.35	.14	.03	☐ 487	Cisco Carlos	.50	.20	.05
☐ 444	White Sox Rookies	.35	.14	.03	☐ 488	J.C. Martin	.50	.20	.05
	Billy Farmer				☐ 489	Eddie Kasko MG	.50	.20	.05
	John Matias				☐ 490	Bill Singer	.50	.20	.05
☐ 445	Vada Pinson	1.00	.40	.10	☐ 491	Graig Nettles	4.00	1.60	.40
☐ 446	Billy Grabarkewitz	.35	.14	.03	☐ 492	Astros Rookies	.50	.20	.05
☐ 447	Lee Stange	.35	.14	.03		Keith Lampard			
☐ 448	Houston Astros	1.00	.40	.10		Scipio Spinks			
	Team Card				☐ 493	Lindy McDaniel	.75	.30	.07
☐ 449	Jim Palmer	8.00	3.25	.80	☐ 494	Larry Stahl	.50	.20	.05
☐ 450	Willie McCovey AS	3.50	1.40	.35	☐ 495	Dave Morehead	.50	.20	.05
☐ 451	Boog Powell AS	.75	.30	.07	☐ 496	Steve Whitaker	.50	.20	.05
☐ 452	Felix Millan AS	.50	.20	.05	☐ 497	Eddie Watt	.50	.20	.05
☐ 453	Rod Carew AS	4.50	1.80	.45	☐ 498	Al Weis	.50	.20	.05
☐ 454	Ron Santo AS	.50	.20	.05	☐ 499	Skip Lockwood	.50	.20	.05
☐ 455	Brooks Robinson AS	3.50	1.40	.35	☐ 500	Hank Aaron	25.00	10.00	2.50
☐ 456	Don Kessinger AS	.50	.20	.05	☐ 501	Chicago White Sox	1.00	.40	.10
☐ 457	Rico Petrocelli AS	.50	.20	.05		Team Card			
☐ 458	Pete Rose AS	9.00	3.75	.90	☐ 502	Rollie Fingers	4.50	1.80	.45
☐ 459	Reggie Jackson AS	8.00	3.25	.80	☐ 503	Dal Maxvill	.75	.30	.07

		NRMT	VG-E	GOOD
☐ 504	Don Pavletich	.50	.20	.05
☐ 505	Ken Holtzman	.75	.30	.07
☐ 506	Ed Stroud	.50	.20	.05
☐ 507	Pat Corrales	.75	.30	.07
☐ 508	Joe Niekro	1.00	.40	.10
☐ 509	Montreal Expos Team Card	1.00	.40	.10
☐ 510	Tony Oliva	1.50	.60	.15
☐ 511	Joe Hoerner	.50	.20	.05
☐ 512	Billy Harris	.50	.20	.05
☐ 513	Preston Gomez MG	.50	.20	.05
☐ 514	Steve Hovley	.50	.20	.05
☐ 515	Don Wilson	.50	.20	.05
☐ 516	Yankees Rookies John Ellis Jim Lyttle	.50	.20	.05
☐ 517	Joe Gibbon	.50	.20	.05
☐ 518	Bill Melton	.50	.20	.05
☐ 519	Don McMahon	.50	.20	.05
☐ 520	Willie Horton	.75	.30	.07
☐ 521	Cal Koonce	.50	.20	.05
☐ 522	Angels Team	1.00	.40	.10
☐ 523	Jose Pena	.50	.20	.05
☐ 524	Alvin Dark MG	.75	.30	.07
☐ 525	Jerry Adair	.50	.20	.05
☐ 526	Ron Herbel	.50	.20	.05
☐ 527	Don Bosch	.50	.20	.05
☐ 528	Elrod Hendricks	.50	.20	.05
☐ 529	Bob Aspromonte	.50	.20	.05
☐ 530	Bob Gibson	7.00	2.80	.70
☐ 531	Ron Clark	.50	.20	.05
☐ 532	Danny Murtaugh MG	.50	.20	.05
☐ 533	Buzz Stephen	.50	.20	.05
☐ 534	Twins Team	1.00	.40	.10
☐ 535	Andy Kosco	.50	.20	.05
☐ 536	Mike Kekich	.50	.20	.05
☐ 537	Joe Morgan	3.50	1.40	.35
☐ 538	Bob Humphreys	.50	.20	.05
☐ 539	Phillies Rookies Dennis Doyle Larry Bowa	4.00	1.60	.40
☐ 540	Gary Peters	.50	.20	.05
☐ 541	Bill Heath	.50	.20	.05
☐ 542	Checklist 6	2.50	.30	.06
☐ 543	Clyde Wright	.50	.20	.05
☐ 544	Cincinnati Reds Team Card	1.25	.50	.12
☐ 545	Ken Harrelson	1.00	.40	.10
☐ 546	Ron Reed	.50	.20	.05

		NRMT	VG-E	GOOD
☐ 547	Rick Monday	1.00	.40	.10
☐ 548	Howie Reed	.85	.34	.08
☐ 549	Cardinals Team	1.50	.60	.15
☐ 550	Frank Howard	1.50	.60	.15
☐ 551	Dock Ellis	.85	.34	.08
☐ 552	Royals Rookies Don O'Riley Dennis Paepke Fred Rico	.85	.34	.08
☐ 553	Jim Lefebvre	1.25	.50	.12
☐ 554	Tom Timmermann	.85	.34	.08
☐ 555	Orlando Cepeda	3.00	1.20	.30
☐ 556	Dave Bristol MG	.85	.34	.08
☐ 557	Ed Kranepool	1.25	.50	.12
☐ 558	Vern Fuller	.85	.34	.08
☐ 559	Tommy Davis	1.25	.50	.12
☐ 560	Gaylord Perry	5.00	2.00	.50
☐ 561	Tom McCraw	.85	.34	.08
☐ 562	Ted Abernathy	.85	.34	.08
☐ 563	Boston Red Sox Team Card	1.50	.60	.15
☐ 564	Johnny Briggs	.85	.34	.08
☐ 565	Jim Hunter	6.00	2.40	.60
☐ 566	Gene Alley	1.25	.50	.12
☐ 567	Bob Oliver	.85	.34	.08
☐ 568	Stan Bahnsen	.85	.34	.08
☐ 569	Cookie Rojas	1.25	.50	.12
☐ 570	Jim Fregosi	1.25	.50	.12
☐ 571	Jim Brewer	.85	.34	.08
☐ 572	Frank Quilici MG	.85	.34	.08
☐ 573	Padres Rookies Mike Corkins Rafael Robles Ron Slocum	.85	.34	.08
☐ 574	Bobby Bolin	.85	.34	.08
☐ 575	Cleon Jones	.85	.34	.08
☐ 576	Milt Pappas	1.25	.50	.12
☐ 577	Bernie Allen	.85	.34	.08
☐ 578	Tom Griffin	.85	.34	.08
☐ 579	Detroit Tigers Team Card	2.00	.80	.17
☐ 580	Pete Rose	75.00	30.00	7.50
☐ 581	Tom Satriano	.85	.34	.08
☐ 582	Mike Paul	.85	.34	.08
☐ 583	Hal Lanier	1.25	.50	.12
☐ 584	Al Downing	1.25	.50	.12
☐ 585	Rusty Staub	1.75	.70	.17
☐ 586	Rickey Clark	.85	.34	.08
☐ 587	Jose Arcia	.85	.34	.08

		NRMT	VG-E	GOOD
☐ 588A	Checklist 7 (666 Adolpho)	3.00	.40	.07
☐ 588B	Checklist 7 (666 Adolfo)	6.00	.60	.10
☐ 589	Joe Keough	.85	.34	.08
☐ 590	Mike Cuellar	1.25	.50	.12
☐ 591	Mike Ryan	.85	.34	.08
☐ 592	Daryl Patterson	.85	.34	.08
☐ 593	Chicago Cubs Team Card	1.50	.60	.15
☐ 594	Jake Gibbs	.85	.34	.08
☐ 595	Maury Wills	2.25	.90	.22
☐ 596	Mike Hershberger	.85	.34	.08
☐ 597	Sonny Siebert	1.25	.50	.12
☐ 598	Joe Pepitone	1.25	.50	.12
☐ 599	Senators Rookies Dick Stelmaszek Gene Martin Dick Such	.85	.34	.08
☐ 600	Willie Mays	32.00	13.00	3.20
☐ 601	Pete Richert	.85	.34	.08
☐ 602	Ted Savage	.85	.34	.08
☐ 603	Ray Oyler	.85	.34	.08
☐ 604	Clarence Gaston	.85	.34	.08
☐ 605	Rick Wise	1.25	.50	.12
☐ 606	Chico Ruiz	.85	.34	.08
☐ 607	Gary Waslewski	.85	.34	.08
☐ 608	Pittsburgh Pirates Team Card	1.75	.70	.15
☐ 609	Buck Martinez	.85	.34	.08
☐ 610	Jerry Koosman	1.50	.60	.15
☐ 611	Norm Cash	1.50	.60	.15
☐ 612	Jim Hickman	.85	.34	.08
☐ 613	Dave Baldwin	.85	.34	.08
☐ 614	Mike Shannon	1.25	.50	.12
☐ 615	Mark Belanger	1.25	.50	.12
☐ 616	Jim Merritt	.85	.34	.08
☐ 617	Jim French	.85	.34	.08
☐ 618	Billy Wynne	.85	.34	.08
☐ 619	Norm Miller	.85	.34	.08
☐ 620	Jim Perry	1.50	.60	.15
☐ 621	Braves Rookies Mike McQueen Darrell Evans Rick Kester	10.00	4.00	1.00
☐ 622	Don Sutton	5.50	2.20	.55
☐ 623	Horace Clarke	.85	.34	.08
☐ 624	Clyde King MG	.85	.34	.08
☐ 625	Dean Chance	1.25	.50	.12
☐ 626	Dave Ricketts	.85	.34	.08
☐ 627	Gary Wagner	.85	.34	.08
☐ 628	Wayne Garrett	.85	.34	.08
☐ 629	Merv Rettenmund	.85	.34	.08
☐ 630	Ernie Banks	12.00	5.00	1.20
☐ 631	Oakland Athletics Team Card	1.50	.60	.15
☐ 632	Gary Sutherland	.85	.34	.08
☐ 633	Roger Nelson	.85	.34	.08
☐ 634	Bud Harrelson	2.50	1.00	.25
☐ 635	Bob Allison	2.50	1.00	.25
☐ 636	Jim Stewart	2.00	.80	.20
☐ 637	Cleveland Indians Team Card	4.00	1.60	.40
☐ 638	Frank Bertaina	2.00	.80	.20
☐ 639	Dave Campbell	2.00	.80	.20
☐ 640	Al Kaline	25.00	10.00	2.50
☐ 641	Al McBean	2.00	.80	.20
☐ 642	Angels Rookies Greg Garrett Gordon Lund Jarvis Tatum	2.00	.80	.20
☐ 643	Jose Pagan	2.00	.80	.20
☐ 644	Gerry Nyman	2.00	.80	.20
☐ 645	Don Money	2.50	1.00	.25
☐ 646	Jim Britton	2.00	.80	.20
☐ 647	Tom Matchick	2.00	.80	.20
☐ 648	Larry Haney	2.00	.80	.20
☐ 649	Jimmie Hall	2.50	1.00	.25
☐ 650	Sam McDowell	3.00	1.20	.30
☐ 651	Jim Gosger	2.00	.80	.20
☐ 652	Rich Rollins	2.50	1.00	.25
☐ 653	Moe Drabowsky	2.00	.80	.20
☐ 654	NL Rookies Oscar Gamble Boots Day Angel Mangual	3.50	1.40	.35
☐ 655	John Roseboro	2.50	1.00	.25
☐ 656	Jim Hardin	2.00	.80	.20
☐ 657	San Diego Padres Team Card	4.50	1.80	.45
☐ 658	Ken Tatum	2.00	.80	.20
☐ 659	Pete Ward	2.00	.80	.20
☐ 660	Johnny Bench	90.00	36.00	9.00
☐ 661	Jerry Robertson	2.00	.80	.20
☐ 662	Frank Lucchesi MG	2.00	.80	.20
☐ 663	Tito Francona	2.50	1.00	.25
☐ 664	Bob Robertson	2.50	1.00	.25
☐ 665	Jim Lonborg	2.50	1.00	.25

		NRMT	VG-E	GOOD
☐ 666	Adolpho Phillips ...	2.00	.80	.20
☐ 667	Bob Meyer	2.00	.80	.20
☐ 668	Bob Tillman	2.00	.80	.20
☐ 669	White Sox Rookies .	2.00	.80	.20
	Bart Johnson			
	Dan Lazar			
	Mickey Scott			
☐ 670	Ron Santo	4.00	1.60	.40
☐ 671	Jim Campanis	2.00	.80	.20
☐ 672	Leon McFadden	2.00	.80	.20
☐ 673	Ted Uhlaender	2.00	.80	.20
☐ 674	Dave Leonhard	2.00	.80	.20
☐ 675	Jose Cardenal	2.00	.80	.20
☐ 676	Senators Team	4.00	1.60	.40
☐ 677	Woodie Fryman	2.00	.80	.20
☐ 678	Dave Duncan	2.00	.80	.20
☐ 679	Ray Sadecki	2.00	.80	.20
☐ 680	Rico Petrocelli	2.50	1.00	.25
☐ 681	Bob Garibaldi	2.00	.80	.20
☐ 682	Dalton Jones	2.00	.80	.20
☐ 683	Reds Rookies	4.00	1.60	.40
	Vern Geishert			
	Hal McRae			
	Wayne Simpson			
☐ 684	Jack Fisher	2.00	.80	.20
☐ 685	Tom Haller	2.50	1.00	.25
☐ 686	Jackie Hernandez ..	2.00	.80	.20
☐ 687	Bob Priddy	2.00	.80	.20
☐ 688	Ted Kubiak	2.00	.80	.20
☐ 689	Frank Tepedino	2.00	.80	.20
☐ 690	Ron Fairly	2.50	1.00	.25
☐ 691	Joe Grzenda	2.00	.80	.20
☐ 692	Duffy Dyer	2.00	.80	.20
☐ 693	Bob Johnson	2.00	.80	.20
☐ 694	Gary Ross	2.00	.80	.20
☐ 695	Bobby Knoop	2.00	.80	.20
☐ 696	San Francisco Giants	4.00	1.60	.40
	Team Card			
☐ 697	Jim Hannan	2.00	.80	.20
☐ 698	Tom Tresh	4.00	1.60	.40
☐ 699	Hank Aguirre	2.00	.80	.20
☐ 700	Frank Robinson ...	25.00	10.00	2.50
☐ 701	Jack Billingham	2.00	.80	.20
☐ 702	AL Rookies	2.00	.80	.20
	Bob Johnson			
	Ron Klimkowski			
	Bill Zepp			
☐ 703	Lou Marone	2.00	.80	.20
☐ 704	Frank Baker	2.00	.80	.20

		NRMT	VG-E	GOOD
☐ 705	Tony Cloninger ...	2.00	.80	.20
☐ 706	John McNamara MG	4.00	1.60	.40
☐ 707	Kevin Collins	2.00	.80	.20
☐ 708	Jose Santiago	2.00	.80	.20
☐ 709	Mike Fiore	2.00	.80	.20
☐ 710	Felix Millan	2.00	.80	.20
☐ 711	Ed Brinkman	2.00	.80	.20
☐ 712	Nolan Ryan	65.00	26.00	6.50
☐ 713	Pilots Team	9.00	3.75	.90
☐ 714	Al Spangler	2.00	.80	.20
☐ 715	Mickey Lolich	4.50	1.80	.45
☐ 716	Cardinals Rookies .	2.50	1.00	.25
	Sal Campisi			
	Reggie Cleveland			
	Santiago Guzman			
☐ 717	Tom Phoebus	2.00	.80	.20
☐ 718	Ed Spiezio	2.00	.80	.20
☐ 719	Jim Roland	2.00	.80	.20
☐ 720	Rick Reichardt	3.00	1.00	.20

1971 Topps

*The cards in this 752-card set measure 2 ½"
by 3 ½". The 1971 Topps set is a challenge
to complete in strict mint condition because
the black obverse border is easily scratched
and damaged. An unusual feature of this set
is that the player is also pictured in black and
white on the back of the card. Featured subsets within this set include League Leaders
(61-72), Playoffs cards (195-202), and World
Series cards (327-332). Cards 524-643 and
the last series (644-752) are somewhat
scarce.*

		NRMT	VG-E	GOOD
Complete Set (752)		1200.00	500.00	175.00
Common Player (1-263)		.30	.12	.03
Common Player (264-393)		.35	.14	.03
Common Player (394-523)		.45	.18	.04
Common Player (524-643)		.85	.34	.08
Common Player (644-752)		2.00	.80	.20
☐ 1	Baltimore Orioles	5.00	1.00	.20
	Team Card			
☐ 2	Dock Ellis	.30	.12	.03
☐ 3	Dick McAuliffe	.30	.12	.03
☐ 4	Vic Davalillo	.30	.12	.03
☐ 5	Thurman Munson	16.00	6.50	1.60
☐ 6	Ed Spiezio	.30	.12	.03
☐ 7	Jim Holt	.30	.12	.03
☐ 8	Mike McQueen	.30	.12	.03
☐ 9	George Scott	.50	.20	.05
☐ 10	Claude Osteen	.50	.20	.05
☐ 11	Elliott Maddox	.30	.12	.03
☐ 12	Johnny Callison	.50	.20	.05
☐ 13	White Sox Rookies	.30	.12	.03
	Charlie Brinkman			
	Dick Moloney			
☐ 14	Dave Concepcion	5.00	2.00	.50
☐ 15	Andy Messersmith	.50	.20	.05
☐ 16	Ken Singleton	1.50	.60	.15
☐ 17	Billy Sorrell	.30	.12	.03
☐ 18	Norm Miller	.30	.12	.03
☐ 19	Skip Pitlock	.30	.12	.03
☐ 20	Reggie Jackson	27.00	11.00	2.70
☐ 21	Dan McGinn	.30	.12	.03
☐ 22	Phil Roof	.30	.12	.03
☐ 23	Oscar Gamble	.50	.20	.05
☐ 24	Rich Hand	.30	.12	.03
☐ 25	Clarence Gaston	.50	.20	.05
☐ 26	Bert Blyleven	10.00	4.00	1.00
☐ 27	Pirates Rookies	.30	.12	.03
	Fred Cambria			
	Gene Clines			
☐ 28	Ron Klimkowski	.30	.12	.03
☐ 29	Don Buford	.50	.20	.05
☐ 30	Phil Niekro	3.50	1.40	.35
☐ 31	Eddie Kasko MG	.30	.12	.03
☐ 32	Jerry DaVanon	.30	.12	.03
☐ 33	Del Unser	.30	.12	.03
☐ 34	Sandy Vance	.30	.12	.03
☐ 35	Lou Piniella	.75	.30	.07
☐ 36	Dean Chance	.50	.20	.05
☐ 37	Rich McKinney	.30	.12	.03
☐ 38	Jim Colborn	.30	.12	.03

		NRMT	VG-E	GOOD
☐ 39	Tiger Rookies	.30	.12	.03
	Lerrin LaGrow			
	Gene Lamont			
☐ 40	Lee May	.50	.20	.05
☐ 41	Rick Austin	.30	.12	.03
☐ 42	Boots Day	.30	.12	.03
☐ 43	Steve Kealey	.30	.12	.03
☐ 44	Johnny Edwards	.30	.12	.03
☐ 45	Jim Hunter	4.00	1.60	.40
☐ 46	Dave Campbell	.30	.12	.03
☐ 47	Johnny Jeter	.30	.12	.03
☐ 48	Dave Baldwin	.30	.12	.03
☐ 49	Don Money	.50	.20	.05
☐ 50	Willie McCovey	5.00	2.00	.50
☐ 51	Steve Kline	.30	.12	.03
☐ 52	Braves Rookies	.50	.20	.05
	Oscar Brown			
	Earl Williams			
☐ 53	Paul Blair	.50	.20	.05
☐ 54	Checklist 1	1.50	.20	.04
☐ 55	Steve Carlton	12.00	5.00	1.20
☐ 56	Duane Josephson	.30	.12	.03
☐ 57	Von Joshua	.30	.12	.03
☐ 58	Bill Lee	.50	.20	.05
☐ 59	Gene Mauch MG	.50	.20	.05
☐ 60	Dick Bosman	.30	.12	.03
☐ 61	AL Batting Leaders	1.50	.60	.15
	Alex Johnson			
	Carl Yastrzemski			
	Tony Oliva			
☐ 62	NL Batting Leaders	1.00	.40	.10
	Rico Carty			
	Joe Torre			
	Manny Sanguillen			
☐ 63	AL RBI Leaders	1.00	.40	.10
	Frank Howard			
	Tony Conigliaro			
	Boog Powell			
☐ 64	NL RBI Leaders	1.75	.70	.17
	Johnny Bench			
	Tony Perez			
	Billy Williams			
☐ 65	AL HR Leaders	1.50	.60	.15
	Frank Howard			
	Harmon Killebrew			
	Carl Yastrzemski			

		NRMT	VG-E	GOOD
☐ 66	NL HR Leaders	1.75	.70	.17
	Johnny Bench			
	Billy Williams			
	Tony Perez			
☐ 67	AL ERA Leaders ...	1.00	.40	.10
	Diego Segui			
	Jim Palmer			
	Clyde Wright			
☐ 68	NL ERA Leaders ...	1.00	.40	.10
	Tom Seaver			
	Wayne Simpson			
	Luke Walker			
☐ 69	AL Pitching Leaders	1.00	.40	.10
	Mike Cuellar			
	Dave McNally			
	Jim Perry			
☐ 70	NL Pitching Leaders	1.50	.60	.15
	Bob Gibson			
	Gaylord Perry			
	Fergie Jenkins			
☐ 71	AL Strikeout Leaders	1.00	.40	.10
	Sam McDowell			
	Mickey Lolich			
	Bob Johnson			
☐ 72	NL Strikeout Leaders	1.50	.60	.15
	Tom Seaver			
	Bob Gibson			
	Fergie Jenkins			
☐ 73	George Brunet	.30	.12	.03
☐ 74	Twins Rookies	.30	.12	.03
	Pete Hamm			
	Jim Nettles			
☐ 75	Gary Nolan	.30	.12	.03
☐ 76	Ted Savage	.30	.12	.03
☐ 77	Mike Compton	.30	.12	.03
☐ 78	Jim Spencer	.30	.12	.03
☐ 79	Wade Blasingame ..	.30	.12	.03
☐ 80	Bill Melton	.30	.12	.03
☐ 81	Felix Millan	.30	.12	.03
☐ 82	Casey Cox	.30	.12	.03
☐ 83	Met Rookies	.50	.20	.05
	Tim Foli			
	Randy Bobb			
☐ 84	Marcel Lachemann .	.50	.20	.05
☐ 85	Billy Grabarkewitz .	.30	.12	.03
☐ 86	Mike Kilkenny	.30	.12	.03
☐ 87	Jack Heidemann ...	.30	.12	.03
☐ 88	Hal King	.30	.12	.03
☐ 89	Ken Brett	.50	.20	.05

		NRMT	VG-E	GOOD
☐ 90	Joe Pepitone	.75	.30	.07
☐ 91	Bob Lemon MG ...	1.25	.50	.12
☐ 92	Fred Wenz	.30	.12	.03
☐ 93	Senators Rookies .	.30	.12	.03
	Norm McRae			
	Denny Riddleberger			
☐ 94	Don Hahn	.30	.12	.03
☐ 95	Luis Tiant	.75	.30	.07
☐ 96	Joe Hague	.30	.12	.03
☐ 97	Floyd Wicker	.30	.12	.03
☐ 98	Joe Decker	.30	.12	.03
☐ 99	Mark Belanger	.50	.20	.05
☐ 100	Pete Rose	45.00	18.00	4.50
☐ 101	Les Cain	.30	.12	.03
☐ 102	Astros Rookies ...	1.00	.40	.10
	Ken Forsch			
	Larry Howard			
☐ 103	Rich Severson	.30	.12	.03
☐ 104	Dan Frisella	.30	.12	.03
☐ 105	Tony Conigliaro ...	1.00	.40	.10
☐ 106	Tom Dukes	.30	.12	.03
☐ 107	Roy Foster	.30	.12	.03
☐ 108	John Cumberland .	.30	.12	.03
☐ 109	Steve Hovley	.30	.12	.03
☐ 110	Bill Mazeroski	.75	.30	.07
☐ 111	Yankee Rookies ..	.30	.12	.03
	Loyd Colson			
	Bobby Mitchell			
☐ 112	Manny Mota	.50	.20	.05
☐ 113	Jerry Crider	.30	.12	.03
☐ 114	Billy Conigliaro ...	.50	.20	.05
☐ 115	Donn Clendenon ..	.50	.20	.05
☐ 116	Ken Sanders	.30	.12	.03
☐ 117	Ted Simmons	7.00	2.80	.70
☐ 118	Cookie Rojas	.50	.20	.05
☐ 119	Frank Lucchesi MG	.30	.12	.03
☐ 120	Willie Horton	.50	.20	.05
☐ 121	Cubs Rookies	.30	.12	.03
	Jim Dunegan			
	Roe Skidmore			
☐ 122	Eddie Watt	.30	.12	.03
☐ 123A	Checklist 2	2.00	.30	.04
	(card number at bottom right)			
☐ 123B	Checklist 2	2.50	.30	.05
	(card number centered)			
☐ 124	Don Gullett	.50	.20	.05
☐ 125	Ray Fosse	.30	.12	.03
☐ 126	Danny Coombs ...	.30	.12	.03
☐ 127	Danny Thompson .	.30	.12	.03

		NRMT	VG-E	GOOD
☐ 128	Frank Johnson	.30	.12	.03
☐ 129	Aurelio Monteagudo	.30	.12	.03
☐ 130	Denis Menke	.30	.12	.03
☐ 131	Curt Blefary	.30	.12	.03
☐ 132	Jose Laboy	.30	.12	.03
☐ 133	Mickey Lolich	1.00	.40	.10
☐ 134	Jose Arcia	.30	.12	.03
☐ 135	Rick Monday	.50	.20	.05
☐ 136	Duffy Dyer	.30	.12	.03
☐ 137	Marcelino Lopez ...	.30	.12	.03
☐ 138	Phillies Rookies	.50	.20	.05
	Joe Lis			
	Willie Montanez			
☐ 139	Paul Casanova	.30	.12	.03
☐ 140	Gaylord Perry	3.50	1.40	.35
☐ 141	Frank Quilici	.30	.12	.03
☐ 142	Mack Jones	.30	.12	.03
☐ 143	Steve Blass	.50	.20	.05
☐ 144	Jackie Hernandez ..	.30	.12	.03
☐ 145	Bill Singer	.30	.12	.03
☐ 146	Ralph Houk MG	.50	.20	.05
☐ 147	Bob Priddy	.30	.12	.03
☐ 148	John Mayberry	.50	.20	.05
☐ 149	Mike Hershberger ..	.30	.12	.03
☐ 150	Sam McDowell	.50	.20	.05
☐ 151	Tommy Davis	.50	.20	.05
☐ 152	Angels Rookies	.30	.12	.03
	Lloyd Allen			
	Winston Llenas			
☐ 153	Gary Ross	.30	.12	.03
☐ 154	Cesar Gutierrez ...	.30	.12	.03
☐ 155	Ken Henderson	.30	.12	.03
☐ 156	Bart Johnson	.30	.12	.03
☐ 157	Bob Bailey	.30	.12	.03
☐ 158	Jerry Reuss	.75	.30	.07
☐ 159	Jarvis Tatum	.30	.12	.03
☐ 160	Tom Seaver	21.00	8.50	2.10
☐ 161	Coin Checklist	1.50	.20	.04
☐ 162	Jack Billingham	.30	.12	.03
☐ 163	Buck Martinez	.30	.12	.03
☐ 164	Reds Rookies	.50	.20	.05
	Frank Duffy			
	Milt Wilcox			
☐ 165	Cesar Tovar	.30	.12	.03
☐ 166	Joe Hoerner	.30	.12	.03
☐ 167	Tom Grieve	.75	.30	.07
☐ 168	Bruce Dal Canton ..	.30	.12	.03
☐ 169	Ed Herrmann	.30	.12	.03
☐ 170	Mike Cuellar	.50	.20	.05

		NRMT	VG-E	GOOD
☐ 171	Bobby Wine	.30	.12	.03
☐ 172	Duke Sims	.30	.12	.03
☐ 173	Gil Garrido	.30	.12	.03
☐ 174	Dave LaRoche	.30	.12	.03
☐ 175	Jim Hickman	.30	.12	.03
☐ 176	Red Sox Rookies ..	.30	.12	.03
	Bob Montgomery			
	Doug Griffin			
☐ 177	Hal McRae	.75	.30	.07
☐ 178	Dave Duncan	.30	.12	.03
☐ 179	Mike Corkins	.30	.12	.03
☐ 180	Al Kaline	6.50	2.60	.65
☐ 181	Hal Lanier	.50	.20	.05
☐ 182	Al Downing	.50	.20	.05
☐ 183	Gil Hodges MG ...	3.00	1.20	.30
☐ 184	Stan Bahnsen	.30	.12	.03
☐ 185	Julian Javier	.50	.20	.05
☐ 186	Bob Spence	.30	.12	.03
☐ 187	Ted Abernathy	.30	.12	.03
☐ 188	Dodgers Rookies ..	2.00	.80	.20
	Bob Valentine			
	Mike Strahler			
☐ 189	George Mitterwald .	.30	.12	.03
☐ 190	Bob Tolan	.50	.20	.05
☐ 191	Mike Andrews	.30	.12	.03
☐ 192	Billy Wilson	.30	.12	.03
☐ 193	Bob Grich	1.75	.70	.17
☐ 194	Mike Lum	.30	.12	.03
☐ 195	AL Playoff Game 1	1.25	.50	.12
	Powell muscles Twins			
☐ 196	AL Playoff Game 2	1.25	.50	.12
	McNally makes it			
	two straight			
☐ 197	AL Playoff Game 3	2.00	.80	.20
	Palmer mows 'em down			
☐ 198	AL Playoff Summary	1.25	.50	.12
	Orioles celebrate			
☐ 199	NL Playoff Game 1	1.25	.50	.12
	Cline pinch-triple			
	decides it			
☐ 200	NL Playoff Game 2	1.25	.50	.12
	Tolan scores for			
	third time			
☐ 201	NL Playoff Game 3	1.25	.50	.12
	Cline scores			
	winning run			
☐ 202	NL Playoff Summary	1.25	.50	.12
	Reds celebrate			
☐ 203	Larry Gura	.75	.30	.07

		NRMT	VG-E	GOOD
☐ 204	Brewers Rookies ... Bernie Smith George Kopacz	.30	.12	.03
☐ 205	Gerry Moses	.30	.12	.03
☐ 206	Checklist 3	1.50	.20	.04
☐ 207	Alan Foster	.30	.12	.03
☐ 208	Billy Martin MG	2.00	.80	.20
☐ 209	Steve Renko	.30	.12	.03
☐ 210	Rod Carew	15.00	6.00	1.50
☐ 211	Phil Hennigan	.30	.12	.03
☐ 212	Rich Hebner	.50	.20	.05
☐ 213	Frank Baker	.30	.12	.03
☐ 214	Al Ferrara	.30	.12	.03
☐ 215	Diego Segui	.30	.12	.03
☐ 216	Cards Rookies .... Reggie Cleveland Luis Melendez	.30	.12	.03
☐ 217	Ed Stroud	.30	.12	.03
☐ 218	Tony Cloninger	.30	.12	.03
☐ 219	Elrod Hendricks ...	.30	.12	.03
☐ 220	Ron Santo	.75	.30	.07
☐ 221	Dave Morehead	.30	.12	.03
☐ 222	Bob Watson	.50	.20	.05
☐ 223	Cecil Upshaw	.30	.12	.03
☐ 224	Alan Gallagher	.30	.12	.03
☐ 225	Gary Peters	.35	.14	.03
☐ 226	Bill Russell	.75	.30	.07
☐ 227	Floyd Weaver	.30	.12	.03
☐ 228	Wayne Garrett	.30	.12	.03
☐ 229	Jim Hannan	.30	.12	.03
☐ 230	Willie Stargell	6.00	2.40	.60
☐ 231	Indians Rookies ... Vince Colbert John Lowenstein	.50	.20	.05
☐ 232	John Strohmayer ...	.30	.12	.03
☐ 233	Larry Bowa	1.75	.70	.17
☐ 234	Jim Lyttle	.30	.12	.03
☐ 235	Nate Colbert	.30	.12	.03
☐ 236	Bob Humphreys	.30	.12	.03
☐ 237	Cesar Cedeno	1.25	.50	.12
☐ 238	Chuck Dobson	.30	.12	.03
☐ 239	Red Schoendienst MG	.75	.30	.07
☐ 240	Clyde Wright	.30	.12	.03
☐ 241	Dave Nelson	.30	.12	.03
☐ 242	Jim Ray	.30	.12	.03
☐ 243	Carlos May	.30	.12	.03
☐ 244	Bob Tillman	.30	.12	.03
☐ 245	Jim Kaat	1.75	.70	.17
☐ 246	Tony Taylor	.30	.12	.03

		NRMT	VG-E	GOOD
☐ 247	Royals Rookies .... Jerry Cram Paul Splittorff	.75	.30	.07
☐ 248	Hoyt Wilhelm	3.50	1.40	.35
☐ 249	Chico Salmon	.30	.12	.03
☐ 250	Johnny Bench	27.00	11.00	2.70
☐ 251	Frank Reberger	.30	.12	.03
☐ 252	Eddie Leon	.30	.12	.03
☐ 253	Bill Sudakis	.30	.12	.03
☐ 254	Cal Koonce	.30	.12	.03
☐ 255	Bob Robertson	.30	.12	.03
☐ 256	Tony Gonzalez	.30	.12	.03
☐ 257	Nelson Briles	.50	.20	.05
☐ 258	Dick Green	.30	.12	.03
☐ 259	Dave Marshall	.30	.12	.03
☐ 260	Tommy Harper	.50	.20	.05
☐ 261	Darold Knowles ...	.30	.12	.03
☐ 262	Padres Rookies ... Jim Williams Dave Robinson	.30	.12	.03
☐ 263	John Ellis	.30	.12	.03
☐ 264	Joe Morgan	3.50	1.40	.35
☐ 265	Jim Northrup	.50	.20	.05
☐ 266	Bill Stoneman	.35	.14	.03
☐ 267	Rich Morales	.35	.14	.03
☐ 268	Phillies Team	1.00	.40	.10
☐ 269	Gail Hopkins	.35	.14	.03
☐ 270	Rico Carty	.75	.30	.07
☐ 271	Bill Zepp	.35	.14	.03
☐ 272	Tommy Helms	.50	.20	.05
☐ 273	Pete Richert	.35	.14	.03
☐ 274	Ron Slocum	.35	.14	.03
☐ 275	Vada Pinson	1.00	.40	.10
☐ 276	Giants Rookies .... Mike Davison George Foster	4.50	1.80	.45
☐ 277	Gary Waslewski ...	.35	.14	.03
☐ 278	Jerry Grote	.35	.14	.03
☐ 279	Lefty Phillips MG ..	.35	.14	.03
☐ 280	Fergie Jenkins	2.50	1.00	.25
☐ 281	Danny Walton	.35	.14	.03
☐ 282	Jose Pagan	.35	.14	.03
☐ 283	Dick Such	.35	.14	.03
☐ 284	Jim Gosger	.35	.14	.03
☐ 285	Sal Bando	.50	.20	.05
☐ 286	Jerry McNertney ...	.35	.14	.03
☐ 287	Mike Fiore	.35	.14	.03
☐ 288	Joe Moeller	.35	.14	.03
☐ 289	White Sox Team ..	1.00	.40	.10

		NRMT	VG-E	GOOD
☐ 290	Tony Oliva	1.75	.70	.17
☐ 291	George Culver	.35	.14	.03
☐ 292	Jay Johnstone	.75	.30	.07
☐ 293	Pat Corrales	.50	.20	.05
☐ 294	Steve Dunning	.35	.14	.03
☐ 295	Bobby Bonds	1.50	.60	.15
☐ 296	Tom Timmermann	.35	.14	.03
☐ 297	Johnny Briggs	.35	.14	.03
☐ 298	Jim Nelson	.35	.14	.03
☐ 299	Ed Kirkpatrick	.35	.14	.03
☐ 300	Brooks Robinson	7.50	2.80	.70
☐ 301	Earl Wilson	.35	.14	.03
☐ 302	Phil Gagliano	.35	.14	.03
☐ 303	Lindy McDaniel	.50	.20	.05
☐ 304	Ron Brand	.35	.14	.03
☐ 305	Reggie Smith	.75	.30	.07
☐ 306	Jim Nash	.35	.14	.03
☐ 307	Don Wert	.35	.14	.03
☐ 308	St. Louis Cardinals Team Card	1.00	.40	.10
☐ 309	Dick Ellsworth	.50	.20	.05
☐ 310	Tommie Agee	.50	.20	.05
☐ 311	Lee Stange	.35	.14	.03
☐ 312	Harry Walker MG	.35	.14	.03
☐ 313	Tom Hall	.35	.14	.03
☐ 314	Jeff Torborg	.50	.20	.05
☐ 315	Ron Fairly	.50	.20	.05
☐ 316	Fred Scherman	.35	.14	.03
☐ 317	Athletic Rookies Jim Driscoll Angel Mangual	.35	.14	.03
☐ 318	Rudy May	.35	.14	.03
☐ 319	Ty Cline	.35	.14	.03
☐ 320	Dave McNally	.50	.20	.05
☐ 321	Tom Matchick	.35	.14	.03
☐ 322	Jim Beauchamp	.35	.14	.03
☐ 323	Billy Champion	.35	.14	.03
☐ 324	Graig Nettles	2.25	.90	.22
☐ 325	Juan Marichal	4.00	1.60	.40
☐ 326	Richie Scheinblum	.35	.14	.03
☐ 327	World Series Game 1 Powell homers to opposite field	1.25	.50	.12
☐ 328	World Series Game 2 Don Buford	1.25	.50	.12
☐ 329	World Series Game 3 Frank Robinson shows muscle	2.00	.80	.20

		NRMT	VG-E	GOOD
☐ 330	World Series Game 4 Reds stay alive	1.25	.50	.12
☐ 331	World Series Game 5 Brooks Robinson commits robbery	2.00	.80	.20
☐ 332	World Series Summary Orioles celebrate	1.25	.50	.12
☐ 333	Clay Kirby	.35	.14	.03
☐ 334	Roberto Pena	.35	.14	.03
☐ 335	Jerry Koosman	.75	.30	.07
☐ 336	Detroit Tigers Team Card	1.00	.40	.10
☐ 337	Jesus Alou	.35	.14	.03
☐ 338	Gene Tenace	.75	.30	.05
☐ 339	Wayne Simpson	.35	.14	.03
☐ 340	Rico Petrocelli	.50	.20	.05
☐ 341	Steve Garvey	75.00	30.00	7.50
☐ 342	Frank Tepedino	.35	.14	.03
☐ 343	Pirates Rookies Ed Acosta Milt May	.35	.14	.03
☐ 344	Ellie Rodriguez	.35	.14	.03
☐ 345	Joel Horlen	.35	.14	.03
☐ 346	Lum Harris MG	.35	.14	.03
☐ 347	Ted Uhlaender	.35	.14	.03
☐ 348	Fred Norman	.35	.14	.03
☐ 349	Rich Reese	.35	.14	.03
☐ 350	Billy Williams	4.00	1.60	.40
☐ 351	Jim Shellenback	.35	.14	.03
☐ 352	Denny Doyle	.35	.14	.03
☐ 353	Carl Taylor	.35	.14	.03
☐ 354	Don McMahon	.35	.14	.03
☐ 355	Bud Harrelson	.50	.20	.05
☐ 356	Bob Locker	.35	.14	.03
☐ 357	Reds Team	1.00	.40	.10
☐ 358	Danny Cater	.35	.14	.03
☐ 359	Ron Reed	.35	.14	.03
☐ 360	Jim Fregosi	.75	.30	.07
☐ 361	Don Sutton	3.50	1.40	.35
☐ 362	Orioles Rookies Mike Adamson Roger Freed	.35	.14	.03
☐ 363	Mike Nagy	.35	.14	.03
☐ 364	Tommy Dean	.35	.14	.03
☐ 365	Bob Johnson	.35	.14	.03
☐ 366	Ron Stone	.35	.14	.03
☐ 367	Dalton Jones	.35	.14	.03
☐ 368	Bob Veale	.50	.20	.05
☐ 369	Checklist 4	1.50	.20	.04

		NRMT	VG-E	GOOD			NRMT	VG-E	GOOD
☐ 370	Joe Torre	2.00	.80	.20	☐ 413	Pat Kelly	.45	.18	.04
☐ 371	Jack Hiatt	.35	.14	.03	☐ 414	Woodie Fryman	.45	.18	.04
☐ 372	Lew Krausse	.35	.14	.03	☐ 415	Mike Hegan	.45	.18	.04
☐ 373	Tom McCraw	.35	.14	.03	☐ 416	Gene Alley	.60	.24	.06
☐ 374	Clete Boyer	.50	.20	.05	☐ 417	Dick Hall	.45	.18	.04
☐ 375	Steve Hargan	.35	.14	.03	☐ 418	Adolfo Phillips	.45	.18	.04
☐ 376	Expos Rookies	.35	.14	.03	☐ 419	Ron Hansen	.45	.18	.04
	Clyde Mashore				☐ 420	Jim Merritt	.45	.18	.04
	Ernie McAnally				☐ 421	John Stephenson	.45	.18	.04
☐ 377	Greg Garrett	.35	.14	.03	☐ 422	Frank Bertaina	.45	.18	.04
☐ 378	Tito Fuentes	.35	.14	.03	☐ 423	Tigers Rookies	.45	.18	.04
☐ 379	Wayne Granger	.35	.14	.03		Dennis Saunders			
☐ 380	Ted Williams MG	5.00	2.00	.50		Tim Marting			
☐ 381	Fred Gladding	.35	.14	.03	☐ 424	R. Rodriquez	.45	.18	.04
☐ 382	Jake Gibbs	.35	.14	.03	☐ 425	Doug Rader	.60	.24	.06
☐ 383	Rod Gaspar	.35	.14	.03	☐ 426	Chris Cannizzaro	.45	.18	.04
☐ 384	Rollie Fingers	3.00	1.20	.30	☐ 427	Bernie Allen	.45	.18	.04
☐ 385	Maury Wills	1.50	.60	.15	☐ 428	Jim McAndrew	.45	.18	.04
☐ 386	Red Sox Team	1.00	.40	.10	☐ 429	Chuck Hinton	.45	.18	.04
☐ 387	Ron Herbel	.35	.14	.03	☐ 430	Wes Parker	.60	.24	.06
☐ 388	Al Oliver	1.75	.70	.17	☐ 431	Tom Burgmeier	.45	.18	.04
☐ 389	Ed Brinkman	.35	.14	.03	☐ 432	Bob Didier	.45	.18	.04
☐ 390	Glenn Beckert	.50	.20	.05	☐ 433	Skip Lockwood	.45	.18	.04
☐ 391	Twins Rookies	.50	.20	.05	☐ 434	Gary Sutherland	.45	.18	.04
	Steve Brye				☐ 435	Jose Cardenal	.45	.18	.04
	Cotton Nash				☐ 436	Wilbur Wood	.60	.24	.06
☐ 392	Grant Jackson	.35	.14	.03	☐ 437	Danny Murtaugh MG	.45	.18	.04
☐ 393	Merv Rettenmund	.35	.14	.03	☐ 438	Mike McCormick	.60	.24	.06
☐ 394	Clay Carroll	.45	.18	.04	☐ 439	Phillies Rookies	2.25	.90	.22
☐ 395	Roy White	.60	.24	.06		Greg Luzinski			
☐ 396	Dick Schofield	.45	.18	.04		Scott Reid			
☐ 397	Alvin Dark MG	.60	.24	.06	☐ 440	Bert Campaneris	.60	.24	.06
☐ 398	Howie Reed	.45	.18	.04	☐ 441	Milt Pappas	.60	.24	.06
☐ 399	Jim French	.45	.18	.04	☐ 442	California Angels	1.00	.40	.10
☐ 400	Hank Aaron	21.00	8.50	2.10		Team Card			
☐ 401	Tom Murphy	.45	.18	.04	☐ 443	Rich Robertson	.45	.18	.04
☐ 402	Dodgers Team	1.00	.40	.10	☐ 444	Jimmie Price	.45	.18	.04
☐ 403	Joe Coleman	.45	.18	.04	☐ 445	Art Shamsky	.45	.18	.04
☐ 404	Astros Rookies	.45	.18	.04	☐ 446	Bobby Bolin	.45	.18	.04
	Buddy Harris				☐ 447	Cesar Geronimo	.45	.18	.04
	Roger Metzger				☐ 448	Dave Roberts	.45	.18	.04
☐ 405	Leo Cardenas	.45	.18	.04	☐ 449	Brant Alyea	.45	.18	.04
☐ 406	Ray Sadecki	.45	.18	.04	☐ 450	Bob Gibson	6.50	2.60	.65
☐ 407	Joe Rudi	.60	.24	.06	☐ 451	Joe Keough	.45	.18	.04
☐ 408	Rafael Robles	.45	.18	.04	☐ 452	John Boccabella	.45	.18	.04
☐ 409	Don Pavletich	.45	.18	.04	☐ 453	Terry Crowley	.45	.18	.04
☐ 410	Ken Holtzman	.60	.24	.06	☐ 454	Mike Paul	.45	.18	.04
☐ 411	George Spriggs	.45	.18	.04	☐ 455	Don Kessinger	.60	.24	.06
☐ 412	Jerry Johnson	.45	.18	.04	☐ 456	Bob Meyer	.45	.18	.04

		NRMT	VG-E	GOOD
☐ 457	Willie Smith	.45	.18	.04
☐ 458	White Sox Rookies	.45	.18	.04
	Ron Lolich			
	Dave Lemonds			
☐ 459	Jim Lefebvre	.75	.30	.07
☐ 460	Fritz Peterson	.45	.18	.04
☐ 461	Jim Ray Hart	.60	.24	.06
☐ 462	Senators Team	1.00	.40	.10
☐ 463	Tom Kelley	.45	.18	.04
☐ 464	Aurelio Rodriguez	.45	.18	.04
☐ 465	Jim McCarver	1.00	.40	.10
☐ 466	Ken Berry	.45	.18	.04
☐ 467	Al Santorini	.45	.18	.04
☐ 468	Frank Fernandez	.45	.18	.04
☐ 469	Bob Aspromonte	.45	.18	.04
☐ 470	Bob Oliver	.45	.18	.04
☐ 471	Tom Griffin	.45	.18	.04
☐ 472	Ken Rudolph	.45	.18	.04
☐ 473	Gary Wagner	.45	.18	.04
☐ 474	Jim Fairey	.45	.18	.04
☐ 475	Ron Perranoski	.60	.24	.06
☐ 476	Dal Maxvill	.60	.24	.06
☐ 477	Earl Weaver MG	1.00	.40	.10
☐ 478	Bernie Carbo	.45	.18	.04
☐ 479	Dennis Higgins	.45	.18	.04
☐ 480	Manny Sanguillen	.60	.24	.06
☐ 481	Daryl Patterson	.45	.18	.04
☐ 482	Padres Team	1.00	.40	.10
☐ 483	Gene Michael	.60	.24	.06
☐ 484	Don Wilson	.45	.18	.04
☐ 485	Ken McMullen	.45	.18	.04
☐ 486	Steve Huntz	.45	.18	.04
☐ 487	Paul Schaal	.45	.18	.04
☐ 488	Jerry Stephenson	.45	.18	.04
☐ 489	Luis Alvarado	.45	.18	.04
☐ 490	Deron Johnson	.45	.18	.04
☐ 491	Jim Hardin	.45	.18	.04
☐ 492	Ken Boswell	.45	.18	.04
☐ 493	Dave May	.45	.18	.04
☐ 494	Braves Rookies	.60	.24	.06
	Ralph Garr			
	Rick Kester			
☐ 495	Felipe Alou	.60	.24	.06
☐ 496	Woody Woodward	.60	.24	.06
☐ 497	Horacio Pina	.45	.18	.04
☐ 498	John Kennedy	.45	.18	.04
☐ 499	Checklist 5	1.50	.20	.04
☐ 500	Jim Perry	.75	.30	.07
☐ 501	Andy Etchebarren	.45	.18	.04

		NRMT	VG-E	GOOD
☐ 502	Cubs Team	1.00	.40	.10
☐ 503	Gates Brown	.60	.24	.06
☐ 504	Ken Wright	.45	.18	.04
☐ 505	Ollie Brown	.45	.18	.04
☐ 506	Bobby Knoop	.45	.18	.04
☐ 507	George Stone	.45	.18	.04
☐ 508	Roger Repoz	.45	.18	.04
☐ 509	Jim Grant	.45	.18	.04
☐ 510	Ken Harrelson	1.00	.40	.10
☐ 511	Chris Short	.45	.18	.04
☐ 512	Red Sox Rookies	.45	.18	.04
	Dick Mills			
	Mike Garman			
☐ 513	Nolan Ryan	27.00	11.00	2.70
☐ 514	Ron Woods	.45	.18	.04
☐ 515	Carl Morton	.45	.18	.04
☐ 516	Ted Kubiak	.45	.18	.04
☐ 517	Charlie Fox MG	.45	.18	.04
☐ 518	Joe Grzenda	.45	.18	.04
☐ 519	Willie Crawford	.45	.18	.04
☐ 520	Tommy John	2.50	1.00	.25
☐ 521	Leron Lee	.45	.18	.04
☐ 522	Twins Team	1.00	.40	.10
☐ 523	John Odom	.45	.18	.04
☐ 524	Mickey Stanley	1.00	.40	.10
☐ 525	Ernie Banks	11.00	4.50	1.10
☐ 526	Ray Jarvis	.85	.34	.08
☐ 527	Cleon Jones	.85	.34	.08
☐ 528	Wally Bunker	.85	.34	.08
☐ 529	NL Rookie Infielders	3.50	1.40	.35
	Enzo Hernandez			
	Bill Buckner			
	Marty Perez			
☐ 530	Carl Yastrzemski	32.00	13.00	3.20
☐ 531	Mike Torrez	1.00	.40	.10
☐ 532	Bill Rigney MG	.85	.34	.08
☐ 533	Mike Ryan	.85	.34	.08
☐ 534	Luke Walker	.85	.34	.08
☐ 535	Curt Flood	1.25	.50	.12
☐ 536	Claude Raymond	.85	.34	.08
☐ 537	Tom Egan	.85	.34	.08
☐ 538	Angel Bravo	.85	.34	.08
☐ 539	Larry Brown	.85	.34	.08
☐ 540	Larry Dierker	1.00	.40	.10
☐ 541	Bob Burda	.85	.34	.08
☐ 542	Bob Miller	.85	.34	.08
☐ 543	New York Yankees	2.50	1.00	.25
	Team Card			
☐ 544	Vida Blue	3.00	1.20	.30

		NRMT	VG-E	GOOD
☐ 545	Dick Dietz	.85	.34	.08
☐ 546	John Matias	.85	.34	.08
☐ 547	Pat Dobson	1.00	.40	.10
☐ 548	Don Mason	.85	.34	.08
☐ 549	Jim Brewer	.85	.34	.08
☐ 550	Harmon Killebrew	10.00	4.00	1.00
☐ 551	Frank Linzy	.85	.34	.08
☐ 552	Buddy Bradford	.85	.34	.08
☐ 553	Kevin Collins	.85	.34	.08
☐ 554	Lowell Palmer	.85	.34	.08
☐ 555	Walt Williams	.85	.34	.08
☐ 556	Jim McGlothlin	.85	.34	.08
☐ 557	Tom Satriano	.85	.34	.08
☐ 558	Hector Torres	.85	.34	.08
☐ 559	AL Rookie Pitchers	.85	.34	.08
	Terry Cox			
	Bill Gogolewski			
	Gary Jones			
☐ 560	Rusty Staub	2.00	.80	.20
☐ 561	Syd O'Brien	.85	.34	.08
☐ 562	Dave Giusti	1.00	.40	.10
☐ 563	Giants Team	1.75	.70	.17
☐ 564	Al Fitzmorris	.85	.34	.08
☐ 565	Jim Wynn	1.25	.50	.12
☐ 566	Tim Cullen	.85	.34	.08
☐ 567	Walt Alston MG	2.50	1.00	.25
☐ 568	Sal Campisi	.85	.34	.08
☐ 569	Ivan Murrell	.85	.34	.08
☐ 570	Jim Palmer	9.00	3.75	.90
☐ 571	Ted Sizemore	1.00	.40	.10
☐ 572	Jerry Kenney	.85	.34	.08
☐ 573	Ed Kranepool	1.00	.40	.10
☐ 574	Jim Bunning	2.50	1.00	.25
☐ 575	Bill Freehan	1.50	.60	.15
☐ 576	Cubs Rookies	.85	.34	.08
	Adrian Garrett			
	Brock Davis			
	Garry Jestadt			
☐ 577	Jim Lonborg	1.25	.50	.12
☐ 578	Ron Hunt	.85	.34	.08
☐ 579	Marty Pattin	.85	.34	.08
☐ 580	Tony Perez	3.00	1.20	.30
☐ 581	Roger Nelson	.85	.34	.08
☐ 582	Dave Cash	1.00	.40	.10
☐ 583	Ron Cook	.85	.34	.08
☐ 584	Indians Team	1.75	.70	.17
☐ 585	Willie Davis	1.25	.50	.12
☐ 586	Dick Woodson	.85	.34	.08
☐ 587	Sonny Jackson	.85	.34	.08

		NRMT	VG-E	GOOD
☐ 588	Tom Bradley	.85	.34	.08
☐ 589	Bob Barton	.85	.34	.08
☐ 590	Alex Johnson	1.00	.40	.10
☐ 591	Jackie Brown	.85	.34	.08
☐ 592	Randy Hundley	1.00	.40	.10
☐ 593	Jack Aker	.85	.34	.08
☐ 594	Cards Rookies	1.50	.60	.15
	Bob Chlupsa			
	Bob Stinson			
	Al Hrabosky			
☐ 595	Dave Johnson	2.00	.80	.20
☐ 596	Mike Jorgensen	.85	.34	.08
☐ 597	Ken Suarez	.85	.34	.08
☐ 598	Rick Wise	1.00	.40	.10
☐ 599	Norm Cash	1.50	.60	.15
☐ 600	Willie Mays	32.00	13.00	3.20
☐ 601	Ken Tatum	.85	.34	.08
☐ 602	Marty Martinez	.85	.34	.08
☐ 603	Pirates Team	1.75	.70	.17
☐ 604	John Gelnar	.85	.34	.08
☐ 605	Orlando Cepeda	3.00	1.20	.30
☐ 606	Chuck Taylor	.85	.34	.08
☐ 607	Paul Ratliff	.85	.34	.08
☐ 608	Mike Wegener	.85	.34	.08
☐ 609	Leo Durocher MG	1.75	.70	.17
☐ 610	Amos Otis	1.25	.50	.12
☐ 611	Tom Phoebus	.85	.34	.08
☐ 612	Indians Rookies	.85	.34	.08
	Lou Camilli			
	Ted Ford			
	Steve Mingori			
☐ 613	Pedro Borbon	.85	.34	.08
☐ 614	Billy Cowan	.85	.34	.08
☐ 615	Mel Stottlemyre	1.50	.60	.15
☐ 616	Larry Hisle	1.00	.40	.10
☐ 617	Clay Dalrymple	.85	.34	.08
☐ 618	Tug McGraw	1.50	.60	.15
☐ 619A	Checklist 6	2.50	.30	.06
	(copyright on back)			
☐ 619B	Checklist 6	3.50	.40	.08
	(no copyright)			
☐ 620	Frank Howard	1.50	.60	.15
☐ 621	Ron Bryant	.85	.34	.08
☐ 622	Joe Lahoud	.85	.34	.08
☐ 623	Pat Jarvis	.85	.34	.08
☐ 624	Athletics Team	1.75	.70	.17
☐ 625	Lou Brock	10.00	4.00	1.00
☐ 626	Freddie Patek	1.00	.40	.10
☐ 627	Steve Hamilton	.85	.34	.08

		NRMT	VG-E	GOOD
☐ 628	John Bateman	.85	.34	.08
☐ 629	John Hiller	1.00	.40	.10
☐ 630	Roberto Clemente ..	22.00	9.00	2.20
☐ 631	Eddie Fisher	.85	.34	.08
☐ 632	Darrel Chaney	.85	.34	.08
☐ 633	AL Rookie Outfielders	.85	.34	.08
	Bobby Brooks			
	Pete Koegel			
	Scott Northey			
☐ 634	Phil Regan	1.00	.40	.10
☐ 635	Bobby Murcer	1.75	.70	.17
☐ 636	Denny Lemaster ...	.85	.34	.08
☐ 637	Dave Bristol MG ...	.85	.34	.08
☐ 638	Stan Williams	.85	.34	.08
☐ 639	Tom Haller	1.00	.40	.10
☐ 640	Frank Robinson ...	12.00	5.00	1.20
☐ 641	New York Mets	3.00	1.20	.30
	Team Card			
☐ 642	Jim Roland	.85	.34	.08
☐ 643	Rick Reichardt	.85	.34	.08
☐ 644	Jim Stewart	2.00	.80	.20
☐ 645	Jim Maloney	2.50	1.00	.25
☐ 646	Bobby Floyd	2.00	.80	.20
☐ 647	Juan Pizarro	2.00	.80	.20
☐ 648	Mets Rookies	4.00	1.60	.40
	Rich Folkers			
	Ted Martinez			
	John Matlack			
☐ 649	Sparky Lyle	3.50	1.40	.35
☐ 650	Rich Allen	7.00	2.80	.70
☐ 651	Jerry Robertson ...	2.00	.80	.20
☐ 652	Braves Team	4.00	1.60	.40
☐ 653	Russ Snyder	2.00	.80	.20
☐ 654	Don Shaw	2.00	.80	.20
☐ 655	Mike Epstein	2.00	.80	.20
☐ 656	Gerry Nyman	2.00	.80	.20
☐ 657	Jose Azcue	2.00	.80	.20
☐ 658	Paul Lindblad	2.00	.80	.20
☐ 659	Byron Browne	2.00	.80	.20
☐ 660	Ray Culp	2.00	.80	.20
☐ 661	Chuck Tanner MG .	3.00	1.20	.30
☐ 662	Mike Hedlund	2.00	.80	.20
☐ 663	Marv Staehle	2.00	.80	.20
☐ 664	Rookie Pitchers	2.50	1.00	.25
	Archie Reynolds			
	Bob Reynolds			
	Ken Reynolds			
☐ 665	Ron Swoboda	2.50	1.00	.25
☐ 666	Gene Brabender ...	2.00	.80	.20

		NRMT	VG-E	GOOD
☐ 667	Pete Ward	2.00	.80	.20
☐ 668	Gary Neibauer	2.00	.80	.20
☐ 669	Ike Brown	2.00	.80	.20
☐ 670	Bill Hands	2.00	.80	.20
☐ 671	Bill Voss	2.00	.80	.20
☐ 672	Ed Crosby	2.00	.80	.20
☐ 673	Gerry Janeski	2.00	.80	.20
☐ 674	Montreal Expos ...	4.50	1.80	.45
	Team Card			
☐ 675	Dave Boswell	2.00	.80	.20
☐ 676	Tommie Reynolds .	2.00	.80	.20
☐ 677	Jack DiLauro	2.00	.80	.20
☐ 678	George Thomas ..	2.00	.80	.20
☐ 679	Don O'Riley	2.00	.80	.20
☐ 680	Don Mincher	2.50	1.00	.25
☐ 681	Bill Butler	2.00	.80	.20
☐ 682	Terry Harmon	2.00	.80	.20
☐ 683	Bill Burbach	2.00	.80	.20
☐ 684	Curt Motton	2.00	.80	.20
☐ 685	Moe Drabowsky ..	2.00	.80	.20
☐ 686	Chico Ruiz	2.00	.80	.20
☐ 687	Ron Taylor	2.00	.80	.20
☐ 688	Sparky Anderson MG	4.50	1.80	.45
☐ 689	Frank Baker	2.00	.80	.20
☐ 690	Bob Moose	2.00	.80	.20
☐ 691	Bobby Heise	2.00	.80	.20
☐ 692	AL Rookie Pitchers	2.00	.80	.20
	Hal Haydel			
	Rogelio Moret			
	Wayne Twitchell			
☐ 693	Jose Pena	2.00	.80	.20
☐ 694	Rick Renick	2.00	.80	.20
☐ 695	Joe Niekro	4.00	1.60	.40
☐ 696	Jerry Morales	2.50	1.00	.25
☐ 697	Rickey Clark	2.00	.80	.20
☐ 698	Milwaukee Brewers	4.50	1.80	.45
	Team Card			
☐ 699	Jim Britton	2.00	.80	.20
☐ 700	Boog Powell	5.00	2.00	.50
☐ 701	Bob Garibaldi	2.00	.80	.20
☐ 702	Milt Ramirez	2.00	.80	.20
☐ 703	Mike Kekich	2.00	.80	.20
☐ 704	J.C. Martin	2.00	.80	.20
☐ 705	Dick Selma	2.00	.80	.20
☐ 706	Joe Foy	2.00	.80	.20
☐ 707	Fred Lasher	2.00	.80	.20
☐ 708	Russ Nagelson ...	2.00	.80	.20

		NRMT	VG-E	GOOD
☐ 709	Rookie Outfielders . Dusty Baker Don Baylor Tom Paciorek	18.00	7.25	1.80
☐ 710	Sonny Siebert	2.50	1.00	.25
☐ 711	Larry Stahl	2.00	.80	.20
☐ 712	Jose Martinez	2.00	.80	.20
☐ 713	Mike Marshall	2.50	1.00	.25
☐ 714	Dick Williams MG	2.50	1.00	.25
☐ 715	Horace Clarke	2.00	.80	.20
☐ 716	Dave Leonhard	2.00	.80	.20
☐ 717	Tommie Aaron	2.50	1.00	.25
☐ 718	Billy Wynne	2.00	.80	.20
☐ 719	Jerry May	2.00	.80	.20
☐ 720	Matty Alou	2.50	1.00	.25
☐ 721	John Morris	2.00	.80	.20
☐ 722	Houston Astros Team Card	4.00	1.60	.40
☐ 723	Vicente Romo	2.00	.80	.20
☐ 724	Tom Tischinski	2.00	.80	.20
☐ 725	Gary Gentry	2.00	.80	.20
☐ 726	Paul Popovich	2.00	.80	.20
☐ 727	Ray Lamb	2.00	.80	.20
☐ 728	NL Rookie Outfielders Wayne Redmond Keith Lampard Bernie Williams	2.00	.80	.20
☐ 729	Dick Billings	2.00	.80	.20
☐ 730	Jim Rooker	2.00	.80	.20
☐ 731	Jim Qualls	2.00	.80	.20
☐ 732	Bob Reed	2.00	.80	.20
☐ 733	Lee Maye	2.00	.80	.20
☐ 734	Rob Gardner	2.00	.80	.20
☐ 735	Mike Shannon	3.50	1.40	.35
☐ 736	Mel Queen	2.00	.80	.20
☐ 737	Preston Gomez MG	2.00	.80	.20
☐ 738	Russ Gibson	2.00	.80	.20
☐ 739	Barry Lersch	2.00	.80	.20
☐ 740	Luis Aparicio	10.00	4.00	1.00
☐ 741	Skip Guinn	2.00	.80	.20
☐ 742	Kansas City Royals Team Card	4.00	1.60	.40
☐ 743	John O'Donoghue	2.00	.80	.20
☐ 744	Chuck Manuel	2.00	.80	.20
☐ 745	Sandy Alomar	2.00	.80	.20
☐ 746	Andy Kosco	2.00	.80	.20

		NRMT	VG-E	GOOD
☐ 747	NL Rookie Pitchers Al Severinsen Scipio Spinks Balor Moore	2.00	.80	.20
☐ 748	John Purdin	2.00	.80	.20
☐ 749	Ken Szotkiewicz	2.00	.80	.20
☐ 750	Denny McLain	5.00	2.00	.50
☐ 751	Al Weis	2.00	.80	.20
☐ 752	Dick Drago	3.00	1.00	.20

1972 Topps

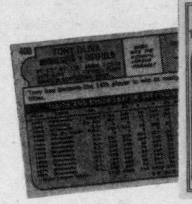

*The cards in this 787-card set measure 2 ½"
by 3 ½". The 1972 Topps set contained the
most cards ever for a Topps set to that point
in time. Features appearing for the first time
were "Boyhood Photos" (KP: 341-348 and
491-498), Awards and Trophy cards (621-
626), "In Action" (distributed throughout the
set) and "Traded Cards" (TR: 751-757).
Other subsets included League Leaders (85-
96), Playoffs cards (221-222), and World
Series cards (223-230). The curved lines of
the color picture are a departure from the
rectangular designs of other years. There is
a series of intermediate scarcity (526-656)
and the usual high numbers (657-787).*

	NRMT	VG-E	GOOD
Complete Set (787)	1300.00	500.00	175.00
Common Player (1-132)	.25	.10	.02
Common Player (133-263)	.30	.12	.03
Common Player (264-394)	.35	.14	.03

		NRMT	VG-E	GOOD
	Common Player (395-525) .	.40	.16	.04
	Common Player (526-656) .	.85	.34	.08
	Common Player (657-787) .	2.00	.80	.20
☐ 1	Pittsburgh Pirates .. Team Card	4.00	.60	.12
☐ 2	Ray Culp	.25	.10	.02
☐ 3	Bob Tolan	.40	.16	.04
☐ 4	Checklist 1	1.25	.15	.03
☐ 5	John Bateman	.25	.10	.02
☐ 6	Fred Scherman	.25	.10	.02
☐ 7	Enzo Hernandez	.25	.10	.02
☐ 8	Ron Swoboda	.40	.16	.04
☐ 9	Stan Williams	.25	.10	.02
☐ 10	Amos Otis	.40	.16	.04
☐ 11	Bobby Valentine ...	.75	.30	.07
☐ 12	Jose Cardenal	.25	.10	.02
☐ 13	Joe Grzenda	.25	.10	.02
☐ 14	Phillies Rookies .... Pete Koegel Mike Anderson Wayne Twitchell	.25	.10	.02
☐ 15	Walt Williams	.25	.10	.02
☐ 16	Mike Jorgensen	.25	.10	.02
☐ 17	Dave Duncan	.25	.10	.02
☐ 18A	Juan Pizarro ...... (yellow underline C and S of Cubs)	.25	.10	.02
☐ 18B	Juan Pizarro ...... (green underline C and S of Cubs)	5.00	2.00	.50
☐ 19	Billy Cowan	.25	.10	.02
☐ 20	Don Wilson	.25	.10	.02
☐ 21	Braves Team	.60	.24	.06
☐ 22	Rob Gardner	.25	.10	.02
☐ 23	Ted Kubiak	.25	.10	.02
☐ 24	Ted Ford	.25	.10	.02
☐ 25	Bill Singer	.40	.16	.04
☐ 26	Andy Etchebarren ...	.25	.10	.02
☐ 27	Bob Johnson	.25	.10	.02
☐ 28	Twins Rookies .... Bob Gebhard Steve Brye Hal Haydel	.25	.10	.02
☐ 29A	Bill Bonham .... (yellow underline C and S of Cubs)	.25	.10	.02
☐ 29B	Bill Bonham .... (green underline C and S of Cubs)	5.00	2.00	.50
☐ 30	Rico Petrocelli	.40	.16	.04
☐ 31	Cleon Jones	.25	.10	.02
☐ 32	Jones In Action	.25	.10	.02
☐ 33	Billy Martin MG ...	1.50	.60	.15
☐ 34	Martin In Action ...	.60	.24	.06
☐ 35	Jerry Johnson	.25	.10	.02
☐ 36	Johnson In Action ..	.25	.10	.02
☐ 37	Carl Yastrzemski ..	15.00	6.00	1.50
☐ 38	Yastrzemski In Action	6.00	2.40	.60
☐ 39	Bob Barton	.25	.10	.02
☐ 40	Barton In Action ...	.25	.10	.02
☐ 41	Tommy Davis	.40	.16	.04
☐ 42	Davis In Action	.25	.10	.02
☐ 43	Rick Wise	.25	.10	.02
☐ 44	Wise In Action	.25	.10	.02
☐ 45A	Glenn Beckert .... (yellow underline C and S of Cubs)	.40	.16	.04
☐ 45B	Glenn Beckert .... (green underline C and S of Cubs)	5.00	2.00	.50
☐ 46	Beckert In Action ..	.25	.10	.02
☐ 47	John Ellis	.25	.10	.02
☐ 48	Ellis In Action	.25	.10	.02
☐ 49	Willie Mays	15.00	6.00	1.50
☐ 50	Mays In Action	6.00	2.40	.60
☐ 51	Harmon Killebrew ..	4.00	1.60	.40
☐ 52	Killebrew In Action .	1.50	.60	.15
☐ 53	Bud Harrelson	.40	.16	.04
☐ 54	Harrelson In Action .	.25	.10	.02
☐ 55	Clyde Wright	.25	.10	.02
☐ 56	Rich Chiles	.25	.10	.02
☐ 57	Bob Oliver	.25	.10	.02
☐ 58	Ernie McAnally	.25	.10	.02
☐ 59	Fred Stanley	.25	.10	.02
☐ 60	Manny Sanguillen .	.40	.16	.04
☐ 61	Cubs Rookies ..... Burt Hooton Gene Hiser Earl Stephenson	.60	.24	.06
☐ 62	Angel Mangual ...	.25	.10	.02
☐ 63	Duke Sims	.25	.10	.02
☐ 64	Pete Broberg	.25	.10	.02
☐ 65	Cesar Cedeno	.60	.24	.06
☐ 66	Ray Corbin	.25	.10	.02
☐ 67	Red Schoendienst MG	.60	.24	.06
☐ 68	Jim York	.25	.10	.02
☐ 69	Roger Freed	.25	.10	.02
☐ 70	Mike Cuellar	.40	.16	.04
☐ 71	Angels Team	.60	.24	.06
☐ 72	Bruce Kison	.60	.24	.06
☐ 73	Steve Huntz	.25	.10	.02
☐ 74	Cecil Upshaw	.25	.10	.02
☐ 75	Bert Campaneris ..	.40	.16	.04

			NRMT	VG-E	GOOD
☐	76	Don Carrithers	.25	.10	.02
☐	77	Ron Theobald	.25	.10	.02
☐	78	Steve Arlin	.25	.10	.02
☐	79	Red Sox Rookies	20.00	8.00	2.00
		Mike Garman			
		Cecil Cooper			
		Carlton Fisk			
☐	80	Tony Perez	2.00	.80	.20
☐	81	Mike Hedlund	.25	.10	.02
☐	82	Ron Woods	.25	.10	.02
☐	83	Dalton Jones	.25	.10	.02
☐	84	Vince Colbert	.25	.10	.02
☐	85	NL Batting Leaders	.75	.30	.07
		Joe Torre			
		Ralph Garr			
		Glenn Beckert			
☐	86	AL Batting Leaders	.75	.30	.07
		Tony Oliva			
		Bobby Murcer			
		Merv Rettenmund			
☐	87	NL RBI Leaders	1.50	.60	.15
		Joe Torre			
		Willie Stargell			
		Hank Aaron			
☐	88	AL RBI Leaders	1.25	.50	.12
		Harmon Killebrew			
		Frank Robinson			
		Reggie Smith			
☐	89	NL Home Run Leaders	1.50	.60	.15
		Willie Stargell			
		Hank Aaron			
		Lee May			
☐	90	AL Home Run Leaders	1.00	.40	.10
		Bill Melton			
		Norm Cash			
		Reggie Jackson			
☐	91	NL ERA Leaders	1.00	.40	.10
		Tom Seaver			
		Dave Roberts			
		(photo actually Danny Coombs)			
		Don Wilson			
☐	92	AL ERA Leaders	.75	.30	.07
		Vida Blue			
		Wilbur Wood			
		Jim Palmer			

			NRMT	VG-E	GOOD
☐	93	NL Pitching Leaders	1.50	.60	.15
		Fergie Jenkins			
		Steve Carlton			
		Al Downing			
		Tom Seaver			
☐	94	AL Pitching Leaders	.75	.30	.07
		Mickey Lolich			
		Vida Blue			
		Wilbur Wood			
☐	95	NL Strikeout Leaders	1.00	.40	.10
		Tom Seaver			
		Fergie Jenkins			
		Bill Stoneman			
☐	96	AL Strikeout Leaders	.75	.30	.07
		Mickey Lolich			
		Vida Blue			
		Joe Coleman			
☐	97	Tom Kelley	.25	.10	.02
☐	98	Chuck Tanner MG	.40	.16	.04
☐	99	Ross Grimsley	.25	.10	.02
☐	100	Frank Robinson	4.00	1.60	.40
☐	101	Astros Rookies	1.50	.60	.15
		Bill Greif			
		J.R. Richard			
		Ray Busse			
☐	102	Lloyd Allen	.25	.10	.02
☐	103	Checklist 2	1.25	.20	.03
☐	104	Toby Harrah	1.25	.50	.12
☐	105	Gary Gentry	.25	.10	.02
☐	106	Brewers Team	.60	.24	.06
☐	107	Jose Cruz	1.50	.60	.15
☐	108	Gary Waslewski	.25	.10	.02
☐	109	Jerry May	.25	.10	.02
☐	110	Ron Hunt	.25	.10	.02
☐	111	Jim Grant	.25	.10	.02
☐	112	Greg Luzinski	1.00	.40	.10
☐	113	Rogelio Moret	.25	.10	.02
☐	114	Bill Buckner	1.50	.60	.15
☐	115	Jim Fregosi	.40	.16	.04
☐	116	Ed Farmer	.25	.10	.02
☐	117A	Cleo James	.25	.10	.02
		(yellow underline C and S of Cubs)			
☐	117B	Cleo James	5.00	2.00	.50
		(green underline C and S of Cubs)			
☐	118	Skip Lockwood	.25	.10	.02
☐	119	Marty Perez	.25	.10	.02
☐	120	Bill Freehan	.60	.24	.06
☐	121	Ed Sprague	.25	.10	.02
☐	122	Larry Biittner	.25	.10	.02

		NRMT	VG-E	GOOD
☐ 123	Ed Acosta	.25	.10	.02
☐ 124	Yankees Rookies	.25	.10	.02
	Alan Closter			
	Rusty Torres			
	Roger Hambright			
☐ 125	Dave Cash	.40	.16	.04
☐ 126	Bart Johnson	.25	.10	.02
☐ 127	Duffy Dyer	.25	.10	.02
☐ 128	Eddie Watt	.25	.10	.02
☐ 129	Charlie Fox MG	.25	.10	.02
☐ 130	Bob Gibson	4.00	1.60	.40
☐ 131	Jim Nettles	.25	.10	.02
☐ 132	Joe Morgan	2.50	1.00	.25
☐ 133	Joe Keough	.30	.12	.03
☐ 134	Carl Morton	.30	.12	.03
☐ 135	Vada Pinson	.75	.30	.07
☐ 136	Darrell Chaney	.30	.12	.03
☐ 137	Dick Williams MG	.50	.20	.05
☐ 138	Mike Kekich	.30	.12	.03
☐ 139	Tim McCarver	.75	.30	.07
☐ 140	Pat Dobson	.50	.20	.05
☐ 141	Mets Rookies	.50	.20	.05
	Buzz Capra			
	Leroy Stanton			
	Jon Matlack			
☐ 142	Chris Chambliss	1.50	.60	.15
☐ 143	Garry Jestadt	.30	.12	.03
☐ 144	Marty Pattin	.30	.12	.03
☐ 145	Don Kessinger	.50	.20	.05
☐ 146	Steve Kealey	.30	.12	.03
☐ 147	Dave Kingman	4.50	1.80	.45
☐ 148	Dick Billings	.30	.12	.03
☐ 149	Gary Neibauer	.30	.12	.03
☐ 150	Norm Cash	1.00	.40	.10
☐ 151	Jim Brewer	.30	.12	.03
☐ 152	Gene Clines	.30	.12	.03
☐ 153	Rick Auerbach	.30	.12	.03
☐ 154	Ted Simmons	1.50	.60	.15
☐ 155	Larry Dierker	.50	.20	.05
☐ 156	Minnesota Twins	.75	.30	.07
	Team Card			
☐ 157	Don Gullett	.50	.20	.05
☐ 158	Jerry Kenney	.30	.12	.03
☐ 159	John Boccabella	.30	.12	.03
☐ 160	Andy Messersmith	.50	.20	.05
☐ 161	Brock Davis	.30	.12	.03
☐ 162	Brewers Rookies	1.00	.40	.10
	Jerry Bell			
	Darrell Porter			
	Bob Reynolds			
	(Porter and Bell photos switched)			
☐ 163	Tug McGraw	.75	.30	.07
☐ 164	McGraw In Action	.50	.20	.05
☐ 165	Chris Speier	.60	.24	.06
☐ 166	Speier In Action	.30	.12	.03
☐ 167	Deron Johnson	.30	.12	.03
☐ 168	Johnson In Action	.30	.12	.03
☐ 169	Vida Blue	.75	.30	.07
☐ 170	Blue In Action	.50	.20	.05
☐ 171	Darrell Evans	1.50	.60	.15
☐ 172	Evans In Action	.50	.20	.05
☐ 173	Clay Kirby	.30	.12	.03
☐ 174	Kirby In Action	.30	.12	.03
☐ 175	Tom Haller	.30	.12	.03
☐ 176	Haller In Action	.30	.12	.03
☐ 177	Paul Schaal	.30	.12	.03
☐ 178	Schaal In Action	.30	.12	.03
☐ 179	Dock Ellis	.30	.12	.03
☐ 180	Ellis In Action	.30	.12	.03
☐ 181	Ed Kranepool	.50	.20	.05
☐ 182	Kranepool In Action	.30	.12	.03
☐ 183	Bill Melton	.30	.12	.03
☐ 184	Melton In Action	.30	.12	.03
☐ 185	Ron Bryant	.30	.12	.03
☐ 186	Bryant In Action	.30	.12	.03
☐ 187	Gates Brown	.50	.20	.05
☐ 188	Frank Lucchesi MG	.30	.12	.03
☐ 189	Gene Tenace	.50	.20	.05
☐ 190	Dave Giusti	.50	.20	.05
☐ 191	Jeff Burroughs	.75	.30	.07
☐ 192	Cubs Team	.75	.30	.07
☐ 193	Kurt Bevacqua	.30	.12	.03
☐ 194	Fred Norman	.30	.12	.03
☐ 195	Orlando Cepeda	1.75	.70	.17
☐ 196	Mel Queen	.30	.12	.03
☐ 197	Johnny Briggs	.30	.12	.03
☐ 198	Dodgers Rookies	1.50	.60	.15
	Charlie Hough			
	Bob O'Brien			
	Mike Strahler			
☐ 199	Mike Fiore	.30	.12	.03
☐ 200	Lou Brock	4.00	1.60	.40
☐ 201	Phil Roof	.30	.12	.03
☐ 202	Scipio Spinks	.30	.12	.03
☐ 203	Ron Blomberg	.30	.12	.03

		NRMT	VG-E	GOOD
☐ 204	Tommy Helms	.50	.20	.05
☐ 205	Dick Drago	.30	.12	.03
☐ 206	Dal Maxvill	.50	.20	.05
☐ 207	Tom Egan	.30	.12	.03
☐ 208	Milt Pappas	.50	.20	.05
☐ 209	Joe Rudi	.50	.20	.05
☐ 210	Denny McLain	1.00	.40	.10
☐ 211	Gary Sutherland	.30	.12	.03
☐ 212	Grant Jackson	.30	.12	.03
☐ 213	Angels Rookies	.30	.12	.03
	Billy Parker			
	Art Kusnyer			
	Tom Silverio			
☐ 214	Mike McQueen	.30	.12	.03
☐ 215	Alex Johnson	.50	.20	.05
☐ 216	Joe Niekro	.75	.30	.07
☐ 217	Roger Metzger	.30	.12	.03
☐ 218	Eddie Kasko MG	.30	.12	.03
☐ 219	Rennie Stennett	.50	.20	.05
☐ 220	Jim Perry	.75	.30	.07
☐ 221	NL Playoffs	.75	.30	.07
	Bucs champs			
☐ 222	AL Playoffs	1.50	.60	.15
	Orioles champs			
	(Brooks Robinson)			
☐ 223	World Series Game 1	.75	.30	.07
	(McNally pitching)			
☐ 224	World Series Game 2	.75	.30	.07
	(Dave Johnson and Mark Belanger)			
☐ 225	World Series Game 3	.75	.30	.07
	(Sanguillen scoring)			
☐ 226	World Series Game 4	2.25	.90	.22
	(Clemente on 2nd)			
☐ 227	World Series Game 5	.75	.30	.07
	(Briles pitching)			
☐ 228	World Series Game 6	1.00	.40	.10
	(Frank Robinson and			
	Manny Sanguillen)			
☐ 229	World Series Game 7	.75	.30	.07
	(Blass pitching)			
☐ 230	World Series Summary	.75	.30	.07
	Pirates celebrate			
☐ 231	Casey Cox	.30	.12	.03
☐ 232	Giants Rookies	.30	.12	.03
	Chris Arnold			
	Jim Barr			
	Dave Rader			
☐ 233	Jay Johnstone	.50	.20	.05
☐ 234	Ron Taylor	.30	.12	.03
☐ 235	Merv Rettenmund	.30	.12	.03
☐ 236	Jim McGlothlin	.30	.12	.03
☐ 237	Yankees Team	1.00	.40	.10
☐ 238	Leron Lee	.30	.12	.03
☐ 239	Tom Timmermann	.30	.12	.03
☐ 240	Rich Allen	1.50	.60	.15
☐ 241	Rollie Fingers	2.50	1.00	.25
☐ 242	Don Mincher	.30	.12	.03
☐ 243	Frank Linzy	.30	.12	.03
☐ 244	Steve Braun	.30	.12	.03
☐ 245	Tommie Agee	.30	.12	.03
☐ 246	Tom Burgmeier	.30	.12	.03
☐ 247	Milt May	.30	.12	.03
☐ 248	Tom Bradley	.30	.12	.03
☐ 249	Harry Walker MG	.30	.12	.03
☐ 250	Boog Powell	1.00	.40	.10
☐ 251	Checklist 3	1.25	.15	.03
☐ 252	Ken Reynolds	.30	.12	.03
☐ 253	Sandy Alomar	.30	.12	.03
☐ 254	Boots Day	.30	.12	.03
☐ 255	Jim Lonborg	.50	.20	.05
☐ 256	George Foster	1.50	.60	.15
☐ 257	Tigers Rookies	.30	.12	.03
	Jim Foor			
	Tim Hosley			
	Paul Jata			
☐ 258	Randy Hundley	.50	.20	.05
☐ 259	Sparky Lyle	.75	.30	.07
☐ 260	Ralph Garr	.50	.20	.05
☐ 261	Steve Mingori	.30	.12	.03
☐ 262	San Diego Padres Team Card	.75	.30	.07
☐ 263	Felipe Alou	.50	.20	.05
☐ 264	Tommy John	2.00	.80	.20
☐ 265	Wes Parker	.50	.20	.05
☐ 266	Bobby Bolin	.35	.14	.03
☐ 267	Dave Concepcion	1.50	.60	.15
☐ 268	A's Rookies	.35	.14	.03
	Dwain Anderson			
	Chris Floethe			
☐ 269	Don Hahn	.35	.14	.03
☐ 270	Jim Palmer	4.50	1.60	.40
☐ 271	Ken Rudolph	.35	.14	.03
☐ 272	Mickey Rivers	1.00	.40	.10
☐ 273	Bobby Floyd	.35	.14	.03
☐ 274	Al Severinsen	.35	.14	.03
☐ 275	Cesar Tovar	.35	.14	.03
☐ 276	Gene Mauch MG	.50	.20	.05
☐ 277	Elliott Maddox	.35	.14	.03

		NRMT	VG-E	GOOD
☐ 278	Dennis Higgins	.35	.14	.03
☐ 279	Larry Brown	.35	.14	.03
☐ 280	Willie McCovey	4.00	1.60	.40
☐ 281	Bill Parsons	.35	.14	.03
☐ 282	Astros Team	.75	.30	.07
☐ 283	Darrell Brandon ...	.35	.14	.03
☐ 284	Ike Brown	.35	.14	.03
☐ 285	Gaylord Perry	4.00	1.60	.40
☐ 286	Gene Alley	.50	.20	.05
☐ 287	Jim Hardin	.35	.14	.03
☐ 288	Johnny Jeter	.35	.14	.03
☐ 289	Syd O'Brien	.35	.14	.03
☐ 290	Sonny Siebert	.50	.20	.05
☐ 291	Hal McRae	.75	.30	.07
☐ 292	McRae In Action ...	.50	.20	.05
☐ 293	Dan Frisella	.35	.14	.03
☐ 294	Frisella In Action ..	.35	.14	.03
☐ 295	Dick Dietz	.35	.14	.03
☐ 296	Dietz In Action	.35	.14	.03
☐ 297	Claude Osteen	.50	.20	.05
☐ 298	Osteen In Action ..	.35	.14	.03
☐ 299	Hank Aaron	15.00	6.00	1.50
☐ 300	Aaron in Action	6.00	2.40	.60
☐ 301	George Mitterwald ..	.35	.14	.03
☐ 302	Mitterwald In Action	.35	.14	.03
☐ 303	Joe Pepitone	.50	.20	.05
☐ 304	Pepitone In Action ..	.35	.14	.03
☐ 305	Ken Boswell	.35	.14	.03
☐ 306	Boswell In Action ..	.35	.14	.03
☐ 307	Steve Renko	.35	.14	.03
☐ 308	Renko In Action ...	.35	.14	.03
☐ 309	Roberto Clemente .	13.00	5.25	1.30
☐ 310	Clemente In Action .	5.00	2.00	.50
☐ 311	Clay Carroll	.35	.14	.03
☐ 312	Carroll In Action ...	.35	.14	.03
☐ 313	Luis Aparicio	3.00	1.20	.30
☐ 314	Aparicio In Action ..	1.25	.50	.12
☐ 315	Paul Splittorff	.50	.20	.05
☐ 316	Cardinals Rookies ..	.50	.20	.05
	Jim Bibby			
	Jorge Roque			
	Santiago Guzman			
☐ 317	Rich Hand	.35	.14	.03
☐ 318	Sonny Jackson	.35	.14	.03
☐ 319	Aurelio Rodriguez ..	.35	.14	.03
☐ 320	Steve Blass	.50	.20	.05
☐ 321	Joe Lahoud	.35	.14	.03
☐ 322	Jose Pena	.35	.14	.03
☐ 323	Earl Weaver MG ...	.75	.30	.07
☐ 324	Mike Ryan	.35	.14	.03
☐ 325	Mel Stottlemyre ...	.75	.30	.07
☐ 326	Pat Kelly	.35	.14	.03
☐ 327	Steve Stone	.75	.30	.07
☐ 328	Red Sox Team ...	.75	.30	.07
☐ 329	Roy Foster	.35	.14	.03
☐ 330	Jim Hunter	3.00	1.20	.30
☐ 331	Stan Swanson	.35	.14	.03
☐ 332	Buck Martinez	.35	.14	.03
☐ 333	Steve Barber	.35	.14	.03
☐ 334	Rangers Rookies ..	.35	.14	.03
	Bill Fahey			
	Jim Mason			
	Tom Ragland			
☐ 335	Bill Hands	.35	.14	.03
☐ 336	Marty Martinez	.35	.14	.03
☐ 337	Mike Kilkenny	.35	.14	.03
☐ 338	Bob Grich	.75	.30	.07
☐ 339	Ron Cook	.35	.14	.03
☐ 340	Roy White	.50	.20	.05
☐ 341	KP: Joe Torre	.50	.20	.05
☐ 342	KP: Wilbur Wood ...	.35	.14	.03
☐ 343	KP: Willie Stargell ..	1.00	.40	.10
☐ 344	KP: Dave McNally ..	.35	.14	.03
☐ 345	KP: Rick Wise	.35	.14	.03
☐ 346	KP: Jim Fregosi ...	.50	.20	.05
☐ 347	KP: Tom Seaver ...	1.50	.60	.15
☐ 348	KP: Sal Bando	.35	.14	.03
☐ 349	Al Fitzmorris	.35	.14	.03
☐ 350	Frank Howard	.75	.30	.07
☐ 351	Braves Rookies ...	.50	.20	.05
	Tom House			
	Rick Kester			
	Jimmy Britton			
☐ 352	Dave LaRoche	.35	.14	.03
☐ 353	Art Shamsky	.35	.14	.03
☐ 354	Tom Murphy	.35	.14	.03
☐ 355	Bob Watson	.50	.20	.05
☐ 356	Gerry Moses	.35	.14	.03
☐ 357	Woodie Fryman ...	.35	.14	.03
☐ 358	Sparky Anderson MG	1.00	.40	.10
☐ 359	Don Pavletich	.35	.14	.03
☐ 360	Dave Roberts	.35	.14	.03
☐ 361	Mike Andrews	.35	.14	.03
☐ 362	New York Mets ...	1.00	.40	.10
	Team Card			
☐ 363	Ron Klimkowski ...	.35	.14	.03
☐ 364	Johnny Callison ...	.50	.20	.05
☐ 365	Dick Bosman	.35	.14	.03

	NRMT	VG-E	GOOD			NRMT	VG-E	GOOD
☐ 366 Jimmy Rosario	.35	.14	.03	☐ 409 Frank Baker	.45	.18	.04
☐ 367 Ron Perranoski	.50	.20	.05	☐ 410 Fergie Jenkins	1.75	.70	.17
☐ 368 Danny Thompson	.35	.14	.03	☐ 411 Bob Montgomery	.45	.18	.04
☐ 369 Jim Lefebvre	.75	.30	.07	☐ 412 Dick Kelley	.45	.18	.04
☐ 370 Don Buford	.50	.20	.05	☐ 413 White Sox Rookies	.45	.18	.04
☐ 371 Denny Lemaster	.35	.14	.03	Don Eddy			
☐ 372 Royals Rookies	.35	.14	.03	Dave Lemonds			
Lance Clemons				☐ 414 Bob Miller	.45	.18	.04
Monty Montgomery				☐ 415 Cookie Rojas	.60	.24	.06
☐ 373 John Mayberry	.50	.20	.05	☐ 416 Johnny Edwards	.45	.18	.04
☐ 374 Jack Heidemann	.35	.14	.03	☐ 417 Tom Hall	.45	.18	.04
☐ 375 Reggie Cleveland	.35	.14	.03	☐ 418 Tom Shopay	.45	.18	.04
☐ 376 Andy Kosco	.35	.14	.03	☐ 419 Jim Spencer	.45	.18	.04
☐ 377 Terry Harmon	.35	.14	.03	☐ 420 Steve Carlton	13.00	5.25	1.30
☐ 378 Checklist 4	1.25	.15	.03	☐ 421 Ellie Rodriguez	.45	.18	.04
☐ 379 Ken Berry	.35	.14	.03	☐ 422 Ray Lamb	.45	.18	.04
☐ 380 Earl Williams	.35	.14	.03	☐ 423 Oscar Gamble	.60	.24	.06
☐ 381 Chicago White Sox	.75	.30	.07	☐ 424 Bill Gogolewski	.45	.18	.04
Team Card				☐ 425 Ken Singleton	.90	.36	.09
☐ 382 Joe Gibbon	.35	.14	.03	☐ 426 Singleton In Action	.60	.24	.06
☐ 383 Brant Alyea	.35	.14	.03	☐ 427 Tito Fuentes	.45	.18	.04
☐ 384 Dave Campbell	.35	.14	.03	☐ 428 Fuentes In Action	.45	.18	.04
☐ 385 Mickey Stanley	.50	.20	.05	☐ 429 Bob Robertson	.45	.18	.04
☐ 386 Jim Colborn	.35	.14	.03	☐ 430 Robertson In Action	.45	.18	.04
☐ 387 Horace Clarke	.35	.14	.03	☐ 431 Clarence Gaston	.45	.18	.04
☐ 388 Charlie Williams	.35	.14	.03	☐ 432 Gaston In Action	.45	.18	.04
☐ 389 Bill Rigney MG	.35	.14	.03	☐ 433 Johnny Bench	20.00	8.00	2.00
☐ 390 Willie Davis	.50	.20	.05	☐ 434 Bench In Action	8.00	3.25	.80
☐ 391 Ken Sanders	.35	.14	.03	☐ 435 Reggie Jackson	18.00	7.25	1.80
☐ 392 Pirates Rookies	.75	.30	.07	☐ 436 Jackson In Action	7.00	2.80	.70
Fred Cambria				☐ 437 Maury Wills	1.25	.50	.12
Richie Zisk				☐ 438 Wills In Action	.60	.24	.06
☐ 393 Curt Motton	.35	.14	.03	☐ 439 Billy Williams	3.00	1.20	.30
☐ 394 Ken Forsch	.50	.20	.05	☐ 440 Williams In Action	1.25	.50	.12
☐ 395 Matty Alou	.60	.24	.06	☐ 441 Thurman Munson	10.00	4.00	1.00
☐ 396 Paul Lindblad	.45	.18	.04	☐ 442 Munson In Action	4.00	1.60	.40
☐ 397 Philadelphia Phillies	.90	.36	.09	☐ 443 Ken Henderson	.45	.18	.04
Team Card				☐ 444 Henderson In Action	.45	.18	.04
☐ 398 Larry Hisle	.60	.24	.06	☐ 445 Tom Seaver	14.00	5.25	1.30
☐ 399 Milt Wilcox	.60	.24	.06	☐ 446 Seaver In Action	5.50	2.00	.50
☐ 400 Tony Oliva	1.50	.60	.15	☐ 447 Willie Stargell	5.00	2.00	.45
☐ 401 Jim Nash	.45	.18	.04	☐ 448 Stargell In Action	2.00	.70	.17
☐ 402 Bobby Heise	.45	.18	.04	☐ 449 Bob Lemon MG	1.00	.40	.10
☐ 403 John Cumberland	.45	.18	.04	☐ 450 Mickey Lolich	1.00	.40	.10
☐ 404 Jeff Torborg	.60	.24	.06	☐ 451 Tony LaRussa	.75	.30	.07
☐ 405 Ron Fairly	.60	.24	.06	☐ 452 Ed Herrmann	.45	.18	.04
☐ 406 George Hendrick	1.00	.40	.10	☐ 453 Barry Lersch	.45	.18	.04
☐ 407 Chuck Taylor	.45	.18	.04	☐ 454 Oakland A's	1.00	.40	.10
☐ 408 Jim Northrup	.60	.24	.06	Team Card			

		NRMT	VG-E	GOOD				NRMT	VG-E	GOOD
☐ 455	Tommy Harper	.60	.24	.06		☐ 496	KP: Bud Harrelson	.45	.18	.04
☐ 456	Mark Belanger	.60	.24	.06		☐ 497	KP: Jim Perry	.45	.18	.04
☐ 457	Padres Rookies ...	.60	.24	.06		☐ 498	KP: Brooks Robinson	1.50	.60	.15
	Darcy Fast					☐ 499	Vicente Romo	.45	.18	.04
	Derrel Thomas					☐ 500	Joe Torre	1.00	.40	.10
	Mike Ivie					☐ 501	Pete Hamm	.45	.18	.04
☐ 458	Aurelio Monteagudo	.45	.18	.04		☐ 502	Jackie Hernandez .	.45	.18	.04
☐ 459	Rick Renick	.45	.18	.04		☐ 503	Gary Peters	.60	.24	.06
☐ 460	Al Downing	.60	.24	.06		☐ 504	Ed Spiezio	.45	.18	.04
☐ 461	Tim Cullen	.45	.18	.04		☐ 505	Mike Marshall	.60	.24	.06
☐ 462	Rickey Clark	.45	.18	.04		☐ 506	Indians Rookies ...	.60	.24	.06
☐ 463	Bernie Carbo	.45	.18	.04			Terry Ley			
☐ 464	Jim Roland	.45	.18	.04			Jim Moyer			
☐ 465	Gil Hodges MG ...	2.50	1.00	.25			Dick Tidrow			
☐ 466	Norm Miller	.45	.18	.04		☐ 507	Fred Gladding	.45	.18	.04
☐ 467	Steve Kline	.45	.18	.04		☐ 508	Elrod Hendricks ...	.45	.18	.04
☐ 468	Richie Scheinblum .	.45	.18	.04		☐ 509	Don McMahon	.45	.18	.04
☐ 469	Ron Herbel	.45	.18	.04		☐ 510	Ted Williams MG ..	5.00	2.00	.50
☐ 470	Ray Fosse	.45	.18	.04		☐ 511	Tony Taylor	.45	.18	.04
☐ 471	Luke Walker	.45	.18	.04		☐ 512	Paul Popovich	.45	.18	.04
☐ 472	Phil Gagliano	.45	.18	.04		☐ 513	Lindy McDaniel ...	.60	.24	.06
☐ 473	Dan McGinn	.45	.18	.04		☐ 514	Ted Sizemore	.45	.18	.04
☐ 474	Orioles Rookies ...	2.00	.80	.20		☐ 515	Bert Blyleven	3.50	1.40	.35
	Don Baylor					☐ 516	Oscar Brown	.45	.18	.04
	Roric Harrison					☐ 517	Ken Brett	.60	.24	.06
	Johnny Oates					☐ 518	Wayne Garrett ...	.45	.18	.04
☐ 475	Gary Nolan	.45	.18	.04		☐ 519	Ted Abernathy ...	.45	.18	.04
☐ 476	Lee Richard	.45	.18	.04		☐ 520	Larry Bowa	1.50	.60	.15
☐ 477	Tom Phoebus	.45	.18	.04		☐ 521	Alan Foster	.45	.18	.04
☐ 478	Checklist 5	1.25	.15	.03		☐ 522	Dodgers Team ...	1.25	.50	.12
☐ 479	Don Shaw	.45	.18	.04		☐ 523	Chuck Dobson ...	.45	.18	.04
☐ 480	Lee May	.60	.24	.06		☐ 524	Reds Rookies	.45	.18	.04
☐ 481	Billy Conigliaro	.60	.24	.06			Ed Armbrister			
☐ 482	Joe Hoerner	.45	.18	.04			Mel Behney			
☐ 483	Ken Suarez	.45	.18	.04		☐ 525	Carlos May	.45	.18	.04
☐ 484	Lum Harris MG	.45	.18	.04		☐ 526	Bob Bailey	.85	.34	.08
☐ 485	Phil Regan	.60	.24	.06		☐ 527	Dave Leonhard ...	.85	.34	.08
☐ 486	John Lowenstein ...	.45	.18	.04		☐ 528	Ron Stone	.85	.34	.08
☐ 487	Tigers Team	1.00	.40	.10		☐ 529	Dave Nelson	.85	.34	.08
☐ 488	Mike Nagy	.45	.18	.04		☐ 530	Don Sutton	3.50	1.40	.35
☐ 489	Expos Rookies	.45	.18	.04		☐ 531	Freddie Patek	1.00	.40	.10
	Terry Humphrey					☐ 532	Fred Kendall	.85	.34	.08
	Keith Lampard					☐ 533	Ralph Houk MG ...	1.00	.40	.10
☐ 490	Dave McNally	.60	.24	.06		☐ 534	Jim Hickman	.85	.34	.08
☐ 491	KP: Lou Piniella ...	.60	.24	.06		☐ 535	Ed Brinkman	.85	.34	.08
☐ 492	KP: Mel Stottlemyre	.45	.18	.04		☐ 536	Doug Rader	1.00	.40	.10
☐ 493	KP: Bob Bailey ...	.45	.18	.04		☐ 537	Bob Locker	.85	.34	.08
☐ 494	KP: Willie Horton ..	.45	.18	.04		☐ 538	Charlie Sands ...	.85	.34	.08
☐ 495	KP: Bill Melton	.45	.18	.04		☐ 539	Terry Forster	1.50	.60	.15

	NRMT	VG-E	GOOD		NRMT	VG-E	GOOD
☐ 540 Felix Millan	.85	.34	.08	☐ 588 Jim Holt	.85	.34	.08
☐ 541 Roger Repoz	.85	.34	.08	☐ 589 Hal Lanier	1.00	.40	.10
☐ 542 Jack Billingham	.85	.34	.08	☐ 590 Graig Nettles	2.50	1.00	.25
☐ 543 Duane Josephson	.85	.34	.08	☐ 591 Paul Casanova	.85	.34	.08
☐ 544 Ted Martinez	.85	.34	.08	☐ 592 Lew Krausse	.85	.34	.08
☐ 545 Wayne Granger	.85	.34	.08	☐ 593 Rich Morales	.85	.34	.08
☐ 546 Joe Hague	.85	.34	.08	☐ 594 Jim Beauchamp	.85	.34	.08
☐ 547 Indians Team	1.75	.70	.17	☐ 595 Nolan Ryan	21.00	8.50	2.10
☐ 548 Frank Reberger	.85	.34	.08	☐ 596 Manny Mota	1.25	.50	.12
☐ 549 Dave May	.85	.34	.08	☐ 597 Jim Magnuson	.85	.34	.08
☐ 550 Brooks Robinson	10.00	4.00	1.00	☐ 598 Hal King	.85	.34	.08
☐ 551 Ollie Brown	.85	.34	.08	☐ 599 Billy Champion	.85	.34	.08
☐ 552 Brown In Action	.85	.34	.08	☐ 600 Al Kaline	12.00	5.00	1.20
☐ 553 Wilbur Wood	1.00	.40	.10	☐ 601 George Stone	.85	.34	.08
☐ 554 Wood In Action	.85	.34	.08	☐ 602 Dave Bristol MG	.85	.34	.08
☐ 555 Ron Santo	1.50	.60	.15	☐ 603 Jim Ray	.85	.34	.08
☐ 556 Santo In Action	1.00	.40	.10	☐ 604A Checklist 6	3.50	.40	.08
☐ 557 John Odom	.85	.34	.08	(copyright on back bottom right)			
☐ 558 Odom In Action	.85	.34	.08	☐ 604B Checklist 6	5.00	.50	.10
☐ 559 Pete Rose	60.00	24.00	6.00	(copyright on back bottom left)			
☐ 560 Rose In Action	20.00	8.00	2.00	☐ 605 Nelson Briles	1.00	.40	.10
☐ 561 Leo Cardenas	.85	.34	.08	☐ 606 Luis Melendez	.85	.34	.08
☐ 562 Cardenas In Action	.85	.34	.08	☐ 607 Frank Duffy	.85	.34	.08
☐ 563 Ray Sadecki	.85	.34	.08	☐ 608 Mike Corkins	.85	.34	.08
☐ 564 Sadecki In Action	.85	.34	.08	☐ 609 Tom Grieve	1.25	.50	.12
☐ 565 Reggie Smith	1.25	.50	.12	☐ 610 Bill Stoneman	.85	.34	.08
☐ 566 Smith In Action	.85	.34	.08	☐ 611 Rich Reese	.85	.34	.08
☐ 567 Juan Marichal	4.50	1.80	.45	☐ 612 Joe Decker	.85	.34	.08
☐ 568 Marichal In Action	1.75	.70	.17	☐ 613 Mike Ferraro	1.00	.40	.10
☐ 569 Ed Kirkpatrick	.85	.34	.08	☐ 614 Ted Uhlaender	.85	.34	.08
☐ 570 Kirkpatrick In Action	.85	.34	.08	☐ 615 Steve Hargan	.85	.34	.08
☐ 571 Nate Colbert	.85	.34	.08	☐ 616 Joe Ferguson	1.00	.40	.10
☐ 572 Colbert In Action	.85	.34	.08	☐ 617 Kansas City Royals	1.75	.70	.17
☐ 573 Fritz Peterson	.85	.34	.08	Team Card			
☐ 574 Peterson In Action	.85	.34	.08	☐ 618 Rich Robertson	.85	.34	.08
☐ 575 Al Oliver	1.75	.70	.17	☐ 619 Rich McKinney	.85	.34	.08
☐ 576 Leo Durocher MG	1.50	.60	.15	☐ 620 Phil Niekro	4.00	1.60	.40
☐ 577 Mike Paul	.85	.34	.08	☐ 621 Commissioners Award	1.00	.40	.10
☐ 578 Billy Grabarkewitz	.85	.34	.08	☐ 622 MVP Award	1.00	.40	.10
☐ 579 Doyle Alexander	3.00	1.20	.30	☐ 623 Cy Young Award	1.00	.40	.10
☐ 580 Lou Piniella	2.00	.80	.20	☐ 624 Minor League Player	1.00	.40	.10
☐ 581 Wade Blasingame	.85	.34	.08	☐ 625 Rookie of the Year	1.00	.40	.10
☐ 582 Montreal Expos	1.75	.70	.17	☐ 626 Babe Ruth Award	1.25	.50	.12
Team Card				☐ 627 Moe Drabowsky	.85	.34	.08
☐ 583 Darold Knowles	.85	.34	.08	☐ 628 Terry Crowley	.85	.34	.08
☐ 584 Jerry McNertney	.85	.34	.08	☐ 629 Paul Doyle	.85	.34	.08
☐ 585 George Scott	1.00	.40	.10	☐ 630 Rich Hebner	1.00	.40	.10
☐ 586 Denis Menke	.85	.34	.08	☐ 631 John Strohmayer	.85	.34	.08
☐ 587 Billy Wilson	.85	.34	.08	☐ 632 Mike Hegan	.85	.34	.08

		NRMT	VG-E	GOOD
☐ 633	Jack Hiatt	.85	.34	.08
☐ 634	Dick Woodson	.85	.34	.08
☐ 635	Don Money	1.00	.40	.10
☐ 636	Bill Lee	1.25	.50	.12
☐ 637	Preston Gomez MG	.85	.34	.08
☐ 638	Ken Wright	.85	.34	.08
☐ 639	J.C. Martin	.85	.34	.08
☐ 640	Joe Coleman	.85	.34	.08
☐ 641	Mike Lum	.85	.34	.08
☐ 642	Dennis Riddleberger	.85	.34	.08
☐ 643	Russ Gibson	.85	.34	.08
☐ 644	Bernie Allen	.85	.34	.08
☐ 645	Jim Maloney	1.00	.40	.10
☐ 646	Chico Salmon	.85	.34	.08
☐ 647	Bob Moose	.85	.34	.08
☐ 648	Jim Lyttle	.85	.34	.08
☐ 649	Pete Richert	.85	.34	.08
☐ 650	Sal Bando	1.00	.40	.10
☐ 651	Cincinnati Reds Team Card	1.75	.70	.17
☐ 652	Marcelino Lopez	.85	.34	.08
☐ 653	Jim Fairey	.85	.34	.08
☐ 654	Horacio Pina	.85	.34	.08
☐ 655	Jerry Grote	.85	.34	.08
☐ 656	Rudy May	.85	.34	.08
☐ 657	Bobby Wine	2.00	.80	.20
☐ 658	Steve Dunning	2.00	.80	.20
☐ 659	Bob Aspromonte	2.00	.80	.20
☐ 660	Paul Blair	2.50	1.00	.25
☐ 661	Bill Virdon	3.00	1.20	.30
☐ 662	Stan Bahnsen	2.00	.80	.20
☐ 663	Fran Healy	2.00	.80	.20
☐ 664	Bobby Knoop	2.00	.80	.20
☐ 665	Chris Short	2.00	.80	.20
☐ 666	Hector Torres	2.00	.80	.20
☐ 667	Ray Newman	2.00	.80	.20
☐ 668	Texas Rangers Team Card	4.50	1.80	.45
☐ 669	Willie Crawford	2.00	.80	.20
☐ 670	Ken Holtzman	2.50	1.00	.25
☐ 671	Donn Clendenon	2.50	1.00	.25
☐ 672	Archie Reynolds	2.00	.80	.20
☐ 673	Dave Marshall	2.00	.80	.20
☐ 674	John Kennedy	2.00	.80	.20
☐ 675	Pat Jarvis	2.00	.80	.20
☐ 676	Danny Cater	2.00	.80	.20
☐ 677	Ivan Murrell	2.00	.80	.20
☐ 678	Steve Luebber	2.00	.80	.20

		NRMT	VG-E	GOOD
☐ 679	Astros Rookies Bob Fenwick Bob Stinson	2.00	.80	.20
☐ 680	Dave Johnson	3.50	1.40	.35
☐ 681	Bobby Pfeil	2.00	.80	.20
☐ 682	Mike McCormick	2.50	1.00	.25
☐ 683	Steve Hovley	2.00	.80	.20
☐ 684	Hal Breeden	2.00	.80	.20
☐ 685	Joel Horlen	2.00	.80	.20
☐ 686	Steve Garvey	75.00	30.00	7.50
☐ 687	Del Unser	2.00	.80	.20
☐ 688	St. Louis Cardinals Team Card	4.00	1.60	.40
☐ 689	Eddie Fisher	2.00	.80	.20
☐ 690	Willie Montanez	2.50	1.00	.25
☐ 691	Curt Blefary	2.00	.80	.20
☐ 692	Blefary In Action	2.00	.80	.20
☐ 693	Alan Gallagher	2.00	.80	.20
☐ 694	Gallagher In Action	2.00	.80	.20
☐ 695	Rod Carew	60.00	24.00	6.00
☐ 696	Carew In Action	20.00	8.00	2.00
☐ 697	Jerry Koosman	5.00	2.00	.50
☐ 698	Koosman In Action	3.00	1.20	.30
☐ 699	Bobby Murcer	5.00	2.00	.50
☐ 700	Murcer In Action	3.00	1.20	.30
☐ 701	Jose Pagan	2.00	.80	.20
☐ 702	Pagan In Action	2.00	.80	.20
☐ 703	Doug Griffin	2.00	.80	.20
☐ 704	Griffin In Action	2.00	.80	.20
☐ 705	Pat Corrales	2.50	1.00	.25
☐ 706	Corrales In Action	2.00	.80	.20
☐ 707	Tim Foli	2.00	.80	.20
☐ 708	Foli In Action	2.00	.80	.20
☐ 709	Jim Kaat	6.00	2.40	.60
☐ 710	Kaat In Action	3.50	1.40	.35
☐ 711	Bobby Bonds	5.00	2.00	.50
☐ 712	Bonds In Action	3.00	1.20	.30
☐ 713	Gene Michael	2.50	1.00	.25
☐ 714	Michael In Action	2.00	.80	.20
☐ 715	Mike Epstein	2.00	.80	.20
☐ 716	Jesus Alou	2.00	.80	.20
☐ 717	Bruce Dal Canton	2.00	.80	.20
☐ 718	Del Rice MG	2.00	.80	.20
☐ 719	Cesar Geronimo	2.00	.80	.20
☐ 720	Sam McDowell	2.50	1.00	.25
☐ 721	Eddie Leon	2.00	.80	.20
☐ 722	Bill Sudakis	2.00	.80	.20
☐ 723	Al Santorini	2.00	.80	.20

		NRMT	VG-E	GOOD
☐ 724	AL Rookie Pitchers .	2.50	1.00	.25
	John Curtis			
	Rich Hinton			
	Mickey Scott			
☐ 725	Dick McAuliffe	2.50	1.00	.25
☐ 726	Dick Selma	2.00	.80	.20
☐ 727	Jose LaBoy	2.00	.80	.20
☐ 728	Gail Hopkins	2.00	.80	.20
☐ 729	Bob Veale	2.50	1.00	.25
☐ 730	Rick Monday	3.00	1.20	.30
☐ 731	Baltimore Orioles ..	4.00	1.60	.40
	Team Card			
☐ 732	George Culver	2.00	.80	.20
☐ 733	Jim Ray Hart	2.50	1.00	.25
☐ 734	Bob Burda	2.00	.80	.20
☐ 735	Diego Segui	2.00	.80	.20
☐ 736	Bill Russell	3.50	1.40	.35
☐ 737	Len Randle	2.00	.80	.20
☐ 738	Jim Merritt	2.00	.80	.20
☐ 739	Don Mason	2.00	.80	.20
☐ 740	Rico Carty	3.00	1.20	.30
☐ 741	Rookie First Basemen	2.50	1.00	.25
	Tom Hutton			
	John Milner			
	Rick Miller			
☐ 742	Jim Rooker	2.00	.80	.20
☐ 743	Cesar Gutierrez ...	2.00	.80	.20
☐ 744	Jim Slaton	2.50	1.00	.25
☐ 745	Julian Javier	2.50	1.00	.25
☐ 746	Lowell Palmer	2.00	.80	.20
☐ 747	Jim Stewart	2.00	.80	.20
☐ 748	Phil Hennigan	2.00	.80	.20
☐ 749	Walter Alston MG ..	4.50	1.80	.45
☐ 750	Willie Horton	2.50	1.00	.25
☐ 751	Steve Carlton TR ..	33.00	12.00	3.00
☐ 752	Joe Morgan TR	13.00	5.25	1.30
☐ 753	Denny McLain TR ..	4.50	1.80	.45
☐ 754	Frank Robinson TR .	13.00	5.25	1.30
☐ 755	Jim Fregosi TR	3.50	1.40	.35
☐ 756	Rick Wise TR	2.50	1.00	.25
☐ 757	Jose Cardenal TR ..	2.50	1.00	.25
☐ 758	Gil Garrido	2.00	.80	.20
☐ 759	Chris Cannizzaro ...	2.00	.80	.20
☐ 760	Bill Mazeroski	4.00	1.60	.40
☐ 761	Rookie Outfielders .	11.00	4.50	1.10
	Ben Oglivie			
	Ron Cey			
	Bernie Williams			
☐ 762	Wayne Simpson ...	2.00	.80	.20

		NRMT	VG-E	GOOD
☐ 763	Ron Hansen	2.00	.80	.20
☐ 764	Dusty Baker	3.50	1.40	.35
☐ 765	Ken McMullen	2.00	.80	.20
☐ 766	Steve Hamilton	2.00	.80	.20
☐ 767	Tom McCraw	2.00	.80	.20
☐ 768	Denny Doyle	2.00	.80	.20
☐ 769	Jack Aker	2.00	.80	.20
☐ 770	Jim Wynn	2.50	1.00	.25
☐ 771	San Francisco Giants	4.00	1.60	.40
	Team Card			
☐ 772	Ken Tatum	2.00	.80	.20
☐ 773	Ron Brand	2.00	.80	.20
☐ 774	Luis Alvarado	2.00	.80	.20
☐ 775	Jerry Reuss	3.50	1.40	.35
☐ 776	Bill Voss	2.00	.80	.20
☐ 777	Hoyt Wilhelm	10.00	4.00	1.00
☐ 778	Twins Rookies	3.50	1.40	.35
	Vic Albury			
	Rick Dempsey			
	Jim Strickland			
☐ 779	Tony Cloninger ...	2.00	.80	.20
☐ 780	Dick Green	2.00	.80	.20
☐ 781	Jim McAndrew	2.00	.80	.20
☐ 782	Larry Stahl	2.00	.80	.20
☐ 783	Les Cain	2.00	.80	.20
☐ 784	Ken Aspromonte ..	2.00	.80	.20
☐ 785	Vic Davalillo	2.00	.80	.20
☐ 786	Chuck Brinkman ...	2.00	.80	.20
☐ 787	Ron Reed	3.00	1.00	.25

1973 Topps

*The cards in this 660-card set measure 2 ½"
by 3 ½". The 1973 Topps set marked the last*

year in which Topps marketed baseball
cards in consecutive series. The last series
(529-660) is more difficult to obtain. Beginning in 1974, all Topps cards were printed at
the same time, thus eliminating the "high
number" factor. The set features team leader
cards featuring small individual pictures of
the coaching staff members with a larger
picture of the manager. The "background"
variations below with respect to these leader
cards are subtle and are best understood
after a side-by-side comparison of the two
varieties. An "All-Time Leaders" series (471-
478) appeared for the first time in this set.
Kid Pictures appeared again for the second
year in a row (341-346). Other topical subsets within the set included League Leaders
(61-68), Playoffs cards (201-202), World
Series cards (203-210), and Rookie
Prospects (601-616).

		NRMT	VG-E	GOOD
Complete Set (660)		650.00	250.00	90.00
Common Player (1-264)		.25	.10	.02
Common Player (265-396)		.25	.10	.02
Common Player (397-528)		.50	.20	.05
Common Player (529-660)		1.25	.50	.12
☐ 1	All-Time HR Leaders	10.00	2.50	.50
	714 Babe Ruth			
	673 Hank Aaron			
	654 Willie Mays			
☐ 2	Rich Hebner	.35	.14	.03
☐ 3	Jim Lonborg	.35	.14	.03
☐ 4	John Milner	.25	.10	.02
☐ 5	Ed Brinkman	.25	.10	.02
☐ 6	Mac Scarce	.25	.10	.02
☐ 7	Texas Rangers Team	.50	.20	.05
☐ 8	Tom Hall	.25	.10	.02
☐ 9	Johnny Oates	.25	.10	.02
☐ 10	Don Sutton	2.00	.80	.20
☐ 11	Chris Chambliss	.50	.20	.05
☐ 12A	Padres Leaders	.35	.14	.03
	Don Zimmer MG			
	Dave Garcia CO			
	Johnny Podres CO			
	Bob Skinner CO			
	Whitey Wietelmann CO			
	(Podres no right ear)			
☐ 12B	Padres Leaders	.75	.30	.07
	(Podres has right ear)			

		NRMT	VG-E	GOOD
☐ 13	George Hendrick	.50	.20	.05
☐ 14	Sonny Siebert	.35	.14	.03
☐ 15	Ralph Garr	.35	.14	.03
☐ 16	Steve Braun	.25	.10	.02
☐ 17	Fred Gladding	.25	.10	.02
☐ 18	Leroy Stanton	.25	.10	.02
☐ 19	Tim Foli	.25	.10	.02
☐ 20	Stan Bahnsen	.25	.10	.02
☐ 21	Randy Hundley	.35	.14	.03
☐ 22	Ted Abernathy	.25	.10	.02
☐ 23	Dave Kingman	1.50	.60	.15
☐ 24	Al Santorini	.25	.10	.02
☐ 25	Roy White	.35	.14	.03
☐ 26	Pittsburgh Pirates	.50	.20	.05
	Team Card			
☐ 27	Bill Gogolewski	.25	.10	.02
☐ 28	Hal McRae	.35	.14	.03
☐ 29	Tony Taylor	.25	.10	.02
☐ 30	Tug McGraw	.75	.30	.07
☐ 31	Buddy Bell	4.00	1.60	.40
☐ 32	Fred Norman	.25	.10	.02
☐ 33	Jim Breazeale	.25	.10	.02
☐ 34	Pat Dobson	.35	.14	.03
☐ 35	Willie Davis	.35	.14	.03
☐ 36	Steve Barber	.25	.10	.02
☐ 37	Bill Robinson	.35	.14	.03
☐ 38	Mike Epstein	.25	.10	.02
☐ 39	Dave Roberts	.25	.10	.02
☐ 40	Reggie Smith	.50	.20	.05
☐ 41	Tom Walker	.25	.10	.02
☐ 42	Mike Andrews	.25	.10	.02
☐ 43	Randy Moffitt	.25	.10	.02
☐ 44	Rick Monday	.35	.14	.03
☐ 45	Ellie Rodriguez	.25	.10	.02
	(photo actually John Felske)			
☐ 46	Lindy McDaniel	.35	.14	.03
☐ 47	Luis Melendez	.25	.10	.02
☐ 48	Paul Splittorff	.35	.14	.03
☐ 49A	Twins Leaders	.35	.14	.03
	Frank Quilici MG			
	Vern Morgan CO			
	Bob Rodgers CO			
	Ralph Rowe CO			
	Al Worthington CO			
	(solid backgrounds)			
☐ 49B	Twins Leaders	.75	.30	.07
	(natural backgrounds)			
☐ 50	Roberto Clemente	12.00	5.00	1.20
☐ 51	Chuck Seelbach	.25	.10	.02

			NRMT	VG-E	GOOD
☐	52	Denis Menke	.25	.10	.02
☐	53	Steve Dunning	.25	.10	.02
☐	54	Checklist 1	1.00	.10	.02
☐	55	Jon Matlack	.35	.14	.03
☐	56	Merv Rettenmund	.25	.10	.02
☐	57	Derrel Thomas	.25	.10	.02
☐	58	Mike Paul	.25	.10	.02
☐	59	Steve Yeager	.50	.20	.05
☐	60	Ken Holtzman	.35	.14	.03
☐	61	Batting Leaders	1.25	.50	.12
		Billy Williams			
		Rod Carew			
☐	62	Home Run Leaders	1.25	.50	.12
		Johnny Bench			
		Dick Allen			
☐	63	RBI Leaders	1.25	.50	.12
		Johnny Bench			
		Dick Allen			
☐	64	Stolen Base Leaders	.75	.30	.07
		Lou Brock			
		Bert Campaneris			
☐	65	ERA Leaders	.75	.30	.07
		Steve Carlton			
		Luis Tiant			
☐	66	Victory Leaders	1.00	.40	.10
		Steve Carlton			
		Gaylord Perry			
		Wilbur Wood			
☐	67	Strikeout Leaders	3.00	1.20	.30
		Steve Carlton			
		Nolan Ryan			
☐	68	Leading Firemen	.50	.20	.05
		Clay Carroll			
		Sparky Lyle			
☐	69	Phil Gagliano	.25	.10	.02
☐	70	Milt Pappas	.35	.14	.03
☐	71	Johnny Briggs	.25	.10	.02
☐	72	Ron Reed	.25	.10	.02
☐	73	Ed Herrmann	.25	.10	.02
☐	74	Billy Champion	.25	.10	.02
☐	75	Vada Pinson	.50	.20	.05
☐	76	Doug Rader	.35	.14	.03
☐	77	Mike Torrez	.35	.14	.03
☐	78	Richie Scheinblum	.25	.10	.02
☐	79	Jim Willoughby	.25	.10	.02
☐	80	Tony Oliva	1.00	.40	.10

			NRMT	VG-E	GOOD
☐	81A	Cubs Leaders	.50	.20	.05
		Whitey Lockman MG			
		Hank Aguirre CO			
		Ernie Banks CO			
		Larry Jansen CO			
		Pete Reiser CO			
		(solid backgrounds)			
☐	81B	Cubs Leaders	.75	.30	.07
		(natural backgrounds)			
☐	82	Fritz Peterson	.25	.10	.02
☐	83	Leron Lee	.25	.10	.02
☐	84	Rollie Fingers	2.00	.80	.20
☐	85	Ted Simmons	1.00	.40	.10
☐	86	Tom McCraw	.25	.10	.02
☐	87	Ken Boswell	.25	.10	.02
☐	88	Mickey Stanley	.35	.14	.03
☐	89	Jack Billingham	.25	.10	.02
☐	90	Brooks Robinson	4.00	1.60	.40
☐	91	Dodgers Team	.75	.30	.07
☐	92	Jerry Bell	.25	.10	.02
☐	93	Jesus Alou	.25	.10	.02
☐	94	Dick Billings	.25	.10	.02
☐	95	Steve Blass	.35	.14	.03
☐	96	Doug Griffin	.25	.10	.02
☐	97	Willie Montanez	.25	.10	.02
☐	98	Dick Woodson	.25	.10	.02
☐	99	Carl Taylor	.25	.10	.02
☐	100	Hank Aaron	13.00	5.25	1.30
☐	101	Ken Henderson	.25	.10	.02
☐	102	Rudy May	.25	.10	.02
☐	103	Celerino Sanchez	.25	.10	.02
☐	104	Reggie Cleveland	.25	.10	.02
☐	105	Carlos May	.25	.10	.02
☐	106	Terry Humphrey	.25	.10	.02
☐	107	Phil Hennigan	.25	.10	.02
☐	108	Bill Russell	.35	.14	.03
☐	109	Doyle Alexander	.75	.30	.07
☐	110	Bob Watson	.35	.14	.03
☐	111	Dave Nelson	.25	.10	.02
☐	112	Gary Ross	.25	.10	.02
☐	113	Jerry Grote	.25	.10	.02
☐	114	Lynn McGlothen	.25	.10	.02
☐	115	Ron Santo	.60	.24	.06

	NRMT	VG-E	GOOD
☐ 116A Yankees Leaders ..	.60	.24	.06
Ralph Houk MG			
Jim Hegan CO			
Elston Howard CO			
Dick Howser CO			
Jim Turner CO			
(solid backgrounds)			
☐ 116B Yankees Leaders ..	1.00	.40	.10
(natural backgrounds)			
☐ 117 Ramon Hernandez .	.25	.10	.02
☐ 118 John Mayberry	.35	.14	.03
☐ 119 Larry Bowa	1.00	.40	.10
☐ 120 Joe Coleman	.25	.10	.02
☐ 121 Dave Rader	.25	.10	.02
☐ 122 Jim Strickland	.25	.10	.02
☐ 123 Sandy Alomar	.25	.10	.02
☐ 124 Jim Hardin	.25	.10	.02
☐ 125 Ron Fairly	.35	.14	.03
☐ 126 Jim Brewer	.25	.10	.02
☐ 127 Brewers Team	.50	.20	.05
☐ 128 Ted Sizemore	.25	.10	.02
☐ 129 Terry Forster	.35	.14	.03
☐ 130 Pete Rose	20.00	8.00	2.00
☐ 131A Red Sox Leaders ..	.35	.14	.03
Eddie Kasko MG			
Doug Camilli CO			
Don Lenhardt CO			
Eddie Popowski CO			
(no right ear)			
Lee Stange CO			
☐ 131B Red Sox Leaders ..	.75	.30	.07
(Popowski has right ear showing)			
☐ 132 Matty Alou	.35	.14	.03
☐ 133 Dave Roberts	.25	.10	.02
☐ 134 Milt Wilcox	.35	.14	.03
☐ 135 Lee May	.35	.14	.03
☐ 136A Orioles Leaders ...	.75	.30	.07
Earl Weaver MG			
George Bamberger CO			
Jim Frey CO			
Billy Hunter CO			
George Staller CO			
(orange backgrounds)			
☐ 136B Orioles Leaders ...	1.00	.40	.10
(dark pale backgrounds)			
☐ 137 Jim Beauchamp ...	.25	.10	.02
☐ 138 Horacio Pina	.25	.10	.02
☐ 139 Carmen Fanzone ..	.25	.10	.02
☐ 140 Lou Piniella	.60	.24	.06

	NRMT	VG-E	GOOD
☐ 141 Bruce Kison	.35	.14	.03
☐ 142 Thurman Munson .	7.00	2.80	.70
☐ 143 John Curtis	.25	.10	.02
☐ 144 Marty Perez	.25	.10	.02
☐ 145 Bobby Bonds	.75	.30	.07
☐ 146 Woodie Fryman ...	.25	.10	.02
☐ 147 Mike Anderson ...	.25	.10	.02
☐ 148 Dave Goltz	.25	.10	.02
☐ 149 Ron Hunt	.25	.10	.02
☐ 150 Wilbur Wood	.35	.14	.03
☐ 151 Wes Parker	.35	.14	.03
☐ 152 Dave May	.25	.10	.02
☐ 153 Al Hrabosky	.50	.20	.05
☐ 154 Jeff Torborg	.35	.14	.03
☐ 155 Sal Bando	.35	.14	.03
☐ 156 Cesar Geronimo ..	.25	.10	.02
☐ 157 Denny Riddleberger	.25	.10	.02
☐ 158 Astros Team	.50	.20	.05
☐ 159 Clarence Gaston ..	.25	.10	.02
☐ 160 Jim Palmer	4.00	1.60	.40
☐ 161 Ted Martinez	.25	.10	.02
☐ 162 Pete Broberg	.25	.10	.02
☐ 163 Vic Davalillo	.25	.10	.02
☐ 164 Monty Montgomery	.25	.10	.02
☐ 165 Luis Aparicio	2.50	1.00	.25
☐ 166 Terry Harmon	.25	.10	.02
☐ 167 Steve Stone	.35	.14	.03
☐ 168 Jim Northrup	.35	.14	.03
☐ 169 Ron Schueler	.25	.10	.02
☐ 170 Harmon Killebrew .	3.50	1.40	.35
☐ 171 Bernie Carbo	.25	.10	.02
☐ 172 Steve Kline	.25	.10	.02
☐ 173 Hal Breeden	.25	.10	.02
☐ 174 Rich Gossage	6.00	2.40	.60
☐ 175 Frank Robinson ...	3.50	1.40	.35
☐ 176 Chuck Taylor	.25	.10	.02
☐ 177 Bill Plummer	.25	.10	.02
☐ 178 Don Rose	.25	.10	.02
☐ 179A A's Leaders	.35	.14	.03
Dick Williams MG			
Jerry Adair CO			
Vern Hoscheit CO			
Irv Noren CO			
Wes Stock CO			
(orange backgrounds)			
☐ 179B A's Leaders	.75	.30	.07
(dark pale backgrounds)			
☐ 180 Fergie Jenkins	1.25	.50	.12
☐ 181 Jack Brohamer ...	.25	.10	.02

		NRMT	VG-E	GOOD
☐ 182	Mike Caldwell	.50	.20	.05
☐ 183	Don Buford	.35	.14	.03
☐ 184	Jerry Koosman	.60	.24	.06
☐ 185	Jim Wynn	.35	.14	.03
☐ 186	Bill Fahey	.25	.10	.02
☐ 187	Luke Walker	.25	.10	.02
☐ 188	Cookie Rojas	.35	.14	.03
☐ 189	Greg Luzinski	.75	.30	.07
☐ 190	Bob Gibson	3.50	1.40	.35
☐ 191	Tigers Team	.60	.24	.06
☐ 192	Pat Jarvis	.25	.10	.02
☐ 193	Carlton Fisk	4.50	1.80	.45
☐ 194	Jorge Orta	.25	.10	.02
☐ 195	Clay Carroll	.25	.10	.02
☐ 196	Ken McMullen	.25	.10	.02
☐ 197	Ed Goodson	.25	.10	.02
☐ 198	Horace Clarke	.25	.10	.02
☐ 199	Bert Blyleven	1.50	.60	.15
☐ 200	Billy Williams	2.75	1.10	.27
☐ 201	A.L. Playoffs A's over Tigers; Hendrick scores winning run	.75	.30	.07
☐ 202	N.L. Playoffs Reds over Pirates Foster's run decides	.75	.30	.07
☐ 203	World Series Game 1 Tenace the Menace	.75	.30	.07
☐ 204	World Series Game 2 A's two straight	.75	.30	.07
☐ 205	World Series Game 3 Reds win squeeker	.75	.30	.07
☐ 206	World Series Game 4 Tenace singles in ninth	.75	.30	.07
☐ 207	World Series Game 5 Odom out at plate	.75	.30	.07
☐ 208	World Series Game 6 Red's slugging ties series	.75	.30	.07
☐ 209	World Series Game 7 Campy stars winning rally	.75	.30	.07
☐ 210	World Series Summary World champions: A's Win	.75	.30	.07
☐ 211	Balor Moore	.25	.10	.02
☐ 212	Joe Lahoud	.25	.10	.02
☐ 213	Steve Garvey	12.00	5.00	1.20

		NRMT	VG-E	GOOD
☐ 214	Steve Hamilton	.25	.10	.02
☐ 215	Dusty Baker	.60	.24	.06
☐ 216	Toby Harrah	.50	.20	.05
☐ 217	Don Wilson	.25	.10	.02
☐ 218	Aurelio Rodriguez	.25	.10	.02
☐ 219	Cardinals Team	.50	.20	.05
☐ 220	Nolan Ryan	10.00	4.00	1.00
☐ 221	Fred Kendall	.25	.10	.02
☐ 222	Rob Gardner	.25	.10	.02
☐ 223	Bud Harrelson	.35	.14	.03
☐ 224	Bill Lee	.35	.14	.03
☐ 225	Al Oliver	1.00	.40	.10
☐ 226	Ray Fosse	.25	.10	.02
☐ 227	Wayne Twitchell	.25	.10	.02
☐ 228	Bobby Darwin	.25	.10	.02
☐ 229	Roric Harrison	.25	.10	.02
☐ 230	Joe Morgan	2.50	1.00	.25
☐ 231	Bill Parsons	.25	.10	.02
☐ 232	Ken Singleton	.50	.20	.03
☐ 233	Ed Kirkpatrick	.25	.10	.02
☐ 234	Bill North	.25	.10	.02
☐ 235	Jim Hunter	2.75	1.10	.27
☐ 236	Tito Fuentes	.25	.10	.02
☐ 237A	Braves Leaders Eddie Mathews MG Lew Burdette CO Jim Busby CO Roy Hartsfield CO Ken Silvestri CO (orange backgrounds)	1.00	.40	.10
☐ 237B	Braves Leaders (dark pale backgrounds)	1.25	.50	.12
☐ 238	Tony Muser	.25	.10	.02
☐ 239	Pete Richert	.25	.10	.02
☐ 240	Bobby Murcer	.60	.24	.06
☐ 241	Dwain Anderson	.25	.10	.02
☐ 242	George Culver	.25	.10	.02
☐ 243	Angels Team	.50	.20	.05
☐ 244	Ed Acosta	.25	.10	.02
☐ 245	Carl Yastrzemski	11.00	4.50	1.10
☐ 246	Ken Sanders	.25	.10	.02
☐ 247	Del Unser	.25	.10	.02
☐ 248	Jerry Johnson	.25	.10	.02
☐ 249	Larry Biittner	.25	.10	.02
☐ 250	Manny Sanguillen	.35	.14	.03
☐ 251	Roger Nelson	.25	.10	.02

		NRMT	VG-E	GOOD
☐ 252A	Giants Leaders	.35	.14	.03
	Charlie Fox MG			
	Joe Amalfitano CO			
	Andy Gilbert CO			
	Don McMahon CO			
	John McNamara CO			
	(orange backgrounds)			
☐ 252B	Giants Leaders	.75	.30	.07
	(dark pale backgrounds)			
☐ 253	Mark Belanger	.35	.14	.03
☐ 254	Bill Stoneman	.25	.10	.02
☐ 255	Reggie Jackson	14.00	5.75	1.40
☐ 256	Chris Zachary	.25	.10	.02
☐ 257A	Mets Leaders	1.50	.60	.15
	Yogi Berra MG			
	Roy McMillan CO			
	Joe Pignatano CO			
	Rube Walker CO			
	Eddie Yost CO			
	(orange backgrounds)			
☐ 257B	Mets Leaders	2.00	.80	.20
	(dark pale backgrounds)			
☐ 258	Tommy John	1.50	.60	.15
☐ 259	Jim Holt	.25	.10	.02
☐ 260	Gary Nolan	.25	.10	.02
☐ 261	Pat Kelly	.25	.10	.02
☐ 262	Jack Aker	.25	.10	.02
☐ 263	George Scott	.35	.14	.03
☐ 264	Checklist 2	1.00	.10	.02
☐ 265	Gene Michael	.40	.16	.04
☐ 266	Mike Lum	.30	.12	.03
☐ 267	Lloyd Allen	.30	.12	.03
☐ 268	Jerry Morales	.30	.12	.03
☐ 269	Tim McCarver	.60	.24	.06
☐ 270	Luis Tiant	.60	.24	.06
☐ 271	Tom Hutton	.30	.12	.03
☐ 272	Ed Farmer	.30	.12	.03
☐ 273	Chris Speier	.40	.16	.04
☐ 274	Darold Knowles	.30	.12	.03
☐ 275	Tony Perez	1.25	.50	.12
☐ 276	Joe Lovitto	.30	.12	.03
☐ 277	Bob Miller	.30	.12	.03
☐ 278	Baltimore Orioles ..	.60	.24	.06
	Team Card			
☐ 279	Mike Strahler	.30	.12	.03
☐ 280	Al Kaline	4.50	1.90	.45
☐ 281	Mike Jorgensen	.30	.12	.03
☐ 282	Steve Hovley	.30	.12	.03
☐ 283	Ray Sadecki	.30	.12	.03
☐ 284	Glenn Borgmann ..	.30	.12	.03
☐ 285	Don Kessinger	.40	.16	.04
☐ 286	Frank Linzy	.30	.12	.03
☐ 287	Eddie Leon	.30	.12	.03
☐ 288	Gary Gentry	.30	.12	.03
☐ 289	Bob Oliver	.30	.12	.03
☐ 290	Cesar Cedeno	.50	.20	.05
☐ 291	Rogelio Moret	.30	.12	.03
☐ 292	Jose Cruz	.50	.20	.05
☐ 293	Bernie Allen	.30	.12	.03
☐ 294	Steve Arlin	.30	.12	.03
☐ 295	Bert Campaneris ..	.40	.16	.04
☐ 296	Reds Leaders	.50	.20	.05
	Sparky Anderson MG			
	Alex Grammas CO			
	Ted Kluszewski CO			
	George Scherger CO			
	Larry Shepard CO			
☐ 297	Walt Williams	.30	.12	.03
☐ 298	Ron Bryant	.30	.12	.03
☐ 299	Ted Ford	.30	.12	.03
☐ 300	Steve Carlton	8.00	3.25	.80
☐ 301	Billy Grabarkewitz .	.30	.12	.03
☐ 302	Terry Crowley	.30	.12	.03
☐ 303	Nelson Briles	.40	.16	.04
☐ 304	Duke Sims	.30	.12	.03
☐ 305	Willie Mays	13.00	5.25	1.30
☐ 306	Tom Burgmeier	.30	.12	.03
☐ 307	Boots Day	.30	.12	.03
☐ 308	Skip Lockwood	.30	.12	.03
☐ 309	Paul Popovich	.30	.12	.03
☐ 310	Dick Allen	.60	.24	.06
☐ 311	Joe Decker	.30	.12	.03
☐ 312	Oscar Brown	.30	.12	.03
☐ 313	Jim Ray	.30	.12	.03
☐ 314	Ron Swoboda	.40	.16	.04
☐ 315	John Odom	.30	.12	.03
☐ 316	San Diego Padres .	.60	.24	.06
	Team Card			
☐ 317	Danny Cater	.30	.12	.03
☐ 318	Jim McGlothlin	.30	.12	.03
☐ 319	Jim Spencer	.30	.12	.03
☐ 320	Lou Brock	3.50	1.40	.35
☐ 321	Rich Hinton	.30	.12	.03
☐ 322	Garry Maddox	.60	.24	.06

		NRMT	VG-E	GOOD
☐ 323	Tigers Leaders	.75	.30	.07
	Billy Martin MG			
	Art Fowler CO			
	Charlie Silvera CO			
	Dick Tracewski CO			
☐ 324	Al Downing	.40	.16	.04
☐ 325	Boog Powell	.75	.30	.07
☐ 326	Darrell Brandon ...	.30	.12	.03
☐ 327	John Lowenstein ...	.30	.12	.03
☐ 328	Bill Bonham	.30	.12	.03
☐ 329	Ed Kranepool	.40	.16	.04
☐ 330	Rod Carew	7.00	2.80	.70
☐ 331	Carl Morton	.30	.12	.03
☐ 332	John Felske	.30	.12	.03
☐ 333	Gene Clines	.30	.12	.03
☐ 334	Freddie Patek	.40	.16	.04
☐ 335	Bob Tolan	.40	.16	.04
☐ 336	Tom Bradley	.30	.12	.03
☐ 337	Dave Duncan	.30	.12	.03
☐ 338	Checklist 3	1.00	.10	.02
☐ 339	Dick Tidrow	.30	.12	.03
☐ 340	Nate Colbert	.30	.12	.03
☐ 341	KP: Jim Palmer ...	1.00	.40	.10
☐ 342	KP: Sam McDowell .	.30	.12	.03
☐ 343	KP: Bobby Murcer ..	.40	.16	.04
☐ 344	KP: Jim Hunter	.75	.30	.07
☐ 345	KP: Chris Speier ...	.30	.12	.03
☐ 346	KP: Gaylord Perry ..	.75	.30	.07
☐ 347	Kansas City Royals	.60	.24	.06
	Team Card			
☐ 348	Rennie Stennett ...	.40	.16	.04
☐ 349	Dick McAuliffe	.40	.16	.04
☐ 350	Tom Seaver	10.00	4.00	1.00
☐ 351	Jimmy Stewart	.30	.12	.03
☐ 352	Don Stanhouse	.30	.12	.03
☐ 353	Steve Brye	.30	.12	.03
☐ 354	Billy Parker	.30	.12	.03
☐ 355	Mike Marshall	.50	.20	.04
☐ 356	White Sox Leaders .	.40	.16	.04
	Chuck Tanner MG			
	Joe Lonnett CO			
	Jim Mahoney CO			
	Al Monchak CO			
	Johnny Sain CO			
☐ 357	Ross Grimsley	.30	.12	.03
☐ 358	Jim Nettles	.30	.12	.03
☐ 359	Cecil Upshaw	.30	.12	.03
☐ 360	Joe Rudi	.40	.16	.04
	(photo actually Gene Tenace)			
☐ 361	Fran Healy	.30	.12	.03
☐ 362	Eddie Watt	.30	.12	.03
☐ 363	Jackie Hernandez .	.30	.12	.03
☐ 364	Rick Wise	.40	.16	.04
☐ 365	Rico Petrocelli ...	.40	.16	.04
☐ 366	Brock Davis	.30	.12	.03
☐ 367	Burt Hooton	.30	.12	.03
☐ 368	Bill Buckner	.75	.30	.07
☐ 369	Lerrin LaGrow	.30	.12	.03
☐ 370	Willie Stargell	3.50	1.40	.35
☐ 371	Mike Kekich	.30	.12	.03
☐ 372	Oscar Gamble	.40	.16	.04
☐ 373	Clyde Wright	.30	.12	.03
☐ 374	Darrell Evans	.75	.30	.07
☐ 375	Larry Dierker	.40	.16	.04
☐ 376	Frank Duffy	.30	.12	.03
☐ 377	Expos Leaders ...	.40	.16	.04
	Gene Mauch MG			
	Dave Bristol CO			
	Larry Doby CO			
	Cal McLish CO			
	Jerry Zimmerman CO			
☐ 378	Len Randle	.30	.12	.03
☐ 379	Cy Acosta	.30	.12	.03
☐ 380	Johnny Bench	12.00	5.00	1.20
☐ 381	Vicente Romo	.30	.12	.03
☐ 382	Mike Hegan	.30	.12	.03
☐ 383	Diego Segui	.30	.12	.03
☐ 384	Don Baylor	1.00	.40	.10
☐ 385	Jim Perry	.50	.20	.05
☐ 386	Don Money	.40	.16	.04
☐ 387	Jim Barr	.30	.12	.03
☐ 388	Ben Oglivie	.50	.20	.05
☐ 389	New York Mets ...	1.50	.60	.15
	Team Card			
☐ 390	Mickey Lolich	.75	.30	.07
☐ 391	Lee Lacy	.50	.20	.05
☐ 392	Dick Drago	.30	.12	.03
☐ 393	Jose Cardenal	.30	.12	.03
☐ 394	Sparky Lyle	.50	.20	.05
☐ 395	Roger Metzger	.30	.12	.03
☐ 396	Grant Jackson	.30	.12	.03
☐ 397	Dave Cash	.50	.20	.05
☐ 398	Rich Hand	.50	.20	.05
☐ 399	George Foster	1.50	.60	.15
☐ 400	Gaylord Perry	2.50	1.00	.25
☐ 401	Clyde Mashore ...	.50	.20	.05
☐ 402	Jack Hiatt	.50	.20	.05
☐ 403	Sonny Jackson ...	.50	.20	.05

		NRMT	VG-E	GOOD
☐ 404	Chuck Brinkman . . .	.50	.20	.05
☐ 405	Cesar Tovar	.50	.20	.05
☐ 406	Paul Lindblad	.50	.20	.05
☐ 407	Felix Millan	.50	.20	.05
☐ 408	Jim Colborn	.50	.20	.05
☐ 409	Ivan Murrell	.50	.20	.05
☐ 410	Willie McCovey	3.50	1.40	.35
	(Bench behind plate)			
☐ 411	Ray Corbin	.50	.20	.05
☐ 412	Manny Mota	.75	.30	.07
☐ 413	Tom Timmermann .	.50	.20	.05
☐ 414	Ken Rudolph	.50	.20	.05
☐ 415	Marty Pattin	.50	.20	.05
☐ 416	Paul Schaal	.50	.20	.05
☐ 417	Scipio Spinks	.50	.20	.05
☐ 418	Bob Grich	.75	.30	.07
☐ 419	Casey Cox	.50	.20	.05
☐ 420	Tommie Agee	.50	.20	.05
☐ 421A	Angels Leaders	.75	.30	.07
	Bobby Winkles MG			
	Tom Morgan CO			
	Salty Parker CO			
	Jimmie Reese CO			
	John Roseboro CO			
	(orange backgrounds)			
☐ 421B	Angels Leaders	1.00	.40	.10
	(dark pale backgrounds)			
☐ 422	Bob Robertson	.50	.20	.05
☐ 423	Johnny Jeter	.50	.20	.05
☐ 424	Denny Doyle	.50	.20	.05
☐ 425	Alex Johnson	.50	.20	.05
☐ 426	Dave LaRoche	.50	.20	.05
☐ 427	Rick Auerbach	.50	.20	.05
☐ 428	Wayne Simpson . . .	.50	.20	.05
☐ 429	Jim Fairey	.50	.20	.05
☐ 430	Vida Blue	.75	.30	.07
☐ 431	Gerry Moses	.50	.20	.05
☐ 432	Dan Frisella	.50	.20	.05
☐ 433	Willie Horton	.75	.30	.07
☐ 434	San Francisco Giants	1.00	.40	.10
	Team Card			
☐ 435	Rico Carty	.75	.30	.07
☐ 436	Jim McAndrew	.50	.20	.05
☐ 437	John Kennedy	.50	.20	.05
☐ 438	Enzo Hernandez . . .	.50	.20	.05
☐ 439	Eddie Fisher	.50	.20	.05
☐ 440	Glenn Beckert	.75	.30	.07
☐ 441	Gail Hopkins	.50	.20	.05
☐ 442	Dick Dietz	.50	.20	.05

		NRMT	VG-E	GOOD
☐ 443	Danny Thompson .	.50	.20	.05
☐ 444	Ken Brett	.50	.20	.05
☐ 445	Ken Berry	.50	.20	.05
☐ 446	Jerry Reuss	.75	.30	.07
☐ 447	Joe Hague	.50	.20	.05
☐ 448	John Hiller	.75	.30	.07
☐ 449A	Indians Leaders . . .	.75	.30	.07
	Ken Aspromonte MG			
	Rocky Colavito CO			
	Joe Lutz CO			
	Warren Spahn CO			
	(Spahn's right ear pointed)			
☐ 449B	Indians Leaders . . .	1.00	.40	.10
	(Spahn's right ear round)			
☐ 450	Joe Torre	1.00	.40	.10
☐ 451	John Vukovich	.50	.20	.05
☐ 452	Paul Casanova . . .	.50	.20	.05
☐ 453	Checklist 4	1.25	.15	.03
☐ 454	Tom Haller	.50	.20	.05
☐ 455	Bill Melton	.50	.20	.05
☐ 456	Dick Green	.50	.20	.05
☐ 457	John Strohmayer . .	.50	.20	.05
☐ 458	Jim Mason	.50	.20	.05
☐ 459	Jimmy Howarth	.50	.20	.05
☐ 460	Bill Freehan	1.00	.40	.10
☐ 461	Mike Corkins	.50	.20	.05
☐ 462	Ron Blomberg	.50	.20	.05
☐ 463	Ken Tatum	.50	.20	.05
☐ 464	Chicago Cubs	1.00	.40	.10
	Team Card			
☐ 465	Dave Giusti	.75	.30	.07
☐ 466	Jose Arcia	.50	.20	.05
☐ 467	Mike Ryan	.50	.20	.05
☐ 468	Tom Griffin	.50	.20	.05
☐ 469	Dan Monzon	.50	.20	.05
☐ 470	Mike Cuellar	.75	.30	.07
☐ 471	Hits Leaders	3.00	1.20	.30
	Ty Cobb 4191			
☐ 472	Grand Slam Leaders	3.00	1.20	.30
	Lou Gehrig 23			
☐ 473	Total Bases Leaders	3.00	1.20	.30
	Hank Aaron 6172			
☐ 474	RBI Leaders	4.50	1.80	.45
	Babe Ruth 2209			
☐ 475	Batting Leaders . . .	3.00	1.20	.30
	Ty Cobb .367			
☐ 476	Shutout Leaders . . .	1.50	.60	.15
	Walter Johnson 113			

		NRMT	VG-E	GOOD
☐ 477	Victory Leaders	1.50	.60	.15
	Cy Young 511			
☐ 478	Strikeout Leaders ..	1.50	.60	.15
	Walter Johnson 3508			
☐ 479	Hal Lanier	.75	.30	.07
☐ 480	Juan Marichal	3.50	1.40	.35
☐ 481	Chicago White Sox .	1.00	.40	.10
	Team Card			
☐ 482	Rick Reuschel	4.00	1.60	.40
☐ 483	Dal Maxvill	.75	.30	.07
☐ 484	Ernie McAnally	.50	.20	.05
☐ 485	Norm Cash	1.00	.40	.10
☐ 486A	Phillies Leaders ...	.75	.30	.07
	Danny Ozark MG			
	Carroll Beringer CO			
	Billy DeMars CO			
	Ray Rippelmeyer CO			
	Bobby Wine CO			
	(orange backgrounds)			
☐ 486B	Phillies Leaders ...	1.00	.40	.10
	(dark pale backgrounds)			
☐ 487	Bruce Dal Canton ..	.50	.20	.05
☐ 488	Dave Campbell	.50	.20	.05
☐ 489	Jeff Burroughs	.75	.30	.07
☐ 490	Claude Osteen	.75	.30	.07
☐ 491	Bob Montgomery ...	.50	.20	.05
☐ 492	Pedro Borbon	.50	.20	.05
☐ 493	Duffy Dyer	.50	.20	.05
☐ 494	Rich Morales	.50	.20	.05
☐ 495	Tommy Helms	.75	.30	.07
☐ 496	Ray Lamb	.50	.20	.05
☐ 497A	Cardinals Leaders ..	.75	.30	.07
	Red Schoendienst MG			
	Vern Benson CO			
	George Kissell CO			
	Barney Schultz CO			
	(orange backgrounds)			
☐ 497B	Cardinals Leaders ..	1.00	.40	.10
	(dark pale backgrounds)			
☐ 498	Graig Nettles	2.25	.90	.22
☐ 499	Bob Moose	.50	.20	.05
☐ 500	Oakland A's Team ..	1.00	.40	.10
☐ 501	Larry Gura	.75	.30	.07
☐ 502	Bobby Valentine	1.00	.40	.10
☐ 503	Phil Niekro	3.50	1.40	.35
☐ 504	Earl Williams	.50	.20	.05
☐ 505	Bob Bailey	.50	.20	.05
☐ 506	Bart Johnson	.50	.20	.05
☐ 507	Darrel Chaney	.50	.20	.05

		NRMT	VG-E	GOOD
☐ 508	Gates Brown	.75	.30	.07
☐ 509	Jim Nash	.50	.20	.05
☐ 510	Amos Otis	.75	.30	.07
☐ 511	Sam McDowell ...	.75	.30	.07
☐ 512	Dalton Jones	.50	.20	.05
☐ 513	Dave Marshall	.50	.20	.05
☐ 514	Jerry Kenney	.50	.20	.05
☐ 515	Andy Messersmith .	.75	.30	.07
☐ 516	Danny Walton	.50	.20	.05
☐ 517A	Pirates Leaders ...	.75	.30	.07
	Bill Virdon MG			
	Don Leppert CO			
	Bill Mazeroski CO			
	Dave Ricketts CO			
	Mel Wright CO			
	(Mazeroski has no right ear)			
☐ 517B	Pirates Leaders ...	1.00	.40	.10
	(Mazeroski has right ear)			
☐ 518	Bob Veale	.75	.30	.07
☐ 519	Johnny Edwards ...	.50	.20	.05
☐ 520	Mel Stottlemyre ...	1.00	.40	.10
☐ 521	Atlanta Braves	1.00	.40	.10
	Team Card			
☐ 522	Leo Cardenas	.50	.20	.05
☐ 523	Wayne Granger	.50	.20	.05
☐ 524	Gene Tenace	.75	.30	.07
☐ 525	Jim Fregosi	.75	.30	.07
☐ 526	Ollie Brown	.50	.20	.05
☐ 527	Dan McGinn	.50	.20	.05
☐ 528	Paul Blair	.75	.30	.07
☐ 529	Milt May	1.25	.50	.12
☐ 530	Jim Kaat	3.50	1.40	.35
☐ 531	Ron Woods	1.25	.50	.12
☐ 532	Steve Mingori	1.25	.50	.12
☐ 533	Larry Stahl	1.25	.50	.12
☐ 534	Dave Lemonds	1.25	.50	.12
☐ 535	Johnny Callison	1.50	.60	.15
☐ 536	Philadelphia Phillies	2.25	.90	.22
	Team Card			
☐ 537	Bill Slayback	1.25	.50	.12
☐ 538	Jim Ray Hart	1.50	.60	.15
☐ 539	Tom Murphy	1.25	.50	.12
☐ 540	Cleon Jones	1.25	.50	.12
☐ 541	Bob Bolin	1.25	.50	.12
☐ 542	Pat Corrales	1.50	.60	.15
☐ 543	Alan Foster	1.25	.50	.12
☐ 544	Von Joshua	1.25	.50	.12
☐ 545	Orlando Cepeda ...	3.00	1.20	.30
☐ 546	Jim York	1.25	.50	.12

		NRMT	VG-E	GOOD
☐ 547	Bobby Heise	1.25	.50	.12
☐ 548	Don Durham	1.25	.50	.12
☐ 549	Rangers Leaders ..	2.25	.90	.22
	Whitey Herzog MG			
	Chuck Estrada CO			
	Chuck Hiller CO			
	Jackie Moore CO			
☐ 550	Dave Johnson	2.50	1.00	.25
☐ 551	Mike Kilkenny	1.25	.50	.12
☐ 552	J.C. Martin	1.25	.50	.12
☐ 553	Mickey Scott	1.25	.50	.12
☐ 554	Dave Concepcion ..	2.50	1.00	.25
☐ 555	Bill Hands	1.25	.50	.12
☐ 556	New York Yankees .	3.50	1.40	.35
	Team Card			
☐ 557	Bernie Williams	1.25	.50	.12
☐ 558	Jerry May	1.25	.50	.12
☐ 559	Barry Lersch	1.25	.50	.12
☐ 560	Frank Howard	2.50	1.00	.25
☐ 561	Jim Geddes	1.25	.50	.12
☐ 562	Wayne Garrett	1.25	.50	.12
☐ 563	Larry Haney	1.25	.50	.12
☐ 564	Mike Thompson	1.25	.50	.12
☐ 565	Jim Hickman	1.25	.50	.12
☐ 566	Lew Krausse	1.25	.50	.12
☐ 567	Bob Fenwick	1.25	.50	.12
☐ 568	Ray Newman	1.25	.50	.12
☐ 569	Dodgers Leaders ..	3.00	1.20	.30
	Walt Alston MG			
	Red Adams CO			
	Monty Basgall CO			
	Jim Gilliam CO			
	Tom Lasorda CO			
☐ 570	Bill Singer	1.25	.50	.12
☐ 571	Rusty Torres	1.25	.50	.12
☐ 572	Gary Sutherland ...	1.25	.50	.12
☐ 573	Fred Beene	1.25	.50	.12
☐ 574	Bob Didier	1.25	.50	.12
☐ 575	Dock Ellis	1.25	.50	.12
☐ 576	Montreal Expos	2.25	.90	.22
	Team Card			
☐ 577	Eric Soderholm	1.25	.50	.12
☐ 578	Ken Wright	1.25	.50	.12
☐ 579	Tom Grieve	1.75	.70	.17
☐ 580	Joe Pepitone	1.50	.60	.15
☐ 581	Steve Kealey	1.25	.50	.12
☐ 582	Darrell Porter	1.50	.60	.15
☐ 583	Bill Grief	1.25	.50	.12
☐ 584	Chris Arnold	1.25	.50	.12

		NRMT	VG-E	GOOD
☐ 585	Joe Niekro	2.50	1.00	.25
☐ 586	Bill Sudakis	1.25	.50	.12
☐ 587	Rich McKinney ...	1.25	.50	.12
☐ 588	Checklist 5	10.00	1.00	.20
☐ 589	Ken Forsch	1.50	.60	.15
☐ 590	Deron Johnson ...	1.25	.50	.12
☐ 591	Mike Hedlund	1.25	.50	.12
☐ 592	John Boccabella ...	1.25	.50	.12
☐ 593	Royals Leaders ...	1.75	.70	.17
	Jack McKeon MG			
	Galen Cisco CO			
	Harry Dunlop CO			
	Charlie Lau CO			
☐ 594	Vic Harris	1.25	.50	.12
☐ 595	Don Gullett	1.50	.60	.15
☐ 596	Red Sox Team ...	2.75	1.10	.27
☐ 597	Mickey Rivers	1.75	.70	.17
☐ 598	Phil Roof	1.25	.50	.12
☐ 599	Ed Crosby	1.25	.50	.12
☐ 600	Dave McNally	1.50	.60	.15
☐ 601	Rookie Catchers ..	1.25	.50	.12
	Sergio Robles			
	George Pena			
	Rick Stelmaszek			
☐ 602	Rookie Pitchers ...	1.25	.50	.12
	Mel Behney			
	Ralph Garcia			
	Doug Rau			
☐ 603	Rookie 3rd Basemen	1.25	.50	.12
	Terry Hughes			
	Bill McNulty			
	Ken Reitz			
☐ 604	Rookie Pitchers ...	1.25	.50	.12
	Jesse Jefferson			
	Dennis O'Toole			
	Bob Strampe			
☐ 605	Rookie 1st Basemen	1.50	.60	.15
	Enos Cabell			
	Pat Bourque			
	Gonzalo Marquez			
☐ 606	Rookie Outfielders .	3.00	1.20	.30
	Gary Matthews			
	Tom Paciorek			
	Jorge Roque			
☐ 607	Rookie Shortstops .	1.25	.50	.12
	Pepe Frias			
	Ray Busse			
	Mario Guerrero			

		NRMT	VG-E	GOOD
☐ 608	Rookie Pitchers	1.50	.60	.15
	Steve Busby			
	Dick Colpaert			
	George Medich			
☐ 609	Rookie 2nd Basemen	3.00	1.20	.30
	Larvell Blanks			
	Pedro Garcia			
	Dave Lopes			
☐ 610	Rookie Pitchers	2.00	.80	.20
	Jimmy Freeman			
	Charlie Hough			
	Hank Webb			
☐ 611	Rookie Outfielders .	1.50	.60	.15
	Rich Coggins			
	Jim Wohlford			
	Richie Zisk			
☐ 612	Rookie Pitchers	1.25	.50	.12
	Steve Lawson			
	Bob Reynolds			
	Brent Strom			
☐ 613	Rookie Catchers ...	8.00	3.25	.80
	Bob Boone			
	Skip Jutze			
	Mike Ivie			
☐ 614	Rookie Outfielders .	40.00	16.00	4.00
	Alonza Bumbry			
	Dwight Evans			
	Charlie Spikes			
☐ 615	Rookie 3rd Basemen	200.00	80.00	20.00
	Ron Cey			
	John Hilton			
	Mike Schmidt			
☐ 616	Rookie Pitchers	1.25	.50	.12
	Norm Angelini			
	Steve Blateric			
	Mike Garman			
☐ 617	Rich Chiles	1.25	.50	.12
☐ 618	Andy Etchebarren ..	1.25	.50	.12
☐ 619	Billy Wilson	1.25	.50	.12
☐ 620	Tommy Harper	1.50	.60	.15
☐ 621	Joe Ferguson	1.50	.60	.15
☐ 622	Larry Hisle	1.50	.60	.15
☐ 623	Steve Renko	1.25	.50	.12
☐ 624	Astros Leaders	2.25	.90	.22
	Leo Durocher MG			
	Preston Gomez CO			
	Grady Hatton CO			
	Hub Kittle CO			
	Jim Owens CO			

		NRMT	VG-E	GOOD
☐ 625	Angel Mangual ...	1.25	.50	.12
☐ 626	Bob Barton	1.25	.50	.12
☐ 627	Luis Alvarado ...	1.25	.50	.12
☐ 628	Jim Slaton	1.25	.50	.12
☐ 629	Indians Team	2.25	.90	.22
☐ 630	Denny McLain ...	2.75	1.10	.27
☐ 631	Tom Matchick	1.25	.50	.12
☐ 632	Dick Selma	1.25	.50	.12
☐ 633	Ike Brown	1.25	.50	.12
☐ 634	Alan Closter	1.25	.50	.12
☐ 635	Gene Alley	1.50	.60	.15
☐ 636	Rickey Clark	1.25	.50	.12
☐ 637	Norm Miller	1.25	.50	.12
☐ 638	Ken Reynolds	1.25	.50	.12
☐ 639	Willie Crawford ...	1.25	.50	.12
☐ 640	Dick Bosman	1.25	.50	.12
☐ 641	Cincinnati Reds ...	2.75	1.10	.27
	Team Card			
☐ 642	Jose LaBoy	1.25	.50	.12
☐ 643	Al Fitzmorris	1.25	.50	.12
☐ 644	Jack Heidemann ..	1.25	.50	.12
☐ 645	Bob Locker	1.25	.50	.12
☐ 646	Brewers Leaders ..	1.75	.70	.17
	Del Crandall MG			
	Harvey Kuenn CO			
	Joe Nossek CO			
	Bob Shaw CO			
	Jim Walton CO			
☐ 647	George Stone	1.25	.50	.12
☐ 648	Tom Egan	1.25	.50	.12
☐ 649	Rich Folkers	1.25	.50	.12
☐ 650	Felipe Alou	1.50	.60	.15
☐ 651	Don Carrithers ...	1.25	.50	.12
☐ 652	Ted Kubiak	1.25	.50	.12
☐ 653	Joe Hoerner	1.25	.50	.12
☐ 654	Twins Team	2.25	.90	.22
☐ 655	Clay Kirby	1.25	.50	.12
☐ 656	John Ellis	1.25	.50	.12
☐ 657	Bob Johnson	1.25	.50	.12
☐ 658	Elliott Maddox ...	1.25	.50	.12
☐ 659	Jose Pagan	1.25	.50	.12
☐ 660	Fred Scherman ...	2.50	.65	.10

1974 Topps

The cards in this 660-card set measure 2 ½ "
by 3 ½ ". This year marked the first time
Topps issued all the cards of its baseball set
at the same time rather than in series. Some
interesting variations were created by the
rumored move of the San Diego Padres to
Washington. Fifteen cards (13 players, the
team card, and the rookie card #599) of the
Padres were printed either as "San Diego"
(SD) or "Washington." The latter are the
scarcer variety and are denoted in the
checklist below by WAS. Each team's
manager and his coaches again have a
combined card with small pictures of each
coach below the larger photo of the team's
manager. The first six cards in the set (1-6)
feature Hank Aaron and his illustrious
career. Other topical subsets included in the
set are League Leaders (201-208), All-Star
selections (331-339), Playoffs cards (470-
471), World Series cards (472-479), and
Rookie Prospects (596-608).

	NRMT	VG-E	GOOD
Complete Set (660)	375.00	150.00	45.00
Common Player (1-660) ...	.25	.10	.02

			NRMT	VG-E	GOOD
☐	1	Hank Aaron	15.00	4.00	.80
		Complete ML record			
☐	2	Aaron Special 54-57	3.50	1.40	.35
		Records on back			
☐	3	Aaron Special 58-61	3.50	1.40	.35
		Memorable homers			
☐	4	Aaron Special 62-65	3.50	1.40	.35
		Life in ML's 1954-63			
☐	5	Aaron Special 66-69	3.50	1.40	.35
		Life in ML's 1964-73			
☐	6	Aaron Special 70-73	3.50	1.40	.35
		Milestone homers			
☐	7	Jim Hunter	2.75	1.10	.27
☐	8	George Theodore .	.25	.10	.02
☐	9	Mickey Lolich	.60	.24	.06
☐	10	Johnny Bench	8.00	3.25	.80
☐	11	Jim Bibby	.25	.10	.02
☐	12	Dave May	.25	.10	.02
☐	13	Tom Hilgendorf ...	.25	.10	.02
☐	14	Paul Popovich	.25	.10	.02
☐	15	Joe Torre	.60	.24	.06
☐	16	Baltimore Orioles ..	.50	.20	.05
		Team Card			
☐	17	Doug Bird	.25	.10	.02
☐	18	Gary Thomasson ..	.25	.10	.02
☐	19	Gerry Moses	.25	.10	.02
☐	20	Nolan Ryan	7.50	3.00	.75
☐	21	Bob Gallagher	.25	.10	.02
☐	22	Cy Acosta	.25	.10	.02
☐	23	Craig Robinson ...	.25	.10	.02
☐	24	John Hiller	.35	.14	.03
☐	25	Ken Singleton	.35	.14	.03
☐	26	Bill Campbell	.35	.14	.03
☐	27	George Scott	.35	.14	.03
☐	28	Manny Sanguillen .	.35	.14	.03
☐	29	Phil Niekro	2.00	.80	.20
☐	30	Bobby Bonds	.50	.20	.05
☐	31	Astros Leaders ...	.35	.14	.03
		Preston Gomez MG			
		Roger Craig CO			
		Hub Kittle CO			
		Grady Hatton CO			
		Bob Lillis CO			
☐	32A	Johnny Grubb SD .	.35	.14	.03
☐	32B	Johnny Grubb WAS	4.00	1.60	.40
☐	33	Don Newhauser ..	.25	.10	.02
☐	34	Andy Kosco	.25	.10	.02
☐	35	Gaylord Perry	2.25	.90	.22
☐	36	St. Louis Cardinals	.50	.20	.05
		Team Card			
☐	37	Dave Sells	.25	.10	.02
☐	38	Don Kessinger ...	.35	.14	.03
☐	39	Ken Suarez	.25	.10	.02
☐	40	Jim Palmer	3.50	1.40	.35
☐	41	Bobby Floyd	.25	.10	.02

		NRMT	VG-E	GOOD
☐ 42	Claude Osteen	.35	.14	.03
☐ 43	Jim Wynn	.35	.14	.03
☐ 44	Mel Stottlemyre	.50	.20	.05
☐ 45	Dave Johnson	.60	.24	.06
☐ 46	Pat Kelly	.25	.10	.02
☐ 47	Dick Ruthven	.25	.10	.02
☐ 48	Dick Sharon	.25	.10	.02
☐ 49	Steve Renko	.25	.10	.02
☐ 50	Rod Carew	6.00	2.40	.60
☐ 51	Bobby Heise	.25	.10	.02
☐ 52	Al Oliver	.75	.30	.07
☐ 53A	Fred Kendall SD	.35	.14	.03
☐ 53B	Fred Kendall WAS	4.00	1.60	.40
☐ 54	Elias Sosa	.25	.10	.02
☐ 55	Frank Robinson	3.50	1.40	.35
☐ 56	New York Mets Team	.75	.30	.07
☐ 57	Darold Knowles	.25	.10	.02
☐ 58	Charlie Spikes	.25	.10	.02
☐ 59	Ross Grimsley	.25	.10	.02
☐ 60	Lou Brock	3.50	1.40	.35
☐ 61	Luis Aparicio	2.00	.80	.20
☐ 62	Bob Locker	.25	.10	.02
☐ 63	Bill Sudakis	.25	.10	.02
☐ 64	Doug Rau	.25	.10	.02
☐ 65	Amos Otis	.35	.14	.03
☐ 66	Sparky Lyle	.50	.20	.05
☐ 67	Tommy Helms	.35	.14	.03
☐ 68	Grant Jackson	.25	.10	.02
☐ 69	Del Unser	.25	.10	.02
☐ 70	Dick Allen	.60	.24	.06
☐ 71	Dan Frisella	.25	.10	.02
☐ 72	Aurelio Rodriguez	.25	.10	.02
☐ 73	Mike Marshall	.50	.20	.05
☐ 74	Twins Team	.50	.20	.05
☐ 75	Jim Colborn	.25	.10	.02
☐ 76	Mickey Rivers	.35	.14	.03
☐ 77A	Rich Troedson SD	.35	.14	.03
☐ 77B	Rich Troedson WAS	4.00	1.60	.40
☐ 78	Giants Leaders	.35	.14	.03
	Charlie Fox MG			
	John McNamara CO			
	Joe Amalfitano CO			
	Andy Gilbert CO			
	Don McMahon CO			
☐ 79	Gene Tenace	.35	.14	.02
☐ 80	Tom Seaver	7.50	2.80	.70
☐ 81	Frank Duffy	.25	.10	.02
☐ 82	Dave Giusti	.25	.10	.02
☐ 83	Orlando Cepeda	1.00	.40	.10

		NRMT	VG-E	GOOD
☐ 84	Rick Wise	.35	.14	.03
☐ 85	Joe Morgan	2.50	1.00	.25
☐ 86	Joe Ferguson	.25	.10	.02
☐ 87	Fergie Jenkins	1.00	.40	.10
☐ 88	Freddie Patek	.35	.14	.03
☐ 89	Jackie Brown	.25	.10	.02
☐ 90	Bobby Murcer	.60	.24	.06
☐ 91	Ken Forsch	.25	.10	.02
☐ 92	Paul Blair	.35	.14	.03
☐ 93	Rod Gilbreath	.25	.10	.02
☐ 94	Tigers Team	.50	.20	.05
☐ 95	Steve Carlton	6.00	2.40	.60
☐ 96	Jerry Hairston	.25	.10	.02
☐ 97	Bob Bailey	.25	.10	.02
☐ 98	Bert Blyleven	.75	.30	.07
☐ 99	Brewers Leaders	.35	.14	.03
	Del Crandall MG			
	Harvey Kuenn CO			
	Joe Nossek CO			
	Jim Walton CO			
	Al Widmar CO			
☐ 100	Willie Stargell	3.00	1.20	.30
☐ 101	Bobby Valentine	.50	.20	.05
☐ 102A	Bill Greif SD	.35	.14	.03
☐ 102B	Bill Greif WAS	4.00	1.60	.40
☐ 103	Sal Bando	.35	.14	.03
☐ 104	Ron Bryant	.25	.10	.02
☐ 105	Carlton Fisk	2.50	1.00	.25
☐ 106	Harry Parker	.25	.10	.02
☐ 107	Alex Johnson	.25	.10	.02
☐ 108	Al Hrabosky	.35	.14	.03
☐ 109	Bob Grich	.50	.20	.03
☐ 110	Billy Williams	2.75	1.10	.27
☐ 111	Clay Carroll	.25	.10	.02
☐ 112	Dave Lopes	.60	.24	.06
☐ 113	Dick Drago	.25	.10	.02
☐ 114	Angels Team	.50	.20	.05
☐ 115	Willie Horton	.35	.14	.03
☐ 116	Jerry Reuss	.35	.14	.03
☐ 117	Ron Blomberg	.25	.10	.02
☐ 118	Bill Lee	.35	.14	.03
☐ 119	Phillies Leaders	.35	.14	.03
	Danny Ozark MG			
	Ray Ripplemeyer CO			
	Bobby Wine CO			
	Carroll Beringer CO			
	Billy DeMars CO			
☐ 120	Wilbur Wood	.35	.14	.03
☐ 121	Larry Lintz	.25	.10	.02

		NRMT	VG-E	GOOD
☐ 122	Jim Holt	.25	.10	.02
☐ 123	Nelson Briles	.35	.14	.03
☐ 124	Bobby Coluccio	.25	.10	.02
☐ 125A	Nate Colbert SD	.35	.14	.03
☐ 125B	Nate Colbert WAS	4.00	1.60	.40
☐ 126	Checklist 1	1.00	.10	.02
☐ 127	Tom Paciorek	.25	.10	.02
☐ 128	John Ellis	.25	.10	.02
☐ 129	Chris Speier	.35	.14	.03
☐ 130	Reggie Jackson	9.00	3.75	.90
☐ 131	Bob Boone	1.00	.40	.10
☐ 132	Felix Millan	.25	.10	.02
☐ 133	David Clyde	.25	.10	.02
☐ 134	Denis Menke	.25	.10	.02
☐ 135	Roy White	.35	.14	.03
☐ 136	Rick Reuschel	.75	.30	.07
☐ 137	Al Bumbry	.25	.10	.02
☐ 138	Eddie Brinkman	.25	.10	.02
☐ 139	Aurelio Monteagudo	.25	.10	.02
☐ 140	Darrell Evans	.60	.25	.05
☐ 141	Pat Bourque	.25	.10	.02
☐ 142	Pedro Garcia	.25	.10	.02
☐ 143	Dick Woodson	.25	.10	.02
☐ 144	Dodgers Leaders	1.00	.40	.10
	Walter Alston MG			
	Tom Lasorda CO			
	Jim Gilliam CO			
	Red Adams CO			
	Monty Basgall CO			
☐ 145	Dock Ellis	.25	.10	.02
☐ 146	Ron Fairly	.35	.14	.03
☐ 147	Bart Johnson	.25	.10	.02
☐ 148A	Dave Hilton SD	.35	.14	.03
☐ 148B	Dave Hilton WAS	4.00	1.60	.40
☐ 149	Mac Scarce	.25	.10	.02
☐ 150	John Mayberry	.35	.14	.03
☐ 151	Diego Segui	.25	.10	.02
☐ 152	Oscar Gamble	.35	.14	.03
☐ 153	Jon Matlack	.35	.14	.03
☐ 154	Astros Team	.50	.20	.05
☐ 155	Bert Campaneris	.35	.14	.03
☐ 156	Randy Moffitt	.25	.10	.02
☐ 157	Vic Harris	.25	.10	.02
☐ 158	Jack Billingham	.25	.10	.02
☐ 159	Jim Ray Hart	.35	.14	.03
☐ 160	Brooks Robinson	3.50	1.40	.35
☐ 161	Ray Burris	.50	.20	.05
☐ 162	Bill Freehan	.50	.20	.05
☐ 163	Ken Berry	.25	.10	.02

		NRMT	VG-E	GOOD
☐ 164	Tom House	.35	.14	.03
☐ 165	Willie Davis	.35	.14	.03
☐ 166	Royals Leaders	.35	.14	.03
	Jack McKeon MG			
	Charlie Lau CO			
	Harry Dunlop CO			
	Galen Cisco CO			
☐ 167	Luis Tiant	.60	.24	.06
☐ 168	Danny Thompson	.25	.10	.02
☐ 169	Steve Rogers	.60	.24	.06
☐ 170	Bill Melton	.25	.10	.02
☐ 171	Eduardo Rodriguez	.25	.10	.02
☐ 172	Gene Clines	.25	.10	.02
☐ 173A	Randy Jones SD	.60	.24	.06
☐ 173B	Randy Jones WAS	4.00	1.60	.40
☐ 174	Bill Robinson	.35	.14	.03
☐ 175	Reggie Cleveland	.25	.10	.02
☐ 176	John Lowenstein	.25	.10	.02
☐ 177	Dave Roberts	.25	.10	.02
☐ 178	Garry Maddox	.35	.14	.03
☐ 179	Mets Leaders	1.25	.50	.12
	Yogi Berra MG			
	Rube Walker CO			
	Eddie Yost CO			
	Roy McMillan CO			
	Joe Pignatano CO			
☐ 180	Ken Holtzman	.35	.14	.03
☐ 181	Cesar Geronimo	.25	.10	.02
☐ 182	Lindy McDaniel	.35	.14	.03
☐ 183	Johnny Oates	.25	.10	.02
☐ 184	Texas Rangers	.50	.20	.05
	Team Card			
☐ 185	Jose Cardenal	.25	.10	.02
☐ 186	Fred Scherman	.25	.10	.02
☐ 187	Don Baylor	1.00	.40	.10
☐ 188	Rudy Meoli	.25	.10	.02
☐ 189	Jim Brewer	.25	.10	.02
☐ 190	Tony Oliva	1.00	.40	.10
☐ 191	Al Fitzmorris	.25	.10	.02
☐ 192	Mario Guerrero	.25	.10	.02
☐ 193	Tom Walker	.25	.10	.02
☐ 194	Darrell Porter	.35	.14	.03
☐ 195	Carlos May	.25	.10	.02
☐ 196	Jim Fregosi	.35	.14	.03
☐ 197A	Vicente Romo SD	.35	.14	.03
☐ 197B	Vicente Romo WAS	4.00	1.60	.40
☐ 198	Dave Cash	.35	.14	.03
☐ 199	Mike Kekich	.25	.10	.02
☐ 200	Cesar Cedeno	.35	.14	.03

		NRMT	VG-E	GOOD
☐ 201	Batting Leaders .... Rod Carew Pete Rose	3.00	1.20	.30
☐ 202	Home Run Leaders Reggie Jackson Willie Stargell	1.75	.70	.17
☐ 203	RBI Leaders ...... Reggie Jackson Willie Stargell	1.75	.70	.17
☐ 204	Stolen Base Leaders Tommy Harper Lou Brock	.60	.24	.06
☐ 205	Victory Leaders .... Wilbur Wood Ron Bryant	.50	.20	.05
☐ 206	ERA Leaders ...... Jim Palmer Tom Seaver	2.25	.90	.22
☐ 207	Strikeout Leaders .. Nolan Ryan Tom Seaver	2.50	1.00	.25
☐ 208	Leading Firemen ... John Hiller Mike Marshall	.50	.20	.05
☐ 209	Ted Sizemore	.25	.10	.02
☐ 210	Bill Singer	.25	.10	.02
☐ 211	Chicago Cubs Team	.50	.20	.05
☐ 212	Rollie Fingers	1.75	.70	.17
☐ 213	Dave Rader	.25	.10	.02
☐ 214	Billy Grabarkewitz ..	.25	.10	.02
☐ 215	Al Kaline	4.00	1.60	.40
☐ 216	Ray Sadecki	.25	.10	.02
☐ 217	Tim Foli	.25	.10	.02
☐ 218	Johnny Briggs	.25	.10	.02
☐ 219	Doug Griffin	.25	.10	.02
☐ 220	Don Sutton	2.00	.80	.20
☐ 221	White Sox Leaders . Chuck Tanner MG Jim Mahoney CO Alex Monchak CO Johnny Sain CO Joe Lonnett CO	.35	.14	.03
☐ 222	Ramon Hernandez .	.25	.10	.02
☐ 223	Jeff Burroughs	.50	.20	.05
☐ 224	Roger Metzger	.25	.10	.02
☐ 225	Paul Splittorff	.35	.14	.03
☐ 226A	Padres Team SD ..	1.00	.40	.10
☐ 226B	Padres Team WAS .	5.00	2.00	.50
☐ 227	Mike Lum	.25	.10	.02
☐ 228	Ted Kubiak	.25	.10	.02
☐ 229	Fritz Peterson	.25	.10	.02
☐ 230	Tony Perez	1.25	.50	.12
☐ 231	Dick Tidrow	.25	.10	.02
☐ 232	Steve Brye	.25	.10	.02
☐ 233	Jim Barr	.25	.10	.02
☐ 234	John Milner	.25	.10	.02
☐ 235	Dave McNally	.35	.14	.03
☐ 236	Cardinals Leaders . Red Schoendienst MG Barney Schultz CO George Kissell CO Johnny Lewis CO Vern Benson CO	.35	.14	.03
☐ 237	Ken Brett	.25	.10	.02
☐ 238	Fran Healy HOR .. (Munson sliding in background)	.35	.14	.03
☐ 239	Bill Russell	.35	.14	.03
☐ 240	Joe Coleman	.25	.10	.02
☐ 241A	Glenn Beckert SD .	.35	.14	.03
☐ 241B	Glenn Beckert WAS	4.00	1.60	.40
☐ 242	Bill Gogolewski ...	.25	.10	.02
☐ 243	Bob Oliver	.25	.10	.02
☐ 244	Carl Morton	.25	.10	.02
☐ 245	Cleon Jones	.25	.10	.02
☐ 246	Athletics Team	.50	.20	.05
☐ 247	Rick Miller	.25	.10	.02
☐ 248	Tom Hall	.25	.10	.02
☐ 249	George Mitterwald .	.25	.10	.02
☐ 250A	Willie McCovey SD	4.00	1.60	.40
☐ 250B	Willie McCovey WAS	21.00	8.50	2.10
☐ 251	Graig Nettles	1.50	.60	.15
☐ 252	Dave Parker	18.00	7.25	1.80
☐ 253	John Boccabella ..	.25	.10	.02
☐ 254	Stan Bahnsen	.25	.10	.02
☐ 255	Larry Bowa	.60	.24	.06
☐ 256	Tom Griffin	.25	.10	.02
☐ 257	Buddy Bell	1.00	.40	.10
☐ 258	Jerry Morales	.25	.10	.02
☐ 259	Bob Reynolds	.25	.10	.02
☐ 260	Ted Simmons	1.00	.40	.10
☐ 261	Jerry Bell	.25	.10	.02
☐ 262	Ed Kirkpatrick	.25	.10	.02
☐ 263	Checklist 2	1.00	.10	.02
☐ 264	Joe Rudi	.35	.14	.03
☐ 265	Tug McGraw	.60	.24	.06
☐ 266	Jim Northrup	.35	.14	.03
☐ 267	Andy Messersmith .	.35	.14	.03
☐ 268	Tom Grieve	.35	.14	.03

		NRMT	VG-E	GOOD
☐ 269	Bob Johnson	.25	.10	.02
☐ 270	Ron Santo	.50	.20	.05
☐ 271	Bill Hands	.25	.10	.02
☐ 272	Paul Casanova	.25	.10	.02
☐ 273	Checklist 3	1.00	.10	.02
☐ 274	Fred Beene	.25	.10	.02
☐ 275	Ron Hunt	.25	.10	.02
☐ 276	Angels Leaders	.35	.14	.03
	Bobby Winkles MG			
	John Roseboro CO			
	Tom Morgan CO			
	Jimmie Reese CO			
	Salty Parker CO			
☐ 277	Gary Nolan	.25	.10	.02
☐ 278	Cookie Rojas	.35	.14	.03
☐ 279	Jim Crawford	.25	.10	.02
☐ 280	Carl Yastrzemski	9.00	3.75	.90
☐ 281	Giants Team	.50	.20	.05
☐ 282	Doyle Alexander	.50	.20	.05
☐ 283	Mike Schmidt	50.00	20.00	5.00
☐ 284	Dave Duncan	.25	.10	.02
☐ 285	Reggie Smith	.50	.20	.05
☐ 286	Tony Muser	.25	.10	.02
☐ 287	Clay Kirby	.25	.10	.02
☐ 288	Gorman Thomas	2.00	.80	.20
☐ 289	Rick Auerbach	.25	.10	.02
☐ 290	Vida Blue	.50	.20	.05
☐ 291	Don Hahn	.25	.10	.02
☐ 292	Chuck Seelbach	.25	.10	.02
☐ 293	Milt May	.25	.10	.02
☐ 294	Steve Foucault	.25	.10	.02
☐ 295	Rick Monday	.35	.14	.03
☐ 296	Ray Corbin	.25	.10	.02
☐ 297	Hal Breeden	.25	.10	.02
☐ 298	Roric Harrison	.25	.10	.02
☐ 299	Gene Michael	.35	.14	.03
☐ 300	Pete Rose	16.00	6.50	1.60
☐ 301	Bob Montgomery	.25	.10	.02
☐ 302	Rudy May	.25	.10	.02
☐ 303	George Hendrick	.35	.14	.03
☐ 304	Don Wilson	.25	.10	.02
☐ 305	Tito Fuentes	.25	.10	.02
☐ 306	Orioles Leaders	.75	.30	.07
	Earl Weaver MG			
	Jim Frey CO			
	George Bamberger CO			
	Billy Hunter CO			
	George Staller CO			
☐ 307	Luis Melendez	.25	.10	.02

		NRMT	VG-E	GOOD
☐ 308	Bruce Dal Canton	.25	.10	.02
☐ 309A	Dave Roberts SD	.35	.14	.03
☐ 309B	Dave Roberts WAS	5.00	2.00	.50
☐ 310	Terry Forster	.35	.14	.03
☐ 311	Jerry Grote	.25	.10	.02
☐ 312	Deron Johnson	.25	.10	.02
☐ 313	Barry Lersch	.25	.10	.02
☐ 314	Milwaukee Brewers	.50	.20	.05
	Team Card			
☐ 315	Ron Cey	1.00	.40	.10
☐ 316	Jim Perry	.35	.14	.03
☐ 317	Richie Zisk	.35	.14	.03
☐ 318	Jim Merritt	.25	.10	.02
☐ 319	Randy Hundley	.35	.14	.03
☐ 320	Dusty Baker	.50	.20	.05
☐ 321	Steve Braun	.25	.10	.02
☐ 322	Ernie McAnally	.25	.10	.02
☐ 323	Richie Scheinblum	.25	.10	.02
☐ 324	Steve Kline	.25	.10	.02
☐ 325	Tommy Harper	.35	.14	.03
☐ 326	Reds Leaders	.60	.24	.06
	Sparky Anderson MG			
	Larry Shephard CO			
	George Scherger CO			
	Alex Grammas CO			
	Ted Kluszewski CO			
☐ 327	Tom Timmermann	.25	.10	.02
☐ 328	Skip Jutze	.25	.10	.02
☐ 329	Mark Belanger	.35	.14	.03
☐ 330	Juan Marichal	2.50	1.00	.25
☐ 331	All-Star Catchers	1.75	.70	.17
	Carlton Fisk			
	Johnny Bench			
☐ 332	All-Star 1B	1.75	.70	.17
	Dick Allen			
	Hank Aaron			
☐ 333	All-Star 2B	1.50	.60	.15
	Rod Carew			
	Joe Morgan			
☐ 334	All-Star 3B	1.00	.40	.10
	Brooks Robinson			
	Ron Santo			
☐ 335	All-Star SS	.35	.14	.03
	Bert Campaneris			
	Chris Speier			
☐ 336	All-Star LF	2.50	1.00	.25
	Bobby Murcer			
	Pete Rose			

		NRMT	VG-E	GOOD
☐ 337	All-Star CF	.35	.14	.03
	Amos Otis			
	Cesar Cedeno			
☐ 338	All-Star RF	2.25	.90	.22
	Reggie Jackson			
	Billy Williams			
☐ 339	All-Star Pitchers	.50	.20	.05
	Jim Hunter			
	Rick Wise			
☐ 340	Thurman Munson	5.00	2.00	.50
☐ 341	Dan Driessen	.75	.30	.07
☐ 342	Jim Lohborg	.35	.14	.03
☐ 343	Royals Team	.50	.20	.05
☐ 344	Mike Caldwell	.35	.14	.03
☐ 345	Bill North	.25	.10	.02
☐ 346	Ron Reed	.25	.10	.02
☐ 347	Sandy Alomar	.25	.10	.02
☐ 348	Pete Richert	.25	.10	.02
☐ 349	John Vukovich	.25	.10	.02
☐ 350	Bob Gibson	3.00	1.20	.30
☐ 351	Dwight Evans	5.50	2.20	.55
☐ 352	Bill Stoneman	.25	.10	.02
☐ 353	Rich Coggins	.25	.10	.02
☐ 354	Cubs Leaders	.35	.14	.03
	Whitey Lockman MG			
	J.C. Martin CO			
	Hank Aguirre CO			
	Al Spangler CO			
	Jim Marshall CO			
☐ 355	Dave Nelson	.25	.10	.02
☐ 356	Jerry Koosman	.50	.20	.05
☐ 357	Buddy Bradford	.25	.10	.02
☐ 358	Dal Maxvill	.35	.14	.03
☐ 359	Brent Strom	.25	.10	.02
☐ 360	Greg Luzinski	.75	.30	.07
☐ 361	Don Carrithers	.25	.10	.02
☐ 362	Hal King	.25	.10	.02
☐ 363	Yankees Team	.60	.24	.06
☐ 364A	Cito Gaston SD	.35	.14	.03
☐ 364B	Cito Gaston WAS	5.00	2.00	.50
☐ 365	Steve Busby	.35	.14	.03
☐ 366	Larry Hisle	.35	.14	.03
☐ 367	Norm Cash	.75	.30	.07
☐ 368	Manny Mota	.35	.14	.03
☐ 369	Paul Lindblad	.25	.10	.02
☐ 370	Bob Watson	.35	.14	.03
☐ 371	Jim Slaton	.25	.10	.02
☐ 372	Ken Reitz	.25	.10	.02
☐ 373	John Curtis	.25	.10	.02

		NRMT	VG-E	GOOD
☐ 374	Marty Perez	.25	.10	.02
☐ 375	Earl Williams	.25	.10	.02
☐ 376	Jorge Orta	.25	.10	.02
☐ 377	Ron Woods	.25	.10	.02
☐ 378	Burt Hooton	.25	.10	.02
☐ 379	Rangers Leaders	.75	.30	.07
	Billy Martin MG			
	Frank Lucchesi CO			
	Art Fowler CO			
	Charlie Silvera CO			
	Jackie Moore CO			
☐ 380	Bud Harrelson	.35	.14	.03
☐ 381	Charlie Sands	.25	.10	.02
☐ 382	Bob Moose	.25	.10	.02
☐ 383	Phillies Team	.50	.20	.05
☐ 384	Chris Chambliss	.50	.20	.05
☐ 385	Don Gullett	.35	.14	.03
☐ 386	Gary Matthews	.50	.20	.05
☐ 387A	Rich Morales SD	.35	.14	.03
☐ 387B	Rich Morales WAS	5.00	2.00	.50
☐ 388	Phil Roof	.25	.10	.02
☐ 389	Gates Brown	.35	.14	.03
☐ 390	Lou Piniella	.50	.20	.05
☐ 391	Billy Champion	.25	.10	.02
☐ 392	Dick Green	.25	.10	.02
☐ 393	Orlando Pena	.25	.10	.02
☐ 394	Ken Henderson	.25	.10	.02
☐ 395	Doug Rader	.35	.14	.03
☐ 396	Tommy Davis	.40	.20	.05
☐ 397	George Stone	.25	.10	.02
☐ 398	Duke Sims	.25	.10	.02
☐ 399	Mike Paul	.25	.10	.02
☐ 400	Harmon Killebrew	3.00	1.20	.30
☐ 401	Elliott Maddox	.25	.10	.02
☐ 402	Jim Rooker	.25	.10	.02
☐ 403	Red Sox Leaders	.35	.14	.03
	Darrell Johnson MG			
	Eddie Popowski CO			
	Lee Stange CO			
	Don Zimmer CO			
	Don Bryant CO			
☐ 404	Jim Howarth	.25	.10	.02
☐ 405	Ellie Rodriguez	.25	.10	.02
☐ 406	Steve Arlin	.25	.10	.02
☐ 407	Jim Wohlford	.25	.10	.02
☐ 408	Charlie Hough	.50	.20	.05
☐ 409	Ike Brown	.25	.10	.02
☐ 410	Pedro Borbon	.25	.10	.02
☐ 411	Frank Baker	.25	.10	.02

		NRMT	VG-E	GOOD
☐ 412	Chuck Taylor	.25	.10	.02
☐ 413	Don Money	.35	.14	.03
☐ 414	Checklist 4	1.00	.10	.02
☐ 415	Gary Gentry	.25	.10	.02
☐ 416	White Sox Team	.50	.20	.05
☐ 417	Rich Folkers	.25	.10	.02
☐ 418	Walt Williams	.25	.10	.02
☐ 419	Wayne Twitchell	.25	.10	.02
☐ 420	Ray Fosse	.25	.10	.02
☐ 421	Dan Fife	.25	.10	.02
☐ 422	Gonzalo Marquez	.25	.10	.02
☐ 423	Fred Stanley	.25	.10	.02
☐ 424	Jim Beauchamp	.25	.10	.02
☐ 425	Pete Broberg	.25	.10	.02
☐ 426	Rennie Stennett	.25	.10	.02
☐ 427	Bobby Bolin	.25	.10	.02
☐ 428	Gary Sutherland	.25	.10	.02
☐ 429	Dick Lange	.25	.10	.02
☐ 430	Matty Alou	.35	.14	.03
☐ 431	Gene Garber	.35	.14	.03
☐ 432	Chris Arnold	.25	.10	.02
☐ 433	Lerrin LaGrow	.25	.10	.02
☐ 434	Ken McMullen	.25	.10	.02
☐ 435	Dave Concepcion	.75	.30	.07
☐ 436	Don Hood	.25	.10	.02
☐ 437	Jim Lyttle	.25	.10	.02
☐ 438	Ed Herrmann	.25	.10	.02
☐ 439	Norm Miller	.25	.10	.02
☐ 440	Jim Kaat	1.00	.40	.10
☐ 441	Tom Ragland	.25	.10	.02
☐ 442	Alan Foster	.25	.10	.02
☐ 443	Tom Hutton	.25	.10	.02
☐ 444	Vic Davalillo	.25	.10	.02
☐ 445	George Medich	.25	.10	.02
☐ 446	Len Randle	.25	.10	.02
☐ 447	Twins Leaders	.35	.14	.03
	Frank Quilici MG			
	Ralph Rowe CO			
	Bob Rodgers CO			
	Vern Morgan CO			
☐ 448	Ron Hodges	.25	.10	.02
☐ 449	Tom McCraw	.25	.10	.02
☐ 450	Rich Hebner	.35	.14	.03
☐ 451	Tommy John	1.50	.60	.15
☐ 452	Gene Hiser	.25	.10	.02
☐ 453	Balor Moore	.25	.10	.02
☐ 454	Kurt Bevacqua	.25	.10	.02
☐ 455	Tom Bradley	.25	.10	.02
☐ 456	Dave Winfield	40.00	16.00	4.00

		NRMT	VG-E	GOOD
☐ 457	Chuck Goggin	.25	.10	.02
☐ 458	Jim Ray	.25	.10	.02
☐ 459	Cincinnati Reds	.60	.24	.06
	Team Card			
☐ 460	Boog Powell	.60	.24	.06
☐ 461	John Odom	.25	.10	.02
☐ 462	Luis Alvarado	.25	.10	.02
☐ 463	Pat Dobson	.35	.14	.03
☐ 464	Jose Cruz	.50	.20	.05
☐ 465	Dick Bosman	.25	.10	.02
☐ 466	Dick Billings	.25	.10	.02
☐ 467	Winston Llenas	.25	.10	.02
☐ 468	Pepe Frias	.25	.10	.02
☐ 469	Joe Decker	.25	.10	.02
☐ 470	AL Playoffs	2.25	.90	.22
	A's over Orioles			
	(Reggie Jackson)			
☐ 471	NL Playoffs	.60	.24	.06
	Mets over Reds			
	(Matlack pitching)			
☐ 472	World Series Game 1	.60	.24	.06
	(Knowles pitching)			
☐ 473	World Series Game 2	2.25	.90	.22
	(Willie Mays batting)			
☐ 474	World Series Game 3	.60	.24	.06
	(Campaneris stealing)			
☐ 475	World Series Game 4	.60	.24	.06
	(Staub batting)			
☐ 476	World Series Game 5	.60	.24	.06
	Cleon Jones scoring)			
☐ 477	World Series Game 6	2.25	.90	.22
	(Reggie Jackson)			
☐ 478	World Series Game 7	.60	.24	.06
	(Campaneris batting)			
☐ 479	World Series Summary	.60	.24	.06
	A's celebrate; win			
	2nd consecutive			
	championship			
☐ 480	Willie Crawford	.25	.10	.02
☐ 481	Jerry Terrell	.25	.10	.02
☐ 482	Bob Didier	.25	.10	.02
☐ 483	Atlanta Braves	.50	.20	.05
	Team Card			
☐ 484	Carmen Fanzone	.25	.10	.02
☐ 485	Felipe Alou	.35	.14	.03
☐ 486	Steve Stone	.35	.14	.03
☐ 487	Ted Martinez	.25	.10	.02
☐ 488	Andy Etchebarren	.25	.10	.02

		NRMT	VG-E	GOOD
☐ 489	Pirates Leaders	.35	.14	.03
	Danny Murtaugh MG			
	Don Osborn CO			
	Don Leppert CO			
	Bill Mazeroski CO			
	Bob Skinner CO			
☐ 490	Vada Pinson	.50	.24	.06
☐ 491	Roger Nelson	.25	.10	.02
☐ 492	Mike Rogodzinski ..	.25	.10	.02
☐ 493	Joe Hoerner	.25	.10	.02
☐ 494	Ed Goodson	.25	.10	.02
☐ 495	Dick McAuliffe	.35	.14	.03
☐ 496	Tom Murphy	.25	.10	.02
☐ 497	Bobby Mitchell	.25	.10	.02
☐ 498	Pat Corrales	.35	.14	.03
☐ 499	Rusty Torres	.25	.10	.02
☐ 500	Lee May	.35	.14	.03
☐ 501	Eddie Leon	.25	.10	.02
☐ 502	Dave LaRoche	.25	.10	.02
☐ 503	Eric Soderholm	.25	.10	.02
☐ 504	Joe Niekro	.50	.20	.05
☐ 505	Bill Buckner	.60	.24	.06
☐ 506	Ed Farmer	.25	.10	.02
☐ 507	Larry Stahl	.25	.10	.02
☐ 508	Expos Team	.50	.20	.05
☐ 509	Jesse Jefferson ...	.25	.10	.02
☐ 510	Wayne Garrett	.25	.10	.02
☐ 511	Toby Harrah	.35	.14	.03
☐ 512	Joe Lahoud	.25	.10	.02
☐ 513	Jim Campanis	.25	.10	.02
☐ 514	Paul Schaal	.25	.10	.02
☐ 515	Willie Montanez ...	.25	.10	.02
☐ 516	Horacio Pina	.25	.10	.02
☐ 517	Mike Hegan	.25	.10	.02
☐ 518	Derrel Thomas	.25	.10	.02
☐ 519	Bill Sharp	.25	.10	.02
☐ 520	Tim McCarver	.60	.24	.06
☐ 521	Indians Leaders ...	.35	.14	.03
	Ken Aspromonte MG			
	Clay Bryant CO			
	Tony Pacheco CO			
☐ 522	J.R. Richard	.50	.20	.05
☐ 523	Cecil Cooper	1.75	.70	.17
☐ 524	Bill Plummer	.25	.10	.02
☐ 525	Clyde Wright	.25	.10	.02
☐ 526	Frank Tepedino ...	.25	.10	.02
☐ 527	Bobby Darwin	.25	.10	.02
☐ 528	Bill Bonham	.25	.10	.02
☐ 529	Horace Clarke	.25	.10	.02

		NRMT	VG-E	GOOD
☐ 530	Mickey Stanley ...	.35	.14	.03
☐ 531	Expos Leaders ...	.35	.14	.03
	Gene Mauch MG			
	Dave Bristol CO			
	Cal McLish CO			
	Larry Doby CO			
	Jerry Zimmerman CO			
☐ 532	Skip Lockwood	.25	.10	.02
☐ 533	Mike Phillips	.25	.10	.02
☐ 534	Eddie Watt	.25	.10	.02
☐ 535	Bob Tolan	.35	.14	.03
☐ 536	Duffy Dyer	.25	.10	.02
☐ 537	Steve Mingori	.25	.10	.02
☐ 538	Cesar Tovar	.25	.10	.02
☐ 539	Lloyd Allen	.25	.10	.02
☐ 540	Bob Robertson	.25	.10	.02
☐ 541	Cleveland Indians .	.50	.20	.05
	Team Card			
☐ 542	Rich Gossage	1.50	.60	.15
☐ 543	Danny Cater	.25	.10	.02
☐ 544	Ron Schueler	.25	.10	.02
☐ 545	Billy Conigliaro ...	.35	.14	.03
☐ 546	Mike Corkins	.25	.10	.02
☐ 547	Glenn Borgmann ..	.25	.10	.02
☐ 548	Sonny Siebert	.35	.14	.03
☐ 549	Mike Jorgensen ...	.25	.10	.02
☐ 550	Sam McDowell	.35	.14	.03
☐ 551	Von Joshua	.25	.10	.02
☐ 552	Denny Doyle	.25	.10	.02
☐ 553	Jim Willoughby ...	.25	.10	.02
☐ 554	Tim Johnson	.25	.10	.02
☐ 555	Woodie Fryman ...	.25	.10	.02
☐ 556	Dave Campbell	.25	.10	.02
☐ 557	Jim McGlothlin	.25	.10	.02
☐ 558	Bill Fahey	.25	.10	.02
☐ 559	Darrell Chaney	.25	.10	.02
☐ 560	Mike Cuellar	.35	.14	.03
☐ 561	Ed Kranepool	.35	.14	.03
☐ 562	Jack Aker	.25	.10	.02
☐ 563	Hal McRae	.35	.14	.03
☐ 564	Mike Ryan	.25	.10	.02
☐ 565	Milt Wilcox	.25	.10	.02
☐ 566	Jackie Hernandez .	.25	.10	.02
☐ 567	Red Sox Team	.50	.20	.05
☐ 568	Mike Torrez	.35	.14	.03
☐ 569	Rick Dempsey	.35	.14	.03
☐ 570	Ralph Garr	.35	.14	.03
☐ 571	Rich Hand	.25	.10	.02
☐ 572	Enzo Hernandez ..	.25	.10	.02

		NRMT	VG-E	GOOD
☐ 573	Mike Adams	.25	.10	.02
☐ 574	Bill Parsons	.25	.10	.02
☐ 575	Steve Garvey	9.00	3.75	.90
☐ 576	Scipio Spinks	.25	.10	.02
☐ 577	Mike Sadek	.25	.10	.02
☐ 578	Ralph Houk MG ...	.35	.14	.03
☐ 579	Cecil Upshaw	.25	.10	.02
☐ 580	Jim Spencer	.25	.10	.02
☐ 581	Fred Norman	.25	.10	.02
☐ 582	Bucky Dent	1.25	.50	.12
☐ 583	Marty Pattin	.25	.10	.02
☐ 584	Ken Rudolph	.25	.10	.02
☐ 585	Merv Rettenmund ..	.25	.10	.02
☐ 586	Jack Brohamer	.25	.10	.02
☐ 587	Larry Christenson ..	.25	.10	.02
☐ 588	Hal Lanier	.35	.14	.03
☐ 589	Boots Day	.25	.10	.02
☐ 590	Roger Moret	.25	.10	.02
☐ 591	Sonny Jackson	.25	.10	.02
☐ 592	Ed Bane	.25	.10	.02
☐ 593	Steve Yeager	.35	.14	.03
☐ 594	Leroy Stanton	.25	.10	.02
☐ 595	Steve Blass	.35	.14	.03
☐ 596	Rookie Pitchers	.35	.14	.03
	Wayne Garland			
	Fred Holdsworth			
	Mark Littell			
	Dick Pole			
☐ 597	Rookie Shortstops .	.60	.24	.06
	Dave Chalk			
	John Gamble			
	Pete MacKanin			
	Manny Trillo			
☐ 598	Rookie Outfielders .	2.50	1.00	.25
	Dave Augustine			
	Ken Griffey			
	Steve Ontiveros			
	Jim Tyrone			
☐ 599A	Rookie Pitchers WAS	.60	.24	.06
	Ron Diorio			
	Dave Freisleben			
	Frank Riccelli			
	Greg Shanahan			
☐ 599B	Rookie Pitchers SD .	3.00	1.20	.30
	(SD in large print)			
☐ 599C	Rookie Pitchers SD .	4.50	1.80	.45
	(SD in small print)			

		NRMT	VG-E	GOOD
☐ 600	Rookie Infielders ..	5.00	2.00	.50
	Ron Cash			
	Jim Cox			
	Bill Madlock			
	Reggie Sanders			
☐ 601	Rookie Outfielders .	2.50	1.00	.25
	Ed Armbrister			
	Rich Bladt			
	Brian Downing			
	Bake McBride			
☐ 602	Rookie Pitchers	.50	.20	.05
	Glen Abbott			
	Rick Henninger			
	Craig Swan			
	Dan Vossler			
☐ 603	Rookie Catchers ..	.50	.20	.05
	Barry Foote			
	Tom Lundstedt			
	Charlie Moore			
	Sergio Robles			
☐ 604	Rookie Infielders ..	4.00	1.60	.40
	Terry Hughes			
	John Knox			
	Andy Thornton			
	Frank White			
☐ 605	Rookie Pitchers	2.00	.80	.20
	Vic Albury			
	Ken Frailing			
	Kevin Kobel			
	Frank Tanana			
☐ 606	Rookie Outfielders .	.35	.14	.03
	Jim Fuller			
	Wilbur Howard			
	Tommy Smith			
	Otto Velez			
☐ 607	Rookie Shortstops .	.35	.14	.03
	Leo Foster			
	Tom Heintzelman			
	Dave Rosello			
	Frank Taveras			
☐ 608A	Rookie Pitchers: ERR	2.00	.80	.20
	Bob Apodaco (sic)			
	Dick Baney			
	John D'Acquisto			
	Mike Wallace			

		NRMT	VG-E	GOOD
☐ 608B	Rookie Pitchers: COR	.35	.14	.03
	Bob Apodaca			
	Dick Baney			
	John D'Acquisto			
	Mike Wallace			
☐ 609	Rico Petrocelli	.35	.14	.03
☐ 610	Dave Kingman	1.00	.40	.10
☐ 611	Rich Stelmaszek	.25	.10	.02
☐ 612	Luke Walker	.25	.10	.02
☐ 613	Dan Monzon	.25	.10	.02
☐ 614	Adrian Devine	.25	.10	.02
☐ 615	Johnny Jeter	.25	.10	.02
☐ 616	Larry Gura	.35	.14	.03
☐ 617	Ted Ford	.25	.10	.02
☐ 618	Jim Mason	.25	.10	.02
☐ 619	Mike Anderson	.25	.10	.02
☐ 620	Al Downing	.35	.14	.03
☐ 621	Bernie Carbo	.25	.10	.02
☐ 622	Phil Gagliano	.25	.10	.02
☐ 623	Celerino Sanchez	.25	.10	.02
☐ 624	Bob Miller	.25	.10	.02
☐ 625	Ollie Brown	.25	.10	.02
☐ 626	Pittsburgh Pirates	.50	.20	.05
	Team Card			
☐ 627	Carl Taylor	.25	.10	.02
☐ 628	Ivan Murrell	.25	.10	.02
☐ 629	Rusty Staub	.60	.24	.06
☐ 630	Tommy Agee	.25	.10	.02
☐ 631	Steve Barber	.25	.10	.02
☐ 632	George Culver	.25	.10	.02
☐ 633	Dave Hamilton	.25	.10	.02
☐ 634	Braves Leaders	1.00	.40	.10
	Eddie Mathews MG			
	Herm Starrette CO			
	Connie Ryan CO			
	Jim Busby CO			
	Ken Silvestri CO			
☐ 635	Johnny Edwards	.25	.10	.02
☐ 636	Dave Goltz	.25	.10	.02
☐ 637	Checklist 5	1.00	.10	.02
☐ 638	Ken Sanders	.25	.10	.02
☐ 639	Joe Lovitto	.25	.10	.02
☐ 640	Milt Pappas	.35	.14	.03
☐ 641	Chuck Brinkman	.25	.10	.02
☐ 642	Terry Harmon	.25	.10	.02
☐ 643	Dodgers Team	.75	.30	.07
☐ 644	Wayne Granger	.25	.10	.02
☐ 645	Ken Boswell	.25	.10	.02
☐ 646	George Foster	1.25	.50	.12

		NRMT	VG-E	GOOD
☐ 647	Juan Beniquez	.75	.30	.07
☐ 648	Terry Crowley	.35	.14	.03
	(Munson blocking plate)			
☐ 649	Fernando Gonzalez	.25	.10	.02
☐ 650	Mike Epstein	.25	.10	.02
☐ 651	Leron Lee	.25	.10	.02
☐ 652	Gail Hopkins	.25	.10	.02
☐ 653	Bob Stinson	.25	.10	.02
☐ 654A	Jesus Alou (outfield)	.35	.14	.03
☐ 654B	Jesus Alou	6.00	2.40	.60
	(no position)			
☐ 655	Mike Tyson	.25	.10	.02
☐ 656	Adrian Garrett	.25	.10	.02
☐ 657	Jim Shellenback	.25	.10	.02
☐ 658	Lee Lacy	.35	.14	.03
☐ 659	Joe Lis	.25	.10	.02
☐ 660	Larry Dierker	.50	.10	.02

1974 Topps Traded

The cards in this 44-card set measure 2 ½"
by 3 ½". The 1974 Topps Traded set contains 43 player cards and one unnumbered
checklist card. The obverses have the word
"traded" in block letters and the backs are
designed in newspaper style. Card numbers
are the same as in the regular set except
they are followed by a "T." No known scarcities exist for this set.

	NRMT	VG-E	GOOD
Complete Set (44)	6.50	2.60	.65
Common Player	.12	.05	.01

1975 Topps

	NRMT	VG-E	GOOD
☐ 23T Craig Robinson	.12	.05	.01
☐ 42T Claude Osteen	.20	.08	.02
☐ 43T Jim Wynn	.20	.08	.02
☐ 51T Bobby Heise	.12	.05	.01
☐ 59T Ross Grimsley	.12	.05	.01
☐ 62T Bob Locker	.12	.05	.01
☐ 63T Bill Sudakis	.12	.05	.01
☐ 73T Mike Marshall	.30	.12	.03
☐ 123T Nelson Briles	.20	.08	.02
☐ 139T Aurelio Monteagudo	.12	.05	.01
☐ 151T Diego Segui	.12	.05	.01
☐ 165T Willie Davis	.25	.10	.02
☐ 175T Reggie Cleveland ..	.12	.05	.01
☐ 182T Lindy McDaniel	.20	.08	.02
☐ 186T Fred Scherman	.12	.05	.01
☐ 249T George Mitterwald .	.12	.05	.01
☐ 262T Ed Kirkpatrick	.12	.05	.01
☐ 269T Bob Johnson	.12	.05	.01
☐ 270T Ron Santo	.40	.16	.04
☐ 313T Barry Lersch	.12	.05	.01
☐ 319T Randy Hundley	.20	.08	.02
☐ 330T Juan Marichal	1.50	.60	.15
☐ 348T Pete Richert	.12	.05	.01
☐ 373T John Curtis	.12	.05	.01
☐ 390T Lou Piniella	.35	.14	.03
☐ 428T Gary Sutherland ...	.12	.05	.01
☐ 454T Kurt Bevacqua	.12	.05	.01
☐ 458T Jim Ray	.12	.05	.01
☐ 485T Felipe Alou	.20	.08	.02
☐ 486T Steve Stone	.20	.08	.02
☐ 496T Tom Murphy	.12	.05	.01
☐ 516T Horacio Pina	.12	.05	.01
☐ 534T Eddie Watt	.12	.05	.01
☐ 538T Cesar Tovar	.12	.05	.01
☐ 544T Ron Schueler	.12	.05	.01
☐ 579T Cecil Upshaw	.12	.05	.01
☐ 585T Merv Rettenmund ..	.12	.05	.01
☐ 612T Luke Walker	.12	.05	.01
☐ 616T Larry Gura	.20	.08	.02
☐ 618T Jim Mason	.12	.05	.01
☐ 630T Tommie Agee	.15	.06	.01
☐ 648T Terry Crowley	.12	.05	.01
☐ 649T Fernando Gonzalez	.12	.05	.01
☐ xxxT= Traded Checklist .. (unnumbered)	.50	.06	.01

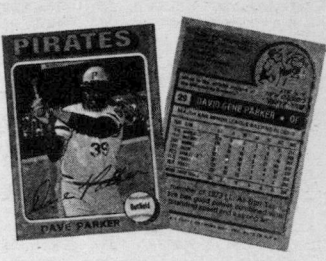

The cards in the 1975 Topps set were issued in two different sizes: a regular standard size (2 ½" by 3 ½") and a mini size (2 ½" by 3 ⅛") which was issued as a test in certain areas of the country. The 660-card Topps baseball set for 1975 was radically different in appearance from sets of the preceding years. The most prominent change was the use of a two-color frame surrounding the picture area rather than a single, subdued color. A facsimile autograph appears on the picture, and the backs are printed in red and green on gray. Cards 189-212 depict the MVP's of both leagues from 1951 through 1974. The first seven cards (1-7) feature players breaking records or achieving milestones during the previous season. Cards 306-313 picture league leaders in various statistical categories. Cards 459-466 depict the results of post-season action. Team cards feature a checklist back for players on that team and show a small inset photo of the manager on the front. The Phillies Team card #46 erroneously lists Terry Harmon as #339 instead of #399. This set is quite popular with collectors, at least in part due to the fact that the rookie cards of Robin Yount, George Brett, Jim Rice, Gary Carter, Fred Lynn, and Keith Hernandez are all in the set. Topps minis have the same checklist and are worth approximately double the prices listed below.

		NRMT	VG-E	GOOD
	Complete Set (660)	525.00	210.00	50.00
	Common Player (1-132) ...	.25	.10	.02
	Common Player (133-660) .	.25	.10	.02
☐ 1	RB: Hank Aaron ...	10.00	2.50	.50
	Sets Homer Mark			
☐ 2	RB: Lou Brock	1.75	.70	.17
	118 Stolen Bases			
☐ 3	RB: Bob Gibson	1.75	.70	.17
	3000th Strikeout			
☐ 4	RB: Al Kaline	2.00	.80	.20
	3000 Hit Club			
☐ 5	RB: Nolan Ryan ...	2.25	.90	.22
	Fans 300 for			
	3rd Year in a Row			
☐ 6	RB: Mike Marshall ..	.50	.20	.05
	Hurls 106 Games			
☐ 7	No Hitters	.60	.24	.06
	Steve Busby			
	Dick Bosman			
	Nolan Ryan			
☐ 8	Rogelio Moret	.25	.10	.02
☐ 9	Frank Tepedino	.25	.10	.02
☐ 10	Willie Davis	.35	.14	.03
☐ 11	Bill Melton	.25	.10	.02
☐ 12	David Clyde	.25	.10	.02
☐ 13	Gene Locklear	.25	.10	.02
☐ 14	Milt Wilcox	.25	.10	.02
☐ 15	Jose Cardenal	.25	.10	.02
☐ 16	Frank Tanana	.60	.24	.06
☐ 17	Dave Concepcion ..	.60	.24	.06
☐ 18	Tigers: Team/Mgr. .	.65	.15	.03
	Ralph Houk			
	(checklist back)			
☐ 19	Jerry Koosman	.50	.20	.05
☐ 20	Thurman Munson ..	4.00	1.60	.40
☐ 21	Rollie Fingers	1.50	.60	.15
☐ 22	Dave Cash	.25	.10	.02
☐ 23	Bill Russell	.35	.14	.03
☐ 24	Al Fitzmorris	.25	.10	.02
☐ 25	Lee May	.35	.14	.03
☐ 26	Dave McNally	.35	.14	.03
☐ 27	Ken Reitz	.25	.10	.02
☐ 28	Tom Murphy	.25	.10	.02
☐ 29	Dave Parker	5.00	2.00	.50
☐ 30	Bert Blyleven	.75	.30	.07
☐ 31	Dave Rader	.25	.10	.02
☐ 32	Reggie Cleveland ..	.25	.10	.02
☐ 33	Dusty Baker	.35	.14	.03
☐ 34	Steve Renko	.25	.10	.02

		NRMT	VG-E	GOOD
☐ 35	Ron Santo	.50	.20	.05
☐ 36	Joe Lovitto	.25	.10	.02
☐ 37	Dave Freisleben ..	.25	.10	.02
☐ 38	Buddy Bell	.75	.30	.07
☐ 39	Andre Thornton ...	.50	.20	.05
☐ 40	Bill Singer	.25	.10	.02
☐ 41	Cesar Geronimo ..	.25	.10	.02
☐ 42	Joe Coleman	.25	.10	.02
☐ 43	Cleon Jones	.25	.10	.02
☐ 44	Pat Dobson	.35	.14	.03
☐ 45	Joe Rudi	.35	.14	.03
☐ 46	Phillies: Team/Mgr.	.65	.15	.03
	Danny Ozark			
	(checklist back)			
☐ 47	Tommy John	1.25	.50	.12
☐ 48	Freddie Patek	.35	.14	.03
☐ 49	Larry Dierker	.35	.14	.03
☐ 50	Brooks Robinson ..	3.50	1.40	.35
☐ 51	Bob Forsch	1.00	.40	.10
☐ 52	Darrell Porter	.35	.14	.03
☐ 53	Dave Giusti	.25	.10	.02
☐ 54	Eric Soderholm ...	.25	.10	.02
☐ 55	Bobby Bonds	.50	.20	.05
☐ 56	Rick Wise	.35	.14	.03
☐ 57	Dave Johnson	.50	.20	.05
☐ 58	Chuck Taylor	.25	.10	.02
☐ 59	Ken Henderson ...	.25	.10	.02
☐ 60	Fergie Jenkins ...	1.00	.40	.10
☐ 61	Dave Winfield	11.00	4.50	1.10
☐ 62	Fritz Peterson	.25	.10	.02
☐ 63	Steve Swisher	.25	.10	.02
☐ 64	Dave Chalk	.25	.10	.02
☐ 65	Don Gullett	.25	.10	.02
☐ 66	Willie Horton	.35	.14	.03
☐ 67	Tug McGraw	.50	.20	.05
☐ 68	Ron Blomberg	.25	.10	.02
☐ 69	John Odom	.25	.10	.02
☐ 70	Mike Schmidt	22.00	9.00	2.20
☐ 71	Charlie Hough	.50	.20	.05
☐ 72	Royals: Team/Mgr.	.65	.15	.03
	Jack McKeon			
	(checklist back)			
☐ 73	J.R. Richard	.35	.14	.03
☐ 74	Mark Belanger	.35	.14	.03
☐ 75	Ted Simmons	.75	.30	.07
☐ 76	Ed Sprague	.25	.10	.02
☐ 77	Richie Zisk	.35	.14	.03
☐ 78	Ray Corbin	.25	.10	.02
☐ 79	Gary Matthews ...	.35	.14	.03

		NRMT	VG-E	GOOD			NRMT	VG-E	GOOD
☐ 80	Carlton Fisk	2.00	.80	.20	☐ 124	Jerry Reuss	.35	.14	.03
☐ 81	Ron Reed	.25	.10	.02	☐ 125	Ken Singleton	.35	.14	.03
☐ 82	Pat Kelly	.25	.10	.02	☐ 126	Checklist 1-132	.90	.10	.02
☐ 83	Jim Merritt	.25	.10	.02	☐ 127	Glenn Borgmann	.25	.10	.02
☐ 84	Enzo Hernandez	.25	.10	.02	☐ 128	Bill Lee	.35	.14	.03
☐ 85	Bill Bonham	.25	.10	.02	☐ 129	Rick Monday	.35	.14	.03
☐ 86	Joe Lis	.25	.10	.02	☐ 130	Phil Niekro	2.00	.80	.20
☐ 87	George Foster	1.25	.50	.12	☐ 131	Toby Harrah	.35	.14	.03
☐ 88	Tom Egan	.25	.10	.02	☐ 132	Randy Moffitt	.25	.10	.02
☐ 89	Jim Ray	.25	.10	.02	☐ 133	Dan Driessen	.35	.14	.03
☐ 90	Rusty Staub	.50	.20	.05	☐ 134	Ron Hodges	.25	.10	.02
☐ 91	Dick Green	.25	.10	.02	☐ 135	Charlie Spikes	.25	.10	.02
☐ 92	Cecil Upshaw	.25	.10	.02	☐ 136	Jim Mason	.25	.10	.02
☐ 93	Dave Lopes	.50	.20	.05	☐ 137	Terry Forster	.35	.14	.03
☐ 94	Jim Lonborg	.35	.14	.03	☐ 138	Del Unser	.25	.10	.02
☐ 95	John Mayberry	.35	.14	.03	☐ 139	Horacio Pina	.25	.10	.02
☐ 96	Mike Cosgrove	.25	.10	.02	☐ 140	Steve Garvey	6.00	2.40	.60
☐ 97	Earl Williams	.25	.10	.02	☐ 141	Mickey Stanley	.35	.14	.03
☐ 98	Rich Folkers	.25	.10	.02	☐ 142	Bob Reynolds	.25	.10	.02
☐ 99	Mike Hegan	.25	.10	.02	☐ 143	Cliff Johnson	.25	.10	.02
☐ 100	Willie Stargell	3.00	1.20	.30	☐ 144	Jim Wohlford	.25	.10	.02
☐ 101	Expos: Team/Mgr. Gene Mauch (checklist back)	.65	.15	.03	☐ 145	Ken Holtzman	.35	.14	.03
					☐ 146	Padres: Team/Mgr. John McNamara (checklist back)	.65	.15	.03
☐ 102	Joe Decker	.25	.10	.02	☐ 147	Pedro Garcia	.25	.10	.02
☐ 103	Rick Miller	.25	.10	.02	☐ 148	Jim Rooker	.25	.10	.02
☐ 104	Bill Madlock	1.25	.50	.12	☐ 149	Tim Foli	.25	.10	.02
☐ 105	Buzz Capra	.25	.10	.02	☐ 150	Bob Gibson	2.50	1.00	.25
☐ 106	Mike Hargrove	.50	.20	.05	☐ 151	Steve Brye	.25	.10	.02
☐ 107	Jim Barr	.25	.10	.02	☐ 152	Mario Guerrero	.25	.10	.02
☐ 108	Tom Hall	.25	.10	.02	☐ 153	Rick Reuschel	.50	.20	.05
☐ 109	George Hendrick	.35	.14	.03	☐ 154	Mike Lum	.25	.10	.02
☐ 110	Wilbur Wood	.35	.14	.03	☐ 155	Jim Bibby	.35	.14	.03
☐ 111	Wayne Garrett	.25	.10	.02	☐ 156	Dave Kingman	1.00	.40	.10
☐ 112	Larry Hardy	.25	.10	.02	☐ 157	Pedro Borbon	.25	.10	.02
☐ 113	Elliott Maddox	.25	.10	.02	☐ 158	Jerry Grote	.25	.10	.02
☐ 114	Dick Lange	.25	.10	.02	☐ 159	Steve Arlin	.25	.10	.02
☐ 115	Joe Ferguson	.25	.10	.02	☐ 160	Graig Nettles	1.25	.50	.12
☐ 116	Lerrin LaGrow	.25	.10	.02	☐ 161	Stan Bahnsen	.25	.10	.02
☐ 117	Orioles: Team/Mgr. Earl Weaver (checklist back)	.65	.15	.03	☐ 162	Willie Montanez	.25	.10	.02
					☐ 163	Jim Brewer	.25	.10	.02
☐ 118	Mike Anderson	.25	.10	.02	☐ 164	Mickey Rivers	.35	.14	.03
☐ 119	Tommy Helms	.35	.14	.03	☐ 165	Doug Rader	.35	.14	.03
☐ 120	Steve Busby (photo actually Fran Healy)	.35	.14	.03	☐ 166	Woodie Fryman	.25	.10	.02
					☐ 167	Rich Coggins	.25	.10	.02
☐ 121	Bill North	.25	.10	.02	☐ 168	Bill Greif	.25	.10	.02
☐ 122	Al Hrabosky	.35	.14	.03	☐ 169	Cookie Rojas	.35	.14	.03
☐ 123	Johnny Briggs	.25	.10	.02	☐ 170	Bert Campaneris	.35	.14	.03

		NRMT	VG-E	GOOD
☐ 171	Ed Kirkpatrick	.25	.10	.02
☐ 172	Red Sox: Team/Mgr.	.65	.15	.03
	Darrell Johnson			
	(checklist back)			
☐ 173	Steve Rogers	.35	.14	.03
☐ 174	Bake McBride	.35	.14	.03
☐ 175	Don Money	.35	.14	.03
☐ 176	Burt Hooton	.25	.10	.02
☐ 177	Vic Correll	.25	.10	.02
☐ 178	Cesar Tovar	.25	.10	.02
☐ 179	Tom Bradley	.25	.10	.02
☐ 180	Joe Morgan	3.50	1.40	.35
☐ 181	Fred Beene	.25	.10	.02
☐ 182	Don Hahn	.25	.10	.02
☐ 183	Mel Stottlemyre	.35	.14	.03
☐ 184	Jorge Orta	.25	.10	.02
☐ 185	Steve Carlton	5.00	2.00	.50
☐ 186	Willie Crawford	.25	.10	.02
☐ 187	Denny Doyle	.25	.10	.02
☐ 188	Tom Griffin	.25	.10	.02
☐ 189	1951 MVP's	1.50	.60	.15
	Larry (Yogi) Berra			
	Roy Campanella			
	(Campy never issued)			
☐ 190	1952 MVP's	.50	.20	.05
	Bobby Shantz			
	Hank Bauer			
☐ 191	1953 MVP's	.60	.24	.06
	Al Rosen			
	Roy Campanella			
☐ 192	1954 MVP's	1.50	.60	.15
	Yogi Berra			
	Willie Mays			
☐ 193	1955 MVP's	1.50	.60	.15
	Yogi Berra			
	Roy Campanella			
	(Campy never issued)			
☐ 194	1956 MVP's	3.00	1.20	.30
	Mickey Mantle			
	Don Newcombe			
☐ 195	1957 MVP's	4.50	1.80	.45
	Mickey Mantle			
	Hank Aaron			
☐ 196	1958 MVP's	.60	.24	.06
	Jackie Jensen			
	Ernie Banks			
☐ 197	1959 MVP's	.60	.24	.06
	Nellie Fox			
	Ernie Banks			

		NRMT	VG-E	GOOD
☐ 198	1960 MVP's	.75	.30	.07
	Roger Maris			
	Dick Groat			
☐ 199	1961 MVP's	1.00	.40	.10
	Roger Maris			
	Frank Robinson			
☐ 200	1962 MVP's	3.00	1.20	.30
	Mickey Mantle			
	Maury Wills			
	(Wills never issued)			
☐ 201	1963 MVP's	.75	.30	.07
	Elston Howard			
	Sandy Koufax			
☐ 202	1964 MVP's	.60	.24	.06
	Brooks Robinson			
	Ken Boyer			
☐ 203	1965 MVP's	.75	.30	.07
	Zoilo Versalles			
	Willie Mays			
☐ 204	1966 MVP's	.90	.36	.09
	Frank Robinson			
	Bob Clemente			
☐ 205	1967 MVP's	.90	.36	.09
	Carl Yastrzemski			
	Orlando Cepeda			
☐ 206	1968 MVP's	.60	.24	.06
	Denny McLain			
	Bob Gibson			
☐ 207	1969 MVP's	.75	.30	.07
	Harmon Killebrew			
	Willie McCovey			
☐ 208	1970 MVP's	.75	.30	.07
	Boog Powell			
	Johnny Bench			
☐ 209	1971 MVP's	.50	.20	.05
	Vida Blue			
	Joe Torre			
☐ 210	1972 MVP's	.75	.30	.07
	Rich Allen			
	Johnny Bench			
☐ 211	1973 MVP's	3.00	1.20	.30
	Reggie Jackson			
	Pete Rose			
☐ 212	1974 MVP's	.60	.24	.06
	Jeff Burroughs			
	Steve Garvey			
☐ 213	Oscar Gamble	.35	.14	.03
☐ 214	Harry Parker	.25	.10	.02
☐ 215	Bobby Valentine	.50	.20	.05

		NRMT	VG-E	GOOD			NRMT	VG-E	GOOD
☐ 216	Giants: Team/Mgr. .	.65	.15	.03	☐ 259	Len Randle	.25	.10	.02
	Wes Westrum				☐ 260	Johnny Bench	7.50	3.00	.75
	(checklist back)				☐ 261	Andy Hassler	.25	.10	.02
☐ 217	Lou Piniella	.50	.20	.05	☐ 262	Rowland Office ...	.25	.10	.02
☐ 218	Jerry Johnson	.25	.10	.02	☐ 263	Jim Perry	.35	.14	.03
☐ 219	Ed Herrmann	.25	.10	.02	☐ 264	John Milner	.25	.10	.02
☐ 220	Don Sutton	1.75	.70	.17	☐ 265	Ron Bryant	.25	.10	.02
☐ 221	Aurelio Rodriguez ..	.25	.10	.02	☐ 266	Sandy Alomar ...	.25	.10	.02
☐ 222	Dan Spillner	.35	.14	.03	☐ 267	Dick Ruthven	.25	.10	.02
☐ 223	Robin Yount	35.00	14.00	3.50	☐ 268	Hal McRae	.35	.14	.03
☐ 224	Ramon Hernandez .	.25	.10	.02	☐ 269	Doug Rau	.25	.10	.02
☐ 225	Bob Grich	.35	.14	.03	☐ 270	Ron Fairly	.35	.14	.03
☐ 226	Bill Campbell	.25	.10	.02	☐ 271	Gerry Moses	.25	.10	.02
☐ 227	Bob Watson	.35	.14	.03	☐ 272	Lynn McGlothen ..	.25	.10	.02
☐ 228	George Brett	60.00	24.00	6.00	☐ 273	Steve Braun	.25	.10	.02
☐ 229	Barry Foote	.25	.10	.02	☐ 274	Vicente Romo	.25	.10	.02
☐ 230	Jim Hunter	2.00	.80	.20	☐ 275	Paul Blair :	.35	.14	.03
☐ 231	Mike Tyson	.25	.10	.02	☐ 276	White Sox Team/Mgr.	.65	.15	.03
☐ 232	Diego Segui	.25	.10	.02		Chuck Tanner			
☐ 233	Billy Grabarkewitz ..	.25	.10	.02		(checklist back)			
☐ 234	Tom Grieve	.35	.14	.03	☐ 277	Frank Taveras	.25	.10	.02
☐ 235	Jack Billingham ...	.25	.10	.02	☐ 278	Paul Lindblad	.25	.10	.02
☐ 236	Angels: Team/Mgr. .	.65	.15	.03	☐ 279	Milt May	.25	.10	.02
	Dick Williams				☐ 280	Carl Yastrzemski ..	7.50	3.00	.75
	(checklist back)				☐ 281	Jim Slaton	.25	.10	.02
☐ 237	Carl Morton	.25	.10	.02	☐ 282	Jerry Morales	.25	.10	.02
☐ 238	Dave Duncan	.25	.10	.02	☐ 283	Steve Foucault ...	.25	.10	.02
☐ 239	George Stone	.25	.10	.02	☐ 284	Ken Griffey	.60	.24	.06
☐ 240	Garry Maddox	.35	.14	.03	☐ 285	Ellie Rodriguez ...	.25	.10	.02
☐ 241	Dick Tidrow	.25	.10	.02	☐ 286	Mike Jorgensen ..	.25	.10	.02
☐ 242	Jay Johnstone	.35	.14	.03	☐ 287	Roric Harrison ...	.25	.10	.02
☐ 243	Jim Kaat	1.00	.40	.10	☐ 288	Bruce Ellingsen ..	.25	.10	.02
☐ 244	Bill Buckner	.50	.20	.05	☐ 289	Ken Rudolph	.25	.10	.02
☐ 245	Mickey Lolich	.50	.20	.05	☐ 290	Jon Matlack	.35	.14	.03
☐ 246	Cardinals: Team/Mgr.	.65	.15	.03	☐ 291	Bill Sudakis	.25	.10	.02
	Red Schoendienst				☐ 292	Ron Schueler	.25	.10	.02
	(checklist back)				☐ 293	Dick Sharon	.25	.10	.02
☐ 247	Enos Cabell	.25	.10	.02	☐ 294	Geoff Zahn	.25	.10	.02
☐ 248	Randy Jones	.35	.14	.03	☐ 295	Vada Pinson	.50	.24	.06
☐ 249	Danny Thompson ..	.25	.10	.02	☐ 296	Alan Foster	.25	.10	.02
☐ 250	Ken Brett	.25	.10	.02	☐ 297	Craig Kusick	.25	.10	.02
☐ 251	Fran Healy	.25	.10	.02	☐ 298	Johnny Grubb	.25	.10	.02
☐ 252	Fred Scherman	.25	.10	.02	☐ 299	Bucky Dent	.50	.20	.05
☐ 253	Jesus Alou	.25	.10	.02	☐ 300	Reggie Jackson ...	7.50	3.00	.75
☐ 254	Mike Torrez	.35	.14	.03	☐ 301	Dave Roberts	.25	.10	.02
☐ 255	Dwight Evans	2.75	1.10	.27	☐ 302	Rick Burleson	.50	.20	.05
☐ 256	Billy Champion	.25	.10	.02	☐ 303	Grant Jackson	.25	.10	.02
☐ 257	Checklist: 133-264 .	.90	.10	.02					
☐ 258	Dave LaRoche	.25	.10	.02					

		NRMT	VG-E	GOOD
☐ 304	Pirates: Team/Mgr. . Danny Murtaugh (checklist back)	.65	.15	.03
☐ 305	Jim Colborn	.25	.10	.02
☐ 306	Batting Leaders . . . . Rod Carew Ralph Garr	.60	.24	.06
☐ 307	Home Run Leaders Dick Allen Mike Schmidt	.90	.36	.09
☐ 308	RBI Leaders . . . . . . Jeff Burroughs Johnny Bench	.75	.30	.07
☐ 309	Stolen Base Leaders Bill North Lou Brock	.60	.24	.06
☐ 310	Victory Leaders . . . . Jim Hunter Fergie Jenkins Andy Messersmith Phil Niekro	.75	.30	.07
☐ 311	ERA Leaders . . . . . Jim Hunter Buzz Capra	.60	.24	.06
☐ 312	Strikeout Leaders . . Nolan Ryan Steve Carlton	2.50	1.00	.25
☐ 313	Leading Firemen . . . Terry Forster Mike Marshall	.50	.20	.05
☐ 314	Buck Martinez	.25	.10	.02
☐ 315	Don Kessinger	.35	.14	.03
☐ 316	Jackie Brown	.25	.10	.02
☐ 317	Joe Lahoud	.25	.10	.02
☐ 318	Ernie McAnally	.25	.10	.02
☐ 319	Johnny Oates	.25	.10	.02
☐ 320	Pete Rose	15.00	6.00	1.50
☐ 321	Rudy May	.25	.10	.02
☐ 322	Ed Goodson	.25	.10	.02
☐ 323	Fred Holdsworth . . .	.25	.10	.02
☐ 324	Ed Kranepool	.35	.14	.03
☐ 325	Tony Oliva	.75	.30	.07
☐ 326	Wayne Twitchell . . .	.25	.10	.02
☐ 327	Jerry Hairston	.25	.10	.02
☐ 328	Sonny Siebert	.35	.14	.03
☐ 329	Ted Kubiak	.25	.10	.02
☐ 330	Mike Marshall	.35	.14	.03

		NRMT	VG-E	GOOD
☐ 331	Indians: Team/Mgr. Frank Robinson (checklist back)	.65	.15	.03
☐ 332	Fred Kendall	.25	.10	.02
☐ 333	Dick Drago	.25	.10	.02
☐ 334	Greg Gross	.25	.10	.02
☐ 335	Jim Palmer	3.50	1.40	.35
☐ 336	Rennie Stennett . . .	.25	.10	.02
☐ 337	Kevin Kobel	.25	.10	.02
☐ 338	Rich Stelmaszek . .	.25	.10	.02
☐ 339	Jim Fregosi	.35	.14	.03
☐ 340	Paul Splittorff	.35	.14	.03
☐ 341	Hal Breeden	.25	.10	.02
☐ 342	Leroy Stanton	.25	.10	.02
☐ 343	Danny Frisella	.25	.10	.02
☐ 344	Ben Oglivie	.35	.14	.03
☐ 345	Clay Carroll	.25	.10	.02
☐ 346	Bobby Darwin	.25	.10	.02
☐ 347	Mike Caldwell	.35	.14	.03
☐ 348	Tony Muser	.25	.10	.02
☐ 349	Ray Sadecki	.25	.10	.02
☐ 350	Bobby Murcer	.50	.20	.05
☐ 351	Bob Boone	.60	.24	.06
☐ 352	Darold Knowles . . .	.25	.10	.02
☐ 353	Luis Melendez	.25	.10	.02
☐ 354	Dick Bosman	.25	.10	.02
☐ 355	Chris Cannizzaro . .	.25	.10	.02
☐ 356	Rico Petrocelli	.35	.14	.03
☐ 357	Ken Forsch	.25	.10	.02
☐ 358	Al Bumbry	.25	.10	.02
☐ 359	Paul Popovich	.25	.10	.02
☐ 360	George Scott	.35	.14	.03
☐ 361	Dodgers: Team/Mgr. Walter Alston (checklist back)	.75	.25	.04
☐ 362	Steve Hargan	.25	.10	.02
☐ 363	Carmen Fanzone .	.25	.10	.02
☐ 364	Doug Bird	.25	.10	.02
☐ 365	Bob Bailey	.25	.10	.02
☐ 366	Ken Sanders	.25	.10	.02
☐ 367	Craig Robinson . . .	.25	.10	.02
☐ 368	Vic Albury	.25	.10	.02
☐ 369	Merv Rettenmund . .	.25	.10	.02
☐ 370	Tom Seaver	6.50	2.60	.65
☐ 371	Gates Brown	.35	.14	.03
☐ 372	John D'Acquisto . . .	.25	.10	.02
☐ 373	Bill Sharp	.25	.10	.02
☐ 374	Eddie Watt	.25	.10	.02
☐ 375	Roy White	.35	.14	.03

		NRMT	VG-E	GOOD
☐ 376	Steve Yeager	.35	.14	.03
☐ 377	Tom Hilgendorf	.25	.10	.02
☐ 378	Derrel Thomas	.25	.10	.02
☐ 379	Bernie Carbo	.25	.10	.02
☐ 380	Sal Bando	.35	.14	.03
☐ 381	John Curtis	.25	.10	.02
☐ 382	Don Baylor	.75	.30	.07
☐ 383	Jim York	.25	.10	.02
☐ 384	Brewers: Team/Mgr.	.65	.15	.03
	Del Crandall			
	(checklist back)			
☐ 385	Dock Ellis	.25	.10	.02
☐ 386	Checklist: 265-396	.90	.10	.02
☐ 387	Jim Spencer	.25	.10	.02
☐ 388	Steve Stone	.35	.14	.03
☐ 389	Tony Solaita	.25	.10	.02
☐ 390	Ron Cey	.60	.24	.06
☐ 391	Don DeMola	.25	.10	.02
☐ 392	Bruce Bochte	.50	.20	.05
☐ 393	Gary Gentry	.25	.10	.02
☐ 394	Larvell Blanks	.25	.10	.02
☐ 395	Bud Harrelson	.35	.14	.03
☐ 396	Fred Norman	.25	.10	.02
☐ 397	Bill Freehan	.50	.20	.05
☐ 398	Elias Sosa	.25	.10	.02
☐ 399	Terry Harmon	.25	.10	.02
☐ 400	Dick Allen	.50	.20	.05
☐ 401	Mike Wallace	.25	.10	.02
☐ 402	Bob Tolan	.35	.14	.03
☐ 403	Tom Buskey	.25	.10	.02
☐ 404	Ted Sizemore	.25	.10	.02
☐ 405	John Montague	.25	.10	.02
☐ 406	Bob Gallagher	.25	.10	.02
☐ 407	Herb Washington	.25	.10	.02
☐ 408	Clyde Wright	.25	.10	.02
☐ 409	Bob Robertson	.25	.10	.02
☐ 410	Mike Cueller	.35	.14	.03
	(sic, Cuellar)			
☐ 411	George Mitterwald	.25	.10	.02
☐ 412	Bill Hands	.25	.10	.02
☐ 413	Marty Pattin	.25	.10	.02
☐ 414	Manny Mota	.35	.14	.03
☐ 415	John Hiller	.35	.14	.03
☐ 416	Larry Lintz	.25	.10	.02
☐ 417	Skip Lockwood	.25	.10	.02
☐ 418	Leo Foster	.25	.10	.02
☐ 419	Dave Goltz	.25	.10	.02
☐ 420	Larry Bowa	.50	.20	.05

		NRMT	VG-E	GOOD
☐ 421	Mets: Team/Mgr.	.75	.25	.04
	Yogi Berra			
	(checklist back)			
☐ 422	Brian Downing	.50	.20	.05
☐ 423	Clay Kirby	.25	.10	.02
☐ 424	John Lowenstein	.25	.10	.02
☐ 425	Tito Fuentes	.25	.10	.02
☐ 426	George Medich	.25	.10	.02
☐ 427	Clarence Gaston	.25	.10	.02
☐ 428	Dave Hamilton	.25	.10	.02
☐ 429	Jim Dwyer	.25	.10	.02
☐ 430	Luis Tiant	.50	.20	.05
☐ 431	Rod Gilbreath	.25	.10	.02
☐ 432	Ken Berry	.25	.10	.02
☐ 433	Larry Demery	.25	.10	.02
☐ 434	Bob Locker	.25	.10	.02
☐ 435	Dave Nelson	.25	.10	.02
☐ 436	Ken Frailing	.25	.10	.02
☐ 437	Al Cowens	.35	.14	.03
☐ 438	Don Carrithers	.25	.10	.02
☐ 439	Ed Brinkman	.25	.10	.02
☐ 440	Andy Messersmith	.35	.14	.03
☐ 441	Bobby Heise	.25	.10	.02
☐ 442	Maximino Leon	.25	.10	.02
☐ 443	Twins: Team/Mgr.	.65	.15	.03
	Frank Quilici			
	(checklist back)			
☐ 444	Gene Garber	.25	.10	.02
☐ 445	Felix Millan	.25	.10	.02
☐ 446	Bart Johnson	.25	.10	.02
☐ 447	Terry Crowley	.25	.10	.02
☐ 448	Frank Duffy	.25	.10	.02
☐ 449	Charlie Williams	.25	.10	.02
☐ 450	Willie McCovey	3.00	1.20	.30
☐ 451	Rick Dempsey	.35	.14	.03
☐ 452	Angel Mangual	.25	.10	.02
☐ 453	Claude Osteen	.35	.14	.03
☐ 454	Doug Griffin	.25	.10	.02
☐ 455	Don Wilson	.25	.10	.02
☐ 456	Bob Coluccio	.25	.10	.02
☐ 457	Mario Mendoza	.25	.10	.02
☐ 458	Ross Grimsley	.25	.10	.02
☐ 459	1974 AL Champs	.50	.20	.05
	A's over Orioles			
	(2B action pictured)			
☐ 460	1974 NL Champs	.75	.30	.07
	Dodgers over Pirates			
	(Taveras/Garvey at 2B)			

		NRMT	VG-E	GOOD
☐ 461	World Series Game 1 (Reggie Jackson)	1.75	.70	.17
☐ 462	World Series Game 2 (Dodger dugout)	.50	.20	.05
☐ 463	World Series Game 3 (Fingers pitching)	.75	.30	.07
☐ 464	World Series Game 4 (A's batter)	.50	.20	.05
☐ 465	World Series Game 5 (Rudi rounding third)	.50	.20	.05
☐ 466	World Series Summary A's do it again; win third straight (A's group picture)	.50	.20	.05
☐ 467	Ed Halicki	.25	.10	.02
☐ 468	Bobby Mitchell	.25	.10	.02
☐ 469	Tom Dettore	.25	.10	.02
☐ 470	Jeff Burroughs	.35	.14	.03
☐ 471	Bob Stinson	.25	.10	.02
☐ 472	Bruce Dal Canton	.25	.10	.02
☐ 473	Ken McMullen	.25	.10	.02
☐ 474	Luke Walker	.25	.10	.02
☐ 475	Darrell Evans	.60	.24	.06
☐ 476	Ed Figueroa	.25	.10	.02
☐ 477	Tom Hutton	.25	.10	.02
☐ 478	Tom Burgmeier	.25	.10	.02
☐ 479	Ken Boswell	.25	.10	.02
☐ 480	Carlos May	.25	.10	.02
☐ 481	Will McEnaney	.25	.10	.02
☐ 482	Tom McCraw	.25	.10	.02
☐ 483	Steve Ontiveros	.25	.10	.02
☐ 484	Glenn Beckert	.35	.14	.03
☐ 485	Sparky Lyle	.50	.20	.05
☐ 486	Ray Fosse	.25	.10	.02
☐ 487	Astros: Team/Mgr. Preston Gomez (checklist back)	.65	.15	.03
☐ 488	Bill Travers	.25	.10	.02
☐ 489	Cecil Cooper	1.00	.40	.10
☐ 490	Reggie Smith	.50	.20	.05
☐ 491	Doyle Alexander	.50	.20	.05
☐ 492	Rich Hebner	.25	.10	.02
☐ 493	Don Stanhouse	.25	.10	.02
☐ 494	Pete LaCock	.25	.10	.02
☐ 495	Nelson Briles	.35	.14	.03
☐ 496	Pepe Frias	.25	.10	.02
☐ 497	Jim Nettles	.25	.10	.02
☐ 498	Al Downing	.35	.14	.03
☐ 499	Marty Perez	.25	.10	.02
☐ 500	Nolan Ryan	6.50	2.60	.65
☐ 501	Bill Robinson	.35	.14	.03
☐ 502	Pat Bourque	.25	.10	.02
☐ 503	Fred Stanley	.25	.10	.02
☐ 504	Buddy Bradford	.25	.10	.02
☐ 505	Chris Speier	.35	.14	.03
☐ 506	Leron Lee	.25	.10	.02
☐ 507	Tom Carroll	.25	.10	.02
☐ 508	Bob Hansen	.25	.10	.02
☐ 509	Dave Hilton	.25	.10	.02
☐ 510	Vida Blue	.50	.20	.05
☐ 511	Rangers: Team/Mgr. Billy Martin (checklist back)	.65	.15	.03
☐ 512	Larry Milbourne	.25	.10	.02
☐ 513	Dick Pole	.25	.10	.02
☐ 514	Jose Cruz	.35	.14	.03
☐ 515	Manny Sanguillen	.35	.14	.03
☐ 516	Don Hood	.25	.10	.02
☐ 517	Checklist: 397-528	.90	.10	.02
☐ 518	Leo Cardenas	.25	.10	.02
☐ 519	Jim Todd	.25	.10	.02
☐ 520	Amos Otis	.35	.14	.03
☐ 521	Dennis Blair	.25	.10	.02
☐ 522	Gary Sutherland	.25	.10	.02
☐ 523	Tom Paciorek	.25	.10	.02
☐ 524	John Doherty	.25	.10	.02
☐ 525	Tom House	.35	.14	.03
☐ 526	Larry Hisle	.35	.14	.03
☐ 527	Mac Scarce	.25	.10	.02
☐ 528	Eddie Leon	.25	.10	.02
☐ 529	Gary Thomasson	.25	.10	.02
☐ 530	Gaylord Perry	2.00	.80	.20
☐ 531	Reds: Team/Mgr. Sparky Anderson (checklist back)	.75	.25	.04
☐ 532	Gorman Thomas	.75	.30	.07
☐ 533	Rudy Meoli	.25	.10	.02
☐ 534	Alex Johnson	.25	.10	.02
☐ 535	Gene Tenace	.35	.14	.03
☐ 536	Bob Moose	.25	.10	.02
☐ 537	Tommy Harper	.35	.14	.03
☐ 538	Duffy Dyer	.25	.10	.02
☐ 539	Jesse Jefferson	.25	.10	.02
☐ 540	Lou Brock	3.00	1.20	.30
☐ 541	Roger Metzger	.25	.10	.02
☐ 542	Pete Broberg	.25	.10	.02
☐ 543	Larry Biittner	.25	.10	.02
☐ 544	Steve Mingori	.25	.10	.02

		NRMT	VG-E	GOOD			NRMT	VG-E	GOOD
☐ 545	Billy Williams	2.25	.90	.22	☐ 590	Cesar Cedeno	.35	.14	.03
☐ 546	John Knox	.25	.10	.02	☐ 591	Glenn Abbott	.25	.10	.02
☐ 547	Von Joshua	.25	.10	.02	☐ 592	Balor Moore	.25	.10	.02
☐ 548	Charlie Sands	.25	.10	.02	☐ 593	Gene Lamont	.25	.10	.02
☐ 549	Bill Butler	.25	.10	.02	☐ 594	Jim Fuller	.25	.10	.02
☐ 550	Ralph Garr	.25	.10	.02	☐ 595	Joe Niekro	.50	.20	.05
☐ 551	Larry Christenson	.25	.10	.02	☐ 596	Ollie Brown	.25	.10	.02
☐ 552	Jack Brohamer	.25	.10	.02	☐ 597	Winston Llenas	.25	.10	.02
☐ 553	John Boccabella	.25	.10	.02	☐ 598	Bruce Kison	.25	.10	.02
☐ 554	Rich Gossage	1.00	.40	.10	☐ 599	Nate Colbert	.25	.10	.02
☐ 555	Al Oliver	.75	.30	.07	☐ 600	Rod Carew	5.00	2.00	.50
☐ 556	Tim Johnson	.25	.10	.02	☐ 601	Juan Beniquez	.25	.10	.02
☐ 557	Larry Gura	.35	.14	.03	☐ 602	John Vukovich	.25	.10	.02
☐ 558	Dave Roberts	.25	.10	.02	☐ 603	Lew Krausse	.25	.10	.02
☐ 559	Bob Montgomery	.25	.10	.02	☐ 604	Oscar Zamora	.25	.10	.02
☐ 560	Tony Perez	1.00	.40	.10	☐ 605	John Ellis	.25	.10	.02
☐ 561	A's: Team/Mgr. Alvin Dark (checklist back)	.65	.15	.03	☐ 606	Bruce Miller	.25	.10	.02
					☐ 607	Jim Holt	.25	.10	.02
					☐ 608	Gene Michael	.35	.14	.03
☐ 562	Gary Nolan	.25	.10	.02	☐ 609	Elrod Hendricks	.25	.10	.02
☐ 563	Wilbur Howard	.25	.10	.02	☐ 610	Ron Hunt	.25	.10	.02
☐ 564	Tommy Davis	.35	.14	.03	☐ 611	Yankees: Team/Mgr. Bill Virdon (checklist back)	.75	.25	.04
☐ 565	Joe Torre	.60	.24	.06					
☐ 566	Ray Burris	.25	.10	.02					
☐ 567	Jim Sundberg	.60	.24	.06	☐ 612	Terry Hughes	.25	.10	.02
☐ 568	Dale Murray	.25	.10	.02	☐ 613	Bill Parsons	.25	.10	.02
☐ 569	Frank White	.75	.30	.07	☐ 614	Rookie Pitchers Jack Kucek Dyar Miller Vern Ruhle Paul Siebert	.35	.14	.03
☐ 570	Jim Wynn	.35	.14	.03					
☐ 571	Dave Lemanczyk	.25	.10	.02					
☐ 572	Roger Nelson	.25	.10	.02					
☐ 573	Orlando Pena	.25	.10	.02					
☐ 574	Tony Taylor	.25	.10	.02	☐ 615	Rookie Pitchers Pat Darcy Dennis Leonard Tom Underwood Hank Webb	1.00	.40	.10
☐ 575	Gene Clines	.25	.10	.02					
☐ 576	Phil Roof	.25	.10	.02					
☐ 577	John Morris	.25	.10	.02					
☐ 578	Dave Tomlin	.25	.10	.02					
☐ 579	Skip Pitlock	.25	.10	.02	☐ 616	Rookie Outfielders Dave Augustine Pepe Mangual Jim Rice John Scott	30.00	12.00	3.00
☐ 580	Frank Robinson	3.00	1.20	.30					
☐ 581	Darrel Chaney	.25	.10	.02					
☐ 582	Eduardo Rodriguez	.25	.10	.02					
☐ 583	Andy Etchebarren	.25	.10	.02					
☐ 584	Mike Garman	.25	.10	.02	☐ 617	Rookie Infielders Mike Cubbage Doug DeCinces Reggie Sanders Manny Trillo	1.75	.70	.17
☐ 585	Chris Chambliss	.50	.20	.05					
☐ 586	Tim McCarver	.50	.20	.05					
☐ 587	Chris Ward	.25	.10	.02					
☐ 588	Rick Auerbach	.25	.10	.02					
☐ 589	Braves: Team/Mgr. Clyde King (checklist back)	.65	.15	.03					

		NRMT	VG-E	GOOD
☐ 618	Rookie Pitchers	2.75	1.10	.27
	Jamie Easterly			
	Tom Johnson			
	Scott McGregor			
	Rick Rhoden			
☐ 619	Rookie Outfielders .	.35	.14	.03
	Benny Ayala			
	Nyls Nyman			
	Tommy Smith			
	Jerry Turner			
☐ 620	Rookie Catcher/OF	40.00	16.00	4.00
	Gary Carter			
	Marc Hill			
	Danny Meyer			
	Leon Roberts			
☐ 621	Rookie Pitchers	.90	.36	.09
	John Denny			
	Rawly Eastwick			
	Jim Kern			
	Juan Veintidos			
☐ 622	Rookie Outfielders .	12.00	5.00	1.20
	Ed Armbrister			
	Fred Lynn			
	Tom Poquette			
	Terry Whitfield			
☐ 623	Rookie Infielders ...	25.00	10.00	2.50
	Phil Garner			
	Keith Hernandez			
	(sic, bats right)			
	Bob Sheldon			
	Tom Veryzer			
☐ 624	Rookie Pitchers	.35	.14	.03
	Doug Konieczny			
	Gary Lavelle			
	Jim Otten			
	Eddie Solomon			
☐ 625	Boog Powell	.50	.20	.05
☐ 626	Larry Haney	.35	.14	.03
	(photo actually Dave Duncan)			
☐ 627	Tom Walker	.25	.10	.02
☐ 628	Ron LeFlore	.50	.20	.05
☐ 629	Joe Hoerner	.25	.10	.02
☐ 630	Greg Luzinski	.60	.24	.06
☐ 631	Lee Lacy	.35	.14	.03
☐ 632	Morris Nettles	.25	.10	.02
☐ 633	Paul Casanova	.25	.10	.02
☐ 634	Cy Acosta	.25	.10	.02
☐ 635	Chuck Dobson	.25	.10	.02
☐ 636	Charlie Moore	.25	.10	.02

		NRMT	VG-E	GOOD
☐ 637	Ted Martinez	.25	.10	.02
☐ 638	Cubs: Team/Mgr..	.65	.15	.03
	Jim Marshall			
	(checklist back)			
☐ 639	Steve Kline	.25	.10	.02
☐ 640	Harmon Killebrew..	3.00	1.20	.30
☐ 641	Jim Northrup	.35	.14	.03
☐ 642	Mike Phillips	.25	.10	.02
☐ 643	Brent Strom	.25	.10	.02
☐ 644	Bill Fahey	.25	.10	.02
☐ 645	Danny Cater	.25	.10	.02
☐ 646	Checklist: 529-660	.90	.10	.02
☐ 647	Claudell Washington	2.75	1.10	.27
☐ 648	Dave Pagan	.25	.10	.02
☐ 649	Jack Heidemann ..	.25	.10	.02
☐ 650	Dave May	.25	.10	.02
☐ 651	John Morlan	.25	.10	.02
☐ 652	Lindy McDaniel ...	.35	.14	.03
☐ 653	Lee Richard	.25	.10	.02
☐ 654	Jerry Terrell	.25	.10	.02
☐ 655	Rico Carty	.35	.14	.03
☐ 656	Bill Plummer	.25	.10	.02
☐ 657	Bob Oliver	.25	.10	.02
☐ 658	Vic Harris	.25	.10	.02
☐ 659	Bob Apodaca	.25	.10	.02
☐ 660	Hank Aaron	10.00	2.50	.50

1976 Topps

The 1976 Topps set of 660 cards (measuring 2 ½" by 3 ½") is known for its sharp color photographs and interesting presentation of subjects. Team cards feature a checklist back for players on that team and show a small inset photo of the manager on the front. A "Father and Son" series (66-70) spotlights five Major Leaguers whose fathers also made the "Big Show." Other subseries include "All Time All Stars" (341-350), "Record Breakers" from the previous season (1-6), League Leaders (191-205), Postseason cards (461-462), and Rookie Prospects (589-599).

			NRMT	VG-E	GOOD
		Complete Set (660)	275.00	110.00	27.00
		Common Player (1-660)	.18	.08	.01
☐	1	RB: Hank Aaron ... Most RBI's, 2262	8.00	2.00	.40
☐	2	RB: Bobby Bonds .. Most leadoff HR's 32; plus three seasons 30 homers/30 steals	.35	.14	.03
☐	3	RB: Mickey Lolich .. Lefthander, Most Strikeouts, 2679	.35	.14	.03
☐	4	RB: Dave Lopes ... Most Consecutive SB attempts, 38	.25	.10	.02
☐	5	RB: Tom Seaver ... Most Cons. seasons with 200 SO's, 8	1.50	.60	.15
☐	6	RB: Rennie Stennett Most Hits in a 9 inning game, 7	.25	.10	.02
☐	7	Jim Umbarger	.18	.08	.01
☐	8	Tito Fuentes	.18	.08	.01
☐	9	Paul Lindblad	.18	.08	.01
☐	10	Lou Brock	2.50	1.00	.25
☐	11	Jim Hughes	.18	.08	.01
☐	12	Richie Zisk	.25	.10	.02
☐	13	John Wockenfuss	.18	.08	.01
☐	14	Gene Garber	.18	.08	.01
☐	15	George Scott	.25	.10	.02
☐	16	Bob Apodaca	.18	.08	.01
☐	17	New York Yankees Team Card (checklist back)	1.00	.25	.04
☐	18	Dale Murray	.18	.08	.01
☐	19	George Brett	16.00	6.50	1.60
☐	20	Bob Watson	.25	.10	.02
☐	21	Dave LaRoche	.18	.08	.01
☐	22	Bill Russell	.25	.10	.02
☐	23	Brian Downing	.35	.14	.03
☐	24	Cesar Geronimo	.18	.08	.01
☐	25	Mike Torrez	.25	.10	.02
☐	26	Andre Thornton	.25	.10	.02
☐	27	Ed Figueroa	.18	.08	.01
☐	28	Dusty Baker	.35	.14	.03
☐	29	Rick Burleson	.25	.10	.02
☐	30	John Montefusco	.35	.14	.03
☐	31	Len Randle	.18	.08	.01
☐	32	Danny Frisella	.18	.08	.01
☐	33	Bill North	.18	.08	.01
☐	34	Mike Garman	.18	.08	.01
☐	35	Tony Oliva	.75	.30	.07
☐	36	Frank Taveras	.18	.08	.01
☐	37	John Hiller	.25	.10	.02
☐	38	Garry Maddox	.25	.10	.02
☐	39	Pete Broberg	.18	.08	.01
☐	40	Dave Kingman	.75	.30	.07
☐	41	Tippy Martinez	.35	.14	.03
☐	42	Barry Foote	.18	.08	.01
☐	43	Paul Splittorff	.25	.10	.02
☐	44	Doug Rader	.35	.14	.03
☐	45	Boog Powell	.50	.20	.05
☐	46	Dodgers Team (checklist back)	.75	.20	.04
☐	47	Jesse Jefferson	.18	.08	.01
☐	48	Dave Concepcion	.50	.20	.05
☐	49	Dave Duncan	.18	.08	.01
☐	50	Fred Lynn	2.25	.90	.22
☐	51	Ray Burris	.18	.08	.01
☐	52	Dave Chalk	.18	.08	.01
☐	53	Mike Beard	.18	.08	.01
☐	54	Dave Rader	.18	.08	.01
☐	55	Gaylord Perry	1.75	.70	.17
☐	56	Bob Tolan	.18	.08	.01
☐	57	Phil Garner	.25	.10	.02
☐	58	Ron Reed	.18	.08	.01
☐	59	Larry Hisle	.25	.10	.02
☐	60	Jerry Reuss	.25	.10	.02
☐	61	Ron LeFlore	.25	.10	.02
☐	62	Johnny Oates	.18	.08	.01
☐	63	Bobby Darwin	.18	.08	.01
☐	64	Jerry Koosman	.50	.20	.05
☐	65	Chris Chambliss	.35	.14	.03
☐	66	Father and Son Gus Bell Buddy Bell	.35	.14	.03

		NRMT	VG-E	GOOD
☐ 67	Father and Son	.25	.10	.02
	Ray Boone			
	Bob Boone			
☐ 68	Father and Son	.25	.10	.02
	Joe Coleman			
	Joe Coleman Jr.			
☐ 69	Father and Son	.25	.10	.02
	Jim Hegan			
	Mike Hegan			
☐ 70	Father and Son	.25	.10	.02
	Roy Smalley			
	Roy Smalley Jr.			
☐ 71	Steve Rogers	.25	.10	.02
☐ 72	Hal McRae	.35	.14	.03
☐ 73	Baltimore Orioles ..	.65	.15	.03
	Team Card			
	(checklist back)			
☐ 74	Oscar Gamble	.25	.10	.02
☐ 75	Larry Dierker	.25	.10	.02
☐ 76	Willie Crawford	.18	.08	.01
☐ 77	Pedro Borbon	.18	.08	.01
☐ 78	Cecil Cooper	.90	.36	.09
☐ 79	Jerry Morales	.18	.08	.01
☐ 80	Jim Kaat	.75	.30	.07
☐ 81	Darrell Evans	.60	.24	.06
☐ 82	Von Joshua	.18	.08	.01
☐ 83	Jim Spencer	.18	.08	.01
☐ 84	Brent Strom	.18	.08	.01
☐ 85	Mickey Rivers	.25	.10	.02
☐ 86	Mike Tyson	.18	.08	.01
☐ 87	Tom Burgmeier	.18	.08	.01
☐ 88	Duffy Dyer	.18	.08	.01
☐ 89	Vern Ruhle	.18	.08	.01
☐ 90	Sal Bando	.35	.14	.03
☐ 91	Tom Hutton	.18	.08	.01
☐ 92	Eduardo Rodriguez .	.18	.08	.01
☐ 93	Mike Phillips	.18	.08	.01
☐ 94	Jim Dwyer	.18	.08	.01
☐ 95	Brooks Robinson ..	2.50	1.00	.25
☐ 96	Doug Bird	.18	.08	.01
☐ 97	Wilbur Howard	.18	.08	.01
☐ 98	Dennis Eckersley ..	4.00	1.60	.40
☐ 99	Lee Lacy	.25	.10	.02
☐ 100	Jim Hunter	2.00	.80	.20
☐ 101	Pete LaCock	.18	.08	.01
☐ 102	Jim Willoughby	.18	.08	.01
☐ 103	Biff Pocoroba	.18	.08	.01
☐ 104	Reds Team	.65	.15	.03
	(checklist back)			
☐ 105	Gary Lavelle	.25	.10	.02
☐ 106	Tom Grieve	.35	.14	.03
☐ 107	Dave Roberts	.18	.08	.01
☐ 108	Don Kirkwood	.18	.08	.01
☐ 109	Larry Lintz	.18	.08	.01
☐ 110	Carlos May	.18	.08	.01
☐ 111	Danny Thompson ..	.18	.08	.01
☐ 112	Kent Tekulve	1.00	.40	.10
☐ 113	Gary Sutherland ..	.18	.08	.01
☐ 114	Jay Johnstone	.35	.14	.03
☐ 115	Ken Holtzman	.25	.10	.02
☐ 116	Charlie Moore	.18	.08	.01
☐ 117	Mike Jorgensen ...	.18	.08	.01
☐ 118	Red Sox Team	.65	.15	.03
	(checklist back)			
☐ 119	Checklist 1-132 ...	.80	.10	.02
☐ 120	Rusty Staub	.50	.20	.05
☐ 121	Tony Solaita	.18	.08	.01
☐ 122	Mike Cosgrove	.18	.08	.01
☐ 123	Walt Williams	.18	.08	.01
☐ 124	Doug Rau	.18	.08	.01
☐ 125	Don Baylor	.60	.24	.06
☐ 126	Tom Dettore	.18	.08	.01
☐ 127	Larvell Blanks	.18	.08	.01
☐ 128	Ken Griffey	.35	.14	.03
☐ 129	Andy Etchebarren .	.18	.08	.01
☐ 130	Luis Tiant	.50	.20	.05
☐ 131	Bill Stein	.18	.08	.01
☐ 132	Don Hood	.18	.08	.01
☐ 133	Gary Matthews ...	.35	.14	.03
☐ 134	Mike Ivie	.18	.08	.01
☐ 135	Bake McBride	.25	.10	.02
☐ 136	Dave Goltz	.18	.08	.01
☐ 137	Bill Robinson	.25	.10	.02
☐ 138	Lerrin LaGrow ...	.18	.08	.01
☐ 139	Gorman Thomas ..	.50	.20	.05
☐ 140	Vida Blue	.35	.14	.03
☐ 141	Larry Parrish	1.50	.60	.15
☐ 142	Dick Drago	.18	.08	.01
☐ 143	Jerry Grote	.18	.08	.01
☐ 144	Al Fitzmorris	.18	.08	.01
☐ 145	Larry Bowa	.50	.20	.05
☐ 146	George Medich	.18	.08	.01
☐ 147	Astros Team	.65	.15	.03
	(checklist back)			
☐ 148	Stan Thomas	.18	.08	.01
☐ 149	Tommy Davis	.35	.14	.03
☐ 150	Steve Garvey	4.50	1.80	.45
☐ 151	Bill Bonham	.18	.08	.01

		NRMT	VG-E	GOOD
☐ 152	Leroy Stanton	.18	.08	.01
☐ 153	Buzz Capra	.18	.08	.01
☐ 154	Bucky Dent	.35	.14	.03
☐ 155	Jack Billingham	.18	.08	.01
☐ 156	Rico Carty	.25	.10	.02
☐ 157	Mike Caldwell	.25	.10	.02
☐ 158	Ken Reitz	.18	.08	.01
☐ 159	Jerry Terrell	.18	.08	.01
☐ 160	Dave Winfield	6.00	2.40	.60
☐ 161	Bruce Kison	.18	.08	.01
☐ 162	Jack Pierce	.18	.08	.01
☐ 163	Jim Slaton	.18	.08	.01
☐ 164	Pepe Mangual	.18	.08	.01
☐ 165	Gene Tenace	.25	.10	.02
☐ 166	Skip Lockwood	.18	.08	.01
☐ 167	Freddie Patek	.18	.08	.01
☐ 168	Tom Hilgendorf	.18	.08	.01
☐ 169	Graig Nettles	1.00	.40	.10
☐ 170	Rick Wise	.25	.10	.02
☐ 171	Greg Gross	.18	.08	.01
☐ 172	Rangers Team (checklist back)	.65	.15	.03
☐ 173	Steve Swisher	.18	.08	.01
☐ 174	Charlie Hough	.35	.14	.03
☐ 175	Ken Singleton	.35	.14	.03
☐ 176	Dick Lange	.18	.08	.01
☐ 177	Marty Perez	.18	.08	.01
☐ 178	Tom Buskey	.18	.08	.01
☐ 179	George Foster	1.00	.40	.10
☐ 180	Rich Gossage	1.00	.40	.10
☐ 181	Willie Montanez	.18	.08	.01
☐ 182	Harry Rasmussen	.18	.08	.01
☐ 183	Steve Braun	.18	.08	.01
☐ 184	Bill Greif	.18	.08	.01
☐ 185	Dave Parker	3.00	1.20	.30
☐ 186	Tom Walker	.18	.08	.01
☐ 187	Pedro Garcia	.18	.08	.01
☐ 188	Fred Scherman	.18	.08	.01
☐ 189	Claudell Washington	.50	.20	.05
☐ 190	Jon Matlack	.25	.10	.02
☐ 191	NL Batting Leaders Bill Madlock Ted Simmons Manny Sanguillen	.35	.14	.03
☐ 192	AL Batting Leaders Rod Carew Fred Lynn Thurman Munson	1.50	.60	.15
☐ 193	NL Home Run Leaders Mike Schmidt Dave Kingman Greg Luzinski	.75	.30	.07
☐ 194	AL Home Run Leaders Reggie Jackson George Scott John Mayberry	.75	.30	.07
☐ 195	NL RBI Leaders Greg Luzinski Johnny Bench Tony Perez	.60	.24	.06
☐ 196	AL RBI Leaders George Scott John Mayberry Fred Lynn	.35	.14	.03
☐ 197	NL Steals Leaders Dave Lopes Joe Morgan Lou Brock	.75	.30	.07
☐ 198	AL Steals Leaders Mickey Rivers Claudell Washington Amos Otis	.35	.14	.03
☐ 199	NL Victory Leaders Tom Seaver Randy Jones Andy Messersmith	.50	.20	.05
☐ 200	AL Victory Leaders Jim Hunter Jim Palmer Vida Blue	.75	.30	.07
☐ 201	NL ERA Leaders Randy Jones Andy Messersmith Tom Seaver	.50	.20	.05
☐ 202	AL ERA Leaders Jim Palmer Jim Hunter Dennis Eckersley	1.00	.40	.10
☐ 203	NL Strikeout Leaders Tom Seaver John Montefusco Andy Messersmith	.50	.20	.05
☐ 204	AL Strikeout Leaders Frank Tanana Bert Blyleven Gaylord Perry	.35	.14	.03

		NRMT	VG-E	GOOD
☐ 205	Leading Firemen ...	.35	.14	.03
	Al Hrabosky			
	Rich Gossage			
☐ 206	Manny Trillo	.18	.08	.01
☐ 207	Andy Hassler	.18	.08	.01
☐ 208	Mike Lum	.18	.08	.01
☐ 209	Alan Ashby	.50	.20	.05
☐ 210	Lee May	.25	.10	.02
☐ 211	Clay Carroll	.18	.08	.01
☐ 212	Pat Kelly	.18	.08	.01
☐ 213	Dave Heaverlo	.18	.08	.01
☐ 214	Eric Soderholm ...	.18	.08	.01
☐ 215	Reggie Smith	.35	.14	.03
☐ 216	Expos Team	.65	.15	.03
	(checklist back)			
☐ 217	Dave Freisleben ...	.18	.08	.01
☐ 218	John Knox	.18	.08	.01
☐ 219	Tom Murphy	.18	.08	.01
☐ 220	Manny Sanguillen ..	.25	.10	.02
☐ 221	Jim Todd	.18	.08	.01
☐ 222	Wayne Garrett	.18	.08	.01
☐ 223	Ollie Brown	.18	.08	.01
☐ 224	Jim York	.18	.08	.01
☐ 225	Roy White	.25	.10	.02
☐ 226	Jim Sundberg	.25	.10	.02
☐ 227	Oscar Zamora	.18	.08	.01
☐ 228	John Hale	.18	.08	.01
☐ 229	Jerry Remy	.35	.14	.03
☐ 230	Carl Yastrzemski ..	6.50	2.60	.65
☐ 231	Tom House	.25	.10	.02
☐ 232	Frank Duffy	.18	.08	.01
☐ 233	Grant Jackson	.18	.08	.01
☐ 234	Mike Sadek	.18	.08	.01
☐ 235	Bert Blyleven	.75	.30	.07
☐ 236	Kansas City Royals	.65	.15	.03
	Team Card			
	(checklist back)			
☐ 237	Dave Hamilton	.18	.08	.01
☐ 238	Larry Biittner	.18	.08	.01
☐ 239	John Curtis	.18	.08	.01
☐ 240	Pete Rose	15.00	6.00	1.50
☐ 241	Hector Torres	.18	.08	.01
☐ 242	Dan Meyer	.18	.08	.01
☐ 243	Jim Rooker	.18	.08	.01
☐ 244	Bill Sharp	.18	.08	.01
☐ 245	Felix Millan	.18	.08	.01
☐ 246	Cesar Tovar	.18	.08	.01
☐ 247	Terry Harmon	.18	.08	.01
☐ 248	Dick Tidrow	.18	.08	.01
☐ 249	Cliff Johnson	.18	.08	.01
☐ 250	Fergie Jenkins	.75	.30	.07
☐ 251	Rick Monday	.25	.10	.02
☐ 252	Tim Nordbrook	.18	.08	.01
☐ 253	Bill Buckner	.35	.14	.03
☐ 254	Rudy Meoli	.18	.08	.01
☐ 255	Fritz Peterson	.18	.08	.01
☐ 256	Rowland Office	.18	.08	.01
☐ 257	Ross Grimsley	.18	.08	.01
☐ 258	Nyls Nyman	.18	.08	.01
☐ 259	Darrel Chaney	.18	.08	.01
☐ 260	Steve Busby	.25	.10	.02
☐ 261	Gary Thomasson ..	.18	.08	.01
☐ 262	Checklist 133-264	.80	.10	.02
☐ 263	Lyman Bostock	.50	.20	.05
☐ 264	Steve Renko	.18	.08	.01
☐ 265	Willie Davis	.25	.10	.02
☐ 266	Alan Foster	.18	.08	.01
☐ 267	Aurelio Rodriguez .	.18	.08	.01
☐ 268	Del Unser	.18	.08	.01
☐ 269	Rick Austin	.18	.08	.01
☐ 270	Willie Stargell	3.00	1.20	.30
☐ 271	Jim Lonborg	.25	.10	.02
☐ 272	Rick Dempsey	.25	.10	.02
☐ 273	Joe Niekro	.35	.14	.03
☐ 274	Tommy Harper ...	.25	.10	.02
☐ 275	Rick Manning	.25	.10	.02
☐ 276	Mickey Scott	.18	.08	.01
☐ 277	Cubs Team	.65	.15	.03
	(checklist back)			
☐ 278	Bernie Carbo	.18	.08	.01
☐ 279	Roy Howell	.18	.08	.01
☐ 280	Burt Hooton	.18	.08	.01
☐ 281	Dave May	.18	.08	.01
☐ 282	Dan Osborn	.18	.08	.01
☐ 283	Merv Rettenmund ..	.18	.08	.01
☐ 284	Steve Ontiveros ...	.18	.08	.01
☐ 285	Mike Cuellar	.25	.10	.02
☐ 286	Jim Wohlford	.18	.08	.01
☐ 287	Pete Mackanin ...	.18	.08	.01
☐ 288	Bill Campbell	.18	.08	.01
☐ 289	Enzo Hernandez ..	.18	.08	.01
☐ 290	Ted Simmons	.75	.30	.07
☐ 291	Ken Sanders	.18	.08	.01
☐ 292	Leon Roberts	.18	.08	.01
☐ 293	Bill Castro	.18	.08	.01
☐ 294	Ed Kirkpatrick	.18	.08	.01
☐ 295	Dave Cash	.18	.08	.01
☐ 296	Pat Dobson	.25	.10	.02

		NRMT	VG-E	GOOD
☐ 297	Roger Metzger	.18	.08	.01
☐ 298	Dick Bosman	.18	.08	.01
☐ 299	Champ Summers ..	.18	.08	.01
☐ 300	Johnny Bench	5.50	2.20	.55
☐ 301	Jackie Brown	.18	.08	.01
☐ 302	Rick Miller	.18	.08	.01
☐ 303	Steve Foucault	.18	.08	.01
☐ 304	Angels Team	.65	.15	.03
	(checklist back)			
☐ 305	Andy Messersmith .	.25	.10	.02
☐ 306	Rod Gilbreath	.18	.08	.01
☐ 307	Al Bumbry	.18	.08	.01
☐ 308	Jim Barr	.18	.08	.01
☐ 309	Bill Melton	.18	.08	.01
☐ 310	Randy Jones	.25	.10	.02
☐ 311	Cookie Rojas	.25	.10	.02
☐ 312	Don Carrithers	.18	.08	.01
☐ 313	Dan Ford	.25	.10	.02
☐ 314	Ed Kranepool	.25	.10	.02
☐ 315	Al Hrabosky	.25	.10	.02
☐ 316	Robin Yount	7.50	3.00	.75
☐ 317	John Candelaria ...	3.00	1.20	.30
☐ 318	Bob Boone	.50	.20	.05
☐ 319	Larry Gura	.25	.10	.02
☐ 320	Willie Horton	.25	.10	.02
☐ 321	Jose Cruz	.35	.14	.03
☐ 322	Glenn Abbott	.18	.08	.01
☐ 323	Rob Sperring	.18	.08	.01
☐ 324	Jim Bibby	.25	.10	.02
☐ 325	Tony Perez	.75	.30	.07
☐ 326	Dick Pole	.18	.08	.01
☐ 327	Dave Moates	.18	.08	.01
☐ 328	Carl Morton	.18	.08	.01
☐ 329	Joe Ferguson	.18	.08	.01
☐ 330	Nolan Ryan	5.50	2.20	.55
☐ 331	San Diego Padres ..	.65	.15	.03
	Team Card			
	(checklist back)			
☐ 332	Charlie Williams ...	.18	.08	.01
☐ 333	Bob Coluccio	.18	.08	.01
☐ 334	Dennis Leonard ...	.25	.10	.02
☐ 335	Bob Grich	.35	.14	.03
☐ 336	Vic Albury	.18	.08	.01
☐ 337	Bud Harrelson	.25	.10	.02
☐ 338	Bob Bailey	.18	.08	.01
☐ 339	John Denny	.35	.14	.03
☐ 340	Jim Rice	8.50	3.50	.85
☐ 341	All-Time 1B	2.50	1.00	.25
	Lou Gehrig			
☐ 342	All-Time 2B	1.50	.60	.15
	Rogers Hornsby			
☐ 343	All-Time 3B	.75	.30	.07
	Pie Traynor			
☐ 344	All-Time SS	1.50	.60	.15
	Honus Wagner			
☐ 345	All-Time OF	4.50	1.80	.45
	Babe Ruth			
☐ 346	All-Time OF	3.00	1.20	.30
	Ty Cobb			
☐ 347	All-Time OF	3.00	1.20	.30
	Ted Williams			
☐ 348	All-Time C	.75	.30	.07
	Mickey Cochrane			
☐ 349	All-Time RHP	1.50	.60	.15
	Walter Johnson			
☐ 350	All-Time LHP	1.25	.50	.12
	Lefty Grove			
☐ 351	Randy Hundley ...	.18	.08	.01
☐ 352	Dave Giusti	.18	.08	.01
☐ 353	Sixto Lezcano	.25	.10	.02
☐ 354	Ron Blomberg	.18	.08	.01
☐ 355	Steve Carlton	4.00	1.60	.40
☐ 356	Ted Martinez	.18	.08	.01
☐ 357	Ken Forsch	.25	.10	.02
☐ 358	Buddy Bell	.50	.20	.05
☐ 359	Rick Reuschel	.50	.20	.05
☐ 360	Jeff Burroughs	.25	.10	.02
☐ 361	Detroit Tigers	.65	.15	.03
	Team Card			
	(checklist back)			
☐ 362	Will McEnaney	.18	.08	.01
☐ 363	Dave Collins	.75	.30	.07
☐ 364	Elias Sosa	.18	.08	.01
☐ 365	Carlton Fisk	1.25	.50	.12
☐ 366	Bobby Valentine ..	.35	.14	.03
☐ 367	Bruce Miller	.18	.08	.01
☐ 368	Wilbur Wood	.25	.10	.02
☐ 369	Frank White	.50	.20	.05
☐ 370	Ron Cey	.50	.20	.05
☐ 371	Elrod Hendricks ...	.18	.08	.01
☐ 372	Rick Baldwin	.18	.08	.01
☐ 373	Johnny Briggs	.18	.08	.01
☐ 374	Dan Warthen	.18	.08	.01
☐ 375	Ron Fairly	.25	.10	.02
☐ 376	Rich Hebner	.25	.10	.02
☐ 377	Mike Hegan	.18	.08	.01
☐ 378	Steve Stone	.25	.10	.02
☐ 379	Ken Boswell	.18	.08	.01

		NRMT	VG-E	GOOD
☐ 380	Bobby Bonds	.35	.14	.03
☐ 381	Denny Doyle	.18	.08	.01
☐ 382	Matt Alexander	.18	.08	.01
☐ 383	John Ellis	.18	.08	.01
☐ 384	Phillies Team	.65	.15	.03
	(checklist back)			
☐ 385	Mickey Lolich	.35	.14	.03
☐ 386	Ed Goodson	.18	.08	.01
☐ 387	Mike Miley	.18	.08	.01
☐ 388	Stan Perzanowski	.18	.08	.01
☐ 389	Glenn Adams	.18	.08	.01
☐ 390	Don Gullett	.25	.10	.02
☐ 391	Jerry Hairston	.18	.08	.01
☐ 392	Checklist 265-396	.80	.10	.02
☐ 393	Paul Mitchell	.18	.08	.01
☐ 394	Fran Healy	.18	.08	.01
☐ 395	Jim Wynn	.25	.10	.02
☐ 396	Bill Lee	.25	.10	.02
☐ 397	Tim Foli	.18	.08	.01
☐ 398	Dave Tomlin	.18	.08	.01
☐ 399	Luis Melendez	.18	.08	.01
☐ 400	Rod Carew	4.00	1.60	.40
☐ 401	Ken Brett	.18	.08	.01
☐ 402	Don Money	.18	.08	.01
☐ 403	Geoff Zahn	.18	.08	.01
☐ 404	Enos Cabell	.18	.08	.01
☐ 405	Rollie Fingers	1.00	.40	.10
☐ 406	Ed Herrmann	.18	.08	.01
☐ 407	Tom Underwood	.18	.08	.01
☐ 408	Charlie Spikes	.18	.08	.01
☐ 409	Dave Lemanczyk	.18	.08	.01
☐ 410	Ralph Garr	.18	.08	.01
☐ 411	Bill Singer	.18	.08	.01
☐ 412	Toby Harrah	.25	.10	.02
☐ 413	Pete Varney	.18	.08	.01
☐ 414	Wayne Garland	.18	.08	.01
☐ 415	Vada Pinson	.35	.14	.03
☐ 416	Tommy John	1.00	.40	.10
☐ 417	Gene Clines	.18	.08	.01
☐ 418	Jose Morales	.18	.08	.01
☐ 419	Reggie Cleveland	.18	.08	.01
☐ 420	Joe Morgan	3.00	1.20	.30
☐ 421	A's Team	.65	.15	.03
	(checklist back)			
☐ 422	Johnny Grubb	.18	.08	.01
☐ 423	Ed Halicki	.18	.08	.01
☐ 424	Phil Roof	.18	.08	.01
☐ 425	Rennie Stennett	.18	.08	.01
☐ 426	Bob Forsch	.25	.10	.02

		NRMT	VG-E	GOOD
☐ 427	Kurt Bevacqua	.18	.08	.01
☐ 428	Jim Crawford	.18	.08	.01
☐ 429	Fred Stanley	.18	.08	.01
☐ 430	Jose Cardenal	.18	.08	.01
☐ 431	Dick Ruthven	.18	.08	.01
☐ 432	Tom Veryzer	.18	.08	.01
☐ 433	Rick Waits	.18	.08	.01
☐ 434	Morris Nettles	.18	.08	.01
☐ 435	Phil Niekro	1.75	.70	.17
☐ 436	Bill Fahey	.18	.08	.01
☐ 437	Terry Forster	.25	.10	.02
☐ 438	Doug DeCinces	.50	.20	.05
☐ 439	Rick Rhoden	.60	.24	.06
☐ 440	John Mayberry	.25	.10	.02
☐ 441	Gary Carter	12.00	5.00	1.20
☐ 442	Hank Webb	.18	.08	.01
☐ 443	Giants Team	.65	.15	.03
	(checklist back)			
☐ 444	Gary Nolan	.18	.08	.01
☐ 445	Rico Petrocelli	.25	.10	.02
☐ 446	Larry Haney	.18	.08	.01
☐ 447	Gene Locklear	.18	.08	.01
☐ 448	Tom Johnson	.18	.08	.01
☐ 449	Bob Robertson	.18	.08	.01
☐ 450	Jim Palmer	3.50	1.40	.35
☐ 451	Buddy Bradford	.18	.08	.01
☐ 452	Tom Hausman	.18	.08	.01
☐ 453	Lou Piniella	.35	.14	.03
☐ 454	Tom Griffin	.18	.08	.01
☐ 455	Dick Allen	.35	.14	.03
☐ 456	Joe Coleman	.18	.08	.01
☐ 457	Ed Crosby	.18	.08	.01
☐ 458	Earl Williams	.18	.08	.01
☐ 459	Jim Brewer	.18	.08	.01
☐ 460	Cesar Cedeno	.25	.10	.02
☐ 461	NL and AL Champs	.35	.14	.03
	Reds sweep Bucs,			
	Bosox surprise A's			
☐ 462	'75 World Series	.35	.14	.03
	Reds Champs			
☐ 463	Steve Hargan	.18	.08	.01
☐ 464	Ken Henderson	.18	.08	.01
☐ 465	Mike Marshall	.25	.10	.02
☐ 466	Bob Stinson	.18	.08	.01
☐ 467	Woodie Fryman	.18	.08	.01
☐ 468	Jesus Alou	.18	.08	.01
☐ 469	Rawly Eastwick	.18	.08	.01
☐ 470	Bobby Murcer	.35	.14	.03
☐ 471	Jim Burton	.18	.08	.01

	NRMT	VG-E	GOOD
☐ 472 Bob Davis	.18	.08	.01
☐ 473 Paul Blair	.25	.10	.02
☐ 474 Ray Corbin	.18	.08	.01
☐ 475 Joe Rudi	.25	.10	.02
☐ 476 Bob Moose	.18	.08	.01
☐ 477 Indians Team (checklist back)	.65	.15	.03
☐ 478 Lynn McGlothen	.18	.08	.01
☐ 479 Bobby Mitchell	.18	.08	.01
☐ 480 Mike Schmidt	14.00	5.75	1.40
☐ 481 Rudy May	.18	.08	.01
☐ 482 Tim Hosley	.18	.08	.01
☐ 483 Mickey Stanley	.25	.10	.02
☐ 484 Eric Raich	.18	.08	.01
☐ 485 Mike Hargrove	.25	.10	.02
☐ 486 Bruce Dal Canton	.18	.08	.01
☐ 487 Leron Lee	.18	.08	.01
☐ 488 Claude Osteen	.25	.10	.02
☐ 489 Skip Jutze	.18	.08	.01
☐ 490 Frank Tanana	.35	.14	.03
☐ 491 Terry Crowley	.18	.08	.01
☐ 492 Marty Pattin	.18	.08	.01
☐ 493 Derrel Thomas	.18	.08	.01
☐ 494 Craig Swan	.25	.10	.02
☐ 495 Nate Colbert	.18	.08	.01
☐ 496 Juan Beniquez	.18	.08	.01
☐ 497 Joe McIntosh	.18	.08	.01
☐ 498 Glenn Borgmann	.18	.08	.01
☐ 499 Mario Guerrero	.18	.08	.01
☐ 500 Reggie Jackson	7.00	2.80	.70
☐ 501 Billy Champion	.18	.08	.01
☐ 502 Tim McCarver	.35	.14	.03
☐ 503 Elliott Maddox	.18	.08	.01
☐ 504 Pirates Team (checklist back)	.65	.15	.03
☐ 505 Mark Belanger	.25	.10	.02
☐ 506 George Mitterwald	.18	.08	.01
☐ 507 Ray Bare	.18	.08	.01
☐ 508 Duane Kuiper	.18	.08	.01
☐ 509 Bill Hands	.18	.08	.01
☐ 510 Amos Otis	.35	.14	.03
☐ 511 Jamie Easterley	.18	.08	.01
☐ 512 Ellie Rodriguez	.18	.08	.01
☐ 513 Bart Johnson	.18	.08	.01
☐ 514 Dan Driessen	.25	.10	.02
☐ 515 Steve Yeager	.18	.08	.01
☐ 516 Wayne Granger	.18	.08	.01
☐ 517 John Milner	.18	.08	.01
☐ 518 Doug Flynn	.18	.08	.01
☐ 519 Steve Brye	.18	.08	.01
☐ 520 Willie McCovey	2.50	1.00	.25
☐ 521 Jim Colborn	.18	.08	.01
☐ 522 Ted Sizemore	.18	.08	.01
☐ 523 Bob Montgomery	.18	.08	.01
☐ 524 Pete Falcone	.18	.08	.01
☐ 525 Billy Williams	1.75	.70	.17
☐ 526 Checklist 397-528	.80	.10	.02
☐ 527 Mike Anderson	.18	.08	.01
☐ 528 Dock Ellis	.18	.08	.01
☐ 529 Deron Johnson	.18	.08	.01
☐ 530 Don Sutton	1.50	.60	.15
☐ 531 New York Mets Team (checklist back)	.75	.20	.04
☐ 532 Milt May	.18	.08	.01
☐ 533 Lee Richard	.18	.08	.01
☐ 534 Stan Bahnsen	.18	.08	.01
☐ 535 Dave Nelson	.18	.08	.01
☐ 536 Mike Thompson	.18	.08	.01
☐ 537 Tony Muser	.18	.08	.01
☐ 538 Pat Darcy	.18	.08	.01
☐ 539 John Balaz	.18	.08	.01
☐ 540 Bill Freehan	.35	.14	.03
☐ 541 Steve Mingori	.18	.08	.01
☐ 542 Keith Hernandez	7.00	2.80	.70
☐ 543 Wayne Twitchell	.18	.08	.01
☐ 544 Pepe Frias	.18	.08	.01
☐ 545 Sparky Lyle	.35	.14	.03
☐ 546 Dave Rosello	.18	.08	.01
☐ 547 Roric Harrison	.18	.08	.01
☐ 548 Manny Mota	.25	.10	.02
☐ 549 Randy Tate	.18	.08	.01
☐ 550 Hank Aaron	9.00	3.75	.90
☐ 551 Jerry DaVanon	.18	.08	.01
☐ 552 Terry Humphrey	.18	.08	.01
☐ 553 Randy Moffitt	.18	.08	.01
☐ 554 Ray Fosse	.18	.08	.01
☐ 555 Dyar Miller	.18	.08	.01
☐ 556 Twins Team (checklist back)	.65	.15	.03
☐ 557 Dan Spillner	.18	.08	.01
☐ 558 Clarence Gaston	.18	.08	.01
☐ 559 Clyde Wright	.18	.08	.01
☐ 560 Jorge Orta	.18	.08	.01
☐ 561 Tom Carroll	.18	.08	.01
☐ 562 Adrian Garrett	.18	.08	.01
☐ 563 Larry Demery	.18	.08	.01

		NRMT	VG-E	GOOD
☐ 564	Bubble Gum Champ Kurt Bevacqua	.25	.10	.02
☐ 565	Tug McGraw	.35	.14	.03
☐ 566	Ken McMullen	.18	.08	.01
☐ 567	George Stone	.18	.08	.01
☐ 568	Rob Andrews	.18	.08	.01
☐ 569	Nelson Briles	.25	.10	.02
☐ 570	George Hendrick	.25	.10	.02
☐ 571	Don DeMola	.18	.08	.01
☐ 572	Rich Coggins	.18	.08	.01
☐ 573	Bill Travers	.18	.08	.01
☐ 574	Don Kessinger	.25	.10	.02
☐ 575	Dwight Evans	1.75	.75	.15
☐ 576	Maximino Leon	.18	.08	.01
☐ 577	Marc Hill	.18	.08	.01
☐ 578	Ted Kubiak	.18	.08	.01
☐ 579	Clay Kirby	.18	.08	.01
☐ 580	Bert Campaneris	.25	.10	.02
☐ 581	Cardinals Team (checklist back)	.65	.15	.03
☐ 582	Mike Kekich	.18	.08	.01
☐ 583	Tommy Helms	.25	.10	.02
☐ 584	Stan Wall	.18	.08	.01
☐ 585	Joe Torre	.50	.20	.05
☐ 586	Ron Schueler	.18	.08	.01
☐ 587	Leo Cardenas	.18	.08	.01
☐ 588	Kevin Kobel	.18	.08	.01
☐ 589	Rookie Pitchers Santo Alcala Mike Flanagan Joe Pactwa Pablo Torrealba	2.50	1.00	.25
☐ 590	Rookie Outfielders Henry Cruz Chet Lemon Ellis Valentine Terry Whitfield	1.25	.50	.12
☐ 591	Rookie Pitchers Steve Grilli Craig Mitchell Jose Sosa George Throop	.25	.10	.02
☐ 592	Rookie Infielders Willie Randolph Dave McKay Jerry Royster Roy Staiger	5.00	2.00	.50

		NRMT	VG-E	GOOD
☐ 593	Rookie Pitchers Larry Anderson Ken Crosby Mark Littell Butch Metzger	.35	.14	.03
☐ 594	Rookie Catchers/OF Andy Merchant Ed Ott Royle Stillman Jerry White	.35	.14	.03
☐ 595	Rookie Pitchers Art DeFillipis Randy Lerch Sid Monge Steve Barr	.35	.14	.03
☐ 596	Rookie Infielders Craig Reynolds Lamar Johnson Johnnie LeMaster Jerry Manuel	.50	.20	.05
☐ 597	Rookie Pitchers Don Aase Jack Kucek Frank LaCorte Mike Pazik	.75	.30	.07
☐ 598	Rookie Outfielders Hector Cruz Jamie Quirk Jerry Turner Joe Wallis	.35	.14	.03
☐ 599	Rookie Pitchers Rob Dressler Ron Guidry Bob McClure Pat Zachry	12.00	5.00	1.20
☐ 600	Tom Seaver	4.50	1.80	.45
☐ 601	Ken Rudolph	.18	.08	.01
☐ 602	Doug Konieczny	.18	.08	.01
☐ 603	Jim Holt	.18	.08	.01
☐ 604	Joe Lovitto	.18	.08	.01
☐ 605	Al Downing	.25	.10	.02
☐ 606	Milwaukee Brewers Team Card (checklist back)	.65	.15	.03
☐ 607	Rich Hinton	.18	.08	.01
☐ 608	Vic Correll	.18	.08	.01
☐ 609	Fred Norman	.18	.08	.01
☐ 610	Greg Luzinski	.50	.20	.05
☐ 611	Rich Folkers	.18	.08	.01

		NRMT	VG-E	GOOD
☐ 612	Joe Lahoud	.18	.08	.01
☐ 613	Tim Johnson	.18	.08	.01
☐ 614	Fernando Arroyo	.18	.08	.01
☐ 615	Mike Cubbage	.18	.08	.01
☐ 616	Buck Martinez	.18	.08	.01
☐ 617	Darold Knowles	.18	.08	.01
☐ 618	Jack Brohamer	.18	.08	.01
☐ 619	Bill Butler	.18	.08	.01
☐ 620	Al Oliver	.50	.20	.05
☐ 621	Tom Hall	.18	.08	.01
☐ 622	Rick Auerbach	.18	.08	.01
☐ 623	Bob Allietta	.18	.08	.01
☐ 624	Tony Taylor	.18	.08	.01
☐ 625	J.R. Richard	.25	.10	.02
☐ 626	Bob Sheldon	.18	.08	.01
☐ 627	Bill Plummer	.18	.08	.01
☐ 628	John D'Acquisto	.18	.08	.01
☐ 629	Sandy Alomar	.18	.08	.01
☐ 630	Chris Speier	.25	.10	.02
☐ 631	Braves Team (checklist back)	.65	.15	.03
☐ 632	Rogelio Moret	.18	.08	.01
☐ 633	John Stearns	.25	.10	.02
☐ 634	Larry Christenson	.18	.08	.01
☐ 635	Jim Fregosi	.35	.14	.03
☐ 636	Joe Decker	.18	.08	.01
☐ 637	Bruce Bochte	.25	.10	.02
☐ 638	Doyle Alexander	.35	.14	.03
☐ 639	Fred Kendall	.18	.08	.01
☐ 640	Bill Madlock	.75	.30	.07
☐ 641	Tom Paciorek	.18	.08	.01
☐ 642	Dennis Blair	.18	.08	.01
☐ 643	Checklist 529-660	.80	.10	.02
☐ 644	Tom Bradley	.18	.08	.01
☐ 645	Darrell Porter	.25	.10	.02
☐ 646	John Lowenstein	.18	.08	.01
☐ 647	Ramon Hernandez	.18	.08	.01
☐ 648	Al Cowens	.25	.10	.02
☐ 649	Dave Roberts	.18	.08	.01
☐ 650	Thurman Munson	5.00	2.00	.50
☐ 651	John Odom	.18	.08	.01
☐ 652	Ed Armbrister	.18	.08	.01
☐ 653	Mike Norris	.25	.10	.02
☐ 654	Doug Griffin	.18	.08	.01
☐ 655	Mike Vail	.18	.08	.01
☐ 656	Chicago White Sox Team Card (checklist back)	.65	.15	.03
☐ 657	Roy Smalley	.60	.24	.06

		NRMT	VG-E	GOOD
☐ 658	Jerry Johnson	.18	.08	.01
☐ 659	Ben Oglivie	.25	.10	.02
☐ 660	Dave Lopes	.65	.12	.02

1976 Topps Traded

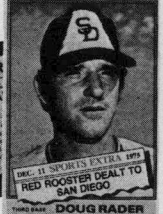

*The cards in this 44-card set measure 2 ½"
by 3 ½". The 1976 Topps Traded set contains 43 players and one unnumbered
checklist card. The individuals pictured were
traded after the Topps regular set was
printed. A "Sports Extra" heading design is
found on each picture and is also used to
introduce the biographical section of the
reverse. Each card is numbered according
to the player's regular 1976 card with the
addition of "T" to indicate his new status.*

	NRMT	VG-E	GOOD
Complete Set (44)	6.50	2.60	.65
Common Player	.12	.05	.01

		NRMT	VG-E	GOOD
☐ 27T	Ed Figueroa	.12	.05	.01
☐ 28T	Dusty Baker	.30	.12	.03
☐ 44T	Doug Rader	.20	.08	.02
☐ 58T	Ron Reed	.15	.06	.01
☐ 74T	Oscar Gamble	.20	.08	.02
☐ 80T	Jim Kaat	.75	.30	.07
☐ 83T	Jim Spencer	.12	.05	.01
☐ 85T	Mickey Rivers	.15	.06	.01
☐ 99T	Lee Lacy	.15	.06	.01
☐ 120T	Rusty Staub	.40	.16	.04
☐ 127T	Larvell Blanks	.12	.05	.01

	NRMT	VG-E	GOOD
☐ 146T George Medich	.12	.05	.01
☐ 158T Ken Reitz	.12	.05	.01
☐ 208T Mike Lum	.12	.05	.01
☐ 211T Clay Carroll	.12	.05	.01
☐ 231T Tom House	.15	.06	.01
☐ 250T Fergie Jenkins	.75	.30	.07
☐ 259T Darrel Chaney	.12	.05	.01
☐ 292T Leon Roberts	.12	.05	.01
☐ 296T Pat Dobson	.15	.06	.01
☐ 309T Bill Melton	.12	.05	.01
☐ 338T Bob Bailey	.12	.05	.01
☐ 380T Bobby Bonds	.30	.12	.03
☐ 383T John Ellis	.12	.05	.01
☐ 385T Mickey Lolich	.30	.12	.03
☐ 401T Ken Brett	.12	.05	.01
☐ 410T Ralph Garr	.15	.06	.01
☐ 411T Bill Singer	.12	.05	.01
☐ 428T Jim Crawford	.12	.05	.01
☐ 434T Morris Nettles	.12	.05	.01
☐ 464T Ken Henderson	.12	.05	.01
☐ 497T Joe McIntosh	.12	.05	.01
☐ 524T Pete Falcone	.12	.05	.01
☐ 527T Mike Anderson	.12	.05	.01
☐ 528T Dock Ellis	.12	.05	.01
☐ 532T Milt May	.12	.05	.01
☐ 554T Ray Fosse	.12	.05	.01
☐ 579T Clay Kirby	.12	.05	.01
☐ 583T Tommy Helms	.15	.06	.01
☐ 592T Willie Randolph	.90	.36	.09
☐ 618T Jack Brohamer	.12	.05	.01
☐ 632T Rogelio Moret	.12	.05	.01
☐ 649T Dave Roberts	.12	.05	.01
☐ xxxT= Traded Checklist ..	.50	.05	.01
(unnumbered)			

1977 Topps

The cards in this 660-card set measure 2 ½"
by 3 ½". In 1977 for the fifth consecutive
year, Topps produced a 660-card baseball
set. The player's name, team affiliation, and
his position are compactly arranged over the
picture area and a facsimile autograph appears on the photo. Team cards feature a
checklist of that team's players in the set and
a small picture of the manager on the front
of the card. Appearing for the first time are
the series "Brothers" (631-634) and "Turn
Back The Clock" (433-437). Other subseries
in the set are League Leaders (1-8), Record
Breakers (231-234), Playoffs cards (276-
277), World Series cards (411-413), and
Rookie Prospects (472-479 and 487-494).
The key card in the set is the rookie card of
Dale Murphy (476). Cards numbered 23 or
lower which feature Yankees and do not follow the numbering checklisted below are not
necessarily error cards. They are probably
Burger King cards, a separate set with its
own pricing and mass distribution. Burger
King cards are indistinguishable from the
corresponding Topps cards except for the
card numbering difference and the fact that
Burger King cards do not have a printing
sheet designation (such as A through F like
the regular Topps) anywhere on the card
back in very small print.

	NRMT	VG-E	GOOD
Complete Set (660)	275.00	110.00	27.00
Common Player (1-660) ..	.15	.06	.01

			NRMT	VG-E	GOOD
☐	1	Batting Leaders	2.00	.00	.00
		George Brett			
		Bill Madlock			
☐	2	Home Run Leaders	.75	.30	.07
		Graig Nettles			
		Mike Schmidt			
☐	3	RBI Leaders	.25	.10	.02
		Lee May			
		George Foster			
☐	4	Stolen Base Leaders	.25	.10	.02
		Bill North			
		Dave Lopes			
☐	5	Victory Leaders	.35	.14	.03
		Jim Palmer			
		Randy Jones			
☐	6	Strikeout Leaders ..	2.00	.80	.20
		Nolan Ryan			
		Tom Seaver			
☐	7	ERA Leaders	.25	.10	.02
		Mark Fidrych			
		John Denny			
☐	8	Leading Firemen ...	.25	.10	.02
		Bill Campbell			
		Rawly Eastwick			
☐	9	Doug Rader	.25	.10	.02
☐	10	Reggie Jackson ...	7.00	2.80	.70
☐	11	Rob Dressler	.15	.06	.01
☐	12	Larry Haney	.15	.06	.01
☐	13	Luis Gomez	.15	.06	.01
☐	14	Tommy Smith	.15	.06	.01
☐	15	Don Gullett	.15	.06	.01
☐	16	Bob Jones	.15	.06	.01
☐	17	Steve Stone	.25	.10	.02
☐	18	Indians Team/Mgr. .	.65	.15	.03
		Frank Robinson			
		(checklist back)			
☐	19	John D'Acquisto	.15	.06	.01
☐	20	Graig Nettles	.75	.30	.07
☐	21	Ken Forsch	.15	.06	.01
☐	22	Bill Freehan	.25	.10	.02
☐	23	Dan Driessen	.25	.10	.02
☐	24	Carl Morton	.15	.06	.01
☐	25	Dwight Evans	1.50	.60	.15
☐	26	Ray Sadecki	.15	.06	.01
☐	27	Bill Buckner	.35	.14	.03
☐	28	Woodie Fryman	.15	.06	.01
☐	29	Bucky Dent	.35	.14	.03
☐	30	Greg Luzinski	.35	.14	.03
☐	31	Jim Todd	.15	.06	.01

			NRMT	VG-E	GOOD
☐	32	Checklist 1	.70	.08	.02
☐	33	Wayne Garland	.15	.06	.01
☐	34	Angels Team/Mgr. .	.65	.15	.03
		Norm Sherry			
		(checklist back)			
☐	35	Rennie Stennett	.15	.06	.01
☐	36	John Ellis	.15	.06	.01
☐	37	Steve Hargan	.15	.06	.01
☐	38	Craig Kusick	.15	.06	.01
☐	39	Tom Griffin	.15	.06	.01
☐	40	Bobby Murcer	.35	.14	.03
☐	41	Jim Kern	.15	.06	.01
☐	42	Jose Cruz	.25	.10	.02
☐	43	Ray Bare	.15	.06	.01
☐	44	Bud Harrelson	.25	.10	.02
☐	45	Rawly Eastwick	.15	.06	.01
☐	46	Buck Martinez	.15	.06	.01
☐	47	Lynn McGlothen	.15	.06	.01
☐	48	Tom Paciorek	.15	.06	.01
☐	49	Grant Jackson	.15	.06	.01
☐	50	Ron Cey	.35	.14	.03
☐	51	Brewers Team/Mgr. .	.65	.15	.03
		Alex Grammas			
		(checklist back)			
☐	52	Ellis Valentine	.15	.06	.01
☐	53	Paul Mitchell	.15	.06	.01
☐	54	Sandy Alomar	.15	.06	.01
☐	55	Jeff Burroughs	.25	.10	.02
☐	56	Rudy May	.15	.06	.01
☐	57	Marc Hill	.15	.06	.01
☐	58	Chet Lemon	.25	.10	.02
☐	59	Larry Christenson .	.15	.06	.01
☐	60	Jim Rice	5.00	2.00	.50
☐	61	Manny Sanguillen .	.25	.10	.02
☐	62	Eric Raich	.15	.06	.01
☐	63	Tito Fuentes	.15	.06	.01
☐	64	Larry Biittner	.15	.06	.01
☐	65	Skip Lockwood	.15	.06	.01
☐	66	Roy Smalley	.25	.10	.02
☐	67	Joaquin Andujar	1.00	.40	.10
☐	68	Bruce Bochte	.15	.06	.01
☐	69	Jim Crawford	.15	.06	.01
☐	70	Johnny Bench	4.50	1.80	.45
☐	71	Dock Ellis	.15	.06	.01
☐	72	Mike Anderson	.15	.06	.01
☐	73	Charlie Williams	.15	.06	.01
☐	74	A's Team/Mgr.	.65	.15	.03
		Jack McKeon			
		(checklist back)			

		NRMT	VG-E	GOOD
☐ 75	Dennis Leonard ...	.25	.10	.02
☐ 76	Tim Foli	.15	.06	.01
☐ 77	Dyar Miller	.15	.06	.01
☐ 78	Bob Davis	.15	.06	.01
☐ 79	Don Money	.15	.06	.01
☐ 80	Andy Messersmith .	.25	.10	.02
☐ 81	Juan Beniquez	.15	.06	.01
☐ 82	Jim Rooker	.15	.06	.01
☐ 83	Kevin Bell	.15	.06	.01
☐ 84	Ollie Brown	.15	.06	.01
☐ 85	Duane Kuiper	.15	.06	.01
☐ 86	Pat Zachry	.15	.06	.01
☐ 87	Glenn Borgmann ...	.15	.06	.01
☐ 88	Stan Wall	.15	.06	.01
☐ 89	Butch Hobson	.15	.06	.01
☐ 90	Cesar Cedeno	.25	.10	.02
☐ 91	John Verhoeven	.15	.06	.01
☐ 92	Dave Rosello	.15	.06	.01
☐ 93	Tom Poquette	.15	.06	.01
☐ 94	Craig Swan	.15	.06	.01
☐ 95	Keith Hernandez ...	3.50	1.40	.35
☐ 96	Lou Piniella	.35	.14	.03
☐ 97	Dave Heaverlo	.15	.06	.01
☐ 98	Milt May	.15	.06	.01
☐ 99	Tom Hausman	.15	.06	.01
☐ 100	Joe Morgan	1.50	.60	.15
☐ 101	Dick Bosman	.15	.06	.01
☐ 102	Jose Morales	.15	.06	.01
☐ 103	Mike Bacsik	.15	.06	.01
☐ 104	Omar Moreno	.25	.10	.02
☐ 105	Steve Yeager	.15	.06	.01
☐ 106	Mike Flanagan	.35	.14	.03
☐ 107	Bill Melton	.15	.06	.01
☐ 108	Alan Foster	.15	.06	.01
☐ 109	Jorge Orta	.15	.06	.01
☐ 110	Steve Carlton	4.00	1.60	.40
☐ 111	Rico Petrocelli	.25	.10	.02
☐ 112	Bill Greif	.15	.06	.01
☐ 113	Blue Jays Leaders .	.50	.10	.02
	Roy Hartsfield MG			
	Don Leppert CO			
	Bob Miller CO			
	Jackie Moore CO			
	Harry Warner CO			
	(checklist back)			
☐ 114	Bruce Dal Canton ..	.15	.06	.01
☐ 115	Rick Manning	.15	.06	.01
☐ 116	Joe Niekro	.35	.14	.03
☐ 117	Frank White	.35	.14	.03

		NRMT	VG-E	GOOD
☐ 118	Rick Jones	.15	.06	.01
☐ 119	John Stearns	.15	.06	.01
☐ 120	Rod Carew	4.00	1.60	.40
☐ 121	Gary Nolan	.15	.06	.01
☐ 122	Ben Oglivie	.25	.10	.02
☐ 123	Fred Stanley	.15	.06	.01
☐ 124	George Mitterwald .	.15	.06	.01
☐ 125	Bill Travers	.15	.06	.01
☐ 126	Rod Gilbreath	.15	.06	.01
☐ 127	Ron Fairly	.15	.06	.01
☐ 128	Tommy John	1.00	.40	.10
☐ 129	Mike Sadek	.15	.06	.01
☐ 130	Al Oliver	.35	.14	.03
☐ 131	Orlando Ramirez ...	.15	.06	.01
☐ 132	Chip Lang	.15	.06	.01
☐ 133	Ralph Garr	.15	.06	.01
☐ 134	Padres Team/Mgr.	.65	.15	.03
	John McNamara			
	(checklist back)			
☐ 135	Mark Belanger	.25	.10	.02
☐ 136	Jerry Mumphrey ...	.35	.14	.03
☐ 137	Jeff Terpko	.15	.06	.01
☐ 138	Bob Stinson	.15	.06	.01
☐ 139	Fred Norman	.15	.06	.01
☐ 140	Mike Schmidt	9.00	3.75	.90
☐ 141	Mark Littell	.15	.06	.01
☐ 142	Steve Dillard	.15	.06	.01
☐ 143	Ed Herrmann	.15	.06	.01
☐ 144	Bruce Sutter	2.50	1.00	.25
☐ 145	Tom Veryzer	.15	.06	.01
☐ 146	Dusty Baker	.25	.10	.02
☐ 147	Jackie Brown	.15	.06	.01
☐ 148	Fran Healy	.15	.06	.01
☐ 149	Mike Cubbage	.15	.06	.01
☐ 150	Tom Seaver	4.00	1.60	.40
☐ 151	Johnny LeMaster ..	.15	.06	.01
☐ 152	Gaylord Perry	1.75	.70	.17
☐ 153	Ron Jackson	.15	.06	.01
☐ 154	Dave Giusti	.15	.06	.01
☐ 155	Joe Rudi	.25	.10	.02
☐ 156	Pete Mackanin	.15	.06	.01
☐ 157	Ken Brett	.15	.06	.01
☐ 158	Ted Kubiak	.15	.06	.01
☐ 159	Bernie Carbo	.15	.06	.01
☐ 160	Will McEnaney	.15	.06	.01
☐ 161	Garry Templeton ..	1.00	.40	.10
☐ 162	Mike Cuellar	.25	.10	.02
☐ 163	Dave Hilton	.15	.06	.01
☐ 164	Tug McGraw	.35	.14	.03

		NRMT	VG-E	GOOD
☐ 165	Jim Wynn	.25	.10	.02
☐ 166	Bill Campbell	.15	.06	.01
☐ 167	Rich Hebner	.25	.10	.02
☐ 168	Charlie Spikes	.15	.06	.01
☐ 169	Darold Knowles	.15	.06	.01
☐ 170	Thurman Munson	4.00	1.60	.40
☐ 171	Ken Sanders	.15	.06	.01
☐ 172	John Milner	.15	.06	.01
☐ 173	Chuck Scrivener	.15	.06	.01
☐ 174	Nelson Briles	.25	.10	.02
☐ 175	Butch Wynegar	.60	.24	.06
☐ 176	Bob Robertson	.15	.06	.01
☐ 177	Bart Johnson	.15	.06	.01
☐ 178	Bombo Rivera	.15	.06	.01
☐ 179	Paul Hartzell	.15	.06	.01
☐ 180	Dave Lopes	.25	.10	.02
☐ 181	Ken McMullen	.15	.06	.01
☐ 182	Dan Spillner	.15	.06	.01
☐ 183	Cardinals Team/Mgr.	.65	.15	.03
	Vern Rapp			
	(checklist back)			
☐ 184	Bo McLaughlin	.15	.06	.01
☐ 185	Sixto Lezcano	.15	.06	.01
☐ 186	Doug Flynn	.15	.06	.01
☐ 187	Dick Pole	.15	.06	.01
☐ 188	Bob Tolan	.15	.06	.01
☐ 189	Rick Dempsey	.25	.10	.02
☐ 190	Ray Burris	.15	.06	.01
☐ 191	Doug Griffin	.15	.06	.01
☐ 192	Clarence Gaston	.15	.06	.01
☐ 193	Larry Gura	.25	.10	.02
☐ 194	Gary Matthews	.25	.10	.02
☐ 195	Ed Figueroa	.15	.06	.01
☐ 196	Len Randle	.15	.06	.01
☐ 197	Ed Ott	.15	.06	.01
☐ 198	Wilbur Wood	.25	.10	.02
☐ 199	Pepe Frias	.15	.06	.01
☐ 200	Frank Tanana	.35	.14	.03
☐ 201	Ed Kranepool	.25	.10	.02
☐ 202	Tom Johnson	.15	.06	.01
☐ 203	Ed Armbrister	.15	.06	.01
☐ 204	Jeff Newman	.15	.06	.01
☐ 205	Pete Falcone	.15	.06	.01
☐ 206	Boog Powell	.35	.14	.03
☐ 207	Glenn Abbott	.15	.06	.01
☐ 208	Checklist 2	.70	.08	.01
☐ 209	Rob Andrews	.15	.06	.01
☐ 210	Fred Lynn	1.50	.60	.15

		NRMT	VG-E	GOOD
☐ 211	Giants Team/Mgr.	.65	.15	.03
	Joe Altobelli			
	(checklist back)			
☐ 212	Jim Mason	.15	.06	.01
☐ 213	Maximino Leon	.15	.06	.01
☐ 214	Darrell Porter	.15	.06	.01
☐ 215	Butch Metzger	.15	.06	.01
☐ 216	Doug DeCinces	.35	.14	.03
☐ 217	Tom Underwood	.15	.06	.01
☐ 218	John Wathan	1.50	.60	.15
☐ 219	Joe Coleman	.15	.06	.01
☐ 220	Chris Chambliss	.35	.14	.03
☐ 221	Bob Bailey	.15	.06	.01
☐ 222	Francisco Barrios	.15	.06	.01
☐ 223	Earl Williams	.15	.06	.01
☐ 224	Rusty Torres	.15	.06	.01
☐ 225	Bob Apodaca	.15	.06	.01
☐ 226	Leroy Stanton	.15	.06	.01
☐ 227	Joe Sambito	.35	.14	.03
☐ 228	Twins Team/Mgr.	.65	.15	.03
	Gene Mauch			
	(checklist back)			
☐ 229	Don Kessinger	.25	.10	.02
☐ 230	Vida Blue	.35	.14	.03
☐ 231	RB: George Brett	2.00	.80	.20
	Most cons. games			
	with 3 or more hits			
☐ 232	RB: Minnie Minoso	.25	.10	.02
	Oldest to hit safely			
☐ 233	RB: Jose Morales, Most	.25	.10	.02
	pinch-hits, season			
☐ 234	RB: Nolan Ryan	1.75	.70	.17
	Most seasons, 300			
	or more strikeouts			
☐ 235	Cecil Cooper	.50	.20	.05
☐ 236	Tom Buskey	.15	.06	.01
☐ 237	Gene Clines	.15	.06	.01
☐ 238	Tippy Martinez	.25	.10	.02
☐ 239	Bill Plummer	.15	.06	.01
☐ 240	Ron LeFlore	.25	.10	.02
☐ 241	Dave Tomlin	.15	.06	.01
☐ 242	Ken Henderson	.15	.06	.01
☐ 243	Ron Reed	.15	.06	.01
☐ 244	John Mayberry	.35	.14	.03
	(cartoon mentions T206 Wagner)			
☐ 245	Rick Rhoden	.35	.14	.03
☐ 246	Mike Vail	.15	.06	.01
☐ 247	Chris Knapp	.15	.06	.01
☐ 248	Wilbur Howard	.15	.06	.01

		NRMT	VG-E	GOOD
☐ 249	Pete Redfern	.15	.06	.01
☐ 250	Bill Madlock	.50	.20	.05
☐ 251	Tony Muser	.15	.06	.01
☐ 252	Dale Murray	.15	.06	.01
☐ 253	John Hale	.15	.06	.01
☐ 254	Doyle Alexander	.35	.14	.03
☐ 255	George Scott	.25	.10	.02
☐ 256	Joe Hoerner	.15	.06	.01
☐ 257	Mike Miley	.15	.06	.01
☐ 258	Luis Tiant	.35	.14	.03
☐ 259	Mets Team/Mgr.	.75	.20	.04
	Joe Frazier			
	(checklist back)			
☐ 260	J.R. Richard	.25	.10	.02
☐ 261	Phil Garner	.25	.10	.02
☐ 262	Al Cowens	.25	.10	.02
☐ 263	Mike Marshall	.25	.10	.02
☐ 264	Tom Hutton	.15	.06	.01
☐ 265	Mark Fidrych	.50	.20	.05
☐ 266	Derrel Thomas	.15	.06	.01
☐ 267	Ray Fosse	.15	.06	.01
☐ 268	Rick Sawyer	.15	.06	.01
☐ 269	Joe Lis	.15	.06	.01
☐ 270	Dave Parker	2.00	.80	.20
☐ 271	Terry Forster	.25	.10	.02
☐ 272	Lee Lacy	.25	.10	.02
☐ 273	Eric Soderholm	.15	.06	.01
☐ 274	Don Stanhouse	.15	.06	.01
☐ 275	Mike Hargrove	.15	.06	.01
☐ 276	AL Champs	.35	.14	.03
	Chambliss' homer			
	decides it			
☐ 277	NL Champs	.35	.14	.03
	Reds sweep Phillies			
☐ 278	Danny Frisella	.15	.06	.01
☐ 279	Joe Wallis	.15	.06	.01
☐ 280	Jim Hunter	1.75	.70	.17
☐ 281	Roy Staiger	.15	.06	.01
☐ 282	Sid Monge	.15	.06	.01
☐ 283	Jerry DaVanon	.15	.06	.01
☐ 284	Mike Norris	.15	.06	.01
☐ 285	Brooks Robinson	2.50	1.00	.25
☐ 286	Johnny Grubb	.15	.06	.01
☐ 287	Reds Team/Mgr.	.75	.20	.04
	Sparky Anderson			
	(checklist back)			
☐ 288	Bob Montgomery	.15	.06	.01
☐ 289	Gene Garber	.15	.06	.01
☐ 290	Amos Otis	.35	.14	.03
☐ 291	Jason Thompson	.35	.14	.03
☐ 292	Rogelio Moret	.15	.06	.01
☐ 293	Jack Brohamer	.15	.06	.01
☐ 294	George Medich	.15	.06	.01
☐ 295	Gary Carter	6.50	2.60	.65
☐ 296	Don Hood	.15	.06	.01
☐ 297	Ken Reitz	.15	.06	.01
☐ 298	Charlie Hough	.25	.10	.02
☐ 299	Otto Velez	.15	.06	.01
☐ 300	Jerry Koosman	.35	.14	.03
☐ 301	Toby Harrah	.25	.10	.02
☐ 302	Mike Garman	.15	.06	.01
☐ 303	Gene Tenace	.25	.10	.02
☐ 304	Jim Hughes	.15	.06	.01
☐ 305	Mickey Rivers	.25	.10	.02
☐ 306	Rick Waits	.15	.06	.01
☐ 307	Gary Sutherland	.15	.06	.01
☐ 308	Gene Pentz	.15	.06	.01
☐ 309	Red Sox Team/Mgr.	.65	.15	.03
	Don Zimmer			
	(checklist back)			
☐ 310	Larry Bowa	.50	.20	.05
☐ 311	Vern Ruhle	.15	.06	.01
☐ 312	Rob Belloir	.15	.06	.01
☐ 313	Paul Blair	.25	.10	.02
☐ 314	Steve Mingori	.15	.06	.01
☐ 315	Dave Chalk	.15	.06	.01
☐ 316	Steve Rogers	.25	.10	.02
☐ 317	Kurt Bevacqua	.15	.06	.01
☐ 318	Duffy Dyer	.15	.06	.01
☐ 319	Rich Gossage	.75	.30	.07
☐ 320	Ken Griffey	.35	.14	.03
☐ 321	Dave Goltz	.15	.06	.01
☐ 322	Bill Russell	.25	.10	.02
☐ 323	Larry Lintz	.15	.06	.01
☐ 324	John Curtis	.15	.06	.01
☐ 325	Mike Ivie	.15	.06	.01
☐ 326	Jesse Jefferson	.15	.06	.01
☐ 327	Astros Team/Mgr.	.65	.15	.03
	Bill Virdon			
	(checklist back)			
☐ 328	Tommy Boggs	.15	.06	.01
☐ 329	Ron Hodges	.15	.06	.01
☐ 330	George Hendrick	.25	.10	.02
☐ 331	Jim Colborn	.15	.06	.01
☐ 332	Elliott Maddox	.15	.06	.01
☐ 333	Paul Reuschel	.15	.06	.01
☐ 334	Bill Stein	.15	.06	.01
☐ 335	Bill Robinson	.25	.10	.02

		NRMT	VG-E	GOOD
☐ 336	Denny Doyle	.15	.06	.01
☐ 337	Ron Schueler	.15	.06	.01
☐ 338	Dave Duncan	.15	.06	.01
☐ 339	Adrian Devine	.15	.06	.01
☐ 340	Hal McRae	.25	.10	.02
☐ 341	Joe Kerrigan	.15	.06	.01
☐ 342	Jerry Remy	.15	.06	.01
☐ 343	Ed Halicki	.15	.06	.01
☐ 344	Brian Downing	.25	.10	.02
☐ 345	Reggie Smith	.35	.14	.03
☐ 346	Bill Singer	.15	.06	.01
☐ 347	George Foster	1.25	.50	.12
☐ 348	Brent Strom	.15	.06	.01
☐ 349	Jim Holt	.15	.06	.01
☐ 350	Larry Dierker	.15	.06	.01
☐ 351	Jim Sundberg	.25	.10	.02
☐ 352	Mike Phillips	.15	.06	.01
☐ 353	Stan Thomas	.15	.06	.01
☐ 354	Pirates Team/Mgr.	.65	.15	.03
	Chuck Tanner			
	(checklist back)			
☐ 355	Lou Brock	2.25	.90	.22
☐ 356	Checklist 3	.70	.08	.01
☐ 357	Tim McCarver	.35	.14	.03
☐ 358	Tom House	.25	.10	.02
☐ 359	Willie Randolph	.60	.24	.06
☐ 360	Rick Monday	.25	.10	.02
☐ 361	Eduardo Rodriguez	.15	.06	.01
☐ 362	Tommy Davis	.25	.10	.02
☐ 363	Dave Roberts	.15	.06	.01
☐ 364	Vic Correll	.15	.06	.01
☐ 365	Mike Torrez	.25	.10	.02
☐ 366	Ted Sizemore	.15	.06	.01
☐ 367	Dave Hamilton	.15	.06	.01
☐ 368	Mike Jorgensen	.15	.06	.01
☐ 369	Terry Humphrey	.15	.06	.01
☐ 370	John Montefusco	.25	.10	.02
☐ 371	Royals Team/Mgr.	.65	.15	.03
	Whitey Herzog			
	(checklist back)			
☐ 372	Rich Folkers	.15	.06	.01
☐ 373	Bert Campaneris	.25	.10	.02
☐ 374	Kent Tekulve	.25	.10	.02
☐ 375	Larry Hisle	.25	.10	.02
☐ 376	Nino Espinosa	.15	.06	.01
☐ 377	Dave McKay	.15	.06	.01
☐ 378	Jim Umbarger	.15	.06	.01
☐ 379	Larry Cox	.15	.06	.01
☐ 380	Lee May	.25	.10	.02

		NRMT	VG-E	GOOD
☐ 381	Bob Forsch	.25	.10	.02
☐ 382	Charlie Moore	.15	.06	.01
☐ 383	Stan Bahnsen	.15	.06	.01
☐ 384	Darrel Chaney	.15	.06	.01
☐ 385	Dave LaRoche	.15	.06	.01
☐ 386	Manny Mota	.25	.10	.02
☐ 387	Yankees Team	.75	.20	.04
	(checklist back)			
☐ 388	Terry Harmon	.15	.06	.01
☐ 389	Ken Kravec	.15	.06	.01
☐ 390	Dave Winfield	4.00	1.60	.40
☐ 391	Dan Warthen	.15	.06	.01
☐ 392	Phil Roof	.15	.06	.01
☐ 393	John Lowenstein	.15	.06	.01
☐ 394	Bill Laxton	.15	.06	.01
☐ 395	Manny Trillo	.15	.06	.01
☐ 396	Tom Murphy	.15	.06	.01
☐ 397	Larry Herndon	.35	.14	.03
☐ 398	Tom Burgmeier	.15	.06	.01
☐ 399	Bruce Boisclair	.15	.06	.01
☐ 400	Steve Garvey	3.50	1.40	.35
☐ 401	Mickey Scott	.15	.06	.01
☐ 402	Tommy Helms	.15	.06	.01
☐ 403	Tom Grieve	.25	.10	.02
☐ 404	Eric Rasmussen	.15	.06	.01
☐ 405	Claudell Washington	.25	.10	.02
☐ 406	Tim Johnson	.15	.06	.01
☐ 407	Dave Freisleben	.15	.06	.01
☐ 408	Cesar Tovar	.15	.06	.01
☐ 409	Pete Broberg	.15	.06	.01
☐ 410	Willie Montanez	.15	.06	.01
☐ 411	W.S. Games 1 and 2	.50	.20	.05
	Morgan homers opener;			
	Bench stars as			
	Reds take 2nd game			
☐ 412	W.S. Games 3 and 4	.50	.20	.05
	Reds stop Yankees;			
	Bench's two homers			
	wrap it up			
☐ 413	World Series Summary	.50	.20	.05
	Cincy wins 2nd			
	straight series			
☐ 414	Tommy Harper	.25	.10	.02
☐ 415	Jay Johnstone	.25	.10	.02
☐ 416	Chuck Hartenstein	.15	.06	.01
☐ 417	Wayne Garrett	.15	.06	.01
☐ 418	White Sox Team/Mgr.	.65	.15	.03
	Bob Lemon			
	(checklist back)			

		NRMT	VG-E	GOOD
☐ 419	Steve Swisher	.15	.06	.01
☐ 420	Rusty Staub	.35	.14	.03
☐ 421	Doug Rau	.15	.06	.01
☐ 422	Freddie Patek	.15	.06	.01
☐ 423	Gary Lavelle	.15	.06	.01
☐ 424	Steve Brye	.15	.06	.01
☐ 425	Joe Torre	.35	.14	.03
☐ 426	Dick Drago	.15	.06	.01
☐ 427	Dave Rader	.15	.06	.01
☐ 428	Rangers Team/Mgr. Frank Lucchesi (checklist back)	.65	.15	.03
☐ 429	Ken Boswell	.15	.06	.01
☐ 430	Fergie Jenkins	.60	.24	.06
☐ 431	Dave Collins (photo actually Bobby Jones)	.25	.10	.02
☐ 432	Buzz Capra	.15	.06	.01
☐ 433	Turn back clock 1972 Nate Colbert	.25	.10	.02
☐ 434	Turn back clock 1967 Yaz Triple Crown	2.00	.80	.20
☐ 435	Turn back clock 1962 Wills 104 steals	.35	.14	.03
☐ 436	Turn back clock 1957 Keegan hurls Majors' only no-hitter	.25	.10	.02
☐ 437	Turn back clock 1952 Kiner leads NL HR's 7th straight year	.35	.14	.03
☐ 438	Marty Perez	.15	.06	.01
☐ 439	Gorman Thomas	.35	.14	.03
☐ 440	Jon Matlack	.25	.10	.02
☐ 441	Larvell Blanks	.15	.06	.01
☐ 442	Braves Team/Mgr. Dave Bristol (checklist back)	.65	.15	.03
☐ 443	Lamar Johnson	.15	.06	.01
☐ 444	Wayne Twitchell	.15	.06	.01
☐ 445	Ken Singleton	.25	.10	.02
☐ 446	Bill Bonham	.15	.06	.01
☐ 447	Jerry Turner	.15	.06	.01
☐ 448	Ellie Rodriguez	.15	.06	.01
☐ 449	Al Fitzmorris	.15	.06	.01
☐ 450	Pete Rose	9.00	3.75	.90
☐ 451	Checklist 4	.70	.08	.01
☐ 452	Mike Caldwell	.15	.06	.01
☐ 453	Pedro Garcia	.15	.06	.01
☐ 454	Andy Etchebarren	.15	.06	.01
☐ 455	Rick Wise	.15	.06	.01

		NRMT	VG-E	GOOD
☐ 456	Leon Roberts	.15	.06	.01
☐ 457	Steve Luebber	.15	.06	.01
☐ 458	Leo Foster	.15	.06	.01
☐ 459	Steve Foucault	.15	.06	.01
☐ 460	Willie Stargell	2.50	1.00	.25
☐ 461	Dick Tidrow	.15	.06	.01
☐ 462	Don Baylor	.60	.24	.06
☐ 463	Jamie Quirk	.15	.06	.01
☐ 464	Randy Moffitt	.15	.06	.01
☐ 465	Rico Carty	.25	.10	.02
☐ 466	Fred Holdsworth	.15	.06	.01
☐ 467	Phillies Team/Mgr. Danny Ozark (checklist back)	.65	.15	.03
☐ 468	Ramon Hernandez	.15	.06	.01
☐ 469	Pat Kelly	.15	.06	.01
☐ 470	Ted Simmons	.50	.20	.05
☐ 471	Del Unser	.15	.06	.01
☐ 472	Rookie Pitchers Don Aase Bob McClure Gil Patterson Dave Wehrmeister	.35	.14	.03
☐ 473	Rookie Outfielders Andre Dawson Gene Richards John Scott Denny Walling	33.00	12.00	3.00
☐ 474	Rookie Shortstops Bob Bailor Kiko Garcia Craig Reynolds Alex Taveras	.25	.10	.02
☐ 475	Rookie Pitchers Chris Batton Rick Camp Scott McGregor Manny Sarmiento	.35	.14	.03
☐ 476	Rookie Catchers Gary Alexander Rick Cerone Dale Murphy Kevin Pasley	65.00	26.00	6.50
☐ 477	Rookie Infielders Doug Ault Rich Dauer Orlando Gonzalez Phil Mankowski	.25	.10	.02

		NRMT	VG-E	GOOD
☐ 478	Rookie Pitchers	.25	.10	.02
	Jim Gideon			
	Leon Hooten			
	Dave Johnson			
	Mark Lemongello			
☐ 479	Rookie Outfielders .	.25	.10	.02
	Brian Asselstine			
	Wayne Gross			
	Sam Mejias			
	Alvis Woods			
☐ 480	Carl Yastrzemski ...	5.00	2.00	.50
☐ 481	Roger Metzger	.15	.06	.01
☐ 482	Tony Solaita	.15	.06	.01
☐ 483	Richie Zisk	.15	.06	.01
☐ 484	Burt Hooton	.15	.06	.01
☐ 485	Roy White	.25	.10	.02
☐ 486	Ed Bane	.15	.06	.01
☐ 487	Rookie Pitchers	.25	.10	.02
	Larry Anderson			
	Ed Glynn			
	Joe Henderson			
	Greg Terlecky			
☐ 488	Rookie Outfielders .	20.00	8.00	2.00
	Jack Clark			
	Ruppert Jones			
	Lee Mazzilli			
	Dan Thomas			
☐ 489	Rookie Pitchers	.35	.14	.03
	Len Barker			
	Randy Lerch			
	Greg Minton			
	Mike Overy			
☐ 490	Rookie Shortstops .	.35	.14	.03
	Billy Almon			
	Mickey Klutts			
	Tommy McMillan			
	Mark Wagner			
☐ 491	Rookie Pitchers	1.00	.40	.10
	Mike Dupree			
	Denny Martinez			
	Craig Mitchell			
	Bob Sykes			
☐ 492	Rookie Outfielders .	1.00	.40	.10
	Tony Armas			
	Steve Kemp			
	Carlos Lopez			
	Gary Woods			

		NRMT	VG-E	GOOD
☐ 493	Rookie Pitchers ...	.75	.30	.07
	Mike Krukow			
	Jim Otten			
	Gary Wheelock			
	Mike Willis			
☐ 494	Rookie Infielders ..	.50	.20	.05
	Juan Bernhardt			
	Mike Champion			
	Jim Gantner			
	Bump Wills			
☐ 495	Al Hrabosky	.25	.10	.02
☐ 496	Gary Thomasson ...	.15	.06	.01
☐ 497	Clay Carroll	.15	.06	.01
☐ 498	Sal Bando	.25	.10	.02
☐ 499	Pablo Torrealba ...	.15	.06	.01
☐ 500	Dave Kingman	.50	.20	.05
☐ 501	Jim Bibby	.15	.06	.01
☐ 502	Randy Hundley ...	.15	.06	.01
☐ 503	Bill Lee	.25	.10	.02
☐ 504	Dodgers Team/Mgr.	.75	.20	.04
	Tom Lasorda			
	(checklist back)			
☐ 505	Oscar Gamble	.25	.10	.02
☐ 506	Steve Grilli	.15	.06	.01
☐ 507	Mike Hegan	.15	.06	.01
☐ 508	Dave Pagan	.15	.06	.01
☐ 509	Cookie Rojas	.25	.10	.02
☐ 510	John Candelaria ..	.75	.30	.07
☐ 511	Bill Fahey	.15	.06	.01
☐ 512	Jack Billingham ...	.15	.06	.01
☐ 513	Jerry Terrell	.15	.06	.01
☐ 514	Cliff Johnson	.15	.06	.01
☐ 515	Chris Speier	.15	.06	.01
☐ 516	Bake McBride	.15	.06	.01
☐ 517	Pete Vuckovich ...	.50	.20	.05
☐ 518	Cubs Team/Mgr. ..	.65	.15	.03
	Herman Franks			
	(checklist back)			
☐ 519	Don Kirkwood	.15	.06	.01
☐ 520	Garry Maddox	.25	.10	.02
☐ 521	Bob Grich	.25	.10	.02
☐ 522	Enzo Hernandez ..	.15	.06	.01
☐ 523	Rollie Fingers	1.00	.40	.10
☐ 524	Rowland Office ...	.15	.06	.01
☐ 525	Dennis Eckersley .	1.00	.40	.10
☐ 526	Larry Parrish	.35	.14	.03
☐ 527	Dan Meyer	.15	.06	.01
☐ 528	Bill Castro	.15	.06	.01
☐ 529	Jim Essian	.15	.06	.01

	NRMT	VG-E	GOOD
☐ 530 Rick Reuschel	.35	.14	.03
☐ 531 Lyman Bostock	.25	.10	.02
☐ 532 Jim Willoughby	.15	.06	.01
☐ 533 Mickey Stanley	.15	.06	.01
☐ 534 Paul Splittorff	.15	.06	.01
☐ 535 Cesar Geronimo	.15	.06	.01
☐ 536 Vic Albury	.15	.06	.01
☐ 537 Dave Roberts	.15	.06	.01
☐ 538 Frank Taveras	.15	.06	.01
☐ 539 Mike Wallace	.15	.06	.01
☐ 540 Bob Watson	.25	.10	.02
☐ 541 John Denny	.25	.10	.02
☐ 542 Frank Duffy	.15	.06	.01
☐ 543 Ron Blomberg	.15	.06	.01
☐ 544 Gary Ross	.15	.06	.01
☐ 545 Bob Boone	.35	.14	.03
☐ 546 Orioles Team/Mgr.	.75	.20	.04
Earl Weaver			
(checklist back)			
☐ 547 Willie McCovey	2.00	.80	.20
☐ 548 Joel Youngblood	.15	.06	.01
☐ 549 Jerry Royster	.15	.06	.01
☐ 550 Randy Jones	.15	.06	.01
☐ 551 Bill North	.15	.06	.01
☐ 552 Pepe Mangual	.15	.06	.01
☐ 553 Jack Heidemann	.15	.06	.01
☐ 554 Bruce Kimm	.15	.06	.01
☐ 555 Dan Ford	.15	.06	.01
☐ 556 Doug Bird	.15	.06	.01
☐ 557 Jerry White	.15	.06	.01
☐ 558 Elias Sosa	.15	.06	.01
☐ 559 Alan Bannister	.15	.06	.01
☐ 560 Dave Concepcion	.35	.14	.03
☐ 561 Pete LaCock	.15	.06	.01
☐ 562 Checklist 5	.70	.08	.01
☐ 563 Bruce Kison	.15	.06	.01
☐ 564 Alan Ashby	.25	.10	.02
☐ 565 Mickey Lolich	.35	.14	.03
☐ 566 Rick Miller	.15	.06	.01
☐ 567 Enos Cabell	.15	.06	.01
☐ 568 Carlos May	.15	.06	.01
☐ 569 Jim Lonborg	.25	.10	.02
☐ 570 Bobby Bonds	.35	.14	.03
☐ 571 Darrell Evans	.50	.20	.05
☐ 572 Ross Grimsley	.15	.06	.01
☐ 573 Joe Ferguson	.15	.06	.01
☐ 574 Aurelio Rodriguez	.15	.06	.01
☐ 575 Dick Ruthven	.15	.06	.01
☐ 576 Fred Kendall	.15	.06	.01

	NRMT	VG-E	GOOD
☐ 577 Jerry Augustine	.15	.06	.01
☐ 578 Bob Randall	.15	.06	.01
☐ 579 Don Carrithers	.15	.06	.01
☐ 580 George Brett	8.00	3.25	.80
☐ 581 Pedro Borbon	.15	.06	.01
☐ 582 Ed Kirkpatrick	.15	.06	.01
☐ 583 Paul Lindblad	.15	.06	.01
☐ 584 Ed Goodson	.15	.06	.01
☐ 585 Rick Burleson	.25	.10	.02
☐ 586 Steve Renko	.15	.06	.01
☐ 587 Rick Baldwin	.15	.06	.01
☐ 588 Dave Moates	.15	.06	.01
☐ 589 Mike Cosgrove	.15	.06	.01
☐ 590 Buddy Bell	.35	.14	.03
☐ 591 Chris Arnold	.15	.06	.01
☐ 592 Dan Briggs	.15	.06	.01
☐ 593 Dennis Blair	.15	.06	.01
☐ 594 Biff Pocoroba	.15	.06	.01
☐ 595 John Hiller	.25	.10	.02
☐ 596 Jerry Martin	.15	.06	.01
☐ 597 Mariners Leaders	.50	.10	.02
Darrell Johnson MG			
Don Bryant CO			
Jim Busby CO			
Vada Pinson CO			
Wes Stock CO			
(checklist back)			
☐ 598 Sparky Lyle	.35	.14	.03
☐ 599 Mike Tyson	.15	.06	.01
☐ 600 Jim Palmer	2.00	.80	.20
☐ 601 Mike Lum	.15	.06	.01
☐ 602 Andy Hassler	.15	.06	.01
☐ 603 Willie Davis	.25	.10	.02
☐ 604 Jim Slaton	.15	.06	.01
☐ 605 Felix Millan	.15	.06	.01
☐ 606 Steve Braun	.15	.06	.01
☐ 607 Larry Demery	.15	.06	.01
☐ 608 Roy Howell	.15	.06	.01
☐ 609 Jim Barr	.15	.06	.01
☐ 610 Jose Cardenal	.15	.06	.01
☐ 611 Dave Lemanczyk	.15	.06	.01
☐ 612 Barry Foote	.15	.06	.01
☐ 613 Reggie Cleveland	.15	.06	.01
☐ 614 Greg Gross	.15	.06	.01
☐ 615 Phil Niekro	1.50	.60	.15
☐ 616 Tommy Sandt	.15	.06	.01
☐ 617 Bobby Darwin	.15	.06	.01
☐ 618 Pat Dobson	.25	.10	.02
☐ 619 Johnny Oates	.15	.06	.01

		NRMT	VG-E	GOOD
☐ 620	Don Sutton	1.50	.60	.15
☐ 621	Tigers Team/Mgr. Ralph Houk (checklist back)	.75	.20	.04
☐ 622	Jim Wohlford	.15	.06	.01
☐ 623	Jack Kucek	.15	.06	.01
☐ 624	Hector Cruz	.15	.06	.01
☐ 625	Ken Holtzman	.25	.10	.02
☐ 626	Al Bumbry	.15	.06	.01
☐ 627	Bob Myrick	.15	.06	.01
☐ 628	Mario Guerrero	.15	.06	.01
☐ 629	Bobby Valentine	.35	.14	.03
☐ 630	Bert Blyleven	.50	.20	.05
☐ 631	Big League Brothers George Brett Ken Brett	1.50	.60	.15
☐ 632	Big League Brothers Bob Forsch Ken Forsch	.25	.10	.02
☐ 633	Big League Brothers Lee May Carlos May	.25	.10	.02
☐ 634	Big League Brothers Paul Reuschel Rick Reuschel (photos switched)	.25	.10	.02
☐ 635	Robin Yount	4.00	1.60	.40
☐ 636	Santo Alcala	.15	.06	.01
☐ 637	Alex Johnson	.15	.06	.01
☐ 638	Jim Kaat	.60	.24	.06
☐ 639	Jerry Morales	.15	.06	.01
☐ 640	Carlton Fisk	.90	.36	.09
☐ 641	Dan Larson	.15	.06	.01
☑ 642	Willie Crawford	.15	.06	.01
☐ 643	Mike Pazik	.15	.06	.01
☐ 644	Matt Alexander	.15	.06	.01
☐ 645	Jerry Reuss	.25	.10	.02
☐ 646	Andres Mora	.15	.06	.01
☐ 647	Expos Team/Mgr. Dick Williams (checklist back)	.65	.15	.03
☐ 648	Jim Spencer	.15	.06	.01
☐ 649	Dave Cash	.15	.06	.01
☐ 650	Nolan Ryan	4.50	1.80	.45
☐ 651	Von Joshua	.15	.06	.01
☐ 652	Tom Walker	.15	.06	.01
☐ 653	Diego Segui	.15	.06	.01
☐ 654	Ron Pruitt	.15	.06	.01
☐ 655	Tony Perez	.75	.30	.07

		NRMT	VG-E	GOOD
☐ 656	Ron Guidry	3.00	1.20	.30
☐ 657	Mick Kelleher	.15	.06	.01
☐ 658	Marty Pattin	.15	.06	.01
☐ 659	Merv Rettenmund	.15	.06	.01
☐ 660	Willie Horton	.25	.10	.02

1978 Topps

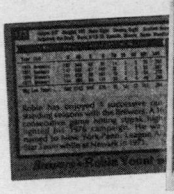

The cards in this 726-card set measure 2 ½ " by 3 ½ ". The 1978 Topps set experienced an increase in number of cards from the previous five regular issue sets of 660. Cards 1 through 7 feature Record Breakers (RB) of the 1977 season. Other subsets within this set include League Leaders (201- 208), Post-season cards (411-413), and Rookie Prospects (701-711). While no scar- cities exist, 66 of the cards are more abun- dant in supply as they were "double printed." These 66 double-printed cards are noted in the checklist by DP. Team cards again fea- ture a checklist of that team's players in the set on the back. Cards numbered 23 or lower which feature Astros, Rangers, Tigers, or Yankees and do not follow the numbering checklisted below are not necessarily error cards. They are probably Burger King cards, a separate set with its own pricing and mass distribution. Burger King cards are indistin- guishable from the corresponding Topps cards except for the card numbering dif- ference and the fact that Burger King cards do not have a printing sheet designation

(such as A through F like the regular Topps) anywhere on the card back in very small print.

		NRMT	VG-E	GOOD
	Complete Set (726)	200.00	80.00	20.00
	Common Player (1-726)	.12	.05	.01
	Common DP's (1-726)	.05	.02	.00
☐ 1	RB: Lou Brock	2.00	.40	.08
	Most steals, lifetime			
☐ 2	RB: Sparky Lyle	.20	.08	.02
	Most games, pure relief, lifetime			
☐ 3	RB: Willie McCovey	.75	.30	.07
	Most times, 2 HR's in inning, lifetime			
☐ 4	RB: Brooks Robinson	.90	.36	.09
	Most consecutive seasons with one club			
☐ 5	RB: Pete Rose	2.25	.90	.22
	Most hits, switch hitter, lifetime			
☐ 6	RB: Nolan Ryan	1.50	.60	.15
	Most games with 10 or more strikeouts, lifetime			
☐ 7	RB: Reggie Jackson	2.00	.80	.20
	Most homers, one World Series			
☐ 8	Mike Sadek	.12	.05	.01
☐ 9	Doug DeCinces	.20	.08	.02
☐ 10	Phil Niekro	1.25	.50	.12
☐ 11	Rick Manning	.12	.05	.01
☐ 12	Don Aase	.12	.05	.01
☐ 13	Art Howe	.20	.08	.02
☐ 14	Lerrin LaGrow	.12	.05	.01
☐ 15	Tony Perez DP	.25	.08	.02
☐ 16	Roy White	.20	.08	.02
☐ 17	Mike Krukow	.20	.08	.02
☐ 18	Bob Grich	.20	.08	.02
☐ 19	Darrell Porter	.12	.05	.01
☐ 20	Pete Rose DP	4.00	1.60	.40
☐ 21	Steve Kemp	.20	.08	.02
☐ 22	Charlie Hough	.20	.08	.02
☐ 23	Bump Wills	.12	.05	.01
☐ 24	Don Money DP	.05	.02	.00
☐ 25	Jon Matlack	.20	.08	.02
☐ 26	Rich Hebner	.20	.08	.02
☐ 27	Geoff Zahn	.12	.05	.01
☐ 28	Ed Ott	.12	.05	.01

		NRMT	VG-E	GOOD
☐ 29	Bob Lacey	.12	.05	.01
☐ 30	George Hendrick	.20	.08	.02
☐ 31	Glenn Abbott	.12	.05	.01
☐ 32	Garry Templeton	.20	.08	.02
☐ 33	Dave Lemanczyk	.12	.05	.01
☐ 34	Willie McCovey	2.00	.80	.20
☐ 35	Sparky Lyle	.30	.12	.03
☐ 36	Eddie Murray	35.00	14.00	3.50
☐ 37	Rick Waits	.12	.05	.01
☐ 38	Willie Montanez	.12	.05	.01
☐ 39	Floyd Bannister	1.25	.50	.12
☐ 40	Carl Yastrzemski	3.50	1.40	.35
☐ 41	Burt Hooton	.12	.05	.01
☐ 42	Jorge Orta	.12	.05	.01
☐ 43	Bill Atkinson	.12	.05	.01
☐ 44	Toby Harrah	.20	.08	.02
☐ 45	Mark Fidrych	.30	.12	.03
☐ 46	Al Cowens	.12	.05	.01
☐ 47	Jack Billingham	.12	.05	.01
☐ 48	Don Baylor	.50	.20	.05
☐ 49	Ed Kranepool	.12	.05	.01
☐ 50	Rick Reuschel	.30	.12	.03
☐ 51	Charlie Moore DP	.05	.02	.00
☐ 52	Jim Lonborg	.20	.08	.02
☐ 53	Phil Garner DP	.05	.02	.00
☐ 54	Tom Johnson	.12	.05	.01
☐ 55	Mitchell Page	.12	.05	.01
☐ 56	Randy Jones	.12	.05	.01
☐ 57	Dan Meyer	.12	.05	.01
☐ 58	Bob Forsch	.20	.08	.02
☐ 59	Otto Velez	.12	.05	.01
☐ 60	Thurman Munson	2.25	.90	.22
☐ 61	Larvell Blanks	.12	.05	.01
☐ 62	Jim Barr	.12	.05	.01
☐ 63	Don Zimmer	.20	.08	.02
☐ 64	Gene Pentz	.12	.05	.01
☐ 65	Ken Singleton	.20	.08	.02
☐ 66	White Sox Team (checklist back)	.50	.10	.02
☐ 67	Claudell Washington	.20	.08	.02
☐ 68	Steve Foucault DP	.05	.02	.00
☐ 69	Mike Vail	.12	.05	.01
☐ 70	Rich Gossage	.60	.24	.06
☐ 71	Terry Humphrey	.12	.05	.01
☐ 72	Andre Dawson	6.50	2.60	.65
☐ 73	Andy Hassler	.12	.05	.01
☐ 74	Checklist 1	.45	.05	.01
☐ 75	Dick Ruthven	.12	.05	.01
☐ 76	Steve Ontiveros	.12	.05	.01

		NRMT	VG-E	GOOD			NRMT	VG-E	GOOD
☐ 77	Ed Kirkpatrick	.12	.05	.01	☐ 123	Manny Trillo	.12	.05	.01
☐ 78	Pablo Torrealba ...	.12	.05	.01	☐ 124	Dave Rozema	.12	.05	.01
☐ 79	Darrell Johnson DP	.05	.02	.00	☐ 125	George Scott	.20	.08	.02
☐ 80	Ken Griffey	.20	.08	.02	☐ 126	Paul Moskau	.12	.05	.01
☐ 81	Pete Redfern	.12	.05	.01	☐ 127	Chet Lemon	.20	.08	.02
☐ 82	Giants Team	.50	.10	.02	☐ 128	Bill Russell	.20	.08	.02
	(checklist back)				☐ 129	Jim Colborn	.12	.05	.01
☐ 83	Bob Montgomery	.12	.05	.01	☐ 130	Jeff Burroughs	.20	.08	.02
☐ 84	Kent Tekulve	.20	.08	.02	☐ 131	Bert Blyleven	.50	.20	.05
☐ 85	Ron Fairly	.12	.05	.01	☐ 132	Enos Cabell	.12	.05	.01
☐ 86	Dave Tomlin	.12	.05	.01	☐ 133	Jerry Augustine	.12	.05	.01
☐ 87	John Lowenstein	.12	.05	.01	☐ 134	Steve Henderson	.12	.05	.01
☐ 88	Mike Phillips	.12	.05	.01	☐ 135	Ron Guidry DP	.60	.24	.06
☐ 89	Ken Clay	.12	.05	.01	☐ 136	Ted Sizemore	.12	.05	.01
☐ 90	Larry Bowa	.30	.12	.03	☐ 137	Craig Kusick	.12	.05	.01
☐ 91	Oscar Zamora	.12	.05	.01	☐ 138	Larry Demery	.12	.05	.01
☐ 92	Adrian Devine	.12	.05	.01	☐ 139	Wayne Gross	.12	.05	.01
☐ 93	Bobby Cox DP	.05	.02	.00	☐ 140	Rollie Fingers	.60	.24	.06
☐ 94	Chuck Scrivener	.12	.05	.01	☐ 141	Ruppert Jones	.12	.05	.01
☐ 95	Jamie Quirk	.12	.05	.01	☐ 142	John Montefusco	.20	.08	.02
☐ 96	Orioles Team	.50	.10	.02	☐ 143	Keith Hernandez	2.50	1.00	.25
	(checklist back)				☐ 144	Jesse Jefferson	.12	.05	.01
☐ 97	Stan Bahnsen	.12	.05	.01	☐ 145	Rick Monday	.12	.05	.01
☐ 98	Jim Essian	.12	.05	.01	☐ 146	Doyle Alexander	.20	.08	.02
☐ 99	Willie Hernandez	1.00	.40	.10	☐ 147	Lee Mazzilli	.12	.05	.01
☐ 100	George Brett	4.00	1.60	.40	☐ 148	Andre Thornton	.20	.08	.02
☐ 101	Sid Monge	.12	.05	.01	☐ 149	Dale Murray	.12	.05	.01
☐ 102	Matt Alexander	.12	.05	.01	☐ 150	Bobby Bonds	.30	.12	.03
☐ 103	Tom Murphy	.12	.05	.01	☐ 151	Milt Wilcox	.12	.05	.01
☐ 104	Lee Lacy	.12	.05	.01	☐ 152	Ivan DeJesus	.12	.05	.01
☐ 105	Reggie Cleveland	.12	.05	.01	☐ 153	Steve Stone	.12	.05	.01
☐ 106	Bill Plummer	.12	.05	.01	☐ 154	Cecil Cooper DP	.20	.08	.02
☐ 107	Ed Halicki	.12	.05	.01	☐ 155	Butch Hobson	.12	.05	.01
☐ 108	Von Joshua	.12	.05	.01	☐ 156	Andy Messersmith	.20	.08	.02
☐ 109	Joe Torre	.30	.12	.03	☐ 157	Pete LaCock DP	.05	.02	.00
☐ 110	Richie Zisk	.12	.05	.01	☐ 158	Joaquin Andujar	.30	.12	.03
☐ 111	Mike Tyson	.12	.05	.01	☐ 159	Lou Piniella	.20	.08	.02
☐ 112	Astros Team	.50	.10	.02	☐ 160	Jim Palmer	2.00	.80	.20
	(checklist back)				☐ 161	Bob Boone	.30	.12	.03
☐ 113	Don Carrithers	.12	.05	.01	☐ 162	Paul Thormodsgard	.12	.05	.01
☐ 114	Paul Blair	.12	.05	.01	☐ 163	Bill North	.12	.05	.01
☐ 115	Gary Nolan	.12	.05	.01	☐ 164	Bob Owchinko	.12	.05	.01
☐ 116	Tucker Ashford	.12	.05	.01	☐ 165	Rennie Stennett	.12	.05	.01
☐ 117	John Montague	.12	.05	.01	☐ 166	Carlos Lopez	.12	.05	.01
☐ 118	Terry Harmon	.12	.05	.01	☐ 167	Tim Foli	.12	.05	.01
☐ 119	Denny Martinez	.20	.08	.02	☐ 168	Reggie Smith	.20	.08	.02
☐ 120	Gary Carter	3.00	1.20	.30	☐ 169	Jerry Johnson	.12	.05	.01
☐ 121	Alvis Woods	.12	.05	.01	☐ 170	Lou Brock	2.00	.80	.20
☐ 122	Dennis Eckersley	.75	.30	.07	☐ 171	Pat Zachry	.12	.05	.01

		NRMT	VG-E	GOOD
☐ 172	Mike Hargrove	.12	.05	.01
☐ 173	Robin Yount	2.50	1.00	.25
☐ 174	Wayne Garland	.12	.05	.01
☐ 175	Jerry Morales	.12	.05	.01
☐ 176	Milt May	.12	.05	.01
☐ 177	Gene Garber DP ..	.05	.02	.00
☐ 178	Dave Chalk	.12	.05	.01
☐ 179	Dick Tidrow	.12	.05	.01
☐ 180	Dave Concepcion ..	.30	.12	.03
☐ 181	Ken Forsch	.12	.05	.01
☐ 182	Jim Spencer	.12	.05	.01
☐ 183	Doug Bird	.12	.05	.01
☐ 184	Checklist 2	.45	.05	.01
☐ 185	Ellis Valentine	.12	.05	.01
☐ 186	Bob Stanley DP ...	.30	.12	.03
☐ 187	Jerry Royster DP ..	.05	.02	.00
☐ 188	Al Bumbry	.12	.05	.01
☐ 189	Tom Lasorda MG ..	.30	.12	.03
☐ 190	John Candelaria ...	.30	.12	.03
☐ 191	Rodney Scott	.12	.05	.01
☐ 192	Padres Team	.50	.10	.02
	(checklist back)			
☐ 193	Rich Chiles	.12	.05	.01
☐ 194	Derrel Thomas	.12	.05	.01
☐ 195	Larry Dierker	.12	.05	.01
☐ 196	Bob Bailor	.12	.05	.01
☐ 197	Nino Espinosa	.12	.05	.01
☐ 198	Ron Pruitt	.12	.05	.01
☐ 199	Craig Reynolds ...	.12	.05	.01
☐ 200	Reggie Jackson ...	3.50	1.40	.35
☐ 201	Batting Leaders	.60	.24	.06
	Dave Parker			
	Rod Carew			
☐ 202	Home Run Leaders DP	.12	.05	.01
	George Foster			
	Jim Rice			
☐ 203	RBI Leaders	.20	.08	.02
	George Foster			
	Larry Hisle			
☐ 204	Steals Leaders DP .	.12	.05	.01
	Frank Taveras			
	Freddie Patek			
☐ 205	Victory Leaders	.50	.20	.05
	Steve Carlton			
	Dave Goltz			
	Dennis Leonard			
	Jim Palmer			

		NRMT	VG-E	GOOD
☐ 206	Strikeout Leaders DP	.20	.08	.02
	Phil Niekro			
	Nolan Ryan			
☐ 207	ERA Leaders DP ..	.12	.05	.01
	John Candelaria			
	Frank Tanana			
☐ 208	Top Firemen	.20	.08	.02
	Rollie Fingers			
	Bill Campbell			
☐ 209	Dock Ellis	.12	.05	.01
☐ 210	Jose Cardenal	.12	.05	.01
☐ 211	Earl Weaver MG DP	.12	.05	.01
☐ 212	Mike Caldwell	.12	.05	.01
☐ 213	Alan Bannister	.12	.05	.01
☐ 214	Angels Team	.50	.10	.02
	(checklist back)			
☐ 215	Darrell Evans	.40	.16	.04
☐ 216	Mike Paxton	.12	.05	.01
☐ 217	Rod Gilbreath	.12	.05	.01
☐ 218	Marty Pattin	.12	.05	.01
☐ 219	Mike Cubbage	.12	.05	.01
☐ 220	Pedro Borbon	.12	.05	.01
☐ 221	Chris Speier	.12	.05	.01
☐ 222	Jerry Martin	.12	.05	.01
☐ 223	Bruce Kison	.12	.05	.01
☐ 224	Jerry Tabb	.12	.05	.01
☐ 225	Don Gullett DP ...	.05	.02	.00
☐ 226	Joe Ferguson	.12	.05	.01
☐ 227	Al Fitzmorris	.12	.05	.01
☐ 228	Manny Mota DP ...	.12	.05	.01
☐ 229	Leo Foster	.12	.05	.01
☐ 230	Al Hrabosky	.12	.05	.01
☐ 231	Wayne Nordhagen ..	.12	.05	.01
☐ 232	Mickey Stanley ...	.12	.05	.01
☐ 233	Dick Pole	.12	.05	.01
☐ 234	Herman Franks MG	.12	.05	.01
☐ 235	Tim McCarver	.30	.12	.03
☐ 236	Terry Whitfield ...	.12	.05	.01
☐ 237	Rich Dauer	.12	.05	.01
☐ 238	Juan Beniquez	.12	.05	.01
☐ 239	Dyar Miller	.12	.05	.01
☐ 240	Gene Tenace	.20	.08	.02
☐ 241	Pete Vuckovich ...	.20	.08	.02
☐ 242	Barry Bonnell DP ..	.12	.05	.01
☐ 243	Bob McClure	.12	.05	.01
☐ 244	Expos Team DP ...	.20	.04	.01
	(checklist back)			
☐ 245	Rick Burleson	.20	.08	.02
☐ 246	Dan Driessen	.12	.05	.01

		NRMT	VG-E	GOOD
☐ 247	Larry Christenson	.12	.05	.01
☐ 248	Frank White DP	.12	.05	.01
☐ 249	Dave Goltz DP	.05	.02	.00
☐ 250	Graig Nettles DP	.20	.07	.01
☐ 251	Don Kirkwood	.12	.05	.01
☐ 252	Steve Swisher DP	.05	.02	.00
☐ 253	Jim Kern	.12	.05	.01
☐ 254	Dave Collins	.12	.05	.01
☐ 255	Jerry Reuss	.20	.08	.02
☐ 256	Joe Altobelli MG	.12	.05	.01
☐ 257	Hector Cruz	.12	.05	.01
☐ 258	John Hiller	.12	.05	.01
☐ 259	Dodgers Team (checklist back)	.50	.10	.02
☐ 260	Bert Campaneris	.20	.08	.02
☐ 261	Tim Hosley	.12	.05	.01
☐ 262	Rudy May	.12	.05	.01
☐ 263	Danny Walton	.12	.05	.01
☐ 264	Jamie Easterly	.12	.05	.01
☐ 265	Sal Bando DP	.12	.05	.01
☐ 266	Bob Shirley	.12	.05	.01
☐ 267	Doug Ault	.12	.05	.01
☐ 268	Gil Flores	.12	.05	.01
☐ 269	Wayne Twitchell	.12	.05	.01
☐ 270	Carlton Fisk	.60	.24	.06
☐ 271	Randy Lerch DP	.05	.02	.00
☐ 272	Royle Stillman	.12	.05	.01
☐ 273	Fred Norman	.12	.05	.01
☐ 274	Freddie Patek	.12	.05	.01
☐ 275	Dan Ford	.12	.05	.01
☐ 276	Bill Bonham DP	.05	.02	.00
☐ 277	Bruce Boisclair	.12	.05	.01
☐ 278	Enrique Romo	.12	.05	.01
☐ 279	Bill Virdon MG	.20	.08	.02
☐ 280	Buddy Bell	.30	.12	.03
☐ 281	Eric Rasmussen DP	.05	.02	.00
☐ 282	Yankees Team (checklist back)	.60	.15	.04
☐ 283	Omar Moreno	.12	.05	.01
☐ 284	Randy Moffitt	.12	.05	.01
☐ 285	Steve Yeager DP	.05	.02	.00
☐ 286	Ben Oglivie	.20	.08	.02
☐ 287	Kiko Garcia	.12	.05	.01
☐ 288	Dave Hamilton	.12	.05	.01
☐ 289	Checklist 3	.45	.05	.01
☐ 290	Willie Horton	.20	.08	.02
☐ 291	Gary Ross	.12	.05	.01
☐ 292	Gene Richards	.12	.05	.01
☐ 293	Mike Willis	.12	.05	.01
☐ 294	Larry Parrish	.20	.08	.02
☐ 295	Bill Lee	.20	.08	.02
☐ 296	Biff Pocoroba	.12	.05	.01
☐ 297	Warren Brusstar DP	.05	.02	.00
☐ 298	Tony Armas	.20	.08	.02
☐ 299	Whitey Herzog MG	.20	.08	.02
☐ 300	Joe Morgan	1.50	.60	.15
☐ 301	Buddy Schultz	.12	.05	.01
☐ 302	Cubs Team (checklist back)	.50	.10	.02
☐ 303	Sam Hinds	.12	.05	.01
☐ 304	John Milner	.12	.05	.01
☐ 305	Rico Carty	.20	.08	.02
☐ 306	Joe Niekro	.30	.12	.03
☐ 307	Glenn Borgmann	.12	.05	.01
☐ 308	Jim Rooker	.12	.05	.01
☐ 309	Cliff Johnson	.12	.05	.01
☐ 310	Don Sutton	1.25	.50	.12
☐ 311	Jose Baez DP	.05	.02	.00
☐ 312	Greg Minton	.12	.05	.01
☐ 313	Andy Etchebarren	.12	.05	.01
☐ 314	Paul Lindblad	.12	.05	.01
☐ 315	Mark Belanger	.20	.08	.02
☐ 316	Henry Cruz DP	.05	.02	.00
☐ 317	Dave Johnson	.30	.12	.03
☐ 318	Tom Griffin	.12	.05	.01
☐ 319	Alan Ashby	.20	.08	.02
☐ 320	Fred Lynn	.75	.30	.07
☐ 321	Santo Alcala	.12	.05	.01
☐ 322	Tom Paciorek	.12	.05	.01
☐ 323	Jim Fregosi DP	.12	.05	.01
☐ 324	Vern Rapp MG	.12	.05	.01
☐ 325	Bruce Sutter	.60	.24	.06
☐ 326	Mike Lum DP	.05	.02	.00
☐ 327	Rick Langford DP	.05	.02	.00
☐ 328	Milwaukee Brewers Team Card (checklist back)	.50	.10	.02
☐ 329	John Verhoeven	.12	.05	.01
☐ 330	Bob Watson	.20	.08	.02
☐ 331	Mark Littell	.12	.05	.01
☐ 332	Duane Kuiper	.12	.05	.01
☐ 333	Jim Todd	.12	.05	.01
☐ 334	John Stearns	.12	.05	.01
☐ 335	Bucky Dent	.20	.08	.02
☐ 336	Steve Busby	.12	.05	.01
☐ 337	Tom Grieve	.20	.08	.02
☐ 338	Dave Heaverlo	.12	.05	.01
☐ 339	Mario Guerrero	.12	.05	.01

		NRMT	VG-E	GOOD
☐ 340	Bake McBride	.12	.05	.01
☐ 341	Mike Flanagan	.20	.08	.02
☐ 342	Aurelio Rodriguez	.12	.05	.01
☐ 343	John Wathan DP	.12	.05	.01
☐ 344	Sam Ewing	.12	.05	.01
☐ 345	Luis Tiant	.30	.12	.02
☐ 346	Larry Biittner	.12	.05	.01
☐ 347	Terry Forster	.20	.08	.02
☐ 348	Del Unser	.12	.05	.01
☐ 349	Rick Camp DP	.05	.02	.00
☐ 350	Steve Garvey	3.00	1.20	.30
☐ 351	Jeff Torborg	.20	.08	.02
☐ 352	Tony Scott	.12	.05	.01
☐ 353	Doug Bair	.12	.05	.01
☐ 354	Cesar Geronimo	.12	.05	.01
☐ 355	Bill Travers	.12	.05	.01
☐ 356	New York Mets Team Card (checklist back)	.50	.10	.02
☐ 357	Tom Poquette	.12	.05	.01
☐ 358	Mark Lemongello	.12	.05	.01
☐ 359	Marc Hill	.12	.05	.01
☐ 360	Mike Schmidt	5.00	2.00	.50
☐ 361	Chris Knapp	.12	.05	.01
☐ 362	Dave May	.12	.05	.01
☐ 363	Bob Randall	.12	.05	.01
☐ 364	Jerry Turner	.12	.05	.01
☐ 365	Ed Figueroa	.12	.05	.01
☐ 366	Larry Milbourne DP	.05	.02	.00
☐ 367	Rick Dempsey	.12	.05	.01
☐ 368	Balor Moore	.12	.05	.01
☐ 369	Tim Nordbrook	.12	.05	.01
☐ 370	Rusty Staub	.30	.12	.03
☐ 371	Ray Burris	.12	.05	.01
☐ 372	Brian Asselstine	.12	.05	.01
☐ 373	Jim Willoughby	.12	.05	.01
☐ 374	Jose Morales	.12	.05	.01
☐ 375	Tommy John	.75	.30	.07
☐ 376	Jim Wohlford	.12	.05	.01
☐ 377	Manny Sarmiento	.12	.05	.01
☐ 378	Bobby Winkles MG	.12	.05	.01
☐ 379	Skip Lockwood	.12	.05	.01
☐ 380	Ted Simmons	.40	.16	.04
☐ 381	Phillies Team (checklist back)	.50	.10	.02
☐ 382	Joe Lahoud	.12	.05	.01
☐ 383	Mario Mendoza	.12	.05	.01
☐ 384	Jack Clark	4.00	1.60	.40
☐ 385	Tito Fuentes	.12	.05	.01
☐ 386	Bob Gorinski	.12	.05	.01
☐ 387	Ken Holtzman	.12	.05	.01
☐ 388	Bill Fahey DP	.05	.02	.00
☐ 389	Julio Gonzalez	.12	.05	.01
☐ 390	Oscar Gamble	.12	.05	.01
☐ 391	Larry Haney	.12	.05	.01
☐ 392	Billy Almon	.12	.05	.01
☐ 393	Tippy Martinez	.12	.05	.01
☐ 394	Roy Howell DP	.05	.02	.00
☐ 395	Jim Hughes	.12	.05	.01
☐ 396	Bob Stinson DP	.05	.02	.00
☐ 397	Greg Gross	.12	.05	.01
☐ 398	Don Hood	.12	.05	.01
☐ 399	Pete Mackanin	.12	.05	.01
☐ 400	Nolan Ryan	3.00	1.20	.30
☐ 401	Sparky Anderson MG	.20	.08	.02
☐ 402	Dave Campbell	.12	.05	.01
☐ 403	Bud Harrelson	.12	.05	.01
☐ 404	Tigers Team (checklist back)	.50	.10	.02
☐ 405	Rawly Eastwick	.12	.05	.01
☐ 406	Mike Jorgensen	.12	.05	.01
☐ 407	Odell Jones	.12	.05	.01
☐ 408	Joe Zdeb	.12	.05	.01
☐ 409	Ron Schueler	.12	.05	.01
☐ 410	Bill Madlock	.40	.16	.04
☐ 411	AL Champs Yankees rally to defeat Royals	.50	.20	.05
☐ 412	NL Champs Dodgers overpower Phillies in four	.50	.20	.05
☐ 413	World Series Reggie and Yankees reign supreme	1.25	.50	.12
☐ 414	Darold Knowles DP	.05	.02	.00
☐ 415	Ray Fosse	.12	.05	.01
☐ 416	Jack Brohamer	.12	.05	.01
☐ 417	Mike Garman DP	.05	.02	.00
☐ 418	Tony Muser	.12	.05	.01
☐ 419	Jerry Garvin	.12	.05	.01
☐ 420	Greg Luzinski	.30	.12	.03
☐ 421	Junior Moore	.12	.05	.01
☐ 422	Steve Braun	.12	.05	.01
☐ 423	Dave Rosello	.12	.05	.01
☐ 424	Boston Red Sox Team Card (checklist back)	.50	.10	.02
☐ 425	Steve Rogers DP	.12	.05	.01

		NRMT	VG-E	GOOD
☐ 426	Fred Kendall	.12	.05	.01
☐ 427	Mario Soto	.75	.30	.07
☐ 428	Joel Youngblood	.12	.05	.01
☐ 429	Mike Barlow	.12	.05	.01
☐ 430	Al Oliver	.30	.12	.03
☐ 431	Butch Metzger	.12	.05	.01
☐ 432	Terry Bulling	.12	.05	.01
☐ 433	Fernando Gonzalez	.12	.05	.01
☐ 434	Mike Norris	.12	.05	.01
☐ 435	Checklist 4	.45	.05	.01
☐ 436	Vic Harris DP	.05	.02	.00
☐ 437	Bo McLaughlin	.12	.05	.01
☐ 438	John Ellis	.12	.05	.01
☐ 439	Ken Kravec	.12	.05	.01
☐ 440	Dave Lopes	.20	.08	.02
☐ 441	Larry Gura	.12	.05	.01
☐ 442	Elliott Maddox	.12	.05	.01
☐ 443	Darrel Chaney	.12	.05	.01
☐ 444	Roy Hartsfield MG	.12	.05	.01
☐ 445	Mike Ivie	.12	.05	.01
☐ 446	Tug McGraw	.30	.12	.03
☐ 447	Leroy Stanton	.12	.05	.01
☐ 448	Bill Castro	.12	.05	.01
☐ 449	Tim Blackwell DP	.05	.02	.00
☐ 450	Tom Seaver	2.50	1.00	.25
☐ 451	Minnesota Twins Team Card (checklist back)	.50	.10	.02
☐ 452	Jerry Mumphrey	.12	.05	.01
☐ 453	Doug Flynn	.12	.05	.01
☐ 454	Dave LaRoche	.12	.05	.01
☐ 455	Bill Robinson	.20	.08	.02
☐ 456	Vern Ruhle	.12	.05	.01
☐ 457	Bob Bailey	.12	.05	.01
☐ 458	Jeff Newman	.12	.05	.01
☐ 459	Charlie Spikes	.12	.05	.01
☐ 460	Jim Hunter	1.50	.60	.15
☐ 461	Rob Andrews DP	.05	.02	.00
☐ 462	Rogelio Moret	.12	.05	.01
☐ 463	Kevin Bell	.12	.05	.01
☐ 464	Jerry Grote	.12	.05	.01
☐ 465	Hal McRae	.20	.08	.02
☐ 466	Dennis Blair	.12	.05	.01
☐ 467	Alvin Dark MG	.12	.05	.01
☐ 468	Warren Cromartie	.12	.05	.01
☐ 469	Rick Cerone	.12	.05	.01
☐ 470	J.R. Richard	.20	.08	.02
☐ 471	Roy Smalley	.12	.05	.01
☐ 472	Ron Reed	.12	.05	.01
☐ 473	Bill Buckner	.30	.12	.03
☐ 474	Jim Slaton	.12	.05	.01
☐ 475	Gary Matthews	.20	.08	.02
☐ 476	Bill Stein	.12	.05	.01
☐ 477	Doug Capilla	.12	.05	.01
☐ 478	Jerry Remy	.12	.05	.01
☐ 479	Cardinals Team (checklist back)	.50	.10	.02
☐ 480	Ron LeFlore	.12	.05	.01
☐ 481	Jackson Todd	.12	.05	.01
☐ 482	Rick Miller	.12	.05	.01
☐ 483	Ken Macha	.12	.05	.01
☐ 484	Jim Norris	.12	.05	.01
☐ 485	Chris Chambliss	.20	.08	.02
☐ 486	John Curtis	.12	.05	.01
☐ 487	Jim Tyrone	.12	.05	.01
☐ 488	Dan Spillner	.12	.05	.01
☐ 489	Rudy Meoli	.12	.05	.01
☐ 490	Amos Otis	.20	.08	.02
☐ 491	Scott McGregor	.20	.08	.02
☐ 492	Jim Sundberg	.12	.05	.01
☐ 493	Steve Renko	.12	.05	.01
☐ 494	Chuck Tanner MG	.12	.05	.01
☐ 495	Dave Cash	.12	.05	.01
☐ 496	Jim Clancy DP	.20	.08	.02
☐ 497	Glenn Adams	.12	.05	.01
☐ 498	Joe Sambito	.12	.05	.01
☐ 499	Seattle Mariners Team Card (checklist back)	.50	.10	.02
☐ 500	George Foster	.60	.24	.06
☐ 501	Dave Roberts	.12	.05	.01
☐ 502	Pat Rockett	.12	.05	.01
☐ 503	Ike Hampton	.12	.05	.01
☐ 504	Roger Freed	.12	.05	.01
☐ 505	Felix Millan	.12	.05	.01
☐ 506	Ron Blomberg	.12	.05	.01
☐ 507	Willie Crawford	.12	.05	.01
☐ 508	Johnny Oates	.12	.05	.01
☐ 509	Brent Strom	.12	.05	.01
☐ 510	Willie Stargell	2.00	.80	.20
☐ 511	Frank Duffy	.12	.05	.01
☐ 512	Larry Herndon	.12	.05	.01
☐ 513	Barry Foote	.12	.05	.01
☐ 514	Rob Sperring	.12	.05	.01
☐ 515	Tim Corcoran	.12	.05	.01
☐ 516	Gary Beare	.12	.05	.01
☐ 517	Andres Mora	.12	.05	.01
☐ 518	Tommy Boggs DP	.05	.02	.00

		NRMT	VG-E	GOOD
☐ 519	Brian Downing	.20	.08	.01
☐ 520	Larry Hisle	.12	.05	.01
☐ 521	Steve Staggs	.12	.05	.01
☐ 522	Dick Williams MG ..	.12	.05	.01
☐ 523	Donnie Moore	.30	.12	.03
☐ 524	Bernie Carbo	.12	.05	.01
☐ 525	Jerry Terrell	.12	.05	.01
☐ 526	Reds Team	.50	.10	.02
	(checklist back)			
☐ 527	Vic Correll	.12	.05	.01
☐ 528	Rob Picciolo	.12	.05	.01
☐ 529	Paul Hartzell	.12	.05	.01
☐ 530	Dave Winfield	2.50	1.00	.25
☐ 531	Tom Underwood	.12	.05	.01
☐ 532	Skip Jutze	.12	.05	.01
☐ 533	Sandy Alomar	.12	.05	.01
☐ 534	Wilbur Howard	.12	.05	.01
☐ 535	Checklist 5	.45	.05	.01
☐ 536	Roric Harrison	.12	.05	.01
☐ 537	Bruce Bochte	.12	.05	.01
☐ 538	Johnny LeMaster ..	.12	.05	.01
☐ 539	Vic Davalillo DP ...	.05	.02	.00
☐ 540	Steve Carlton	2.50	1.00	.25
☐ 541	Larry Cox	.12	.05	.01
☐ 542	Tim Johnson	.12	.05	.01
☐ 543	Larry Harlow DP ...	.05	.02	.00
☐ 544	Len Randle DP	.05	.02	.00
☐ 545	Bill Campbell	.12	.05	.01
☐ 546	Ted Martinez	.12	.05	.01
☐ 547	John Scott	.12	.05	.01
☐ 548	Billy Hunter MG DP	.05	.02	.00
☐ 549	Joe Kerrigan	.12	.05	.01
☐ 550	John Mayberry	.20	.08	.02
☐ 551	Atlanta Braves	.50	.10	.02
	Team Card			
	(checklist back)			
☐ 552	Francisco Barrios ..	.12	.05	.01
☐ 553	Terry Puhl	.40	.16	.04
☐ 554	Joe Coleman	.12	.05	.01
☐ 555	Butch Wynegar	.12	.05	.01
☐ 556	Ed Armbrister	.12	.05	.01
☐ 557	Tony Solaita	.12	.05	.01
☐ 558	Paul Mitchell	.12	.05	.01
☐ 559	Phil Mankowski	.12	.05	.01
☐ 560	Dave Parker	1.75	.70	.17
☐ 561	Charlie Williams ...	.12	.05	.01
☐ 562	Glenn Burke	.12	.05	.01
☐ 563	Dave Rader	.12	.05	.01
☐ 564	Mick Kelleher	.12	.05	.01

		NRMT	VG-E	GOOD
☐ 565	Jerry Koosman ...	.20	.08	.02
☐ 566	Merv Rettenmund .	.12	.05	.01
☐ 567	Dick Drago	.12	.05	.01
☐ 568	Tom Hutton	.12	.05	.01
☐ 569	Lary Sorensen	.12	.05	.01
☐ 570	Dave Kingman	.50	.20	.05
☐ 571	Buck Martinez	.12	.05	.01
☐ 572	Rick Wise	.12	.05	.01
☐ 573	Luis Gomez	.12	.05	.01
☐ 574	Bob Lemon MG ...	.30	.12	.03
☐ 575	Pat Dobson	.20	.08	.01
☐ 576	Sam Mejias	.12	.05	.01
☐ 577	Oakland A's	.50	.10	.02
	Team Card			
	(checklist back)			
☐ 578	Buzz Capra	.12	.05	.01
☐ 579	Rance Mulliniks ...	.20	.08	.02
☐ 580	Rod Carew	2.50	1.00	.25
☐ 581	Lynn McGlothen ...	.12	.05	.01
☐ 582	Fran Healy	.12	.05	.01
☐ 583	George Medich ...	.12	.05	.01
☐ 584	John Hale	.12	.05	.01
☐ 585	Woodie Fryman DP	.05	.02	.00
☐ 586	Ed Goodson	.12	.05	.01
☐ 587	John Urrea	.12	.05	.01
☐ 588	Jim Mason	.12	.05	.01
☐ 589	Bob Knepper	1.75	.70	.17
☐ 590	Bobby Murcer	.30	.12	.03
☐ 591	George Zeber	.12	.05	.01
☐ 592	Bob Apodaca	.12	.05	.01
☐ 593	Dave Skaggs	.12	.05	.01
☐ 594	Dave Freisleben ..	.12	.05	.01
☐ 595	Sixto Lezcano	.12	.05	.01
☐ 596	Gary Wheelock ...	.12	.05	.01
☐ 597	Steve Dillard	.12	.05	.01
☐ 598	Eddie Solomon ...	.12	.05	.01
☐ 599	Gary Woods	.12	.05	.01
☐ 600	Frank Tanana	.20	.08	.02
☐ 601	Gene Mauch MG ..	.12	.05	.01
☐ 602	Eric Soderholm ...	.12	.05	.01
☐ 603	Will McEnaney ...	.12	.05	.01
☐ 604	Earl Williams	.12	.05	.01
☐ 605	Rick Rhoden	.30	.12	.03
☐ 606	Pirates Team	.50	.10	.02
	(checklist back)			
☐ 607	Fernando Arroyo ..	.12	.05	.01
☐ 608	Johnny Grubb	.12	.05	.01
☐ 609	John Denny	.20	.08	.02
☐ 610	Garry Maddox	.12	.05	.01

		NRMT	VG-E	GOOD
☐ 611	Pat Scanlon	.12	.05	.01
☐ 612	Ken Henderson	.12	.05	.01
☐ 613	Marty Perez	.12	.05	.01
☐ 614	Joe Wallis	.12	.05	.01
☐ 615	Clay Carroll	.12	.05	.01
☐ 616	Pat Kelly	.12	.05	.01
☐ 617	Joe Nolan	.12	.05	.01
☐ 618	Tommy Helms	.12	.05	.01
☐ 619	Thad Bosley DP	.12	.05	.01
☐ 620	Willie Randolph	.40	.18	.03
☐ 621	Craig Swan DP	.12	.05	.01
☐ 622	Champ Summers	.12	.05	.01
☐ 623	Eduardo Rodriguez	.12	.05	.01
☐ 624	Gary Alexander DP	.05	.02	.00
☐ 625	Jose Cruz	.20	.08	.02
☐ 626	Blue Jays Team DP (checklist back)	.20	.05	.01
☐ 627	David Johnson	.12	.05	.01
☐ 628	Ralph Garr	.12	.05	.01
☐ 629	Don Stanhouse	.12	.05	.01
☐ 630	Ron Cey	.30	.12	.03
☐ 631	Danny Ozark MG	.12	.05	.01
☐ 632	Rowland Office	.12	.05	.01
☐ 633	Tom Veryzer	.12	.05	.01
☐ 634	Len Barker	.12	.05	.01
☐ 635	Joe Rudi	.20	.08	.02
☐ 636	Jim Bibby	.12	.05	.01
☐ 637	Duffy Dyer	.12	.05	.01
☐ 638	Paul Splittorff	.12	.05	.01
☐ 639	Gene Clines	.12	.05	.01
☐ 640	Lee May DP	.12	.05	.01
☐ 641	Doug Rau	.12	.05	.01
☐ 642	Denny Doyle	.12	.05	.01
☐ 643	Tom House	.12	.05	.01
☐ 644	Jim Dwyer	.12	.05	.01
☐ 645	Mike Torrez	.12	.05	.01
☐ 646	Rick Auerbach DP	.05	.02	.00
☐ 647	Steve Dunning	.12	.05	.01
☐ 648	Gary Thomasson	.12	.05	.01
☐ 649	Moose Haas	.30	.12	.03
☐ 650	Cesar Cedeno	.20	.08	.02
☐ 651	Doug Rader	.20	.08	.02
☐ 652	Checklist 6	.45	.05	.01
☐ 653	Ron Hodges DP	.05	.02	.00
☐ 654	Pepe Frias	.12	.05	.01
☐ 655	Lyman Bostock	.20	.08	.02
☐ 656	Dave Garcia MG	.12	.05	.01
☐ 657	Bombo Rivera	.12	.05	.01
☐ 658	Manny Sanguillen	.20	.08	.02

		NRMT	VG-E	GOOD
☐ 659	Rangers Team (checklist back)	.50	.10	.02
☐ 660	Jason Thompson	.20	.08	.02
☐ 661	Grant Jackson	.12	.05	.01
☐ 662	Paul Dade	.12	.05	.01
☐ 663	Paul Reuschel	.12	.05	.01
☐ 664	Fred Stanley	.12	.05	.01
☐ 665	Dennis Leonard	.20	.08	.02
☐ 666	Billy Smith	.12	.05	.01
☐ 667	Jeff Byrd	.12	.05	.01
☐ 668	Dusty Baker	.20	.08	.02
☐ 669	Pete Falcone	.12	.05	.01
☐ 670	Jim Rice	3.50	1.40	.35
☐ 671	Gary Lavelle	.12	.05	.01
☐ 672	Don Kessinger	.12	.05	.01
☐ 673	Steve Brye	.12	.05	.01
☐ 674	Ray Knight	1.25	.50	.12
☐ 675	Jay Johnstone	.20	.08	.02
☐ 676	Bob Myrick	.12	.05	.01
☐ 677	Ed Herrmann	.12	.05	.01
☐ 678	Tom Burgmeier	.12	.05	.01
☐ 679	Wayne Garrett	.12	.05	.01
☐ 680	Vida Blue	.20	.08	.02
☐ 681	Rob Belloir	.12	.05	.01
☐ 682	Ken Brett	.12	.05	.01
☐ 683	Mike Champion	.12	.05	.01
☐ 684	Ralph Houk MG	.20	.08	.02
☐ 685	Frank Taveras	.12	.05	.01
☐ 686	Gaylord Perry	1.75	.70	.17
☐ 687	Julio Cruz	.20	.08	.02
☐ 688	George Mitterwald	.12	.05	.01
☐ 689	Indians Team (checklist back)	.50	.10	.02
☐ 690	Mickey Rivers	.20	.08	.02
☐ 691	Ross Grimsley	.12	.05	.01
☐ 692	Ken Reitz	.12	.05	.01
☐ 693	Lamar Johnson	.12	.05	.01
☐ 694	Elias Sosa	.12	.05	.01
☐ 695	Dwight Evans	1.00	.40	.10
☐ 696	Steve Mingori	.12	.05	.01
☐ 697	Roger Metzger	.12	.05	.01
☐ 698	Juan Bernhardt	.12	.05	.01
☐ 699	Jackie Brown	.12	.05	.01
☐ 700	Johnny Bench	3.00	1.20	.30
☐ 701	Rookie Pitchers Tom Hume Larry Landreth Steve McCatty Bruce Taylor	.30	.12	.03

		NRMT	VG-E	GOOD
☐ 702	Rookie Catchers ...	.20	.08	.02
	Bill Nahorodony			
	Kevin Pasley			
	Rick Sweet			
	Don Werner			
☐ 703	Rookie Pitchers DP .	6.50	2.60	.65
	Larry Andersen			
	Tim Jones			
	Mickey Mahler			
	Jack Morris			
☐ 704	Rookie 2nd Basemen	7.50	3.00	.75
	Garth Iorg			
	Dave Oliver			
	Sam Perlozzo			
	Lou Whitaker			
☐ 705	Rookie Outfielders .	.30	.12	.03
	Dave Bergman			
	Miguel Dilone			
	Clint Hurdle			
	Willie Norwood			
☐ 706	Rookie 1st Basemen	.20	.08	.02
	Wayne Cage			
	Ted Cox			
	Pat Putnam			
	Dave Revering			
☐ 707	Rookie Shortstops .	35.00	14.00	3.50
	Mickey Klutts			
	Paul Molitor			
	Alan Trammell			
	U.L. Washington			
☐ 708	Rookie Catchers ...	35.00	14.00	3.50
	Bo Diaz			
	Dale Murphy			
	Lance Parrish			
	Ernie Whitt			
☐ 709	Rookie Pitchers	.30	.12	.03
	Steve Burke			
	Matt Keough			
	Lance Rautzhan			
	Dan Schatzeder			
☐ 710	Rookie Outfielders .	.75	.30	.07
	Dell Alston			
	Rick Bosetti			
	Mike Easler			
	Keith Smith			

		NRMT	VG-E	GOOD
☐ 711	Rookie Pitchers DP	.12	.05	.01
	Cardell Camper			
	Dennis Lamp			
	Craig Mitchell			
	Roy Thomas			
☐ 712	Bobby Valentine ..	.30	.12	.03
☐ 713	Bob Davis	.12	.05	.01
☐ 714	Mike Anderson ...	.12	.05	.01
☐ 715	Jim Kaat	.50	.20	.05
☐ 716	Clarence Gaston ..	.12	.05	.01
☐ 717	Nelson Briles	.12	.05	.01
☐ 718	Ron Jackson	.12	.05	.01
☐ 719	Randy Elliott	.12	.05	.01
☐ 720	Fergie Jenkins ...	.40	.16	.04
☐ 721	Billy Martin MG ...	.40	.16	.04
☐ 722	Pete Broberg	.12	.05	.01
☐ 723	John Wockenfuss ..	.12	.05	.01
☐ 724	Kansas City Royals	.50	.10	.02
	Team Card			
	(checklist back)			
☐ 725	Kurt Bevacqua	.12	.05	.01
☐ 726	Wilbur Wood	.20	.08	.02

1979 Topps

*The cards in this 726-card set measure 2 ½"
by 3 ½". Topps continued with the same
number of cards as in 1978. Various series
spotlight League Leaders (1-8), "Season
and Career Record Holders" (411-418),
"Record Breakers of 1978" (201-206) and
one "Prospects" card for each team (701-
726). Team cards feature a checklist on*

back of that team's players in the set and a small picture of the manager on the front of the card. There are 66 cards that were double printed and these are noted in the checklist by the abbreviation DP. Bump Wills was initially depicted in a Ranger uniform but with a Blue Jays affiliation; later printings correctly labeled him with Texas. The set price listed does not include the scarcer Wills (Rangers) card. Cards numbered 23 or lower which feature Phillies or Yankees and do not follow the numbering checklisted below are not necessarily error cards. They are probably Burger King cards, a separate set with its own pricing and mass distribution. Burger King cards are indistinguishable from the corresponding Topps cards except for the card numbering difference and the fact that Burger King cards do not have a printing sheet designation (such as A through F like the regular Topps) anywhere on the card back in very small print.

		NRMT	VG-E	GOOD
Complete Set (726)		140.00	56.00	14.00
Common Player (1-726)		.10	.04	.01
Common DP's (1-726)		.04	.02	.00
☐ 1	Batting Leaders .... Rod Carew Dave Parker	1.50	.40	.08
☐ 2	Home Run Leaders Jim Rice George Foster	.30	.12	.03
☐ 3	RBI Leaders .... Jim Rice George Foster	.30	.12	.03
☐ 4	Stolen Base Leaders Ron LeFlore Omar Moreno	.20	.08	.02
☐ 5	Victory Leaders .... Ron Guidry Gaylord Perry	.30	.12	.03
☐ 6	Strikeout Leaders .. Nolan Ryan J.R. Richard	.40	.16	.04
☐ 7	ERA Leaders ...... Ron Guidry Craig Swan	.20	.08	.02

		NRMT	VG-E	GOOD
☐ 8	Leading Firemen .. Rich Gossage Rollie Fingers	.20	.08	.02
☐ 9	Dave Campbell ...	.10	.04	.01
☐ 10	Lee May	.20	.08	.02
☐ 11	Marc Hill	.10	.04	.01
☐ 12	Dick Drago	.10	.04	.01
☐ 13	Paul Dade	.10	.04	.01
☐ 14	Rafael Landestoy .	.10	.04	.01
☐ 15	Ross Grimsley	.10	.04	.01
☐ 16	Fred Stanley	.10	.04	.01
☐ 17	Donnie Moore	.20	.08	.02
☐ 18	Tony Solaita	.10	.04	.01
☐ 19	Larry Gura DP	.10	.04	.01
☐ 20	Joe Morgan DP ...	.50	.15	.03
☐ 21	Kevin Kobel	.10	.04	.01
☐ 22	Mike Jorgensen ...	.10	.04	.01
☐ 23	Terry Forster	.20	.08	.02
☐ 24	Paul Molitor	3.50	1.40	.35
☐ 25	Steve Carlton	2.25	.90	.22
☐ 26	Jamie Quirk	.10	.04	.01
☐ 27	Dave Goltz	.10	.04	.01
☐ 28	Steve Brye	.10	.04	.01
☐ 29	Rick Langford	.10	.04	.01
☐ 30	Dave Winfield	2.50	1.00	.25
☐ 31	Tom House DP	.10	.04	.01
☐ 32	Jerry Mumphrey ..	.10	.04	.01
☐ 33	Dave Rozema	.10	.04	.01
☐ 34	Rob Andrews	.10	.04	.01
☐ 35	Ed Figueroa	.10	.04	.01
☐ 36	Alan Ashby	.10	.04	.01
☐ 37	Joe Kerrigan DP ..	.04	.02	.00
☐ 38	Bernie Carbo	.10	.04	.01
☐ 39	Dale Murphy	8.50	3.50	.85
☐ 40	Dennis Eckersley .	.60	.25	.05
☐ 41	Twins Team/Mgr... Gene Mauch (checklist back)	.40	.10	.02
☐ 42	Ron Blomberg	.10	.04	.01
☐ 43	Wayne Twitchell ..	.10	.04	.01
☐ 44	Kurt Bevacqua ...	.10	.04	.01
☐ 45	Al Hrabosky	.10	.04	.01
☐ 46	Ron Hodges	.10	.04	.01
☐ 47	Fred Norman	.10	.04	.01
☐ 48	Merv Rettenmund .	.10	.04	.01
☐ 49	Vern Ruhle	.10	.04	.01
☐ 50	Steve Garvey DP .	1.25	.50	.12
☐ 51	Ray Fosse DP	.04	.02	.00
☐ 52	Randy Lerch	.10	.04	.01

			NRMT	VG-E	GOOD
☐	53	Mick Kelleher	.10	.04	.01
☐	54	Dell Alston DP	.04	.02	.00
☐	55	Willie Stargell	2.00	.80	.20
☐	56	John Hale	.10	.04	.01
☐	57	Eric Rasmussen	.10	.04	.01
☐	58	Bob Randall DP	.04	.02	.00
☐	59	John Denny DP	.10	.04	.01
☐	60	Mickey Rivers	.20	.08	.01
☐	61	Bo Diaz	.20	.08	.02
☐	62	Randy Moffitt	.10	.04	.01
☐	63	Jack Brohamer	.10	.04	.01
☐	64	Tom Underwood	.10	.04	.01
☐	65	Mark Belanger	.20	.08	.02
☐	66	Tigers Team/Mgr. Les Moss (checklist back)	.40	.10	.02
☐	67	Jim Mason	.04	.02	.00
☐	68	Joe Niekro DP	.10	.04	.01
☐	69	Elliott Maddox	.10	.04	.01
☐	70	John Candelaria	.30	.12	.03
☐	71	Brian Downing	.20	.08	.02
☐	72	Steve Mingori	.10	.04	.01
☐	73	Ken Henderson	.10	.04	.01
☐	74	Shane Rawley	1.00	.40	.10
☐	75	Steve Yeager	.10	.04	.01
☐	76	Warren Cromartie	.10	.04	.01
☐	77	Dan Briggs DP	.04	.02	.00
☐	78	Elias Sosa	.10	.04	.01
☐	79	Ted Cox	.10	.04	.01
☐	80	Jason Thompson	.10	.04	.01
☐	81	Roger Erickson	.10	.04	.01
☐	82	Mets Team/Mgr. Joe Torre (checklist back)	.40	.10	.02
☐	83	Fred Kendall	.10	.04	.01
☐	84	Greg Minton	.10	.04	.01
☐	85	Gary Matthews	.20	.08	.02
☐	86	Rodney Scott	.10	.04	.01
☐	87	Pete Falcone	.10	.04	.01
☐	88	Bob Molinaro	.10	.04	.01
☐	89	Dick Tidrow	.10	.04	.01
☐	90	Bob Boone	.30	.12	.03
☐	91	Terry Crowley	.10	.04	.01
☐	92	Jim Bibby	.10	.04	.01
☐	93	Phil Mankowski	.10	.04	.01
☐	94	Len Barker	.10	.04	.01
☐	95	Robin Yount	2.25	.90	.22

			NRMT	VG-E	GOOD
☐	96	Indians Team/Mgr. Jeff Torborg (checklist back)	.40	.10	.02
☐	97	Sam Mejias	.10	.04	.01
☐	98	Ray Burris	.10	.04	.01
☐	99	John Wathan	.30	.12	.03
☐	100	Tom Seaver DP	1.25	.50	.12
☐	101	Roy Howell	.10	.04	.01
☐	102	Mike Anderson	.10	.04	.01
☐	103	Jim Todd	.10	.04	.01
☐	104	Johnny Oates DP	.04	.02	.00
☐	105	Rick Camp DP	.04	.02	.00
☐	106	Frank Duffy	.10	.04	.01
☐	107	Jesus Alou DP	.04	.02	.00
☐	108	Eduardo Rodriguez	.10	.04	.01
☐	109	Joel Youngblood	.10	.04	.01
☐	110	Vida Blue	.20	.08	.02
☐	111	Roger Freed	.10	.04	.01
☐	112	Phillies Team/Mgr. Danny Ozark (checklist back)	.40	.10	.02
☐	113	Pete Redfern	.10	.04	.01
☐	114	Cliff Johnson	.10	.04	.01
☐	115	Nolan Ryan	2.25	.90	.22
☐	116	Ozzie Smith	18.00	7.25	1.80
☐	117	Grant Jackson	.10	.04	.01
☐	118	Bud Harrelson	.10	.04	.01
☐	119	Don Stanhouse	.10	.04	.01
☐	120	Jim Sundberg	.10	.04	.01
☐	121	Checklist 1 DP	.15	.03	.00
☐	122	Mike Paxton	.10	.04	.01
☐	123	Lou Whitaker	2.00	.80	.20
☐	124	Dan Schatzeder	.10	.04	.01
☐	125	Rick Burleson	.20	.08	.02
☐	126	Doug Bair	.10	.04	.01
☐	127	Thad Bosley	.10	.04	.01
☐	128	Ted Martinez	.10	.04	.01
☐	129	Marty Pattin DP	.04	.02	.00
☐	130	Bob Watson DP	.10	.04	.01
☐	131	Jim Clancy	.10	.04	.01
☐	132	Rowland Office	.10	.04	.01
☐	133	Bill Castro	.10	.04	.01
☐	134	Alan Bannister	.10	.04	.01
☐	135	Bobby Murcer	.30	.12	.02
☐	136	Jim Kaat	.40	.16	.04
☐	137	Larry Wolfe DP	.04	.02	.00
☐	138	Mark Lee	.10	.04	.01
☐	139	Luis Pujols	.10	.04	.01
☐	140	Don Gullett	.10	.04	.01

		NRMT	VG-E	GOOD
☐ 141	Tom Paciorek	.10	.04	.01
☐ 142	Charlie Williams ...	.10	.04	.01
☐ 143	Tony Scott	.10	.04	.01
☐ 144	Sandy Alomar	.10	.04	.01
☐ 145	Rick Rhoden	.30	.12	.03
☐ 146	Duane Kuiper	.10	.04	.01
☐ 147	Dave Hamilton	.10	.04	.01
☐ 148	Bruce Boisclair ...	.10	.04	.01
☐ 149	Manny Sarmiento ..	.10	.04	.01
☐ 150	Wayne Cage	.10	.04	.01
☐ 151	John Hiller	.10	.04	.01
☐ 152	Rick Cerone	.10	.04	.01
☐ 153	Dennis Lamp	.10	.04	.01
☐ 154	Jim Gantner DP ...	.10	.04	.01
☐ 155	Dwight Evans	1.00	.40	.10
☐ 156	Buddy Solomon ...	.10	.04	.01
☐ 157	U.L. Washington ...	.10	.04	.01
☐ 158	Joe Sambito	.10	.04	.01
☐ 159	Roy White	.20	.08	.02
☐ 160	Mike Flanagan	.30	.12	.03
☐ 161	Barry Foote	.10	.04	.01
☐ 162	Tom Johnson	.10	.04	.01
☐ 163	Glenn Burke	.10	.04	.01
☐ 164	Mickey Lolich	.30	.12	.03
☐ 165	Frank Taveras	.10	.04	.01
☐ 166	Leon Roberts	.10	.04	.01
☐ 167	Roger Metzger DP .	.04	.02	:00
☐ 168	Dave Freisleben ...	.10	.04	.01
☐ 169	Bill Nahorodny	.10	.04	.01
☐ 170	Don Sutton	1.25	.50	.12
☐ 171	Gene Clines	.10	.04	.01
☐ 172	Miko Bruhrict	.10	.04	.01
☐ 173	John Lowenstein ...	.10	.04	.01
☐ 174	Rick Auerbach	.10	.04	.01
☐ 175	George Hendrick ...	.20	.08	.02
☐ 176	Aurelio Rodriguez ..	.10	.04	.01
☐ 177	Ron Reed	.10	.04	.01
☐ 178	Alvis Woods	.10	.04	.01
☐ 179	Jim Beattie DP	.10	.04	.01
☐ 180	Larry Hisle	.10	.04	.01
☐ 181	Mike Garman	.10	.04	.01
☐ 182	Tim Johnson	.10	.04	.01
☐ 183	Paul Splittorff	.10	.04	.01
☐ 184	Darrel Chaney	.10	.04	.01
☐ 185	Mike Torrez	.10	.04	.01
☐ 186	Eric Soderholm	.10	.04	.01
☐ 187	Mark Lemongello ..	.10	.04	.01
☐ 188	Pat Kelly	.10	.04	.01
☐ 189	Eddie Whitson	.50	.20	.05
☐ 190	Ron Cey	.30	.12	.03
☐ 191	Mike Norris	.10	.04	.01
☐ 192	Cardinals Team/Mgr.	.40	.10	.02
	Ken Boyer			
	(checklist back)			
☐ 193	Glenn Adams	.10	.04	.01
☐ 194	Randy Jones	.10	.04	.01
☐ 195	Bill Madlock	.30	.12	.03
☐ 196	Steve Kemp DP ...	.10	.04	.01
☐ 197	Bob Apodaca	.10	.04	.01
☐ 198	Johnny Grubb	.10	.04	.01
☐ 199	Larry Milbourne ...	.10	.04	.01
☐ 200	Johnny Bench DP .	1.25	.50	.12
☐ 201	RB: Mike Edwards..	.10	.04	.01
	Most unassisted DP's,			
	second basemen			
☐ 202	RB: Ron Guidry, Most	.30	.12	.03
	strikeouts, lefthander,			
	nine inning game			
☐ 203	RB: J.R. Richard ..	.20	.08	.02
	Most strikeouts,			
	season, righthander			
☐ 204	RB: Pete Rose ...	1.50	.60	.15
	Most consecutive			
	games batting safely			
☐ 205	RB: John Stearns .	.10	.04	.01
	Most SB's by			
	catcher, season			
☐ 206	RB: Sammy Stewart	.10	.04	.01
	7 straight SO's,			
	first ML game			
☐ 207	Dave Lemanczyk ..	.10	.04	.01
☐ 208	Clarence Gaston ..	.10	.04	.01
☐ 209	Reggie Cleveland .	.10	.04	.01
☐ 210	Larry Bowa	.30	.12	.03
☐ 211	Denny Martinez ...	.20	.08	.02
☐ 212	Carney Lansford ..	2.75	1.10	.27
☐ 213	Bill Travers	.10	.04	.01
☐ 214	Red Sox Team/Mgr.	.40	.10	.02
	Don Zimmer			
	(checklist back)			
☐ 215	Willie McCovey ...	1.50	.60	.15
☐ 216	Wilbur Wood	.10	.04	.01
☐ 217	Steve Dillard	.10	.04	.01
☐ 218	Dennis Leonard ...	.20	.08	.02
☐ 219	Roy Smalley	.10	.04	.01
☐ 220	Cesar Geronimo ..	.10	.04	.01
☐ 221	Jesse Jefferson ...	.10	.04	.01
☐ 222	Bob Beall	.10	.04	.01

		NRMT	VG-E	GOOD			NRMT	VG-E	GOOD
☐ 223	Kent Tekulve	.20	.08	.02	☐ 268	Julio Gonzalez	.10	.04	.01
☐ 224	Dave Revering	.10	.04	.01	☐ 269	Woodie Fryman	.10	.04	.01
☐ 225	Rich Gossage	.50	.20	.05	☐ 270	Butch Hobson	.10	.04	.01
☐ 226	Ron Pruitt	.10	.04	.01	☐ 271	Rawly Eastwick	.10	.04	.01
☐ 227	Steve Stone	.10	.04	.01	☐ 272	Tim Corcoran	.10	.04	.01
☐ 228	Vic Davalillo	.10	.04	.01	☐ 273	Jerry Terrell	.10	.04	.01
☐ 229	Doug Flynn	.10	.04	.01	☐ 274	Willie Norwood	.10	.04	.01
☐ 230	Bob Forsch	.10	.04	.01	☐ 275	Junior Moore	.10	.04	.01
☐ 231	John Wockenfuss	.10	.04	.01	☐ 276	Jim Colborn	.10	.04	.01
☐ 232	Jimmy Sexton	.10	.04	.01	☐ 277	Tom Grieve	.20	.08	.02
☐ 233	Paul Mitchell	.10	.04	.01	☐ 278	Andy Messersmith	.20	.08	.02
☐ 234	Toby Harrah	.20	.08	.02	☐ 279	Jerry Grote DP	.04	.02	.00
☐ 235	Steve Rogers	.10	.04	.01	☐ 280	Andre Thornton	.20	.08	.02
☐ 236	Jim Dwyer	.10	.04	.01	☐ 281	Vic Correll DP	.04	.02	.00
☐ 237	Billy Smith	.10	.04	.01	☐ 282	Blue Jays Team/Mgr.	.30	.08	.01
☐ 238	Balor Moore	.10	.04	.01		Roy Hartsfield			
☐ 239	Willie Horton	.20	.08	.02		(checklist back)			
☐ 240	Rick Reuschel	.30	.12	.03	☐ 283	Ken Kravec	.10	.04	.01
☐ 241	Checklist 2 DP	.15	.03	.00	☐ 284	Johnnie LeMaster	.10	.04	.01
☐ 242	Pablo Torrealba	.10	.04	.01	☐ 285	Bobby Bonds	.30	.12	.03
☐ 243	Buck Martinez DP	.04	.02	.00	☐ 286	Duffy Dyer	.10	.04	.01
☐ 244	Pirates Team/Mgr.	.40	.10	.02	☐ 287	Andres Mora	.10	.04	.01
	Chuck Tanner				☐ 288	Milt Wilcox	.10	.04	.01
	(checklist back)				☐ 289	Jose Cruz	.20	.08	.02
☐ 245	Jeff Burroughs	.10	.04	.01	☐ 290	Dave Lopes	.20	.08	.02
☐ 246	Darrell Jackson	.10	.04	.01	☐ 291	Tom Griffin	.10	.04	.01
☐ 247	Tucker Ashford DP	.04	.02	.00	☐ 292	Don Reynolds	.10	.04	.01
☐ 248	Pete LaCock	.10	.04	.01	☐ 293	Jerry Garvin	.10	.04	.01
☐ 249	Paul Thormodsgard	.10	.04	.01	☐ 294	Pepe Frias	.10	.04	.01
☐ 250	Willie Randolph	.30	.12	.03	☐ 295	Mitchell Page	.10	.04	.01
☐ 251	Jack Morris	2.75	1.10	.27	☐ 296	Preston Hanna	.10	.04	.01
☐ 252	Bob Stinson	.10	.04	.01	☐ 297	Ted Sizemore	.10	.04	.01
☐ 253	Rick Wise	.10	.04	.01	☐ 298	Rich Gale	.10	.04	.01
☐ 254	Luis Gomez	.10	.04	.01	☐ 299	Steve Ontiveros	.10	.04	.01
☐ 255	Tommy John	.60	.24	.06	☐ 300	Rod Carew	2.25	.90	.22
☐ 256	Mike Sadek	.10	.04	.01	☐ 301	Tom Hume	.10	.04	.01
☐ 257	Adrian Devine	.10	.04	.01	☐ 302	Braves Team/Mgr.	.40	.10	.02
☐ 258	Mike Phillips	.10	.04	.01		Bobby Cox			
☐ 259	Reds Team/Mgr.	.40	.10	.02		(checklist back)			
	Sparky Anderson				☐ 303	Lary Sorensen	.10	.04	.01
	(checklist back)				☐ 304	Steve Swisher	.10	.04	.01
☐ 260	Richie Zisk	.10	.04	.01	☐ 305	Willie Montanez	.10	.04	.01
☐ 261	Mario Guerrero	.10	.04	.01	☐ 306	Floyd Bannister	.20	.08	.02
☐ 262	Nelson Briles	.10	.04	.01	☐ 307	Larvell Blanks	.10	.04	.01
☐ 263	Oscar Gamble	.10	.04	.01	☐ 308	Bert Blyleven	.40	.16	.04
☐ 264	Don Robinson	.75	.30	.07	☐ 309	Ralph Garr	.10	.04	.01
☐ 265	Don Money	.10	.04	.01	☐ 310	Thurman Munson	2.00	.80	.20
☐ 266	Jim Willoughby	.10	.04	.01	☐ 311	Gary Lavelle	.10	.04	.01
☐ 267	Joe Rudi	.20	.08	.02	☐ 312	Bob Robertson	.10	.04	.01

		NRMT	VG-E	GOOD			NRMT	VG-E	GOOD
☐ 313	Dyar Miller	.10	.04	.01	☐ 358	Alan Trammell	6.00	2.40	.60
☐ 314	Larry Harlow	.10	.04	.01	☐ 359	Dan Spillner DP	.04	.02	.00
☐ 315	Jon Matlack	.10	.04	.01	☐ 360	Amos Otis	.20	.08	.02
☐ 316	Milt May	.10	.04	.01	☐ 361	Tom Dixon	.10	.04	.01
☐ 317	Jose Cardenal	.10	.04	.01	☐ 362	Mike Cubbage	.10	.04	.01
☐ 318	Bob Welch	2.75	1.10	.27	☐ 363	Craig Skok	.10	.04	.01
☐ 319	Wayne Garrett	.10	.04	.01	☐ 364	Gene Richards	.10	.04	.01
☐ 320	Carl Yastrzemski	3.00	1.20	.30	☐ 365	Sparky Lyle	.30	.12	.03
☐ 321	Gaylord Perry	1.50	.60	.15	☐ 366	Juan Bernhardt	.10	.04	.01
☐ 322	Danny Goodwin	.10	.04	.01	☐ 367	Dave Skaggs	.10	.04	.01
☐ 323	Lynn McGlothen	.10	.04	.01	☐ 368	Don Aase	.10	.04	.01
☐ 324	Mike Tyson	.10	.04	.01	☐ 369A	Bump Wills ERR	3.00	1.20	.30
☐ 325	Cecil Cooper	.40	.16	.04		(Blue Jays)			
☐ 326	Pedro Borbon	.10	.04	.01	☐ 369B	Bump Wills COR	4.00	1.60	.40
☐ 327	Art Howe	.20	.08	.01		(Rangers)			
☐ 328	Oakland A's Team/Mgr.	.40	.10	.02	☐ 370	Dave Kingman	.40	.16	.04
	Jack McKeon				☐ 371	Jeff Holly	.10	.04	.01
	(checklist back)				☐ 372	Lamar Johnson	.10	.04	.01
☐ 329	Joe Coleman	.10	.04	.01	☐ 373	Lance Rautzhan	.10	.04	.01
☐ 330	George Brett	3.50	1.40	.35	☐ 374	Ed Herrmann	.10	.04	.01
☐ 331	Mickey Mahler	.10	.04	.01	☐ 375	Bill Campbell	.10	.04	.01
☐ 332	Gary Alexander	.10	.04	.01	☐ 376	Gorman Thomas	.30	.12	.03
☐ 333	Chet Lemon	.20	.08	.02	☐ 377	Paul Moskau	.10	.04	.01
☐ 334	Craig Swan	.10	.04	.01	☐ 378	Rob Picciolo DP	.04	.02	.00
☐ 335	Chris Chambliss	.20	.08	.02	☐ 379	Dale Murray	.10	.04	.01
☐ 336	Bobby Thompson	.10	.04	.01	☐ 380	John Mayberry	.20	.08	.02
☐ 337	John Montague	.10	.04	.01	☐ 381	Astros Team/Mgr.	.40	.10	.02
☐ 338	Vic Harris	.10	.04	.01		Bill Virdon			
☐ 339	Ron Jackson	.10	.04	.01		(checklist back)			
☐ 340	Jim Palmer	1.50	.60	.15	☐ 382	Jerry Martin	.10	.04	.01
☐ 341	Willie Upshaw	.50	.20	.05	☐ 383	Phil Garner	.10	.04	.01
☐ 342	Dave Roberts	.10	.04	.01	☐ 384	Tommy Boggs	.10	.04	.01
☐ 343	Ed Glynn	.10	.04	.01	☐ 385	Dan Ford	.10	.04	.01
☐ 344	Jerry Royster	.10	.04	.01	☐ 386	Francisco Barrios	.10	.04	.01
☐ 345	Tug McGraw	.30	.12	.03	☐ 387	Gary Thomasson	.10	.04	.01
☐ 346	Bill Buckner	.30	.12	.03	☐ 388	Jack Billingham	.10	.04	.01
☐ 347	Doug Rau	.10	.04	.01	☐ 389	Joe Zdeb	.10	.04	.01
☐ 348	Andre Dawson	5.00	2.00	.50	☐ 390	Rollie Fingers	.60	.24	.06
☐ 349	Jim Wright	.10	.04	.01	☐ 391	Al Oliver	.30	.12	.03
☐ 350	Garry Templeton	.20	.08	.02	☐ 392	Doug Ault	.10	.04	.01
☐ 351	Wayne Nordhagen	.10	.04	.01	☐ 393	Scott McGregor	.20	.08	.02
☐ 352	Steve Renko	.10	.04	.01	☐ 394	Randy Stein	.10	.04	.01
☐ 353	Checklist 3	.40	.05	.01	☐ 395	Dave Cash	.10	.04	.01
☐ 354	Bill Bonham	.10	.04	.01	☐ 396	Bill Plummer	.10	.04	.01
☐ 355	Lee Mazzilli	.10	.04	.01	☐ 397	Sergio Ferrer	.10	.04	.01
☐ 356	Giants Team/Mgr.	.40	.10	.02	☐ 398	Ivan DeJesus	.10	.04	.01
	Joe Altobelli				☐ 399	David Clyde	.10	.04	.01
	(checklist back)				☐ 400	Jim Rice	2.50	1.00	.25
☐ 357	Jerry Augustine	.10	.04	.01	☐ 401	Ray Knight	.30	.12	.03

		NRMT	VG-E	GOOD
☐ 402	Paul Hartzell	.10	.04	.01
☐ 403	Tim Foli	.10	.04	.01
☐ 404	White Sox Team/Mgr Don Kessinger (checklist back)	.40	.10	.02
☐ 405	Butch Wynegar DP	.04	.02	.00
☐ 406	Joe Wallis DP	.04	.02	.00
☐ 407	Pete Vuckovich	.10	.04	.01
☐ 408	Charlie Moore DP	.04	.02	.00
☐ 409	Willie Wilson	1.50	.60	.15
☐ 410	Darrell Evans	.30	.12	.03
☐ 411	Hits Record Season: G.Sisler Career: Ty Cobb	.40	.16	.04
☐ 412	RBI Record Season: Hack Wilson Career: Hank Aaron	.40	.16	.04
☐ 413	Home Run Record Season: Roger Maris Career: Hank Aaron	.50	.20	.05
☐ 414	Batting Record Season: R.Hornsby Career: Ty Cobb	.40	.16	.04
☐ 415	Steals Record Season: Lou Brock Career: Lou Brock	.40	.16	.04
☐ 416	Wins Record Season: Jack Chesbro Career: Cy Young	.20	.08	.02
☐ 417	Strikeout Record DP Season: Nolan Ryan Career: W.Johnson	.15	.06	.01
☐ 418	ERA Record DP Season: Dutch Leonard Career: W.Johnson	.10	.04	.01
☐ 419	Dick Ruthven	.10	.04	.01
☐ 420	Ken Griffey	.20	.08	.02
☐ 421	Doug DeCinces	.20	.08	.02
☐ 422	Ruppert Jones	.10	.04	.01
☐ 423	Bob Montgomery	.10	.04	.01
☐ 424	Angels Team/Mgr. Jim Fregosi (checklist back)	.40	.10	.02
☐ 425	Rick Manning	.10	.04	.01
☐ 426	Chris Speier	.10	.04	.01
☐ 427	Andy Replogle	.10	.04	.01
☐ 428	Bobby Valentine	.20	.08	.02
☐ 429	John Urrea DP	.04	.02	.00
☐ 430	Dave Parker	1.25	.50	.12
☐ 431	Glenn Borgmann	.10	.04	.01
☐ 432	Dave Heaverlo	.10	.04	.01
☐ 433	Larry Biittner	.10	.04	.01
☐ 434	Ken Clay	.10	.04	.01
☐ 435	Gene Tenace	.10	.04	.01
☐ 436	Hector Cruz	.10	.04	.01
☐ 437	Rick Williams	.10	.04	.01
☐ 438	Horace Speed	.10	.04	.01
☐ 439	Frank White	.20	.08	.02
☐ 440	Rusty Staub	.30	.12	.03
☐ 441	Lee Lacy	.10	.04	.01
☐ 442	Doyle Alexander	.20	.08	.02
☐ 443	Bruce Bochte	.10	.04	.01
☐ 444	Aurelio Lopez	.20	.08	.02
☐ 445	Steve Henderson	.10	.04	.01
☐ 446	Jim Lonborg	.10	.04	.01
☐ 447	Manny Sanguillen	.10	.04	.01
☐ 448	Moose Haas	.10	.04	.01
☐ 449	Bombo Rivera	.10	.04	.01
☐ 450	Dave Concepcion	.20	.08	.02
☐ 451	Royals Team/Mgr. Whitey Herzog (checklist back)	.40	.10	.02
☐ 452	Jerry Morales	.10	.04	.01
☐ 453	Chris Knapp	.10	.04	.01
☐ 454	Len Randle	.10	.04	.01
☐ 455	Bill Lee DP	.10	.04	.01
☐ 456	Chuck Baker	.10	.04	.01
☐ 457	Bruce Sutter	.60	.24	.06
☐ 458	Jim Essian	.10	.04	.01
☐ 459	Sid Monge	.10	.04	.01
☐ 460	Graig Nettles	.40	.16	.04
☐ 461	Jim Barr DP	.04	.02	.00
☐ 462	Otto Velez	.10	.04	.01
☐ 463	Steve Comer	.10	.04	.01
☐ 464	Joe Nolan	.10	.04	.01
☐ 465	Reggie Smith	.20	.08	.02
☐ 466	Mark Littell	.10	.04	.01
☐ 467	Don Kessinger DP	.10	.04	.01
☐ 468	Stan Bahnsen DP	.04	.02	.00
☐ 469	Lance Parrish	3.00	1.20	.30
☐ 470	Garry Maddox DP	.10	.04	.01
☐ 471	Joaquin Andujar	.20	.08	.02
☐ 472	Craig Kusick	.10	.04	.01
☐ 473	Dave Roberts	.10	.04	.01
☐ 474	Dick Davis	.10	.04	.01
☐ 475	Dan Driessen	.10	.04	.01
☐ 476	Tom Poquette	.10	.04	.01
☐ 477	Bob Grich	.20	.08	.02

		NRMT	VG-E	GOOD			NRMT	VG-E	GOOD
☐ 478	Juan Beniquez	.10	.04	.01	☐ 522	Ken Holtzman	.10	.04	.01
☐ 479	Padres Team/Mgr.	.40	.10	.02	☐ 523	John Milner	.10	.04	.01
	Roger Craig				☐ 524	Tom Burgmeier	.10	.04	.01
	(checklist back)				☐ 525	Freddie Patek	.10	.04	.01
☐ 480	Fred Lynn	.70	.28	.07	☐ 526	Dodgers Team/Mgr.	.50	.12	.02
☐ 481	Skip Lockwood	.10	.04	.01		Tom Lasorda			
☐ 482	Craig Reynolds	.10	.04	.01		(checklist back)			
☐ 483	Checklist 4 DP	.15	.03	.00	☐ 527	Lerrin LaGrow	.10	.04	.01
☐ 484	Rick Waits	.10	.04	.01	☐ 528	Wayne Gross DP	.04	.02	.00
☐ 485	Bucky Dent	.20	.08	.02	☐ 529	Brian Asselstine	.10	.04	.01
☐ 486	Bob Knepper	.30	.12	.03	☐ 530	Frank Tanana	.20	.08	.02
☐ 487	Miguel Dilone	.10	.04	.01	☐ 531	Fernando Gonzalez	.10	.04	.01
☐ 488	Bob Owchinko	.10	.04	.01	☐ 532	Buddy Schultz	.10	.04	.01
☐ 489	Larry Cox	.10	.04	.01	☐ 533	Leroy Stanton	.10	.04	.01
	(photo actually Dave Rader)				☐ 534	Ken Forsch	.10	.04	.01
☐ 490	Al Cowens	.10	.04	.01	☐ 535	Ellis Valentine	.10	.04	.01
☐ 491	Tippy Martinez	.10	.04	.01	☐ 536	Jerry Reuss	.20	.08	.02
☐ 492	Bob Bailor	.10	.04	.01	☐ 537	Tom Veryzer	.10	.04	.01
☐ 493	Larry Christenson	.10	.04	.01	☐ 538	Mike Ivie DP	.04	.02	.00
☐ 494	Jerry White	.10	.04	.01	☐ 539	John Ellis	.10	.04	.01
☐ 495	Tony Perez	.50	.20	.05	☐ 540	Greg Luzinski	.30	.12	.03
☐ 496	Barry Bonnell DP	.04	.02	.00	☐ 541	Jim Slaton	.10	.04	.01
☐ 497	Glenn Abbott	.10	.04	.01	☐ 542	Rick Bosetti	.10	.04	.01
☐ 498	Rich Chiles	.10	.04	.01	☐ 543	Kiko Garcia	.10	.04	.01
☐ 499	Rangers Team/Mgr.	.40	.10	.02	☐ 544	Fergie Jenkins	.40	.16	.04
	Pat Corrales				☐ 545	John Stearns	.10	.04	.01
	(checklist back)				☐ 546	Bill Russell	.20	.08	.01
☐ 500	Ron Guidry	1.00	.40	.10	☐ 547	Clint Hurdle	.10	.04	.01
☐ 501	Junior Kennedy	.10	.04	.01	☐ 548	Enrique Romo	.10	.04	.01
☐ 502	Steve Braun	.10	.04	.01	☐ 549	Bob Bailey	.10	.04	.01
☐ 503	Terry Humphrey	.10	.04	.01	☐ 550	Sal Bando	.20	.08	.02
☐ 504	Larry McWilliams	.30	.12	.03	☐ 551	Cubs Team/Mgr.	.40	.10	.02
☐ 505	Ed Kranepool	.10	.04	.01		Herman Franks			
☐ 506	John D'Acquisto	.10	.04	.01		(checklist back)			
☐ 507	Tony Armas	.20	.08	.02	☐ 552	Jose Morales	.10	.04	.01
☐ 508	Charlie Hough	.20	.08	.02	☐ 553	Denny Walling	.10	.04	.01
☐ 509	Mario Mendoza	.10	.04	.01	☐ 554	Matt Keough	.10	.04	.01
☐ 510	Ted Simmons	.40	.18	.03	☐ 555	Biff Pocoroba	.10	.04	.01
☐ 511	Paul Reuschel DP	.04	.02	.00	☐ 556	Mike Lum	.10	.04	.01
☐ 512	Jack Clark	2.50	1.00	.25	☐ 557	Ken Brett	.10	.04	.01
☐ 513	Dave Johnson	.20	.08	.02	☐ 558	Jay Johnstone	.20	.08	.02
☐ 514	Mike Proly	.10	.04	.01	☐ 559	Greg Pryor	.10	.04	.01
☐ 515	Enos Cabell	.10	.04	.01	☐ 560	John Montefusco	.20	.08	.02
☐ 516	Champ Summers DP	.04	.02	.00	☐ 561	Ed Ott	.10	.04	.01
☐ 517	Al Bumbry	.10	.04	.01	☐ 562	Dusty Baker	.20	.08	.02
☐ 518	Jim Umbarger	.10	.04	.01	☐ 563	Roy Thomas	.10	.04	.01
☐ 519	Ben Oglivie	.20	.08	.01	☐ 564	Jerry Turner	.10	.04	.01
☐ 520	Gary Carter	2.50	1.00	.25	☐ 565	Rico Carty	.20	.08	.02
☐ 521	Sam Ewing	.10	.04	.01	☐ 566	Nino Espinosa	.10	.04	.01

		NRMT	VG-E	GOOD
☐ 567	Richie Hebner	.10	.04	.01
☐ 568	Carlos Lopez	.10	.04	.01
☐ 569	Bob Sykes	.10	.04	.01
☐ 570	Cesar Cedeno	.20	.08	.02
☐ 571	Darrell Porter	.10	.04	.01
☐ 572	Rod Gilbreath	.10	.04	.01
☐ 573	Jim Kern	.10	.04	.01
☐ 574	Claudell Washington	.20	.08	.02
☐ 575	Luis Tiant	.30	.12	.03
☐ 576	Mike Parrott	.10	.04	.01
☐ 577	Brewers Team/Mgr.	.40	.10	.02
	George Bamberger			
	(checklist back)			
☐ 578	Pete Broberg	.10	.04	.01
☐ 579	Greg Gross	.10	.04	.01
☐ 580	Ron Fairly	.10	.04	.01
☐ 581	Darold Knowles	.10	.04	.01
☐ 582	Paul Blair	.10	.04	.01
☐ 583	Julio Cruz	.10	.04	.01
☐ 584	Jim Rooker	.10	.04	.01
☐ 585	Hal McRae	.20	.08	.02
☐ 586	Bob Horner	2.50	1.00	.25
☐ 587	Ken Reitz	.10	.04	.01
☐ 588	Tom Murphy	.10	.04	.01
☐ 589	Terry Whitfield	.10	.04	.01
☐ 590	J.R. Richard	.20	.08	.02
☐ 591	Mike Hargrove	.10	.04	.01
☐ 592	Mike Krukow	.20	.08	.02
☐ 593	Rick Dempsey	.10	.04	.01
☐ 594	Bob Shirley	.10	.04	.01
☐ 595	Phil Niekro	1.25	.50	.12
☐ 596	Jim Wohlford	.10	.04	.01
☐ 597	Bob Stanley	.10	.04	.01
☐ 598	Mark Wagner	.10	.04	.01
☐ 599	Jim Spencer	.10	.04	.01
☐ 600	George Foster	.50	.20	.05
☐ 601	Dave LaRoche	.10	.04	.01
☐ 602	Checklist 5	.45	.05	.01
☐ 603	Rudy May	.10	.04	.01
☐ 604	Jeff Newman	.10	.04	.01
☐ 605	Rick Monday DP	.10	.04	.01
☐ 606	Expos Team/Mgr.	.40	.10	.02
	Dick Williams			
	(checklist back)			
☐ 607	Omar Moreno	.10	.04	.01
☐ 608	Dave McKay	.10	.04	.01
☐ 609	Silvio Martinez	.10	.04	.01
☐ 610	Mike Schmidt	4.00	1.60	.40
☐ 611	Jim Norris	.10	.04	.01
☐ 612	Rick Honeycutt	.50	.20	.05
☐ 613	Mike Edwards	.10	.04	.01
☐ 614	Willie Hernandez	.40	.16	.04
☐ 615	Ken Singleton	.20	.08	.02
☐ 616	Billy Almon	.10	.04	.01
☐ 617	Terry Puhl	.10	.04	.01
☐ 618	Jerry Remy	.10	.04	.01
☐ 619	Ken Landreaux	.30	.12	.03
☐ 620	Bert Campaneris	.10	.04	.01
☐ 621	Pat Zachry	.10	.04	.01
☐ 622	Dave Collins	.10	.04	.01
☐ 623	Bob McClure	.10	.04	.01
☐ 624	Larry Herndon	.10	.04	.01
☐ 625	Mark Fidrych	.20	.08	.02
☐ 626	Yankees Team/Mgr.	.50	.12	.02
	Bob Lemon			
	(checklist back)			
☐ 627	Gary Serum	.10	.04	.01
☐ 628	Del Unser	.10	.04	.01
☐ 629	Gene Garber	.10	.04	.01
☐ 630	Bake McBride	.10	.04	.01
☐ 631	Jorge Orta	.10	.04	.01
☐ 632	Don Kirkwood	.10	.04	.01
☐ 633	Rob Wilfong DP	.04	.02	.00
☐ 634	Paul Lindblad	.10	.04	.01
☐ 635	Don Baylor	.75	.30	.07
☐ 636	Wayne Garland	.10	.04	.01
☐ 637	Bill Robinson	.20	.08	.02
☐ 638	Al Fitzmorris	.10	.04	.01
☐ 639	Manny Trillo	.10	.04	.01
☐ 640	Eddie Murray	6.00	2.40	.60
☐ 641	Bobby Castillo	.10	.04	.01
☐ 642	Wilbur Howard DP	.04	.02	.00
☐ 643	Tom Hausman	.10	.04	.01
☐ 644	Manny Mota	.10	.04	.01
☐ 645	George Scott DP	.10	.04	.01
☐ 646	Rick Sweet	.10	.04	.01
☐ 647	Bob Lacey	.10	.04	.01
☐ 648	Lou Piniella	.20	.08	.02
☐ 649	John Curtis	.10	.04	.01
☐ 650	Pete Rose	4.50	1.80	.45
☐ 651	Mike Caldwell	.10	.04	.01
☐ 652	Stan Papi	.10	.04	.01
☐ 653	Warren Brusstar DP	.04	.02	.00
☐ 654	Rick Miller	.10	.04	.01
☐ 655	Jerry Koosman	.20	.08	.02
☐ 656	Hosken Powell	.10	.04	.01
☐ 657	George Medich	.10	.04	.01
☐ 658	Taylor Duncan	.10	.04	.01

		NRMT	VG-E	GOOD			NRMT	VG-E	GOOD
☐ 659	Mariners Team/Mgr. Darrell Johnson (checklist back)	.40	.10	.02	☐ 701	Orioles Prospects . Mark Corey John Flinn Sammy Stewart	.20	.08	.02
☐ 660	Ron LeFlore DP ...	.10	.04	.01					
☐ 661	Bruce Kison	.10	.04	.01	☐ 702	Red Sox Prospects Joel Finch Garry Hancock Allen Ripley	.20	.08	.02
☐ 662	Kevin Bell	.10	.04	.01					
☐ 663	Mike Vail	.10	.04	.01					
☐ 664	Doug Bird	.10	.04	.01	☐ 703	Angels Prospects . Jim Anderson Dave Frost Bob Slater	.10	.04	.01
☐ 665	Lou Brock	1.50	.60	.15					
☐ 666	Rich Dauer	.10	.04	.01					
☐ 667	Don Hood	.10	.04	.01	☐ 704	White Sox Prospects Ross Baumgarten Mike Colbern Mike Squires	.10	.04	.01
☐ 668	Bill North	.10	.04	.01					
☐ 669	Checklist 6	.45	.05	.01					
☐ 670	Jim Hunter DP ...	.60	.20	.05	☐ 705	Indians Prospects . Alfredo Griffin Tim Norrid Dave Oliver	1.00	.40	.10
☐ 671	Joe Ferguson DP ..	.04	.02	.00					
☐ 672	Ed Halicki	.10	.04	.01					
☐ 673	Tom Hutton	.10	.04	.01	☐ 706	Tigers Prospects .. Dave Stegman Dave Tobik Kip Young	.10	.04	.01
☐ 674	Dave Tomlin	.10	.04	.01					
☐ 675	Tim McCarver	.30	.12	.03					
☐ 676	Johnny Sutton	.10	.04	.01	☐ 707	Royals Prospects . Randy Bass Jim Gaudet Randy McGilberry	.20	.08	.02
☐ 677	Larry Parrish	.20	.08	.02					
☐ 678	Geoff Zahn	.10	.04	.01					
☐ 679	Derrel Thomas	.10	.04	.01	☐ 708	Brewers Prospects Kevin Bass Eddie Romero Ned Yost	1.50	.60	.15
☐ 680	Carlton Fisk	.60	.24	.06					
☐ 681	John Henry Johnson	.10	.04	.01					
☐ 682	Dave Chalk	.10	.04	.01	☐ 709	Twins Prospects .. Sam Perlozzo Rick Sofield Kevin Stanfield	.10	.04	.01
☐ 683	Dan Meyer DP	.04	.02	.00					
☐ 684	Jamie Easterly DP .	.04	.02	.00					
☐ 685	Sixto Lezcano	.10	.04	.01	☐ 710	Yankees Prospects Brian Doyle Mike Heath Dave Rajsich	.30	.12	.03
☐ 686	Ron Schueler DP ..	.04	.02	.00					
☐ 687	Rennie Stennett ...	.10	.04	.01					
☐ 688	Mike Willis	.10	.04	.01	☐ 711	A's Prospects .... Dwayne Murphy Bruce Robinson Alan Wirth	.30	.12	.03
☐ 689	Orioles Team/Mgr. Earl Weaver (checklist back)	.50	.12	.02					
☐ 690	Buddy Bell DP	.10	.04	.01	☐ 712	Mariners Prospects Bud Anderson Greg Biercevicz Byron McLaughlin	.10	.04	.01
☐ 691	Dock Ellis DP	.04	.02	.00					
☐ 692	Mickey Stanley	.10	.04	.01					
☐ 693	Dave Rader	.10	.04	.01					
☐ 694	Burt Hooton	.10	.04	.01					
☐ 695	Keith Hernandez ...	2.25	.90	.22					
☐ 696	Andy Hassler	.10	.04	.01					
☐ 697	Dave Bergman	.10	.04	.01					
☐ 698	Bill Stein	.10	.04	.01					
☐ 699	Hal Dues	.10	.04	.01					
☐ 700	Reggie Jackson DP	1.50	.60	.15					

	NRMT	VG-E	GOOD
☐ 713 Rangers Prospects . Danny Darwin Pat Putnam Billy Sample	.30	.12	.03
☐ 714 Blue Jays Prospects Victor Cruz Pat Kelly Ernie Whitt	.30	.12	.03
☐ 715 Braves Prospects .. Bruce Benedict Glenn Hubbard Larry Whisenton	.30	.12	.03
☐ 716 Cubs Prospects .... Dave Geisel Karl Pagel Scot Thompson	.10	.04	.01
☐ 717 Reds Prospects .... Mike LaCoss Ron Oester Harry Spilman	.40	.16	.04
☐ 718 Astros Prospects ... Bruce Bochy Mike Fischlin Don Pisker	.10	.04	.01
☐ 719 Dodgers Prospects . Pedro Guerrero Rudy Law Joe Simpson	7.00	2.80	.70
☐ 720 Expos Prospects .... Jerry Fry Jerry Pirtle Scott Sanderson	.30	.12	.03
☐ 721 Mets Prospects .... Juan Berenguer Dwight Bernard Dan Norman	.30	.12	.03
☐ 722 Phillies Prospects .. Jim Morrison Lonnie Smith Jim Wright	.30	.12	.03
☐ 723 Pirates Prospects .. Dale Berra Eugenio Cotes Ben Wiltbank	.30	.12	.03
☐ 724 Cardinals Prospects Tom Bruno George Frazier Terry Kennedy	.30	.12	.03

	NRMT	VG-E	GOOD
☐ 725 Padres Prospects . Jim Beswick Steve Mura Broderick Perkins	.10	.04	.01
☐ 726 Giants Prospects .. Greg Johnston Joe Strain John Tamargo	.20	.08	.02

1980 Topps

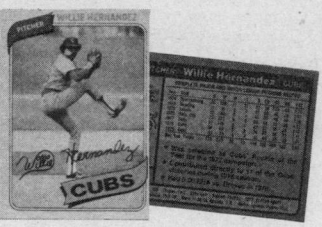

The cards in this 726-card set measure 2 ½ "
by 3 ½ ". In 1980 Topps released another set
of the same size and number of cards as the
previous two years. As with these sets,
Topps again has produced 66 double-
printed cards in the set; they are noted by DP
in the checklist below. The player's name
appears over the picture and his position
and team are found in pennant design.
Every card carries a facsimile autograph.
Team cards feature a team checklist of
players in the set on the back and the
manager's name on the front. Cards 1-6
show Highlights (HL) of the 1979 season,
cards 201-207 are League Leaders, and
cards 661-686 feature American and National League rookie "Future Stars," one card for
each team showing three young prospects.

	MINT	EXC	G-VG
Complete Set (726)	140.00	56.00	14.00
Common Player (1-726) .	.10	.04	.01
Common DP's (1-726) ...	.04	.02	.00

		MINT	EXC	G-VG
☐ 1	HL: Brock and Yaz, . Enter 3000 hit circle	1.50	.40	.08
☐ 2	HL: Willie McCovey, 512th homer sets new mark for NL lefties	.65	.26	.06
☐ 3	HL: Manny Mota, All-time pinch-hits, 145	.20	.08	.02
☐ 4	HL: Pete Rose, Career Record 10th season with 200 or more hits	2.00	.80	.20
☐ 5	HL: Garry Templeton, First with 100 hits from each side of plate	.20	.08	.02
☐ 6	HL: Del Unser, 3rd . cons. pinch homer sets new ML standard	.10	.04	.01
☐ 7	Mike Lum	.10	.04	.01
☐ 8	Craig Swan	.10	.04	.01
☐ 9	Steve Braun	.10	.04	.01
☐ 10	Denny Martinez	.20	.08	.02
☐ 11	Jimmy Sexton	.10	.04	.01
☐ 12	John Curtis DP	.04	.02	.00
☐ 13	Ron Pruitt	.10	.04	.01
☐ 14	Dave Cash	.10	.04	.01
☐ 15	Bill Campbell	.10	.04	.01
☐ 16	Jerry Narron	.10	.04	.01
☐ 17	Bruce Sutter	.40	.16	.04
☐ 18	Ron Jackson	.10	.04	.01
☐ 19	Balor Moore	.10	.04	.01
☐ 20	Dan Ford	.10	.04	.01
☐ 21	Manny Sarmiento	.10	.04	.01
☐ 22	Pat Putnam	.10	.04	.01
☐ 23	Derrel Thomas	.10	.04	.01
☐ 24	Jim Slaton	.10	.04	.01
☐ 25	Lee Mazzilli	.10	.04	.01
☐ 26	Marty Pattin	.10	.04	.01
☐ 27	Del Unser	.10	.04	.01
☐ 28	Bruce Kison	.10	.04	.01
☐ 29	Mark Wagner	.10	.04	.01
☐ 30	Vida Blue	.20	.08	.02
☐ 31	Jay Johnstone	.20	.08	.02
☐ 32	Julio Cruz DP	.10	.04	.01
☐ 33	Tony Scott	.10	.04	.01
☐ 34	Jeff Newman DP	.04	.02	.00
☐ 35	Luis Tiant	.20	.08	.02
☐ 36	Rusty Torres	.10	.04	.01
☐ 37	Kiko Garcia	.10	.04	.01
☐ 38	Dan Spillner DP	.04	.02	.00
☐ 39	Rowland Office	.10	.04	.01
☐ 40	Carlton Fisk	.50	.20	.05
☐ 41	Rangers Team/Mgr. Pat Corrales (checklist back)	.35	.10	.02
☐ 42	David Palmer	.40	.16	.04
☐ 43	Bombo Rivera	.10	.04	.01
☐ 44	Bill Fahey	.10	.04	.01
☐ 45	Frank White	.30	.12	.03
☐ 46	Rico Carty	.20	.08	.02
☐ 47	Bill Bonham DP	.04	.02	.00
☐ 48	Rick Miller	.10	.04	.01
☐ 49	Mario Guerrero	.10	.04	.01
☐ 50	J.R. Richard	.20	.08	.02
☐ 51	Joe Ferguson DP	.04	.02	.00
☐ 52	Warren Brusstar	.10	.04	.01
☐ 53	Ben Oglivie	.20	.08	.02
☐ 54	Dennis Lamp	.10	.04	.01
☐ 55	Bill Madlock	.30	.12	.03
☐ 56	Bobby Valentine	.20	.08	.02
☐ 57	Pete Vuckovich	.10	.04	.01
☐ 58	Doug Flynn	.10	.04	.01
☐ 59	Eddy Putman	.10	.04	.01
☐ 60	Bucky Dent	.20	.08	.02
☐ 61	Gary Serum	.10	.04	.01
☐ 62	Mike Ivie	.10	.04	.01
☐ 63	Bob Stanley	.10	.04	.01
☐ 64	Joe Nolan	.10	.04	.01
☐ 65	Al Bumbry	.10	.04	.01
☐ 66	Royals Team/Mgr. Jim Frey (checklist back)	.35	.10	.02
☐ 67	Doyle Alexander	.20	.08	.02
☐ 68	Larry Harlow	.10	.04	.01
☐ 69	Rick Williams	.10	.04	.01
☐ 70	Gary Carter	2.00	.80	.20
☐ 71	John Milner DP	.04	.02	.00
☐ 72	Fred Howard DP	.04	.02	.00
☐ 73	Dave Collins	.10	.04	.01
☐ 74	Sid Monge	.10	.04	.01
☐ 75	Bill Russell	.20	.08	.02
☐ 76	John Stearns	.10	.04	.01
☐ 77	Dave Stieb	3.50	1.40	.35
☐ 78	Ruppert Jones	.10	.04	.01
☐ 79	Bob Owchinko	.10	.04	.01
☐ 80	Ron LeFlore	.10	.04	.01
☐ 81	Ted Sizemore	.10	.04	.01
☐ 82	Astros Team/Mgr. Bill Virdon (checklist back)	.35	.10	.02

		MINT	EXC	G-VG			MINT	EXC	G-VG
☐ 83	Steve Trout	.30	.12	.03	☐ 128	Tom Burgmeier	.10	.04	.01
☐ 84	Gary Lavelle	.10	.04	.01	☐ 129	Craig Reynolds	.10	.04	.01
☐ 85	Ted Simmons	.40	.16	.04	☐ 130	Amos Otis	.20	.08	.02
☐ 86	Dave Hamilton	.10	.04	.01	☐ 131	Paul Mitchell	.10	.04	.01
☐ 87	Pepe Frias	.10	.04	.01	☐ 132	Biff Pocoroba	.10	.04	.01
☐ 88	Ken Landreaux	.10	.04	.01	☐ 133	Jerry Turner	.10	.04	.01
☐ 89	Don Hood	.10	.04	.01	☐ 134	Matt Keough	.10	.04	.01
☐ 90	Manny Trillo	.10	.04	.01	☐ 135	Bill Buckner	.30	.12	.03
☐ 91	Rick Dempsey	.10	.04	.01	☐ 136	Dick Ruthven	.10	.04	.01
☐ 92	Rick Rhoden	.20	.08	.02	☐ 137	John Castino	.10	.04	.01
☐ 93	Dave Roberts DP	.04	.02	.00	☐ 138	Ross Baumgarten	.10	.04	.01
☐ 94	Neil Allen	.40	.16	.04	☐ 139	Dane Iorg	.20	.08	.02
☐ 95	Cecil Cooper	.30	.12	.03	☐ 140	Rich Gossage	.50	.20	.05
☐ 96	A's Team/Mgr.	.35	.10	.02	☐ 141	Gary Alexander	.10	.04	.01
	Jim Marshall				☐ 142	Phil Huffman	.10	.04	.01
	(checklist back)				☐ 143	Bruce Bochte DP	.10	.04	.01
☐ 97	Bill Lee	.10	.04	.01	☐ 144	Steve Comer	.10	.04	.01
☐ 98	Jerry Terrell	.10	.04	.01	☐ 145	Darrell Evans	.30	.12	.03
☐ 99	Victor Cruz	.10	.04	.01	☐ 146	Bob Welch	.50	.20	.05
☐ 100	Johnny Bench	2.50	1.00	.25	☐ 147	Terry Puhl	.10	.04	.01
☐ 101	Aurelio Lopez	.10	.04	.01	☐ 148	Manny Sanguillen	.20	.08	.02
☐ 102	Rich Dauer	.10	.04	.01	☐ 149	Tom Hume	.10	.04	.01
☐ 103	Bill Caudill	.30	.12	.03	☐ 150	Jason Thompson	.10	.04	.01
☐ 104	Manny Mota	.10	.04	.01	☐ 151	Tom Hausman DP	.04	.02	.00
☐ 105	Frank Tanana	.20	.08	.02	☐ 152	John Fulgham	.10	.04	.01
☐ 106	Jeff Leonard	1.50	.60	.15	☐ 153	Tim Blackwell	.10	.04	.01
☐ 107	Francisco Barrios	.10	.04	.01	☐ 154	Lary Sorensen	.10	.04	.01
☐ 108	Bob Horner	.90	.36	.09	☐ 155	Jerry Remy	.10	.04	.01
☐ 109	Bill Travers	.10	.04	.01	☐ 156	Tony Brizzolara	.10	.04	.01
☐ 110	Fred Lynn DP	.30	.12	.03	☐ 157	Willie Wilson DP	.20	.08	.02
☐ 111	Bob Knepper	.20	.08	.02	☐ 158	Rob Picciolo DP	.04	.02	.00
☐ 112	White Sox Team/Mgr.	.35	.10	.02	☐ 159	Ken Clay	.10	.04	.01
	Tony LaRussa				☐ 160	Eddie Murray	3.50	1.40	.35
	(checklist back)				☐ 161	Larry Christenson	.10	.04	.01
☐ 113	Geoff Zahn	.10	.04	.01	☐ 162	Bob Randall	.10	.04	.01
☐ 114	Juan Beniquez	.10	.04	.01	☐ 163	Steve Swisher	.10	.04	.01
☐ 115	Sparky Lyle	.20	.08	.02	☐ 164	Greg Pryor	.10	.04	.01
☐ 116	Larry Cox	.10	.04	.01	☐ 165	Omar Moreno	.10	.04	.01
☐ 117	Dock Ellis	.10	.04	.01	☐ 166	Glenn Abbott	.10	.04	.01
☐ 118	Phil Garner	.10	.04	.01	☐ 167	Jack Clark	2.00	.80	.20
☐ 119	Sammy Stewart	.10	.04	.01	☐ 168	Rick Waits	.10	.04	.01
☐ 120	Greg Luzinski	.20	.08	.02	☐ 169	Luis Gomez	.10	.04	.01
☐ 121	Checklist 1	.25	.03	.00	☐ 170	Burt Hooton	.10	.04	.01
☐ 122	Dave Rosello DP	.04	.02	.00	☐ 171	Fernando Gonzalez	.10	.04	.01
☐ 123	Lynn Jones	.10	.04	.01	☐ 172	Ron Hodges	.10	.04	.01
☐ 124	Dave Lemanczyk	.10	.04	.01	☐ 173	John Henry Johnson	.10	.04	.01
☐ 125	Tony Perez	.40	.16	.04	☐ 174	Ray Knight	.20	.08	.02
☐ 126	Dave Tomlin	.10	.04	.01	☐ 175	Rick Reuschel	.20	.08	.02
☐ 127	Gary Thomasson	.10	.04	.01	☐ 176	Champ Summers	.10	.04	.01

		MINT	EXC	G-VG
☐ 177	Dave Heaverlo	.10	.04	.01
☐ 178	Tim McCarver	.30	.12	.03
☐ 179	Ron Davis	.20	.08	.02
☐ 180	Warren Cromartie	.10	.04	.01
☐ 181	Moose Haas	.10	.04	.01
☐ 182	Ken Reitz	.10	.04	.01
☐ 183	Jim Anderson DP	.04	.02	.00
☐ 184	Steve Renko DP	.04	.02	.00
☐ 185	Hal McRae	.20	.08	.02
☐ 186	Junior Moore	.10	.04	.01
☐ 187	Alan Ashby	.10	.04	.01
☐ 188	Terry Crowley	.10	.04	.01
☐ 189	Kevin Kobel	.10	.04	.01
☐ 190	Buddy Bell	.30	.12	.03
☐ 191	Ted Martinez	.10	.04	.01
☐ 192	Braves Team/Mgr. Bobby Cox (checklist back)	.35	.10	.02
☐ 193	Dave Goltz	.10	.04	.01
☐ 194	Mike Easler	.20	.08	.02
☐ 195	John Montefusco	.20	.08	.02
☐ 196	Lance Parrish	1.50	.60	.15
☐ 197	Byron McLaughlin	.10	.04	.01
☐ 198	Dell Alston DP	.04	.02	.00
☐ 199	Mike LaCoss	.20	.08	.02
☐ 200	Jim Rice	1.50	.60	.15
☐ 201	Batting Leaders Keith Hernandez Fred Lynn	.30	.12	.03
☐ 202	Home Run Leaders Dave Kingman Gorman Thomas	.20	.08	.02
☐ 203	RBI Leaders Dave Winfield Don Baylor	.30	.12	.03
☐ 204	Stolen Base Leaders Omar Moreno Willie Wilson	.20	.08	.02
☐ 205	Victory Leaders Joe Niekro Phil Niekro Mike Flanagan	.20	.08	.02
☐ 206	Strikeout Leaders J.R. Richard Nolan Ryan	.30	.12	.03
☐ 207	ERA Leaders J.R. Richard Ron Guidry	.20	.08	.02
☐ 208	Wayne Cage	.10	.04	.01

		MINT	EXC	G-VG
☐ 209	Von Joshua	.10	.04	.01
☐ 210	Steve Carlton	2.00	.80	.20
☐ 211	Dave Skaggs DP	.04	.02	.00
☐ 212	Dave Roberts	.10	.04	.01
☐ 213	Mike Jorgensen DP	.04	.02	.00
☐ 214	Angels Team/Mgr. Jim Fregosi (checklist back)	.35	.10	.02
☐ 215	Sixto Lezcano	.10	.04	.01
☐ 216	Phil Mankowski	.10	.04	.01
☐ 217	Ed Halicki	.10	.04	.01
☐ 218	Jose Morales	.10	.04	.01
☐ 219	Steve Mingori	.10	.04	.01
☐ 220	Dave Concepcion	.30	.12	.03
☐ 221	Joe Cannon	.10	.04	.01
☐ 222	Ron Hassey	.30	.12	.03
☐ 223	Bob Sykes	.10	.04	.01
☐ 224	Willie Montanez	.10	.04	.01
☐ 225	Lou Piniella	.20	.08	.02
☐ 226	Bill Stein	.10	.04	.01
☐ 227	Len Barker	.10	.04	.01
☐ 228	Johnny Oates	.10	.04	.01
☐ 229	Jim Bibby	.10	.04	.01
☐ 230	Dave Winfield	2.00	.80	.20
☐ 231	Steve McCatty	.10	.04	.01
☐ 232	Alan Trammell	2.50	1.00	.25
☐ 233	LaRue Washington	.10	.04	.01
☐ 234	Vern Ruhle	.10	.04	.01
☐ 235	Andre Dawson	2.50	1.00	.25
☐ 236	Marc Hill	.10	.04	.01
☐ 237	Scott McGregor	.20	.08	.02
☐ 238	Rob Wilfong	.10	.04	.01
☐ 239	Don Aase	.10	.04	.01
☐ 240	Dave Kingman	.30	.12	.03
☐ 241	Checklist 2	.25	.03	.00
☐ 242	Lamar Johnson	.10	.04	.01
☐ 243	Jerry Augustine	.10	.04	.01
☐ 244	Cardinals Team/Mgr. Ken Boyer (checklist back)	.35	.10	.02
☐ 245	Phil Niekro	.90	.36	.09
☐ 246	Tim Foli DP	.04	.02	.00
☐ 247	Frank Riccelli	.10	.04	.01
☐ 248	Jamie Quirk	.10	.04	.01
☐ 249	Jim Clancy	.10	.04	.01
☐ 250	Jim Kaat	.40	.16	.04
☐ 251	Kip Young	.10	.04	.01
☐ 252	Ted Cox	.10	.04	.01
☐ 253	John Montague	.10	.04	.01

		MINT	EXC	G-VG
☐ 254	Paul Dade DP	.04	.02	.00
☐ 255	Dusty Baker DP	.10	.04	.01
☐ 256	Roger Erickson	.10	.04	.01
☐ 257	Larry Herndon	.10	.04	.01
☐ 258	Paul Moskau	.10	.04	.01
☐ 259	Mets Team/Mgr.	.40	.10	.02
	Joe Torre			
	(checklist back)			
☐ 260	Al Oliver	.30	.12	.03
☐ 261	Dave Chalk	.10	.04	.01
☐ 262	Benny Ayala	.10	.04	.01
☐ 263	Dave LaRoche DP	.04	.02	.00
☐ 264	Bill Robinson	.20	.08	.02
☐ 265	Robin Yount	1.75	.70	.17
☐ 266	Bernie Carbo	.10	.04	.01
☐ 267	Dan Schatzeder	.10	.04	.01
☐ 268	Rafael Landestoy	.10	.04	.01
☐ 269	Dave Tobik	.10	.04	.01
☐ 270	Mike Schmidt DP	1.50	.60	.15
☐ 271	Dick Drago DP	.04	.02	.00
☐ 272	Ralph Garr	.10	.04	.01
☐ 273	Eduardo Rodriguez	.10	.04	.01
☐ 274	Dale Murphy	6.00	2.40	.60
☐ 275	Jerry Koosman	.20	.08	.02
☐ 276	Tom Veryzer	.10	.04	.01
☐ 277	Rick Bosetti	.10	.04	.01
☐ 278	Jim Spencer	.10	.04	.01
☐ 279	Rob Andrews	.10	.04	.01
☐ 280	Gaylord Perry	.90	.36	.09
☐ 281	Paul Blair	.10	.04	.01
☐ 282	Mariners Team/Mgr.	.30	.10	.02
	Darrell Johnson			
	(checklist back)			
☐ 283	John Ellis	.10	.04	.01
☐ 284	Larry Murray DP	.04	.02	.00
☐ 285	Don Baylor	.40	.16	.04
☐ 286	Darold Knowles DP	.04	.02	.00
☐ 287	John Lowenstein	.10	.04	.01
☐ 288	Dave Rozema	.10	.04	.01
☐ 289	Bruce Bochy	.10	.04	.01
☐ 290	Steve Garvey	2.00	.80	.20
☐ 291	Randy Scarberry	.10	.04	.01
☐ 292	Dale Berra	.10	.04	.01
☐ 293	Elias Sosa	.10	.04	.01
☐ 294	Charlie Spikes	.10	.04	.01
☐ 295	Larry Gura	.10	.04	.01
☐ 296	Dave Rader	.10	.04	.01
☐ 297	Tim Johnson	.10	.04	.01
☐ 298	Ken Holtzman	.10	.04	.01

		MINT	EXC	G-VG
☐ 299	Steve Henderson	.10	.04	.01
☐ 300	Ron Guidry	.65	.26	.06
☐ 301	Mike Edwards	.10	.04	.01
☐ 302	Dodgers Team/Mgr.	.45	.12	.02
	Tom Lasorda			
	(checklist back)			
☐ 303	Bill Castro	.10	.04	.01
☐ 304	Butch Wynegar	.10	.04	.01
☐ 305	Randy Jones	.10	.04	.01
☐ 306	Denny Walling	.10	.04	.01
☐ 307	Rick Honeycutt	.10	.04	.01
☐ 308	Mike Hargrove	.10	.04	.01
☐ 309	Larry McWilliams	.10	.04	.01
☐ 310	Dave Parker	.90	.36	.09
☐ 311	Roger Metzger	.10	.04	.01
☐ 312	Mike Barlow	.10	.04	.01
☐ 313	Johnny Grubb	.10	.04	.01
☐ 314	Tim Stoddard	.20	.08	.02
☐ 315	Steve Kemp	.20	.08	.02
☐ 316	Bob Lacey	.10	.04	.01
☐ 317	Mike Anderson DP	.04	.02	.00
☐ 318	Jerry Reuss	.20	.08	.02
☐ 319	Chris Speier	.10	.04	.01
☐ 320	Dennis Eckersley	.50	.20	.05
☐ 321	Keith Hernandez	1.50	.60	.15
☐ 322	Claudell Washington	.20	.08	.02
☐ 323	Mick Kelleher	.10	.04	.01
☐ 324	Tom Underwood	.10	.04	.01
☐ 325	Dan Driessen	.10	.04	.01
☐ 326	Bo McLaughlin	.10	.04	.01
☐ 327	Ray Fosse DP	.04	.02	.00
☐ 328	Twins Team/Mgr.	.35	.10	.02
	Gene Mauch			
	(checklist back)			
☐ 329	Bert Roberge	.10	.04	.01
☐ 330	Al Cowens	.10	.04	.01
☐ 331	Richie Hebner	.10	.04	.01
☐ 332	Enrique Romo	.10	.04	.01
☐ 333	Jim Norris DP	.04	.02	.00
☐ 334	Jim Beattie	.10	.04	.01
☐ 335	Willie McCovey	1.50	.60	.15
☐ 336	George Medich	.10	.04	.01
☐ 337	Carney Lansford	.60	.24	.06
☐ 338	John Wockenfuss	.10	.04	.01
☐ 339	John D'Acquisto	.10	.04	.01
☐ 340	Ken Singleton	.20	.08	.02
☐ 341	Jim Essian	.10	.04	.01
☐ 342	Odell Jones	.10	.04	.01
☐ 343	Mike Vail	.10	.04	.01

		MINT	EXC	G-VG
☐ 344	Randy Lerch	.10	.04	.01
☐ 345	Larry Parrish	.20	.08	.02
☐ 346	Buddy Solomon	.10	.04	.01
☐ 347	Harry Chappas	.10	.04	.01
☐ 348	Checklist 3	.25	.03	.00
☐ 349	Jack Brohamer	.10	.04	.01
☐ 350	George Hendrick	.20	.08	.02
☐ 351	Bob Davis	.10	.04	.01
☐ 352	Dan Briggs	.10	.04	.01
☐ 353	Andy Hassler	.10	.04	.01
☐ 354	Rick Auerbach	.10	.04	.01
☐ 355	Gary Matthews	.20	.08	.02
☐ 356	Padres Team/Mgr. Jerry Coleman (checklist back)	.35	.10	.02
☐ 357	Bob McClure	.10	.04	.01
☐ 358	Lou Whitaker	1.00	.40	.10
☐ 359	Randy Moffitt	.10	.04	.01
☐ 360	Darrell Porter DP	.10	.04	.01
☐ 361	Wayne Garland	.10	.04	.01
☐ 362	Danny Goodwin	.10	.04	.01
☐ 363	Wayne Gross	.10	.04	.01
☐ 364	Ray Burris	.10	.04	.01
☐ 365	Bobby Murcer	.30	.12	.03
☐ 366	Rob Dressler	.10	.04	.01
☐ 367	Billy Smith	.10	.04	.01
☐ 368	Willie Aikens	.20	.08	.02
☐ 369	Jim Kern	.10	.04	.01
☐ 370	Cesar Cedeno	.20	.08	.02
☐ 371	Jack Morris	1.50	.60	.15
☐ 372	Joel Youngblood	.10	.04	.01
☐ 373	Dan Petry DP	.60	.24	.06
☐ 374	Jim Gantner	.10	.04	.01
☐ 375	Ross Grimsley	.10	.04	.01
☐ 376	Gary Allenson	.10	.04	.01
☐ 377	Junior Kennedy	.10	.04	.01
☐ 378	Jerry Mumphrey	.10	.04	.01
☐ 379	Kevin Bell	.10	.04	.01
☐ 380	Garry Maddox	.10	.04	.01
☐ 381	Cubs Team/Mgr. Preston Gomez (checklist back)	.35	.10	.02
☐ 382	Dave Freisleben	.10	.04	.01
☐ 383	Ed Ott	.10	.04	.01
☐ 384	Joey McLaughlin	.10	.04	.01
☐ 385	Enos Cabell	.10	.04	.01
☐ 386	Darrell Jackson	.10	.04	.01
☐ 387A	Fred Stanley (yellow name on front)	1.00	.40	.10

		MINT	EXC	G-VG
☐ 387B	Fred Stanley (red name on front)	.10	.04	.01
☐ 388	Mike Paxton	.10	.04	.01
☐ 389	Pete LaCock	.10	.04	.01
☐ 390	Fergie Jenkins	.40	.16	.04
☐ 391	Tony Armas DP	.10	.04	.01
☐ 392	Milt Wilcox	.10	.04	.01
☐ 393	Ozzie Smith	3.00	1.20	.30
☐ 394	Reggie Cleveland	.10	.04	.01
☐ 395	Ellis Valentine	.10	.04	.01
☐ 396	Dan Meyer	.10	.04	.01
☐ 397	Roy Thomas DP	.04	.02	.00
☐ 398	Barry Foote	.10	.04	.01
☐ 399	Mike Proly DP	.04	.02	.00
☐ 400	George Foster	.50	.20	.05
☐ 401	Pete Falcone	.10	.04	.01
☐ 402	Merv Rettenmund	.10	.04	.01
☐ 403	Pete Redfern DP	.04	.02	.00
☐ 404	Orioles Team/Mgr. Earl Weaver (checklist back)	.40	.10	.02
☐ 405	Dwight Evans	.80	.32	.08
☐ 406	Paul Molitor	1.50	.60	.15
☐ 407	Tony Solaita	.10	.04	.01
☐ 408	Bill North	.10	.04	.01
☐ 409	Paul Splittorff	.10	.04	.01
☐ 410	Bobby Bonds	.20	.08	.02
☐ 411	Frank LaCorte	.10	.04	.01
☐ 412	Thad Bosley	.10	.04	.01
☐ 413	Allen Ripley	.10	.04	.01
☐ 414	George Scott	.10	.04	.01
☐ 415	Bill Atkinson	.10	.04	.01
☐ 416	Tom Brookens	.10	.04	.01
☐ 417	Craig Chamberlain DP	.04	.02	.00
☐ 418	Roger Freed DP	.04	.02	.00
☐ 419	Vic Correll	.10	.04	.01
☐ 420	Butch Hobson	.10	.04	.01
☐ 421	Doug Bird	.10	.04	.01
☐ 422	Larry Milbourne	.10	.04	.01
☐ 423	Dave Frost	.10	.04	.01
☐ 424	Yankees Team/Mgr. Dick Howser (checklist back)	.40	.10	.02
☐ 425	Mark Belanger	.20	.08	.02
☐ 426	Grant Jackson	.10	.04	.01
☐ 427	Tom Hutton DP	.04	.02	.00
☐ 428	Pat Zachry	.10	.04	.01
☐ 429	Duane Kuiper	.10	.04	.01
☐ 430	Larry Hisle DP	.10	.04	.01

		MINT	EXC	G-VG
☐ 431	Mike Krukow	.20	.08	.02
☐ 432	Willie Norwood	.10	.04	.01
☐ 433	Rich Gale	.10	.04	.01
☐ 434	Johnnie LeMaster	.10	.04	.01
☐ 435	Don Gullett	.10	.04	.01
☐ 436	Billy Almon	.10	.04	.01
☐ 437	Joe Niekro	.20	.08	.02
☐ 438	Dave Revering	.10	.04	.01
☐ 439	Mike Phillips	.10	.04	.01
☐ 440	Don Sutton	.80	.32	.08
☐ 441	Eric Soderholm	.10	.04	.01
☐ 442	Jorge Orta	.10	.04	.01
☐ 443	Mike Parrott	.10	.04	.01
☐ 444	Alvis Woods	.10	.04	.01
☐ 445	Mark Fidrych	.20	.08	.02
☐ 446	Duffy Dyer	.10	.04	.01
☐ 447	Nino Espinosa	.10	.04	.01
☐ 448	Jim Wohlford	.10	.04	.01
☐ 449	Doug Bair	.10	.04	.01
☐ 450	George Brett	3.75	1.50	.37
☐ 451	Indians Team/Mgr. Dave Garcia (checklist back)	.35	.10	.02
☐ 452	Steve Dillard	.10	.04	.01
☐ 453	Mike Bacsik	.10	.04	.01
☐ 454	Tom Donohue	.10	.04	.01
☐ 455	Mike Torrez	.10	.04	.01
☐ 456	Frank Taveras	.10	.04	.01
☐ 457	Bert Blyleven	.40	.16	.04
☐ 458	Billy Sample	.10	.04	.01
☐ 459	Mickey Lolich DP	.10	.04	.01
☐ 460	Willie Randolph	.30	.12	.03
☐ 461	Dwayne Murphy	.15	.06	.01
☐ 462	Mike Sadek DP	.04	.02	.00
☐ 463	Jerry Royster	.10	.04	.01
☐ 464	John Denny	.10	.04	.01
☐ 465	Rick Monday	.10	.04	.01
☐ 466	Mike Squires	.10	.04	.01
☐ 467	Jesse Jefferson	.10	.04	.01
☐ 468	Aurelio Rodriguez	.10	.04	.01
☐ 469	Randy Niemann DP	.04	.02	.00
☐ 470	Bob Boone	.30	.12	.03
☐ 471	Hosken Powell DP	.04	.02	.00
☐ 472	Willie Hernandez	.30	.12	.03
☐ 473	Bump Wills	.10	.04	.01
☐ 474	Steve Busby	.10	.04	.01
☐ 475	Cesar Geronimo	.10	.04	.01
☐ 476	Bob Shirley	.10	.04	.01
☐ 477	Buck Martinez	.10	.04	.01

		MINT	EXC	G-VG
☐ 478	Gil Flores	.10	.04	.01
☐ 479	Expos Team/Mgr. Dick Williams (checklist back)	.30	.10	.02
☐ 480	Bob Watson	.20	.08	.02
☐ 481	Tom Paciorek	.10	.04	.01
☐ 482	Rickey Henderson	27.00	11.00	2.70
☐ 483	Bo Diaz	.10	.04	.01
☐ 484	Checklist 4	.25	.03	.00
☐ 485	Mickey Rivers	.20	.08	.02
☐ 486	Mike Tyson DP	.04	.02	.00
☐ 487	Wayne Nordhagen	.10	.04	.01
☐ 488	Roy Howell	.10	.04	.01
☐ 489	Preston Hanna DP	.04	.02	.00
☐ 490	Lee May	.10	.04	.01
☐ 491	Steve Mura DP	.04	.02	.00
☐ 492	Todd Cruz	.10	.04	.01
☐ 493	Jerry Martin	.10	.04	.01
☐ 494	Craig Minetto	.10	.04	.01
☐ 495	Bake McBride	.10	.04	.01
☐ 496	Silvio Martinez	.10	.04	.01
☐ 497	Jim Mason	.10	.04	.01
☐ 498	Danny Darwin	.10	.04	.01
☐ 499	Giants Team/Mgr. Dave Bristol (checklist back)	.35	.10	.02
☐ 500	Tom Seaver	1.75	.70	.17
☐ 501	Rennie Stennett	.10	.04	.01
☐ 502	Rich Wortham DP	.04	.02	.00
☐ 503	Mike Cubbage	.10	.04	.01
☐ 504	Gene Garber	.10	.04	.01
☐ 505	Bert Campaneris	.10	.04	.01
☐ 506	Tom Buskey	.10	.04	.01
☐ 507	Leon Roberts	.10	.04	.01
☐ 508	U.L. Washington	.10	.04	.01
☐ 509	Ed Glynn	.10	.04	.01
☐ 510	Ron Cey	.30	.12	.03
☐ 511	Eric Wilkins	.10	.04	.01
☐ 512	Jose Cardenal	.10	.04	.01
☐ 513	Tom Dixon DP	.04	.02	.00
☐ 514	Steve Ontiveros	.10	.04	.01
☐ 515	Mike Caldwell	.10	.04	.01
☐ 516	Hector Cruz	.10	.04	.01
☐ 517	Don Stanhouse	.10	.04	.01
☐ 518	Nelson Norman	.10	.04	.01
☐ 519	Steve Nicosia	.10	.04	.01
☐ 520	Steve Rogers	.10	.04	.01
☐ 521	Ken Brett	.10	.04	.01
☐ 522	Jim Morrison	.10	.04	.01

		MINT	EXC	G-VG
☐ 523	Ken Henderson	.10	.04	.01
☐ 524	Jim Wright DP	.04	.02	.00
☐ 525	Clint Hurdle	.10	.04	.01
☐ 526	Phillies Team/Mgr. .	.40	.10	.02
	Dallas Green			
	(checklist back)			
☐ 527	Doug Rau DP	.04	.02	.00
☐ 528	Adrian Devine	.10	.04	.01
☐ 529	Jim Barr	.10	.04	.01
☐ 530	Jim Sundberg DP ..	.10	.04	.01
☐ 531	Eric Rasmussen ...	.10	.04	.01
☐ 532	Willie Horton	.20	.08	.02
☐ 533	Checklist 5	.25	.03	.00
☐ 534	Andre Thornton	.20	.08	.02
☐ 535	Bob Forsch	.10	.04	.01
☐ 536	Lee Lacy	.10	.04	.01
☐ 537	Alex Trevino	.20	.08	.02
☐ 538	Joe Strain	.10	.04	.01
☐ 539	Rudy May	.10	.04	.01
☐ 540	Pete Rose	4.00	1.60	.40
☐ 541	Miguel Dilone	.10	.04	.01
☐ 542	Joe Coleman	.10	.04	.01
☐ 543	Pat Kelly	.10	.04	.01
☐ 544	Rick Sutcliffe	2.75	1.10	.27
☐ 545	Jeff Burroughs	.10	.04	.01
☐ 546	Rick Langford	.10	.04	.01
☐ 547	John Wathan	.20	.08	.02
☐ 548	Dave Rajsich	.10	.04	.01
☐ 549	Larry Wolfe	.10	.04	.01
☐ 550	Ken Griffey	.20	.08	.02
☐ 551	Pirates Team/Mgr. .	.35	.10	.02
	Chuck Tanner			
	(checklist back)			
☐ 552	Bill Nahorodny	.10	.04	.01
☐ 553	Dick Davis	.10	.04	.01
☐ 554	Art Howe	.20	.08	.02
☐ 555	Ed Figueroa	.10	.04	.01
☐ 556	Joe Rudi	.20	.08	.02
☐ 557	Mark Lee	.10	.04	.01
☐ 558	Alfredo Griffin	.30	.12	.03
☐ 559	Dale Murray	.10	.04	.01
☐ 560	Dave Lopes	.20	.08	.02
☐ 561	Eddie Whitson	.20	.08	.02
☐ 562	Joe Wallis	.10	.04	.01
☐ 563	Will McEnaney	.10	.04	.01
☐ 564	Rick Manning	.10	.04	.01
☐ 565	Dennis Leonard ...	.20	.08	.02
☐ 566	Bud Harrelson	.10	.04	.01
☐ 567	Skip Lockwood	.10	.04	.01
☐ 568	Gary Roenicke	.20	.08	.02
☐ 569	Terry Kennedy	.20	.08	.02
☐ 570	Roy Smalley	.10	.04	.01
☐ 571	Joe Sambito	.10	.04	.01
☐ 572	Jerry Morales DP ..	.04	.02	.00
☐ 573	Kent Tekulve	.20	.08	.02
☐ 574	Scot Thompson	.10	.04	.01
☐ 575	Ken Kravec	.10	.04	.01
☐ 576	Jim Dwyer	.10	.04	.01
☐ 577	Blue Jays Team/Mgr.	.30	.10	.02
	Bobby Mattick			
	(checklist back)			
☐ 578	Scott Sanderson ..	.20	.08	.02
☐ 579	Charlie Moore	.10	.04	.01
☐ 580	Nolan Ryan	2.00	.80	.20
☐ 581	Bob Bailor	.10	.04	.01
☐ 582	Brian Doyle	.10	.04	.01
☐ 583	Bob Stinson	.10	.04	.01
☐ 584	Kurt Bevacqua	.10	.04	.01
☐ 585	Al Hrabosky	.10	.04	.01
☐ 586	Mitchell Page	.10	.04	.01
☐ 587	Garry Templeton ...	.20	.08	.02
☐ 588	Greg Minton	.10	.04	.01
☐ 589	Chet Lemon	.10	.04	.01
☐ 590	Jim Palmer	1.25	.50	.12
☐ 591	Rick Cerone	.10	.04	.01
☐ 592	Jon Matlack	.10	.04	.01
☐ 593	Jesus Alou	.10	.04	.01
☐ 594	Dick Tidrow	.10	.04	.01
☐ 595	Don Money	.10	.04	.01
☐ 596	Rick Matula	.10	.04	.01
☐ 597	Tom Poquette	.10	.04	.01
☐ 598	Fred Kendall DP ...	.04	.02	.00
☐ 599	Mike Norris	.10	.04	.01
☐ 600	Reggie Jackson ...	2.50	1.00	.25
☐ 601	Buddy Schultz	.10	.04	.01
☐ 602	Brian Downing	.20	.08	.02
☐ 603	Jack Billingham DP	.04	.02	.00
☐ 604	Glenn Adams	.10	.04	.01
☐ 605	Terry Forster	.20	.08	.02
☐ 606	Reds Team/Mgr. ...	.35	.10	.02
	John McNamara			
	(checklist back)			
☐ 607	Woodie Fryman ...	.10	.04	.01
☐ 608	Alan Bannister	.10	.04	.01
☐ 609	Ron Reed	.10	.04	.01
☐ 610	Willie Stargell	1.50	.60	.15
☐ 611	Jerry Garvin DP ...	.04	.02	.00
☐ 612	Cliff Johnson	.10	.04	.01

		MINT	EXC	G-VG
☐ 613	Randy Stein	.10	.04	.01
☐ 614	John Hiller	.10	.04	.01
☐ 615	Doug DeCinces	.20	.08	.02
☐ 616	Gene Richards	.10	.04	.01
☐ 617	Joaquin Andujar	.20	.08	.02
☐ 618	Bob Montgomery DP	.04	.02	.00
☐ 619	Sergio Ferrer	.10	.04	.01
☐ 620	Richie Zisk	.10	.04	.01
☐ 621	Bob Grich	.20	.08	.02
☐ 622	Mario Soto	.20	.08	.02
☐ 623	Gorman Thomas	.20	.08	.02
☐ 624	Lerrin LaGrow	.10	.04	.01
☐ 625	Chris Chambliss	.20	.08	.02
☐ 626	Tigers Team/Mgr.	.40	.10	.02
	Sparky Anderson			
	(checklist back)			
☐ 627	Pedro Borbon	.10	.04	.01
☐ 628	Doug Capilla	.10	.04	.01
☐ 629	Jim Todd	.10	.04	.01
☐ 630	Larry Bowa	.30	.12	.03
☐ 631	Mark Littell	.10	.04	.01
☐ 632	Barry Bonnell	.10	.04	.01
☐ 633	Bob Apodaca	.10	.04	.01
☐ 634	Glenn Borgmann DP	.04	.02	.00
☐ 635	John Candelaria	.30	.12	.03
☐ 636	Toby Harrah	.20	.08	.02
☐ 637	Joe Simpson	.10	.04	.01
☐ 638	Mark Clear	.20	.08	.02
☐ 639	Larry Biittner	.10	.04	.01
☐ 640	Mike Flanagan	.20	.08	.02
☐ 641	Ed Kranepool	.10	.04	.01
☐ 642	Ken Forsch DP	.10	.04	.01
☐ 643	John Mayberry	.20	.08	.02
☐ 644	Charlie Hough	.20	.08	.02
☐ 645	Rick Burleson	.20	.08	.02
☐ 646	Checklist 6	.25	.03	.00
☐ 647	Milt May	.10	.04	.01
☐ 648	Roy White	.20	.08	.02
☐ 649	Tom Griffin	.10	.04	.01
☐ 650	Joe Morgan	1.00	.40	.10
☐ 651	Rollie Fingers	.50	.20	.05
☐ 652	Mario Mendoza	.10	.04	.01
☐ 653	Stan Bahnsen	.10	.04	.01
☐ 654	Bruce Boisclair DP	.04	.02	.00
☐ 655	Tug McGraw	.20	.08	.02
☐ 656	Larvell Blanks	.10	.04	.01
☐ 657	Dave Edwards	.10	.04	.01
☐ 658	Chris Knapp	.10	.04	.01

		MINT	EXC	G-VG
☐ 659	Brewers Team/Mgr.	.35	.10	.02
	George Bamberger			
	(checklist back)			
☐ 660	Rusty Staub	.30	.12	.03
☐ 661	Orioles Rookies	.15	.06	.01
	Mark Corey			
	Dave Ford			
	Wayne Krenchicki			
☐ 662	Red Sox Rookies	.15	.06	.01
	Joel Finch			
	Mike O'Berry			
	Chuck Rainey			
☐ 663	Angels Rookies	.50	.20	.05
	Ralph Botting			
	Bob Clark			
	Dickie Thon			
☐ 664	White Sox Rookies	.15	.06	.01
	Mike Colbern			
	Guy Hoffman			
	Dewey Robinson			
☐ 665	Indians Rookies	.25	.10	.02
	Larry Andersen			
	Bobby Cuellar			
	Sandy Wihtol			
☐ 666	Tigers Rookies	.15	.06	.01
	Mike Chris			
	Al Greene			
	Bruce Robbins			
☐ 667	Royals Rookies	1.50	.60	.15
	Renie Martin			
	Bill Paschall			
	Dan Quisenberry			
☐ 668	Brewers Rookies	.20	.08	.02
	Danny Boitano			
	Willie Mueller			
	Lenn Sakata			
☐ 669	Twins Rookies	.50	.20	.05
	Dan Graham			
	Rick Sofield			
	Gary Ward			
☐ 670	Yankees Rookies	.15	.06	.01
	Bobby Brown			
	Brad Gulden			
	Darryl Jones			
☐ 671	A's Rookies	.25	.10	.02
	Derek Bryant			
	Brian Kingman			
	Mike Morgan			

		MINT	EXC	G-VG
☐ 672	Mariners Rookies	.15	.06	.01
	Charlie Beamon			
	Rodney Craig			
	Rafael Vasquez			
☐ 673	Rangers Rookies	.15	.06	.01
	Brian Allard			
	Jerry Don Gleaton			
	Greg Mahlberg			
☐ 674	Blue Jays Rookies	.15	.06	.01
	Butch Edge			
	Pat Kelly			
	Ted Wilborn			
☐ 675	Braves Rookies	.20	.08	.02
	Bruce Benedict			
	Larry Bradford			
	Eddie Miller			
☐ 676	Cubs Rookies	.15	.06	.01
	Dave Geisel			
	Steve Macko			
	Karl Pagel			
☐ 677	Reds Rookies	.15	.06	.01
	Art DeFreites			
	Frank Pastore			
	Harry Spilman			
☐ 678	Astros Rookies	.20	.08	.02
	Reggie Baldwin			
	Alan Knicely			
	Pete Ladd			
☐ 679	Dodgers Rookies	.60	.24	.06
	Joe Beckwith			
	Mickey Hatcher			
	Dave Patterson			
☐ 680	Expos Rookies	.35	.14	.03
	Tony Bernazard			
	Randy Miller			
	John Tamargo			
☐ 681	Mets Rookies	7.00	2.80	.70
	Dan Norman			
	Jesse Orosco			
	Mike Scott			
☐ 682	Phillies Rookies	.20	.08	.02
	Ramon Aviles			
	Dickie Noles			
	Kevin Saucier			
☐ 683	Pirates Rookies	.15	.06	.01
	Dorian Boyland			
	Alberto Lois			
	Harry Saferight			

		MINT	EXC	G-VG
☐ 684	Cardinals Rookies	.70	.28	.07
	George Frazier			
	Tom Herr			
	Dan O'Brien			
☐ 685	Padres Rookies	.20	.08	.02
	Tim Flannery			
	Brian Greer			
	Jim Wilhelm			
☐ 686	Giants Rookies	.15	.06	.01
	Greg Johnston			
	Dennis Littlejohn			
	Phil Nastu			
☐ 687	Mike Heath DP	.04	.02	.00
☐ 688	Steve Stone	.10	.04	.01
☐ 689	Red Sox Team/Mgr.	.35	.10	.02
	Don Zimmer			
	(checklist back)			
☐ 690	Tommy John	.50	.20	.05
☐ 691	Ivan DeJesus	.10	.04	.01
☐ 692	Rawly Eastwick DP	.04	.02	.00
☐ 693	Craig Kusick	.10	.04	.01
☐ 694	Jim Rooker	.10	.04	.01
☐ 695	Reggie Smith	.20	.08	.02
☐ 696	Julio Gonzalez	.10	.04	.01
☐ 697	David Clyde	.10	.04	.01
☐ 698	Oscar Gamble	.10	.04	.01
☐ 699	Floyd Bannister	.20	.08	.02
☐ 700	Rod Carew DP	1.00	.40	.10
☐ 701	Ken Oberkfell	.30	.12	.03
☐ 702	Ed Farmer	.10	.04	.01
☐ 703	Otto Velez	.10	.04	.01
☐ 704	Gene Tenace	.10	.04	.01
☐ 705	Freddie Patek	.10	.04	.01
☐ 706	Tippy Martinez	.10	.04	.01
☐ 707	Elliott Maddox	.10	.04	.01
☐ 708	Bob Tolan	.10	.04	.01
☐ 709	Pat Underwood	.10	.04	.01
☐ 710	Graig Nettles	.30	.12	.03
☐ 711	Bob Galasso	.10	.04	.01
☐ 712	Rodney Scott	.10	.04	.01
☐ 713	Terry Whitfield	.10	.04	.01
☐ 714	Fred Norman	.10	.04	.01
☐ 715	Sal Bando	.15	.06	.01
☐ 716	Lynn McGlothen	.10	.04	.01
☐ 717	Mickey Klutts DP	.04	.02	.00
☐ 718	Greg Gross	.10	.04	.01
☐ 719	Don Robinson	.20	.08	.02
☐ 720	Carl Yastrzemski DP	1.50	.60	.15
☐ 721	Paul Hartzell	.10	.04	.01

		MINT	EXC	G-VG
☐ 722	Jose Cruz	.20	.08	.02
☐ 723	Shane Rawley	.20	.08	.02
☐ 724	Jerry White	.10	.04	.01
☐ 725	Rick Wise	.10	.04	.01
☐ 726	Steve Yeager	.20	.08	.02

1981 Topps

*The cards in this 726-card set measure 2 ½"
by 3 ½". League Leaders (1-8), Record
Breakers (201-208), and Post-season cards
(401-404) are topical subsets found in this
set marketed by Topps in 1981. The team
cards are all grouped together (661-686) and
feature team checklist backs and a very
small photo of the team's manager in the
upper right corner of the obverse. The obverses carry the player's position and team in a
baseball cap design, and the company name
is printed in a small baseball. The backs are
red and gray. The 66 double-printed cards
are noted in the checklist by DP. The set is
quite popular with collectors partly due to the
presence of rookie cards of Fernando Valen-
zuela, Tim Raines, Kirk Gibson, Harold
Baines, John Tudor, Lloyd Moseby, Hubie
Brooks, Mike Boddicker, and Tony Pena.*

	MINT	EXC	G-VG
Complete Set (726)	85.00	34.00	8.50
Common Player (1-726)	.07	.03	.01
Common DP's (1-726)	.03	.01	.00

			MINT	EXC	G-VG
☐	1	Batting Leaders ... George Brett Bill Buckner	.65	.10	.02
☐	2	Home Run Leaders Reggie Jackson Ben Oglivie Mike Schmidt	.35	.14	.03
☐	3	RBI Leaders Cecil Cooper Mike Schmidt	.20	.08	.02
☐	4	Stolen Base Leaders Rickey Henderson Ron LeFlore	.18	.08	.01
☐	5	Victory Leaders ... Steve Stone Steve Carlton	.15	.06	.01
☐	6	Strikeout Leaders . Len Barker Steve Carlton	.15	.06	.01
☐	7	ERA Leaders Rudy May Don Sutton	.10	.04	.01
☐	8	Leading Firemen .. Dan Quisenberry Rollie Fingers Tom Hume	.10	.04	.01
☐	9	Pete LaCock DP ..	.03	.01	.00
☐	10	Mike Flanagan	.10	.04	.01
☐	11	Jim Wohlford DP ..	.03	.01	.00
☐	12	Mark Clear	.07	.03	.01
☐	13	Joe Charboneau ..	.10	.04	.01
☐	14	John Tudor	1.75	.70	.17
☐	15	Larry Parrish	.10	.04	.01
☐	16	Ron Davis	.07	.03	.01
☐	17	Cliff Johnson	.07	.03	.01
☐	18	Glenn Adams	.07	.03	.01
☐	19	Jim Clancy	.10	.04	.01
☐	20	Jeff Burroughs	.10	.04	.01
☐	21	Ron Oester	.10	.04	.01
☐	22	Danny Darwin	.07	.03	.01
☐	23	Alex Trevino	.07	.03	.01
☐	24	Don Stanhouse	.07	.03	.01
☐	25	Sixto Lezcano	.07	.03	.01
☐	26	U.L. Washington	.07	.03	.01
☐	27	Champ Summers DP	.03	.01	.00
☐	28	Enrique Romo	.07	.03	.01
☐	29	Gene Tenace	.10	.04	.01
☐	30	Jack Clark	.60	.24	.06
☐	31	Checklist 1-121 DP	.07	.01	.00

			MINT	EXC	G-VG				MINT	EXC	G-VG
☐	32	Ken Oberkfell	.07	.03	.01	☐	75	Reggie Smith	.15	.06	.01
☐	33	Rick Honeycutt	.07	.03	.01	☐	76	Mario Mendoza	.07	.03	.01
☐	34	Aurelio Rodriguez	.07	.03	.01	☐	77	Mike Barlow	.07	.03	.01
☐	35	Mitchell Page	.07	.03	.01	☐	78	Steve Dillard	.07	.03	.01
☐	36	Ed Farmer	.07	.03	.01	☐	79	Bruce Robbins	.07	.03	.01
☐	37	Gary Roenicke	.07	.03	.01	☐	80	Rusty Staub	.20	.08	.02
☐	38	Win Remmerswaal	.07	.03	.01	☐	81	Dave Stapleton	.10	.04	.01
☐	39	Tom Veryzer	.07	.03	.01	☐	82	Astros Rookies DP	.10	.04	.01
☐	40	Tug McGraw	.15	.06	.01			Danny Heep			
☐	41	Ranger Rookies	.10	.04	.01			Alan Knicely			
		Bob Babcock						Bobby Sprowl			
		John Butcher				☐	83	Mike Proly	.07	.03	.01
		Jerry Don Gleaton				☐	84	Johnnie LeMaster	.07	.03	.01
☐	42	Jerry White DP	.03	.01	.00	☐	85	Mike Caldwell	.07	.03	.01
☐	43	Jose Morales	.07	.03	.01	☐	86	Wayne Gross	.07	.03	.01
☐	44	Larry McWilliams	.07	.03	.01	☐	87	Rick Camp	.07	.03	.01
☐	45	Enos Cabell	.07	.03	.01	☐	88	Joe Lefebvre	.10	.04	.01
☐	46	Rick Bosetti	.07	.03	.01	☐	89	Darrell Jackson	.07	.03	.01
☐	47	Ken Brett	.07	.03	.01	☐	90	Bake McBride	.07	.03	.01
☐	48	Dave Skaggs	.07	.03	.01	☐	91	Tim Stoddard DP	.07	.03	.01
☐	49	Bob Shirley	.07	.03	.01	☐	92	Mike Easler	.10	.04	.01
☐	50	Dave Lopes	.15	.06	.01	☐	93	Ed Glynn DP	.03	.01	.00
☐	51	Bill Robinson DP	.03	.01	.00	☐	94	Harry Spilman DP	.03	.01	.00
☐	52	Hector Cruz	.07	.03	.01	☐	95	Jim Sundberg	.10	.04	.01
☐	53	Kevin Saucier	.07	.03	.01	☐	96	A's Rookies	.15	.06	.01
☐	54	Ivan DeJesus	.07	.03	.01			Dave Beard			
☐	55	Mike Norris	.07	.03	.01			Ernie Camacho			
☐	56	Buck Martinez	.07	.03	.01			Pat Dempsey			
☐	57	Dave Roberts	.07	.03	.01	☐	97	Chris Speier	.07	.03	.01
☐	58	Joel Youngblood	.07	.03	.01	☐	98	Clint Hurdle	.07	.03	.01
☐	59	Dan Petry	.10	.04	.01	☐	99	Eric Wilkins	.07	.03	.01
☐	60	Willie Randolph	.15	.06	.01	☐	100	Rod Carew	1.25	.50	.12
☐	61	Butch Wynegar	.07	.03	.01	☐	101	Benny Ayala	.07	.03	.01
☐	62	Joe Pettini	.07	.03	.01	☐	102	Dave Tobik	.07	.03	.01
☐	63	Steve Renko DP	.03	.01	.00	☐	103	Jerry Martin	.07	.03	.01
☐	64	Brian Asselstine	.07	.03	.01	☐	104	Terry Forster	.10	.04	.01
☐	65	Scott McGregor	.10	.04	.01	☐	105	Jose Cruz	.15	.06	.01
☐	66	Royals Rookies	.10	.04	.01	☐	106	Don Money	.07	.03	.01
		Manny Castillo				☐	107	Rich Wortham	.07	.03	.01
		Tim Ireland				☐	108	Bruce Benedict	.07	.03	.01
		Mike Jones				☐	109	Mike Scott	1.25	.50	.12
☐	67	Ken Kravec	.07	.03	.01	☐	110	Carl Yastrzemski	1.75	.70	.17
☐	68	Matt Alexander DP	.03	.01	.00	☐	111	Greg Minton	.07	.03	.01
☐	69	Ed Halicki	.07	.03	.01	☐	112	White Sox Rookies	.10	.04	.01
☐	70	Al Oliver DP	.10	.04	.01			Rusty Kuntz			
☐	71	Hal Dues	.07	.03	.01			Fran Mullin			
☐	72	Barry Evans DP	.03	.01	.00			Leo Sutherland			
☐	73	Doug Bair	.07	.03	.01	☐	113	Mike Phillips	.07	.03	.01
☐	74	Mike Hargrove	.07	.03	.01	☐	114	Tom Underwood	.07	.03	.01

		MINT	EXC	G-VG
☐ 115	Roy Smalley	.07	.03	.01
☐ 116	Joe Simpson	.07	.03	.01
☐ 117	Pete Falcone	.07	.03	.01
☐ 118	Kurt Bevacqua	.07	.03	.01
☐ 119	Tippy Martinez	.07	.03	.01
☐ 120	Larry Bowa	.15	.06	.01
☐ 121	Larry Harlow	.07	.03	.01
☐ 122	John Denny	.10	.04	.01
☐ 123	Al Cowens	.07	.03	.01
☐ 124	Jerry Garvin	.07	.03	.01
☐ 125	Andre Dawson	1.00	.40	.10
☐ 126	Charlie Leibrandt	.45	.18	.04
☐ 127	Rudy Law	.07	.03	.01
☐ 128	Gary Allenson DP	.03	.01	.00
☐ 129	Art Howe	.15	.06	.01
☐ 130	Larry Gura	.10	.04	.01
☐ 131	Keith Moreland	.40	.16	.04
☐ 132	Tommy Boggs	.07	.03	.01
☐ 133	Jeff Cox	.07	.03	.01
☐ 134	Steve Mura	.07	.03	.01
☐ 135	Gorman Thomas	.20	.08	.02
☐ 136	Doug Capilla	.07	.03	.01
☐ 137	Hosken Powell	.07	.03	.01
☐ 138	Rich Dotson DP	.35	.14	.03
☐ 139	Oscar Gamble	.07	.03	.01
☐ 140	Bob Forsch	.07	.03	.01
☐ 141	Miguel Dilone	.07	.03	.01
☐ 142	Jackson Todd	.07	.03	.01
☐ 143	Dan Meyer	.07	.03	.01
☐ 144	Allen Ripley	.07	.03	.01
☐ 145	Mickey Rivers	.10	.04	.01
☐ 146	Bobby Castillo	.07	.03	.01
☐ 147	Dale Berra	.07	.03	.01
☐ 148	Randy Niemann	.07	.03	.01
☐ 149	Joe Nolan	.07	.03	.01
☐ 150	Mark Fidrych	.15	.06	.01
☐ 151	Claudell Washington	.15	.06	.01
☐ 152	John Urrea	.07	.03	.01
☐ 153	Tom Poquette	.07	.03	.01
☐ 154	Rick Langford	.07	.03	.01
☐ 155	Chris Chambliss	.15	.06	.01
☐ 156	Bob McClure	.07	.03	.01
☐ 157	John Wathan	.15	.06	.01
☐ 158	Fergie Jenkins	.25	.10	.02
☐ 159	Brian Doyle	.07	.03	.01
☐ 160	Garry Maddox	.10	.04	.01
☐ 161	Dan Graham	.07	.03	.01
☐ 162	Doug Corbett	.10	.04	.01
☐ 163	Bill Almon	.07	.03	.01
☐ 164	LaMarr Hoyt	.25	.10	.02
☐ 165	Tony Scott	.07	.03	.01
☐ 166	Floyd Bannister	.10	.04	.01
☐ 167	Terry Whitfield	.07	.03	.01
☐ 168	Don Robinson DP	.03	.01	.00
☐ 169	John Mayberry	.10	.04	.01
☐ 170	Ross Grimsley	.07	.03	.01
☐ 171	Gene Richards	.07	.03	.01
☐ 172	Gary Woods	.07	.03	.01
☐ 173	Bump Wills	.07	.03	.01
☐ 174	Doug Rau	.07	.03	.01
☐ 175	Dave Collins	.07	.03	.01
☐ 176	Mike Krukow	.10	.04	.01
☐ 177	Rick Peters	.07	.03	.01
☐ 178	Jim Essian DP	.03	.01	.00
☐ 179	Rudy May	.07	.03	.01
☐ 180	Pete Rose	3.50	1.40	.35
☐ 181	Elias Sosa	.07	.03	.01
☐ 182	Bob Grich	.15	.06	.01
☐ 183	Dick Davis DP	.03	.01	.00
☐ 184	Jim Dwyer	.07	.03	.01
☐ 185	Dennis Leonard	.10	.04	.01
☐ 186	Wayne Nordhagen	.07	.03	.01
☐ 187	Mike Parrott	.07	.03	.01
☐ 188	Doug DeCinces	.15	.06	.01
☐ 189	Craig Swan	.10	.04	.01
☐ 190	Cesar Cedeno	.15	.06	.01
☐ 191	Rick Sutcliffe	.60	.24	.06
☐ 192	Braves Rookies	.30	.12	.03
	Terry Harper			
	Ed Miller			
	Rafael Ramirez			
☐ 193	Pete Vuckovich	.10	.04	.01
☐ 194	Rod Scurry	.10	.04	.01
☐ 195	Rich Murray	.07	.03	.01
☐ 196	Duffy Dyer	.07	.03	.01
☐ 197	Jim Kern	.07	.03	.01
☐ 198	Jerry Dybzinski	.07	.03	.01
☐ 199	Chuck Rainey	.07	.03	.01
☐ 200	George Foster	.25	.10	.02
☐ 201	RB: Johnny Bench	.40	.16	.04
	Most homers, lifetime, catcher			
☐ 202	RB: Steve Carlton	.35	.14	.03
	Most strikeouts, lefthander, lifetime			
☐ 203	RB: Bill Gullickson	.10	.04	.01
	Most strikeouts, game, rookie			

		MINT	EXC	G-VG
☐ 204	RB: Ron LeFlore and Rodney Scott Most stolen bases, teammates, season	.10	.04	.01
☐ 205	RB: Pete Rose .... Most cons. seasons 600 or more at-bats	.75	.30	.07
☐ 206	RR: Mike Schmidt .. Most homers, third baseman, season	.45	.18	.04
☐ 207	RB: Ozzie Smith ... Most assists season, shortstop	.15	.06	.01
☐ 208	RB: Willie Wilson .. Most at-bats, season	.10	.04	.01
☐ 209	Dickie Thon DP	.10	.04	.01
☐ 210	Jim Palmer	.80	.32	.08
☐ 211	Derrel Thomas	.07	.03	.01
☐ 212	Steve Nicosia	.07	.03	.01
☐ 213	Al Holland	.10	.04	.01
☐ 214	Angels Rookies .... Ralph Botting Jim Dorsey John Harris	.10	.04	.01
☐ 215	Larry Hisle	.10	.04	.01
☐ 216	John Henry Johnson	.07	.03	.01
☐ 217	Rich Hebner	.07	.03	.01
☐ 218	Paul Splittorff	.07	.03	.01
☐ 219	Ken Landreaux	.07	.03	.01
☐ 220	Tom Seaver	1.25	.50	.12
☐ 221	Bob Davis	.07	.03	.01
☐ 222	Jorge Orta	.07	.03	.01
☐ 223	Roy Lee Jackson ..	.07	.03	.01
☐ 224	Pat Zachry	.07	.03	.01
☐ 225	Ruppert Jones	.07	.03	.01
☐ 226	Manny Sanguillen DP	.07	.03	.01
☐ 227	Fred Martinez	.07	.03	.01
☐ 228	Tom Paciorek	.07	.03	.01
☐ 229	Rollie Fingers	.50	.20	.05
☐ 230	George Hendrick ...	.10	.04	.01
☐ 231	Joe Beckwith	.07	.03	.01
☐ 232	Mickey Klutts	.07	.03	.01
☐ 233	Skip Lockwood	.07	.03	.01
☐ 234	Lou Whitaker	.40	.16	.04
☐ 235	Scott Sanderson ...	.10	.04	.01
☐ 236	Mike Ivie	.07	.03	.01
☐ 237	Charlie Moore	.07	.03	.01
☐ 238	Willie Hernandez ...	.20	.08	.02
☐ 239	Rick Miller DP	.03	.01	.00

		MINT	EXC	G-VG
☐ 240	Nolan Ryan	1.50	.60	.15
☐ 241	Checklist 122-242 DP	.07	.01	.00
☐ 242	Chet Lemon	.10	.04	.01
☐ 243	Sal Butera	.07	.03	.01
☐ 244	Cardinals Rookies . Tito Landrum Al Olmsted Andy Rincon	.15	.06	.01
☐ 245	Ed Figueroa	.07	.03	.01
☐ 246	Ed Ott DP	.03	.01	.00
☐ 247	Glenn Hubbard DP	.03	.01	.00
☐ 248	Joey McLaughlin ...	.07	.03	.01
☐ 249	Larry Cox	.07	.03	.01
☐ 250	Ron Guidry	.40	.16	.04
☐ 251	Tom Brookens	.07	.03	.01
☐ 252	Victor Cruz	.07	.03	.01
☐ 253	Dave Bergman	.07	.03	.01
☐ 254	Ozzie Smith	1.25	.50	.12
☐ 255	Mark Littell	.07	.03	.01
☐ 256	Bombo Rivera	.07	.03	.01
☐ 257	Rennie Stennett ...	.07	.03	.01
☐ 258	Joe Price	.10	.04	.01
☐ 259	Mets Rookies ..... Juan Berenguer Hubie Brooks Mookie Wilson	1.75	.70	.17
☐ 260	Ron Cey	.20	.08	.02
☐ 261	Rickey Henderson .	4.00	1.60	.40
☐ 262	Sammy Stewart ...	.07	.03	.01
☐ 263	Brian Downing	.10	.04	.01
☐ 264	Jim Norris	.07	.03	.01
☐ 265	John Candelaria ..	.15	.06	.01
☐ 266	Tom Herr	.20	.08	.02
☐ 267	Stan Bahnsen	.07	.03	.01
☐ 268	Jerry Royster	.07	.03	.01
☐ 269	Ken Forsch	.07	.03	.01
☐ 270	Greg Luzinski	.20	.08	.02
☐ 271	Bill Castro	.07	.03	.01
☐ 272	Bruce Kimm	.07	.03	.01
☐ 273	Stan Papi	.07	.03	.01
☐ 274	Craig Chamberlain .	.07	.03	.01
☐ 275	Dwight Evans	.40	.16	.04
☐ 276	Dan Spillner	.07	.03	.01
☐ 277	Alfredo Griffin	.15	.06	.01
☐ 278	Rick Sofield	.07	.03	.01
☐ 279	Bob Knepper	.15	.06	.01
☐ 280	Ken Griffey	.15	.06	.01
☐ 281	Fred Stanley	.07	.03	.01

		MINT	EXC	G-VG
☐ 282	Mariners Rookies ..	.10	.04	.01
	Rick Anderson			
	Greg Biercevicz			
	Rodney Craig			
☐ 283	Billy Sample	.07	.03	.01
☐ 284	Brian Kingman	.07	.03	.01
☐ 285	Jerry Turner	.07	.03	.01
☐ 286	Dave Frost	.07	.03	.01
☐ 287	Lenn Sakata	.07	.03	.01
☐ 288	Bob Clark	.07	.03	.01
☐ 289	Mickey Hatcher	.15	.06	.01
☐ 290	Bob Boone DP	.10	.04	.01
☐ 291	Aurelio Lopez	.07	.03	.01
☐ 292	Mike Squires	.07	.03	.01
☐ 293	Charlie Lea	.20	.08	.02
☐ 294	Mike Tyson DP	.03	.01	.00
☐ 295	Hal McRae	.10	.04	.01
☐ 296	Bill Nahorodny DP	.03	.01	.00
☐ 297	Bob Bailor	.07	.03	.01
☐ 298	Buddy Solomon	.07	.03	.01
☐ 299	Elliott Maddox	.07	.03	.01
☐ 300	Paul Molitor	.45	.18	.04
☐ 301	Matt Keough	.07	.03	.01
☐ 302	Dodgers Rookies ..	6.00	2.40	.60
	Jack Perconte			
	Mike Scioscia			
	Fernando Valenzuela			
☐ 303	Johnny Oates	.07	.03	.01
☐ 304	John Castino	.07	.03	.01
☐ 305	Ken Clay	.07	.03	.01
☐ 306	Juan Beniquez DP	.03	.01	.00
☐ 307	Gene Garber	.07	.03	.01
☐ 308	Rick Manning	.07	.03	.01
☐ 309	Luis Salazar	.20	.08	.02
☐ 310	Vida Blue DP ..:.	.10	.04	.01
☐ 311	Freddie Patek	.07	.03	.01
☐ 312	Rick Rhoden	.15	.06	.01
☐ 313	Luis Pujols	.07	.03	.01
☐ 314	Rich Dauer	.07	.03	.01
☐ 315	Kirk Gibson	6.50	2.60	.65
☐ 316	Craig Minetto	.07	.03	.01
☐ 317	Lonnie Smith	.10	.04	.01
☐ 318	Steve Yeager	.07	.03	.01
☐ 319	Rowland Office	.07	.03	.01
☐ 320	Tom Burgmeier	.07	.03	.01
☐ 321	Leon Durham	.50	.20	.05
☐ 322	Rich Dauer	.10	.04	.01
☐ 323	Jim Morrison DP	.07	.03	.01
☐ 324	Mike Willis	.07	.03	.01
☐ 325	Ray Knight	.20	.08	.02
☐ 326	Biff Pocoroba	.07	.03	.01
☐ 327	Moose Haas	.10	.04	.01
☐ 328	Twins Rookies	.20	.08	.02
	Dave Engle			
	Greg Johnston			
	Gary Ward			
☐ 329	Joaquin Andujar	.15	.06	.01
☐ 330	Frank White	.15	.06	.01
☐ 331	Dennis Lamp	.07	.03	.01
☐ 332	Lee Lacy DP	.07	.03	.01
☐ 333	Sid Monge	.07	.03	.01
☐ 334	Dane Iorg	.07	.03	.01
☐ 335	Rick Cerone	.07	.03	.01
☐ 336	Eddie Whitson	.10	.04	.01
☐ 337	Lynn Jones	.07	.03	.01
☐ 338	Checklist 243-363	.15	.02	.00
☐ 339	John Ellis	.07	.03	.01
☐ 340	Bruce Kison	.07	.03	.01
☐ 341	Dwayne Murphy	.07	.03	.01
☐ 342	Eric Rasmussen DP	.03	.01	.00
☐ 343	Frank Taveras	.07	.03	.01
☐ 344	Byron McLaughlin	.07	.03	.01
☐ 345	Warren Cromartie	.07	.03	.01
☐ 346	Larry Christenson DP	.03	.01	.00
☐ 347	Harold Baines	2.50	1.00	.25
☐ 348	Bob Sykes	.07	.03	.01
☐ 349	Glenn Hoffman	.07	.03	.01
☐ 350	J.R. Richard	.15	.06	.01
☐ 351	Otto Velez	.07	.03	.01
☐ 352	Dick Tidrow DP	.03	.01	.00
☐ 353	Terry Kennedy	.10	.04	.01
☐ 354	Mario Soto	.15	.06	.01
☐ 355	Bob Horner	.35	.14	.03
☐ 356	Padres Rookies	.10	.04	.01
	George Stablein			
	Craig Stimac			
	Tom Tellmann			
☐ 357	Jim Slaton	.07	.03	.01
☐ 358	Mark Wagner	.07	.03	.01
☐ 359	Tom Hausman	.07	.03	.01
☐ 360	Willie Wilson	.20	.08	.02
☐ 361	Joe Strain	.07	.03	.01
☐ 362	Bo Diaz	.10	.04	.01
☐ 363	Geoff Zahn	.07	.03	.01
☐ 364	Mike Davis	.45	.18	.04
☐ 365	Graig Nettles DP	.10	.04	.01
☐ 366	Mike Ramsey	.07	.03	.01
☐ 367	Dennis Martinez	.10	.04	.01

		MINT	EXC	G-VG
☐ 368	Leon Roberts	.07	.03	.01
☐ 369	Frank Tanana	.15	.06	.01
☐ 370	Dave Winfield	1.25	.50	.12
☐ 371	Charlie Hough	.15	.06	.01
☐ 372	Jay Johnstone	.15	.06	.01
☐ 373	Pat Underwood	.07	.03	.01
☐ 374	Tommy Hutton	.07	.03	.01
☐ 375	Dave Concepcion	.15	.06	.01
☐ 376	Ron Reed	.07	.03	.01
☐ 377	Jerry Morales	.07	.03	.01
☐ 378	Dave Rader	.07	.03	.01
☐ 379	Lary Sorensen	.07	.03	.01
☐ 380	Willie Stargell	1.00	.40	.10
☐ 381	Cubs Rookies	.10	.04	.01
	Carlos Lezcano			
	Steve Macko			
	Randy Martz			
☐ 382	Paul Mirabella	.07	.03	.01
☐ 383	Eric Soderholm DP	.03	.01	.00
☐ 384	Mike Sadek	.07	.03	.01
☐ 385	Joe Sambito	.07	.03	.01
☐ 386	Dave Edwards	.07	.03	.01
☐ 387	Phil Niekro	.70	.28	.07
☐ 388	Andre Thornton	.10	.04	.01
☐ 389	Marty Pattin	.07	.03	.01
☐ 390	Cesar Geronimo	.07	.03	.01
☐ 391	Dave Lemanczyk DP	.03	.01	.00
☐ 392	Lance Parrish	.65	.26	.06
☐ 393	Broderick Perkins	.07	.03	.01
☐ 394	Woodie Fryman	.07	.03	.01
☐ 395	Scot Thompson	.07	.03	.01
☐ 396	Bill Campbell	.07	.03	.01
☐ 397	Julio Cruz	.07	.03	.01
☐ 398	Ross Baumgarten	.07	.03	.01
☐ 399	Orioles Rookies	1.50	.60	.15
	Mike Boddicker			
	Mark Corey			
	Floyd Rayford			
☐ 400	Reggie Jackson	1.50	.60	.15
☐ 401	AL Champs	.50	.20	.05
	Royals sweep Yanks			
	(Brett swinging)			
☐ 402	NL Champs	.20	.08	.02
	Phillies squeak			
	past Astros			
☐ 403	1980 World Series	.20	.08	.02
	Phillies beat			
	Royals in six			

		MINT	EXC	G-VG
☐ 404	1980 World Series	.20	.08	.02
	Phillies win first			
	World Series			
☐ 405	Nino Espinosa	.07	.03	.01
☐ 406	Dickie Noles	.07	.03	.01
☐ 407	Ernie Whitt	.15	.06	.01
☐ 408	Fernando Arroyo	.07	.03	.01
☐ 409	Larry Herndon	.07	.03	.01
☐ 410	Bert Campaneris	.10	.04	.01
☐ 411	Terry Puhl	.10	.04	.01
☐ 412	Britt Burns	.25	.10	.02
☐ 413	Tony Bernazard	.10	.04	.01
☐ 414	John Pacella DP	.03	.01	.00
☐ 415	Ben Oglivie	.10	.04	.01
☐ 416	Gary Alexander	.07	.03	.01
☐ 417	Dan Schatzeder	.07	.03	.01
☐ 418	Bobby Brown	.07	.03	.01
☐ 419	Tom Hume	.07	.03	.01
☐ 420	Keith Hernandez	.75	.30	.01
☐ 421	Bob Stanley	.07	.03	.01
☐ 422	Dan Ford	.07	.03	.01
☐ 423	Shane Rawley	.15	.06	.01
☐ 424	Yankees Rookies	.10	.04	.01
	Tim Lollar			
	Bruce Robinson			
	Dennis Werth			
☐ 425	Al Bumbry	.07	.03	.01
☐ 426	Warren Brusstar	.07	.03	.01
☐ 427	John D'Acquisto	.07	.03	.01
☐ 428	John Stearns	.07	.03	.01
☐ 429	Mick Kelleher	.07	.03	.01
☐ 430	Jim Bibby	.07	.03	.01
☐ 431	Dave Roberts	.07	.03	.01
☐ 432	Len Barker	.07	.03	.01
☐ 433	Rance Mulliniks	.07	.03	.01
☐ 434	Roger Erickson	.07	.03	.01
☐ 435	Jim Spencer	.07	.03	.01
☐ 436	Gary Lucas	.10	.04	.01
☐ 437	Mike Heath DP	.03	.01	.00
☐ 438	John Montefusco	.10	.04	.01
☐ 439	Denny Walling	.07	.03	.01
☐ 440	Jerry Reuss	.15	.06	.01
☐ 441	Ken Reitz	.07	.03	.01
☐ 442	Ron Pruitt	.07	.03	.01
☐ 443	Jim Beattie DP	.03	.01	.00
☐ 444	Garth Iorg	.07	.03	.01
☐ 445	Ellis Valentine	.07	.03	.01
☐ 446	Checklist 364-484	.15	.02	.01
☐ 447	Junior Kennedy DP	.03	.01	.00

	MINT	EXC	G-VG		MINT	EXC	G-VG
☐ 448 Tim Corcoran	.07	.03	.01	☐ 491 Gordy Pladson	.07	.03	.01
☐ 449 Paul Mitchell	.07	.03	.01	☐ 492 Barry Foote	.07	.03	.01
☐ 450 Dave Kingman DP	.10	.04	.01	☐ 493 Dan Quisenberry	.25	.10	.02
☐ 451 Indians Rookies	.10	.04	.01	☐ 494 Bob Walk	.30	.12	.03
Chris Bando				☐ 495 Dusty Baker	.10	.04	.01
Tom Brennan				☐ 496 Paul Dade	.07	.03	.01
Sandy Wihtol				☐ 497 Fred Norman	.07	.03	.01
☐ 452 Renie Martin	.07	.03	.01	☐ 498 Pat Putnam	.07	.03	.01
☐ 453 Rob Wilfong DP	.03	.01	.00	☐ 499 Frank Pastore	.07	.03	.01
☐ 454 Andy Hassler	.07	.03	.01	☐ 500 Jim Rice	.70	.28	.07
☐ 455 Rick Burleson	.10	.04	.01	☐ 501 Tim Foli DP	.03	.01	.00
☐ 456 Jeff Reardon	.90	.36	.09	☐ 502 Giants Rookies	.10	.04	.01
☐ 457 Mike Lum	.07	.03	.01	Chris Bourjos			
☐ 458 Randy Jones	.07	.03	.01	Al Hargesheimer			
☐ 459 Greg Gross	.07	.03	.01	Mike Rowland			
☐ 460 Rich Gossage	.30	.12	.03	☐ 503 Steve McCatty	.07	.03	.01
☐ 461 Dave McKay	.07	.03	.01	☐ 504 Dale Murphy	2.50	1.00	.25
☐ 462 Jack Brohamer	.07	.03	.01	☐ 505 Jason Thompson	.07	.03	.01
☐ 463 Milt May	.07	.03	.01	☐ 506 Phil Huffman	.07	.03	.01
☐ 464 Adrian Devine	.07	.03	.01	☐ 507 Jamie Quirk	.07	.03	.01
☐ 465 Bill Russell	.10	.04	.01	☐ 508 Rob Dressler	.07	.03	.01
☐ 466 Bob Molinaro	.07	.03	.01	☐ 509 Pete Mackanin	.07	.03	.01
☐ 467 Dave Stieb	.45	.18	.04	☐ 510 Lee Mazzilli	.07	.03	.01
☐ 468 John Wockenfuss	.07	.03	.01	☐ 511 Wayne Garland	.07	.03	.01
☐ 469 Jeff Leonard	.25	.10	.02	☐ 512 Gary Thomasson	.07	.03	.01
☐ 470 Manny Trillo	.07	.03	.01	☐ 513 Frank LaCorte	.07	.03	.01
☐ 471 Mike Vail	.07	.03	.01	☐ 514 George Riley	.07	.03	.01
☐ 472 Dyar Miller DP	.03	.01	.00	☐ 515 Robin Yount	1.00	.40	.10
☐ 473 Jose Cardenal	.07	.03	.01	☐ 516 Doug Bird	.07	.03	.01
☐ 474 Mike LaCoss	.07	.03	.01	☐ 517 Richie Zisk	.10	.04	.01
☐ 475 Buddy Bell	.20	.08	.02	☐ 518 Grant Jackson	.07	.03	.01
☐ 476 Jerry Koosman	.15	.06	.01	☐ 519 John Tamargo DP	.03	.01	.00
☐ 477 Luis Gomez	.07	.03	.01	☐ 520 Steve Stone	.10	.04	.01
☐ 478 Juan Eichelberger	.07	.03	.01	☐ 521 Sam Mejias	.07	.03	.01
☐ 479 Expos Rookies	8.50	3.50	.85	☐ 522 Mike Colbern	.07	.03	.01
Tim Raines				☐ 523 John Fulgham	.07	.03	.01
Roberto Ramos				☐ 524 Willie Aikens	.07	.03	.01
Bobby Pate				☐ 525 Mike Torrez	.07	.03	.01
☐ 480 Carlton Fisk	.35	.14	.03	☐ 526 Phillies Rookies	.15	.06	.01
☐ 481 Bob Lacey DP	.03	.01	.00	Marty Bystrom			
☐ 482 Jim Gantner	.07	.03	.01	Jay Loviglio			
☐ 483 Mike Griffin	.07	.03	.01	Jim Wright			
☐ 484 Max Venable DP	.03	.01	.00	☐ 527 Danny Goodwin	.07	.03	.01
☐ 485 Garry Templeton	.15	.06	.01	☐ 528 Gary Matthews	.10	.04	.01
☐ 486 Marc Hill	.07	.03	.01	☐ 529 Dave LaRoche	.07	.03	.01
☐ 487 Dewey Robinson	.07	.03	.01	☐ 530 Steve Garvey	1.25	.50	.12
☐ 488 Damaso Garcia	.15	.06	.01	☐ 531 John Curtis	.07	.03	.01
☐ 489 John Littlefield	.07	.03	.01	☐ 532 Bill Stein	.07	.03	.01
☐ 490 Eddie Murray	1.50	.60	.15	☐ 533 Jesus Figueroa	.07	.03	.01

		MINT	EXC	G-VG
☐ 534	Dave Smith	.45	.18	.04
☐ 535	Omar Moreno	.07	.03	.01
☐ 536	Bob Owchinko DP	.03	.01	.00
☐ 537	Ron Hodges	.07	.03	.01
☐ 538	Tom Griffin	.07	.03	.01
☐ 539	Rodney Scott	.07	.03	.01
☐ 540	Mike Schmidt DP	1.00	.40	.10
☐ 541	Steve Swisher	.07	.03	.01
☐ 542	Larry Bradford DP	.03	.01	.00
☐ 543	Terry Crowley	.07	.03	.01
☐ 544	Rich Gale	.07	.03	.01
☐ 545	Johnny Grubb	.07	.03	.01
☐ 546	Paul Moskau	.07	.03	.01
☐ 547	Mario Guerrero	.07	.03	.01
☐ 548	Dave Goltz	.07	.03	.01
☐ 549	Jerry Remy	.07	.03	.01
☐ 550	Tommy John	.35	.14	.03
☐ 551	Pirates Rookies	2.25	.90	.22
	Vance Law			
	Tony Pena			
	Pascual Perez			
☐ 552	Steve Trout	.10	.04	.01
☐ 553	Tim Blackwell	.07	.03	.01
☐ 554	Bert Blyleven	.30	.12	.03
☐ 555	Cecil Cooper	.25	.10	.02
☐ 556	Jerry Mumphrey	.07	.03	.01
☐ 557	Chris Knapp	.07	.03	.01
☐ 558	Barry Bonnell	.07	.03	.01
☐ 559	Willie Montanez	.07	.03	.01
☐ 560	Joe Morgan	.60	.24	.06
☐ 561	Dennis Littlejohn	.07	.03	.01
☐ 562	Checklist 485-605	.15	.02	.00
☐ 563	Jim Kaat	.25	.10	.02
☐ 564	Ron Hassey DP	.07	.03	.01
☐ 565	Burt Hooton	.07	.03	.01
☐ 566	Del Unser	.07	.03	.01
☐ 567	Mark Bomback	.07	.03	.01
☐ 568	Dave Revering	.07	.03	.01
☐ 569	Al Williams DP	.03	.01	.00
☐ 570	Ken Singleton	.15	.06	.01
☐ 571	Todd Cruz	.07	.03	.01
☐ 572	Jack Morris	.60	.24	.06
☐ 573	Phil Garner	.07	.03	.01
☐ 574	Bill Caudill	.07	.03	.01
☐ 575	Tony Perez	.30	.12	.03
☐ 576	Reggie Cleveland	.07	.03	.01

		MINT	EXC	G-VG
☐ 577	Blue Jays Rookies	.15	.06	.01
	Luis Leal			
	Brian Milner			
	Ken Schrom			
☐ 578	Bill Gullickson	.30	.12	.03
☐ 579	Tim Flannery	.07	.03	.01
☐ 580	Don Baylor	.25	.10	.02
☐ 581	Roy Howell	.07	.03	.01
☐ 582	Gaylord Perry	.50	.20	.05
☐ 583	Larry Milbourne	.07	.03	.01
☐ 584	Randy Lerch	.07	.03	.01
☐ 585	Amos Otis	.15	.06	.01
☐ 586	Silvio Martinez	.07	.03	.01
☐ 587	Jeff Newman	.07	.03	.01
☐ 588	Gary Lavelle	.07	.03	.01
☐ 589	Lamar Johnson	.07	.03	.01
☐ 590	Bruce Sutter	.20	.08	.02
☐ 591	John Lowenstein	.07	.03	.01
☐ 592	Steve Comer	.07	.03	.01
☐ 593	Steve Kemp	.10	.04	.01
☐ 594	Preston Hanna DP	.03	.01	.00
☐ 595	Butch Hobson	.07	.03	.01
☐ 596	Jerry Augustine	.07	.03	.01
☐ 597	Rafael Landestoy	.07	.03	.01
☐ 598	George Vukovich DP	.03	.01	.00
☐ 599	Dennis Kinney	.07	.03	.01
☐ 600	Johnny Bench	1.25	.50	.12
☐ 601	Don Aase	.07	.03	.01
☐ 602	Bobby Murcer	.15	.06	.01
☐ 603	John Verhoeven	.07	.03	.01
☐ 604	Rob Picciolo	.07	.03	.01
☐ 605	Don Sutton	.50	.20	.05
☐ 606	Reds Rookies DP	.07	.03	.01
	Bruce Berenyi			
	Geoff Combe			
	Paul Householder			
☐ 607	David Palmer	.10	.04	.01
☐ 608	Greg Pryor	.07	.03	.01
☐ 609	Lynn McGlothen	.07	.03	.01
☐ 610	Darrell Porter	.07	.03	.01
☐ 611	Rick Matula DP	.03	.01	.00
☐ 612	Duane Kuiper	.07	.03	.01
☐ 613	Jim Anderson	.07	.03	.01
☐ 614	Dave Rozema	.07	.03	.01
☐ 615	Rick Dempsey	.07	.03	.01
☐ 616	Rick Wise	.07	.03	.01
☐ 617	Craig Reynolds	.07	.03	.01
☐ 618	John Milner	.07	.03	.01
☐ 619	Steve Henderson	.07	.03	.01

	MINT	EXC	G-VG
☐ 620 Dennis Eckersley ..	.30	.12	.03
☐ 621 Tom Donohue	.07	.03	.01
☐ 622 Randy Moffitt	.07	.03	.01
☐ 623 Sal Bando	.10	.04	.01
☐ 624 Bob Welch	.20	.08	.02
☐ 625 Bill Buckner	.20	.08	.02
☐ 626 Tigers Rookies	.10	.04	.01
Dave Steffen			
Jerry Ujdur			
Roger Weaver			
☐ 627 Luis Tiant	.15	.06	.01
☐ 628 Vic Correll	.07	.03	.01
☐ 629 Tony Armas	.15	.06	.01
☐ 630 Steve Carlton	1.00	.40	.10
☐ 631 Ron Jackson	.07	.03	.01
☐ 632 Alan Bannister	.07	.03	.01
☐ 633 Bill Lee	.10	.04	.01
☐ 634 Doug Flynn	.07	.03	.01
☐ 635 Bobby Bonds	.15	.06	.01
☐ 636 Al Hrabosky	.10	.04	.01
☐ 637 Jerry Narron	.07	.03	.01
☐ 638 Checklist 606-726 ..	.15	.02	.00
☐ 639 Carney Lansford ...	.30	.12	.03
☐ 640 Dave Parker	.50	.20	.05
☐ 641 Mark Belanger	.10	.04	.01
☐ 642 Vern Ruhle	.07	.03	.01
☐ 643 Lloyd Moseby	1.25	.50	.12
☐ 644 Ramon Aviles DP ..	.03	.01	.00
☐ 645 Rick Reuschel	.20	.08	.02
☐ 646 Marvis Foley	.07	.03	.01
☐ 647 Dick Drago	.07	.03	.01
☐ 648 Darrell Evans	.25	.10	.02
☐ 649 Manny Sarmiento ..	.07	.03	.01
☐ 650 Bucky Dent	.15	.06	.01
☐ 651 Pedro Guerrero	1.50	.60	.15
☐ 652 John Montague	.07	.03	.01
☐ 653 Bill Fahey	.07	.03	.01
☐ 654 Ray Burris	.07	.03	.01
☐ 655 Dan Driessen	.07	.03	.01
☐ 656 Jon Matlack	.07	.03	.01
☐ 657 Mike Cubbage DP ..	.03	.01	.00
☐ 658 Milt Wilcox	.07	.03	.01
☐ 659 Brewers Rookies ...	.10	.04	.01
John Flinn			
Ed Romero			
Ned Yost			
☐ 660 Gary Carter	1.50	.60	.15

	MINT	EXC	G-VG
☐ 661 Orioles Team/Mgr. .	.25	.05	.01
Earl Weaver			
(checklist back)			
☐ 662 Red Sox Team/Mgr.	.20	.05	.01
Ralph Houk			
(checklist back)			
☐ 663 Angels Team/Mgr. .	.20	.05	.01
Jim Fregosi			
(checklist back)			
☐ 664 White Sox Team/Mgr.	.20	.05	.01
Tony LaRussa			
(checklist back)			
☐ 665 Indians Team/Mgr. .	.20	.05	.01
Dave Garcia			
(checklist back)			
☐ 666 Tigers Team/Mgr. .	.25	.05	.01
Sparky Anderson			
(checklist back)			
☐ 667 Royals Team/Mgr. .	.20	.05	.01
Jim Frey			
(checklist back)			
☐ 668 Brewers Team/Mgr.	.20	.05	.01
Bob Rodgers			
(checklist back)			
☐ 669 Twins Team/Mgr...	.20	.05	.01
John Goryl			
(checklist back)			
☐ 670 Yankees Team/Mgr.	.25	.05	.01
Gene Michael			
(checklist back)			
☐ 671 A's Team/Mgr.	.25	.05	.01
Billy Martin			
(checklist back)			
☐ 672 Mariners Team/Mgr.	.20	.05	.01
Maury Wills			
(checklist back)			
☐ 673 Rangers Team/Mgr.	.20	.05	.01
Don Zimmer			
(checklist back)			
☐ 674 Blue Jays Team/Mgr.	.20	.05	.01
Bobby Mattick			
(checklist back)			
☐ 675 Braves Team/Mgr. .	.20	.05	.01
Bobby Cox			
(checklist back)			
☐ 676 Cubs Team/Mgr. ...	.20	.05	.01
Joe Amalfitano			
(checklist back)			

		MINT	EXC	G-VG
☐ 677	Reds Team/Mgr. John McNamara (checklist back)	.20	.05	.01
☐ 678	Astros Team/Mgr. Bill Virdon (checklist back)	.20	.05	.01
☐ 679	Dodgers Team/Mgr. Tom Lasorda (checklist back)	.25	.05	.01
☐ 680	Expos Team/Mgr. Dick Williams (checklist back)	.20	.05	.01
☐ 681	Mets Team/Mgr. Joe Torre (checklist back)	.25	.05	.01
☐ 682	Phillies Team/Mgr. Dallas Green (checklist back)	.20	.05	.01
☐ 683	Pirates Team/Mgr. Chuck Tanner (checklist back)	.20	.05	.01
☐ 684	Cardinals Team/Mgr. Whitey Herzog (checklist back)	.20	.05	.01
☐ 685	Padres Team/Mgr. Frank Howard (checklist back)	.20	.05	.01
☐ 686	Giants Team/Mgr. Dave Bristol (checklist back)	.20	.05	.01
☐ 687	Jeff Jones	.07	.03	.01
☐ 688	Kiko Garcia	.07	.03	.01
☐ 689	Red Sox Rookies Bruce Hurst Keith MacWhorter Reid Nichols	2.25	.90	.22
☐ 690	Bob Watson	.10	.04	.01
☐ 691	Dick Ruthven	.07	.03	.01
☐ 692	Lenny Randle	.07	.03	.01
☐ 693	Steve Howe	.15	.06	.01
☐ 694	Bud Harrelson DP	.03	.01	.00
☐ 695	Kent Tekulve	.10	.04	.01
☐ 696	Alan Ashby	.10	.04	.01
☐ 697	Rick Waits	.07	.03	.01
☐ 698	Mike Jorgensen	.07	.03	.01
☐ 699	Glenn Abbott	.07	.03	.01
☐ 700	George Brett	2.00	.80	.20
☐ 701	Joe Rudi	.10	.04	.01
☐ 702	George Medich	.07	.03	.01

		MINT	EXC	G-VG
☐ 703	Alvis Woods	.07	.03	.01
☐ 704	Bill Travers DP	.03	.01	.00
☐ 705	Ted Simmons	.20	.08	.02
☐ 706	Dave Ford	.07	.03	.01
☐ 707	Dave Cash	.07	.03	.01
☐ 708	Doyle Alexander	.15	.06	.01
☐ 709	Alan Trammell DP	.30	.12	.03
☐ 710	Ron LeFlore DP	.07	.03	.01
☐ 711	Joe Ferguson	.07	.03	.01
☐ 712	Bill Bonham	.07	.03	.01
☐ 713	Bill North	.07	.03	.01
☐ 714	Pete Redfern	.07	.03	.01
☐ 715	Bill Madlock	.15	.06	.01
☐ 716	Glenn Borgmann	.07	.03	.01
☐ 717	Jim Barr DP	.03	.01	.00
☐ 718	Larry Biittner	.07	.03	.01
☐ 719	Sparky Lyle	.15	.06	.01
☐ 720	Fred Lynn	.25	.10	.02
☐ 721	Toby Harrah	.10	.04	.01
☐ 722	Joe Niekro	.15	.06	.01
☐ 723	Bruce Bochte	.07	.03	.01
☐ 724	Lou Piniella	.15	.06	.01
☐ 725	Steve Rogers	.10	.04	.01
☐ 726	Rick Monday	.20	.08	.02

1981 Topps Traded

The cards in this 132-card set measure 2 ½ " by 3 ½ ". For the first time since 1976, Topps issued a "traded" set in 1981. Unlike the small traded sets of 1974 and 1976, this set contains a larger number of cards and was sequentially numbered, alphabetically, from

727 to 858. Thus, this set gives the impression it is a continuation of their regular issue of this year. The sets were issued only through hobby card dealers and were boxed in complete sets of 132 cards.

	MINT	EXC	G-VG
Complete Set (132)	22.00	9.00	2.20
Common Player (727-858)	.08	.03	.01

		MINT	EXC	G-VG
☐ 727	Danny Ainge	.65	.26	.06
☐ 728	Doyle Alexander	.20	.08	.02
☐ 729	Gary Alexander	.08	.03	.01
☐ 730	Bill Almon	.08	.03	.01
☐ 731	Joaquin Andujar	.15	.06	.01
☐ 732	Bob Bailor	.08	.03	.01
☐ 733	Juan Beniquez	.08	.03	.01
☐ 734	Dave Bergman	.08	.03	.01
☐ 735	Tony Bernazard	.08	.03	.01
☐ 736	Larry Biittner	.08	.03	.01
☐ 737	Doug Bird	.08	.03	.01
☐ 738	Bert Blyleven	.40	.16	.04
☐ 739	Mark Bomback	.08	.03	.01
☐ 740	Bobby Bonds	.20	.08	.02
☐ 741	Rick Bosetti	.08	.03	.01
☐ 742	Hubie Brooks	1.25	.50	.12
☐ 743	Rick Burleson	.15	.06	.01
☐ 744	Ray Burris	.08	.03	.01
☐ 745	Jeff Burroughs	.15	.06	.01
☐ 746	Enos Cabell	.08	.03	.01
☐ 747	Ken Clay	.08	.03	.01
☐ 748	Mark Clear	.08	.03	.01
☐ 749	Larry Cox	.08	.03	.01
☐ 750	Hector Cruz	.08	.03	.01
☐ 751	Victor Cruz	.08	.03	.01
☐ 752	Mike Cubbage	.08	.03	.01
☐ 753	Dick Davis	.08	.03	.01
☐ 754	Brian Doyle	.08	.03	.01
☐ 755	Dick Drago	.08	.03	.01
☐ 756	Leon Durham	.50	.20	.05
☐ 757	Jim Dwyer	.08	.03	.01
☐ 758	Dave Edwards	.08	.03	.01
☐ 759	Jim Essian	.08	.03	.01
☐ 760	Bill Fahey	.08	.03	.01
☐ 761	Rollie Fingers	.85	.34	.08
☐ 762	Carlton Fisk	.70	.28	.07
☐ 763	Barry Foote	.08	.03	.01
☐ 764	Ken Forsch	.08	.03	.01
☐ 765	Kiko Garcia	.08	.03	.01
☐ 766	Cesar Geronimo	.08	.03	.01
☐ 767	Gary Gray	.08	.03	.01
☐ 768	Mickey Hatcher	.20	.08	.02
☐ 769	Steve Henderson	.08	.03	.01
☐ 770	Marc Hill	.08	.03	.01
☐ 771	Butch Hobson	.08	.03	.01
☐ 772	Rick Honeycutt	.08	.03	.01
☐ 773	Roy Howell	.08	.03	.01
☐ 774	Mike Ivie	.08	.03	.01
☐ 775	Roy Lee Jackson	.08	.03	.01
☐ 776	Cliff Johnson	.08	.03	.01
☐ 777	Randy Jones	.15	.06	.01
☐ 778	Ruppert Jones	.08	.03	.01
☐ 779	Mick Kelleher	.08	.03	.01
☐ 780	Terry Kennedy	.15	.06	.01
☐ 781	Dave Kingman	.35	.14	.03
☐ 782	Bob Knepper	.20	.08	.02
☐ 783	Ken Kravec	.08	.03	.01
☐ 784	Bob Lacey	.08	.03	.01
☐ 785	Dennis Lamp	.08	.03	.01
☐ 786	Rafael Landestoy	.08	.03	.01
☐ 787	Ken Landreaux	.15	.06	.01
☐ 788	Carney Lansford	.35	.14	.03
☐ 789	Dave LaRoche	.08	.03	.01
☐ 790	Joe Lefebvre	.08	.03	.01
☐ 791	Ron LeFlore	.15	.06	.01
☐ 792	Randy Lerch	.08	.03	.01
☐ 793	Sixto Lezcano	.08	.03	.01
☐ 794	John Littlefield	.08	.03	.01
☐ 795	Mike Lum	.08	.03	.01
☐ 796	Greg Luzinski	.30	.12	.03
☐ 797	Fred Lynn	.50	.20	.05
☐ 798	Jerry Martin	.08	.03	.01
☐ 799	Buck Martinez	.08	.03	.01
☐ 800	Gary Matthews	.15	.06	.01
☐ 801	Mario Mendoza	.08	.03	.01
☐ 802	Larry Milbourne	.08	.03	.01
☐ 803	Rick Miller	.08	.03	.01
☐ 804	John Montefusco	.15	.06	.01
☐ 805	Jerry Morales	.08	.03	.01
☐ 806	Jose Morales	.08	.03	.01
☐ 807	Joe Morgan	1.25	.50	.12
☐ 808	Jerry Mumphrey	.08	.03	.01
☐ 809	Gene Nelson	.35	.14	.03
☐ 810	Ed Ott	.08	.03	.01
☐ 811	Bob Owchinko	.08	.03	.01
☐ 812	Gaylord Perry	1.25	.50	.12
☐ 813	Mike Phillips	.08	.03	.01
☐ 814	Darrell Porter	.15	.06	.01
☐ 815	Mike Proly	.08	.03	.01
☐ 816	Tim Raines	7.00	2.80	.70

1982 Topps

		MINT	EXC	G-VG
☐ 817	Lenny Randle	.08	.03	.01
☐ 818	Doug Rau	.08	.03	.01
☐ 819	Jeff Reardon	.60	.24	.06
☐ 820	Ken Reitz	.08	.03	.01
☐ 821	Steve Renko	.08	.03	.01
☐ 822	Rick Reuschel	.25	.10	.02
☐ 823	Dave Revering	.08	.03	.01
☐ 024	Dave Roberts	.08	.03	.01
☐ 825	Leon Roberts	.08	.03	.01
☐ 826	Joe Rudi	.15	.06	.01
☐ 827	Kevin Saucier	.08	.03	.01
☐ 828	Tony Scott	.08	.03	.01
☐ 829	Bob Shirley	.08	.03	.01
☐ 830	Ted Simmons	.45	.18	.04
☐ 831	Lary Sorensen	.08	.03	.01
☐ 832	Jim Spencer	.08	.03	.01
☐ 833	Harry Spilman	.08	.03	.01
☐ 834	Fred Stanley	.08	.03	.01
☐ 835	Rusty Staub	.25	.10	.02
☐ 836	Bill Stein	.08	.03	.01
☐ 837	Joe Strain	.08	.03	.01
☐ 838	Bruce Sutter	.40	.16	.04
☐ 839	Don Sutton	1.00	.40	.10
☐ 840	Steve Swisher	.08	.03	.01
☐ 841	Frank Tanana	.20	.08	.02
☐ 842	Gene Tenace	.15	.06	.01
☐ 843	Jason Thompson	.08	.03	.01
☐ 844	Dickie Thon	.20	.08	.02
☐ 845	Bill Travers	.08	.03	.01
☐ 846	Tom Underwood	.08	.03	.01
☐ 847	John Urrea	.08	.03	.01
☐ 848	Mike Vail	.08	.03	.01
☐ 849	Ellis Valentine	.08	.03	.01
☐ 850	Fernando Valenzuela	4.50	1.80	.45
☐ 851	Pete Vuckovich	.15	.06	.01
☐ 852	Mark Wagner	.08	.03	.01
☐ 853	Bob Walk	.25	.10	.02
☐ 854	Claudell Washington	.20	.08	.02
☐ 855	Dave Winfield	2.00	.80	.20
☐ 856	Geoff Zahn	.08	.03	.01
☐ 857	Richie Zisk	.15	.06	.01
☐ 858	Checklist 727-858	.08	.01	.00

*The cards in this 792-card set measure 2 ½"
by 3 ½". The 1982 baseball series is the
largest set Topps has ever issued at one
printing. The 66-card increase from the previous year's total eliminated the "double
print" practice which had occurred in every
regular issue since 1978. Cards 1-6 depict
Highlights (HL) of the 1981 season, cards
161-168 picture League Leaders, and there
are mini-series of AL (547-557) and NL (337-
347) All-Stars (AS). The abbreviation "SA" in
the checklist is given for the 40 "Super Action" cards introduced in this set. The team
cards are actually Team Leader (TL) cards
picturing the batting and pitching leader for
that team with a checklist back.*

		MINT	EXC	G-VG
	Complete Set (792)	85.00	34.00	8.50
	Common Player (1-792)	.06	.02	.00
☐ 1	HL: Steve Carlton Sets new NL strikeout record	.45	.10	.02
☐ 2	HL: Ron Davis Fans 8 straight in relief	.10	.04	.01
☐ 3	HL: Tim Raines Swipes 71 bases as rookie	.25	.10	.02
☐ 4	HL: Pete Rose Sets NL career hits mark	.75	.30	.07

			MINT	EXC	G-VG
☐	5	HL: Nolan Ryan ... Pitches fifth career no-hitter	.40	.16	.04
☐	6	HL: Fern. Valenzuela 8 shutouts as rookie	.20	.08	.02
☐	7	Scott Sanderson ...	.06	.02	.00
☐	8	Rich Dauer	.06	.02	.00
☐	9	Ron Guidry	.30	.12	.03
☐	10	SA: Ron Guidry	.15	.06	.01
☐	11	Gary Alexander	.06	.02	.00
☐	12	Moose Haas	.06	.02	.00
☐	13	Lamar Johnson ...	.06	.02	.00
☐	14	Steve Howe	.06	.02	.00
☐	15	Ellis Valentine	.06	.02	.00
☐	16	Steve Comer	.06	.02	.00
☐	17	Darrell Evans	.15	.06	.01
☐	18	Fernando Arroyo ...	.06	.02	.00
☐	19	Ernie Whitt	.10	.04	.01
☐	20	Garry Maddox	.10	.04	.01
☐	21	Orioles Rookies ... Bob Bonner Cal Ripken Jeff Schneider	11.00	4.50	1.10
☐	22	Jim Beattie	.06	.02	.00
☐	23	Willie Hernandez ...	.20	.08	.02
☐	24	Dave Frost	.06	.02	.00
☐	25	Jerry Remy	.06	.02	.00
☐	26	Jorge Orta	.06	.02	.00
☐	27	Tom Herr	.15	.06	.01
☐	28	John Urrea	.06	.02	.00
☐	29	Dwayne Murphy ...	.06	.02	.00
☐	30	Tom Seaver	.65	.26	.06
☐	31	SA: Tom Seaver ...	.30	.12	.03
☐	32	Gene Garber	.06	.02	.00
☐	33	Jerry Morales	.06	.02	.00
☐	34	Joe Sambito	.06	.02	.00
☐	35	Willie Aikens	.06	.02	.00
☐	36	Rangers TL ...... Mgr. Don Zimmer Batting: Al Oliver Pitching: Doc Medich	.15	.04	.01
☐	37	Dan Graham	.06	.02	.00
☐	38	Charlie Lea	.10	.04	.01
☐	39	Lou Whitaker	.25	.10	.02
☐	40	Dave Parker	.30	.12	.03
☐	41	SA: Dave Parker ...	.15	.06	.01
☐	42	Rick Sofield	.06	.02	.00
☐	43	Mike Cubbage	.06	.02	.00
☐	44	Britt Burns	.06	.02	.00
☐	45	Rick Cerone	.06	.02	.00
☐	46	Jerry Augustine ...	.06	.02	.00
☐	47	Jeff Leonard	.10	.04	.01
☐	48	Bobby Castillo ...	.06	.02	.00
☐	49	Alvis Woods	.06	.02	.00
☐	50	Buddy Bell	.15	.06	.01
☐	51	Cubs Rookies .... Jay Howell Carlos Lezcano Ty Waller	.35	.14	.03
☐	52	Larry Andersen ...	.06	.02	.00
☐	53	Greg Gross	.06	.02	.00
☐	54	Ron Hassey	.10	.04	.01
☐	55	Rick Burleson	.10	.04	.01
☐	56	Mark Littell	.06	.02	.00
☐	57	Craig Reynolds ...	.06	.02	.00
☐	58	John D'Acquisto ..	.06	.02	.00
☐	59	Rich Gedman	.50	.20	.05
☐	60	Tony Armas	.10	.04	.01
☐	61	Tommy Boggs	.06	.02	.00
☐	62	Mike Tyson	.06	.02	.00
☐	63	Mario Soto	.10	.04	.01
☐	64	Lynn Jones	.06	.02	.00
☐	65	Terry Kennedy	.10	.04	.01
☐	66	Astros TL .... Mgr. Bill Virdon Batting: Art Howe Pitching: Nolan Ryan	.20	.06	.01
☐	67	Rich Gale	.06	.02	.00
☐	68	Roy Howell	.06	.02	.00
☐	69	Al Williams	.06	.02	.00
☐	70	Tim Raines	2.00	.80	.20
☐	71	Roy Lee Jackson ..	.06	.02	.00
☐	72	Rick Auerbach ...	.06	.02	.00
☐	73	Buddy Solomon ...	.06	.02	.00
☐	74	Bob Clark	.06	.02	.00
☐	75	Tommy John	.25	.10	.02
☐	76	Greg Pryor	.06	.02	.00
☐	77	Miguel Dilone	.06	.02	.00
☐	78	George Medich ...	.06	.02	.00
☐	79	Bob Bailor	.06	.02	.00
☐	80	Jim Palmer	.55	.22	.05
☐	81	SA: Jim Palmer ...	.25	.10	.02
☐	82	Bob Welch	.15	.06	.01
☐	83	Yankees Rookies . Steve Balboni Andy McGaffigan Andre Robertson	.35	.14	.03
☐	84	Rennie Stennett ...	.06	.02	.00

		MINT	EXC	G-VG
☐ 85	Lynn McGlothen ...	.06	.02	.00
☐ 86	Dane Iorg	.06	.02	.00
☐ 87	Matt Keough	.06	.02	.00
☐ 88	Biff Pocoroba	.06	.02	.00
☐ 89	Steve Henderson ..	.06	.02	.00
☐ 90	Nolan Ryan	.85	.34	.08
☐ 91	Carney Lansford ...	.20	.08	.02
☐ 92	Brad Havens	.06	.02	.00
☐ 93	Larry Hisle	.06	.02	.00
☐ 94	Andy Hassler	.06	.02	.00
☐ 95	Ozzie Smith	.45	.18	.04
☐ 96	Royals TL	.20	.06	.01
	Mgr. Jim Frey			
	Batting: George Brett			
	Pitching: Larry Gura			
☐ 97	Paul Moskau	.06	.02	.00
☐ 98	Terry Bulling	.06	.02	.00
☐ 99	Barry Bonnell	.06	.02	.00
☐ 100	Mike Schmidt ..	1.25	.50	.12
☐ 101	SA: Mike Schmidt ..	.50	.20	.05
☐ 102	Dan Briggs	.06	.02	.00
☐ 103	Bob Lacey	.06	.02	.00
☐ 104	Rance Mulliniks	.06	.02	.00
☐ 105	Kirk Gibson	1.25	.50	.12
☐ 106	Enrique Romo	.06	.02	.00
☐ 107	Wayne Krenchicki ..	.06	.02	.00
☐ 108	Bob Sykes	.06	.02	.00
☐ 109	Dave Revering	.06	.02	.00
☐ 110	Carlton Fisk	.30	.12	.03
☐ 111	SA: Carlton Fisk ...	.15	.06	.01
☐ 112	Billy Sample	.06	.02	.00
☐ 113	Steve McCatty	.06	.02	.00
☐ 114	Ken Landreaux	.06	.02	.00
☐ 115	Gaylord Perry	.35	.14	.03
☐ 116	Jim Wohlford	.06	.02	.00
☐ 117	Rawly Eastwick ...	.06	.02	.00
☐ 118	Expos Rookies ...	.35	.14	.03
	Terry Francona			
	Brad Mills			
	Bryn Smith			
☐ 119	Joe Pittman	.06	.02	.00
☐ 120	Gary Lucas	.06	.02	.00
☐ 121	Ed Lynch	.10	.04	.01
☐ 122	Jamie Easterly	.06	.02	.00
	(photo actually Reggie Cleveland)			
☐ 123	Danny Goodwin	.06	.02	.00
☐ 124	Reid Nichols	.06	.02	.00
☐ 125	Danny Ainge	.15	.06	.01

		MINT	EXC	G-VG
☐ 126	Braves TL	.15	.04	.01
	Mgr. Bobby Cox			
	Batting: C.Washington			
	Pitching: Rick Mahler			
☐ 127	Lonnie Smith	.10	.04	.01
☐ 128	Frank Pastore	.06	.02	.00
☐ 129	Checklist 1-132 ...	.10	.01	.00
☐ 130	Julio Cruz	.06	.02	.00
☐ 131	Stan Bahnsen	.06	.02	.00
☐ 132	Lee May	.06	.02	.00
☐ 133	Pat Underwood ...	.06	.02	.00
☐ 134	Dan Ford	.06	.02	.00
☐ 135	Andy Rincon	.06	.02	.00
☐ 136	Lenn Sakata	.06	.02	.00
☐ 137	George Cappuzzello	.06	.02	.00
☐ 138	Tony Pena	.25	.10	.02
☐ 139	Jeff Jones	.06	.02	.00
☐ 140	Ron LeFlore	.10	.04	.01
☐ 141	Indians Rookies ...	1.25	.50	.12
	Chris Bando			
	Tom Brennan			
	Von Hayes			
☐ 142	Dave LaRoche ...	.06	.02	.00
☐ 143	Mookie Wilson	.15	.06	.01
☐ 144	Fred Breining	.06	.02	.00
☐ 145	Bob Horner	.25	.10	.02
☐ 146	Mike Griffin	.06	.02	.00
☐ 147	Denny Walling	.06	.02	.00
☐ 148	Mickey Klutts	.06	.02	.00
☐ 149	Pat Putnam	.06	.02	.00
☐ 150	Ted Simmons	.20	.08	.02
☐ 151	Dave Edwards	.06	.02	.00
☐ 152	Ramon Aviles	.06	.02	.00
☐ 153	Roger Erickson ...	.06	.02	.00
☐ 154	Dennis Werth	.06	.02	.00
☐ 155	Otto Velez	.06	.02	.00
☐ 156	Oakland A's TL ...	.20	.06	.01
	Mgr. Billy Martin			
	Batting: R.Henderson			
	Pitching: S. McCatty			
☐ 157	Steve Crawford ...	.06	.02	.00
☐ 158	Brian Downing	.10	.04	.01
☐ 159	Larry Biittner	.06	.02	.00
☐ 160	Luis Tiant	.15	.06	.01
☐ 161	Batting Leaders ...	.15	.06	.01
	Bill Madlock			
	Carney Lansford			

		MINT	EXC	G-VG
☐ 162	Home Run Leaders	.20	.08	.02
	Mike Schmidt			
	Tony Armas			
	Dwight Evans			
	Bobby Grich			
	Eddie Murray			
☐ 163	RBI Leaders	.30	.12	.03
	Mike Schmidt			
	Eddie Murray			
☐ 164	Stolen Base Leaders	.30	.12	.03
	Tim Raines			
	Rickey Henderson			
☐ 165	Victory Leaders	.15	.06	.01
	Tom Seaver			
	Denny Martinez			
	Steve McCatty			
	Jack Morris			
	Pete Vuckovich			
☐ 166	Strikeout Leaders	.15	.06	.01
	Fernando Valenzuela			
	Len Barker			
☐ 167	ERA Leaders	.15	.06	.01
	Nolan Ryan			
	Steve McCatty			
☐ 168	Leading Firemen	.15	.06	.01
	Bruce Sutter			
	Rollie Fingers			
☐ 169	Charlie Leibrandt	.10	.04	.01
☐ 170	Jim Bibby	.06	.02	.00
☐ 171	Giants Rookies	1.25	.50	.12
	Bob Brenly			
	Chili Davis			
	Bob Tufts			
☐ 172	Bill Gullickson	.10	.04	.01
☐ 173	Jamie Quirk	.06	.02	.00
☐ 174	Dave Ford	.06	.02	.00
☐ 175	Jerry Mumphrey	.06	.02	.00
☐ 176	Dewey Robinson	.06	.02	.00
☐ 177	John Ellis	.06	.02	.00
☐ 178	Dyar Miller	.06	.02	.00
☐ 179	Steve Garvey	.85	.34	.08
☐ 180	SA: Steve Garvey	.40	.16	.04
☐ 181	Silvio Martinez	.06	.02	.00
☐ 182	Larry Herndon	.06	.02	.00
☐ 183	Mike Proly	.06	.02	.00
☐ 184	Mick Kelleher	.06	.02	.00
☐ 185	Phil Niekro	.45	.18	.04

		MINT	EXC	G-VG
☐ 186	Cardinals TL	.15	.04	.01
	Mgr. Whitey Herzog			
	Batting K. Hernandez			
	Pitching Bob Forsch			
☐ 187	Jeff Newman	.06	.02	.00
☐ 188	Randy Martz	.06	.02	.00
☐ 189	Glenn Hoffman	.06	.02	.00
☐ 190	J.R. Richard	.10	.04	.01
☐ 191	Tim Wallach	1.25	.50	.12
☐ 192	Broderick Perkins	.06	.02	.00
☐ 193	Darrell Jackson	.06	.02	.00
☐ 194	Mike Vail	.06	.02	.00
☐ 195	Paul Molitor	.35	.14	.03
☐ 196	Willie Upshaw	.06	.02	.00
☐ 197	Shane Rawley	.10	.04	.01
☐ 198	Chris Speier	.06	.02	.00
☐ 199	Don Aase	.06	.02	.00
☐ 200	George Brett	1.50	.60	.15
☐ 201	SA: George Brett	.60	.24	.06
☐ 202	Rick Manning	.06	.02	.00
☐ 203	Blue Jays Rookies	3.50	1.40	.35
	Jesse Barfield			
	Brian Milner			
	Boomer Wells			
☐ 204	Gary Roenicke	.06	.02	.00
☐ 205	Neil Allen	.10	.04	.01
☐ 206	Tony Bernazard	.06	.02	.00
☐ 207	Rod Scurry	.06	.02	.00
☐ 208	Bobby Murcer	.15	.06	.01
☐ 209	Gary Lavelle	.06	.02	.00
☐ 210	Keith Hernandez	.50	.20	.05
☐ 211	Dan Petry	.10	.04	.01
☐ 212	Mario Mendoza	.06	.02	.00
☐ 213	Dave Stewart	1.50	.60	.15
☐ 214	Brian Asselstine	.06	.02	.00
☐ 215	Mike Krukow	.10	.04	.01
☐ 216	White Sox TL	.15	.04	.01
	Mgr. Tony LaRussa			
	Batting: Chet Lemon			
	Pitching: Dennis Lamp			
☐ 217	Bo McLaughlin	.06	.02	.00
☐ 218	Dave Roberts	.06	.02	.00
☐ 219	John Curtis	.06	.02	.00
☐ 220	Manny Trillo	.06	.02	.00
☐ 221	Jim Slaton	.06	.02	.00
☐ 222	Butch Wynegar	.06	.02	.00
☐ 223	Lloyd Moseby	.20	.08	.02
☐ 224	Bruce Bochte	.06	.02	.00
☐ 225	Mike Torrez	.06	.02	.00

		MINT	EXC	G-VG			MINT	EXC	G-VG
☐ 226	Checklist 133-264 ..	.10	.01	.00	☐ 266	Rick Leach	.06	.02	.00
☐ 227	Ray Burris	.06	.02	.00	☐ 267	Kurt Bevacqua	.06	.02	.00
☐ 228	Sam Mejias	.06	.02	.00	☐ 268	Rickey Keeton	.06	.02	.00
☐ 229	Geoff Zahn	.06	.02	.00	☐ 269	Jim Essian	.06	.02	.00
☐ 230	Willie Wilson	.20	.08	.02	☐ 270	Rusty Staub	.15	.06	.01
☐ 231	Phillies Rookies ...	.40	.16	.04	☐ 271	Larry Bradford	.06	.02	.00
	Mark Davis				☐ 272	Bump Wills	.06	.02	.00
	Bob Dornier				☐ 273	Doug Bird	.06	.02	.00
	Ozzie Virgil				☐ 274	Bob Ojeda	.65	.26	.06
☐ 232	Terry Crowley	.06	.02	.00	☐ 275	Bob Watson	.10	.04	.01
☐ 233	Duane Kuiper	.06	.02	.00	☐ 276	Angels TL	.20	.06	.01
☐ 234	Ron Hodges	.06	.02	.00		Mgr. Gene Mauch			
☐ 235	Mike Easler	.06	.02	.00		Batting: Rod Carew			
☐ 236	John Martin	.06	.02	.00		Pitching: Ken Forsch			
☐ 237	Rusty Kuntz	.06	.02	.00	☐ 277	Terry Puhl	.06	.02	.00
☐ 238	Kevin Saucier	.06	.02	.00	☐ 278	John Littlefield	.06	.02	.00
☐ 239	Jon Matlack	.06	.02	.00	☐ 279	Bill Russell	.10	.04	.01
☐ 240	Bucky Dent	.10	.04	.01	☐ 280	Ben Oglivie	.10	.04	.01
☐ 241	SA: Bucky Dent	.06	.02	.00	☐ 281	John Verhoeven ...	.06	.02	.00
☐ 242	Milt May	.06	.02	.00	☐ 282	Ken Macha	.06	.02	.00
☐ 243	Bob Owchinko	.06	.02	.00	☐ 283	Brian Allard	.06	.02	.00
☐ 244	Rufino Linares	.06	.02	.00	☐ 284	Bob Grich	.10	.04	.01
☐ 245	Ken Reitz	.06	.02	.00	☐ 285	Sparky Lyle	.15	.06	.01
☐ 246	New York Mets TL ..	.20	.06	.01	☐ 286	Bill Fahey	.06	.02	.00
	Mgr. Joe Torre				☐ 287	Alan Bannister	.06	.02	.00
	Batting: Hubie Brooks				☐ 288	Garry Templeton ..	.10	.04	.01
	Pitching: Mike Scott				☐ 289	Bob Stanley	.06	.02	.00
☐ 247	Pedro Guerrero	.75	.30	.07	☐ 290	Ken Singleton	.10	.04	.01
☐ 248	Frank LaCorte	.06	.02	.00	☐ 291	Pirates Rookies ...	1.25	.50	.12
☐ 249	Tim Flannery	.06	.02	.00		Vance Law			
☐ 250	Tug McGraw	.15	.06	.01		Bob Long			
☐ 251	Fred Lynn	.30	.12	.03		Johnny Ray			
☐ 252	SA: Fred Lynn	.15	.06	.01	☐ 292	David Palmer	.06	.02	.00
☐ 253	Chuck Baker	.06	.02	.00	☐ 293	Rob Picciolo	.06	.02	.00
☐ 254	Jorge Bell	8.00	3.25	.80	☐ 294	Mike LaCoss	.06	.02	.00
☐ 255	Tony Perez	.25	.10	.02	☐ 295	Jason Thompson ..	.06	.02	.00
☐ 256	SA: Tony Perez	.10	.04	.01	☐ 296	Bob Walk	.10	.04	.01
☐ 257	Larry Harlow	.06	.02	.00	☐ 297	Clint Hurdle	.06	.02	.00
☐ 258	Bo Diaz	.10	.04	.01	☐ 298	Danny Darwin	.06	.02	.00
☐ 259	Rodney Scott	.06	.02	.00	☐ 299	Steve Trout	.06	.02	.00
☐ 260	Bruce Sutter	.20	.08	.02	☐ 300	Reggie Jackson ...	1.25	.50	.12
☐ 261	Tigers Rookies	.10	.04	.01	☐ 301	SA: Reggie Jackson	.50	.20	.05
	Howard Bailey				☐ 302	Doug Flynn	.06	.02	.00
	Marty Castillo				☐ 303	Bill Caudill	.06	.02	.00
	Dave Rucker				☐ 304	Johnnie LeMaster .	.06	.02	.00
☐ 262	Doug Bair	.06	.02	.00	☐ 305	Don Sutton	.40	.16	.04
☐ 263	Victor Cruz	.06	.02	.00	☐ 306	SA: Don Sutton ...	.20	.08	.02
☐ 264	Dan Quisenberry ...	.20	.08	.02	☐ 307	Randy Bass	.10	.04	.01
☐ 265	Al Bumbry	.06	.02	.00	☐ 308	Charlie Moore	.06	.02	.00

	MINT	EXC	G-VG
☐ 309 Pete Redfern	.06	.02	.00
☐ 310 Mike Hargrove	.06	.02	.00
☐ 311 Dodgers TL	.15	.04	.01
Mgr. Tom Lasorda			
Batting: Dusty Baker			
Pitching: Burt Hooton			
☐ 312 Lenny Randle	.06	.02	.00
☐ 313 John Harris	.06	.02	.00
☐ 314 Buck Martinez	.06	.02	.00
☐ 315 Burt Hooton	.06	.02	.00
☐ 316 Steve Braun	.06	.02	.00
☐ 317 Dick Ruthven	.06	.02	.00
☐ 318 Mike Heath	.06	.02	.00
☐ 319 Dave Rozema	.06	.02	.00
☐ 320 Chris Chambliss	.10	.04	.01
☐ 321 SA: Chris Chambliss	.06	.02	.00
☐ 322 Garry Hancock	.06	.02	.00
☐ 323 Bill Lee	.10	.04	.01
☐ 324 Steve Dillard	.06	.02	.00
☐ 325 Jose Cruz	.10	.04	.01
☐ 326 Pete Falcone	.06	.02	.00
☐ 327 Joe Nolan	.06	.02	.00
☐ 328 Ed Farmer	.06	.02	.00
☐ 329 U.L. Washington	.06	.02	.00
☐ 330 Rick Wise	.06	.02	.00
☐ 331 Benny Ayala	.06	.02	.00
☐ 332 Don Robinson	.06	.02	.00
☐ 333 Brewers Rookies	.10	.04	.01
Frank DiPino			
Marshall Edwards			
Chuck Porter			
☐ 334 Aurelio Rodriguez	.06	.02	.00
☐ 335 Jim Sundberg	.10	.04	.01
☐ 336 Mariners TL	.10	.03	.01
Mgr. Rene Lachemann			
Batting: Tom Paciorek			
Pitching: Glenn Abbott			
☐ 337 Pete Rose AS	.75	.30	.07
☐ 338 Dave Lopes AS	.10	.04	.01
☐ 339 Mike Schmidt AS	.40	.16	.04
☐ 340 Dave Concepcion AS	.10	.04	.01
☐ 341 Andre Dawson AS	.20	.08	.02
☐ 342A George Foster AS	.25	.10	.02
(with autograph)			
☐ 342B George Foster AS	1.75	.70	.17
(w/o autograph)			
☐ 343 Dave Parker AS	.15	.06	.01
☐ 344 Gary Carter AS	.25	.10	.02
☐ 345 Fern. Valenzuela AS	.15	.06	.01

	MINT	EXC	G-VG
☐ 346 Tom Seaver AS	.25	.10	.02
☐ 347 Bruce Sutter AS	.10	.04	.01
☐ 348 Derrel Thomas	.06	.02	.00
☐ 349 George Frazier	.06	.02	.00
☐ 350 Thad Bosley	.06	.02	.00
☐ 351 Reds Rookies	.10	.04	.01
Scott Brown			
Geoff Coumbe			
Paul Householder			
☐ 352 Dick Davis	.06	.02	.00
☐ 353 Jack O'Connor	.06	.02	.00
☐ 354 Roberto Ramos	.06	.02	.00
☐ 355 Dwight Evans	.25	.10	.02
☐ 356 Denny Lewallyn	.06	.02	.00
☐ 357 Butch Hobson	.06	.02	.00
☐ 358 Mike Parrott	.06	.02	.00
☐ 359 Jim Dwyer	.06	.02	.00
☐ 360 Len Barker	.06	.02	.00
☐ 361 Rafael Landestoy	.06	.02	.00
☐ 362 Jim Wright	.06	.02	.00
☐ 363 Bob Molinaro	.06	.02	.00
☐ 364 Doyle Alexander	.10	.04	.01
☐ 365 Bill Madlock	.15	.06	.01
☐ 366 Padres TL	.10	.03	.01
Mgr. Frank Howard			
Batting: Luis Salazar			
Pitching: Eichelberger			
☐ 367 Jim Kaat	.15	.06	.01
☐ 368 Alex Trevino	.06	.02	.00
☐ 369 Champ Summers	.06	.02	.00
☐ 370 Mike Norris	.06	.02	.00
☐ 371 Jerry Don Gleaton	.06	.02	.00
☐ 372 Luis Gomez	.06	.02	.00
☐ 373 Gene Nelson	.15	.06	.01
☐ 374 Tim Blackwell	.06	.02	.00
☐ 375 Dusty Baker	.10	.04	.01
☐ 376 Chris Welsh	.06	.02	.00
☐ 377 Kiko Garcia	.06	.02	.00
☐ 378 Mike Caldwell	.06	.02	.00
☐ 379 Rob Wilfong	.06	.02	.00
☐ 380 Dave Stieb	.20	.08	.02
☐ 381 Red Sox Rookies	.50	.20	.05
Bruce Hurst			
Dave Schmidt			
Julio Valdez			
☐ 382 Joe Simpson	.06	.02	.00
☐ 383A Pascual Perez ERR	30.00	12.00	3.00
(no position on front)			
☐ 383B Pascual Perez COR	.15	.06	.01

		MINT	EXC	G-VG			MINT	EXC	G-VG
☐ 384	Keith Moreland	.10	.04	.01	☐ 426	Orioles TL	.20	.06	.01
☐ 385	Ken Forsch	.06	.02	.00		Mgr. Earl Weaver			
☐ 386	Jerry White	.06	.02	.00		Batting: Eddie Murray			
☐ 387	Tom Veryzer	.06	.02	.00		Pitching: Sam Stewart			
☐ 388	Joe Rudi	.10	.04	.01	☐ 427	Ron Oester	.06	.02	.00
☐ 389	George Vukovich ..	.06	.02	.00	☐ 428	LaMarr Hoyt	.10	.04	.01
☐ 390	Eddie Murray	1.25	.50	.12	☐ 429	John Wathan	.10	.04	.01
☐ 391	Dave Tobik	.06	.02	.00	☐ 430	Vida Blue	.10	.04	.01
☐ 392	Rick Bosetti	.06	.02	.00	☐ 431	SA: Vida Blue	.06	.02	.00
☐ 393	Al Hrabosky	.10	.04	.01	☐ 432	Mike Scott	.40	.16	.04
☐ 394	Checklist 265-396 ..	.10	.01	.00	☐ 433	Alan Ashby	.06	.02	.00
☐ 395	Omar Moreno	.06	.02	.00	☐ 434	Joe Lefebvre	.06	.02	.00
☐ 396	Twins TL	.10	.03	.01	☐ 435	Robin Yount	.75	.30	.07
	Mgr. Billy Gardner				☐ 436	Joe Strain	.06	.02	.00
	Batting: John Castino				☐ 437	Juan Berenguer ...	.06	.02	.00
	Pitching: F. Arroyo				☐ 438	Pete Mackanin ...	.06	.02	.00
☐ 397	Ken Brett	.06	.02	.00	☐ 439	Dave Righetti	2.25	.90	.22
☐ 398	Mike Squires	.06	.02	.00	☐ 440	Jeff Burroughs	.10	.04	.01
☐ 399	Pat Zachry	.06	.02	.00	☐ 441	Astros Rookies ...	.10	.04	.01
☐ 400	Johnny Bench	1.00	.40	.10		Danny Heep			
☐ 401	SA: Johnny Bench ..	.40	.16	.04		Billy Smith			
☐ 402	Bill Stein	.06	.02	.00		Bobby Sprowl			
☐ 403	Jim Tracy	.06	.02	.00	☐ 442	Bruce Kison	.06	.02	.00
☐ 404	Dickie Thon	.10	.04	.01	☐ 443	Mark Wagner	.06	.02	.00
☐ 405	Rick Reuschel	.15	.06	.01	☐ 444	Terry Forster	.10	.04	.01
☐ 406	Al Holland	.06	.02	.00	☐ 445	Larry Parrish	.10	.04	.01
☐ 407	Danny Boone	.06	.02	.00	☐ 446	Wayne Garland ...	.06	.02	.00
☐ 408	Ed Romero	.06	.02	.00	☐ 447	Darrell Porter	.06	.02	.00
☐ 409	Don Cooper	.06	.02	.00	☐ 448	SA: Darrell Porter .	.06	.02	.00
☐ 410	Ron Cey	.15	.06	.01	☐ 449	Luis Aguayo	.06	.02	.00
☐ 411	SA: Ron Cey	.10	.04	.01	☐ 450	Jack Morris	.45	.18	.04
☐ 412	Luis Leal	.06	.02	.00	☐ 451	Ed Miller	.06	.02	.00
☐ 413	Dan Meyer	.06	.02	.00	☐ 452	Lee Smith	.80	.32	.08
☐ 414	Elias Sosa	.06	.02	.00	☐ 453	Art Howe	.10	.04	.01
☐ 415	Don Baylor	.15	.06	.01	☐ 454	Rick Langford	.06	.02	.00
☐ 416	Marty Bystrom	.06	.02	.00	☐ 455	Tom Burgmeier ...	.06	.02	.00
☐ 417	Pat Kelly	.06	.02	.00	☐ 456	Chicago Cubs TL ..	.10	.03	.01
☐ 418	Rangers Rookies ..	.30	.12	.03		Mgr. Joe Amalfitano			
	John Butcher					Batting: Bill Buckner			
	Bobby Johnson					Pitching: Randy Martz			
	Dave Schmidt				☐ 457	Tim Stoddard	.06	.02	.00
☐ 419	Steve Stone	.10	.04	.01	☐ 458	Willie Montanez ...	.06	.02	.00
☐ 420	George Hendrick ...	.10	.04	.01	☐ 459	Bruce Berenyi	.06	.02	.00
☐ 421	Mark Clear	.06	.02	.00	☐ 460	Jack Clark	.40	.16	.04
☐ 422	Cliff Johnson	.06	.02	.00	☐ 461	Rich Dotson	.10	.04	.01
☐ 423	Stan Papi	.06	.02	.00	☐ 462	Dave Chalk	.06	.02	.00
☐ 424	Bruce Benedict	.06	.02	.00	☐ 463	Jim Kern	.06	.02	.00
☐ 425	John Candelaria ...	.10	.04	.01	☐ 464	Juan Bonilla	.06	.02	.00
					☐ 465	Lee Mazzilli	.06	.02	.00

		MINT	EXC	G-VG
☐ 466	Randy Lerch	.06	.02	.00
☐ 467	Mickey Hatcher	.15	.06	.01
☐ 468	Floyd Bannister	.06	.02	.00
☐ 469	Ed Ott	.06	.02	.00
☐ 470	John Mayberry	.10	.04	.01
☐ 471	Royals Rookies	.20	.08	.02
	Atlee Hammaker			
	Mike Jones			
	Darryl Motley			
☐ 472	Oscar Gamble	.06	.02	.00
☐ 473	Mike Stanton	.06	.02	.00
☐ 474	Ken Oberkfell	.06	.02	.00
☐ 475	Alan Trammell	.50	.20	.05
☐ 476	Brian Kingman	.06	.02	.00
☐ 477	Steve Yeager	.06	.02	.00
☐ 478	Ray Searage	.06	.02	.00
☐ 479	Rowland Office	.06	.02	.00
☐ 480	Steve Carlton	.90	.36	.09
☐ 481	SA: Steve Carlton	.40	.16	.04
☐ 482	Glenn Hubbard	.06	.02	.00
☐ 483	Gary Woods	.06	.02	.00
☐ 484	Ivan DeJesus	.06	.02	.00
☐ 485	Kent Tekulve	.10	.04	.01
☐ 486	Yankees TL	.15	.04	.01
	Mgr. Bob Lemon			
	Batting: J. Mumphrey			
	Pitching: Tommy John			
☐ 487	Bob McClure	.06	.02	.00
☐ 488	Ron Jackson	.06	.02	.00
☐ 489	Rick Dempsey	.06	.02	.00
☐ 490	Dennis Eckersley	.20	.08	.02
☐ 491	Checklist 397-528	.10	.01	.00
☐ 492	Joe Price	.06	.02	.00
☐ 493	Chet Lemon	.10	.04	.01
☐ 494	Hubie Brooks	.20	.08	.02
☐ 495	Dennis Leonard	.10	.04	.01
☐ 496	Johnny Grubb	.06	.02	.00
☐ 497	Jim Anderson	.06	.02	.00
☐ 498	Dave Bergman	.06	.02	.00
☐ 499	Paul Mirabella	.06	.02	.00
☐ 500	Rod Carew	.85	.34	.08
☐ 501	SA: Rod Carew	.40	.16	.04
☐ 502	Braves Rookies	1.50	.60	.15
	Steve Bedrosian			
	Brett Butler			
	Larry Owen			
☐ 503	Julio Gonzalez	.06	.02	.00
☐ 504	Rick Peters	.06	.02	.00
☐ 505	Graig Nettles	.20	.08	.02
☐ 506	SA: Graig Nettles	.10	.04	.01
☐ 507	Terry Harper	.06	.02	.00
☐ 508	Jody Davis	.60	.24	.06
☐ 509	Harry Spilman	.06	.02	.00
☐ 510	Fernando Valenzuela	1.00	.40	.10
☐ 511	Ruppert Jones	.06	.02	.00
☐ 512	Jerry Dybzinski	.06	.02	.00
☐ 513	Rick Rhoden	.10	.04	.01
☐ 514	Joe Ferguson	.06	.02	.00
☐ 515	Larry Bowa	.15	.06	.01
☐ 516	SA: Larry Bowa	.06	.02	.00
☐ 517	Mark Brouhard	.06	.02	.00
☐ 518	Garth Iorg	.06	.02	.00
☐ 519	Glenn Adams	.06	.02	.00
☐ 520	Mike Flanagan	.10	.04	.01
☐ 521	Bill Almon	.06	.02	.00
☐ 522	Chuck Rainey	.06	.02	.00
☐ 523	Gary Gray	.06	.02	.00
☐ 524	Tom Hausman	.06	.02	.00
☐ 525	Ray Knight	.10	.04	.01
☐ 526	Expos TL	.10	.03	.01
	Mgr. Jim Fanning			
	Batting: W.Cromartie			
	Pitching: B.Gullickson			
☐ 527	John Henry Johnson	.06	.02	.00
☐ 528	Matt Alexander	.06	.02	.00
☐ 529	Allen Ripley	.06	.02	.00
☐ 530	Dickie Noles	.06	.02	.00
☐ 531	A's Rookies	.10	.04	.01
	Rich Bordi			
	Mark Budaska			
	Kelvin Moore			
☐ 532	Toby Harrah	.10	.04	.01
☐ 533	Joaquin Andujar	.10	.04	.01
☐ 534	Dave McKay	.06	.02	.00
☐ 535	Lance Parrish	.30	.12	.03
☐ 536	Rafael Ramirez	.06	.02	.00
☐ 537	Doug Capilla	.06	.02	.00
☐ 538	Lou Piniella	.10	.04	.01
☐ 539	Vern Ruhle	.06	.02	.00
☐ 540	Andre Dawson	.45	.18	.04
☐ 541	Barry Evans	.06	.02	.00
☐ 542	Ned Yost	.06	.02	.00
☐ 543	Bill Robinson	.10	.04	.01
☐ 544	Larry Christenson	.06	.02	.00
☐ 545	Reggie Smith	.10	.04	.01
☐ 546	SA: Reggie Smith	.06	.02	.00
☐ 547	Rod Carew AS	.25	.10	.02
☐ 548	Willie Randolph AS	.10	.04	.01

	MINT	EXC	G-VG			MINT	EXC	G-VG
☐ 549 George Brett AS ...	.40	.16	.04	☐ 589 Dave Stapleton ...		.06	.02	.00
☐ 550 Bucky Dent AS	.10	.04	.01	☐ 590 Al Oliver		.15	.06	.01
☐ 551 Reggie Jackson AS	.40	.16	.04	☐ 591 SA: Al Oliver		.06	.02	.00
☐ 552 Ken Singleton AS .	.06	.02	.00	☐ 592 Craig Swan		.06	.02	.00
☐ 553 Dave Winfield AS ..	.30	.12	.03	☐ 593 Billy Smith		.06	.02	.00
☐ 554 Carlton Fisk AS ...	.15	.06	.01	☐ 594 Renie Martin		.06	.02	.00
☐ 555 Scott McGregor AS .	.10	.04	.01	☐ 595 Dave Collins		.06	.02	.00
☐ 556 Jack Morris AS	.15	.06	.01	☐ 596 Damaso Garcia ...		.10	.04	.01
☐ 557 Rich Gossage AS ..	.10	.04	.01	☐ 597 Wayne Nordhagen .		.06	.02	.00
☐ 558 John Tudor	.35	.14	.03	☐ 598 Bob Galasso		.06	.02	.00
☐ 559 Indians TL	.10	.03	.01	☐ 599 White Sox Rookies .		.10	.04	.01
Mgr. Dave Garcia				Jay Loviglio				
Batting: Mike Hargrove				Reggie Patterson				
Pitching: Bert Blyleven				Leo Sutherland				
☐ 560 Doug Corbett	.06	.02	.00	☐ 600 Dave Winfield		.70	.26	.06
☐ 561 Cardinals Rookies ..	.10	.04	.01	☐ 601 Sid Monge		.06	.02	.00
Glenn Brummer				☐ 602 Freddie Patek		.06	.02	.00
Luis DeLeon				☐ 603 Rich Hebner		.06	.02	.00
Gene Roof				☐ 604 Orlando Sanchez .		.06	.02	.00
☐ 562 Mike O'Berry	.06	.02	.00	☐ 605 Steve Rogers		.06	.02	.00
☐ 563 Ross Baumgarten ..	.06	.02	.00	☐ 606 Blue Jays TL		.10	.03	.01
☐ 564 Doug DeCinces	.10	.04	.01	Mgr. Bobby Mattick				
☐ 565 Jackson Todd	.06	.02	.00	Batting: J.Mayberry				
☐ 566 Mike Jorgensen ...	.06	.02	.00	Pitching: Dave Stieb				
☐ 567 Bob Babcock	.06	.02	.00	☐ 607 Leon Durham		.10	.04	.01
☐ 568 Joe Pettini	.06	.02	.00	☐ 608 Jerry Royster		.06	.02	.00
☐ 569 Willie Randolph	.10	.04	.01	☐ 609 Rick Sutcliffe		.25	.10	.02
☐ 570 SA: Willie Randolph .	.06	.02	.00	☐ 610 Rickey Henderson .		1.75	.70	.17
☐ 571 Glenn Abbott	.06	.02	.00	☐ 611 Joe Niekro		.15	.06	.01
☐ 572 Juan Beniquez	.06	.02	.00	☐ 612 Gary Ward		.10	.04	.01
☐ 573 Rick Waits	.06	.02	.00	☐ 613 Jim Gantner		.06	.02	.00
☐ 574 Mike Ramsey	.06	.02	.00	☐ 614 Juan Eichelberger .		.06	.02	.00
☐ 575 Al Cowens	.06	.02	.00	☐ 615 Bob Boone		.15	.06	.01
☐ 576 Giants TL	.10	.03	.01	☐ 616 SA: Bob Boone		.06	.02	.00
Mgr. Frank Robinson				☐ 617 Scott McGregor ...		.10	.04	.01
Batting: Milt May				☐ 618 Tim Foli		.06	.02	.00
Pitching: Vida Blue				☐ 619 Bill Campbell		.06	.02	.00
☐ 577 Rick Monday	.10	.04	.01	☐ 620 Ken Griffey		.10	.04	.01
☐ 578 Shooty Babitt	.06	.02	.00	☐ 621 SA: Ken Griffey ...		.06	.02	.00
☐ 579 Rick Mahler	.30	.12	.03	☐ 622 Dennis Lamp		.06	.02	.00
☐ 580 Bobby Bonds	.15	.06	.01	☐ 623 Mets Rookies		1.25	.50	.12
☐ 581 Ron Reed	.06	.02	.00	Ron Gardenhire				
☐ 582 Luis Pujols	.06	.02	.00	Terry Leach				
☐ 583 Tippy Martinez	.06	.02	.00	Tim Leary				
☐ 584 Hosken Powell	.06	.02	.00	☐ 624 Fergie Jenkins		.20	.08	.02
☐ 585 Rollie Fingers	.25	.10	.02	☐ 625 Hal McRae		.10	.04	.01
☐ 586 SA: Rollie Fingers ..	.15	.06	.01	☐ 626 Randy Jones		.06	.02	.00
☐ 587 Tim Lollar	.06	.02	.00	☐ 627 Enos Cabell		.06	.02	.00
☐ 588 Dale Berra	.06	.02	.00	☐ 628 Bill Travers		.06	.02	.00

		MINT	EXC	G-VG
☐ 629	John Wockenfuss ..	.06	.02	.00
☐ 630	Joe Charboneau ...	.10	.04	.01
☐ 631	Gene Tenace	.06	.02	.00
☐ 632	Bryan Clark	.06	.02	.00
☐ 633	Mitchell Page	.06	.02	.00
☐ 634	Checklist 529-660 ..	.10	.01	.00
☐ 635	Ron Davis	.06	.02	.00
☐ 636	Phillies TL	.35	.09	.02
	Mgr. Dallas Green			
	Batting: Pete Rose			
	Pitching: S.Carlton			
☐ 637	Rick Camp	.06	.02	.00
☐ 638	John Milner	.06	.02	.00
☐ 639	Ken Kravec	.06	.02	.00
☐ 640	Cesar Cedeno	.10	.04	.01
☐ 641	Steve Mura	.06	.02	.00
☐ 642	Mike Scioscia	.10	.04	.01
☐ 643	Pete Vuckovich ...	.10	.04	.01
☐ 644	John Castino	.06	.02	.00
☐ 645	Frank White	.10	.04	.01
☐ 646	SA: Frank White ...	.06	.02	.00
☐ 647	Warren Brusstar ...	.06	.02	.00
☐ 648	Jose Morales	.06	.02	.00
☐ 649	Ken Clay	.06	.02	.00
☐ 650	Carl Yastrzemski ...	1.50	.60	.15
☐ 651	SA: Carl Yastrzemski	.60	.24	.06
☐ 652	Steve Nicosia	.06	.02	.00
☐ 653	Angels Rookies	2.50	1.00	.25
	Tom Brunansky			
	Luis Sanchez			
	Daryl Sconiers			
☐ 654	Jim Morrison	.06	.02	.00
☐ 655	Joel Youngblood ...	.06	.02	.00
☐ 656	Eddie Whitson	.10	.04	.01
☐ 657	Tom Poquette	.06	.02	.00
☐ 658	Tito Landrum	.06	.02	.00
☐ 659	Fred Martinez	.06	.02	.00
☐ 660	Dave Concepcion ..	.15	.06	.01
☐ 661	SA: Dave Concepcion	.06	.02	.00
☐ 662	Luis Salazar	.10	.04	.01
☐ 663	Hector Cruz	.06	.02	.00
☐ 664	Dan Spillner	.06	.02	.00
☐ 665	Jim Clancy	.10	.04	.01
☐ 666	Tigers TL	.10	.03	.01
	Mgr. Sparky Anderson			
	Batting: Steve Kemp			
	Pitching: Dan Petry			
☐ 667	Jeff Reardon	.25	.10	.02
☐ 668	Dale Murphy	2.00	.80	.20

		MINT	EXC	G-VG
☐ 669	Larry Milbourne ...	.06	.02	.00
☐ 670	Steve Kemp	.10	.04	.01
☐ 671	Mike Davis	.10	.04	.01
☐ 672	Bob Knepper	.10	.04	.01
☐ 673	Keith Drumwright ..	.06	.02	.00
☐ 674	Dave Goltz	.06	.02	.00
☐ 675	Cecil Cooper	.20	.08	.02
☐ 676	Sal Butera	.06	.02	.00
☐ 677	Alfredo Griffin	.10	.04	.01
☐ 678	Tom Paciorek	.06	.02	.00
☐ 679	Sammy Stewart ...	.06	.02	.00
☐ 680	Gary Matthews ...	.10	.04	.01
☐ 681	Dodgers Rookies ..	4.00	1.60	.40
	Mike Marshall			
	Ron Roenicke			
	Steve Sax			
☐ 682	Jesse Jefferson ...	.06	.02	.00
☐ 683	Phil Garner	.06	.02	.00
☐ 684	Harold Baines	.50	.20	.05
☐ 685	Bert Blyleven	.20	.08	.02
☐ 686	Gary Allenson	.06	.02	.00
☐ 687	Greg Minton	.06	.02	.00
☐ 688	Leon Roberts	.06	.02	.00
☐ 689	Lary Sorensen	.06	.02	.00
☐ 690	Dave Kingman	.20	.08	.02
☐ 691	Dan Schatzeder ...	.06	.02	.00
☐ 692	Wayne Gross	.06	.02	.00
☐ 693	Cesar Geronimo ...	.06	.02	.00
☐ 694	Dave Wehrmeister ..	.06	.02	.00
☐ 695	Warren Cromartie .	.06	.02	.00
☐ 696	Pirates TL	.10	.03	.01
	Mgr. Chuck Tanner			
	Batting: Bill Madlock			
	Pitching:Eddie Solomon			
☐ 697	John Montefusco ..	.10	.04	.01
☐ 698	Tony Scott	.06	.02	.00
☐ 699	Dick Tidrow	.06	.02	.00
☐ 700	George Foster	.25	.10	.02
☐ 701	SA: George Foster .	.10	.04	.01
☐ 702	Steve Renko	.06	.02	.00
☐ 703	Brewers TL	.10	.03	.01
	Mgr. Bob Rodgers			
	Batting: Cecil Cooper			
	Pitching: P.Vuckovich			
☐ 704	Mickey Rivers	.10	.04	.01
☐ 705	SA: Mickey Rivers .	.06	.02	.00
☐ 706	Barry Foote	.06	.02	.00
☐ 707	Mark Bomback	.06	.02	.00
☐ 708	Gene Richards ...	.06	.02	.00

	MINT	EXC	G-VG
☐ 709 Don Money	.06	.02	.00
☐ 710 Jerry Reuss	.10	.04	.01
☐ 711 Mariners Rookies	1.00	.40	.10
Dave Edler			
Dave Henderson			
Reggie Walton			
☐ 712 Dennis Martinez	.10	.04	.01
☐ 713 Del Unser	.06	.02	.00
☐ 714 Jerry Koosman	.15	.06	.01
☐ 715 Willie Stargell	.60	.24	.06
☐ 716 SA: Willie Stargell	.25	.10	.02
☐ 717 Rick Miller	.06	.02	.00
☐ 718 Charlie Hough	.10	.04	.01
☐ 719 Jerry Narron	.06	.02	.00
☐ 720 Greg Luzinski	.15	.06	.01
☐ 721 SA: Greg Luzinski	.10	.04	.01
☐ 722 Jerry Martin	.06	.02	.00
☐ 723 Junior Kennedy	.06	.02	.00
☐ 724 Dave Rosello	.06	.02	.00
☐ 725 Amos Otis	.10	.04	.01
☐ 726 SA: Amos Otis	.06	.02	.00
☐ 727 Sixto Lezcano	.06	.02	.00
☐ 728 Aurelio Lopez	.06	.02	.00
☐ 729 Jim Spencer	.06	.02	.00
☐ 730 Gary Carter	.80	.32	.08
☐ 731 Padres Rookies	.10	.04	.01
Mike Armstrong			
Doug Gwosdz			
Fred Kuhaulua			
☐ 732 Mike Lum	.06	.02	.00
☐ 733 Larry McWilliams	.06	.02	.00
☐ 734 Mike Ivie	.06	.02	.00
☐ 735 Rudy May	.06	.02	.00
☐ 736 Jerry Turner	.06	.02	.00
☐ 737 Reggie Cleveland	.06	.02	.00
☐ 738 Dave Engle	.06	.02	.00
☐ 739 Joey McLaughlin	.06	.02	.00
☐ 740 Dave Lopes	.10	.04	.01
☐ 741 SA: Dave Lopes	.06	.02	.00
☐ 742 Dick Drago	.06	.02	.00
☐ 743 John Stearns	.06	.02	.00
☐ 744 Mike Witt	1.00	.40	.10
☐ 745 Bake McBride	.06	.02	.00
☐ 746 Andre Thornton	.10	.04	.01
☐ 747 John Lowenstein	.06	.02	.00
☐ 748 Marc Hill	.06	.02	.00
☐ 749 Bob Shirley	.06	.02	.00
☐ 750 Jim Rice	.60	.24	.06
☐ 751 Rick Honeycutt	.06	.02	.00

	MINT	EXC	G-VG
☐ 752 Lee Lacy	.06	.02	.00
☐ 753 Tom Brookens	.06	.02	.00
☐ 754 Joe Morgan	.40	.16	.04
☐ 755 SA: Joe Morgan	.15	.06	.01
☐ 756 Reds TL	.20	.06	.01
Mgr. John McNamara			
Batting: Ken Griffey			
Pitching: Tom Seaver			
☐ 757 Tom Underwood	.06	.02	.00
☐ 758 Claudell Washington	.10	.04	.01
☐ 759 Paul Splittorff	.06	.02	.00
☐ 760 Bill Buckner	.15	.06	.01
☐ 761 Dave Smith	.10	.04	.01
☐ 762 Mike Phillips	.06	.02	.00
☐ 763 Tom Hume	.06	.02	.00
☐ 764 Steve Swisher	.06	.02	.00
☐ 765 Gorman Thomas	.15	.06	.01
☐ 766 Twins Rookies	4.50	1.80	.45
Lenny Faedo			
Kent Hrbek			
Tim Laudner			
☐ 767 Roy Smalley	.06	.02	.00
☐ 768 Jerry Garvin	.06	.02	.00
☐ 769 Richie Zisk	.10	.04	.01
☐ 770 Rich Gossage	.25	.10	.02
☐ 771 SA: Rich Gossage	.10	.04	.01
☐ 772 Bert Campaneris	.10	.04	.01
☐ 773 John Denny	.10	.04	.01
☐ 774 Jay Johnstone	.10	.04	.01
☐ 775 Bob Forsch	.06	.02	.00
☐ 776 Mark Belanger	.10	.04	.01
☐ 777 Tom Griffin	.06	.02	.00
☐ 778 Kevin Hickey	.06	.02	.00
☐ 779 Grant Jackson	.06	.02	.00
☐ 780 Pete Rose	2.25	.90	.22
☐ 781 SA: Pete Rose	.75	.30	.07
☐ 782 Frank Taveras	.06	.02	.00
☐ 783 Greg Harris	.25	.10	.02
☐ 784 Milt Wilcox	.06	.02	.00
☐ 785 Dan Driessen	.06	.02	.00
☐ 786 Red Sox TL	.10	.03	.01
Mgr. Ralph Houk			
Batting: C.Lansford			
Pitching: Mike Torrez			
☐ 787 Fred Stanley	.06	.02	.00
☐ 788 Woodie Fryman	.06	.02	.00
☐ 789 Checklist 661-792	.10	.01	.00
☐ 790 Larry Gura	.06	.02	.00
☐ 791 Bobby Brown	.06	.02	.00
☐ 792 Frank Tanana	.15	.06	.01

1982 Topps Traded

The cards in this 132-card set measure 2 ½" by 3 ½". The 1982 Topps Traded or extended series is distinguished by a "T" printed after the number (located on the reverse). Of the total cards, 70 players represent the American League and 61 represent the National League, with the remaining card a numbered checklist (132T). The Cubs lead the pack with 12 changes, while the Red Sox are the only team in either league to have no new additions. All 131 player photos used in the set are completely new. Of this total, 112 individuals are seen in the uniform of their new team, 11 others have been elevated to single card status from "Future Stars" cards, and eight more are entirely new to the 1982 Topps lineup. The backs are almost completely red in color with black print.

	MINT	EXC	G-VG
Complete Set (132)	22.00	9.00	2.20
Common Player (1-132)	.08	.03	.01

		MINT	EXC	G-VG
☐	1T Doyle Alexander	.20	.08	.02
☐	2T Jesse Barfield	2.00	.80	.20
☐	3T Ross Baumgarten	.08	.03	.01
☐	4T Steve Bedrosian	.85	.34	.08
☐	5T Mark Belanger	.15	.06	.01
☐	6T Kurt Bevacqua	.08	.03	.01
☐	7T Tim Blackwell	.08	.03	.01
☐	8T Vida Blue	.15	.06	.01
☐	9T Bob Boone	.20	.08	.02
☐	10T Larry Bowa	.20	.08	.02

		MINT	EXC	G-VG
☐	11T Dan Briggs	.08	.03	.01
☐	12T Bobby Brown	.08	.03	.01
☐	13T Tom Brunansky	1.50	.60	.15
☐	14T Jeff Burroughs	.15	.06	.01
☐	15T Enos Cabell	.08	.03	.01
☐	16T Bill Campbell	.08	.03	.01
☐	17T Bobby Castillo	.08	.03	.01
☐	18T Bill Caudill	.08	.03	.01
☐	19T Cesar Cedeno	.20	.08	.02
☐	20T Dave Collins	.08	.03	.01
☐	21T Doug Corbett	.08	.03	.01
☐	22T Al Cowens	.08	.03	.01
☐	23T Chili Davis	1.50	.60	.15
☐	24T Dick Davis	.08	.03	.01
☐	25T Ron Davis	.08	.03	.01
☐	26T Doug DeCinces	.20	.08	.02
☐	27T Ivan DeJesus	.08	.03	.01
☐	28T Bob Dernier	.20	.08	.02
☐	29T Bo Diaz	.15	.06	.01
☐	30T Roger Erickson	.08	.03	.01
☐	31T Jim Essian	.08	.03	.01
☐	32T Ed Farmer	.08	.03	.01
☐	33T Doug Flynn	.08	.03	.01
☐	34T Tim Foli	.08	.03	.01
☐	35T Dan Ford	.08	.03	.01
☐	36T George Foster	.40	.16	.04
☐	37T Dave Frost	.08	.03	.01
☐	38T Rich Gale	.08	.03	.01
☐	39T Ron Gardenhire	.15	.06	.01
☐	40T Ken Griffey	.20	.08	.02
☐	41T Greg Harris	.15	.06	.01
☐	42T Von Hayes	1.50	.60	.15
☐	43T Larry Herndon	.08	.03	.01
☐	44T Kent Hrbek	4.50	1.80	.45
☐	45T Mike Ivie	.08	.03	.01
☐	46T Grant Jackson	.08	.03	.01
☐	47T Reggie Jackson	2.50	1.00	.25
☐	48T Ron Jackson	.08	.03	.01
☐	49T Fergie Jenkins	.40	.16	.04
☐	50T Lamar Johnson	.08	.03	.01
☐	51T Randy Johnson	.08	.03	.01
☐	52T Jay Johnstone	.20	.08	.02
☐	53T Mick Kelleher	.08	.03	.01
☐	54T Steve Kemp	.15	.06	.01
☐	55T Junior Kennedy	.08	.03	.01
☐	56T Jim Kern	.08	.03	.01
☐	57T Ray Knight	.25	.10	.02
☐	58T Wayne Krenchicki	.08	.03	.01
☐	59T Mike Krukow	.15	.06	.01

	MINT	EXC	G-VG
☐ 60T Duane Kuiper	.08	.03	.01
☐ 61T Mike LaCoss	.08	.03	.01
☐ 62T Chet Lemon	.15	.06	.01
☐ 63T Sixto Lezcano	.08	.03	.01
☐ 64T Dave Lopes	.20	.08	.02
☐ 65T Jerry Martin	.08	.03	.01
☐ 66T Renie Martin	.08	.03	.01
☐ 67T John Mayberry	.15	.06	.01
☐ 68T Lee Mazzilli	.08	.03	.01
☐ 69T Bake McBride	.08	.03	.01
☐ 70T Dan Meyer	.08	.03	.01
☐ 71T Larry Milbourne	.08	.03	.01
☐ 72T Eddie Milner	.15	.06	.01
☐ 73T Sid Monge	.08	.03	.01
☐ 74T John Montefusco	.15	.06	.01
☐ 75T Jose Morales	.08	.03	.01
☐ 76T Keith Moreland	.15	.06	.01
☐ 77T Jim Morrison	.08	.03	.01
☐ 78T Rance Mulliniks	.08	.03	.01
☐ 79T Steve Mura	.08	.03	.01
☐ 80T Gene Nelson	.15	.06	.01
☐ 81T Joe Nolan	.08	.03	.01
☐ 82T Dickie Noles	.08	.03	.01
☐ 83T Al Oliver	.20	.08	.02
☐ 84T Jorge Orta	.08	.03	.01
☐ 85T Tom Paciorek	.08	.03	.01
☐ 86T Larry Parrish	.15	.06	.01
☐ 87T Jack Perconte	.08	.03	.01
☐ 88T Gaylord Perry	1.00	.40	.10
☐ 89T Rob Picciolo	.08	.03	.01
☐ 90T Joe Pittman	.08	.03	.01
☐ 91T Hosken Powell	.08	.03	.01
☐ 92T Mike Proly	.08	.03	.01
☐ 93T Greg Pryor	.08	.03	.01
☐ 94T Charlie Puleo	.15	.06	.01
☐ 95T Shane Rawley	.15	.06	.01
☐ 96T Johnny Ray	.90	.36	.09
☐ 97T Dave Revering	.08	.03	.01
☐ 98T Cal Ripken	8.50	3.50	.85
☐ 99T Allen Ripley	.08	.03	.01
☐ 100T Bill Robinson	.15	.06	.01
☐ 101T Aurelio Rodriguez	.08	.03	.01
☐ 102T Joe Rudi	.15	.06	.01
☐ 103T Steve Sax	2.50	1.00	.25
☐ 104T Dan Schatzeder	.08	.03	.01
☐ 105T Bob Shirley	.08	.03	.01
☐ 106T Eric Show	.75	.30	.07
☐ 107T Roy Smalley	.15	.06	.01
☐ 108T Lonnie Smith	.15	.06	.01

	MINT	EXC	G-VG
☐ 109T Ozzie Smith	2.50	1.00	.25
☐ 110T Reggie Smith	.20	.08	.02
☐ 111T Lary Sorensen	.08	.03	.01
☐ 112T Elias Sosa	.08	.03	.01
☐ 113T Mike Stanton	.08	.03	.01
☐ 114T Steve Stroughter	.08	.03	.01
☐ 115T Champ Summers	.08	.03	.01
☐ 116T Rick Sutcliffe	.35	.14	.03
☐ 117T Frank Tanana	.15	.06	.01
☐ 118T Frank Taveras	.08	.03	.01
☐ 119T Garry Templeton	.15	.06	.01
☐ 120T Alex Trevino	.08	.03	.01
☐ 121T Jerry Turner	.08	.03	.01
☐ 122T Ed VandeBerg	.15	.06	.01
☐ 123T Tom Veryzer	.08	.03	.01
☐ 124T Ron Washington	.08	.03	.01
☐ 125T Bob Watson	.15	.06	.01
☐ 126T Dennis Werth	.08	.03	.01
☐ 127T Eddie Whitson	.15	.06	.01
☐ 128T Rob Wilfong	.08	.03	.01
☐ 129T Bump Wills	.08	.03	.01
☐ 130T Gary Woods	.08	.03	.01
☐ 131T Butch Wynegar	.15	.06	.01
☐ 132T Checklist: 1-132	.08	.01	.00

1983 Topps

*The cards in this 792-card set measure 2 ½"
by 3 ½". Each regular card of the Topps set
for 1983 features a large action shot of a
player with a small cameo portrait at bottom
right. There are special series for AL and NL
All Stars (386-407), League Leaders (701-*

708) and Record Breakers (1-6). In addition, there are 34 "Super Veteran" (SV) cards and six numbered checklist cards. The Super Veteran cards are oriented horizontally and show two pictures of the featured player, a recent picture and a picture showing the player as a rookie when he broke in. The cards are numbered on the reverse at the upper left corner. The team cards are actually Team Leader (TL) cards picturing the batting and pitching leader for that team with a checklist back.

		MINT	EXC	G-VG
	Complete Set (792)	90.00	36.00	9.00
	Common Player (1-792) ...	.06	.02	.00
☐ 1	RB: Tony Armas ... 11 putouts by rightfielder	.12	.03	.01
☐ 2	RB: Rickey Henderson Sets modern record for steals, season	.30	.12	.03
☐ 3	RB: Greg Minton ... 269 1/3 homerless innings streak	.10	.04	.01
☐ 4	RB: Lance Parrish .. Threw out three baserunners in All-Star game	.15	.06	.01
☐ 5	RB: Manny Trillo ... 479 consecutive errorless chances, second baseman	.10	.04	.01
☐ 6	RB: John Wathan .. ML steals record for catchers, 31	.10	.04	.01
☐ 7	Gene Richards	.06	.02	.00
☐ 8	Steve Balboni	.10	.04	.01
☐ 9	Joey McLaughlin ...	.06	.02	.00
☐ 10	Gorman Thomas ...	.15	.06	.01
☐ 11	Billy Gardner MG ...	.06	.02	.00
☐ 12	Paul Mirabella	.06	.02	.00
☐ 13	Larry Herndon	.06	.02	.00
☐ 14	Frank LaCorte	.06	.02	.00
☐ 15	Ron Cey	.15	.06	.01
☐ 16	George Vukovich ...	.06	.02	.00
☐ 17	Kent Tekulve	.10	.04	.01
☐ 18	SV: Kent Tekulve ...	.06	.02	.00
☐ 19	Oscar Gamble	.06	.02	.00
☐ 20	Carlton Fisk	.20	.08	.02

		MINT	EXC	G-VG
☐ 21	Baltimore Orioles TL BA: Eddie Murray ERA: Jim Palmer	.25	.07	.01
☐ 22	Randy Martz	.06	.02	.00
☐ 23	Mike Heath	.06	.02	.00
☐ 24	Steve Mura	.06	.02	.00
☐ 25	Hal McRae	.10	.04	.01
☐ 26	Jerry Royster	.06	.02	.00
☐ 27	Doug Corbett	.06	.02	.00
☐ 28	Bruce Bochte	.06	.02	.00
☐ 29	Randy Jones	.06	.02	.00
☐ 30	Jim Rice	.35	.14	.03
☐ 31	Bill Gullickson	.10	.04	.01
☐ 32	Dave Bergman	.06	.02	.00
☐ 33	Jack O'Connor	.06	.02	.00
☐ 34	Paul Householder ..	.06	.02	.00
☐ 35	Rollie Fingers	.25	.10	.02
☐ 36	SV: Rollie Fingers .	.10	.04	.01
☐ 37	Darrell Johnson MG	.06	.02	.00
☐ 38	Tim Flannery	.06	.02	.00
☐ 39	Terry Puhl	.06	.02	.00
☐ 40	Fernando Valenzuela	.40	.16	.04
☐ 41	Jerry Turner	.06	.02	.00
☐ 42	Dale Murray	.06	.02	.00
☐ 43	Bob Dernier	.06	.02	.00
☐ 44	Don Robinson	.06	.02	.00
☐ 45	John Mayberry	.10	.04	.01
☐ 46	Richard Dotson ...	.10	.04	.01
☐ 47	Dave McKay	.06	.02	.00
☐ 48	Lary Sorensen	.06	.02	.00
☐ 49	Willie McGee	2.50	1.00	.25
☐ 50	Bob Horner .... ('82 RBI total 7)	.25	.10	.02
☐ 51	Chicago Cubs TL BA: Leon Durham ERA: Fergie Jenkins	.15	.04	.01
☐ 52	Onix Concepcion ..	.06	.02	.00
☐ 53	Mike Witt	.20	.08	.02
☐ 54	Jim Maler	.06	.02	.00
☐ 55	Mookie Wilson	.10	.04	.01
☐ 56	Chuck Rainey	.06	.02	.00
☐ 57	Tim Blackwell	.06	.02	.00
☐ 58	Al Holland	.06	.02	.00
☐ 59	Benny Ayala	.06	.02	.00
☐ 60	Johnny Bench	.65	.26	.06
☐ 61	SV: Johnny Bench .	.25	.10	.02
☐ 62	Bob McClure	.06	.02	.00
☐ 63	Rick Monday	.06	.02	.00
☐ 64	Bill Stein	.06	.02	.00

		MINT	EXC	G-VG
☐ 65	Jack Morris	.30	.12	.03
☐ 66	Bob Lillis MG	.06	.02	.00
☐ 67	Sal Butera	.06	.02	.00
☐ 68	Eric Show	.40	.16	.04
☐ 69	Lee Lacy	.06	.02	.00
☐ 70	Steve Carlton	.55	.22	.05
☐ 71	SV: Steve Carlton	.25	.10	.02
☐ 72	Tom Paciorek	.06	.02	.00
☐ 73	Allen Ripley	.06	.02	.00
☐ 74	Julio Gonzalez	.06	.02	.00
☐ 75	Amos Otis	.10	.04	.01
☐ 76	Rick Mahler	.10	.04	.01
☐ 77	Hosken Powell	.06	.02	.00
☐ 78	Bill Caudill	.06	.02	.00
☐ 79	Mick Kelleher	.06	.02	.00
☐ 80	George Foster	.20	.08	.02
☐ 81	Yankees TL	.15	.04	.01
	BA: Jerry Mumphrey			
	ERA: Dave Righetti			
☐ 82	Bruce Hurst	.30	.12	.03
☐ 83	Ryne Sandberg	5.50	2.20	.55
☐ 84	Milt May	.06	.02	.00
☐ 85	Ken Singleton	.10	.04	.01
☐ 86	Tom Hume	.06	.02	.00
☐ 87	Joe Rudi	.10	.04	.01
☐ 88	Jim Gantner	.06	.02	.00
☐ 89	Leon Roberts	.06	.02	.00
☐ 90	Jerry Reuss	.10	.04	.01
☐ 91	Larry Milbourne	.06	.02	.00
☐ 92	Mike LaCoss	.06	.02	.00
☐ 93	John Castino	.06	.02	.00
☐ 94	Dave Edwards	.06	.02	.00
☐ 95	Alan Trammell	.40	.16	.04
☐ 96	Dick Howser MG	.10	.04	.01
☐ 97	Ross Baumgarten	.06	.02	.00
☐ 98	Vance Law	.15	.06	.01
☐ 99	Dickie Noles	.06	.02	.00
☐ 100	Pete Rose	2.00	.80	.20
☐ 101	SV: Pete Rose	.75	.30	.07
☐ 102	Dave Beard	.06	.02	.00
☐ 103	Darrell Porter	.06	.02	.00
☐ 104	Bob Walk	.10	.04	.01
☐ 105	Don Baylor	.15	.06	.01
☐ 106	Gene Nelson	.06	.02	.00
☐ 107	Mike Jorgensen	.06	.02	.00
☐ 108	Glenn Hoffman	.06	.02	.00
☐ 109	Luis Leal	.06	.02	.00
☐ 110	Ken Griffey	.10	.04	.01

		MINT	EXC	G-VG
☐ 111	Montreal Expos TL	.10	.03	.01
	BA: Al Oliver			
	ERA: Steve Rogers			
☐ 112	Bob Shirley	.06	.02	.00
☐ 113	Ron Roenicke	.06	.02	.00
☐ 114	Jim Slaton	.06	.02	.00
☐ 115	Chili Davis	.15	.06	.01
☐ 116	Dave Schmidt	.10	.04	.01
☐ 117	Alan Knicely	.06	.02	.00
☐ 118	Chris Welsh	.06	.02	.00
☐ 119	Tom Brookens	.06	.02	.00
☐ 120	Len Barker	.06	.02	.00
☐ 121	Mickey Hatcher	.10	.04	.01
☐ 122	Jimmy Smith	.06	.02	.00
☐ 123	George Frazier	.06	.02	.00
☐ 124	Marc Hill	.06	.02	.00
☐ 125	Leon Durham	.10	.04	.01
☐ 126	Joe Torre MG	.10	.04	.01
☐ 127	Preston Hanna	.06	.02	.00
☐ 128	Mike Ramsey	.06	.02	.00
☐ 129	Checklist: 1-132	.10	.01	.00
☐ 130	Dave Stieb	.20	.08	.02
☐ 131	Ed Ott	.06	.02	.00
☐ 132	Todd Cruz	.06	.02	.00
☐ 133	Jim Barr	.06	.02	.00
☐ 134	Hubie Brooks	.15	.06	.01
☐ 135	Dwight Evans	.20	.08	.02
☐ 136	Willie Aikens	.06	.02	.00
☐ 137	Woodie Fryman	.06	.02	.00
☐ 138	Rick Dempsey	.06	.02	.00
☐ 139	Bruce Berenyi	.06	.02	.00
☐ 140	Willie Randolph	.10	.04	.01
☐ 141	Indians TL	.10	.03	.01
	BA: Toby Harrah			
	ERA: Rick Sutcliffe			
☐ 142	Mike Caldwell	.06	.02	.00
☐ 143	Joe Pettini	.06	.02	.00
☐ 144	Mark Wagner	.06	.02	.00
☐ 145	Don Sutton	.35	.14	.03
☐ 146	SV: Don Sutton	.15	.06	.01
☐ 147	Rick Leach	.06	.02	.00
☐ 148	Dave Roberts	.06	.02	.00
☐ 149	Johnny Ray	.15	.06	.01
☐ 150	Bruce Sutter	.15	.06	.01
☐ 151	SV: Bruce Sutter	.10	.04	.01
☐ 152	Jay Johnstone	.10	.04	.01
☐ 153	Jerry Koosman	.10	.04	.01
☐ 154	Johnnie LeMaster	.06	.02	.00
☐ 155	Dan Quisenberry	.15	.06	.01

	MINT	EXC	G-VG
☐ 156 Billy Martin MG	.15	.06	.01
☐ 157 Steve Bedrosian ...	.20	.08	.01
☐ 158 Rob Wilfong	.06	.02	.00
☐ 159 Mike Stanton	.06	.02	.00
☐ 160 Dave Kingman	.15	.06	.01
☐ 161 SV: Dave Kingman .	.10	.04	.01
☐ 162 Mark Clear	.06	.02	.00
☐ 163 Cal Ripken	2.00	.80	.20
☐ 164 David Palmer	.06	.02	.00
☐ 165 Dan Driessen	.06	.02	.00
☐ 166 John Pacella	.06	.02	.00
☐ 167 Mark Brouhard ...	.06	.02	.00
☐ 168 Juan Eichelberger .	.06	.02	.00
☐ 169 Doug Flynn	.06	.02	.00
☐ 170 Steve Howe	.06	.02	.00
☐ 171 Giants TL	.15	.04	.01
BA: Joe Morgan			
ERA: Bill Laskey			
☐ 172 Vern Ruhle	.06	.02	.00
☐ 173 Jim Morrison	.06	.02	.00
☐ 174 Jerry Ujdur	.06	.02	.00
☐ 175 Bo Diaz	.06	.02	.00
☐ 176 Dave Righetti	.30	.12	.03
☐ 177 Harold Baines	.25	.10	.02
☐ 178 Luis Tiant	.10	.04	.01
☐ 179 SV: Luis Tiant	.06	.02	.00
☐ 180 Rickey Henderson .	.80	.32	.08
☐ 181 Terry Felton	.06	.02	.00
☐ 182 Mike Fischlin	.06	.02	.00
☐ 183 Ed VandeBerg	.10	.04	.01
☐ 184 Bob Clark	.06	.02	.00
☐ 185 Tim Lollar	.06	.02	.00
☐ 186 Whitey Herzog MG .	.06	.02	.00
☐ 187 Terry Leach	.20	.08	.02
☐ 188 Rick Miller	.06	.02	.00
☐ 189 Dan Schatzeder ...	.06	.02	.00
☐ 190 Cecil Cooper	.15	.06	.01
☐ 191 Joe Price	.06	.02	.00
☐ 192 Floyd Rayford	.06	.02	.00
☐ 193 Harry Spilman	.06	.02	.00
☐ 194 Cesar Geronimo ...	.06	.02	.00
☐ 195 Bob Stoddard	.06	.02	.00
☐ 196 Bill Fahey	.06	.02	.00
☐ 197 Jim Eisenreich ...	.20	.08	.02
☐ 198 Kiko Garcia	.06	.02	.00
☐ 199 Marty Bystrom	.06	.02	.00
☐ 200 Rod Carew	.65	.26	.06
☐ 201 SV: Rod Carew	.25	.10	.02

	MINT	EXC	G-VG
☐ 202 Blue Jays TL	.10	.03	.01
BA: Damaso Garcia			
ERA: Dave Stieb			
☐ 203 Mike Morgan	.06	.02	.00
☐ 204 Junior Kennedy ...	.06	.02	.00
☐ 205 Dave Parker	.25	.10	.02
☐ 206 Ken Oberkfell	.06	.02	.00
☐ 207 Rick Camp	.06	.02	.00
☐ 208 Dan Meyer	.06	.02	.00
☐ 209 Mike Moore	.45	.18	.04
☐ 210 Jack Clark	.35	.14	.03
☐ 211 John Denny	.10	.04	.01
☐ 212 John Stearns	.06	.02	.00
☐ 213 Tom Burgmeier ...	.06	.02	.00
☐ 214 Jerry White	.06	.02	.00
☐ 215 Mario Soto	.10	.04	.01
☐ 216 Tony LaRussa MG ..	.10	.04	.01
☐ 217 Tim Stoddard	.06	.02	.00
☐ 218 Roy Howell	.06	.02	.00
☐ 219 Mike Armstrong ...	.06	.02	.00
☐ 220 Dusty Baker	.10	.04	.01
☐ 221 Joe Niekro	.10	.04	.01
☐ 222 Damaso Garcia ...	.06	.02	.00
☐ 223 John Montefusco ..	.06	.02	.00
☐ 224 Mickey Rivers	.10	.04	.01
☐ 225 Enos Cabell	.06	.02	.00
☐ 226 Enrique Romo	.06	.02	.00
☐ 227 Chris Bando	.06	.02	.00
☐ 228 Joaquin Andujar ..	.10	.04	.01
☐ 229 Phillies TL	.15	.04	.01
BA: Bo Diaz			
ERA: Steve Carlton			
☐ 230 Fergie Jenkins	.15	.06	.01
☐ 231 SV: Fergie Jenkins .	.10	.04	.01
☐ 232 Tom Brunansky ...	.35	.14	.03
☐ 233 Wayne Gross	.06	.02	.00
☐ 234 Larry Andersen ...	.06	.02	.00
☐ 235 Claudell Washington	.10	.04	.01
☐ 236 Steve Renko	.06	.02	.00
☐ 237 Dan Norman	.06	.02	.00
☐ 238 Bud Black	.20	.08	.02
☐ 239 Dave Stapleton ...	.06	.02	.00
☐ 240 Rich Gossage	.20	.08	.02
☐ 241 SV: Rich Gossage .	.10	.04	.01
☐ 242 Joe Nolan	.06	.02	.00
☐ 243 Duane Walker	.06	.02	.00
☐ 244 Dwight Bernard ...	.06	.02	.00
☐ 245 Steve Sax	.40	.16	.04
☐ 246 George Bamberger MG	.06	.02	.00

		MINT	EXC	G-VG
☐ 247	Dave Smith	.10	.04	.01
☐ 248	Bake McBride	.06	.02	.00
☐ 249	Checklist: 133-264	.10	.01	.00
☐ 250	Bill Buckner	.15	.06	.01
☐ 251	Alan Wiggins	.15	.06	.01
☐ 252	Luis Aguayo	.06	.02	.00
☐ 253	Larry McWilliams	.06	.02	.00
☐ 254	Rick Cerone	.06	.02	.00
☐ 255	Gene Garber	.06	.02	.00
☐ 256	SV: Gene Garber	.06	.02	.00
☐ 257	Jesse Barfield	.60	.24	.06
☐ 258	Manny Castillo	.06	.02	.00
☐ 259	Jeff Jones	.06	.02	.00
☐ 260	Steve Kemp	.10	.04	.01
☐ 261	Tigers TL	.10	.01	.00
	BA: Larry Herndon			
	ERA: Dan Petry			
☐ 262	Ron Jackson	.06	.02	.00
☐ 263	Renie Martin	.06	.02	.00
☐ 264	Jamie Quirk	.06	.02	.00
☐ 265	Joel Youngblood	.06	.02	.00
☐ 266	Paul Boris	.06	.02	.00
☐ 267	Terry Francona	.06	.02	.00
☐ 268	Storm Davis	.75	.30	.07
☐ 269	Ron Oester	.06	.02	.00
☐ 270	Dennis Eckersley	.20	.08	.02
☐ 271	Ed Romero	.06	.02	.00
☐ 272	Frank Tanana	.10	.04	.01
☐ 273	Mark Belanger	.10	.04	.01
☐ 274	Terry Kennedy	.10	.04	.01
☐ 275	Ray Knight	.10	.04	.01
☐ 276	Gene Mauch MG	.06	.02	.00
☐ 277	Rance Mulliniks	.06	.02	.00
☐ 278	Kevin Hickey	.06	.02	.00
☐ 279	Greg Gross	.06	.02	.00
☐ 280	Bert Blyleven	.15	.06	.01
☐ 281	Andre Robertson	.06	.02	.00
☐ 282	Reggie Smith	.15	.06	.01
	(Ryne Sandberg ducking back)			
☐ 283	SV: Reggie Smith	.06	.02	.00
☐ 284	Jeff Lahti	.06	.02	.00
☐ 285	Lance Parrish	.30	.12	.03
☐ 286	Rick Langford	.06	.02	.00
☐ 287	Bobby Brown	.06	.02	.00
☐ 288	Joe Cowley	.10	.04	.01
☐ 289	Jerry Dybzinski	.06	.02	.00
☐ 290	Jeff Reardon	.15	.06	.01

		MINT	EXC	G-VG
☐ 291	Pirates TL	.10	.03	.01
	BA: Bill Madlock			
	ERA: John Candelaria			
☐ 292	Craig Swan	.06	.02	.00
☐ 293	Glenn Gulliver	.06	.02	.00
☐ 294	Dave Engle	.06	.02	.00
☐ 295	Jerry Remy	.06	.02	.00
☐ 296	Greg Harris	.06	.02	.00
☐ 297	Ned Yost	.06	.02	.00
☐ 298	Floyd Chiffer	.06	.02	.00
☐ 299	George Wright	.06	.02	.00
☐ 300	Mike Schmidt	.90	.36	.09
☐ 301	SV: Mike Schmidt	.35	.14	.03
☐ 302	Ernie Whitt	.06	.02	.00
☐ 303	Miguel Dilone	.06	.02	.00
☐ 304	Dave Rucker	.06	.02	.00
☐ 305	Larry Bowa	.10	.04	.01
☐ 306	Tom Lasorda MG	.10	.04	.01
☐ 307	Lou Piniella	.10	.04	.01
☐ 308	Jesus Vega	.06	.02	.00
☐ 309	Jeff Leonard	.10	.04	.01
☐ 310	Greg Luzinski	.10	.04	.01
☐ 311	Glenn Brummer	.06	.02	.00
☐ 312	Brian Kingman	.06	.02	.00
☐ 313	Gary Gray	.06	.02	.00
☐ 314	Ken Dayley	.10	.04	.01
☐ 315	Rick Burleson	.10	.04	.01
☐ 316	Paul Splittorff	.06	.02	.00
☐ 317	Gary Rajsich	.06	.02	.00
☐ 318	John Tudor	.30	.12	.03
☐ 319	Lenn Sakata	.06	.02	.00
☐ 320	Steve Rogers	.06	.02	.00
☐ 321	Brewers TL	.15	.04	.01
	BA: Robin Yount			
	ERA: Pete Vuckovich			
☐ 322	Dave Van Gorder	.06	.02	.00
☐ 323	Luis DeLeon	.06	.02	.00
☐ 324	Mike Marshall	.35	.14	.03
☐ 325	Von Hayes	.30	.12	.03
☐ 326	Garth Iorg	.06	.02	.00
☐ 327	Bobby Castillo	.06	.02	.00
☐ 328	Craig Reynolds	.06	.02	.00
☐ 329	Randy Niemann	.06	.02	.00
☐ 330	Buddy Bell	.15	.06	.01
☐ 331	Mike Krukow	.10	.04	.01
☐ 332	Glenn Wilson	.35	.14	.03
☐ 333	Dave LaRoche	.06	.02	.00
☐ 334	SV: Dave LaRoche	.06	.02	.00
☐ 335	Steve Henderson	.06	.02	.00

	MINT	EXC	G-VG
☐ 336 Rene Lachemann MG	.06	.02	.00
☐ 337 Tito Landrum	.06	.02	.00
☐ 338 Bob Owchinko	.06	.02	.00
☐ 339 Terry Harper	.06	.02	.00
☐ 340 Larry Gura	.06	.02	.00
☐ 341 Doug DeCinces	.10	.04	.01
☐ 342 Atlee Hammaker	.10	.04	.01
☐ 343 Bob Bailor	.06	.02	.00
☐ 344 Roger LaFrancois	.06	.02	.00
☐ 345 Jim Clancy	.06	.02	.00
☐ 346 Joe Pittman	.06	.02	.00
☐ 347 Sammy Stewart	.06	.02	.00
☐ 348 Alan Bannister	.06	.02	.00
☐ 349 Checklist: 265-396	.10	.01	.00
☐ 350 Robin Yount	.50	.20	.05
☐ 351 Reds TL	.10	.03	.01
BA: Cesar Cedeno			
ERA: Mario Soto			
☐ 352 Mike Scioscia	.10	.04	.01
☐ 353 Steve Comer	.06	.02	.00
☐ 354 Randy Johnson	.06	.02	.00
☐ 355 Jim Bibby	.06	.02	.00
☐ 356 Gary Woods	.06	.02	.00
☐ 357 Len Matuszek	.06	.02	.00
☐ 358 Jerry Garvin	.06	.02	.00
☐ 359 Dave Collins	.06	.02	.00
☐ 360 Nolan Ryan	.60	.24	.06
☐ 361 SV: Nolan Ryan	.25	.10	.02
☐ 362 Bill Almon	.06	.02	.00
☐ 363 John Stuper	.06	.02	.00
☐ 364 Brett Butler	.10	.04	.01
☐ 365 Dave Lopes	.10	.04	.01
☐ 366 Dick Williams MG	.06	.02	.00
☐ 367 Bud Anderson	.06	.02	.00
☐ 368 Richie Zisk	.06	.02	.00
☐ 369 Jesse Orosco	.06	.02	.00
☐ 370 Gary Carter	.50	.20	.05
☐ 371 Mike Richardt	.06	.02	.00
☐ 372 Terry Crowley	.06	.02	.00
☐ 373 Kevin Saucier	.06	.02	.00
☐ 374 Wayne Krenchicki	.06	.02	.00
☐ 375 Pete Vuckovich	.10	.04	.01
☐ 376 Ken Landreaux	.06	.02	.00
☐ 377 Lee May	.06	.02	.00
☐ 378 SV: Lee May	.06	.02	.00
☐ 379 Guy Sularz	.06	.02	.00
☐ 380 Ron Davis	.06	.02	.00

	MINT	EXC	G-VG
☐ 381 Red Sox TL	.15	.04	.01
BA: Jim Rice			
ERA: Bob Stanley			
☐ 382 Bob Knepper	.10	.04	.01
☐ 383 Ozzie Virgil	.06	.02	.00
☐ 384 Dave Dravecky	.40	.16	.04
☐ 385 Mike Easler	.06	.02	.00
☐ 386 Rod Carew AS	.20	.08	.02
☐ 387 Bob Grich AS	.10	.04	.01
☐ 388 George Brett AS	.35	.14	.03
☐ 389 Robin Yount AS	.20	.08	.02
☐ 390 Reggie Jackson AS	.30	.12	.03
☐ 391 Rickey Henderson AS	.35	.14	.03
☐ 392 Fred Lynn AS	.10	.04	.01
☐ 393 Carlton Fisk AS	.10	.04	.01
☐ 394 Pete Vuckovich AS	.06	.02	.00
☐ 395 Larry Gura AS	.06	.02	.00
☐ 396 Dan Quisenberry AS	.10	.04	.01
☐ 397 Pete Rose AS	.55	.22	.05
☐ 398 Manny Trillo AS	.06	.02	.00
☐ 399 Mike Schmidt AS	.30	.12	.03
☐ 400 Dave Concepcion AS	.06	.02	.00
☐ 401 Dale Murphy AS	.45	.18	.04
☐ 402 Andre Dawson AS	.20	.08	.02
☐ 403 Tim Raines AS	.20	.08	.02
☐ 404 Gary Carter AS	.20	.08	.02
☐ 405 Steve Rogers AS	.06	.02	.00
☐ 406 Steve Carlton AS	.20	.08	.02
☐ 407 Bruce Sutter AS	.10	.04	.01
☐ 408 Rudy May	.06	.02	.00
☐ 409 Marvis Foley	.06	.02	.00
☐ 410 Phil Niekro	.35	.14	.03
☐ 411 SV: Phil Niekro	.15	.06	.01
☐ 412 Rangers TL	.10	.03	.01
BA: Buddy Bell			
ERA: Charlie Hough			
☐ 413 Matt Keough	.06	.02	.00
☐ 414 Julio Cruz	.06	.02	.00
☐ 415 Bob Forsch	.06	.02	.00
☐ 416 Joe Ferguson	.06	.02	.00
☐ 417 Tom Hausman	.06	.02	.00
☐ 418 Greg Pryor	.06	.02	.00
☐ 419 Steve Crawford	.06	.02	.00
☐ 420 Al Oliver	.10	.04	.01
☐ 421 SV: Al Oliver	.06	.02	.00
☐ 422 George Cappuzzello	.06	.02	.00
☐ 423 Tom Lawless	.10	.04	.01
☐ 424 Jerry Augustine	.06	.02	.00
☐ 425 Pedro Guerrero	.45	.18	.04

		MINT	EXC	G-VG
☐ 426	Earl Weaver MG ...	.06	.02	.00
☐ 427	Roy Lee Jackson ...	.06	.02	.00
☐ 428	Champ Summers ..	.06	.02	.00
☐ 429	Eddie Whitson	.06	.02	.00
☐ 430	Kirk Gibson	.50	.20	.04
☐ 431	Gary Gaetti	4.50	1.80	.45
☐ 432	Porfirio Altamirano .	.06	.02	.00
☐ 433	Dale Berra	.06	.02	.00
☐ 434	Dennis Lamp	.06	.02	.00
☐ 435	Tony Armas	.10	.04	.01
☐ 436	Bill Campbell	.06	.02	.00
☐ 437	Rick Sweet	.06	.02	.00
☐ 438	Dave LaPoint	.45	.18	.04
☐ 439	Rafael Ramirez	.06	.02	.00
☐ 440	Ron Guidry	.20	.08	.02
☐ 441	Astros TL	.10	.03	.01
	BA: Ray Knight			
	ERA: Joe Niekro			
☐ 442	Brian Downing	.10	.04	.01
☐ 443	Don Hood	.06	.02	.00
☐ 444	Wally Backman	.20	.08	.02
☐ 445	Mike Flanagan	.10	.04	.01
☐ 446	Reid Nichols	.06	.02	.00
☐ 447	Bryn Smith	.10	.04	.01
☐ 448	Darrell Evans	.15	.06	.01
☐ 449	Eddie Milner	.10	.04	.01
☐ 450	Ted Simmons	.15	.06	.01
☐ 451	SV: Ted Simmons ..	.10	.04	.01
☐ 452	Lloyd Moseby	.15	.06	.01
☐ 453	Lamar Johnson	.06	.02	.00
☐ 454	Bob Welch	.10	.04	.01
☐ 455	Sixto Lezcano	.06	.02	.00
☐ 456	Lee Elia MG	.06	.02	.00
☐ 457	Milt Wilcox	.06	.02	.00
☐ 458	Ron Washington ...	.06	.02	.00
☐ 459	Ed Farmer	.06	.02	.00
☐ 460	Roy Smalley	.06	.02	.00
☐ 461	Steve Trout	.06	.02	.00
☐ 462	Steve Nicosia	.06	.02	.00
☐ 463	Gaylord Perry	.30	.12	.03
☐ 464	SV: Gaylord Perry ..	.15	.06	.01
☐ 465	Lonnie Smith	.10	.04	.01
☐ 466	Tom Underwood	.06	.02	.00
☐ 467	Rufino Linares	.06	.02	.00
☐ 468	Dave Goltz	.06	.02	.00
☐ 469	Ron Gardenhire ...	.06	.02	.00
☐ 470	Greg Minton	.06	.02	.00

		MINT	EXC	G-VG
☐ 471	K.C. Royals TL	.10	.03	.01
	BA: Willie Wilson			
	ERA: Vida Blue			
☐ 472	Gary Allenson	.06	.02	.00
☐ 473	John Lowenstein ..	.06	.02	.00
☐ 474	Ray Burris	.06	.02	.00
☐ 475	Cesar Cedeno	.10	.04	.01
☐ 476	Rob Picciolo	.06	.02	.00
☐ 477	Tom Niedenfuer ...	.10	.04	.01
☐ 478	Phil Garner	.06	.02	.00
☐ 479	Charlie Hough	.10	.04	.01
☐ 480	Toby Harrah	.10	.04	.01
☐ 481	Scot Thompson ...	.06	.02	.00
☐ 482	Tony Gwynn	16.00	6.50	1.60
☐ 483	Lynn Jones	.06	.02	.00
☐ 484	Dick Ruthven	.06	.02	.00
☐ 485	Omar Moreno	.06	.02	.00
☐ 486	Clyde King MG ...	.06	.02	.00
☐ 487	Jerry Hairston ...	.06	.02	.00
☐ 488	Alfredo Griffin ...	.10	.04	.01
☐ 489	Tom Herr	.10	.04	.01
☐ 490	Jim Palmer	.45	.18	.04
☐ 491	SV: Jim Palmer ...	.20	.08	.02
☐ 492	Paul Serna	.06	.02	.00
☐ 493	Steve McCatty ...	.06	.02	.00
☐ 494	Bob Brenly	.06	.02	.00
☐ 495	Warren Cromartie .	.06	.02	.00
☐ 496	Tom Veryzer	.06	.02	.00
☐ 497	Rick Sutcliffe ...	.15	.06	.01
☐ 498	Wade Boggs	32.00	13.00	3.20
☐ 499	Jeff Little	.06	.02	.00
☐ 500	Reggie Jackson ...	.85	.34	.08
☐ 501	SV: Reggie Jackson	.35	.14	.03
☐ 502	Atlanta Braves TL .	.25	.07	.01
	BA: Dale Murphy			
	ERA: Phil Niekro			
☐ 503	Moose Haas	.06	.02	.00
☐ 504	Don Werner	.06	.02	.00
☐ 505	Garry Templeton ..	.10	.04	.01
☐ 506	Jim Gott	.40	.16	.04
☐ 507	Tony Scott	.06	.02	.00
☐ 508	Tom Filer	.15	.06	.01
☐ 509	Lou Whitaker	.25	.10	.02
☐ 510	Tug McGraw	.10	.04	.01
☐ 511	SV: Tug McGraw ..	.06	.02	.00
☐ 512	Doyle Alexander ..	.10	.04	.01
☐ 513	Fred Stanley	.06	.02	.00
☐ 514	Rudy Law	.06	.02	.00
☐ 515	Gene Tenace	.06	.02	.00

	MINT	EXC	G-VG
☐ 516 Bill Virdon MG	.06	.02	.00
☐ 517 Gary Ward	.10	.04	.01
☐ 518 Bill Laskey	.06	.02	.00
☐ 519 Terry Bulling	.06	.02	.00
☐ 520 Fred Lynn	.25	.10	.02
☐ 521 Bruce Benedict	.06	.02	.00
☐ 522 Pat Zachry	.06	.02	.00
☐ 523 Carney Lansford	.15	.06	.01
☐ 524 Tom Brennan	.06	.02	.00
☐ 525 Frank White	.10	.04	.01
☐ 526 Checklist: 397-528	.10	.01	.00
☐ 527 Larry Biittner	.06	.02	.00
☐ 528 Jamie Easterly	.06	.02	.00
☐ 529 Tim Laudner	.10	.04	.01
☐ 530 Eddie Murray	.75	.30	.07
☐ 531 Oakland A's TL	.15	.04	.01
BA: Rickey Henderson			
ERA: Rick Langford			
☐ 532 Dave Stewart	.20	.08	.02
☐ 533 Luis Salazar	.10	.04	.01
☐ 534 John Butcher	.06	.02	.00
☐ 535 Manny Trillo	.06	.02	.00
☐ 536 John Wockenfuss	.06	.02	.00
☐ 537 Rod Scurry	.06	.02	.00
☐ 538 Danny Heep	.06	.02	.00
☐ 539 Roger Erickson	.06	.02	.00
☐ 540 Ozzie Smith	.40	.16	.04
☐ 541 Britt Burns	.10	.04	.01
☐ 542 Jody Davis	.10	.04	.01
☐ 543 Alan Fowlkes	.06	.02	.00
☐ 544 Larry Whisenton	.06	.02	.00
☐ 545 Floyd Bannister	.06	.02	.00
☐ 546 Dave Garcia MG	.06	.02	.00
☐ 547 Geoff Zahn	.06	.02	.00
☐ 548 Brian Giles	.06	.02	.00
☐ 549 Charlie Puleo	.06	.02	.00
☐ 550 Carl Yastrzemski	1.00	.40	.10
☐ 551 SV: Carl Yastrzemski	.40	.16	.04
☐ 552 Tim Wallach	.20	.08	.02
☐ 553 Dennis Martinez	.10	.04	.01
☐ 554 Mike Vail	.06	.02	.00
☐ 555 Steve Yeager	.06	.02	.00
☐ 556 Willie Upshaw	.10	.04	.01
☐ 557 Rick Honeycutt	.06	.02	.00
☐ 558 Dickie Thon	.10	.04	.01
☐ 559 Pete Redfern	.06	.02	.00
☐ 560 Ron LeFlore	.10	.04	.01

	MINT	EXC	G-VG
☐ 561 Cardinals TL	.10	.03	.01
BA: Lonnie Smith			
ERA: Joaquin Andujar			
☐ 562 Dave Rozema	.06	.02	.00
☐ 563 Juan Bonilla	.06	.02	.00
☐ 564 Sid Monge	.06	.02	.00
☐ 565 Bucky Dent	.10	.04	.01
☐ 566 Manny Sarmiento	.06	.02	.00
☐ 567 Joe Simpson	.06	.02	.00
☐ 568 Willie Hernandez	.10	.04	.01
☐ 569 Jack Perconte	.06	.02	.00
☐ 570 Vida Blue	.10	.04	.01
☐ 571 Mickey Klutts	.06	.02	.00
☐ 572 Bob Watson	.10	.04	.01
☐ 573 Andy Hassler	.06	.02	.00
☐ 574 Glenn Adams	.06	.02	.00
☐ 575 Neil Allen	.06	.02	.00
☐ 576 Frank Robinson MG	.15	.06	.01
☐ 577 Luis Aponte	.06	.02	.00
☐ 578 David Green	.06	.02	.00
☐ 579 Rich Dauer	.06	.02	.00
☐ 580 Tom Seaver	.60	.24	.06
☐ 581 SV: Tom Seaver	.25	.10	.02
☐ 582 Marshall Edwards	.06	.02	.00
☐ 583 Terry Forster	.10	.04	.01
☐ 584 Dave Hostetler	.06	.02	.00
☐ 585 Jose Cruz	.10	.04	.01
☐ 586 Frank Viola	5.50	2.20	.55
☐ 587 Ivan DeJesus	.06	.02	.00
☐ 588 Pat Underwood	.06	.02	.00
☐ 589 Alvis Woods	.06	.02	.00
☐ 590 Tony Pena	.20	.08	.02
☐ 591 White Sox TL	.10	.03	.01
BA: Greg Luzinski			
ERA: LaMarr Hoyt			
☐ 592 Shane Rawley	.10	.04	.01
☐ 593 Broderick Perkins	.06	.02	.00
☐ 594 Eric Rasmussen	.06	.02	.00
☐ 595 Tim Raines	.80	.32	.08
☐ 596 Randy Johnson	.06	.02	.00
☐ 597 Mike Proly	.06	.02	.00
☐ 598 Dwayne Murphy	.06	.02	.00
☐ 599 Don Aase	.06	.02	.00
☐ 600 George Brett	1.00	.40	.10
☐ 601 Ed Lynch	.06	.02	.00
☐ 602 Rich Gedman	.15	.06	.01
☐ 603 Joe Morgan	.35	.14	.03
☐ 604 SV: Joe Morgan	.15	.06	.01
☐ 605 Gary Roenicke	.06	.02	.00

		MINT	EXC	G-VG
☐ 606	Bobby Cox MG	.06	.02	.00
☐ 607	Charlie Leibrandt ..	.06	.02	.00
☐ 608	Don Money	.06	.02	.00
☐ 609	Danny Darwin	.06	.02	.00
☐ 610	Steve Garvey	.70	.28	.07
☐ 611	Bert Roberge	.06	.02	.00
☐ 612	Steve Swisher	.06	.02	.00
☐ 613	Mike Ivie	.06	.02	.00
☐ 614	Ed Glynn	.06	.02	.00
☐ 615	Garry Maddox	.10	.04	.01
☐ 616	Bill Nahorodny	.06	.02	.00
☐ 617	Butch Wynegar	.06	.02	.00
☐ 618	LaMarr Hoyt	.10	.04	.01
☐ 619	Keith Moreland	.10	.04	.01
☐ 620	Mike Norris	.06	.02	.00
☐ 621	New York Mets TL	.10	.03	.01
	BA: Mookie Wilson			
	ERA: Craig Swan			
☐ 622	Dave Edler	.06	.02	.00
☐ 623	Luis Sanchez	.06	.02	.00
☐ 624	Glenn Hubbard	.06	.02	.00
☐ 625	Ken Forsch	.06	.02	.00
☐ 626	Jerry Martin	.06	.02	.00
☐ 627	Doug Bair	.06	.02	.00
☐ 628	Julio Valdez	.06	.02	.00
☐ 629	Charlie Lea	.06	.02	.00
☐ 630	Paul Molitor	.25	.10	.02
☐ 631	Tippy Martinez	.06	.02	.00
☐ 632	Alex Trevino	.06	.02	.00
☐ 633	Vicente Romo	.06	.02	.00
☐ 634	Max Venable	.06	.02	.00
☐ 635	Graig Nettles	.15	.06	.01
☐ 636	SV: Graig Nettles ..	.10	.04	.01
☐ 637	Pat Corrales MG ...	.06	.02	.00
☐ 638	Dan Petry	.10	.04	.01
☐ 639	Art Howe	.10	.04	.01
☐ 640	Andre Thornton	.10	.04	.01
☐ 641	Billy Sample	.06	.02	.00
☐ 642	Checklist: 529-660 .	.10	.01	.00
☐ 643	Bump Wills	.06	.02	.00
☐ 644	Joe Lefebvre	.06	.02	.00
☐ 645	Bill Madlock	.15	.06	.01
☐ 646	Jim Essian	.06	.02	.00
☐ 647	Bobby Mitchell	.06	.02	.00
☐ 648	Jeff Burroughs	.10	.04	.01
☐ 649	Tommy Boggs	.06	.02	.00
☐ 650	George Hendrick ...	.10	.04	.01

		MINT	EXC	G-VG
☐ 651	Angels TL	.20	.06	.01
	BA: Rod Carew			
	ERA: Mike Witt			
☐ 652	Butch Hobson	.06	.02	.00
☐ 653	Ellis Valentine	.06	.02	.00
☐ 654	Bob Ojeda	.15	.06	.01
☐ 655	Al Bumbry	.06	.02	.00
☐ 656	Dave Frost	.06	.02	.00
☐ 657	Mike Gates	.06	.02	.00
☐ 658	Frank Pastore	.06	.02	.00
☐ 659	Charlie Moore	.06	.02	.00
☐ 660	Mike Hargrove	.06	.02	.00
☐ 661	Bill Russell	.10	.04	.01
☐ 662	Joe Sambito	.06	.02	.00
☐ 663	Tom O'Malley	.06	.02	.00
☐ 664	Bob Molinaro	.06	.02	.00
☐ 665	Jim Sundberg	.10	.04	.01
☐ 666	Sparky Anderson MG	.10	.04	.01
☐ 667	Dick Davis	.06	.02	.00
☐ 668	Larry Christenson .	.06	.02	.00
☐ 669	Mike Squires	.06	.02	.00
☐ 670	Jerry Mumphrey ...	.06	.02	.00
☐ 671	Lenny Faedo	.06	.02	.00
☐ 672	Jim Kaat	.15	.06	.01
☐ 673	SV: Jim Kaat	.10	.04	.01
☐ 674	Kurt Bevacqua	.06	.02	.00
☐ 675	Jim Beattie	.06	.02	.00
☐ 676	Biff Pocoroba	.06	.02	.00
☐ 677	Dave Revering	.06	.02	.00
☐ 678	Juan Beniquez	.06	.02	.00
☐ 679	Mike Scott	.35	.14	.03
☐ 680	Andre Dawson	.45	.18	.04
☐ 681	Dodgers Leaders ..	.20	.06	.01
	BA: Pedro Guerrero			
	ERA: Fern.Valenzuela			
☐ 682	Bob Stanley	.06	.02	.00
☐ 683	Dan Ford	.06	.02	.00
☐ 684	Rafael Landestoy ..	.06	.02	.00
☐ 685	Lee Mazzilli	.06	.02	.00
☐ 686	Randy Lerch	.06	.02	.00
☐ 687	U.L. Washington ..	.06	.02	.00
☐ 688	Jim Wohlford	.06	.02	.00
☐ 689	Ron Hassey	.06	.02	.00
☐ 690	Kent Hrbek	.70	.28	.07
☐ 691	Dave Tobik	.06	.02	.00
☐ 692	Denny Walling	.06	.02	.00
☐ 693	Sparky Lyle	.10	.04	.01
☐ 694	SV: Sparky Lyle ...	.06	.02	.00
☐ 695	Ruppert Jones	.06	.02	.00

		MINT	EXC	G-VG
☐ 696	Chuck Tanner MG	.06	.02	.00
☐ 697	Barry Foote	.06	.02	.00
☐ 698	Tony Bernazard	.06	.02	.00
☐ 699	Lee Smith	.15	.06	.01
☐ 700	Keith Hernandez	.45	.18	.04
☐ 701	Batting Leaders	.10	.04	.01
	AL: Willie Wilson			
	NL: Al Oliver			
☐ 702	Home Run Leaders	.15	.06	.01
	AL: Reggie Jackson			
	AL: Gorman Thomas			
	NL: Dave Kingman			
☐ 703	RBI Leaders	.15	.06	.01
	AL: Hal McRae			
	NL: Dale Murphy			
	NL: Al Oliver			
☐ 704	SB Leaders	.25	.10	.02
	AL: Rickey Henderson			
	NL: Tim Raines			
☐ 705	Victory Leaders	.12	.05	.01
	AL: LaMarr Hoyt			
	NL: Steve Carlton			
☐ 706	Strikeout Leaders	.12	.05	.01
	AL: Floyd Bannister			
	NL: Steve Carlton			
☐ 707	ERA Leaders	.10	.04	.01
	AL: Rick Sutcliffe			
	NL: Steve Rogers			
☐ 708	Leading Firemen	.10	.04	.01
	AL: Dan Quisenberry			
	NL: Bruce Sutter			
☐ 709	Jimmy Sexton	.06	.02	.00
☐ 710	Willie Wilson	.15	.06	.01
☐ 711	Mariners TL	.10	.04	.01
	BA: Bruce Bochte			
	ERA: Jim Beattie			
☐ 712	Bruce Kison	.06	.02	.00
☐ 713	Ron Hodges	.06	.02	.00
☐ 714	Wayne Nordhagen	.06	.02	.00
☐ 715	Tony Perez	.20	.08	.02
☐ 716	SV: Tony Perez	.10	.04	.01
☐ 717	Scott Sanderson	.06	.02	.00
☐ 718	Jim Dwyer	.06	.02	.00
☐ 719	Rich Gale	.06	.02	.00
☐ 720	Dave Concepcion	.15	.06	.01
☐ 721	John Martin	.06	.02	.00
☐ 722	Jorge Orta	.06	.02	.00
☐ 723	Randy Moffitt	.06	.02	.00
☐ 724	Johnny Grubb	.06	.02	.00

		MINT	EXC	G-VG
☐ 725	Dan Spillner	.06	.02	.00
☐ 726	Harvey Kuenn MG	.06	.02	.00
☐ 727	Chet Lemon	.10	.04	.01
☐ 728	Ron Reed	.06	.02	.00
☐ 729	Jerry Morales	.06	.02	.00
☐ 730	Jason Thompson	.06	.02	.00
☐ 731	Al Williams	.06	.02	.00
☐ 732	Dave Henderson	.20	.08	.02
☐ 733	Buck Martinez	.06	.02	.00
☐ 734	Steve Braun	.06	.02	.00
☐ 735	Tommy John	.20	.08	.02
☐ 736	SV: Tommy John	.10	.04	.01
☐ 737	Mitchell Page	.06	.02	.00
☐ 738	Tim Foli	.06	.02	.00
☐ 739	Rick Ownbey	.06	.02	.00
☐ 740	Rusty Staub	.15	.06	.01
☐ 741	SV: Rusty Staub	.10	.04	.01
☐ 742	Padres TL	.10	.03	.01
	BA: Terry Kennedy			
	ERA: Tim Lollar			
☐ 743	Mike Torrez	.06	.02	.00
☐ 744	Brad Mills	.06	.02	.00
☐ 745	Scott McGregor	.10	.04	.01
☐ 746	John Wathan	.10	.04	.01
☐ 747	Fred Breining	.06	.02	.00
☐ 748	Derrel Thomas	.06	.02	.00
☐ 749	Jon Matlack	.06	.02	.00
☐ 750	Ben Oglivie	.10	.04	.01
☐ 751	Brad Havens	.06	.02	.00
☐ 752	Luis Pujols	.06	.02	.00
☐ 753	Elias Sosa	.06	.02	.00
☐ 754	Bill Robinson	.10	.04	.01
☐ 755	John Candelaria	.10	.04	.01
☐ 756	Russ Nixon MG	.06	.02	.00
☐ 757	Rick Manning	.06	.02	.00
☐ 758	Aurelio Rodriguez	.06	.02	.00
☐ 759	Doug Bird	.06	.02	.00
☐ 760	Dale Murphy	1.50	.60	.15
☐ 761	Gary Lucas	.06	.02	.00
☐ 762	Cliff Johnson	.06	.02	.00
☐ 763	Al Cowens	.06	.02	.00
☐ 764	Pete Falcone	.06	.02	.00
☐ 765	Bob Boone	.15	.06	.01
☐ 766	Barry Bonnell	.06	.02	.00
☐ 767	Duane Kuiper	.06	.02	.00
☐ 768	Chris Speier	.06	.02	.00
☐ 769	Checklist: 661-792	.10	.01	.00
☐ 770	Dave Winfield	.55	.22	.05

		MINT	EXC	G-VG
☐ 771	Twins TL	.10	.03	.01
	BA: Kent Hrbek			
	ERA: Bobby Castillo			
☐ 772	Jim Kern	.06	.02	.00
☐ 773	Larry Hisle	.06	.02	.00
☐ 774	Alan Ashby	.06	.02	.00
☐ 775	Burt Hooton	.06	.02	.00
☐ 776	Larry Parrish	.10	.04	.01
☐ 777	John Curtis	.06	.02	.00
☐ 778	Rich Hebner	.06	.02	.00
☐ 779	Rick Waits	.06	.02	.00
☐ 780	Gary Matthews	.10	.04	.01
☐ 781	Rick Rhoden	.10	.04	.01
☐ 782	Bobby Murcer	.10	.04	.01
☐ 783	SV: Bobby Murcer ..	.06	.02	.00
☐ 784	Jeff Newman	.06	.02	.00
☐ 785	Dennis Leonard ...	.10	.04	.01
☐ 786	Ralph Houk MG ...	.06	.02	.00
☐ 787	Dick Tidrow	.06	.02	.00
☐ 788	Dane Iorg	.06	.02	.00
☐ 789	Bryan Clark	.06	.02	.00
☐ 790	Bob Grich	.10	.04	.01
☐ 791	Gary Lavelle	.06	.02	.00
☐ 792	Chris Chambliss ...	.15	.05	.01

1983 Topps Traded

RON KITTLE

The cards in this 132-card set measure 2 ½" by 3 ½". For the third year in a row, Topps issued a 132-card Traded (or extended) set featuring some of the year's top rookies and players who had changed teams during the year, but were featured with their old team in

the Topps regular issue of 1983. The cards were available through hobby dealers only and were printed in Ireland by the Topps affiliate in that country. The set is numbered alphabetically by the last name of the player of the card.

		MINT	EXC	G-VG
Complete Set (132)		65.00	26.00	6.50
Common Player (1-132) ..		.07	.03	.01
☐	1T Neil Allen	.15	.06	.01
☐	2T Bill Almon	.07	.03	.01
☐	3T Joe Altobelli MG ..	.07	.03	.01
☐	4T Tony Armas	.15	.06	.01
☐	5T Doug Bair	.07	.03	.01
☐	6T Steve Baker	.07	.03	.01
☐	7T Floyd Bannister ..	.15	.06	.01
☐	8T Don Baylor	.25	.10	.02
☐	9T Tony Bernazard ...	.07	.03	.01
☐	10T Larry Biittner	.07	.03	.01
☐	11T Dann Bilardello ...	.07	.03	.01
☐	12T Doug Bird	.07	.03	.01
☐	13T Steve Boros MG ...	.07	.03	.01
☐	14T Greg Brock	.35	.14	.03
☐	15T Mike Brown	.15	.06	.01
	(Red Sox pitcher)			
☐	16T Tom Burgmeier ...	.07	.03	.01
☐	17T Randy Bush	.40	.16	.04
☐	18T Bert Campaneris ..	.15	.06	.01
☐	19T Ron Cey	.20	.08	.02
☐	20T Chris Codiroli	.15	.06	.01
☐	21T Dave Collins	.07	.03	.01
☐	22T Terry Crowley	.07	.03	.01
☐	23T Julio Cruz	.07	.03	.01
☐	24T Mike Davis	.15	.06	.01
☐	25T Frank DiPino	.07	.03	.01
☐	26T Bill Doran	1.50	.60	.15
☐	27T Jerry Dybzinski ...	.07	.03	.01
☐	28T Jamie Easterly ...	.07	.03	.01
☐	29T Juan Eichelberger .	.07	.03	.01
☐	30T Jim Essian	.07	.03	.01
☐	31T Pete Falcone	.07	.03	.01
☐	32T Mike Ferraro MG ...	.07	.03	.01
☐	33T Terry Forster	.15	.06	.01
☐	34T Julio Franco	1.50	.60	.15
☐	35T Rich Gale	.07	.03	.01
☐	36T Kiko Garcia	.07	.03	.01
☐	37T Steve Garvey	1.50	.60	.15
☐	38T Johnny Grubb	.07	.03	.01
☐	39T Mel Hall	.70	.28	.07

	MINT	EXC	G-VG
☐ 40T Von Hayes	.70	.28	.07
☐ 41T Danny Heep	.15	.06	.01
☐ 42T Steve Henderson	.07	.03	.01
☐ 43T Keith Hernandez	1.00	.40	.10
☐ 44T Leo Hernandez	.20	.08	.02
☐ 45T Willie Hernandez	.20	.08	.02
☐ 46T Al Holland	.07	.03	.01
☐ 47T Frank Howard MG	.15	.06	.01
☐ 48T Bobby Johnson	.07	.03	.01
☐ 49T Cliff Johnson	.07	.03	.01
☐ 50T Odell Jones	.07	.03	.01
☐ 51T Mike Jorgensen	.07	.03	.01
☐ 52T Bob Kearney	.07	.03	.01
☐ 53T Steve Kemp	.15	.06	.01
☐ 54T Matt Keough	.07	.03	.01
☐ 55T Ron Kittle	.60	.24	.06
☐ 56T Mickey Klutts	.07	.03	.01
☐ 57T Alan Knicely	.07	.03	.01
☐ 58T Mike Krukow	.15	.06	.01
☐ 59T Rafael Landestoy	.07	.03	.01
☐ 60T Carney Lansford	.25	.10	.02
☐ 61T Joe Lefebvre	.07	.03	.01
☐ 62T Bryan Little	.07	.03	.01
☐ 63T Aurelio Lopez	.07	.03	.01
☐ 64T Mike Madden	.07	.03	.01
☐ 65T Rick Manning	.07	.03	.01
☐ 66T Billy Martin MG	.20	.08	.02
☐ 67T Lee Mazzilli	.07	.03	.01
☐ 68T Andy McGaffigan	.07	.03	.01
☐ 69T Craig McMurtry	.15	.06	.01
☐ 70T John McNamara MG	.07	.03	.01
☐ 71T Orlando Mercado	.15	.06	.01
☐ 72T Larry Milbourne	.07	.03	.01
☐ 73T Randy Moffitt	.07	.03	.01
☐ 74T Sid Monge	.07	.03	.01
☐ 75T Jose Morales	.07	.03	.01
☐ 76T Omar Moreno	.07	.03	.01
☐ 77T Joe Morgan	1.00	.40	.10
☐ 78T Mike Morgan	.07	.03	.01
☐ 79T Dale Murray	.07	.03	.01
☐ 80T Jeff Newman	.07	.03	.01
☐ 81T Pete O'Brien	1.75	.70	.17
☐ 82T Jorge Orta	.07	.03	.01
☐ 83T Alejandro Pena	.65	.26	.06
☐ 84T Pascual Perez	.20	.08	.02
☐ 85T Tony Perez	.55	.22	.05
☐ 86T Broderick Perkins	.07	.03	.01
☐ 87T Tony Phillips	.20	.08	.02
☐ 88T Charlie Puleo	.07	.03	.01

	MINT	EXC	G-VG
☐ 89T Pat Putnam	.07	.03	.01
☐ 90T Jamie Quirk	.07	.03	.01
☐ 91T Doug Rader MG	.15	.06	.01
☐ 92T Chuck Rainey	.07	.03	.01
☐ 93T Bobby Ramos	.07	.03	.01
☐ 94T Gary Redus	.45	.18	.04
☐ 95T Steve Renko	.07	.03	.01
☐ 96T Leon Roberts	.07	.03	.01
☐ 97T Aurelio Rodriguez	.07	.03	.01
☐ 98T Dick Ruthven	.07	.03	.01
☐ 99T Daryl Sconiers	.07	.03	.01
☐ 100T Mike Scott	1.00	.40	.10
☐ 101T Tom Seaver	1.50	.60	.15
☐ 102T John Shelby	.75	.30	.07
☐ 103T Bob Shirley	.07	.03	.01
☐ 104T Joe Simpson	.07	.03	.01
☐ 105T Doug Sisk	.15	.06	.01
☐ 106T Mike Smithson	.15	.06	.01
☐ 107T Elias Sosa	.07	.03	.01
☐ 108T Darryl Strawberry	50.00	20.00	5.00
☐ 109T Tom Tellmann	.07	.03	.01
☐ 110T Gene Tenace	.15	.06	.01
☐ 111T Gorman Thomas	.20	.08	.02
☐ 112T Dick Tidrow	.07	.03	.01
☐ 113T Dave Tobik	.07	.03	.01
☐ 114T Wayne Tolleson	.15	.06	.01
☐ 115T Mike Torrez	.07	.03	.01
☐ 116T Manny Trillo	.07	.03	.01
☐ 117T Steve Trout	.07	.03	.01
☐ 118T Lee Tunnell	.20	.08	.02
☐ 119T Mike Vail	.07	.03	.01
☐ 120T Ellis Valentine	.07	.03	.01
☐ 121T Tom Veryzer	.07	.03	.01
☐ 122T George Vukovich	.07	.03	.01
☐ 123T Rick Waits	.07	.03	.01
☐ 124T Greg Walker	.70	.28	.07
☐ 125T Chris Welsh	.07	.03	.01
☐ 126T Len Whitehouse	.07	.03	.01
☐ 127T Eddie Whitson	.07	.03	.01
☐ 128T Jim Wohlford	.07	.03	.01
☐ 129T Matt Young	.20	.08	.02
☐ 130T Joel Youngblood	.07	.03	.01
☐ 131T Pat Zachry	.07	.03	.01
☐ 132T Checklist 1T-132T	.07	.01	.00

1984 Topps

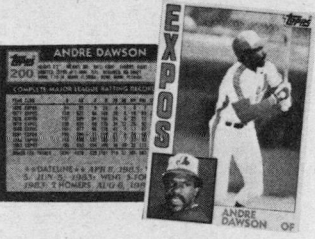

The cards in this 792-card set measure 2 ½"
by 3 ½". For the second year in a row, Topps
utilized a dual picture on the front of the card.
A portrait is shown in a square insert and an
action shot is featured in the main photo.
Card numbers 1-6 feature 1983 Highlights
(HL), cards 131-138 depict League Leaders,
card numbers 386-407 feature All-Stars and
card numbers 701-718 feature active Major
League career leaders in various statistical
categories. Each team leader (TL) card features the team's leading hitter and pitcher
pictured on the front with a team checklist
back. There are six numerical checklist
cards in the set. The player cards feature
team logos in the upper right corner of the
reverse. Topps also produced a specially
boxed "glossy" edition frequently referred to
as the Topps Tiffany set. There were supposedly only 10,000 sets of the Tiffany cards
produced; they were marketed to hobby
dealers. The checklist of cards (792 regular
and 132 Traded) is identical to that of the
normal non-glossy cards. There are two
primary distinguishing features of the Tiffany
cards, white card stock reverses and high
gloss obverses. These Tiffany cards are
valued at approximately six times the values
listed below.

	MINT	EXC	G-VG
Complete Set (792)	100.00	40.00	10.00
Common Player (1-792)	.05	.02	.00

			MINT	EXC	G-VG
☐	1	HL: Steve Carlton 300th win and all-time SO king	.30	.10	.02
☐	2	HL: Rickey Henderson 100 stolen bases, three times	.25	.10	.02
☐	3	HL: Dan Quisenberry Sets save record	.10	.04	.01
☐	4	HL: Nolan Ryan, Steve Carlton, and Gaylord Perry (All surpass Johnson)	.25	.10	.02
☐	5	HL: Dave Righetti, Bob Forsch, and Mike Warren (All pitch no-hitters)	.10	.04	.01
☐	6	HL: Johnny Bench Gaylord Perry, and Carl Yastrzemski (Superstars retire)	.30	.12	.03
☐	7	Gary Lucas	.05	.02	.00
☐	8	Don Mattingly	27.00	11.00	2.70
☐	9	Jim Gott	.10	.04	.01
☐	10	Robin Yount	.40	.16	.04
☐	11	Minnesota Twins TL Kent Hrbek Ken Schrom	.10	.03	.01
☐	12	Billy Sample	.05	.02	.00
☐	13	Scott Holman	.05	.02	.00
☐	14	Tom Brookens	.05	.02	.00
☐	15	Burt Hooton	.05	.02	.00
☐	16	Omar Moreno	.05	.02	.00
☐	17	John Denny	.08	.03	.01
☐	18	Dale Berra	.05	.02	.00
☐	19	Ray Fontenot	.08	.03	.01
☐	20	Greg Luzinski	.10	.04	.01
☐	21	Joe Altobelli MG	.05	.02	.00
☐	22	Bryan Clark	.05	.02	.00
☐	23	Keith Moreland	.05	.02	.00
☐	24	John Martin	.05	.02	.00
☐	25	Glenn Hubbard	.05	.02	.00
☐	26	Bud Black	.05	.02	.00
☐	27	Daryl Sconiers	.05	.02	.00
☐	28	Frank Viola	.80	.32	.08
☐	29	Danny Heep	.05	.02	.00
☐	30	Wade Boggs	7.00	2.80	.70
☐	31	Andy McGaffigan	.05	.02	.00
☐	32	Bobby Ramos	.05	.02	.00
☐	33	Tom Burgmeier	.05	.02	.00

		MINT	EXC	G-VG
☐ 34	Eddie Milner	.05	.02	.00
☐ 35	Don Sutton	.30	.12	.03
☐ 36	Denny Walling	.05	.02	.00
☐ 37	Texas Rangers TL	.10	.03	.01
	Buddy Bell			
	Rick Honeycutt			
☐ 38	Luis DeLeon	.05	.02	.00
☐ 39	Garth Iorg	.05	.02	.00
☐ 40	Dusty Baker	.08	.03	.01
☐ 41	Tony Bernazard	.05	.02	.00
☐ 42	Johnny Grubb	.05	.02	.00
☐ 43	Ron Reed	.05	.02	.00
☐ 44	Jim Morrison	.05	.02	.00
☐ 45	Jerry Mumphrey	.05	.02	.00
☐ 46	Ray Smith	.05	.02	.00
☐ 47	Rudy Law	.05	.02	.00
☐ 48	Julio Franco	.45	.18	.04
☐ 49	John Stuper	.05	.02	.00
☐ 50	Chris Chambliss	.10	.04	.01
☐ 51	Jim Frey MG	.05	.02	.00
☐ 52	Paul Splittorff	.05	.02	.00
☐ 53	Juan Beniquez	.05	.02	.00
☐ 54	Jesse Orosco	.05	.02	.00
☐ 55	Dave Concepcion	.10	.04	.01
☐ 56	Gary Allenson	.05	.02	.00
☐ 57	Dan Schatzeder	.05	.02	.00
☐ 58	Max Venable	.05	.02	.00
☐ 59	Sammy Stewart	.05	.02	.00
☐ 60	Paul Molitor	.15	.06	.01
☐ 61	Chris Codiroli	.08	.03	.01
☐ 62	Dave Hostetler	.05	.02	.00
☐ 63	Ed VandeBerg	.05	.02	.00
☐ 64	Mike Scioscia	.08	.03	.01
☐ 65	Kirk Gibson	.35	.14	.03
☐ 66	Houston Astros TL	.15	.04	.01
	Jose Cruz			
	Nolan Ryan			
☐ 67	Gary Ward	.08	.03	.01
☐ 68	Luis Salazar	.08	.03	.01
☐ 69	Rod Scurry	.05	.02	.00
☐ 70	Gary Matthews	.08	.03	.01
☐ 71	Leo Hernandez	.08	.03	.01
☐ 72	Mike Squires	.05	.02	.00
☐ 73	Jody Davis	.08	.03	.01
☐ 74	Jerry Martin	.05	.02	.00
☐ 75	Bob Forsch	.05	.02	.00
☐ 76	Alfredo Griffin	.08	.03	.01
☐ 77	Brett Butler	.10	.04	.01
☐ 78	Mike Torrez	.05	.02	.00
☐ 79	Rob Wilfong	.05	.02	.00
☐ 80	Steve Rogers	.05	.02	.00
☐ 81	Billy Martin MG	.10	.04	.01
☐ 82	Doug Bird	.05	.02	.00
☐ 83	Richie Zisk	.05	.02	.00
☐ 84	Lenny Faedo	.05	.02	.00
☐ 85	Atlee Hammaker	.05	.02	.00
☐ 86	John Shelby	.35	.14	.03
☐ 87	Frank Pastore	.05	.02	.00
☐ 88	Rob Picciolo	.05	.02	.00
☐ 89	Mike Smithson	.08	.03	.01
☐ 90	Pedro Guerrero	.35	.14	.03
☐ 91	Dan Spillner	.05	.02	.00
☐ 92	Lloyd Moseby	.15	.06	.01
☐ 93	Bob Knepper	.10	.04	.01
☐ 94	Mario Ramirez	.05	.02	.00
☐ 95	Aurelio Lopez	.05	.02	.00
☐ 96	K.C. Royals TL	.10	.03	.01
	Hal McRae			
	Larry Gura			
☐ 97	LaMarr Hoyt	.08	.03	.01
☐ 98	Steve Nicosia	.05	.02	.00
☐ 99	Craig Lefferts	.15	.06	.01
☐ 100	Reggie Jackson	.60	.24	.06
☐ 101	Porfirio Altamirano	.05	.02	.00
☐ 102	Ken Oberkfell	.05	.02	.00
☐ 103	Dwayne Murphy	.05	.02	.00
☐ 104	Ken Dayley	.05	.02	.00
☐ 105	Tony Armas	.08	.03	.01
☐ 106	Tim Stoddard	.05	.02	.00
☐ 107	Ned Yost	.05	.02	.00
☐ 108	Randy Moffitt	.05	.02	.00
☐ 109	Brad Wellman	.05	.02	.00
☐ 110	Ron Guidry	.20	.08	.02
☐ 111	Bill Virdon MG	.05	.02	.00
☐ 112	Tom Niedenfuer	.08	.03	.01
☐ 113	Kelly Paris	.08	.03	.01
☐ 114	Checklist 1-132	.08	.01	.00
☐ 115	Andre Thornton	.08	.03	.01
☐ 116	George Bjorkman	.05	.02	.00
☐ 117	Tom Veryzer	.05	.02	.00
☐ 118	Charlie Hough	.08	.03	.01
☐ 119	John Wockenfuss	.05	.02	.00
☐ 120	Keith Hernandez	.35	.14	.03
☐ 121	Pat Sheridan	.20	.08	.02
☐ 122	Cecilio Guante	.08	.03	.01
☐ 123	Butch Wynegar	.05	.02	.00
☐ 124	Damaso Garcia	.05	.02	.00
☐ 125	Britt Burns	.05	.02	.00

		MINT	EXC	G-VG
☐ 126	Atlanta Braves TL ..	.15	.04	.01
	Dale Murphy			
	Craig McMurtry			
☐ 127	Mike Madden	.05	.02	.00
☐ 128	Rick Manning	.05	.02	.00
☐ 129	Bill Laskey	.05	.02	.00
☐ 130	Ozzie Smith	.30	.12	.03
☐ 131	Batting Leaders	.25	.10	.02
	Bill Madlock			
	Wade Boggs			
☐ 132	Home Run Leaders	.25	.10	.02
	Mike Schmidt			
	Jim Rice			
☐ 133	RBI Leaders	.20	.08	.02
	Dale Murphy			
	Cecil Cooper			
	Jim Rice			
☐ 134	Stolen Base Leaders	.25	.10	.02
	Tim Raines			
	Rickey Henderson			
☐ 135	Victory Leaders	.08	.03	.01
	John Denny			
	LaMarr Hoyt			
☐ 136	Strikeout Leaders ..	.15	.06	.01
	Steve Carlton			
	Jack Morris			
☐ 137	ERA Leaders	.08	.03	.01
	Atlee Hammaker			
	Rick Honeycutt			
☐ 138	Leading Firemen ...	.08	.03	.01
	Al Holland			
	Dan Quisenberry			
☐ 139	Bert Campaneris ...	.08	.03	.01
☐ 140	Storm Davis	.10	.04	.01
☐ 141	Pat Corrales MG ...	.05	.02	.00
☐ 142	Rich Gale	.05	.02	.00
☐ 143	Jose Morales	.05	.02	.00
☐ 144	Brian Harper	.08	.03	.01
☐ 145	Gary Lavelle	.05	.02	.00
☐ 146	Ed Romero	.05	.02	.00
☐ 147	Dan Petry	.08	.03	.01
☐ 148	Joe Lefebvre	.05	.02	.00
☐ 149	Jon Matlack	.05	.02	.00
☐ 150	Dale Murphy	1.00	.40	.10
☐ 151	Steve Trout	.05	.02	.00
☐ 152	Glenn Brummer ...	.05	.02	.00
☐ 153	Dick Tidrow	.05	.02	.00
☐ 154	Dave Henderson ...	.15	.06	.01
☐ 155	Frank White	.10	.04	.01

		MINT	EXC	G-VG
☐ 156	Oakland A's TL ...	.12	.04	.01
	Rickey Henderson			
	Tim Conroy			
☐ 157	Gary Gaetti	.65	.26	.06
☐ 158	John Curtis	.05	.02	.00
☐ 159	Darryl Cias	.05	.02	.00
☐ 160	Mario Soto	.05	.02	.00
☐ 161	Junior Ortiz	.05	.02	.00
☐ 162	Bob Ojeda	.10	.04	.01
☐ 163	Lorenzo Gray	.05	.02	.00
☐ 164	Scott Sanderson ..	.05	.02	.00
☐ 165	Ken Singleton	.10	.04	.01
☐ 166	Jamie Nelson	.05	.02	.00
☐ 167	Marshall Edwards ..	.05	.02	.00
☐ 168	Juan Bonilla	.05	.02	.00
☐ 169	Larry Parrish	.08	.03	.01
☐ 170	Jerry Reuss	.08	.03	.01
☐ 171	Frank Robinson MG	.10	.04	.01
☐ 172	Frank DiPino	.05	.02	.00
☐ 173	Marvell Wynne	.10	.04	.01
☐ 174	Juan Berenguer ...	.05	.02	.00
☐ 175	Graig Nettles	.15	.06	.01
☐ 176	Lee Smith	.10	.04	.01
☐ 177	Jerry Hairston	.05	.02	.00
☐ 178	Bill Krueger	.05	.02	.00
☐ 179	Buck Martinez	.05	.02	.00
☐ 180	Manny Trillo	.05	.02	.00
☐ 181	Roy Thomas	.05	.02	.00
☐ 182	Darryl Strawberry ..	12.00	5.00	1.20
☐ 183	Al Williams	.05	.02	.00
☐ 184	Mike O'Berry	.05	.02	.00
☐ 185	Sixto Lezcano	.05	.02	.00
☐ 186	Cardinal TL	.10	.03	.01
	Lonnie Smith			
	John Stuper			
☐ 187	Luis Aponte	.05	.02	.00
☐ 188	Bryan Little	.05	.02	.00
☐ 189	Tim Conroy	.08	.03	.01
☐ 190	Ben Oglivie	.08	.03	.01
☐ 191	Mike Boddicker ...	.10	.04	.01
☐ 192	Nick Esasky	.35	.14	.03
☐ 193	Darrell Brown	.05	.02	.00
☐ 194	Domingo Ramos ..	.05	.02	.00
☐ 195	Jack Morris	.20	.08	.02
☐ 196	Don Slaught	.15	.06	.01
☐ 197	Garry Hancock	.05	.02	.00
☐ 198	Bill Doran	.70	.28	.07
☐ 199	Willie Hernandez ..	.20	.08	.02
☐ 200	Andre Dawson	.40	.16	.04

		MINT	EXC	G-VG
☐ 201	Bruce Kison	.05	.02	.00
☐ 202	Bobby Cox MG	.05	.02	.00
☐ 203	Matt Keough	.05	.02	.00
☐ 204	Bobby Meacham . . .	.10	.04	.01
☐ 205	Greg Minton	.05	.02	.00
☐ 206	Andy Van Slyke . . .	2.50	1.00	.25
☐ 207	Donnie Moore	.05	.02	.00
☐ 208	Jose Oquendo	.35	.14	.03
☐ 209	Manny Sarmiento . .	.05	.02	.00
☐ 210	Joe Morgan	.25	.10	.02
☐ 211	Rick Sweet	.05	.02	.00
☐ 212	Broderick Perkins . .	.05	.02	.00
☐ 213	Bruce Hurst	.15	.06	.01
☐ 214	Paul Householder . .	.05	.02	.00
☐ 215	Tippy Martinez	.05	.02	.00
☐ 216	White Sox TL	.10	.03	.01
	Carlton Fisk			
	Richard Dotson			
☐ 217	Alan Ashby	.05	.02	.00
☐ 218	Rick Waits	.05	.02	.00
☐ 219	Joe Simpson	.05	.02	.00
☐ 220	Fernando Valenzuela	.30	.12	.03
☐ 221	Cliff Johnson	.05	.02	.00
☐ 222	Rick Honeycutt	.05	.02	.00
☐ 223	Wayne Krenchicki . .	.05	.02	.00
☐ 224	Sid Monge	.05	.02	.00
☐ 225	Lee Mazzilli	.05	.02	.00
☐ 226	Juan Eichelberger . .	.05	.02	.00
☐ 227	Steve Braun	.05	.02	.00
☐ 228	John Rabb	.05	.02	.00
☐ 229	Paul Owens MG . . .	.05	.02	.00
☐ 230	Rickey Henderson . .	.60	.24	.06
☐ 231	Gary Woods	.05	.02	.00
☐ 232	Tim Wallach	.15	.06	.01
☐ 233	Checklist 133-264 . .	.08	.01	.00
☐ 234	Rafael Ramirez . . .	.05	.02	.00
☐ 235	Matt Young	.10	.04	.01
☐ 236	Ellis Valentine	.05	.02	.00
☐ 237	John Castino	.05	.02	.00
☐ 238	Reid Nichols	.05	.02	.00
☐ 239	Jay Howell	.10	.04	.01
☐ 240	Eddie Murray	.60	.22	.05
☐ 241	Bill Almon	.05	.02	.00
☐ 242	Alex Trevino	.05	.02	.00
☐ 243	Pete Ladd	.05	.02	.00
☐ 244	Candy Maldonado . .	.30	.12	.03
☐ 245	Rick Sutcliffe	.25	.10	.02

		MINT	EXC	G-VG
☐ 246	New York Mets TL	.12	.04	.01
	Mookie Wilson			
	Tom Seaver			
☐ 247	Onix Concepcion . .	.05	.02	.00
☐ 248	Bill Dawley	.10	.04	.01
☐ 249	Jay Johnstone	.08	.03	.01
☐ 250	Bill Madlock	.10	.04	.01
☐ 251	Tony Gwynn	2.50	1.00	.25
☐ 252	Larry Christenson .	.05	.02	.00
☐ 253	Jim Wohlford	.05	.02	.00
☐ 254	Shane Rawley	.10	.04	.01
☐ 255	Bruce Benedict . . .	.05	.02	.00
☐ 256	Dave Geisel	.05	.02	.00
☐ 257	Julio Cruz	.05	.02	.00
☐ 258	Luis Sanchez	.05	.02	.00
☐ 259	Sparky Anderson MG	.05	.02	.00
☐ 260	Scott McGregor . . .	.08	.03	.01
☐ 261	Bobby Brown	.05	.02	.00
☐ 262	Tom Candiotti	.20	.08	.02
☐ 263	Jack Fimple	.05	.02	.00
☐ 264	Doug Frobel	.05	.02	.00
☐ 265	Donnie Hill	.10	.04	.01
☐ 266	Steve Lubratich . . .	.05	.02	.00
☐ 267	Carmelo Martinez . .	.25	.10	.02
☐ 268	Jack O'Connor	.05	.02	.00
☐ 269	Aurelio Rodriguez . .	.05	.02	.00
☐ 270	Jeff Russell	.25	.10	.02
☐ 271	Moose Haas	.05	.02	.00
☐ 272	Rick Dempsey	.05	.02	.00
☐ 273	Charlie Puleo	.05	.02	.00
☐ 274	Rick Monday	.08	.03	.01
☐ 275	Len Matuszek	.05	.02	.00
☐ 276	Angels TL	.12	.04	.01
	Rod Carew			
	Geoff Zahn			
☐ 277	Eddie Whitson	.08	.03	.01
☐ 278	Jorge Bell	1.25	.50	.12
☐ 279	Ivan DeJesus	.05	.02	.00
☐ 280	Floyd Bannister . . .	.05	.02	.00
☐ 281	Larry Milbourne . . .	.05	.02	.00
☐ 282	Jim Barr	.05	.02	.00
☐ 283	Larry Biittner	.05	.02	.00
☐ 284	Howard Bailey	.05	.02	.00
☐ 285	Darrell Porter	.05	.02	.00
☐ 286	Lary Sorensen	.05	.02	.00
☐ 287	Warren Cromartie . .	.05	.02	.00
☐ 288	Jim Beattie	.05	.02	.00
☐ 289	Randy Johnson . . .	.05	.02	.00
☐ 290	Dave Dravecky . . .	.08	.03	.01

		MINT	EXC	G-VG
☐ 291	Chuck Tanner MG	.05	.02	.00
☐ 292	Tony Scott	.05	.02	.00
☐ 293	Ed Lynch	.05	.02	.00
☐ 294	U.L. Washington	.05	.02	.00
☐ 295	Mike Flanagan	.08	.03	.01
☐ 296	Jeff Newman	.05	.02	.00
☐ 297	Bruce Berenyi	.05	.02	.00
☐ 298	Jim Gantner	.05	.02	.00
☐ 299	John Butcher	.05	.02	.00
☐ 300	Pete Rose	1.50	.60	.15
☐ 301	Frank LaCorte	.05	.02	.00
☐ 302	Barry Bonnell	.05	.02	.00
☐ 303	Marty Castillo	.05	.02	.00
☐ 304	Warren Brusstar	.05	.02	.00
☐ 305	Roy Smalley	.05	.02	.00
☐ 306	Dodgers TL	.10	.03	.01
	Pedro Guerrero			
	Bob Welch			
☐ 307	Bobby Mitchell	.05	.02	.00
☐ 308	Ron Hassey	.08	.03	.01
☐ 309	Tony Phillips	.08	.03	.01
☐ 310	Willie McGee	.35	.14	.03
☐ 311	Jerry Koosman	.10	.04	.01
☐ 312	Jorge Orta	.05	.02	.00
☐ 313	Mike Jorgensen	.05	.02	.00
☐ 314	Orlando Mercado	.05	.02	.00
☐ 315	Bob Grich	.08	.03	.01
☐ 316	Mark Bradley	.05	.02	.00
☐ 317	Greg Pryor	.05	.02	.00
☐ 318	Bill Gullickson	.05	.02	.00
☐ 319	Al Bumbry	.05	.02	.00
☐ 320	Bob Stanley	.05	.02	.00
☐ 321	Harvey Kuenn MG	.05	.02	.00
☐ 322	Ken Schrom	.05	.02	.00
☐ 323	Alan Knicely	.05	.02	.00
☐ 324	Alejandro Pena	.35	.14	.03
☐ 325	Darrell Evans	.15	.06	.01
☐ 326	Bob Kearney	.05	.02	.00
☐ 327	Ruppert Jones	.05	.02	.00
☐ 328	Vern Ruhle	.05	.02	.00
☐ 329	Pat Tabler	.25	.10	.02
☐ 330	John Candelaria	.10	.04	.01
☐ 331	Bucky Dent	.08	.03	.01
☐ 332	Kevin Gross	.35	.14	.03
☐ 333	Larry Herndon	.05	.02	.00
☐ 334	Chuck Rainey	.05	.02	.00
☐ 335	Don Baylor	.12	.05	.01

		MINT	EXC	G-VG
☐ 336	Seattle Mariners TL	.10	.03	.01
	Pat Putnam			
	Matt Young			
☐ 337	Kevin Hagen	.05	.02	.00
☐ 338	Mike Warren	.10	.04	.01
☐ 339	Roy Lee Jackson	.05	.02	.00
☐ 340	Hal McRae	.08	.03	.01
☐ 341	Dave Tobik	.05	.02	.00
☐ 342	Tim Foli	.05	.02	.00
☐ 343	Mark Davis	.08	.03	.01
☐ 344	Rick Miller	.05	.02	.00
☐ 345	Kent Hrbek	.35	.14	.03
☐ 346	Kurt Bevacqua	.05	.02	.00
☐ 347	Allan Ramirez	.05	.02	.00
☐ 348	Toby Harrah	.05	.02	.00
☐ 349	Bob L. Gibson	.08	.03	.01
	(Brewers Pitcher)			
☐ 350	George Foster	.15	.06	.01
☐ 351	Russ Nixon MG	.05	.02	.00
☐ 352	Dave Stewart	.15	.06	.01
☐ 353	Jim Anderson	.05	.02	.00
☐ 354	Jeff Burroughs	.05	.02	.00
☐ 355	Jason Thompson	.05	.02	.00
☐ 356	Glenn Abbott	.05	.02	.00
☐ 357	Ron Cey	.10	.04	.01
☐ 358	Bob Dernier	.05	.02	.00
☐ 359	Jim Acker	.08	.03	.01
☐ 360	Willie Randolph	.10	.04	.01
☐ 361	Dave Smith	.08	.03	.01
☐ 362	David Green	.05	.02	.00
☐ 363	Tim Laudner	.08	.03	.01
☐ 364	Scott Fletcher	.20	.08	.02
☐ 365	Steve Bedrosian	.15	.06	.01
☐ 366	Padres TL	.10	.03	.01
	Terry Kennedy			
	Dave Dravecky			
☐ 367	Jamie Easterly	.05	.02	.00
☐ 368	Hubie Brooks	.10	.04	.01
☐ 369	Steve McCatty	.05	.02	.00
☐ 370	Tim Raines	.50	.20	.05
☐ 371	Dave Gumpert	.05	.02	.00
☐ 372	Gary Roenicke	.05	.02	.00
☐ 373	Bill Scherrer	.05	.02	.00
☐ 374	Don Money	.05	.02	.00
☐ 375	Dennis Leonard	.08	.03	.01
☐ 376	Dave Anderson	.15	.06	.01
☐ 377	Danny Darwin	.05	.02	.00
☐ 378	Bob Brenly	.05	.02	.00
☐ 379	Checklist 265-396	.08	.01	.00

	MINT	EXC	G-VG			MINT	EXC	G-VG
☐ 380 Steve Garvey	.50	.20	.05	☐ 427 Rick Leach	.05	.02	.00
☐ 381 Ralph Houk MG	.05	.02	.00	☐ 428 Fred Breining	.05	.02	.00
☐ 382 Chris Nyman	.05	.02	.00	☐ 429 Randy Bush	.20	.08	.01
☐ 383 Terry Puhl	.05	.02	.00	☐ 430 Rusty Staub	.10	.04	.01
☐ 384 Lee Tunnell	.10	.04	.01	☐ 431 Chris Bando	.05	.02	.00
☐ 385 Tony Perez	.15	.06	.01	☐ 432 Charles Hudson	.20	.08	.02
☐ 386 George Hendrick AS	.08	.03	.01	☐ 433 Rich Hebner	.05	.02	.00
☐ 387 Johnny Ray AS	.08	.03	.01	☐ 434 Harold Baines	.20	.08	.02
☐ 388 Mike Schmidt AS	.30	.12	.03	☐ 435 Neil Allen	.05	.02	.00
☐ 389 Ozzie Smith AS	.15	.06	.01	☐ 436 Rick Peters	.05	.02	.00
☐ 390 Tim Raines AS	.15	.06	.01	☐ 437 Mike Proly	.05	.02	.00
☐ 391 Dale Murphy AS	.35	.14	.03	☐ 438 Biff Pocoroba	.05	.02	.00
☐ 392 Andre Dawson AS	.15	.06	.01	☐ 439 Bob Stoddard	.05	.02	.00
☐ 393 Gary Carter AS	.20	.08	.02	☐ 440 Steve Kemp	.08	.03	.01
☐ 394 Steve Rogers AS	.08	.03	.01	☐ 441 Bob Lillis MG	.05	.02	.00
☐ 395 Steve Carlton AS	.20	.08	.02	☐ 442 Byron McLaughlin	.05	.02	.00
☐ 396 Jesse Orosco AS	.08	.03	.01	☐ 443 Benny Ayala	.05	.02	.00
☐ 397 Eddie Murray AS	.15	.06	.01	☐ 444 Steve Renko	.05	.02	.00
☐ 398 Lou Whitaker AS	.10	.04	.01	☐ 445 Jerry Remy	.05	.02	.00
☐ 399 George Brett AS	.30	.12	.03	☐ 446 Luis Pujols	.05	.02	.00
☐ 400 Cal Ripken AS	.20	.08	.02	☐ 447 Tom Brunansky	.25	.10	.02
☐ 401 Jim Rice AS	.15	.06	.01	☐ 448 Ben Hayes	.05	.02	.00
☐ 402 Dave Winfield AS	.15	.06	.01	☐ 449 Joe Pettini	.05	.02	.00
☐ 403 Lloyd Moseby AS	.08	.03	.01	☐ 450 Gary Carter	.40	.16	.04
☐ 404 Ted Simmons AS	.08	.03	.01	☐ 451 Bob Jones	.05	.02	.00
☐ 405 LaMarr Hoyt AS	.08	.03	.01	☐ 452 Chuck Porter	.05	.02	.00
☐ 406 Ron Guidry AS	.10	.04	.01	☐ 453 Willie Upshaw	.05	.02	.00
☐ 407 Dan Quisenberry AS	.08	.03	.01	☐ 454 Joe Beckwith	.05	.02	.00
☐ 408 Lou Piniella AS	.08	.03	.01	☐ 455 Terry Kennedy	.05	.02	.00
☐ 409 Juan Agosto	.15	.06	.01	☐ 456 Chicago Cubs TL	.10	.03	.01
☐ 410 Claudell Washington	.08	.03	.01	Keith Moreland			
☐ 411 Houston Jimenez	.08	.03	.01	Fergie Jenkins			
☐ 412 Doug Rader MG	.05	.02	.00	☐ 457 Dave Rozema	.05	.02	.00
☐ 413 Spike Owen	.20	.08	.02	☐ 458 Kiko Garcia	.05	.02	.00
☐ 414 Mitchell Page	.05	.02	.00	☐ 459 Kevin Hickey	.05	.02	.00
☐ 415 Tommy John	.15	.06	.01	☐ 460 Dave Winfield	.45	.18	.04
☐ 416 Dane Iorg	.05	.02	.00	☐ 461 Jim Maler	.05	.02	.00
☐ 417 Mike Armstrong	.05	.02	.00	☐ 462 Lee Lacy	.05	.02	.00
☐ 418 Ron Hodges	.05	.02	.00	☐ 463 Dave Engle	.05	.02	.00
☐ 419 John Henry Johnson	.05	.02	.00	☐ 464 Jeff A. Jones	.05	.02	.00
☐ 420 Cecil Cooper	.12	.05	.01	(A's Pitcher)			
☐ 421 Charlie Lea	.05	.02	.00	☐ 465 Mookie Wilson	.08	.03	.01
☐ 422 Jose Cruz	.10	.04	.01	☐ 466 Gene Garber	.05	.02	.00
☐ 423 Mike Morgan	.05	.02	.00	☐ 467 Mike Ramsey	.05	.02	.00
☐ 424 Dann Bilardello	.05	.02	.00	☐ 468 Geoff Zahn	.05	.02	.00
☐ 425 Steve Howe	.05	.02	.00	☐ 469 Tom O'Malley	.05	.02	.00
☐ 426 Orioles TL	.15	.04	.01	☐ 470 Nolan Ryan	.45	.18	.04
Cal Ripken				☐ 471 Dick Howser MG	.08	.03	.01
Mike Boddicker							

		MINT	EXC	G-VG
☐ 472	Mike Brown (Red Sox Pitcher)	.08	.03	.01
☐ 473	Jim Dwyer	.05	.02	.00
☐ 474	Greg Bargar	.05	.02	.00
☐ 475	Gary Redus	.25	.10	.02
☐ 476	Tom Tellmann	.05	.02	.00
☐ 477	Rafael Landestoy	.05	.02	.00
☐ 478	Alan Bannister	.05	.02	.00
☐ 479	Frank Tanana	.08	.03	.01
☐ 480	Ron Kittle	.25	.10	.02
☐ 481	Mark Thurmond	.10	.04	.01
☐ 482	Enos Cabell	.05	.02	.00
☐ 483	Fergie Jenkins	.15	.06	.01
☐ 484	Ozzie Virgil	.05	.02	.00
☐ 485	Rick Rhoden	.10	.04	.01
☐ 486	N.Y. Yankees TL Don Baylor Ron Guidry	.10	.03	.01
☐ 487	Ricky Adams	.05	.02	.00
☐ 488	Jesse Barfield	.30	.12	.03
☐ 489	Dave Von Ohlen	.05	.02	.00
☐ 490	Cal Ripken	.75	.30	.07
☐ 491	Bobby Castillo	.05	.02	.00
☐ 492	Tucker Ashford	.05	.02	.00
☐ 493	Mike Norris	.05	.02	.00
☐ 494	Chili Davis	.15	.06	.01
☐ 495	Rollie Fingers	.20	.08	.02
☐ 496	Terry Francona	.05	.02	.00
☐ 497	Bud Anderson	.05	.02	.00
☐ 498	Rich Gedman	.10	.04	.01
☐ 499	Mike Witt	.12	.05	.01
☐ 500	George Brett	.75	.30	.07
☐ 501	Steve Henderson	.05	.02	.00
☐ 502	Joe Torre MG	.08	.03	.01
☐ 503	Elias Sosa	.05	.02	.00
☐ 504	Mickey Rivers	.08	.03	.01
☐ 505	Pete Vuckovich	.08	.03	.01
☐ 506	Ernie Whitt	.05	.02	.00
☐ 507	Mike LaCoss	.05	.02	.00
☐ 508	Mel Hall	.25	.10	.02
☐ 509	Brad Havens	.05	.02	.00
☐ 510	Alan Trammell	.35	.14	.03
☐ 511	Marty Bystrom	.05	.02	.00
☐ 512	Oscar Gamble	.05	.02	.00
☐ 513	Dave Beard	.05	.02	.00
☐ 514	Floyd Rayford	.05	.02	.00
☐ 515	Gorman Thomas	.10	.04	.01
☐ 516	Montreal Expos TL Al Oliver Charlie Lea	.10	.03	.01
☐ 517	John Moses	.08	.03	.01
☐ 518	Greg Walker	.45	.18	.04
☐ 519	Ron Davis	.05	.02	.00
☐ 520	Bob Boone	.10	.04	.01
☐ 521	Pete Falcone	.05	.02	.00
☐ 522	Dave Bergman	.05	.02	.00
☐ 523	Glenn Hoffman	.05	.02	.00
☐ 524	Carlos Diaz	.05	.02	.00
☐ 525	Willie Wilson	.12	.05	.01
☐ 526	Ron Oester	.05	.02	.00
☐ 527	Checklist 397-528	.08	.01	.00
☐ 528	Mark Brouhard	.05	.02	.00
☐ 529	Keith Atherton	.05	.02	.00
☐ 530	Dan Ford	.05	.02	.00
☐ 531	Steve Boros MG	.05	.02	.00
☐ 532	Eric Show	.08	.03	.01
☐ 533	Ken Landreaux	.05	.02	.00
☐ 534	Pete O'Brien	1.00	.40	.10
☐ 535	Bo Diaz	.05	.02	.00
☐ 536	Doug Bair	.05	.02	.00
☐ 537	Johnny Ray	.12	.05	.01
☐ 538	Kevin Bass	.10	.04	.01
☐ 539	George Frazier	.05	.02	.00
☐ 540	George Hendrick	.08	.03	.01
☐ 541	Dennis Lamp	.05	.02	.00
☐ 542	Duane Kuiper	.05	.02	.00
☐ 543	Craig McMurtry	.08	.03	.01
☐ 544	Cesar Geronimo	.05	.02	.00
☐ 545	Bill Buckner	.10	.04	.01
☐ 546	Indians TL Mike Hargrove Lary Sorensen	.10	.03	.01
☐ 547	Mike Moore	.10	.04	.01
☐ 548	Ron Jackson	.05	.02	.00
☐ 549	Walt Terrell	.35	.14	.03
☐ 550	Jim Rice	.30	.12	.03
☐ 551	Scott Ullger	.05	.02	.00
☐ 552	Ray Burris	.05	.02	.00
☐ 553	Joe Nolan	.05	.02	.00
☐ 554	Ted Power	.05	.02	.00
☐ 555	Greg Brock	.12	.05	.01
☐ 556	Joey McLaughlin	.05	.02	.00
☐ 557	Wayne Tolleson	.10	.04	.01
☐ 558	Mike Davis	.08	.03	.01
☐ 559	Mike Scott	.25	.10	.02
☐ 560	Carlton Fisk	.15	.06	.01

	MINT	EXC	G-VG		MINT	EXC	G-VG
☐ 561 Whitey Herzog MG .	.05	.02	.00	☐ 606 Blue Jays TL	.10	.03	.01
☐ 562 Manny Castillo	.05	.02	.00	Lloyd Moseby			
☐ 563 Glenn Wilson	.08	.03	.01	Dave Stieb			
☐ 564 Al Holland	.05	.02	.00	☐ 607 Tom Hume	.05	.02	.00
☐ 565 Leon Durham	.08	.03	.01	☐ 608 Bobby Johnson	.05	.02	.00
☐ 566 Jim Bibby	.05	.02	.00	☐ 609 Dan Meyer	.05	.02	.00
☐ 567 Mike Heath	.05	.02	.00	☐ 610 Steve Sax	.25	.10	.02
☐ 568 Pete Filson	.05	.02	.00	☐ 611 Chet Lemon	.08	.03	.01
☐ 569 Bake McBride	.05	.02	.00	☐ 612 Harry Spilman	.05	.02	.00
☐ 570 Dan Quisenberry ...	.12	.05	.01	☐ 613 Greg Gross	.05	.02	.00
☐ 571 Bruce Bochy	.05	.02	.00	☐ 614 Len Barker	.05	.02	.00
☐ 572 Jerry Royster	.05	.02	.00	☐ 615 Garry Templeton ..	.08	.03	.01
☐ 573 Dave Kingman	.15	.06	.01	☐ 616 Don Robinson	.05	.02	.00
☐ 574 Brian Downing	.08	.03	.01	☐ 617 Rick Cerone	.05	.02	.00
☐ 575 Jim Clancy	.08	.03	.01	☐ 618 Dickie Noles	.05	.02	.00
☐ 576 Giants TL	.10	.03	.01	☐ 619 Jerry Dybzinski ...	.05	.02	.00
Jeff Leonard				☐ 620 Al Oliver	.10	.04	.01
Atlee Hammaker				☐ 621 Frank Howard MG .	.05	.02	.00
☐ 577 Mark Clear	.05	.02	.00	☐ 622 Al Cowens	.05	.02	.00
☐ 578 Lenn Sakata	.05	.02	.00	☐ 623 Ron Washington ..	.05	.02	.00
☐ 579 Bob James	.20	.08	.02	☐ 624 Terry Harper	.05	.02	.00
☐ 580 Lonnie Smith	.08	.03	.01	☐ 625 Larry Gura	.05	.02	.00
☐ 581 Jose DeLeon	.25	.10	.02	☐ 626 Bob Clark	.05	.02	.00
☐ 582 Bob McClure	.05	.02	.00	☐ 627 Dave LaPoint	.08	.03	.01
☐ 583 Derrel Thomas	.05	.02	.00	☐ 628 Ed Jurak	.05	.02	.00
☐ 584 Dave Schmidt	.08	.03	.01	☐ 629 Rick Langford	.05	.02	.00
☐ 585 Dan Driessen	.05	.02	.00	☐ 630 Ted Simmons	.12	.05	.01
☐ 586 Joe Niekro	.10	.04	.01	☐ 631 Dennis Martinez ..	.08	.03	.01
☐ 587 Von Hayes	.18	.08	.01	☐ 632 Tom Foley	.05	.02	.00
☐ 588 Milt Wilcox	.05	.02	.00	☐ 633 Mike Krukow	.08	.03	.01
☐ 589 Mike Easler	.05	.02	.00	☐ 634 Mike Marshall	.15	.06	.01
☐ 590 Dave Stieb	.15	.06	.01	☐ 635 Dave Righetti	.18	.08	.01
☐ 591 Tony LaRussa MG .	.05	.02	.00	☐ 636 Pat Putnam	.05	.02	.00
☐ 592 Andre Robertson ...	.05	.02	.00	☐ 637 Phillies TL	.10	.03	.01
☐ 593 Jeff Lahti	.05	.02	.00	Gary Matthews			
☐ 594 Gene Richards	.05	.02	.00	John Denny			
☐ 595 Jeff Reardon	.10	.04	.01	☐ 638 George Vukovich ..	.05	.02	.00
☐ 596 Ryne Sandberg	1.00	.40	.10	☐ 639 Rick Lysander	.05	.02	.00
☐ 597 Rick Camp	.05	.02	.00	☐ 640 Lance Parrish	.25	.10	.02
☐ 598 Rusty Kuntz	.05	.02	.00	☐ 641 Mike Richardt	.05	.02	.00
☐ 599 Doug Sisk	.08	.03	.01	☐ 642 Tom Underwood ...	.05	.02	.00
☐ 600 Rod Carew	.45	.18	.04	☐ 643 Mike Brown	.08	.03	.01
☐ 601 John Tudor	.15	.06	.01	(Angels OF)			
☐ 602 John Wathan	.05	.02	.00	☐ 644 Tim Lollar	.05	.02	.00
☐ 603 Renie Martin	.05	.02	.00	☐ 645 Tony Pena	.12	.05	.01
☐ 604 John Lowenstein ...	.05	.02	.00	☐ 646 Checklist 529-660	.08	.01	.00
☐ 605 Mike Caldwell	.05	.02	.00	☐ 647 Ron Roenicke	.05	.02	.00
				☐ 648 Len Whitehouse ..	.05	.02	.00
				☐ 649 Tom Herr	.08	.03	.01

		MINT	EXC	G-VG
☐ 650	Phil Niekro	.20	.08	.02
☐ 651	John McNamara MG	.05	.02	.00
☐ 652	Rudy May	.05	.02	.00
☐ 653	Dave Stapleton	.05	.02	.00
☐ 654	Bob Bailor	.05	.02	.00
☐ 655	Amos Otis	.08	.03	.01
☐ 656	Bryn Smith	.08	.03	.01
☐ 657	Thad Bosley	.05	.02	.00
☐ 658	Jerry Augustine	.05	.02	.00
☐ 659	Duane Walker	.05	.02	.00
☐ 660	Ray Knight	.10	.04	.01
☐ 661	Steve Yeager	.05	.02	.00
☐ 662	Tom Brennan	.05	.02	.00
☐ 663	Johnnie LeMaster	.05	.02	.00
☐ 664	Dave Stegman	.05	.02	.00
☐ 665	Buddy Bell	.12	.05	.01
☐ 666	Detroit Tigers TL	.12	.03	.01
	Lou Whitaker			
	Jack Morris			
☐ 667	Vance Law	.08	.03	.01
☐ 668	Larry McWilliams	.05	.02	.00
☐ 669	Dave Lopes	.08	.03	.01
☐ 670	Rich Gossage	.15	.06	.01
☐ 671	Jamie Quirk	.05	.02	.00
☐ 672	Ricky Nelson	.05	.02	.00
☐ 673	Mike Walters	.05	.02	.00
☐ 674	Tim Flannery	.05	.02	.00
☐ 675	Pascual Perez	.10	.04	.01
☐ 676	Brian Giles	.05	.02	.00
☐ 677	Doyle Alexander	.08	.03	.01
☐ 678	Chris Speier	.05	.02	.00
☐ 679	Art Howe	.08	.03	.01
☐ 680	Fred Lynn	.20	.08	.02
☐ 681	Tom Lasorda MG	.08	.03	.01
☐ 682	Dan Morogiello	.05	.02	.00
☐ 683	Marty Barrett	1.75	.70	.17
☐ 684	Bob Shirley	.05	.02	.00
☐ 685	Willie Aikens	.05	.02	.00
☐ 686	Joe Price	.05	.02	.00
☐ 687	Roy Howell	.05	.02	.00
☐ 688	George Wright	.05	.02	.00
☐ 689	Mike Fischlin	.05	.02	.00
☐ 690	Jack Clark	.30	.12	.03
☐ 691	Steve Lake	.05	.02	.00
☐ 692	Dickie Thon	.05	.02	.00
☐ 693	Alan Wiggins	.05	.02	.00
☐ 694	Mike Stanton	.05	.02	.00
☐ 695	Lou Whitaker	.18	.08	.01

		MINT	EXC	G-VG
☐ 696	Pirates TL	.10	.03	.01
	Bill Madlock			
	Rick Rhoden			
☐ 697	Dale Murray	.05	.02	.00
☐ 698	Marc Hill	.05	.02	.00
☐ 699	Dave Rucker	.05	.02	.00
☐ 700	Mike Schmidt	.60	.24	.06
☐ 701	NL Active Batting	.20	.08	.02
	Bill Madlock			
	Pete Rose			
	Dave Parker			
☐ 702	NL Active Hits	.20	.08	.02
	Pete Rose			
	Rusty Staub			
	Tony Perez			
☐ 703	NL Active Home Run	.15	.06	.01
	Mike Schmidt			
	Tony Perez			
	Dave Kingman			
☐ 704	NL Active RBI	.10	.04	.01
	Tony Perez			
	Rusty Staub			
	Al Oliver			
☐ 705	NL Active Steals	.10	.04	.01
	Joe Morgan			
	Cesar Cedeno			
	Larry Bowa			
☐ 706	NL Active Victory	.20	.08	.02
	Steve Carlton			
	Fergie Jenkins			
	Tom Seaver			
☐ 707	NL Active Strikeout	.20	.08	.02
	Steve Carlton			
	Nolan Ryan			
	Tom Seaver			
☐ 708	NL Active ERA	.18	.08	.01
	Tom Seaver			
	Steve Carlton			
	Steve Rogers			
☐ 709	NL Active Save	.10	.04	.01
	Bruce Sutter			
	Tug McGraw			
	Gene Garber			
☐ 710	AL Active Batting	.20	.08	.02
	Rod Carew			
	George Brett			
	Cecil Cooper			

	MINT	EXC	G-VG			MINT	EXC	G-VG
☐ 711 AL Active Hits	.18	.08	.01	☐ 734 Odell Jones	.05	.02	.00
Rod Carew				☐ 735 Rick Burleson	.08	.03	.01
Bert Campaneris				☐ 736 Dick Ruthven	.05	.02	.00
Reggie Jackson				☐ 737 Jim Essian	.05	.02	.00
☐ 712 AL Active Home Run	.15	.06	.01	☐ 738 Bill Schroeder	.10	.04	.01
Reggie Jackson				☐ 739 Bob Watson	.08	.03	.01
Graig Nettles				☐ 740 Tom Seaver	.40	.16	.04
Greg Luzinski				☐ 741 Wayne Gross	.05	.02	.00
☐ 713 AL Active RBI	.15	.06	.01	☐ 742 Dick Williams MG	.05	.02	.00
Reggie Jackson				☐ 743 Don Hood	.05	.02	.00
Ted Simmons				☐ 744 Jamie Allen	.05	.02	.00
Graig Nettles				☐ 745 Dennis Eckersley	.15	.06	.01
☐ 714 AL Active Steals	.08	.03	.01	☐ 746 Mickey Hatcher	.08	.03	.01
Bert Campaneris				☐ 747 Pat Zachry	.05	.02	.00
Dave Lopes				☐ 748 Jeff Leonard	.10	.04	.01
Omar Moreno				☐ 749 Doug Flynn	.05	.02	.00
☐ 715 AL Active Victory	.18	.08	.01	☐ 750 Jim Palmer	.35	.14	.03
Jim Palmer				☐ 751 Charlie Moore	.05	.02	.00
Don Sutton				☐ 752 Phil Garner	.05	.02	.00
Tommy John				☐ 753 Doug Gwosdz	.05	.02	.00
☐ 716 AL Active Strikeout	.08	.03	.01	☐ 754 Kent Tekulve	.08	.03	.01
Don Sutton				☐ 755 Garry Maddox	.08	.03	.01
Bert Blyleven				☐ 756 Reds TL	.10	.03	.01
Jerry Koosman				Ron Oester			
☐ 717 AL Active ERA	.15	.06	.01	Mario Soto			
Jim Palmer				☐ 757 Larry Bowa	.10	.04	.01
Rollie Fingers				☐ 758 Bill Stein	.05	.02	.00
Ron Guidry				☐ 759 Richard Dotson	.08	.03	.01
☐ 718 AL Active Save	.12	.05	.01	☐ 760 Bob Horner	.18	.08	.01
Rollie Fingers				☐ 761 John Montefusco	.05	.02	.00
Rich Gossage				☐ 762 Rance Mulliniks	.05	.02	.00
Dan Quisenberry				☐ 763 Craig Swan	.05	.02	.00
☐ 719 Andy Hassler	.05	.02	.00	☐ 764 Mike Hargrove	.05	.02	.00
☐ 720 Dwight Evans	.15	.06	.01	☐ 765 Ken Forsch	.05	.02	.00
☐ 721 Del Crandall MG	.05	.02	.00	☐ 766 Mike Vail	.05	.02	.00
☐ 722 Bob Welch	.08	.03	.01	☐ 767 Carney Lansford	.10	.04	.01
☐ 723 Rich Dauer	.05	.02	.00	☐ 768 Champ Summers	.05	.02	.00
☐ 724 Eric Rasmussen	.05	.02	.00	☐ 769 Bill Caudill	.05	.02	.00
☐ 725 Cesar Cedeno	.08	.03	.01	☐ 770 Ken Griffey	.08	.03	.01
☐ 726 Brewers TL	.10	.03	.01	☐ 771 Billy Gardner MG	.05	.02	.00
Ted Simmons				☐ 772 Jim Slaton	.05	.02	.00
Moose Haas				☐ 773 Todd Cruz	.05	.02	.00
☐ 727 Joel Youngblood	.05	.02	.00	☐ 774 Tom Gorman	.08	.03	.01
☐ 728 Tug McGraw	.10	.04	.01	☐ 775 Dave Parker	.18	.08	.01
☐ 729 Gene Tenace	.08	.03	.01	☐ 776 Craig Reynolds	.05	.02	.00
☐ 730 Bruce Sutter	.12	.05	.01	☐ 777 Tom Paciorek	.05	.02	.00
☐ 731 Lynn Jones	.05	.02	.00	☐ 778 Andy Hawkins	.40	.16	.04
☐ 732 Terry Crowley	.05	.02	.00	☐ 779 Jim Sundberg	.08	.03	.01
☐ 733 Dave Collins	.05	.02	.00	☐ 780 Steve Carlton	.35	.14	.03

		MINT	EXC	G-VG
☐	781 Checklist 661-792 ..	.08	.01	.00
☐	782 Steve Balboni	.08	.03	.01
☐	783 Luis Leal	.05	.02	.00
☐	784 Leon Roberts	.05	.02	.00
☐	785 Joaquin Andujar ...	.10	.04	.01
☐	786 Red Sox TL	.25	.08	.01
	Wade Boggs			
	Bob Ojeda			
☐	787 Bill Campbell	.05	.02	.00
☐	788 Milt May	.05	.02	.00
☐	789 Bert Blyleven	.12	.05	.01
☐	790 Doug DeCinces	.08	.03	.01
☐	791 Terry Forster	.08	.03	.01
☐	792 Bill Russell	.15	.04	.01

1984 Topps Traded

*The cards in this 132-card set measure 2 ½"
by 3 ½". In its now standard procedure,
Topps issued its Traded (or extended) set for
the fourth year in a row. Because all photos
and statistics of its regular set for the year
were developed during the fall and winter
months of the preceding year, players who
changed teams during the fall, winter, and
spring months are portrayed with the teams
they were with in 1983. The Traded set
amends the shortcomings of the regular set
by presenting the players with their proper
teams for the current year. Rookies not contained in the regular set are also picked up
in the Traded set. Again this year, the Topps
affiliate in Ireland printed the cards, and the*

*cards were available through hobby chan-
nels only.*

		MINT	EXC	G-VG
	Complete Set (132)	85.00	34.00	8.50
	Common Player (1-132) ..	.10	.04	.01
☐	1T Willie Aikens	.10	.04	.01
☐	2T Luis Aponte	.10	.04	.01
☐	3T Mike Armstrong ...	.10	.04	.01
☐	4T Bob Bailor	.10	.04	.01
☐	5T Dusty Baker	.20	.08	.02
☐	6T Steve Balboni	.20	.08	.02
☐	7T Alan Bannister ...	.10	.04	.01
☐	8T Dave Beard	.10	.04	.01
☐	9T Joe Beckwith	.10	.04	.01
☐	10T Bruce Berenyi	.10	.04	.01
☐	11T Dave Bergman	.10	.04	.01
☐	12T Tony Bernazard ...	.10	.04	.01
☐	13T Yogi Berra MG	.40	.16	.04
☐	14T Barry Bonnell	.10	.04	.01
☐	15T Phil Bradley	1.75	.70	.17
☐	16T Fred Breining	.10	.04	.01
☐	17T Bill Buckner	.30	.12	.03
☐	18T Ray Burris	.10	.04	.01
☐	19T John Butcher	.10	.04	.01
☐	20T Brett Butler	.30	.12	.03
☐	21T Enos Cabell	.10	.04	.01
☐	22T Bill Campbell	.10	.04	.01
☐	23T Bill Caudill	.10	.04	.01
☐	24T Bob Clark	.10	.04	.01
☐	25T Bryan Clark	.10	.04	.01
☐	26T Jaime Cocanower ..	.20	.08	.02
☐	27T Ron Darling	6.00	2.40	.60
☐	28T Alvin Davis	4.00	1.60	.40
☐	29T Ken Dayley	.20	.08	.02
☐	30T Jeff Dedmon	.20	.08	.02
☐	31T Bob Dernier	.20	.08	.02
☐	32T Carlos Diaz	.10	.04	.01
☐	33T Mike Easler	.10	.04	.01
☐	34T Dennis Eckersley ..	.50	.20	.05
☐	35T Jim Essian	.10	.04	.01
☐	36T Darrell Evans	.30	.12	.03
☐	37T Mike Fitzgerald ...	.20	.08	.02
☐	38T Tim Foli	.10	.04	.01
☐	39T George Frazier	.10	.04	.01
☐	40T Rich Gale	.10	.04	.01
☐	41T Barbaro Garbey ...	.20	.08	.02
☐	42T Dwight Gooden	40.00	16.00	4.00
☐	43T Rich Gossage	.30	.12	.03
☐	44T Wayne Gross	.10	.04	.01

	MINT	EXC	G-VG		MINT	EXC	G-VG
☐ 45T Mark Gubicza	2.00	.80	.20	☐ 94T Rob Picciolo	.10	.04	.01
☐ 46T Jackie Gutierrez	.20	.08	.02	☐ 95T Vern Rapp MG	.10	.04	.01
☐ 47T Mel Hall	.30	.12	.03	☐ 96T Floyd Rayford	.10	.04	.01
☐ 48T Toby Harrah	.20	.08	.02	☐ 97T Randy Ready	.35	.14	.03
☐ 49T Ron Hassey	.20	.08	.02	☐ 98T Ron Reed	.10	.04	.01
☐ 50T Rich Hebner	.10	.04	.01	☐ 99T Gene Richards	.10	.04	.01
☐ 51T Willie Hernandez	.30	.12	.03	☐ 100T Jose Rijo	1.00	.40	.10
☐ 52T Ricky Horton	.40	.16	.04	☐ 101T Jeff Robinson	.40	.16	.04
☐ 53T Art Howe	.20	.08	.02	(Giants pitcher)			
☐ 54T Dane Iorg	.10	.04	.01	☐ 102T Ron Romanick	.20	.08	.02
☐ 55T Brook Jacoby	1.50	.60	.15	☐ 103T Pete Rose	7.00	2.80	.70
☐ 56T Mike Jeffcoat	.20	.08	.02	☐ 104T Bret Saberhagen	8.00	3.25	.80
☐ 57T Dave Johnson MG	.30	.12	.03	☐ 105T Juan Samuel	3.00	1.20	.30
☐ 58T Lynn Jones	.10	.04	.01	☐ 106T Scott Sanderson	.10	.04	.01
☐ 59T Ruppert Jones	.10	.04	.01	☐ 107T Dick Schofield	.60	.24	.06
☐ 60T Mike Jorgensen	.10	.04	.01	☐ 108T Tom Seaver	3.00	1.20	.30
☐ 61T Bob Kearney	.10	.04	.01	☐ 109T Jim Slaton	.10	.04	.01
☐ 62T Jimmy Key	3.00	1.20	.30	☐ 110T Mike Smithson	.10	.04	.01
☐ 63T Dave Kingman	.30	.12	.03	☐ 111T Lary Sorensen	.10	.04	.01
☐ 64T Jerry Koosman	.20	.08	.02	☐ 112T Tim Stoddard	.10	.04	.01
☐ 65T Wayne Krenchicki	.10	.04	.01	☐ 113T Champ Summers	.10	.04	.01
☐ 66T Rusty Kuntz	.10	.04	.01	☐ 114T Jim Sundberg	.20	.08	.02
☐ 67T Rene Lachemann MG	.10	.04	.01	☐ 115T Rick Sutcliffe	.45	.18	.04
☐ 68T Frank LaCorte	.10	.04	.01	☐ 116T Craig Swan	.10	.04	.01
☐ 69T Dennis Lamp	.10	.04	.01	☐ 117T Tim Teufel	.35	.14	.03
☐ 70T Mark Langston	3.50	1.40	.35	☐ 118T Derrel Thomas	.10	.04	.01
☐ 71T Rick Leach	.10	.04	.01	☐ 119T Gorman Thomas	.30	.12	.03
☐ 72T Craig Lefferts	.10	.04	.01	☐ 120T Alex Trevino	.10	.04	.01
☐ 73T Gary Lucas	.10	.04	.01	☐ 121T Manny Trillo	.10	.04	.01
☐ 74T Jerry Martin	.10	.04	.01	☐ 122T John Tudor	.40	.16	.04
☐ 75T Carmelo Martinez	.20	.08	.02	☐ 123T Tom Underwood	.10	.04	.01
☐ 76T Mike Mason	.20	.08	.02	☐ 124T Mike Vail	.10	.04	.01
☐ 77T Gary Matthews	.20	.08	.02	☐ 125T Tom Waddell	.20	.08	.02
☐ 78T Andy McGaffigan	.10	.04	.01	☐ 126T Gary Ward	.20	.08	.02
☐ 79T Larry Milbourne	.10	.04	.01	☐ 127T Curt Wilkerson	.20	.08	.02
☐ 80T Sid Monge	.10	.04	.01	☐ 128T Frank Williams	.30	.12	.03
☐ 81T Jackie Moore MG	.10	.04	.01	☐ 129T Glenn Wilson	.20	.08	.02
☐ 82T Joe Morgan	1.00	.40	.10	☐ 130T John Wockenfuss	.10	.04	.01
☐ 83T Graig Nettles	.40	.16	.04	☐ 131T Ned Yost	.10	.04	.01
☐ 84T Phil Niekro	1.00	.40	.10	☐ 132T Checklist: 1-132	.10	.01	.00
☐ 85T Ken Oberkfell	.10	.04	.01				
☐ 86T Mike O'Berry	.10	.04	.01				
☐ 87T Al Oliver	.20	.08	.02				
☐ 88T Jorge Orta	.10	.04	.01				
☐ 89T Amos Otis	.20	.08	.02				
☐ 90T Dave Parker	.70	.28	.07				
☐ 91T Tony Perez	.60	.24	.06				
☐ 92T Gerald Perry	1.50	.60	.15				
☐ 93T Gary Pettis	.40	.16	.04				

1985 Topps

The cards in this 792-card set measure 2 ½ " by 3 ½". The 1985 Topps set contains full color cards. The fronts feature both the Topps and team logos along with the team name, player's name, and his position. The backs feature player statistics with ink colors of light green and maroon on a gray stock. A trivia quiz is included on the lower portion of the backs. The first ten cards (1-10) are Record Breakers (RB), cards 131-143 are Father and Son (FS) cards, and cards 701 to 722 portray All-Star selections (AS). Cards 271 to 282 represent "First Draft Picks" still active in the Major Leagues and cards 389-404 feature the coach and players on the 1984 U.S. Olympic Baseball Team. The manager cards in the set are important in that they contain the checklist of that team's players on the back. Topps also produced a specially boxed "glossy" edition frequently referred to as the Topps Tiffany set. There were supposedly only 5,000 sets of the Tiffany cards produced; they were marketed to hobby dealers. The checklist of cards (792 regular and 132 Traded) is identical to that of the normal non-glossy cards. There are two primary distinguishing features of the Tiffany cards, white card stock reverses and high gloss obverses. These Tiffany cards are valued at approximately six times the values listed below.

	MINT	EXC	G-VG
Complete Set (792)	100.00	40.00	10.00
Common Player (1-792) ...	.04	.02	.00

			MINT	EXC	G-VG
☐	1	Carlton Fisk RB ... Longest game by catcher	.15	.04	.01
☐	2	Steve Garvey RB . Consecutive errorless games, 1B	.20	.08	.02
☐	3	Dwight Gooden RB Most strikeouts, rookie, season	.75	.30	.07
☐	4	Cliff Johnson RB .. Most pinch homers, lifetime	.04	.02	.00
☐	5	Joe Morgan RB ... Most homers, 2B, lifetime	.10	.04	.01
☐	6	Pete Rose RB .... Most singles, lifetime	.50	.20	.05
☐	7	Nolan Ryan RB ... Most strikeouts, lifetime	.20	.08	.02
☐	8	Juan Samuel RB .. Most stolen bases, rookie, season	.15	.06	.01
☐	9	Bruce Sutter RB .. Most saves, season, NL	.07	.03	.01
☐	10	Don Sutton RB ... Most seasons, 100 or more K's	.10	.04	.01
☐	11	Ralph Houk MG ... (checklist back)	.07	.02	.00
☐	12	Dave Lopes	.07	.03	.01
☐	13	Tim Lollar	.04	.02	.00
☐	14	Chris Bando	.04	.02	.00
☐	15	Jerry Koosman ...	.07	.03	.01
☐	16	Bobby Meacham ..	.04	.02	.00
☐	17	Mike Scott	.30	.12	.03
☐	18	Mickey Hatcher ...	.07	.03	.01
☐	19	George Frazier ...	.04	.02	.00
☐	20	Chet Lemon	.07	.03	.01
☐	21	Lee Tunnell	.04	.02	.00
☐	22	Duane Kuiper	.04	.02	.00
☐	23	Bret Saberhagen ..	2.50	1.00	.25
☐	24	Jesse Barfield ...	.25	.10	.02
☐	25	Steve Bedrosian ..	.12	.05	.01
☐	26	Roy Smalley	.04	.02	.00
☐	27	Bruce Berenyi ...	.04	.02	.00
☐	28	Dann Bilardello ..	.04	.02	.00
☐	29	Odell Jones	.04	.02	.00

		MINT	EXC	G-VG			MINT	EXC	G-VG
☐ 30	Cal Ripken	.50	.20	.05	☐ 77	Joe Beckwith	.04	.02	.00
☐ 31	Terry Whitfield	.04	.02	.00	☐ 78	Scott Fletcher	.07	.03	.01
☐ 32	Chuck Porter	.04	.02	.00	☐ 79	Rick Mahler	.04	.02	.00
☐ 33	Tito Landrum	.04	.02	.00	☐ 80	Keith Hernandez	.30	.12	.03
☐ 34	Ed Nunez	.07	.03	.01	☐ 81	Lenn Sakata	.04	.02	.00
☐ 35	Graig Nettles	.10	.04	.01	☐ 82	Joe Price	.04	.02	.00
☐ 36	Fred Breining	.04	.02	.00	☐ 83	Charlie Moore	.04	.02	.00
☐ 37	Reid Nichols	.04	.02	.00	☐ 84	Spike Owen	.04	.02	.00
☐ 38	Jackie Moore MG	.07	.02	.00	☐ 85	Mike Marshall	.12	.05	.01
	(checklist back)				☐ 86	Don Aase	.04	.02	.00
☐ 39	John Wockenfuss	.04	.02	.00	☐ 87	David Green	.04	.02	.00
☐ 40	Phil Niekro	.18	.08	.01	☐ 88	Bryn Smith	.04	.02	.00
☐ 41	Mike Fischlin	.04	.02	.00	☐ 89	Jackie Gutierrez	.07	.03	.01
☐ 42	Luis Sanchez	.04	.02	.00	☐ 90	Rich Gossage	.12	.05	.01
☐ 43	Andre David	.07	.03	.01	☐ 91	Jeff Burroughs	.04	.02	.00
☐ 44	Dickie Thon	.04	.02	.00	☐ 92	Paul Owens MG	.07	.02	.00
☐ 45	Greg Minton	.04	.02	.00		(checklist back)			
☐ 46	Gary Woods	.04	.02	.00	☐ 93	Don Schulze	.04	.02	.00
☐ 47	Dave Rozema	.04	.02	.00	☐ 94	Toby Harrah	.04	.02	.00
☐ 48	Tony Fernandez	1.25	.50	.12	☐ 95	Jose Cruz	.10	.04	.01
☐ 49	Butch Davis	.07	.03	.01	☐ 96	Johnny Ray	.10	.04	.01
☐ 50	John Candelaria	.07	.03	.01	☐ 97	Pete Filson	.04	.02	.00
☐ 51	Bob Watson	.07	.03	.01	☐ 98	Steve Lake	.04	.02	.00
☐ 52	Jerry Dybzinski	.04	.02	.00	☐ 99	Milt Wilcox	.04	.02	.00
☐ 53	Tom Gorman	.04	.02	.00	☐ 100	George Brett	.50	.20	.05
☐ 54	Cesar Cedeno	.07	.03	.01	☐ 101	Jim Acker	.04	.02	.00
☐ 55	Frank Tanana	.07	.03	.01	☐ 102	Tommy Dunbar	.04	.02	.00
☐ 56	Jim Dwyer	.04	.02	.00	☐ 103	Randy Lerch	.04	.02	.00
☐ 57	Pat Zachry	.04	.02	.00	☐ 104	Mike Fitzgerald	.04	.02	.00
☐ 58	Orlando Mercado	.04	.02	.00	☐ 105	Ron Kittle	.12	.05	.01
☐ 59	Rick Waits	.04	.02	.00	☐ 106	Pascual Perez	.07	.03	.01
☐ 60	George Hendrick	.07	.03	.01	☐ 107	Tom Foley	.04	.02	.00
☐ 61	Curt Kaufman	.07	.03	.01	☐ 108	Darnell Coles	.10	.04	.01
☐ 62	Mike Ramsey	.04	.02	.00	☐ 109	Gary Roenicke	.04	.02	.00
☐ 63	Steve McCatty	.04	.02	.00	☐ 110	Alejandro Pena	.07	.03	.01
☐ 64	Mark Bailey	.07	.03	.01	☐ 111	Doug DeCinces	.07	.03	.01
☐ 65	Bill Buckner	.10	.04	.01	☐ 112	Tom Tellmann	.04	.02	.00
☐ 66	Dick Williams MG	.07	.02	.00	☐ 113	Tom Herr	.07	.03	.01
	(checklist back)				☐ 114	Bob James	.04	.02	.00
☐ 67	Rafael Santana	.25	.10	.02	☐ 115	Rickey Henderson	.45	.18	.04
☐ 68	Von Hayes	.15	.06	.01	☐ 116	Dennis Boyd	.20	.08	.02
☐ 69	Jim Winn	.07	.03	.01	☐ 117	Greg Gross	.04	.02	.00
☐ 70	Don Baylor	.10	.04	.01	☐ 118	Eric Show	.07	.03	.01
☐ 71	Tim Laudner	.04	.02	.00	☐ 119	Pat Corrales MG	.07	.02	.00
☐ 72	Rick Sutcliffe	.12	.05	.01		(checklist back)			
☐ 73	Rusty Kuntz	.04	.02	.00	☐ 120	Steve Kemp	.07	.03	.01
☐ 74	Mike Krukow	.04	.02	.00	☐ 121	Checklist: 1-132	.07	.01	.00
☐ 75	Willie Upshaw	.04	.02	.00	☐ 122	Tom Brunansky	.18	.08	.01
☐ 76	Alan Bannister	.04	.02	.00	☐ 123	Dave Smith	.07	.03	.01

		MINT	EXC	G-VG
☐ 124	Rich Hebner	.04	.02	.00
☐ 125	Kent Tekulve	.07	.03	.01
☐ 126	Ruppert Jones	.04	.02	.00
☐ 127	Mark Gubicza	.75	.30	.07
☐ 128	Ernie Whitt	.04	.02	.00
☐ 129	Gene Garber	.04	.02	.00
☐ 130	Al Oliver	.10	.04	.01
☐ 131	Buddy/Gus Bell FS	.07	.03	.01
☐ 132	Dale/Yogi Berra FS	.12	.05	.01
☐ 133	Bob/Ray Boone FS	.07	.03	.01
☐ 134	Terry/Tito Francona FS	.07	.03	.01
☐ 135	Terry/Bob Kennedy FS	.07	.03	.01
☐ 136	Jeff/Jim Kunkel FS	.07	.03	.01
☐ 137	Vance/Vern Law FS	.07	.03	.01
☐ 138	Dick/Dick Schofield FS	.07	.03	.01
☐ 139	Joel/Bob Skinner FS	.07	.03	.01
☐ 140	Roy/Roy Smalley FS	.07	.03	.01
☐ 141	Mike/D.Stenhouse FS	.07	.03	.01
☐ 142	Steve/Dizzy Trout FS	.07	.03	.01
☐ 143	Ozzie/Ozzie Virgil FS	.07	.03	.01
☐ 144	Ron Gardenhire	.04	.02	.00
☐ 145	Alvin Davis	1.50	.60	.15
☐ 146	Gary Redus	.04	.02	.00
☐ 147	Bill Swaggerty	.04	.02	.00
☐ 148	Steve Yeager	.04	.02	.00
☐ 149	Dickie Noles	.04	.02	.00
☐ 150	Jim Rice	.25	.10	.02
☐ 151	Moose Haas	.04	.02	.00
☐ 152	Steve Braun	.04	.02	.00
☐ 153	Frank LaCorte	.04	.02	.00
☐ 154	Argenis Salazar	.04	.02	.00
☐ 155	Yogi Berra MG (checklist back)	.12	.04	.01
☐ 156	Craig Reynolds	.04	.02	.00
☐ 157	Tug McGraw	.10	.04	.01
☐ 158	Pat Tabler	.07	.03	.01
☐ 159	Carlos Diaz	.04	.02	.00
☐ 160	Lance Parrish	.18	.08	.01
☐ 161	Ken Schrom	.04	.02	.00
☐ 162	Benny Distefano	.10	.04	.01
☐ 163	Dennis Eckersley	.15	.06	.01
☐ 164	Jorge Orta	.04	.02	.00
☐ 165	Dusty Baker	.07	.03	.01
☐ 166	Keith Atherton	.04	.02	.00
☐ 167	Rufino Linares	.04	.02	.00
☐ 168	Garth Iorg	.04	.02	.00
☐ 169	Dan Spillner	.04	.02	.00
☐ 170	George Foster	.10	.04	.01
☐ 171	Bill Stein	.04	.02	.00
☐ 172	Jack Perconte	.04	.02	.00
☐ 173	Mike Young	.10	.04	.01
☐ 174	Rick Honeycutt	.04	.02	.00
☐ 175	Dave Parker	.15	.06	.01
☐ 176	Bill Schroeder	.04	.02	.00
☐ 177	Dave Von Ohlen	.04	.02	.00
☐ 178	Miguel Dilone	.04	.02	.00
☐ 179	Tommy John	.15	.06	.01
☐ 180	Dave Winfield	.35	.14	.03
☐ 181	Roger Clemens	10.00	4.00	1.00
☐ 182	Tim Flannery	.04	.02	.00
☐ 183	Larry McWilliams	.04	.02	.00
☐ 184	Carmen Castillo	.04	.02	.00
☐ 185	Al Holland	.04	.02	.00
☐ 186	Bob Lillis MG (checklist back)	.07	.02	.00
☐ 187	Mike Walters	.04	.02	.00
☐ 188	Greg Pryor	.04	.02	.00
☐ 189	Warren Brusstar	.04	.02	.00
☐ 190	Rusty Staub	.10	.04	.01
☐ 191	Steve Nicosia	.04	.02	.00
☐ 192	Howard Johnson	1.50	.60	.15
☐ 193	Jimmy Key	1.25	.50	.12
☐ 194	Dave Stegman	.04	.02	.00
☐ 195	Glenn Hubbard	.04	.02	.00
☐ 196	Pete O'Brien	.10	.04	.01
☐ 197	Mike Warren	.04	.02	.00
☐ 198	Eddie Milner	.04	.02	.00
☐ 199	Dennis Martinez	.07	.03	.01
☐ 200	Reggie Jackson	.45	.18	.04
☐ 201	Burt Hooton	.04	.02	.00
☐ 202	Gorman Thomas	.10	.04	.01
☐ 203	Bob McClure	.04	.02	.00
☐ 204	Art Howe	.07	.03	.01
☐ 205	Steve Rogers	.04	.02	.00
☐ 206	Phil Garner	.07	.02	.00
☐ 207	Mark Clear	.04	.02	.00
☐ 208	Champ Summers	.04	.02	.00
☐ 209	Bill Campbell	.04	.02	.00
☐ 210	Gary Matthews	.07	.03	.01
☐ 211	Clay Christiansen	.04	.02	.00
☐ 212	George Vukovich	.04	.02	.00
☐ 213	Billy Gardner MG (checklist back)	.07	.02	.00
☐ 214	John Tudor	.15	.06	.01
☐ 215	Bob Brenly	.04	.02	.00
☐ 216	Jerry Don Gleaton	.04	.02	.00
☐ 217	Leon Roberts	.04	.02	.00
☐ 218	Doyle Alexander	.07	.03	.01

		MINT	EXC	G-VG			MINT	EXC	G-VG
☐ 219	Gerald Perry	.45	.18	.04	☐ 266	Frank Viola	.30	.12	.03
☐ 220	Fred Lynn	.15	.06	.01	☐ 267	Henry Cotto	.10	.04	.01
☐ 221	Ron Reed	.04	.02	.00	☐ 268	Chuck Tanner MG	.07	.02	.00
☐ 222	Hubie Brooks	.10	.04	.01		(checklist back)			
☐ 223	Tom Hume	.04	.02	.00	☐ 269	Doug Baker	.04	.02	.00
☐ 224	Al Cowens	.04	.02	.00	☐ 270	Dan Quisenberry	.12	.05	.01
☐ 225	Mike Boddicker	.10	.04	.01	☐ 271	Tim Foli FDP68	.04	.02	.00
☐ 226	Juan Beniquez	.04	.02	.00	☐ 272	Jeff Burroughs FDP69	.04	.02	.00
☐ 227	Danny Darwin	.04	.02	.00	☐ 273	Bill Almon FDP74	.04	.02	.00
☐ 228	Dion James	.15	.06	.01	☐ 274	Floyd Bannister FDP76	.04	.02	.00
☐ 229	Dave LaPoint	.07	.03	.01	☐ 275	Harold Baines FDP77	.10	.04	.01
☐ 230	Gary Carter	.35	.14	.03	☐ 276	Bob Horner FDP78	.12	.05	.01
☐ 231	Dwayne Murphy	.04	.02	.00	☐ 277	Al Chambers FDP79	.04	.02	.00
☐ 232	Dave Beard	.04	.02	.00	☐ 278	D.Strawberry FDP80	.75	.30	.07
☐ 233	Ed Jurak	.04	.02	.00	☐ 279	Mike Moore FDP81	.07	.03	.01
☐ 234	Jerry Narron	.04	.02	.00	☐ 280	Sh.Dunston FDP82	.75	.30	.07
☐ 235	Garry Maddox	.07	.03	.01	☐ 281	Tim Belcher FDP83	.60	.24	.06
☐ 236	Mark Thurmond	.04	.02	.00	☐ 282	Shawn Abner FDP84	.45	.18	.04
☐ 237	Julio Franco	.12	.05	.01	☐ 283	Fran Mullins	.04	.02	.00
☐ 238	Jose Rijo	.35	.14	.03	☐ 284	Marty Bystrom	.04	.02	.00
☐ 239	Tim Teufel	.10	.04	.01	☐ 285	Dan Driessen	.04	.02	.00
☐ 240	Dave Stieb	.12	.05	.01	☐ 286	Rudy Law	.04	.02	.00
☐ 241	Jim Frey MG	.07	.02	.00	☐ 287	Walt Terrell	.04	.02	.00
	(checklist back)				☐ 288	Jeff Kunkel	.07	.03	.01
☐ 242	Greg Harris	.04	.02	.00	☐ 289	Tom Underwood	.04	.02	.00
☐ 243	Barbaro Garbey	.04	.02	.00	☐ 290	Cecil Cooper	.10	.04	.01
☐ 244	Mike Jones	.04	.02	.00	☐ 291	Bob Welch	.07	.03	.01
☐ 245	Chili Davis	.10	.04	.01	☐ 292	Brad Komminsk	.04	.02	.00
☐ 246	Mike Norris	.04	.02	.00	☐ 293	Curt Young	.35	.14	.03
☐ 247	Wayne Tolleson	.04	.02	.00	☐ 294	Tom Nieto	.04	.02	.00
☐ 248	Terry Forster	.07	.03	.01	☐ 295	Joe Niekro	.07	.03	.01
☐ 249	Harold Baines	.15	.06	.01	☐ 296	Ricky Nelson	.04	.02	.00
☐ 250	Jesse Orosco	.04	.02	.00	☐ 297	Gary Lucas	.04	.02	.00
☐ 251	Brad Gulden	.04	.02	.00	☐ 298	Marty Barrett	.12	.05	.01
☐ 252	Dan Ford	.04	.02	.00	☐ 299	Andy Hawkins	.07	.03	.01
☐ 253	Sid Bream	.30	.12	.03	☐ 300	Rod Carew	.35	.14	.03
☐ 254	Pete Vuckovich	.04	.02	.00	☐ 301	John Montefusco	.04	.02	.00
☐ 255	Lonnie Smith	.04	.02	.00	☐ 302	Tim Corcoran	.04	.02	.00
☐ 256	Mike Stanton	.04	.02	.00	☐ 303	Mike Jeffcoat	.04	.02	.00
☐ 257	Bryan Little	.04	.02	.00	☐ 304	Gary Gaetti	.30	.12	.03
☐ 258	Mike Brown	.04	.02	.00	☐ 305	Dale Berra	.04	.02	.00
	(Angels OF)				☐ 306	Rick Reuschel	.10	.04	.01
☐ 259	Gary Allenson	.04	.02	.00	☐ 307	Sparky Anderson MG	.07	.03	.01
☐ 260	Dave Righetti	.12	.05	.01		(checklist back)			
☐ 261	Checklist: 133-264	.07	.01	.00	☐ 308	John Wathan	.04	.02	.00
☐ 262	Greg Booker	.04	.02	.00	☐ 309	Mike Witt	.10	.04	.01
☐ 263	Mel Hall	.10	.04	.01	☐ 310	Manny Trillo	.04	.02	.00
☐ 264	Joe Sambito	.04	.02	.00	☐ 311	Jim Gott	.04	.02	.00
☐ 265	Juan Samuel	.50	.20	.05	☐ 312	Marc Hill	.04	.02	.00

		MINT	EXC	G-VG
☐ 313	Dave Schmidt	.07	.03	.01
☐ 314	Ron Oester	.04	.02	.00
☐ 315	Doug Sisk	.04	.02	.00
☐ 316	John Lowenstein	.04	.02	.00
☐ 317	Jack Lazorko	.04	.02	.00
☐ 318	Ted Simmons	.10	.04	.01
☐ 319	Jeff Jones	.04	.02	.00
☐ 320	Dale Murphy	.60	.24	.06
☐ 321	Ricky Horton	.25	.10	.02
☐ 322	Dave Stapleton	.04	.02	.00
☐ 323	Andy McGaffigan	.04	.02	.00
☐ 324	Bruce Bochy	.04	.02	.00
☐ 325	John Denny	.07	.03	.01
☐ 326	Kevin Bass	.10	.04	.01
☐ 327	Brook Jacoby	.25	.10	.02
☐ 328	Bob Shirley	.04	.02	.00
☐ 329	Ron Washington	.04	.02	.00
☐ 330	Leon Durham	.07	.03	.01
☐ 331	Bill Laskey	.04	.02	.00
☐ 332	Brian Harper	.04	.02	.00
☐ 333	Willie Hernandez	.10	.04	.01
☐ 334	Dick Howser MG	.07	.02	.00
	(checklist back)			
☐ 335	Bruce Benedict	.04	.02	.00
☐ 336	Rance Mulliniks	.04	.02	.00
☐ 337	Billy Sample	.04	.02	.00
☐ 338	Britt Burns	.04	.02	.00
☐ 339	Danny Heep	.04	.02	.00
☐ 340	Robin Yount	.35	.14	.03
☐ 341	Floyd Rayford	.04	.02	.00
☐ 342	Ted Power	.04	.02	.00
☐ 343	Bill Russell	.07	.03	.01
☐ 344	Dave Henderson	.10	.04	.01
☐ 345	Charlie Lea	.04	.02	.00
☐ 346	Terry Pendleton	.45	.18	.04
☐ 347	Rick Langford	.04	.02	.00
☐ 348	Bob Boone	.10	.04	.01
☐ 349	Domingo Ramos	.04	.02	.00
☐ 350	Wade Boggs	3.50	1.40	.35
☐ 351	Juan Agosto	.04	.02	.00
☐ 352	Joe Morgan	.18	.08	.01
☐ 353	Julio Solano	.04	.02	.00
☐ 354	Andre Robertson	.04	.02	.00
☐ 355	Bert Blyleven	.10	.04	.01
☐ 356	Dave Meier	.07	.03	.01
☐ 357	Rich Bordi	.04	.02	.00
☐ 358	Tony Pena	.10	.04	.01
☐ 359	Pat Sheridan	.04	.02	.00
☐ 360	Steve Carlton	.30	.12	.03

		MINT	EXC	G-VG
☐ 361	Alfredo Griffin	.07	.03	.01
☐ 362	Craig McMurtry	.04	.02	.00
☐ 363	Ron Hodges	.04	.02	.00
☐ 364	Richard Dotson	.07	.03	.01
☐ 365	Danny Ozark MG	.07	.01	.00
	(checklist back)			
☐ 366	Todd Cruz	.04	.02	.00
☐ 367	Keefe Cato	.04	.02	.00
☐ 368	Dave Bergman	.04	.02	.00
☐ 369	R.J. Reynolds	.20	.08	.02
☐ 370	Bruce Sutter	.12	.05	.01
☐ 371	Mickey Rivers	.07	.03	.01
☐ 372	Roy Howell	.04	.02	.00
☐ 373	Mike Moore	.07	.03	.01
☐ 374	Brian Downing	.07	.03	.01
☐ 375	Jeff Reardon	.10	.04	.01
☐ 376	Jeff Newman	.04	.02	.00
☐ 377	Checklist: 265-396	.07	.01	.00
☐ 378	Alan Wiggins	.04	.02	.00
☐ 379	Charles Hudson	.04	.02	.00
☐ 380	Ken Griffey	.07	.03	.01
☐ 381	Roy Smith	.04	.02	.00
☐ 382	Denny Walling	.04	.02	.00
☐ 383	Rick Lysander	.04	.02	.00
☐ 384	Jody Davis	.07	.03	.01
☐ 385	Jose DeLeon	.04	.02	.00
☐ 386	Dan Gladden	.35	.14	.03
☐ 387	Buddy Biancalana	.07	.03	.01
☐ 388	Bert Roberge	.04	.02	.00
☐ 389	Rod Dedeaux OLY CO	.04	.02	.00
☐ 390	Sid Akins OLY	.10	.04	.01
☐ 391	Flavio Alfaro OLY	.07	.03	.01
☐ 392	Don August OLY	.45	.18	.04
☐ 393	Scott Bankhead OLY	.30	.12	.03
☐ 394	Bob Caffrey OLY	.10	.04	.01
☐ 395	Mike Dunne OLY	.90	.36	.09
☐ 396	Gary Green OLY	.15	.06	.01
☐ 397	John Hoover OLY	.15	.06	.01
☐ 398	Shane Mack OLY	.45	.18	.04
☐ 399	John Marzano OLY	.35	.14	.03
☐ 400	Oddibe McDowell OLY	.65	.26	.06
☐ 401	Mark McGwire OLY	17.00	7.00	1.70
☐ 402	Pat Pacillo OLY	.25	.10	.02
☐ 403	Cory Snyder OLY	7.00	2.80	.70
☐ 404	Billy Swift OLY	.20	.08	.02
☐ 405	Tom Veryzer	.04	.02	.00
☐ 406	Len Whitehouse	.04	.02	.00
☐ 407	Bobby Ramos	.04	.02	.00
☐ 408	Sid Monge	.04	.02	.00

		MINT	EXC	G-VG
☐ 409	Brad Wellman	.04	.02	.00
☐ 410	Bob Horner	.15	.06	.01
☐ 411	Bobby Cox MG (checklist back)	.07	.01	.00
☐ 412	Bud Black	.04	.02	.00
☐ 413	Vance Law	.07	.03	.01
☐ 414	Gary Ward	.07	.03	.01
☐ 415	Ron Darling UER (no trivia answer)	1.00	.40	.10
☐ 416	Wayne Gross	.04	.02	.00
☐ 417	John Franco	.85	.34	.08
☐ 418	Ken Landreaux	.04	.02	.00
☐ 419	Mike Caldwell	.04	.02	.00
☐ 420	Andre Dawson	.30	.12	.03
☐ 421	Dave Rucker	.04	.02	.00
☐ 422	Carney Lansford	.10	.04	.01
☐ 423	Barry Bonnell	.04	.02	.00
☐ 424	Al Nipper	.15	.06	.01
☐ 425	Mike Hargrove	.04	.02	.00
☐ 426	Vern Ruhle	.04	.02	.00
☐ 427	Mario Ramirez	.04	.02	.00
☐ 428	Larry Andersen	.04	.02	.00
☐ 429	Rick Cerone	.04	.02	.00
☐ 430	Ron Davis	.04	.02	.00
☐ 431	U.L. Washington	.04	.02	.00
☐ 432	Thad Bosley	.04	.02	.00
☐ 433	Jim Morrison	.04	.02	.00
☐ 434	Gene Richards	.04	.02	.00
☐ 435	Dan Petry	.07	.03	.01
☐ 436	Willie Aikens	.04	.02	.00
☐ 437	Al Jones	.04	.02	.00
☐ 438	Joe Torre MG (checklist back)	.07	.01	.00
☐ 439	Junior Ortiz	.04	.02	.00
☐ 440	Fernando Valenzuela	.25	.10	.02
☐ 441	Duane Walker	.04	.02	.00
☐ 442	Ken Forsch	.04	.02	.00
☐ 443	George Wright	.04	.02	.00
☐ 444	Tony Phillips	.04	.02	.00
☐ 445	Tippy Martinez	.04	.02	.00
☐ 446	Jim Sundberg	.04	.02	.00
☐ 447	Jeff Lahti	.04	.02	.00
☐ 448	Derrel Thomas	.04	.02	.00
☐ 449	Phil Bradley	.65	.26	.06
☐ 450	Steve Garvey	.35	.14	.03
☐ 451	Bruce Hurst	.15	.06	.01
☐ 452	John Castino	.04	.02	.00
☐ 453	Tom Waddell	.07	.03	.01
☐ 454	Glenn Wilson	.07	.03	.01
☐ 455	Bob Knepper	.07	.03	.01
☐ 456	Tim Foli	.04	.02	.00
☐ 457	Cecilio Guante	.04	.02	.00
☐ 458	Randy Johnson	.04	.02	.00
☐ 459	Charlie Leibrandt	.04	.02	.00
☐ 460	Ryne Sandberg	.40	.16	.04
☐ 461	Marty Castillo	.04	.02	.00
☐ 462	Gary Lavelle	.04	.02	.00
☐ 463	Dave Collins	.04	.02	.00
☐ 464	Mike Mason	.07	.03	.01
☐ 465	Bob Grich	.07	.03	.01
☐ 466	Tony LaRussa MG (checklist back)	.07	.02	.00
☐ 467	Ed Lynch	.04	.02	.00
☐ 468	Wayne Krenchicki	.04	.02	.00
☐ 469	Sammy Stewart	.04	.02	.00
☐ 470	Steve Sax	.25	.10	.02
☐ 471	Pete Ladd	.04	.02	.00
☐ 472	Jim Essian	.04	.02	.00
☐ 473	Tim Wallach	.12	.05	.01
☐ 474	Kurt Kepshire	.07	.03	.01
☐ 475	Andre Thornton	.07	.03	.01
☐ 476	Jeff Stone	.15	.06	.01
☐ 477	Bob Ojeda	.10	.04	.01
☐ 478	Kurt Bevacqua	.04	.02	.00
☐ 479	Mike Madden	.04	.02	.00
☐ 480	Lou Whitaker	.15	.06	.01
☐ 481	Dale Murray	.04	.02	.00
☐ 482	Harry Spilman	.04	.02	.00
☐ 483	Mike Smithson	.04	.02	.00
☐ 484	Larry Bowa	.10	.04	.01
☐ 485	Matt Young	.04	.02	.00
☐ 486	Steve Balboni	.04	.02	.00
☐ 487	Frank Williams	.15	.06	.01
☐ 488	Joel Skinner	.07	.03	.01
☐ 489	Bryan Clark	.04	.02	.00
☐ 490	Jason Thompson	.04	.02	.00
☐ 491	Rick Camp	.04	.02	.00
☐ 492	Dave Johnson MG (checklist back)	.07	.02	.00
☐ 493	Orel Hershiser	6.50	2.60	.65
☐ 494	Rich Dauer	.04	.02	.00
☐ 495	Mario Soto	.04	.02	.00
☐ 496	Donnie Scott	.04	.02	.00
☐ 497	Gary Pettis (photo actually Gary's little brother, Lynn)	.25	.10	.02
☐ 498	Ed Romero	.04	.02	.00
☐ 499	Danny Cox	.20	.08	.02

	MINT	EXC	G-VG			MINT	EXC	G-VG
☐ 500 Mike Schmidt	.45	.18	.04	☐ 547 Pete Rose MG	.45	.12	.03
☐ 501 Dan Schatzeder	.04	.02	.00	(checklist back)			
☐ 502 Rick Miller	.04	.02	.00	☐ 548 Larry Parrish	.04	.02	.00
☐ 503 Tim Conroy	.04	.02	.00	☐ 549 Mike Scioscia	.07	.03	.01
☐ 504 Jerry Willard	.04	.02	.00	☐ 550 Scott McGregor	.07	.03	.01
☐ 505 Jim Beattie	.04	.02	.00	☐ 551 Andy Van Slyke	.35	.14	.03
☐ 506 Franklin Stubbs	.35	.14	.03	☐ 552 Chris Codiroli	.04	.02	.00
☐ 507 Ray Fontenot	.04	.02	.00	☐ 553 Bob Clark	.04	.02	.00
☐ 508 John Shelby	.04	.02	.00	☐ 554 Doug Flynn	.04	.02	.00
☐ 509 Milt May	.04	.02	.00	☐ 555 Bob Stanley	.04	.02	.00
☐ 510 Kent Hrbek	.25	.10	.02	☐ 556 Sixto Lezcano	.04	.02	.00
☐ 511 Lee Smith	.07	.03	.01	☐ 557 Len Barker	.04	.02	.00
☐ 512 Tom Brookens	.04	.02	.00	☐ 558 Carmelo Martinez	.04	.02	.00
☐ 513 Lynn Jones	.04	.02	.00	☐ 559 Jay Howell	.07	.03	.01
☐ 514 Jeff Cornell	.04	.02	.00	☐ 560 Bill Madlock	.07	.03	.01
☐ 515 Dave Concepcion	.07	.03	.01	☐ 561 Darryl Motley	.04	.02	.00
☐ 516 Roy Lee Jackson	.04	.02	.00	☐ 562 Houston Jimenez	.04	.02	.00
☐ 517 Jerry Martin	.04	.02	.00	☐ 563 Dick Ruthven	.04	.02	.00
☐ 518 Chris Chambliss	.07	.03	.01	☐ 564 Alan Ashby	.04	.02	.00
☐ 519 Doug Rader MG	.07	.02	.00	☐ 565 Kirk Gibson	.30	.12	.03
(checklist back)				☐ 566 Ed VandeBerg	.04	.02	.00
☐ 520 LaMarr Hoyt	.07	.03	.01	☐ 567 Joel Youngblood	.04	.02	.00
☐ 521 Rick Dempsey	.04	.02	.00	☐ 568 Cliff Johnson	.04	.02	.00
☐ 522 Paul Molitor	.15	.06	.01	☐ 569 Ken Oberkfell	.04	.02	.00
☐ 523 Candy Maldonado	.10	.04	.01	☐ 570 Darryl Strawberry	2.50	1.00	.25
☐ 524 Rob Wilfong	.04	.02	.00	☐ 571 Charlie Hough	.07	.03	.01
☐ 525 Darrell Porter	.04	.02	.00	☐ 572 Tom Paciorek	.04	.02	.00
☐ 526 David Palmer	.04	.02	.00	☐ 573 Jay Tibbs	.15	.06	.01
☐ 527 Checklist: 397-528	.07	.01	.00	☐ 574 Joe Altobelli MG	.07	.02	.00
☐ 528 Bill Krueger	.04	.02	.00	(checklist back)			
☐ 529 Rich Gedman	.10	.04	.01	☐ 575 Pedro Guerrero	.25	.10	.02
☐ 530 Dave Dravecky	.07	.03	.01	☐ 576 Jaime Cocanower	.04	.02	.00
☐ 531 Joe Lefebvre	.04	.02	.00	☐ 577 Chris Speier	.04	.02	.00
☐ 532 Frank DiPino	.04	.02	.00	☐ 578 Terry Francona	.04	.02	.00
☐ 533 Tony Bernazard	.04	.02	.00	☐ 579 Ron Romanick	.07	.03	.01
☐ 534 Brian Dayett	.04	.02	.00	☐ 580 Dwight Evans	.12	.05	.01
☐ 535 Pat Putnam	.04	.02	.00	☐ 581 Mark Wagner	.04	.02	.00
☐ 536 Kirby Puckett	8.50	3.50	.85	☐ 582 Ken Phelps	.25	.10	.02
☐ 537 Don Robinson	.04	.02	.00	☐ 583 Bobby Brown	.04	.02	.00
☐ 538 Keith Moreland	.04	.02	.00	☐ 584 Kevin Gross	.04	.02	.00
☐ 539 Aurelio Lopez	.04	.02	.00	☐ 585 Butch Wynegar	.04	.02	.00
☐ 540 Claudell Washington	.07	.03	.01	☐ 586 Bill Scherrer	.04	.02	.00
☐ 541 Mark Davis	.07	.03	.01	☐ 587 Doug Frobel	.04	.02	.00
☐ 542 Don Slaught	.04	.02	.00	☐ 588 Bobby Castillo	.04	.02	.00
☐ 543 Mike Squires	.04	.02	.00	☐ 589 Bob Dernier	.04	.02	.00
☐ 544 Bruce Kison	.04	.02	.00	☐ 590 Ray Knight	.07	.03	.01
☐ 545 Lloyd Moseby	.10	.04	.01	☐ 591 Larry Herndon	.04	.02	.00
☐ 546 Brent Gaff	.04	.02	.00	☐ 592 Jeff Robinson	.25	.10	.02
				(Giants pitcher)			

		MINT	EXC	G-VG
☐ 593	Rick Leach	.04	.02	.00
☐ 594	Curt Wilkerson	.04	.02	.00
☐ 595	Larry Gura	.04	.02	.00
☐ 596	Jerry Hairston	.04	.02	.00
☐ 597	Brad Lesley	.04	.02	.00
☐ 598	Jose Oquendo	.07	.03	.01
☐ 599	Storm Davis	.07	.03	.01
☐ 600	Pete Rose	1.00	.40	.10
☐ 601	Tom Lasorda MG (checklist back)	.07	.02	.00
☐ 602	Jeff Dedmon	.04	.02	.00
☐ 603	Rick Manning	.04	.02	.00
☐ 604	Daryl Sconiers	.04	.02	.00
☐ 605	Ozzie Smith	.20	.08	.02
☐ 606	Rich Gale	.04	.02	.00
☐ 607	Bill Almon	.04	.02	.00
☐ 608	Craig Lefferts	.04	.02	.00
☐ 609	Broderick Perkins	.04	.02	.00
☐ 610	Jack Morris	.15	.06	.01
☐ 611	Ozzie Virgil	.04	.02	.00
☐ 612	Mike Armstrong	.04	.02	.00
☐ 613	Terry Puhl	.04	.02	.00
☐ 614	Al Williams	.04	.02	.00
☐ 615	Marvell Wynne	.04	.02	.00
☐ 616	Scott Sanderson	.04	.02	.00
☐ 617	Willie Wilson	.10	.04	.01
☐ 618	Pete Falcone	.04	.02	.00
☐ 619	Jeff Leonard	.07	.03	.01
☐ 620	Dwight Gooden	8.50	3.50	.85
☐ 621	Marvis Foley	.04	.02	.00
☐ 622	Luis Leal	.04	.02	.00
☐ 623	Greg Walker	.07	.03	.01
☐ 624	Benny Ayala	.04	.02	.00
☐ 625	Mark Langston	1.25	.50	.12
☐ 626	German Rivera	.07	.03	.01
☐ 627	Eric Davis	13.50	5.00	1.00
☐ 628	Rene Lachemann MG (checklist back)	.07	.02	.00
☐ 629	Dick Schofield	.12	.05	.01
☐ 630	Tim Raines	.35	.14	.03
☐ 631	Bob Forsch	.04	.02	.00
☐ 632	Bruce Bochte	.04	.02	.00
☐ 633	Glenn Hoffman	.04	.02	.00
☐ 634	Bill Dawley	.04	.02	.00
☐ 635	Terry Kennedy	.04	.02	.00
☐ 636	Shane Rawley	.07	.03	.01
☐ 637	Brett Butler	.07	.03	.01
☐ 638	Mike Pagliarulo	1.25	.50	.12
☐ 639	Ed Hodge	.04	.02	.00

		MINT	EXC	G-VG
☐ 640	Steve Henderson	.10	.04	.01
☐ 641	Rod Scurry	.04	.02	.00
☐ 642	Dave Owen	.04	.02	.00
☐ 643	Johnny Grubb	.04	.02	.00
☐ 644	Mark Huismann	.04	.02	.00
☐ 645	Damaso Garcia	.04	.02	.00
☐ 646	Scot Thompson	.04	.02	.00
☐ 647	Rafael Ramirez	.04	.02	.00
☐ 648	Bob Jones	.04	.02	.00
☐ 649	Sid Fernandez	.90	.36	.09
☐ 650	Greg Luzinski	.10	.04	.01
☐ 651	Jeff Russell	.04	.02	.00
☐ 652	Joe Nolan	.04	.02	.00
☐ 653	Mark Brouhard	.04	.02	.00
☐ 654	Dave Anderson	.04	.02	.00
☐ 655	Joaquin Andujar	.10	.04	.01
☐ 656	Chuck Cottier MG (checklist back)	.07	.02	.00
☐ 657	Jim Slaton	.04	.02	.00
☐ 658	Mike Stenhouse	.07	.03	.01
☐ 659	Checklist: 529-660	.07	.01	.00
☐ 660	Tony Gwynn	1.00	.40	.10
☐ 661	Steve Crawford	.04	.02	.00
☐ 662	Mike Heath	.04	.02	.00
☐ 663	Luis Aguayo	.04	.02	.00
☐ 664	Steve Farr	.20	.08	.02
☐ 665	Don Mattingly	9.00	3.75	.90
☐ 666	Mike LaCoss	.04	.02	.00
☐ 667	Dave Engle	.04	.02	.00
☐ 668	Steve Trout	.04	.02	.00
☐ 669	Lee Lacy	.04	.02	.00
☐ 670	Tom Seaver	.30	.12	.03
☐ 671	Dane Iorg	.04	.02	.00
☐ 672	Juan Berenguer	.04	.02	.00
☐ 673	Buck Martinez	.04	.02	.00
☐ 674	Atlee Hammaker	.04	.02	.00
☐ 675	Tony Perez	.12	.05	.01
☐ 676	Albert Hall	.10	.04	.01
☐ 677	Wally Backman	.07	.03	.01
☐ 678	Joey McLaughlin	.04	.02	.00
☐ 679	Bob Kearney	.04	.02	.00
☐ 680	Jerry Reuss	.07	.03	.01
☐ 681	Ben Oglivie	.07	.03	.01
☐ 682	Doug Corbett	.04	.02	.00
☐ 683	Whitey Herzog MG (checklist back)	.07	.02	.00
☐ 684	Bill Doran	.10	.04	.01
☐ 685	Bill Caudill	.04	.02	.00
☐ 686	Mike Easler	.04	.02	.00

	MINT	EXC	G-VG		MINT	EXC	G-VG
☐ 687 Bill Gullickson	.04	.02	.00	☐ 735 Garry Templeton	.07	.03	.01
☐ 688 Len Matuszek	.04	.02	.00	☐ 736 Jerry Mumphrey	.04	.02	.00
☐ 689 Luis DeLeon	.04	.02	.00	☐ 737 Bo Diaz	.04	.02	.00
☐ 690 Alan Trammell	.30	.12	.03	☐ 738 Omar Moreno	.04	.02	.00
☐ 691 Dennis Rasmussen	.25	.10	.02	☐ 739 Ernie Camacho	.04	.02	.00
☐ 692 Randy Bush	.07	.03	.01	☐ 740 Jack Clark	.25	.10	.02
☐ 693 Tim Stoddard	.04	.02	.00	☐ 741 John Butcher	.04	.02	.00
☐ 694 Joe Carter	1.75	.70	.17	☐ 742 Ron Hassey	.04	.02	.00
☐ 695 Rick Rhoden	.07	.03	.01	☐ 743 Frank White	.07	.03	.01
☐ 696 John Rabb	.04	.02	.00	☐ 744 Doug Bair	.04	.02	.00
☐ 697 Onix Concepcion	.04	.02	.00	☐ 745 Buddy Bell	.10	.04	.01
☐ 698 Jorge Bell	.50	.20	.05	☐ 746 Jim Clancy	.04	.02	.00
☐ 699 Donnie Moore	.04	.02	.00	☐ 747 Alex Trevino	.04	.02	.00
☐ 700 Eddie Murray	.45	.18	.04	☐ 748 Lee Mazzilli	.04	.02	.00
☐ 701 Eddie Murray AS	.15	.06	.01	☐ 749 Julio Cruz	.04	.02	.00
☐ 702 Damaso Garcia AS	.04	.02	.00	☐ 750 Rollie Fingers	.15	.06	.01
☐ 703 George Brett AS	.25	.10	.02	☐ 751 Kelvin Chapman	.04	.02	.00
☐ 704 Cal Ripken AS	.20	.08	.02	☐ 752 Bob Owchinko	.04	.02	.00
☐ 705 Dave Winfield AS	.15	.06	.01	☐ 753 Greg Brock	.04	.02	.00
☐ 706 Rickey Henderson AS	.25	.10	.02	☐ 754 Larry Milbourne	.04	.02	.00
☐ 707 Tony Armas AS	.07	.03	.01	☐ 755 Ken Singleton	.07	.03	.01
☐ 708 Lance Parrish AS	.10	.04	.01	☐ 756 Rob Picciolo	.04	.02	.00
☐ 709 Mike Boddicker AS	.07	.03	.01	☐ 757 Willie McGee	.30	.12	.03
☐ 710 Frank Viola AS	.10	.04	.01	☐ 758 Ray Burris	.04	.02	.00
☐ 711 Dan Quisenberry AS	.07	.03	.01	☐ 759 Jim Fanning MG	.07	.02	.00
☐ 712 Keith Hernandez AS	.15	.06	.01	(checklist back)			
☐ 713 Ryne Sandberg AS	.15	.06	.01	☐ 760 Nolan Ryan	.40	.16	.04
☐ 714 Mike Schmidt AS	.25	.12	.03	☐ 761 Jerry Remy	.04	.02	.00
☐ 715 Ozzie Smith AS	.15	.06	.01	☐ 762 Eddie Whitson	.04	.02	.00
☐ 716 Dale Murphy AS	.30	.14	.03	☐ 763 Kiko Garcia	.04	.02	.00
☐ 717 Tony Gwynn AS	.25	.12	.03	☐ 764 Jamie Easterly	.04	.02	.00
☐ 718 Jeff Leonard AS	.07	.03	.01	☐ 765 Willie Randolph	.07	.03	.01
☐ 719 Gary Carter AS	.15	.06	.01	☐ 766 Paul Mirabella	.04	.02	.00
☐ 720 Rick Sutcliffe AS	.07	.04	.01	☐ 767 Darrell Brown	.04	.02	.00
☐ 721 Bob Knepper AS	.07	.03	.01	☐ 768 Ron Cey	.10	.04	.01
☐ 722 Bruce Sutter AS	.07	.03	.01	☐ 769 Joe Cowley	.04	.02	.00
☐ 723 Dave Stewart	.10	.04	.01	☐ 770 Carlton Fisk	.15	.06	.01
☐ 724 Oscar Gamble	.04	.02	.00	☐ 771 Geoff Zahn	.04	.02	.00
☐ 725 Floyd Bannister	.04	.02	.00	☐ 772 Johnnie LeMaster	.04	.02	.00
☐ 726 Al Bumbry	.04	.02	.00	☐ 773 Hal McRae	.07	.03	.01
☐ 727 Frank Pastore	.04	.02	.00	☐ 774 Dennis Lamp	.04	.02	.00
☐ 728 Bob Bailor	.04	.02	.00	☐ 775 Mookie Wilson	.07	.03	.01
☐ 729 Don Sutton	.25	.10	.02	☐ 776 Jerry Royster	.04	.02	.00
☐ 730 Dave Kingman	.10	.04	.01	☐ 777 Ned Yost	.04	.02	.00
☐ 731 Neil Allen	.04	.02	.00	☐ 778 Mike Davis	.07	.03	.01
☐ 732 John McNamara MG	.07	.02	.00	☐ 779 Nick Esasky	.07	.03	.01
(checklist back)				☐ 780 Mike Flanagan	.07	.03	.01
☐ 733 Tony Scott	.04	.02	.00	☐ 781 Jim Gantner	.04	.02	.00
☐ 734 John Henry Johnson	.04	.02	.00	☐ 782 Tom Niedenfuer	.04	.02	.00

		MINT	EXC	G-VG
☐ 783	Mike Jorgensen ...	.04	.02	.00
☐ 784	Checklist: 661-792	.07	.01	.00
☐ 785	Tony Armas	.07	.03	.01
☐ 786	Enos Cabell	.04	.02	.00
☐ 787	Jim Wohlford	.04	.02	.00
☐ 788	Steve Comer	.04	.02	.00
☐ 789	Luis Salazar	.04	.02	.00
☐ 790	Ron Guidry	.15	.06	.01
☐ 791	Ivan DeJesus	.04	.02	.00
☐ 792	Darrell Evans	.15	.06	.01

1985 Topps Traded

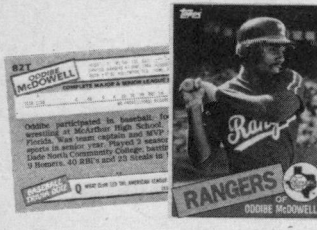

*The cards in this 132-card set measure 2 ½"
by 3 ½". In its now standard procedure,
Topps issued its Traded (or extended) set for
the fifth year in a row. Because all photos
and statistics of its regular set for the year
were developed during the fall and winter
months of the preceding year, players who
changed teams during the fall, winter, and
spring months are portrayed in the 1985
regular issue set with the teams they were
with in 1984. The Traded set amends the
shortcomings of the regular set by presenting the players with their proper teams for
the current year. Rookies not contained in
the regular set are also picked up in the
Traded set. Again this year, the Topps affiliate in Ireland printed the cards, and the
cards were available through hobby channels only.*

		MINT	EXC	G-VG
	Complete Set (132)	14.00	5.75	1.40
	Common Player (1-132) ..	.06	.02	.00
☐	1T Don Aase	.10	.04	.01
☐	2T Bill Almon	.06	.02	.00
☐	3T Benny Ayala	.06	.02	.00
☐	4T Dusty Baker	.10	.04	.01
☐	5T G.Bamberger MG .	.10	.04	.01
☐	6T Dale Berra	.06	.02	.00
☐	7T Rich Bordi	.06	.02	.00
☐	8T Daryl Boston	.10	.04	.01
☐	9T Hubie Brooks	.20	.08	.02
☐	10T Chris Brown	.45	.18	.04
☐	11T Tom Browning	1.25	.50	.12
☐	12T Al Bumbry	.06	.02	.00
☐	13T Ray Burris	.06	.02	.00
☐	14T Jeff Burroughs ...	.10	.04	.01
☐	15T Bill Campbell	.06	.02	.00
☐	16T Don Carman	.30	.12	.03
☐	17T Gary Carter	.70	.28	.07
☐	18T Bobby Castillo ...	.06	.02	.00
☐	19T Bill Caudill	.06	.02	.00
☐	20T Rick Cerone	.06	.02	.00
☐	21T Bryan Clark	.06	.02	.00
☐	22T Jack Clark	.40	.16	.04
☐	23T Pat Clements	.15	.06	.01
☐	24T Vince Coleman ...	5.00	2.00	.50
☐	25T Dave Collins	.06	.02	.00
☐	26T Danny Darwin	.06	.02	.00
☐	27T Jim Davenport MG .	.06	.02	.00
☐	28T Jerry Davis	.10	.04	.01
☐	29T Brian Dayett	.06	.02	.00
☐	30T Ivan DeJesus	.06	.02	.00
☐	31T Ken Dixon	.15	.06	.01
☐	32T Mariano Duncan ..	.20	.08	.02
☐	33T John Felske MG ..	.06	.02	.00
☐	34T Mike Fitzgerald ..	.06	.02	.00
☐	35T Ray Fontenot	.06	.02	.00
☐	36T Greg Gagne	.30	.12	.03
☐	37T Oscar Gamble ...	.06	.02	.00
☐	38T Scott Garrelts ...	.20	.08	.02
☐	39T Bob L. Gibson ...	.06	.02	.00
☐	40T Jim Gott	.06	.02	.00
☐	41T David Green	.06	.02	.00
☐	42T Alfredo Griffin ...	.15	.06	.01
☐	43T Ozzie Guillen	.65	.26	.06
☐	44T Eddie Haas MG ..	.06	.02	.00
☐	45T Terry Harper	.06	.02	.00
☐	46T Toby Harrah	.10	.04	.01
☐	47T Greg Harris	.06	.02	.00

	MINT	EXC	G-VG
☐ 48T Ron Hassey	.06	.02	.00
☐ 49T Rickey Henderson	1.00	.40	.10
☐ 50T Steve Henderson	.06	.02	.00
☐ 51T George Hendrick	.10	.04	.01
☐ 52T Joe Hesketh	.20	.08	.02
☐ 53T Teddy Higuera	2.50	1.00	.25
☐ 54T Donnie Hill	.10	.04	.01
☐ 55T Al Holland	.06	.02	.00
☐ 56T Burt Hooton	.06	.02	.00
☐ 57T Jay Howell	.10	.04	.01
☐ 58T Ken Howell	.20	.08	.02
☐ 59T LaMarr Hoyt	.10	.04	.01
☐ 60T Tim Hulett	.15	.06	.01
☐ 61T Bob James	.10	.04	.01
☐ 62T Steve Jeltz	.15	.06	.01
☐ 63T Cliff Johnson	.06	.02	.00
☐ 64T Howard Johnson	1.00	.40	.10
☐ 65T Ruppert Jones	.06	.02	.00
☐ 66T Steve Kemp	.10	.04	.01
☐ 67T Bruce Kison	.06	.02	.00
☐ 68T Alan Knicely	.06	.02	.00
☐ 69T Mike LaCoss	.06	.02	.00
☐ 70T Lee Lacy	.06	.02	.00
☐ 71T Dave LaPoint	.10	.04	.01
☐ 72T Gary Lavelle	.06	.02	.00
☐ 73T Vance Law	.10	.04	.01
☐ 74T Johnnie LeMaster	.06	.02	.00
☐ 75T Sixto Lezcano	.06	.02	.00
☐ 76T Tim Lollar	.06	.02	.00
☐ 77T Fred Lynn	.25	.10	.02
☐ 78T Billy Martin MG	.15	.06	.01
☐ 79T Ron Mathis	.10	.04	.01
☐ 80T Len Matuszek	.06	.02	.00
☐ 81T Gene Mauch MG	.06	.02	.00
☐ 82T Oddibe McDowell	.50	.20	.05
☐ 83T Roger McDowell	.85	.34	.08
☐ 84T John McNamara MG	.06	.02	.00
☐ 85T Donnie Moore	.06	.02	.00
☐ 86T Gene Nelson	.06	.02	.00
☐ 87T Steve Nicosia	.06	.02	.00
☐ 88T Al Oliver	.15	.06	.01
☐ 89T Joe Orsulak	.20	.08	.02
☐ 90T Rob Picciolo	.06	.02	.00
☐ 91T Chris Pittaro	.10	.04	.01
☐ 92T Jim Presley	.75	.30	.07
☐ 93T Rick Reuschel	.15	.06	.01
☐ 94T Bert Roberge	.06	.02	.00
☐ 95T Bob Rodgers MG	.06	.02	.00
☐ 96T Jerry Royster	.06	.02	.00
☐ 97T Dave Rozema	.06	.02	.00
☐ 98T Dave Rucker	.06	.02	.00
☐ 99T Vern Ruhle	.06	.02	.00
☐ 100T Paul Runge	.10	.04	.01
☐ 101T Mark Salas	.15	.06	.01
☐ 102T Luis Salazar	.06	.02	.00
☐ 103T Joe Sambito	.06	.02	.00
☐ 104T Rick Schu	.15	.06	.01
☐ 105T Donnie Scott	.06	.02	.00
☐ 106T Larry Sheets	.45	.18	.04
☐ 107T Don Slaught	.06	.02	.00
☐ 108T Roy Smalley	.06	.02	.00
☐ 109T Lonnie Smith	.10	.04	.01
☐ 110T Nate Snell	.15	.06	.01
(headings on back for a batter)			
☐ 111T Chris Speier	.06	.02	.00
☐ 112T Mike Stenhouse	.10	.04	.01
☐ 113T Tim Stoddard	.06	.02	.00
☐ 114T Jim Sundberg	.10	.04	.01
☐ 115T Bruce Sutter	.25	.10	.02
☐ 116T Don Sutton	.60	.24	.06
☐ 117T Kent Tekulve	.10	.04	.01
☐ 118T Tom Tellmann	.06	.02	.00
☐ 119T Walt Terrell	.10	.04	.01
☐ 120T Mickey Tettleton	.10	.04	.01
☐ 121T Derrel Thomas	.06	.02	.00
☐ 122T Rich Thompson	.10	.04	.01
☐ 123T Alex Trevino	.06	.02	.00
☐ 124T John Tudor	.25	.10	.02
☐ 125T Jose Uribe	.30	.12	.03
☐ 126T Bobby Valentine MG	.10	.04	.01
☐ 127T Dave Von Ohlen	.06	.02	.00
☐ 128T U.L. Washington	.06	.02	.00
☐ 129T Earl Weaver MG	.10	.04	.01
☐ 130T Eddie Whitson	.10	.04	.01
☐ 131T Herm Winningham	.15	.06	.01
☐ 132T Checklist 1-132	.06	.01	.00

1986 Topps

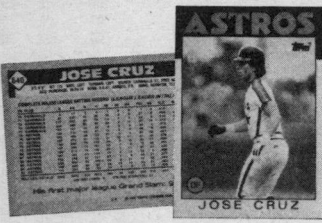

The cards in this 792-card set are standard-size (2 ½" by 3 ½"). The first seven cards are a tribute to Pete Rose and his career. Cards 2-7 show small photos of Pete's Topps cards of the given years on the front with biographical information pertaining to those years on the back. The team leader cards were done differently with a simple player action shot on a white background; the player pictured is dubbed the "Dean" of that team, i.e., the player with the longest continuous service with that team. Topps again features a "Turn Back The Clock" series (401-405). Record breakers of the previous year are acknowledged on cards 201 to 207. Cards 701-722 feature All-Star selections from each league. Manager cards feature the team checklist on the reverse. Ryne Sandberg (#690) is the only player card in the set without a Topps logo on the front of the card; this omission was never corrected by Topps. There are two other un-corrected errors involving misnumbered cards; see card numbers 51, 57, 141, and 171 in the checklist below. The backs of all the cards have a distinctive red background. Topps also produced a specially boxed "glossy" edition frequently referred to as the Topps Tiffany set. There were supposedly only 5,000 sets of the Tiffany cards produced; they were marketed to hobby dealers. The checklist of cards (792 regular and 132 Traded) is identical to that of the normal non-glossy cards. There are two

primary distinguishing features of the Tiffany cards, white card stock reverses and high gloss obverses. These Tiffany cards are valued at approximately six times the values listed below.

		MINT	EXC	G-VG
	Complete Set (792)	28.00	11.50	2.80
	Common Player (1-792) ..	.03	.01	.00
☐ 1	Pete Rose	1.00	.20	.04
☐ 2	Rose Special: '63-'66	.30	.12	.03
☐ 3	Rose Special: '67-'70	.30	.12	.03
☐ 4	Rose Special: '71-'74	.30	.12	.03
☐ 5	Rose Special: '75-'78	.30	.12	.03
☐ 6	Rose Special: '79-'82	.30	.12	.03
☐ 7	Rose Special: '83-'85	.30	.12	.03
☐ 8	Dwayne Murphy ..	.03	.01	.00
☐ 9	Roy Smith	.03	.01	.00
☐ 10	Tony Gwynn	.60	.24	.06
☐ 11	Bob Ojeda	.08	.03	.01
☐ 12	Jose Uribe	.25	.10	.02
☐ 13	Bob Kearney	.03	.01	.00
☐ 14	Julio Cruz	.03	.01	.00
☐ 15	Eddie Whitson ...	.03	.01	.00
☐ 16	Rick Schu	.06	.02	.00
☐ 17	Mike Stenhouse ..	.03	.01	.00
☐ 18	Brent Gaff	.03	.01	.00
☐ 19	Rich Hebner	.03	.01	.00
☐ 20	Lou Whitaker	.10	.04	.01
☐ 21	G.Bamberger MG . (checklist back)	.06	.01	.00
☐ 22	Duane Walker	.03	.01	.00
☐ 23	Manny Lee	.10	.04	.01
☐ 24	Len Barker	.03	.01	.00
☐ 25	Willie Wilson	.10	.04	.01
☐ 26	Frank DiPino	.03	.01	.00
☐ 27	Ray Knight	.06	.02	.00
☐ 28	Eric Davis	2.50	1.00	.25
☐ 29	Tony Phillips	.03	.01	.00
☐ 30	Eddie Murray	.30	.12	.03
☐ 31	Jamie Easterly ...	.03	.01	.00
☐ 32	Steve Yeager	.03	.01	.00
☐ 33	Jeff Lahti	.03	.01	.00
☐ 34	Ken Phelps	.06	.02	.00
☐ 35	Jeff Reardon	.06	.02	.00
☐ 36	Tigers Leaders ... Lance Parrish	.10	.04	.00
☐ 37	Mark Thurmond ...	.03	.01	.00
☐ 38	Glenn Hoffman ...	.03	.01	.00
☐ 39	Dave Rucker	.03	.01	.00

		MINT	EXC	G-VG
☐ 40	Ken Griffey	.06	.02	.00
☐ 41	Brad Wellman	.03	.01	.00
☐ 42	Geoff Zahn	.03	.01	.00
☐ 43	Dave Engle	.03	.01	.00
☐ 44	Lance McCullers	.30	.12	.03
☐ 45	Damaso Garcia	.03	.01	.00
☐ 46	Billy Hatcher	.15	.06	.01
☐ 47	Juan Berenguer	.03	.01	.00
☐ 48	Bill Almon	.03	.01	.00
☐ 49	Rick Manning	.03	.01	.00
☐ 50	Dan Quisenberry	.10	.04	.01
☐ 51	Bobby Wine MG ERR	.10	.03	.01
	(checklist back)			
	(number of card on			
	back is actually 57)			
☐ 52	Chris Welsh	.03	.01	.00
☐ 53	Len Dykstra	.70	.28	.07
☐ 54	John Franco	.10	.04	.01
☐ 55	Fred Lynn	.12	.05	.01
☐ 56	Tom Niedenfuer	.03	.01	.00
☐ 57	Bill Doran	.10	.04	.01
	(see also 51)			
☐ 58	Bill Krueger	.03	.01	.00
☐ 59	Andre Thornton	.06	.02	.00
☐ 60	Dwight Evans	.12	.05	.01
☐ 61	Karl Best	.10	.04	.01
☐ 62	Bob Boone	.06	.02	.00
☐ 63	Ron Roenicke	.03	.01	.00
☐ 64	Floyd Bannister	.03	.01	.00
☐ 65	Dan Driessen	.03	.01	.00
☐ 66	Cardinals Leaders	.03	.01	.00
	Bob Forsch			
☐ 67	Carmelo Martinez	.03	.01	.00
☐ 68	Ed Lynch	.03	.01	.00
☐ 69	Luis Aguayo	.03	.01	.00
☐ 70	Dave Winfield	.25	.10	.02
☐ 71	Ken Schrom	.03	.01	.00
☐ 72	Shawon Dunston	.10	.04	.01
☐ 73	Randy O'Neal	.03	.01	.00
☐ 74	Rance Mulliniks	.03	.01	.00
☐ 75	Jose DeLeon	.03	.01	.00
☐ 76	Dion James	.03	.01	.00
☐ 77	Charlie Leibrandt	.03	.01	.00
☐ 78	Bruce Benedict	.03	.01	.00
☐ 79	Dave Schmidt	.03	.01	.00
☐ 80	Darryl Strawberry	.75	.30	.07
☐ 81	Gene Mauch MG	.06	.01	.00
	(checklist back)			
☐ 82	Tippy Martinez	.03	.01	.00
☐ 83	Phil Garner	.03	.01	.00
☐ 84	Curt Young	.03	.01	.00
☐ 85	Tony Perez	.20	.08	.02
	(Eric Davis also shown on card)			
☐ 86	Tom Waddell	.03	.01	.00
☐ 87	Candy Maldonado	.08	.03	.01
☐ 88	Tom Nieto	.03	.01	.00
☐ 89	Randy St.Claire	.03	.01	.00
☐ 90	Garry Templeton	.06	.02	.00
☐ 91	Steve Crawford	.03	.01	.00
☐ 92	Al Cowens	.03	.01	.00
☐ 93	Scot Thompson	.03	.01	.00
☐ 94	Rich Bordi	.03	.01	.00
☐ 95	Ozzie Virgil	.03	.01	.00
☐ 96	Blue Jays Leaders	.03	.01	.00
	Jim Clancy			
☐ 97	Gary Gaetti	.12	.05	.01
☐ 98	Dick Ruthven	.03	.01	.00
☐ 99	Buddy Biancalana	.03	.01	.00
☐ 100	Nolan Ryan	.30	.12	.03
☐ 101	Dave Bergman	.03	.01	.00
☐ 102	Joe Orsulak	.10	.04	.01
☐ 103	Luis Salazar	.03	.01	.00
☐ 104	Sid Fernandez	.12	.05	.01
☐ 105	Gary Ward	.03	.01	.00
☐ 106	Ray Burris	.03	.01	.00
☐ 107	Rafael Ramirez	.03	.01	.00
☐ 108	Ted Power	.03	.01	.00
☐ 109	Len Matuszek	.03	.01	.00
☐ 110	Scott McGregor	.06	.02	.00
☐ 111	Roger Craig MG	.06	.01	.00
	(checklist back)			
☐ 112	Bill Campbell	.03	.01	.00
☐ 113	U.L. Washington	.03	.01	.00
☐ 114	Mike Brown	.03	.01	.00
	(Pirates OF)			
☐ 115	Jay Howell	.06	.02	.00
☐ 116	Brook Jacoby	.08	.03	.01
☐ 117	Bruce Kison	.03	.01	.00
☐ 118	Jerry Royster	.03	.01	.00
☐ 119	Barry Bonnell	.03	.01	.00
☐ 120	Steve Carlton	.20	.08	.02
☐ 121	Nelson Simmons	.08	.03	.01
☐ 122	Pete Filson	.03	.01	.00
☐ 123	Greg Walker	.08	.03	.01
☐ 124	Luis Sanchez	.03	.01	.00
☐ 125	Dave Lopes	.06	.02	.00
☐ 126	Mets Leaders	.03	.01	.00
	Mookie Wilson			

		MINT	EXC	G-VG
☐ 127	Jack Howell	.30	.12	.03
☐ 128	John Wathan	.03	.01	.00
☐ 129	Jeff Dedmon	.03	.01	.00
☐ 130	Alan Trammell	.20	.08	.02
☐ 131	Checklist: 1-132	.06	.01	.00
☐ 132	Razor Shines	.06	.02	.00
☐ 133	Andy McGaffigan	.03	.01	.00
☐ 134	Carney Lansford	.06	.02	.00
☐ 135	Joe Niekro	.08	.03	.01
☐ 136	Mike Hargrove	.03	.01	.00
☐ 137	Charlie Moore	.03	.01	.00
☐ 138	Mark Davis	.06	.02	.00
☐ 139	Daryl Boston	.06	.02	.00
☐ 140	John Candelaria	.06	.02	.00
☐ 141	Chuck Cottier MG (checklist back) (see also 171)	.10	.03	.01
☐ 142	Bob Jones	.03	.01	.00
☐ 143	Dave Van Gorder	.03	.01	.00
☐ 144	Doug Sisk	.03	.01	.00
☐ 145	Pedro Guerrero	.20	.08	.02
☐ 146	Jack Perconte	.03	.01	.00
☐ 147	Larry Sheets	.12	.05	.01
☐ 148	Mike Heath	.03	.01	.00
☐ 149	Brett Butler	.08	.03	.01
☐ 150	Joaquin Andujar	.08	.03	.01
☐ 151	Dave Stapleton	.03	.01	.00
☐ 152	Mike Morgan	.03	.01	.00
☐ 153	Ricky Adams	.03	.01	.00
☐ 154	Bert Roberge	.03	.01	.00
☐ 155	Bob Grich	.06	.02	.00
☐ 156	White Sox Leaders Richard Dotson	.03	.01	.00
☐ 157	Ron Hassey	.03	.01	.00
☐ 158	Derrel Thomas	.03	.01	.00
☐ 159	Orel Hershiser	1.25	.50	.12
☐ 160	Chet Lemon	.06	.02	.00
☐ 161	Lee Tunnell	.03	.01	.00
☐ 162	Greg Gagne	.10	.04	.01
☐ 163	Pete Ladd	.03	.01	.00
☐ 164	Steve Balboni	.03	.01	.00
☐ 165	Mike Davis	.03	.01	.00
☐ 166	Dickie Thon	.03	.01	.00
☐ 167	Zane Smith	.12	.05	.01
☐ 168	Jeff Burroughs	.03	.01	.00
☐ 169	George Wright	.03	.01	.00
☐ 170	Gary Carter	.25	.10	.02

		MINT	EXC	G-VG
☐ 171	Bob Rodgers MG ERR (checklist back) (number of card on back actually 141)	.10	.03	.01
☐ 172	Jerry Reed	.03	.01	.00
☐ 173	Wayne Gross	.03	.01	.00
☐ 174	Brian Snyder	.03	.01	.00
☐ 175	Steve Sax	.15	.06	.01
☐ 176	Jay Tibbs	.03	.01	.00
☐ 177	Joel Youngblood	.03	.01	.00
☐ 178	Ivan DeJesus	.03	.01	.00
☐ 179	Stu Cliburn	.08	.03	.01
☐ 180	Don Mattingly	3.00	1.20	.30
☐ 181	Al Nipper	.03	.01	.00
☐ 182	Bobby Brown	.03	.01	.00
☐ 183	Larry Andersen	.03	.01	.00
☐ 184	Tim Laudner	.03	.01	.00
☐ 185	Rollie Fingers	.12	.05	.01
☐ 186	Astros Leaders Jose Cruz	.03	.01	.00
☐ 187	Scott Fletcher	.06	.02	.00
☐ 188	Bob Dernier	.03	.01	.00
☐ 189	Mike Mason	.03	.01	.00
☐ 190	George Hendrick	.06	.02	.00
☐ 191	Wally Backman	.06	.02	.00
☐ 192	Milt Wilcox	.03	.01	.00
☐ 193	Daryl Sconiers	.03	.01	.00
☐ 194	Craig McMurtry	.03	.01	.00
☐ 195	Dave Concepcion	.06	.02	.00
☐ 196	Doyle Alexander	.06	.02	.00
☐ 197	Enos Cabell	.03	.01	.00
☐ 198	Ken Dixon	.06	.02	.00
☐ 199	Dick Howser MG (checklist back)	.06	.01	.00
☐ 200	Mike Schmidt	.40	.16	.04
☐ 201	RB: Vince Coleman Most stolen bases, season, rookie	.20	.08	.02
☐ 202	RB: Dwight Gooden Youngest 20 game winner	.30	.12	.03
☐ 203	RB: Keith Hernandez Most game-winning RBI's	.15	.06	.01
☐ 204	RB: Phil Niekro Oldest shutout pitcher	.10	.04	.01
☐ 205	RB: Tony Perez Oldest grand slammer	.10	.04	.01

	MINT	EXC	G-VG			MINT	EXC	G-VG
☐ 206 RB: Pete Rose	.35	.14	.03	☐ 248 Spike Owen	.03	.01	.00
Most hits, lifetime				☐ 249 Rob Deer	.20	.08	.02
☐ 207 RB: Fern.Valenzuela	.12	.05	.01	☐ 250 Dwight Gooden ...	1.50	.60	.15
Most cons. innings,				☐ 251 Rich Dauer	.03	.01	.00
start of season,				☐ 252 Bobby Castillo	.03	.01	.00
no earned runs				☐ 253 Dann Bilardello ...	.03	.01	.00
☐ 208 Ramon Romero	.03	.01	.00	☐ 254 Ozzie Guillen	.30	.12	.03
☐ 209 Randy Ready	.06	.02	.00	☐ 255 Tony Armas	.06	.02	.00
☐ 210 Calvin Schiraldi	.08	.03	.01	☐ 256 Kurt Kepshire	.03	.01	.00
☐ 211 Ed Wojna	.08	.03	.01	☐ 257 Doug DeCinces ...	.06	.02	.00
☐ 212 Chris Speier	.03	.01	.00	☐ 258 Tim Burke	.25	.10	.02
☐ 213 Bob Shirley	.03	.01	.00	☐ 259 Dan Pasqua	.15	.06	.01
☐ 214 Randy Bush	.03	.01	.00	☐ 260 Tony Pena	.08	.03	.01
☐ 215 Frank White	.06	.02	.00	☐ 261 Bobby Valentine MG	.06	.01	.00
☐ 216 A's Leaders	.03	.01	.00	(checklist back)			
Dwayne Murphy				☐ 262 Mario Ramirez	.03	.01	.00
☐ 217 Bill Scherrer	.03	.01	.00	☐ 263 Checklist: 133-264	.06	.01	.00
☐ 218 Randy Hunt	.03	.01	.00	☐ 264 Darren Daulton ...	.10	.04	.01
☐ 219 Dennis Lamp	.03	.01	.00	☐ 265 Ron Davis	.03	.01	.00
☐ 220 Bob Horner	.10	.04	.01	☐ 266 Keith Moreland ...	.03	.01	.00
☐ 221 Dave Henderson ...	.06	.02	.00	☐ 267 Paul Molitor	.12	.05	.01
☐ 222 Craig Gerber	.03	.01	.00	☐ 268 Mike Scott	.25	.10	.02
☐ 223 Atlee Hammaker ...	.03	.01	.00	☐ 269 Dane Iorg	.03	.01	.00
☐ 224 Cesar Cedeno	.06	.02	.00	☐ 270 Jack Morris	.12	.05	.01
☐ 225 Ron Darling	.20	.08	.02	☐ 271 Dave Collins	.03	.01	.00
☐ 226 Lee Lacy	.03	.01	.00	☐ 272 Tim Tolman	.03	.01	.00
☐ 227 Al Jones	.03	.01	.00	☐ 273 Jerry Willard	.03	.01	.00
☐ 228 Tom Lawless	.03	.01	.00	☐ 274 Ron Gardenhire ...	.03	.01	.00
☐ 229 Bill Gullickson	.03	.01	.00	☐ 275 Charlie Hough	.06	.02	.00
☐ 230 Terry Kennedy	.03	.01	.00	☐ 276 Yankees Leaders .	.03	.01	.00
☐ 231 Jim Frey MG	.06	.01	.00	Willie Randolph			
(checklist back)				Jaime Cocanower			
☐ 232 Rick Rhoden	.06	.02	.00	☐ 277 Jaime Cocanower ...	.03	.01	.00
☐ 233 Steve Lyons	.06	.02	.00	☐ 278 Sixto Lezcano	.03	.01	.00
☐ 234 Doug Corbett	.03	.01	.00	☐ 279 Al Pardo	.03	.01	.00
☐ 235 Butch Wynegar	.03	.01	.00	☐ 280 Tim Raines	.25	.10	.02
☐ 236 Frank Eufemia	.03	.01	.00	☐ 281 Steve Mura	.03	.01	.00
☐ 237 Ted Simmons	.08	.03	.01	☐ 282 Jerry Mumphrey ...	.03	.01	.00
☐ 238 Larry Parrish	.03	.01	.00	☐ 283 Mike Fischlin	.03	.01	.00
☐ 239 Joel Skinner	.03	.01	.00	☐ 284 Brian Dayett	.03	.01	.00
☐ 240 Tommy John	.10	.04	.01	☐ 285 Buddy Bell	.08	.03	.01
☐ 241 Tony Fernandez ...	.20	.08	.02	☐ 286 Luis DeLeon	.03	.01	.00
☐ 242 Rich Thompson	.03	.01	.00	☐ 287 John Christensen ..	.03	.01	.00
☐ 243 Johnny Grubb	.03	.01	.00	☐ 288 Don Aase	.03	.01	.00
☐ 244 Craig Lefferts	.03	.01	.00	☐ 289 Johnnie LeMaster .	.03	.01	.00
☐ 245 Jim Sundberg	.03	.01	.00	☐ 290 Carlton Fisk	.12	.05	.01
☐ 246 Phillies Leaders ...	.12	.05	.01	☐ 291 Tom Lasorda MG ..	.10	.03	.01
Steve Carlton				(checklist back)			
☐ 247 Terry Harper	.03	.01	.00	☐ 292 Chuck Porter	.03	.01	.00
				☐ 293 Chris Chambliss ..	.06	.02	.00

		MINT	EXC	G-VG			MINT	EXC	G-VG
☐ 294	Danny Cox	.08	.03	.01	☐ 340	Cal Ripken	.30	.12	.03
☐ 295	Kirk Gibson	.25	.10	.02	☐ 341	Frank Williams	.03	.01	.00
☐ 296	Geno Petralli	.03	.01	.00	☐ 342	Gary Redus	.03	.01	.00
☐ 297	Tim Lollar	.03	.01	.00	☐ 343	Carlos Diaz	.03	.01	.00
☐ 298	Craig Reynolds	.03	.01	.00	☐ 344	Jim Wohlford	.03	.01	.00
☐ 299	Bryn Smith	.03	.01	.00	☐ 345	Donnie Moore	.03	.01	.00
☐ 300	George Brett	.40	.16	.04	☐ 346	Bryan Little	.03	.01	.00
☐ 301	Dennis Rasmussen	.06	.02	.00	☐ 347	Teddy Higuera	.90	.36	.09
☐ 302	Greg Gross	.03	.01	.00	☐ 348	Cliff Johnson	.03	.01	.00
☐ 303	Curt Wardle	.03	.01	.00	☐ 349	Mark Clear	.03	.01	.00
☐ 304	Mike Gallego	.03	.01	.00	☐ 350	Jack Clark	.20	.08	.02
☐ 305	Phil Bradley	.08	.03	.01	☐ 351	Chuck Tanner MG	.06	.01	.00
☐ 306	Padres Leaders	.03	.01	.00		(checklist back)			
	Terry Kennedy				☐ 352	Harry Spilman	.03	.01	.00
☐ 307	Dave Sax	.03	.01	.00	☐ 353	Keith Atherton	.03	.01	.00
☐ 308	Ray Fontenot	.03	.01	.00	☐ 354	Tony Bernazard	.03	.01	.00
☐ 309	John Shelby	.03	.01	.00	☐ 355	Lee Smith	.06	.02	.00
☐ 310	Greg Minton	.03	.01	.00	☐ 356	Mickey Hatcher	.06	.02	.00
☐ 311	Dick Schofield	.03	.01	.00	☐ 357	Ed VandeBerg	.03	.01	.00
☐ 312	Tom Filer	.03	.01	.00	☐ 358	Rick Dempsey	.03	.01	.00
☐ 313	Joe DeSa	.03	.01	.00	☐ 359	Mike LaCoss	.03	.01	.00
☐ 314	Frank Pastore	.03	.01	.00	☐ 360	Lloyd Moseby	.08	.03	.01
☐ 315	Mookie Wilson	.06	.02	.00	☐ 361	Shane Rawley	.06	.02	.00
☐ 316	Sammy Khalifa	.08	.03	.01	☐ 362	Tom Paciorek	.03	.01	.00
☐ 317	Ed Romero	.03	.01	.00	☐ 363	Terry Forster	.06	.02	.00
☐ 318	Terry Whitfield	.03	.01	.00	☐ 364	Reid Nichols	.03	.01	.00
☐ 319	Rick Camp	.03	.01	.00	☐ 365	Mike Flanagan	.06	.02	.00
☐ 320	Jim Rice	.18	.08	.02	☐ 366	Reds Leaders	.03	.01	.00
☐ 321	Earl Weaver MG	.06	.01	.00		Dave Concepcion			
	(checklist back)				☐ 367	Aurelio Lopez	.03	.01	.00
☐ 322	Bob Forsch	.03	.01	.00	☐ 368	Greg Brock	.03	.01	.00
☐ 323	Jerry Davis	.03	.01	.00	☐ 369	Al Holland	.03	.01	.00
☐ 324	Dan Schatzeder	.03	.01	.00	☐ 370	Vince Coleman	1.50	.60	.15
☐ 325	Juan Beniquez	.03	.01	.00	☐ 371	Bill Stein	.03	.01	.00
☐ 326	Kent Tekulve	.03	.01	.00	☐ 372	Ben Oglivie	.06	.02	.00
☐ 327	Mike Pagliarulo	.10	.04	.01	☐ 373	Urbano Lugo	.03	.01	.00
☐ 328	Pete O'Brien	.08	.03	.01	☐ 374	Terry Francona	.03	.01	.00
☐ 329	Kirby Puckett	1.25	.50	.12	☐ 375	Rich Gedman	.06	.02	.00
☐ 330	Rick Sutcliffe	.10	.04	.01	☐ 376	Bill Dawley	.03	.01	.00
☐ 331	Alan Ashby	.03	.01	.00	☐ 377	Joe Carter	.30	.12	.03
☐ 332	Darryl Motley	.03	.01	.00	☐ 378	Bruce Bochte	.03	.01	.00
☐ 333	Tom Henke	.10	.04	.01	☐ 379	Bobby Meacham	.03	.01	.00
☐ 334	Ken Oberkfell	.03	.01	.00	☐ 380	LaMarr Hoyt	.06	.02	.00
☐ 335	Don Sutton	.15	.06	.01	☐ 381	Ray Miller MG	.06	.01	.00
☐ 336	Indians Leaders	.03	.01	.00		(checklist back)			
	Andre Thornton				☐ 382	Ivan Calderon	.60	.24	.06
☐ 337	Darnell Coles	.03	.01	.00	☐ 383	Chris Brown	.35	.14	.03
☐ 338	Jorge Bell	.20	.08	.02	☐ 384	Steve Trout	.03	.01	.00
☐ 339	Bruce Berenyi	.03	.01	.00	☐ 385	Cecil Cooper	.08	.03	.01

		MINT	EXC	G-VG
☐ 386	Cecil Fielder	.15	.06	.01
☐ 387	Steve Kemp	.03	.01	.00
☐ 388	Dickie Noles	.03	.01	.00
☐ 389	Glenn Davis	1.25	.50	.12
☐ 390	Tom Seaver	.30	.12	.03
☐ 391	Julio Franco	.10	.04	.01
☐ 392	John Russell	.03	.01	.00
☐ 393	Chris Pittaro	.03	.01	.00
☐ 394	Checklist: 265-396	.06	.01	.00
☐ 395	Scott Garrelts	.06	.02	.00
☐ 396	Red Sox Leaders	.08	.03	.01
	Dwight Evans			
☐ 397	Steve Buechele	.20	.08	.02
☐ 398	Earnie Riles	.20	.08	.02
☐ 399	Bill Swift	.06	.02	.00
☐ 400	Rod Carew	.30	.12	.03
☐ 401	Turn Back 5 Years	.10	.04	.01
	Fern.Valenzuela '81			
☐ 402	Turn Back 10 Years	.15	.06	.01
	Tom Seaver '76			
☐ 403	Turn Back 15 Years	.15	.06	.01
	Willie Mays '71			
☐ 404	Turn Back 20 Years	.10	.04	.01
	Frank Robinson '66			
☐ 405	Turn Back 25 Years	.15	.06	.01
	Roger Maris '61			
☐ 406	Scott Sanderson	.03	.01	.00
☐ 407	Sal Butera	.03	.01	.00
☐ 408	Dave Smith	.06	.02	.00
☐ 409	Paul Runge	.03	.01	.00
☐ 410	Dave Kingman	.08	.03	.01
☐ 411	Sparky Anderson MG	.06	.01	.00
	(checklist back)			
☐ 412	Jim Clancy	.03	.01	.00
☐ 413	Tim Flannery	.03	.01	.00
☐ 414	Tom Gorman	.03	.01	.00
☐ 415	Hal McRae	.06	.02	.00
☐ 416	Dennis Martinez	.06	.02	.00
☐ 417	R.J. Reynolds	.03	.01	.00
☐ 418	Alan Knicely	.03	.01	.00
☐ 419	Frank Wills	.03	.01	.00
☐ 420	Von Hayes	.08	.03	.01
☐ 421	David Palmer	.03	.01	.00
☐ 422	Mike Jorgensen	.03	.01	.00
☐ 423	Dan Spillner	.03	.01	.00
☐ 424	Rick Miller	.03	.01	.00
☐ 425	Larry McWilliams	.03	.01	.00
☐ 426	Brewers Leaders	.03	.01	.00
	Charlie Moore			

		MINT	EXC	G-VG
☐ 427	Joe Cowley	.03	.01	.00
☐ 428	Max Venable	.03	.01	.00
☐ 429	Greg Booker	.03	.01	.00
☐ 430	Kent Hrbek	.15	.06	.01
☐ 431	George Frazier	.03	.01	.00
☐ 432	Mark Bailey	.03	.01	.00
☐ 433	Chris Codiroli	.03	.01	.00
☐ 434	Curt Wilkerson	.03	.01	.00
☐ 435	Bill Caudill	.03	.01	.00
☐ 436	Doug Flynn	.03	.01	.00
☐ 437	Rick Mahler	.03	.01	.00
☐ 438	Clint Hurdle	.03	.01	.00
☐ 439	Rick Honeycutt	.03	.01	.00
☐ 440	Alvin Davis	.15	.06	.01
☐ 441	Whitey Herzog MG	.06	.01	.00
	(checklist back)			
☐ 442	Ron Robinson	.08	.03	.01
☐ 443	Bill Buckner	.06	.02	.00
☐ 444	Alex Trevino	.03	.01	.00
☐ 445	Bert Blyleven	.08	.03	.01
☐ 446	Lenn Sakata	.03	.01	.00
☐ 447	Jerry Don Gleaton	.03	.01	.00
☐ 448	Herm Winningham	.10	.04	.01
☐ 449	Rod Scurry	.03	.01	.00
☐ 450	Graig Nettles	.10	.04	.01
☐ 451	Mark Brown	.06	.02	.00
☐ 452	Bob Clark	.03	.01	.00
☐ 453	Steve Jeltz	.03	.01	.00
☐ 454	Burt Hooton	.03	.01	.00
☐ 455	Willie Randolph	.06	.02	.00
☐ 456	Braves Leaders	.15	.06	.01
	Dale Murphy			
☐ 457	Mickey Tettleton	.08	.03	.01
☐ 458	Kevin Bass	.08	.03	.01
☐ 459	Luis Leal	.03	.01	.00
☐ 460	Leon Durham	.06	.02	.00
☐ 461	Walt Terrell	.03	.01	.00
☐ 462	Domingo Ramos	.03	.01	.00
☐ 463	Jim Gott	.03	.01	.00
☐ 464	Ruppert Jones	.03	.01	.00
☐ 465	Jesse Orosco	.03	.01	.00
☐ 466	Tom Foley	.03	.01	.00
☐ 467	Bob James	.03	.01	.00
☐ 468	Mike Scioscia	.03	.01	.00
☐ 469	Storm Davis	.06	.02	.00
☐ 470	Bill Madlock	.08	.03	.00
☐ 471	Bobby Cox MG	.06	.01	.00
	(checklist back)			
☐ 472	Joe Hesketh	.06	.02	.00

		MINT	EXC	G-VG
☐ 473	Mark Brouhard	.03	.01	.00
☐ 474	John Tudor	.10	.04	.01
☐ 475	Juan Samuel	.12	.05	.01
☐ 476	Ron Mathis	.08	.03	.01
☐ 477	Mike Easler	.03	.01	.00
☐ 478	Andy Hawkins	.06	.02	.00
☐ 479	Bob Melvin	.10	.04	.01
☐ 480	Oddibe McDowell	.15	.06	.01
☐ 481	Scott Bradley	.10	.04	.01
☐ 482	Rick Lysander	.03	.01	.00
☐ 483	George Vukovich	.03	.01	.00
☐ 484	Donnie Hill	.03	.01	.00
☐ 485	Gary Matthews	.06	.02	.00
☐ 486	Angels Leaders	.03	.01	.00
	Bobby Grich			
☐ 487	Bret Saberhagen	.30	.12	.03
☐ 488	Lou Thornton	.08	.03	.01
☐ 489	Jim Winn	.03	.01	.00
☐ 490	Jeff Leonard	.08	.03	.01
☐ 491	Pascual Perez	.06	.02	.00
☐ 492	Kelvin Chapman	.03	.01	.00
☐ 493	Gene Nelson	.03	.01	.00
☐ 494	Gary Roenicke	.03	.01	.00
☐ 495	Mark Langston	.10	.04	.01
☐ 496	Jay Johnstone	.06	.02	.00
☐ 497	John Stuper	.03	.01	.00
☐ 498	Tito Landrum	.03	.01	.00
☐ 499	Bob L. Gibson	.03	.01	.00
☐ 500	Rickey Henderson	.35	.14	.03
☐ 501	Dave Johnson MG	.06	.01	.00
	(checklist back)			
☐ 502	Glen Cook	.08	.03	.01
☐ 503	Mike Fitzgerald	.03	.01	.00
☐ 504	Denny Walling	.03	.01	.00
☐ 505	Jerry Koosman	.06	.02	.00
☐ 506	Bill Russell	.06	.02	.00
☐ 507	Steve Ontiveros	.08	.03	.01
☐ 508	Alan Wiggins	.03	.01	.00
☐ 509	Ernie Camacho	.03	.01	.00
☐ 510	Wade Boggs	2.00	.80	.20
☐ 511	Ed Nunez	.03	.01	.00
☐ 512	Thad Bosley	.03	.01	.00
☐ 513	Ron Washington	.03	.01	.00
☐ 514	Mike Jones	.03	.01	.00
☐ 515	Darrell Evans	.08	.03	.01
☐ 516	Giants Leaders	.03	.01	.00
	Greg Minton			
☐ 517	Milt Thompson	.25	.10	.02
☐ 518	Buck Martinez	.03	.01	.00
☐ 519	Danny Darwin	.03	.01	.00
☐ 520	Keith Hernandez	.25	.10	.02
☐ 521	Nate Snell	.08	.03	.01
☐ 522	Bob Bailor	.03	.01	.00
☐ 523	Joe Price	.03	.01	.00
☐ 524	Darrell Miller	.08	.03	.01
☐ 525	Marvell Wynne	.03	.01	.00
☐ 526	Charlie Lea	.03	.01	.00
☐ 527	Checklist: 397-528	.06	.01	.00
☐ 528	Terry Pendleton	.06	.02	.00
☐ 529	Marc Sullivan	.03	.01	.00
☐ 530	Rich Gossage	.10	.04	.01
☐ 531	Tony LaRussa MG	.06	.01	.00
	(checklist back)			
☐ 532	Don Carman	.20	.08	.02
☐ 533	Billy Sample	.03	.01	.00
☐ 534	Jeff Calhoun	.03	.01	.00
☐ 535	Toby Harrah	.03	.01	.00
☐ 536	Jose Rijo	.06	.02	.00
☐ 537	Mark Salas	.03	.01	.00
☐ 538	Dennis Eckersley	.10	.04	.01
☐ 539	Glenn Hubbard	.03	.01	.00
☐ 540	Dan Petry	.06	.02	.00
☐ 541	Jorge Orta	.03	.01	.00
☐ 542	Don Schulze	.03	.01	.00
☐ 543	Jerry Narron	.03	.01	.00
☐ 544	Eddie Milner	.03	.01	.00
☐ 545	Jimmy Key	.10	.04	.01
☐ 546	Mariners Leaders	.03	.01	.00
	Dave Henderson			
☐ 547	Roger McDowell	.45	.18	.04
☐ 548	Mike Young	.08	.03	.01
☐ 549	Bob Welch	.06	.02	.00
☐ 550	Tom Herr	.06	.02	.00
☐ 551	Dave LaPoint	.06	.02	.00
☐ 552	Marc Hill	.03	.01	.00
☐ 553	Jim Morrison	.03	.01	.00
☐ 554	Paul Householder	.03	.01	.00
☐ 555	Hubie Brooks	.08	.03	.01
☐ 556	John Denny	.06	.02	.00
☐ 557	Gerald Perry	.12	.05	.01
☐ 558	Tim Stoddard	.03	.01	.00
☐ 559	Tommy Dunbar	.03	.01	.00
☐ 560	Dave Righetti	.10	.04	.01
☐ 561	Bob Lillis MG	.06	.01	.00
	(checklist back)			
☐ 562	Joe Beckwith	.03	.01	.00
☐ 563	Alejandro Sanchez	.03	.01	.00
☐ 564	Warren Brusstar	.03	.01	.00

		MINT	EXC	G-VG			MINT	EXC	G-VG
☐ 565	Tom Brunansky	.12	.05	.01	☐ 611	Gary Woods	.03	.01	.00
☐ 566	Alfredo Griffin	.06	.02	.00	☐ 612	Richard Dotson	.06	.02	.00
☐ 567	Jeff Barkley	.03	.01	.00	☐ 613	Roy Smalley	.03	.01	.00
☐ 568	Donnie Scott	.03	.01	.00	☐ 614	Rick Waits	.03	.01	.00
☐ 569	Jim Acker	.03	.01	.00	☐ 615	Johnny Ray	.08	.03	.01
☐ 570	Rusty Staub	.08	.03	.01	☐ 616	Glenn Brummer	.03	.01	.00
☐ 571	Mike Jeffcoat	.03	.01	.00	☐ 617	Lonnie Smith	.03	.01	.00
☐ 572	Paul Zuvella	.03	.01	.00	☐ 618	Jim Pankovits	.03	.01	.00
☐ 573	Tom Hume	.03	.01	.00	☐ 619	Danny Heep	.03	.01	.00
☐ 574	Ron Kittle	.10	.04	.01	☐ 620	Bruce Sutter	.10	.04	.01
☐ 575	Mike Boddicker	.08	.03	.01	☐ 621	John Felske MG	.06	.01	.00
☐ 576	Expos Leaders	.12	.05	.01		(checklist back)			
	Andre Dawson				☐ 622	Gary Lavelle	.03	.01	.00
☐ 577	Jerry Reuss	.06	.02	.00	☐ 623	Floyd Rayford	.03	.01	.00
☐ 578	Lee Mazzilli	.03	.01	.00	☐ 624	Steve McCatty	.03	.01	.00
☐ 579	Jim Slaton	.03	.01	.00	☐ 625	Bob Brenly	.03	.01	.00
☐ 580	Willie McGee	.15	.06	.01	☐ 626	Roy Thomas	.03	.01	.00
☐ 581	Bruce Hurst	.12	.05	.01	☐ 627	Ron Oester	.03	.01	.00
☐ 582	Jim Gantner	.03	.01	.00	☐ 628	Kirk McCaskill	.30	.12	.03
☐ 583	Al Bumbry	.03	.01	.00	☐ 629	Mitch Webster	.25	.10	.02
☐ 584	Brian Fisher	.25	.10	.02	☐ 630	Fernando Valenzuela	.20	.08	.02
☐ 585	Garry Maddox	.06	.02	.00	☐ 631	Steve Braun	.03	.01	.00
☐ 586	Greg Harris	.03	.01	.00	☐ 632	Dave Von Ohlen	.03	.01	.00
☐ 587	Rafael Santana	.03	.01	.00	☐ 633	Jackie Gutierrez	.03	.01	.00
☐ 588	Steve Lake	.03	.01	.00	☐ 634	Roy Lee Jackson	.03	.01	.00
☐ 589	Sid Bream	.03	.01	.00	☐ 635	Jason Thompson	.03	.01	.00
☐ 590	Bob Knepper	.06	.02	.00	☐ 636	Cubs Leaders	.03	.01	.00
☐ 591	Jackie Moore MG	.06	.01	.00		Lee Smith			
	(checklist back)				☐ 637	Rudy Law	.03	.01	.00
☐ 592	Frank Tanana	.06	.02	.00	☐ 638	John Butcher	.03	.01	.00
☐ 593	Jesse Barfield	.20	.08	.02	☐ 639	Bo Diaz	.03	.01	.00
☐ 594	Chris Bando	.03	.01	.00	☐ 640	Jose Cruz	.08	.03	.01
☐ 595	Dave Parker	.15	.06	.01	☐ 641	Wayne Tolleson	.03	.01	.00
☐ 596	Onix Concepcion	.03	.01	.00	☐ 642	Ray Searage	.03	.01	.00
☐ 597	Sammy Stewart	.03	.01	.00	☐ 643	Tom Brookens	.03	.01	.00
☐ 598	Jim Presley	.20	.08	.02	☐ 644	Mark Gubicza	.08	.03	.01
☐ 599	Rick Aguilera	.25	.10	.02	☐ 645	Dusty Baker	.06	.02	.00
☐ 600	Dale Murphy	.40	.16	.04	☐ 646	Mike Moore	.06	.02	.00
☐ 601	Gary Lucas	.03	.01	.00	☐ 647	Mel Hall	.06	.02	.00
☐ 602	Mariano Duncan	.15	.06	.01	☐ 648	Steve Bedrosian	.10	.04	.01
☐ 603	Bill Laskey	.03	.01	.00	☐ 649	Ronn Reynolds	.03	.01	.00
☐ 604	Gary Pettis	.06	.02	.00	☐ 650	Dave Stieb	.10	.04	.01
☐ 605	Dennis Boyd	.08	.03	.01	☐ 651	Billy Martin MG	.10	.03	.01
☐ 606	Royals Leaders	.03	.01	.00		(checklist back)			
	Hal McRae				☐ 652	Tom Browning	.15	.06	.01
☐ 607	Ken Dayley	.03	.01	.00	☐ 653	Jim Dwyer	.03	.01	.00
☐ 608	Bruce Bochy	.03	.01	.00	☐ 654	Ken Howell	.03	.01	.00
☐ 609	Barbaro Garbey	.03	.01	.00	☐ 655	Manny Trillo	.03	.01	.00
☐ 610	Ron Guidry	.10	.04	.01	☐ 656	Brian Harper	.03	.01	.00

		MINT	EXC	G-VG
☐ 657	Juan Agosto	.03	.01	.00
☐ 658	Rob Wilfong	.03	.01	.00
☐ 659	Checklist: 529-660	.06	.01	.00
☐ 660	Steve Garvey	.35	.14	.03
☐ 661	Roger Clemens	2.00	.80	.20
☐ 662	Bill Schroeder	.03	.01	.00
☐ 663	Neil Allen	.03	.01	.00
☐ 664	Tim Corcoran	.03	.01	.00
☐ 665	Alejandro Pena	.03	.01	.00
☐ 666	Rangers Leaders	.03	.01	.00
	Charlie Hough			
☐ 667	Tim Teufel	.03	.01	.00
☐ 668	Cecilio Guante	.03	.01	.00
☐ 669	Ron Cey	.06	.02	.00
☐ 670	Willie Hernandez	.08	.03	.01
☐ 671	Lynn Jones	.03	.01	.00
☐ 672	Rob Picciolo	.03	.01	.00
☐ 673	Ernie Whitt	.03	.01	.00
☐ 674	Pat Tabler	.08	.03	.01
☐ 675	Claudell Washington	.06	.02	.00
☐ 676	Matt Young	.03	.01	.00
☐ 677	Nick Esasky	.03	.01	.00
☐ 678	Dan Gladden	.06	.02	.00
☐ 679	Britt Burns	.03	.01	.00
☐ 680	George Foster	.10	.04	.01
☐ 681	Dick Williams MG	.06	.01	.00
	(checklist back)			
☐ 682	Junior Ortiz	.03	.01	.00
☐ 683	Andy Van Slyke	.20	.08	.02
☐ 684	Bob McClure	.03	.01	.00
☐ 685	Tim Wallach	.08	.03	.01
☐ 686	Jeff Stone	.03	.01	.00
☐ 687	Mike Trujillo	.03	.01	.00
☐ 688	Larry Herndon	.03	.01	.00
☐ 689	Dave Stewart	.10	.04	.01
☐ 690	Ryne Sandberg	.25	.10	.02
	(no Topps logo on front)			
☐ 691	Mike Madden	.03	.01	.00
☐ 692	Dale Berra	.03	.01	.00
☐ 693	Tom Tellmann	.03	.01	.00
☐ 694	Garth Iorg	.03	.01	.00
☐ 695	Mike Smithson	.03	.01	.00
☐ 696	Dodgers Leaders	.03	.01	.00
	Bill Russell			
☐ 697	Bud Black	.03	.01	.00
☐ 698	Brad Komminsk	.03	.01	.00
☐ 699	Pat Corrales MG	.06	.01	.00
	(checklist back)			
☐ 700	Reggie Jackson	.35	.14	.03

		MINT	EXC	G-VG
☐ 701	Keith Hernandez AS	.12	.06	.01
☐ 702	Tom Herr AS	.06	.02	.00
☐ 703	Tim Wallach AS	.06	.02	.00
☐ 704	Ozzie Smith AS	.10	.05	.01
☐ 705	Dale Murphy AS	.25	.12	.03
☐ 706	Pedro Guerrero AS	.10	.05	.01
☐ 707	Willie McGee AS	.10	.04	.01
☐ 708	Gary Carter AS	.15	.06	.01
☐ 709	Dwight Gooden AS	.30	.12	.03
☐ 710	John Tudor AS	.06	.02	.00
☐ 711	Jeff Reardon AS	.06	.02	.00
☐ 712	Don Mattingly AS	.80	.32	.08
☐ 713	Damaso Garcia AS	.06	.02	.00
☐ 714	George Brett AS	.20	.10	.02
☐ 715	Cal Ripken AS	.15	.08	.02
☐ 716	Rickey Henderson AS	.20	.10	.02
☐ 717	Dave Winfield AS	.15	.06	.01
☐ 718	Jorge Bell AS	.10	.05	.01
☐ 719	Carlton Fisk AS	.10	.04	.01
☐ 720	Bret Saberhagen AS	.10	.04	.01
☐ 721	Ron Guidry AS	.06	.04	.01
☐ 722	Dan Quisenberry AS	.06	.02	.00
☐ 723	Marty Bystrom	.03	.01	.00
☐ 724	Tim Hulett	.03	.01	.00
☐ 725	Mario Soto	.03	.01	.00
☐ 726	Orioles Leaders	.03	.01	.00
	Rick Dempsey			
☐ 727	David Green	.03	.01	.00
☐ 728	Mike Marshall	.10	.04	.01
☐ 729	Jim Beattie	.03	.01	.00
☐ 730	Ozzie Smith	.15	.06	.01
☐ 731	Don Robinson	.03	.01	.00
☐ 732	Floyd Youmans	.30	.12	.03
☐ 733	Ron Romanick	.03	.01	.00
☐ 734	Marty Barrett	.08	.03	.01
☐ 735	Dave Dravecky	.03	.01	.00
☐ 736	Glenn Wilson	.03	.01	.00
☐ 737	Pete Vuckovich	.03	.01	.00
☐ 738	Andre Robertson	.03	.01	.00
☐ 739	Dave Rozema	.03	.01	.00
☐ 740	Lance Parrish	.12	.05	.01
☐ 741	Pete Rose MG	.35	.12	.02
	(checklist back)			
☐ 742	Frank Viola	.25	.10	.02
☐ 743	Pat Sheridan	.03	.01	.00
☐ 744	Lary Sorensen	.03	.01	.00
☐ 745	Willie Upshaw	.03	.01	.00
☐ 746	Denny Gonzalez	.03	.01	.00
☐ 747	Rick Cerone	.03	.01	.00

1986 Topps Traded

		MINT	EXC	G-VG
☐ 748	Steve Henderson ..	.03	.01	.00
☐ 749	Ed Jurak	.03	.01	.00
☐ 750	Gorman Thomas ...	.06	.02	.00
☐ 751	Howard Johnson ...	.20	.08	.02
☐ 752	Mike Krukow	.03	.01	.00
☐ 753	Dan Ford	.03	.01	.00
☐ 754	Pat Clements	.10	.04	.01
☐ 755	Harold Baines	.10	.04	.01
☐ 756	Pirates Leaders	.03	.01	.00
	Rick Rhoden			
☐ 757	Darrell Porter	.03	.01	.00
☐ 758	Dave Anderson	.03	.01	.00
☐ 759	Moose Haas	.03	.01	.00
☐ 760	Andre Dawson	.25	.10	.02
☐ 761	Don Slaught	.03	.01	.00
☐ 762	Eric Show	.06	.02	.00
☐ 763	Terry Puhl	.03	.01	.00
☐ 764	Kevin Gross	.03	.01	.00
☐ 765	Don Baylor	.10	.04	.01
☐ 766	Rick Langford	.03	.01	.00
☐ 767	Jody Davis	.08	.03	.01
☐ 768	Vern Ruhle	.03	.01	.00
☐ 769	Harold Reynolds ...	.35	.14	.03
☐ 770	Vida Blue	.06	.02	.00
☐ 771	John McNamara MG	.06	.01	.00
	(checklist back)			
☐ 772	Brian Downing	.06	.02	.00
☐ 773	Greg Pryor	.03	.01	.00
☐ 774	Terry Leach	.08	.03	.01
☐ 775	Al Oliver	.08	.03	.01
☐ 776	Gene Garber	.03	.01	.00
☐ 777	Wayne Krenchicki ..	.03	.01	.00
☐ 778	Jerry Hairston	.03	.01	.00
☐ 779	Rick Reuschel	.06	.02	.00
☐ 780	Robin Yount	.25	.10	.02
☐ 781	Joe Nolan	.03	.01	.00
☐ 782	Ken Landreaux	.03	.01	.00
☐ 783	Ricky Horton	.03	.01	.00
☐ 784	Alan Bannister	.03	.01	.00
☐ 785	Bob Stanley	.03	.01	.00
☐ 786	Twins Leaders	.03	.01	.00
	Mickey Hatcher			
☐ 787	Vance Law	.06	.02	.00
☐ 788	Marty Castillo	.03	.01	.00
☐ 789	Kurt Bevacqua	.03	.01	.00
☐ 790	Phil Niekro	.15	.06	.01
☐ 791	Checklist: 661-792	.06	.01	.00
☐ 792	Charles Hudson ...	.06	.02	.00

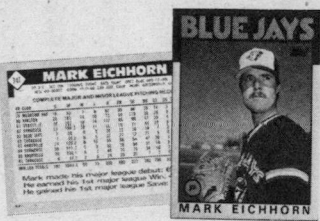

This 132-card Traded or extended set was distributed by Topps to dealers in a special red and white box as a complete set. The card fronts are identical in style to the Topps regular issue and are also 2 ½ " by 3 ½ ". The backs are printed in red and black on white card stock. Cards are numbered (with a T suffix) alphabetically according to the name of the player.

		MINT	EXC	G-VG
Complete Set (132)		17.00	7.00	1.70
Common Player (1-132) ..		.05	.02	.00
☐	1T Andy Allanson	.15	.06	.01
☐	2T Neil Allen	.05	.02	.00
☐	3T Joaquin Andujar ...	.10	.04	.01
☐	4T Paul Assenmacher ..	.15	.06	.01
☐	5T Scott Bailes	.15	.06	.01
☐	6T Don Baylor	.15	.06	.01
☐	7T Steve Bedrosian ..	.15	.06	.01
☐	8T Juan Beniquez	.05	.02	.00
☐	9T Juan Berenguer ...	.05	.02	.00
☐	10T Mike Bielecki	.10	.04	.01
☐	11T Barry Bonds	1.00	.40	.10
☐	12T Bobby Bonilla	1.00	.40	.10
☐	13T Juan Bonilla	.05	.02	.00
☐	14T Rich Bordi	.05	.02	.00
☐	15T Steve Boros MG ...	.05	.02	.00
☐	16T Rick Burleson	.10	.04	.01
☐	17T Bill Campbell	.05	.02	.00
☐	18T Tom Candiotti	.10	.04	.01
☐	19T John Cangelosi ...	.15	.06	.01
☐	20T Jose Canseco	8.00	3.25	.80

	MINT	EXC	G-VG
☐ 21T Carmen Castillo ...	.05	.02	.00
☐ 22T Rick Cerone	.05	.02	.00
☐ 23T John Cerutti	.15	.06	.01
☐ 24T Will Clark	3.50	1.40	.35
☐ 25T Mark Clear	.05	.02	.00
☐ 26T Darnell Coles	.10	.04	.01
☐ 27T Dave Collins	.05	.02	.00
☐ 28T Tim Conroy	.05	.02	.00
☐ 29T Joe Cowley	.05	.02	.00
☐ 30T Joel Davis	.15	.06	.01
☐ 31T Rob Deer	.15	.06	.01
☐ 32T John Denny	.10	.04	.01
☐ 33T Mike Easler	.05	.02	.00
☐ 34T Mark Eichhorn	.15	.06	.01
☐ 35T Steve Farr	.05	.02	.00
☐ 36T Scott Fletcher	.15	.06	.01
☐ 37T Terry Forster	.10	.04	.01
☐ 38T Terry Francona	.05	.02	.00
☐ 39T Jim Fregosi MG	.05	.02	.00
☐ 40T Andres Galarraga ..	1.25	.50	.12
☐ 41T Ken Griffey	.10	.04	.01
☐ 42T Bill Gullickson	.05	.02	.00
☐ 43T Jose Guzman	.20	.08	.02
☐ 44T Moose Haas	.05	.02	.00
☐ 45T Billy Hatcher	.15	.06	.01
☐ 46T Mike Heath	.05	.02	.00
☐ 47T Tom Hume	.05	.02	.00
☐ 48T Pete Incaviglia	.70	.28	.07
☐ 49T Dane Iorg	.05	.02	.00
☐ 50T Bo Jackson	1.75	.70	.17
☐ 51T Wally Joyner	2.00	.80	.20
☐ 52T Charlie Kerfeld	.15	.06	.01
☐ 53T Eric King	.15	.06	.01
☐ 54T Bob Kipper	.05	.02	.00
☐ 55T Wayne Krenchicki ..	.05	.02	.00
☐ 56T John Kruk	.35	.14	.03
☐ 57T Mike LaCoss	.05	.02	.00
☐ 58T Pete Ladd	.05	.02	.00
☐ 59T Mike Laga	.10	.04	.01
☐ 60T Hal Lanier MG	.05	.02	.00
☐ 61T Dave LaPoint	.10	.04	.01
☐ 62T Rudy Law	.05	.02	.00
☐ 63T Rick Leach	.05	.02	.00
☐ 64T Tim Leary	.20	.08	.02
☐ 65T Dennis Leonard	.10	.04	.01
☐ 66T Jim Leyland MG ...	.05	.02	.00
☐ 67T Steve Lyons	.05	.02	.00
☐ 68T Mickey Mahler	.05	.02	.00
☐ 69T Candy Maldonado ..	.15	.06	.01

	MINT	EXC	G-VG
☐ 70T Roger Mason	.10	.04	.01
☐ 71T Bob McClure	.05	.02	.00
☐ 72T Andy McGaffigan ..	.05	.02	.00
☐ 73T Gene Michael MG .	.05	.02	.00
☐ 74T Kevin Mitchell	.30	.12	.03
☐ 75T Omar Moreno	.05	.02	.00
☐ 76T Jerry Mumphrey ...	.05	.02	.00
☐ 77T Phil Niekro	.30	.12	.03
☐ 78T Randy Niemann ...	.05	.02	.00
☐ 79T Juan Nieves	.15	.06	.01
☐ 80T Otis Nixon	.15	.06	.01
☐ 81T Bob Ojeda	.15	.06	.01
☐ 82T Jose Oquendo	.10	.04	.01
☐ 83T Tom Paciorek	.05	.02	.00
☐ 84T David Palmer	.05	.02	.00
☐ 85T Frank Pastore	.05	.02	.00
☐ 86T Lou Piniella MG ...	.10	.04	.01
☐ 87T Dan Plesac	.30	.12	.03
☐ 88T Darrell Porter	.05	.02	.00
☐ 89T Rey Quinones	.20	.08	.02
☐ 90T Gary Redus	.05	.02	.00
☐ 91T Bip Roberts	.10	.04	.01
☐ 92T Billy Jo Robidoux ..	.10	.04	.01
☐ 93T Jeff Robinson	.15	.06	.01
(Giants pitcher)			
☐ 94T Gary Roenicke	.05	.02	.00
☐ 95T Ed Romero	.05	.02	.00
☐ 96T Argenis Salazar ...	.05	.02	.00
☐ 97T Joe Sambito	.05	.02	.00
☐ 98T Billy Sample	.05	.02	.00
☐ 99T Dave Schmidt	.10	.04	.01
☐ 100T Ken Schrom	.05	.02	.00
☐ 101T Tom Seaver	.40	.16	.04
☐ 102T Ted Simmons	.15	.06	.01
☐ 103T Sammy Stewart ...	.05	.02	.00
☐ 104T Kurt Stillwell	.30	.12	.03
☐ 105T Franklin Stubbs ...	.05	.02	.00
☐ 106T Dale Sveum	.30	.12	.03
☐ 107T Chuck Tanner MG .	.05	.02	.00
☐ 108T Danny Tartabull ...	.75	.30	.07
☐ 109T Tim Teufel	.05	.02	.00
☐ 110T Bob Tewksbury ..	.15	.06	.01
☐ 111T Andres Thomas ...	.20	.08	.02
☐ 112T Milt Thompson ...	.10	.04	.01
☐ 113T Robby Thompson .	.30	.12	.03
☐ 114T Jay Tibbs	.05	.02	.00
☐ 115T Wayne Tolleson ..	.05	.02	.00
☐ 116T Alex Trevino	.05	.02	.00
☐ 117T Manny Trillo	.05	.02	.00

	MINT	EXC	G-VG
☐ 118T Ed VandeBerg	.05	.02	.00
☐ 119T Ozzie Virgil	.05	.02	.00
☐ 120T Bob Walk..........	.10	.04	.01
☐ 121T Gene Walter	.10	.04	.01
☐ 122T Claudell Washington	.10	.04	.01
☐ 123T Bill Wegman	.15	.06	.01
☐ 124T Dick Williams MG ..	.05	.02	.00
☐ 125T Mitch Williams	.20	.08	.02
☐ 126T Bobby Witt	.40	.16	.04
☐ 127T Todd Worrell	.50	.20	.05
☐ 128T George Wright	.05	.02	.00
☐ 129T Ricky Wright	.05	.02	.00
☐ 130T Steve Yeager	.05	.02	.00
☐ 131T Paul Zuvella	.05	.02	.00
☐ 132T Checklist 1-132	.05	.01	.00

1987 Topps

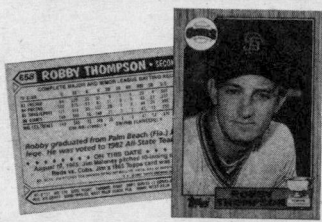

This 792-card set is reminiscent of the 1962 Topps baseball cards with their simulated wood grain borders. The backs are printed in yellow and blue on gray card stock. The manager cards contain a checklist of the respective team's players on the back. Subsets in the set include Record Breakers (1-7), Turn Back The Clock (311-315), and All-Star selections (595-616). The Team Leader cards typically show players conferring on the mound inside a white cloud. The wax pack wrapper gives details of "Spring Fever Baseball" where a lucky collector can win a trip for four to Spring Training. Topps also produced a specially boxed "glossy"

edition frequently referred to as the Topps Tiffany set. This year Topps did not disclose the number of sets they produced or sold; it is apparent from the availability that there were many more sets produced this year compared to the 1984-86 Tiffany sets. The checklist of cards (792 regular and 132 Traded) is identical to that of the normal nonglossy cards. There are two primary distinguishing features of the Tiffany cards, white card stock reverses and high gloss obverses. These Tiffany cards are valued at approximately four times the values listed below.

			MINT	EXC	G-VG
Complete Set (792)			27.00	11.00	2.70
Common Player (1-792) ..			.03	.01	.00
☐	1	RB: Roger Clemens Most strikeouts, nine inning game	.40	.10	.02
☐	2	RB: Jim Deshaies . Most cons. K's, start of game	.06	.02	.00
☐	3	RB: Dwight Evans . Earliest home run, season	.08	.03	.01
☐	4	RB: Davey Lopes . Most steals, season, 40-year-old	.06	.02	.00
☐	5	RB: Dave Righetti . Most saves, season	.08	.03	.01
☐	6	RB: Ruben Sierra . Youngest player to switch hit homers in game	.12	.05	.01
☐	7	RB: Todd Worrell .. Most saves, season, rookie	.10	.04	.01
☐	8	Terry Pendleton ...	.03	.01	.00
☐	9	Jay Tibbs	.03	.01	.00
☐	10	Cecil Cooper	.08	.03	.01
☐	11	Indians Team ...... (mound conference)	.03	.01	.00
☐	12	Jeff Sellers	.12	.05	.01
☐	13	Nick Esasky	.03	.01	.00
☐	14	Dave Stewart	.08	.03	.01
☐	15	Claudell Washington	.06	.02	.00
☐	16	Pat Clements	.03	.01	.00
☐	17	Pete O'Brien	.08	.03	.01

		MINT	EXC	G-VG
☐ 18	Dick Howser MG ... (checklist back)	.06	.01	.00
☐ 19	Matt Young	.03	.01	.00
☐ 20	Gary Carter	.20	.08	.02
☐ 21	Mark Davis	.06	.02	.00
☐ 22	Doug DeCinces ...	.06	.02	.00
☐ 23	Lee Smith	.06	.02	.00
☐ 24	Tony Walker	.08	.03	.01
☐ 25	Bert Blyleven	.08	.03	.01
☐ 26	Greg Brock	.03	.01	.00
☐ 27	Joe Cowley	.03	.01	.00
☐ 28	Rick Dempsey	.03	.01	.00
☐ 29	Jimmy Key	.08	.03	.01
☐ 30	Tim Raines	.20	.08	.02
☐ 31	Braves Team	.03	.01	.00
	(Hubbard/Ramirez)			
☐ 32	Tim Leary	.06	.02	.00
☐ 33	Andy Van Slyke ...	.15	.06	.01
☐ 34	Jose Rijo	.06	.02	.00
☐ 35	Sid Bream	.03	.01	.00
☐ 36	Eric King	.10	.04	.01
☐ 37	Marvell Wynne	.03	.01	.00
☐ 38	Dennis Leonard ...	.03	.01	.00
☐ 39	Marty Barrett	.08	.03	.01
☐ 40	Dave Righetti	.10	.04	.01
☐ 41	Bo Diaz	.03	.01	.00
☐ 42	Gary Redus	.03	.01	.00
☐ 43	Gene Michael MG ..	.06	.01	.00
	(checklist back)			
☐ 44	Greg Harris	.03	.01	.00
☐ 45	Jim Presley	.08	.03	.01
☐ 46	Dan Gladden	.06	.02	.00
☐ 47	Dennis Powell	.03	.01	.00
☐ 48	Wally Backman ...	.06	.02	.00
☐ 49	Terry Harper	.03	.01	.00
☐ 50	Dave Smith	.03	.01	.00
☐ 51	Mel Hall	.06	.02	.00
☐ 52	Keith Atherton	.03	.01	.00
☐ 53	Ruppert Jones	.03	.01	.00
☐ 54	Bill Dawley	.03	.01	.00
☐ 55	Tim Wallach	.08	.03	.01
☐ 56	Brewers Team	.03	.01	.00
	(mound conference)			
☐ 57	Scott Nielsen	.10	.04	.01
☐ 58	Thad Bosley	.03	.01	.00
☐ 59	Ken Dayley	.03	.01	.00
☐ 60	Tony Pena	.08	.03	.01
☐ 61	Bobby Thigpen	.25	.10	.02
☐ 62	Bobby Meacham ...	.03	.01	.00

		MINT	EXC	G-VG
☐ 63	Fred Toliver	.03	.01	.00
☐ 64	Harry Spilman	.03	.01	.00
☐ 65	Tom Browning	.12	.05	.01
☐ 66	Marc Sullivan	.03	.01	.00
☐ 67	Bill Swift	.03	.01	.00
☐ 68	Tony LaRussa MG .	.06	.01	.00
	(checklist back)			
☐ 69	Lonnie Smith	.03	.01	.00
☐ 70	Charlie Hough	.06	.02	.00
☐ 71	Mike Aldrete	.20	.08	.02
☐ 72	Walt Terrell	.03	.01	.00
☐ 73	Dave Anderson ...	.03	.01	.00
☐ 74	Dan Pasqua	.06	.02	.00
☐ 75	Ron Darling	.15	.06	.01
☐ 76	Rafael Ramirez ...	.03	.01	.00
☐ 77	Bryan Oelkers	.03	.01	.00
☐ 78	Tom Foley	.03	.01	.00
☐ 79	Juan Nieves	.10	.04	.01
☐ 80	Wally Joyner	1.25	.50	.12
☐ 81	Padres Team	.03	.01	.00
	(Hawkins/Kennedy)			
☐ 82	Rob Murphy	.20	.08	.02
☐ 83	Mike Davis	.03	.01	.00
☐ 84	Steve Lake	.03	.01	.00
☐ 85	Kevin Bass	.06	.02	.00
☐ 86	Nate Snell	.03	.01	.00
☐ 87	Mark Salas	.03	.01	.00
☐ 88	Ed Wojna	.03	.01	.00
☐ 89	Ozzie Guillen	.06	.02	.00
☐ 90	Dave Stieb	.10	.04	.01
☐ 91	Harold Reynolds ..	.06	.02	.00
☐ 92A	Urbano Lugo	.25	.10	.02
	ERR (no trademark)			
☐ 92B	Urbano Lugo COR	.06	.02	.00
☐ 93	Jim Leyland MG ..	.06	.01	.00
	(checklist back)			
☐ 94	Calvin Schiraldi ..	.06	.02	.00
☐ 95	Oddibe McDowell .	.08	.03	.01
☐ 96	Frank Williams ...	.03	.01	.00
☐ 97	Glenn Wilson	.03	.01	.00
☐ 98	Bill Scherrer	.03	.01	.00
☐ 99	Darryl Motley	.03	.01	.00
☐ 100	Steve Garvey	.25	.10	.02
☐ 101	Carl Willis	.06	.02	.00
☐ 102	Paul Zuvella	.03	.01	.00
☐ 103	Rick Aguilera	.03	.01	.00
☐ 104	Billy Sample	.03	.01	.00
☐ 105	Floyd Youmans ...	.06	.02	.00

		MINT	EXC	G-VG
☐ 106	Blue Jays Team ..... (Bell/Barfield)	.12	.05	.01
☐ 107	John Butcher	.03	.01	.00
☐ 108	Jim Gantner .... (Brewers logo reversed) ERR	.06	.02	.00
☐ 109	R.J. Reynolds	.03	.01	.00
☐ 110	John Tudor	.10	.04	.01
☐ 111	Alfredo Griffin	.06	.02	.00
☐ 112	Alan Ashby	.03	.01	.00
☐ 113	Neil Allen	.03	.01	.00
☐ 114	Billy Beane	.06	.02	.00
☐ 115	Donnie Moore	.03	.01	.00
☐ 116	Bill Russell	.03	.01	.00
☐ 117	Jim Beattie	.03	.01	.00
☐ 118	Bobby Valentine MG (checklist back)	.06	.01	.00
☐ 119	Ron Robinson	.03	.01	.00
☐ 120	Eddie Murray	.20	.08	.02
☐ 121	Kevin Romine	.10	.04	.01
☐ 122	Jim Clancy	.03	.01	.00
☐ 123	John Kruk	.30	.12	.03
☐ 124	Ray Fontenot	.03	.01	.00
☐ 125	Bob Brenly	.03	.01	.00
☐ 126	Mike Loynd	.08	.03	.01
☐ 127	Vance Law	.03	.01	.00
☐ 128	Checklist 1-132	.06	.01	.00
☐ 129	Rick Cerone	.03	.01	.00
☐ 130	Dwight Gooden	.70	.28	.07
☐ 131	Pirates Team ...... (Bream/Pena)	.03	.01	.00
☐ 132	Paul Assenmacher	.08	.03	.01
☐ 133	Jose Oquendo	.03	.01	.00
☐ 134	Rich Yett	.03	.01	.00
☐ 135	Mike Easler	.03	.01	.00
☐ 136	Ron Romanick	.03	.01	.00
☐ 137	Jerry Willard	.03	.01	.00
☐ 138	Roy Lee Jackson ...	.03	.01	.00
☐ 139	Devon White	.70	.28	.07
☐ 140	Bret Saberhagen ...	.18	.08	.01
☐ 141	Herm Winningham ...	.03	.01	.00
☐ 142	Rick Sutcliffe	.10	.04	.01
☐ 143	Steve Boros MG .... (checklist back)	.06	.01	.00
☐ 144	Mike Scioscia	.03	.01	.00
☐ 145	Charlie Kerfeld	.03	.01	.00
☐ 146	Tracy Jones	.30	.12	.03
☐ 147	Randy Niemann	.03	.01	.00
☐ 148	Dave Collins	.03	.01	.00
☐ 149	Ray Searage	.03	.01	.00

		MINT	EXC	G-VG
☐ 150	Wade Boggs	1.00	.40	.10
☐ 151	Mike LaCoss	.03	.01	.00
☐ 152	Toby Harrah	.03	.01	.00
☐ 153	Duane Ward	.08	.03	.01
☐ 154	Tom O'Malley	.03	.01	.00
☐ 155	Eddie Whitson	.03	.01	.00
☐ 156	Mariners Team .... (mound conference)	.03	.01	.00
☐ 157	Danny Darwin	.03	.01	.00
☐ 158	Tim Teufel	.03	.01	.00
☐ 159	Ed Olwine	.08	.03	.01
☐ 160	Julio Franco	.08	.03	.01
☐ 161	Steve Ontiveros	.03	.01	.00
☐ 162	Mike LaValliere ...	.12	.05	.01
☐ 163	Kevin Gross	.03	.01	.00
☐ 164	Sammy Khalifa	.03	.01	.00
☐ 165	Jeff Reardon	.06	.02	.01
☐ 166	Bob Boone	.06	.02	.00
☐ 167	Jim Deshaies	.15	.06	.01
☐ 168	Lou Piniella MG .... (checklist back)	.08	.02	.00
☐ 169	Ron Washington	.03	.01	.00
☐ 170	Bo Jackson	.90	.36	.09
☐ 171	Chuck Cary	.10	.04	.01
☐ 172	Ron Oester	.03	.01	.00
☐ 173	Alex Trevino	.03	.01	.00
☐ 174	Henry Cotto	.03	.01	.00
☐ 175	Bob Stanley	.03	.01	.00
☐ 176	Steve Buechele ...	.03	.01	.00
☐ 177	Keith Moreland	.03	.01	.00
☐ 178	Cecil Fielder	.06	.02	.00
☐ 179	Bill Wegman	.06	.02	.00
☐ 180	Chris Brown	.08	.03	.01
☐ 181	Cardinals Team .... (mound conference)	.03	.01	.00
☐ 182	Lee Lacy	.03	.01	.00
☐ 183	Andy Hawkins	.06	.02	.00
☐ 184	Bobby Bonilla	.70	.28	.07
☐ 185	Roger McDowell ...	.06	.02	.00
☐ 186	Bruce Benedict ...	.03	.01	.00
☐ 187	Mark Huismann ...	.03	.01	.00
☐ 188	Tony Phillips	.03	.01	.00
☐ 189	Joe Hesketh	.03	.01	.00
☐ 190	Jim Sundberg	.03	.01	.00
☐ 191	Charles Hudson ...	.03	.01	.00
☐ 192	Cory Snyder	.60	.24	.06
☐ 193	Roger Craig MG ... (checklist back)	.06	.01	.00
☐ 194	Kirk McCaskill	.03	.01	.00

		MINT	EXC	G-VG
☐ 195	Mike Pagliarulo	.08	.03	.01
☐ 196	Randy O'Neal	.03	.01	.00
	(wrong ML career W-L totals)			
☐ 197	Mark Bailey	.03	.01	.00
☐ 198	Lee Mazzilli	.03	.01	.00
☐ 199	Mariano Duncan ...	.03	.01	.00
☐ 200	Pete Rose	.40	.16	.04
☐ 201	John Cangelosi	.08	.03	.01
☐ 202	Ricky Wright	.03	.01	.00
☐ 203	Mike Kingery	.08	.03	.01
☐ 204	Sammy Stewart	.03	.01	.00
☐ 205	Graig Nettles	.08	.03	.01
☐ 206	Twins Team	.06	.02	.00
	(Frank Viola and Tim Laudner)			
☐ 207	George Frazier	.03	.01	.00
☐ 208	John Shelby	.03	.01	.00
☐ 209	Rick Schu	.03	.01	.00
☐ 210	Lloyd Moseby	.08	.03	.01
☐ 211	John Morris	.03	.01	.00
☐ 212	Mike Fitzgerald	.03	.01	.00
☐ 213	Randy Myers	.40	.16	.04
☐ 214	Omar Moreno	.03	.01	.00
☐ 215	Mark Langston	.10	.04	.01
☐ 216	B.J. Surhoff	.35	.14	.03
☐ 217	Chris Codiroli	.03	.01	.00
☐ 218	Sparky Anderson MG	.06	.01	.00
	(checklist back)			
☐ 219	Cecilio Guante	.03	.01	.00
☐ 220	Joe Carter	.18	.08	.01
☐ 221	Vern Ruhle	.03	.01	.00
☐ 222	Denny Walling	.03	.01	.00
☐ 223	Charlie Leibrandt ..	.03	.01	.00
☐ 224	Wayne Tolleson ...	.03	.01	.00
☐ 225	Mike Smithson	.03	.01	.00
☐ 226	Max Venable	.03	.01	.00
☐ 227	Jamie Moyer	.15	.06	.01
☐ 228	Curt Wilkerson	.03	.01	.00
☐ 229	Mike Birkbeck	.10	.04	.01
☐ 230	Don Baylor	.08	.03	.01
☐ 231	Giants Team	.03	.01	.00
	(Bob Brenly and Jim Gott)			
☐ 232	Reggie Williams ...	.08	.03	.01
☐ 233	Russ Morman	.10	.04	.01
☐ 234	Pat Sheridan	.03	.01	.00
☐ 235	Alvin Davis	.10	.04	.01
☐ 236	Tommy John	.10	.04	.01
☐ 237	Jim Morrison	.03	.01	.00
☐ 238	Bill Krueger	.03	.01	.00
☐ 239	Juan Espino	.03	.01	.00

		MINT	EXC	G-VG
☐ 240	Steve Balboni	.03	.01	.00
☐ 241	Danny Heep	.03	.01	.00
☐ 242	Rick Mahler	.03	.01	.00
☐ 243	Whitey Herzog MG	.06	.01	.00
	(checklist back)			
☐ 244	Dickie Noles	.03	.01	.00
☐ 245	Willie Upshaw	.03	.01	.00
☐ 246	Jim Dwyer	.03	.01	.00
☐ 247	Jeff Reed	.03	.01	.00
☐ 248	Gene Walter	.03	.01	.00
☐ 249	Jim Pankovits	.03	.01	.00
☐ 250	Teddy Higuera	.15	.06	.01
☐ 251	Rob Wilfong	.03	.01	.00
☐ 252	Dennis Martinez ...	.03	.01	.00
☐ 253	Eddie Milner	.03	.01	.00
☐ 254	Bob Tewksbury	.10	.04	.01
☐ 255	Juan Samuel	.10	.05	.01
☐ 256	Royals Team	.10	.04	.01
	(Brett/F.White)			
☐ 257	Bob Forsch	.03	.01	.00
☐ 258	Steve Yeager	.03	.01	.00
☐ 259	Mike Greenwell	4.00	1.60	.40
☐ 260	Vida Blue	.06	.02	.00
☐ 261	Ruben Sierra	.90	.36	.09
☐ 262	Jim Winn	.03	.01	.00
☐ 263	Stan Javier	.06	.02	.00
☐ 264	Checklist 133-264 ..	.06	.01	.00
☐ 265	Darrell Evans	.08	.03	.01
☐ 266	Jeff Hamilton	.15	.06	.01
☐ 267	Howard Johnson ..	.10	.04	.01
☐ 268	Pat Corrales MG ...	.06	.01	.00
	(checklist back)			
☐ 269	Cliff Speck	.06	.02	.00
☐ 270	Jody Davis	.06	.02	.00
☐ 271	Mike Brown	.03	.01	.00
	(Mariners pitcher)			
☐ 272	Andres Galarraga ..	.90	.36	.09
☐ 273	Gene Nelson	.03	.01	.00
☐ 274	Jeff Hearron	.10	.04	.01
	(duplicate 1986 stat line on back)			
☐ 275	LaMarr Hoyt	.06	.02	.00
☐ 276	Jackie Gutierrez ...	.03	.01	.00
☐ 277	Juan Agosto	.03	.01	.00
☐ 278	Gary Pettis	.03	.01	.00
☐ 279	Dan Plesac	.20	.08	.02
☐ 280	Jeff Leonard	.06	.02	.00
☐ 281	Reds Team	.10	.04	.01
	(Pete Rose, Bo Diaz, and Bill Gullickson)			

		MINT	EXC	G-VG
☐ 282	Jeff Calhoun	.03	.01	.00
☐ 283	Doug Drabek	.20	.08	.02
☐ 284	John Moses	.03	.01	.00
☐ 285	Dennis Boyd	.06	.02	.00
☐ 286	Mike Woodard	.03	.01	.00
☐ 287	Dave Von Ohlen	.03	.01	.00
☐ 288	Tito Landrum	.03	.01	.00
☐ 289	Bob Kipper	.03	.01	.00
☐ 290	Leon Durham	.06	.02	.00
☐ 291	Mitch Williams	.20	.08	.02
☐ 292	Franklin Stubbs	.03	.01	.00
☐ 293	Bob Rodgers MG	.06	.01	.00
	(checklist back)			
☐ 294	Steve Jeltz	.03	.01	.00
☐ 295	Len Dykstra	.10	.04	.01
☐ 296	Andres Thomas	.12	.05	.01
☐ 297	Don Schulze	.03	.01	.00
☐ 298	Larry Herndon	.03	.01	.00
☐ 299	Joel Davis	.03	.01	.00
☐ 300	Reggie Jackson	.30	.12	.03
☐ 301	Luis Aquino	.06	.02	.00
	UER (no trademark, never corrected)			
☐ 302	Bill Schroeder	.03	.01	.00
☐ 303	Juan Berenguer	.03	.01	.00
☐ 304	Phil Garner	.03	.01	.00
☐ 305	John Franco	.08	.03	.01
☐ 306	Red Sox Team	.06	.02	.00
	(Tom Seaver, John McNamara, and Rich Gedman)			
☐ 307	Lee Guetterman	.12	.05	.01
☐ 308	Don Slaught	.03	.01	.00
☐ 309	Mike Young	.03	.01	.00
☐ 310	Frank Viola	.15	.06	.01
☐ 311	Turn Back 1982	.12	.05	.01
	Rickey Henderson			
☐ 312	Turn Back 1977	.12	.05	.01
	Reggie Jackson			
☐ 313	Turn Back 1972	.12	.05	.01
	Roberto Clemente			
☐ 314	Turn Back 1967 UER	.12	.05	.01
	Carl Yastrzemski			
	(sic, 112 RBI's on back)			
☐ 315	Turn Back 1962	.06	.02	.00
	Maury Wills			
☐ 316	Brian Fisher	.03	.01	.00
☐ 317	Clint Hurdle	.03	.01	.00
☐ 318	Jim Fregosi MG	.06	.01	.00
	(checklist back)			
☐ 319	Greg Swindell	.45	.18	.04

		MINT	EXC	G-VG
☐ 320	Barry Bonds	.70	.28	.07
☐ 321	Mike Laga	.03	.01	.00
☐ 322	Chris Bando	.03	.01	.00
☐ 323	Al Newman	.06	.02	.00
☐ 324	David Palmer	.03	.01	.00
☐ 325	Garry Templeton	.06	.02	.00
☐ 326	Mark Gubicza	.08	.03	.01
☐ 327	Dale Sveum	.20	.08	.02
☐ 328	Bob Welch	.06	.02	.00
☐ 329	Ron Roenicke	.03	.01	.00
☐ 330	Mike Scott	.20	.08	.02
☐ 331	Mets Team	.15	.06	.01
	(Gary Carter and Darryl Strawberry)			
☐ 332	Joe Price	.03	.01	.00
☐ 333	Ken Phelps	.06	.02	.00
☐ 334	Ed Correa	.15	.06	.01
☐ 335	Candy Maldonado	.06	.02	.00
☐ 336	Allan Anderson	.25	.10	.02
☐ 337	Darrell Miller	.03	.01	.00
☐ 338	Tim Conroy	.03	.01	.00
☐ 339	Donnie Hill	.03	.01	.00
☐ 340	Roger Clemens	.90	.36	.09
☐ 341	Mike Brown	.03	.01	.00
	(Pirates OF)			
☐ 342	Bob James	.03	.01	.00
☐ 343	Hal Lanier MG	.06	.01	.00
	(checklist back)			
☐ 344A	Joe Niekro	.10	.04	.01
	(copyright inside righthand border)			
☐ 344B	Joe Niekro	.30	.12	.03
	(copyright outside righthand border)			
☐ 345	Andre Dawson	.25	.10	.02
☐ 346	Shawon Dunston	.08	.03	.01
☐ 347	Mickey Brantley	.10	.04	.01
☐ 348	Carmelo Martinez	.03	.01	.00
☐ 349	Storm Davis	.06	.02	.00
☐ 350	Keith Hernandez	.20	.08	.02
☐ 351	Gene Garber	.03	.01	.00
☐ 352	Mike Felder	.06	.02	.00
☐ 353	Ernie Camacho	.03	.01	.00
☐ 354	Jamie Quirk	.03	.01	.00
☐ 355	Don Carman	.03	.01	.00
☐ 356	White Sox Team	.03	.01	.00
	(mound conference)			
☐ 357	Steve Fireovid	.06	.02	.00
☐ 358	Sal Butera	.03	.01	.00
☐ 359	Doug Corbett	.03	.01	.00
☐ 360	Pedro Guerrero	.15	.06	.01
☐ 361	Mark Thurmond	.03	.01	.00

	MINT	EXC	G-VG
☐ 362 Luis Quinones	.08	.03	.01
☐ 363 Jose Guzman	.08	.03	.01
☐ 364 Randy Bush	.03	.01	.00
☐ 365 Rick Rhoden	.06	.02	.00
☐ 366 Mark McGwire	2.50	1.00	.25
☐ 367 Jeff Lahti	.03	.01	.00
☐ 368 John McNamara MG (checklist back)	.06	.01	.00
☐ 369 Brian Dayett	.03	.01	.00
☐ 370 Fred Lynn	.10	.04	.01
☐ 371 Mark Eichhorn	.08	.03	.01
☐ 372 Jerry Mumphrey	.03	.01	.00
☐ 373 Jeff Dedmon	.03	.01	.00
☐ 374 Glenn Hoffman	.03	.01	.00
☐ 375 Ron Guidry	.10	.04	.01
☐ 376 Scott Bradley	.03	.01	.00
☐ 377 John Henry Johnson	.03	.01	.00
☐ 378 Rafael Santana	.03	.01	.00
☐ 379 John Russell	.03	.01	.00
☐ 380 Rich Gossage	.08	.03	.01
☐ 381 Expos Team (mound conference)	.03	.01	.00
☐ 382 Rudy Law	.03	.01	.00
☐ 383 Ron Davis	.03	.01	.00
☐ 384 Johnny Grubb	.03	.01	.00
☐ 385 Orel Hershiser	.30	.12	.03
☐ 386 Dickie Thon	.03	.01	.00
☐ 387 T.R. Bryden	.06	.02	.00
☐ 388 Geno Petralli	.03	.01	.00
☐ 389 Jeff Robinson (Giants pitcher)	.06	.02	.00
☐ 390 Gary Matthews	.03	.01	.00
☐ 391 Jay Howell	.06	.02	.00
☐ 392 Checklist 265-396 .	.06	.01	.00
☐ 393 Pete Rose MG (checklist back)	.35	.14	.03
☐ 394 Mike Bielecki	.03	.01	.00
☐ 395 Damaso Garcia	.03	.01	.00
☐ 396 Tim Lollar	.03	.01	.00
☐ 397 Greg Walker	.06	.02	.00
☐ 398 Brad Havens	.03	.01	.00
☐ 399 Curt Ford	.08	.03	.01
☐ 400 George Brett	.30	.12	.03
☐ 401 Billy Jo Robidoux ..	.06	.02	.00
☐ 402 Mike Trujillo	.03	.01	.00
☐ 403 Jerry Royster	.03	.01	.00
☐ 404 Doug Sisk	.03	.01	.00
☐ 405 Brook Jacoby	.08	.03	.01

	MINT	EXC	G-VG
☐ 406 Yankees Team ... (Henderson/Mattingly)	.25	.10	.02
☐ 407 Jim Acker	.03	.01	.00
☐ 408 John Mizerock	.03	.01	.00
☐ 409 Milt Thompson	.06	.02	.00
☐ 410 Fernando Valenzuela	.18	.08	.01
☐ 411 Darnell Coles	.03	.01	.00
☐ 412 Eric Davis	.90	.36	.09
☐ 413 Moose Haas	.03	.01	.00
☐ 414 Joe Orsulak	.03	.01	.00
☐ 415 Bobby Witt	.25	.10	.02
☐ 416 Tom Nieto	.03	.01	.00
☐ 417 Pat Perry	.03	.01	.00
☐ 418 Dick Williams MG . (checklist back)	.06	.01	.00
☐ 419 Mark Portugal	.06	.02	.00
☐ 420 Will Clark	1.75	.70	.17
☐ 421 Jose DeLeon	.03	.01	.00
☐ 422 Jack Howell	.03	.01	.00
☐ 423 Jaime Cocanower .	.03	.01	.00
☐ 424 Chris Speier	.03	.01	.00
☐ 425 Tom Seaver	.25	.10	.02
☐ 426 Floyd Rayford	.03	.01	.00
☐ 427 Edwin Nunez	.03	.01	.00
☐ 428 Bruce Bochy	.03	.01	.00
☐ 429 Tim Pyznarski	.10	.04	.01
☐ 430 Mike Schmidt	.35	.14	.03
☐ 431 Dodgers Team ..... (mound conference)	.03	.01	.00
☐ 432 Jim Slaton	.03	.01	.00
☐ 433 Ed Hearn	.06	.02	.00
☐ 434 Mike Fischlin	.03	.01	.00
☐ 435 Bruce Sutter	.08	.03	.01
☐ 436 Andy Allanson	.08	.03	.01
☐ 437 Ted Power	.03	.01	.00
☐ 438 Kelly Downs	.25	.10	.02
☐ 439 Karl Best	.03	.01	.00
☐ 440 Willie McGee	.12	.05	.01
☐ 441 Dave Leiper	.06	.02	.00
☐ 442 Mitch Webster	.03	.01	.00
☐ 443 John Felske MG .. (checklist back)	.06	.01	.00
☐ 444 Jeff Russell	.03	.01	.00
☐ 445 Dave Lopes	.06	.02	.00
☐ 446 Chuck Finley	.08	.03	.01
☐ 447 Bill Almon	.03	.01	.00
☐ 448 Chris Bosio	.10	.04	.01
☐ 449 Pat Dodson	.10	.04	.01
☐ 450 Kirby Puckett	.45	.18	.04

		MINT	EXC	G-VG
☐ 451	Joe Sambito	.03	.01	.00
☐ 452	Dave Henderson	.06	.02	.00
☐ 453	Scott Terry	.10	.04	.01
☐ 454	Luis Salazar	.03	.01	.00
☐ 455	Mike Boddicker	.06	.02	.00
☐ 456	A's Team	.03	.01	.00
	(mound conference)			
☐ 457	Len Matuszek	.03	.01	.00
☐ 458	Kelly Gruber	.03	.01	.00
☐ 459	Dennis Eckersley	.10	.04	.01
☐ 460	Darryl Strawberry	.45	.18	.04
☐ 461	Craig McMurtry	.03	.01	.00
☐ 462	Scott Fletcher	.06	.02	.00
☐ 463	Tom Candiotti	.03	.01	.00
☐ 464	Butch Wynegar	.03	.01	.00
☐ 465	Todd Worrell	.18	.08	.01
☐ 466	Kal Daniels	.90	.36	.09
☐ 467	Randy St.Claire	.03	.01	.00
☐ 468	George Bamberger MG	.06	.01	.00
	(checklist back)			
☐ 469	Mike Diaz	.10	.04	.01
☐ 470	Dave Dravecky	.03	.01	.00
☐ 471	Ronn Reynolds	.03	.01	.00
☐ 472	Bill Doran	.08	.03	.01
☐ 473	Steve Farr	.03	.01	.00
☐ 474	Jerry Narron	.03	.01	.00
☐ 475	Scott Garrelts	.03	.01	.00
☐ 476	Danny Tartabull	.75	.30	.07
☐ 477	Ken Howell	.03	.01	.00
☐ 478	Tim Laudner	.03	.01	.00
☐ 479	Bob Sebra	.10	.04	.01
☐ 480	Jim Rice	.15	.06	.01
☐ 481	Phillies Team	.06	.02	.00
	(Glenn Wilson, Juan Samuel, and			
	Von Hayes)			
☐ 482	Daryl Boston	.03	.01	.00
☐ 483	Dwight Lowry	.08	.03	.01
☐ 484	Jim Traber	.06	.02	.00
☐ 485	Tony Fernandez	.10	.04	.01
☐ 486	Otis Nixon	.08	.03	.01
☐ 487	Dave Gumpert	.03	.01	.00
☐ 488	Ray Knight	.06	.02	.00
☐ 489	Bill Gullickson	.03	.01	.00
☐ 490	Dale Murphy	.40	.16	.04
☐ 491	Ron Karkovice	.06	.02	.00
☐ 492	Mike Heath	.03	.01	.00
☐ 493	Tom Lasorda MG	.08	.02	.00
	(checklist back)			
☐ 494	Barry Jones	.10	.04	.01

		MINT	EXC	G-VG
☐ 495	Gorman Thomas	.08	.03	.01
☐ 496	Bruce Bochte	.03	.01	.00
☐ 497	Dale Mohorcic	.15	.06	.01
☐ 498	Bob Kearney	.03	.01	.00
☐ 499	Bruce Ruffin	.15	.06	.01
☐ 500	Don Mattingly	1.50	.60	.15
☐ 501	Craig Lefferts	.03	.01	.00
☐ 502	Dick Schofield	.03	.01	.00
☐ 503	Larry Andersen	.03	.01	.00
☐ 504	Mickey Hatcher	.06	.02	.00
☐ 505	Bryn Smith	.03	.01	.00
☐ 506	Orioles Team	.03	.01	.00
	(mound conference)			
☐ 507	Dave Stapleton	.03	.01	.00
	(infielder)			
☐ 508	Scott Bankhead	.06	.02	.00
☐ 509	Enos Cabell	.03	.01	.00
☐ 510	Tom Henke	.06	.02	.00
☐ 511	Steve Lyons	.03	.01	.00
☐ 512	Dave Magadan	.40	.16	.04
☐ 513	Carmen Castillo	.03	.01	.00
☐ 514	Orlando Mercado	.03	.01	.00
☐ 515	Willie Hernandez	.08	.03	.01
☐ 516	Ted Simmons	.08	.03	.01
☐ 517	Mario Soto	.03	.01	.00
☐ 518	Gene Mauch MG	.06	.01	.00
	(checklist back)			
☐ 519	Curt Young	.03	.01	.00
☐ 520	Jack Clark	.18	.08	.01
☐ 521	Rick Reuschel	.06	.02	.00
☐ 522	Checklist 397-528	.06	.01	.00
☐ 523	Earnie Riles	.03	.01	.00
☐ 524	Bob Shirley	.03	.01	.00
☐ 525	Phil Bradley	.08	.03	.01
☐ 526	Roger Mason	.03	.01	.00
☐ 527	Jim Wohlford	.03	.01	.00
☐ 528	Ken Dixon	.03	.01	.00
☐ 529	Alvaro Espinoza	.03	.01	.00
☐ 530	Tony Gwynn	.35	.14	.03
☐ 531	Astros Team	.08	.03	.01
	(Y.Berra conference)			
☐ 532	Jeff Stone	.03	.01	.00
☐ 533	Argenis Salazar	.03	.01	.00
☐ 534	Scott Sanderson	.03	.01	.00
☐ 535	Tony Armas	.06	.02	.00
☐ 536	Terry Mulholland	.10	.04	.01
☐ 537	Rance Mulliniks	.03	.01	.00
☐ 538	Tom Niedenfuer	.03	.01	.00
☐ 539	Reid Nichols	.03	.01	.00

	MINT	EXC	G-VG		MINT	EXC	G-VG
☐ 540 Terry Kennedy	.03	.01	.00	☐ 585 Scott Bailes	.10	.04	.01
☐ 541 Rafael Belliard	.08	.03	.01	☐ 586 Ben Oglivie	.06	.02	.00
☐ 542 Ricky Horton	.03	.01	.00	☐ 587 Eric Plunk	.06	.02	.00
☐ 543 Dave Johnson MG	.08	.02	.00	☐ 588 Wallace Johnson	.06	.02	.00
(checklist back)				☐ 589 Steve Crawford	.03	.01	.00
☐ 544 Zane Smith	.08	.03	.01	☐ 590 Vince Coleman	.25	.10	.02
☐ 545 Buddy Bell	.08	.03	.01	☐ 591 Spike Owen	.03	.01	.00
☐ 546 Mike Morgan	.03	.01	.00	☐ 592 Chris Welsh	.03	.01	.00
☐ 547 Rob Deer	.12	.05	.01	☐ 593 Chuck Tanner MG	.06	.01	.00
☐ 548 Bill Mooneyham	.06	.02	.00	(checklist back)			
☐ 549 Bob Melvin	.03	.01	.00	☐ 594 Rick Anderson	.08	.03	.01
☐ 550 Pete Incaviglia	.65	.26	.06	☐ 595 Keith Hernandez AS	.10	.04	.01
☐ 551 Frank Wills	.03	.01	.00	☐ 596 Steve Sax AS	.08	.03	.01
☐ 552 Larry Sheets	.08	.03	.01	☐ 597 Mike Schmidt AS	.20	.08	.02
☐ 553 Mike Maddux	.15	.06	.01	☐ 598 Ozzie Smith AS	.10	.04	.01
☐ 554 Buddy Biancalana	.03	.01	.00	☐ 599 Tony Gwynn AS	.15	.06	.01
☐ 555 Dennis Rasmussen	.06	.02	.00	☐ 600 Dave Parker AS	.08	.03	.01
☐ 556 Angels Team	.06	.02	.00	☐ 601 Darryl Strawberry AS	.20	.08	.02
(Lachemann/Witt/Boone)				☐ 602 Gary Carter AS	.12	.05	.01
☐ 557 John Cerutti	.12	.05	.01	☐ 603A Dwight Gooden AS	.75	.30	.07
☐ 558 Greg Gagne	.03	.01	.00	ERR (no trademark)			
☐ 559 Lance McCullers	.06	.02	.00	☐ 603B Dwight Gooden AS COR	.30	.12	.03
☐ 560 Glenn Davis	.25	.10	.02	☐ 604 Fern. Valenzuela AS	.10	.04	.01
☐ 561 Rey Quinones	.15	.06	.01	☐ 605 Todd Worrell AS	.08	.03	.01
☐ 562 Bryan Clutterbuck	.06	.02	.00	☐ 606A Don Mattingly AS	1.50	.60	.15
☐ 563 John Stefero	.03	.01	.00	ERR (no trademark)			
☐ 564 Larry McWilliams	.03	.01	.00	☐ 606B Don Mattingly AS COR	.60	.24	.06
☐ 565 Dusty Baker	.06	.02	.00	☐ 607 Tony Bernazard AS	.06	.02	.00
☐ 566 Tim Hulett	.03	.01	.00	☐ 608 Wade Boggs AS	.35	.14	.03
☐ 567 Greg Mathews	.20	.08	.02	☐ 609 Cal Ripken AS	.12	.05	.01
☐ 568 Earl Weaver MG	.08	.02	.00	☐ 610 Jim Rice AS	.10	.04	.01
(checklist back)				☐ 611 Kirby Puckett AS	.20	.08	.02
☐ 569 Wade Rowdon	.06	.02	.00	☐ 612 George Bell AS	.10	.04	.01
☐ 570 Sid Fernandez	.10	.04	.01	☐ 613 Lance Parrish AS	.08	.03	.01
☐ 571 Ozzie Virgil	.03	.01	.00	☐ 614 Roger Clemens AS	.25	.10	.02
☐ 572 Pete Ladd	.03	.01	.00	☐ 615 Teddy Higuera AS	.08	.03	.01
☐ 573 Hal McRae	.06	.02	.00	☐ 616 Dave Righetti AS	.08	.03	.01
☐ 574 Manny Lee	.03	.01	.00	☐ 617 Al Nipper	.03	.01	.00
☐ 575 Pat Tabler	.06	.02	.00	☐ 618 Tom Kelly MG	.08	.02	.00
☐ 576 Frank Pastore	.03	.01	.00	(checklist back)			
☐ 577 Dann Bilardello	.03	.01	.00	☐ 619 Jerry Reed	.03	.01	.00
☐ 578 Billy Hatcher	.08	.03	.01	☐ 620 Jose Canseco	4.50	1.80	.45
☐ 579 Rick Burleson	.06	.02	.00	☐ 621 Danny Cox	.06	.02	.00
☐ 580 Mike Krukow	.03	.01	.00	☐ 622 Glenn Braggs	.25	.10	.02
☐ 581 Cubs Team	.03	.01	.00	☐ 623 Kurt Stillwell	.20	.08	.02
(Cey/Trout)				☐ 624 Tim Burke	.03	.01	.00
☐ 582 Bruce Berenyi	.03	.01	.00	☐ 625 Mookie Wilson	.06	.02	.00
☐ 583 Junior Ortiz	.03	.01	.00	☐ 626 Joel Skinner	.03	.01	.00
☐ 584 Ron Kittle	.08	.03	.01	☐ 627 Ken Oberkfell	.03	.01	.00

		MINT	EXC	G-VG			MINT	EXC	G-VG
☐ 628	Bob Walk	.03	.01	.00	☐ 672	Chili Davis	.08	.03	.01
☐ 629	Larry Parrish	.03	.01	.00	☐ 673	Don Sutton	.12	.05	.01
☐ 630	John Candelaria	.06	.02	.00	☐ 674	Bill Campbell	.03	.01	.00
☐ 631	Tigers Team	.03	.01	.00	☐ 675	Ed Romero	.03	.01	.00
	(mound conference)				☐ 676	Charlie Moore	.03	.01	.00
☐ 632	Rob Woodward	.06	.02	.00	☐ 677	Bob Grich	.06	.02	.00
☐ 633	Jose Uribe	.03	.01	.00	☐ 678	Carney Lansford	.06	.02	.00
☐ 634	Rafael Palmeiro	.90	.36	.09	☐ 679	Kent Hrbek	.15	.06	.01
☐ 635	Ken Schrom	.03	.01	.00	☐ 680	Ryne Sandberg	.20	.08	.02
☐ 636	Darren Daulton	.03	.01	.00	☐ 681	George Bell	.20	.08	.02
☐ 637	Bip Roberts	.06	.02	.00	☐ 682	Jerry Reuss	.03	.01	.00
☐ 638	Rich Bordi	.03	.01	.00	☐ 683	Gary Roenicke	.03	.01	.00
☐ 639	Gerald Perry	.08	.03	.01	☐ 684	Kent Tekulve	.03	.01	.00
☐ 640	Mark Clear	.03	.01	.00	☐ 685	Jerry Hairston	.03	.01	.00
☐ 641	Domingo Ramos	.03	.01	.00	☐ 686	Doyle Alexander	.03	.01	.00
☐ 642	Al Pulido	.06	.02	.00	☐ 687	Alan Trammell	.15	.06	.01
☐ 643	Ron Shepherd	.06	.02	.00	☐ 688	Juan Beniquez	.03	.01	.00
☐ 644	John Denny	.03	.01	.00	☐ 689	Darrell Porter	.03	.01	.00
☐ 645	Dwight Evans	.10	.04	.01	☐ 690	Dane Iorg	.03	.01	.00
☐ 646	Mike Mason	.03	.01	.00	☐ 691	Dave Parker	.12	.05	.01
☐ 647	Tom Lawless	.03	.01	.00	☐ 692	Frank White	.06	.02	.00
☐ 648	Barry Larkin	.90	.36	.09	☐ 693	Terry Puhl	.03	.01	.00
☐ 649	Mickey Tettleton	.03	.01	.00	☐ 694	Phil Niekro	.12	.05	.01
☐ 650	Hubie Brooks	.08	.03	.01	☐ 695	Chico Walker	.08	.03	.01
☐ 651	Benny Distefano	.06	.02	.00	☐ 696	Gary Lucas	.03	.01	.00
☐ 652	Terry Forster	.06	.02	.00	☐ 697	Ed Lynch	.03	.01	.00
☐ 653	Kevin Mitchell	.25	.10	.02	☐ 698	Ernie Whitt	.03	.01	.00
☐ 654	Checklist 529-660	.06	.01	.00	☐ 699	Ken Landreaux	.03	.01	.00
☐ 655	Jesse Barfield	.15	.06	.01	☐ 700	Dave Bergman	.03	.01	.00
☐ 656	Rangers Team	.03	.01	.00	☐ 701	Willie Randolph	.06	.02	.00
	(Valentine/R.Wright)				☐ 702	Greg Gross	.03	.01	.00
☐ 657	Tom Waddell	.03	.01	.00	☐ 703	Dave Schmidt	.06	.02	.00
☐ 658	Robby Thompson	.20	.08	.02	☐ 704	Jesse Orosco	.03	.01	.00
☐ 659	Aurelio Lopez	.03	.01	.00	☐ 705	Bruce Hurst	.10	.04	.01
☐ 660	Bob Horner	.10	.04	.01	☐ 706	Rick Manning	.03	.01	.00
☐ 661	Lou Whitaker	.10	.04	.01	☐ 707	Bob McClure	.03	.01	.00
☐ 662	Frank DiPino	.03	.01	.00	☐ 708	Scott McGregor	.06	.02	.00
☐ 663	Cliff Johnson	.03	.01	.00	☐ 709	Dave Kingman	.08	.03	.01
☐ 664	Mike Marshall	.10	.04	.01	☐ 710	Gary Gaetti	.10	.04	.01
☐ 665	Rod Scurry	.03	.01	.00	☐ 711	Ken Griffey	.06	.02	.00
☐ 666	Von Hayes	.08	.03	.01	☐ 712	Don Robinson	.03	.01	.00
☐ 667	Ron Hassey	.03	.01	.00	☐ 713	Tom Brookens	.03	.01	.00
☐ 668	Juan Bonilla	.03	.01	.00	☐ 714	Dan Quisenberry	.08	.03	.01
☐ 669	Bud Black	.03	.01	.00	☐ 715	Bob Dernier	.03	.01	.00
☐ 670	Jose Cruz	.06	.02	.00	☐ 716	Rick Leach	.03	.01	.00
☐ 671A	Ray Soff ERR	.08	.03	.01	☐ 717	Ed VandeBerg	.03	.01	.00
	(no D* before copyright line)				☐ 718	Steve Carlton	.20	.08	.02
☐ 671B	Ray Soff COR	.08	.03	.01	☐ 719	Tom Hume	.03	.01	.00
	(D* before copyright line)				☐ 720	Richard Dotson	.06	.02	.00

		MINT	EXC	G-VG
☐ 721	Tom Herr	.06	.02	.00
☐ 722	Bob Knepper	.06	.02	.00
☐ 723	Brett Butler	.06	.02	.00
☐ 724	Greg Minton	.03	.01	.00
☐ 725	George Hendrick	.03	.01	.00
☐ 726	Frank Tanana	.03	.01	.00
☐ 727	Mike Moore	.03	.01	.00
☐ 728	Tippy Martinez	.03	.01	.00
☐ 729	Tom Paciorek	.03	.01	.00
☐ 730	Eric Show	.06	.02	.00
☐ 731	Dave Concepcion	.06	.02	.00
☐ 732	Manny Trillo	.03	.01	.00
☐ 733	Bill Caudill	.03	.01	.00
☐ 734	Bill Madlock	.08	.03	.01
☐ 735	Rickey Henderson	.25	.10	.02
☐ 736	Steve Bedrosian	.10	.04	.01
☐ 737	Floyd Bannister	.03	.01	.00
☐ 738	Jorge Orta	.03	.01	.00
☐ 739	Chet Lemon	.03	.01	.00
☐ 740	Rich Gedman	.06	.02	.00
☐ 741	Paul Molitor	.10	.04	.01
☐ 742	Andy McGaffigan	.03	.01	.00
☐ 743	Dwayne Murphy	.03	.01	.00
☐ 744	Roy Smalley	.03	.01	.00
☐ 745	Glenn Hubbard	.03	.01	.00
☐ 746	Bob Ojeda	.06	.02	.00
☐ 747	Johnny Ray	.06	.02	.00
☐ 748	Mike Flanagan	.06	.02	.00
☐ 749	Ozzie Smith	.15	.06	.01
☐ 750	Steve Trout	.03	.01	.00
☐ 751	Garth Iorg	.03	.01	.00
☐ 752	Dan Petry	.06	.02	.00
☐ 753	Rick Honeycutt	.03	.01	.00
☐ 754	Dave LaPoint	.06	.02	.00
☐ 755	Luis Aguayo	.03	.01	.00
☐ 756	Carlton Fisk	.10	.04	.01
☐ 757	Nolan Ryan	.25	.10	.02
☐ 758	Tony Bernazard	.03	.01	.00
☐ 759	Joel Youngblood	.03	.01	.00
☐ 760	Mike Witt	.08	.03	.01
☐ 761	Greg Pryor	.03	.01	.00
☐ 762	Gary Ward	.03	.01	.00
☐ 763	Tim Flannery	.03	.01	.00
☐ 764	Bill Buckner	.06	.02	.00
☐ 765	Kirk Gibson	.15	.06	.01
☐ 766	Don Aase	.03	.01	.00
☐ 767	Ron Cey	.06	.02	.00
☐ 768	Dennis Lamp	.03	.01	.00
☐ 769	Steve Sax	.12	.05	.01

		MINT	EXC	G-VG
☐ 770	Dave Winfield	.25	.10	.02
☐ 771	Shane Rawley	.06	.02	.00
☐ 772	Harold Baines	.10	.04	.01
☐ 773	Robin Yount	.25	.10	.02
☐ 774	Wayne Krenchicki	.03	.01	.00
☐ 775	Joaquin Andujar	.06	.02	.00
☐ 776	Tom Brunansky	.10	.04	.01
☐ 777	Chris Chambliss	.06	.02	.00
☐ 778	Jack Morris	.12	.05	.01
☐ 779	Craig Reynolds	.03	.01	.00
☐ 780	Andre Thornton	.06	.02	.00
☐ 781	Atlee Hammaker	.03	.01	.00
☐ 782	Brian Downing	.06	.02	.00
☐ 783	Willie Wilson	.08	.03	.01
☐ 784	Cal Ripken	.20	.08	.02
☐ 785	Terry Francona	.03	.01	.00
☐ 786	Jimy Williams MG	.06	.01	.00
	(checklist back)			
☐ 787	Alejandro Pena	.03	.01	.00
☐ 788	Tim Stoddard	.03	.01	.00
☐ 789	Dan Schatzeder	.03	.01	.00
☐ 790	Julio Cruz	.03	.01	.00
☐ 791	Lance Parrish	.15	.06	.01
	UER (no trademark, never corrected)			
☐ 792	Checklist 661-792	.06	.01	.00

1987 Topps Traded

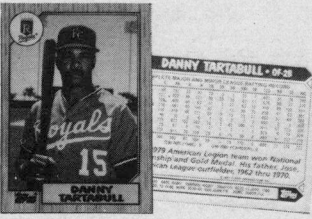

This 132-card Traded or extended set was distributed by Topps to dealers in a special green and white box as a complete set. The card fronts are identical in style to the Topps regular issue and are also 2 ½ " by 3 ½ ". The *backs are printed in yellow and blue on white card stock. Cards are numbered (with a T suffix) alphabetically according to the name of the player.*

	MINT	EXC	G-VG
Complete Set (132)	12.00	5.00	1.20
Common Player (1-132) ...	.05	.02	.00

		MINT	EXC	G-VG
☐	1T Bill Almon	.05	.02	.00
☐	2T Scott Bankhead	.10	.04	.01
☐	3T Eric Bell	.10	.04	.01
☐	4T Juan Beniquez	.05	.02	.00
☐	5T Juan Berenguer	.05	.02	.00
☐	6T Greg Booker	.05	.02	.00
☐	7T Thad Bosley	.05	.02	.00
☐	8T Larry Bowa MG	.10	.04	.01
☐	9T Greg Brock	.10	.04	.01
☐	10T Bob Brower	.15	.06	.01
☐	11T Jerry Browne	.10	.04	.01
☐	12T Ralph Bryant	.10	.04	.01
☐	13T DeWayne Buice ...	.10	.04	.01
☐	14T Ellis Burks	1.75	.70	.17
☐	15T Ivan Calderon	.20	.08	.02
☐	16T Jeff Calhoun	.05	.02	.00
☐	17T Casey Candaele ...	.10	.04	.01
☐	18T John Cangelosi ...	.10	.04	.01
☐	19T Steve Carlton	.20	.08	.02
☐	20T Juan Castillo	.10	.04	.01
☐	21T Rick Cerone	.05	.02	.00
☐	22T Ron Cey	.10	.04	.01
☐	23T John Christensen ..	.05	.02	.00
☐	24T David Cone	2.00	.80	.20
☐	25T Chuck Crim	.10	.04	.01
☐	26T Storm Davis	.10	.04	.01
☐	27T Andre Dawson	.35	.14	.03
☐	28T Rick Dempsey	.10	.04	.01
☐	29T Doug Drabek	.10	.04	.01
☐	30T Mike Dunne	.20	.08	.02
☐	31T Dennis Eckersley ..	.20	.08	.02
☐	32T Lee Elia MG	.05	.02	.00
☐	33T Brian Fisher	.10	.04	.01
☐	34T Terry Francona	.05	.02	.00
☐	35T Willie Fraser	.10	.04	.01
☐	36T Billy Gardner MG ..	.05	.02	.00
☐	37T Ken Gerhart	.15	.06	.01
☐	38T Dan Gladden	.10	.04	.01
☐	39T Jim Gott	.10	.04	.01
☐	40T Cecilio Guante	.05	.02	.00
☐	41T Albert Hall	.10	.04	.01
☐	42T Terry Harper	.05	.02	.00

		MINT	EXC	G-VG
☐	43T Mickey Hatcher ...	.10	.04	.01
☐	44T Brad Havens	.05	.02	.00
☐	45T Neal Heaton	.05	.02	.00
☐	46T Mike Henneman ..	.30	.12	.03
☐	47T Donnie Hill	.05	.02	.00
☐	48T Guy Hoffman	.05	.02	.00
☐	49T Brian Holton	.15	.06	.01
☐	50T Charles Hudson ..	.05	.02	.00
☐	51T Danny Jackson ...	.25	.10	.02
☐	52T Reggie Jackson ...	.45	.18	.04
☐	53T Chris James	.45	.18	.04
☐	54T Dion James	.10	.04	.01
☐	55T Stan Jefferson	.25	.10	.02
☐	56T Joe Johnson	.10	.04	.01
☐	57T Terry Kennedy	.10	.04	.01
☐	58T Mike Kingery	.10	.04	.01
☐	59T Ray Knight	.10	.04	.01
☐	60T Gene Larkin	.30	.12	.03
☐	61T Mike LaValliere ...	.10	.04	.01
☐	62T Jack Lazorko	.05	.02	.00
☐	63T Terry Leach	.15	.06	.01
☐	64T Tim Leary	.20	.08	.02
☐	65T Jim Lindeman	.20	.08	.02
☐	66T Steve Lombardozzi	.10	.04	.01
☐	67T Bill Long	.15	.06	.01
☐	68T Barry Lyons	.15	.06	.01
☐	69T Shane Mack	.20	.08	.02
☐	70T Greg Maddux	.60	.24	.06
☐	71T Bill Madlock	.10	.04	.01
☐	72T Joe Magrane	.50	.20	.05
☐	73T Dave Martinez	.20	.08	.02
☐	74T Fred McGriff	1.50	.60	.15
☐	75T Mark McLemore ...	.05	.02	.00
☐	76T Kevin McReynolds ..	.25	.10	.02
☐	77T Dave Meads	.10	.04	.01
☐	78T Eddie Milner	.05	.02	.00
☐	79T Greg Minton	.05	.02	.00
☐	80T John Mitchell	.15	.06	.01
☐	81T Kevin Mitchell	.15	.06	.01
☐	82T Charlie Moore	.05	.02	.00
☐	83T Jeff Musselman ...	.15	.06	.01
☐	84T Gene Nelson	.05	.02	.00
☐	85T Graig Nettles	.15	.06	.01
☐	86T Al Newman	.05	.02	.00
☐	87T Reid Nichols	.05	.02	.00
☐	88T Tom Niedenfuer ..	.05	.02	.00
☐	89T Joe Niekro	.10	.04	.01
☐	90T Tom Nieto	.05	.02	.00
☐	91T Matt Nokes	.60	.26	.06

		MINT	EXC	G-VG
☐	92T Dickie Noles	.05	.02	.00
☐	93T Pat Pacillo	.15	.06	.01
☐	94T Lance Parrish	.15	.06	.01
☐	95T Tony Pena	.15	.06	.01
☐	96T Luis Polonia	.25	.10	.02
☐	97T Randy Ready	.10	.04	.01
☐	98T Jeff Reardon	.15	.06	.01
☐	99T Gary Redus	.05	.02	.00
☐	100T Jeff Reed	.05	.02	.00
☐	101T Rick Rhoden	.10	.04	.01
☐	102T Cal Ripken Sr. MG	.05	.02	.00
☐	103T Wally Ritchie	.10	.04	.01
☐	104T Jeff Robinson (Tigers pitcher)	.45	.18	.04
☐	105T Gary Roenicke	.05	.02	.00
☐	106T Jerry Royster	.05	.02	.00
☐	107T Mark Salas	.05	.02	.00
☐	108T Luis Salazar	.05	.02	.00
☐	109T Benny Santiago	1.00	.40	.10
☐	110T Dave Schmidt	.10	.04	.01
☐	111T Kevin Seitzer	1.50	.60	.15
☐	112T John Shelby	.05	.02	.00
☐	113T Steve Shields	.10	.04	.01
☐	114T John Smiley	.35	.14	.03
☐	115T Chris Speier	.05	.02	.00
☐	116T Mike Stanley	.20	.08	.02
☐	117T Terry Steinbach	.40	.16	.04
☐	118T Les Straker	.15	.06	.01
☐	119T Jim Sundberg	.10	.04	.01
☐	120T Danny Tartabull	.30	.12	.03
☐	121T Tom Trebelhorn MG	.05	.02	.00
☐	122T Dave Valle	.05	.02	.00
☐	123T Ed VandeBerg	.05	.02	.00
☐	124T Andy Van Slyke	.25	.10	.02
☐	125T Gary Ward	.10	.04	.01
☐	126T Alan Wiggins	.05	.02	.00
☐	127T Bill Wilkinson	.15	.06	.01
☐	128T Frank Williams	.05	.02	.00
☐	129T Matt Williams	.45	.18	.04
☐	130T Jim Winn	.05	.02	.00
☐	131T Matt Young	.05	.02	.00
☐	132T Checklist	.05	.01	.00

1988 Topps

This 792-card set features backs which are printed in orange and black on white card stock. The manager cards contain a checklist of the respective team's players on the back. Subsets in the set include Record Breakers (1-7), Turn Back The Clock (661-665), and All-Star selections (386-407). The Team Leader cards typically show two players together inside a white cloud. Topps also produced a specially boxed "glossy" edition frequently referred to as the Topps Tiffany set. This year, again, Topps did not disclose the number of sets they produced or sold; it is apparent from the availability that there were many more sets produced this year compared to the 1984-86 Tiffany sets. The checklist of cards (792 regular and 132 Traded) is identical to that of the normal non-glossy cards. There are two primary distinguishing features of the Tiffany cards, white card stock reverses and high gloss obverses. These Tiffany cards are valued at approximately four times the values listed below.

		MINT	EXC	G-VG
	Complete Set (792)	24.00	10.00	2.40
	Common Player (1-792)	.03	.01	.00
☐	1 Vince Coleman RB 100 Steals for Third Cons. Season	.25	.07	.01
☐	2 Don Mattingly RB Six Grand Slams	.40	.16	.04

		MINT	EXC	G-VG
☐	**3A** Mark McGwire RB ERR **1.00**		.40	.10
	Rookie Homer Record			
	(white spot behind left foot)			
☐	**3B** Mark McGwire RB COR .40		.16	.04
	Rookie Homer Record			
	(no white spot)			
☐	**4A** Eddie Murray RB ERR 2.00		.80	.20
	Switch Home Runs,			
	Two Straight Games			
	(caption in box on card front)			
☐	**4B** Eddie Murray RB COR .25		.10	.02
	Switch Home Runs,			
	Two Straight Games			
	(no caption on front)			
☐	**5** Phil/Joe Niekro RB . .06		.02	.00
	Brothers Win Record			
☐	**6** Nolan Ryan RB ..... .15		.06	.01
	11th Season with			
	200 Strikeouts			
☐	**7** Benito Santiago RB .20		.08	.02
	34-Game Hitting Streak,			
	Rookie Record			
☐	**8** Kevin Elster .... .20		.08	.02
☐	**9** Andy Hawkins ..... .03		.01	.00
☐	**10** Ryne Sandberg .... .15		.06	.01
☐	**11** Mike Young .... .03		.01	.00
☐	**12** Bill Schroeder ..... .03		.01	.00
☐	**13** Andres Thomas ... .03		.01	.00
☐	**14** Sparky Anderson MG .06		.01	.00
	(checklist back)			
☐	**15** Chili Davis .... .06		.02	.00
☐	**16** Kirk McCaskill .... .03		.01	.00
☐	**17** Ron Oester .... .03		.01	.00
☐	**18A** Al Leiter ERR 1.25		.50	.12
	(photo actually Jeff George,			
	right ear visible)			
☐	**18B** Al Leiter COR 1.00		.40	.10
	(left ear visible)			
☐	**19** Mark Davidson ..... .12		.05	.01
☐	**20** Kevin Gross .... .03		.01	.00
☐	**21** Red Sox TL .... .12		.05	.01
	Wade Boggs and			
	Spike Owen			
☐	**22** Greg Swindell ..... .10		.04	.01
☐	**23** Ken Landreaux ..... .03		.01	.00
☐	**24** Jim Deshaies ..... .03		.01	.00
☐	**25** Andres Galarraga .. .20		.08	.02
☐	**26** Mitch Williams ..... .03		.01	.00
☐	**27** R.J. Reynolds ...... .03		.01	.00
☐	**28** Jose Nunez .... .10		.04	.01
☐	**29** Argenis Salazar ... .03		.01	.00
☐	**30** Sid Fernandez .... .08		.03	.01
☐	**31** Bruce Bochy ...... .03		.01	.00
☐	**32** Mike Morgan ..... .03		.01	.00
☐	**33** Rob Deer .... .08		.03	.01
☐	**34** Ricky Horton ..... .03		.01	.00
☐	**35** Harold Baines .... .08		.03	.01
☐	**36** Jamie Moyer ..... .03		.01	.00
☐	**37** Ed Romero ...... .03		.01	.00
☐	**38** Jeff Calhoun ..... .03		.01	.00
☐	**39** Gerald Perry ..... .08		.03	.01
☐	**40** Orel Hershiser .... .20		.08	.02
☐	**41** Bob Melvin ...... .03		.01	.00
☐	**42** Bill Landrum ..... .10		.04	.01
☐	**43** Dick Schofield .... .03		.01	.00
☐	**44** Lou Piniella MG ... .06		.01	.00
	(checklist back)			
☐	**45** Kent Hrbek ...... .12		.05	.01
☐	**46** Darnell Coles ..... .03		.01	.00
☐	**47** Joaquin Andujar .. .06		.02	.00
☐	**48** Alan Ashby ...... .03		.01	.00
☐	**49** Dave Clark .... .08		.03	.01
☐	**50** Hubie Brooks ..... .06		.02	.00
☐	**51** Orioles TL .... .15		.06	.01
	Eddie Murray and			
	Cal Ripken			
☐	**52** Don Robinson ..... .03		.01	.00
☐	**53** Curt Wilkerson ... .03		.01	.00
☐	**54** Jim Clancy ...... .03		.01	.00
☐	**55** Phil Bradley ..... .08		.03	.01
☐	**56** Ed Hearn .... .03		.01	.00
☐	**57** Tim Crews ...... .10		.04	.01
☐	**58** Dave Magadan .... .08		.03	.01
☐	**59** Danny Cox ...... .06		.02	.00
☐	**60** Rickey Henderson . .25		.10	.02
☐	**61** Mark Knudson .... .10		.04	.01
☐	**62** Jeff Hamilton .... .06		.02	.00
☐	**63** Jimmy Jones ..... .10		.04	.01
☐	**64** Ken Caminiti ..... .18		.08	.01
☐	**65** Leon Durham ..... .03		.01	.00
☐	**66** Shane Rawley .... .03		.01	.00
☐	**67** Ken Oberkfell .... .03		.01	.00
☐	**68** Dave Dravecky ... .08		.03	.01
☐	**69** Mike Hart .... .08		.03	.01
☐	**70** Roger Clemens ... .50		.20	.05
☐	**71** Gary Pettis ...... .03		.01	.00
☐	**72** Dennis Eckersley .. .10		.04	.01
☐	**73** Randy Bush ...... .03		.01	.00

		MINT	EXC	G-VG
☐ 74	Tom Lasorda MG (checklist back)	.08	.02	.00
☐ 75	Joe Carter	.12	.05	.01
☐ 76	Dennis Martinez	.03	.01	.00
☐ 77	Tom O'Malley	.03	.01	.00
☐ 78	Dan Petry	.03	.01	.00
☐ 79	Ernie Whitt	.03	.01	.00
☐ 80	Mark Langston	.08	.03	.01
☐ 81	Reds TL Ron Robinson and John Franco	.03	.01	.00
☐ 82	Darrel Akerfelds	.10	.04	.01
☐ 83	Jose Oquendo	.03	.01	.00
☐ 84	Cecilio Guante	.03	.01	.00
☐ 85	Howard Johnson	.08	.03	.01
☐ 86	Ron Karkovice	.03	.01	.00
☐ 87	Mike Mason	.03	.01	.00
☐ 88	Earnie Riles	.03	.01	.00
☐ 89	Gary Thurman	.20	.08	.02
☐ 90	Dale Murphy	.25	.10	.02
☐ 91	Joey Cora	.10	.04	.01
☐ 92	Len Matuszek	.03	.01	.00
☐ 93	Bob Sebra	.03	.01	.00
☐ 94	Chuck Jackson	.10	.04	.01
☐ 95	Lance Parrish	.08	.03	.01
☐ 96	Todd Benzinger	.25	.10	.02
☐ 97	Scott Garrelts	.03	.01	.00
☐ 98	Rene Gonzales	.12	.05	.01
☐ 99	Chuck Finley	.03	.01	.00
☐ 100	Jack Clark	.15	.06	.01
☐ 101	Allan Anderson	.06	.02	.00
☐ 102	Barry Larkin	.12	.05	.01
☐ 103	Curt Young	.03	.01	.00
☐ 104	Dick Williams MG (checklist back)	.06	.01	.00
☐ 105	Jesse Orosco	.03	.01	.00
☐ 106	Jim Walewander	.15	.06	.01
☐ 107	Scott Bailes	.03	.01	.00
☐ 108	Steve Lyons	.03	.01	.00
☐ 109	Joel Skinner	.03	.01	.00
☐ 110	Teddy Higuera	.08	.03	.01
☐ 111	Expos TL Hubie Brooks and Vance Law	.03	.01	.00
☐ 112	Les Lancaster	.10	.04	.01
☐ 113	Kelly Gruber	.03	.01	.00
☐ 114	Jeff Russell	.03	.01	.00
☐ 115	Johnny Ray	.06	.02	.00
☐ 116	Jerry Don Gleaton	.03	.01	.00
☐ 117	James Steels	.08	.03	.01
☐ 118	Bob Welch	.06	.02	.00
☐ 119	Robbie Wine	.12	.05	.01
☐ 120	Kirby Puckett	.30	.12	.03
☐ 121	Checklist 1-132	.06	.01	.00
☐ 122	Tony Bernazard	.03	.01	.00
☐ 123	Tom Candiotti	.03	.01	.00
☐ 124	Ray Knight	.06	.02	.00
☐ 125	Bruce Hurst	.10	.04	.01
☐ 126	Steve Jeltz	.03	.01	.00
☐ 127	Jim Gott	.03	.01	.00
☐ 128	Johnny Grubb	.03	.01	.00
☐ 129	Greg Minton	.03	.01	.00
☐ 130	Buddy Bell	.08	.03	.01
☐ 131	Don Schulze	.03	.01	.00
☐ 132	Donnie Hill	.03	.01	.00
☐ 133	Greg Mathews	.03	.01	.00
☐ 134	Chuck Tanner MG (checklist back)	.06	.01	.00
☐ 135	Dennis Rasmussen	.06	.02	.00
☐ 136	Brian Dayett	.03	.01	.00
☐ 137	Chris Bosio	.03	.01	.00
☐ 138	Mitch Webster	.03	.01	.00
☐ 139	Jerry Browne	.03	.01	.00
☐ 140	Jesse Barfield	.12	.05	.01
☐ 141	Royals TL George Brett and Bret Saberhagen	.15	.06	.01
☐ 142	Andy Van Slyke	.15	.06	.01
☐ 143	Mickey Tettleton	.03	.01	.00
☐ 144	Don Gordon	.10	.04	.01
☐ 145	Bill Madlock	.06	.02	.00
☐ 146	Donnell Nixon	.10	.04	.01
☐ 147	Bill Buckner	.06	.02	.00
☐ 148	Carmelo Martinez	.03	.01	.00
☐ 149	Ken Howell	.03	.01	.00
☐ 150	Eric Davis	.60	.24	.06
☐ 151	Bob Knepper	.03	.01	.00
☐ 152	Jody Reed	.35	.14	.03
☐ 153	John Habyan	.03	.01	.00
☐ 154	Jeff Stone	.03	.01	.00
☐ 155	Bruce Sutter	.08	.03	.01
☐ 156	Gary Matthews	.03	.01	.00
☐ 157	Atlee Hammaker	.03	.01	.00
☐ 158	Tim Hulett	.03	.01	.00
☐ 159	Brad Arnsberg	.10	.04	.01
☐ 160	Willie McGee	.10	.04	.01
☐ 161	Bryn Smith	.03	.01	.00
☐ 162	Mark McLemore	.03	.01	.00

		MINT	EXC	G-VG
☐ 163	Dale Mohorcic	.03	.01	.00
☐ 164	Dave Johnson MG . (checklist back)	.06	.01	.00
☐ 165	Robin Yount	.20	.08	.02
☐ 166	Rick Rodriquez	.10	.04	.01
☐ 167	Rance Mulliniks	.03	.01	.00
☐ 168	Barry Jones	.03	.01	.00
☐ 169	Ross Jones	.10	.04	.01
☐ 170	Rich Gossage	.08	.03	.01
☐ 171	Cubs TL	.03	.01	.00
	Shawon Dunston and Manny Trillo			
☐ 172	Lloyd McClendon ..	.10	.04	.01
☐ 173	Eric Plunk	.03	.01	.00
☐ 174	Phil Garner	.03	.01	.00
☐ 175	Kevin Bass	.06	.02	.00
☐ 176	Jeff Reed	.03	.01	.00
☐ 177	Frank Tanana	.03	.01	.00
☐ 178	Dwayne Henry	.06	.02	.00
☐ 179	Charlie Puleo	.03	.01	.00
☐ 180	Terry Kennedy	.03	.01	.00
☐ 181	David Cone	1.00	.40	.10
☐ 182	Ken Phelps	.06	.02	.00
☐ 183	Tom Lawless	.03	.01	.00
☐ 184	Ivan Calderon	.08	.03	.01
☐ 185	Rick Rhoden	.03	.01	.00
☐ 186	Rafael Palmeiro ...	.25	.10	.02
☐ 187	Steve Kiefer	.03	.01	.00
☐ 188	John Russell	.03	.01	.00
☐ 189	Wes Gardner	.20	.08	.02
☐ 190	Candy Maldonado ..	.06	.02	.00
☐ 191	John Cerutti	.03	.01	.00
☐ 192	Devon White	.12	.05	.01
☐ 193	Brian Fisher	.03	.01	.00
☐ 194	Tom Kelly MG ..... (checklist back)	.06	.01	.00
☐ 195	Dan Quisenberry ...	.08	.03	.01
☐ 196	Dave Engle	.03	.01	.00
☐ 197	Lance McCullers ...	.06	.02	.00
☐ 198	Franklin Stubbs	.03	.01	.00
☐ 199	Dave Meads	.10	.04	.01
☐ 200	Wade Boggs	.70	.28	.07
☐ 201	Rangers TL	.06	.02	.00
	Bobby Valentine, Pete O'Brien, Pete Incaviglia, and Steve Buechele			
☐ 202	Glenn Hoffman	.03	.01	.00
☐ 203	Fred Toliver	.03	.01	.00

		MINT	EXC	G-VG
☐ 204	Paul O'Neill	.08	.03	.01
☐ 205	Nelson Liriano	.12	.05	.01
☐ 206	Domingo Ramos ..	.03	.01	.00
☐ 207	John Mitchell	.12	.05	.01
☐ 208	Steve Lake	.03	.01	.00
☐ 209	Richard Dotson ...	.06	.02	.00
☐ 210	Willie Randolph ...	.06	.02	.00
☐ 211	Frank DiPino	.03	.01	.00
☐ 212	Greg Brock	.03	.01	.00
☐ 213	Albert Hall	.03	.01	.00
☐ 214	Dave Schmidt	.03	.01	.00
☐ 215	Von Hayes	.08	.03	.01
☐ 216	Jerry Reuss	.03	.01	.00
☐ 217	Harry Spilman	.03	.01	.00
☐ 218	Dan Schatzeder ...	.03	.01	.00
☐ 219	Mike Stanley	.06	.02	.00
☐ 220	Tom Henke	.06	.02	.00
☐ 221	Rafael Belliard ...	.03	.01	.00
☐ 222	Steve Farr	.03	.01	.00
☐ 223	Stan Jefferson ...	.10	.04	.01
☐ 224	Tom Trebelhorn MG (checklist back)	.06	.01	.00
☐ 225	Mike Scioscia	.03	.01	.00
☐ 226	Dave Lopes	.06	.02	.00
☐ 227	Ed Correa	.03	.01	.00
☐ 228	Wallace Johnson ..	.03	.01	.00
☐ 229	Jeff Musselman ...	.08	.03	.01
☐ 230	Pat Tabler	.06	.02	.00
☐ 231	Pirates TL	.10	.04	.01
	Barry Bonds and Bobby Bonilla			
☐ 232	Bob James	.03	.01	.00
☐ 233	Rafael Santana ...	.03	.01	.00
☐ 234	Ken Dayley	.03	.01	.00
☐ 235	Gary Ward	.03	.01	.00
☐ 236	Ted Power	.03	.01	.00
☐ 237	Mike Heath	.03	.01	.00
☐ 238	Luis Polonia	.20	.08	.02
☐ 239	Roy Smalley	.03	.01	.00
☐ 240	Lee Smith	.06	.02	.00
☐ 241	Damaso Garcia ...	.03	.01	.00
☐ 242	Tom Niedenfuer ...	.03	.01	.00
☐ 243	Mark Ryal	.08	.03	.01
☐ 244	Jeff D. Robinson .. (Pirates pitcher)	.03	.01	.00
☐ 245	Rich Gedman	.06	.02	.00
☐ 246	Mike Campbell	.15	.06	.01
☐ 247	Thad Bosley	.03	.01	.00
☐ 248	Storm Davis	.06	.02	.00

		MINT	EXC	G-VG
☐ 249	Mike Marshall	.08	.03	.01
☐ 250	Nolan Ryan	.25	.10	.02
☐ 251	Tom Foley	.03	.01	.00
☐ 252	Bob Brower	.10	.04	.01
☐ 253	Checklist 133-264	.06	.01	.00
☐ 254	Lee Elia MG (checklist back)	.06	.01	.00
☐ 255	Mookie Wilson	.03	.01	.00
☐ 256	Ken Schrom	.03	.01	.00
☐ 257	Jerry Royster	.03	.01	.00
☐ 258	Ed Nunez	.03	.01	.00
☐ 259	Ron Kittle	.08	.03	.01
☐ 260	Vince Coleman	.18	.08	.01
☐ 261	Giants TL (five players)	.03	.01	.00
☐ 262	Drew Hall	.10	.04	.01
☐ 263	Glenn Braggs	.06	.02	.00
☐ 264	Les Straker	.10	.04	.01
☐ 265	Bo Diaz	.03	.01	.00
☐ 266	Paul Assenmacher	.03	.01	.00
☐ 267	Billy Bean	.15	.06	.01
☐ 268	Bruce Ruffin	.03	.01	.00
☐ 269	Ellis Burks	1.00	.40	.10
☐ 270	Mike Witt	.08	.03	.01
☐ 271	Ken Gerhart	.08	.03	.01
☐ 272	Steve Ontiveros	.03	.01	.00
☐ 273	Garth Iorg	.03	.01	.00
☐ 274	Junior Ortiz	.03	.01	.00
☐ 275	Kevin Seitzer	.90	.36	.09
☐ 276	Luis Salazar	.03	.01	.00
☐ 277	Alejandro Pena	.03	.01	.00
☐ 278	Jose Cruz	.06	.02	.00
☐ 279	Randy St.Claire	.03	.01	.00
☐ 280	Pete Incaviglia	.15	.06	.01
☐ 281	Jerry Hairston	.03	.01	.00
☐ 282	Pat Perry	.03	.01	.00
☐ 283	Phil Lombardi	.08	.03	.01
☐ 284	Larry Bowa MG (checklist back)	.06	.01	.00
☐ 285	Jim Presley	.06	.02	.00
☐ 286	Chuck Crim	.10	.04	.01
☐ 287	Manny Trillo	.03	.01	.00
☐ 288	Pat Pacillo	.06	.02	.00
☐ 289	Dave Bergman	.03	.01	.00
☐ 290	Tony Fernandez	.10	.04	.01
☐ 291	Astros TL Billy Hatcher and Kevin Bass	.06	.02	.00
☐ 292	Carney Lansford	.06	.02	.00
☐ 293	Doug Jones	.25	.10	.02
☐ 294	Al Pedrique	.10	.04	.01
☐ 295	Bert Blyleven	.08	.03	.01
☐ 296	Floyd Rayford	.03	.01	.00
☐ 297	Zane Smith	.06	.02	.00
☐ 298	Milt Thompson	.03	.01	.00
☐ 299	Steve Crawford	.03	.01	.00
☐ 300	Don Mattingly	1.25	.50	.12
☐ 301	Bud Black	.03	.01	.00
☐ 302	Jose Uribe	.03	.01	.00
☐ 303	Eric Show	.03	.01	.00
☐ 304	George Hendrick	.03	.01	.00
☐ 305	Steve Sax	.10	.04	.01
☐ 306	Billy Hatcher	.06	.02	.00
☐ 307	Mike Trujillo	.03	.01	.00
☐ 308	Lee Mazzilli	.03	.01	.00
☐ 309	Bill Long	.10	.04	.01
☐ 310	Tom Herr	.06	.02	.00
☐ 311	Scott Sanderson	.03	.01	.00
☐ 312	Joey Meyer	.20	.08	.02
☐ 313	Bob McClure	.03	.01	.00
☐ 314	Jimy Williams MG (checklist back)	.06	.01	.00
☐ 315	Dave Parker	.10	.04	.01
☐ 316	Jose Rijo	.03	.01	.00
☐ 317	Tom Nieto	.03	.01	.00
☐ 318	Mel Hall	.03	.01	.00
☐ 319	Mike Loynd	.03	.01	.00
☐ 320	Alan Trammell	.15	.06	.01
☐ 321	White Sox TL Harold Baines and Carlton Fisk	.08	.03	.01
☐ 322	Vicente Palacios	.12	.05	.01
☐ 323	Rick Leach	.03	.01	.00
☐ 324	Danny Jackson	.15	.06	.01
☐ 325	Glenn Hubbard	.03	.01	.00
☐ 326	Al Nipper	.03	.01	.00
☐ 327	Larry Sheets	.08	.03	.01
☐ 328	Greg Cadaret	.12	.05	.01
☐ 329	Chris Speier	.03	.01	.00
☐ 330	Eddie Whitson	.03	.01	.00
☐ 331	Brian Downing	.03	.01	.00
☐ 332	Jerry Reed	.03	.01	.00
☐ 333	Wally Backman	.03	.01	.00
☐ 334	Dave LaPoint	.03	.01	.00
☐ 335	Claudell Washington	.06	.02	.00
☐ 336	Ed Lynch	.03	.01	.00
☐ 337	Jim Gantner	.03	.01	.00
☐ 338	Brian Holton	.08	.03	.01

		MINT	EXC	G-VG
☐ 339	Kurt Stillwell	.03	.01	.00
☐ 340	Jack Morris	.10	.04	.01
☐ 341	Carmen Castillo	.03	.01	.00
☐ 342	Larry Andersen	.03	.01	.00
☐ 343	Greg Gagne	.03	.01	.00
☐ 344	Tony LaRussa MG	.06	.01	.00
	(checklist back)			
☐ 345	Scott Fletcher	.03	.01	.00
☐ 346	Vance Law	.03	.01	.00
☐ 347	Joe Johnson	.03	.01	.00
☐ 348	Jim Eisenreich	.03	.01	.00
☐ 349	Bob Walk	.03	.01	.00
☐ 350	Will Clark	.60	.24	.06
☐ 351	Cardinals TL	.03	.01	.00
	Red Schoendienst			
	and Tony Pena			
☐ 352	Billy Ripken	.15	.06	.01
☐ 353	Ed Olwine	.03	.01	.00
☐ 354	Marc Sullivan	.03	.01	.00
☐ 355	Roger McDowell	.06	.02	.00
☐ 356	Luis Aguayo	.03	.01	.00
☐ 357	Floyd Bannister	.03	.01	.00
☐ 358	Rey Quinones	.03	.01	.00
☐ 359	Tim Stoddard	.03	.01	.00
☐ 360	Tony Gwynn	.30	.12	.03
☐ 361	Greg Maddux	.35	.14	.03
☐ 362	Juan Castillo	.08	.03	.01
☐ 363	Willie Fraser	.03	.01	.00
☐ 364	Nick Esasky	.03	.01	.00
☐ 365	Floyd Youmans	.03	.01	.00
☐ 366	Chet Lemon	.03	.01	.00
☐ 367	Tim Leary	.06	.02	.00
☐ 368	Gerald Young	.25	.10	.02
☐ 369	Greg Harris	.03	.01	.00
☐ 370	Jose Canseco	1.50	.60	.15
☐ 371	Joe Hesketh	.03	.01	.00
☐ 372	Matt Williams	.30	.12	.03
☐ 373	Checklist 265-396	.06	.01	.00
☐ 374	Doc Edwards MG	.06	.01	.00
	(checklist back)			
☐ 375	Tom Brunansky	.08	.03	.01
☐ 376	Bill Wilkinson	.10	.04	.01
☐ 377	Sam Horn	.25	.10	.02
☐ 378	Todd Frohwirth	.10	.04	.01
☐ 379	Rafael Ramirez	.03	.01	.00
☐ 380	Joe Magrane	.25	.10	.02
☐ 381	Angels TL	.12	.05	.01
	Wally Joyner and			
	Jack Howell			

		MINT	EXC	G-VG
☐ 382	Keith Miller	.20	.08	.02
	(New York Mets)			
☐ 383	Eric Bell	.03	.01	.00
☐ 384	Neil Allen	.03	.01	.00
☐ 385	Carlton Fisk	.08	.03	.01
☐ 386	Don Mattingly AS	.40	.16	.04
☐ 387	Willie Randolph AS	.06	.02	.00
☐ 388	Wade Boggs AS	.30	.12	.03
☐ 389	Alan Trammell AS	.08	.03	.01
☐ 390	George Bell AS	.10	.04	.01
☐ 391	Kirby Puckett AS	.15	.06	.01
☐ 392	Dave Winfield AS	.12	.05	.01
☐ 393	Matt Nokes AS	.15	.06	.01
☐ 394	Roger Clemens AS	.20	.08	.02
☐ 395	Jimmy Key AS	.06	.02	.00
☐ 396	Tom Henke AS	.06	.02	.00
☐ 397	Jack Clark AS	.10	.04	.01
☐ 398	Juan Samuel AS	.06	.02	.00
☐ 399	Tim Wallach AS	.06	.02	.00
☐ 400	Ozzie Smith AS	.10	.04	.01
☐ 401	Andre Dawson AS	.12	.05	.01
☐ 402	Tony Gwynn AS	.12	.05	.01
☐ 403	Tim Raines AS	.12	.05	.01
☐ 404	Benny Santiago AS	.15	.06	.01
☐ 405	Dwight Gooden AS	.20	.08	.02
☐ 406	Shane Rawley AS	.06	.02	.00
☐ 407	Steve Bedrosian AS	.06	.02	.00
☐ 408	Dion James	.03	.01	.00
☐ 409	Joel McKeon	.03	.01	.00
☐ 410	Tony Pena	.06	.02	.00
☐ 411	Wayne Tolleson	.03	.01	.00
☐ 412	Randy Myers	.08	.03	.01
☐ 413	John Christensen	.03	.01	.00
☐ 414	John McNamara MG	.06	.01	.00
	(checklist back)			
☐ 415	Don Carman	.03	.01	.00
☐ 416	Keith Moreland	.03	.01	.00
☐ 417	Mark Ciardi	.08	.03	.01
☐ 418	Joel Youngblood	.03	.01	.00
☐ 419	Scott McGregor	.03	.01	.00
☐ 420	Wally Joyner	.35	.14	.03
☐ 421	Ed VandeBerg	.03	.01	.00
☐ 422	Dave Concepcion	.06	.02	.00
☐ 423	John Smiley	.20	.08	.02
☐ 424	Dwayne Murphy	.03	.01	.00
☐ 425	Jeff Reardon	.06	.02	.00
☐ 426	Randy Ready	.03	.01	.00
☐ 427	Paul Kilgus	.12	.05	.01
☐ 428	John Shelby	.03	.01	.00

		MINT	EXC	G-VG
☐ 429	Tigers TL	.15	.06	.01
	Alan Trammell and			
	Kirk Gibson			
☐ 430	Glenn Davis	.12	.05	.01
☐ 431	Casey Candaele	.03	.01	.00
☐ 432	Mike Moore	.03	.01	.00
☐ 433	Bill Pecota	.10	.04	.01
☐ 434	Rick Aguilera	.03	.01	.00
☐ 435	Mike Pagliarulo	.08	.03	.01
☐ 436	Mike Bielecki	.03	.01	.00
☐ 437	Fred Manrique	.10	.04	.01
☐ 438	Rob Ducey	.15	.06	.01
☐ 439	Dave Martinez	.08	.03	.01
☐ 440	Steve Bedrosian	.08	.03	.01
☐ 441	Rick Manning	.03	.01	.00
☐ 442	Tom Bolton	.10	.04	.01
☐ 443	Ken Griffey	.06	.02	.00
☐ 444	Cal Ripken, Sr. MG	.06	.01	.00
	(checklist back)			
	UER (two copyrights)			
☐ 445	Mike Krukow	.03	.01	.00
☐ 446	Doug DeCinces	.03	.01	.00
☐ 447	Jeff Montgomery	.15	.06	.01
☐ 448	Mike Davis	.03	.01	.00
☐ 449	Jeff M. Robinson	.30	.12	.03
	(Tigers pitcher)			
☐ 450	Barry Bonds	.15	.06	.01
☐ 451	Keith Atherton	.03	.01	.00
☐ 452	Willie Wilson	.08	.03	.01
☐ 453	Dennis Powell	.03	.01	.00
☐ 454	Marvell Wynne	.03	.01	.00
☐ 455	Shawn Hillegas	.15	.06	.01
☐ 456	Dave Anderson	.03	.01	.00
☐ 457	Terry Leach	.06	.02	.00
☐ 458	Ron Hassey	.03	.01	.00
☐ 459	Yankees TL	.08	.03	.01
	Dave Winfield and			
	Willie Randolph			
☐ 460	Ozzie Smith	.12	.05	.01
☐ 461	Danny Darwin	.03	.01	.00
☐ 462	Don Slaught	.03	.01	.00
☐ 463	Fred McGriff	.40	.16	.04
☐ 464	Jay Tibbs	.03	.01	.00
☐ 465	Paul Molitor	.10	.04	.01
☐ 466	Jerry Mumphrey	.03	.01	.00
☐ 467	Don Aase	.03	.01	.00
☐ 468	Darren Daulton	.03	.01	.00
☐ 469	Jeff Dedmon	.03	.01	.00
☐ 470	Dwight Evans	.10	.04	.01

		MINT	EXC	G-VG
☐ 471	Donnie Moore	.03	.01	.00
☐ 472	Robby Thompson	.03	.01	.00
☐ 473	Joe Niekro	.06	.02	.00
☐ 474	Tom Brookens	.03	.01	.00
☐ 475	Pete Rose MG	.30	.10	.02
	(checklist back)			
☐ 476	Dave Stewart	.08	.03	.01
☐ 477	Jamie Quirk	.03	.01	.00
☐ 478	Sid Bream	.03	.01	.00
☐ 479	Brett Butler	.06	.02	.00
☐ 480	Dwight Gooden	.35	.14	.03
☐ 481	Mariano Duncan	.03	.01	.00
☐ 482	Mark Davis	.06	.02	.00
☐ 483	Rod Booker	.10	.04	.01
☐ 484	Pat Clements	.03	.01	.00
☐ 485	Harold Reynolds	.03	.01	.00
☐ 486	Pat Keedy	.10	.04	.01
☐ 487	Jim Pankovits	.03	.01	.00
☐ 488	Andy McGaffigan	.03	.01	.00
☐ 489	Dodgers TL	.12	.05	.01
	Pedro Guerrero and			
	Fernando Valenzuela			
☐ 490	Larry Parrish	.03	.01	.00
☐ 491	B.J. Surhoff	.08	.03	.01
☐ 492	Doyle Alexander	.03	.01	.00
☐ 493	Mike Greenwell	1.25	.50	.12
☐ 494	Wally Ritchie	.10	.04	.01
☐ 495	Eddie Murray	.20	.08	.02
☐ 496	Guy Hoffman	.03	.01	.00
☐ 497	Kevin Mitchell	.06	.02	.00
☐ 498	Bob Boone	.06	.02	.00
☐ 499	Eric King	.03	.01	.00
☐ 500	Andre Dawson	.20	.08	.02
☐ 501	Tim Birtsas	.03	.01	.00
☐ 502	Dan Gladden	.06	.02	.00
☐ 503	Junior Noboa	.08	.03	.01
☐ 504	Bob Rodgers MG	.06	.01	.00
	(checklist back)			
☐ 505	Willie Upshaw	.03	.01	.00
☐ 506	John Cangelosi	.03	.01	.00
☐ 507	Mark Gubicza	.08	.03	.01
☐ 508	Tim Teufel	.03	.01	.00
☐ 509	Bill Dawley	.03	.01	.00
☐ 510	Dave Winfield	.20	.08	.02
☐ 511	Joel Davis	.03	.01	.00
☐ 512	Alex Trevino	.03	.01	.00
☐ 513	Tim Flannery	.03	.01	.00
☐ 514	Pat Sheridan	.03	.01	.00
☐ 515	Juan Nieves	.03	.01	.00

		MINT	EXC	G-VG
☐ 516	Jim Sundberg	.03	.01	.00
☐ 517	Ron Robinson	.03	.01	.00
☐ 518	Greg Gross	.03	.01	.00
☐ 519	Mariners TL	.03	.01	.00
	Harold Reynolds and			
	Phil Bradley			
☐ 520	Dave Smith	.03	.01	.00
☐ 521	Jim Dwyer	.03	.01	.00
☐ 522	Bob Patterson	.10	.04	.01
☐ 523	Gary Roenicke	.03	.01	.00
☐ 524	Gary Lucas	.03	.01	.00
☐ 525	Marty Barrett	.06	.02	.00
☐ 526	Juan Berenguer	.03	.01	.00
☐ 527	Steve Henderson	.03	.01	.00
☐ 528A	Checklist 397-528	.50	.10	.02
	ERR (455 S. Carlton)			
☐ 528B	Checklist 397-528	.06	.01	.00
	COR (455 S. Hillegas)			
☐ 529	Tim Burke	.03	.01	.00
☐ 530	Gary Carter	.20	.08	.02
☐ 531	Rich Yett	.03	.01	.00
☐ 532	Mike Kingery	.03	.01	.00
☐ 533	John Farrell	.20	.08	.02
☐ 534	John Wathan MG	.06	.01	.00
	(checklist back)			
☐ 535	Ron Guidry	.08	.03	.01
☐ 536	John Morris	.03	.01	.00
☐ 537	Steve Buechele	.03	.01	.00
☐ 538	Bill Wegman	.03	.01	.00
☐ 539	Mike LaValliere	.03	.01	.00
☐ 540	Bret Saberhagen	.10	.04	.01
☐ 541	Juan Beniquez	.03	.01	.00
☐ 542	Paul Noce	.10	.04	.01
☐ 543	Kent Tekulve	.03	.01	.00
☐ 544	Jim Traber	.03	.01	.00
☐ 545	Don Baylor	.08	.03	.01
☐ 546	John Candelaria	.06	.02	.00
☐ 547	Felix Fermin	.10	.04	.01
☐ 548	Shane Mack	.10	.04	.01
☐ 549	Braves TL	.06	.02	.00
	Albert Hall,			
	Dale Murphy,			
	Ken Griffey,			
	and Dion James			
☐ 550	Pedro Guerrero	.15	.06	.01
☐ 551	Terry Steinbach	.15	.06	.01
☐ 552	Mark Thurmond	.03	.01	.00
☐ 553	Tracy Jones	.06	.02	.00
☐ 554	Mike Smithson	.03	.01	.00

		MINT	EXC	G-VG
☐ 555	Brook Jacoby	.08	.03	.01
☐ 556	Stan Clarke	.08	.03	.01
☐ 557	Craig Reynolds	.03	.01	.00
☐ 558	Bob Ojeda	.06	.02	.00
☐ 559	Ken Williams	.20	.08	.02
☐ 560	Tim Wallach	.08	.03	.01
☐ 561	Rick Cerone	.03	.01	.00
☐ 562	Jim Lindeman	.06	.02	.00
☐ 563	Jose Guzman	.03	.01	.00
☐ 564	Frank Lucchesi MG	.06	.01	.00
	(checklist back)			
☐ 565	Lloyd Moseby	.08	.03	.01
☐ 566	Charlie O'Brien	.10	.04	.01
☐ 567	Mike Diaz	.03	.01	.00
☐ 568	Chris Brown	.06	.02	.00
☐ 569	Charlie Leibrandt	.03	.01	.00
☐ 570	Jeffrey Leonard	.06	.02	.00
☐ 571	Mark Williamson	.10	.04	.01
☐ 572	Chris James	.18	.08	.01
☐ 573	Bob Stanley	.03	.01	.00
☐ 574	Graig Nettles	.08	.03	.01
☐ 575	Don Sutton	.10	.04	.01
☐ 576	Tommy Hinzo	.10	.04	.01
☐ 577	Tom Browning	.08	.03	.01
☐ 578	Gary Gaetti	.10	.04	.01
☐ 579	Mets TL	.15	.06	.01
	Gary Carter and			
	Kevin McReynolds			
☐ 580	Mark McGwire	1.00	.40	.10
☐ 581	Tito Landrum	.03	.01	.00
☐ 582	Mike Henneman	.20	.08	.02
☐ 583	Dave Valle	.06	.02	.00
☐ 584	Steve Trout	.03	.01	.00
☐ 585	Ozzie Guillen	.06	.02	.00
☐ 586	Bob Forsch	.03	.01	.00
☐ 587	Terry Puhl	.03	.01	.00
☐ 588	Jeff Parrett	.15	.06	.01
☐ 589	Geno Petralli	.03	.01	.00
☐ 590	George Bell	.15	.06	.01
☐ 591	Doug Drabek	.03	.01	.00
☐ 592	Dale Sveum	.03	.01	.00
☐ 593	Bob Tewksbury	.03	.01	.00
☐ 594	Bobby Valentine MG	.06	.01	.00
	(checklist back)			
☐ 595	Frank White	.06	.02	.00
☐ 596	John Kruk	.08	.03	.01
☐ 597	Gene Garber	.03	.01	.00
☐ 598	Lee Lacy	.03	.01	.00
☐ 599	Calvin Schiraldi	.03	.01	.00

		MINT	EXC	G-VG
☐ 600	Mike Schmidt	.25	.10	.02
☐ 601	Jack Lazorko	.03	.01	.00
☐ 602	Mike Aldrete	.06	.02	.00
☐ 603	Rob Murphy	.03	.01	.00
☐ 604	Chris Bando	.03	.01	.00
☐ 605	Kirk Gibson	.15	.06	.01
☐ 606	Moose Haas	.03	.01	.00
☐ 607	Mickey Hatcher	.06	.02	.00
☐ 608	Charlie Kerfeld	.03	.01	.00
☐ 609	Twins TL	.10	.04	.01
	Gary Gaetti and			
	Kent Hrbek			
☐ 610	Keith Hernandez	.15	.06	.01
☐ 611	Tommy John	.08	.03	.01
☐ 612	Curt Ford	.03	.01	.00
☐ 613	Bobby Thigpen	.06	.02	.00
☐ 614	Herm Winningham	.03	.01	.00
☐ 615	Jody Davis	.06	.02	.00
☐ 616	Jay Aldrich	.10	.04	.01
☐ 617	Oddibe McDowell	.08	.03	.01
☐ 618	Cecil Fielder	.03	.01	.00
☐ 619	Mike Dunne	.12	.05	.01
	(inconsistent design,			
	black name on front)			
☐ 620	Cory Snyder	.18	.08	.01
☐ 621	Gene Nelson	.03	.01	.00
☐ 622	Kal Daniels	.18	.08	.01
☐ 623	Mike Flanagan	.03	.01	.00
☐ 624	Jim Leyland MG	.06	.01	.00
	(checklist back)			
☐ 625	Frank Viola	.15	.06	.01
☐ 626	Glenn Wilson	.03	.01	.00
☐ 627	Joe Boever	.10	.04	.01
☐ 628	Dave Henderson	.06	.02	.00
☐ 629	Kelly Downs	.03	.01	.00
☐ 630	Darrell Evans	.06	.02	.00
☐ 631	Jack Howell	.03	.01	.00
☐ 632	Steve Shields	.03	.01	.00
☐ 633	Barry Lyons	.10	.04	.01
☐ 634	Jose DeLeon	.03	.01	.00
☐ 635	Terry Pendleton	.03	.01	.00
☐ 636	Charles Hudson	.03	.01	.00
☐ 637	Jay Bell	.15	.06	.01
☐ 638	Steve Balboni	.03	.01	.00
☐ 639	Brewers TL	.03	.01	.00
	Glenn Braggs			
	and Tony Muser CO			
☐ 640	Garry Templeton	.06	.02	.00
	(inconsistent design, green border)			

		MINT	EXC	G-VG
☐ 641	Rick Honeycutt	.03	.01	.00
☐ 642	Bob Dernier	.03	.01	.00
☐ 643	Rocky Childress	.08	.03	.01
☐ 644	Terry McGriff	.08	.03	.01
☐ 645	Matt Nokes	.45	.18	.04
☐ 646	Checklist 529-660	.06	.01	.00
☐ 647	Pascual Perez	.06	.02	.00
☐ 648	Al Newman	.03	.01	.00
☐ 649	DeWayne Buice	.10	.04	.01
☐ 650	Cal Ripken	.18	.08	.01
☐ 651	Mike Jackson	.15	.06	.01
☐ 652	Bruce Benedict	.03	.01	.00
☐ 653	Jeff Sellers	.03	.01	.00
☐ 654	Roger Craig MG	.06	.01	.00
	(checklist back)			
☐ 655	Len Dykstra	.08	.03	.01
☐ 656	Lee Guetterman	.03	.01	.00
☐ 657	Gary Redus	.03	.01	.00
☐ 658	Tim Conroy	.03	.01	.00
	(inconsistent design, name in white)			
☐ 659	Bobby Meacham	.03	.01	.00
☐ 660	Rick Reuschel	.06	.02	.00
☐ 661	Turn Back Clock 1983	.15	.06	.01
	Nolan Ryan			
☐ 662	Turn Back Clock 1978	.08	.03	.01
	Jim Rice			
☐ 663	Turn Back Clock 1973	.03	.01	.00
	Ron Blomberg			
☐ 664	Turn Back Clock 1968	.10	.04	.01
	Bob Gibson			
☐ 665	Turn Back Clock 1963	.15	.06	.01
	Stan Musial			
☐ 666	Mario Soto	.03	.01	.00
☐ 667	Luis Quinones	.03	.01	.00
☐ 668	Walt Terrell	.03	.01	.00
☐ 669	Phillies TL	.06	.02	.00
	Lance Parrish			
	and Mike Ryan CO			
☐ 670	Dan Plesac	.06	.02	.00
☐ 671	Tim Laudner	.03	.01	.00
☐ 672	John Davis	.12	.05	.01
☐ 673	Tony Phillips	.03	.01	.00
☐ 674	Mike Fitzgerald	.03	.01	.00
☐ 675	Jim Rice	.12	.05	.01
☐ 676	Ken Dixon	.03	.01	.00
☐ 677	Eddie Milner	.03	.01	.00
☐ 678	Jim Acker	.03	.01	.00
☐ 679	Darrell Miller	.03	.01	.00
☐ 680	Charlie Hough	.03	.01	.00

		MINT	EXC	G-VG			MINT	EXC	G-VG
☐ 681	Bobby Bonilla	.15	.06	.01	☐ 726	Alfredo Griffin	.06	.02	.00
☐ 682	Jimmy Key	.08	.03	.01	☐ 727	Greg Booker	.03	.01	.00
☐ 683	Julio Franco	.08	.03	.01	☐ 728	Andy Allanson	.03	.01	.00
☐ 684	Hal Lanier MG (checklist back)	.06	.01	.00	☐ 729	Blue Jays TL George Bell and Fred McGriff	.10	.04	.01
☐ 685	Ron Darling	.10	.04	.01					
☐ 686	Terry Francona	.03	.01	.00	☐ 730	John Franco	.06	.02	.00
☐ 687	Mickey Brantley	.08	.03	.01	☐ 731	Rick Schu	.03	.01	.00
☐ 688	Jim Winn	.03	.01	.00	☐ 732	David Palmer	.03	.01	.00
☐ 689	Tom Pagnozzi	.12	.05	.01	☐ 733	Spike Owen	.03	.01	.00
☐ 690	Jay Howell	.03	.01	.00	☐ 734	Craig Lefferts	.03	.01	.00
☐ 691	Dan Pasqua	.06	.02	.00	☐ 735	Kevin McReynolds	.20	.08	.02
☐ 692	Mike Birkbeck	.03	.01	.00	☐ 736	Matt Young	.03	.01	.00
☐ 693	Benny Santiago	.60	.24	.06	☐ 737	Butch Wynegar	.03	.01	.00
☐ 694	Eric Nolte	.12	.05	.01	☐ 738	Scott Bankhead	.03	.01	.00
☐ 695	Shawon Dunston	.06	.02	.00	☐ 739	Daryl Boston	.03	.01	.00
☐ 696	Duane Ward	.03	.01	.00	☐ 740	Rick Sutcliffe	.08	.03	.01
☐ 697	Steve Lombardozzi	.03	.01	.00	☐ 741	Mike Easler	.03	.01	.00
☐ 698	Brad Havens	.03	.01	.00	☐ 742	Mark Clear	.03	.01	.00
☐ 699	Padres TL Benito Santiago and Tony Gwynn	.20	.08	.02	☐ 743	Larry Herndon	.03	.01	.00
					☐ 744	Whitey Herzog MG (checklist back)	.06	.01	.00
☐ 700	George Brett	.25	.10	.02	☐ 745	Bill Doran	.06	.02	.00
☐ 701	Sammy Stewart	.03	.01	.00	☐ 746	Gene Larkin	.20	.08	.02
☐ 702	Mike Gallego	.03	.01	.00	☐ 747	Bobby Witt	.06	.02	.00
☐ 703	Bob Brenly	.03	.01	.00	☐ 748	Reid Nichols	.03	.01	.00
☐ 704	Dennis Boyd	.06	.02	.00	☐ 749	Mark Eichhorn	.03	.01	.00
☐ 705	Juan Samuel	.08	.03	.01	☐ 750	Bo Jackson	.30	.12	.03
☐ 706	Rick Mahler	.03	.01	.00	☐ 751	Jim Morrison	.03	.01	.00
☐ 707	Fred Lynn	.10	.04	.01	☐ 752	Mark Grant	.03	.01	.00
☐ 708	Gus Polidor	.06	.02	.00	☐ 753	Danny Heep	.03	.01	.00
☐ 709	George Frazier	.03	.01	.00	☐ 754	Mike LaCoss	.03	.01	.00
☐ 710	Darryl Strawberry	.35	.14	.03	☐ 755	Ozzie Virgil	.03	.01	.00
☐ 711	Bill Gullickson	.03	.01	.00	☐ 756	Mike Maddux	.03	.01	.00
☐ 712	John Moses	.03	.01	.00	☐ 757	John Marzano	.08	.03	.01
☐ 713	Willie Hernandez	.06	.02	.00	☐ 758	Eddie Williams	.12	.05	.01
☐ 714	Jim Fregosi MG (checklist back)	.06	.01	.00	☐ 759	A's TL Mark McGwire and Jose Canseco	.35	.14	.03
☐ 715	Todd Worrell	.10	.04	.01	☐ 760	Mike Scott	.12	.05	.01
☐ 716	Lenn Sakata	.03	.01	.00	☐ 761	Tony Armas	.06	.02	.00
☐ 717	Jay Baller	.03	.01	.00	☐ 762	Scott Bradley	.03	.01	.00
☐ 718	Mike Felder	.03	.01	.00	☐ 763	Doug Sisk	.03	.01	.00
☐ 719	Denny Walling	.03	.01	.00	☐ 764	Greg Walker	.06	.02	.00
☐ 720	Tim Raines	.18	.08	.01	☐ 765	Neal Heaton	.03	.01	.00
☐ 721	Pete O'Brien	.06	.02	.00	☐ 766	Henry Cotto	.03	.01	.00
☐ 722	Manny Lee	.03	.01	.00	☐ 767	Jose Lind	.18	.08	.01
☐ 723	Bob Kipper	.03	.01	.00	☐ 768	Dickie Noles	.03	.01	.00
☐ 724	Danny Tartabull	.20	.08	.02	☐ 769	Cecil Cooper	.08	.03	.01
☐ 725	Mike Boddicker	.06	.02	.00					

		MINT	EXC	G-VG
☐ 770	Lou Whitaker	.08	.03	.01
☐ 771	Ruben Sierra	.18	.08	.01
☐ 772	Sal Butera	.03	.01	.00
☐ 773	Frank Williams	.03	.01	.00
☐ 774	Gene Mauch MG	.06	.01	.00
	(checklist back)			
☐ 775	Dave Stieb	.08	.03	.01
☐ 776	Checklist 661-792	.06	.01	.00
☐ 777	Lonnie Smith	.03	.01	.00
☐ 778A	Keith Comstock ERR	6.00	2.40	.60
	(white "Padres")			
☐ 778B	Keith Comstock COR	.15	.06	.01
	(blue "Padres")			
☐ 779	Tom Glavine	.15	.06	.01
☐ 780	Fernando Valenzuela	.12	.05	.01
☐ 781	Keith Hughes	.15	.06	.01
☐ 782	Jeff Ballard	.12	.05	.01
☐ 783	Ron Roenicke	.03	.01	.00
☐ 784	Joe Sambito	.03	.01	.00
☐ 785	Alvin Davis	.08	.03	.01
☐ 786	Joe Price	.03	.01	.00
	(inconsistent design,			
	orange team name)			
☐ 787	Bill Almon	.03	.01	.00
☐ 788	Ray Searage	.03	.01	.00
☐ 789	Indians' TL	.10	.04	.01
	Joe Carter and			
	Cory Snyder			
☐ 790	Dave Righetti	.08	.03	.01
☐ 791	Ted Simmons	.08	.03	.01
☐ 792	John Tudor	.10	.04	.01

1988 Topps Big Cards

This set of 264 cards was issued as three separately distributed series of 88 cards each. Cards were distributed in wax packs with seven cards for a suggested retail of 40 cents. These cards are very reminiscent in style of the 1956 Topps card set and are popular with collectors perhaps for that reason. The cards measure approximately 2⅝" by 3¾" and are oriented horizontally.

	MINT	EXC	G-VG
Complete Set (264)	27.00	11.00	2.70
Common Player (1-88)	.05	.02	.00
Common Player (89-176)	.05	.02	.00
Common Player (177-264)	.05	.02	.00

		MINT	EXC	G-VG
☐ 1	Paul Molitor	.12	.04	.01
☐ 2	Milt Thompson	.05	.02	.00
☐ 3	Billy Hatcher	.05	.02	.00
☐ 4	Mike Witt	.05	.02	.00
☐ 5	Vince Coleman	.12	.05	.01
☐ 6	Dwight Evans	.12	.05	.01
☐ 7	Tim Wallach	.08	.03	.01
☐ 8	Alan Trammell	.15	.06	.01
☐ 9	Will Clark	.75	.30	.07
☐ 10	Jeff Reardon	.08	.03	.01
☐ 11	Dwight Gooden	.50	.20	.05
☐ 12	Benny Santiago	.15	.06	.01
☐ 13	Jose Canseco	1.75	.70	.17
☐ 14	Dale Murphy	.40	.16	.04
☐ 15	George Bell	.20	.08	.02
☐ 16	Ryne Sandberg	.20	.08	.02
☐ 17	Brook Jacoby	.08	.03	.01
☐ 18	Fernando Valenzuela	.12	.05	.01

			MINT	EXC	G-VG				MINT	EXC	G-VG
☐	19	Scott Fletcher	.05	.02	.00	☐	68	Andres Thomas	.08	.03	.01
☐	20	Eric Davis	.75	.30	.07	☐	69	Jeff Musselman	.05	.02	.00
☐	21	Willie Wilson	.10	.04	.01	☐	70	Jerry Mumphrey	.05	.02	.00
☐	22	B.J. Surhoff	.10	.04	.01	☐	71	Joe Carter	.15	.06	.01
☐	23	Steve Bedrosian	.10	.04	.01	☐	72	Mike Scioscia	.05	.02	.00
☐	24	Dave Winfield	.35	.14	.03	☐	73	Pete Incaviglia	.20	.08	.02
☐	25	Bobby Bonilla	.15	.06	.01	☐	74	Barry Larkin	.15	.06	.01
☐	26	Larry Sheets	.08	.03	.01	☐	75	Frank White	.08	.03	.01
☐	27	Ozzie Guillen	.08	.03	.01	☐	76	Willie Randolph	.08	.03	.01
☐	28	Checklist 1-88	.05	.01	.00	☐	77	Kevin Bass	.08	.03	.01
☐	29	Nolan Ryan	.35	.14	.03	☐	78	Brian Downing	.08	.03	.01
☐	30	Bob Boone	.08	.03	.01	☐	79	Willie McGee	.12	.05	.01
☐	31	Tom Herr	.08	.03	.01	☐	80	Ellis Burks	.50	.20	.05
☐	32	Wade Boggs	1.00	.40	.10	☐	81	Hubie Brooks	.08	.03	.01
☐	33	Neal Heaton	.05	.02	.00	☐	82	Darrell Evans	.08	.03	.01
☐	34	Doyle Alexander	.05	.02	.00	☐	83	Robby Thompson	.08	.03	.01
☐	35	Candy Maldonado	.05	.02	.00	☐	84	Kent Hrbek	.15	.06	.01
☐	36	Kirby Puckett	.50	.20	.05	☐	85	Ron Darling	.12	.05	.01
☐	37	Gary Carter	.25	.10	.02	☐	86	Stan Jefferson	.10	.04	.01
☐	38	Lance McCullers	.08	.03	.01	☐	87	Teddy Higuera	.10	.04	.01
☐	39	Terry Steinbach	.12	.05	.01	☐	88	Mike Schmidt	.40	.16	.04
☐	40	Gerald Perry	.10	.04	.01	☐	89	Barry Bonds	.15	.06	.01
☐	41	Tom Henke	.05	.02	.00	☐	90	Jim Presley	.10	.04	.01
☐	42	Leon Durham	.05	.02	.00	☐	91	Orel Hershiser	.75	.30	.07
☐	43	Cory Snyder	.15	.06	.01	☐	92	Jesse Barfield	.20	.08	.02
☐	44	Dale Sveum	.05	.02	.00	☐	93	Tom Candiotti	.05	.02	.00
☐	45	Lance Parrish	.12	.05	.01	☐	94	Bret Saberhagen	.15	.06	.01
☐	46	Steve Sax	.15	.06	.01	☐	95	Jose Uribe	.08	.03	.01
☐	47	Charlie Hough	.05	.02	.00	☐	96	Tom Browning	.12	.05	.01
☐	48	Kal Daniels	.20	.08	.02	☐	97	Johnny Ray	.08	.03	.01
☐	49	Bo Jackson	.35	.14	.03	☐	98	Mike Morgan	.05	.02	.00
☐	50	Ron Guidry	.12	.05	.01	☐	99	Lou Whitaker	.10	.04	.01
☐	51	Bill Doran	.08	.03	.01	☐	100	Jim Sundberg	.05	.02	.00
☐	52	Wally Joyner	.50	.20	.05	☐	101	Roger McDowell	.08	.03	.01
☐	53	Terry Pendleton	.08	.03	.01	☐	102	Randy Ready	.05	.02	.00
☐	54	Marty Barrett	.08	.03	.01	☐	103	Mike Gallego	.05	.02	.00
☐	55	Andres Galarraga	.20	.08	.02	☐	104	Steve Buechele	.05	.02	.00
☐	56	Larry Herndon	.05	.02	.00	☐	105	Greg Walker	.08	.03	.01
☐	57	Kevin Mitchell	.08	.03	.01	☐	106	Jose Lind	.10	.04	.01
☐	58	Greg Gagne	.05	.02	.00	☐	107	Steve Trout	.05	.02	.00
☐	59	Keith Hernandez	.25	.10	.02	☐	108	Rick Rhoden	.08	.03	.01
☐	60	John Kruk	.10	.04	.01	☐	109	Jim Pankovits	.05	.02	.00
☐	61	Mike LaValliere	.05	.02	.00	☐	110	Ken Griffey	.08	.03	.01
☐	62	Cal Ripken	.30	.12	.03	☐	111	Danny Cox	.08	.03	.01
☐	63	Ivan Calderon	.10	.04	.01	☐	112	Franklin Stubbs	.05	.02	.00
☐	64	Alvin Davis	.10	.04	.01	☐	113	Lloyd Moseby	.08	.03	.01
☐	65	Luis Polonia	.08	.03	.01	☐	114	Mel Hall	.08	.03	.01
☐	66	Robin Yount	.25	.10	.02	☐	115	Kevin Seitzer	.30	.12	.03
☐	67	Juan Samuel	.10	.04	.01	☐	116	Tim Raines	.25	.10	.02

		MINT	EXC	G-VG			MINT	EXC	G-VG
☐ 117	Juan Castillo	.05	.02	.00	☐ 166	Brett Butler	.10	.04	.01
☐ 118	Roger Clemens	.75	.30	.07	☐ 167	Nick Esasky	.08	.03	.01
☐ 119	Mike Aldrete	.08	.03	.01	☐ 168	Kirk McCaskill	.08	.03	.01
☐ 120	Mario Soto	.05	.02	.00	☐ 169	Fred Lynn	.12	.05	.01
☐ 121	Jack Howell	.08	.03	.01	☐ 170	Jack Morris	.12	.05	.01
☐ 122	Rick Schu	.05	.02	.00	☐ 171	Pedro Guerrero	.15	.06	.01
☐ 123	Jeff Robinson	.08	.03	.01	☐ 172	Dave Stieb	.10	.04	.01
☐ 124	Doug Drabek	.05	.02	.00	☐ 173	Pat Tabler	.08	.03	.01
☐ 125	Henry Cotto	.05	.02	.00	☐ 174	Floyd Bannister	.05	.02	.00
☐ 126	Checklist 89-176	.05	.01	.00	☐ 175	Rafael Belliard	.05	.02	.00
☐ 127	Gary Gaetti	.15	.06	.01	☐ 176	Mark Langston	.10	.04	.01
☐ 128	Rick Sutcliffe	.10	.04	.01	☐ 177	Greg Mathews	.08	.03	.01
☐ 129	Howard Johnson	.12	.05	.01	☐ 178	Claudell Washington	.08	.03	.01
☐ 130	Chris Brown	.08	.03	.01	☐ 179	Mark McGwire	1.00	.40	.10
☐ 131	Dave Henderson	.08	.03	.01	☐ 180	Bert Blyleven	.08	.03	.01
☐ 132	Curt Wilkerson	.05	.02	.00	☐ 181	Jim Rice	.15	.06	.01
☐ 133	Mike Marshall	.10	.04	.01	☐ 182	Mookie Wilson	.08	.03	.01
☐ 134	Kelly Gruber	.05	.02	.00	☐ 183	Willie Fraser	.05	.02	.00
☐ 135	Julio Franco	.08	.03	.01	☐ 184	Andy Van Slyke	.15	.06	.01
☐ 136	Kurt Stillwell	.08	.03	.01	☐ 185	Matt Nokes	.20	.08	.02
☐ 137	Donnie Hill	.05	.02	.00	☐ 186	Eddie Whitson	.05	.02	.00
☐ 138	Mike Pagliarulo	.10	.04	.01	☐ 187	Tony Fernandez	.10	.04	.01
☐ 139	Von Hayes	.10	.04	.01	☐ 188	Rick Reuschel	.08	.03	.01
☐ 140	Mike Scott	.12	.05	.01	☐ 189	Ken Phelps	.08	.03	.01
☐ 141	Bob Kipper	.05	.02	.00	☐ 190	Juan Nieves	.05	.02	.00
☐ 142	Harold Reynolds	.08	.03	.01	☐ 191	Kirk Gibson	.25	.10	.02
☐ 143	Bob Brenley	.05	.02	.00	☐ 192	Glenn Davis	.20	.08	.02
☐ 144	Dave Concepcion	.10	.04	.01	☐ 193	Zane Smith	.08	.03	.01
☐ 145	Devon White	.10	.04	.01	☐ 194	Jose DeLeon	.05	.02	.00
☐ 146	Jeff Stone	.05	.02	.00	☐ 195	Gary Ward	.05	.02	.00
☐ 147	Chet Lemon	.08	.03	.01	☐ 196	Pascual Perez	.08	.03	.01
☐ 148	Ozzie Virgil	.05	.02	.00	☐ 197	Carlton Fisk	.12	.05	.01
☐ 149	Todd Worrell	.12	.05	.01	☐ 198	Oddibe McDowell	.08	.03	.01
☐ 150	Mitch Webster	.05	.02	.00	☐ 199	Mark Gubicza	.10	.04	.01
☐ 151	Rob Deer	.08	.03	.01	☐ 200	Glenn Hubbard	.05	.02	.00
☐ 152	Rich Gedman	.08	.03	.01	☐ 201	Frank Viola	.20	.08	.02
☐ 153	Andre Dawson	.20	.08	.02	☐ 202	Jody Reed	.10	.04	.01
☐ 154	Mike Davis	.05	.02	.00	☐ 203	Len Dykstra	.08	.03	.01
☐ 155	Nelson Liriano	.05	.02	.00	☐ 204	Dick Schofield	.05	.02	.00
☐ 156	Greg Swindell	.12	.05	.01	☐ 205	Sid Bream	.05	.02	.00
☐ 157	George Brett	.35	.14	.03	☐ 206	Guillermo Hernandez	.08	.03	.01
☐ 158	Kevin McReynolds	.25	.10	.02	☐ 207	Keith Moreland	.05	.02	.00
☐ 159	Brian Fisher	.08	.03	.01	☐ 208	Mark Eichhorn	.05	.02	.00
☐ 160	Mike Kingery	.05	.02	.00	☐ 209	Rene Gonzalez	.08	.03	.01
☐ 161	Tony Gwynn	.35	.14	.03	☐ 210	Dave Valle	.05	.02	.00
☐ 162	Don Baylor	.10	.04	.01	☐ 211	Tom Brunansky	.10	.04	.01
☐ 163	Jerry Browne	.05	.02	.00	☐ 212	Charles Hudson	.05	.02	.00
☐ 164	Dan Pasqua	.08	.03	.01	☐ 213	John Farrell	.08	.03	.01
☐ 165	Rickey Henderson	.40	.16	.04	☐ 214	Jeff Treadway	.10	.04	.01

1988 Topps Traded

		MINT	EXC	G-VG
☐ 215	Eddie Murray	.30	.12	.03
☐ 216	Checklist 177-264	.05	.01	.00
☐ 217	Greg Brock	.05	.02	.00
☐ 218	John Shelby	.05	.02	.00
☐ 219	Craig Reynolds	.05	.02	.00
☐ 220	Dion James	.05	.02	.00
☐ 221	Carney Lansford	.08	.03	.01
☐ 222	Juan Berenguer	.05	.02	.00
☐ 223	Luis Rivera	.05	.02	.00
☐ 224	Harold Baines	.10	.04	.01
☐ 225	Shawon Dunston	.10	.04	.01
☐ 226	Luis Aguayo	.05	.02	.00
☐ 227	Pete O'Brien	.08	.03	.01
☐ 228	Ozzie Smith	.15	.06	.01
☐ 229	Don Mattingly	1.50	.60	.15
☐ 230	Danny Tartabull	.35	.14	.03
☐ 231	Andy Allanson	.05	.02	.00
☐ 232	John Franco	.08	.03	.01
☐ 233	Mike Greenwell	1.25	.50	.12
☐ 234	Bob Ojeda	.08	.03	.01
☐ 235	Chili Davis	.08	.03	.01
☐ 236	Mike Dunne	.10	.04	.01
☐ 237	Jim Morrison	.05	.02	.00
☐ 238	Carmelo Martinez	.05	.02	.00
☐ 239	Ernie Whitt	.05	.02	.00
☐ 240	Scott Garrelts	.05	.02	.00
☐ 241	Mike Moore	.08	.03	.01
☐ 242	Dave Parker	.12	.05	.01
☐ 243	Tim Laudner	.05	.02	.00
☐ 244	Bill Wegman	.05	.02	.00
☐ 245	Bob Horner	.10	.04	.01
☐ 246	Rafael Santana	.08	.03	.01
☐ 247	Alfredo Griffin	.08	.03	.01
☐ 248	Mark Bailey	.05	.02	.00
☐ 249	Ron Gant	.25	.10	.02
☐ 250	Bryn Smith	.05	.02	.00
☐ 251	Lance Johnson	.08	.03	.01
☐ 252	Sam Horn	.15	.06	.01
☐ 253	Darryl Strawberry	.75	.30	.07
☐ 254	Chuck Finley	.05	.02	.00
☐ 255	Darnell Coles	.05	.02	.00
☐ 256	Mike Henneman	.10	.04	.01
☐ 257	Andy Hawkins	.08	.03	.01
☐ 258	Jim Clancy	.05	.02	.00
☐ 259	Atlee Hammaker	.05	.02	.00
☐ 260	Glenn Wilson	.05	.02	.00
☐ 261	Larry McWilliams	.05	.02	.00
☐ 262	Jack Clark	.15	.06	.01
☐ 263	Walt Weiss	.50	.20	.05
☐ 264	Gene Larkin	.15	.06	.01

1988 Topps Traded

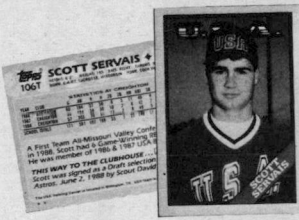

This 132-card Traded or extended set was distributed by Topps to dealers in a special blue and white box as a complete set. The card fronts are identical in style to the Topps regular issue and are also 2 ½" by 3 ½". The backs are printed in orange and black on white card stock. Cards are numbered (with a T suffix) alphabetically according to the name of the player. This set has generated additional interest due to the inclusion of the 1988 U.S. Olympic Baseball team members. These Olympians are indicated in the checklist below by OLY.

		MINT	EXC	G-VG
Complete Set (132)		14.00	5.75	1.40
Common Player (1-132)		.05	.02	.00
☐ 1T	Jim Abbott OLY	1.00	.40	.10
☐ 2T	Juan Agosto	.05	.02	.00
☐ 3T	Luis Alicea	.15	.06	.01
☐ 4T	Roberto Alomar	.35	.14	.03
☐ 5T	Brady Anderson	.35	.14	.03
☐ 6T	Jack Armstrong	.25	.10	.02
☐ 7T	Don August	.15	.06	.01
☐ 8T	Floyd Bannister	.05	.02	.00
☐ 9T	Bret Barberie OLY	.20	.08	.02
☐ 10T	Jose Bautista	.15	.06	.01
☐ 11T	Don Baylor	.10	.04	.01
☐ 12T	Tim Belcher	.15	.06	.01
☐ 13T	Buddy Bell	.10	.04	.01
☐ 14T	Andy Benes OLY	.65	.26	.06
☐ 15T	Damon Berryhill	.35	.14	.03
☐ 16T	Bud Black	.05	.02	.00
☐ 17T	Pat Borders	.15	.06	.01

	MINT	EXC	G-VG		MINT	EXC	G-VG
☐ 18T Phil Bradley	.10	.04	.01	☐ 67T Billy Masse OLY	.25	.10	.02
☐ 19T Jeff Branson OLY	.20	.08	.02	☐ 68T Jack McDowell	.15	.06	.01
☐ 20T Tom Brunansky	.10	.04	.01	☐ 69T Jack McKeon MG	.05	.02	.00
☐ 21T Jay Buhner	.35	.14	.03	☐ 70T Larry McWilliams	.05	.02	.00
☐ 22T Brett Butler	.10	.04	.01	☐ 71T Mickey Morandini OLY	.25	.10	.02
☐ 23T Jim Campanis OLY	.20	.08	.02	☐ 72T Keith Moreland	.05	.02	.00
☐ 24T Sil Campusano	.25	.10	.02	☐ 73T Mike Morgan	.05	.02	.00
☐ 25T John Candelaria	.10	.04	.01	☐ 74T Charles Nagy OLY	.25	.10	.02
☐ 26T Jose Cecena	.15	.06	.01	☐ 75T Al Nipper	.05	.02	.00
☐ 27T Rick Cerone	.05	.02	.00	☐ 76T Russ Nixon MG	.05	.02	.00
☐ 28T Jack Clark	.15	.06	.01	☐ 77T Jesse Orosco	.05	.02	.00
☐ 29T Kevin Coffman	.10	.04	.01	☐ 78T Joe Orsulak	.05	.02	.00
☐ 30T Pat Combs OLY	.20	.08	.02	☐ 79T Dave Palmer	.05	.02	.00
☐ 31T Henry Cotto	.05	.02	.00	☐ 80T Mark Parent	.15	.06	.01
☐ 32T Chili Davis	.10	.04	.01	☐ 81T Dave Parker	.10	.04	.01
☐ 33T Mike Davis	.05	.02	.00	☐ 82T Dan Pasqua	.10	.04	.01
☐ 34T Jose DeLeon	.05	.02	.00	☐ 83T Melido Perez	.25	.10	.02
☐ 35T Richard Dotson	.10	.04	.01	☐ 84T Steve Peters	.15	.06	.01
☐ 36T Cecil Espy	.15	.06	.01	☐ 85T Dan Petry	.05	.02	.00
☐ 37T Tom Filer	.05	.02	.00	☐ 86T Gary Pettis	.05	.02	.00
☐ 38T Mike Fiore OLY	.30	.12	.03	☐ 87T Jeff Pico	.15	.06	.01
☐ 39T Ron Gant	.45	.18	.04	☐ 88T Jim Poole OLY	.20	.08	.02
☐ 40T Kirk Gibson	.20	.08	.02	☐ 89T Ted Power	.05	.02	.00
☐ 41T Rich Gossage	.10	.04	.01	☐ 90T Rafael Ramirez	.05	.02	.00
☐ 42T Mark Grace	1.50	.60	.15	☐ 91T Dennis Rasmussen	.10	.04	.01
☐ 43T Alfredo Griffin	.10	.04	.01	☐ 92T Jose Rijo	.10	.04	.01
☐ 44T Ty Griffin OLY	1.00	.40	.10	☐ 93T Ernie Riles	.05	.02	.00
☐ 45T Bryan Harvey	.30	.12	.03	☐ 94T Luis Rivera	.10	.04	.01
☐ 46T Ron Hassey	.05	.02	.00	☐ 95T Doug Robbins OLY	.20	.08	.02
☐ 47T Ray Hayward	.10	.04	.01	☐ 96T Frank Robinson MG	.10	.04	.01
☐ 48T Dave Henderson	.10	.04	.01	☐ 97T Cookie Rojas MG	.05	.02	.00
☐ 49T Tom Herr	.10	.04	.01	☐ 98T Chris Sabo	1.75	.70	.17
☐ 50T Bob Horner	.10	.04	.01	☐ 99T Mark Salas	.05	.02	.00
☐ 51T Ricky Horton	.05	.02	.00	☐ 100T Luis Salazar	.05	.02	.00
☐ 52T Jay Howell	.05	.02	.00	☐ 101T Rafael Santana	.05	.02	.00
☐ 53T Glenn Hubbard	.05	.02	.00	☐ 102T Nelson Santovenia	.15	.06	.01
☐ 54T Jeff Innis	.20	.08	.02	☐ 103T Mackey Sasser	.25	.10	.02
☐ 55T Danny Jackson	.15	.06	.01	☐ 104T Calvin Schiraldi	.05	.02	.00
☐ 56T Darrin Jackson	.20	.08	.02	☐ 105T Mike Schooler	.15	.06	.01
☐ 57T Roberto Kelly	.35	.14	.03	☐ 106T Scott Servais OLY	.20	.08	.02
☐ 58T Ron Kittle	.10	.04	.01	☐ 107T Dave Silvestri OLY	.20	.08	.02
☐ 59T Ray Knight	.10	.04	.01	☐ 108T Don Slaught	.05	.02	.00
☐ 60T Vance Law	.10	.04	.01	☐ 109T Joe Slusarski OLY	.20	.08	.02
☐ 61T Jeffrey Leonard	.10	.04	.01	☐ 110T Lee Smith	.10	.04	.01
☐ 62T Mike Macfarlane	.20	.08	.02	☐ 111T Pete Smith	.15	.06	.01
☐ 63T Scotti Madison	.15	.06	.01	☐ 112T Jim Snyder MG	.05	.02	.00
☐ 64T Kirt Manwaring	.15	.06	.01	☐ 113T Ed Sprague OLY	.30	.12	.03
☐ 65T Mark Marquess OLY	.05	.02	.00	☐ 114T Pete Stanicek	.15	.06	.01
☐ 66T Tino Martinez OLY	1.00	.40	.10	☐ 115T Kurt Stillwell	.10	.04	.01

	MINT	EXC	G-VG
☐ 116T Todd Stottlemyre ..	.15	.06	.01
☐ 117T Bill Swift	.10	.04	.01
☐ 118T Pat Tabler	.05	.02	.00
☐ 119T Scott Terry	.05	.02	.00
☐ 120T Mickey Tettleton ...	.05	.02	.00
☐ 121T Dickie Thon	.05	.02	.00
☐ 122T Jeff Treadway	.20	.08	.02
☐ 123T Willie Upshaw	.05	.02	.00
☐ 124T Robin Ventura OLY.	1.25	.50	.12
☐ 125T Ron Washington	.05	.02	.00
☐ 126T Walt Weiss	1.25	.50	.12
☐ 127T Bob Welch	.10	.04	.01
☐ 128T David Wells	.15	.06	.01
☐ 129T Glenn Wilson	.05	.02	.00
☐ 130T Ted Wood OLY	.35	.14	.03
☐ 131T Don Zimmer MG ...	.05	.02	.00
☐ 132T Checklist 1T-132T ..	.05	.01	.00

1989 Topps

This 792-card set features backs which are printed in pink and black on gray card stock. The manager cards contain a checklist of the respective team's players on the back. Subsets in the set include Record Breakers (1-7), Turn Back the Clock (661-665), and All-Star selections (386-407). The bonus cards distributed throughout the set that are indicated on the Topps checklist cards are actually Team Leader (TL) cards. Also sprinkled throughout the set are Future Stars (FS) and First Draft Picks (FDP).

			MINT	EXC	G-VG
		Complete Set (792)	24.00	10.00	2.40
		Common Player (1-792) ..	.03	.01	.00
☐	1	George Bell RB ... Slams 3 HR on Opening Day	.12	.03	.01
☐	2	Wade Boggs RB .. Gets 200 Hits 6th Straight Season	.15	.06	.01
☐	3	Gary Carter RB ... Sets Record for Career Putouts	.10	.04	.01
☐	4	Andre Dawson RB . Logs Double Figures in HR and SB	.10	.04	.01
☐	5	Orel Hershiser RB . Pitches 59 Scoreless Innings	.12	.05	.01
☐	6	Doug Jones RB ... Earns His 15th Straight Save (photo actually Chris Codiroli)	.06	.02	.00
☐	7	Kevin McReynolds RB Steals 21 Without Being Caught	.08	.03	.01
☐	8	Dave Eiland	.12	.05	.01
☐	9	Tim Teufel	.03	.01	.00
☐	10	Andre Dawson	.10	.04	.01
☐	11	Bruce Sutter	.08	.03	.01
☐	12	Dale Sveum	.03	.01	.00
☐	13	Doug Sisk	.03	.01	.00
☐	14	Tom Kelly MG .... (team checklist back)	.06	.01	.00
☐	15	Robby Thompson ..	.03	.01	.00
☐	16	Ron Robinson	.03	.01	.00
☐	17	Brian Downing	.03	.01	.00
☐	18	Rick Rhoden	.03	.01	.00
☐	19	Greg Gagne	.03	.01	.00
☐	20	Steve Bedrosian ..	.08	.03	.01
☐	21	Chicago White Sox TL Greg Walker	.03	.01	.00
☐	22	Tim Crews	.03	.01	.00
☐	23	Mike Fitzgerald ... Montreal Expos	.03	.01	.00
☐	24	Larry Andersen ...	.03	.01	.00
☐	25	Frank White	.06	.02	.00
☐	26	Dale Mohorcic	.03	.01	.00
☐	27	Orestes Destrade .	.20	.08	.02
☐	28	Mike Moore	.03	.01	.00
☐	29	Kelly Gruber	.03	.01	.00

		MINT	EXC	G-VG
☐ 30	Doc Gooden	.30	.12	.03
☐ 31	Terry Francona	.03	.01	.00
☐ 32	Dennis Rasmussen .	.06	.02	.00
☐ 33	B.J. Surhoff	.06	.02	.00
☐ 34	Ken Williams	.03	.01	.00
☐ 35	John Tudor	.08	.03	.01
☐ 36	Mitch Webster	.03	.01	.00
☐ 37	Bob Stanley	.03	.01	.00
☐ 38	Paul Runge	.03	.01	.00
☐ 39	Mike Maddux	.03	.01	.00
☐ 40	Steve Sax	.10	.04	.01
☐ 41	Terry Mulholland ...	.03	.01	.00
☐ 42	Jim Eppard	.08	.03	.01
☐ 43	Guillermo Hernandez	.06	.02	.00
☐ 44	Jim Snyder MG	.06	.01	.00
	(team checklist back)			
☐ 45	Kal Daniels	.10	.04	.01
☐ 46	Mark Portugal	.03	.01	.00
☐ 47	Carney Lansford ...	.06	.02	.00
☐ 48	Tim Burke	.03	.01	.00
☐ 49	Craig Biggio	.12	.05	.01
☐ 50	George Bell	.10	.04	.01
☐ 51	California Angels TL	.03	.01	.00
	Mark McLemore			
☐ 52	Bob Brenly	.03	.01	.00
☐ 53	Ruben Sierra	.10	.04	.01
☐ 54	Steve Trout	.03	.01	.00
☐ 55	Julio Franco	.06	.02	.00
☐ 56	Pat Tabler	.06	.02	.00
☐ 57	Alejandro Pena	.03	.01	.00
☐ 58	Lee Mazzilli	.03	.01	.00
☐ 59	Mark Davis	.06	.02	.00
☐ 60	Tom Brunansky	.08	.03	.01
☐ 61	Neil Allen	.03	.01	.00
☐ 62	Alfredo Griffin	.06	.02	.00
☐ 63	Mark Clear	.03	.01	.00
☐ 64	Alex Trevino	.03	.01	.00
☐ 65	Rick Reuschel	.06	.02	.00
☐ 66	Manny Trillo	.03	.01	.00
☐ 67	Dave Palmer	.03	.01	.00
☐ 68	Darrell Miller	.03	.01	.00
☐ 69	Jeff Ballard	.03	.01	.00
☐ 70	Mark McGwire	.40	.16	.04
☐ 71	Mike Boddicker ...	.06	.02	.00
☐ 72	John Moses	.03	.01	.00
☐ 73	Pascual Perez	.06	.02	.00
☐ 74	Nick Leyva MG	.06	.01	.00
	(team checklist back)			
☐ 75	Tom Henke	.03	.01	.00

		MINT	EXC	G-VG
☐ 76	Terry Blocker	.12	.05	.01
☐ 77	Doyle Alexander ..	.03	.01	.00
☐ 78	Jim Sundberg	.03	.01	.00
☐ 79	Scott Bankhead ...	.03	.01	.00
☐ 80	Cory Snyder	.12	.05	.01
☐ 81	Montreal Expos TL	.08	.03	.01
	Tim Raines			
☐ 82	Dave Leiper	.03	.01	.00
☐ 83	Jeff Blauser	.10	.04	.01
☐ 84	Bill Bene FDP	.25	.10	.02
☐ 85	Kevin McReynolds .	.12	.05	.01
☐ 86	Al Nipper	.03	.01	.00
☐ 87	Larry Owen	.03	.01	.00
☐ 88	Darryl Hamilton ...	.20	.08	.02
☐ 89	Dave LaPoint	.03	.01	.00
☐ 90	Vince Coleman	.12	.05	.01
☐ 91	Floyd Youmans ...	.03	.01	.00
☐ 92	Jeff Kunkel	.03	.01	.00
☐ 93	Ken Howell	.03	.01	.00
☐ 94	Chris Speier	.03	.01	.00
☐ 95	Gerald Young	.06	.02	.00
☐ 96	Rick Cerone	.03	.01	.00
☐ 97	Greg Mathews	.03	.01	.00
☐ 98	Larry Sheets	.06	.02	.00
☐ 99	Sherman Corbett ..	.10	.04	.01
☐ 100	Mike Schmidt	.20	.08	.02
☐ 101	Les Straker	.03	.01	.00
☐ 102	Mike Gallego	.03	.01	.00
☐ 103	Tim Birtsas	.03	.01	.00
☐ 104	Dallas Green MG ..	.06	.01	.00
	(team checklist back)			
☐ 105	Ron Darling	.08	.03	.01
☐ 106	Willie Upshaw	.03	.01	.00
☐ 107	Jose DeLeon	.03	.01	.00
☐ 108	Fred Manrique	.03	.01	.00
☐ 109	Hipolito Pena	.12	.05	.01
☐ 110	Paul Molitor	.10	.04	.01
☐ 111	Cincinnati Reds TL	.10	.04	.01
	Eric Davis			
	(swinging bat)			
☐ 112	Jim Presley	.06	.02	.00
☐ 113	Lloyd Moseby	.06	.02	.00
☐ 114	Bob Kipper	.03	.01	.00
☐ 115	Jody Davis	.06	.02	.00
☐ 116	Jeff Montgomery ...	.20	.08	.02
☐ 117	Dave Anderson	.03	.01	.00
☐ 118	Checklist 1-132 ...	.06	.01	.00
☐ 119	Terry Puhl	.03	.01	.00
☐ 120	Frank Viola	.12	.05	.01

		MINT	EXC	G-VG
☐ 121	Garry Templeton . . .	.06	.02	.00
☐ 122	Lance Johnson	.10	.04	.01
☐ 123	Spike Owen	.03	.01	.00
☐ 124	Jim Traber	.03	.01	.00
☐ 125	Mike Krukow	.03	.01	.00
☐ 126	Sid Bream	.03	.01	.00
☐ 127	Walt Terrell	.03	.01	.00
☐ 128	Milt Thompson	.03	.01	.00
☐ 129	Terry Clark	.15	.06	.01
☐ 130	Gerald Perry	.08	.03	.01
☐ 131	Dave Otto	.10	.04	.01
☐ 132	Curt Ford	.03	.01	.00
☐ 133	Bill Long	.03	.01	.00
☐ 134	Don Zimmer MG . . .	.06	.01	.00
	(team checklist back)			
☐ 135	Jose Rijo	.03	.01	.00
☐ 136	Joey Meyer	.10	.04	.01
☐ 137	Geno Petralli	.03	.01	.00
☐ 138	Wallace Johnson . . .	.03	.01	.00
☐ 139	Mike Flanagan	.03	.01	.00
☐ 140	Shawon Dunston . . .	.06	.02	.00
☐ 141	Cleveland Indians TL	.06	.02	.00
	Brook Jacoby			
☐ 142	Mike Diaz	.03	.01	.00
☐ 143	Mike Campbell	.03	.01	.00
☐ 144	Jay Bell	.03	.01	.00
☐ 145	Dave Stewart	.06	.02	.00
☐ 146	Gary Pettis	.03	.01	.00
☐ 147	DeWayne Buice . . .	.03	.01	.00
☐ 148	Bill Pecota	.03	.01	.00
☐ 149	Doug Dascenzo	.15	.06	.01
☐ 150	Fernando Valenzuela	.10	.04	.01
☐ 151	Terry McGriff	.03	.01	.00
☐ 152	Mark Thurmond	.03	.01	.00
☐ 153	Jim Pankovits	.03	.01	.00
☐ 154	Don Carman	.03	.01	.00
☐ 155	Marty Barrett	.06	.02	.00
☐ 156	Dave Gallagher	.15	.06	.01
☐ 157	Tom Glavine	.03	.01	.00
☐ 158	Mike Aldrete	.03	.01	.00
☐ 159	Pat Clements	.03	.01	.00
☐ 160	Jeffrey Leonard	.06	.02	.00
☐ 161	Gregg Olson FDP . .	.30	.12	.03
☐ 162	John Davis	.03	.01	.00
☐ 163	Bob Forsch	.03	.01	.00
☐ 164	Hal Lanier MG	.06	.01	.00
	(team checklist back)			
☐ 165	Mike Dunne	.06	.02	.00
☐ 166	Doug Jennings	.20	.08	.02
☐ 167	Steve Searcy FS . .	.25	.10	.02
☐ 168	Willie Wilson	.08	.03	.01
☐ 169	Mike Jackson	.03	.01	.00
☐ 170	Tony Fernandez . . .	.10	.04	.01
☐ 171	Atlanta Braves TL .	.03	.01	.00
	Andres Thomas			
☐ 172	Frank Williams	.03	.01	.00
☐ 173	Mel Hall	.03	.01	.00
☐ 174	Todd Burns	.20	.08	.02
☐ 175	John Shelby	.03	.01	.00
☐ 176	Jeff Parrett	.03	.01	.00
☐ 177	Monty Fariss FDP .	.30	.12	.03
☐ 178	Mark Grant	.03	.01	.00
☐ 179	Ozzie Virgil	.03	.01	.00
☐ 180	Mike Scott	.10	.04	.01
☐ 181	Craig Worthington .	.20	.08	.02
☐ 182	Bob McClure	.03	.01	.00
☐ 183	Oddibe McDowell .	.06	.02	.00
☐ 184	John Costello	.10	.04	.01
☐ 185	Claudell Washington	.06	.02	.00
☐ 186	Pat Perry	.03	.01	.00
☐ 187	Darren Daulton	.03	.01	.00
☐ 188	Dennis Lamp	.03	.01	.00
☐ 189	Kevin Mitchell	.06	.02	.00
☐ 190	Mike Witt	.08	.03	.01
☐ 191	Sil Campusano	.20	.08	.02
☐ 192	Paul Mirabella	.03	.01	.00
☐ 193	Sparky Anderson MG	.06	.01	.00
	(team checklist back)			
☐ 194	Greg W. Harris . . .	.20	.08	.02
	San Diego Padres			
☐ 195	Ozzie Guillen	.06	.02	.00
☐ 196	Denny Walling	.03	.01	.00
☐ 197	Neal Heaton	.03	.01	.00
☐ 198	Danny Heep	.03	.01	.00
☐ 199	Mike Schooler	.12	.05	.01
☐ 200	George Brett	.20	.08	.02
☐ 201	Blue Jays TL	.03	.01	.00
	Kelly Gruber			
☐ 202	Brad Moore	.15	.06	.01
☐ 203	Rob Ducey	.06	.02	.00
☐ 204	Brad Havens	.03	.01	.00
☐ 205	Dwight Evans	.08	.03	.01
☐ 206	Roberto Alomar . . .	.20	.08	.02
☐ 207	Terry Leach	.06	.02	.00
☐ 208	Tom Pagnozzi	.03	.01	.00
☐ 209	Jeff Bittiger	.12	.05	.01
☐ 210	Dale Murphy	.20	.08	.02
☐ 211	Mike Pagliarulo . . .	.06	.02	.00

		MINT	EXC	G-VG			MINT	EXC	G-VG
☐ 212	Scott Sanderson ...	.03	.01	.00	☐ 257	Rick Aguilera	.03	.01	.00
☐ 213	Rene Gonzales	.03	.01	.00	☐ 258	Checklist 133-264 .	.06	.01	.00
☐ 214	Charlie O'Brien	.03	.01	.00	☐ 259	Larry McWilliams ..	.03	.01	.00
☐ 215	Kevin Gross	.03	.01	.00	☐ 260	Dave Winfield	.15	.06	.01
☐ 216	Jack Howell	.03	.01	.00	☐ 261	St.Louis Cardinals TL	.06	.02	.00
☐ 217	Joe Price	.03	.01	.00		Tom Brunansky			
☐ 218	Mike LaValliere	.03	.01	.00		(with Luis Alicea)			
☐ 219	Jim Clancy	.03	.01	.00	☐ 262	Jeff Pico	.10	.04	.01
☐ 220	Gary Gaetti	.10	.04	.01	☐ 263	Mike Felder	.03	.01	.00
☐ 221	Cecil Espy	.10	.04	.01	☐ 264	Rob Dibble	.12	.05	.01
☐ 222	Mark Lewis FDP ...	.30	.12	.03	☐ 265	Kent Hrbek	.10	.04	.01
☐ 223	Jay Buhner	.15	.06	.01	☐ 266	Luis Aquino	.03	.01	.00
☐ 224	Tony LaRussa MG .	.06	.01	.00	☐ 267	Jeff Robinson	.08	.03	.01
	(team checklist back)					Detroit Tigers			
☐ 225	Ramon Martinez ...	.25	.10	.02	☐ 268	Keith Miller	.15	.06	.01
☐ 226	Bill Doran	.06	.02	.00		Philadelphia Phillies			
☐ 227	John Farrell	.03	.01	.00	☐ 269	Tom Bolton	.03	.01	.00
☐ 228	Nelson Santovenia .	.10	.04	.01	☐ 270	Wally Joyner	.15	.06	.01
☐ 229	Jimmy Key	.06	.02	.00	☐ 271	Jay Tibbs	.03	.01	.00
☐ 230	Ozzie Smith	.10	.04	.01	☐ 272	Ron Hassey	.03	.01	.00
☐ 231	San Diego Padres TL	.10	.04	.01	☐ 273	Jose Lind	.03	.01	.00
	Roberto Alomar				☐ 274	Mark Eichhorn	.03	.01	.00
	(G.Carter at plate)				☐ 275	Danny Tartabull ...	.12	.05	.01
☐ 232	Ricky Horton	.03	.01	.00	☐ 276	Paul Kilgus	.03	.01	.00
☐ 233	Gregg Jefferies FS .	2.50	1.00	.25	☐ 277	Mike Davis	.03	.01	.00
☐ 234	Tom Browning	.08	.03	.01	☐ 278	Andy McGaffigan ..	.03	.01	.00
☐ 235	John Kruk	.06	.02	.00	☐ 279	Scott Bradley	.03	.01	.00
☐ 236	Charles Hudson ...	.03	.01	.00	☐ 280	Bob Knepper	.03	.01	.00
☐ 237	Glenn Hubbard	.03	.01	.00	☐ 281	Gary Redus	.03	.01	.00
☐ 238	Eric King	.03	.01	.00	☐ 282	Cris Carpenter	.20	.08	.02
☐ 239	Tim Laudner	.03	.01	.00	☐ 283	Andy Allanson	.03	.01	.00
☐ 240	Greg Maddux	.10	.04	.01	☐ 284	Jim Leyland MG ...	.06	.01	.00
☐ 241	Brett Butler	.06	.02	.00		(team checklist back)			
☐ 242	Ed Vandeberg	.03	.01	.00	☐ 285	John Candelaria ...	.06	.02	.00
☐ 243	Bob Boone	.06	.02	.00	☐ 286	Darrin Jackson	.15	.06	.01
☐ 244	Jim Acker	.03	.01	.00	☐ 287	Juan Nieves	.03	.01	.00
☐ 245	Jim Rice	.10	.04	.01	☐ 288	Pat Sheridan	.03	.01	.00
☐ 246	Rey Quinones	.03	.01	.00	☐ 289	Ernie Whitt	.03	.01	.00
☐ 247	Shawn Hillegas ...	.03	.01	.00	☐ 290	John Franco	.06	.02	.00
☐ 248	Tony Phillips	.03	.01	.00	☐ 291	New York Mets TL	.12	.05	.01
☐ 249	Tim Leary	.06	.02	.00		Darryl Strawberry			
☐ 250	Cal Ripken	.15	.06	.01		(with K.Hernandez			
☐ 251	John Dopson	.12	.05	.01		and K.McReynolds)			
☐ 252	Billy Hatcher	.06	.02	.00	☐ 292	Jim Corsi	.15	.06	.01
☐ 253	Jose Alvarez	.10	.04	.01	☐ 293	Glenn Wilson	.03	.01	.00
☐ 254	Tom Lasorda MG ..	.06	.01	.00	☐ 294	Juan Berenguer ...	.03	.01	.00
	(team checklist back)				☐ 295	Scott Fletcher	.03	.01	.00
☐ 255	Ron Guidry	.08	.03	.01	☐ 296	Ron Gant	.25	.10	.02
☐ 256	Benny Santiago ...	.12	.05	.01	☐ 297	Oswald Peraza ...	.12	.05	.01

		MINT	EXC	G-VG
☐ 298	Chris James	.06	.02	.00
☐ 299	Steve Ellsworth	.12	.05	.01
☐ 300	Darryl Strawberry	.30	.12	.03
☐ 301	Charlie Leibrandt	.03	.01	.00
☐ 302	Gary Ward	.03	.01	.00
☐ 303	Felix Fermin	.03	.01	.00
☐ 304	Joel Youngblood	.03	.01	.00
☐ 305	Dave Smith	.03	.01	.00
☐ 306	Tracy Woodson	.10	.04	.01
☐ 307	Lance McCullers	.06	.02	.00
☐ 308	Ron Karkovice	.03	.01	.00
☐ 309	Mario Diaz	.08	.03	.01
☐ 310	Rafael Palmeiro	.10	.04	.01
☐ 311	Chris Bosio	.03	.01	.00
☐ 312	Tom Lawless	.03	.01	.00
☐ 313	Dennis Martinez	.03	.01	.00
☐ 314	Bobby Valentine MG	.06	.01	.00
	(team checklist back)			
☐ 315	Greg Swindell	.08	.03	.01
☐ 316	Walt Weiss	.40	.16	.04
☐ 317	Jack Armstrong	.20	.08	.02
☐ 318	Gene Larkin	.06	.02	.00
☐ 319	Greg Booker	.03	.01	.00
☐ 320	Lou Whitaker	.08	.03	.01
☐ 321	Boston Red Sox TL	.08	.03	.01
	Jody Reed			
☐ 322	John Smiley	.03	.01	.00
☐ 323	Gary Thurman	.03	.01	.00
☐ 324	Bob Milacki	.20	.08	.02
☐ 325	Jesse Barfield	.10	.04	.01
☐ 326	Dennis Boyd	.06	.02	.00
☐ 327	Mark Lemke	.20	.08	.02
☐ 328	Rick Honeycutt	.03	.01	.00
☐ 329	Bob Melvin	.03	.01	.00
☐ 330	Eric Davis	.25	.10	.02
☐ 331	Curt Wilkerson	.03	.01	.00
☐ 332	Tony Armas	.06	.02	.00
☐ 333	Bob Ojeda	.06	.02	.00
☐ 334	Steve Lyons	.03	.01	.00
☐ 335	Dave Righetti	.08	.03	.01
☐ 336	Steve Balboni	.03	.01	.00
☐ 337	Calvin Schiraldi	.03	.01	.00
☐ 338	Jim Adduci	.03	.01	.00
☐ 339	Scott Bailes	.03	.01	.00
☐ 340	Kirk Gibson	.15	.06	.01
☐ 341	Jim Deshaies	.03	.01	.00
☐ 342	Tom Brookens	.03	.01	.00
☐ 343	Gary Sheffield FS	1.50	.60	.15

		MINT	EXC	G-VG
☐ 344	Tom Trebelhorn MG	.06	.01	.00
	(team checklist back)			
☐ 345	Charlie Hough	.03	.01	.00
☐ 346	Rex Hudler	.03	.01	.00
☐ 347	John Cerutti	.03	.01	.00
☐ 348	Ed Hearn	.03	.01	.00
☐ 349	Ron Jones	.30	.12	.03
☐ 350	Andy Van Slyke	.10	.04	.01
☐ 351	San Fran. Giants TL	.03	.01	.00
	Bob Melvin			
	(with Bill Fahey CO)			
☐ 352	Rick Schu	.03	.01	.00
☐ 353	Marvell Wynne	.03	.01	.00
☐ 354	Larry Parrish	.03	.01	.00
☐ 355	Mark Langston	.08	.03	.01
☐ 356	Kevin Elster	.06	.02	.00
☐ 357	Jerry Reuss	.03	.01	.00
☐ 358	Ricky Jordan	1.25	.50	.12
☐ 359	Tommy John	.08	.03	.01
☐ 360	Ryne Sandberg	.15	.06	.01
☐ 361	Kelly Downs	.03	.01	.00
☐ 362	Jack Lazorko	.03	.01	.00
☐ 363	Rich Yett	.03	.01	.00
☐ 364	Rob Deer	.06	.02	.00
☐ 365	Mike Henneman	.03	.01	.00
☐ 366	Herm Winningham	.03	.01	.00
☐ 367	Johnny Paredes	.10	.04	.01
☐ 368	Brian Holton	.03	.01	.00
☐ 369	Ken Caminiti	.03	.01	.00
☐ 370	Dennis Eckersley	.08	.03	.01
☐ 371	Manny Lee	.03	.01	.00
☐ 372	Craig Lefferts	.03	.01	.00
☐ 373	Tracy Jones	.06	.02	.00
☐ 374	John Wathan MG	.06	.01	.00
	(team checklist back)			
☐ 375	Terry Pendleton	.03	.01	.00
☐ 376	Steve Lombardozzi	.03	.01	.00
☐ 377	Mike Smithson	.03	.01	.00
☐ 378	Checklist 265-396	.03	.01	.00
☐ 379	Tim Flannery	.03	.01	.00
☐ 380	Rickey Henderson	.20	.08	.02
☐ 381	Baltimore Orioles TL	.03	.01	.00
	Larry Sheets			
☐ 382	John Smoltz	.20	.08	.02
☐ 383	Howard Johnson	.08	.03	.01
☐ 384	Mark Salas	.03	.01	.00
☐ 385	Von Hayes	.08	.03	.01
☐ 386	Andres Galarraga AS	.10	.04	.01
☐ 387	Ryne Sandberg AS	.10	.04	.01

		MINT	EXC	G-VG
☐ 388	Bobby Bonilla AS	.08	.03	.01
☐ 389	Ozzie Smith AS	.08	.03	.01
☐ 390	Darryl Strawberry AS	.15	.06	.01
☐ 391	Andre Dawson AS	.10	.04	.01
☐ 392	Andy Van Slyke AS	.08	.03	.01
☐ 393	Gary Carter AS	.12	.05	.01
☐ 394	Orel Hershiser AS	.12	.05	.01
☐ 395	Danny Jackson AS	.08	.03	.01
☐ 396	Kirk Gibson AS	.10	.04	.01
☐ 397	Don Mattingly AS	.25	.10	.02
☐ 398	Julio Franco AS	.08	.03	.01
☐ 399	Wade Boggs AS	.20	.08	.02
☐ 400	Alan Trammell AS	.08	.03	.01
☐ 401	Jose Canseco AS	.30	.12	.03
☐ 402	Mike Greenwell AS	.20	.08	.02
☐ 403	Kirby Puckett AS	.12	.05	.01
☐ 404	Bob Boone AS	.08	.03	.01
☐ 405	Roger Clemens AS	.15	.06	.01
☐ 406	Frank Viola AS	.08	.03	.01
☐ 407	Dave Winfield AS	.10	.04	.01
☐ 408	Greg Walker	.06	.02	.00
☐ 409	Ken Dayley	.03	.01	.00
☐ 410	Jack Clark	.10	.04	.01
☐ 411	Mitch Williams	.03	.01	.00
☐ 412	Barry Lyons	.03	.01	.00
☐ 413	Mike Kingery	.03	.01	.00
☐ 414	Jim Fregosi MG (team checklist back)	.06	.01	.00
☐ 415	Rich Gossage	.08	.03	.01
☐ 416	Fred Lynn	.08	.03	.01
☐ 417	Mike LaCoss	.03	.01	.00
☐ 418	Bob Dernier	.03	.01	.00
☐ 419	Tom Filer	.03	.01	.00
☐ 420	Joe Carter	.10	.04	.01
☐ 421	Kirk McCaskill	.03	.01	.00
☐ 422	Bo Diaz	.03	.01	.00
☐ 423	Brian Fisher	.03	.01	.00
☐ 424	Luis Polonia	.03	.01	.00
☐ 425	Jay Howell	.03	.01	.00
☐ 426	Dan Gladden	.06	.02	.00
☐ 427	Eric Show	.03	.01	.00
☐ 428	Craig Reynolds	.03	.01	.00
☐ 429	Minnesota Twins TL Greg Gagne (taking throw at 2nd)	.03	.01	.00
☐ 430	Mark Gubicza	.06	.02	.00
☐ 431	Luis Rivera	.03	.01	.00
☐ 432	Chad Kreuter	.20	.08	.02
☐ 433	Albert Hall	.03	.01	.00
☐ 434	Ken Patterson	.10	.04	.01
☐ 435	Len Dykstra	.08	.03	.01
☐ 436	Bobby Meacham	.03	.01	.00
☐ 437	Andy Benes FDP	.35	.14	.03
☐ 438	Greg Gross	.03	.01	.00
☐ 439	Frank DiPino	.03	.01	.00
☐ 440	Bobby Bonilla	.10	.04	.01
☐ 441	Jerry Reed	.03	.01	.00
☐ 442	Jose Oquendo	.03	.01	.00
☐ 443	Rod Nichols	.10	.04	.01
☐ 444	Moose Stubing MG (team checklist back)	.06	.01	.00
☐ 445	Matt Nokes	.10	.04	.01
☐ 446	Rob Murphy	.03	.01	.00
☐ 447	Donell Nixon	.03	.01	.00
☐ 448	Eric Plunk	.03	.01	.00
☐ 449	Carmelo Martinez	.03	.01	.00
☐ 450	Roger Clemens	.25	.10	.02
☐ 451	Mark Davidson	.03	.01	.00
☐ 452	Israel Sanchez	.10	.04	.01
☐ 453	Tom Prince	.10	.04	.01
☐ 454	Paul Assenmacher	.03	.01	.00
☐ 455	Johnny Ray	.06	.02	.00
☐ 456	Tim Belcher	.06	.02	.00
☐ 457	Mackey Sasser	.08	.03	.01
☐ 458	Donn Pall	.10	.04	.01
☐ 459	Seattle Mariners TL Dave Valle	.03	.01	.00
☐ 460	Dave Stieb	.08	.03	.01
☐ 461	Buddy Bell	.08	.03	.01
☐ 462	Jose Guzman	.03	.01	.00
☐ 463	Steve Lake	.03	.01	.00
☐ 464	Bryn Smith	.03	.01	.00
☐ 465	Mark Grace	.85	.34	.08
☐ 466	Chuck Crim	.03	.01	.00
☐ 467	Jim Walewander	.03	.01	.00
☐ 468	Henry Cotto	.03	.01	.00
☐ 469	Jose Bautista	.10	.04	.01
☐ 470	Lance Parrish	.08	.03	.01
☐ 471	Steve Curry	.12	.05	.01
☐ 472	Brian Harper	.03	.01	.00
☐ 473	Don Robinson	.03	.01	.00
☐ 474	Bob Rodgers MG (team checklist back)	.06	.01	.00
☐ 475	Dave Parker	.08	.03	.01
☐ 476	Jon Perlman	.08	.03	.01
☐ 477	Dick Schofield	.03	.01	.00
☐ 478	Doug Drabek	.03	.01	.00
☐ 479	Mike Macfarlane	.12	.05	.01

		MINT	EXC	G-VG
☐ 480	Keith Hernandez ...	.12	.05	.01
☐ 481	Chris Brown	.06	.02	.00
☐ 482	Steve Peters	.12	.05	.01
☐ 483	Mickey Hatcher ...	.06	.02	.00
☐ 484	Steve Shields	.03	.01	.00
☐ 485	Hubie Brooks	.06	.02	.00
☐ 486	Jack McDowell	.15	.06	.01
☐ 487	Scott Lusader	.10	.04	.01
☐ 488	Kevin Coffman	.10	.04	.01
☐ 489	Phila. Phillies TL ...	.12	.05	.01
	Mike Schmidt			
☐ 490	Chris Sabo	.85	.34	.08
☐ 491	Mike Birkbeck	.03	.01	.00
☐ 492	Alan Ashby	.03	.01	.00
☐ 493	Todd Benzinger ...	.06	.02	.00
☐ 494	Shane Rawley	.03	.01	.00
☐ 495	Candy Maldonado ..	.06	.02	.00
☐ 496	Dwayne Henry	.03	.01	.00
☐ 497	Pete Stanicek	.10	.04	.01
☐ 498	Dave Valle	.03	.01	.00
☐ 499	Don Heinkel	.10	.04	.01
☐ 500	Jose Canseco	1.00	.40	.10
☐ 501	Vance Law	.03	.01	.00
☐ 502	Duane Ward	.03	.01	.00
☐ 503	Al Newman	.03	.01	.00
☐ 504	Bob Walk	.03	.01	.00
☐ 505	Pete Rose MG	.25	.07	.01
	(team checklist back)			
☐ 506	Kirt Manwaring	.10	.04	.01
☐ 507	Steve Farr	.03	.01	.00
☐ 508	Wally Backman	.03	.01	.00
☐ 509	Bud Black	.03	.01	.00
☐ 510	Bob Horner	.08	.03	.01
☐ 511	Richard Dotson ...	.06	.02	.00
☐ 512	Donnie Hill	.03	.01	.00
☐ 513	Jesse Orosco	.03	.01	.00
☐ 514	Chet Lemon	.03	.01	.00
☐ 515	Barry Larkin	.08	.03	.01
☐ 516	Eddie Whitson	.03	.01	.00
☐ 517	Greg Brock	.03	.01	.00
☐ 518	Bruce Ruffin	.03	.01	.00
☐ 519	New York Yankees TL	.03	.01	.00
	Willie Randolph			
☐ 520	Rick Sutcliffe	.08	.03	.01
☐ 521	Mickey Tettleton ...	.03	.01	.00
☐ 522	Randy Kramer	.10	.04	.01
☐ 523	Andres Thomas ...	.03	.01	.00
☐ 524	Checklist 397-528 ..	.06	.01	.00
☐ 525	Chili Davis	.06	.02	.00
☐ 526	Wes Gardner	.03	.01	.00
☐ 527	Dave Henderson ..	.06	.02	.00
☐ 528	Luis Medina	.35	.14	.03
☐ 529	Tom Foley	.03	.01	.00
☐ 530	Nolan Ryan	.15	.06	.01
☐ 531	Dave Hengel	.10	.04	.01
☐ 532	Jerry Browne	.03	.01	.00
☐ 533	Andy Hawkins	.03	.01	.00
☐ 534	Doc Edwards MG .	.06	.01	.00
	(team checklist back)			
☐ 535	Todd Worrell	.08	.03	.01
☐ 536	Joel Skinner	.03	.01	.00
☐ 537	Pete Smith	.10	.04	.01
☐ 538	Juan Castillo	.03	.01	.00
☐ 539	Barry Jones	.03	.01	.00
☐ 540	Bo Jackson	.15	.06	.01
☐ 541	Cecil Fielder	.03	.01	.00
☐ 542	Todd Frohwirth	.03	.01	.00
☐ 543	Damon Berryhill ...	.15	.06	.01
☐ 544	Jeff Sellers	.03	.01	.00
☐ 545	Mookie Wilson	.03	.01	.00
☐ 546	Mark Williamson ...	.03	.01	.00
☐ 547	Mark McLemore ...	.03	.01	.00
☐ 548	Bobby Witt	.06	.02	.00
☐ 549	Chicago Cubs TL .	.03	.01	.00
	Jamie Moyer			
	(pitching)			
☐ 550	Orel Hershiser	.20	.08	.02
☐ 551	Randy Ready	.03	.01	.00
☐ 552	Greg Cadaret	.03	.01	.00
☐ 553	Luis Salazar	.03	.01	.00
☐ 554	Nick Esasky	.03	.01	.00
☐ 555	Bert Blyleven	.08	.03	.01
☐ 556	Bruce Fields	.03	.01	.00
☐ 557	Keith Miller	.03	.01	.00
	New York Mets			
☐ 558	Dan Pasqua	.06	.02	.00
☐ 559	Juan Agosto	.03	.01	.00
☐ 560	Tim Raines	.12	.05	.01
☐ 561	Luis Aguayo	.03	.01	.00
☐ 562	Danny Cox	.06	.02	.00
☐ 563	Bill Schroeder	.03	.01	.00
☐ 564	Russ Nixon MG ...	.06	.01	.00
	(team checklist back)			
☐ 565	Jeff Russell	.03	.01	.00
☐ 566	Al Pedrique	.03	.01	.00
☐ 567	David Wells	.08	.03	.01
☐ 568	Mickey Brantley ...	.06	.02	.00
☐ 569	German Jimenez ..	.10	.04	.01

	MINT	EXC	G-VG		MINT	EXC	G-VG
☐ 570 Tony Gwynn	.15	.06	.01	☐ 614 Joe Hesketh	.03	.01	.00
☐ 571 Billy Ripken	.03	.01	.00	☐ 615 Robin Yount	.12	.05	.01
☐ 572 Atlee Hammaker	.03	.01	.00	☐ 616 Steve Rosenberg	.10	.04	.01
☐ 573 Jim Abbott FDP	.75	.30	.07	☐ 617 Mark Parent	.10	.04	.01
☐ 574 Dave Clark	.06	.02	.00	☐ 618 Rance Mulliniks	.03	.01	.00
☐ 575 Juan Samuel	.08	.03	.01	☐ 619 Checklist 529-660	.06	.01	.00
☐ 576 Greg Minton	.03	.01	.00	☐ 620 Barry Bonds	.10	.04	.01
☐ 577 Randy Bush	.03	.01	.00	☐ 621 Rick Mahler	.03	.01	.00
☐ 578 John Morris	.03	.01	.00	☐ 622 Stan Javier	.03	.01	.00
☐ 579 Houston Astros TL	.06	.02	.00	☐ 623 Fred Toliver	.03	.01	.00
Glenn Davis				☐ 624 Jack McKeon MG	.06	.01	.00
(batting stance)				(team checklist back)			
☐ 580 Harold Reynolds	.03	.01	.00	☐ 625 Eddie Murray	.15	.06	.01
☐ 581 Gene Nelson	.03	.01	.00	☐ 626 Jeff Reed	.03	.01	.00
☐ 582 Mike Marshall	.08	.03	.01	☐ 627 Greg Harris	.03	.01	.00
☐ 583 Paul Gibson	.10	.04	.01	Philadelphia Phillies			
☐ 584 Randy Velarde	.08	.03	.01	☐ 628 Matt Williams	.08	.03	.01
☐ 585 Harold Baines	.08	.03	.01	☐ 629 Pete O'Brien	.06	.02	.00
☐ 586 Joe Boever	.03	.01	.00	☐ 630 Mike Greenwell	.50	.20	.05
☐ 587 Mike Stanley	.03	.01	.00	☐ 631 Dave Bergman	.03	.01	.00
☐ 588 Luis Alicea	.10	.04	.01	☐ 632 Bryan Harvey	.25	.10	.02
☐ 589 Dave Meads	.03	.01	.00	☐ 633 Daryl Boston	.03	.01	.00
☐ 590 Andres Galarraga	.12	.05	.01	☐ 634 Marvin Freeman	.03	.01	.00
☐ 591 Jeff Musselman	.03	.01	.00	☐ 635 Willie Randolph	.06	.02	.00
☐ 592 John Cangelosi	.03	.01	.00	☐ 636 Bill Wilkinson	.03	.01	.00
☐ 593 Drew Hall	.03	.01	.00	☐ 637 Carmen Castillo	.03	.01	.00
☐ 594 Jimy Williams MG	.06	.01	.00	☐ 638 Floyd Bannister	.03	.01	.00
(team checklist back)				☐ 639 Oakland A's TL	.12	.05	.01
☐ 595 Teddy Higuera	.08	.03	.01	Walt Weiss			
☐ 596 Kurt Stillwell	.03	.01	.00	☐ 640 Willie McGee	.08	.03	.01
☐ 597 Terry Taylor	.15	.06	.01	☐ 641 Curt Young	.03	.01	.00
☐ 598 Ken Gerhart	.03	.01	.00	☐ 642 Argenis Salazar	.03	.01	.00
☐ 599 Tom Candiotti	.03	.01	.00	☐ 643 Louie Meadows	.10	.04	.01
☐ 600 Wade Boggs	.40	.16	.04	☐ 644 Lloyd McClendon	.03	.01	.00
☐ 601 Dave Dravecky	.03	.01	.00	☐ 645 Jack Morris	.10	.04	.01
☐ 602 Devon White	.08	.03	.01	☐ 646 Kevin Bass	.06	.02	.00
☐ 603 Frank Tanana	.03	.01	.00	☐ 647 Randy Johnson	.20	.08	.02
☐ 604 Paul O'Neill	.03	.01	.00	☐ 648 Sandy Alomar FS	.90	.36	.09
☐ 605 Bob Welch	.06	.02	.00	☐ 649 Stewart Cliburn	.03	.01	.00
☐ 606 Rick Dempsey	.03	.01	.00	☐ 650 Kirby Puckett	.20	.08	.02
☐ 607 Willie Ansley FDP	.30	.12	.03	☐ 651 Tom Niedenfuer	.03	.01	.00
☐ 608 Phil Bradley	.06	.02	.00	☐ 652 Rich Gedman	.06	.02	.00
☐ 609 Detroit Tigers TL	.06	.02	.00	☐ 653 Tommy Barrett	.12	.05	.01
Frank Tanana				☐ 654 Whitey Herzog MG	.06	.01	.00
(with Alan Trammell and Mike Heath)				(team checklist back)			
☐ 610 Randy Myers	.06	.02	.00	☐ 655 Dave Magadan	.06	.02	.00
☐ 611 Don Slaught	.03	.01	.00	☐ 656 Ivan Calderon	.06	.02	.00
☐ 612 Dan Quisenberry	.08	.03	.01	☐ 657 Joe Magrane	.06	.02	.00
☐ 613 Gary Varsho	.15	.06	.01	☐ 658 R.J. Reynolds	.03	.01	.00

		MINT	EXC	G-VG
☐ 659	Al Leiter	.15	.06	.01
☐ 660	Will Clark	.25	.10	.02
☐ 661	Dwight Gooden TBC84	.12	.05	.01
☐ 662	Lou Brock TBC79 ..	.08	.03	.01
☐ 663	Hank Aaron TBC74	.10	.04	.01
☐ 664	Gil Hodges TBC69	.08	.03	.01
☐ 665	Tony Oliva TBC64 .	.08	.03	.01
	(fabricated card)			
☐ 666	Randy St.Claire ...	.03	.01	.00
☐ 667	Dwayne Murphy ...	.03	.01	.00
☐ 668	Mike Bielecki	.03	.01	.00
☐ 669	L.A. Dodgers TL ...	.15	.06	.01
	Orel Hershiser			
	(mound conference			
	with Mike Scioscia)			
☐ 670	Kevin Seitzer	.15	.06	.01
☐ 671	Jim Gantner	.03	.01	.00
☐ 672	Allan Anderson	.06	.02	.00
☐ 673	Don Baylor	.06	.02	.00
☐ 674	Otis Nixon	.03	.01	.00
☐ 675	Bruce Hurst	.08	.03	.01
☐ 676	Ernie Riles	.03	.01	.00
☐ 677	Dave Schmidt	.03	.01	.00
☐ 678	Dion James	.03	.01	.00
☐ 679	Willie Fraser	.03	.01	.00
☐ 680	Gary Carter	.15	.06	.01
☐ 681	Jeff Robinson	.03	.01	.00
	Pittsburgh Pirates			
☐ 682	Rick Leach	.03	.01	.00
☐ 683	Jose Cecena	.10	.04	.01
☐ 684	Dave Johnson MG ..	.06	.01	.00
	(team checklist back)			
☐ 685	Jeff Treadway	.10	.04	.01
☐ 686	Scott Terry	.03	.01	.00
☐ 687	Alvin Davis	.08	.03	.01
☐ 688	Zane Smith	.06	.02	.00
☐ 689	Stan Jefferson	.06	.02	.00
☐ 690	Doug Jones	.06	.02	.00
☐ 691	Roberto Kelly	.15	.06	.01
☐ 692	Steve Ontiveros ...	.03	.01	.00
☐ 693	Pat Borders	.15	.06	.01
☐ 694	Les Lancaster	.03	.01	.00
☐ 695	Carlton Fisk	.08	.03	.01
☐ 696	Don August	.06	.02	.00
☐ 697	Franklin Stubbs ...	.03	.01	.00
☐ 698	Keith Atherton	.03	.01	.00
☐ 699	Pittsburgh Pirates TL	.06	.02	.00
	Al Pedrique			
	(Tony Gwynn sliding)			

		MINT	EXC	G-VG
☐ 700	Don Mattingly	.75	.30	.07
☐ 701	Storm Davis	.06	.02	.00
☐ 702	Jamie Quirk	.03	.01	.00
☐ 703	Scott Garrelts	.03	.01	.00
☐ 704	Carlos Quintana ..	.30	.12	.03
☐ 705	Terry Kennedy	.03	.01	.00
☐ 706	Pete Incaviglia ...	.10	.04	.01
☐ 707	Steve Jeltz	.03	.01	.00
☐ 708	Chuck Finley	.03	.01	.00
☐ 709	Tom Herr	.06	.02	.00
☐ 710	David Cone	.20	.08	.02
☐ 711	Candy Sierra	.12	.05	.01
☐ 712	Bill Swift	.03	.01	.00
☐ 713	Ty Griffin FDP	.50	.20	.05
☐ 714	Joe Morgan MG ..	.06	.02	.00
	(team checklist back)			
☐ 715	Tony Pena	.06	.02	.00
☐ 716	Wayne Tolleson ..	.03	.01	.00
☐ 717	Jamie Moyer	.03	.01	.00
☐ 718	Glenn Braggs	.03	.01	.00
☐ 719	Danny Darwin	.03	.01	.00
☐ 720	Tim Wallach	.06	.02	.00
☐ 721	Ron Tingley	.10	.04	.01
☐ 722	Todd Stottlemyre ..	.15	.06	.01
☐ 723	Rafael Belliard ...	.03	.01	.00
☐ 724	Jerry Don Gleaton .	.03	.01	.00
☐ 725	Terry Steinbach ..	.08	.03	.01
☐ 726	Dickie Thon	.03	.01	.00
☐ 727	Joe Orsulak	.03	.01	.00
☐ 728	Charlie Puleo	.03	.01	.00
☐ 729	Texas Rangers TL .	.03	.01	.00
	Steve Buechele			
☐ 730	Danny Jackson ...	.10	.04	.01
☐ 731	Mike Young	.03	.01	.00
☐ 732	Steve Buechele ...	.03	.01	.00
☐ 733	Randy Bockus	.10	.04	.01
☐ 734	Jody Reed	.08	.03	.01
☐ 735	Roger McDowell ..	.06	.02	.00
☐ 736	Jeff Hamilton	.03	.01	.00
☐ 737	Norm Charlton ...	.12	.05	.01
☐ 738	Darnell Coles	.03	.01	.00
☐ 739	Brook Jacoby	.06	.02	.00
☐ 740	Dan Plesac	.06	.02	.00
☐ 741	Ken Phelps	.06	.02	.00
☐ 742	Mike Harkey FS ...	.45	.18	.04
☐ 743	Mike Heath	.03	.01	.00
☐ 744	Roger Craig MG ..	.06	.01	.00
	(team checklist back)			
☐ 745	Fred McGriff	.15	.06	.01

		MINT	EXC	G-VG
☐ 746	German Gonzalez ..	.10	.04	.01
☐ 747	Will Tejada	.03	.01	.00
☐ 748	Jimmy Jones	.06	.02	.00
☐ 749	Rafael Ramirez	.03	.01	.00
☐ 750	Bret Saberhagen ...	.10	.04	.01
☐ 751	Ken Oberkfell	.03	.01	.00
☐ 752	Jim Gott	.03	.01	.00
☐ 753	Jose Uribe	.03	.01	.00
☐ 754	Bob Brower	.03	.01	.00
☐ 755	Mike Scioscia	.03	.01	.00
☐ 756	Scott Medvin	.10	.04	.01
☐ 757	Brady Anderson	.20	.08	.02
☐ 758	Gene Walter	.03	.01	.00
☐ 759	Milwaukee Brewers TL Rob Deer	.06	.02	.00
☐ 760	Lee Smith	.06	.02	.00
☐ 761	Dante Bichette	.20	.08	.02
☐ 762	Bobby Thigpen	.06	.02	.00
☐ 763	Dave Martinez	.03	.01	.00
☐ 764	Robin Ventura FDP .	.85	.34	.08
☐ 765	Glenn Davis	.10	.04	.01
☐ 766	Cecilio Guante	.03	.01	.00
☐ 767	Mike Capel	.12	.05	.01
☐ 768	Bill Wegman	.03	.01	.00
☐ 769	Junior Ortiz	.03	.01	.00
☐ 770	Alan Trammell	.12	.05	.01
☐ 771	Ron Kittle	.06	.02	.00
☐ 772	Ron Oester	.03	.01	.00
☐ 773	Keith Moreland	.03	.01	.00
☐ 774	Frank Robinson MG (team checklist back)	.08	.02	.00
☐ 775	Jeff Reardon	.06	.02	.00
☐ 776	Nelson Liriano	.03	.01	.00
☐ 777	Ted Power	.03	.01	.00
☐ 778	Bruce Benedict	.03	.01	.00
☐ 779	Craig McMurtry	.03	.01	.00
☐ 780	Pedro Guerrero	.10	.04	.01
☐ 781	Greg Briley	.12	.05	.01
☐ 782	Checklist 661-792 ..	.06	.01	.00
☐ 783	Trevor Wilson	.15	.06	.01
☐ 784	Steve Avery FDP ...	.25	.10	.02
☐ 785	Ellis Burks	.20	.08	.02
☐ 786	Melido Perez	.15	.06	.01
☐ 787	Dave West	.45	.18	.04
☐ 788	Mike Morgan	.03	.01	.00
☐ 789	Kansas City Royals TL Bo Jackson (throwing)	.10	.04	.01
☐ 790	Sid Fernandez	.08	.03	.01

		MINT	EXC	G-VG
☐ 791	Jim Lindeman	.03	.01	.00
☐ 792	Rafael Santana ...	.06	.02	.00

1948 Bowman

The 48-card Bowman set of 1948 was the first major set of the post-war period. Each 2 1/16" by 2 1/2" card had a black and white photo of a current player, with his biographical information printed in black ink on a gray back. Due to the printing process and the 36-card sheet size upon which Bowman was then printing, the 12 cards marked with an SP in the checklist are scarcer numerically, as they were removed from the printing sheet in order to make room for the 12 high numbers (37-48). Many cards are found with over-printed, transposed, or blank backs.

	NRMT	VG-E	GOOD
Complete Set	1700.00	750.00	275.00
Common Player (1-36) ...	12.00	5.00	1.20
Common Player (37-48) ..	20.00	8.00	2.00
Common Player Sp	30.00	12.00	3.00

		NRMT	VG-E	GOOD
☐ 1	Bob Elliott	60.00	8.00	1.50
☐ 2	Ewell Blackwell ...	22.00	9.00	2.20
☐ 3	Ralph Kiner	70.00	28.00	7.00
☐ 4	Johnny Mize	50.00	20.00	5.00
☐ 5	Bob Feller	80.00	32.00	8.00
☐ 6	Yogi Berra	325.00	130.00	32.00
☐ 7	Pete Reiser SP ...	36.00	15.00	3.60
☐ 8	Phil Rizzuto SP ...	135.00	54.00	13.50

		NRMT	VG-E	GOOD
☐ 9	Walker Cooper	12.00	5.00	1.20
☐ 10	Buddy Rosar	12.00	5.00	1.20
☐ 11	Johnny Lindell	12.00	5.00	1.20
☐ 12	Johnny Sain	27.00	11.00	2.70
☐ 13	Willard Marshall SP	30.00	12.00	3.00
☐ 14	Allie Reynolds	32.00	13.00	3.20
☐ 15	Eddie Joost	12.00	5.00	1.20
☐ 16	Jack Lohrke SP	30.00	12.00	3.00
☐ 17	Enos Slaughter	50.00	20.00	5.00
☐ 18	Warren Spahn	110.00	45.00	11.00
☐ 19	Tommy Henrich	20.00	8.00	2.00
☐ 20	Buddy Kerr SP	30.00	12.00	3.00
☐ 21	Ferris Fain	15.00	6.00	1.50
☐ 22	Floyd Bevens SP ...	30.00	12.00	3.00
☐ 23	Larry Jansen	12.00	5.00	1.20
☐ 24	Dutch Leonard SP .	30.00	12.00	3.00
☐ 25	Barney McCosky ...	12.00	5.00	1.20
☐ 26	Frank Shea SP	30.00	12.00	3.00
☐ 27	Sid Gordon	12.00	5.00	1.20
☐ 28	Emil Verban SP	30.00	12.00	3.00
☐ 29	Joe Page SP	35.00	14.00	3.50
☐ 30	Whitey Lockman SP	35.00	14.00	3.50
☐ 31	Bill McCahan	12.00	5.00	1.20
☐ 32	Bill Rigney	12.00	5.00	1.20
☐ 33	Bill Johnson	12.00	5.00	1.20
☐ 34	Sheldon Jones SP ..	30.00	12.00	3.00
☐ 35	Snuffy Stirnweiss ..	15.00	6.00	1.50
☐ 36	Stan Musial	425.00	170.00	42.00
☐ 37	Clint Hartung	20.00	8.00	2.00
☐ 38	Red Schoendienst ..	45.00	18.00	4.50
☐ 39	Augie Galan	20.00	8.00	2.00
☐ 40	Marty Marion	45.00	18.00	4.50
☐ 41	Rex Barney	20.00	8.00	2.00
☐ 42	Ray Poat	20.00	8.00	2.00
☐ 43	Bruce Edwards	20.00	8.00	2.00
☐ 44	Johnny Wyrostek ...	20.00	8.00	2.00
☐ 45	Hank Sauer	30.00	12.00	3.00
☐ 46	Herman Wehmeier ..	20.00	8.00	2.00
☐ 47	Bobby Thomson	45.00	18.00	4.50
☐ 48	Dave Kosla	45.00	12.00	2.50

1949 Bowman

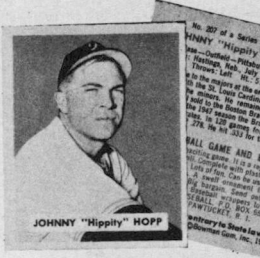

JOHNNY "Hippity" HOPP

*The cards in this 240-card set measure 2 1⁄16"
by 2 1⁄2". In 1949 Bowman took an intermediate step between black and white and
full color with this set of tinted photos on
colored backgrounds. Collectors should note
the series price variations which reflect some
inconsistencies in the printing process.
There are four major varieties in name printing which are noted in the checklist below:
NOF: name on front; NNOF: no name on
front; PR: printed name on back; and SCR:
script name on back. These variations
resulted when Bowman used twelve of the
lower numbers to fill out the last press sheet
of 36 cards adding to numbers 217-240.
Cards 1-3 and 5-73 can be found with either
gray or white backs.*

	NRMT	VG-E	GOOD
Complete Set	11500.00	5000.00	2000.00
Common Card 1-3/5-36/73	12.50	5.00	1.25
Common Card (37-72) ...	13.50	6.00	1.50
Common Card (4/74-108) .	11.00	4.50	1.10
Common Card (109-144) .	10.00	4.00	1.00
Common Card (145-180) .	75.00	30.00	7.50
Common Card (181-216) .	70.00	28.00	7.00
Common Card (217-240) .	70.00	28.00	7.00

		NRMT	VG-E	GOOD
☐ 1	Vern Bickford	50.00	9.00	2.00
☐ 2	Whitey Lockman	12.50	5.00	1.25
☐ 3	Bob Porterfield	12.50	5.00	1.25
☐ 4A	Jerry Priddy NNOF	11.00	4.50	1.10
☐ 4B	Jerry Priddy NOF .	35.00	14.00	3.50
☐ 5	Hank Sauer	15.00	6.00	1.50

			NRMT	VG-E	GOOD
☐	6	Phil Cavarretta	15.00	6.00	1.50
☐	7	Joe Dobson	12.50	5.00	1.25
☐	8	Murry Dickson	12.50	5.00	1.25
☐	9	Ferris Fain	15.00	6.00	1.50
☐	10	Ted Gray	12.50	5.00	1.25
☐	11	Lou Boudreau	36.00	15.00	3.60
☐	12	Cass Michaels	12.50	5.00	1.25
☐	13	Bob Chesnes	12.50	5.00	1.25
☐	14	Curt Simmons	20.00	8.00	2.00
☐	15	Ned Garver	12.50	5.00	1.25
☐	16	Al Kozar	12.50	5.00	1.25
☐	17	Earl Torgeson	12.50	5.00	1.25
☐	18	Bobby Thomson	18.00	7.25	1.80
☐	19	Bobby Brown	25.00	10.00	2.50
☐	20	Gene Hermanski	12.50	5.00	1.25
☐	21	Frank Baumholtz	12.50	5.00	1.25
☐	22	Peanuts Lowrey	12.50	5.00	1.25
☐	23	Bobby Doerr	40.00	16.00	4.00
☐	24	Stan Musial	350.00	140.00	35.00
☐	25	Carl Scheib	12.50	5.00	1.25
☐	26	George Kell	40.00	16.00	4.00
☐	27	Bob Feller	85.00	34.00	8.50
☐	28	Don Kolloway	12.50	5.00	1.25
☐	29	Ralph Kiner	45.00	18.00	4.50
☐	30	Andy Seminick	12.50	5.00	1.25
☐	31	Dick Kokos	12.50	5.00	1.25
☐	32	Eddie Yost	12.50	5.00	1.25
☐	33	Warren Spahn	80.00	32.00	8.00
☐	34	Dave Koslo	12.50	5.00	1.25
☐	35	Vic Raschi	25.00	10.00	2.50
☐	36	Pee Wee Reese	100.00	40.00	10.00
☐	37	Johnny Wyrostek	13.50	6.00	1.50
☐	38	Emil Verban	13.50	6.00	1.50
☐	39	Billy Goodman	15.00	6.00	1.50
☐	40	Red Munger	13.50	6.00	1.50
☐	41	Lou Brissie	13.50	6.00	1.50
☐	42	Hoot Evers	13.50	6.00	1.50
☐	43	Dale Mitchell	15.00	6.00	1.50
☐	44	Dave Philley	13.50	6.00	1.50
☐	45	Wally Westlake	13.50	6.00	1.50
☐	46	Robin Roberts	125.00	50.00	12.50
☐	47	Johnny Sain	22.00	9.00	2.00
☐	48	Willard Marshall	13.50	6.00	1.50
☐	49	Frank Shea	13.50	6.00	1.50
☐	50	Jackie Robinson	450.00	180.00	45.00
☐	51	Herman Wehmeier	13.50	6.00	1.50
☐	52	Johnny Schmitz	13.50	6.00	1.50
☐	53	Jack Kramer	13.50	6.00	1.50
☐	54	Marty Marion	18.00	7.25	1.80
☐	55	Eddie Joost	13.50	6.00	1.50
☐	56	Pat Mullin	13.50	6.00	1.50
☐	57	Gene Bearden	13.50	6.00	1.50
☐	58	Bob Elliott	15.00	6.00	1.50
☐	59	Jack Lohrke	13.50	6.00	1.50
☐	60	Yogi Berra	225.00	90.00	22.00
☐	61	Rex Barney	13.50	6.00	1.50
☐	62	Grady Hatton	13.50	6.00	1.50
☐	63	Andy Pafko	15.00	6.00	1.50
☐	64	Dom DiMaggio	21.00	8.50	2.00
☐	65	Enos Slaughter	45.00	18.00	4.50
☐	66	Elmer Valo	13.50	6.00	1.50
☐	67	Alvin Dark	18.00	7.25	1.80
☐	68	Sheldon Jones	13.50	6.00	1.50
☐	69	Tommy Henrich	18.00	7.25	1.80
☐	70	Carl Furillo	40.00	16.00	4.00
☐	71	Vern Stephens	15.00	6.00	1.50
☐	72	Tommy Holmes	15.00	6.00	1.50
☐	73	Billy Cox	18.00	7.25	1.80
☐	74	Tom McBride	11.00	4.50	1.10
☐	75	Eddie Mayo	11.00	4.50	1.10
☐	76	Bill Nicholson	11.00	4.50	1.10
☐	77	Ernie Bonham	11.00	4.50	1.10
☐	78A	Sam Zoldak NNOF	11.00	4.50	1.10
☐	78B	Sam Zoldak NOF	35.00	14.00	3.50
☐	79	Ron Northey	11.00	4.50	1.10
☐	80	Bill McCahan	11.00	4.50	1.10
☐	81	Virgil Stallcup	11.00	4.50	1.10
☐	82	Joe Page	18.00	7.25	1.80
☐	83A	Bob Scheffing NNOF	11.00	4.50	1.10
☐	83B	Bob Scheffing NOF	35.00	14.00	3.50
☐	84	Roy Campanella	400.00	160.00	40.00
☐	85A	Johnny Mize NNOF	50.00	20.00	5.00
☐	85B	Johnny Mize NOF	100.00	40.00	10.00
☐	86	Johnny Pesky	11.00	4.50	1.10
☐	87	Randy Gumpert	11.00	4.50	1.10
☐	88A	Bill Salkeld NNOF	11.00	4.50	1.10
☐	88B	Bill Salkeld NOF	35.00	14.00	3.50
☐	89	Mizell Platt	11.00	4.50	1.10
☐	90	Gil Coan	11.00	4.50	1.10
☐	91	Dick Wakefield	11.00	4.50	1.10
☐	92	Willie Jones	11.00	4.50	1.10
☐	93	Ed Stevens	11.00	4.50	1.10
☐	94	Mickey Vernon	20.00	8.00	2.00
☐	95	Howie Pollet	11.00	4.50	1.10
☐	96	Taft Wright	11.00	4.50	1.10
☐	97	Danny Litwhiler	11.00	4.50	1.10
☐	98A	Phil Rizzuto NNOF	75.00	30.00	7.50
☐	98B	Phil Rizzuto NOF	150.00	60.00	15.00

		NRMT	VG-E	GOOD
☐ 99	Frank Gustine	11.00	4.50	1.10
☐ 100	Gil Hodges	125.00	50.00	12.50
☐ 101	Sid Gordon	11.00	4.50	1.10
☐ 102	Stan Spence	11.00	4.50	1.10
☐ 103	Joe Tipton	11.00	4.50	1.10
☐ 104	Eddie Stanky	16.00	6.50	1.60
☐ 105	Bill Kennedy	11.00	4.50	1.10
☐ 106	Jake Early	11.00	4.50	1.10
☐ 107	Eddie Lake	11.00	4.50	1.10
☐ 108	Ken Heintzelman	11.00	4.50	1.10
☐ 109A	Ed Fitzgerald SCR	10.00	4.00	1.00
☐ 109B	Ed Fitzgerald PR	30.00	12.00	3.00
☐ 110	Early Wynn	80.00	32.00	8.00
☐ 111	Red Schoendienst	21.00	8.50	2.00
☐ 112	Sam Chapman	10.00	4.00	1.00
☐ 113	Ray LaManno	10.00	4.00	1.00
☐ 114	Allie Reynolds	24.00	10.00	2.40
☐ 115	Dutch Leonard	10.00	4.00	1.00
☐ 116	Joe Hatton	10.00	4.00	1.00
☐ 117	Walker Cooper	10.00	4.00	1.00
☐ 118	Sam Mele	10.00	4.00	1.00
☐ 119	Floyd Baker	10.00	4.00	1.00
☐ 120	Cliff Fannin	10.00	4.00	1.00
☐ 121	Mark Christman	10.00	4.00	1.00
☐ 122	George Vico	10.00	4.00	1.00
☐ 123	Johnny Blatnick	10.00	4.00	1.00
☐ 124A	Danny Murtaugh SCR	10.00	4.00	1.00
☐ 124B	Danny Murtaugh PR	30.00	12.00	3.00
☐ 125	Ken Keltner	10.00	4.00	1.00
☐ 126A	Al Brazle SCR	10.00	4.00	1.00
☐ 126B	Al Brazle PR	30.00	12.00	3.00
☐ 127A	Hank Majeski SCR	10.00	4.00	1.00
☐ 127B	Hank Majeski PR	30.00	12.00	3.00
☐ 128	Johnny VanderMeer	16.00	6.50	1.60
☐ 129	Bill Johnson	10.00	4.00	1.00
☐ 130	Harry Walker	10.00	4.00	1.00
☐ 131	Paul Lehner	10.00	4.00	1.00
☐ 132A	Al Evans SCR	10.00	4.00	1.00
☐ 132B	Al Evans PR	30.00	12.00	3.00
☐ 133	Aaron Robinson	10.00	4.00	1.00
☐ 134	Hank Borowy	10.00	4.00	1.00
☐ 135	Stan Rojek	10.00	4.00	1.00
☐ 136	Hank Edwards	10.00	4.00	1.00
☐ 137	Ted Wilks	10.00	4.00	1.00
☐ 138	Buddy Rosar	10.00	4.00	1.00
☐ 139	Hank Arft	10.00	4.00	1.00
☐ 140	Ray Scarborough	10.00	4.00	1.00
☐ 141	Ulysses Lupien	10.00	4.00	1.00
☐ 142	Eddie Waitkus	10.00	4.00	1.00

		NRMT	VG-E	GOOD
☐ 143A	Bob Dillinger SCR	10.00	4.00	1.00
☐ 143B	Bob Dillinger PR	30.00	12.00	3.00
☐ 144	Mickey Haefner	10.00	4.00	1.00
☐ 145	Sylvester Donnelly	75.00	30.00	7.50
☐ 146	Mike McCormick	75.00	30.00	7.50
☐ 147	Bert Singleton	75.00	30.00	7.50
☐ 148	Bob Swift	75.00	30.00	7.50
☐ 149	Roy Partee	75.00	30.00	7.50
☐ 150	Allie Clark	75.00	30.00	7.50
☐ 151	Mickey Harris	75.00	30.00	7.50
☐ 152	Clarence Maddern	75.00	30.00	7.50
☐ 153	Phil Masi	75.00	30.00	7.50
☐ 154	Clint Hartung	75.00	30.00	7.50
☐ 155	Mickey Guerra	75.00	30.00	7.50
☐ 156	Al Zarilla	75.00	30.00	7.50
☐ 157	Walt Masterson	75.00	30.00	7.50
☐ 158	Harry Brecheen	75.00	30.00	7.50
☐ 159	Glen Moulder	75.00	30.00	7.50
☐ 160	Jim Blackburn	75.00	30.00	7.50
☐ 161	Jocko Thompson	75.00	30.00	7.50
☐ 162	Preacher Roe	75.00	30.00	7.50
☐ 163	Clyde McCullough	75.00	30.00	7.50
☐ 164	Vic Wertz	90.00	36.00	9.00
☐ 165	Snuffy Stirnweiss	90.00	36.00	9.00
☐ 166	Mike Tresh	75.00	30.00	7.50
☐ 167	Babe Martin	75.00	30.00	7.50
☐ 168	Doyle Lade	75.00	30.00	7.50
☐ 169	Jeff Heath	75.00	30.00	7.50
☐ 170	Bill Rigney	75.00	30.00	7.50
☐ 171	Dick Fowler	75.00	30.00	7.50
☐ 172	Eddie Pellagrini	75.00	30.00	7.50
☐ 173	Eddie Stewart	75.00	30.00	7.50
☐ 174	Terry Moore	100.00	40.00	10.00
☐ 175	Luke Appling	110.00	45.00	11.00
☐ 176	Ken Raffensberger	75.00	30.00	7.50
☐ 177	Stan Lopata	75.00	30.00	7.50
☐ 178	Tom Brown	75.00	30.00	7.50
☐ 179	Hugh Casey	90.00	36.00	9.00
☐ 180	Connie Berry	75.00	30.00	7.50
☐ 181	Gus Niarhos	70.00	28.00	7.00
☐ 182	Hal Peck	70.00	28.00	7.00
☐ 183	Lou Stringer	70.00	28.00	7.00
☐ 184	Bob Chipman	70.00	28.00	7.00
☐ 185	Pete Reiser	90.00	36.00	9.00
☐ 186	Buddy Kerr	70.00	28.00	7.00
☐ 187	Phil Marchildon	70.00	28.00	7.00
☐ 188	Karl Drews	70.00	28.00	7.00
☐ 189	Earl Wooten	70.00	28.00	7.00
☐ 190	Jim Hearn	70.00	28.00	7.00

	NRMT	VG-E	GOOD
☐ 191 Joe Haynes	70.00	28.00	7.00
☐ 192 Harry Gumbert	70.00	28.00	7.00
☐ 193 Ken Trinkle	70.00	28.00	7.00
☐ 194 Ralph Branca	100.00	40.00	10.00
☐ 195 Eddie Bockman	70.00	28.00	7.00
☐ 196 Fred Hutchinson	90.00	36.00	9.00
☐ 197 Johnny Lindell	70.00	28.00	7.00
☐ 198 Steve Gromek	70.00	28.00	7.00
☐ 199 Tex Hughson	70.00	28.00	7.00
☐ 200 Jess Dobernic	70.00	28.00	7.00
☐ 201 Sibby Sisti	70.00	28.00	7.00
☐ 202 Larry Jansen	70.00	28.00	7.00
☐ 203 Barney McCosky	70.00	28.00	7.00
☐ 204 Bob Savage	70.00	28.00	7.00
☐ 205 Dick Sisler	70.00	28.00	7.00
☐ 206 Bruce Edwards	70.00	28.00	7.00
☐ 207 Johnny Hopp	80.00	32.00	8.00
☐ 208 Dizzy Trout	80.00	32.00	8.00
☐ 209 Charlie Keller	90.00	36.00	9.00
☐ 210 Joe Gordon	90.00	36.00	9.00
☐ 211 Boo Ferriss	70.00	28.00	7.00
☐ 212 Ralph Hamner	70.00	28.00	7.00
☐ 213 Red Barrett	70.00	28.00	7.00
☐ 214 Richie Ashburn	375.00	150.00	37.00
☐ 215 Kirby Higbe	70.00	28.00	7.00
☐ 216 Schoolboy Rowe	80.00	32.00	8.00
☐ 217 Marino Pieretti	70.00	28.00	7.00
☐ 218 Dick Kryhoski	70.00	28.00	7.00
☐ 219 Virgil "Fire" Trucks	80.00	32.00	8.00
☐ 220 Johnny McCarthy	70.00	28.00	7.00
☐ 221 Bob Muncrief	70.00	28.00	7.00
☐ 222 Alex Kellner	70.00	28.00	7.00
☐ 223 Bobby Hofman	70.00	28.00	7.00
☐ 224 Satchell Paige	1000.00	400.00	100.00
☐ 225 Gerry Coleman	90.00	36.00	9.00
☐ 226 Duke Snider	800.00	320.00	80.00
☐ 227 Fritz Ostermueller	70.00	28.00	7.00
☐ 228 Jackie Mayo	70.00	28.00	7.00
☐ 229 Ed Lopat	110.00	45.00	11.00
☐ 230 Augie Galan	70.00	28.00	7.00
☐ 231 Earl Johnson	70.00	28.00	7.00
☐ 232 George McQuinn	70.00	28.00	7.00
☐ 233 Larry Doby	110.00	45.00	11.00
☐ 234 Rip Sewell	70.00	28.00	7.00
☐ 235 Jim Russell	70.00	28.00	7.00
☐ 236 Fred Sanford	70.00	28.00	7.00
☐ 237 Monte Kennedy	70.00	28.00	7.00
☐ 238 Bob Lemon	200.00	80.00	20.00
☐ 239 Frank McCormick	80.00	32.00	8.00

	NRMT	VG-E	GOOD
☐ 240 Babe Young	100.00	40.00	8.00
(photo actually Bobby Young)			

1950 Bowman

The cards in this 252-card set measure 2 1/16"
by 2 1/2". This set, marketed in 1950 by Bowman, represented a major improvement in
terms of quality over their previous efforts.
Each card was a beautifully colored line
drawing developed from a simple
photograph. The first 72 cards are the scarcest in the set, while the final 72 cards may
be found with or without the copyright line.
This was the only Bowman sports set to
carry the famous "5-Star" logo.

	NRMT	VG-E	GOOD
Complete Set	6500.00	3000.00	900.00
Common Player (1-72)	30.00	12.00	3.00
Common Player (73-252)	12.00	5.00	1.20
☐ 1 Mel Parnell	200.00	20.00	4.00
☐ 2 Vern Stephens	32.00	13.00	3.20
☐ 3 Dom DiMaggio	40.00	16.00	4.00
☐ 4 Gus Zernial	35.00	14.00	3.50
☐ 5 Bob Kuzava	30.00	12.00	3.00
☐ 6 Bob Feller	100.00	40.00	10.00
☐ 7 Jim Hegan	32.00	13.00	3.20
☐ 8 George Kell	50.00	20.00	5.00
☐ 9 Vic Wertz	32.00	13.00	3.20
☐ 10 Tommy Henrich	35.00	14.00	3.50
☐ 11 Phil Rizzuto	80.00	32.00	8.00

			NRMT	VG-E	GOOD				NRMT	VG-E	GOOD
☐	12	Joe Page	35.00	14.00	3.50	☐	61	Bob Rush	30.00	12.00	3.00
☐	13	Ferris Fain	32.00	13.00	3.20	☐	62	Ted Kluszewski	40.00	16.00	4.00
☐	14	Alex Kellner	30.00	12.00	3.00	☐	63	Ewell Blackwell	35.00	14.00	3.50
☐	15	Al Kozar	30.00	12.00	3.00	☐	64	Alvin Dark	35.00	14.00	3.50
☐	16	Roy Sievers	35.00	14.00	3.50	☐	65	Dave Koslo	30.00	12.00	3.00
☐	17	Sid Hudson	30.00	12.00	3.00	☐	66	Larry Jansen	30.00	12.00	3.00
☐	18	Eddie Robinson	30.00	12.00	3.00	☐	67	Willie Jones	30.00	12.00	3.00
☐	19	Warren Spahn	90.00	36.00	9.00	☐	68	Curt Simmons	32.00	13.00	3.20
☐	20	Bob Elliott	32.00	13.00	3.20	☐	69	Wally Westlake	30.00	12.00	3.00
☐	21	Pee Wee Reese	100.00	40.00	10.00	☐	70	Bob Chesnes	30.00	12.00	3.00
☐	22	Jackie Robinson	450.00	180.00	45.00	☐	71	Red Schoendienst	35.00	14.00	3.50
☐	23	Don Newcombe	55.00	22.00	5.50	☐	72	Howie Pollet	30.00	12.00	3.00
☐	24	Johnny Schmitz	30.00	12.00	3.00	☐	73	Willard Marshall	12.00	5.00	1.20
☐	25	Hank Sauer	32.00	13.00	3.20	☐	74	Johnny Antonelli	16.00	6.50	1.60
☐	26	Grady Hatton	30.00	12.00	3.00	☐	75	Roy Campanella	250.00	100.00	25.00
☐	27	Herman Wehmeier	30.00	12.00	3.00	☐	76	Rex Barney	12.00	5.00	1.20
☐	28	Bobby Thomson	35.00	14.00	3.50	☐	77	Duke Snider	200.00	80.00	20.00
☐	29	Eddie Stanky	32.00	13.00	3.20	☐	78	Mickey Owen	14.00	5.75	1.40
☐	30	Eddie Waltkus	30.00	12.00	3.00	☐	79	Johnny VanderMeer	16.00	6.50	1.60
☐	31	Del Ennis	32.00	13.00	3.20	☐	80	Howard Fox	12.00	5.00	1.20
☐	32	Robin Roberts	65.00	26.00	6.50	☐	81	Ron Northey	12.00	5.00	1.20
☐	33	Ralph Kiner	55.00	22.00	5.50	☐	82	Whitey Lockman	14.00	5.75	1.40
☐	34	Murry Dickson	30.00	12.00	3.00	☐	83	Sheldon Jones	12.00	5.00	1.20
☐	35	Enos Slaughter	50.00	20.00	5.00	☐	84	Richie Ashburn	40.00	16.00	4.00
☐	36	Eddie Kazak	30.00	12.00	3.00	☐	85	Ken Heintzelman	12.00	5.00	1.20
☐	37	Luke Appling	45.00	18.00	4.50	☐	86	Stan Rojek	12.00	5.00	1.20
☐	38	Bill Wight	30.00	12.00	3.00	☐	87	Bill Werle	12.00	5.00	1.20
☐	39	Larry Doby	40.00	16.00	4.00	☐	88	Marty Marion	16.00	6.50	1.60
☐	40	Bob Lemon	50.00	20.00	5.00	☐	89	Red Munger	12.00	5.00	1.20
☐	41	Hoot Evers	30.00	12.00	3.00	☐	90	Harry Brecheen	12.00	5.00	1.20
☐	42	Art Houtteman	30.00	12.00	3.00	☐	91	Cass Michaels	12.00	5.00	1.20
☐	43	Bobby Doerr	50.00	20.00	5.00	☐	92	Hank Majeski	12.00	5.00	1.20
☐	44	Joe Dobson	30.00	12.00	3.00	☐	93	Gene Bearden	12.00	5.00	1.20
☐	45	Al Zarilla	30.00	12.00	3.00	☐	94	Lou Boudreau	35.00	14.00	3.50
☐	46	Yogi Berra	300.00	120.00	30.00	☐	95	Aaron Robinson	12.00	5.00	1.20
☐	47	Jerry Coleman	35.00	14.00	3.50	☐	96	Virgil Trucks	14.00	5.75	1.40
☐	48	Lou Brissie	30.00	12.00	3.00	☐	97	Maurice McDermott	12.00	5.00	1.20
☐	49	Elmer Valo	30.00	12.00	3.00	☐	98	Ted Williams	450.00	180.00	45.00
☐	50	Dick Kokos	30.00	12.00	3.00	☐	99	Billy Goodman	14.00	5.75	1.40
☐	51	Ned Garver	30.00	12.00	3.00	☐	100	Vic Raschi	20.00	8.00	2.00
☐	52	Sam Mele	30.00	12.00	3.00	☐	101	Bobby Brown	20.00	8.00	2.00
☐	53	Clyde Vollmer	30.00	12.00	3.00	☐	102	Billy Johnson	12.00	5.00	1.20
☐	54	Gil Coan	30.00	12.00	3.00	☐	103	Eddie Joost	12.00	5.00	1.20
☐	55	Buddy Kerr	30.00	12.00	3.00	☐	104	Sam Chapman	12.00	5.00	1.20
☐	56	Del Crandall	35.00	14.00	3.50	☐	105	Bob Dillinger	12.00	5.00	1.20
☐	57	Vern Bickford	30.00	12.00	3.00	☐	106	Cliff Fannin	12.00	5.00	1.20
☐	58	Carl Furillo	40.00	16.00	4.00	☐	107	Sam Dente	12.00	5.00	1.20
☐	59	Ralph Branca	35.00	14.00	3.50	☐	108	Ray Scarborough	12.00	5.00	1.20
☐	60	Andy Pafko	32.00	13.00	3.20	☐	109	Sid Gordon	12.00	5.00	1.20

	NRMT	VG-E	GOOD		NRMT	VG-E	GOOD
☐ 110 Tommy Holmes	14.00	5.75	1.40	☐ 159 Joe Tipton	12.00	5.00	1.20
☐ 111 Walker Cooper	12.00	5.00	1.20	☐ 160 Mickey Harris	12.00	5.00	1.20
☐ 112 Gil Hodges	60.00	24.00	6.00	☐ 161 Sherry Robertson	12.00	5.00	1.20
☐ 113 Gene Hermanski	12.00	5.00	1.20	☐ 162 Eddie Yost	12.00	5.00	1.20
☐ 114 Wayne Terwilliger	12.00	5.00	1.20	☐ 163 Earl Torgeson	12.00	5.00	1.20
☐ 115 Roy Smalley	12.00	5.00	1.20	☐ 164 Sibby Sisti	12.00	5.00	1.20
☐ 116 Virgil Stallcup	12.00	5.00	1.20	☐ 165 Bruce Edwards	12.00	5.00	1.20
☐ 117 Bill Rigney	12.00	5.00	1.20	☐ 166 Joe Hatton	12.00	5.00	1.20
☐ 118 Clint Hartung	12.00	5.00	1.20	☐ 167 Preacher Roe	22.00	9.00	2.20
☐ 119 Dick Sisler	12.00	5.00	1.20	☐ 168 Bob Scheffing	12.00	5.00	1.20
☐ 120 John Thompson	12.00	5.00	1.20	☐ 169 Hank Edwards	12.00	5.00	1.20
☐ 121 Andy Seminick	12.00	5.00	1.20	☐ 170 Dutch Leonard	12.00	5.00	1.20
☐ 122 Johnny Hopp	12.00	5.00	1.20	☐ 171 Harry Gumbert	12.00	5.00	1.20
☐ 123 Dino Restelli	12.00	5.00	1.20	☐ 172 Peanuts Lowrey	12.00	5.00	1.20
☐ 124 Clyde McCullough	12.00	5.00	1.20	☐ 173 Lloyd Merriman	12.00	5.00	1.20
☐ 125 Del Rice	12.00	5.00	1.20	☐ 174 Hank Thompson	14.00	5.75	1.40
☐ 126 Al Brazle	12.00	5.00	1.20	☐ 175 Monte Kennedy	12.00	5.00	1.20
☐ 127 Dave Philley	12.00	5.00	1.20	☐ 176 Sylvester Donnelly	12.00	5.00	1.20
☐ 128 Phil Masi	12.00	5.00	1.20	☐ 177 Hank Borowy	12.00	5.00	1.20
☐ 129 Joe Gordon	16.00	6.75	1.60	☐ 178 Ed Fitzgerald	12.00	5.00	1.20
☐ 130 Dale Mitchell	14.00	5.75	1.40	☐ 179 Chuck Diering	12.00	5.00	1.20
☐ 131 Steve Gromek	12.00	5.00	1.20	☐ 180 Harry Walker	12.00	5.00	1.20
☐ 132 James"Mickey" Vernon	14.00	5.75	1.40	☐ 181 Marino Pieretti	12.00	5.00	1.20
☐ 133 Don Kolloway	12.00	5.00	1.20	☐ 182 Sam Zoldak	12.00	5.00	1.20
☐ 134 Paul Trout	12.00	5.00	1.20	☐ 183 Mickey Haefner	12.00	5.00	1.20
☐ 135 Pat Mullin	12.00	5.00	1.20	☐ 184 Randy Gumpert	12.00	5.00	1.20
☐ 136 Warren Rosar	12.00	5.00	1.20	☐ 185 Howie Judson	12.00	5.00	1.20
☐ 137 Johnny Pesky	12.00	5.00	1.20	☐ 186 Ken Keltner	12.00	5.00	1.20
☐ 138 Allie Reynolds	22.00	9.00	2.20	☐ 187 Lou Stringer	12.00	5.00	1.20
☐ 139 Johnny Mize	45.00	18.00	4.50	☐ 188 Earl Johnson	12.00	5.00	1.20
☐ 140 Pete Suder	12.00	5.00	1.20	☐ 189 Owen Friend	12.00	5.00	1.20
☐ 141 Joe Coleman	12.00	5.00	1.20	☐ 190 Ken Wood	12.00	5.00	1.20
☐ 142 Sherm Lollar	12.00	5.00	1.20	☐ 191 Dick Starr	12.00	5.00	1.20
☐ 143 Eddie Stewart	12.00	5.00	1.20	☐ 192 Bob Chipman	12.00	5.00	1.20
☐ 144 Al Evans	12.00	5.00	1.20	☐ 193 Pete Reiser	14.00	5.75	1.40
☐ 145 Jack Graham	12.00	5.00	1.20	☐ 194 Billy Cox	14.00	5.75	1.40
☐ 146 Floyd Baker	12.00	5.00	1.20	☐ 195 Phil Cavarretta	14.00	5.75	1.40
☐ 147 Mike Garcia	14.00	5.75	1.40	☐ 196 Doyle Lade	12.00	5.00	1.20
☐ 148 Early Wynn	40.00	16.00	4.00	☐ 197 Johnny Wyrostek	12.00	5.00	1.20
☐ 149 Bob Swift	12.00	5.00	1.20	☐ 198 Danny Litwhiler	12.00	5.00	1.20
☐ 150 George Vico	12.00	5.00	1.20	☐ 199 Jack Kramer	12.00	5.00	1.20
☐ 151 Fred Hutchinson	14.00	5.75	1.40	☐ 200 Kirby Higbe	12.00	5.00	1.20
☐ 152 Ellis Kinder	12.00	5.00	1.20	☐ 201 Pete Castiglione	12.00	5.00	1.20
☐ 153 Walt Masterson	12.00	5.00	1.20	☐ 202 Cliff Chambers	12.00	5.00	1.20
☐ 154 Gus Niarhos	12.00	5.00	1.20	☐ 203 Danny Murtaugh	12.00	5.00	1.20
☐ 155 Frank Shea	12.00	5.00	1.20	☐ 204 Granny Hamner	12.00	5.00	1.20
☐ 156 Fred Sanford	12.00	5.00	1.20	☐ 205 Mike Goliat	12.00	5.00	1.20
☐ 157 Mike Guerra	12.00	5.00	1.20	☐ 206 Stan Lopata	12.00	5.00	1.20
☐ 158 Paul Lehner	12.00	5.00	1.20	☐ 207 Max Lanier	12.00	5.00	1.20

		NRMT	VG-E	GOOD
☐ 208	Jim Hearn	12.00	5.00	1.20
☐ 209	Johnny Lindell	12.00	5.00	1.20
☐ 210	Ted Gray	12.00	5.00	1.20
☐ 211	Charley Keller	14.00	5.75	1.40
☐ 212	Jerry Priddy	12.00	5.00	1.20
☐ 213	Carl Scheib	12.00	5.00	1.20
☐ 214	Dick Fowler	12.00	5.00	1.20
☐ 215	Ed Lopat	25.00	10.00	2.50
☐ 216	Bob Porterfield	12.00	5.00	1.20
☐ 217	Casey Stengel MG	80.00	32.00	8.00
☐ 218	Cliff Mapes	12.00	5.00	1.20
☐ 219	Hank Bauer	40.00	16.00	4.00
☐ 220	Leo Durocher MG	35.00	14.00	3.50
☐ 221	Don Mueller	21.00	8.50	2.10
☐ 222	Bobby Morgan	12.00	5.00	1.20
☐ 223	Jim Russell	12.00	5.00	1.20
☐ 224	Jack Banta	12.00	5.00	1.20
☐ 225	Eddie Sawyer MG	14.00	5.75	1.40
☐ 226	Jim Konstanty	21.00	8.50	2.10
☐ 227	Bob Miller	12.00	5.00	1.20
☐ 228	Bill Nicholson	12.00	5.00	1.20
☐ 229	Frank Frisch	35.00	14.00	3.50
☐ 230	Bill Serena	12.00	5.00	1.20
☐ 231	Preston Ward	12.00	5.00	1.20
☐ 232	Al Rosen	35.00	14.00	3.50
☐ 233	Allie Clark	12.00	5.00	1.20
☐ 234	Bobby Shantz	18.00	7.25	1.80
☐ 235	Harold Gilbert	12.00	5.00	1.20
☐ 236	Bob Cain	12.00	5.00	1.20
☐ 237	Bill Salkeld	12.00	5.00	1.20
☐ 238	Vernal Jones	12.00	5.00	1.20
☐ 239	Bill Howerton	12.00	5.00	1.20
☐ 240	Eddie Lake	12.00	5.00	1.20
☐ 241	Neil Berry	12.00	5.00	1.20
☐ 242	Dick Kryhoski	12.00	5.00	1.20
☐ 243	Johnny Groth	12.00	5.00	1.20
☐ 244	Dale Coogan	12.00	5.00	1.20
☐ 245	Al Papai	12.00	5.00	1.20
☐ 246	Walt Dropo	18.00	7.25	1.80
☐ 247	Irv Noren	12.00	5.00	1.20
☐ 248	Sam Jethroe	14.00	5.75	1.40
☐ 249	Snuffy Stirnweiss	14.00	5.75	1.40
☐ 250	Ray Coleman	12.00	5.00	1.20
☐ 251	John Moss	12.00	5.00	1.20
☐ 252	Billy DeMars	60.00	8.00	1.50

1951 Bowman

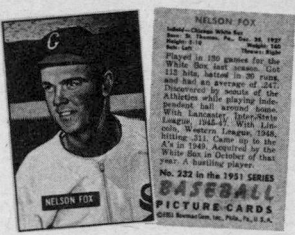

The cards in this 324-card set measure 2 1/16"
by 3 1/8". Many of the obverses of the cards
appearing in the 1951 Bowman set are en-
largements of those appearing in the previous year. The high number series
(253-324) is highly valued and contains the
true "Rookie" cards of Mickey Mantle and
Willie Mays. Card number 195 depicts Paul
Richards in caricature. George Kell's card
(#46) incorrectly lists him as being in the
"1941" Bowman series. Player names are
found printed in a panel on the front of the
card. These cards were supposedly also
sold in sheets in variety stores in the
Philadelphia area.

	NRMT	VG-E	GOOD
Complete Set (324)	13000.00	5500.00	1800.00
Common Player (1-36)	13.50	6.00	1.50
Common Player (37-72)	12.00	5.00	1.20
Common Player (73-252)	10.00	4.00	1.00
Common Player (253-324)	40.00	16.00	4.00

☐ 1	Whitey Ford	750.00	100.00	20.00
☐ 2	Yogi Berra	250.00	100.00	25.00
☐ 3	Robin Roberts	45.00	18.00	4.50
☐ 4	Del Ennis	15.00	6.00	1.50
☐ 5	Dale Mitchell	15.00	6.00	1.50
☐ 6	Don Newcombe	20.00	8.00	2.00
☐ 7	Gil Hodges	45.00	18.00	4.50
☐ 8	Paul Lehner	13.50	6.00	1.50
☐ 9	Sam Chapman	13.50	6.00	1.50
☐ 10	Red Schoendienst	20.00	9.25	1.80
☐ 11	Red Munger	13.50	6.00	1.50

		NRMT	VG-E	GOOD			NRMT	VG-E	GOOD
☐	12 Hank Majeski	13.50	6.00	1.50	☐ 60 Chico Carrasquel .	12.00	5.00	1.20
☐	13 Eddie Stanky	15.00	6.00	1.50	☐ 61 Jim Hearn	12.00	5.00	1.20
☐	14 Alvin Dark	16.00	6.50	1.60	☐ 62 Lou Boudreau	33.00	15.00	4.00
☐	15 Johnny Pesky	13.50	6.00	1.50	☐ 63 Bob Dillinger	12.00	5.00	1.20
☐	16 Maurice McDermott	13.50	6.00	1.50	☐ 64 Bill Werle	12.00	5.00	1.20
☐	17 Pete Castiglione	13.50	6.00	1.50	☐ 65 Mickey Vernon	15.00	6.00	1.50
☐	18 Gil Coan	13.50	6.00	1.50	☐ 66 Bob Elliott	14.00	5.75	1.40
☐	19 Sid Gordon	13.50	6.00	1.50	☐ 67 Roy Sievers	14.00	5.75	1.40
☐	20 Del Crandell	15.00	6.00	1.50	☐ 68 Dick Kokos	12.00	5.00	1.20
	(sic, Crandall)				☐ 69 Johnny Schmitz	12.00	5.00	1.20
☐	21 Snuffy Stirnweiss	15.00	6.00	1.50	☐ 70 Ron Northey	12.00	5.00	1.20
☐	22 Hank Sauer	15.00	6.00	1.50	☐ 71 Jerry Priddy	12.00	5.00	1.20
☐	23 Hoot Evers	13.50	6.00	1.50	☐ 72 Lloyd Merriman	12.00	5.00	1.20
☐	24 Ewell Blackwell	15.00	6.00	1.50	☐ 73 Tommy Byrne	12.00	5.00	1.20
☐	25 Vic Raschi	20.00	8.00	2.00	☐ 74 Billy Johnson	12.00	5.00	1.20
☐	26 Phil Rizzuto	50.00	20.00	5.00	☐ 75 Russ Meyer	10.00	4.00	1.00
☐	27 Jim Konstanty	16.00	6.50	1.60	☐ 76 Stan Lopata	10.00	4.00	1.00
☐	28 Eddie Waitkus	13.50	6.00	1.50	☐ 77 Mike Goliat	10.00	4.00	1.00
☐	29 Allie Clark	13.50	6.00	1.50	☐ 78 Early Wynn	35.00	14.00	3.50
☐	30 Bob Feller	80.00	32.00	8.00	☐ 79 Jim Hegan	12.00	5.00	1.20
☐	31 Roy Campanella	175.00	70.00	18.00	☐ 80 Pee Wee Reese	90.00	36.00	9.00
☐	32 Duke Snider	135.00	54.00	13.50	☐ 81 Carl Furillo	21.00	8.50	2.10
☐	33 Bob Hooper	13.50	6.00	1.50	☐ 82 Joe Tipton	10.00	4.00	1.00
☐	34 Marty Marion	16.00	6.50	1.60	☐ 83 Carl Scheib	10.00	4.00	1.00
☐	35 Al Zarilla	13.50	6.00	1.50	☐ 84 Barney McCosky	10.00	4.00	1.00
☐	36 Joe Dobson	13.50	6.00	1.50	☐ 85 Eddie Kazak	10.00	4.00	1.00
☐	37 Whitey Lockman	13.50	6.00	1.50	☐ 86 Harry Brecheen	10.00	4.00	1.00
☐	38 Al Evans	12.00	5.00	1.20	☐ 87 Floyd Baker	10.00	4.00	1.00
☐	39 Ray Scarborough	12.00	5.00	1.20	☐ 88 Eddie Robinson	10.00	4.00	1.00
☐	40 Gus Bell	16.00	6.50	1.60	☐ 89 Hank Thompson	12.00	5.00	1.20
☐	41 Eddie Yost	12.00	5.00	1.20	☐ 90 Dave Koslo	10.00	4.00	1.00
☐	42 Vern Bickford	12.00	5.00	1.20	☐ 91 Clyde Vollmer	10.00	4.00	1.00
☐	43 Billy DeMars	12.00	5.00	1.20	☐ 92 Vern Stephens	12.00	5.00	1.20
☐	44 Roy Smalley	12.00	5.00	1.20	☐ 93 Danny O'Connell	10.00	4.00	1.00
☐	45 Art Houtteman	12.00	5.00	1.20	☐ 94 Clyde McCullough	10.00	4.00	1.00
☐	46 George Kell 1941	40.00	16.00	4.00	☐ 95 Sherry Robertson	10.00	4.00	1.00
☐	47 Grady Hatton	12.00	5.00	1.20	☐ 96 Sandy Consuegra	10.00	4.00	1.00
☐	48 Ken Raffensberger	12.00	5.00	1.20	☐ 97 Bob Kuzava	10.00	4.00	1.00
☐	49 Jerry Coleman	14.00	5.75	1.40	☐ 98 Willard Marshall	10.00	4.00	1.00
☐	50 Johnny Mize	45.00	18.00	4.50	☐ 99 Earl Torgeson	10.00	4.00	1.00
☐	51 Andy Seminick	12.00	5.00	1.20	☐ 100 Sherm Lollar	12.00	5.00	1.20
☐	52 Dick Sisler	12.00	5.00	1.20	☐ 101 Owen Friend	10.00	4.00	1.00
☐	53 Bob Lemon	35.00	14.00	3.50	☐ 102 Dutch Leonard	10.00	4.00	1.00
☐	54 Ray Boone	14.00	5.75	1.40	☐ 103 Andy Pafko	12.00	5.00	1.20
☐	55 Gene Hermanski	12.00	5.00	1.20	☐ 104 Virgil Trucks	12.00	5.00	1.20
☐	56 Ralph Branca	16.00	6.50	1.60	☐ 105 Don Kolloway	10.00	4.00	1.00
☐	57 Alex Kellner	12.00	5.00	1.20	☐ 106 Pat Mullin	10.00	4.00	1.00
☐	58 Enos Slaughter	40.00	18.00	4.00	☐ 107 Johnny Wyrostek	10.00	4.00	1.00
☐	59 Randy Gumpert	12.00	5.00	1.20	☐ 108 Virgil Stallcup	10.00	4.00	1.00

		NRMT	VG-E	GOOD
☐ 109	Allie Reynolds	21.00	8.50	2.10
☐ 110	Bobby Brown	20.00	8.00	2.00
☐ 111	Curt Simmons	12.00	5.00	1.20
☐ 112	Willie Jones	10.00	4.00	1.00
☐ 113	Bill Nicholson	10.00	4.00	1.00
☐ 114	Sam Zoldak	10.00	4.00	1.00
☐ 115	Steve Gromek	10.00	4.00	1.00
☐ 116	Bruce Edwards	10.00	4.00	1.00
☐ 117	Eddie Miksis	10.00	4.00	1.00
☐ 118	Preacher Roe	18.00	7.25	1.80
☐ 119	Eddie Joost	10.00	4.00	1.00
☐ 120	Joe Coleman	10.00	4.00	1.00
☐ 121	Jerry Staley	10.00	4.00	1.00
☐ 122	Joe Garagiola	80.00	32.00	8.00
☐ 123	Howie Judson	10.00	4.00	1.00
☐ 124	Gus Niarhos	10.00	4.00	1.00
☐ 125	Bill Rigney	10.00	4.00	1.00
☐ 126	Bobby Thomson	20.00	8.00	2.00
☐ 127	Sal Maglie	25.00	10.00	2.50
☐ 128	Ellis Kinder	10.00	4.00	1.00
☐ 129	Matt Batts	10.00	4.00	1.00
☐ 130	Tom Saffell	10.00	4.00	1.00
☐ 131	Cliff Chambers	10.00	4.00	1.00
☐ 132	Cass Michaels	10.00	4.00	1.00
☐ 133	Sam Dente	10.00	4.00	1.00
☐ 134	Warren Spahn	60.00	24.00	6.00
☐ 135	Walker Cooper	10.00	4.00	1.00
☐ 136	Ray Coleman	10.00	4.00	1.00
☐ 137	Dick Starr	10.00	4.00	1.00
☐ 138	Phil Cavarretta	12.00	5.00	1.20
☐ 139	Doyle Lade	10.00	4.00	1.00
☐ 140	Eddie Lake	10.00	4.00	1.00
☐ 141	Fred Hutchinson	12.00	5.00	1.20
☐ 142	Aaron Robinson	10.00	4.00	1.00
☐ 143	Ted Kluszewski	20.00	8.00	2.00
☐ 144	Herman Wehmeier	10.00	4.00	1.00
☐ 145	Fred Sanford	10.00	4.00	1.00
☐ 146	Johnny Hopp	12.00	5.00	1.20
☐ 147	Ken Heintzelman	10.00	4.00	1.00
☐ 148	Granny Hamner	10.00	4.00	1.00
☐ 149	Bubba Church	10.00	4.00	1.00
☐ 150	Mike Garcia	12.00	5.00	1.20
☐ 151	Larry Doby	16.00	6.50	1.60
☐ 152	Cal Abrams	10.00	4.00	1.00
☐ 153	Rex Barney	10.00	4.00	1.00
☐ 154	Pete Suder	10.00	4.00	1.00
☐ 155	Lou Brissie	10.00	4.00	1.00
☐ 156	Del Rice	10.00	4.00	1.00
☐ 157	Al Brazle	10.00	4.00	1.00
☐ 158	Chuck Diering	10.00	4.00	1.00
☐ 159	Eddie Stewart	10.00	4.00	1.00
☐ 160	Phil Masi	10.00	4.00	1.00
☐ 161	Wes Westrum	10.00	4.00	1.00
☐ 162	Larry Jansen	10.00	4.00	1.00
☐ 163	Monte Kennedy	10.00	4.00	1.00
☐ 164	Bill Wight	10.00	4.00	1.00
☐ 165	Ted Williams	375.00	150.00	37.00
☐ 166	Stan Rojek	10.00	4.00	1.00
☐ 167	Murry Dickson	10.00	4.00	1.00
☐ 168	Sam Mele	10.00	4.00	1.00
☐ 169	Sid Hudson	10.00	4.00	1.00
☐ 170	Sibby Sisti	10.00	4.00	1.00
☐ 171	Buddy Kerr	10.00	4.00	1.00
☐ 172	Ned Garver	10.00	4.00	1.00
☐ 173	Hank Arft	10.00	4.00	1.00
☐ 174	Mickey Owen	12.00	5.00	1.20
☐ 175	Wayne Terwilliger	10.00	4.00	1.00
☐ 176	Vic Wertz	12.00	5.00	1.20
☐ 177	Charlie Keller	12.00	5.00	1.20
☐ 178	Ted Gray	10.00	4.00	1.00
☐ 179	Danny Litwhiler	10.00	4.00	1.00
☐ 180	Howie Fox	10.00	4.00	1.00
☐ 181	Casey Stengel MG	70.00	28.00	7.00
☐ 182	Tom Ferrick	10.00	4.00	1.00
☐ 183	Hank Bauer	21.00	8.50	2.10
☐ 184	Eddie Sawyer MG	12.00	5.00	1.20
☐ 185	Jimmy Bloodworth	10.00	4.00	1.00
☐ 186	Richie Ashburn	30.00	12.00	3.00
☐ 187	Al Rosen	17.00	7.00	1.70
☐ 188	Bobby Avila	12.00	5.00	1.20
☐ 189	Erv Palica	10.00	4.00	1.00
☐ 190	Joe Hatton	10.00	4.00	1.00
☐ 191	Billy Hitchcock	10.00	4.00	1.00
☐ 192	Hank Wyse	10.00	4.00	1.00
☐ 193	Ted Wilks	10.00	4.00	1.00
☐ 194	Peanuts Lowrey	10.00	4.00	1.00
☐ 195	Paul Richards (caricature)	15.00	6.00	1.50
☐ 196	Billy Pierce	18.00	7.25	1.80
☐ 197	Bob Cain	10.00	4.00	1.00
☐ 198	Monte Irvin	45.00	18.00	4.50
☐ 199	Sheldon Jones	10.00	4.00	1.00
☐ 200	Jack Kramer	10.00	4.00	1.00
☐ 201	Steve O'Neill	10.00	4.00	1.00
☐ 202	Mike Guerra	10.00	4.00	1.00
☐ 203	Vernon Law	15.00	6.00	1.50
☐ 204	Vic Lombardi	10.00	4.00	1.00
☐ 205	Mickey Grasso	10.00	4.00	1.00

		NRMT	VG-E	GOOD
☐ 206	Conrado Marrero	10.00	4.00	1.00
☐ 207	Billy Southworth	10.00	4.00	1.00
☐ 208	Blix Donnelly	10.00	4.00	1.00
☐ 209	Ken Wood	10.00	4.00	1.00
☐ 210	Les Moss	10.00	4.00	1.00
☐ 211	Hal Jeffcoat	10.00	4.00	1.00
☐ 212	Bob Rush	10.00	4.00	1.00
☐ 213	Neil Berry	10.00	4.00	1.00
☐ 214	Bob Swift	10.00	4.00	1.00
☐ 215	Ken Peterson	10.00	4.00	1.00
☐ 216	Connie Ryan	10.00	4.00	1.00
☐ 217	Joe Page	15.00	6.00	1.50
☐ 218	Ed Lopat	25.00	10.00	2.50
☐ 219	Gene Woodling	27.00	11.00	2.70
☐ 220	Bob Miller	10.00	4.00	1.00
☐ 221	Dick Whitman	10.00	4.00	1.00
☐ 222	Thurman Tucker	10.00	4.00	1.00
☐ 223	Johnny VanderMeer	15.00	6.00	1.50
☐ 224	Billy Cox	12.00	5.00	1.20
☐ 225	Dan Bankhead	12.00	5.00	1.20
☐ 226	Jimmy Dykes	12.00	5.00	1.20
☐ 227	Bobby Schantz (sic, Shantz)	14.00	5.75	1.40
☐ 228	Cloyd Boyer	12.00	5.00	1.20
☐ 229	Bill Howerton	10.00	4.00	1.00
☐ 230	Max Lanier	10.00	4.00	1.00
☐ 231	Luis Aloma	10.00	4.00	1.00
☐ 232	Nelson Fox	50.00	20.00	5.00
☐ 233	Leo Durocher MG	35.00	14.00	3.50
☐ 234	Clint Hartung	10.00	4.00	1.00
☐ 235	Jack Lohrke	10.00	4.00	1.00
☐ 236	Warren Rosar	10.00	4.00	1.00
☐ 237	Billy Goodman	12.00	5.00	1.20
☐ 238	Pete Reiser	14.00	5.75	1.40
☐ 239	Bill MacDonald	10.00	4.00	1.00
☐ 240	Joe Haynes	10.00	4.00	1.00
☐ 241	Irv Noren	10.00	4.00	1.00
☐ 242	Sam Jethroe	10.00	4.00	1.00
☐ 243	Johnny Antonelli	12.00	5.00	1.20
☐ 244	Cliff Fannin	10.00	4.00	1.00
☐ 245	John Berardino	12.00	5.00	1.20
☐ 246	Bill Serena	10.00	4.00	1.00
☐ 247	Bob Ramazotti	10.00	4.00	1.00
☐ 248	Johnny Klippstein	10.00	4.00	1.00
☐ 249	Johnny Groth	10.00	4.00	1.00
☐ 250	Hank Borowy	10.00	4.00	1.00
☐ 251	Willard Ramsdell	10.00	4.00	1.00
☐ 252	Dixie Howell	10.00	4.00	1.00
☐ 253	Mickey Mantle	5500.00	2000.00	400.00
☐ 254	Jackie Jensen	90.00	36.00	9.00
☐ 255	Milo Candini	40.00	16.00	4.00
☐ 256	Ken Sylvestri	40.00	16.00	4.00
☐ 257	Birdie Tebbetts	45.00	18.00	4.50
☐ 258	Luke Easter	45.00	18.00	4.50
☐ 259	Chuck Dressen MG	50.00	20.00	5.00
☐ 260	Carl Erskine	80.00	32.00	8.00
☐ 261	Wally Moses	45.00	18.00	4.50
☐ 262	Gus Zernial	45.00	18.00	4.50
☐ 263	Howie Pollet	40.00	16.00	4.00
☐ 264	Don Richmond	40.00	16.00	4.00
☐ 265	Steve Bilko	40.00	16.00	4.00
☐ 266	Harry Dorish	40.00	16.00	4.00
☐ 267	Ken Holcombe	40.00	16.00	4.00
☐ 268	Don Mueller	45.00	18.00	4.50
☐ 269	Ray Noble	40.00	16.00	4.00
☐ 270	Willard Nixon	40.00	16.00	4.00
☐ 271	Tommy Wright	40.00	16.00	4.00
☐ 272	Billy Meyer MG	40.00	16.00	4.00
☐ 273	Danny Murtaugh	45.00	18.00	4.50
☐ 274	George Metkovich	40.00	16.00	4.00
☐ 275	Bucky Harris MG	55.00	22.00	5.50
☐ 276	Frank Quinn	40.00	16.00	4.00
☐ 277	Roy Hartsfield	40.00	16.00	4.00
☐ 278	Norman Roy	40.00	16.00	4.00
☐ 279	Jim Delsing	40.00	16.00	4.00
☐ 280	Frank Overmire	40.00	16.00	4.00
☐ 281	Al Widmar	40.00	16.00	4.00
☐ 282	Frank Frisch	60.00	24.00	6.00
☐ 283	Walt Dubiel	40.00	16.00	4.00
☐ 284	Gene Bearden	40.00	16.00	4.00
☐ 285	Johnny Lipon	40.00	16.00	4.00
☐ 286	Bob Usher	40.00	16.00	4.00
☐ 287	Jim Blackburn	40.00	16.00	4.00
☐ 288	Bobby Adams	40.00	16.00	4.00
☐ 289	Cliff Mapes	45.00	18.00	4.50
☐ 290	Bill Dickey	150.00	60.00	15.00
☐ 291	Tommy Henrich	60.00	24.00	6.00
☐ 292	Eddie Pellegrini	40.00	16.00	4.00
☐ 293	Ken Johnson	40.00	16.00	4.00
☐ 294	Jocko Thompson	40.00	16.00	4.00
☐ 295	Al Lopez MG	70.00	28.00	7.00
☐ 296	Bob Kennedy	45.00	18.00	4.50
☐ 297	Dave Philley	40.00	16.00	4.00
☐ 298	Joe Astroth	40.00	16.00	4.00
☐ 299	Clyde King	45.00	18.00	4.50
☐ 300	Hal Rice	40.00	16.00	4.00
☐ 301	Tommy Glaviano	40.00	16.00	4.00
☐ 302	Jim Busby	40.00	16.00	4.00

		NRMT	VG-E	GOOD
☐ 303	Marv Rotblatt	40.00	16.00	4.00
☐ 304	Al Gettell	40.00	16.00	4.00
☐ 305	Willie Mays	1600.00	600.00	200.00
☐ 306	Jim Piersall	80.00	32.00	8.00
☐ 307	Walt Masterson	40.00	16.00	4.00
☐ 308	Ted Beard	40.00	16.00	4.00
☐ 309	Mel Queen	40.00	16.00	4.00
☐ 310	Erv Dusak	40.00	16.00	4.00
☐ 311	Mickey Harris	40.00	16.00	4.00
☐ 312	Gene Mauch	50.00	20.00	5.00
☐ 313	Ray Mueller	40.00	16.00	4.00
☐ 314	Johnny Sain	50.00	20.00	5.00
☐ 315	Zack Taylor	40.00	16.00	4.00
☐ 316	Duane Pillette	40.00	16.00	4.00
☐ 317	Smokey Burgess	50.00	20.00	5.00
☐ 318	Warren Hacker	40.00	16.00	4.00
☐ 319	Red Rolfe	45.00	18.00	4.50
☐ 320	Hal White	40.00	16.00	4.00
☐ 321	Earl Johnson	40.00	16.00	4.00
☐ 322	Luke Sewell	45.00	18.00	4.50
☐ 323	Joe Adcock	60.00	24.00	6.00
☐ 324	Johnny Pramesa	75.00	25.00	5.00

1952 Bowman

The cards in this 252-card set measure 2 ⅛"
by 3 ⅛". While the Bowman set of 1952
retained the card size introduced in 1951, it
employed a modification of color tones from
the two preceding years. The cards also appeared with a facsimile autograph on the
front and, for the first time since 1949,
premium advertising on the back. The 1952

set was sold in sheets as well as in gum
packs. Artwork for 15 cards that were never
issued was recently discovered.

		NRMT	VG-E	GOOD
Complete Set (252)		7000.00	3000.00	900.00
Common Player (1-36)		15.00	6.00	1.50
Common Player (37-144)		12.00	5.00	1.20
Common Player (145-180)		11.00	4.50	1.10
Common Player (181-216)		10.00	4.00	1.00
Common Player (217-252)		25.00	10.00	2.50

			NRMT	VG-E	GOOD
☐ 1	Yogi Berra		400.00	100.00	20.00
☐ 2	Bobby Thomson		22.00	9.00	2.20
☐ 3	Fred Hutchinson		18.00	7.25	1.80
☐ 4	Robin Roberts		45.00	20.00	4.00
☐ 5	Minnie Minoso		30.00	12.00	3.00
☐ 6	Virgil Stallcup		15.00	6.00	1.50
☐ 7	Mike Garcia		18.00	7.25	1.80
☐ 8	Pee Wee Reese		80.00	32.00	8.00
☐ 9	Vern Stephens		18.00	7.25	1.80
☐ 10	Bob Hooper		15.00	6.00	1.50
☐ 11	Ralph Kiner		36.00	15.00	3.60
☐ 12	Max Surkont		15.00	6.00	1.50
☐ 13	Cliff Mapes		15.00	6.00	1.50
☐ 14	Cliff Chambers		15.00	6.00	1.50
☐ 15	Sam Mele		15.00	6.00	1.50
☐ 16	Turk Lown		15.00	6.00	1.50
☐ 17	Ed Lopat		24.00	10.00	2.40
☐ 18	Don Mueller		18.00	7.25	1.80
☐ 19	Bob Cain		15.00	6.00	1.50
☐ 20	Willie Jones		15.00	6.00	1.50
☐ 21	Nellie Fox		27.00	11.00	2.70
☐ 22	Willard Ramsdell		15.00	6.00	1.50
☐ 23	Bob Lemon		35.00	14.00	3.50
☐ 24	Carl Furillo		22.00	9.00	2.20
☐ 25	Mickey McDermott		15.00	6.00	1.50
☐ 26	Eddie Joost		15.00	6.00	1.50
☐ 27	Joe Garagiola		50.00	20.00	5.00
☐ 28	Roy Hartsfield		15.00	6.00	1.50
☐ 29	Ned Garver		15.00	6.00	1.50
☐ 30	Red Schoendienst		21.00	8.50	2.10
☐ 31	Eddie Yost		15.00	6.00	1.50
☐ 32	Eddie Miksis		15.00	6.00	1.50
☐ 33	Gil McDougald		40.00	16.00	4.00
☐ 34	Alvin Dark		18.00	7.25	1.80
☐ 35	Granny Hamner		15.00	6.00	1.50
☐ 36	Cass Michaels		15.00	6.00	1.50
☐ 37	Vic Raschi		16.00	6.50	1.60
☐ 38	Whitey Lockman		13.50	6.00	1.50
☐ 39	Vic Wertz		13.50	6.00	1.50

		NRMT	VG-E	GOOD			NRMT	VG-E	GOOD
☐ 40	Bubba Church	12.00	5.00	1.20	☐ 89	Billy Hitchcock	12.00	5.00	1.20
☐ 41	Chico Carrasquel	12.00	5.00	1.20	☐ 90	Larry Jansen	12.00	5.00	1.20
☐ 42	Johnny Wyrostek	12.00	5.00	1.20	☐ 91	Don Kolloway	12.00	5.00	1.20
☐ 43	Bob Feller	75.00	30.00	7.50	☐ 92	Eddie Waitkus	12.00	5.00	1.20
☐ 44	Roy Campanella	150.00	60.00	15.00	☐ 93	Paul Richards	13.50	6.00	1.50
☐ 45	Johnny Pesky	12.00	5.00	1.20	☐ 94	Luke Sewell	13.50	6.00	1.50
☐ 46	Carl Scheib	12.00	5.00	1.20	☐ 95	Luke Easter	13.50	6.00	1.50
☐ 47	Pete Castiglione	12.00	5.00	1.20	☐ 96	Ralph Branca	16.00	6.50	1.60
☐ 48	Vern Bickford	12.00	5.00	1.20	☐ 97	Willard Marshall	12.00	5.00	1.20
☐ 49	Jim Hearn	12.00	5.00	1.20	☐ 98	Jimmy Dykes	13.50	6.00	1.50
☐ 50	Jerry Staley	12.00	5.00	1.20	☐ 99	Clyde McCullough	12.00	5.00	1.20
☐ 51	Gil Coan	12.00	5.00	1.20	☐ 100	Sibby Sisti	12.00	5.00	1.20
☐ 52	Phil Rizzuto	50.00	20.00	5.00	☐ 101	Mickey Mantle	1500.00	600.00	125.00
☐ 53	Richie Ashburn	27.00	11.00	2.70	☐ 102	Peanuts Lowrey	12.00	5.00	1.20
☐ 54	Billy Pierce	15.00	6.00	1.50	☐ 103	Joe Haynes	12.00	5.00	1.20
☐ 55	Ken Raffensberger	12.00	5.00	1.20	☐ 104	Hal Jeffcoat	12.00	5.00	1.20
☐ 56	Clyde King	13.50	6.00	1.50	☐ 105	Bobby Brown	18.00	7.25	1.80
☐ 57	Clyde Vollmer	12.00	5.00	1.20	☐ 106	Randy Gumpert	12.00	5.00	1.20
☐ 58	Hank Majeski	12.00	5.00	1.20	☐ 107	Del Rice	12.00	5.00	1.20
☐ 59	Murry Dickson	12.00	5.00	1.20	☐ 108	George Metkovich	12.00	5.00	1.20
☐ 60	Sid Gordon	12.00	5.00	1.20	☐ 109	Tom Morgan	12.00	5.00	1.20
☐ 61	Tommy Byrne	12.00	5.00	1.20	☐ 110	Max Lanier	12.00	5.00	1.20
☐ 62	Joe Presko	12.00	5.00	1.20	☐ 111	Hoot Evers	12.00	5.00	1.20
☐ 63	Irv Noren	12.00	5.00	1.20	☐ 112	Smokey Burgess	13.50	6.00	1.50
☐ 64	Roy Smalley	12.00	5.00	1.20	☐ 113	Al Zarilla	12.00	5.00	1.20
☐ 65	Hank Bauer	20.00	8.00	2.00	☐ 114	Frank Hiller	12.00	5.00	1.20
☐ 66	Sal Maglie	16.00	6.50	1.60	☐ 115	Larry Doby	16.00	6.50	1.60
☐ 67	Johnny Groth	12.00	5.00	1.20	☐ 116	Duke Snider	110.00	45.00	10.00
☐ 68	Jim Busby	12.00	5.00	1.20	☐ 117	Bill Wight	12.00	5.00	1.20
☐ 69	Joe Adcock	13.50	6.00	1.50	☐ 118	Ray Murray	12.00	5.00	1.20
☐ 70	Carl Erskine	18.00	7.25	1.80	☐ 119	Bill Howerton	12.00	5.00	1.20
☐ 71	Vernon Law	13.50	6.00	1.50	☐ 120	Chet Nichols	12.00	5.00	1.20
☐ 72	Earl Torgeson	12.00	5.00	1.20	☐ 121	Al Corwin	12.00	5.00	1.20
☐ 73	Gerry Coleman	13.50	6.00	1.50	☐ 122	Billy Johnson	12.00	5.00	1.20
☐ 74	Wes Westrum	12.00	5.00	1.20	☐ 123	Sid Hudson	12.00	5.00	1.20
☐ 75	George Kell	35.00	15.00	3.20	☐ 124	Birdie Tebbetts	13.50	6.00	1.50
☐ 76	Del Ennis	13.50	6.00	1.50	☐ 125	Howie Fox	12.00	5.00	1.20
☐ 77	Eddie Robinson	12.00	5.00	1.20	☐ 126	Phil Cavarretta	13.50	6.00	1.50
☐ 78	Lloyd Merriman	12.00	5.00	1.20	☐ 127	Dick Sisler	12.00	5.00	1.20
☐ 79	Lou Brissie	12.00	5.00	1.20	☐ 128	Don Newcombe	18.00	7.25	1.80
☐ 80	Gil Hodges	45.00	18.00	4.50	☐ 129	Gus Niarhos	12.00	5.00	1.20
☐ 81	Billy Goodman	13.50	6.00	1.50	☐ 130	Allie Clark	12.00	5.00	1.20
☐ 82	Gus Zernial	13.50	6.00	1.50	☐ 131	Bob Swift	12.00	5.00	1.20
☐ 83	Howie Pollet	12.00	5.00	1.20	☐ 132	Dave Cole	12.00	5.00	1.20
☐ 84	Sam Jethroe	12.00	5.00	1.20	☐ 133	Dick Kryhoski	12.00	5.00	1.20
☐ 85	Marty Marion	15.00	6.00	1.50	☐ 134	Al Brazle	12.00	5.00	1.20
☐ 86	Cal Abrams	12.00	5.00	1.20	☐ 135	Mickey Harris	12.00	5.00	1.20
☐ 87	Mickey Vernon	13.50	6.00	1.50	☐ 136	Gene Hermanski	12.00	5.00	1.20
☐ 88	Bruce Edwards	12.00	5.00	1.20	☐ 137	Stan Rojek	12.00	5.00	1.20

		NRMT	VG-E	GOOD			NRMT	VG-E	GOOD
☐ 138	Ted Wilks	12.00	5.00	1.20	☐ 187	Jim Hegan	12.00	5.00	1.20
☐ 139	Jerry Priddy	12.00	5.00	1.20	☐ 188	Charlie Dressen MG	13.50	6.00	1.50
☐ 140	Ray Scarborough	12.00	5.00	1.20	☐ 189	Jim Piersall	14.00	5.75	1.40
☐ 141	Hank Edwards	12.00	5.00	1.20	☐ 190	Dick Fowler	10.00	4.00	1.00
☐ 142	Early Wynn	32.00	13.00	3.20	☐ 191	Bob Friend	14.00	5.75	1.40
☐ 143	Sandy Consuegra	12.00	5.00	1.20	☐ 192	John Cusick	10.00	4.00	1.00
☐ 144	Joe Hatton	12.00	5.00	1.20	☐ 193	Bobby Young	10.00	4.00	1.00
☐ 145	Johnny Mize	45.00	18.00	4.50	☐ 194	Bob Porterfield	10.00	4.00	1.00
☐ 146	Leo Durocher MG	30.00	12.00	3.00	☐ 195	Frank Baumholtz	10.00	4.00	1.00
☐ 147	Marlin Stuart	11.00	4.50	1.10	☐ 196	Stan Musial	325.00	130.00	32.00
☐ 148	Ken Heintzelman	11.00	4.50	1.10	☐ 197	Charlie Silvera	10.00	4.00	1.00
☐ 149	Howie Judson	11.00	4.50	1.10	☐ 198	Chuck Diering	10.00	4.00	1.00
☐ 150	Herman Wehmeier	11.00	4.50	1.10	☐ 199	Ted Gray	10.00	4.00	1.00
☐ 151	Al Rosen	17.00	7.00	1.70	☐ 200	Ken Silvestri	10.00	4.00	1.00
☐ 152	Billy Cox	13.50	6.00	1.50	☐ 201	Ray Coleman	10.00	4.00	1.00
☐ 153	Fred Hatfield	11.00	4.50	1.10	☐ 202	Harry Perkowski	10.00	4.00	1.00
☐ 154	Ferris Fain	13.50	6.00	1.50	☐ 203	Steve Gromek	10.00	4.00	1.00
☐ 155	Billy Meyer	11.00	4.50	1.10	☐ 204	Andy Pafko	10.00	4.00	1.00
☐ 156	Warren Spahn	50.00	20.00	5.00	☐ 205	Walt Masterson	10.00	4.00	1.00
☐ 157	Jim Delsing	11.00	4.50	1.10	☐ 206	Elmer Valo	10.00	4.00	1.00
☐ 158	Bucky Harris MG	25.00	10.00	2.50	☐ 207	George Strickland	10.00	4.00	1.00
☐ 159	Dutch Leonard	11.00	4.50	1.10	☐ 208	Walker Cooper	10.00	4.00	1.00
☐ 160	Eddie Stanky	13.50	6.00	1.50	☐ 209	Dick Littlefield	10.00	4.00	1.00
☐ 161	Jackie Jensen	21.00	8.50	2.10	☐ 210	Archie Wilson	10.00	4.00	1.00
☐ 162	Monte Irvin	30.00	12.00	3.00	☐ 211	Paul Minner	10.00	4.00	1.00
☐ 163	Johnny Lipon	11.00	4.50	1.10	☐ 212	Solly Hemus	10.00	4.00	1.00
☐ 164	Connie Ryan	11.00	4.50	1.10	☐ 213	Monte Kennedy	10.00	4.00	1.00
☐ 165	Saul Rogovin	11.00	4.50	1.10	☐ 214	Ray Boone	10.00	4.00	1.00
☐ 166	Bobby Adams	11.00	4.50	1.10	☐ 215	Sheldon Jones	10.00	4.00	1.00
☐ 167	Bobby Avila	13.50	6.00	1.50	☐ 216	Matt Batts	10.00	4.00	1.00
☐ 168	Preacher Roe	18.00	7.25	1.80	☐ 217	Casey Stengel MG	100.00	40.00	10.00
☐ 169	Walt Dropo	13.50	6.00	1.50	☐ 218	Willie Mays	750.00	325.00	75.00
☐ 170	Joe Astroth	11.00	4.50	1.10	☐ 219	Neil Berry	25.00	10.00	2.50
☐ 171	Mel Queen	11.00	4.50	1.10	☐ 220	Russ Meyer	25.00	10.00	2.50
☐ 172	Ebba St.Claire	11.00	4.50	1.10	☐ 221	Lou Kretlow	25.00	10.00	2.50
☐ 173	Gene Bearden	11.00	4.50	1.10	☐ 222	Dixie Howell	25.00	10.00	2.50
☐ 174	Mickey Grasso	11.00	4.50	1.10	☐ 223	Harry Simpson	25.00	10.00	2.50
☐ 175	Randy Jackson	11.00	4.50	1.10	☐ 224	Johnny Schmitz	25.00	10.00	2.50
☐ 176	Harry Brecheen	11.00	4.50	1.10	☐ 225	Del Wilber	25.00	10.00	2.50
☐ 177	Gene Woodling	16.00	6.50	1.60	☐ 226	Alex Kellner	25.00	10.00	2.50
☐ 178	Dave Williams	13.50	6.00	1.50	☐ 227	Clyde Sukeforth	25.00	10.00	2.50
☐ 179	Pete Suder	11.00	4.50	1.10	☐ 228	Bob Chipman	25.00	10.00	2.50
☐ 180	Ed Fitzgerald	11.00	4.50	1.10	☐ 229	Hank Arft	25.00	10.00	2.50
☐ 181	Joe Collins	13.50	6.00	1.50	☐ 230	Frank Shea	25.00	10.00	2.50
☐ 182	Dave Koslo	10.00	4.00	1.00	☐ 231	Dee Fondy	25.00	10.00	2.50
☐ 183	Pat Mullin	10.00	4.00	1.00	☐ 232	Enos Slaughter	60.00	24.00	6.00
☐ 184	Curt Simmons	13.50	6.00	1.50	☐ 233	Bob Kuzava	25.00	10.00	2.50
☐ 185	Eddie Stewart	10.00	4.00	1.00	☐ 234	Fred Fitzsimmons	25.00	10.00	2.50
☐ 186	Frank Smith	10.00	4.00	1.00	☐ 235	Steve Souchock	25.00	10.00	2.50

		NRMT	VG-E	GOOD
☐ 236	Tommy Brown	25.00	10.00	2.50
☐ 237	Sherm Lollar	30.00	12.00	3.00
☐ 238	Roy McMillan	30.00	12.00	3.00
☐ 239	Dale Mitchell	30.00	12.00	3.00
☐ 240	Billy Loes	30.00	12.00	3.00
☐ 241	Mel Parnell	30.00	12.00	3.00
☐ 242	Everett Kell	25.00	10.00	2.50
☐ 243	Red Munger	25.00	10.00	2.50
☐ 244	Lew Burdette	45.00	18.00	4.50
☐ 245	George Schmees	25.00	10.00	2.50
☐ 246	Jerry Snyder	25.00	10.00	2.50
☐ 247	Johnny Pramesa	25.00	10.00	2.50
☐ 248	Bill Werle	25.00	10.00	2.50
☐ 249	Hank Thompson	30.00	12.00	3.00
☐ 250	Ike Delock	25.00	10.00	2.50
☐ 251	Jack Lohrke	25.00	10.00	2.50
☐ 252	Frank Crosetti	100.00	15.00	3.00

1953 Bowman Color

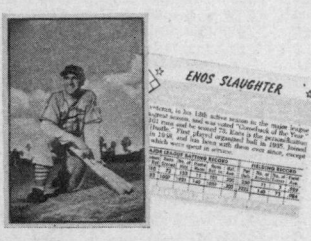

The cards in this 160-card set measure 2 ½ " by 3 ¾ ". The 1953 Bowman Color set, considered by many to be the best looking set of the modern era, contains Kodachrome photographs with no names or facsimile autographs on the face. Numbers 113 to 160 are somewhat more difficult to obtain. There are two cards of Al Corwin (126 and 149). Card number 159 is actually a picture of Floyd Baker.

	NRMT	VG-E	GOOD
Complete Set (160)	8000.00	3600.00	1200.00
Common Player (1-96)	21.00	8.50	2.10

	NRMT	VG-E	GOOD
Common Player (97-112)	25.00	10.00	2.50
Common Player (113-128)	40.00	16.00	4.00
Common Player (129-160)	30.00	12.00	3.00

		NRMT	VG-E	GOOD
☐ 1	Dave Williams	80.00	12.00	2.50
☐ 2	Vic Wertz	23.00	9.50	2.30
☐ 3	Sam Jethroe	21.00	8.50	2.10
☐ 4	Art Houtteman	21.00	8.50	2.10
☐ 5	Sid Gordon	21.00	8.50	2.10
☐ 6	Joe Ginsberg	21.00	8.50	2.10
☐ 7	Harry Chiti	21.00	8.50	2.10
☐ 8	Al Rosen	30.00	12.00	3.00
☐ 9	Phil Rizzuto	60.00	24.00	6.00
☐ 10	Richie Ashburn	36.00	15.00	3.60
☐ 11	Bobby Shantz	25.00	10.00	2.50
☐ 12	Carl Erskine	28.00	11.50	2.80
☐ 13	Gus Zernial	23.00	9.50	2.30
☐ 14	Billy Loes	23.00	9.50	2.30
☐ 15	Jim Busby	21.00	8.50	2.10
☐ 16	Bob Friend	23.00	9.50	2.30
☐ 17	Jerry Staley	21.00	8.50	2.10
☐ 18	Nellie Fox	33.00	15.00	3.50
☐ 19	Alvin Dark	23.00	9.50	2.30
☐ 20	Don Lenhardt	21.00	8.50	2.10
☐ 21	Joe Garagiola	50.00	20.00	5.00
☐ 22	Bob Porterfield	21.00	8.50	2.10
☐ 23	Herman Wehmeier	21.00	8.50	2.10
☐ 24	Jackie Jensen	28.00	11.50	2.80
☐ 25	Hoot Evers	21.00	8.50	2.10
☐ 26	Roy McMillan	21.00	8.50	2.10
☐ 27	Vic Raschi	28.00	11.50	2.80
☐ 28	Smokey Burgess	23.00	9.50	2.30
☐ 29	Bobby Avila	23.00	9.50	2.30
☐ 30	Phil Cavarretta	23.00	9.50	2.30
☐ 31	Jimmy Dykes	23.00	9.50	2.30
☐ 32	Stan Musial	350.00	140.00	32.00
☐ 33	Pee Wee Reese HOR	175.00	70.00	18.00
☐ 34	Gil Coan	21.00	8.50	2.10
☐ 35	Maurice McDermott	21.00	8.50	2.10
☐ 36	Minnie Minoso	27.00	11.00	2.70
☐ 37	Jim Wilson	21.00	8.50	2.10
☐ 38	Harry Byrd	21.00	8.50	2.10
☐ 39	Paul Richards MG	23.00	9.50	2.30
☐ 40	Larry Doby	25.00	10.00	2.50
☐ 41	Sammy White	21.00	8.50	2.10
☐ 42	Tommy Brown	21.00	8.50	2.10
☐ 43	Mike Garcia	23.00	9.50	2.30
☐ 44	Berra/Bauer/Mantle	325.00	130.00	32.00
☐ 45	Walt Dropo	21.00	8.50	2.10

			NRMT	VG-E	GOOD				NRMT	VG-E	GOOD
☐	46	Roy Campanella	175.00	70.00	18.00	☐	94	Bob Addis	21.00	8.50	2.10
☐	47	Ned Garver	21.00	8.50	2.10	☐	95	Wally Moses	21.00	8.50	2.10
☐	48	Hank Sauer	23.00	9.50	2.30	☐	96	Sal Maglie	25.00	10.00	2.50
☐	49	Eddie Stanky	23.00	9.50	2.30	☐	97	Eddie Mathews	125.00	50.00	12.50
☐	50	Lou Kretlow	21.00	8.50	2.10	☐	98	Hector Rodriguez	25.00	10.00	2.50
☐	51	Monte Irvin	45.00	18.00	4.50	☐	99	Warren Spahn	100.00	40.00	10.00
☐	52	Marty Marion	28.00	11.50	2.80	☐	100	Bill Wight	25.00	10.00	2.50
☐	53	Del Rice	21.00	8.50	2.10	☐	101	Red Schoendienst	30.00	12.00	3.00
☐	54	Chico Carrasquel	21.00	8.50	2.10	☐	102	Jim Hegan	27.00	11.00	2.70
☐	55	Leo Durocher MG	45.00	18.00	4.50	☐	103	Del Ennis	27.00	11.00	2.70
☐	56	Bob Cain	21.00	8.50	2.10	☐	104	Luke Easter	27.00	11.00	2.70
☐	57	Lou Boudreau MG	45.00	18.00	4.50	☐	105	Eddie Joost	25.00	10.00	2.50
☐	58	Willard Marshall	21.00	8.50	2.10	☐	106	Ken Raffensberger	25.00	10.00	2.50
☐	59	Mickey Mantle	1350.00	500.00	125.00	☐	107	Alex Kellner	25.00	10.00	2.50
☐	60	Granny Hamner	21.00	8.50	2.10	☐	108	Bobby Adams	25.00	10.00	2.50
☐	61	George Kell	50.00	20.00	5.00	☐	109	Ken Wood	25.00	10.00	2.50
☐	62	Ted Kluszewski	30.00	12.00	3.00	☐	110	Bob Rush	25.00	10.00	2.50
☐	63	Gil McDougald	30.00	12.00	3.00	☐	111	Jim Dyck	25.00	10.00	2.50
☐	64	Curt Simmons	25.00	10.00	2.50	☐	112	Toby Atwell	25.00	10.00	2.50
☐	65	Robin Roberts	50.00	20.00	5.00	☐	113	Karl Drews	40.00	16.00	4.00
☐	66	Mel Parnell	23.00	9.50	2.30	☐	114	Bob Feller	200.00	80.00	20.00
☐	67	Mel Clark	21.00	8.50	2.10	☐	115	Cloyd Boyer	40.00	16.00	4.00
☐	68	Allie Reynolds	30.00	12.00	3.00	☐	116	Eddie Yost	40.00	16.00	4.00
☐	69	Charlie Grimm MG	23.00	9.50	2.30	☐	117	Duke Snider	450.00	180.00	45.00
☐	70	Clint Courtney	21.00	8.50	2.10	☐	118	Billy Martin	175.00	70.00	18.00
☐	71	Paul Minner	21.00	8.50	2.10	☐	119	Dale Mitchell	45.00	18.00	4.50
☐	72	Ted Gray	21.00	8.50	2.10	☐	120	Marlin Stuart	40.00	16.00	4.00
☐	73	Billy Pierce	25.00	10.00	2.50	☐	121	Yogi Berra	450.00	180.00	45.00
☐	74	Don Mueller	23.00	9.50	2.30	☐	122	Bill Serena	40.00	16.00	4.00
☐	75	Saul Rogovin	21.00	8.50	2.10	☐	123	Johnny Lipon	40.00	16.00	4.00
☐	76	Jim Hearn	21.00	8.50	2.10	☐	124	Charlie Dressen MG	50.00	20.00	5.00
☐	77	Mickey Grasso	21.00	8.50	2.10	☐	125	Fred Hatfield	40.00	16.00	4.00
☐	78	Carl Furillo	30.00	12.00	3.00	☐	126	Al Corwin	40.00	16.00	4.00
☐	79	Ray Boone	23.00	9.50	2.30	☐	127	Dick Kryhoski	40.00	16.00	4.00
☐	80	Ralph Kiner	50.00	20.00	5.00	☐	128	Whitey Lockman	45.00	18.00	4.50
☐	81	Enos Slaughter	50.00	20.00	5.00	☐	129	Russ Meyer	30.00	12.00	3.00
☐	82	Joe Astroth	21.00	8.50	2.10	☐	130	Cass Michaels	30.00	12.00	3.00
☐	83	Jack Daniels	21.00	8.50	2.10	☐	131	Connie Ryan	30.00	12.00	3.00
☐	84	Hank Bauer	28.00	11.50	2.80	☐	132	Fred Hutchinson	35.00	14.00	3.50
☐	85	Solly Hemus	21.00	8.50	2.10	☐	133	Willie Jones	30.00	12.00	3.00
☐	86	Harry Simpson	21.00	8.50	2.10	☐	134	Johnny Pesky	30.00	12.00	3.00
☐	87	Harry Perkowski	21.00	8.50	2.10	☐	135	Bobby Morgan	30.00	12.00	3.00
☐	88	Joe Dobson	21.00	8.50	2.10	☐	136	Jim Brideweser	30.00	12.00	3.00
☐	89	Sandy Consuegra	21.00	8.50	2.10	☐	137	Sam Dente	30.00	12.00	3.00
☐	90	Joe Nuxhall	23.00	9.50	2.30	☐	138	Bubba Church	30.00	12.00	3.00
☐	91	Steve Souchock	21.00	8.50	2.10	☐	139	Pete Runnels	35.00	14.00	3.50
☐	92	Gil Hodges	80.00	32.00	8.00	☐	140	Al Brazle	30.00	12.00	3.00
☐	93	Phil Rizzuto and Billy Martin	125.00	50.00	12.50	☐	141	Frank Shea	30.00	12.00	3.00
						☐	142	Larry Miggins	30.00	12.00	3.00

	NRMT	VG-E	GOOD
☐ 143 Al Lopez MG	60.00	24.00	6.00
☐ 144 Warren Hacker	30.00	12.00	3.00
☐ 145 George Shuba	35.00	14.00	3.50
☐ 146 Early Wynn	90.00	36.00	9.00
☐ 147 Clem Koshorek	30.00	12.00	3.00
☐ 148 Billy Goodman	35.00	14.00	3.50
☐ 149 Al Corwin	30.00	12.00	3.00
☐ 150 Carl Scheib	30.00	12.00	3.00
☐ 151 Joe Adcock	40.00	16.00	4.00
☐ 152 Clyde Vollmer	30.00	12.00	3.00
☐ 153 Whitey Ford	350.00	140.00	35.00
☐ 154 Turk Lown	30.00	12.00	3.00
☐ 155 Allie Clark	30.00	12.00	3.00
☐ 156 Max Surkont	30.00	12.00	3.00
☐ 157 Sherm Lollar	35.00	14.00	3.50
☐ 158 Howard Fox	30.00	12.00	3.00
☐ 159 Mickey Vernon	35.00	14.00	3.50
(photo actually Floyd Baker)			
☐ 160 Cal Abrams	50.00	15.00	3.00

1953 Bowman BW

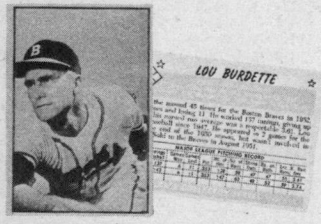

LOU BURDETTE

The cards in this 64-card set measure 2 ½" by 3 ¾". Some collectors believe that the high cost of producing the 1953 color series forced Bowman to issue this set in black and white, since the two sets are identical in design except for the element of color. This set was also produced in fewer numbers than its color counterpart, and is popular among collectors for the challenge involved in completing it.

	NRMT	VG-E	GOOD
Complete Set (64)	1900.00	850.00	250.00
Common Player (1-64)	25.00	10.00	2.50
☐ 1 Gus Bell	80.00	15.00	3.00
☐ 2 Willard Nixon	25.00	10.00	2.50
☐ 3 Bill Rigney	25.00	10.00	2.50
☐ 4 Pat Mullin	25.00	10.00	2.50
☐ 5 Dee Fondy	25.00	10.00	2.50
☐ 6 Ray Murray	25.00	10.00	2.50
☐ 7 Andy Seminick	25.00	10.00	2.50
☐ 8 Pete Suder	25.00	10.00	2.50
☐ 9 Walt Masterson	25.00	10.00	2.50
☐ 10 Dick Sisler	25.00	10.00	2.50
☐ 11 Dick Gernert	25.00	10.00	2.50
☐ 12 Randy Jackson	25.00	10.00	2.50
☐ 13 Joe Tipton	25.00	10.00	2.50
☐ 14 Bill Nicholson	25.00	10.00	2.50
☐ 15 Johnny Mize	100.00	40.00	10.00
☐ 16 Stu Miller	30.00	12.00	3.00
☐ 17 Virgil Trucks	30.00	12.00	3.00
☐ 18 Billy Hoeft	30.00	12.00	3.00
☐ 19 Paul LaPalme	25.00	10.00	2.50
☐ 20 Eddie Robinson	25.00	10.00	2.50
☐ 21 Clarence Podbielan	25.00	10.00	2.50
☐ 22 Matt Batts	25.00	10.00	2.50
☐ 23 Wilmer Mizell	25.00	10.00	2.50
☐ 24 Del Wilber	25.00	10.00	2.50
☐ 25 Johnny Sain	50.00	20.00	5.00
☐ 26 Preacher Roe	50.00	20.00	5.00
☐ 27 Bob Lemon	90.00	36.00	9.00
☐ 28 Hoyt Wilhelm	90.00	36.00	9.00
☐ 29 Sid Hudson	25.00	10.00	2.50
☐ 30 Walker Cooper	25.00	10.00	2.50
☐ 31 Gene Woodling	40.00	16.00	4.00
☐ 32 Rocky Bridges	25.00	10.00	2.50
☐ 33 Bob Kuzava	25.00	10.00	2.50
☐ 34 Ebba St.Claire	25.00	10.00	2.50
☐ 35 Johnny Wyrostek	25.00	10.00	2.50
☐ 36 Jim Piersall	40.00	16.00	4.00
☐ 37 Hal Jeffcoat	25.00	10.00	2.50
☐ 38 Dave Cole	25.00	10.00	2.50
☐ 39 Casey Stengel MG	250.00	100.00	25.00
☐ 40 Larry Jansen	25.00	10.00	2.50
☐ 41 Bob Ramazotti	25.00	10.00	2.50
☐ 42 Howie Judson	25.00	10.00	2.50
☐ 43 Hal Bevan	25.00	10.00	2.50
☐ 44 Jim Delsing	25.00	10.00	2.50
☐ 45 Irv Noren	30.00	12.00	3.00
☐ 46 Bucky Harris	50.00	20.00	5.00
☐ 47 Jack Lohrke	25.00	10.00	2.50

		NRMT	VG-E	GOOD
☐ 48	Steve Ridzik	25.00	10.00	2.50
☐ 49	Floyd Baker	25.00	10.00	2.50
☐ 50	Dutch Leonard	25.00	10.00	2.50
☐ 51	Lou Burdette	40.00	16.00	4.00
☐ 52	Ralph Branca	35.00	14.00	3.50
☐ 53	Morrie Martin	25.00	10.00	2.50
☐ 54	Bill Miller	25.00	10.00	2.50
☐ 55	Don Johnson	25.00	10.00	2.50
☐ 56	Roy Smalley	25.00	10.00	2.50
☐ 57	Andy Pafko	25.00	10.00	2.50
☐ 58	Jim Konstanty	30.00	12.00	3.00
☐ 59	Duane Pillette	25.00	10.00	2.50
☐ 60	Billy Cox	30.00	12.00	3.00
☐ 61	Tom Gorman	25.00	10.00	2.50
☐ 62	Keith Thomas	25.00	10.00	2.50
☐ 63	Steve Gromek	25.00	10.00	2.50
☐ 64	Andy Hansen	40.00	15.00	3.00

1954 Bowman

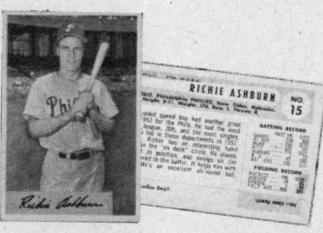

The cards in this 224-card set measure 2 ½ " by 3 ¾ ". A contractual problem apparently resulted in the deletion of the number 66 Ted Williams card from this Bowman set, thereby creating a scarcity which is highly valued among collectors. The set price below does NOT include number 66 Williams. Many errors in players' statistics exist (and some were corrected) while a few players' names were printed on the front, instead of appearing as a facsimile autograph.

		NRMT	VG-E	GOOD
Complete Set (224)		3000.00	1250.00	450.00
Common Player (1-128)		5.00	2.00	.50
Common Player (129-224)		6.00	2.40	.60
☐ 1	Phil Rizzuto	125.00	20.00	4.00
☐ 2	Jackie Jensen	9.00	3.75	.90
☐ 3	Marion Fricano	5.00	2.00	.50
☐ 4	Bob Hooper	5.00	2.00	.50
☐ 5	Billy Hunter	5.00	2.00	.50
☐ 6	Nellie Fox	11.00	4.50	1.10
☐ 7	Walt Dropo	5.00	2.00	.50
☐ 8	Jim Busby	5.00	2.00	.50
☐ 9	Davey Williams	6.00	2.40	.60
☐ 10	Carl Erskine	9.00	3.75	.90
☐ 11	Sid Gordon	5.00	2.00	.50
☐ 12	Roy McMillan	5.00	2.00	.50
☐ 13	Paul Minner	5.00	2.00	.50
☐ 14	Jerry Staley	5.00	2.00	.50
☐ 15	Richie Ashburn	12.00	5.00	.1.20
☐ 16	Jim Wilson	5.00	2.00	.50
☐ 17	Tom Gorman	5.00	2.00	.50
☐ 18	Hoot Evers	5.00	2.00	.50
☐ 19	Bobby Shantz	7.00	2.80	.70
☐ 20	Art Houtteman	5.00	2.00	.50
☐ 21	Vic Wertz	6.00	2.40	.60
☐ 22	Sam Mele	5.00	2.00	.50
☐ 23	Harvey Kuenn	16.00	6.50	1.60
☐ 24	Bob Porterfield	5.00	2.00	.50
☐ 25	Wes Westrum	5.00	2.00	.50
☐ 26	Billy Cox	6.00	2.40	.60
☐ 27	Dick Cole	5.00	2.00	.50
☐ 28	Jim Greengrass	5.00	2.00	.50
☐ 29	Johnny Klippstein	5.00	2.00	.50
☐ 30	Del Rice	5.00	2.00	.50
☐ 31	Smoky Burgess	6.00	2.40	.60
☐ 32	Del Crandall	6.00	2.40	.60
☐ 33A	Vic Raschi	9.00	3.75	.90
	(no mention of trade on back)			
☐ 33B	Vic Raschi	18.00	7.25	1.80
	(traded to St.Louis)			
☐ 34	Sammy White	5.00	2.00	.50
☐ 35	Eddie Joost	5.00	2.00	.50
☐ 36	George Strickland	5.00	2.00	.50
☐ 37	Dick Kokos	5.00	2.00	.50
☐ 38	Minnie Minoso	8.50	3.75	.80
☐ 39	Ned Garver	5.00	2.00	.50
☐ 40	Gil Coan	5.00	2.00	.50
☐ 41	Alvin Dark	7.00	2.80	.70
☐ 42	Billy Loes	5.00	2.00	.50
☐ 43	Bob Friend	6.00	2.40	.60

		NRMT	VG-E	GOOD			NRMT	VG-E	GOOD
☐ 44	Harry Perkowski	5.00	2.00	.50	☐ 92	Ken Raffensberger	5.00	2.00	.50
☐ 45	Ralph Kiner	25.00	10.00	2.50	☐ 93	Bill Serena	5.00	2.00	.50
☐ 46	Rip Repulski	5.00	2.00	.50	☐ 94	Solly Hemus	5.00	2.00	.50
☐ 47	Granny Hamner	5.00	2.00	.50	☐ 95	Robin Roberts	22.00	9.00	2.20
☐ 48	Jack Dittmer	5.00	2.00	.50	☐ 96	Joe Adcock	6.00	2.40	.60
☐ 49	Harry Byrd	5.00	2.00	.50	☐ 97	Gil McDougald	10.00	4.00	1.00
☐ 50	George Kell	22.00	9.00	2.20	☐ 98	Ellis Kinder	5.00	2.00	.50
☐ 51	Alex Kellner	5.00	2.00	.50	☐ 99	Pete Suder	5.00	2.00	.50
☐ 52	Joe Ginsberg	5.00	2.00	.50	☐ 100	Mike Garcia	6.00	2.40	.60
☐ 53	Don Lenhardt	5.00	2.00	.50	☐ 101	Don Larsen	15.00	6.00	1.50
☐ 54	Chico Carrasquel	5.00	2.00	.50	☐ 102	Billy Pierce	6.00	2.40	.60
☐ 55	Jim Delsing	5.00	2.00	.50	☐ 103	Steve Souchock	5.00	2.00	.50
☐ 56	Maurice McDermott	5.00	2.00	.50	☐ 104	Frank Shea	5.00	2.00	.50
☐ 57	Hoyt Wilhelm	22.00	9.00	2.20	☐ 105	Sal Maglie	8.50	3.50	.85
☐ 58	Pee Wee Reese	45.00	18.00	4.50	☐ 106	Clem Labine	6.00	2.40	.60
☐ 59	Bob Schultz	5.00	2.00	.50	☐ 107	Paul LaPalme	5.00	2.00	.50
☐ 60	Fred Baczewski	5.00	2.00	.50	☐ 108	Bobby Adams	5.00	2.00	.50
☐ 61	Eddie Miksis	5.00	2.00	.50	☐ 109	Roy Smalley	5.00	2.00	.50
☐ 62	Enos Slaughter	22.00	9.00	2.20	☐ 110	Red Schoendienst	9.00	4.00	.85
☐ 63	Earl Torgeson	5.00	2.00	.50	☐ 111	Murry Dickson	5.00	2.00	.50
☐ 64	Eddie Mathews	35.00	14.00	3.50	☐ 112	Andy Pafko	5.00	2.00	.50
☐ 65	Mickey Mantle	700.00	280.00	70.00	☐ 113	Allie Reynolds	12.00	5.00	1.20
☐ 66A	Ted Williams	2100.00	800.00	200.00	☐ 114	Willard Nixon	5.00	2.00	.50
☐ 66B	Jim Piersall	100.00	40.00	10.00	☐ 115	Don Bollweg	5.00	2.00	.50
☐ 67	Carl Scheib	5.00	2.00	.50	☐ 116	Luke Easter	5.00	2.00	.50
☐ 68	Bobby Avila	5.00	2.00	.50	☐ 117	Dick Kryhoski	5.00	2.00	.50
☐ 69	Clint Courtney	5.00	2.00	.50	☐ 118	Bob Boyd	5.00	2.00	.50
☐ 70	Willard Marshall	5.00	2.00	.50	☐ 119	Fred Hatfield	5.00	2.00	.50
☐ 71	Ted Gray	5.00	2.00	.50	☐ 120	Mel Hoderlein	5.00	2.00	.50
☐ 72	Eddie Yost	5.00	2.00	.50	☐ 121	Ray Katt	5.00	2.00	.50
☐ 73	Don Mueller	6.00	2.40	.60	☐ 122	Carl Furillo	11.00	4.50	1.10
☐ 74	Jim Gilliam	9.00	3.75	.90	☐ 123	Toby Atwell	5.00	2.00	.50
☐ 75	Max Surkont	5.00	2.00	.50	☐ 124	Gus Bell	6.00	2.40	.60
☐ 76	Joe Nuxhall	6.00	2.40	.60	☐ 125	Warren Hacker	5.00	2.00	.50
☐ 77	Bob Rush	5.00	2.00	.50	☐ 126	Cliff Chambers	5.00	2.00	.50
☐ 78	Sal Yvars	5.00	2.00	.50	☐ 127	Del Ennis	6.00	2.40	.60
☐ 79	Curt Simmons	6.00	2.40	.60	☐ 128	Ebba St.Claire	5.00	2.00	.50
☐ 80	Johnny Logan	6.00	2.40	.60	☐ 129	Hank Bauer	11.00	4.50	1.10
☐ 81	Jerry Coleman	7.00	2.80	.70	☐ 130	Milt Bolling	6.00	2.40	.60
☐ 82	Billy Goodman	6.00	2.40	.60	☐ 131	Joe Astroth	6.00	2.40	.60
☐ 83	Ray Murray	5.00	2.00	.50	☐ 132	Bob Feller	50.00	20.00	5.00
☐ 84	Larry Doby	9.00	4.00	.85	☐ 133	Duane Pillette	6.00	2.40	.60
☐ 85	Jim Dyck	5.00	2.00	.50	☐ 134	Luis Aloma	6.00	2.40	.60
☐ 86	Harry Dorish	5.00	2.00	.50	☐ 135	Johnny Pesky	7.00	2.80	.70
☐ 87	Don Lund	5.00	2.00	.50	☐ 136	Clyde Vollmer	6.00	2.40	.60
☐ 88	Tom Umphlett	5.00	2.00	.50	☐ 137	Al Corwin	6.00	2.40	.60
☐ 89	Willie Mays	250.00	100.00	25.00	☐ 138	Gil Hodges	35.00	14.00	3.50
☐ 90	Roy Campanella	90.00	36.00	9.00	☐ 139	Preston Ward	6.00	2.40	.60
☐ 91	Cal Abrams	5.00	2.00	.50	☐ 140	Saul Rogovin	6.00	2.40	.60

		NRMT	VG-E	GOOD			NRMT	VG-E	GOOD
☐ 141	Joe Garagiola	28.00	11.50	2.80	☐ 187 Vernon Law	7.00	2.80	.70
☐ 142	Al Brazle	6.00	2.40	.60	☐ 188 Frank Smith	6.00	2.40	.60
☐ 143	Willie Jones	6.00	2.40	.60	☐ 189 Randy Jackson	6.00	2.40	.60
☐ 144	Ernie Johnson	6.00	2.40	.60	☐ 190 Joe Presko	6.00	2.40	.60
☐ 145	Billy Martin	35.00	14.00	3.50	☐ 191 Karl Drews	6.00	2.40	.60
☐ 146	Dick Gernert	6.00	2.40	.60	☐ 192 Lou Burdette	8.50	3.50	.85
☐ 147	Joe DeMaestri	6.00	2.40	.60	☐ 193 Eddie Robinson	6.00	2.40	.60
☐ 148	Dale Mitchell	7.00	2.80	.70	☐ 194 Sid Hudson	6.00	2.40	.60
☐ 149	Bob Young	6.00	2.40	.60	☐ 195 Bob Cain	6.00	2.40	.60
☐ 150	Cass Michaels	6.00	2.40	.60	☐ 196 Bob Lemon	22.00	9.00	2.20
☐ 151	Pat Mullin	6.00	2.40	.60	☐ 197 Lou Kretlow	6.00	2.40	.60
☐ 152	Mickey Vernon	7.00	2.80	.70	☐ 198 Virgil Trucks	7.00	2.80	.70
☐ 153	Whitey Lockman	7.00	2.80	.70	☐ 199 Steve Gromek	6.00	2.40	.60
☐ 154	Don Newcombe	11.00	4.50	1.10	☐ 200 Conrado Marrero	6.00	2.40	.60
☐ 155	Frank Thomas	7.00	2.80	.70	☐ 201 Bobby Thomson	9.00	3.75	.90
☐ 156	Rocky Bridges	6.00	2.40	.60	☐ 202 George Shuba	7.00	2.80	.70
☐ 157	Turk Lown	6.00	2.40	.60	☐ 203 Vic Janowicz	7.00	2.80	.70
☐ 158	Stu Miller	6.00	2.40	.60	☐ 204 Jack Collum	6.00	2.40	.60
☐ 159	Johnny Lindell	6.00	2.40	.60	☐ 205 Hal Jeffcoat	6.00	2.40	.60
☐ 160	Danny O'Connell	6.00	2.40	.60	☐ 206 Steve Bilko	6.00	2.40	.60
☐ 161	Yogi Berra	100.00	40.00	10.00	☐ 207 Stan Lopata	6.00	2.40	.60
☐ 162	Ted Lepcio	6.00	2.40	.60	☐ 208 Johnny Antonelli	7.00	2.80	.70
☐ 163A	Dave Philley	7.00	2.80	.70	☐ 209 Gene Woodling	9.00	3.75	.90
	(no mention of trade on back)				☐ 210 Jim Piersall	9.00	3.75	.90
☐ 163B	Dave Philley	17.00	7.00	1.70	☐ 211 Al Robertson	6.00	2.40	.60
	(traded to Cleveland)				☐ 212 Owen Friend	6.00	2.40	.60
☐ 164	Early Wynn	22.00	9.00	2.20	☐ 213 Dick Littlefield	6.00	2.40	.60
☐ 165	Johnny Groth	6.00	2.40	.60	☐ 214 Ferris Fain	7.00	2.80	.70
☐ 166	Sandy Consuegra	6.00	2.40	.60	☐ 215 Johnny Bucha	6.00	2.40	.60
☐ 167	Billy Hoeft	6.00	2.40	.60	☐ 216 Jerry Snyder	6.00	2.40	.60
☐ 168	Ed Fitzgerald	6.00	2.40	.60	☐ 217 Hank Thompson	7.00	2.80	.70
☐ 169	Larry Jansen	6.00	2.40	.60	☐ 218 Preacher Roe	10.00	4.00	1.00
☐ 170	Duke Snider	80.00	32.00	8.00	☐ 219 Hal Rice	6.00	2.40	.60
☐ 171	Carlos Bernier	6.00	2.40	.60	☐ 220 Hobie Landrith	6.00	2.40	.60
☐ 172	Andy Seminick	6.00	2.40	.00	☐ 221 Frank Baumholtz	6.00	2.40	.60
☐ 173	Dee Fondy	6.00	2.40	.60	☐ 222 Memo Luna	6.00	2.40	.60
☐ 174	Pete Castiglione	6.00	2.40	.60	☐ 223 Steve Ridzik	6.00	2.40	.60
☐ 175	Mel Clark	6.00	2.40	.60	☐ 224 Bill Bruton	20.00	4.00	.75
☐ 176	Vern Bickford	6.00	2.40	.60				
☐ 177	Whitey Ford	45.00	18.00	4.50				
☐ 178	Del Wilber	6.00	2.40	.60				
☐ 179	Morrie Martin	6.00	2.40	.60				
☐ 180	Joe Tipton	6.00	2.40	.60				
☐ 181	Les Moss	6.00	2.40	.60				
☐ 182	Sherm Lollar	7.00	2.80	.70				
☐ 183	Matt Batts	6.00	2.40	.60				
☐ 184	Mickey Grasso	6.00	2.40	.60				
☐ 185	Daryl Spencer	6.00	2.40	.60				
☐ 186	Russ Meyer	6.00	2.40	.60				

1955 Bowman

*The cards in this 320-card set measure 2 ½"
by 3 ¾". The Bowman set of 1955 is known
as the "TV set" because each player
photograph is cleverly shown within a
television set design. The set contains um-
pire cards, some transposed pictures (e.g.,
Johnsons and Bollings), an incorrect spelling
for Harvey Kuenn, and a traded line for
Palica (all of which are noted in the checklist
below). Some three-card advertising strips
exist.*

	NRMT	VG-E	GOOD
Complete Set (320)	3750.00	1650.00	550.00
Common Player (1-96)	5.00	2.00	.50
Common Player (97-224)	4.00	1.60	.40
Common Player (225-320)	10.00	4.00	1.00
Common Umpires (225-320)	15.00	6.00	1.50

			NRMT	VG-E	GOOD
☐	1	Hoyt Wilhelm	75.00	10.00	2.00
☐	2	Alvin Dark	7.00	2.80	.70
☐	3	Joe Coleman	5.00	2.00	.50
☐	4	Eddie Waitkus	5.00	2.00	.50
☐	5	Jim Robertson	5.00	2.00	.50
☐	6	Pete Suder	5.00	2.00	.50
☐	7	Gene Baker	5.00	2.00	.50
☐	8	Warren Hacker	5.00	2.00	.50
☐	9	Gil McDougald	10.00	4.00	1.00
☐	10	Phil Rizzuto	33.00	13.00	3.00
☐	11	Bill Bruton	6.00	2.40	.60
☐	12	Andy Pafko	6.00	2.40	.60
☐	13	Clyde Vollmer	5.00	2.00	.50
☐	14	Gus Keriazakos	5.00	2.00	.50
☐	15	Frank Sullivan	5.00	2.00	.50
☐	16	Jim Piersall	8.00	3.25	.80
☐	17	Del Ennis	6.00	2.40	.60
☐	18	Stan Lopata	5.00	2.00	.50
☐	19	Bobby Avila	6.00	2.40	.60
☐	20	Al Smith	5.00	2.00	.50
☐	21	Don Hoak	6.00	2.40	.60
☐	22	Roy Campanella	75.00	30.00	7.50
☐	23	Al Kaline	75.00	30.00	7.50
☐	24	Al Aber	5.00	2.00	.50
☐	25	Minnie Minoso	8.00	3.25	.80
☐	26	Virgil Trucks	6.00	2.40	.60
☐	27	Preston Ward	5.00	2.00	.50
☐	28	Dick Cole	5.00	2.00	.50
☐	29	Red Schoendienst	9.00	3.75	.90
☐	30	Bill Sarni	5.00	2.00	.50
☐	31	Johnny Temple	6.00	2.40	.60
☐	32	Wally Post	6.00	2.40	.60
☐	33	Nellie Fox	11.00	4.50	1.10
☐	34	Clint Courtney	5.00	2.00	.50
☐	35	Bill Tuttle	5.00	2.00	.50
☐	36	Wayne Belardi	5.00	2.00	.50
☐	37	Pee Wee Reese	40.00	16.00	4.00
☐	38	Early Wynn	18.00	7.25	1.80
☐	39	Bob Darnell	5.00	2.00	.50
☐	40	Vic Wertz	6.00	2.40	.60
☐	41	Mel Clark	5.00	2.00	.50
☐	42	Bob Greenwood	5.00	2.00	.50
☐	43	Bob Buhl	5.00	2.00	.50
☐	44	Danny O'Connell	5.00	2.00	.50
☐	45	Tom Umphlett	5.00	2.00	.50
☐	46	Mickey Vernon	6.00	2.40	.60
☐	47	Sammy White	5.00	2.00	.50
☐	48A	Milt Bolling ERR	6.00	2.40	.60
		(name on back is Frank Bolling)			
☐	48B	Milt Bolling COR	20.00	8.00	2.00
☐	49	Jim Greengrass	5.00	2.00	.50
☐	50	Hobie Landrith	5.00	2.00	.50
☐	51	Elvin Tappe	5.00	2.00	.50
☐	52	Hal Rice	5.00	2.00	.50
☐	53	Alex Kellner	5.00	2.00	.50
☐	54	Don Bollweg	5.00	2.00	.50
☐	55	Cal Abrams	6.00	2.40	.60
☐	56	Billy Cox	7.00	2.80	.70
☐	57	Bob Friend	6.00	2.40	.60
☐	58	Frank Thomas	6.00	2.40	.60
☐	59	Whitey Ford	40.00	16.00	4.00
☐	60	Enos Slaughter	20.00	8.00	2.00
☐	61	Paul LaPalme	5.00	2.00	.50
☐	62	Royce Lint	5.00	2.00	.50

		NRMT	VG-E	GOOD
☐ 63	Irv Noren	6.00	2.40	.60
☐ 64	Curt Simmons	6.00	2.40	.60
☐ 65	Don Zimmer	10.00	4.00	1.00
☐ 66	George Shuba	6.00	2.40	.60
☐ 67	Don Larsen	11.00	4.50	1.10
☐ 68	Elston Howard	20.00	8.00	2.00
☐ 69	Billy Hunter	5.00	2.00	.50
☐ 70	Lou Burdette	8.00	3.25	.80
☐ 71	Dave Jolly	5.00	2.00	.50
☐ 72	Chet Nichols	5.00	2.00	.50
☐ 73	Eddie Yost	5.00	2.00	.50
☐ 74	Jerry Snyder	5.00	2.00	.50
☐ 75	Brooks Lawrence	5.00	2.00	.50
☐ 76	Tom Poholsky	5.00	2.00	.50
☐ 77	Jim McDonald	5.00	2.00	.50
☐ 78	Gil Coan	5.00	2.00	.50
☐ 79	Willie Miranda	5.00	2.00	.50
☐ 80	Lou Limmer	5.00	2.00	.50
☐ 81	Bobby Morgan	5.00	2.00	.50
☐ 82	Lee Walls	5.00	2.00	.50
☐ 83	Max Surkont	5.00	2.00	.50
☐ 84	George Freese	5.00	2.00	.50
☐ 85	Cass Michaels	5.00	2.00	.50
☐ 86	Ted Gray	5.00	2.00	.50
☐ 87	Randy Jackson	5.00	2.00	.50
☐ 88	Steve Bilko	5.00	2.00	.50
☐ 89	Lou Boudreau MG	18.00	7.25	1.80
☐ 90	Art Ditmar	5.00	2.00	.50
☐ 91	Dick Marlowe	5.00	2.00	.50
☐ 92	George Zuverink	5.00	2.00	.50
☐ 93	Andy Seminick	5.00	2.00	.50
☐ 94	Hank Thompson	6.00	2.40	.60
☐ 95	Sal Maglie	8.00	3.25	.80
☐ 96	Ray Narleski	5.00	2.00	.50
☐ 97	Johnny Podres	10.00	4.00	1.00
☐ 98	Jim Gilliam	9.00	3.75	.90
☐ 99	Jerry Coleman	6.00	2.40	.60
☐ 100	Tom Morgan	5.00	2.00	.50
☐ 101A	Don Johnson ERR	5.00	2.00	.50
	(photo actually Ernie Johnson)			
☐ 101B	Don Johnson COR	15.00	6.00	1.50
☐ 102	Bobby Thomson	7.00	2.80	.70
☐ 103	Eddie Mathews	30.00	12.00	3.00
☐ 104	Bob Porterfield	4.00	1.60	.40
☐ 105	Johnny Schmitz	4.00	1.60	.40
☐ 106	Del Rice	4.00	1.60	.40
☐ 107	Solly Hemus	4.00	1.60	.40
☐ 108	Lou Kretlow	4.00	1.60	.40
☐ 109	Vern Stephens	5.00	2.00	.50
☐ 110	Bob Miller	4.00	1.60	.40
☐ 111	Steve Ridzik	4.00	1.60	.40
☐ 112	Granny Hamner	4.00	1.60	.40
☐ 113	Bob Hall	4.00	1.60	.40
☐ 114	Vic Janowicz	5.00	2.00	.50
☐ 115	Roger Bowman	4.00	1.60	.40
☐ 116	Sandy Consuegra	4.00	1.60	.40
☐ 117	Johnny Groth	4.00	1.60	.40
☐ 118	Bobby Adams	4.00	1.60	.40
☐ 119	Joe Astroth	4.00	1.60	.40
☐ 120	Ed Burtschy	4.00	1.60	.40
☐ 121	Rufus Crawford	4.00	1.60	.40
☐ 122	Al Corwin	4.00	1.60	.40
☐ 123	Marv Grissom	4.00	1.60	.40
☐ 124	Johnny Antonelli	6.00	2.40	.60
☐ 125	Paul Giel	4.00	1.60	.40
☐ 126	Billy Goodman	5.00	2.00	.50
☐ 127	Hank Majeski	4.00	1.60	.40
☐ 128	Mike Garcia	6.00	2.40	.60
☐ 129	Hal Naragon	4.00	1.60	.40
☐ 130	Richie Ashburn	11.00	4.50	1.10
☐ 131	Willard Marshall	4.00	1.60	.40
☐ 132A	Harvey Kueen ERR	7.00	2.80	.70
	(sic, Kuenn)			
☐ 132B	Harvey Kuenn COR	16.00	6.50	1.60
☐ 133	Charles King	4.00	1.60	.40
☐ 134	Bob Feller	40.00	16.00	4.00
☐ 135	Lloyd Merriman	4.00	1.60	.40
☐ 136	Rocky Bridges	4.00	1.60	.40
☐ 137	Bob Talbot	4.00	1.60	.40
☐ 138	Davey Williams	5.00	2.00	.50
☐ 139	Shantz Brothers	6.00	2.40	.60
	Wilmer and Bobby			
☐ 140	Bobby Shantz	6.00	2.40	.60
☐ 141	Wes Westrum	5.00	2.00	.50
☐ 142	Rudy Regalado	4.00	1.60	.40
☐ 143	Don Newcombe	8.00	3.25	.80
☐ 144	Art Houtteman	4.00	1.60	.40
☐ 145	Bob Nieman	4.00	1.60	.40
☐ 146	Don Liddle	4.00	1.60	.40
☐ 147	Sam Mele	4.00	1.60	.40
☐ 148	Bob Chakales	4.00	1.60	.40
☐ 149	Cloyd Boyer	4.00	1.60	.40
☐ 150	Billy Klaus	4.00	1.60	.40
☐ 151	Jim Brideweser	4.00	1.60	.40
☐ 152	Johnny Klippstein	4.00	1.60	.40
☐ 153	Eddie Robinson	4.00	1.60	.40
☐ 154	Frank Lary	6.00	2.40	.60
☐ 155	Jerry Staley	4.00	1.60	.40

		NRMT	VG-E	GOOD
☐ 156	Jim Hughes	4.00	1.60	.40
☐ 157A	Ernie Johnson ERR	5.00	2.00	.50
	(photo actually Don Johnson)			
☐ 157B	Ernie Johnson COR	15.00	6.00	1.50
☐ 158	Gil Hodges	28.00	11.50	2.80
☐ 159	Harry Byrd	5.00	2.00	.50
☐ 160	Bill Skowron	10.00	4.00	1.00
☐ 161	Matt Batts	4.00	1.60	.40
☐ 162	Charlie Maxwell	4.00	1.60	.40
☐ 163	Sid Gordon	4.00	1.60	.40
☐ 164	Toby Atwell	4.00	1.60	.40
☐ 165	Maurice McDermott	4.00	1.60	.40
☐ 166	Jim Busby	4.00	1.60	.40
☐ 167	Bob Grim	6.00	2.40	.60
☐ 168	Yogi Berra	75.00	30.00	7.50
☐ 169	Carl Furillo	10.00	4.00	1.00
☐ 170	Carl Erskine	8.00	3.25	.80
☐ 171	Robin Roberts	18.00	7.25	1.80
☐ 172	Willie Jones	4.00	1.60	.40
☐ 173	Chico Carrasquel	4.00	1.60	.40
☐ 174	Sherm Lollar	5.00	2.00	.50
☐ 175	Wilmer Shantz	4.00	1.60	.40
☐ 176	Joe DeMaestri	4.00	1.60	.40
☐ 177	Willard Nixon	4.00	1.60	.40
☐ 178	Tom Brewer	4.00	1.60	.40
☐ 179	Hank Aaron	160.00	65.00	15.00
☐ 180	Johnny Logan	5.00	2.00	.50
☐ 181	Eddie Miksis	4.00	1.60	.40
☐ 182	Bob Rush	4.00	1.60	.40
☐ 183	Ray Katt	4.00	1.60	.40
☐ 184	Willie Mays	160.00	65.00	15.00
☐ 185	Vic Raschi	7.00	2.80	.70
☐ 186	Alex Grammas	4.00	1.60	.40
☐ 187	Fred Hatfield	4.00	1.60	.40
☐ 188	Ned Garver	4.00	1.60	.40
☐ 189	Jack Collum	4.00	1.60	.40
☐ 190	Fred Baczewski	4.00	1.60	.40
☐ 191	Bob Lemon	18.00	7.25	1.80
☐ 192	George Strickland	4.00	1.60	.40
☐ 193	Howie Judson	4.00	1.60	.40
☐ 194	Joe Nuxhall	5.00	2.00	.50
☐ 195A	Erv Palica	5.00	2.00	.50
	(without trade)			
☐ 195B	Erv Palica	15.00	6.00	1.50
	(with trade)			
☐ 196	Russ Meyer	4.00	1.60	.40
☐ 197	Ralph Kiner	22.00	9.00	2.20
☐ 198	Dave Pope	4.00	1.60	.40
☐ 199	Vernon Law	6.00	2.40	.60
☐ 200	Dick Littlefield	4.00	1.60	.40
☐ 201	Allie Reynolds	11.00	4.50	1.10
☐ 202	Mickey Mantle	375.00	150.00	35.00
☐ 203	Steve Gromek	4.00	1.60	.40
☐ 204A	Frank Bolling ERR	5.00	2.00	.50
	(name on back is Milt Bolling)			
☐ 204B	Frank Bolling COR	15.00	6.00	1.50
☐ 205	Rip Repulski	4.00	1.60	.40
☐ 206	Ralph Beard	4.00	1.60	.40
☐ 207	Frank Shea	4.00	1.60	.40
☐ 208	Ed Fitzgerald	4.00	1.60	.40
☐ 209	Smokey Burgess	5.00	2.00	.50
☐ 210	Earl Torgeson	4.00	1.60	.40
☐ 211	Sonny Dixon	4.00	1.60	.40
☐ 212	Jack Dittmer	4.00	1.60	.40
☐ 213	George Kell	18.00	7.25	1.80
☐ 214	Billy Pierce	6.00	2.40	.60
☐ 215	Bob Kuzava	4.00	1.60	.40
☐ 216	Preacher Roe	7.00	2.80	.70
☐ 217	Del Crandall	5.00	2.00	.50
☐ 218	Joe Adcock	6.00	2.40	.60
☐ 219	Whitey Lockman	5.00	2.00	.50
☐ 220	Jim Hearn	4.00	1.60	.40
☐ 221	Hector Brown	4.00	1.60	.40
☐ 222	Russ Kemmerer	4.00	1.60	.40
☐ 223	Hal Jeffcoat	4.00	1.60	.40
☐ 224	Dee Fondy	4.00	1.60	.40
☐ 225	Paul Richards	12.00	5.00	1.20
☐ 226	W. McKinley UMP	15.00	6.00	1.50
☐ 227	Frank Baumholtz	10.00	4.00	1.00
☐ 228	John Phillips	10.00	4.00	1.00
☐ 229	Jim Brosnan	12.00	5.00	1.20
☐ 230	Al Brazle	10.00	4.00	1.00
☐ 231	Jim Konstanty	12.00	5.00	1.20
☐ 232	Birdie Tebbetts	12.00	5.00	1.20
☐ 233	Bill Serena	10.00	4.00	1.00
☐ 234	Dick Bartell	10.00	4.00	1.00
☐ 235	J. Paparella UMP	15.00	6.00	1.50
☐ 236	Murry Dickson	10.00	4.00	1.00
☐ 237	Johnny Wyrostek	10.00	4.00	1.00
☐ 238	Eddie Stanky	12.00	5.00	1.20
☐ 239	Edwin Rommel UMP	15.00	6.00	1.50
☐ 240	Billy Loes	12.00	5.00	1.20
☐ 241	Johnny Pesky	12.00	5.00	1.20
☐ 242	Ernie Banks	250.00	100.00	25.00
☐ 243	Gus Bell	12.00	5.00	1.20
☐ 244	Duane Pillette	10.00	4.00	1.00
☐ 245	Bill Miller	10.00	4.00	1.00
☐ 246	Hank Bauer	20.00	8.00	2.00

		NRMT	VG-E	GOOD
☐ 247	Dutch Leonard	10.00	4.00	1.00
☐ 248	Harry Dorish	10.00	4.00	1.00
☐ 249	Billy Gardner	12.00	5.00	1.20
☐ 250	Larry Napp UMP	15.00	6.00	1.50
☐ 251	Stan Jok	10.00	4.00	1.00
☐ 252	Roy Smalley	10.00	4.00	1.00
☐ 253	Jim Wilson	10.00	4.00	1.00
☐ 254	Bennett Flowers	10.00	4.00	1.00
☐ 255	Pete Runnels	12.00	5.00	1.20
☐ 256	Owen Friend	10.00	4.00	1.00
☐ 257	Tom Alston	10.00	4.00	1.00
☐ 258	John Stevens UMP	15.00	6.00	1.50
☐ 259	Don Mossi	12.00	5.00	1.20
☐ 260	Edwin Hurley UMP	15.00	6.00	1.50
☐ 261	Walt Moryn	10.00	4.00	1.00
☐ 262	Jim Lemon	12.00	5.00	1.20
☐ 263	Eddie Joost	10.00	4.00	1.00
☐ 264	Bill Henry	10.00	4.00	1.00
☐ 265	Albert Barlick UMP	15.00	6.00	1.50
☐ 266	Mike Fornieles	10.00	4.00	1.00
☐ 267	Jim Honochick UMP	40.00	16.00	4.00
☐ 268	Roy Lee Hawes	10.00	4.00	1.00
☐ 269	Joe Amalfitano	10.00	4.00	1.00
☐ 270	Chico Fernandez	10.00	4.00	1.00
☐ 271	Bob Hooper	10.00	4.00	1.00
☐ 272	John Flaherty UMP	15.00	6.00	1.50
☐ 273	Bubba Church	10.00	4.00	1.00
☐ 274	Jim Delsing	10.00	4.00	1.00
☐ 275	William Grieve UMP	15.00	6.00	1.50
☐ 276	Ike Delock	10.00	4.00	1.00
☐ 277	Ed Runge UMP	15.00	6.00	1.50
☐ 278	Charlie Neal	15.00	6.00	1.50
☐ 279	Hank Soar UMP	15.00	6.00	1.50
☐ 280	Clyde McCullough	10.00	4.00	1.00
☐ 281	Charles Berry UMP	15.00	6.00	1.50
☐ 282	Phil Cavarretta	12.00	5.00	1.20
☐ 283	Nestor Chylak UMP	15.00	6.00	1.50
☐ 284	Bill Jackowski UMP	15.00	6.00	1.50
☐ 285	Walt Dropo	12.00	5.00	1.20
☐ 286	Frank Secory UMP	15.00	6.00	1.50
☐ 287	Ron Mrozinski	10.00	4.00	1.00
☐ 288	Dick Smith	10.00	4.00	1.00
☐ 289	Arthur Gore UMP	15.00	6.00	1.50
☐ 290	Hershell Freeman	10.00	4.00	1.00
☐ 291	Frank Dascoli UMP	15.00	6.00	1.50
☐ 292	Marv Blaylock	10.00	4.00	1.00
☐ 293	Thomas Gorman UMP	15.00	6.00	1.50
☐ 294	Wally Moses	12.00	5.00	1.20
☐ 295	Lee Ballanfant UMP	15.00	6.00	1.50

		NRMT	VG-E	GOOD
☐ 296	Bill Virdon	30.00	12.00	3.00
☐ 297	Dusty Boggess UMP	15.00	6.00	1.50
☐ 298	Charlie Grimm	12.00	5.00	1.20
☐ 299	Lon Warneke UMP	15.00	6.00	1.50
☐ 300	Tommy Byrne	12.00	5.00	1.20
☐ 301	William Engeln UMP	15.00	6.00	1.50
☐ 302	Frank Malzone	16.00	6.50	1.60
☐ 303	Jocko Conlan UMP	45.00	18.00	4.50
☐ 304	Harry Chiti	10.00	4.00	1.00
☐ 305	Frank Umont UMP	15.00	6.00	1.50
☐ 306	Bob Cerv	15.00	6.00	1.50
☐ 307	Babe Pinelli UMP	15.00	6.00	1.50
☐ 308	Al Lopez MG	35.00	14.00	3.50
☐ 309	Hal Dixon UMP	15.00	6.00	1.50
☐ 310	Ken Lehman	10.00	4.00	1.00
☐ 311	Lawrence Goetz UMP	15.00	6.00	1.50
☐ 312	Bill Wight	10.00	4.00	1.00
☐ 313	Augie Donatelli UMP	20.00	8.00	2.00
☐ 314	Dale Mitchell	12.00	5.00	1.20
☐ 315	Cal Hubbard UMP	45.00	18.00	4.50
☐ 316	Marion Fricano	10.00	4.00	1.00
☐ 317	William Summers UMP	15.00	6.00	1.50
☐ 318	Sid Hudson	10.00	4.00	1.00
☐ 319	Al Schroll	10.00	4.00	1.00
☐ 320	George Susce Jr.	20.00	8.00	1.00

1981 Donruss

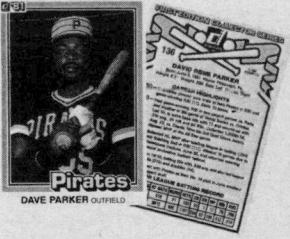

DAVE PARKER OUTFIELD

*The cards in this 605-card set measure 2 ½"
by 3 ½". In 1981 Donruss launched itself into
the baseball card market with a set containing 600 numbered cards and five unnumbered checklists. Even though the five*

checklist cards are unnumbered, they are numbered below (601-605) for convenience in reference. The cards are printed on thin stock and more than one pose exists for several popular players. The numerous errors of the first print run were later corrected by the company. These are marked P1 and P2 in the checklist below.

	MINT	EXC	G-VG
Complete Set (P1)	28.00	11.50	2.80
Complete Set (P2)	24.00	10.00	2.40
Common Player (1-605)	.03	.01	.00

		MINT	EXC	G-VG
☐	1 Ozzie Smith	.50	.10	.02
☐	2 Rollie Fingers	.30	.12	.03
☐	3 Rick Wise	.03	.01	.00
☐	4 Gene Richards	.03	.01	.00
☐	5 Alan Trammell	.45	.18	.04
☐	6 Tom Brookens	.03	.01	.00
☐	7A Duffy Dyer P1	.10	.04	.01
	1980 batting average has decimal point			
☐	7B Duffy Dyer P2	.06	.02	.00
	1980 batting average has no decimal point			
☐	8 Mark Fidrych	.10	.04	.01
☐	9 Dave Rozema	.03	.01	.00
☐	10 Ricky Peters	.03	.01	.00
☐	11 Mike Schmidt	1.00	.40	.10
☐	12 Willie Stargell	.35	.14	.03
☐	13 Tim Foli	.03	.01	.00
☐	14 Manny Sanguillen	.06	.02	.00
☐	15 Grant Jackson	.03	.01	.00
☐	16 Eddie Solomon	.03	.01	.00
☐	17 Omar Moreno	.03	.01	.00
☐	18 Joe Morgan	.30	.12	.03
☐	19 Rafael Landestoy	.03	.01	.00
☐	20 Bruce Bochy	.03	.01	.00
☐	21 Joe Sambito	.03	.01	.00
☐	22 Manny Trillo	.03	.01	.00
☐	23A Dave Smith P1	.35	.14	.03
	Line box around stats is not complete			
☐	23B Dave Smith P2	.35	.14	.03
	Box totally encloses stats at top			
☐	24 Terry Puhl	.06	.02	.00
☐	25 Bump Wills	.03	.01	.00
☐	26A John Ellis P1 ERR	.60	.24	.06
	Photo on front shows Danny Walton			
☐	26B John Ellis P2 COR	.10	.04	.01
☐	27 Jim Kern	.03	.01	.00
☐	28 Richie Zisk	.06	.02	.00
☐	29 John Mayberry	.06	.02	.00
☐	30 Bob Davis	.03	.01	.00
☐	31 Jackson Todd	.03	.01	.00
☐	32 Alvis Woods	.03	.01	.00
☐	33 Steve Carlton	.60	.24	.06
☐	34 Lee Mazzilli	.03	.01	.00
☐	35 John Stearns	.03	.01	.00
☐	36 Roy Lee Jackson	.03	.01	.00
☐	37 Mike Scott	.60	.24	.06
☐	38 Lamar Johnson	.03	.01	.00
☐	39 Kevin Bell	.03	.01	.00
☐	40 Ed Farmer	.03	.01	.00
☐	41 Ross Baumgarten	.03	.01	.00
☐	42 Leo Sutherland	.03	.01	.00
☐	43 Dan Meyer	.03	.01	.00
☐	44 Ron Reed	.03	.01	.00
☐	45 Mario Mendoza	.03	.01	.00
☐	46 Rick Honeycutt	.03	.01	.00
☐	47 Glenn Abbott	.03	.01	.00
☐	48 Leon Roberts	.03	.01	.00
☐	49 Rod Carew	.60	.24	.06
☐	50 Bert Campaneris	.06	.02	.00
☐	51A Tom Donahue P1 ERR	.15	.06	.01
	Name on front misspelled Donahue			
☐	51B Tom Donohue P2 COR	.10	.04	.01
☐	52 Dave Frost	.03	.01	.00
☐	53 Ed Halicki	.03	.01	.00
☐	54 Dan Ford	.03	.01	.00
☐	55 Garry Maddox	.06	.02	.00
☐	56A Steve Garvey P1	1.25	.50	.12
	"Surpassed 25 HR"			
☐	56B Steve Garvey P2	.60	.24	.06
	"Surpassed 21 HR"			
☐	57 Bill Russell	.06	.02	.00
☐	58 Don Sutton	.30	.12	.03
☐	59 Reggie Smith	.10	.04	.01
☐	60 Rick Monday	.06	.02	.00
☐	61 Ray Knight	.10	.04	.01
☐	62 Johnny Bench	.65	.26	.06
☐	63 Mario Soto	.10	.04	.01
☐	64 Doug Bair	.03	.01	.00

		MINT	EXC	G-VG
☐ 65	George Foster	.20	.08	.02
☐ 66	Jeff Burroughs	.06	.02	.00
☐ 67	Keith Hernandez	.35	.14	.03
☐ 68	Tom Herr	.15	.06	.01
☐ 69	Bob Forsch	.06	.02	.00
☐ 70	John Fulgham	.03	.01	.00
☐ 71A	Bobby Bonds P1 ERR 986 lifetime HR	.30	.12	.03
☐ 71B	Bobby Bonds P2 COR 326 lifetime HR	.10	.04	.01
☐ 72A	Rennie Stennett P1 . "breaking broke leg"	.10	.04	.01
☐ 72B	Rennie Stennett P2 . Word "broke" deleted	.06	.02	.00
☐ 73	Joe Strain	.03	.01	.00
☐ 74	Ed Whitson	.06	.02	.00
☐ 75	Tom Griffin	.03	.01	.00
☐ 76	Billy North	.03	.01	.00
☐ 77	Gene Garber	.03	.01	.00
☐ 78	Mike Hargrove	.03	.01	.00
☐ 79	Dave Rosello	.03	.01	.00
☐ 80	Ron Hassey	.06	.02	.00
☐ 81	Sid Monge	.03	.01	.00
☐ 82A	Joe Charboneau P1 '78 highlights, "For some reason"	.15	.06	.01
☐ 82B	Joe Charboneau P2 phrase "For some reason" deleted	.10	.04	.01
☐ 83	Cecil Cooper	.15	.06	.01
☐ 84	Sal Bando	.06	.02	.00
☐ 85	Moose Haas	.06	.02	.00
☐ 86	Mike Caldwell	.03	.01	.00
☐ 87A	Larry Hisle P1 '77 highlights, llne ends with "28 RBI"	.15	.06	.01
☐ 87B	Larry Hisle P2 correct line "28 HR"	.10	.04	.01
☐ 88	Luis Gomez	.03	.01	.00
☐ 89	Larry Parrish	.06	.02	.00
☐ 90	Gary Carter	.60	.24	.06
☐ 91	Bill Gullickson	.25	.10	.02
☐ 92	Fred Norman	.03	.01	.00
☐ 93	Tommy Hutton	.03	.01	.00
☐ 94	Carl Yastrzemski	1.00	.40	.10
☐ 95	Glenn Hoffman	.03	.01	.00
☐ 96	Dennis Eckersley	.20	.08	.02
☐ 97A	Tom Burgmeier P1 ERR Throws: Right	.10	.04	.01
☐ 97B	Tom Burgmeier P2 COR Throws: Left	.06	.02	.00
☐ 98	Win Remmerswaal	.03	.01	.00
☐ 99	Bob Horner	.20	.08	.02
☐ 100	George Brett	.80	.32	.08
☐ 101	Dave Chalk	.03	.01	.00
☐ 102	Dennis Leonard	.06	.02	.00
☐ 103	Renie Martin	.03	.01	.00
☐ 104	Amos Otis	.10	.04	.01
☐ 105	Graig Nettles	.15	.06	.01
☐ 106	Eric Soderholm	.03	.01	.00
☐ 107	Tommy John	.20	.08	.02
☐ 108	Tom Underwood	.03	.01	.00
☐ 109	Lou Piniella	.10	.04	.01
☐ 110	Mickey Klutts	.03	.01	.00
☐ 111	Bobby Murcer	.10	.04	.01
☐ 112	Eddie Murray	.80	.32	.08
☐ 113	Rick Dempsey	.06	.02	.00
☐ 114	Scott McGregor	.06	.02	.00
☐ 115	Ken Singleton	.10	.04	.01
☐ 116	Gary Roenicke	.03	.01	.00
☐ 117	Dave Revering	.03	.01	.00
☐ 118	Mike Norris	.03	.01	.00
☐ 119	Rickey Henderson	1.75	.70	.17
☐ 120	Mike Heath	.03	.01	.00
☐ 121	Dave Cash	.03	.01	.00
☐ 122	Randy Jones	.03	.01	.00
☐ 123	Eric Rasmussen	.03	.01	.00
☐ 124	Jerry Mumphrey	.03	.01	.00
☐ 125	Richie Hebner	.03	.01	.00
☐ 126	Mark Wagner	.03	.01	.00
☐ 127	Jack Morris	.30	.12	.03
☐ 128	Dan Petry	.10	.04	.01
☐ 129	Bruce Robbins	.03	.01	.00
☐ 130	Champ Summers	.03	.01	.00
☐ 131A	Pete Rose P1 last line ends with "see card 251"	2.00	.80	.20
☐ 131B	Pete Rose P2 last line corrected "see card 371"	1.25	.50	.12
☐ 132	Willie Stargell	.35	.14	.03
☐ 133	Ed Ott	.03	.01	.00
☐ 134	Jim Bibby	.03	.01	.00
☐ 135	Bert Blyleven	.15	.06	.01
☐ 136	Dave Parker	.30	.12	.03
☐ 137	Bill Robinson	.06	.02	.00
☐ 138	Enos Cabell	.03	.01	.00
☐ 139	Dave Bergman	.03	.01	.00

		MINT	EXC	G-VG
☐ 140	J.R. Richard	.10	.04	.01
☐ 141	Ken Forsch	.03	.01	.00
☐ 142	Larry Bowa	.15	.06	.01
☐ 143	Frank LaCorte	.03	.01	.00
	(photo actually Randy Niemann)			
☐ 144	Denny Walling	.03	.01	.00
☐ 145	Buddy Bell	.15	.06	.01
☐ 146	Ferguson Jenkins	.18	.08	.01
☐ 147	Dannny Darwin	.03	.01	.00
☐ 148	John Grubb	.03	.01	.00
☐ 149	Alfredo Griffin	.10	.04	.01
☐ 150	Jerry Garvin	.03	.01	.00
☐ 151	Paul Mirabella	.03	.01	.00
☐ 152	Rick Bosetti	.03	.01	.00
☐ 153	Dick Ruthven	.03	.01	.00
☐ 154	Frank Taveras	.03	.01	.00
☐ 155	Craig Swan	.03	.01	.00
☐ 156	Jeff Reardon	.60	.24	.06
☐ 157	Steve Henderson	.03	.01	.00
☐ 158	Jim Morrison	.03	.01	.00
☐ 159	Glenn Borgmann	.03	.01	.00
☐ 160	LaMarr Hoyt	.25	.10	.02
☐ 161	Rich Wortham	.03	.01	.00
☐ 162	Thad Bosley	.03	.01	.00
☐ 163	Julio Cruz	.03	.01	.00
☐ 164A	Del Unser P1	.10	.04	.01
	no "3B" heading			
☐ 164B	Del Unser P2	.06	.02	.00
	Batting record on back			
	corrected ("3B")			
☐ 165	Jim Anderson	.03	.01	.00
☐ 166	Jim Beattie	.03	.01	.00
☐ 167	Shane Rawley	.10	.04	.01
☐ 168	Joe Simpson	.03	.01	.00
☐ 169	Rod Carew	.60	.24	.06
☐ 170	Fred Patek	.06	.02	.00
☐ 171	Frank Tanana	.10	.04	.01
☐ 172	Alfredo Martinez	.03	.01	.00
☐ 173	Chris Knapp	.03	.01	.00
☐ 174	Joe Rudi	.06	.02	.00
☐ 175	Greg Luzinski	.15	.06	.01
☐ 176	Steve Garvey	.65	.26	.06
☐ 177	Joe Ferguson	.03	.01	.00
☐ 178	Bob Welch	.15	.06	.01
☐ 179	Dusty Baker	.10	.04	.01
☐ 180	Rudy Law	.03	.01	.00
☐ 181	Dave Concepcion	.15	.06	.01
☐ 182	Johnny Bench	.65	.26	.06
☐ 183	Mike LaCoss	.03	.01	.00
☐ 184	Ken Griffey	.10	.04	.01
☐ 185	Dave Collins	.03	.01	.00
☐ 186	Brian Asselstine	.03	.01	.00
☐ 187	Garry Templeton	.10	.04	.01
☐ 188	Mike Phillips	.03	.01	.00
☐ 189	Pete Vuckovich	.06	.02	.00
☐ 190	John Urrea	.03	.01	.00
☐ 191	Tony Scott	.03	.01	.00
☐ 192	Darrell Evans	.15	.06	.01
☐ 193	Milt May	.03	.01	.00
☐ 194	Bob Knepper	.10	.04	.01
☐ 195	Randy Moffitt	.03	.01	.00
☐ 196	Larry Herndon	.03	.01	.00
☐ 197	Rick Camp	.03	.01	.00
☐ 198	Andre Thornton	.06	.02	.00
☐ 199	Tom Veryzer	.03	.01	.00
☐ 200	Gary Alexander	.03	.01	.00
☐ 201	Rick Waits	.03	.01	.00
☐ 202	Rick Manning	.03	.01	.00
☐ 203	Paul Molitor	.25	.10	.02
☐ 204	Jim Gantner	.03	.01	.00
☐ 205	Paul Mitchell	.03	.01	.00
☐ 206	Reggie Cleveland	.03	.01	.00
☐ 207	Sixto Lezcano	.03	.01	.00
☐ 208	Bruce Benedict	.03	.01	.00
☐ 209	Rodney Scott	.03	.01	.00
☐ 210	John Tamargo	.03	.01	.00
☐ 211	Bill Lee	.06	.02	.00
☐ 212	Andre Dawson	.40	.16	.04
☐ 213	Rowland Office	.03	.01	.00
☐ 214	Carl Yastrzemski	1.00	.40	.10
☐ 215	Jerry Remy	.03	.01	.00
☐ 216	Mike Torrez	.06	.02	.00
☐ 217	Skip Lockwood	.03	.01	.00
☐ 218	Fred Lynn	.20	.08	.02
☐ 219	Chris Chambliss	.10	.04	.01
☐ 220	Willie Aikens	.03	.01	.00
☐ 221	John Wathan	.10	.04	.01
☐ 222	Dan Quisenberry	.15	.06	.01
☐ 223	Willie Wilson	.15	.06	.01
☐ 224	Clint Hurdle	.03	.01	.00
☐ 225	Bob Watson	.06	.02	.00
☐ 226	Jim Spencer	.03	.01	.00
☐ 227	Ron Guidry	.20	.08	.02
☐ 228	Reggie Jackson	.85	.34	.08
☐ 229	Oscar Gamble	.06	.02	.00
☐ 230	Jeff Cox	.03	.01	.00
☐ 231	Luis Tiant	.10	.04	.01
☐ 232	Rich Dauer	.03	.01	.00

		MINT	EXC	G-VG
☐ 233	Dan Graham	.03	.01	.00
☐ 234	Mike Flanagan	.10	.04	.01
☐ 235	John Lowenstein	.03	.01	.00
☐ 236	Benny Ayala	.03	.01	.00
☐ 237	Wayne Gross	.03	.01	.00
☐ 238	Rick Langford	.03	.01	.00
☐ 239	Tony Armas	.10	.04	.01
☐ 240A	Bob Lacy P1 ERR	.30	.12	.03
	Name misspelled			
	Bob "Lacy"			
☐ 240B	Bob Lacey P2 COR	.10	.04	.01
☐ 241	Gene Tenace	.06	.02	.00
☐ 242	Bob Shirley	.03	.01	.00
☐ 243	Gary Lucas	.06	.02	.00
☐ 244	Jerry Turner	.03	.01	.00
☐ 245	John Wockenfuss	.03	.01	.00
☐ 246	Stan Papi	.03	.01	.00
☐ 247	Milt Wilcox	.03	.01	.00
☐ 248	Dan Schatzeder	.03	.01	.00
☐ 249	Steve Kemp	.10	.04	.01
☐ 250	Jim Lentine	.03	.01	.00
☐ 251	Pete Rose	1.25	.50	.12
☐ 252	Bill Madlock	.15	.06	.01
☐ 253	Dale Berra	.03	.01	.00
☐ 254	Kent Tekulve	.06	.02	.00
☐ 255	Enrique Romo	.03	.01	.00
☐ 256	Mike Easler	.06	.02	.00
☐ 257	Chuck Tanner MG	.06	.02	.00
☐ 258	Art Howe	.10	.04	.01
☐ 259	Alan Ashby	.06	.02	.00
☐ 260	Nolan Ryan	.60	.24	.06
☐ 261A	Vern Ruhle P1 ERR	.60	.24	.06
	Photo on front			
	actually Ken Forsch			
☐ 261B	Vern Ruhle P2 COR	.10	.04	.01
☐ 262	Bob Boone	.15	.06	.01
☐ 263	Cesar Cedeno	.10	.04	.01
☐ 264	Jeff Leonard	.15	.06	.01
☐ 265	Pat Putnam	.03	.01	.00
☐ 266	Jon Matlack	.03	.01	.00
☐ 267	Dave Rajsich	.03	.01	.00
☐ 268	Billy Sample	.03	.01	.00
☐ 269	Damaso Garcia	.10	.04	.01
☐ 270	Tom Buskey	.03	.01	.00
☐ 271	Joey McLaughlin	.03	.01	.00
☐ 272	Barry Bonnell	.03	.01	.00
☐ 273	Tug McGraw	.10	.04	.01
☐ 274	Mike Jorgensen	.03	.01	.00
☐ 275	Pat Zachry	.03	.01	.00
☐ 276	Neil Allen	.06	.02	.00
☐ 277	Joel Youngblood	.03	.01	.00
☐ 278	Greg Pryor	.03	.01	.00
☐ 279	Britt Burns	.20	.08	.02
☐ 280	Rich Dotson	.45	.18	.04
☐ 281	Chet Lemon	.06	.02	.00
☐ 282	Rusty Kuntz	.03	.01	.00
☐ 283	Ted Cox	.03	.01	.00
☐ 284	Sparky Lyle	.10	.04	.01
☐ 285	Larry Cox	.03	.01	.00
☐ 286	Floyd Bannister	.06	.02	.00
☐ 287	Byron McLaughlin	.03	.01	.00
☐ 288	Rodney Craig	.03	.01	.00
☐ 289	Bobby Grich	.10	.04	.01
☐ 290	Dickie Thon	.10	.04	.01
☐ 291	Mark Clear	.06	.02	.00
☐ 292	Dave Lemanczyk	.03	.01	.00
☐ 293	Jason Thompson	.03	.01	.00
☐ 294	Rick Miller	.03	.01	.00
☐ 295	Lonnie Smith	.06	.02	.00
☐ 296	Ron Cey	.10	.04	.01
☐ 297	Steve Yeager	.03	.01	.00
☐ 298	Bobby Castillo	.03	.01	.00
☐ 299	Manny Mota	.06	.02	.00
☐ 300	Jay Johnstone	.06	.02	.00
☐ 301	Dan Driessen	.03	.01	.00
☐ 302	Joe Nolan	.03	.01	.00
☐ 303	Paul Householder	.03	.01	.00
☐ 304	Harry Spilman	.03	.01	.00
☐ 305	Cesar Geronimo	.03	.01	.00
☐ 306A	Gary Mathews P1 ERR	.30	.12	.03
	Name misspelled			
☐ 306B	Gary Matthews P2 COR	.10	.04	.01
☐ 307	Ken Roitz	.03	.01	.00
☐ 308	Ted Simmons	.15	.06	.01
☐ 309	John Littlefield	.03	.01	.00
☐ 310	George Frazier	.03	.01	.00
☐ 311	Dane Iorg	.03	.01	.00
☐ 312	Mike Ivie	.03	.01	.00
☐ 313	Dennis Littlejohn	.03	.01	.00
☐ 314	Gary Lavelle	.03	.01	.00
☐ 315	Jack Clark	.30	.12	.03
☐ 316	Jim Wohlford	.03	.01	.00
☐ 317	Rick Matula	.03	.01	.00
☐ 318	Toby Harrah	.06	.02	.00
☐ 319A	Dwane Kuiper P1 ERR	.15	.06	.01
	Name misspelled			
☐ 319B	Duane Kuiper P2 COR	.10	.04	.01

	MINT	EXC	G-VG		MINT	EXC	G-VG
☐ 320 Len Barker	.03	.01	.00	☐ 358 Matt Keough	.03	.01	.00
☐ 321 Victor Cruz	.03	.01	.00	☐ 359 Dwayne Murphy	.03	.01	.00
☐ 322 Dell Alston	.03	.01	.00	☐ 360 Brian Kingman	.03	.01	.00
☐ 323 Robin Yount	.40	.16	.04	☐ 361 Bill Fahey	.03	.01	.00
☐ 324 Charlie Moore	.03	.01	.00	☐ 362 Steve Mura	.03	.01	.00
☐ 325 Lary Sorensen	.03	.01	.00	☐ 363 Dennis Kinney	.03	.01	.00
☐ 326A Gorman Thomas P1	.30	.12	.03	☐ 364 Dave Winfield	.50	.20	.05
2nd line on back:				☐ 365 Lou Whitaker	.25	.10	.02
"30 HR mark 4th"				☐ 366 Lance Parrish	.30	.14	.03
☐ 326B Gorman Thomas P2	.10	.04	.01	☐ 367 Tim Corcoran	.03	.01	.00
"30 HR mark 3rd"				☐ 368 Pat Underwood	.03	.01	.00
☐ 327 Bob Rodgers MG	.06	.02	.00	☐ 369 Al Cowens	.03	.01	.00
☐ 328 Phil Niekro	.30	.12	.03	☐ 370 Sparky Anderson MG	.06	.02	.00
☐ 329 Chris Speier	.03	.01	.00	☐ 371 Pete Rose	1.25	.50	.12
☐ 330A Steve Rodgers P1	.30	.12	.03	☐ 372 Phil Garner	.03	.01	.00
ERR Name misspelled				☐ 373 Steve Nicosia	.03	.01	.00
☐ 330B Steve Rogers P2 COR	.10	.04	.01	☐ 374 John Candelaria	.10	.04	.01
☐ 331 Woodie Fryman	.03	.01	.00	☐ 375 Don Robinson	.06	.02	.00
☐ 332 Warren Cromartie	.03	.01	.00	☐ 376 Lee Lacy	.03	.01	.00
☐ 333 Jerry White	.03	.01	.00	☐ 377 John Milner	.03	.01	.00
☐ 334 Tony Perez	.20	.08	.02	☐ 378 Craig Reynolds	.03	.01	.00
☐ 335 Carlton Fisk	.20	.08	.02	☐ 379A Luis Pujols P1 ERR	.15	.06	.01
☐ 336 Dick Drago	.03	.01	.00	Name misspelled			
☐ 337 Steve Renko	.03	.01	.00	☐ 379B Luis Pujols P2 COR	.06	.02	.00
☐ 338 Jim Rice	.30	.12	.03	☐ 380 Joe Niekro	.10	.04	.01
☐ 339 Jerry Royster	.03	.01	.00	☐ 381 Joaquin Andujar	.10	.04	.01
☐ 340 Frank White	.10	.04	.01	☐ 382 Keith Moreland	.35	.14	.03
☐ 341 Jamie Quirk	.03	.01	.00	☐ 383 Jose Cruz	.10	.04	.01
☐ 342A Paul Spittorff P1 ERR	.15	.06	.01	☐ 384 Bill Virdon MG	.06	.02	.00
Name misspelled				☐ 385 Jim Sundberg	.06	.02	.00
☐ 342B Paul Splittorff	.10	.04	.01	☐ 386 Doc Medich	.03	.01	.00
P2 COR				☐ 387 Al Oliver	.12	.06	.01
☐ 343 Marty Pattin	.03	.01	.00	☐ 388 Jim Norris	.03	.01	.00
☐ 344 Pete LaCock	.03	.01	.00	☐ 389 Bob Bailor	.03	.01	.00
☐ 345 Willie Randolph	.10	.04	.01	☐ 390 Ernie Whitt	.06	.02	.00
☐ 346 Rick Cerone	.03	.01	.00	☐ 391 Otto Velez	.03	.01	.00
☐ 347 Rich Gossage	.15	.06	.01	☐ 392 Roy Howell	.03	.01	.00
☐ 348 Reggie Jackson	.85	.34	.08	☐ 393 Bob Walk	.30	.12	.03
☐ 349 Ruppert Jones	.03	.01	.00	☐ 394 Doug Flynn	.03	.01	.00
☐ 350 Dave McKay	.03	.01	.00	☐ 395 Pete Falcone	.03	.01	.00
☐ 351 Yogi Berra CO	.20	.08	.02	☐ 396 Tom Hausman	.03	.01	.00
☐ 352 Doug DeCinces	.06	.02	.00	☐ 397 Elliott Maddox	.03	.01	.00
☐ 353 Jim Palmer	.40	.16	.04	☐ 398 Mike Squires	.03	.01	.00
☐ 354 Tippy Martinez	.03	.01	.00	☐ 399 Marvis Foley	.03	.01	.00
☐ 355 Al Bumbry	.03	.01	.00	☐ 400 Steve Trout	.06	.02	.00
☐ 356 Earl Weaver MG	.10	.04	.01	☐ 401 Wayne Nordhagen	.03	.01	.00
☐ 357A Bob Picciolo P1 ERR	.15	.06	.01	☐ 402 Tony LaRussa MG	.06	.02	.00
Name misspelled				☐ 403 Bruce Bochte	.03	.01	.00
☐ 357B Rob Picciolo P2 COR	.06	.02	.00	☐ 404 Bake McBride	.03	.01	.00

		MINT	EXC	G-VG
☐ 405	Jerry Narron	.03	.01	.00
☐ 406	Rob Dressler	.03	.01	.00
☐ 407	Dave Heaverlo	.03	.01	.00
☐ 408	Tom Paciorek	.03	.01	.00
☐ 409	Carney Lansford	.15	.06	.01
☐ 410	Brian Downing	.06	.02	.00
☐ 411	Don Aase	.03	.01	.00
☐ 412	Jim Barr	.03	.01	.00
☐ 413	Don Baylor	.15	.06	.01
☐ 414	Jim Fregosi	.06	.02	.00
☐ 415	Dallas Green MG	.10	.04	.01
☐ 416	Dave Lopes	.10	.04	.01
☐ 417	Jerry Reuss	.06	.02	.00
☐ 418	Rick Sutcliffe	.25	.10	.02
☐ 419	Derrel Thomas	.03	.01	.00
☐ 420	Tom Lasorda MG	.10	.04	.01
☐ 421	Charles Leibrandt	.35	.14	.03
☐ 422	Tom Seaver	.50	.20	.05
☐ 423	Ron Oester	.06	.02	.00
☐ 424	Junior Kennedy	.03	.01	.00
☐ 425	Tom Seaver	.50	.20	.05
☐ 426	Bobby Cox MG	.03	.01	.00
☐ 427	Leon Durham	.35	.14	.03
☐ 428	Terry Kennedy	.06	.02	.00
☐ 429	Silvio Martinez	.03	.01	.00
☐ 430	George Hendrick	.06	.02	.00
☐ 431	Red Schoendienst MG	.06	.02	.00
☐ 432	Johnnie LeMaster	.03	.01	.00
☐ 433	Vida Blue	.10	.04	.01
☐ 434	John Montefusco	.06	.02	.00
☐ 435	Terry Whitfield	.03	.01	.00
☐ 436	Dave Bristol MG	.03	.01	.00
☐ 437	Dale Murphy	1.25	.50	.12
☐ 438	Jerry Dybzinski	.03	.01	.00
☐ 439	Jorge Orta	.03	.01	.00
☐ 440	Wayne Garland	.03	.01	.00
☐ 441	Miguel Dilone	.03	.01	.00
☐ 442	Dave Garcia MG	.03	.01	.00
☐ 443	Don Money	.03	.01	.00
☐ 444A	Buck Martinez P1 ERR (reverse negative)	.15	.06	.01
☐ 444B	Buck Martinez P2 COR	.06	.02	.00
☐ 445	Jerry Augustine	.03	.01	.00
☐ 446	Ben Oglivie	.06	.02	.00
☐ 447	Jim Slaton	.03	.01	.00
☐ 448	Doyle Alexander	.10	.04	.01
☐ 449	Tony Bernazard	.06	.02	.00
☐ 450	Scott Sanderson	.06	.02	.00
☐ 451	David Palmer	.06	.02	.00
☐ 452	Stan Bahnsen	.03	.01	.00
☐ 453	Dick Williams MG	.06	.02	.00
☐ 454	Rick Burleson	.06	.02	.00
☐ 455	Gary Allenson	.03	.01	.00
☐ 456	Bob Stanley	.03	.01	.00
☐ 457A	John Tudor P1 ERR lifetime W-L "9.7"	1.25	.50	.12
☐ 457B	John Tudor P2 COR corrected "9-7"	1.00	.40	.10
☐ 458	Dwight Evans	.25	.10	.02
☐ 459	Glenn Hubbard	.03	.01	.00
☐ 460	U.L. Washington	.03	.01	.00
☐ 461	Larry Gura	.03	.01	.00
☐ 462	Rich Gale	.03	.01	.00
☐ 463	Hal McRae	.06	.02	.00
☐ 464	Jim Frey MG	.03	.01	.00
☐ 465	Bucky Dent	.10	.04	.01
☐ 466	Dennis Werth	.03	.01	.00
☐ 467	Ron Davis	.03	.01	.00
☐ 468	Reggie Jackson	.85	.34	.08
☐ 469	Bobby Brown	.03	.01	.00
☐ 470	Mike Davis	.30	.12	.03
☐ 471	Gaylord Perry	.30	.12	.03
☐ 472	Mark Belanger	.06	.02	.00
☐ 473	Jim Palmer	.40	.16	.04
☐ 474	Sammy Stewart	.03	.01	.00
☐ 475	Tim Stoddard	.03	.01	.00
☐ 476	Steve Stone	.06	.02	.00
☐ 477	Jeff Newman	.03	.01	.00
☐ 478	Steve McCatty	.03	.01	.00
☐ 479	Billy Martin MG	.15	.06	.01
☐ 480	Mitchell Page	.03	.01	.00
☐ 481	Cy Young Winner 1980 Steve Carlton	.30	.12	.03
☐ 482	Bill Buckner	.15	.06	.01
☐ 483A	Ivan DeJesus P1 ERR lifetime hits "702"	.10	.04	.01
☐ 483B	Ivan DeJesus P2 COR lifetime hits "642"	.06	.02	.00
☐ 484	Cliff Johnson	.03	.01	.00
☐ 485	Lenny Randle	.03	.01	.00
☐ 486	Larry Milbourne	.03	.01	.00
☐ 487	Roy Smalley	.03	.01	.00
☐ 488	John Castino	.03	.01	.00
☐ 489	Ron Jackson	.03	.01	.00
☐ 490A	Dave Roberts P1 Career Highlights: "Showed pop in"	.10	.04	.01

		MINT	EXC	G-VG
☐ 490B	Dave Roberts P2 ..	.06	.02	.00
	"Declared himself"			
☐ 491	MVP: George Brett .	.50	.20	.05
☐ 492	Mike Cubbage	.03	.01	.00
☐ 493	Rob Wilfong	.03	.01	.00
☐ 494	Danny Goodwin ...	.03	.01	.00
☐ 495	Jose Morales	.03	.01	.00
☐ 496	Mickey Rivers	.06	.02	.00
☐ 497	Mike Edwards	.03	.01	.00
☐ 498	Mike Sadek	.03	.01	.00
☐ 499	Lenn Sakata	.03	.01	.00
☐ 500	Gene Michael MG ..	.03	.01	.00
☐ 501	Dave Roberts	.03	.01	.00
☐ 502	Steve Dillard	.03	.01	.00
☐ 503	Jim Essian	.03	.01	.00
☐ 504	Rance Mulliniks	.03	.01	.00
☐ 505	Darrell Porter	.03	.01	.00
☐ 506	Joe Torre MG	.10	.04	.01
☐ 507	Terry Crowley	.03	.01	.00
☐ 508	Bill Travers	.03	.01	.00
☐ 509	Nelson Norman	.03	.01	.00
☐ 510	Bob McClure	.03	.01	.00
☐ 511	Steve Howe	.10	.04	.01
☐ 512	Dave Rader	.03	.01	.00
☐ 513	Mick Kelleher	.03	.01	.00
☐ 514	Kiko Garcia	.03	.01	.00
☐ 515	Larry Biittner	.03	.01	.00
☐ 516A	Willie Norwood P1 ..	.10	.04	.01
	Career Highlights			
	"Spent most of"			
☐ 516B	Willie Norwood P2 ..	.06	.02	.00
	"Traded to Seattle"			
☐ 517	Bo Diaz	.06	.02	.00
☐ 518	Juan Beniquez	.03	.01	.00
☐ 519	Scot Thompson	.03	.01	.00
☐ 520	Jim Tracy	.03	.01	.00
☐ 521	Carlos Lezcano	.03	.01	.00
☐ 522	Joe Amalfitano MG .	.03	.01	.00
☐ 523	Preston Hanna	.03	.01	.00
☐ 524A	Ray Burris P1	.10	.04	.01
	Career Highlights:			
	"Went on ..."			
☐ 524B	Ray Burris P2	.06	.02	.00
	"Drafted by ..."			
☐ 525	Broderick Perkins ..	.03	.01	.00
☐ 526	Mickey Hatcher	.10	.04	.01
☐ 527	John Goryl MG	.03	.01	.00
☐ 528	Dick Davis	.03	.01	.00
☐ 529	Butch Wynegar	.03	.01	.00

		MINT	EXC	G-VG
☐ 530	Sal Butera	.03	.01	.00
☐ 531	Jerry Koosman ...	.08	.04	.01
☐ 532A	Geoff Zahn P1	.10	.04	.01
	Career Highlights:			
	"Was 2nd in"			
☐ 532B	Geoff Zahn P2	.06	.02	.00
	"Signed a 3 year"			
☐ 533	Dennis Martinez ...	.06	.02	.00
☐ 534	Gary Thomasson ..	.03	.01	.00
☐ 535	Steve Macko	.03	.01	.00
☐ 536	Jim Kaat	.18	.08	.01
☐ 537	Best Hitters	1.25	.50	.12
	George Brett			
	Rod Carew			
☐ 538	Tim Raines	5.00	2.00	.50
☐ 539	Keith Smith	.03	.01	.00
☐ 540	Ken Macha	.03	.01	.00
☐ 541	Burt Hooton	.03	.01	.00
☐ 542	Butch Hobson	.03	.01	.00
☐ 543	Bill Stein	.03	.01	.00
☐ 544	Dave Stapleton ...	.03	.01	.00
☐ 545	Bob Pate	.03	.01	.00
☐ 546	Doug Corbett	.06	.02	.00
☐ 547	Darrell Jackson ...	.03	.01	.00
☐ 548	Pete Redfern	.03	.01	.00
☐ 549	Roger Erickson ...	.03	.01	.00
☐ 550	Al Hrabosky	.06	.02	.00
☐ 551	Dick Tidrow	.03	.01	.00
☐ 552	Dave Ford	.03	.01	.00
☐ 553	Dave Kingman	.15	.06	.01
☐ 554A	Mike Vail P1	.10	.04	.01
	Career Highlights:			
	"After two ..."			
☐ 554B	Mike Vail P2	.06	.02	.00
	"Traded to ..."			
☐ 555A	Jerry Martin P1 ...	.10	.04	.01
	Career Highlights:			
	"Overcame a ..."			
☐ 555B	Jerry Martin P2 ...	.06	.02	.00
	"Traded to ..."			
☐ 556A	Jesus Figueroa P1	.10	.04	.01
	Career Highlights:			
	"Had an ..."			
☐ 556B	Jesus Figueroa P2	.06	.02	.00
	"Traded to ..."			
☐ 557	Don Stanhouse ...	.03	.01	.00
☐ 558	Barry Foote	.03	.01	.00
☐ 559	Tim Blackwell	.03	.01	.00
☐ 560	Bruce Sutter	.15	.06	.01

		MINT	EXC	G-VG
☐ 561	Rick Reuschel	.10	.04	.01
☐ 562	Lynn McGlothen	.03	.01	.00
☐ 563A	Bob Owchinko P1	.10	.04	.01
	Career Highlights:			
	"Traded to ..."			
☐ 563B	Bob Owchinko P2	.06	.02	.00
	"Involved in a "			
☐ 564	John Verhoeven	.03	.01	.00
☐ 565	Ken Landreaux	.03	.01	.00
☐ 566A	Glen Adams P1 ERR	.15	.06	.01
	Name misspelled			
☐ 566B	Glenn Adams P2 COR	.06	.02	.00
☐ 567	Hosken Powell	.03	.01	.00
☐ 568	Dick Noles	.03	.01	.00
☐ 569	Danny Ainge	.35	.14	.03
☐ 570	Bobby Mattick MG	.03	.01	.00
☐ 571	Joe Lefebvre	.06	.02	.00
☐ 572	Bobby Clark	.03	.01	.00
☐ 573	Dennis Lamp	.03	.01	.00
☐ 574	Randy Lerch	.03	.01	.00
☐ 575	Mookie Wilson	.40	.16	.04
☐ 576	Ron LeFlore	.06	.02	.00
☐ 577	Jim Dwyer	.03	.01	.00
☐ 578	Bill Castro	.03	.01	.00
☐ 579	Greg Minton	.03	.01	.00
☐ 580	Mark Littell	.03	.01	.00
☐ 581	Andy Hassler	.03	.01	.00
☐ 582	Dave Stieb	.30	.12	.03
☐ 583	Ken Oberkfell	.03	.01	.00
☐ 584	Larry Bradford	.03	.01	.00
☐ 585	Fred Stanley	.03	.01	.00
☐ 586	Bill Caudill	.03	.01	.00
☐ 587	Doug Capilla	.03	.01	.00
☐ 588	George Riley	.03	.01	.00
☐ 589	Willie Hernandez	.15	.06	.01
☐ 590	MVP: Mike Schmidt	.50	.20	.05
☐ 591	Cy Young Winner 1980:	.06	.02	.00
	Steve Stone			
☐ 592	Rick Sofield	.03	.01	.00
☐ 593	Bombo Rivera	.03	.01	.00
☐ 594	Gary Ward	.06	.02	.00
☐ 595A	Dave Edwards P1	.10	.04	.01
	Career Highlights:			
	"Sidelined the"			
☐ 595B	Dave Edwards P2	.06	.02	.00
	"Traded to ..."			
☐ 596	Mike Proly	.03	.01	.00
☐ 597	Tommy Boggs	.03	.01	.00
☐ 598	Greg Gross	.03	.01	.00

		MINT	EXC	G-VG
☐ 599	Elias Sosa	.03	.01	.00
☐ 600	Pat Kelly	.03	.01	.00
☐ 601A	Checklist 1 P1 ERR	.10	.01	.00
	unnumbered			
	(51 Donahue)			
☐ 601B	Checklist 1 P2 COR	.75	.10	.01
	unnumbered			
	(51 Donohue)			
☐ 602	Checklist 2	.08	.01	.00
	unnumbered			
☐ 603A	Checklist 3 P1 ERR	.10	.01	.00
	unnumbered			
	(306 Mathews)			
☐ 603B	Checklist 3 P2 COR	.10	.01	.00
	unnumbered			
	(306 Matthews)			
☐ 604A	Checklist 4 P1 ERR	.10	.01	.00
	unnumbered			
	(379 Pujois)			
☐ 604B	Checklist 4 P2 COR	.10	.01	.00
	unnumbered			
	(379 Pujols)			
☐ 605A	Checklist 5 P1 ERR	.10	.01	.00
	unnumbered			
	(566 Glen Adams)			
☐ 605B	Checklist 5 P2 COR	.10	.01	.00
	unnumbered			
	(566 Glenn Adams)			

1982 Donruss

The 1982 Donruss set contains 653 numbered cards and the seven unnumbered checklists; each card measures 2½" by 3½". The first 26 cards of this set are entitled Donruss Diamond Kings (DK) and feature the artwork of Dick Perez of Perez-Steele Galleries. The set was marketed with puzzle pieces rather than with bubble gum. There are 63 pieces to the puzzle, which when put together make a collage of Babe Ruth entitled "Hall of Fame Diamond King." The card stock in this year's Donruss cards is considerably thicker than that of the 1981 cards. The seven unnumbered checklist cards are arbitrarily assigned numbers 654 through 660 and are listed at the end of the list below.

		MINT	EXC	G-VG
	Complete Set (660)	30.00	12.00	3.00
	Common Player (1-660) ...	.03	.01	.00
☐	1 Pete Rose DK	1.50	.60	.15
☐	2 Gary Carter DK	.50	.20	.05
☐	3 Steve Garvey DK ..	.55	.22	.05
☐	4 Vida Blue DK	.10	.04	.01
☐	5A Alan Trammel DK ERR	1.00	.40	.10
	(name misspelled)			
☐	5B Alan Trammell DK ..	.40	.16	.04
	COR			
☐	6 Len Barker DK	.08	.03	.01
☐	7 Dwight Evans DK ..	.20	.08	.02
☐	8 Rod Carew DK	.50	.20	.05
☐	9 George Hendrick DK	.08	.03	.01
☐	10 Phil Niekro DK	.30	.12	.03
☐	11 Richie Zisk DK	.08	.03	.01
☐	12 Dave Parker DK ...	.30	.12	.03
☐	13 Nolan Ryan DK	.55	.22	.05
☐	14 Ivan DeJesus DK ..	.08	.03	.01
☐	15 George Brett DK ...	.75	.30	.07
☐	16 Tom Seaver DK	.50	.20	.05
☐	17 Dave Kingman DK .	.12	.05	.01
☐	18 Dave Winfield DK ..	.50	.20	.05
☐	19 Mike Norris DK	.08	.03	.01
☐	20 Carlton Fisk DK ...	.20	.08	.02
☐	21 Ozzie Smith DK ...	.25	.10	.02
☐	22 Roy Smalley DK ...	.08	.03	.01
☐	23 Buddy Bell DK	.10	.04	.01
☐	24 Ken Singleton DK ..	.10	.04	.01
☐	25 John Mayberry DK .	.08	.03	.01
☐	26 Gorman Thomas DK	.10	.04	.01
☐	27 Earl Weaver MG ...	.06	.02	.00
☐	28 Rollie Fingers	.20	.08	.02

		MINT	EXC	G-VG
☐	29 Sparky Anderson MG	.06	.02	.00
☐	30 Dennis Eckersley .	.20	.08	.02
☐	31 Dave Winfield	.50	.20	.05
☐	32 Burt Hooton	.03	.01	.00
☐	33 Rick Waits	.03	.01	.00
☐	34 George Brett	.65	.26	.06
☐	35 Steve McCatty	.03	.01	.00
☐	36 Steve Rogers	.03	.01	.00
☐	37 Bill Stein	.03	.01	.00
☐	38 Steve Renko	.03	.01	.00
☐	39 Mike Squires	.03	.01	.00
☐	40 George Hendrick ..	.06	.02	.00
☐	41 Bob Knepper	.10	.04	.01
☐	42 Steve Carlton	.50	.20	.05
☐	43 Larry Biittner	.03	.01	.00
☐	44 Chris Welsh	.03	.01	.00
☐	45 Steve Nicosia	.03	.01	.00
☐	46 Jack Clark	.25	.10	.02
☐	47 Chris Chambliss ..	.06	.02	.00
☐	48 Ivan DeJesus	.03	.01	.00
☐	49 Lee Mazzilli	.03	.01	.00
☐	50 Julio Cruz	.03	.01	.00
☐	51 Pete Redfern	.03	.01	.00
☐	52 Dave Stieb	.20	.08	.02
☐	53 Doug Corbett	.03	.01	.00
☐	54 Jorge Bell	6.00	2.40	.60
☐	55 Joe Simpson	.03	.01	.00
☐	56 Rusty Staub	.12	.05	.01
☐	57 Hector Cruz	.03	.01	.00
☐	58 Claudell Washington	.08	.03	.01
☐	59 Enrique Romo	.03	.01	.00
☐	60 Gary Lavelle	.03	.01	.00
☐	61 Tim Flannery	.03	.01	.00
☐	62 Joe Nolan	.03	.01	.00
☐	63 Larry Bowa	.15	.06	.01
☐	64 Sixto Lezcano	.03	.01	.00
☐	65 Joe Sambito	.03	.01	.00
☐	66 Bruce Kison	.03	.01	.00
☐	67 Wayne Nordhagen .	.03	.01	.00
☐	68 Woodie Fryman ...	.03	.01	.00
☐	69 Billy Sample	.03	.01	.00
☐	70 Amos Otis	.08	.03	.01
☐	71 Matt Keough	.03	.01	.00
☐	72 Toby Harrah	.06	.02	.00
☐	73 Dave Righetti	1.50	.60	.15
☐	74 Carl Yastrzemski ..	1.00	.40	.10
☐	75 Bob Welch	.10	.04	.01
☐	76A Alan Trammel ERR	1.00	.40	.10
	(name misspelled)			

		MINT	EXC	G-VG
☐ 76B	Alan Trammell CORR	.35	.14	.03
☐ 77	Rick Dempsey	.03	.01	.00
☐ 78	Paul Molitor	.25	.10	.02
☐ 79	Dennis Martinez	.06	.02	.00
☐ 80	Jim Slaton	.03	.01	.00
☐ 81	Champ Summers	.03	.01	.00
☐ 82	Carney Lansford	.12	.05	.01
☐ 83	Barry Foote	.03	.01	.00
☐ 84	Steve Garvey	.50	.20	.05
☐ 85	Rick Manning	.03	.01	.00
☐ 86	John Wathan	.06	.02	.00
☐ 87	Brian Kingman	.03	.01	.00
☐ 88	Andre Dawson	.35	.14	.03
☐ 89	Jim Kern	.03	.01	.00
☐ 90	Bobby Grich	.08	.03	.01
☐ 91	Bob Forsch	.03	.01	.00
☐ 92	Art Howe	.08	.03	.01
☐ 93	Marty Bystrom	.03	.01	.00
☐ 94	Ozzie Smith	.30	.12	.03
☐ 95	Dave Parker	.25	.10	.02
☐ 96	Doyle Alexander	.08	.03	.01
☐ 97	Al Hrabosky	.06	.02	.00
☐ 98	Frank Taveras	.03	.01	.00
☐ 99	Tim Blackwell	.03	.01	.00
☐ 100	Floyd Bannister	.06	.02	.00
☐ 101	Alfredo Griffin	.08	.03	.01
☐ 102	Dave Engle	.03	.01	.00
☐ 103	Mario Soto	.06	.02	.00
☐ 104	Ross Baumgarten	.03	.01	.00
☐ 105	Ken Singleton	.08	.03	.01
☐ 106	Ted Simmons	.15	.06	.01
☐ 107	Jack Morris	.20	.08	.02
☐ 108	Bob Watson	.06	.02	.00
☐ 109	Dwight Evans	.18	.08	.01
☐ 110	Tom Lasorda MG	.08	.03	.01
☐ 111	Bert Blyleven	.15	.06	.01
☐ 112	Dan Quisenberry	.12	.05	.01
☐ 113	Rickey Henderson	.75	.30	.07
☐ 114	Gary Carter	.45	.18	.04
☐ 115	Brian Downing	.06	.02	.00
☐ 116	Al Oliver	.10	.04	.01
☐ 117	LaMarr Hoyt	.08	.03	.01
☐ 118	Cesar Cedeno	.08	.03	.01
☐ 119	Keith Moreland	.06	.02	.00
☐ 120	Bob Shirley	.03	.01	.00
☐ 121	Terry Kennedy	.06	.02	.00
☐ 122	Frank Pastore	.03	.01	.00
☐ 123	Gene Garber	.03	.01	.00
☐ 124	Tony Pena	.30	.12	.03
☐ 125	Allen Ripley	.03	.01	.00
☐ 126	Randy Martz	.03	.01	.00
☐ 127	Richie Zisk	.06	.02	.00
☐ 128	Mike Scott	.30	.12	.03
☐ 129	Lloyd Moseby	.25	.10	.02
☐ 130	Rob Wilfong	.03	.01	.00
☐ 131	Tim Stoddard	.03	.01	.00
☐ 132	Gorman Thomas	.12	.05	.01
☐ 133	Dan Petry	.06	.02	.00
☐ 134	Bob Stanley	.03	.01	.00
☐ 135	Lou Piniella	.10	.04	.01
☐ 136	Pedro Guerrero	.40	.16	.04
☐ 137	Len Barker	.03	.01	.00
☐ 138	Rich Gale	.03	.01	.00
☐ 139	Wayne Gross	.03	.01	.00
☐ 140	Tim Wallach	.90	.36	.09
☐ 141	Gene Mauch MG	.03	.01	.00
☐ 142	Doc Medich	.03	.01	.00
☐ 143	Tony Bernazard	.03	.01	.00
☐ 144	Bill Virdon MG	.03	.01	.00
☐ 145	John Littlefield	.03	.01	.00
☐ 146	Dave Bergman	.03	.01	.00
☐ 147	Dick Davis	.03	.01	.00
☐ 148	Tom Seaver	.45	.18	.04
☐ 149	Matt Sinatro	.03	.01	.00
☐ 150	Chuck Tanner MG	.03	.01	.00
☐ 151	Leon Durham	.08	.03	.01
☐ 152	Gene Tenace	.03	.01	.00
☐ 153	Al Bumbry	.03	.01	.00
☐ 154	Mark Brouhard	.03	.01	.00
☐ 155	Rick Peters	.03	.01	.00
☐ 156	Jerry Remy	.03	.01	.00
☐ 157	Rick Reuschel	.10	.04	.01
☐ 158	Steve Howe	.03	.01	.00
☐ 159	Alan Bannister	.03	.01	.00
☐ 160	U.L. Washington	.03	.01	.00
☐ 161	Rick Langford	.03	.01	.00
☐ 162	Bill Gullickson	.06	.02	.00
☐ 163	Mark Wagner	.03	.01	.00
☐ 164	Geoff Zahn	.03	.01	.00
☐ 165	Ron LeFlore	.06	.02	.00
☐ 166	Dane Iorg	.03	.01	.00
☐ 167	Joe Niekro	.10	.04	.01
☐ 168	Pete Rose	1.25	.50	.12
☐ 169	Dave Collins	.03	.01	.00
☐ 170	Rick Wise	.03	.01	.00
☐ 171	Jim Bibby	.03	.01	.00
☐ 172	Larry Herndon	.03	.01	.00
☐ 173	Bob Horner	.18	.08	.01

		MINT	EXC	G-VG			MINT	EXC	G-VG
☐ 174	Steve Dillard	.03	.01	.00	☐ 223	Rick Camp	.03	.01	.00
☐ 175	Mookie Wilson	.10	.04	.01	☐ 224	Mike Jorgensen	.03	.01	.00
☐ 176	Dan Meyer	.03	.01	.00	☐ 225	Jody Davis	.35	.14	.03
☐ 177	Fernando Arroyo	.03	.01	.00	☐ 226	Mike Parrott	.03	.01	.00
☐ 178	Jackson Todd	.03	.01	.00	☐ 227	Jim Clancy	.06	.02	.00
☐ 179	Darrell Jackson	.03	.01	.00	☐ 228	Hosken Powell	.03	.01	.00
☐ 180	Alvis Woods	.03	.01	.00	☐ 229	Tom Hume	.03	.01	.00
☐ 181	Jim Anderson	.03	.01	.00	☐ 230	Britt Burns	.06	.02	.00
☐ 182	Dave Kingman	.15	.06	.01	☐ 231	Jim Palmer	.35	.14	.03
☐ 183	Steve Henderson	.03	.01	.00	☐ 232	Bob Rodgers MG	.03	.01	.00
☐ 184	Brian Asselstine	.03	.01	.00	☐ 233	Milt Wilcox	.03	.01	.00
☐ 185	Rod Scurry	.03	.01	.00	☐ 234	Dave Revering	.03	.01	.00
☐ 186	Fred Breining	.03	.01	.00	☐ 235	Mike Torrez	.03	.01	.00
☐ 187	Danny Boone	.03	.01	.00	☐ 236	Robert Castillo	.03	.01	.00
☐ 188	Junior Kennedy	.03	.01	.00	☐ 237	Von Hayes	.90	.36	.09
☐ 189	Sparky Lyle	.10	.04	.01	☐ 238	Renie Martin	.03	.01	.00
☐ 190	Whitey Herzog MG	.06	.02	.00	☐ 239	Dwayne Murphy	.03	.01	.00
☐ 191	Dave Smith	.08	.03	.01	☐ 240	Rodney Scott	.03	.01	.00
☐ 192	Ed Ott	.03	.01	.00	☐ 241	Fred Patek	.03	.01	.00
☐ 193	Greg Luzinski	.12	.05	.01	☐ 242	Mickey Rivers	.06	.02	.00
☐ 194	Bill Lee	.06	.02	.00	☐ 243	Steve Trout	.03	.01	.00
☐ 195	Don Zimmer MG	.03	.01	.00	☐ 244	Jose Cruz	.10	.04	.01
☐ 196	Hal McRae	.06	.02	.00	☐ 245	Manny Trillo	.03	.01	.00
☐ 197	Mike Norris	.03	.01	.00	☐ 246	Lary Sorensen	.03	.01	.00
☐ 198	Duane Kuiper	.03	.01	.00	☐ 247	Dave Edwards	.03	.01	.00
☐ 199	Rick Cerone	.03	.01	.00	☐ 248	Dan Driessen	.03	.01	.00
☐ 200	Jim Rice	.30	.12	.03	☐ 249	Tommy Boggs	.03	.01	.00
☐ 201	Steve Yeager	.03	.01	.00	☐ 250	Dale Berra	.03	.01	.00
☐ 202	Tom Brookens	.03	.01	.00	☐ 251	Ed Whitson	.06	.02	.00
☐ 203	Jose Morales	.03	.01	.00	☐ 252	Lee Smith	.55	.22	.05
☐ 204	Roy Howell	.03	.01	.00	☐ 253	Tom Paciorek	.03	.01	.00
☐ 205	Tippy Martinez	.03	.01	.00	☐ 254	Pat Zachry	.03	.01	.00
☐ 206	Moose Haas	.03	.01	.00	☐ 255	Luis Leal	.03	.01	.00
☐ 207	Al Cowens	.03	.01	.00	☐ 256	John Castino	.03	.01	.00
☐ 208	Dave Stapleton	.03	.01	.00	☐ 257	Rich Dauer	.03	.01	.00
☐ 209	Bucky Dent	.08	.03	.01	☐ 258	Cecil Cooper	.15	.06	.01
☐ 210	Ron Cey	.10	.04	.01	☐ 259	Dave Rozema	.03	.01	.00
☐ 211	Jorge Orta	.03	.01	.00	☐ 260	John Tudor	.20	.08	.02
☐ 212	Jamie Quirk	.03	.01	.00	☐ 261	Jerry Mumphrey	.03	.01	.00
☐ 213	Jeff Jones	.03	.01	.00	☐ 262	Jay Johnstone	.06	.02	.00
☐ 214	Tim Raines	.90	.36	.09	☐ 263	Bo Diaz	.06	.02	.00
☐ 215	Jon Matlack	.03	.01	.00	☐ 264	Dennis Leonard	.06	.02	.00
☐ 216	Rod Carew	.50	.20	.05	☐ 265	Jim Spencer	.03	.01	.00
☐ 217	Jim Kaat	.15	.06	.01	☐ 266	John Milner	.03	.01	.00
☐ 218	Joe Pittman	.03	.01	.00	☐ 267	Don Aase	.03	.01	.00
☐ 219	Larry Christenson	.03	.01	.00	☐ 268	Jim Sundberg	.06	.02	.00
☐ 220	Juan Bonilla	.03	.01	.00	☐ 269	Lamar Johnson	.03	.01	.00
☐ 221	Mike Easler	.03	.01	.00	☐ 270	Frank LaCorte	.03	.01	.00
☐ 222	Vida Blue	.08	.03	.01	☐ 271	Barry Evans	.03	.01	.00

		MINT	EXC	G-VG
☐ 272	Enos Cabell	.03	.01	.00
☐ 273	Del Unser	.03	.01	.00
☐ 274	George Foster	.12	.05	.01
☐ 275	Brett Butler	.60	.24	.06
☐ 276	Lee Lacy	.03	.01	.00
☐ 277	Ken Reitz	.03	.01	.00
☐ 278	Keith Hernandez	.35	.14	.03
☐ 279	Doug DeCinces	.08	.03	.01
☐ 280	Charlie Moore	.03	.01	.00
☐ 281	Lance Parrish	.25	.10	.02
☐ 282	Ralph Houk MG	.03	.01	.00
☐ 283	Rich Gossage	.15	.06	.01
☐ 284	Jerry Reuss	.06	.02	.00
☐ 285	Mike Stanton	.03	.01	.00
☐ 286	Frank White	.08	.03	.01
☐ 287	Bob Owchinko	.03	.01	.00
☐ 288	Scott Sanderson	.03	.01	.00
☐ 289	Bump Wills	.03	.01	.00
☐ 290	Dave Frost	.03	.01	.00
☐ 291	Chet Lemon	.06	.02	.00
☐ 292	Tito Landrum	.03	.01	.00
☐ 293	Vern Ruhle	.03	.01	.00
☐ 294	Mike Schmidt	.75	.30	.07
☐ 295	Sam Mejias	.03	.01	.00
☐ 296	Gary Lucas	.03	.01	.00
☐ 297	John Candelaria	.08	.03	.01
☐ 298	Jerry Martin	.03	.01	.00
☐ 299	Dale Murphy	.90	.36	.09
☐ 300	Mike Lum	.03	.01	.00
☐ 301	Tom Hausman	.03	.01	.00
☐ 302	Glenn Abbott	.03	.01	.00
☐ 303	Roger Erickson	.03	.01	.00
☐ 304	Otto Velez	.03	.01	.00
☐ 305	Danny Goodwin	.03	.01	.00
☐ 306	John Mayberry	.06	.02	.00
☐ 307	Lenny Randle	.03	.01	.00
☐ 308	Bob Bailor	.03	.01	.00
☐ 309	Jerry Morales	.03	.01	.00
☐ 310	Rufino Linares	.03	.01	.00
☐ 311	Kent Tekulve	.06	.02	.00
☐ 312	Joe Morgan	.30	.12	.03
☐ 313	John Urrea	.03	.01	.00
☐ 314	Paul Householder	.03	.01	.00
☐ 315	Garry Maddox	.06	.02	.00
☐ 316	Mike Ramsey	.03	.01	.00
☐ 317	Alan Ashby	.03	.01	.00
☐ 318	Bob Clark	.03	.01	.00
☐ 319	Tony LaRussa MG	.06	.02	.00
☐ 320	Charlie Lea	.06	.02	.00
☐ 321	Danny Darwin	.03	.01	.00
☐ 322	Cesar Geronimo	.03	.01	.00
☐ 323	Tom Underwood	.03	.01	.00
☐ 324	Andre Thornton	.06	.02	.00
☐ 325	Rudy May	.03	.01	.00
☐ 326	Frank Tanana	.08	.03	.01
☐ 327	Dave Lopes	.08	.03	.01
☐ 328	Richie Hebner	.03	.01	.00
☐ 329	Mike Flanagan	.08	.03	.01
☐ 330	Mike Caldwell	.03	.01	.00
☐ 331	Scott McGregor	.06	.02	.00
☐ 332	Jerry Augustine	.03	.01	.00
☐ 333	Stan Papi	.03	.01	.00
☐ 334	Rick Miller	.03	.01	.00
☐ 335	Graig Nettles	.12	.05	.01
☐ 336	Dusty Baker	.06	.02	.00
☐ 337	Dave Garcia MG	.03	.01	.00
☐ 338	Larry Gura	.03	.01	.00
☐ 339	Cliff Johnson	.03	.01	.00
☐ 340	Warren Cromartie	.03	.01	.00
☐ 341	Steve Comer	.03	.01	.00
☐ 342	Rick Burleson	.06	.02	.00
☐ 343	John Martin	.03	.01	.00
☐ 344	Craig Reynolds	.03	.01	.00
☐ 345	Mike Proly	.03	.01	.00
☐ 346	Ruppert Jones	.03	.01	.00
☐ 347	Omar Moreno	.03	.01	.00
☐ 348	Greg Minton	.03	.01	.00
☐ 349	Rick Mahler	.25	.10	.02
☐ 350	Alex Trevino	.03	.01	.00
☐ 351	Mike Krukow	.06	.02	.00
☐ 352A	Shane Rawley ERR (photo actually Jim Anderson)	.75	.30	.07
☐ 352B	Shane Rawley COR	.10	.04	.01
☐ 353	Garth Iorg	.03	.01	.00
☐ 354	Pete Mackanin	.03	.01	.00
☐ 355	Paul Moskau	.03	.01	.00
☐ 356	Richard Dotson	.08	.03	.01
☐ 357	Steve Stone	.06	.02	.00
☐ 358	Larry Hisle	.06	.02	.00
☐ 359	Aurelio Lopez	.03	.01	.00
☐ 360	Oscar Gamble	.03	.01	.00
☐ 361	Tom Burgmeier	.03	.01	.00
☐ 362	Terry Forster	.06	.02	.00
☐ 363	Joe Charboneau	.06	.02	.00
☐ 364	Ken Brett	.03	.01	.00
☐ 365	Tony Armas	.08	.03	.01
☐ 366	Chris Speier	.03	.01	.00
☐ 367	Fred Lynn	.18	.08	.01

		MINT	EXC	G-VG
☐ 368	Buddy Bell	.12	.05	.01
☐ 369	Jim Essian	.03	.01	.00
☐ 370	Terry Puhl	.03	.01	.00
☐ 371	Greg Gross	.03	.01	.00
☐ 372	Bruce Sutter	.15	.06	.01
☐ 373	Joe Lefebvre	.03	.01	.00
☐ 374	Ray Knight	.08	.03	.01
☐ 375	Bruce Benedict	.03	.01	.00
☐ 376	Tim Foli	.03	.01	.00
☐ 377	Al Holland	.03	.01	.00
☐ 378	Ken Kravec	.03	.01	.00
☐ 379	Jeff Burroughs	.03	.01	.00
☐ 380	Pete Falcone	.03	.01	.00
☐ 381	Ernie Whitt	.06	.02	.00
☐ 382	Brad Havens	.03	.01	.00
☐ 383	Terry Crowley	.03	.01	.00
☐ 384	Don Money	.03	.01	.00
☐ 385	Dan Schatzeder	.03	.01	.00
☐ 386	Gary Allenson	.03	.01	.00
☐ 387	Yogi Berra MG	.15	.06	.01
☐ 388	Ken Landreaux	.03	.01	.00
☐ 389	Mike Hargrove	.03	.01	.00
☐ 390	Darryl Motley	.06	.02	.00
☐ 391	Dave McKay	.03	.01	.00
☐ 392	Stan Bahnsen	.03	.01	.00
☐ 393	Ken Forsch	.03	.01	.00
☐ 394	Mario Mendoza	.03	.01	.00
☐ 395	Jim Morrison	.03	.01	.00
☐ 396	Mike Ivie	.03	.01	.00
☐ 397	Broderick Perkins	.03	.01	.00
☐ 398	Darrell Evans	.12	.05	.01
☐ 399	Ron Reed	.03	.01	.00
☐ 400	Johnny Bench	.55	.22	.05
☐ 401	Steve Bedrosian	.90	.36	.09
☐ 402	Bill Robinson	.06	.02	.00
☐ 403	Bill Buckner	.12	.05	.01
☐ 404	Ken Oberkfell	.03	.01	.00
☐ 405	Cal Ripken Jr.	7.50	3.00	.75
☐ 406	Jim Gantner	.03	.01	.00
☐ 407	Kirk Gibson	1.50	.60	.15
☐ 408	Tony Perez	.15	.06	.01
☐ 409	Tommy John	.18	.08	.01
☐ 410	Dave Stewart	1.00	.40	.10
☐ 411	Dan Spillner	.03	.01	.00
☐ 412	Willie Aikens	.03	.01	.00
☐ 413	Mike Heath	.03	.01	.00
☐ 414	Ray Burris	.03	.01	.00
☐ 415	Leon Roberts	.03	.01	.00
☐ 416	Mike Witt	.85	.34	.08

		MINT	EXC	G-VG
☐ 417	Bob Molinaro	.03	.01	.00
☐ 418	Steve Braun	.03	.01	.00
☐ 419	Nolan Ryan	.50	.20	.05
☐ 420	Tug McGraw	.10	.04	.01
☐ 421	Dave Concepcion	.12	.05	.01
☐ 422A	Juan Eichelberger ERR (photo actually Gary Lucas)	.65	.26	.06
☐ 422B	Juan Eichelberger COR	.08	.03	.01
☐ 423	Rick Rhoden	.10	.04	.01
☐ 424	Frank Robinson MG	.12	.05	.01
☐ 425	Eddie Miller	.03	.01	.00
☐ 426	Bill Caudill	.03	.01	.00
☐ 427	Doug Flynn	.03	.01	.00
☐ 428	Larry Andersen UER (misspelled Anderson on card front)	.03	.01	.00
☐ 429	Al Williams	.03	.01	.00
☐ 430	Jerry Garvin	.03	.01	.00
☐ 431	Glenn Adams	.03	.01	.00
☐ 432	Barry Bonnell	.03	.01	.00
☐ 433	Jerry Narron	.03	.01	.00
☐ 434	John Stearns	.03	.01	.00
☐ 435	Mike Tyson	.03	.01	.00
☐ 436	Glenn Hubbard	.03	.01	.00
☐ 437	Eddie Solomon	.03	.01	.00
☐ 438	Jeff Leonard	.08	.03	.01
☐ 439	Randy Bass	.06	.02	.00
☐ 440	Mike LaCoss	.03	.01	.00
☐ 441	Gary Matthews	.06	.02	.00
☐ 442	Mark Littell	.03	.01	.00
☐ 443	Don Sutton	.25	.10	.02
☐ 444	John Harris	.03	.01	.00
☐ 445	Vada Pinson CO	.06	.02	.00
☐ 446	Elias Sosa	.03	.01	.00
☐ 447	Charlie Hough	.08	.03	.01
☐ 448	Willie Wilson	.12	.05	.01
☐ 449	Fred Stanley	.03	.01	.00
☐ 450	Tom Veryzer	.03	.01	.00
☐ 451	Ron Davis	.03	.01	.00
☐ 452	Mark Clear	.03	.01	.00
☐ 453	Bill Russell	.06	.02	.00
☐ 454	Lou Whitaker	.15	.06	.01
☐ 455	Dan Graham	.03	.01	.00
☐ 456	Reggie Cleveland	.03	.01	.00
☐ 457	Sammy Stewart	.03	.01	.00
☐ 458	Pete Vuckovich	.08	.03	.01
☐ 459	John Wockenfuss	.03	.01	.00
☐ 460	Glenn Hoffman	.03	.01	.00
☐ 461	Willie Randolph	.10	.04	.01

		MINT	EXC	G-VG
☐ 462	Fernando Valenzuela	.70	.28	.07
☐ 463	Ron Hassey	.03	.01	.00
☐ 464	Paul Splittorff	.03	.01	.00
☐ 465	Rob Picciolo	.03	.01	.00
☐ 466	Larry Parrish	.06	.02	.00
☐ 467	Johnny Grubb	.03	.01	.00
☐ 468	Dan Ford	.03	.01	.00
☐ 469	Silvio Martinez	.03	.01	.00
☐ 470	Kiko Garcia	.03	.01	.00
☐ 471	Bob Boone	.12	.05	.01
☐ 472	Luis Salazar	.10	.04	.01
☐ 473	Randy Niemann	.03	.01	.00
☐ 474	Tom Griffin	.03	.01	.00
☐ 475	Phil Niekro	.30	.12	.03
☐ 476	Hubie Brooks	.30	.12	.03
☐ 477	Dick Tidrow	.03	.01	.00
☐ 478	Jim Beattie	.03	.01	.00
☐ 479	Damaso Garcia	.06	.02	.00
☐ 480	Mickey Hatcher	.08	.03	.01
☐ 481	Joe Price	.03	.01	.00
☐ 482	Ed Farmer	.03	.01	.00
☐ 483	Eddie Murray	.65	.26	.06
☐ 484	Ben Oglivie	.06	.02	.00
☐ 485	Kevin Saucier	.03	.01	.00
☐ 486	Bobby Murcer	.10	.04	.01
☐ 487	Bill Campbell	.03	.01	.00
☐ 488	Reggie Smith	.10	.04	.01
☐ 489	Wayne Garland	.03	.01	.00
☐ 490	Jim Wright	.03	.01	.00
☐ 491	Billy Martin MG	.15	.06	.01
☐ 492	Jim Fanning MG	.03	.01	.00
☐ 493	Don Baylor	.15	.06	.01
☐ 494	Rick Honeycutt	.03	.01	.00
☐ 495	Carlton Fisk	.18	.08	.01
☐ 496	Denny Walling	.03	.01	.00
☐ 497	Bake McBride	.03	.01	.00
☐ 498	Darrell Porter	.03	.01	.00
☐ 499	Gene Richards	.03	.01	.00
☐ 500	Ron Oester	.03	.01	.00
☐ 501	Ken Dayley	.20	.08	.02
☐ 502	Jason Thompson	.03	.01	.00
☐ 503	Milt May	.03	.01	.00
☐ 504	Doug Bird	.03	.01	.00
☐ 505	Bruce Bochte	.03	.01	.00
☐ 506	Neil Allen	.06	.02	.00
☐ 507	Joey McLaughlin	.03	.01	.00
☐ 508	Butch Wynegar	.03	.01	.00
☐ 509	Gary Roenicke	.03	.01	.00
☐ 510	Robin Yount	.50	.20	.05

		MINT	EXC	G-VG
☐ 511	Dave Tobik	.03	.01	.00
☐ 512	Rich Gedman	.40	.16	.04
☐ 513	Gene Nelson	.08	.03	.01
☐ 514	Rick Monday	.06	.02	.00
☐ 515	Miguel Dilone	.03	.01	.00
☐ 516	Clint Hurdle	.03	.01	.00
☐ 517	Jeff Newman	.03	.01	.00
☐ 518	Grant Jackson	.03	.01	.00
☐ 519	Andy Hassler	.03	.01	.00
☐ 520	Pat Putnam	.03	.01	.00
☐ 521	Greg Pryor	.03	.01	.00
☐ 522	Tony Scott	.03	.01	.00
☐ 523	Steve Mura	.03	.01	.00
☐ 524	Johnnie LeMaster	.03	.01	.00
☐ 525	Dick Ruthven	.03	.01	.00
☐ 526	John McNamara MG	.03	.01	.00
☐ 527	Larry McWilliams	.03	.01	.00
☐ 528	Johnny Ray	.75	.30	.07
☐ 529	Pat Tabler	.65	.26	.06
☐ 530	Tom Herr	.10	.04	.01
☐ 531A	San Diego Chicken (with TM)	.90	.36	.09
☐ 531B	San Diego Chicken (without TM)	.70	.28	.07
☐ 532	Sal Butera	.03	.01	.00
☐ 533	Mike Griffin	.03	.01	.00
☐ 534	Kelvin Moore	.03	.01	.00
☐ 535	Reggie Jackson	.60	.22	.05
☐ 536	Ed Romero	.03	.01	.00
☐ 537	Derrel Thomas	.03	.01	.00
☐ 538	Mike O'Berry	.03	.01	.00
☐ 539	Jack O'Connor	.03	.01	.00
☐ 540	Bob Ojeda	.50	.20	.05
☐ 541	Roy Lee Jackson	.03	.01	.00
☐ 542	Lynn Jones	.03	.01	.00
☐ 543	Gaylord Perry	.30	.12	.03
☐ 544A	Phil Garner ERR (reverse negative)	.75	.30	.07
☐ 544B	Phil Garner COR	.10	.04	.01
☐ 545	Garry Templeton	.08	.03	.01
☐ 546	Rafael Ramirez	.03	.01	.00
☐ 547	Jeff Reardon	.12	.05	.01
☐ 548	Ron Guidry	.20	.08	.02
☐ 549	Tim Laudner	.30	.12	.03
☐ 550	John Henry Johnson	.03	.01	.00
☐ 551	Chris Bando	.03	.01	.00
☐ 552	Bobby Brown	.03	.01	.00
☐ 553	Larry Bradford	.03	.01	.00
☐ 554	Scott Fletcher	.60	.24	.06

		MINT	EXC	G-VG
☐ 555	Jerry Royster	.03	.01	.00
☐ 556	Shooty Babitt	.03	.01	.00
	(spelled Babbitt on front)			
☐ 557	Kent Hrbek	3.00	1.20	.30
☐ 558	Yankee Winners	.12	.05	.01
	Ron Guidry			
	Tommy John			
☐ 559	Mark Bomback	.03	.01	.00
☐ 560	Julio Valdez	.03	.01	.00
☐ 561	Buck Martinez	.03	.01	.00
☐ 562	Mike Marshall	1.25	.50	.12
	(Dodger hitter)			
☐ 563	Rennie Stennett	.03	.01	.00
☐ 564	Steve Crawford	.03	.01	.00
☐ 565	Bob Babcock	.03	.01	.00
☐ 566	Johnny Podres CO	.06	.02	.00
☐ 567	Paul Serna	.03	.01	.00
☐ 568	Harold Baines	.50	.18	.04
☐ 569	Dave LaRoche	.03	.01	.00
☐ 570	Lee May	.03	.01	.00
☐ 571	Gary Ward	.06	.02	.00
☐ 572	John Denny	.06	.02	.00
☐ 573	Roy Smalley	.03	.01	.00
☐ 574	Bob Brenly	.20	.08	.02
☐ 575	Bronx Bombers	.45	.18	.04
	Reggie Jackson			
	Dave Winfield			
☐ 576	Luis Pujols	.03	.01	.00
☐ 577	Butch Hobson	.03	.01	.00
☐ 578	Harvey Kuenn MG	.06	.02	.00
☐ 579	Cal Ripken Sr. CO	.08	.03	.01
☐ 580	Juan Berenguer	.03	.01	.00
☐ 581	Benny Ayala	.03	.01	.00
☐ 582	Vance Law	.20	.08	.02
☐ 583	Rick Leach	.03	.01	.00
☐ 584	George Frazier	.03	.01	.00
☐ 585	Phillies Finest	.75	.30	.07
	Pete Rose			
	Mike Schmidt			
☐ 586	Joe Rudi	.06	.02	.00
☐ 587	Juan Beniquez	.03	.01	.00
☐ 588	Luis DeLeon	.08	.03	.01
☐ 589	Craig Swan	.03	.01	.00
☐ 590	Dave Chalk	.03	.01	.00
☐ 591	Billy Gardner MG	.03	.01	.00
☐ 592	Sal Bando	.06	.02	.00
☐ 593	Bert Campaneris	.06	.02	.00
☐ 594	Steve Kemp	.06	.02	.00

		MINT	EXC	G-VG
☐ 595A	Randy Lerch ERR	.65	.26	.06
	(Braves)			
☐ 595B	Randy Lerch COR	.06	.02	.00
	(Brewers)			
☐ 596	Bryan Clark	.03	.01	.00
☐ 597	Dave Ford	.03	.01	.00
☐ 598	Mike Scioscia	.15	.06	.01
☐ 599	John Lowenstein	.03	.01	.00
☐ 600	Rene Lachemann MG	.06	.02	.00
☐ 601	Mick Kelleher	.03	.01	.00
☐ 602	Ron Jackson	.03	.01	.00
☐ 603	Jerry Koosman	.08	.03	.01
☐ 604	Dave Goltz	.03	.01	.00
☐ 605	Ellis Valentine	.03	.01	.00
☐ 606	Lonnie Smith	.06	.02	.00
☐ 607	Joaquin Andujar	.10	.04	.01
☐ 608	Garry Hancock	.03	.01	.00
☐ 609	Jerry Turner	.03	.01	.00
☐ 610	Bob Bonner	.03	.01	.00
☐ 611	Jim Dwyer	.03	.01	.00
☐ 612	Terry Bulling	.03	.01	.00
☐ 613	Joel Youngblood	.03	.01	.00
☐ 614	Larry Milbourne	.03	.01	.00
☐ 615	Gene Roof	.06	.02	.00
	(name on front is Phil Roof)			
☐ 616	Keith Drumwright	.03	.01	.00
☐ 617	Dave Rosello	.03	.01	.00
☐ 618	Rickey Keeton	.03	.01	.00
☐ 619	Dennis Lamp	.03	.01	.00
☐ 620	Sid Monge	.03	.01	.00
☐ 621	Jerry White	.03	.01	.00
☐ 622	Luis Aguayo	.03	.01	.00
☐ 623	Jamie Easterly	.03	.01	.00
☐ 624	Steve Sax	2.25	.90	.22
☐ 625	Dave Roberts	.03	.01	.00
☐ 626	Rick Bosetti	.03	.01	.00
☐ 627	Terry Francona	.10	.04	.01
☐ 628	Pride of Reds	.35	.14	.03
	Tom Seaver			
	Johnny Bench			
☐ 629	Paul Mirabella	.03	.01	.00
☐ 630	Rance Mulliniks	.03	.01	.00
☐ 631	Kevin Hickey	.03	.01	.00
☐ 632	Reid Nichols	.03	.01	.00
☐ 633	Dave Geisel	.03	.01	.00
☐ 634	Ken Griffey	.06	.02	.00
☐ 635	Bob Lemon MG	.10	.04	.01
☐ 636	Orlando Sanchez	.03	.01	.00
☐ 637	Bill Almon	.03	.01	.00

1983 Donruss

		MINT	EXC	G-VG
☐ 638	Danny Ainge	.12	.05	.01
☐ 639	Willie Stargell	.35	.14	.03
☐ 640	Bob Sykes	.03	.01	.00
☐ 641	Ed Lynch	.08	.03	.01
☐ 642	John Ellis	.03	.01	.00
☐ 643	Ferguson Jenkins	.15	.06	.01
☐ 644	Lenn Sakata	.03	.01	.00
☐ 645	Julio Gonzalez	.03	.01	.00
☐ 646	Jesse Orosco	.08	.03	.01
☐ 647	Jerry Dybzinski	.03	.01	.00
☐ 648	Tommy Davis	.06	.02	.00
☐ 649	Ron Gardenhire	.06	.02	.00
☐ 650	Felipe Alou CO	.06	.02	.00
☐ 651	Harvey Haddix CO	.03	.01	.00
☐ 652	Willie Upshaw	.06	.02	.00
☐ 653	Bill Madlock	.10	.04	.01
☐ 654A	DK Checklist (unnumbered) (with Trammel)	.25	.04	.00
☐ 654B	DK Checklist (unnumbered) (with Trammell)	.12	.01	.00
☐ 655	Checklist 1 (unnumbered)	.08	.01	.00
☐ 656	Checklist 2 (unnumbered)	.08	.01	.00
☐ 657	Checklist 3 (unnumbered)	.08	.01	.00
☐ 658	Checklist 4 (unnumbered)	.08	.01	.00
☐ 659	Checklist 5 (unnumbered)	.08	.01	.00
☐ 660	Checklist 6 (unnumbered)	.08	.01	.00

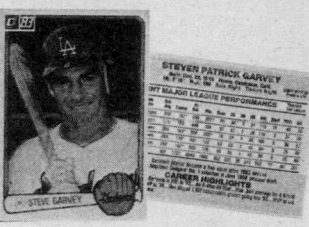

The cards in this 660-card set measure 2 ½" by 3 ½". The 1983 Donruss baseball set, issued with a 63-piece Diamond King puzzle, again leads off with a 26-card Diamond Kings (DK) series. Of the remaining 634 cards, two are combination cards, one portrays the San Diego Chicken, one shows the completed Ty Cobb puzzle, and seven are unnumbered checklist cards. The seven unnumbered checklist cards are arbitrarily assigned numbers 654 through 660 and are listed at the end of the list below. The Donruss logo and the year of issue are shown in the upper left corner of the obverse. The card backs have black print on yellow and white and are numbered on a small ball design. The complete set price below includes only the more common of each variation pair.

		MINT	EXC	G-VG
Complete Set (660)		45.00	18.00	4.50
Common Player (1-660)		.03	.01	.00
☐ 1	Fern. Valenzuela DK	.50	.15	.03
☐ 2	Rollie Fingers DK	.20	.08	.02
☐ 3	Reggie Jackson DK	.50	.20	.05
☐ 4	Jim Palmer DK	.35	.14	.03
☐ 5	Jack Morris DK	.25	.10	.02
☐ 6	George Foster DK	.12	.05	.01
☐ 7	Jim Sundberg DK	.08	.03	.01
☐ 8	Willie Stargell DK	.35	.14	.03
☐ 9	Dave Stieb DK	.15	.06	.01
☐ 10	Joe Niekro DK	.10	.04	.01

			MINT	EXC	G-VG				MINT	EXC	G-VG
☐	11	Rickey Henderson DK	.60	.24	.06	☐	60	Gary Lavelle	.03	.01	.00
☐	12	Dale Murphy DK	.75	.30	.07	☐	61	Tim Lollar	.03	.01	.00
☐	13	Toby Harrah DK	.08	.03	.01	☐	62	Frank Pastore	.03	.01	.00
☐	14	Bill Buckner DK	.10	.04	.01	☐	63	Garry Maddox	.06	.02	.00
☐	15	Willie Wilson DK	.12	.05	.01	☐	64	Bob Forsch	.03	.01	.00
☐	16	Steve Carlton DK	.40	.16	.04	☐	65	Harry Spilman	.03	.01	.00
☐	17	Ron Guidry DK	.20	.08	.02	☐	66	Geoff Zahn	.03	.01	.00
☐	18	Steve Rogers DK	.08	.03	.01	☐	67	Salome Barojas	.03	.01	.00
☐	19	Kent Hrbek DK	.40	.16	.04	☐	68	David Palmer	.03	.01	.00
☐	20	Keith Hernandez DK	.35	.14	.03	☐	69	Charlie Hough	.08	.03	.01
☐	21	Floyd Bannister DK	.08	.03	.01	☐	70	Dan Quisenberry	.12	.06	.01
☐	22	Johnny Bench DK	.45	.18	.04	☐	71	Tony Armas	.08	.03	.01
☐	23	Britt Burns DK	.08	.03	.01	☐	72	Rick Sutcliffe	.15	.06	.01
☐	24	Joe Morgan DK	.30	.12	.03	☐	73	Steve Balboni	.08	.03	.01
☐	25	Carl Yastrzemski DK	.85	.34	.08	☐	74	Jerry Remy	.03	.01	.00
☐	26	Terry Kennedy DK	.08	.03	.01	☐	75	Mike Scioscia	.06	.02	.00
☐	27	Gary Roenicke	.03	.01	.00	☐	76	John Wockenfuss	.03	.01	.00
☐	28	Dwight Bernard	.03	.01	.00	☐	77	Jim Palmer	.35	.14	.03
☐	29	Pat Underwood	.03	.01	.00	☐	78	Rollie Fingers	.20	.08	.02
☐	30	Gary Allenson	.03	.01	.00	☐	79	Joe Nolan	.03	.01	.00
☐	31	Ron Guidry	.18	.08	.01	☐	80	Pete Vuckovich	.06	.02	.00
☐	32	Burt Hooton	.03	.01	.00	☐	81	Rick Leach	.03	.01	.00
☐	33	Chris Bando	.03	.01	.00	☐	82	Rick Miller	.03	.01	.00
☐	34	Vida Blue	.08	.03	.01	☐	83	Graig Nettles	.12	.05	.01
☐	35	Rickey Henderson	.55	.22	.05	☐	84	Ron Cey	.10	.04	.01
☐	36	Ray Burris	.03	.01	.00	☐	85	Miguel Dilone	.03	.01	.00
☐	37	John Butcher	.03	.01	.00	☐	86	John Wathan	.06	.02	.00
☐	38	Don Aase	.03	.01	.00	☐	87	Kelvin Moore	.03	.01	.00
☐	39	Jerry Koosman	.08	.03	.01	☐	88A	Byrn Smith ERR	.15	.06	.01
☐	40	Bruce Sutter	.15	.06	.01			(sic, Bryn)			
☐	41	Jose Cruz	.08	.03	.01	☐	88B	Bryn Smith COR	.75	.30	.07
☐	42	Pete Rose	1.00	.40	.10	☐	89	Dave Hostetler	.06	.02	.00
☐	43	Cesar Cedeno	.08	.03	.01	☐	90	Rod Carew	.45	.18	.04
☐	44	Floyd Chiffer	.03	.01	.00	☐	91	Lonnie Smith	.06	.02	.00
☐	45	Larry McWilliams	.03	.01	.00	☐	92	Bob Knepper	.08	.03	.01
☐	46	Alan Fowlkes	.03	.01	.00	☐	93	Marty Bystrom	.03	.01	.00
☐	47	Dale Murphy	.85	.34	.08	☐	94	Chris Welsh	.03	.01	.00
☐	48	Doug Bird	.03	.01	.00	☐	95	Jason Thompson	.03	.01	.00
☐	49	Hubie Brooks	.08	.03	.01	☐	96	Tom O'Malley	.03	.01	.00
☐	50	Floyd Bannister	.06	.02	.00	☐	97	Phil Niekro	.25	.10	.02
☐	51	Jack O'Connor	.03	.01	.00	☐	98	Neil Allen	.03	.01	.00
☐	52	Steve Senteney	.03	.01	.00	☐	99	Bill Buckner	.10	.04	.01
☐	53	Gary Gaetti	3.00	1.20	.30	☐	100	Ed VandeBerg	.03	.01	.00
☐	54	Damaso Garcia	.06	.02	.00	☐	101	Jim Clancy	.03	.01	.00
☐	55	Gene Nelson	.03	.01	.00	☐	102	Robert Castillo	.03	.01	.00
☐	56	Mookie Wilson	.08	.03	.01	☐	103	Bruce Berenyi	.03	.01	.00
☐	57	Allen Ripley	.03	.01	.00	☐	104	Carlton Fisk	.15	.06	.01
☐	58	Bob Horner	.18	.08	.01	☐	105	Mike Flanagan	.08	.03	.01
☐	59	Tony Pena	.15	.06	.01	☐	106	Cecil Cooper	.15	.06	.01

		MINT	EXC	G-VG
☐ 107	Jack Morris	.20	.08	.02
☐ 108	Mike Morgan	.03	.01	.00
☐ 109	Luis Aponte	.03	.01	.00
☐ 110	Pedro Guerrero	.30	.12	.03
☐ 111	Len Barker	.03	.01	.00
☐ 112	Willie Wilson	.12	.05	.01
☐ 113	Dave Beard	.03	.01	.00
☐ 114	Mike Gates	.03	.01	.00
☐ 115	Reggie Jackson	.50	.20	.05
☐ 116	George Wright	.03	.01	.00
☐ 117	Vance Law	.06	.02	.00
☐ 118	Nolan Ryan	.40	.16	.04
☐ 119	Mike Krukow	.06	.02	.00
☐ 120	Ozzie Smith	.25	.10	.02
☐ 121	Broderick Perkins	.03	.01	.00
☐ 122	Tom Seaver	.40	.16	.04
☐ 123	Chris Chambliss	.06	.02	.00
☐ 124	Chuck Tanner MG	.03	.01	.00
☐ 125	Johnnie LeMaster	.03	.01	.00
☐ 126	Mel Hall	.55	.22	.05
☐ 127	Bruce Bochte	.03	.01	.00
☐ 128	Charlie Puleo	.03	.01	.00
☐ 129	Luis Leal	.03	.01	.00
☐ 130	John Pacella	.03	.01	.00
☐ 131	Glenn Gulliver	.03	.01	.00
☐ 132	Don Money	.03	.01	.00
☐ 133	Dave Rozema	.03	.01	.00
☐ 134	Bruce Hurst	.30	.12	.03
☐ 135	Rudy May	.03	.01	.00
☐ 136	Tom Lasorda MG	.06	.02	.00
☐ 137	Dan Spillner	.06	.02	.00
	(photo actually Ed Whitson)			
☐ 138	Jerry Martin	.03	.01	.00
☐ 139	Mike Norris	.03	.01	.00
☐ 140	Al Oliver	.10	.04	.01
☐ 141	Daryl Sconiers	.03	.01	.00
☐ 142	Lamar Johnson	.03	.01	.00
☐ 143	Harold Baines	.20	.08	.02
☐ 144	Alan Ashby	.03	.01	.00
☐ 145	Garry Templeton	.06	.02	.00
☐ 146	Al Holland	.03	.01	.00
☐ 147	Bo Diaz	.06	.02	.00
☐ 148	Dave Concepcion	.10	.04	.01
☐ 149	Rick Camp	.03	.01	.00
☐ 150	Jim Morrison	.03	.01	.00
☐ 151	Randy Martz	.03	.01	.00
☐ 152	Keith Hernandez	.35	.14	.03
☐ 153	John Lowenstein	.03	.01	.00
☐ 154	Mike Caldwell	.03	.01	.00
☐ 155	Milt Wilcox	.03	.01	.00
☐ 156	Rich Gedman	.10	.04	.01
☐ 157	Rich Gossage	.15	.06	.01
☐ 158	Jerry Reuss	.06	.02	.00
☐ 159	Ron Hassey	.03	.01	.00
☐ 160	Larry Gura	.03	.01	.00
☐ 161	Dwayne Murphy	.03	.01	.00
☐ 162	Woodie Fryman	.03	.01	.00
☐ 163	Steve Comer	.03	.01	.00
☐ 164	Ken Forsch	.03	.01	.00
☐ 165	Dennis Lamp	.03	.01	.00
☐ 166	David Green	.03	.01	.00
☐ 167	Terry Puhl	.03	.01	.00
☐ 168	Mike Schmidt	.60	.24	.06
☐ 169	Eddie Milner	.10	.04	.01
☐ 170	John Curtis	.03	.01	.00
☐ 171	Don Robinson	.03	.01	.00
☐ 172	Rich Gale	.03	.01	.00
☐ 173	Steve Bedrosian	.25	.10	.02
☐ 174	Willie Hernandez	.12	.05	.01
☐ 175	Ron Gardenhire	.03	.01	.00
☐ 176	Jim Beattie	.03	.01	.00
☐ 177	Tim Laudner	.06	.02	.00
☐ 178	Buck Martinez	.03	.01	.00
☐ 179	Kent Hrbek	.40	.14	.03
☐ 180	Alfredo Griffin	.08	.03	.01
☐ 181	Larry Andersen	.03	.01	.00
☐ 182	Pete Falcone	.03	.01	.00
☐ 183	Jody Davis	.10	.04	.01
☐ 184	Glenn Hubbard	.03	.01	.00
☐ 185	Dale Berra	.03	.01	.00
☐ 186	Greg Minton	.03	.01	.00
☐ 187	Gary Lucas	.03	.01	.00
☐ 188	Dave Van Gorder	.03	.01	.00
☐ 189	Bob Dernier	.03	.01	.00
☐ 190	Willie McGee	1.75	.70	.17
☐ 191	Dickie Thon	.03	.01	.00
☐ 192	Bob Boone	.10	.04	.01
☐ 193	Britt Burns	.03	.01	.00
☐ 194	Jeff Reardon	.10	.04	.01
☐ 195	Jon Matlack	.03	.01	.00
☐ 196	Don Slaught	.30	.12	.03
☐ 197	Fred Stanley	.03	.01	.00
☐ 198	Rick Manning	.03	.01	.00
☐ 199	Dave Righetti	.20	.08	.02
☐ 200	Dave Stapleton	.03	.01	.00
☐ 201	Steve Yeager	.03	.01	.00
☐ 202	Enos Cabell	.03	.01	.00
☐ 203	Sammy Stewart	.03	.01	.00

		MINT	EXC	G-VG
☐ 204	Moose Haas	.03	.01	.00
☐ 205	Lenn Sakata	.03	.01	.00
☐ 206	Charlie Moore	.03	.01	.00
☐ 207	Alan Trammell	.30	.12	.03
☐ 208	Jim Rice	.25	.10	.02
☐ 209	Roy Smalley	.03	.01	.00
☐ 210	Bill Russell	.06	.02	.00
☐ 211	Andre Thornton	.06	.02	.00
☐ 212	Willie Aikens	.03	.01	.00
☐ 213	Dave McKay	.03	.01	.00
☐ 214	Tim Blackwell	.03	.01	.00
☐ 215	Buddy Bell	.08	.03	.01
☐ 216	Doug DeCinces	.08	.03	.01
☐ 217	Tom Herr	.08	.03	.01
☐ 218	Frank LaCorte	.03	.01	.00
☐ 219	Steve Carlton	.35	.14	.03
☐ 220	Terry Kennedy	.06	.02	.00
☐ 221	Mike Easler	.03	.01	.00
☐ 222	Jack Clark	.25	.10	.02
☐ 223	Gene Garber	.03	.01	.00
☐ 224	Scott Holman	.03	.01	.00
☐ 225	Mike Proly	.03	.01	.00
☐ 226	Terry Bulling	.03	.01	.00
☐ 227	Jerry Garvin	.03	.01	.00
☐ 228	Ron Davis	.03	.01	.00
☐ 229	Tom Hume	.03	.01	.00
☐ 230	Marc Hill	.03	.01	.00
☐ 231	Dennis Martinez	.06	.02	.00
☐ 232	Jim Gantner	.03	.01	.00
☐ 233	Larry Pashnick	.03	.01	.00
☐ 234	Dave Collins	.03	.01	.00
☐ 235	Tom Burgmeier	.03	.01	.00
☐ 236	Ken Landreaux	.03	.01	.00
☐ 237	John Denny	.08	.03	.01
☐ 238	Hal McRae	.06	.02	.00
☐ 239	Matt Keough	.03	.01	.00
☐ 240	Doug Flynn	.03	.01	.00
☐ 241	Fred Lynn	.18	.08	.01
☐ 242	Billy Sample	.03	.01	.00
☐ 243	Tom Paciorek	.03	.01	.00
☐ 244	Joe Sambito	.03	.01	.00
☐ 245	Sid Monge	.03	.01	.00
☐ 246	Ken Oberkfell	.03	.01	.00
☐ 247	Joe Pittman	.08	.03	.01
	(photo actually Juan Eichelberger)			
☐ 248	Mario Soto	.06	.02	.00
☐ 249	Claudell Washington	.08	.03	.01
☐ 250	Rick Rhoden	.08	.03	.01
☐ 251	Darrell Evans	.10	.04	.01

		MINT	EXC	G-VG
☐ 252	Steve Henderson	.03	.01	.00
☐ 253	Manny Castillo	.03	.01	.00
☐ 254	Craig Swan	.03	.01	.00
☐ 255	Joey McLaughlin	.03	.01	.00
☐ 256	Pete Redfern	.03	.01	.00
☐ 257	Ken Singleton	.08	.03	.01
☐ 258	Robin Yount	.30	.12	.03
☐ 259	Elias Sosa	.03	.01	.00
☐ 260	Bob Ojeda	.10	.04	.01
☐ 261	Bobby Murcer	.08	.03	.01
☐ 262	Candy Maldonado	.60	.24	.06
☐ 263	Rick Waits	.03	.01	.00
☐ 264	Greg Pryor	.03	.01	.00
☐ 265	Bob Owchinko	.03	.01	.00
☐ 266	Chris Speier	.03	.01	.00
☐ 267	Bruce Kison	.03	.01	.00
☐ 268	Mark Wagner	.03	.01	.00
☐ 269	Steve Kemp	.06	.02	.00
☐ 270	Phil Garner	.03	.01	.00
☐ 271	Gene Richards	.03	.01	.00
☐ 272	Renie Martin	.03	.01	.00
☐ 273	Dave Roberts	.03	.01	.00
☐ 274	Dan Driessen	.03	.01	.00
☐ 275	Rufino Linares	.03	.01	.00
☐ 276	Lee Lacy	.03	.01	.00
☐ 277	Ryne Sandberg	4.00	1.60	.40
☐ 278	Darrell Porter	.03	.01	.00
☐ 279	Cal Ripken	1.00	.40	.10
☐ 280	Jamie Easterly	.03	.01	.00
☐ 281	Bill Fahey	.03	.01	.00
☐ 282	Glenn Hoffman	.03	.01	.00
☐ 283	Willie Randolph	.08	.03	.01
☐ 284	Fernando Valenzuela	.25	.10	.02
☐ 285	Alan Bannister	.03	.01	.00
☐ 286	Paul Splittorff	.03	.01	.00
☐ 287	Joe Rudi	.06	.02	.00
☐ 288	Bill Gullickson	.03	.01	.00
☐ 289	Danny Darwin	.03	.01	.00
☐ 290	Andy Hassler	.03	.01	.00
☐ 291	Ernesto Escarrega	.03	.01	.00
☐ 292	Steve Mura	.03	.01	.00
☐ 293	Tony Scott	.03	.01	.00
☐ 294	Manny Trillo	.03	.01	.00
☐ 295	Greg Harris	.03	.01	.00
☐ 296	Luis DeLeon	.03	.01	.00
☐ 297	Kent Tekulve	.06	.02	.00
☐ 298	Atlee Hammaker	.06	.02	.00
☐ 299	Bruce Benedict	.03	.01	.00
☐ 300	Fergie Jenkins	.12	.05	.01

		MINT	EXC	G-VG			MINT	EXC	G-VG
☐ 301	Dave Kingman	.12	.05	.01	☐ 347	Omar Moreno	.03	.01	.00
☐ 302	Bill Caudill	.03	.01	.00	☐ 348	Chili Davis	.35	.14	.03
☐ 303	John Castino	.03	.01	.00	☐ 349	Tommy Boggs	.03	.01	.00
☐ 304	Ernie Whitt	.06	.02	.00	☐ 350	Rusty Staub	.10	.04	.01
☐ 305	Randy Johnson	.03	.01	.00	☐ 351	Bump Wills	.03	.01	.00
☐ 306	Garth Iorg	.03	.01	.00	☐ 352	Rick Sweet	.03	.01	.00
☐ 307	Gaylord Perry	.25	.10	.02	☐ 353	Jim Gott	.30	.12	.03
☐ 308	Ed Lynch	.03	.01	.00	☐ 354	Terry Felton	.03	.01	.00
☐ 309	Keith Moreland	.06	.02	.00	☐ 355	Jim Kern	.03	.01	.00
☐ 310	Rafael Ramirez	.03	.01	.00	☐ 356	Bill Almon	.03	.01	.00
☐ 311	Bill Madlock	.10	.04	.01	☐ 357	Tippy Martinez	.03	.01	.00
☐ 312	Milt May	.03	.01	.00	☐ 358	Roy Howell	.03	.01	.00
☐ 313	John Montefusco	.06	.02	.00	☐ 359	Dan Petry	.08	.03	.01
☐ 314	Wayne Krenchicki	.03	.01	.00	☐ 360	Jerry Mumphrey	.03	.01	.00
☐ 315	George Vukovich	.03	.01	.00	☐ 361	Mark Clear	.03	.01	.00
☐ 316	Joaquin Andujar	.10	.04	.01	☐ 362	Mike Marshall	.25	.10	.02
☐ 317	Craig Reynolds	.03	.01	.00	☐ 363	Lary Sorensen	.03	.01	.00
☐ 318	Rick Burleson	.06	.02	.00	☐ 364	Amos Otis	.08	.03	.01
☐ 319	Richard Dotson	.08	.03	.01	☐ 365	Rick Langford	.03	.01	.00
☐ 320	Steve Rogers	.03	.01	.00	☐ 366	Brad Mills	.03	.01	.00
☐ 321	Dave Schmidt	.15	.06	.01	☐ 367	Brian Downing	.06	.02	.00
☐ 322	Bud Black	.20	.08	.02	☐ 368	Mike Richardt	.03	.01	.00
☐ 323	Jeff Burroughs	.06	.02	.00	☐ 369	Aurelio Rodriguez	.03	.01	.00
☐ 324	Von Hayes	.20	.08	.02	☐ 370	Dave Smith	.06	.02	.00
☐ 325	Butch Wynegar	.03	.01	.00	☐ 371	Tug McGraw	.10	.04	.01
☐ 326	Carl Yastrzemski	.75	.30	.07	☐ 372	Doug Bair	.03	.01	.00
☐ 327	Ron Roenicke	.03	.01	.00	☐ 373	Ruppert Jones	.03	.01	.00
☐ 328	Howard Johnson	2.25	.90	.22	☐ 374	Alex Trevino	.03	.01	.00
☐ 329	Rick Dempsey	.03	.01	.00	☐ 375	Ken Dayley	.06	.02	.00
☐ 330A	Jim Slaton	.06	.02	.00	☐ 376	Rod Scurry	.03	.01	.00
	(bio printed black on white)				☐ 377	Bob Brenly	.06	.02	.00
☐ 330B	Jim Slaton	.10	.04	.01	☐ 378	Scot Thompson	.03	.01	.00
	(bio printed black on yellow)				☐ 379	Julio Cruz	.03	.01	.00
☐ 331	Benny Ayala	.03	.01	.00	☐ 380	John Stearns	.03	.01	.00
☐ 332	Ted Simmons	.12	.05	.01	☐ 381	Dale Murray	.03	.01	.00
☐ 333	Lou Whitaker	.15	.06	.01	☐ 382	Frank Viola	3.75	1.50	.37
☐ 334	Chuck Rainey	.03	.01	.00	☐ 383	Al Bumbry	.03	.01	.00
☐ 335	Lou Piniella	.10	.04	.01	☐ 384	Ben Oglivie	.06	.02	.00
☐ 336	Steve Sax	.35	.14	.03	☐ 385	Dave Tobik	.03	.01	.00
☐ 337	Toby Harrah	.06	.02	.00	☐ 386	Bob Stanley	.03	.01	.00
☐ 338	George Brett	.65	.26	.06	☐ 387	Andre Robertson	.03	.01	.00
☐ 339	Dave Lopes	.08	.03	.01	☐ 388	Jorge Orta	.03	.01	.00
☐ 340	Gary Carter	.40	.16	.04	☐ 389	Ed Whitson	.06	.02	.00
☐ 341	John Grubb	.03	.01	.00	☐ 390	Don Hood	.03	.01	.00
☐ 342	Tim Foli	.03	.01	.00	☐ 391	Tom Underwood	.03	.01	.00
☐ 343	Jim Kaat	.12	.05	.01	☐ 392	Tim Wallach	.18	.08	.01
☐ 344	Mike LaCoss	.03	.01	.00	☐ 393	Steve Renko	.03	.01	.00
☐ 345	Larry Christenson	.03	.01	.00	☐ 394	Mickey Rivers	.06	.02	.00
☐ 346	Juan Bonilla	.03	.01	.00	☐ 395	Greg Luzinski	.10	.04	.01

		MINT	EXC	G-VG
☐ 396	Art Howe	.08	.03	.01
☐ 397	Alan Wiggins	.15	.06	.01
☐ 398	Jim Barr	.03	.01	.00
☐ 399	Ivan DeJesus	.03	.01	.00
☐ 400	Tom Lawless	.06	.02	.00
☐ 401	Bob Walk	.08	.03	.01
☐ 402	Jimmy Smith	.03	.01	.00
☐ 403	Lee Smith	.12	.05	.01
☐ 404	George Hendrick	.06	.02	.00
☐ 405	Eddie Murray	.50	.20	.05
☐ 406	Marshall Edwards	.03	.01	.00
☐ 407	Lance Parrish	.25	.10	.02
☐ 408	Carney Lansford	.15	.06	.01
☐ 409	Dave Winfield	.40	.16	.04
☐ 410	Bob Welch	.10	.04	.01
☐ 411	Larry Milbourne	.03	.01	.00
☐ 412	Dennis Leonard	.06	.02	.00
☐ 413	Dan Meyer	.03	.01	.00
☐ 414	Charlie Lea	.03	.01	.00
☐ 415	Rick Honeycutt	.03	.01	.00
☐ 416	Mike Witt	.20	.08	.02
☐ 417	Steve Trout	.03	.01	.00
☐ 418	Glenn Brummer	.03	.01	.00
☐ 419	Denny Walling	.03	.01	.00
☐ 420	Gary Matthews	.06	.02	.00
☐ 421	Charlie Leibrandt	.08	.03	.01
	(Liebrandt on front of card)			
☐ 422	Juan Eichelberger	.06	.02	.00
	(photo actually Joe Pittman)			
☐ 423	Matt Guante	.06	.02	.00
☐ 424	Bill Laskey	.03	.01	.00
☐ 425	Jerry Royster	.03	.01	.00
☐ 426	Dickie Noles	.03	.01	.00
☐ 427	George Foster	.12	.05	.01
☐ 428	Mike Moore	.35	.14	.03
☐ 429	Gary Ward	.06	.02	.00
☐ 430	Barry Bonnell	.03	.01	.00
☐ 431	Ron Washington	.03	.01	.00
☐ 432	Rance Mulliniks	.03	.01	.00
☐ 433	Mike Stanton	.03	.01	.00
☐ 434	Jesse Orosco	.08	.03	.01
☐ 435	Larry Bowa	.12	.05	.01
☐ 436	Biff Pocoroba	.03	.01	.00
☐ 437	Johnny Ray	.15	.06	.01
☐ 438	Joe Morgan	.30	.12	.03
☐ 439	Eric Show	.35	.14	.03
☐ 440	Larry Biittner	.03	.01	.00
☐ 441	Greg Gross	.03	.01	.00
☐ 442	Gene Tenace	.06	.02	.00

		MINT	EXC	G-VG
☐ 443	Danny Heep	.03	.01	.00
☐ 444	Bobby Clark	.03	.01	.00
☐ 445	Kevin Hickey	.03	.01	.00
☐ 446	Scott Sanderson	.03	.01	.00
☐ 447	Frank Tanana	.08	.03	.01
☐ 448	Cesar Geronimo	.03	.01	.00
☐ 449	Jimmy Sexton	.03	.01	.00
☐ 450	Mike Hargrove	.03	.01	.00
☐ 451	Doyle Alexander	.08	.03	.01
☐ 452	Dwight Evans	.18	.08	.01
☐ 453	Terry Forster	.08	.03	.01
☐ 454	Tom Brookens	.03	.01	.00
☐ 455	Rich Dauer	.03	.01	.00
☐ 456	Rob Picciolo	.03	.01	.00
☐ 457	Terry Crowley	.03	.01	.00
☐ 458	Ned Yost	.03	.01	.00
☐ 459	Kirk Gibson	.40	.16	.04
☐ 460	Reid Nichols	.03	.01	.00
☐ 461	Oscar Gamble	.03	.01	.00
☐ 462	Dusty Baker	.06	.02	.00
☐ 463	Jack Perconte	.03	.01	.00
☐ 464	Frank White	.08	.03	.01
☐ 465	Mickey Klutts	.03	.01	.00
☐ 466	Warren Cromartie	.03	.01	.00
☐ 467	Larry Parrish	.06	.02	.00
☐ 468	Bobby Grich	.08	.03	.01
☐ 469	Dane Iorg	.03	.01	.00
☐ 470	Joe Niekro	.10	.04	.01
☐ 471	Ed Farmer	.03	.01	.00
☐ 472	Tim Flannery	.03	.01	.00
☐ 473	Dave Parker	.20	.08	.02
☐ 474	Jeff Leonard	.08	.03	.01
☐ 475	Al Hrabosky	.06	.02	.00
☐ 476	Ron Hodges	.03	.01	.00
☐ 477	Leon Durham	.06	.02	.00
☐ 478	Jim Essian	.03	.01	.00
☐ 479	Roy Lee Jackson	.03	.01	.00
☐ 480	Brad Havens	.03	.01	.00
☐ 481	Joe Price	.03	.01	.00
☐ 482	Tony Bernazard	.03	.01	.00
☐ 483	Scott McGregor	.06	.02	.00
☐ 484	Paul Molitor	.18	.08	.01
☐ 485	Mike Ivie	.03	.01	.00
☐ 486	Ken Griffey	.06	.02	.00
☐ 487	Dennis Eckersley	.15	.06	.01
☐ 488	Steve Garvey	.40	.16	.04
☐ 489	Mike Fischlin	.03	.01	.00
☐ 490	U.L. Washington	.03	.01	.00
☐ 491	Steve McCatty	.03	.01	.00

		MINT	EXC	G-VG
☐ 492	Roy Johnson	.03	.01	.00
☐ 493	Don Baylor	.12	.05	.01
☐ 494	Bobby Johnson	.03	.01	.00
☐ 495	Mike Squires	.03	.01	.00
☐ 496	Bert Roberge	.03	.01	.00
☐ 497	Dick Ruthven	.03	.01	.00
☐ 498	Tito Landrum	.03	.01	.00
☐ 499	Sixto Lezcano	.03	.01	.00
☐ 500	Johnny Bench	.45	.18	.04
☐ 501	Larry Whisenton	.03	.01	.00
☐ 502	Manny Sarmiento	.03	.01	.00
☐ 503	Fred Breining	.03	.01	.00
☐ 504	Bill Campbell	.03	.01	.00
☐ 505	Todd Cruz	.03	.01	.00
☐ 506	Bob Bailor	.03	.01	.00
☐ 507	Dave Stieb	.18	.08	.01
☐ 508	Al Williams	.03	.01	.00
☐ 509	Dan Ford	.03	.01	.00
☐ 510	Gorman Thomas	.10	.04	.01
☐ 511	Chet Lemon	.06	.02	.00
☐ 512	Mike Torrez	.03	.01	.00
☐ 513	Shane Rawley	.06	.02	.00
☐ 514	Mark Belanger	.06	.02	.00
☐ 515	Rodney Craig	.03	.01	.00
☐ 516	Onix Concepcion	.03	.01	.00
☐ 517	Mike Heath	.03	.01	.00
☐ 518	Andre Dawson	.35	.14	.03
☐ 519	Luis Sanchez	.03	.01	.00
☐ 520	Terry Bogener	.03	.01	.00
☐ 521	Rudy Law	.03	.01	.00
☐ 522	Ray Knight	.08	.03	.01
☐ 523	Joe Lefebvre	.03	.01	.00
☐ 524	Jim Wohlford	.03	.01	.00
☐ 525	Julio Franco	1.75	.70	.17
☐ 526	Ron Oester	.03	.01	.00
☐ 527	Hick Mahler	.06	.02	.00
☐ 528	Steve Nicosia	.03	.01	.00
☐ 529	Junior Kennedy	.03	.01	.00
☐ 530A	Whitey Herzog MG	.10	.04	.01
	(bio printed black on white)			
☐ 530B	Whitey Herzog MG	.10	.04	.01
	(bio printed black on yellow)			
☐ 531A	Don Sutton	.40	.16	.04
	(blue border on photo)			
☐ 531B	Don Sutton	.40	.16	.04
	(green border on photo)			
☐ 532	Mark Brouhard	.03	.01	.00
☐ 533A	Sparky Anderson MG	.10	.04	.01
	(bio printed black on white)			
☐ 533B	Sparky Anderson MG	.10	.04	.01
	(bio printed black on yellow)			
☐ 534	Roger LaFrancois	.03	.01	.00
☐ 535	George Frazier	.03	.01	.00
☐ 536	Tom Niedenfuer	.08	.03	.01
☐ 537	Ed Glynn	.03	.01	.00
☐ 538	Lee May	.03	.01	.00
☐ 539	Bob Kearney	.03	.01	.00
☐ 540	Tim Raines	.45	.18	.04
☐ 541	Paul Mirabella	.03	.01	.00
☐ 542	Luis Tiant	.08	.03	.01
☐ 543	Ron LeFlore	.06	.02	.00
☐ 544	Dave LaPoint	.35	.14	.03
☐ 545	Randy Moffitt	.03	.01	.00
☐ 546	Luis Aguayo	.03	.01	.00
☐ 547	Brad Lesley	.03	.01	.00
☐ 548	Luis Salazar	.06	.02	.00
☐ 549	John Candelaria	.08	.03	.01
☐ 550	Dave Bergman	.03	.01	.00
☐ 551	Bob Watson	.06	.02	.00
☐ 552	Pat Tabler	.12	.05	.01
☐ 553	Brent Gaff	.03	.01	.00
☐ 554	Al Cowens	.03	.01	.00
☐ 555	Tom Brunansky	.50	.20	.05
☐ 556	Lloyd Moseby	.12	.05	.01
☐ 557A	Pascual Perez ERR	2.00	.80	.20
	(Twins in glove)			
☐ 557B	Pascual Perez COR	.10	.04	.01
	(Braves in glove)			
☐ 558	Willie Upshaw	.06	.02	.00
☐ 559	Richie Zisk	.06	.02	.00
☐ 560	Pat Zachry	.03	.01	.00
☐ 561	Jay Johnstone	.08	.03	.01
☐ 562	Carlos Diaz	.06	.02	.00
☐ 563	John Tudor	15	.06	.01
☐ 564	Frank Robinson MG	.12	.05	.01
☐ 565	Dave Edwards	.03	.01	.00
☐ 566	Paul Householder	.03	.01	.00
☐ 567	Ron Reed	.03	.01	.00
☐ 568	Mike Ramsey	.03	.01	.00
☐ 569	Kiko Garcia	.03	.01	.00
☐ 570	Tommy John	.15	.06	.01
☐ 571	Tony LaRussa MG	.06	.02	.00
☐ 572	Joel Youngblood	.03	.01	.00
☐ 573	Wayne Tolleson	.20	.08	.02
☐ 574	Keith Creel	.03	.01	.00
☐ 575	Billy Martin MG	.12	.05	.01
☐ 576	Jerry Dybzinski	.03	.01	.00
☐ 577	Rick Cerone	.03	.01	.00

	MINT	EXC	G-VG
☐ 578 Tony Perez	.15	.06	.01
☐ 579 Greg Brock	.35	.14	.03
☐ 580 Glenn Wilson	.30	.12	.03
☐ 581 Tim Stoddard	.03	.01	.00
☐ 582 Bob McClure	.03	.01	.00
☐ 583 Jim Dwyer	.03	.01	.00
☐ 584 Ed Romero	.03	.01	.00
☐ 585 Larry Herndon	.03	.01	.00
☐ 586 Wade Boggs	17.00	7.00	1.70
☐ 587 Jay Howell	.06	.02	.00
☐ 588 Dave Stewart	.15	.06	.01
☐ 589 Bert Blyleven	.15	.06	.01
☐ 590 Dick Howser MG	.08	.03	.01
☐ 591 Wayne Gross	.03	.01	.00
☐ 592 Terry Francona	.03	.01	.00
☐ 593 Don Werner	.03	.01	.00
☐ 594 Bill Stein	.03	.01	.00
☐ 595 Jesse Barfield	.65	.26	.06
☐ 596 Bob Molinaro	.03	.01	.00
☐ 597 Mike Vail	.03	.01	.00
☐ 598 Tony Gwynn	9.00	3.75	.90
☐ 599 Gary Rajsich	.03	.01	.00
☐ 600 Jerry Ujdur	.03	.01	.00
☐ 601 Cliff Johnson	.03	.01	.00
☐ 602 Jerry White	.03	.01	.00
☐ 603 Bryan Clark	.03	.01	.00
☐ 604 Joe Ferguson	.03	.01	.00
☐ 605 Guy Sularz	.03	.01	.00
☐ 606A Ozzie Virgil	.10	.04	.01
(green border on photo)			
☐ 606B Ozzie Virgil	.10	.04	.01
(orange border on photo)			
☐ 607 Terry Harper	.03	.01	.00
☐ 608 Harvey Kuenn MG	.06	.02	.00
☐ 609 Jim Sundberg	.06	.02	.00
☐ 610 Willie Stargell	.35	.14	.03
☐ 611 Reggie Smith	.08	.03	.01
☐ 612 Rob Wilfong	.03	.01	.00
☐ 613 The Niekro Brothers	.12	.05	.01
Joe Niekro			
Phil Niekro			
☐ 614 Lee Elia MG	.03	.01	.00
☐ 615 Mickey Hatcher	.08	.03	.01
☐ 616 Jerry Hairston	.03	.01	.00
☐ 617 John Martin	.03	.01	.00
☐ 618 Wally Backman	.20	.08	.02
☐ 619 Storm Davis	.45	.18	.04
☐ 620 Alan Knicely	.03	.01	.00
☐ 621 John Stuper	.03	.01	.00

	MINT	EXC	G-VG
☐ 622 Matt Sinatro	.03	.01	.00
☐ 623 Geno Petralli	.06	.02	.00
☐ 624 Duane Walker	.03	.01	.00
☐ 625 Dick Williams MG	.03	.01	.00
☐ 626 Pat Corrales MG	.03	.01	.00
☐ 627 Vern Ruhle	.03	.01	.00
☐ 628 Joe Torre MG	.08	.03	.01
☐ 629 Anthony Johnson	.03	.01	.00
☐ 630 Steve Howe	.03	.01	.00
☐ 631 Gary Woods	.03	.01	.00
☐ 632 LaMarr Hoyt	.08	.03	.01
☐ 633 Steve Swisher	.03	.01	.00
☐ 634 Terry Leach	.25	.10	.02
☐ 635 Jeff Newman	.03	.01	.00
☐ 636 Brett Butler	.12	.05	.01
☐ 637 Gary Gray	.03	.01	.00
☐ 638 Lee Mazzilli	.03	.01	.00
☐ 639A Ron Jackson ERR	10.00	4.00	1.00
(A's in glove)			
☐ 639B Ron Jackson COR	.15	.06	.01
(Angels in glove, red border on photo)			
☐ 639C Ron Jackson COR	.50	.20	.05
(Angels in glove, green border on photo)			
☐ 640 Juan Beniquez	.03	.01	.00
☐ 641 Dave Rucker	.03	.01	.00
☐ 642 Luis Pujols	.03	.01	.00
☐ 643 Rick Monday	.06	.02	.00
☐ 644 Hosken Powell	.03	.01	.00
☐ 645 The Chicken	.20	.08	.02
☐ 646 Dave Engle	.03	.01	.00
☐ 647 Dick Davis	.03	.01	.00
☐ 648 Frank Robinson	.12	.05	.01
Vida Blue			
Joe Morgan			
☐ 649 Al Chambers	.03	.01	.00
☐ 650 Jesus Vega	.03	.01	.00
☐ 651 Jeff Jones	.03	.01	.00
☐ 652 Marvis Foley	.03	.01	.00
☐ 653 Ty Cobb Puzzle Card	.03	.01	.00
☐ 654A Dick Perez/Diamond	.15	.02	.00
King Checklist			
(unnumbered)			
(word "checklist" omitted from back)			
☐ 654B Dick Perez/Diamond	.15	.02	.00
King Checklist			
(unnumbered)			
(word "checklist" is on back)			

		MINT	EXC	G-VG
☐ 655	Checklist 1 .... (unnumbered)	.07	.01	.00
☐ 656	Checklist 2 .... (unnumbered)	.07	.01	.00
☐ 657	Checklist 3 .... (unnumbered)	.07	.01	.00
☐ 658	Checklist 4 .... (unnumbered)	.07	.01	.00
☐ 659	Checklist 5 .... (unnumbered)	.07	.01	.00
☐ 660	Checklist 6 .... (unnumbered)	.07	.01	.00

1984 Donruss

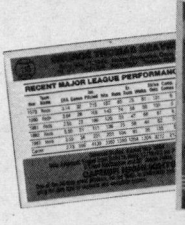

The 1984 Donruss set contains a total of 660 cards, each measuring 2 ½" by 3 ½"; however, only 658 are numbered. The first 26 cards in the set are again Diamond Kings (DK), although the drawings this year were styled differently and are easily differentiated from other DK issues. A new feature, Rated Rookies (RR), was introduced with this set with Bill Madden's 20 selections comprising numbers 27 through 46. Two "Living Legend" cards designated A (featuring Gaylord Perry and Rollie Fingers) and B (featuring Johnny Bench and Carl Yastrzemski) were issued as bonus cards in wax packs, but were not issued in the vending sets sold to hobby dealers. The seven unnumbered checklist cards are arbitrarily assigned numbers 652 through 658 and are

listed at the end of the list below. The designs on the fronts of the Donruss cards changed considerably from the past two years. The backs contain statistics and are printed in green and black ink. The cards were distributed with a 63-piece puzzle of Duke Snider. There are no extra variation cards included in the complete set price below.

		MINT	EXC	G-VG
	Complete Set (658)	225.00	90.00	22.00
	Common Player (1-660) ..	.10	.04	.01
☐ 1A	Robin Yount DK ERR (Perez Steel)	.75	.20	.04
☐ 1B	Robin Yount DK COR	1.50	.60	.15
☐ 2A	Dave Concepcion DK ERR (Perez Steel)	.15	.06	.01
☐ 2B	Dave Concepcion DK COR	.30	.12	.03
☐ 3A	Dwayne Murphy DK ERR (Perez Steel)	.15	.06	.01
☐ 3B	Dwayne Murphy DK COR	.30	.12	.03
☐ 4A	John Castino DK ERR (Perez Steel)	.15	.06	.01
☐ 4B	John Castino DK COR	.30	.12	.03
☐ 5A	Leon Durham DK ERR (Perez Steel)	.15	.06	.01
☐ 5B	Leon Durham DK COR	.30	.12	.03
☐ 6A	Rusty Staub DK ERR (Perez Steel)	.15	.06	.01
☐ 6B	Rusty Staub DK COR	.30	.12	.03
☐ 7A	Jack Clark DK ERR (Perez Steel)	.40	.16	.04
☐ 7B	Jack Clark DK COR	.80	.32	.08
☐ 8A	Dave Dravecky DK ERR (Perez Steel)	.15	.06	.01
☐ 8B	Dave Dravecky DK COR	.30	.12	.03
☐ 9A	Al Oliver DK ERR . (Perez Steel)	.15	.06	.01
☐ 9B	Al Oliver DK COR .	.30	.12	.03
☐ 10A	Dave Righetti DK .. ERR (Perez Steel)	.25	.10	.02
☐ 10B	Dave Righetti DK .. COR	.50	.20	.05
☐ 11A	Hal McRae DK ERR (Perez Steel)	.15	.06	.01
☐ 11B	Hal McRae DK COR	.30	.12	.03

		MINT	EXC	G-VG
☐	12A Ray Knight DK ERR (Perez Steel)	.15	.06	.01
☐	12B Ray Knight DK COR	.30	.12	.03
☐	13A Bruce Sutter DK ERR (Perez Steel)	.15	.06	.01
☐	13B Bruce Sutter DK COR	.30	.12	.03
☐	14A Bob Horner DK ERR (Perez Steel)	.20	.08	.02
☐	14B Bob Horner DK COR	.40	.16	.04
☐	15A Lance Parrish DK .. ERR (Perez Steel)	.30	.12	.03
☐	15B Lance Parrish DK .. COR	.60	.24	.06
☐	16A Matt Young DK ERR (Perez Steel)	.15	.06	.01
☐	16B Matt Young DK COR	.30	.12	.03
☐	17A Fred Lynn DK ERR . (Perez Steel) (A's logo on back)	.20	.08	.02
☐	17B Fred Lynn DK COR	.40	.16	.04
☐	18A Ron Kittle DK ERR . (Perez Steel)	.20	.08	.02
☐	18B Ron Kittle DK COR .	.40	.16	.04
☐	19A Jim Clancy DK ERR . (Perez Steel)	.15	.06	.01
☐	19B Jim Clancy DK COR	.30	.12	.03
☐	20A Bill Madlock DK ERR (Perez Steel)	.15	.06	.01
☐	20B Bill Madlock DK COR	.30	.12	.03
☐	21A Larry Parrish DK ... ERR (Perez Steel)	.15	.06	.01
☐	21B Larry Parrish DK ... COR	.30	.12	.03
☐	22A Eddie Murray DK ERR (Perez Steel)	1.00	.40	.10
☐	22B Eddie Murray DK COR	2.00	.80	.20
☐	23A Mike Schmidt DK ERR (Perez Steel)	1.25	.50	.12
☐	23B Mike Schmidt DK COR	2.50	1.00	.25
☐	24A Pedro Guerrero DK . ERR (Perez Steel)	.30	.12	.03
☐	24B Pedro Guerrero DK . COR	.60	.24	.06
☐	25A Andre Thornton DK . ERR (Perez Steel)	.15	.06	.01
☐	25B Andre Thornton DK . COR	.30	.12	.03
☐	26A Wade Boggs DK ERR (Perez Steel)	3.50	1.40	.35
☐	26B Wade Boggs DK COR	6.00	2.40	.60
☐	27 Joel Skinner RR . .	.25	.10	.02
☐	28 Tommy Dunbar RR	.15	.06	.01
☐	29A Mike Stenhouse RR ERR (no back number)	.25	.10	.02
☐	29B Mike Stenhouse RR COR (number on back)	2.50	1.00	.25
☐	30A Ron Darling RR ERR (no number on back)	6.00	2.40	.60
☐	30B Ron Darling RR COR	10.00	4.00	1.00
☐	31 Dion James RR ...	.75	.30	.07
☐	32 Tony Fernandez RR	7.50	3.00	.75
☐	33 Angel Salazar RR . .	.15	.06	.01
☐	34 Kevin McReynolds RR	11.00	4.50	1.10
☐	35 Dick Schofield RR . .	.75	.30	.07
☐	36 Brad Komminsk RR .	.20	.08	.02
☐	37 Tim Teufel RR	.45	.18	.04
☐	38 Doug Frobel RR	.15	.06	.01
☐	39 Greg Gagne RR	.45	.18	.04
☐	40 Mike Fuentes RR	.15	.06	.01
☐	41 Joe Carter RR	11.00	4.50	1.10
☐	42 Mike Brown RR ... (Angels OF)	.15	.06	.01
☐	43 Mike Jeffcoat RR ...	.15	.06	.01
☐	44 Sid Fernandez RR ..	5.00	2.00	.50
☐	45 Brian Dayett RR ...	.20	.08	.02
☐	46 Chris Smith RR	.15	.06	.01
☐	47 Eddie Murray	1.00	.40	.10
☐	48 Robin Yount	.65	.26	.06
☐	49 Lance Parrish	.35	.14	.03
☐	50 Jim Rice	.45	.18	.04
☐	51 Dave Winfield	.85	.34	.08
☐	52 Fernando Valenzuela	.45	.18	.04
☐	53 George Brett	1.25	.50	.12
☐	54 Rickey Henderson .	1.25	.50	.12
☐	55 Gary Carter	.65	.26	.06
☐	56 Buddy Bell	.15	.06	.01
☐	57 Reggie Jackson ...	1.25	.50	.12
☐	58 Harold Baines	.25	.10	.02
☐	59 Ozzie Smith	.40	.16	.04
☐	60 Nolan Ryan	.85	.34	.08
☐	61 Pete Rose	2.50	1.00	.25
☐	62 Ron Oester	.10	.04	.01
☐	63 Steve Garvey	.80	.32	.08
☐	64 Jason Thompson ..	.10	.04	.01
☐	65 Jack Clark	.35	.14	.03
☐	66 Dale Murphy	1.50	.60	.15
☐	67 Leon Durham	.15	.06	.01
☐	68 Darryl Strawberry .	27.00	10.00	2.50

		MINT	EXC	G-VG
☐ 69	Richie Zisk	.10	.04	.01
☐ 70	Kent Hrbek	.50	.20	.05
☐ 71	Dave Stieb	.25	.10	.02
☐ 72	Ken Schrom	.10	.04	.01
☐ 73	George Bell	1.50	.60	.15
☐ 74	John Moses	.15	.06	.01
☐ 75	Ed Lynch	.10	.04	.01
☐ 76	Chuck Rainey	.10	.04	.01
☐ 77	Biff Pocoroba	.10	.04	.01
☐ 78	Cecilio Guante	.10	.04	.01
☐ 79	Jim Barr	.10	.04	.01
☐ 80	Kurt Bevacqua	.10	.04	.01
☐ 81	Tom Foley	.10	.04	.01
☐ 82	Joe Lefebvre	.10	.04	.01
☐ 83	Andy Van Slyke	4.00	1.60	.40
☐ 84	Bob Lillis MG	.10	.04	.01
☐ 85	Ricky Adams	.10	.04	.01
☐ 86	Jerry Hairston	.10	.04	.01
☐ 87	Bob James	.20	.08	.02
☐ 88	Joe Altobelli MG	.10	.04	.01
☐ 89	Ed Romero	.10	.04	.01
☐ 90	John Grubb	.10	.04	.01
☐ 91	John Henry Johnson	.10	.04	.01
☐ 92	Juan Espino	.10	.04	.01
☐ 93	Candy Maldonado	.25	.10	.02
☐ 94	Andre Thornton	.15	.06	.01
☐ 95	Onix Concepcion	.10	.04	.01
☐ 96	Donnie Hill	.15	.06	.01
	(listed as P, should be 2B)			
☐ 97	Andre Dawson UER	.65	.26	.06
	(wrong middle name, should be Nolan)			
☐ 98	Frank Tanana	.15	.06	.01
☐ 99	Curt Wilkerson	.15	.06	.01
☐ 100	Larry Gura	.10	.04	.01
☐ 101	Dwayne Murphy	.10	.04	.01
☐ 102	Tom Brennan	.10	.04	.01
☐ 103	Dave Righetti	.30	.12	.03
☐ 104	Steve Sax	.40	.16	.04
☐ 105	Dan Petry	.15	.06	.01
☐ 106	Cal Ripken	1.25	.50	.12
☐ 107	Paul Molitor	.30	.12	.03
☐ 108	Fred Lynn	.25	.10	.02
☐ 109	Neil Allen	.10	.04	.01
☐ 110	Joe Niekro	.15	.06	.01
☐ 111	Steve Carlton	.65	.26	.06
☐ 112	Terry Kennedy	.15	.06	.01
☐ 113	Bill Madlock	.20	.08	.02
☐ 114	Chili Davis	.25	.10	.02

		MINT	EXC	G-VG
☐ 115	Jim Gantner	.10	.04	.01
☐ 116	Tom Seaver	.75	.30	.07
☐ 117	Bill Buckner	.20	.08	.02
☐ 118	Bill Caudill	.10	.04	.01
☐ 119	Jim Clancy	.10	.04	.01
☐ 120	John Castino	.10	.04	.01
☐ 121	Dave Concepcion	.20	.08	.02
☐ 122	Greg Luzinski	.20	.08	.02
☐ 123	Mike Boddicker	.20	.08	.02
☐ 124	Pete Ladd	.10	.04	.01
☐ 125	Juan Berenguer	.10	.04	.01
☐ 126	John Montefusco	.10	.04	.01
☐ 127	Ed Jurak	.10	.04	.01
☐ 128	Tom Niedenfuer	.15	.06	.01
☐ 129	Bert Blyleven	.20	.08	.02
☐ 130	Bud Black	.10	.04	.01
☐ 131	Gorman Heimueller	.10	.04	.01
☐ 132	Dan Schatzeder	.10	.04	.01
☐ 133	Ron Jackson	.10	.04	.01
☐ 134	Tom Henke	.85	.34	.08
☐ 135	Kevin Hickey	.10	.04	.01
☐ 136	Mike Scott	.35	.14	.03
☐ 137	Bo Diaz	.10	.04	.01
☐ 138	Glenn Brummer	.10	.04	.01
☐ 139	Sid Monge	.10	.04	.01
☐ 140	Rich Gale	.10	.04	.01
☐ 141	Brett Butler	.20	.08	.02
☐ 142	Brian Harper	.15	.06	.01
☐ 143	John Rabb	.10	.04	.01
☐ 144	Gary Woods	.10	.04	.01
☐ 145	Pat Putnam	.10	.04	.01
☐ 146	Jim Acker	.15	.06	.01
☐ 147	Mickey Hatcher	.20	.08	.02
☐ 148	Todd Cruz	.10	.04	.01
☐ 149	Tom Tellmann	.10	.04	.01
☐ 150	John Wockenfuss	.10	.04	.01
☐ 151	Wade Boggs	10.00	4.00	1.00
☐ 152	Don Baylor	.20	.08	.02
☐ 153	Bob Welch	.15	.06	.01
☐ 154	Alan Bannister	.10	.04	.01
☐ 155	Willie Aikens	.10	.04	.01
☐ 156	Jeff Burroughs	.10	.04	.01
☐ 157	Bryan Little	.10	.04	.01
☐ 158	Bob Boone	.20	.08	.02
☐ 159	Dave Hostetler	.10	.04	.01
☐ 160	Jerry Dybzinski	.10	.04	.01
☐ 161	Mike Madden	.10	.04	.01
☐ 162	Luis DeLeon	.10	.04	.01
☐ 163	Willie Hernandez	.25	.10	.02

		MINT	EXC	G-VG			MINT	EXC	G-VG
☐ 164	Frank Pastore	.10	.04	.01	☐ 213	Bruce Hurst	.30	.12	.03
☐ 165	Rick Camp	.10	.04	.01	☐ 214	Bob Shirley	.10	.04	.01
☐ 166	Lee Mazzilli	.10	.04	.01	☐ 215	Pat Zachry	.10	.04	.01
☐ 167	Scot Thompson	.10	.04	.01	☐ 216	Julio Franco	.30	.12	.03
☐ 168	Bob Forsch	.10	.04	.01	☐ 217	Mike Armstrong	.10	.04	.01
☐ 169	Mike Flanagan	.15	.06	.01	☐ 218	Dave Beard	.10	.04	.01
☐ 170	Rick Manning	.10	.04	.01	☐ 219	Steve Rogers	.10	.04	.01
☐ 171	Chet Lemon	.15	.06	.01	☐ 220	John Butcher	.10	.04	.01
☐ 172	Jerry Remy	.10	.04	.01	☐ 221	Mike Smithson	.15	.06	.01
☐ 173	Ron Guidry	.25	.10	.02	☐ 222	Frank White	.15	.06	.01
☐ 174	Pedro Guerrero	.45	.18	.04	☐ 223	Mike Heath	.10	.04	.01
☐ 175	Willie Wilson	.20	.08	.02	☐ 224	Chris Bando	.10	.04	.01
☐ 176	Carney Lansford	.20	.08	.02	☐ 225	Roy Smalley	.10	.04	.01
☐ 177	Al Oliver	.20	.08	.02	☐ 226	Dusty Baker	.15	.06	.01
☐ 178	Jim Sundberg	.10	.04	.01	☐ 227	Lou Whitaker	.25	.10	.02
☐ 179	Bobby Grich	.15	.06	.01	☐ 228	John Lowenstein	.10	.04	.01
☐ 180	Rich Dotson	.15	.06	.01	☐ 229	Ben Oglivie	.15	.06	.01
☐ 181	Joaquin Andujar	.15	.06	.01	☐ 230	Doug DeCinces	.15	.06	.01
☐ 182	Jose Cruz	.15	.06	.01	☐ 231	Lonnie Smith	.15	.06	.01
☐ 183	Mike Schmidt	1.50	.60	.15	☐ 232	Ray Knight	.15	.06	.01
☐ 184	Gary Redus	.40	.16	.04	☐ 233	Gary Matthews	.15	.06	.01
☐ 185	Garry Templeton	.15	.06	.01	☐ 234	Juan Bonilla	.10	.04	.01
☐ 186	Tony Pena	.20	.08	.02	☐ 235	Rod Scurry	.10	.04	.01
☐ 187	Greg Minton	.10	.04	.01	☐ 236	Atlee Hammaker	.10	.04	.01
☐ 188	Phil Niekro	.40	.16	.04	☐ 237	Mike Caldwell	.10	.04	.01
☐ 189	Ferguson Jenkins	.20	.08	.02	☐ 238	Keith Hernandez	.45	.18	.04
☐ 190	Mookie Wilson	.15	.06	.01	☐ 239	Larry Bowa	.15	.06	.01
☐ 191	Jim Beattie	.10	.04	.01	☐ 240	Tony Bernazard	.10	.04	.01
☐ 192	Gary Ward	.15	.06	.01	☐ 241	Damaso Garcia	.10	.04	.01
☐ 193	Jesse Barfield	.40	.16	.04	☐ 242	Tom Brunansky	.30	.12	.03
☐ 194	Pete Filson	.10	.04	.01	☐ 243	Dan Driessen	.10	.04	.01
☐ 195	Roy Lee Jackson	.10	.04	.01	☐ 244	Ron Kittle	.30	.12	.03
☐ 196	Rick Sweet	.10	.04	.01	☐ 245	Tim Stoddard	.10	.04	.01
☐ 197	Jesse Orosco	.10	.04	.01	☐ 246	Bob L. Gibson	.15	.06	.01
☐ 198	Steve Lake	.10	.04	.01		(Brewers Pitcher)			
☐ 199	Ken Dayley	.10	.04	.01	☐ 247	Marty Castillo	.10	.04	.01
☐ 200	Manny Sarmiento	.10	.04	.01	☐ 248	Don Mattingly	65.00	26.00	6.50
☐ 201	Mark Davis	.20	.08	.02		("trailing" on back)			
☐ 202	Tim Flannery	.10	.04	.01	☐ 249	Jeff Newman	.10	.04	.01
☐ 203	Bill Scherrer	.10	.04	.01	☐ 250	Alejandro Pena	.45	.18	.04
☐ 204	Al Holland	.10	.04	.01	☐ 251	Toby Harrah	.15	.06	.01
☐ 205	Dave Von Ohlen	.10	.04	.01	☐ 252	Cesar Geronimo	.10	.04	.01
☐ 206	Mike LaCoss	.10	.04	.01	☐ 253	Tom Underwood	.10	.04	.01
☐ 207	Juan Beniquez	.10	.04	.01	☐ 254	Doug Flynn	.10	.04	.01
☐ 208	Juan Agosto	.10	.04	.01	☐ 255	Andy Hassler	.10	.04	.01
☐ 209	Bobby Ramos	.10	.04	.01	☐ 256	Odell Jones	.10	.04	.01
☐ 210	Al Bumbry	.10	.04	.01	☐ 257	Rudy Law	.10	.04	.01
☐ 211	Mark Brouhard	.10	.04	.01	☐ 258	Harry Spilman	.10	.04	.01
☐ 212	Howard Bailey	.10	.04	.01	☐ 259	Marty Bystrom	.10	.04	.01

		MINT	EXC	G-VG			MINT	EXC	G-VG
☐ 260	Dave Rucker	.10	.04	.01	☐ 308	Johnny Ray	.25	.10	.02
☐ 261	Ruppert Jones	.10	.04	.01	☐ 309	Andy McGaffigan	.10	.04	.01
☐ 262	Jeff R. Jones	.10	.04	.01	☐ 310	Claudell Washington	.15	.06	.01
	(Reds OF)				☐ 311	Ryne Sandberg	2.00	.80	.20
☐ 263	Gerald Perry	2.00	.80	.20	☐ 312	George Foster	.25	.10	.02
☐ 264	Gene Tenace	.15	.06	.01	☐ 313	Spike Owen	.30	.12	.03
☐ 265	Brad Wellman	.10	.04	.01	☐ 314	Gary Gaetti	.90	.36	.09
☐ 266	Dickie Noles	.10	.04	.01	☐ 315	Willie Upshaw	.15	.06	.01
☐ 267	Jamie Allen	.10	.04	.01	☐ 316	Al Williams	.10	.04	.01
☐ 268	Jim Gott	.15	.06	.01	☐ 317	Jorge Orta	.10	.04	.01
☐ 269	Ron Davis	.10	.04	.01	☐ 318	Orlando Mercado	.10	.04	.01
☐ 270	Benny Ayala	.10	.04	.01	☐ 319	Junior Ortiz	.10	.04	.01
☐ 271	Ned Yost	.10	.04	.01	☐ 320	Mike Proly	.10	.04	.01
☐ 272	Dave Rozema	.10	.04	.01	☐ 321	Randy Johnson	.10	.04	.01
☐ 273	Dave Stapleton	.10	.04	.01	☐ 322	Jim Morrison	.10	.04	.01
☐ 274	Lou Piniella	.15	.06	.01	☐ 323	Max Venable	.10	.04	.01
☐ 275	Jose Morales	.10	.04	.01	☐ 324	Tony Gwynn	4.00	1.60	.40
☐ 276	Broderick Perkins	.10	.04	.01	☐ 325	Duane Walker	.10	.04	.01
☐ 277	Butch Davis	.15	.06	.01	☐ 326	Ozzie Virgil	.10	.04	.01
☐ 278	Tony Phillips	.15	.06	.01	☐ 327	Jeff Lahti	.10	.04	.01
☐ 279	Jeff Reardon	.15	.06	.01	☐ 328	Bill Dawley	.15	.06	.01
☐ 280	Ken Forsch	.10	.04	.01	☐ 329	Rob Wilfong	.10	.04	.01
☐ 281	Pete O'Brien	1.75	.70	.17	☐ 330	Marc Hill	.10	.04	.01
☐ 282	Tom Paciorek	.10	.04	.01	☐ 331	Ray Burris	.10	.04	.01
☐ 283	Frank LaCorte	.10	.04	.01	☐ 332	Allan Ramirez	.10	.04	.01
☐ 284	Tim Lollar	.10	.04	.01	☐ 333	Chuck Porter	.10	.04	.01
☐ 285	Greg Gross	.10	.04	.01	☐ 334	Wayne Krenchicki	.10	.04	.01
☐ 286	Alex Trevino	.10	.04	.01	☐ 335	Gary Allenson	.10	.04	.01
☐ 287	Gene Garber	.10	.04	.01	☐ 336	Bobby Meacham	.15	.06	.01
☐ 288	Dave Parker	.30	.12	.03	☐ 337	Joe Beckwith	.10	.04	.01
☐ 289	Lee Smith	.20	.08	.02	☐ 338	Rick Sutcliffe	.25	.10	.02
☐ 290	Dave LaPoint	.15	.06	.01	☐ 339	Mark Huismann	.15	.06	.01
☐ 291	John Shelby	.60	.24	.06	☐ 340	Tim Conroy	.15	.06	.01
☐ 292	Charlie Moore	.10	.04	.01	☐ 341	Scott Sanderson	.10	.04	.01
☐ 293	Alan Trammell	.50	.20	.05	☐ 342	Larry Biittner	.10	.04	.01
☐ 294	Tony Armas	.15	.06	.01	☐ 343	Dave Stewart	.25	.10	.02
☐ 295	Shane Rawley	.15	.06	.01	☐ 344	Darryl Motley	.10	.04	.01
☐ 296	Greg Brock	.15	.06	.01	☐ 345	Chris Codiroli	.15	.06	.01
☐ 297	Hal McRae	.15	.06	.01	☐ 346	Rich Behenna	.10	.04	.01
☐ 298	Mike Davis	.15	.06	.01	☐ 347	Andre Robertson	.10	.04	.01
☐ 299	Tim Raines	.75	.30	.07	☐ 348	Mike Marshall	.25	.08	.02
☐ 300	Bucky Dent	.15	.06	.01	☐ 349	Larry Herndon	.10	.04	.01
☐ 301	Tommy John	.25	.10	.02	☐ 350	Rich Dauer	.10	.04	.01
☐ 302	Carlton Fisk	.25	.10	.02	☐ 351	Cecil Cooper	.15	.06	.01
☐ 303	Darrell Porter	.10	.04	.01	☐ 352	Rod Carew	.65	.26	.06
☐ 304	Dickie Thon	.15	.06	.01	☐ 353	Willie McGee	.40	.16	.04
☐ 305	Garry Maddox	.15	.06	.01	☐ 354	Phil Garner	.10	.04	.01
☐ 306	Cesar Cedeno	.15	.06	.01	☐ 355	Joe Morgan	.40	.16	.04
☐ 307	Gary Lucas	.10	.04	.01	☐ 356	Luis Salazar	.15	.06	.01

		MINT	EXC	G-VG			MINT	EXC	G-VG
☐ 357	John Candelaria	.15	.06	.01	☐ 406	Eric Show	.15	.06	.01
☐ 358	Bill Laskey	.10	.04	.01	☐ 407	John Denny	.15	.06	.01
☐ 359	Bob McClure	.10	.04	.01	☐ 408	Dann Bilardello	.10	.04	.01
☐ 360	Dave Kingman	.20	.08	.02	☐ 409	Bruce Benedict	.10	.04	.01
☐ 361	Ron Cey	.15	.06	.01	☐ 410	Kent Tekulve	.15	.06	.01
☐ 362	Matt Young	.15	.06	.01	☐ 411	Mel Hall	.20	.08	.01
☐ 363	Lloyd Moseby	.20	.08	.02	☐ 412	John Stuper	.10	.04	.01
☐ 364	Frank Viola	1.00	.40	.10	☐ 413	Rick Dempsey	.10	.04	.01
☐ 365	Eddie Milner	.10	.04	.01	☐ 414	Don Sutton	.40	.16	.04
☐ 366	Floyd Bannister	.10	.04	.01	☐ 415	Jack Morris	.35	.14	.03
☐ 367	Dan Ford	.10	.04	.01	☐ 416	John Tudor	.30	.12	.03
☐ 368	Moose Haas	.10	.04	.01	☐ 417	Willie Randolph	.20	.08	.02
☐ 369	Doug Bair	.10	.04	.01	☐ 418	Jerry Reuss	.15	.06	.01
☐ 370	Ray Fontenot	.10	.04	.01	☐ 419	Don Slaught	.15	.06	.01
☐ 371	Luis Aponte	.10	.04	.01	☐ 420	Steve McCatty	.10	.04	.01
☐ 372	Jack Fimple	.10	.04	.01	☐ 421	Tim Wallach	.25	.10	.02
☐ 373	Neal Heaton	.20	.08	.02	☐ 422	Larry Parrish	.15	.06	.01
☐ 374	Greg Pryor	.10	.04	.01	☐ 423	Brian Downing	.15	.06	.01
☐ 375	Wayne Gross	.10	.04	.01	☐ 424	Britt Burns	.15	.06	.01
☐ 376	Charlie Lea	.10	.04	.01	☐ 425	David Green	.10	.04	.01
☐ 377	Steve Lubratich	.10	.04	.01	☐ 426	Jerry Mumphrey	.10	.04	.01
☐ 378	Jon Matlack	.10	.04	.01	☐ 427	Ivan DeJesus	.10	.04	.01
☐ 379	Julio Cruz	.10	.04	.01	☐ 428	Mario Soto	.10	.04	.01
☐ 380	John Mizerock	.10	.04	.01	☐ 429	Gene Richards	.10	.04	.01
☐ 381	Kevin Gross	.40	.16	.04	☐ 430	Dale Berra	.10	.04	.01
☐ 382	Mike Ramsey	.10	.04	.01	☐ 431	Darrell Evans	.20	.08	.02
☐ 383	Doug Gwosdz	.10	.04	.01	☐ 432	Glenn Hubbard	.10	.04	.01
☐ 384	Kelly Paris	.15	.06	.01	☐ 433	Jody Davis	.15	.06	.01
☐ 385	Pete Falcone	.10	.04	.01	☐ 434	Danny Heep	.10	.04	.01
☐ 386	Milt May	.10	.04	.01	☐ 435	Ed Nunez	.20	.08	.02
☐ 387	Fred Breining	.10	.04	.01	☐ 436	Bobby Castillo	.10	.04	.01
☐ 388	Craig Lefferts	.15	.06	.01	☐ 437	Ernie Whitt	.15	.06	.01
☐ 389	Steve Henderson	.10	.04	.01	☐ 438	Scott Ullger	.10	.04	.01
☐ 390	Randy Moffitt	.10	.04	.01	☐ 439	Doyle Alexander	.20	.08	.02
☐ 391	Ron Washington	.10	.04	.01	☐ 440	Domingo Ramos	.10	.04	.01
☐ 392	Gary Roenicke	.10	.04	.01	☐ 441	Craig Swan	.10	.04	.01
☐ 393	Tom Candiotti	.35	.14	.03	☐ 442	Warren Brusstar	.10	.04	.01
☐ 394	Larry Pashnick	.10	.04	.01	☐ 443	Len Barker	.10	.04	.01
☐ 395	Dwight Evans	.25	.10	.02	☐ 444	Mike Easler	.10	.04	.01
☐ 396	Goose Gossage	.20	.08	.02	☐ 445	Renie Martin	.10	.04	.01
☐ 397	Derrel Thomas	.10	.04	.01	☐ 446	Dennis Rasmussen	.90	.36	.09
☐ 398	Juan Eichelberger	.10	.04	.01	☐ 447	Ted Power	.15	.06	.01
☐ 399	Leon Roberts	.10	.04	.01	☐ 448	Charles Hudson	.30	.12	.03
☐ 400	Dave Lopes	.15	.06	.01	☐ 449	Danny Cox	.75	.30	.07
☐ 401	Bill Gullickson	.10	.04	.01	☐ 450	Kevin Bass	.25	.10	.02
☐ 402	Geoff Zahn	.10	.04	.01	☐ 451	Daryl Sconiers	.10	.04	.01
☐ 403	Billy Sample	.10	.04	.01	☐ 452	Scott Fletcher	.25	.10	.02
☐ 404	Mike Squires	.10	.04	.01	☐ 453	Bryn Smith	.15	.06	.01
☐ 405	Craig Reynolds	.10	.04	.01	☐ 454	Jim Dwyer	.10	.04	.01

		MINT	EXC	G-VG
☐ 455	Rob Picciolo	.10	.04	.01
☐ 456	Enos Cabell	.10	.04	.01
☐ 457	Dennis Boyd	.85	.34	.08
☐ 458	Butch Wynegar	.10	.04	.01
☐ 459	Burt Hooton	.10	.04	.01
☐ 460	Ron Hassey	.10	.04	.01
☐ 461	Danny Jackson	3.50	1.40	.35
☐ 462	Bob Kearney	.10	.04	.01
☐ 463	Terry Francona	.10	.04	.01
☐ 464	Wayne Tolleson	.10	.04	.01
☐ 465	Mickey Rivers	.10	.04	.01
☐ 466	John Wathan	.10	.04	.01
☐ 467	Bill Almon	.10	.04	.01
☐ 468	George Vukovich	.10	.04	.01
☐ 469	Steve Kemp	.15	.06	.01
☐ 470	Ken Landreaux	.10	.04	.01
☐ 471	Milt Wilcox	.10	.04	.01
☐ 472	Tippy Martinez	.10	.04	.01
☐ 473	Ted Simmons	.20	.08	.02
☐ 474	Tim Foli	.10	.04	.01
☐ 475	George Hendrick	.15	.06	.01
☐ 476	Terry Puhl	.10	.04	.01
☐ 477	Von Hayes	.20	.08	.02
☐ 478	Bobby Brown	.10	.04	.01
☐ 479	Lee Lacy	.10	.04	.01
☐ 480	Joel Youngblood	.10	.04	.01
☐ 481	Jim Slaton	.10	.04	.01
☐ 482	Mike Fitzgerald	.10	.04	.01
☐ 483	Keith Moreland	.10	.04	.01
☐ 484	Ron Roenicke	.10	.04	.01
☐ 485	Luis Leal	.10	.04	.01
☐ 486	Bryan Oelkers	.10	.04	.01
☐ 487	Bruce Berenyi	.10	.04	.01
☐ 488	LaMarr Hoyt	.15	.06	.01
☐ 489	Joe Nolan	.10	.04	.01
☐ 490	Marshall Edwards	.10	.04	.01
☐ 491	Mike Laga	.10	.04	.01
☐ 492	Rick Cerone	.10	.04	.01
☐ 493	Rick Miller	.10	.04	.01
	(listed as Mike on card front)			
☐ 494	Rick Honeycutt	.10	.04	.01
☐ 495	Mike Hargrove	.10	.04	.01
☐ 496	Joe Simpson	.10	.04	.01
☐ 497	Keith Atherton	.10	.04	.01
☐ 498	Chris Welsh	.10	.04	.01
☐ 499	Bruce Kison	.10	.04	.01
☐ 500	Bobby Johnson	.10	.04	.01
☐ 501	Jerry Koosman	.15	.06	.01
☐ 502	Frank DiPino	.10	.04	.01
☐ 503	Tony Perez	.25	.08	.02
☐ 504	Ken Oberkfell	.10	.04	.01
☐ 505	Mark Thurmond	.15	.06	.01
☐ 506	Joe Price	.10	.04	.01
☐ 507	Pascual Perez	.20	.08	.02
☐ 508	Marvell Wynne	.15	.06	.01
☐ 509	Mike Krukow	.15	.06	.01
☐ 510	Dick Ruthven	.10	.04	.01
☐ 511	Al Cowens	.10	.04	.01
☐ 512	Cliff Johnson	.10	.04	.01
☐ 513	Randy Bush	.30	.12	.03
☐ 514	Sammy Stewart	.10	.04	.01
☐ 515	Bill Schroeder	.15	.06	.01
☐ 516	Aurelio Lopez	.10	.04	.01
☐ 517	Mike Brown	.15	.06	.01
	(Red Sox pitcher)			
☐ 518	Graig Nettles	.20	.08	.02
☐ 519	Dave Sax	.10	.04	.01
☐ 520	Jerry Willard	.10	.04	.01
☐ 521	Paul Splittorff	.10	.04	.01
☐ 522	Tom Burgmeier	.10	.04	.01
☐ 523	Chris Speier	.10	.04	.01
☐ 524	Bobby Clark	.10	.04	.01
☐ 525	George Wright	.10	.04	.01
☐ 526	Dennis Lamp	.10	.04	.01
☐ 527	Tony Scott	.10	.04	.01
☐ 528	Ed Whitson	.10	.04	.01
☐ 529	Ron Reed	.10	.04	.01
☐ 530	Charlie Puleo	.10	.04	.01
☐ 531	Jerry Royster	.10	.04	.01
☐ 532	Don Robinson	.10	.04	.01
☐ 533	Steve Trout	.10	.04	.01
☐ 534	Bruce Sutter	.20	.08	.02
☐ 535	Bob Horner	.20	.08	.02
☐ 536	Pat Tabler	.20	.08	.02
☐ 537	Chris Chambliss	.15	.06	.01
☐ 538	Bob Ojeda	.20	.08	.02
☐ 539	Alan Ashby	.10	.04	.01
☐ 540	Jay Johnstone	.15	.06	.01
☐ 541	Bob Dernier	.10	.04	.01
☐ 542	Brook Jacoby	1.75	.70	.17
☐ 543	U.L. Washington	.10	.04	.01
☐ 544	Danny Darwin	.10	.04	.01
☐ 545	Kiko Garcia	.10	.04	.01
☐ 546	Vance Law	.15	.06	.01
☐ 547	Tug McGraw	.20	.08	.02
☐ 548	Dave Smith	.15	.06	.01
☐ 549	Len Matuszek	.10	.04	.01
☐ 550	Tom Hume	.10	.04	.01

		MINT	EXC	G-VG			MINT	EXC	G-VG
☐ 551	Dave Dravecky	.15	.06	.01	☐ 598	Dave Engle	.10	.04	.01
☐ 552	Rick Rhoden	.15	.06	.01	☐ 599	Craig McMurtry	.15	.06	.01
☐ 553	Duane Kuiper	.10	.04	.01	☐ 600	Carlos Diaz	.10	.04	.01
☐ 554	Rusty Staub	.20	.08	.02	☐ 601	Tom O'Malley	.10	.04	.01
☐ 555	Bill Campbell	.10	.04	.01	☐ 602	Nick Esasky	.40	.16	.04
☐ 556	Mike Torrez	.10	.04	.01	☐ 603	Ron Hodges	.10	.04	.01
☐ 557	Dave Henderson	.30	.12	.03	☐ 604	Ed VandeBerg	.10	.04	.01
☐ 558	Len Whitehouse	.10	.04	.01	☐ 605	Alfredo Griffin	.15	.06	.01
☐ 559	Barry Bonnell	.10	.04	.01	☐ 606	Glenn Hoffman	.10	.04	.01
☐ 560	Rick Lysander	.10	.04	.01	☐ 607	Hubie Brooks	.20	.08	.02
☐ 561	Garth Iorg	.10	.04	.01	☐ 608	Richard Barnes	.10	.04	.01
☐ 562	Bryan Clark	.10	.04	.01	☐ 609	Greg Walker	.50	.20	.05
☐ 563	Brian Giles	.10	.04	.01	☐ 610	Ken Singleton	.15	.06	.01
☐ 564	Vern Ruhle	.10	.04	.01	☐ 611	Mark Clear	.10	.04	.01
☐ 565	Steve Bedrosian	.30	.12	.03	☐ 612	Buck Martinez	.10	.04	.01
☐ 566	Larry McWilliams	.10	.04	.01	☐ 613	Ken Griffey	.15	.06	.01
☐ 567	Jeff Leonard UER	.20	.08	.02	☐ 614	Reid Nichols	.10	.04	.01
	(listed as P on card front)				☐ 615	Doug Sisk	.10	.04	.01
☐ 568	Alan Wiggins	.10	.04	.01	☐ 616	Bob Brenly	.10	.04	.01
☐ 569	Jeff Russell	.30	.12	.03	☐ 617	Joey McLaughlin	.10	.04	.01
☐ 570	Salome Barojas	.10	.04	.01	☐ 618	Glenn Wilson	.15	.06	.01
☐ 571	Dane Iorg	.10	.04	.01	☐ 619	Bob Stoddard	.10	.04	.01
☐ 572	Bob Knepper	.15	.06	.01	☐ 620	Lenn Sakata UER	.10	.04	.01
☐ 573	Gary Lavelle	.10	.04	.01		(listed as Len on card front)			
☐ 574	Gorman Thomas	.15	.06	.01	☐ 621	Mike Young	.45	.18	.04
☐ 575	Manny Trillo	.10	.04	.01	☐ 622	John Stefero	.15	.06	.01
☐ 576	Jim Palmer	.50	.20	.05	☐ 623	Carmelo Martinez	.30	.12	.03
☐ 577	Dale Murray	.10	.04	.01	☐ 624	Dave Bergman	.10	.04	.01
☐ 578	Tom Brookens	.10	.04	.01	☐ 625	Runnin' Reds	.25	.10	.02
☐ 579	Rich Gedman	.15	.06	.01		(sic, Redbirds)			
☐ 580	Bill Doran	1.50	.60	.15		David Green			
☐ 581	Steve Yeager	.10	.04	.01		Willie McGee			
☐ 582	Dan Spillner	.10	.04	.01		Lonnie Smith			
☐ 583	Dan Quisenberry	.20	.08	.02		Ozzie Smith			
☐ 584	Rance Mulliniks	.10	.04	.01	☐ 626	Rudy May	.10	.04	.01
☐ 585	Storm Davis	.15	.06	.01	☐ 627	Matt Keough	.10	.04	.01
☐ 586	Dave Schmidt	.15	.06	.01	☐ 628	Jose DeLeon	.40	.16	.04
☐ 587	Bill Russell	.15	.06	.01	☐ 629	Jim Essian	.10	.04	.01
☐ 588	Pat Sheridan	.20	.08	.02	☐ 630	Darnell Coles	.40	.16	.04
☐ 589	Rafael Ramirez	.15	.06	.01	☐ 631	Mike Warren	.15	.06	.01
	ERR (A's on front)				☐ 632	Del Crandall MG	.10	.04	.01
☐ 590	Bud Anderson	.10	.04	.01	☐ 633	Dennis Martinez	.15	.06	.01
☐ 591	George Frazier	.10	.04	.01	☐ 634	Mike Moore	.15	.06	.01
☐ 592	Lee Tunnell	.15	.06	.01	☐ 635	Lary Sorensen	.10	.04	.01
☐ 593	Kirk Gibson	.60	.24	.06	☐ 636	Ricky Nelson	.10	.04	.01
☐ 594	Scott McGregor	.15	.06	.01	☐ 637	Omar Moreno	.10	.04	.01
☐ 595	Bob Bailor	.10	.04	.01	☐ 638	Charlie Hough	.15	.06	.01
☐ 596	Tommy Herr	.15	.06	.01	☐ 639	Dennis Eckersley	.30	.12	.03
☐ 597	Luis Sanchez	.10	.04	.01	☐ 640	Walt Terrell	.35	.14	.03

		MINT	EXC	G-VG
☐ 641	Denny Walling	.10	.04	.01
☐ 642	Dave Anderson	.25	.10	.02
☐ 643	Jose Oquendo	.40	.16	.04
☐ 644	Bob Stanley	.10	.04	.01
☐ 645	Dave Geisel	.10	.04	.01
☐ 646	Scott Garrelts	.35	.14	.03
☐ 647	Gary Pettis	.45	.18	.04
☐ 648	Duke Snider Puzzle Card	.10	.04	.01
☐ 649	Johnnie LeMaster	.10	.04	.01
☐ 650	Dave Collins	.10	.04	.01
☐ 651	The Chicken	.20	.08	.02
☐ 652	DK Checklist (unnumbered)	.10	.01	.00
☐ 653	Checklist 1-130 (unnumbered)	.08	.01	.00
☐ 654	Checklist 131-234 (unnumbered)	.08	.01	.00
☐ 655	Checklist 235-338 (unnumbered)	.08	.01	.00
☐ 656	Checklist 339-442 (unnumbered)	.08	.01	.00
☐ 657	Checklist 443-546 (unnumbered)	.08	.01	.00
☐ 658	Checklist 547-651 (unnumbered)	.08	.01	.00
☐ A	Living Legends Gaylord Perry Rollie Fingers	2.00	.80	.20
☐ B	Living Legends Carl Yastrzemski Johnny Bench	5.00	2.00	.50

1985 Donruss

 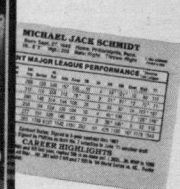

The cards in this 660-card set measure 2 ½" by 3 ½". The 1985 Donruss regular issue cards have fronts that feature jet black borders on which orange lines have been placed. The fronts contain the standard team logo, player's name, position, and Donruss logo. The cards were distributed with puzzle pieces from a Dick Perez rendition of Lou Gehrig. The first 26 cards of the set feature Diamond Kings (DK), for the fourth year in a row; the artwork on the Diamond Kings was again produced by the Perez-Steele Galleries. Cards 27-46 feature Rated Rookies (RR). The unnumbered checklist cards are arbitrarily numbered below as numbers 654 through 660.

		MINT	EXC	G-VG
Complete Set (660)		135.00	54.00	13.50
Common Player (1-660)		.06	.02	.00
☐ 1	Ryne Sandberg DK	.60	.15	.03
☐ 2	Doug DeCinces DK	.10	.04	.01
☐ 3	Richard Dotson DK	.10	.04	.01
☐ 4	Bert Blyleven DK	.15	.06	.01
☐ 5	Lou Whitaker DK	.20	.08	.02
☐ 6	Dan Quisenberry DK	.15	.06	.01
☐ 7	Don Mattingly DK	6.00	2.40	.60
☐ 8	Carney Lansford DK	.15	.06	.01
☐ 9	Frank Tanana DK	.10	.04	.01
☐ 10	Willie Upshaw DK	.10	.04	.01
☐ 11	Claudell Washington DK	.10	.04	.01
☐ 12	Mike Marshall DK	.15	.06	.01
☐ 13	Joaquin Andujar DK	.10	.04	.01

		MINT	EXC	G-VG
☐ 14	Cal Ripken DK	.50	.20	.05
☐ 15	Jim Rice DK	.35	.14	.03
☐ 16	Don Sutton DK	.25	.10	.02
☐ 17	Frank Viola DK	.45	.18	.04
☐ 18	Alvin Davis DK	.40	.16	.04
☐ 19	Mario Soto DK	.10	.04	.01
☐ 20	Jose Cruz DK	.10	.04	.01
☐ 21	Charlie Lea DK	.10	.04	.01
☐ 22	Jesse Orosco DK	.10	.04	.01
☐ 23	Juan Samuel DK	.30	.12	.03
☐ 24	Tony Pena DK	.15	.06	.01
☐ 25	Tony Gwynn DK	.75	.30	.07
☐ 26	Bob Brenly DK	.10	.04	.01
☐ 27	Danny Tartabull RR	7.00	2.80	.70
☐ 28	Mike Bielecki RR	.15	.06	.01
☐ 29	Steve Lyons RR	.15	.06	.01
☐ 30	Jeff Reed RR	.10	.04	.01
☐ 31	Tony Brewer RR	.10	.04	.01
☐ 32	John Morris RR	.15	.06	.01
☐ 33	Daryl Boston RR	.20	.08	.02
☐ 34	Al Pulido RR	.10	.04	.01
☐ 35	Steve Kiefer RR	.15	.06	.01
☐ 36	Larry Sheets RR	.75	.30	.07
☐ 37	Scott Bradley RR	.30	.12	.03
☐ 38	Calvin Schiraldi RR	.30	.12	.03
☐ 39	Shawon Dunston RR	1.25	.50	.12
☐ 40	Charlie Mitchell RR	.10	.04	.01
☐ 41	Billy Hatcher RR	.90	.36	.09
☐ 42	Russ Stephans RR	.10	.04	.01
☐ 43	Alejandro Sanchez RR	.10	.04	.01
☐ 44	Steve Jeltz RR	.10	.04	.01
☐ 45	Jim Traber RR	.35	.14	.03
☐ 46	Doug Loman RR	.15	.06	.01
☐ 47	Eddie Murray	.50	.20	.05
☐ 48	Robin Yount	.35	.14	.03
☐ 49	Lance Parrish	.25	.10	.02
☐ 50	Jim Rice	.30	.12	.03
☐ 51	Dave Winfield	.40	.16	.04
☐ 52	Fernando Valenzuela	.25	.10	.02
☐ 53	George Brett	.60	.24	.06
☐ 54	Dave Kingman	.15	.06	.01
☐ 55	Gary Carter	.35	.14	.03
☐ 56	Buddy Bell	.12	.05	.01
☐ 57	Reggie Jackson	.50	.20	.05
☐ 58	Harold Baines	.18	.08	.01
☐ 59	Ozzie Smith	.25	.10	.02
☐ 60	Nolan Ryan	.45	.18	.04
☐ 61	Mike Schmidt	.75	.30	.07
☐ 62	Dave Parker	.18	.08	.01

		MINT	EXC	G-VG
☐ 63	Tony Gwynn	1.00	.40	.10
☐ 64	Tony Pena	.12	.05	.01
☐ 65	Jack Clark	.25	.10	.02
☐ 66	Dale Murphy	.80	.32	.08
☐ 67	Ryne Sandberg	.40	.16	.04
☐ 68	Keith Hernandez	.35	.14	.03
☐ 69	Alvin Davis	2.00	.80	.20
☐ 70	Kent Hrbek	.35	.14	.03
☐ 71	Willie Upshaw	.06	.02	.00
☐ 72	Dave Engle	.06	.02	.00
☐ 73	Alfredo Griffin	.10	.04	.01
☐ 74A	Jack Perconte (Career Highlights, four lines)	.15	.06	.01
☐ 74B	Jack Perconte (Career Highlights, three lines)	.15	.06	.01
☐ 75	Jesse Orosco	.06	.02	.00
☐ 76	Jody Davis	.10	.04	.01
☐ 77	Bob Horner	.15	.06	.01
☐ 78	Larry McWilliams	.06	.02	.00
☐ 79	Joel Youngblood	.06	.02	.00
☐ 80	Alan Wiggins	.06	.02	.00
☐ 81	Ron Oester	.06	.02	.00
☐ 82	Ozzie Virgil	.06	.02	.00
☐ 83	Ricky Horton	.20	.08	.02
☐ 84	Bill Doran	.15	.06	.01
☐ 85	Rod Carew	.45	.18	.04
☐ 86	LaMarr Hoyt	.10	.04	.01
☐ 87	Tim Wallach	.15	.06	.01
☐ 88	Mike Flanagan	.10	.04	.01
☐ 89	Jim Sundberg	.06	.02	.00
☐ 90	Chet Lemon	.10	.04	.01
☐ 91	Bob Stanley	.06	.02	.00
☐ 92	Willie Randolph	.10	.04	.01
☐ 93	Bill Russell	.10	.04	.01
☐ 94	Julio Franco	.15	.06	.01
☐ 95	Dan Quisenberry	.15	.06	.01
☐ 96	Bill Caudill	.06	.02	.00
☐ 97	Bill Gullickson	.06	.02	.00
☐ 98	Danny Darwin	.06	.02	.00
☐ 99	Curtis Wilkerson	.06	.02	.00
☐ 100	Bud Black	.06	.02	.00
☐ 101	Tony Phillips	.06	.02	.00
☐ 102	Tony Bernazard	.06	.02	.00
☐ 103	Jay Howell	.10	.04	.01
☐ 104	Burt Hooton	.06	.02	.00
☐ 105	Milt Wilcox	.06	.02	.00
☐ 106	Rich Dauer	.06	.02	.00
☐ 107	Don Sutton	.25	.10	.02
☐ 108	Mike Witt	.12	.05	.01

		MINT	EXC	G-VG
☐ 109	Bruce Sutter	.12	.05	.01
☐ 110	Enos Cabell	.06	.02	.00
☐ 111	John Denny	.10	.04	.01
☐ 112	Dave Dravecky	.10	.04	.01
☐ 113	Marvell Wynne	.06	.02	.00
☐ 114	Johnnie LeMaster	.06	.02	.00
☐ 115	Chuck Porter	.06	.02	.00
☐ 116	John Gibbons	.10	.04	.01
☐ 117	Keith Moreland	.06	.02	.00
☐ 118	Darnell Coles	.10	.04	.01
☐ 119	Dennis Lamp	.06	.02	.00
☐ 120	Ron Davis	.06	.02	.00
☐ 121	Nick Esasky	.10	.04	.01
☐ 122	Vance Law	.10	.04	.01
☐ 123	Gary Roenicke	.06	.02	.00
☐ 124	Bill Schroeder	.06	.02	.00
☐ 125	Dave Rozema	.06	.02	.00
☐ 126	Bobby Meacham	.06	.02	.00
☐ 127	Marty Barrett	.30	.12	.03
☐ 128	R.J. Reynolds	.25	.10	.02
☐ 129	Ernie Camacho	.06	.02	.00
	(photo actually Rich Thompson)			
☐ 130	Jorge Orta	.06	.02	.00
☐ 131	Lary Sorensen	.06	.02	.00
☐ 132	Terry Francona	.06	.02	.00
☐ 133	Fred Lynn	.15	.06	.01
☐ 134	Bob Jones	.06	.02	.00
☐ 135	Jerry Hairston	.06	.02	.00
☐ 136	Kevin Bass	.12	.05	.01
☐ 137	Garry Maddox	.10	.04	.01
☐ 138	Dave LaPoint	.10	.04	.01
☐ 139	Kevin McReynolds	1.00	.40	.10
☐ 140	Wayne Krenchicki	.06	.02	.00
☐ 141	Rafael Ramirez	.06	.02	.00
☐ 142	Rod Scurry	.06	.02	.00
☐ 143	Greg Minton	.06	.02	.00
☐ 144	Tim Stoddard	.06	.02	.00
☐ 145	Steve Henderson	.06	.02	.00
☐ 146	George Bell	.60	.24	.06
☐ 147	Dave Meier	.10	.04	.01
☐ 148	Sammy Stewart	.06	.02	.00
☐ 149	Mark Brouhard	.06	.02	.00
☐ 150	Larry Herndon	.06	.02	.00
☐ 151	Oil Can Boyd	.10	.04	.01
☐ 152	Brian Dayett	.06	.02	.00
☐ 153	Tom Niedenfuer	.06	.02	.00
☐ 154	Brook Jacoby	.15	.06	.01
☐ 155	Onix Concepcion	.06	.02	.00
☐ 156	Tim Conroy	.06	.02	.00

		MINT	EXC	G-VG
☐ 157	Joe Hesketh	.15	.06	.01
☐ 158	Brian Downing	.10	.04	.01
☐ 159	Tommy Dunbar	.06	.02	.00
☐ 160	Marc Hill	.06	.02	.00
☐ 161	Phil Garner	.06	.02	.00
☐ 162	Jerry Davis	.06	.02	.00
☐ 163	Bill Campbell	.06	.02	.00
☐ 164	John Franco	1.00	.40	.10
☐ 165	Len Barker	.06	.02	.00
☐ 166	Benny Distefano	.10	.04	.01
☐ 167	George Frazier	.06	.02	.00
☐ 168	Tito Landrum	.06	.02	.00
☐ 169	Cal Ripken	.50	.20	.05
☐ 170	Cecil Cooper	.12	.05	.01
☐ 171	Alan Trammell	.30	.12	.03
☐ 172	Wade Boggs	5.50	2.20	.55
☐ 173	Don Baylor	.15	.06	.01
☐ 174	Pedro Guerrero	.30	.12	.03
☐ 175	Frank White	.10	.04	.01
☐ 176	Rickey Henderson	.60	.24	.06
☐ 177	Charlie Lea	.06	.02	.00
☐ 178	Pete O'Brien	.15	.06	.01
☐ 179	Doug DeCinces	.10	.04	.01
☐ 180	Ron Kittle	.20	.08	.02
☐ 181	George Hendrick	.10	.04	.01
☐ 182	Joe Niekro	.10	.04	.01
☐ 183	Juan Samuel	1.00	.40	.10
☐ 184	Mario Soto	.06	.02	.00
☐ 185	Goose Gossage	.15	.06	.01
☐ 186	Johnny Ray	.15	.06	.01
☐ 187	Bob Brenly	.06	.02	.00
☐ 188	Craig McMurtry	.06	.02	.00
☐ 189	Leon Durham	.10	.04	.01
☐ 190	Dwight Gooden	11.00	4.50	1.10
☐ 191	Barry Bonnell	.06	.02	.00
☐ 192	Tim Teufel	.10	.04	.01
☐ 193	Dave Stieb	.15	.06	.01
☐ 194	Mickey Hatcher	.10	.04	.01
☐ 195	Jesse Barfield	.25	.10	.02
☐ 196	Al Cowens	.06	.02	.00
☐ 197	Hubie Brooks	.10	.04	.01
☐ 198	Steve Trout	.06	.02	.00
☐ 199	Glenn Hubbard	.06	.02	.00
☐ 200	Bill Madlock	.10	.04	.01
☐ 201	Jeff Robinson	.30	.12	.03
	(Giants pitcher)			
☐ 202	Eric Show	.06	.02	.00
☐ 203	Dave Concepcion	.10	.04	.00
☐ 204	Ivan DeJesus	.06	.02	.00

		MINT	EXC	G-VG
☐ 205	Neil Allen	.06	.02	.00
☐ 206	Jerry Mumphrey	.06	.02	.00
☐ 207	Mike Brown	.06	.02	.00
	(Angels OF)			
☐ 208	Carlton Fisk	.15	.06	.01
☐ 209	Bryn Smith	.06	.02	.00
☐ 210	Tippy Martinez	.06	.02	.00
☐ 211	Dion James	.10	.04	.01
☐ 212	Willie Hernandez	.10	.04	.01
☐ 213	Mike Easler	.06	.02	.00
☐ 214	Ron Guidry	.20	.08	.02
☐ 215	Rick Honeycutt	.06	.02	.00
☐ 216	Brett Butler	.10	.04	.01
☐ 217	Larry Gura	.06	.02	.00
☐ 218	Ray Burris	.06	.02	.00
☐ 219	Steve Rogers	.06	.02	.00
☐ 220	Frank Tanana	.10	.04	.01
☐ 221	Ned Yost	.06	.02	.00
☐ 222	Bret Saberhagen	4.00	1.60	.40
☐ 223	Mike Davis	.10	.04	.01
☐ 224	Bert Blyleven	.15	.06	.01
☐ 225	Steve Kemp	.10	.04	.01
☐ 226	Jerry Reuss	.10	.04	.01
☐ 227	Darrell Evans	.15	.06	.01
☐ 228	Wayne Gross	.06	.02	.00
☐ 229	Jim Gantner	.06	.02	.00
☐ 230	Bob Boone	.15	.06	.01
☐ 231	Lonnie Smith	.10	.04	.01
☐ 232	Frank DiPino	.06	.02	.00
☐ 233	Jerry Koosman	.10	.04	.01
☐ 234	Graig Nettles	.15	.06	.01
☐ 235	John Tudor	.15	.06	.01
☐ 236	John Rabb	.06	.02	.00
☐ 237	Rick Manning	.06	.02	.00
☐ 238	Mike Fitzgerald	.06	.02	.00
☐ 239	Gary Matthews	.10	.04	.01
☐ 240	Jim Presley	1.00	.40	.10
☐ 241	Dave Collins	.06	.02	.00
☐ 242	Gary Gaetti	.40	.16	.04
☐ 243	Dann Bilardello	.06	.02	.00
☐ 244	Rudy Law	.06	.02	.00
☐ 245	John Lowenstein	.06	.02	.00
☐ 246	Tom Tellmann	.06	.02	.00
☐ 247	Howard Johnson	.65	.26	.06
☐ 248	Ray Fontenot	.06	.02	.00
☐ 249	Tony Armas	.10	.04	.01
☐ 250	Candy Maldonado	.10	.04	.01
☐ 251	Mike Jeffcoat	.06	.02	.00
☐ 252	Dane Iorg	.06	.02	.00
☐ 253	Bruce Bochte	.06	.02	.00
☐ 254	Pete Rose	1.50	.60	.15
☐ 255	Don Aase	.06	.02	.00
☐ 256	George Wright	.06	.02	.00
☐ 257	Britt Burns	.06	.02	.00
☐ 258	Mike Scott	.30	.12	.03
☐ 259	Len Matuszek	.06	.02	.00
☐ 260	Dave Rucker	.06	.02	.00
☐ 261	Craig Lefferts	.06	.02	.00
☐ 262	Jay Tibbs	.15	.06	.01
☐ 263	Bruce Benedict	.06	.02	.00
☐ 264	Don Robinson	.06	.02	.00
☐ 265	Gary Lavelle	.06	.02	.00
☐ 266	Scott Sanderson	.06	.02	.00
☐ 267	Matt Young	.06	.02	.00
☐ 268	Ernie Whitt	.06	.02	.00
☐ 269	Houston Jimenez	.06	.02	.00
☐ 270	Ken Dixon	.10	.04	.01
☐ 271	Pete Ladd	.06	.02	.00
☐ 272	Juan Berenguer	.06	.02	.00
☐ 273	Roger Clemens	14.00	5.75	1.40
☐ 274	Rick Cerone	.06	.02	.00
☐ 275	Dave Anderson	.06	.02	.00
☐ 276	George Vukovich	.06	.02	.00
☐ 277	Greg Pryor	.06	.02	.00
☐ 278	Mike Warren	.06	.02	.00
☐ 279	Bob James	.06	.02	.00
☐ 280	Bobby Grich	.10	.04	.01
☐ 281	Mike Mason	.06	.02	.00
☐ 282	Ron Reed	.06	.02	.00
☐ 283	Alan Ashby	.06	.02	.00
☐ 284	Mark Thurmond	.06	.02	.00
☐ 285	Joe Lefebvre	.06	.02	.00
☐ 286	Ted Power	.06	.02	.00
☐ 287	Chris Chambliss	.10	.04	.01
☐ 288	Lee Tunnell	.06	.02	.00
☐ 289	Rich Bordi	.06	.02	.00
☐ 290	Glenn Brummer	.06	.02	.00
☐ 291	Mike Boddicker	.12	.05	.01
☐ 292	Rollie Fingers	.18	.08	.01
☐ 293	Lou Whitaker	.18	.08	.01
☐ 294	Dwight Evans	.18	.08	.01
☐ 295	Don Mattingly	14.00	5.75	1.40
☐ 296	Mike Marshall	.15	.06	.01
☐ 297	Willie Wilson	.12	.05	.01
☐ 298	Mike Heath	.06	.02	.00
☐ 299	Tim Raines	.45	.18	.04
☐ 300	Larry Parrish	.10	.04	.01
☐ 301	Geoff Zahn	.06	.02	.00

		MINT	EXC	G-VG			MINT	EXC	G-VG
☐ 302	Rich Dotson	.10	.04	.01	☐ 351	Charlie Moore	.06	.02	.00
☐ 303	David Green	.06	.02	.00	☐ 352	Luis Sanchez	.06	.02	.00
☐ 304	Jose Cruz	.10	.04	.01	☐ 353	Darrell Porter	.06	.02	.00
☐ 305	Steve Carlton	.40	.16	.04	☐ 354	Bill Dawley	.06	.02	.00
☐ 306	Gary Redus	.06	.02	.00	☐ 355	Charles Hudson	.06	.02	.00
☐ 307	Steve Garvey	.45	.18	.04	☐ 356	Garry Templeton	.10	.04	.01
☐ 308	Jose DeLeon	.06	.02	.00	☐ 357	Cecilio Guante	.06	.02	.00
☐ 309	Randy Lerch	.06	.02	.00	☐ 358	Jeff Leonard	.10	.04	.01
☐ 310	Claudell Washington	.10	.04	.01	☐ 359	Paul Molitor	.20	.08	.02
☐ 311	Lee Smith	.10	.04	.01	☐ 360	Ron Gardenhire	.06	.02	.00
☐ 312	Darryl Strawberry	4.00	1.60	.40	☐ 361	Larry Bowa	.10	.04	.01
☐ 313	Jim Beattie	.06	.02	.00	☐ 362	Bob Kearney	.06	.02	.00
☐ 314	John Butcher	.06	.02	.00	☐ 363	Garth Iorg	.06	.02	.00
☐ 315	Damaso Garcia	.06	.02	.00	☐ 364	Tom Brunansky	.20	.08	.02
☐ 316	Mike Smithson	.06	.02	.00	☐ 365	Brad Gulden	.06	.02	.00
☐ 317	Luis Leal	.06	.02	.00	☐ 366	Greg Walker	.10	.04	.01
☐ 318	Ken Phelps	.35	.14	.03	☐ 367	Mike Young	.10	.04	.01
☐ 319	Wally Backman	.10	.04	.01	☐ 368	Rick Waits	.06	.02	.00
☐ 320	Ron Cey	.10	.04	.01	☐ 369	Doug Bair	.06	.02	.00
☐ 321	Brad Komminsk	.06	.02	.00	☐ 370	Bob Shirley	.06	.02	.00
☐ 322	Jason Thompson	.06	.02	.00	☐ 371	Bob Ojeda	.10	.04	.01
☐ 323	Frank Williams	.15	.06	.01	☐ 372	Bob Welch	.10	.04	.01
☐ 324	Tim Lollar	.06	.02	.00	☐ 373	Neal Heaton	.06	.02	.00
☐ 325	Eric Davis	17.00	7.00	1.70	☐ 374	Danny Jackson UER	.30	.12	.03
☐ 326	Von Hayes	.15	.06	.01		(photo actually Frank Wills)			
☐ 327	Andy Van Slyke	.50	.20	.05	☐ 375	Donnie Hill	.06	.02	.00
☐ 328	Craig Reynolds	.06	.02	.00	☐ 376	Mike Stenhouse	.06	.02	.00
☐ 329	Dick Schofield	.10	.04	.01	☐ 377	Bruce Kison	.06	.02	.00
☐ 330	Scott Fletcher	.10	.04	.01	☐ 378	Wayne Tolleson	.06	.02	.00
☐ 331	Jeff Reardon	.10	.04	.01	☐ 379	Floyd Bannister	.06	.02	.00
☐ 332	Rick Dempsey	.06	.02	.00	☐ 380	Vern Ruhle	.06	.02	.00
☐ 333	Ben Oglivie	.10	.04	.01	☐ 381	Tim Corcoran	.06	.02	.00
☐ 334	Dan Petry	.10	.04	.01	☐ 382	Kurt Kepshire	.06	.02	.00
☐ 335	Jackie Gutierrez	.06	.02	.00	☐ 383	Bobby Brown	.06	.02	.00
☐ 336	Dave Righetti	.15	.06	.01	☐ 384	Dave Van Gorder	.06	.02	.00
☐ 337	Alejandro Pena	.10	.04	.01	☐ 385	Rick Mahler	.06	.02	.00
☐ 338	Mel Hall	.10	.04	.01	☐ 386	Lee Mazzilli	.06	.02	.00
☐ 339	Pat Sheridan	.06	.02	.00	☐ 387	Bill Laskey	.06	.02	.00
☐ 340	Keith Atherton	.06	.02	.00	☐ 388	Thad Bosley	.06	.02	.00
☐ 341	David Palmer	.06	.02	.00	☐ 389	Al Chambers	.06	.02	.00
☐ 342	Gary Ward	.10	.04	.01	☐ 390	Tony Fernandez	.45	.18	.04
☐ 343	Dave Stewart	.15	.06	.01	☐ 391	Ron Washington	.06	.02	.00
☐ 344	Mark Gubicza	1.00	.40	.10	☐ 392	Bill Swaggerty	.06	.02	.00
☐ 345	Carney Lansford	.12	.05	.01	☐ 393	Bob L. Gibson	.06	.02	.00
☐ 346	Jerry Willard	.06	.02	.00	☐ 394	Marty Castillo	.06	.02	.00
☐ 347	Ken Griffey	.10	.04	.01	☐ 395	Steve Crawford	.06	.02	.00
☐ 348	Franklin Stubbs	.35	.14	.03	☐ 396	Clay Christiansen	.06	.02	.00
☐ 349	Aurelio Lopez	.06	.02	.00	☐ 397	Bob Bailor	.06	.02	.00
☐ 350	Al Bumbry	.06	.02	.00	☐ 398	Mike Hargrove	.06	.02	.00

		MINT	EXC	G-VG			MINT	EXC	G-VG
☐ 399	Charlie Leibrandt	.06	.02	.00	☐ 446	Ed Whitson	.06	.02	.00
☐ 400	Tom Burgmeier	.06	.02	.00	☐ 447	Cesar Cedeno	.10	.04	.01
☐ 401	Razor Shines	.10	.04	.01	☐ 448	Rick Schu	.20	.08	.02
☐ 402	Rob Wilfong	.06	.02	.00	☐ 449	Joaquin Andujar	.10	.04	.01
☐ 403	Tom Henke	.15	.06	.01	☐ 450	Mark Bailey	.10	.04	.01
☐ 404	Al Jones	.06	.02	.00	☐ 451	Ron Romanick	.10	.04	.01
☐ 405	Mike LaCoss	.06	.02	.00	☐ 452	Julio Cruz	.06	.02	.00
☐ 406	Luis DeLeon	.06	.02	.00	☐ 453	Miguel Dilone	.06	.02	.00
☐ 407	Greg Gross	.06	.02	.00	☐ 454	Storm Davis	.10	.04	.01
☐ 408	Tom Hume	.06	.02	.00	☐ 455	Jaime Cocanower	.10	.04	.01
☐ 409	Rick Camp	.06	.02	.00	☐ 456	Barbaro Garbey	.06	.02	.00
☐ 410	Milt May	.06	.02	.00	☐ 457	Rich Gedman	.10	.04	.01
☐ 411	Henry Cotto	.10	.04	.01	☐ 458	Phil Niekro	.25	.10	.02
☐ 412	David Von Ohlen	.06	.02	.00	☐ 459	Mike Scioscia	.10	.04	.01
☐ 413	Scott McGregor	.10	.04	.01	☐ 460	Pat Tabler	.10	.04	.01
☐ 414	Ted Simmons	.10	.04	.01	☐ 461	Darryl Motley	.06	.02	.00
☐ 415	Jack Morris	.20	.08	.02	☐ 462	Chris Codiroli	.06	.02	.00
☐ 416	Bill Buckner	.10	.04	.01	☐ 463	Doug Flynn	.06	.02	.00
☐ 417	Butch Wynegar	.06	.02	.00	☐ 464	Billy Sample	.06	.02	.00
☐ 418	Steve Sax	.25	.08	.02	☐ 465	Mickey Rivers	.06	.02	.00
☐ 419	Steve Balboni	.06	.02	.00	☐ 466	John Wathan	.06	.02	.00
☐ 420	Dwayne Murphy	.06	.02	.00	☐ 467	Bill Krueger	.06	.02	.00
☐ 421	Andre Dawson	.30	.12	.03	☐ 468	Andre Thornton	.10	.04	.01
☐ 422	Charlie Hough	.10	.04	.01	☐ 469	Rex Hudler	.20	.08	.02
☐ 423	Tommy John	.15	.06	.01	☐ 470	Sid Bream	.35	.14	.03
☐ 424A	Tom Seaver ERR	.90	.36	.09	☐ 471	Kirk Gibson	.35	.14	.03
	(photo actually Floyd Bannister)				☐ 472	John Shelby	.06	.02	.00
☐ 424B	Tom Seaver COR	4.50	1.80	.45	☐ 473	Moose Haas	.06	.02	.00
☐ 425	Tommy Herr	.10	.04	.01	☐ 474	Doug Corbett	.06	.02	.00
☐ 426	Terry Puhl	.06	.02	.00	☐ 475	Willie McGee	.35	.14	.03
☐ 427	Al Holland	.06	.02	.00	☐ 476	Bob Knepper	.10	.04	.01
☐ 428	Eddie Milner	.06	.02	.00	☐ 477	Kevin Gross	.06	.02	.00
☐ 429	Terry Kennedy	.06	.02	.00	☐ 478	Carmelo Martinez	.06	.02	.00
☐ 430	John Candelaria	.10	.04	.01	☐ 479	Kent Tekulve	.10	.04	.01
☐ 431	Manny Trillo	.06	.02	.00	☐ 480	Chili Davis	.10	.04	.01
☐ 432	Ken Oberkfell	.06	.02	.00	☐ 481	Bobby Clark	.06	.02	.00
☐ 433	Rick Sutcliffe	.20	.08	.02	☐ 482	Mookie Wilson	.10	.04	.01
☐ 434	Ron Darling	.90	.36	.09	☐ 483	Dave Owen	.06	.02	.00
☐ 435	Spike Owen	.06	.02	.00	☐ 484	Ed Nunez	.06	.02	.00
☐ 436	Frank Viola	.45	.18	.04	☐ 485	Rance Mulliniks	.06	.02	.00
☐ 437	Lloyd Moseby	.15	.06	.01	☐ 486	Ken Schrom	.06	.02	.00
☐ 438	Kirby Puckett	11.00	4.50	1.10	☐ 487	Jeff Russell	.06	.02	.00
☐ 439	Jim Clancy	.06	.02	.00	☐ 488	Tom Paciorek	.06	.02	.00
☐ 440	Mike Moore	.10	.04	.00	☐ 489	Dan Ford	.06	.02	.00
☐ 441	Doug Sisk	.06	.02	.00	☐ 490	Mike Caldwell	.06	.02	.00
☐ 442	Dennis Eckersley	.20	.08	.02	☐ 491	Scottie Earl	.06	.02	.00
☐ 443	Gerald Perry	.20	.08	.02	☐ 492	Jose Rijo	.40	.16	.04
☐ 444	Dale Berra	.06	.02	.00	☐ 493	Bruce Hurst	.15	.06	.01
☐ 445	Dusty Baker	.10	.04	.01	☐ 494	Ken Landreaux	.06	.02	.00

		MINT	EXC	G-VG			MINT	EXC	G-VG
☐ 495	Mike Fischlin	.06	.02	.00	☐ 542	Jeff Burroughs	.06	.02	.00
☐ 496	Don Slaught	.06	.02	.00	☐ 543	Dan Schatzeder	.06	.02	.00
☐ 497	Steve McCatty	.06	.02	.00	☐ 544	Donnie Scott	.06	.02	.00
☐ 498	Gary Lucas	.06	.02	.00	☐ 545	Jim Slaton	.06	.02	.00
☐ 499	Gary Pettis	.10	.04	.01	☐ 546	Greg Luzinski	.12	.05	.01
☐ 500	Marvis Foley	.06	.02	.00	☐ 547	Mark Salas	.15	.06	.01
☐ 501	Mike Squires	.06	.02	.00	☐ 548	Dave Smith	.06	.02	.00
☐ 502	Jim Pankovits	.06	.02	.00	☐ 549	John Wockenfuss	.06	.02	.00
☐ 503	Luis Aguayo	.06	.02	.00	☐ 550	Frank Pastore	.06	.02	.00
☐ 504	Ralph Citarella	.06	.02	.00	☐ 551	Tim Flannery	.06	.02	.00
☐ 505	Bruce Bochy	.06	.02	.00	☐ 552	Rick Rhoden	.10	.04	.01
☐ 506	Bob Owchinko	.06	.02	.00	☐ 553	Mark Davis	.10	.04	.01
☐ 507	Pascual Perez	.10	.04	.01	☐ 554	Jeff Dedmon	.10	.04	.01
☐ 508	Lee Lacy	.06	.02	.00	☐ 555	Gary Woods	.06	.02	.00
☐ 509	Atlee Hammaker	.06	.02	.00	☐ 556	Danny Heep	.06	.02	.00
☐ 510	Bob Dernier	.06	.02	.00	☐ 557	Mark Langston	2.00	.80	.20
☐ 511	Ed VandeBerg	.06	.02	.00	☐ 558	Darrell Brown	.06	.02	.00
☐ 512	Cliff Johnson	.06	.02	.00	☐ 559	Jimmy Key	2.00	.80	.20
☐ 513	Len Whitehouse	.06	.02	.00	☐ 560	Rick Lysander	.06	.02	.00
☐ 514	Dennis Martinez	.10	.04	.01	☐ 561	Doyle Alexander	.10	.04	.00
☐ 515	Ed Romero	.06	.02	.00	☐ 562	Mike Stanton	.06	.02	.00
☐ 516	Rusty Kuntz	.06	.02	.00	☐ 563	Sid Fernandez	.65	.26	.06
☐ 517	Rick Miller	.06	.02	.00	☐ 564	Richie Hebner	.06	.02	.00
☐ 518	Dennis Rasmussen	.15	.06	.01	☐ 565	Alex Trevino	.06	.02	.00
☐ 519	Steve Yeager	.06	.02	.00	☐ 566	Brian Harper	.06	.02	.00
☐ 520	Chris Bando	.06	.02	.00	☐ 567	Dan Gladden	.45	.18	.04
☐ 521	U.L. Washington	.06	.02	.00	☐ 568	Luis Salazar	.10	.04	.01
☐ 522	Curt Young	.40	.16	.04	☐ 569	Tom Foley	.06	.02	.00
☐ 523	Angel Salazar	.06	.02	.00	☐ 570	Larry Andersen	.06	.02	.00
☐ 524	Curt Kaufman	.06	.02	.00	☐ 571	Danny Cox	.10	.04	.01
☐ 525	Odell Jones	.06	.02	.00	☐ 572	Joe Sambito	.06	.02	.00
☐ 526	Juan Agosto	.06	.02	.00	☐ 573	Juan Beniquez	.06	.02	.00
☐ 527	Denny Walling	.06	.02	.00	☐ 574	Joel Skinner	.06	.02	.00
☐ 528	Andy Hawkins	.10	.04	.01	☐ 575	Randy St.Claire	.06	.02	.00
☐ 529	Sixto Lezcano	.06	.02	.00	☐ 576	Floyd Rayford	.06	.02	.00
☐ 530	Skeeter Barnes	.06	.02	.00	☐ 577	Roy Howell	.06	.02	.00
☐ 531	Randy Johnson	.06	.02	.00	☐ 578	John Grubb	.06	.02	.00
☐ 532	Jim Morrison	.06	.02	.00	☐ 579	Ed Jurak	.06	.02	.00
☐ 533	Warren Brusstar	.06	.02	.00	☐ 580	John Montefusco	.06	.02	.00
☐ 534A	Jeff Pendleton ERR (wrong first name)	.80	.32	.08	☐ 581	Orel Hershiser	11.00	4.50	1.10
☐ 534B	Terry Pendleton COR	2.50	1.00	.25	☐ 582	Tom Waddell	.10	.04	.01
☐ 535	Vic Rodriguez	.10	.04	.01	☐ 583	Mark Huismann	.06	.02	.00
☐ 536	Bob McClure	.06	.02	.00	☐ 584	Joe Morgan	.25	.10	.02
☐ 537	Dave Bergman	.06	.02	.00	☐ 585	Jim Wohlford	.06	.02	.00
☐ 538	Mark Clear	.06	.02	.00	☐ 586	Dave Schmidt	.10	.04	.00
☐ 539	Mike Pagliarulo	1.75	.70	.17	☐ 587	Jeff Kunkel	.10	.04	.01
☐ 540	Terry Whitfield	.06	.02	.00	☐ 588	Hal McRae	.10	.04	.01
☐ 541	Joe Beckwith	.06	.02	.00	☐ 589	Bill Almon	.06	.02	.00
					☐ 590	Carmen Castillo	.06	.02	.00

		MINT	EXC	G-VG
☐ 591	Omar Moreno	.06	.02	.00
☐ 592	Ken Howell	.15	.06	.01
☐ 593	Tom Brookens	.06	.02	.00
☐ 594	Joe Nolan	.06	.02	.00
☐ 595	Willie Lozado	.10	.04	.01
☐ 596	Tom Nieto	.10	.04	.01
☐ 597	Walt Terrell	.06	.02	.00
☐ 598	Al Oliver	.10	.04	.01
☐ 599	Shane Rawley	.10	.04	.01
☐ 600	Denny Gonzalez	.10	.04	.01
☐ 601	Mark Grant	.10	.04	.01
☐ 602	Mike Armstrong	.06	.02	.00
☐ 603	George Foster	.12	.05	.01
☐ 604	Dave Lopes	.10	.04	.01
☐ 605	Salome Barojas	.06	.02	.00
☐ 606	Roy Lee Jackson	.06	.02	.00
☐ 607	Pete Filson	.06	.02	.00
☐ 608	Duane Walker	.06	.02	.00
☐ 609	Glenn Wilson	.10	.04	.01
☐ 610	Rafael Santana	.30	.12	.03
☐ 611	Roy Smith	.10	.04	.01
☐ 612	Ruppert Jones	.06	.02	.00
☐ 613	Joe Cowley	.06	.02	.00
☐ 614	Al Nipper	.20	.08	.02
	(photo actually Mike Brown)			
☐ 615	Gene Nelson	.06	.02	.00
☐ 616	Joe Carter	1.50	.60	.15
☐ 617	Ray Knight	.10	.04	.01
☐ 618	Chuck Rainey	.06	.02	.00
☐ 619	Dan Driessen	.06	.02	.00
☐ 620	Daryl Sconiers	.06	.02	.00
☐ 621	Bill Stein	.06	.02	.00
☐ 622	Roy Smalley	.06	.02	.00
☐ 623	Ed Lynch	.06	.02	.00
☐ 624	Jeff Stone	.15	.06	.01
☐ 625	Bruce Berenyi	.06	.02	.00
☐ 626	Kelvin Chapman	.10	.04	.01
☐ 627	Joe Price	.06	.02	.00
☐ 628	Steve Bedrosian	.15	.06	.01
☐ 629	Vic Mata	.10	.04	.01
☐ 630	Mike Krukow	.06	.02	.00
☐ 631	Phil Bradley	1.00	.40	.10
☐ 632	Jim Gott	.10	.04	.01
☐ 633	Randy Bush	.10	.04	.01
☐ 634	Tom Browning	1.50	.60	.15
☐ 635	Lou Gehrig	.06	.02	.00
	Puzzle Card			
☐ 636	Reid Nichols	.06	.02	.00
☐ 637	Dan Pasqua	.75	.30	.07

		MINT	EXC	G-VG
☐ 638	German Rivera	.10	.04	.01
☐ 639	Don Schulze	.06	.02	.00
☐ 640A	Mike Jones	.10	.04	.01
	(Career Highlights, five lines)			
☐ 640B	Mike Jones	.10	.04	.01
	(Career Highlights, four lines)			
☐ 641	Pete Rose	1.00	.40	.10
☐ 642	Wade Rowdon	.10	.04	.01
☐ 643	Jerry Narron	.06	.02	.00
☐ 644	Darrell Miller	.10	.04	.01
☐ 645	Tim Hulett	.10	.04	.01
☐ 646	Andy McGaffigan	.06	.02	.00
☐ 647	Kurt Bevacqua	.06	.02	.00
☐ 648	John Russell	.10	.04	.01
☐ 649	Ron Robinson	.20	.08	.02
☐ 650	Donnie Moore	.06	.02	.00
☐ 651A	Two for the Title	5.00	2.00	.50
	Dave Winfield			
	Don Mattingly			
	(yellow letters)			
☐ 651B	Two for the Title	6.00	2.40	.60
	Dave Winfield			
	Don Mattingly			
	(white letters)			
☐ 652	Tim Laudner	.06	.02	.00
☐ 653	Steve Farr	.10	.04	.01
☐ 654	DK Checklist 1-26	.09	.01	.00
	(unnumbered)			
☐ 655	Checklist 27-130	.07	.01	.00
	(unnumbered)			
☐ 656	Checklist 131-234	.07	.01	.00
	(unnumbered)			
☐ 657	Checklist 235-338	.07	.01	.00
	(unnumbered)			
☐ 658	Checklist 339-442	.07	.01	.00
	(unnumbered)			
☐ 659	Checklist 443-546	.07	.01	.00
	(unnumbered)			
☐ 660	Checklist 547-653	.07	.01	.00
	(unnumbered)			

1985 Donruss Highlights

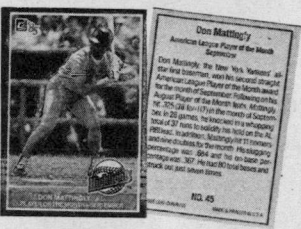

This 56-card set features the players and pitchers of the month for each league as well as a number of highlight cards commemorating the 1985 season. The Donruss Company dedicated the last two cards to their own selections for Rookies of the Year (ROY). This set proved to be more popular than the Donruss Company had predicted, as their first and only print run was exhausted before card dealers' initial orders were filled.

		MINT	EXC	G-VG
	Complete Set (56)	21.00	8.50	2.10
	Common Player (1-56)	.10	.04	.01
☐ 1	Tom Seaver: Sets Opening Day Record	.40	.16	.04
☐ 2	Rollie Fingers: Sets AL Save Mark	.15	.06	.01
☐ 3	Mike Davis: AL Player April	.10	.04	.01
☐ 4	Charlie Leibrandt: AL Pitcher April	.10	.04	.01
☐ 5	Dale Murphy: NL Player April	.75	.30	.07
☐ 6	Fernando Valenzuela: NL Pitcher April	.25	.10	.02
☐ 7	Larry Bowa: NL Shortstop Record	.10	.04	.01
☐ 8	Dave Concepcion: Joins Reds' 2000 Hit Club	.10	.04	.01
☐ 9	Tony Perez: Eldest Grand Slammer	.15	.06	.01
☐ 10	Pete Rose: NL Career Run Leader	1.25	.50	.12
☐ 11	George Brett: AL Player May	.75	.30	.07
☐ 12	Dave Stieb: AL Pitcher May	.15	.06	.01
☐ 13	Dave Parker: NL Player May	.15	.06	.01
☐ 14	Andy Hawkins: NL Pitcher May	.10	.04	.01
☐ 15	Andy Hawkins: Records 11th Straight Win	.10	.04	.01
☐ 16	Von Hayes: Two Homers in First Inning	.15	.06	.01
☐ 17	Rickey Henderson: AL Player June	.75	.30	.07
☐ 18	Jay Howell: AL Pitcher June	.10	.04	.01
☐ 19	Pedro Guerrero: NL Player June	.20	.08	.02
☐ 20	John Tudor: NL Pitcher June	.15	.06	.01
☐ 21	Hernandez/Carter: Marathon Game Iron Men	.30	.12	.03
☐ 22	Nolan Ryan: Records 4000th K	.50	.20	.05
☐ 23	LaMarr Hoyt: All-Star Game MVP	.10	.04	.01
☐ 24	Oddibe McDowell: 1st Ranger to Hit for Cycle	.30	.12	.03
☐ 25	George Brett: AL Player July	.75	.30	.07
☐ 26	Bret Saberhagen: AL Pitcher July	.50	.20	.05
☐ 27	Keith Hernandez: NL Player July	.25	.10	.02
☐ 28	Fernando Valenzuela: NL Pitcher July	.25	.10	.02
☐ 29	W.McGee/V.Coleman: Record Setting Base Stealers	.75	.30	.07
☐ 30	Tom Seaver: Notches 300th Career Win	.35	.14	.03
☐ 31	Rod Carew: Strokes 3000th Hit	.35	.14	.03

		MINT	EXC	G-VG
☐ 32	Dwight Gooden: ... Establishes Met Record	1.25	.50	.12
☐ 33	Dwight Gooden: ... Achieves Strikeout Milestone	1.25	.50	.12
☐ 34	Eddie Murray: ..... Explodes for 9 RBI	.50	.20	.05
☐ 35	Don Baylor: .... AL Career HBP Leader	.15	.06	.01
☐ 36	Don Mattingly: ..... AL Player August	2.50	1.00	.25
☐ 37	Dave Righetti: ..... AL Pitcher August	.15	.06	.01
☐ 38	Willie McGee: ..... NL Player August	.25	.10	.02
☐ 39	Shane Rawley: ..... NL Pitcher August	.10	.04	.01
☐ 40	Pete Rose: .... Ty-Breaking Hit	1.25	.50	.12
☐ 41	Andre Dawson: Hits 3 HR's Drives in 8 Runs	.25	.10	.02
☐ 42	Rickey Henderson: . Sets Yankee Theft Mark	.75	.30	.07
☐ 43	Tom Browning: 20 Wins in Rookie Season	.20	.08	.02
☐ 44	Don Mattingly: Yankee Milestone for Hits	2.50	1.00	.25
☐ 45	Don Mattingly: AL .. Player September	2.50	1.00	.25
☐ 46	Charlie Leibrandt: AL Pitcher September	.10	.04	.01
☐ 47	Gary Carter: NL ... Player September	.30	.12	.03
☐ 48	Dwight Gooden: NL Pitcher September	1.25	.50	.12
☐ 49	Wade Boggs: Major League Record Setter	2.00	.80	.20
☐ 50	Phil Niekro: Hurls .. Shutout for 300th Win	.20	.08	.02
☐ 51	Darrell Evans: ..... Venerable HR King	.10	.04	.01
☐ 52	Willie McGee: NL .. Switch-Hitting Record	.20	.08	.02
☐ 53	Dave Winfield: ..... Equals DiMaggio Feat	.35	.14	.03
☐ 54	Vince Coleman: .... Donruss NL ROY	2.00	.80	.20

		MINT	EXC	G-VG
☐ 55	Ozzie Guillen: .... Donruss AL ROY	.40	.16	.04
☐ 56	Checklist card .... (unnumbered)	.10	.01	.00

1986 Donruss

The cards in this 660-card set measure 2 ½" by 3 ½". The 1986 Donruss regular issue cards have fronts that feature blue borders. The fronts contain the standard team logo, player's name, position, and Donruss logo. The cards were distributed with puzzle pieces from a Dick Perez rendition of Hank Aaron. The first 26 cards of the set are Diamond Kings (DK), for the fifth year in a row; the artwork on the Diamond Kings was again produced by the Perez-Steele Galleries. Cards 27-46 again feature Rated Rookies (RR); Danny Tartabull is included in this subset for the second year in a row. The unnumbered checklist cards are arbitrarily numbered below as numbers 654 through 660.

	MINT	EXC	G-VG
Complete Set (660)	110.00	45.00	11.00
Common Player (1-660) ..	.05	.02	.00

		MINT	EXC	G-VG
☐ 1	Kirk Gibson DK ...	.35	.12	.02
☐ 2	Goose Gossage DK	.15	.06	.01
☐ 3	Willie McGee DK ...	.25	.10	.02
☐ 4	George Bell DK ...	.25	.10	.02

			MINT	EXC	G-VG
☐	5	Tony Armas DK	.10	.04	.01
☐	6	Chili Davis DK	.10	.04	.01
☐	7	Cecil Cooper DK	.12	.05	.01
☐	8	Mike Boddicker DK	.10	.04	.01
☐	9	Dave Lopes DK	.10	.04	.01
☐	10	Bill Doran DK	.10	.04	.01
☐	11	Bret Saberhagen DK	.30	.12	.03
☐	12	Brett Butler DK	.10	.04	.01
☐	13	Harold Baines DK	.15	.06	.01
☐	14	Mike Davis DK	.10	.04	.01
☐	15	Tony Perez DK	.15	.06	.01
☐	16	Willie Randolph DK	.12	.05	.01
☐	17	Bob Boone DK	.12	.05	.01
☐	18	Orel Hershiser DK	1.00	.40	.10
☐	19	Johnny Ray DK	.12	.05	.01
☐	20	Gary Ward DK	.10	.04	.01
☐	21	Rick Mahler DK	.10	.04	.01
☐	22	Phil Bradley DK	.20	.08	.02
☐	23	Jerry Koosman DK	.10	.04	.01
☐	24	Tom Brunansky DK	.20	.08	.02
☐	25	Andre Dawson DK	.30	.12	.03
☐	26	Dwight Gooden DK	1.00	.40	.10
☐	27	Kal Daniels RR	4.50	1.80	.45
☐	28	Fred McGriff RR	5.00	2.00	.50
☐	29	Cory Snyder RR	3.50	1.40	.35
☐	30	Jose Guzman RR	.35	.14	.03
☐	31	Ty Gainey RR	.15	.06	.01
☐	32	Johnny Abrego RR	.10	.04	.01
☐	33A	Andres Galarraga RR (no accent)	4.50	1.80	.45
☐	33B	Andrés Galarraga RR (accent over e)	5.00	2.00	.50
☐	34	Dave Shipanoff RR	.10	.04	.01
☐	35	Mark McLemore RR	.10	.04	.01
☐	36	Marty Clary RR	.10	.04	.01
☐	37	Paul O'Neill RR	.30	.12	.03
☐	38	Danny Tartabull RR	1.50	.60	.15
☐	39	Jose Canseco RR	55.00	22.00	5.50
☐	40	Juan Nieves RR	.30	.12	.03
☐	41	Lance McCullers RR	.45	.18	.04
☐	42	Rick Surhoff RR	.10	.04	.01
☐	43	Todd Worrell RR	.80	.32	.08
☐	44	Bob Kipper RR	.10	.04	.01
☐	45	John Habyan RR	.10	.04	.01
☐	46	Mike Woodard RR	.10	.04	.01
☐	47	Mike Boddicker	.08	.03	.01
☐	48	Robin Yount	.35	.14	.03
☐	49	Lou Whitaker	.12	.05	.01
☐	50	Oil Can Boyd	.08	.03	.01

			MINT	EXC	G-VG
☐	51	Rickey Henderson	.40	.16	.04
☐	52	Mike Marshall	.12	.05	.01
☐	53	George Brett	.50	.20	.05
☐	54	Dave Kingman	.10	.04	.01
☐	55	Hubie Brooks	.08	.03	.01
☐	56	Oddibe McDowell	.25	.10	.02
☐	57	Doug DeCinces	.08	.03	.01
☐	58	Britt Burns	.05	.02	.00
☐	59	Ozzie Smith	.20	.08	.02
☐	60	Jose Cruz	.08	.03	.01
☐	61	Mike Schmidt	.50	.20	.05
☐	62	Pete Rose	.75	.30	.07
☐	63	Steve Garvey	.40	.16	.04
☐	64	Tony Pena	.08	.03	.01
☐	65	Chili Davis	.10	.04	.01
☐	66	Dale Murphy	.50	.20	.05
☐	67	Ryne Sandberg	.30	.12	.03
☐	68	Gary Carter	.30	.12	.03
☐	69	Alvin Davis	.15	.06	.01
☐	70	Kent Hrbek	.20	.08	.02
☐	71	George Bell	.30	.12	.03
☐	72	Kirby Puckett	2.25	.90	.22
☐	73	Lloyd Moseby	.10	.04	.01
☐	74	Bob Kearney	.05	.02	.00
☐	75	Dwight Gooden	2.25	.90	.22
☐	76	Gary Matthews	.08	.03	.01
☐	77	Rick Mahler	.05	.02	.00
☐	78	Benny Distefano	.05	.02	.00
☐	79	Jeff Leonard	.12	.05	.01
☐	80	Kevin McReynolds	.50	.20	.05
☐	81	Ron Oester	.05	.02	.00
☐	82	John Russell	.05	.02	.00
☐	83	Tommy Herr	.10	.04	.01
☐	84	Jerry Mumphrey	.05	.02	.00
☐	85	Ron Romanick	.05	.02	.00
☐	86	Daryl Boston	.05	.02	.00
☐	87	Andre Dawson	.30	.12	.03
☐	88	Eddie Murray	.35	.14	.03
☐	89	Dion James	.05	.02	.00
☐	90	Chet Lemon	.08	.03	.01
☐	91	Bob Stanley	.05	.02	.00
☐	92	Willie Randolph	.08	.03	.01
☐	93	Mike Scioscia	.08	.03	.01
☐	94	Tom Waddell	.05	.02	.00
☐	95	Danny Jackson	.30	.12	.03
☐	96	Mike Davis	.08	.03	.01
☐	97	Mike Fitzgerald	.05	.02	.00
☐	98	Gary Ward	.08	.03	.01
☐	99	Pete O'Brien	.10	.04	.01

	MINT	EXC	G-VG		MINT	EXC	G-VG
☐ 100 Bret Saberhagen ...	.45	.18	.04	☐ 149 Danny Darwin	.05	.02	.00
☐ 101 Alfredo Griffin	.08	.03	.01	☐ 150 Chris Pittaro	.05	.02	.00
☐ 102 Brett Butler	.08	.03	.01	☐ 151 Bill Buckner	.08	.03	.01
☐ 103 Ron Guidry	.15	.06	.01	☐ 152 Mike Pagliarulo ...	.15	.06	.01
☐ 104 Jerry Reuss	.08	.03	.01	☐ 153 Bill Russell	.08	.03	.01
☐ 105 Jack Morris	.15	.06	.01	☐ 154 Brook Jacoby	.12	.05	.01
☐ 106 Rick Dempsey	.05	.02	.00	☐ 155 Pat Sheridan	.05	.02	.00
☐ 107 Ray Burris	.05	.02	.00	☐ 156 Mike Gallego	.05	.02	.00
☐ 108 Brian Downing	.08	.03	.01	☐ 157 Jim Wohlford	.05	.02	.00
☐ 109 Willie McGee	.18	.08	.01	☐ 158 Gary Pettis	.05	.02	.00
☐ 110 Bill Doran	.10	.04	.01	☐ 159 Toby Harrah	.08	.03	.01
☐ 111 Kent Tekulve	.05	.02	.00	☐ 160 Richard Dotson ...	.08	.03	.01
☐ 112 Tony Gwynn	.75	.30	.07	☐ 161 Bob Knepper	.08	.03	.01
☐ 113 Marvell Wynne	.05	.02	.00	☐ 162 Dave Dravecky ...	.05	.02	.00
☐ 114 David Green	.05	.02	.00	☐ 163 Greg Gross	.05	.02	.00
☐ 115 Jim Gantner	.05	.02	.00	☐ 164 Eric Davis	3.50	1.40	.35
☐ 116 George Foster	.12	.05	.01	☐ 165 Gerald Perry	.15	.06	.01
☐ 117 Steve Trout	.05	.02	.00	☐ 166 Rick Rhoden	.08	.03	.01
☐ 118 Mark Langston	.15	.06	.01	☐ 167 Keith Moreland ...	.05	.02	.00
☐ 119 Tony Fernandez ...	.20	.08	.01	☐ 168 Jack Clark	.25	.10	.02
☐ 120 John Butcher	.05	.02	.00	☐ 169 Storm Davis	.08	.03	.01
☐ 121 Ron Robinson	.05	.02	.00	☐ 170 Cecil Cooper	.10	.04	.01
☐ 122 Dan Spillner	.05	.02	.00	☐ 171 Alan Trammell ...	.25	.10	.02
☐ 123 Mike Young	.08	.03	.01	☐ 172 Roger Clemens ...	3.50	1.40	.35
☐ 124 Paul Molitor	.15	.06	.01	☐ 173 Don Mattingly	5.50	2.20	.55
☐ 125 Kirk Gibson	.25	.10	.02	☐ 174 Pedro Guerrero ...	.25	.10	.02
☐ 126 Ken Griffey	.08	.03	.01	☐ 175 Willie Wilson	.10	.04	.01
☐ 127 Tony Armas	.08	.03	.01	☐ 176 Dwayne Murphy ...	.05	.02	.00
☐ 128 Mariano Duncan ...	.15	.06	.01	☐ 177 Tim Raines	.30	.12	.03
☐ 129 Pat Tabler	.08	.03	.01	☐ 178 Larry Parrish	.05	.02	.00
☐ 130 Frank White	.08	.03	.01	☐ 179 Mike Witt	.10	.04	.01
☐ 131 Carney Lansford ...	.10	.04	.01	☐ 180 Harold Baines	.15	.06	.01
☐ 132 Vance Law	.08	.03	.01	☐ 181 Vince Coleman ...	2.25	.90	.22
☐ 133 Dick Schofield	.08	.03	.01	(BA 2.67 on back)			
☐ 134 Wayne Tolleson ...	.05	.02	.00	☐ 182 Jeff Heathcock	.05	.02	.00
☐ 135 Greg Walker	.08	.03	.01	☐ 183 Steve Carlton	.30	.12	.03
☐ 136 Denny Walling	.05	.02	.00	☐ 184 Mario Soto	.05	.02	.00
☐ 137 Ozzie Virgil	.05	.02	.00	☐ 185 Goose Gossage . .	.12	.05	.01
☐ 138 Ricky Horton	.05	.02	.00	☐ 186 Johnny Ray	.10	.04	.01
☐ 139 LaMarr Hoyt	.08	.03	.01	☐ 187 Dan Gladden	.08	.03	.01
☐ 140 Wayne Krenchicki ..	.05	.02	.00	☐ 188 Bob Horner	.15	.06	.01
☐ 141 Glenn Hubbard	.05	.02	.00	☐ 189 Rick Sutcliffe	.12	.05	.01
☐ 142 Cecilio Guante	.05	.02	.00	☐ 190 Keith Hernandez ..	.30	.12	.03
☐ 143 Mike Krukow	.05	.02	.00	☐ 191 Phil Bradley	.12	.05	.01
☐ 144 Lee Smith	.08	.03	.01	☐ 192 Tom Brunansky ...	.15	.06	.01
☐ 145 Edwin Nunez	.05	.02	.00	☐ 193 Jesse Barfield	.25	.10	.02
☐ 146 Dave Stieb	.12	.05	.01	☐ 194 Frank Viola	.35	.14	.03
☐ 147 Mike Smithson	.05	.02	.00	☐ 195 Willie Upshaw	.05	.02	.00
☐ 148 Ken Dixon	.05	.02	.00	☐ 196 Jim Beattie	.05	.02	.00

		MINT	EXC	G-VG
☐ 197	Darryl Strawberry	1.75	.70	.17
☐ 198	Ron Cey	.10	.04	.01
☐ 199	Steve Bedrosian	.12	.05	.01
☐ 200	Steve Kemp	.08	.03	.01
☐ 201	Manny Trillo	.05	.02	.00
☐ 202	Garry Templeton	.08	.03	.01
☐ 203	Dave Parker	.15	.06	.01
☐ 204	John Denny	.08	.03	.01
☐ 205	Terry Pendleton	.08	.03	.01
☐ 206	Terry Puhl	.05	.02	.00
☐ 207	Bobby Grich	.08	.03	.01
☐ 208	Ozzie Guillen	.40	.16	.04
☐ 209	Jeff Reardon	.10	.04	.01
☐ 210	Cal Ripken	.40	.16	.04
☐ 211	Bill Schroeder	.05	.02	.00
☐ 212	Dan Petry	.08	.03	.01
☐ 213	Jim Rice	.20	.08	.02
☐ 214	Dave Righetti	.12	.05	.01
☐ 215	Fernando Valenzuela	.25	.10	.02
☐ 216	Julio Franco	.12	.05	.01
☐ 217	Darryl Motley	.05	.02	.00
☐ 218	Dave Collins	.05	.02	.00
☐ 219	Tim Wallach	.10	.04	.01
☐ 220	George Wright	.05	.02	.00
☐ 221	Tommy Dunbar	.05	.02	.00
☐ 222	Steve Balboni	.05	.02	.00
☐ 223	Jay Howell	.08	.03	.01
☐ 224	Joe Carter	.35	.14	.03
☐ 225	Ed Whitson	.05	.02	.00
☐ 226	Orel Hershiser	1.75	.70	.17
☐ 227	Willie Hernandez	.10	.04	.01
☐ 228	Lee Lacy	.05	.02	.00
☐ 229	Rollie Fingers	.15	.06	.01
☐ 230	Bob Boone	.10	.04	.01
☐ 231	Joaquin Andujar	.10	.04	.01
☐ 232	Craig Reynolds	.05	.02	.00
☐ 233	Shane Rawley	.08	.03	.01
☐ 234	Eric Show	.08	.03	.01
☐ 235	Jose DeLeon	.05	.02	.00
☐ 236	Jose Uribe	.30	.12	.03
☐ 237	Moose Haas	.05	.02	.00
☐ 238	Wally Backman	.08	.03	.01
☐ 239	Dennis Eckersley	.15	.06	.01
☐ 240	Mike Moore	.08	.03	.01
☐ 241	Damaso Garcia	.05	.02	.00
☐ 242	Tim Teufel	.05	.02	.00
☐ 243	Dave Concepcion	.10	.04	.01
☐ 244	Floyd Bannister	.05	.02	.00
☐ 245	Fred Lynn	.15	.06	.01
☐ 246	Charlie Moore	.05	.02	.00
☐ 247	Walt Terrell	.05	.02	.00
☐ 248	Dave Winfield	.30	.12	.03
☐ 249	Dwight Evans	.15	.06	.01
☐ 250	Dennis Powell	.10	.04	.01
☐ 251	Andre Thornton	.08	.03	.01
☐ 252	Onix Concepcion	.05	.02	.00
☐ 253	Mike Heath	.05	.02	.00
☐ 254A	David Palmer ERR (position 2B)	.10	.04	.01
☐ 254B	David Palmer COR (position P)	.60	.24	.06
☐ 255	Donnie Moore	.05	.02	.00
☐ 256	Curtis Wilkerson	.05	.02	.00
☐ 257	Julio Cruz	.05	.02	.00
☐ 258	Nolan Ryan	.35	.14	.03
☐ 259	Jeff Stone	.05	.02	.00
☐ 260	John Tudor	.12	.05	.01
☐ 261	Mark Thurmond	.05	.02	.00
☐ 262	Jay Tibbs	.05	.02	.00
☐ 263	Rafael Ramirez	.05	.02	.00
☐ 264	Larry McWilliams	.05	.02	.00
☐ 265	Mark Davis	.08	.03	.01
☐ 266	Bob Dernier	.05	.02	.00
☐ 267	Matt Young	.05	.02	.00
☐ 268	Jim Clancy	.05	.02	.00
☐ 269	Mickey Hatcher	.08	.03	.01
☐ 270	Sammy Stewart	.05	.02	.00
☐ 271	Bob L. Gibson	.05	.02	.00
☐ 272	Nelson Simmons	.08	.03	.01
☐ 273	Rich Gedman	.08	.03	.01
☐ 274	Butch Wynegar	.05	.02	.00
☐ 275	Ken Howell	.05	.02	.01
☐ 276	Mel Hall	.08	.03	.01
☐ 277	Jim Sundberg	.05	.02	.00
☐ 278	Chris Codiroli	.05	.02	.00
☐ 279	Herm Winningham	.10	.04	.01
☐ 280	Rod Carew	.35	.14	.03
☐ 281	Don Slaught	.05	.02	.00
☐ 282	Scott Fletcher	.08	.03	.01
☐ 283	Bill Dawley	.05	.02	.00
☐ 284	Andy Hawkins	.08	.03	.01
☐ 285	Glenn Wilson	.08	.03	.01
☐ 286	Nick Esasky	.08	.03	.01
☐ 287	Claudell Washington	.08	.03	.01
☐ 288	Lee Mazzilli	.05	.02	.00
☐ 289	Jody Davis	.08	.03	.01
☐ 290	Darrell Porter	.05	.02	.00
☐ 291	Scott McGregor	.08	.03	.01

		MINT	EXC	G-VG			MINT	EXC	G-VG
☐ 292	Ted Simmons	.10	.04	.01	☐ 341	Joe Hesketh	.05	.02	.00
☐ 293	Aurelio Lopez	.05	.02	.00	☐ 342	Charlie Hough	.08	.03	.01
☐ 294	Marty Barrett	.12	.05	.01	☐ 343	Dave Rozema	.05	.02	.00
☐ 295	Dale Berra	.05	.02	.00	☐ 344	Greg Pryor	.05	.02	.00
☐ 296	Greg Brock	.05	.02	.00	☐ 345	Mickey Tettleton	.08	.03	.01
☐ 297	Charlie Leibrandt	.05	.02	.00	☐ 346	George Vukovich	.05	.02	.00
☐ 298	Bill Krueger	.05	.02	.00	☐ 347	Don Baylor	.10	.04	.01
☐ 299	Bryn Smith	.05	.02	.00	☐ 348	Carlos Diaz	.05	.02	.00
☐ 300	Burt Hooton	.05	.02	.00	☐ 349	Barbaro Garbey	.05	.02	.00
☐ 301	Stu Cliburn	.08	.03	.01	☐ 350	Larry Sheets	.12	.05	.01
☐ 302	Luis Salazar	.05	.02	.00	☐ 351	Ted Higuera	1.50	.60	.15
☐ 303	Ken Dayley	.05	.02	.00	☐ 352	Juan Beniquez	.05	.02	.00
☐ 304	Frank DiPino	.05	.02	.00	☐ 353	Bob Forsch	.05	.02	.00
☐ 305	Von Hayes	.12	.05	.01	☐ 354	Mark Bailey	.05	.02	.00
☐ 306	Gary Redus	.05	.02	.00	☐ 355	Larry Andersen	.05	.02	.00
☐ 307	Craig Lefferts	.05	.02	.00	☐ 356	Terry Kennedy	.05	.02	.00
☐ 308	Sammy Khalifa	.08	.03	.01	☐ 357	Don Robinson	.05	.02	.00
☐ 309	Scott Garrelts	.08	.03	.01	☐ 358	Jim Gott	.05	.02	.00
☐ 310	Rick Cerone	.05	.02	.00	☐ 359	Earnie Riles	.25	.10	.02
☐ 311	Shawon Dunston	.10	.04	.01	☐ 360	John Christensen	.05	.02	.00
☐ 312	Howard Johnson	.25	.10	.02	☐ 361	Ray Fontenot	.05	.02	.00
☐ 313	Jim Presley	.15	.06	.01	☐ 362	Spike Owen	.05	.02	.00
☐ 314	Gary Gaetti	.25	.10	.02	☐ 363	Jim Acker	.05	.02	.00
☐ 315	Luis Leal	.05	.02	.00	☐ 364	Ron Davis	.08	.03	.01
☐ 316	Mark Salas	.05	.02	.00	☐ 365	Tom Hume	.05	.02	.00
☐ 317	Bill Caudill	.05	.02	.00	☐ 366	Carlton Fisk	.15	.06	.01
☐ 318	Dave Henderson	.10	.04	.01	☐ 367	Nate Snell	.05	.02	.00
☐ 319	Rafael Santana	.05	.02	.00	☐ 368	Rick Manning	.05	.02	.00
☐ 320	Leon Durham	.08	.03	.01	☐ 369	Darrell Evans	.10	.04	.01
☐ 321	Bruce Sutter	.12	.05	.01	☐ 370	Ron Hassey	.05	.02	.00
☐ 322	Jason Thompson	.05	.02	.00	☐ 371	Wade Boggs	3.00	1.20	.30
☐ 323	Bob Brenly	.05	.02	.00	☐ 372	Rick Honeycutt	.05	.02	.00
☐ 324	Carmelo Martinez	.05	.02	.00	☐ 373	Chris Bando	.05	.02	.00
☐ 325	Eddie Milner	.05	.02	.00	☐ 374	Bud Black	.05	.02	.00
☐ 326	Juan Samuel	.15	.06	.01	☐ 375	Steve Henderson	.05	.02	.00
☐ 327	Tom Nieto	.05	.02	.00	☐ 376	Charlie Lea	.05	.02	.00
☐ 328	Dave Smith	.08	.03	.01	☐ 377	Reggie Jackson	.45	.18	.04
☐ 329	Urbano Lugo	.05	.02	.00	☐ 378	Dave Schmidt	.08	.03	.01
☐ 330	Joel Skinner	.05	.02	.00	☐ 379	Bob James	.05	.02	.00
☐ 331	Bill Gullickson	.05	.02	.00	☐ 380	Glenn Davis	2.00	.80	.20
☐ 332	Floyd Rayford	.05	.02	.00	☐ 381	Tim Corcoran	.05	.02	.00
☐ 333	Ben Oglivie	.08	.03	.01	☐ 382	Danny Cox	.10	.04	.01
☐ 334	Lance Parrish	.15	.06	.01	☐ 383	Tim Flannery	.05	.02	.00
☐ 335	Jackie Gutierrez	.05	.02	.00	☐ 384	Tom Browning	.20	.08	.02
☐ 336	Dennis Rasmussen	.10	.04	.01	☐ 385	Rick Camp	.05	.02	.00
☐ 337	Terry Whitfield	.05	.02	.00	☐ 386	Jim Morrison	.05	.02	.00
☐ 338	Neal Heaton	.05	.02	.00	☐ 387	Dave LaPoint	.08	.03	.01
☐ 339	Jorge Orta	.05	.02	.00	☐ 388	Dave Lopes	.08	.03	.01
☐ 340	Donnie Hill	.05	.02	.00	☐ 389	Al Cowens	.05	.02	.00

		MINT	EXC	G-VG			MINT	EXC	G-VG
☐ 390	Doyle Alexander	.08	.03	.01	☐ 439	Tom Filer	.05	.02	.00
☐ 391	Tim Laudner	.05	.02	.00	☐ 440	Gorman Thomas	.10	.04	.01
☐ 392	Don Aase	.05	.02	.00	☐ 441	Rick Aguilera	.25	.10	.02
☐ 393	Jaime Cocanower	.05	.02	.00	☐ 442	Scott Sanderson	.05	.02	.00
☐ 394	Randy O'Neal	.05	.02	.00	☐ 443	Jeff Dedmon	.05	.02	.00
☐ 395	Mike Easler	.05	.02	.00	☐ 444	Joe Orsulak	.12	.05	.01
☐ 396	Scott Bradley	.05	.02	.00	☐ 445	Atlee Hammaker	.05	.02	.00
☐ 397	Tom Niedenfuer	.05	.02	.00	☐ 446	Jerry Royster	.05	.02	.00
☐ 398	Jerry Willard	.05	.02	.00	☐ 447	Buddy Bell	.10	.04	.01
☐ 399	Lonnie Smith	.05	.02	.00	☐ 448	Dave Rucker	.05	.02	.00
☐ 400	Bruce Bochte	.05	.02	.00	☐ 449	Ivan DeJesus	.05	.02	.00
☐ 401	Terry Francona	.05	.02	.00	☐ 450	Jim Pankovits	.05	.02	.00
☐ 402	Jim Slaton	.05	.02	.00	☐ 451	Jerry Narron	.05	.02	.00
☐ 403	Bill Stein	.05	.02	.00	☐ 452	Bryan Little	.05	.02	.00
☐ 404	Tim Hulett	.05	.02	.00	☐ 453	Gary Lucas	.05	.02	.00
☐ 405	Alan Ashby	.05	.02	.00	☐ 454	Dennis Martinez	.08	.03	.01
☐ 406	Tim Stoddard	.05	.02	.00	☐ 455	Ed Romero	.05	.02	.00
☐ 407	Garry Maddox	.08	.03	.01	☐ 456	Bob Melvin	.10	.04	.01
☐ 408	Ted Power	.05	.02	.00	☐ 457	Glenn Hoffman	.05	.02	.00
☐ 409	Len Barker	.05	.02	.00	☐ 458	Bob Shirley	.05	.02	.00
☐ 410	Denny Gonzalez	.05	.02	.00	☐ 459	Bob Welch	.08	.03	.01
☐ 411	George Frazier	.05	.02	.00	☐ 460	Carmen Castillo	.05	.02	.00
☐ 412	Andy Van Slyke	.25	.10	.02	☐ 461	Dave Leeper	.08	.03	.01
☐ 413	Jim Dwyer	.05	.02	.00		(outfielder)			
☐ 414	Paul Householder	.05	.02	.00	☐ 462	Tim Birtsas	.12	.05	.01
☐ 415	Alejandro Sanchez	.05	.02	.00	☐ 463	Randy St.Claire	.05	.02	.00
☐ 416	Steve Crawford	.05	.02	.00	☐ 464	Chris Welsh	.05	.02	.00
☐ 417	Dan Pasqua	.10	.04	.01	☐ 465	Greg Harris	.05	.02	.00
☐ 418	Enos Cabell	.05	.02	.00	☐ 466	Lynn Jones	.05	.02	.00
☐ 419	Mike Jones	.05	.02	.00	☐ 467	Dusty Baker	.08	.03	.01
☐ 420	Steve Kiefer	.05	.02	.00	☐ 468	Roy Smith	.05	.02	.00
☐ 421	Tim Burke	.25	.10	.02	☐ 469	Andre Robertson	.05	.02	.00
☐ 422	Mike Mason	.05	.02	.00	☐ 470	Ken Landreaux	.05	.02	.00
☐ 423	Ruppert Jones	.05	.02	.00	☐ 471	Dave Bergman	.05	.02	.00
☐ 424	Jerry Hairston	.05	.02	.00	☐ 472	Gary Roenicke	.05	.02	.00
☐ 425	Tito Landrum	.05	.02	.00	☐ 473	Pete Vuckovich	.05	.02	.00
☐ 426	Jeff Calhoun	.05	.02	.00	☐ 474	Kirk McCaskill	.35	.14	.03
☐ 427	Don Carman	.25	.10	.02	☐ 475	Jeff Lahti	.05	.02	.00
☐ 428	Tony Perez	.12	.05	.01	☐ 476	Mike Scott	.35	.14	.03
☐ 429	Jerry Davis	.05	.02	.00	☐ 477	Darren Daulton	.15	.06	.01
☐ 430	Bob Walk	.08	.03	.01	☐ 478	Graig Nettles	.10	.04	.01
☐ 431	Brad Wellman	.05	.02	.00	☐ 479	Bill Almon	.05	.02	.00
☐ 432	Terry Forster	.08	.03	.01	☐ 480	Greg Minton	.05	.02	.00
☐ 433	Billy Hatcher	.12	.05	.01	☐ 481	Randy Ready	.05	.02	.00
☐ 434	Clint Hurdle	.05	.02	.00	☐ 482	Len Dykstra	1.00	.40	.10
☐ 435	Ivan Calderon	.85	.34	.08	☐ 483	Thad Bosley	.05	.02	.00
☐ 436	Pete Filson	.05	.02	.00	☐ 484	Harold Reynolds	.45	.18	.04
☐ 437	Tom Henke	.12	.05	.01	☐ 485	Al Oliver	.10	.04	.01
☐ 438	Dave Engle	.05	.02	.00	☐ 486	Roy Smalley	.05	.02	.00

		MINT	EXC	G-VG			MINT	EXC	G-VG
☐ 487	John Franco	.15	.06	.01	☐ 536	Ray Searage	.05	.02	.00
☐ 488	Juan Agosto	.05	.02	.00	☐ 537	Tom Brookens	.05	.02	.00
☐ 489	Al Pardo	.05	.02	.00	☐ 538	Al Nipper	.05	.02	.00
☐ 490	Bill Wegman	.12	.05	.01	☐ 539	Billy Sample	.05	.02	.00
☐ 491	Frank Tanana	.08	.03	.01	☐ 540	Steve Sax	.15	.06	.01
☐ 492	Brian Fisher	.30	.12	.03	☐ 541	Dan Quisenberry	.10	.04	.01
☐ 493	Mark Clear	.05	.02	.00	☐ 542	Tony Phillips	.05	.02	.00
☐ 494	Len Matuszek	.05	.02	.00	☐ 543	Floyd Youmans	.40	.16	.04
☐ 495	Ramon Romero	.05	.02	.00	☐ 544	Steve Buechele	.25	.10	.02
☐ 496	John Wathan	.05	.02	.00	☐ 545	Craig Gerber	.05	.02	.00
☐ 497	Rob Picciolo	.05	.02	.00	☐ 546	Joe DeSa	.05	.02	.00
☐ 498	U.L. Washington	.05	.02	.00	☐ 547	Brian Harper	.05	.02	.00
☐ 499	John Candelaria	.08	.03	.01	☐ 548	Kevin Bass	.08	.03	.01
☐ 500	Duane Walker	.05	.02	.00	☐ 549	Tom Foley	.05	.02	.00
☐ 501	Gene Nelson	.05	.02	.00	☐ 550	Dave Van Gorder	.05	.02	.00
☐ 502	John Mizerock	.05	.02	.00	☐ 551	Bruce Bochy	.05	.02	.00
☐ 503	Luis Aguayo	.05	.02	.00	☐ 552	R.J. Reynolds	.05	.02	.00
☐ 504	Kurt Kepshire	.05	.02	.00	☐ 553	Chris Brown	.45	.18	.04
☐ 505	Ed Wojna	.10	.04	.01	☐ 554	Bruce Benedict	.05	.02	.00
☐ 506	Joe Price	.05	.02	.00	☐ 555	Warren Brusstar	.05	.02	.00
☐ 507	Milt Thompson	.30	.12	.03	☐ 556	Danny Heep	.05	.02	.00
☐ 508	Junior Ortiz	.05	.02	.00	☐ 557	Darnell Coles	.05	.02	.00
☐ 509	Vida Blue	.08	.03	.01	☐ 558	Greg Gagne	.08	.03	.00
☐ 510	Steve Engel	.05	.02	.00	☐ 559	Ernie Whitt	.05	.02	.00
☒ 511	Karl Best	.05	.02	.00	☐ 560	Ron Washington	.05	.02	.00
☐ 512	Cecil Fielder	.20	.08	.02	☐ 561	Jimmy Key	.15	.06	.01
☐ 513	Frank Eufemia	.08	.03	.01	☐ 562	Billy Swift	.10	.04	.01
☐ 514	Tippy Martinez	.05	.02	.00	☐ 563	Ron Darling	.30	.12	.03
☐ 515	Billy Jo Robidoux	.10	.04	.01	☐ 564	Dick Ruthven	.05	.02	.00
☐ 516	Bill Scherrer	.05	.02	.00	☐ 565	Zane Smith	.25	.10	.02
☐ 517	Bruce Hurst	.15	.06	.01	☐ 566	Sid Bream	.05	.02	.00
☐ 518	Rich Bordi	.05	.02	.00	☐ 567A	Joel Youngblood ERR	.10	.04	.01
☐ 519	Steve Yeager	.05	.02	.00		(position P)			
☐ 520	Tony Bernazard	.05	.02	.00	☐ 567B	Joel Youngblood COR	.60	.24	.06
☐ 521	Hal McRae	.08	.03	.01		(position IF)			
☐ 522	Jose Rijo	.08	.03	.01	☐ 568	Mario Ramirez	.05	.02	.00
☐ 523	Mitch Webster	.35	.14	.03	☐ 569	Tom Runnels	.05	.02	.00
☐ 524	Jack Howell	.35	.14	.03	☐ 570	Rick Schu	.05	.02	.00
☐ 525	Alan Bannister	.05	.02	.00	☐ 571	Bill Campbell	.05	.02	.00
☐ 526	Ron Kittle	.10	.04	.01	☐ 572	Dickie Thon	.05	.02	.00
☐ 527	Phil Garner	.05	.02	.00	☐ 573	Al Holland	.05	.02	.00
☐ 528	Kurt Bevacqua	.05	.02	.00	☐ 574	Reid Nichols	.05	.02	.00
☐ 529	Kevin Gross	.05	.02	.00	☐ 575	Bert Roberge	.05	.02	.00
☐ 530	Bo Diaz	.05	.02	.00	☐ 576	Mike Flanagan	.08	.03	.01
☐ 531	Ken Oberkfell	.05	.02	.00	☐ 577	Tim Leary	.35	.14	.03
☐ 532	Rick Reuschel	.10	.04	.01	☐ 578	Mike Laga	.05	.02	.00
☐ 533	Ron Meridith	.08	.03	.01	☐ 579	Steve Lyons	.05	.02	.00
☐ 534	Steve Braun	.05	.02	.00	☐ 580	Phil Niekro	.20	.08	.02
☐ 535	Wayne Gross	.05	.02	.00	☐ 581	Gilberto Reyes	.10	.04	.01

		MINT	EXC	G-VG
☐ 582	Jamie Easterly	.05	.02	.00
☐ 583	Mark Gubicza	.12	.05	.01
☐ 584	Stan Javier	.25	.10	.02
☐ 585	Bill Laskey	.05	.02	.00
☐ 586	Jeff Russell	.05	.02	.00
☐ 587	Dickie Noles	.05	.02	.00
☐ 588	Steve Farr	.05	.02	.00
☐ 589	Steve Ontiveros ...	.12	.05	.01
☐ 590	Mike Hargrove	.05	.02	.00
☐ 591	Marty Bystrom	.05	.02	.00
☐ 592	Franklin Stubbs ...	.08	.03	.01
☐ 593	Larry Herndon	.05	.02	.00
☐ 594	Bill Swaggerty	.05	.02	.00
☐ 595	Carlos Ponce	.05	.02	.00
☐ 596	Pat Perry	.10	.04	.01
☐ 597	Ray Knight	.08	.03	.01
☐ 598	Steve Lombardozzi ..	.15	.06	.01
☐ 599	Brad Havens	.05	.02	.00
☐ 600	Pat Clements	.12	.05	.01
☐ 601	Joe Niekro	.08	.03	.01
☐ 602	Hank Aaron	.08	.03	.01
	Puzzle Card			
☐ 603	Dwayne Henry	.08	.03	.01
☐ 604	Mookie Wilson	.08	.03	.01
☐ 605	Buddy Biancalana ..	.05	.02	.00
☐ 606	Rance Mulliniks ...	.05	.02	.00
☐ 607	Alan Wiggins	.05	.02	.00
☐ 608	Joe Cowley	.05	.02	.00
☐ 609A	Tom Seaver	.40	.16	.04
	(green borders on name)			
☐ 609B	Tom Seaver	1.25	.50	.12
	(yellow borders on name)			
☐ 610	Neil Allen	.05	.02	.00
☐ 611	Don Sutton	.25	.10	.02
☐ 612	Fred Toliver	.10	.04	.01
☐ 613	Jay Baller	.08	.03	.01
☐ 614	Marc Sullivan	.08	.03	.01
☐ 615	John Grubb	.05	.02	.00
☐ 616	Bruce Kison	.05	.02	.00
☐ 617	Bill Madlock	.10	.04	.01
☐ 618	Chris Chambliss ...	.08	.03	.01
☐ 619	Dave Stewart	.12	.05	.01
☐ 620	Tim Lollar	.05	.02	.00
☐ 621	Gary Lavelle	.05	.02	.00
☐ 622	Charles Hudson ...	.05	.02	.00
☐ 623	Joel Davis	.12	.05	.01
☐ 624	Joe Johnson	.12	.05	.01
☐ 625	Sid Fernandez	.15	.06	.01
☐ 626	Dennis Lamp	.05	.02	.00
☐ 627	Terry Harper	.05	.02	.00

		MINT	EXC	G-VG
☐ 628	Jack Lazorko	.05	.02	.00
☐ 629	Roger McDowell ..	.60	.24	.06
☐ 630	Mark Funderburk ..	.10	.04	.01
☐ 631	Ed Lynch	.05	.02	.00
☐ 632	Rudy Law	.05	.02	.00
☐ 633	Roger Mason	.10	.04	.01
☐ 634	Mike Felder	.12	.05	.01
☐ 635	Ken Schrom	.05	.02	.00
☐ 636	Bob Ojeda	.08	.03	.01
☐ 637	Ed VandeBerg	.05	.02	.00
☐ 638	Bobby Meacham ...	.05	.02	.00
☐ 639	Cliff Johnson	.05	.02	.00
☐ 640	Garth Iorg	.05	.02	.00
☐ 641	Dan Driessen	.05	.02	.00
☐ 642	Mike Brown OF ...	.05	.02	.00
☐ 643	John Shelby	.05	.02	.00
☐ 644	Pete Rose	.35	.14	.03
	(Ty-Breaking)			
☐ 645	The Knuckle Brothers	.10	.04	.01
	Phil Niekro			
	Joe Niekro			
☐ 646	Jesse Orosco	.05	.02	.00
☐ 647	Billy Beane	.15	.06	.01
☐ 648	Cesar Cedeno	.08	.03	.01
☐ 649	Bert Blyleven	.10	.04	.01
☐ 650	Max Venable	.05	.02	.00
☐ 651	Fleet Feet	.30	.12	.03
	Vince Coleman			
	Willie McGee			
☐ 652	Calvin Schiraldi ...	.08	.03	.01
☐ 653	King of Kings	.65	.26	.06
	(Pete Rose)			
☐ 654	CL: Diamond Kings	.08	.01	.00
	(unnumbered)			
☐ 655A	CL 1: 27-130	.10	.01	.00
	(unnumbered)			
	(45 Beane ERR)			
☐ 655B	CL 1: 27-130	.50	.05	.01
	(unnumbered)			
	(45 Habyan COR)			
☐ 656	CL 2: 131-234	.06	.01	.00
	(unnumbered)			
☐ 657	CL 3: 235-338	.06	.01	.00
	(unnumbered)			
☐ 658	CL 4: 339-442	.06	.01	.00
	(unnumbered)			
☐ 659	CL 5: 443-546	.06	.01	.00
	(unnumbered)			
☐ 660	CL 6: 547-653	.06	.01	.00
	(unnumbered)			

1986 Donruss Rookies

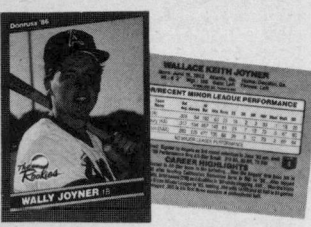

The 1986 Donruss "The Rookies" set features 56 cards plus a 15-piece puzzle of Hank Aaron. Cards are in full color and are standard size, 2½" by 3½". The set was distributed in a small green box with gold lettering. Although the set was wrapped in cellophane, the top card was #1 Joyner, resulting in a percentage of (Joyner) cards arriving in less than perfect condition. Card fronts are similar in design to the 1986 Donruss regular issue except for the presence of "The Rookies" logo in the lower left corner and a bluish green border instead of a blue border.

		MINT	EXC	G-VG
Complete Set (56)		21.00	8.50	2.10
Common Player (1-56)		.08	.03	.01

			MINT	EXC	G-VG
☐	1	Wally Joyner	4.00	1.00	.20
☐	2	Tracy Jones	.55	.22	.05
☐	3	Allan Anderson	.40	.16	.04
☐	4	Ed Correa	.20	.08	.02
☐	5	Reggie Williams	.15	.06	.01
☐	6	Charlie Kerfeld	.15	.06	.01
☐	7	Andres Galarraga	.90	.36	.09
☐	8	Bob Tewksbury	.15	.06	.01
☐	9	Al Newman	.15	.06	.01
☐	10	Andres Thomas	.25	.10	.02
☐	11	Barry Bonds	1.25	.50	.12
☐	12	Juan Nieves	.15	.06	.01
☐	13	Mark Eichhorn	.15	.06	.01
☐	14	Dan Plesac	.35	.14	.03
☐	15	Cory Snyder	1.25	.50	.12
☐	16	Kelly Gruber	.08	.03	.01
☐	17	Kevin Mitchell	.45	.18	.04
☐	18	Steve Lombardozzi	.08	.03	.01
☐	19	Mitch Williams	.25	.10	.02
☐	20	John Cerutti	.20	.08	.02
☐	21	Todd Worrell	.45	.18	.04
☐	22	Jose Canseco	7.50	3.00	.75
☐	23	Pete Incaviglia	.85	.34	.08
☐	24	Jose Guzman	.15	.06	.01
☐	25	Scott Bailes	.15	.06	.01
☐	26	Greg Mathews	.30	.12	.03
☐	27	Eric King	.20	.08	.02
☐	28	Paul Assenmacher	.15	.06	.01
☐	29	Jeff Sellers	.20	.08	.02
☐	30	Bobby Bonilla	1.25	.50	.12
☐	31	Doug Drabek	.35	.14	.03
☐	32	Will Clark	4.00	1.60	.40
☐	33	Bip Roberts	.15	.06	.01
☐	34	Jim Deshaies	.35	.14	.03
☐	35	Mike LaValliere	.25	.10	.02
☐	36	Scott Bankhead	.20	.08	.02
☐	37	Dale Sveum	.30	.12	.03
☐	38	Bo Jackson	2.50	1.00	.25
☐	39	Rob Thompson	.35	.14	.03
☐	40	Eric Plunk	.20	.08	.02
☐	41	Bill Bathe	.15	.06	.01
☐	42	John Kruk	.50	.20	.05
☐	43	Andy Allanson	.15	.06	.01
☐	44	Mark Portugal	.15	.06	.01
☐	45	Danny Tartabull	.85	.34	.08
☐	46	Bob Kipper	.08	.03	.01
☐	47	Gene Walter	.15	.06	.01
☐	48	Rey Quinones	.25	.10	.02
☐	49	Bobby Witt	.50	.20	.05
☐	50	Bill Mooneyham	.15	.06	.01
☐	51	John Cangelosi	.20	.08	.02
☐	52	Ruben Sierra	1.75	.70	.17
☐	53	Rob Woodward	.15	.06	.01
☐	54	Ed Hearn	.15	.06	.01
☐	55	Joel McKeon	.15	.06	.01
☐	56	Checklist card	.08	.01	.00

1986 Donruss Highlights

Donruss' second edition of Highlights was
released late in 1986. The cards are standard size, measuring 2 ½ " by 3 ½ ", and are
glossy in appearance. Cards commemorate
events during the 1986 season, as well as
players and pitchers of the month from each
league. The set was distributed in its own
red, white, blue, and gold box along with a
small Hank Aaron puzzle. Card fronts are
similar to the regular 1986 Donruss issue
except that the Highlights logo is positioned
in the lower left-hand corner and the borders
are in gold instead of blue. The backs are
printed in black and gold on white card stock.

		MINT	EXC	G-VG
Complete Set (56)		7.50	3.00	.75
Common Player (1-56)		.06	.02	.00
☐	1 Will Clark . . . . Homers in First At-Bat	.50	.20	.05
☐	2 Jose Rijo . . . . Oakland Milestone for Strikeouts	.06	.02	.00
☐	3 George Brett . . . . Royals' All-Time Hit Man	.25	.10	.02
☐	4 Mike Schmidt . . . . . Phillies RBI Leader	.30	.12	.03
☐	5 Roger Clemens . . . . KKKKKKKKKK KKKKKKKKKK	.40	.16	.04
☐	6 Roger Clemens . . . AL Pitcher April	.40	.16	.04
☐	7 Kirby Puckett . . . . . AL Player April	.35	.14	.03
☐	8 Dwight Gooden . . . . NL Pitcher April	.40	.16	.04
☐	9 Johnny Ray . . . . NL Player April	.06	.02	.00
☐	10 Reggie Jackson . . . Eclipses Mantle HR Record	.35	.14	.03
☐	11 Wade Boggs . . . . . . First Five Hit Game of Career	.65	.26	.06
☐	12 Don Aase . . . . AL Pitcher May	.06	.02	.00
☐	13 Wade Boggs . . . . . . AL Player May	.65	.26	.06
☐	14 Jeff Reardon . . . . . . NL Pitcher May	.06	.02	.00
☐	15 Hubie Brooks . . . . . . NL Player May	.06	.02	.00
☐	16 Don Sutton . . . . Notches 300th	.10	.04	.01
☐	17 Roger Clemens . . . Starts 14-0	.40	.16	.04
☐	18 Roger Clemens . . . AL Pitcher June	.40	.16	.04
☐	19 Kent Hrbek . . . . AL Player June	.15	.06	.01
☐	20 Rick Rhoden . . . . . NL Pitcher June	.06	.02	.00
☐	21 Kevin Bass . . . . NL Player June	.06	.02	.00
☐	22 Bob Horner . . . . Blasts four HRs in one Game	.10	.04	.01
☐	23 Wally Joyner . . . . . . Starting All-Star Rookie	.60	.24	.06
☐	24 Darryl Strawberry . Starts Third Straight All-Star Game	.45	.18	.04
☐	25 Fernando Valenzuela Ties All-Star Game Record	.15	.06	.01
☐	26 Roger Clemens . . . All-Star Game MVP	.40	.16	.04

			MINT	EXC	G-VG
☐	27	Jack Morris AL Pitcher July	.10	.04	.01
☐	28	Scott Fletcher AL Player July	.06	.02	.00
☐	29	Todd Worrell NL Pitcher July	.10	.04	.01
☐	30	Eric Davis NL Player July	.65	.26	.06
☐	31	Bert Blyleven Records 3000th Strikeout	.10	.04	.01
☐	32	Bobby Doerr '86 HOF Inductee	.15	.06	.01
☐	33	Ernie Lombardi '86 HOF Inductee	.15	.06	.01
☐	34	Willie McCovey '86 HOF Inductee	.20	.08	.02
☐	35	Steve Carlton Notches 4000th K	.20	.08	.02
☐	36	Mike Schmidt Surpasses DiMaggio Record	.30	.12	.03
☐	37	Juan Samuel Records 3rd "Quadruple Double"	.10	.04	.01
☐	38	Mike Witt AL Pitcher August	.10	.04	.01
☐	39	Doug DeCinces AL Player August	.06	.02	.00
☐	40	Bill Gullickson NL Pitcher August	.06	.02	.00
☐	41	Dale Murphy NL Player August	.35	.14	.03
☐	42	Joe Carter Sets Tribe Offensive Record	.15	.06	.01
☐	43	Bo Jackson Longest HR in Royals Stadium	.65	.26	.06
☐	44	Joe Cowley Majors 1st No- Hitter in 2 Years	.06	.02	.00
☐	45	Jim Deshaies Sets ML Strikeout Record	.06	.02	.00
☐	46	Mike Scott No Hitter Clinches Division	.15	.06	.01

			MINT	EXC	G-VG
☐	47	Bruce Hurst AL Pitcher September	.10	.04	.01
☐	48	Don Mattingly AL Player September	.90	.36	.09
☐	49	Mike Krukow NL Pitcher September	.06	.02	.00
☐	50	Steve Sax NL Player September	.15	.06	.01
☐	51	John Cangelosi AL Rookie Steals Record	.10	.04	.01
☐	52	Dave Righetti ML Save Mark	.10	.04	.01
☐	53	Don Mattingly Yankee Record for Hits and Doubles	.90	.36	.09
☐	54	Todd Worrell Donruss NL ROY	.15	.06	.01
☐	55	Jose Canseco Donruss AL ROY	1.25	.50	.12
☐	56	Checklist card	.06	.01	.00

1987 Donruss

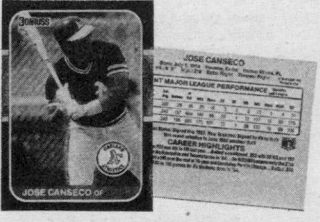

This 660-card set was distributed along with a puzzle of Roberto Clemente. The checklist cards are numbered throughout the set as multiples of 100. The wax pack boxes again contain a separate four cards printed on the bottom of the box. Cards measure 2½" by 3½" and feature a black and gold border on the front; the backs are also done in black and gold on white card stock. The popular

Diamond King subset returns for the sixth consecutive year. Some of the Diamond King (1-26) selections are repeats from prior years; Perez-Steele Galleries has indicated that a five-year rotation will be maintained in order to avoid depleting the pool of available worthy "kings" on some of the teams. Three of the Diamond Kings have a variation (on the reverse) where the yellow strip behind the words "Donruss Diamond Kings" is not printed and hence the background is white.

			MINT	EXC	G-VG
	Complete Set (660)		40.00	15.00	4.00
	Common Player (1-660)		.03	.01	.00
☐	1	Wally Joyner DK	1.25	.40	.08
☐	2	Roger Clemens DK	.65	.26	.06
☐	3	Dale Murphy DK	.50	.20	.05
☐	4	Darryl Strawberry DK	.50	.20	.05
☐	5	Ozzie Smith DK	.15	.06	.01
☐	6	Jose Canseco DK	2.00	.80	.20
☐	7	Charlie Hough DK	.08	.03	.01
☐	8	Brook Jacoby DK	.08	.03	.01
☐	9	Fred Lynn DK	.15	.06	.01
☐	10	Rick Rhoden DK	.08	.03	.01
☐	11	Chris Brown DK	.12	.05	.01
☐	12	Von Hayes DK	.10	.04	.01
☐	13	Jack Morris DK	.15	.06	.01
☐	14A	Kevin McReynolds DK	.85	.34	.08
	(yellow strip missing on back)				
☐	14B	Kevin McReynolds DK	.35	.14	.03
☐	15	George Brett DK	.40	.16	.04
☐	16	Ted Higuera DK	.20	.08	.02
☐	17	Hubie Brooks DK	.08	.03	.01
☐	18	Mike Scott DK	.25	.10	.02
☐	19	Kirby Puckett DK	.40	.16	.04
☐	20	Dave Winfield DK	.30	.12	.03
☐	21	Lloyd Moseby DK	.10	.04	.01
☐	22A	Eric Davis DK	2.50	1.00	.25
	(yellow strip missing on back)				
☐	22B	Eric Davis DK	1.00	.40	.10
☐	23	Jim Presley DK	.10	.04	.01
☐	24	Keith Moreland DK	.08	.03	.01
☐	25A	Greg Walker DK	.50	.20	.05
	(yellow strip missing on back)				
☐	25B	Greg Walker DK	.12	.05	.01
☐	26	Steve Sax DK	.20	.08	.02
☐	27	DK Checklist 1-26	.09	.01	.00
☐	28	B.J. Surhoff RR	.45	.18	.04
☐	29	Randy Myers RR	.60	.24	.06
☐	30	Ken Gerhart RR	.25	.10	.02
☐	31	Benito Santiago RR	1.50	.60	.15
☐	32	Greg Swindell RR	.80	.32	.08
☐	33	Mike Birkbeck RR	.15	.06	.01
☐	34	Terry Steinbach RR	.50	.20	.05
☐	35	Bo Jackson RR	1.25	.50	.12
☐	36	Greg Maddux RR	1.00	.40	.10
☐	37	Jim Lindeman RR	.20	.08	.02
☐	38	Devon White RR	.90	.36	.09
☐	39	Eric Bell RR	.10	.04	.01
☐	40	Willie Fraser RR	.10	.04	.01
☐	41	Jerry Browne RR	.10	.04	.01
☐	42	Chris James RR	.75	.30	.07
☐	43	Rafael Palmeiro RR	1.50	.60	.15
☐	44	Pat Dodson RR	.15	.06	.01
☐	45	Duane Ward RR	.15	.06	.01
☐	46	Mark McGwire RR	7.00	2.80	.70
☐	47	Bruce Fields RR	.10	.04	.01
	(photo actually Darnell Coles).				
☐	48	Eddie Murray	.25	.10	.02
☐	49	Ted Higuera	.18	.08	.01
☐	50	Kirk Gibson	.25	.10	.02
☐	51	Oil Can Boyd	.06	.02	.00
☐	52	Don Mattingly	2.25	.90	.22
☐	53	Pedro Guerrero	.15	.06	.01
☐	54	George Brett	.30	.12	.03
☐	55	Jose Rijo	.06	.02	.00
☐	56	Tim Raines	.25	.10	.02
☐	57	Ed Correa	.20	.08	.02
☐	58	Mike Witt	.10	.04	.01
☐	59	Greg Walker	.08	.03	.01
☐	60	Ozzie Smith	.20	.08	.02
☐	61	Glenn Davis	.25	.10	.02
☐	62	Glenn Wilson	.03	.01	.00
☐	63	Tom Browning	.12	.05	.01
☐	64	Tony Gwynn	.45	.18	.04
☐	65	R.J. Reynolds	.03	.01	.00
☐	66	Will Clark	2.50	1.00	.25
☐	67	Ozzie Virgil	.03	.01	.00
☐	68	Rick Sutcliffe	.10	.04	.01
☐	69	Gary Carter	.25	.10	.02
☐	70	Mike Moore	.03	.01	.00
☐	71	Bert Blyleven	.08	.03	.01
☐	72	Tony Fernandez	.15	.06	.01
☐	73	Kent Hrbek	.18	.08	.01
☐	74	Lloyd Moseby	.08	.03	.01
☐	75	Alvin Davis	.12	.05	.01
☐	76	Keith Hernandez	.25	.10	.02
☐	77	Ryne Sandberg	.20	.08	.02

			MINT	EXC	G-VG				MINT	EXC	G-VG
☐	78	Dale Murphy	.45	.18	.04	☐	127	Alan Trammell	.20	.08	.02
☐	79	Sid Bream	.03	.01	.00	☐	128	Dave Righetti	.10	.04	.01
☐	80	Chris Brown	.08	.03	.01	☐	129	Dwight Evans	.10	.04	.01
☐	81	Steve Garvey	.30	.12	.03	☐	130	Mike Scioscia	.03	.01	.00
☐	82	Mario Soto	.03	.01	.00	☐	131	Julio Franco	.08	.03	.01
☐	83	Shane Rawley	.06	.02	.00	☐	132	Bret Saberhagen	.20	.08	.02
☐	84	Willie McGee	.12	.05	.01	☐	133	Mike Davis	.03	.01	.00
☐	85	Jose Cruz	.08	.03	.01	☐	134	Joe Hesketh	.03	.01	.00
☐	86	Brian Downing	.06	.02	.00	☐	135	Wally Joyner	1.75	.70	.17
☐	87	Ozzie Guillen	.08	.03	.01	☐	136	Don Slaught	.03	.01	.00
☐	88	Hubie Brooks	.08	.03	.01	☐	137	Daryl Boston	.03	.01	.00
☐	89	Cal Ripken	.30	.12	.03	☐	138	Nolan Ryan	.30	.12	.03
☐	90	Juan Nieves	.06	.02	.00	☐	139	Mike Schmidt	.40	.16	.04
☐	91	Lance Parrish	.12	.05	.01	☐	140	Tommy Herr	.06	.02	.00
☐	92	Jim Rice	.18	.08	.01	☐	141	Garry Templeton	.06	.02	.00
☐	93	Ron Guidry	.12	.05	.01	☐	142	Kal Daniels	.90	.36	.09
☐	94	Fernando Valenzuela	.18	.08	.01	☐	143	Billy Sample	.03	.01	.00
☐	95	Andy Allanson	.08	.03	.01	☐	144	Johnny Ray	.08	.03	.01
☐	96	Willie Wilson	.10	.04	.01	☐	145	Rob Thompson	.25	.10	.02
☐	97	Jose Canseco	6.50	2.60	.65	☐	146	Bob Dernier	.03	.01	.00
☐	98	Jeff Reardon	.08	.03	.01	☐	147	Danny Tartabull	.30	.12	.03
☐	99	Bobby Witt	.30	.12	.03	☐	148	Ernie Whitt	.03	.01	.00
☐	100	Checklist	.06	.01	.00	☐	149	Kirby Puckett	.55	.22	.05
☐	101	Jose Guzman	.06	.02	.00	☐	150	Mike Young	.03	.01	.00
☐	102	Steve Balboni	.03	.01	.00	☐	151	Ernest Riles	.03	.01	.00
☐	103	Tony Phillips	.03	.01	.00	☐	152	Frank Tanana	.06	.02	.00
☐	104	Brook Jacoby	.08	.03	.01	☐	153	Rich Gedman	.06	.02	.00
☐	105	Dave Winfield	.30	.12	.03	☐	154	Willie Randolph	.06	.02	.00
☐	106	Orel Hershiser	.35	.14	.03	☐	155	Bill Madlock	.08	.03	.01
☐	107	Lou Whitaker	.10	.04	.01	☐	156	Joe Carter	.20	.08	.02
☐	108	Fred Lynn	.12	.05	.01	☐	157	Danny Jackson	.15	.06	.01
☐	109	Bill Wegman	.06	.02	.00	☐	158	Carney Lansford	.08	.03	.01
☐	110	Donnie Moore	.03	.01	.00	☐	159	Bryn Smith	.03	.01	.00
☐	111	Jack Clark	.18	.08	.01	☐	160	Gary Pettis	.03	.01	.00
☐	112	Bob Knepper	.06	.02	.00	☐	161	Oddibe McDowell	.10	.04	.01
☐	113	Von Hayes	.08	.03	.01	☐	162	John Cangelosi	.10	.04	.01
☐	114	Bip Roberts	.08	.03	.01	☐	163	Mike Scott	.20	.08	.02
☐	115	Tony Pena	.08	.03	.01	☐	164	Eric Show	.06	.02	.00
☐	116	Scott Garrelts	.03	.01	.00	☐	165	Juan Samuel	.12	.05	.01
☐	117	Paul Molitor	.12	.05	.01	☐	166	Nick Esasky	.03	.01	.00
☐	118	Darryl Strawberry	.75	.30	.07	☐	167	Zane Smith	.06	.02	.00
☐	119	Shawon Dunston	.08	.03	.01	☐	168	Mike Brown	.03	.01	.00
☐	120	Jim Presley	.08	.03	.01			(Pirates OF)			
☐	121	Jesse Barfield	.15	.06	.01	☐	169	Keith Moreland	.03	.01	.00
☐	122	Gary Gaetti	.15	.06	.01	☐	170	John Tudor	.10	.04	.01
☐	123	Kurt Stillwell	.25	.10	.02	☐	171	Ken Dixon	.03	.01	.00
☐	124	Joel Davis	.03	.01	.00	☐	172	Jim Gantner	.03	.01	.00
☐	125	Mike Boddicker	.06	.02	.00	☐	173	Jack Morris	.12	.05	.01
☐	126	Robin Yount	.30	.12	.03	☐	174	Bruce Hurst	.12	.05	.01

		MINT	EXC	G-VG
☐ 175	Dennis Rasmussen .	.06	.02	.00
☐ 176	Mike Marshall	.10	.04	.01
☐ 177	Dan Quisenberry . . .	.10	.04	.01
☐ 178	Eric Plunk	.08	.03	.01
☐ 179	Tim Wallach	.08	.03	.01
☐ 180	Steve Buechele	.03	.01	.00
☐ 181	Don Sutton	.15	.06	.01
☐ 182	Dave Schmidt	.06	.02	.00
☐ 183	Terry Pendleton	.06	.02	.00
☐ 184	Jim Deshaies	.15	.06	.01
☐ 185	Steve Bedrosian . . .	.12	.05	.01
☐ 186	Pete Rose	.55	.22	.05
☐ 187	Dave Dravecky	.03	.01	.00
☐ 188	Rick Reuschel	.06	.02	.00
☐ 189	Dan Gladden	.06	.02	.00
☐ 190	Rick Mahler	.03	.01	.00
☐ 191	Thad Bosley	.03	.01	.00
☐ 192	Ron Darling	.18	.08	.01
☐ 193	Matt Young	.03	.01	.00
☐ 194	Tom Brunansky	.12	.05	.01
☐ 195	Dave Stieb	.10	.04	.01
☐ 196	Frank Viola	.15	.06	.01
☐ 197	Tom Henke	.08	.03	.01
☐ 198	Karl Best	.03	.01	.00
☐ 199	Dwight Gooden	.75	.30	.07
☐ 200	Checklist	.06	.01	.00
☐ 201	Steve Trout	.03	.01	.00
☐ 202	Rafael Ramirez	.03	.01	.00
☐ 203	Bob Walk	.06	.02	.00
☐ 204	Roger Mason	.03	.01	.00
☐ 205	Terry Kennedy	.03	.01	.00
☐ 206	Ron Oester	.03	.01	.00
☐ 207	John Russell	.03	.01	.00
☐ 208	Greg Mathews	.20	.08	.02
☐ 209	Charlie Kerfeld	.03	.01	.00
☐ 210	Reggie Jackson	.40	.16	.04
☐ 211	Floyd Bannister	.03	.01	.00
☐ 212	Vance Law	.06	.02	.00
☐ 213	Rich Bordi	.03	.01	.00
☐ 214	Dan Plesac	.30	.12	.03
☐ 215	Dave Collins	.03	.01	.00
☐ 216	Bob Stanley	.03	.01	.00
☐ 217	Joe Niekro	.08	.03	.01
☐ 218	Tom Niedenfuer	.03	.01	.00
☐ 219	Brett Butler	.08	.03	.01
☐ 220	Charlie Leibrandt . .	.03	.01	.00
☐ 221	Steve Ontiveros	.03	.01	.00
☐ 222	Tim Burke	.03	.01	.00
☐ 223	Curtis Wilkerson . . .	.03	.01	.00
☐ 224	Pete Incaviglia	.75	.30	.07
☐ 225	Lonnie Smith	.03	.01	.00
☐ 226	Chris Codiroli	.03	.01	.00
☐ 227	Scott Bailes	.10	.04	.01
☐ 228	Rickey Henderson .	.35	.14	.03
☐ 229	Ken Howell	.03	.01	.00
☐ 230	Darnell Coles	.03	.01	.00
☐ 231	Don Aase	.03	.01	.00
☐ 232	Tim Leary	.10	.04	.01
☐ 233	Bob Boone	.08	.03	.01
☐ 234	Ricky Horton	.03	.01	.00
☐ 235	Mark Bailey	.03	.01	.00
☐ 236	Kevin Gross	.03	.01	.00
☐ 237	Lance McCullers . . .	.06	.02	.00
☐ 238	Cecilio Guante	.03	.01	.00
☐ 239	Bob Melvin	.03	.01	.00
☐ 240	Billy Jo Robidoux . .	.03	.01	.00
☐ 241	Roger McDowell . . .	.08	.03	.01
☐ 242	Leon Durham	.06	.02	.00
☐ 243	Ed Nunez	.03	.01	.00
☐ 244	Jimmy Key	.10	.04	.01
☐ 245	Mike Smithson	.03	.01	.00
☐ 246	Bo Diaz	.03	.01	.00
☐ 247	Carlton Fisk	.12	.05	.01
☐ 248	Larry Sheets	.08	.03	.01
☐ 249	Juan Castillo	.03	.01	.00
☐ 250	Eric King	.12	.05	.01
☐ 251	Doug Drabek	.25	.10	.02
☐ 252	Wade Boggs	1.50	.60	.15
☐ 253	Mariano Duncan . . .	.03	.01	.00
☐ 254	Pat Tabler	.06	.02	.00
☐ 255	Frank White	.06	.02	.00
☐ 256	Alfredo Griffin	.06	.02	.00
☐ 257	Floyd Youmans	.08	.03	.01
☐ 258	Rob Wilfong	.03	.01	.00
☐ 259	Pete O'Brien	.08	.03	.01
☐ 260	Tim Hulett	.03	.01	.00
☐ 261	Dickie Thon	.03	.01	.00
☐ 262	Darren Daulton	.03	.01	.00
☐ 263	Vince Coleman	.40	.16	.04
☐ 264	Andy Hawkins	.06	.02	.00
☐ 265	Eric Davis	1.50	.60	.15
☐ 266	Andres Thomas	.18	.08	.01
☐ 267	Mike Diaz	.10	.04	.01
☐ 268	Chili Davis	.08	.03	.01
☐ 269	Jody Davis	.06	.02	.00
☐ 270	Phil Bradley	.08	.03	.01
☐ 271	George Bell	.25	.10	.02
☐ 272	Keith Atherton	.03	.01	.00

		MINT	EXC	G-VG			MINT	EXC	G-VG
☐ 273	Storm Davis	.06	.02	.00	☐ 322	Lee Guetterman	.12	.05	.01
☐ 274	Rob Deer	.15	.06	.01	☐ 323	Sid Fernandez	.12	.05	.01
☐ 275	Walt Terrell	.03	.01	.00	☐ 324	Jerry Mumphrey	.03	.01	.00
☐ 276	Roger Clemens	1.50	.60	.15	☐ 325	David Palmer	.03	.01	.00
☐ 277	Mike Easler	.03	.01	.00	☐ 326	Bill Almon	.03	.01	.00
☐ 278	Steve Sax	.15	.06	.01	☐ 327	Candy Maldonado	.08	.03	.01
☐ 279	Andre Thornton	.06	.02	.00	☐ 328	John Kruk	.35	.14	.03
☐ 280	Jim Sundberg	.03	.01	.00	☐ 329	John Denny	.03	.01	.00
☐ 281	Bill Bathe	.08	.03	.01	☐ 330	Milt Thompson	.06	.02	.00
☐ 282	Jay Tibbs	.03	.01	.00	☐ 331	Mike LaValliere	.20	.08	.02
☐ 283	Dick Schofield	.03	.01	.00	☐ 332	Alan Ashby	.03	.01	.00
☐ 284	Mike Mason	.03	.01	.00	☐ 333	Doug Corbett	.03	.01	.00
☐ 285	Jerry Hairston	.03	.01	.00	☐ 334	Ron Karkovice	.06	.02	.00
☐ 286	Bill Doran	.08	.03	.01	☐ 335	Mitch Webster	.06	.02	.00
☐ 287	Tim Flannery	.03	.01	.00	☐ 336	Lee Lacy	.03	.01	.00
☐ 288	Gary Redus	.03	.01	.00	☐ 337	Glenn Braggs	.35	.14	.03
☐ 289	John Franco	.08	.03	.01	☐ 338	Dwight Lowry	.10	.04	.01
☐ 290	Paul Assenmacher	.08	.03	.01	☐ 339	Don Baylor	.08	.03	.01
☐ 291	Joe Orsulak	.03	.01	.00	☐ 340	Brian Fisher	.06	.02	.00
☐ 292	Lee Smith	.06	.02	.00	☐ 341	Reggie Williams	.10	.04	.01
☐ 293	Mike Laga	.03	.01	.00	☐ 342	Tom Candiotti	.03	.01	.00
☐ 294	Rick Dempsey	.03	.01	.00	☐ 343	Rudy Law	.03	.01	.00
☐ 295	Mike Felder	.06	.02	.00	☐ 344	Curt Young	.03	.01	.00
☐ 296	Tom Brookens	.03	.01	.00	☐ 345	Mike Fitzgerald	.03	.01	.00
☐ 297	Al Nipper	.03	.01	.00	☐ 346	Ruben Sierra	1.25	.50	.12
☐ 298	Mike Pagliarulo	.08	.03	.01	☐ 347	Mitch Williams	.20	.08	.02
☐ 299	Franklin Stubbs	.06	.02	.00	☐ 348	Jorge Orta	.03	.01	.00
☐ 300	Checklist	.06	.01	.00	☐ 349	Mickey Tettleton	.03	.01	.00
☐ 301	Steve Farr	.03	.01	.00	☐ 350	Ernie Camacho	.03	.01	.00
☐ 302	Bill Mooneyham	.06	.02	.00	☐ 351	Ron Kittle	.08	.03	.01
☐ 303	Andres Galarraga	.35	.14	.03	☐ 352	Ken Landreaux	.03	.01	.00
☐ 304	Scott Fletcher	.06	.02	.00	☐ 353	Chet Lemon	.03	.01	.00
☐ 305	Jack Howell	.06	.02	.00	☐ 354	John Shelby	.03	.01	.00
☐ 306	Russ Morman	.12	.05	.01	☐ 355	Mark Clear	.03	.01	.00
☐ 307	Todd Worrell	.18	.08	.01	☐ 356	Doug DeCinces	.06	.02	.00
☐ 308	Dave Smith	.06	.02	.00	☐ 357	Ken Dayley	.03	.01	.00
☐ 309	Jeff Stone	.03	.01	.00	☐ 358	Phil Garner	.03	.01	.00
☐ 310	Ron Robinson	.03	.01	.00	☐ 359	Steve Jeltz	.03	.01	.00
☐ 311	Bruce Bochy	.03	.01	.00	☐ 360	Ed Whitson	.03	.01	.00
☐ 312	Jim Winn	.03	.01	.00	☐ 361	Barry Bonds	.90	.36	.09
☐ 313	Mark Davis	.06	.02	.00	☐ 362	Vida Blue	.06	.02	.00
☐ 314	Jeff Dedmon	.03	.01	.00	☐ 363	Cecil Cooper	.08	.03	.01
☐ 315	Jamie Moyer	.20	.08	.02	☐ 364	Bob Ojeda	.08	.03	.01
☐ 316	Wally Backman	.06	.02	.00	☐ 365	Dennis Eckersley	.12	.05	.01
☐ 317	Ken Phelps	.08	.03	.01	☐ 366	Mike Morgan	.03	.01	.00
☐ 318	Steve Lombardozzi	.03	.01	.00	☐ 367	Willie Upshaw	.03	.01	.00
☐ 319	Rance Mulliniks	.03	.01	.00	☐ 368	Allan Anderson	.35	.14	.03
☐ 320	Tim Laudner	.03	.01	.00	☐ 369	Bill Gullickson	.03	.01	.00
☐ 321	Mark Eichhorn	.12	.05	.01	☐ 370	Bobby Thigpen	.30	.12	.03

		MINT	EXC	G-VG			MINT	EXC	G-VG
☐ 371	Juan Beniquez	.03	.01	.00	☐ 420	Dave Bergman	.03	.01	.00
☐ 372	Charlie Moore	.03	.01	.00	☐ 421	Joe Sambito	.03	.01	.00
☐ 373	Dan Petry	.06	.02	.00	☐ 422	Bob Tewksbury	.10	.04	.01
☐ 374	Rod Scurry	.03	.01	.00	☐ 423	Len Matuszek	.03	.01	.00
☐ 375	Tom Seaver	.30	.12	.03	☐ 424	Mike Kingery	.12	.05	.01
☐ 376	Ed VandeBerg	.03	.01	.00	☐ 425	Dave Kingman	.08	.03	.01
☐ 377	Tony Bernazard	.03	.01	.00	☐ 426	Al Newman	.08	.03	.01
☐ 378	Greg Pryor	.03	.01	.00	☐ 427	Gary Ward	.03	.01	.00
☐ 379	Dwayne Murphy	.03	.01	.00	☐ 428	Ruppert Jones	.03	.01	.00
☐ 380	Andy McGaffigan	.03	.01	.00	☐ 429	Harold Baines	.10	.04	.01
☐ 381	Kirk McCaskill	.03	.01	.00	☐ 430	Pat Perry	.03	.01	.00
☐ 382	Greg Harris	.03	.01	.00	☐ 431	Terry Puhl	.03	.01	.00
☐ 383	Rich Dotson	.06	.02	.00	☐ 432	Don Carman	.03	.01	.00
☐ 384	Craig Reynolds	.03	.01	.00	☐ 433	Eddie Milner	.03	.01	.00
☐ 385	Greg Gross	.03	.01	.00	☐ 434	LaMarr Hoyt	.06	.02	.00
☐ 386	Tito Landrum	.03	.01	.00	☐ 435	Rick Rhoden	.06	.02	.00
☐ 387	Craig Lefferts	.03	.01	.00	☐ 436	Jose Uribe	.03	.01	.00
☐ 388	Dave Parker	.12	.05	.01	☐ 437	Ken Oberkfell	.03	.01	.00
☐ 389	Bob Horner	.10	.04	.01	☐ 438	Ron Davis	.03	.01	.00
☐ 390	Pat Clements	.03	.01	.00	☐ 439	Jesse Orosco	.03	.01	.00
☐ 391	Jeff Leonard	.08	.03	.01	☐ 440	Scott Bradley	.03	.01	.00
☐ 392	Chris Speier	.03	.01	.00	☐ 441	Randy Bush	.03	.01	.00
☐ 393	John Moses	.03	.01	.00	☐ 442	John Cerutti	.12	.05	.01
☐ 394	Garth Iorg	.03	.01	.00	☐ 443	Roy Smalley	.03	.01	.00
☐ 395	Greg Gagne	.03	.01	.00	☐ 444	Kelly Gruber	.03	.01	.00
☐ 396	Nate Snell	.03	.01	.00	☐ 445	Bob Kearney	.03	.01	.00
☐ 397	Bryan Clutterbuck	.06	.02	.00	☐ 446	Ed Hearn	.06	.02	.00
☐ 398	Darrell Evans	.08	.03	.01	☐ 447	Scott Sanderson	.03	.01	.00
☐ 399	Steve Crawford	.03	.01	.00	☐ 448	Bruce Benedict	.03	.01	.00
☐ 400	Checklist	.06	.01	.00	☐ 449	Junior Ortiz	.03	.01	.00
☐ 401	Phil Lombardi	.10	.04	.01	☐ 450	Mike Aldrete	.25	.10	.02
☐ 402	Rick Honeycutt	.03	.01	.00	☐ 451	Kevin McReynolds	.30	.12	.03
☐ 403	Ken Schrom	.03	.01	.00	☐ 452	Rob Murphy	.25	.10	.02
☐ 404	Bud Black	.03	.01	.00	☐ 453	Kent Tekulve	.03	.01	.00
☐ 405	Donnie Hill	.03	.01	.00	☐ 454	Curt Ford	.10	.04	.01
☐ 406	Wayne Krenchicki	.03	.01	.00	☐ 455	Dave Lopes	.06	.02	.00
☐ 407	Chuck Finley	.06	.02	.00	☐ 456	Bob Grich	.06	.02	.00
☐ 408	Toby Harrah	.03	.01	.00	☐ 457	Jose DeLeon	.03	.01	.00
☐ 409	Steve Lyons	.03	.01	.00	☐ 458	Andre Dawson	.25	.10	.02
☐ 410	Kevin Bass	.06	.02	.00	☐ 459	Mike Flanagan	.06	.02	.00
☐ 411	Marvell Wynne	.03	.01	.00	☐ 460	Joey Meyer	.65	.26	.06
☐ 412	Ron Roenicke	.03	.01	.00	☐ 461	Chuck Cary	.12	.05	.01
☐ 413	Tracy Jones	.30	.12	.03	☐ 462	Bill Buckner	.08	.03	.01
☐ 414	Gene Garber	.03	.01	.00	☐ 463	Bob Shirley	.03	.01	.00
☐ 415	Mike Bielecki	.03	.01	.00	☐ 464	Jeff Hamilton	.25	.10	.02
☐ 416	Frank DiPino	.03	.01	.00	☐ 465	Phil Niekro	.15	.06	.01
☐ 417	Andy Van Slyke	.20	.08	.02	☐ 466	Mark Gubicza	.08	.03	.01
☐ 418	Jim Dwyer	.03	.01	.00	☐ 467	Jerry Willard	.03	.01	.00
☐ 419	Ben Oglivie	.06	.02	.00	☐ 468	Bob Sebra	.10	.04	.01

		MINT	EXC	G-VG
☐ 469	Larry Parrish	.03	.01	.00
☐ 470	Charlie Hough	.06	.02	.00
☐ 471	Hal McRae	.06	.02	.00
☐ 472	Dave Leiper	.06	.02	.00
☐ 473	Mel Hall	.06	.02	.00
☐ 474	Dan Pasqua	.08	.03	.01
☐ 475	Bob Welch	.06	.02	.00
☐ 476	Johnny Grubb	.03	.01	.00
☐ 477	Jim Traber	.06	.02	.00
☐ 478	Chris Bosio	.15	.06	.01
☐ 479	Mark McLemore	.03	.01	.00
☐ 480	John Morris	.03	.01	.00
☐ 481	Billy Hatcher	.08	.03	.01
☐ 482	Dan Schatzeder	.03	.01	.00
☐ 483	Rich Gossage	.10	.04	.01
☐ 484	Jim Morrison	.03	.01	.00
☐ 485	Bob Brenly	.03	.01	.00
☐ 486	Bill Schroeder	.03	.01	.00
☐ 487	Mookie Wilson	.06	.02	.00
☐ 488	Dave Martinez	.20	.08	.02
☐ 489	Harold Reynolds	.06	.02	.00
☐ 490	Jeff Hearron	.08	.03	.01
☐ 491	Mickey Hatcher	.06	.02	.00
☐ 492	Barry Larkin	1.00	.40	.10
☐ 493	Bob James	.03	.01	.00
☐ 494	John Habyan	.03	.01	.00
☐ 495	Jim Adduci	.12	.05	.01
☐ 496	Mike Heath	.03	.01	.00
☐ 497	Tim Stoddard	.03	.01	.00
☐ 498	Tony Armas	.06	.02	.00
☐ 499	Dennis Powell	.03	.01	.00
☐ 500	Checklist	.06	.01	.00
☐ 501	Chris Bando	.03	.01	.00
☐ 502	David Cone	4.00	1.60	.40
☐ 503	Jay Howell	.06	.02	.00
☐ 504	Tom Foley	.03	.01	.00
☐ 505	Ray Chadwick	.06	.02	.00
☐ 506	Mike Loynd	.08	.03	.01
☐ 507	Neil Allen	.03	.01	.00
☐ 508	Danny Darwin	.03	.01	.00
☐ 509	Rick Schu	.03	.01	.00
☐ 510	Jose Oquendo	.03	.01	.00
☐ 511	Gene Walter	.03	.01	.00
☐ 512	Terry McGriff	.12	.05	.01
☐ 513	Ken Griffey	.06	.02	.00
☐ 514	Benny Distefano	.03	.01	.00
☐ 515	Terry Mulholland	.08	.03	.01
☐ 516	Ed Lynch	.03	.01	.00
☐ 517	Bill Swift	.03	.01	.00
☐ 518	Manny Lee	.06	.02	.00
☐ 519	Andre David	.03	.01	.00
☐ 520	Scott McGregor	.06	.02	.00
☐ 521	Rick Manning	.03	.01	.00
☐ 522	Willie Hernandez	.08	.03	.01
☐ 523	Marty Barrett	.08	.03	.01
☐ 524	Wayne Tolleson	.03	.01	.00
☐ 525	Jose Gonzalez	.20	.08	.02
☐ 526	Cory Snyder	.75	.30	.07
☐ 527	Buddy Biancalana	.03	.01	.00
☐ 528	Moose Haas	.03	.01	.00
☐ 529	Wilfredo Tejada	.06	.02	.00
☐ 530	Stu Cliburn	.03	.01	.00
☐ 531	Dale Mohorcic	.15	.06	.01
☐ 532	Ron Hassey	.03	.01	.00
☐ 533	Ty Gainey	.03	.01	.00
☐ 534	Jerry Royster	.03	.01	.00
☐ 535	Mike Maddux	.15	.06	.01
☐ 536	Ted Power	.03	.01	.00
☐ 537	Ted Simmons	.10	.04	.01
☐ 538	Rafael Belliard	.08	.03	.01
☐ 539	Chico Walker	.08	.03	.01
☐ 540	Bob Forsch	.03	.01	.00
☐ 541	John Stefero	.03	.01	.00
☐ 542	Dale Sveum	.20	.08	.02
☐ 543	Mark Thurmond	.03	.01	.00
☐ 544	Jeff Sellers	.15	.06	.01
☐ 545	Joel Skinner	.03	.01	.00
☐ 546	Alex Trevino	.03	.01	.00
☐ 547	Randy Kutcher	.08	.03	.01
☐ 548	Joaquin Andujar	.08	.03	.01
☐ 549	Casey Candaele	.12	.05	.01
☐ 550	Jeff Russell	.03	.01	.00
☐ 551	John Candelaria	.06	.02	.00
☐ 552	Joe Cowley	.03	.01	.00
☐ 553	Danny Cox	.06	.02	.00
☐ 554	Denny Walling	.03	.01	.00
☐ 555	Bruce Ruffin	.20	.08	.02
☐ 556	Buddy Bell	.08	.03	.01
☐ 557	Jimmy Jones	.35	.14	.03
☐ 558	Bobby Bonilla	1.00	.40	.10
☐ 559	Jeff Robinson (Giants pitcher)	.06	.02	.00
☐ 560	Ed Olwine	.06	.02	.00
☐ 561	Glenallen Hill	.12	.05	.00
☐ 562	Lee Mazzilli	.03	.01	.00
☐ 563	Mike Brown (pitcher)	.03	.01	.00
☐ 564	George Frazier	.03	.01	.00

		MINT	EXC	G-VG
☐ 565	Mike Sharperson . . .	.08	.03	.01
☐ 566	Mark Portugal	.08	.03	.01
☐ 567	Rick Leach	.03	.01	.00
☐ 568	Mark Langston	.10	.04	.01
☐ 569	Rafael Santana	.03	.01	.00
☐ 570	Manny Trillo	.03	.01	.00
☐ 571	Cliff Speck	.06	.02	.00
☐ 572	Bob Kipper	.03	.01	.00
☐ 573	Kelly Downs	.30	.12	.03
☐ 574	Randy Asadoor	.08	.03	.01
☐ 575	Dave Magadan	.45	.18	.04
☐ 576	Marvin Freeman	.15	.06	.01
☐ 577	Jeff Lahti	.03	.01	.00
☐ 578	Jeff Calhoun	.03	.01	.00
☐ 579	Gus Polidor	.03	.01	.00
☐ 580	Gene Nelson	.03	.01	.00
☐ 581	Tim Teufel	.03	.01	.00
☐ 582	Odell Jones	.03	.01	.00
☐ 583	Mark Ryal	.08	.03	.01
☐ 584	Randy O'Neal	.03	.01	.00
☐ 585	Mike Greenwell	8.00	3.25	.80
☐ 586	Ray Knight	.06	.02	.00
☐ 587	Ralph Bryant	.12	.05	.01
☐ 588	Carmen Castillo . . .	.03	.01	.00
☐ 589	Ed Wojna	.03	.01	.00
☐ 590	Stan Javier	.06	.02	.00
☐ 591	Jeff Musselman	.15	.06	.01
☐ 592	Mike Stanley	.20	.08	.02
☐ 593	Darrell Porter	.03	.01	.00
☐ 594	Drew Hall	.12	.05	.01
☐ 595	Rob Nelson	.15	.06	.01
☐ 596	Bryan Oelkers	.03	.01	.00
☐ 597	Scott Nielsen	.15	.06	.01
☐ 598	Brian Holton	.20	.08	.02
☐ 599	Kevin Mitchell	.30	.12	.03
☐ 600	Checklist	.06	.01	.00
☐ 601	Jackie Gutierrez . . .	.03	.01	.00
☐ 602	Barry Jones	.15	.06	.01
☐ 603	Jerry Narron	.03	.01	.00
☐ 604	Steve Lake	.03	.01	.00
☐ 605	Jim Pankovits	.03	.01	.00
☐ 606	Ed Romero	.03	.01	.00
☐ 607	Dave LaPoint	.06	.02	.00
☐ 608	Don Robinson	.03	.01	.00
☐ 609	Mike Krukow	.03	.01	.00
☐ 610	Dave Valle	.03	.01	.00
☐ 611	Len Dykstra	.10	.04	.01
☐ 612	Roberto Clemente . . Puzzle Card	.06	.02	.00
☐ 613	Mike Trujillo	.03	.01	.00
☐ 614	Damaso Garcia . . .	.03	.01	.00
☐ 615	Neal Heaton	.03	.01	.00
☐ 616	Juan Berenguer . . .	.03	.01	.00
☐ 617	Steve Carlton	.20	.08	.02
☐ 618	Gary Lucas	.03	.01	.00
☐ 619	Geno Petralli	.03	.01	.00
☐ 620	Rick Aguilera	.03	.01	.00
☐ 621	Fred McGriff	.75	.30	.07
☐ 622	Dave Henderson . .	.06	.02	.00
☐ 623	Dave Clark	.20	.08	.02
☐ 624	Angel Salazar	.03	.01	.00
☐ 625	Randy Hunt	.03	.01	.00
☐ 626	John Gibbons	.03	.01	.00
☐ 627	Kevin Brown	.15	.06	.01
☐ 628	Bill Dawley	.03	.01	.00
☐ 629	Aurelio Lopez	.03	.01	.00
☐ 630	Charles Hudson . . .	.03	.01	.00
☐ 631	Ray Soff	.06	.02	.00
☐ 632	Ray Hayward	.08	.03	.01
☐ 633	Spike Owen	.03	.01	.00
☐ 634	Glenn Hubbard	.03	.01	.00
☐ 635	Kevin Elster	.60	.24	.06
☐ 636	Mike LaCoss	.03	.01	.00
☐ 637	Dwayne Henry	.03	.01	.00
☐ 638	Rey Quinones	.20	.08	.02
☐ 639	Jim Clancy	.03	.01	.00
☐ 640	Larry Andersen	.03	.01	.00
☐ 641	Calvin Schiraldi . . .	.06	.02	.00
☐ 642	Stan Jefferson	.30	.12	.03
☐ 643	Marc Sullivan	.03	.01	.00
☐ 644	Mark Grant	.03	.01	.00
☐ 645	Cliff Johnson	.03	.01	.00
☐ 646	Howard Johnson . .	.12	.05	.01
☐ 647	Dave Sax	.03	.01	.00
☐ 648	Dave Stewart	.08	.03	.01
☐ 649	Danny Heep	.03	.01	.00
☐ 650	Joe Johnson	.03	.01	.00
☐ 651	Bob Brower	.20	.08	.02
☐ 652	Rob Woodward	.03	.01	.00
☐ 653	John Mizerock	.03	.01	.00
☐ 654	Tim Pyznarski	.10	.04	.01
☐ 655	Luis Aquino	.06	.02	.00
☐ 656	Mickey Brantley . . .	.15	.06	.01
☐ 657	Doyle Alexander . . .	.06	.02	.00
☐ 658	Sammy Stewart . . .	.03	.01	.00
☐ 659	Jim Acker	.03	.01	.00
☐ 660	Pete Ladd	.03	.01	.00

1987 Donruss Opening Day

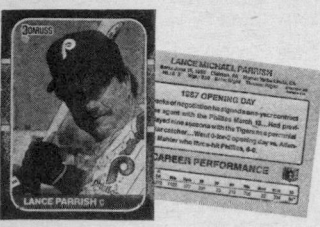

This innovative set of 272 cards features a card for each of the players in the starting line-ups of all the teams on Opening Day 1987. Cards are the standard size, 2 ½" by 3 ½", and are packaged as a complete set in a specially designed box. Cards are very similar in design to the 1987 regular Donruss issue except that these "OD" cards have a maroon border instead of a black border. The set features the first card in a Major League uniform of Joey Cora, Mark Davidson, Donnell Nixon, Bob Patterson, and Alonzo Powell. Teams in the same city share a checklist card. A 15-piece puzzle of Roberto Clemente is also included with every complete set. The error on Bobby Bonds was corrected very early in the press run; supposedly less than one percent of the sets have the error.

		MINT	EXC	G-VG
	Complete Set (272)	18.00	7.25	1.80
	Common Player (1-248)	.05	.02	.00
	Common Logo (249-272)	.03	.01	.00
☐ 1	Doug DeCinces	.05	.02	.00
☐ 2	Mike Witt	.10	.04	.01
☐ 3	George Hendrick	.05	.02	.00
☐ 4	Dick Schofield	.05	.02	.00
☐ 5	Devon White	.60	.24	.06
☐ 6	Butch Wynegar	.05	.02	.00
☐ 7	Wally Joyner	1.00	.40	.10
☐ 8	Mark McLemore	.05	.02	.00
☐ 9	Brian Downing	.05	.02	.00
☐ 10	Gary Pettis	.05	.02	.00
☐ 11	Bill Doran	.10	.04	.01
☐ 12	Phil Garner	.05	.02	.00
☐ 13	Jose Cruz	.10	.04	.01
☐ 14	Kevin Bass	.10	.04	.01
☐ 15	Mike Scott	.20	.08	.02
☐ 16	Glenn Davis	.15	.06	.01
☐ 17	Alan Ashby	.05	.02	.00
☐ 18	Billy Hatcher	.15	.06	.01
☐ 19	Craig Reynolds	.05	.02	.00
☐ 20	Carney Lansford	.10	.04	.01
☐ 21	Mike Davis	.05	.02	.00
☐ 22	Reggie Jackson	.35	.14	.03
☐ 23	Mickey Tettleton	.05	.02	.00
☐ 24	Jose Canseco	2.50	1.00	.25
☐ 25	Rob Nelson	.05	.02	.00
☐ 26	Tony Phillips	.05	.02	.00
☐ 27	Dwayne Murphy	.05	.02	.00
☐ 28	Alfredo Griffin	.05	.02	.00
☐ 29	Curt Young	.05	.02	.00
☐ 30	Willie Upshaw	.05	.02	.00
☐ 31	Mike Sharperson	.05	.02	.00
☐ 32	Rance Mulliniks	.05	.02	.00
☐ 33	Ernie Whitt	.05	.02	.00
☐ 34	Jesse Barfield	.15	.06	.01
☐ 35	Tony Fernandez	.15	.06	.01
☐ 36	Lloyd Moseby	.10	.04	.01
☐ 37	Jimmy Key	.10	.04	.01
☐ 38	Fred McGriff	.40	.16	.04
☐ 39	George Bell	.25	.10	.02
☐ 40	Dale Murphy	.35	.14	.03
☐ 41	Rick Mahler	.05	.02	.00
☐ 42	Ken Griffey	.10	.04	.01
☐ 43	Andres Thomas	.05	.02	.00
☐ 44	Dion James	.05	.02	.00
☐ 45	Ozzie Virgil	.05	.02	.00
☐ 46	Ken Oberkfell	.05	.02	.00
☐ 47	Gary Roenicke	.05	.02	.00
☐ 48	Glenn Hubbard	.05	.02	.00
☐ 49	Bill Schroeder	.05	.02	.00
☐ 50	Greg Brock	.05	.02	.00
☐ 51	Billy Jo Robidoux	.05	.02	.00
☐ 52	Glenn Braggs	.15	.06	.01
☐ 53	Jim Gantner	.05	.02	.00
☐ 54	Paul Molitor	.15	.06	.01
☐ 55	Dale Sveum	.10	.04	.01
☐ 56	Ted Higuera	.15	.06	.01
☐ 57	Rob Deer	.10	.04	.01
☐ 58	Robin Yount	.25	.10	.02

		MINT	EXC	G-VG			MINT	EXC	G-VG
☐ 59	Jim Lindeman	.10	.04	.01	☐ 108	Andre Thornton	.05	.02	.00
☐ 60	Vince Coleman	.30	.12	.03	☐ 109	Joe Carter	.15	.06	.01
☐ 61	Tommy Herr	.05	.02	.00	☐ 110	Tony Bernazard	.05	.02	.00
☐ 62	Terry Pendleton	.05	.02	.00	☐ 111	Julio Franco	.10	.04	.01
☐ 63	John Tudor	.15	.06	.01	☐ 112	Brook Jacoby	.10	.04	.01
☐ 64	Tony Pena	.10	.04	.01	☐ 113	Brett Butler	.10	.04	.01
☐ 65	Ozzie Smith	.20	.08	.02	☐ 114	Donnell Nixon	.10	.04	.01
☐ 66	Tito Landrum	.05	.02	.00	☐ 115	Alvin Davis	.15	.06	.01
☐ 67	Jack Clark	.20	.08	.02	☐ 116	Mark Langston	.20	.08	.02
☐ 68	Bob Dernier	.05	.02	.00	☐ 117	Harold Reynolds	.10	.04	.01
☐ 69	Rick Sutcliffe	.10	.04	.01	☐ 118	Ken Phelps	.05	.02	.00
☐ 70	Andre Dawson	.25	.10	.02	☐ 119	Mike Kingery	.05	.02	.00
☐ 71	Keith Moreland	.05	.02	.00	☐ 120	Dave Valle	.05	.02	.00
☐ 72	Jody Davis	.05	.02	.00	☐ 121	Rey Quinones	.05	.02	.00
☐ 73	Brian Dayett	.05	.02	.00	☐ 122	Phil Bradley	.10	.04	.01
☐ 74	Leon Durham	.05	.02	.00	☐ 123	Jim Presley	.10	.04	.01
☐ 75	Ryne Sandberg	.20	.08	.02	☐ 124	Keith Hernandez	.25	.10	.02
☐ 76	Shawon Dunston	.10	.04	.01	☐ 125	Kevin McReynolds	.25	.10	.02
☐ 77	Mike Marshall	.15	.06	.01	☐ 126	Rafael Santana	.05	.02	.00
☐ 78	Bill Madlock	.05	.02	.00	☐ 127	Bob Ojeda	.10	.04	.01
☐ 79	Orel Hershiser	.60	.24	.06	☐ 128	Darryl Strawberry	.75	.30	.07
☐ 80	Mike Ramsey	.10	.04	.01	☐ 129	Mookie Wilson	.05	.02	.00
☐ 81	Ken Landreaux	.05	.02	.00	☐ 130	Gary Carter	.25	.10	.02
☐ 82	Mike Scioscia	.05	.02	.00	☐ 131	Tim Teufel	.05	.02	.00
☐ 83	Franklin Stubbs	.05	.02	.00	☐ 132	Howard Johnson	.15	.06	.01
☐ 84	Mariano Duncan	.05	.02	.00	☐ 133	Cal Ripken	.30	.12	.03
☐ 85	Steve Sax	.15	.06	.01	☐ 134	Rick Burleson	.05	.02	.00
☐ 86	Mitch Webster	.05	.02	.00	☐ 135	Fred Lynn	.10	.04	.01
☐ 87	Reid Nichols	.05	.02	.00	☐ 136	Eddie Murray	.25	.10	.02
☐ 88	Tim Wallach	.10	.04	.01	☐ 137	Ray Knight	.05	.02	.00
☐ 89	Floyd Youmans	.10	.04	.01	☐ 138	Alan Wiggins	.05	.02	.00
☐ 90	Andres Galarraga	.35	.14	.03	☐ 139	John Shelby	.05	.02	.00
☐ 91	Hubie Brooks	.05	.02	.00	☐ 140	Mike Boddicker	.10	.04	.01
☐ 92	Jeff Reed	.05	.02	.00	☐ 141	Ken Gerhart	.10	.04	.01
☐ 93	Alonzo Powell	.10	.04	.01	☐ 142	Terry Kennedy	.05	.02	.00
☐ 94	Vance Law	.05	.02	.00	☐ 143	Steve Garvey	.30	.12	.03
☐ 95	Bob Brenly	.05	.02	.00	☐ 144	Marvell Wynne	.05	.02	.00
☐ 96	Will Clark	1.00	.40	.10	☐ 145	Kevin Mitchell	.10	.04	.01
☐ 97	Chili Davis	.10	.04	.01	☐ 146	Tony Gwynn	.60	.24	.06
☐ 98	Mike Krukow	.05	.02	.00	☐ 147	Joey Cora	.10	.04	.01
☐ 99	Jose Uribe	.05	.02	.00	☐ 148	Benito Santiago	.75	.30	.07
☐ 100	Chris Brown	.10	.04	.01	☐ 149	Eric Show	.10	.04	.01
☐ 101	Rob Thompson	.10	.04	.01	☐ 150	Garry Templeton	.10	.04	.01
☐ 102	Candy Maldonado	.10	.04	.01	☐ 151	Carmelo Martinez	.05	.02	.00
☐ 103	Jeff Leonard	.10	.04	.01	☐ 152	Von Hayes	.10	.04	.01
☐ 104	Tom Candiotti	.05	.02	.00	☐ 153	Lance Parrish	.10	.04	.01
☐ 105	Chris Bando	.05	.02	.00	☐ 154	Milt Thompson	.05	.02	.00
☐ 106	Cory Snyder	.50	.20	.05	☐ 155	Mike Easler	.05	.02	.00
☐ 107	Pat Tabler	.05	.02	.00	☐ 156	Juan Samuel	.15	.06	.01

		MINT	EXC	G-VG			MINT	EXC	G-VG
☐ 157	Steve Jeltz	.05	.02	.00	☐ 204	Frank White	.10	.04	.01
☐ 158	Glenn Wilson	.05	.02	.00	☐ 205	Bo Jackson	.60	.24	.06
☐ 159	Shane Rawley	.05	.02	.00	☐ 206	George Brett	.35	.14	.03
☐ 160	Mike Schmidt	.30	.12	.03	☐ 207	Kevin Seitzer	1.50	.60	.15
☐ 161	Andy Van Slyke	.20	.08	.02	☐ 208	Willie Wilson	.10	.04	.01
☐ 162	Johnny Ray	.10	.04	.01	☐ 209	Orlando Mercado	.05	.02	.00
☐ 163A	Barry Bonds ERR	100.00	40.00	10.00	☐ 210	Darrell Evans	.10	.04	.01
	(photo actually Johnny Ray)				☐ 211	Larry Herndon	.05	.02	.00
☐ 163B	Barry Bonds COR	.25	.10	.02	☐ 212	Jack Morris	.15	.06	.01
☐ 164	Junior Ortiz	.05	.02	.00	☐ 213	Chet Lemon	.05	.02	.00
☐ 165	Rafael Belliard	.05	.02	.00	☐ 214	Mike Heath	.05	.02	.00
☐ 166	Bob Patterson	.10	.04	.01	☐ 215	Darnell Coles	.05	.02	.00
☐ 167	Bobby Bonilla	.20	.08	.02	☐ 216	Alan Trammell	.25	.10	.02
☐ 168	Sid Bream	.05	.02	.00	☐ 217	Terry Harper	.05	.02	.00
☐ 169	Jim Morrison	.05	.02	.00	☐ 218	Lou Whitaker	.10	.04	.01
☐ 170	Jerry Browne	.05	.02	.00	☐ 219	Gary Gaetti	.20	.08	.02
☐ 171	Scott Fletcher	.05	.02	.00	☐ 220	Tom Nieto	.05	.02	.00
☐ 172	Ruben Sierra	.75	.30	.07	☐ 221	Kirby Puckett	.50	.20	.05
☐ 173	Larry Parrish	.05	.02	.00	☐ 222	Tom Brunansky	.10	.04	.01
☐ 174	Pete O'Brien	.10	.04	.01	☐ 223	Greg Gagne	.05	.02	.00
☐ 175	Pete Incaviglia	.35	.14	.03	☐ 224	Dan Gladden	.05	.02	.00
☐ 176	Don Slaught	.05	.02	.00	☐ 225	Mark Davidson	.10	.04	.01
☐ 177	Oddibe McDowell	.10	.04	.01	☐ 226	Bert Blyleven	.10	.04	.01
☐ 178	Charlie Hough	.05	.02	.00	☐ 227	Steve Lombardozzi	.05	.02	.00
☐ 179	Steve Buechele	.05	.02	.00	☐ 228	Kent Hrbek	.25	.10	.02
☐ 180	Bob Stanley	.05	.02	.00	☐ 229	Gary Redus	.05	.02	.00
☐ 181	Wade Boggs	1.00	.40	.10	☐ 230	Ivan Calderon	.10	.04	.01
☐ 182	Jim Rice	.20	.08	.02	☐ 231	Tim Hulett	.05	.02	.00
☐ 183	Bill Buckner	.10	.04	.01	☐ 232	Carlton Fisk	.15	.06	.01
☐ 184	Dwight Evans	.15	.06	.01	☐ 233	Greg Walker	.10	.04	.01
☐ 185	Spike Owen	.05	.02	.00	☐ 234	Ron Karkovice	.05	.02	.00
☐ 186	Don Baylor	.10	.04	.01	☐ 235	Ozzie Guillen	.15	.06	.01
☐ 187	Marc Sullivan	.05	.02	.00	☐ 236	Harold Baines	.15	.06	.01
☐ 188	Marty Barrett	.10	.04	.01	☐ 237	Donnie Hill	.05	.02	.00
☐ 189	Dave Henderson	.05	.02	.00	☐ 238	Rich Dotson	.10	.04	.01
☐ 190	Bo Diaz	.05	.02	.00	☐ 239	Mike Pagliarulo	.10	.04	.01
☐ 191	Barry Larkin	.25	.10	.02	☐ 240	Joel Skinner	.05	.02	.00
☐ 192	Kal Daniels	.50	.20	.05	☐ 241	Don Mattingly	1.50	.60	.15
☐ 193	Terry Francona	.05	.02	.00	☐ 242	Gary Ward	.05	.02	.00
☐ 194	Tom Browning	.15	.06	.01	☐ 243	Dave Winfield	.25	.10	.02
☐ 195	Ron Oester	.05	.02	.00	☐ 244	Dan Pasqua	.10	.04	.01
☐ 196	Buddy Bell	.10	.04	.01	☐ 245	Wayne Tolleson	.05	.02	.00
☐ 197	Eric Davis	1.00	.40	.10	☐ 246	Willie Randolph	.10	.04	.01
☐ 198	Dave Parker	.15	.06	.01	☐ 247	Dennis Rasmussen	.10	.04	.01
☐ 199	Steve Balboni	.05	.02	.00	☐ 248	Rickey Henderson	.40	.16	.04
☐ 200	Danny Tartabull	.25	.10	.02	☐ 249	Angels Logo	.03	.01	.00
☐ 201	Ed Hearn	.05	.02	.00	☐ 250	Astros Logo	.03	.01	.00
☐ 202	Buddy Biancalana	.05	.02	.00	☐ 251	A's Logo	.03	.01	.00
☐ 203	Danny Jackson	.20	.08	.02	☐ 252	Blue Jays Logo	.03	.01	.00

		MINT	EXC	G-VG
☐ 253	Braves Logo	.03	.01	.00
☐ 254	Brewers Logo	.03	.01	.00
☐ 255	Cardinals Logo	.03	.01	.00
☐ 256	Dodgers Logo	.03	.01	.00
☐ 257	Expos Logo	.03	.01	.00
☐ 258	Giants Logo	.03	.01	.00
☐ 259	Indians Logo	.03	.01	.00
☐ 260	Mariners Logo	.03	.01	.00
☐ 261	Orioles Logo	.03	.01	.00
☐ 262	Padres Logo	.03	.01	.00
☐ 263	Phillies Logo	.03	.01	.00
☐ 264	Pirates Logo	.03	.01	.00
☐ 265	Rangers Logo	.03	.01	.00
☐ 266	Red Sox Logo	.03	.01	.00
☐ 267	Reds Logo	.03	.01	.00
☐ 268	Royals Logo	.03	.01	.00
☐ 269	Tigers Logo	.03	.01	.00
☐ 270	Twins Logo	.03	.01	.00
☐ 271	Chicago Logos	.03	.01	.00
☐ 272	New York Logos	.03	.01	.00

1987 Donruss Rookies

The 1987 Donruss "The Rookies" set features 56 cards plus a 15-piece puzzle of Roberto Clemente. Cards are in full color and are standard size, 2 ½ " by 3 ½ ". The set was distributed in a small green and black box with gold lettering. Card fronts are similar in design to the 1987 Donruss regular issue except for the presence of "The Rookies" logo in the lower left corner and a green border instead of a black border.

		MINT	EXC	G-VG
	Complete Set (56)	12.50	5.00	1.25
	Common Player (1-56)	.05	.02	.00
☐ 1	Mark McGwire	2.50	1.00	.20
☐ 2	Eric Bell	.05	.02	.00
☐ 3	Mark Williamson	.15	.06	.01
☐ 4	Mike Greenwell	3.00	1.20	.30
☐ 5	Ellis Burks	1.75	.70	.17
☐ 6	DeWayne Buice	.15	.06	.01
☐ 7	Mark McLemore	.05	.02	.00
☐ 8	Devon White	.35	.14	.03
☐ 9	Willie Fraser	.05	.02	.00
☐ 10	Les Lancaster	.10	.04	.01
☐ 11	Ken Williams	.25	.10	.02
☐ 12	Matt Nokes	.65	.26	.06
☐ 13	Jeff Robinson (Tigers pitcher)	.45	.18	.04
☐ 14	Bo Jackson	.60	.24	.06
☐ 15	Kevin Seitzer	1.50	.60	.15
☐ 16	Billy Ripken	.25	.10	.02
☐ 17	B.J. Surhoff	.15	.06	.01
☐ 18	Chuck Crim	.15	.06	.01
☐ 19	Mike Birkbeck	.05	.02	.00
☐ 20	Chris Bosio	.05	.02	.00
☐ 21	Les Straker	.15	.06	.01
☐ 22	Mark Davidson	.15	.06	.01
☐ 23	Gene Larkin	.35	.14	.03
☐ 24	Ken Gerhart	.10	.04	.01
☐ 25	Luis Polonia	.30	.12	.03
☐ 26	Terry Steinbach	.25	.10	.02
☐ 27	Mickey Brantley	.20	.08	.02
☐ 28	Mike Stanley	.15	.06	.01
☐ 29	Jerry Browne	.05	.02	.00
☐ 30	Todd Benzinger	.45	.18	.04
☐ 31	Fred McGriff	.75	.30	.07
☐ 32	Mike Henneman	.35	.14	.03
☐ 33	Casey Candaele	.10	.04	.01
☐ 34	Dave Magadan	.25	.10	.02
☐ 35	David Cone	1.25	.50	.12
☐ 36	Mike Jackson	.20	.08	.02
☐ 37	John Mitchell	.15	.06	.01
☐ 38	Mike Dunne	.25	.10	.02
☐ 39	John Smiley	.35	.14	.03
☐ 40	Joe Magrane	.50	.20	.05
☐ 41	Jim Lindeman	.15	.06	.01
☐ 42	Shane Mack	.30	.12	.03
☐ 43	Stan Jefferson	.20	.08	.02
☐ 44	Benito Santiago	.65	.26	.06
☐ 45	Matt Williams	.45	.18	.04
☐ 46	Dave Meads	.10	.04	.01

			MINT	EXC	G-VG
☐	47	Rafael Palmeiro ...	.60	.24	.06
☐	48	Bill Long	.12	.05	.01
☐	49	Bob Brower	.10	.04	.01
☐	50	James Steels	.10	.04	.01
☐	51	Paul Noce	.15	.06	.01
☐	52	Greg Maddux	.35	.14	.03
☐	53	Jeff Musselman	.10	.04	.01
☐	54	Brian Holton	.10	.04	.01
☐	55	Chuck Jackson	.15	.06	.01
☐	56	Checklist Card	.05	.01	.00

1987 Donruss Highlights

Donruss' third (and last) edition of Highlights was released late in 1987. The cards are standard size, measuring 2 ½" by 3 ½", and are glossy in appearance. Cards commemorate events during the 1987 season, as well as players and pitchers of the month from each league. The set was distributed in its own red, black, blue, and gold box along with a small Roberto Clemente puzzle. Card fronts are similar to the regular 1987 Donruss issue except that the Highlights logo is positioned in the lower right-hand corner and the borders are in blue instead of black. The backs are printed in black and gold on white card stock.

	MINT	EXC	G-VG
Complete Set (56)	7.50	3.00	.75
Common Player (1-56)	.06	.02	.00

			MINT	EXC	G-VG
☐	1	Juan Nieves .... First No-Hitter	.06	.02	.00
☐	2	Mike Schmidt ..... Hits 500th Homer	.25	.10	.02
☐	3	Eric Davis .... NL Player April	.35	.14	.03
☐	4	Sid Fernandez ..... NL Pitcher April	.10	.04	.01
☐	5	Brian Downing .... AL Player April	.06	.02	.00
☐	6	Bret Saberhagen .. AL Pitcher April	.15	.06	.01
☐	7	Tim Raines .... Free Agent Returns	.15	.06	.01
☐	8	Eric Davis .... NL Player May	.35	.14	.03
☐	9	Steve Bedrosian ... NL Pitcher May	.06	.02	.00
☐	10	Larry Parrish ..... AL Player May	.06	.02	.00
☐	11	Jim Clancy .... AL Pitcher May	.06	.02	.00
☐	12	Tony Gwynn ..... NL Player June ERR (over "20" hits)	.20	.08	.02
☐	13	Orel Hershiser .... NL Pitcher June	.35	.14	.03
☐	14	Wade Boggs ..... AL Player June	.50	.20	.05
☐	15	Steve Ontiveros ... AL Pitcher June	.06	.02	.00
☐	16	Tim Raines .... All Star Game Hero	.15	.06	.01
☐	17	Don Mattingly .... Consecutive Game Homerun Streak	.65	.26	.06
☐	18	Ray Dandridge .... 1987 HOF Inductee	.15	.06	.01
☐	19	Jim "Catfish" Hunter 1987 HOF Inductee	.15	.06	.01
☐	20	Billy Williams ..... 1987 HOF Inductee	.15	.06	.01
☐	21	Bo Diaz .... NL Player July	.06	.02	.00
☐	22	Floyd Youmans .... NL Pitcher July	.06	.02	.00
☐	23	Don Mattingly .... AL Player July	.65	.26	.06

		MINT	EXC	G-VG
☐ 24	Frank Viola ...... AL Pitcher July	.15	.06	.01
☐ 25	Bobby Witt .... Strikes Out Four Batters in One Inning	.15	.06	.01
☐ 26	Kevin Seitzer ...... Ties AL 9 Inning Game Hit Mark	.50	.20	.05
☐ 27	Mark McGwire ..... Sets Rookie HR Record	.75	.30	.07
☐ 28	Andre Dawson .... Sets Cubs' 1st Year Homer Mark	.20	.08	.02
☐ 29	Paul Molitor ...... Hits in 39 Straight Games	.15	.06	.01
☐ 30	Kirby Puckett ...... Record Weekend	.35	.14	.03
☐ 31	Andre Dawson .... NL Player August	.20	.08	.02
☐ 32	Doug Drabek ...... NL Pitcher August	.06	.02	.00
☐ 33	Dwight Evans ..... AL Player August	.10	.04	.01
☐ 34	Mark Langston .... AL Pitcher August	.10	.04	.01
☐ 35	Wally Joyner ...... 100 RBI in 1st Two Major League Seasons	.30	.12	.03
☐ 36	Vince Coleman .... 100 SB in 1st Three Major League Seasons	.20	.08	.02
☐ 37	Eddie Murray ...... Orioles' All Time Homer King	.20	.08	.02
☐ 38	Cal Ripken .... Ends Consecutive Innings Streak	.20	.08	.02
☐ 39	Blue Jays .... Hit Record 10 Homers In One Game (McGriff/Ducey/Whitt)	.06	.02	.00
☐ 40	McGwire/Canseco .. Equal A's RBI Marks	.90	.36	.09
☐ 41	Bob Boone .... Sets All-Time Catching Record	.06	.02	.00

		MINT	EXC	G-VG
☐ 42	Darryl Strawberry . Sets Mets' One-Season Home Run Mark	.35	.14	.03
☐ 43	Howard Johnson .. NL's All-Time Switchhit HR King	.15	.06	.01
☐ 44	Wade Boggs ..... Five Straight 200 Hit Seasons	.50	.20	.05
☐ 45	Benito Santiago ... Eclipses Rookie Game Hitting Streak	.35	.14	.03
☐ 46	Mark McGwire .... Eclipses Jackson's A's HR Record	.75	.30	.07
☐ 47	Kevin Seitzer ..... 13th Rookie to Collect 200 Hits	.50	.20	.05
☐ 48	Don Mattingly .... Sets Slam Record	.75	.30	.07
☐ 49	Darryl Strawberry . NL Player September	.35	.14	.03
☐ 50	Pascual Perez .... NL Pitcher September	.06	.02	.00
☐ 51	Alan Trammell .... AL Player September	.15	.06	.01
☐ 52	Doyle Alexander .. AL Pitcher September	.06	.02	.00
☐ 53	Nolan Ryan .... Strikeout King Again	.25	.10	.02
☐ 54	Mark McGwire .... Donruss AL ROY	.75	.30	.07
☐ 55	Benito Santiago ... Donruss NL ROY	.50	.20	.05
☐ 56	Checklist Card	.06	.01	.00

1988 Donruss

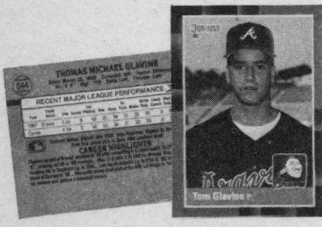

This 660-card set was distributed along with a puzzle of Stan Musial. The six regular checklist cards are numbered throughout the set as multiples of 100. Cards measure 2 ½" by 3 ½" and feature a distinctive black and blue border on the front. The popular Diamond King subset returns for the seventh consecutive year. Rated Rookies are featured again as cards 28-47. Cards marked as SP (short printed) from 648-660 are more difficult to find than the other 13 SP's in the lower 600s. These 26 cards listed as SP were apparently pulled from the printing sheet to make room for the 26 Bonus MVP cards. Six of the checklist cards were done two different ways to reflect the inclusion or exclusion of the Bonus MVP cards in the wax packs. In the checklist below, the A variations (for the checklist cards) are from the wax packs and the B variations are from the factory-collated sets.

		MINT	EXC	G-VG
	Complete Set (660)	28.00	11.50	2.80
	Common Player (1-660) ...	.03	.01	.00
☐	1 Mark McGwire DK ..	1.00	.25	.05
☐	2 Tim Raines DK	.20	.08	.02
☐	3 Benito Santiago DK	.35	.14	.03
☐	4 Alan Trammell DK .	.20	.08	.02
☐	5 Danny Tartabull DK	.20	.08	.02
☐	6 Ron Darling DK ...	.15	.06	.01
☐	7 Paul Molitor DK ...	.15	.06	.01
☐	8 Devon White DK ...	.20	.08	.02

		MINT	EXC	G-VG
☐	9 Andre Dawson DK .	.25	.10	.02
☐	10 Julio Franco DK ...	.08	.03	.01
☐	11 Scott Fletcher DK .	.08	.03	.01
☐	12 Tony Fernandez DK .	.15	.06	.01
☐	13 Shane Rawley DK .	.10	.04	.01
☐	14 Kal Daniels DK	.20	.08	.02
☐	15 Jack Clark DK	.20	.08	.02
☐	16 Dwight Evans DK ..	.15	.06	.01
☐	17 Tommy John DK ..	.15	.06	.01
☐	18 Andy Van Slyke DK	.20	.08	.02
☐	19 Gary Gaetti DK ...	.20	.08	.02
☐	20 Mark Langston DK .	.12	.05	.01
☐	21 Will Clark DK	.60	.24	.06
☐	22 Glenn Hubbard DK .	.08	.03	.01
☐	23 Billy Hatcher DK ..	.10	.04	.01
☐	24 Bob Welch DK	.08	.03	.01
☐	25 Ivan Calderon DK .	.10	.04	.01
☐	26 Cal Ripken Jr. DK .	.25	.10	.02
☐	27 DK Checklist 1-26 .	.06	.01	.00
☐	28 Mackey Sasser RR	.30	.12	.03
☐	29 Jeff Treadway RR .	.35	.14	.03
☐	30 Mike Campbell RR	.20	.08	.02
☐	31 Lance Johnson RR	.20	.08	.02
☐	32 Nelson Liriano RR .	.20	.08	.02
☐	33 Shawn Abner RR .	.30	.12	.03
☐	34 Roberto Alomar RR	.70	.28	.07
☐	35 Shawn Hillegas RR	.20	.08	.02
☐	36 Joey Meyer RR ...	.20	.08	.02
☐	37 Kevin Elster RR ...	.20	.08	.02
☐	38 Jose Lind RR	.30	.12	.03
☐	39 Kirt Manwaring RR	.30	.12	.03
☐	40 Mark Grace RR ...	3.00	1.20	.30
☐	41 Jody Reed RR	.50	.20	.05
☐	42 John Farrell RR ...	.25	.10	.02
☐	43 Al Leiter RR	1.00	.40	.10
☐	44 Gary Thurman RR .	.30	.12	.03
☐	45 Vicente Palacios RR	.15	.06	.01
☐	46 Eddie Williams RR .	.15	.06	.01
☐	47 Jack McDowell RR	.25	.10	.02
☐	48 Ken Dixon	.03	.01	.00
☐	49 Mike Birkbeck	.03	.01	.00
☐	50 Eric King	.03	.01	.00
☐	51 Roger Clemens ...	.50	.20	.05
☐	52 Pat Clements	.03	.01	.00
☐	53 Fernando Valenzuela	.15	.06	.01
☐	54 Mark Gubicza	.08	.03	.01
☐	55 Jay Howell	.03	.01	.00
☐	56 Floyd Youmans ...	.03	.01	.00
☐	57 Ed Correa	.03	.01	.00

		MINT	EXC	G-VG
☐ 58	DeWayne Buice	.10	.04	.01
☐ 59	Jose DeLeon	.03	.01	.00
☐ 60	Danny Cox	.06	.02	.00
☐ 61	Nolan Ryan	.30	.12	.03
☐ 62	Steve Bedrosian	.08	.03	.01
☐ 63	Tom Browning	.10	.04	.01
☐ 64	Mark Davis	.06	.02	.00
☐ 65	R.J. Reynolds	.03	.01	.00
☐ 66	Kevin Mitchell	.08	.03	.01
☐ 67	Ken Oberkfell	.03	.01	.00
☐ 68	Rick Sutcliffe	.08	.03	.01
☐ 69	Dwight Gooden	.45	.18	.04
☐ 70	Scott Bankhead	.08	.03	.01
☐ 71	Bert Blyleven	.08	.03	.01
☐ 72	Jimmy Key	.08	.03	.01
☐ 73	Les Straker	.10	.04	.01
☐ 74	Jim Clancy	.03	.01	.00
☐ 75	Mike Moore	.03	.01	.00
☐ 76	Ron Darling	.12	.05	.01
☐ 77	Ed Lynch	.03	.01	.00
☐ 78	Dale Murphy	.35	.14	.03
☐ 79	Doug Drabek	.06	.02	.00
☐ 80	Scott Garrelts	.03	.01	.00
☐ 81	Ed Whitson	.03	.01	.00
☐ 82	Rob Murphy	.03	.01	.00
☐ 83	Shane Rawley	.03	.01	.00
☐ 84	Greg Mathews	.03	.01	.00
☐ 85	Jim Deshaies	.06	.02	.00
☐ 86	Mike Witt	.08	.03	.01
☐ 87	Donnie Hill	.03	.01	.00
☐ 88	Jeff Reed	.03	.01	.00
☐ 89	Mike Boddicker	.06	.02	.00
☐ 90	Ted Higuera	.10	.04	.01
☐ 91	Walt Terrell	.03	.01	.00
☐ 92	Bob Stanley	.03	.01	.00
☐ 93	Dave Righetti	.08	.03	.01
☐ 94	Orel Hershiser	.25	.10	.02
☐ 95	Chris Bando	.03	.01	.00
☐ 96	Bret Saberhagen	.12	.05	.01
☐ 97	Curt Young	.03	.01	.00
☐ 98	Tim Burke	.03	.01	.00
☐ 99	Charlie Hough	.03	.01	.00
☐ 100A	Checklist 28-137	.06	.01	.00
☐ 100B	Checklist 28-133	.06	.01	.00
☐ 101	Bobby Witt	.08	.03	.01
☐ 102	George Brett	.30	.12	.03
☐ 103	Mickey Tettleton	.03	.01	.00
☐ 104	Scott Bailes	.03	.01	.00
☐ 105	Mike Pagliarulo	.08	.03	.01
☐ 106	Mike Scioscia	.03	.01	.00
☐ 107	Tom Brookens	.03	.01	.00
☐ 108	Ray Knight	.06	.02	.00
☐ 109	Dan Plesac	.06	.02	.00
☐ 110	Wally Joyner	.45	.18	.04
☐ 111	Bob Forsch	.03	.01	.00
☐ 112	Mike Scott	.15	.06	.01
☐ 113	Kevin Gross	.03	.01	.00
☐ 114	Benito Santiago	.30	.12	.03
☐ 115	Bob Kipper	.03	.01	.00
☐ 116	Mike Krukow	.03	.01	.00
☐ 117	Chris Bosio	.03	.01	.00
☐ 118	Sid Fernandez	.08	.03	.01
☐ 119	Jody Davis	.06	.02	.00
☐ 120	Mike Morgan	.03	.01	.00
☐ 121	Mark Eichhorn	.03	.01	.00
☐ 122	Jeff Reardon	.08	.03	.01
☐ 123	John Franco	.08	.03	.01
☐ 124	Richard Dotson	.06	.02	.00
☐ 125	Eric Bell	.03	.01	.00
☐ 126	Juan Nieves	.03	.01	.00
☐ 127	Jack Morris	.12	.05	.01
☐ 128	Rick Rhoden	.03	.01	.00
☐ 129	Rich Gedman	.06	.02	.00
☐ 130	Ken Howell	.03	.01	.00
☐ 131	Brook Jacoby	.08	.03	.01
☐ 132	Danny Jackson	.15	.06	.01
☐ 133	Gene Nelson	.03	.01	.00
☐ 134	Neal Heaton	.03	.01	.00
☐ 135	Willie Fraser	.03	.01	.00
☐ 136	Jose Guzman	.03	.01	.00
☐ 137	Ozzie Guillen	.06	.02	.00
☐ 138	Bob Knepper	.06	.02	.00
☐ 139	Mike Jackson	.15	.06	.01
☐ 140	Joe Magrane	.30	.12	.03
☐ 141	Jimmy Jones	.06	.02	.00
☐ 142	Ted Power	.03	.01	.00
☐ 143	Ozzie Virgil	.03	.01	.00
☐ 144	Felix Fermin	.10	.04	.01
☐ 145	Kelly Downs	.06	.02	.00
☐ 146	Shawon Dunston	.06	.02	.00
☐ 147	Scott Bradley	.03	.01	.00
☐ 148	Dave Stieb	.08	.03	.01
☐ 149	Frank Viola	.15	.06	.01
☐ 150	Terry Kennedy	.03	.01	.00
☐ 151	Bill Wegman	.03	.01	.00
☐ 152	Matt Nokes	.50	.20	.05
☐ 153	Wade Boggs	.90	.36	.09
☐ 154	Wayne Tolleson	.03	.01	.00

		MINT	EXC	G-VG
☐ 155	Mariano Duncan	.03	.01	.00
☐ 156	Julio Franco	.08	.03	.01
☐ 157	Charlie Leibrandt	.03	.01	.00
☐ 158	Terry Steinbach	.12	.05	.01
☐ 159	Mike Fitzgerald	.03	.01	.00
☐ 160	Jack Lazorko	.03	.01	.00
☐ 161	Mitch Williams	.03	.01	.00
☐ 162	Greg Walker	.08	.03	.01
☐ 163	Alan Ashby	.03	.01	.00
☐ 164	Tony Gwynn	.30	.12	.03
☐ 165	Bruce Ruffin	.03	.01	.00
☐ 166	Ron Robinson	.03	.01	.00
☐ 167	Zane Smith	.06	.02	.00
☐ 168	Junior Ortiz	.03	.01	.00
☐ 169	Jamie Moyer	.03	.01	.00
☐ 170	Tony Pena	.08	.03	.01
☐ 171	Cal Ripken	.20	.08	.02
☐ 172	B.J. Surhoff	.10	.04	.01
☐ 173	Lou Whitaker	.10	.04	.01
☐ 174	Ellis Burks	1.25	.50	.12
☐ 175	Ron Guidry	.10	.04	.01
☐ 176	Steve Sax	.12	.05	.01
☐ 177	Danny Tartabull	.20	.08	.02
☐ 178	Carney Lansford	.06	.02	.00
☐ 179	Casey Candaele	.03	.01	.00
☐ 180	Scott Fletcher	.03	.01	.00
☐ 181	Mark McLemore	.03	.01	.00
☐ 182	Ivan Calderon	.08	.03	.01
☐ 183	Jack Clark	.15	.06	.01
☐ 184	Glenn Davis	.15	.06	.01
☐ 185	Luis Aguayo	.03	.01	.00
☐ 186	Bo Diaz	.03	.01	.00
☐ 187	Stan Jefferson	.06	.02	.00
☐ 188	Sid Bream	.03	.01	.00
☐ 189	Bob Brenly	.03	.01	.00
☐ 190	Dion James	.03	.01	.00
☐ 191	Leon Durham	.03	.01	.00
☐ 192	Jesse Orosco	.03	.01	.00
☐ 193	Alvin Davis	.08	.03	.01
☐ 194	Gary Gaetti	.12	.05	.01
☐ 195	Fred McGriff	.35	.14	.03
☐ 196	Steve Lombardozzi	.03	.01	.00
☐ 197	Rance Mulliniks	.03	.01	.00
☐ 198	Rey Quinones	.03	.01	.00
☐ 199	Gary Carter	.25	.10	.02
☐ 200A	Checklist 138-247	.06	.01	.00
☐ 200B	Checklist 134-239	.06	.01	.00
☐ 201	Keith Moreland	.03	.01	.00
☐ 202	Ken Griffey	.06	.02	.00
☐ 203	Tommy Gregg	.15	.06	.01
☐ 204	Will Clark	.75	.30	.07
☐ 205	John Kruk	.10	.04	.01
☐ 206	Buddy Bell	.08	.03	.01
☐ 207	Von Hayes	.08	.03	.01
☐ 208	Tommy Herr	.06	.02	.00
☐ 209	Craig Reynolds	.03	.01	.00
☐ 210	Gary Pettis	.03	.01	.00
☐ 211	Harold Baines	.08	.03	.01
☐ 212	Vance Law	.03	.01	.00
☐ 213	Ken Gerhart	.03	.01	.00
☐ 214	Jim Gantner	.03	.01	.00
☐ 215	Chet Lemon	.03	.01	.00
☐ 216	Dwight Evans	.10	.04	.01
☐ 217	Don Mattingly	1.25	.50	.12
☐ 218	Franklin Stubbs	.03	.01	.00
☐ 219	Pat Tabler	.06	.02	.00
☐ 220	Bo Jackson	.40	.16	.04
☐ 221	Tony Phillips	.03	.01	.00
☐ 222	Tim Wallach	.08	.03	.01
☐ 223	Ruben Sierra	.25	.10	.02
☐ 224	Steve Buechele	.03	.01	.00
☐ 225	Frank White	.06	.02	.00
☐ 226	Alfredo Griffin	.06	.02	.00
☐ 227	Greg Swindell	.10	.04	.01
☐ 228	Willie Randolph	.06	.02	.00
☐ 229	Mike Marshall	.10	.04	.01
☐ 230	Alan Trammell	.15	.06	.01
☐ 231	Eddie Murray	.20	.08	.02
☐ 232	Dale Sveum	.03	.01	.00
☐ 233	Dick Schofield	.03	.01	.00
☐ 234	Jose Oquendo	.03	.01	.00
☐ 235	Bill Doran	.06	.02	.00
☐ 236	Milt Thompson	.03	.01	.00
☐ 237	Marvell Wynne	.03	.01	.00
☐ 238	Bobby Bonilla	.18	.08	.01
☐ 239	Chris Speier	.03	.01	.00
☐ 240	Glenn Braggs	.08	.03	.01
☐ 241	Wally Backman	.03	.01	.00
☐ 242	Ryne Sandberg	.20	.08	.02
☐ 243	Phil Bradley	.08	.03	.01
☐ 244	Kelly Gruber	.03	.01	.00
☐ 245	Tom Brunansky	.10	.04	.01
☐ 246	Ron Oester	.03	.01	.00
☐ 247	Bobby Thigpen	.06	.02	.00
☐ 248	Fred Lynn	.12	.05	.01
☐ 249	Paul Molitor	.12	.05	.01
☐ 250	Darrell Evans	.08	.03	.01
☐ 251	Gary Ward	.03	.01	.00

		MINT	EXC	G-VG			MINT	EXC	G-VG
☐ 252	Bruce Hurst	.10	.04	.01	☐ 300A	Checklist 248-357	.06	.01	.00
☐ 253	Bob Welch	.06	.02	.00	☐ 300B	Checklist 240-345	.06	.01	.00
☐ 254	Joe Carter	.12	.05	.01	☐ 301	Bud Black	.03	.01	.00
☐ 255	Willie Wilson	.08	.03	.01	☐ 302	Jose Canseco	1.75	.70	.17
☐ 256	Mark McGwire	1.25	.50	.12	☐ 303	Tom Foley	.03	.01	.00
☐ 257	Mitch Webster	.03	.01	.00	☐ 304	Pete Incaviglia	.18	.08	.01
☐ 258	Brian Downing	.03	.01	.00	☐ 305	Bob Boone	.06	.02	.00
☐ 259	Mike Stanley	.08	.03	.01	☐ 306	Bill Long	.10	.04	.01
☐ 260	Carlton Fisk	.10	.04	.01	☐ 307	Willie McGee	.10	.04	.01
☐ 261	Billy Hatcher	.08	.03	.01	☐ 308	Ken Caminiti	.20	.08	.02
☐ 262	Glenn Wilson	.03	.01	.00	☐ 309	Darren Daulton	.03	.01	.00
☐ 263	Ozzie Smith	.12	.05	.01	☐ 310	Tracy Jones	.08	.03	.01
☐ 264	Randy Ready	.03	.01	.00	☐ 311	Greg Booker	.03	.01	.00
☐ 265	Kurt Stillwell	.03	.01	.00	☐ 312	Mike LaValliere	.08	.03	.01
☐ 266	David Palmer	.03	.01	.00	☐ 313	Chili Davis	.08	.03	.01
☐ 267	Mike Diaz	.03	.01	.00	☐ 314	Glenn Hubbard	.03	.01	.00
☐ 268	Rob Thompson	.06	.02	.00	☐ 315	Paul Noce	.10	.04	.01
☐ 269	Andre Dawson	.20	.08	.02	☐ 316	Keith Hernandez	.18	.08	.01
☐ 270	Lee Guetterman	.03	.01	.00	☐ 317	Mark Langston	.08	.03	.01
☐ 271	Willie Upshaw	.03	.01	.00	☐ 318	Keith Atherton	.03	.01	.00
☐ 272	Randy Bush	.03	.01	.00	☐ 319	Tony Fernandez	.10	.04	.01
☐ 273	Larry Sheets	.08	.03	.01	☐ 320	Kent Hrbek	.12	.05	.01
☐ 274	Rob Deer	.08	.03	.01	☐ 321	John Cerutti	.03	.01	.00
☐ 275	Kirk Gibson	.18	.08	.01	☐ 322	Mike Kingery	.03	.01	.00
☐ 276	Marty Barrett	.08	.03	.01	☐ 323	Dave Magadan	.10	.04	.01
☐ 277	Rickey Henderson	.25	.10	.02	☐ 324	Rafael Palmeiro	.30	.12	.03
☐ 278	Pedro Guerrero	.15	.06	.01	☐ 325	Jeff Dedmon	.03	.01	.00
☐ 279	Brett Butler	.06	.02	.00	☐ 326	Barry Bonds	.20	.08	.02
☐ 280	Kevin Seitzer	1.00	.40	.10	☐ 327	Jeffrey Leonard	.06	.02	.00
☐ 281	Mike Davis	.03	.01	.00	☐ 328	Tim Flannery	.03	.01	.00
☐ 282	Andres Galarraga	.30	.12	.03	☐ 329	Dave Concepcion	.08	.03	.01
☐ 283	Devon White	.18	.08	.01	☐ 330	Mike Schmidt	.30	.12	.03
☐ 284	Pete O'Brien	.08	.03	.01	☐ 331	Bill Dawley	.03	.01	.00
☐ 285	Jerry Hairston	.03	.01	.00	☐ 332	Larry Andersen	.03	.01	.00
☐ 286	Kevin Bass	.06	.02	.00	☐ 333	Jack Howell	.03	.01	.00
☐ 287	Carmelo Martinez	.03	.01	.00	☐ 334	Ken Williams	.20	.08	.02
☐ 288	Juan Samuel	.08	.03	.01	☐ 335	Bryn Smith	.03	.01	.00
☐ 289	Kal Daniels	.25	.10	.02	☐ 336	Billy Ripken	.15	.06	.01
☐ 290	Albert Hall	.03	.01	.00	☐ 337	Greg Brock	.03	.01	.00
☐ 291	Andy Van Slyke	.15	.06	.01	☐ 338	Mike Heath	.03	.01	.00
☐ 292	Lee Smith	.06	.02	.00	☐ 339	Mike Greenwell	1.25	.50	.12
☐ 293	Vince Coleman	.20	.08	.02	☐ 340	Claudell Washington	.06	.02	.00
☐ 294	Tom Niedenfuer	.03	.01	.00	☐ 341	Jose Gonzalez	.03	.01	.00
☐ 295	Robin Yount	.20	.08	.02	☐ 342	Mel Hall	.03	.01	.00
☐ 296	Jeff Robinson	.30	.12	.03	☐ 343	Jim Eisenreich	.06	.02	.00
	(Tigers pitcher)				☐ 344	Tony Bernazard	.03	.01	.00
☐ 297	Todd Benzinger	.40	.16	.04	☐ 345	Tim Raines	.20	.08	.02
☐ 298	Dave Winfield	.20	.08	.02	☐ 346	Bob Brower	.03	.01	.00
☐ 299	Mickey Hatcher	.06	.02	.00	☐ 347	Larry Parrish	.03	.01	.00

		MINT	EXC	G-VG			MINT	EXC	G-VG
☐ 348	Thad Bosley	.03	.01	.00	☐ 397	Mike Felder	.03	.01	.00
☐ 349	Dennis Eckersley	.10	.04	.01	☐ 398	Willie Hernandez	.06	.02	.00
☐ 350	Cory Snyder	.20	.08	.02	☐ 399	Jim Rice	.15	.06	.01
☐ 351	Rick Cerone	.03	.01	.00	☐ 400A	Checklist 358-467	.06	.01	.00
☐ 352	John Shelby	.03	.01	.00	☐ 400B	Checklist 346-451	.06	.01	.00
☐ 353	Larry Herndon	.03	.01	.00	☐ 401	Tommy John	.10	.04	.01
☐ 354	John Habyan	.03	.01	.00	☐ 402	Brian Holton	.03	.01	.00
☐ 355	Chuck Crim	.08	.03	.01	☐ 403	Carmen Castillo	.03	.01	.00
☐ 356	Gus Polidor	.03	.01	.00	☐ 404	Jamie Quirk	.03	.01	.00
☐ 357	Ken Dayley	.03	.01	.00	☐ 405	Dwayne Murphy	.03	.01	.00
☐ 358	Danny Darwin	.03	.01	.00	☐ 406	Jeff Parrett	.15	.06	.01
☐ 359	Lance Parrish	.10	.04	.01	☐ 407	Don Sutton	.12	.05	.01
☐ 360	James Steels	.10	.04	.01	☐ 408	Jerry Browne	.03	.01	.00
☐ 361	Al Pedrique	.10	.04	.01	☐ 409	Jim Winn	.03	.01	.00
☐ 362	Mike Aldrete	.06	.02	.00	☐ 410	Dave Smith	.03	.01	.00
☐ 363	Juan Castillo	.03	.01	.00	☐ 411	Shane Mack	.15	.06	.01
☐ 364	Len Dykstra	.08	.03	.01	☐ 412	Greg Gross	.03	.01	.00
☐ 365	Luis Quinones	.06	.02	.00	☐ 413	Nick Esasky	.03	.01	.00
☐ 366	Jim Presley	.08	.03	.01	☐ 414	Damaso Garcia	.03	.01	.00
☐ 367	Lloyd Moseby	.08	.03	.01	☐ 415	Brian Fisher	.03	.01	.00
☐ 368	Kirby Puckett	.35	.14	.03	☐ 416	Brian Dayett	.03	.01	.00
☐ 369	Eric Davis	.75	.30	.07	☐ 417	Curt Ford	.03	.01	.00
☐ 370	Gary Redus	.03	.01	.00	☐ 418	Mark Williamson	.10	.04	.01
☐ 371	Dave Schmidt	.03	.01	.00	☐ 419	Bill Schroeder	.03	.01	.00
☐ 372	Mark Clear	.03	.01	.00	☐ 420	Mike Henneman	.20	.08	.02
☐ 373	Dave Bergman	.03	.01	.00	☐ 421	John Marzano	.10	.04	.01
☐ 374	Charles Hudson	.03	.01	.00	☐ 422	Ron Kittle	.08	.03	.01
☐ 375	Calvin Schiraldi	.03	.01	.00	☐ 423	Matt Young	.03	.01	.00
☐ 376	Alex Trevino	.03	.01	.00	☐ 424	Steve Balboni	.03	.01	.00
☐ 377	Tom Candiotti	.03	.01	.00	☐ 425	Luis Polonia	.20	.08	.02
☐ 378	Steve Farr	.03	.01	.00	☐ 426	Randy St.Claire	.03	.01	.00
☐ 379	Mike Gallego	.03	.01	.00	☐ 427	Greg Harris	.03	.01	.00
☐ 380	Andy McGaffigan	.03	.01	.00	☐ 428	Johnny Ray	.06	.02	.01
☐ 381	Kirk McCaskill	.03	.01	.00	☐ 429	Ray Searage	.03	.01	.00
☐ 382	Oddibe McDowell	.08	.03	.01	☐ 430	Ricky Horton	.03	.01	.00
☐ 383	Floyd Bannister	.03	.01	.00	☐ 431	Gerald Young	.35	.14	.03
☐ 384	Denny Walling	.03	.01	.00	☐ 432	Rick Schu	.03	.01	.00
☐ 385	Don Carman	.03	.01	.00	☐ 433	Paul O'Neill	.06	.02	.00
☐ 386	Todd Worrell	.10	.04	.01	☐ 434	Rich Gossage	.08	.03	.01
☐ 387	Eric Show	.03	.01	.00	☐ 435	John Cangelosi	.03	.01	.00
☐ 388	Dave Parker	.10	.04	.01	☐ 436	Mike LaCoss	.03	.01	.00
☐ 389	Rick Mahler	.03	.01	.00	☐ 437	Gerald Perry	.08	.03	.01
☐ 390	Mike Dunne	.15	.06	.01	☐ 438	Dave Martinez	.06	.02	.00
☐ 391	Candy Maldonado	.08	.03	.01	☐ 439	Darryl Strawberry	.40	.16	.04
☐ 392	Bob Dernier	.03	.01	.00	☐ 440	John Moses	.03	.01	.00
☐ 393	Dave Valle	.03	.01	.00	☐ 441	Greg Gagne	.03	.01	.00
☐ 394	Ernie Whitt	.03	.01	.00	☐ 442	Jesse Barfield	.12	.05	.01
☐ 395	Juan Berenguer	.03	.01	.00	☐ 443	George Frazier	.03	.01	.00
☐ 396	Mike Young	.03	.01	.00	☐ 444	Garth Iorg	.03	.01	.00

	MINT	EXC	G-VG		MINT	EXC	G-VG
☐ 445 Ed Nunez	.03	.01	.00	☐ 494 Mike Griffin	.03	.01	.00
☐ 446 Rick Aguilera	.03	.01	.00	☐ 495 Mark Knudson	.10	.04	.01
☐ 447 Jerry Mumphrey	.03	.01	.00	☐ 496 Bill Madlock	.06	.02	.00
☐ 448 Rafael Ramirez	.03	.01	.00	☐ 497 Tim Stoddard	.03	.01	.00
☐ 449 John Smiley	.20	.08	.02	☐ 498 Sam Horn	.35	.14	.03
☐ 450 Atlee Hammaker	.03	.01	.00	☐ 499 Tracy Woodson	.20	.08	.02
☐ 451 Lance McCullers	.06	.02	.00	☐ 500A Checklist 468-577	.06	.01	.00
☐ 452 Guy Hoffman	.03	.01	.00	☐ 500B Checklist 452-557	.06	.01	.00
☐ 453 Chris James	.10	.04	.01	☐ 501 Ken Schrom	.03	.01	.00
☐ 454 Terry Pendleton	.03	.01	.00	☐ 502 Angel Salazar	.03	.01	.00
☐ 455 Dave Meads	.10	.04	.01	☐ 503 Eric Plunk	.03	.01	.00
☐ 456 Bill Buckner	.08	.03	.01	☐ 504 Joe Hesketh	.03	.01	.00
☐ 457 John Pawlowski	.10	.04	.01	☐ 505 Greg Minton	.03	.01	.00
☐ 458 Bob Sebra	.03	.01	.00	☐ 506 Geno Petralli	.03	.01	.00
☐ 459 Jim Dwyer	.03	.01	.00	☐ 507 Bob James	.03	.01	.00
☐ 460 Jay Aldrich	.10	.04	.01	☐ 508 Robbie Wine	.10	.04	.01
☐ 461 Frank Tanana	.03	.01	.00	☐ 509 Jeff Calhoun	.03	.01	.00
☐ 462 Oil Can Boyd	.03	.01	.00	☐ 510 Steve Lake	.03	.01	.00
☐ 463 Dan Pasqua	.06	.02	.00	☐ 511 Mark Grant	.03	.01	.00
☐ 464 Tim Crews	.10	.04	.01	☐ 512 Frank Williams	.03	.01	.00
☐ 465 Andy Allanson	.03	.01	.00	☐ 513 Jeff Blauser	.20	.08	.02
☐ 466 Bill Pecota	.10	.04	.01	☐ 514 Bob Walk	.03	.01	.00
☐ 467 Steve Ontiveros	.03	.01	.00	☐ 515 Craig Lefferts	.03	.01	.00
☐ 468 Hubie Brooks	.06	.02	.00	☐ 516 Manny Trillo	.03	.01	.00
☐ 469 Paul Kilgus	.15	.06	.01	☐ 517 Jerry Reed	.03	.01	.00
☐ 470 Dale Mohorcic	.03	.01	.00	☐ 518 Rick Leach	.03	.01	.00
☐ 471 Dan Quisenberry	.08	.03	.01	☐ 519 Mark Davidson	.15	.06	.01
☐ 472 Dave Stewart	.08	.03	.01	☐ 520 Jeff Ballard	.15	.06	.01
☐ 473 Dave Clark	.06	.02	.00	☐ 521 Dave Stapleton	.06	.02	.00
☐ 474 Joel Skinner	.03	.01	.00	☐ 522 Pat Sheridan	.03	.01	.00
☐ 475 Dave Anderson	.03	.01	.00	☐ 523 Al Nipper	.03	.01	.00
☐ 476 Dan Petry	.03	.01	.00	☐ 524 Steve Trout	.03	.01	.00
☐ 477 Carl Nichols	.10	.04	.01	☐ 525 Jeff Hamilton	.06	.02	.00
☐ 478 Ernest Riles	.03	.01	.00	☐ 526 Tommy Hinzo	.10	.04	.01
☐ 479 George Hendrick	.06	.02	.00	☐ 527 Lonnie Smith	.03	.01	.00
☐ 480 John Morris	.03	.01	.00	☐ 528 Greg Cadaret	.15	.06	.01
☐ 481 Manny Hernandez	.10	.04	.01	☐ 529 Bob McClure	.03	.01	.00
☐ 482 Jeff Stone	.03	.01	.00	("Rob" on front)			
☐ 483 Chris Brown	.06	.02	.00	☐ 530 Chuck Finley	.03	.01	.00
☐ 484 Mike Bielecki	.03	.01	.00	☐ 531 Jeff Russell	.03	.01	.00
☐ 485 Dave Dravecky	.03	.01	.00	☐ 532 Steve Lyons	.03	.01	.00
☐ 486 Rick Manning	.03	.01	.00	☐ 533 Terry Puhl	.03	.01	.00
☐ 487 Bill Almon	.03	.01	.00	☐ 534 Eric Nolte	.15	.06	.01
☐ 488 Jim Sundberg	.03	.01	.00	☐ 535 Kent Tekulve	.03	.01	.00
☐ 489 Ken Phelps	.06	.02	.00	☐ 536 Pat Pacillo	.08	.03	.01
☐ 490 Tom Henke	.06	.02	.00	☐ 537 Charlie Puleo	.03	.01	.00
☐ 491 Dan Gladden	.06	.02	.00	☐ 538 Tom Prince	.12	.05	.01
☐ 492 Barry Larkin	.15	.06	.01	☐ 539 Greg Maddux	.20	.08	.02
☐ 493 Fred Manrique	.10	.04	.01	☐ 540 Jim Lindeman	.03	.01	.00

	MINT	EXC	G-VG		MINT	EXC	G-VG
☐ 541 Pete Stanicek	.25	.10	.02	☐ 586 Bill Gullickson	.03	.01	.00
☐ 542 Steve Kiefer	.03	.01	.00	☐ 587 Tim Belcher	.20	.08	.02
☐ 543A Jim Morrison ERR ..	.06	.02	.00	☐ 588 Doug Jones	.35	.14	.03
(no decimal before lifetime average)				☐ 589 Melido Perez	.30	.12	.03
☐ 543B Jim Morrison COR .	.06	.02	.00	☐ 590 Rick Honeycutt ...	.03	.01	.00
☐ 544 Spike Owen	.03	.01	.00	☐ 591 Pascual Perez	.06	.02	.00
☐ 545 Jay Buhner	.50	.20	.05	☐ 592 Curt Wilkerson	.03	.01	.00
☐ 546 Mike Devereaux ...	.30	.12	.03	☐ 593 Steve Howe	.03	.01	.00
☐ 547 Jerry Don Gleaton ..	.03	.01	.00	☐ 594 John Davis	.15	.06	.01
☐ 548 Jose Rijo	.03	.01	.00	☐ 595 Storm Davis	.06	.02	.00
☐ 549 Dennis Martinez ...	.03	.01	.00	☐ 596 Sammy Stewart ...	.03	.01	.00
☐ 550 Mike Loynd	.03	.01	.00	☐ 597 Neil Allen	.03	.01	.00
☐ 551 Darrell Miller	.03	.01	.00	☐ 598 Alejandro Pena ...	.03	.01	.00
☐ 552 Dave LaPoint	.03	.01	.00	☐ 599 Mark Thurmond ...	.03	.01	.00
☐ 553 John Tudor	.08	.03	.01	☐ 600A Checklist 578-BC26	.06	.01	.00
☐ 554 Rocky Childress ...	.10	.04	.01	☐ 600B Checklist 558-660 .	.06	.01	.00
☐ 555 Wally Ritchie	.10	.04	.01	☐ 601 Jose Mesa	.20	.08	.02
☐ 556 Terry McGriff	.06	.02	.00	☐ 602 Don August	.25	.10	.02
☐ 557 Dave Leiper	.03	.01	.00	☐ 603 Terry Leach SP	.10	.04	.01
☐ 558 Jeff Robinson	.06	.02	.00	☐ 604 Tom Newell	.15	.06	.01
(Pirates pitcher)				☐ 605 Randall Byers SP ..	.20	.08	.02
☐ 559 Jose Uribe	.03	.01	.00	☐ 606 Jim Gott	.03	.01	.00
☐ 560 Ted Simmons	.08	.03	.01	☐ 607 Harry Spilman	.03	.01	.00
☐ 561 Les Lancaster	.10	.04	.01	☐ 608 John Candelaria ...	.06	.02	.00
☐ 562 Keith Miller	.20	.08	.02	☐ 609 Mike Brumley	.15	.06	.01
(New York Mets)				☐ 610 Mickey Brantley ...	.08	.03	.01
☐ 563 Harold Reynolds ...	.03	.01	.00	☐ 611 Jose Nunez SP	.20	.08	.02
☐ 564 Gene Larkin	.25	.10	.02	☐ 612 Tom Nieto	.03	.01	.00
☐ 565 Cecil Fielder	.03	.01	.00	☐ 613 Rick Reuschel	.06	.02	.00
☐ 566 Roy Smalley	.03	.01	.00	☐ 614 Lee Mazzilli SP	.06	.02	.00
☐ 567 Duane Ward	.03	.01	.00	☐ 615 Scott Lusader	.20	.08	.02
☐ 568 Bill Wilkinson	.10	.04	.01	☐ 616 Bobby Meacham ...	.03	.01	.00
☐ 569 Howard Johnson ...	.10	.04	.01	☐ 617 Kevin McReynolds SP	.20	.08	.01
☐ 570 Frank DiPino	.03	.01	.00	☐ 618 Gene Garber	.03	.01	.00
☐ 571 Pete Smith	.15	.06	.01	☐ 619 Barry Lyons SP	.20	.08	.02
☐ 572 Darnell Coles	.03	.01	.00	☐ 620 Randy Myers	.10	.04	.01
☐ 573 Don Robinson	.03	.01	.00	☐ 621 Donnie Moore	.03	.01	.00
☐ 574 Rob Nelson	.03	.01	.00	☐ 622 Domingo Ramos ..	.03	.01	.00
☐ 575 Dennis Rasmussen .	.06	.02	.00	☐ 623 Ed Romero	.03	.01	.00
☐ 576 Steve Jeltz	.03	.01	.00	☐ 624 Greg Myers	.15	.06	.01
☐ 577 Tom Pagnozzi	.15	.06	.01	☐ 625 Ripken Family	.08	.03	.01
☐ 578 Ty Gainey	.03	.01	.00	☐ 626 Pat Perry	.03	.01	.00
☐ 579 Gary Lucas	.03	.01	.00	☐ 627 Andres Thomas SP	.06	.02	.00
☐ 580 Ron Hassey	.03	.01	.00	☐ 628 Matt Williams SP ...	.35	.14	.03
☐ 581 Herm Winningham .	.03	.01	.00	☐ 629 Dave Hengel	.20	.08	.02
☐ 582 Rene Gonzales	.12	.05	.01	☐ 630 Jeff Musselman SP .	.06	.02	.00
☐ 583 Brad Komminsk	.03	.01	.00	☐ 631 Tim Laudner	.03	.01	.00
☐ 584 Doyle Alexander ...	.03	.01	.00	☐ 632 Bob Ojeda SP	.08	.03	.01
☐ 585 Jeff Sellers	.03	.01	.00	☐ 633 Rafael Santana ...	.03	.01	.00

		MINT	EXC	G-VG
☐ 634	Wes Gardner	.25	.10	.02
☐ 635	Roberto Kelly SP . . .	.50	.20	.05
☐ 636	Mike Flanagan SP . .	.06	.02	.00
☐ 637	Jay Bell	.20	.08	.02
☐ 638	Bob Melvin	.03	.01	.00
☐ 639	Damon Berryhill . . .	.35	.14	.03
☐ 640	David Wells SP	.25	.10	.02
☐ 641	Puzzle Card	.03	.01	.00
	(Stan Musial)			
☐ 642	Doug Sisk	.03	.01	.00
☐ 643	Keith Hughes	.20	.08	.02
☐ 644	Tom Glavine	.15	.06	.01
☐ 645	Al Newman	.03	.01	.00
☐ 646	Scott Sanderson . . .	.03	.01	.00
☐ 647	Scott Terry	.10	.04	.01
☐ 648	Tim Teufel SP	.08	.03	.01
☐ 649	Garry Templeton SP	.08	.03	.01
☐ 650	Manny Lee SP	.08	.03	.01
☐ 651	Roger McDowell SP	.10	.04	.01
☐ 652	Mookie Wilson SP . .	.10	.04	.01
☐ 653	David Cone SP	.80	.32	.08
☐ 654	Ron Gant SP	1.00	.40	.10
☐ 655	Joe Price SP	.08	.03	.01
☐ 656	George Bell SP	.25	.10	.02
☐ 657	Gregg Jefferies SP .	7.00	2.80	.70
☐ 658	Todd Stottlemyre SP	.40	.16	.04
☐ 659	Geronimo Berroa SP	.45	.18	.04
☐ 660	Jerry Royster SP . . .	.08	.03	.01

1988 Donruss Bonus MVP's

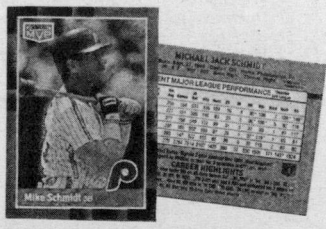

This 26-card set was distributed along with the regular 1988 Donruss issue as random

inserts with the rack and wax packs. These bonus cards are numbered with the prefix BC for bonus cards and were supposedly produced in the same quantities as the other 660 regular issue cards. The "most valuable" player was selected from each of the 26 teams. Cards measure 2½" by 3½" and feature the same distinctive black and blue border on the front as the regular issue. The cards are distinguished by the MVP logo in the upper left corner of the obverse. The last 13 cards numerically are considered to be somewhat tougher to find than the first 13 cards.

		MINT	EXC	G-VG
	Complete Set (26)	10.00	4.00	1.00
	Common Card (BC1-BC13)	.07	.03	.01
	Common Card (BC14-BC26)	.15	.06	.01
☐ BC1	Cal Ripken	.25	.10	.02
☐ BC2	Eric Davis	.70	.28	.07
☐ BC3	Paul Molitor	.15	.06	.01
☐ BC4	Mike Schmidt . . .	.35	.14	.03
☐ BC5	Ivan Calderon . . .	.07	.03	.01
☐ BC6	Tony Gwynn	.40	.16	.04
☐ BC7	Wade Boggs	.85	.34	.08
☐ BC8	Andy Van Slyke .	.15	.06	.01
☐ BC9	Joe Carter	.15	.06	.01
☐ BC10	Andre Dawson . .	.20	.08	.02
☐ BC11	Alan Trammell . .	.20	.08	.02
☐ BC12	Mike Scott	.15	.06	.01
☐ BC13	Wally Joyner . . .	.50	.20	.05
☐ BC14	Dale Murphy . . .	.40	.16	.04
☐ BC15	Kirby Puckett . . .	.50	.20	.05
☐ BC16	Pedro Guerrero .	.20	.08	.02
☐ BC17	Kevin Seitzer . . .	.70	.28	.07
☐ BC18	Tim Raines	.25	.10	.02
☐ BC19	George Bell	.20	.08	.02
☐ BC20	Darryl Strawberry	.75	.30	.07
☐ BC21	Don Mattingly . . .	1.50	.60	.15
☐ BC22	Ozzie Smith	.20	.08	.02
☐ BC23	Mark McGwire . .	1.00	.40	.10
☐ BC24	Will Clark	.75	.30	.07
☐ BC25	Alvin Davis	.15	.06	.01
☐ BC26	Ruben Sierra . . .	.20	.08	.02

1988 Donruss Rookies

The 1988 Donruss "The Rookies" set features 56 cards plus a 15-piece puzzle of Stan Musial. Cards are in full color and are standard size, 2½" by 3½". The set was distributed in a small green and black box with gold lettering. Card fronts are similar in design to the 1988 Donruss regular issue except for the presence of "The Rookies" logo in the lower right corner and a green and black border instead of a blue and black border on the fronts.

		MINT	EXC	G-VG
	Complete Set (56)	11.00	4.50	1.10
	Common Player (1-56)	.05	.02	.00
☐ 1	Mark Grace	1.75	.75	.15
☐ 2	Mike Campbell	.10	.04	.01
☐ 3	Todd Frohwirth	.10	.04	.01
☐ 4	Dave Stapleton	.05	.02	.00
☐ 5	Shawn Abner	.15	.06	.01
☐ 6	Jose Cecena	.12	.05	.01
☐ 7	Dave Gallagher	.25	.10	.02
☐ 8	Mark Parent	.12	.05	.01
☐ 9	Cecil Espy	.15	.06	.01
☐ 10	Pete Smith	.08	.03	.01
☐ 11	Jay Buhner	.20	.08	.02
☐ 12	Pat Borders	.25	.10	.02
☐ 13	Doug Jennings	.25	.10	.02
☐ 14	Brady Anderson	.35	.14	.03
☐ 15	Pete Stanicek	.15	.06	.01
☐ 16	Roberto Kelly	.20	.08	.02
☐ 17	Jeff Treadway	.15	.06	.01
☐ 18	Walt Weiss	1.00	.40	.10
☐ 19	Paul Gibson	.15	.06	.01
☐ 20	Tim Crews	.05	.02	.00
☐ 21	Melido Perez	.15	.06	.01
☐ 22	Steve Peters	.15	.06	.01
☐ 23	Craig Worthington	.25	.10	.02
☐ 24	John Trautwein	.15	.06	.01
☐ 25	DeWayne Vaughn	.10	.04	.01
☐ 26	David Wells	.08	.03	.01
☐ 27	Al Leiter	.25	.10	.02
☐ 28	Tim Belcher	.20	.08	.02
☐ 29	Johnny Paredes	.15	.06	.01
☐ 30	Chris Sabo	1.75	.70	.17
☐ 31	Damon Berryhill	.25	.10	.02
☐ 32	Randy Milligan	.20	.08	.02
☐ 33	Gary Thurman	.15	.06	.01
☐ 34	Kevin Elster	.20	.08	.02
☐ 35	Roberto Alomar	.30	.12	.03
☐ 36	Edgar Martinez UER (photo actually Edwin Nunez)	.30	.12	.03
☐ 37	Todd Stottlemyre	.15	.06	.01
☐ 38	Joey Meyer	.20	.08	.02
☐ 39	Carl Nichols	.05	.02	.00
☐ 40	Jack McDowell	.15	.06	.01
☐ 41	Jose Bautista	.15	.06	.01
☐ 42	Sil Campusano	.25	.10	.02
☐ 43	John Dopson	.20	.08	.02
☐ 44	Jody Reed	.25	.10	.02
☐ 45	Darrin Jackson	.25	.10	.02
☐ 46	Mike Capel	.15	.06	.01
☐ 47	Ron Gant	.30	.12	.03
☐ 48	John Davis	.05	.02	.00
☐ 49	Kevin Coffman	.12	.05	.01
☐ 50	Cris Carpenter	.30	.12	.03
☐ 51	Mackey Sasser	.20	.08	.02
☐ 52	Luis Alicea	.15	.06	.01
☐ 53	Bryan Harvey	.35	.14	.03
☐ 54	Steve Ellsworth	.15	.06	.01
☐ 55	Mike Macfarlane	.25	.10	.02
☐ 56	Checklist Card	.05	.01	.00

1988 Donruss Baseball's Best

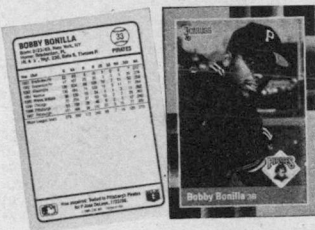

This innovative set of 336 cards was released by Donruss very late in the 1988 season to be sold in large national retail chains as a complete packaged set. Cards are the standard size, 2 ½ " by 3 ½ ", and are packaged as a complete set in a specially designed box. Cards are very similar in design to the 1988 regular Donruss issue except that these cards have orange and black borders instead of blue and black borders. Six (2 ½ " by 3 ½ ") 15-piece puzzles of Stan Musial are also included with every complete set.

		MINT	EXC	G-VG
	Complete Set (336)	24.00	10.00	2.40
	Common Player (1-336) ...	.05	.02	.00
☐ 1	Don Mattingly	1.00	.40	.10
☐ 2	Ron Gant	.35	.14	.03
☐ 3	Bob Boone	.10	.04	.01
☐ 4	Mark Grace	.75	.30	.07
☐ 5	Andy Allanson	.05	.02	.00
☐ 6	Kal Daniels	.20	.08	.02
☐ 7	Floyd Bannister	.05	.02	.00
☐ 8	Alan Ashby	.05	.02	.00
☐ 9	Marty Barrett	.10	.04	.01
☐ 10	Tim Belcher	.15	.06	.01
☐ 11	Harold Baines	.10	.04	.01
☐ 12	Hubie Brooks	.05	.02	.00
☐ 13	Doyle Alexander ...	.05	.02	.00
☐ 14	Gary Carter	.20	.08	.02

		MINT	EXC	G-VG
☐ 15	Glenn Braggs	.10	.04	.01
☐ 16	Steve Bedrosian ..	.10	.04	.01
☐ 17	Barry Bonds	.20	.08	.02
☐ 18	Bert Blyleven	.10	.04	.01
☐ 19	Tom Brunansky ...	.10	.04	.01
☐ 20	John Candelaria ...	.05	.02	.00
☐ 21	Shawn Abner	.15	.06	.01
☐ 22	Jose Canseco	1.50	.60	.15
☐ 23	Brett Butler	.10	.04	.01
☐ 24	Scott Bradley	.05	.02	.00
☐ 25	Ivan Calderon	.10	.04	.01
☐ 26	Rich Gossage	.10	.04	.01
☐ 27	Brian Downing	.05	.02	.00
☐ 28	Jim Rice	.15	.06	.01
☐ 29	Dion James	.05	.02	.00
☐ 30	Terry Kennedy	.05	.02	.00
☐ 31	George Bell	.15	.06	.01
☐ 32	Scott Fletcher	.05	.02	.00
☐ 33	Bobby Bonilla	.15	.06	.01
☐ 34	Tim Burke	.05	.02	.00
☐ 35	Darrell Evans	.10	.04	.01
☐ 36	Mike Davis	.05	.02	.00
☐ 37	Shawon Dunston ..	.10	.04	.01
☐ 38	Kevin Bass	.10	.04	.01
☐ 39	George Brett	.25	.10	.02
☐ 40	David Cone	.30	.12	.03
☐ 41	Ron Darling	.15	.06	.01
☐ 42	Roberto Alomar ...	.25	.10	.02
☐ 43	Dennis Eckersley .	.10	.04	.01
☐ 44	Vince Coleman ...	.20	.08	.02
☐ 45	Sid Bream	.05	.02	.00
☐ 46	Gary Gaetti	.15	.06	.01
☐ 47	Phil Bradley	.10	.04	.01
☐ 48	Jim Clancy	.05	.02	.00
☐ 49	Jack Clark	.15	.06	.01
☐ 50	Mike Krukow	.05	.02	.00
☐ 51	Henry Cotto	.05	.02	.00
☐ 52	Rich Dotson	.05	.02	.00
☐ 53	Jim Gantner	.05	.02	.00
☐ 54	John Franco	.05	.02	.00
☐ 55	Pete Incaviglia ...	.15	.06	.01
☐ 56	Joe Carter	.15	.06	.01
☐ 57	Roger Clemens ...	.50	.20	.05
☐ 58	Gerald Perry	.05	.02	.00
☐ 59	Jack Howell	.05	.02	.00
☐ 60	Vance Law	.05	.02	.00
☐ 61	Jay Bell	.05	.02	.00
☐ 62	Eric Davis	.50	.20	.05
☐ 63	Gene Garber	.05	.02	.00

			MINT	EXC	G-VG				MINT	EXC	G-VG
☐	64	Glenn Davis	.15	.06	.01	☐	113	Dale Murphy	.35	.14	.03
☐	65	Wade Boggs	.75	.30	.07	☐	114	Rick Mahler	.05	.02	.00
☐	66	Kirk Gibson	.25	.10	.02	☐	115	Wally Joyner	.50	.20	.05
☐	67	Carlton Fisk	.10	.04	.01	☐	116	Ryne Sandberg	.25	.10	.02
☐	68	Casey Candaele	.05	.02	.00	☐	117	John Farrell	.10	.04	.01
☐	69	Mike Heath	.05	.02	.00	☐	118	Nick Esasky	.05	.02	.00
☐	70	Kevin Elster	.10	.04	.01	☐	119	Bo Jackson	.35	.14	.03
☐	71	Greg Brock	.05	.02	.00	☐	120	Bill Doran	.10	.04	.01
☐	72	Don Carman	.05	.02	.00	☐	121	Ellis Burks	.50	.20	.05
☐	73	Doug Drabek	.05	.02	.00	☐	122	Pedro Guerrero	.20	.08	.02
☐	74	Greg Gagne	.05	.02	.00	☐	123	Dave LaPoint	.10	.04	.01
☐	75	Danny Cox	.10	.04	.01	☐	124	Neal Heaton	.05	.02	.00
☐	76	Rickey Henderson	.35	.14	.03	☐	125	Willie Hernandez	.10	.04	.01
☐	77	Chris Brown	.05	.02	.00	☐	126	Roger McDowell	.10	.04	.01
☐	78	Terry Steinbach	.10	.04	.01	☐	127	Ted Higuera	.10	.04	.01
☐	79	Will Clark	.50	.20	.05	☐	128	Von Hayes	.10	.04	.01
☐	80	Mickey Brantley	.10	.04	.01	☐	129	Mike LaValliere	.05	.02	.00
☐	81	Ozzie Guillen	.10	.04	.01	☐	130	Dan Gladden	.05	.02	.00
☐	82	Greg Maddux	.15	.06	.01	☐	131	Willie McGee	.15	.06	.01
☐	83	Kirk McCaskill	.05	.02	.00	☐	132	Al Leiter	.20	.08	.02
☐	84	Dwight Evans	.15	.06	.01	☐	133	Mark Grant	.05	.02	.00
☐	85	Ozzie Virgil	.05	.02	.00	☐	134	Bob Welch	.05	.02	.00
☐	86	Mike Morgan	.05	.02	.00	☐	135	Dave Dravecky	.05	.02	.00
☐	87	Tony Fernandez	.10	.04	.01	☐	136	Mark Langston	.10	.04	.01
☐	88	Jose Guzman	.05	.02	.00	☐	137	Dan Pasqua	.10	.04	.01
☐	89	Mike Dunne	.10	.04	.01	☐	138	Rick Sutcliffe	.10	.04	.01
☐	90	Andres Galarraga	.25	.10	.02	☐	139	Dan Petry	.05	.02	.00
☐	91	Mike Henneman	.10	.04	.01	☐	140	Rich Gedman	.10	.04	.01
☐	92	Alfredo Griffin	.05	.02	.00	☐	141	Ken Griffey Sr.	.10	.04	.01
☐	93	Rafael Palmeiro	.25	.10	.02	☐	142	Eddie Murray	.25	.10	.02
☐	94	Jim Deshaies	.05	.02	.00	☐	143	Jimmy Key	.10	.04	.01
☐	95	Mark Gubicza	.10	.04	.01	☐	144	Dale Mohorcic	.05	.02	.00
☐	96	Dwight Gooden	.50	.20	.05	☐	145	Jose Lind	.10	.04	.01
☐	97	Howard Johnson	.15	.06	.01	☐	146	Dennis Martinez	.05	.02	.00
☐	98	Mark Davis	.05	.02	.00	☐	147	Chet Lemon	.05	.02	.00
☐	99	Dave Stewart	.10	.04	.01	☐	148	Orel Hershiser	.35	.14	.03
☐	100	Joe Magrane	.10	.04	.01	☐	149	Dave Martinez	.05	.02	.00
☐	101	Brian Fisher	.05	.02	.00	☐	150	Billy Hatcher	.10	.04	.01
☐	102	Kent Hrbek	.05	.02	.00	☐	151	Charlie Leibrandt	.05	.02	.00
☐	103	Kevin Gross	.05	.02	.00	☐	152	Keith Hernandez	.20	.08	.02
☐	104	Tom Henke	.05	.02	.00	☐	153	Kevin McReynolds	.25	.10	.02
☐	105	Mike Pagliarulo	.10	.04	.01	☐	154	Tony Gwynn	.35	.14	.03
☐	106	Kelly Downs	.05	.02	.00	☐	155	Stan Javier	.05	.02	.00
☐	107	Alvin Davis	.10	.04	.01	☐	156	Tony Pena	.05	.02	.00
☐	108	Willie Randolph	.10	.04	.01	☐	157	Andy Van Slyke	.15	.06	.01
☐	109	Rob Deer	.10	.04	.01	☐	158	Gene Larkin	.10	.04	.01
☐	110	Bo Diaz	.05	.02	.00	☐	159	Chris James	.10	.04	.01
☐	111	Paul Kilgus	.05	.02	.00	☐	160	Fred McGriff	.35	.14	.03
☐	112	Tom Candiotti	.05	.02	.00	☐	161	Rick Rhoden	.10	.04	.01

		MINT	EXC	G-VG			MINT	EXC	G-VG
☐ 162	Scott Garrelts	.05	.02	.00	☐ 211	Rick Honeycutt	.05	.02	.00
☐ 163	Mike Campbell	.10	.04	.01	☐ 212	John Tudor	.15	.06	.01
☐ 164	Dave Righetti	.10	.04	.01	☐ 213	Jim Gott	.05	.02	.00
☐ 165	Paul Molitor	.15	.06	.01	☐ 214	Frank Viola	.20	.08	.02
☐ 166	Danny Jackson	.15	.06	.01	☐ 215	Juan Samuel	.10	.04	.01
☐ 167	Pete O'Brien	.10	.04	.01	☐ 216	Jesse Barfield	.15	.06	.01
☐ 168	Julio Franco	.10	.04	.01	☐ 217	Claudell Washington	.05	.02	.00
☐ 169	Mark McGwire	.75	.30	.07	☐ 218	Rick Reuschel	.10	.04	.01
☐ 170	Zane Smith	.10	.04	.01	☐ 219	Jim Presley	.10	.04	.01
☐ 171	Johnny Ray	.10	.04	.01	☐ 220	Tommy John	.15	.06	.01
☐ 172	Lester Lancaster	.05	.02	.00	☐ 221	Dan Plesac	.05	.02	.00
☐ 173	Mel Hall	.10	.04	.01	☐ 222	Barry Larkin	.15	.06	.01
☐ 174	Tracy Jones	.10	.04	.01	☐ 223	Mike Stanley	.05	.02	.00
☐ 175	Kevin Seitzer	.45	.18	.04	☐ 224	Cory Snyder	.20	.08	.02
☐ 176	Bob Knepper	.05	.02	.00	☐ 225	Andre Dawson	.25	.10	.02
☐ 177	Mike Greenwell	1.25	.50	.12	☐ 226	Ken Oberkfell	.05	.02	.00
☐ 178	Mike Marshall	.10	.04	.01	☐ 227	Devon White	.15	.06	.01
☐ 179	Melido Perez	.15	.06	.01	☐ 228	Jamie Moyer	.10	.04	.01
☐ 180	Tim Raines	.25	.10	.02	☐ 229	Brook Jacoby	.10	.04	.01
☐ 181	Jack Morris	.10	.04	.01	☐ 230	Rob Murphy	.10	.04	.01
☐ 182	Darryl Strawberry	.50	.20	.05	☐ 231	Bret Saberhagen	.15	.06	.01
☐ 183	Robin Yount	.25	.10	.02	☐ 232	Nolan Ryan	.30	.12	.03
☐ 184	Lance Parrish	.10	.04	.01	☐ 233	Bruce Hurst	.15	.06	.01
☐ 185	Darnell Coles	.05	.02	.00	☐ 234	Jesse Orosco	.05	.02	.00
☐ 186	Kirby Puckett	.50	.20	.05	☐ 235	Bobby Thigpen	.10	.04	.01
☐ 187	Terry Pendleton	.05	.02	.00	☐ 236	Pascual Perez	.05	.02	.00
☐ 188	Don Slaught	.05	.02	.00	☐ 237	Matt Nokes	.20	.08	.02
☐ 189	Jimmy Jones	.10	.04	.01	☐ 238	Bob Ojeda	.10	.04	.01
☐ 190	Dave Parker	.15	.06	.01	☐ 239	Joey Meyer	.10	.04	.01
☐ 191	Mike Aldrete	.05	.02	.00	☐ 240	Shane Rawley	.05	.02	.00
☐ 192	Mike Moore	.05	.02	.00	☐ 241	Jeff Robinson	.10	.04	.01
☐ 193	Greg Walker	.10	.04	.01	☐ 242	Jeff Reardon	.10	.04	.01
☐ 194	Calvin Schiraldi	.05	.02	.00	☐ 243	Ozzie Smith	.15	.06	.01
☐ 195	Dick Schofield	.05	.02	.00	☐ 244	Dave Winfield	.25	.10	.02
☐ 196	Jody Reed	.15	.06	.01	☐ 245	John Kruk	.10	.04	.01
☐ 197	Pete Smith	.10	.04	.01	☐ 246	Carney Lansford	.10	.04	.01
☐ 198	Cal Ripken	.25	.10	.02	☐ 247	Candy Maldonado	.10	.04	.01
☐ 199	Lloyd Moseby	.10	.04	.01	☐ 248	Ken Phelps	.10	.04	.01
☐ 200	Ruben Sierra	.15	.06	.01	☐ 249	Ken Williams	.10	.04	.01
☐ 201	R.J. Reynolds	.05	.02	.00	☐ 250	Al Nipper	.05	.02	.00
☐ 202	Bryn Smith	.05	.02	.00	☐ 251	Mark McLemore	.05	.02	.00
☐ 203	Gary Pettis	.05	.02	.00	☐ 252	Lee Smith	.05	.02	.00
☐ 204	Steve Sax	.15	.06	.01	☐ 253	Albert Hall	.05	.02	.00
☐ 205	Frank DiPino	.05	.02	.00	☐ 254	Billy Ripken	.10	.04	.01
☐ 206	Mike Scott	.15	.06	.01	☐ 255	Kelly Gruber	.05	.02	.00
☐ 207	Kurt Stillwell	.10	.04	.01	☐ 256	Charlie Hough	.05	.02	.00
☐ 208	Mookie Wilson	.05	.02	.00	☐ 257	John Smiley	.10	.04	.01
☐ 209	Lee Mazzilli	.05	.02	.00	☐ 258	Tim Wallach	.10	.04	.01
☐ 210	Lance McCullers	.10	.04	.01	☐ 259	Frank Tanana	.10	.04	.01

		MINT	EXC	G-VG
☐ 260	Mike Scioscia	.05	.02	.00
☐ 261	Damon Berryhill	.15	.06	.01
☐ 262	Dave Smith	.05	.02	.00
☐ 263	Willie Wilson	.10	.04	.01
☐ 264	Len Dykstra	.10	.04	.01
☐ 265	Randy Myers	.10	.04	.01
☐ 266	Keith Moreland	.05	.02	.00
☐ 267	Eric Plunk	.05	.02	.00
☐ 268	Todd Worrell	.10	.04	.01
☐ 269	Bob Walk	.05	.02	.00
☐ 270	Keith Atherton	.05	.02	.00
☐ 271	Mike Schmidt	.35	.14	.03
☐ 272	Mike Flanagan	.05	.02	.00
☐ 273	Rafael Santana	.05	.02	.00
☐ 274	Rob Thompson	.10	.04	.01
☐ 275	Rey Quinones	.05	.02	.00
☐ 276	Cecilio Guante	.05	.02	.00
☐ 277	B.J. Surhoff	.10	.04	.01
☐ 278	Chris Sabo	.75	.30	.07
☐ 279	Mitch Williams	.05	.02	.00
☐ 280	Greg Swindell	.10	.04	.01
☐ 281	Alan Trammell	.15	.06	.01
☐ 282	Storm Davis	.10	.04	.01
☐ 283	Chuck Finley	.05	.02	.00
☐ 284	Dave Stieb	.10	.04	.01
☐ 285	Scott Bailes	.05	.02	.00
☐ 286	Larry Sheets	.10	.04	.01
☐ 287	Danny Tartabull	.20	.08	.02
☐ 288	Checklist	.05	.02	.00
☐ 289	Todd Benzinger	.15	.06	.01
☐ 290	John Shelby	.05	.02	.00
☐ 291	Steve Lyons	.05	.02	.00
☐ 292	Mitch Webster	.05	.02	.00
☐ 293	Walt Terrell	.05	.02	.00
☐ 294	Pete Stanicek	.05	.02	.00
☐ 295	Chris Bosio	.05	.02	.00
☐ 296	Milt Thompson	.05	.02	.00
☐ 297	Fred Lynn	.10	.04	.01
☐ 298	Juan Berenguer	.05	.02	.00
☐ 299	Ken Dayley	.05	.02	.00
☐ 300	Joel Skinner	.05	.02	.00
☐ 301	Benito Santiago	.35	.14	.03
☐ 302	Ron Hassey	.05	.02	.00
☐ 303	Jose Uribe	.05	.02	.00
☐ 304	Harold Reynolds	.10	.04	.01
☐ 305	Dale Sveum	.05	.02	.00
☐ 306	Glenn Wilson	.05	.02	.00
☐ 307	Mike Witt	.10	.04	.01
☐ 308	Ron Robinson	.05	.02	.00

		MINT	EXC	G-VG
☐ 309	Denny Walling	.05	.02	.00
☐ 310	Joe Orsulak	.05	.02	.00
☐ 311	David Wells	.05	.02	.00
☐ 312	Steve Buechele	.05	.02	.00
☐ 313	Jose Oquendo	.05	.02	.00
☐ 314	Floyd Youmans	.05	.02	.00
☐ 315	Lou Whitaker	.10	.04	.01
☐ 316	Fernando Valenzuela	.15	.06	.01
☐ 317	Mike Boddicker	.10	.04	.01
☐ 318	Gerald Young	.10	.04	.01
☐ 319	Frank White	.10	.04	.01
☐ 320	Bill Wegman	.05	.02	.00
☐ 321	Tom Niedenfuer	.05	.02	.00
☐ 322	Ed Whitson	.05	.02	.00
☐ 323	Curt Young	.05	.02	.00
☐ 324	Greg Mathews	.05	.02	.00
☐ 325	Doug Jones	.15	.06	.01
☐ 326	Tommy Herr	.10	.04	.01
☐ 327	Kent Tekulve	.05	.02	.00
☐ 328	Rance Mulliniks	.05	.02	.00
☐ 329	Checklist	.05	.02	.00
☐ 330	Craig Lefferts	.05	.02	.00
☐ 331	Franklin Stubbs	.05	.02	.00
☐ 332	Rick Cerone	.05	.02	.00
☐ 333	Dave Schmidt	.05	.02	.00
☐ 334	Larry Parrish	.05	.02	.00
☐ 335	Tom Browning	.10	.04	.01
☐ 336	Checklist	.05	.02	.00

1989 Donruss

This 660-card set was distributed along with a puzzle of Warren Spahn. The six regular *checklist cards are numbered throughout the set as multiples of 100. Cards measure 2 ½" by 3 ½" and feature a distinctive black side border with an alternating coating. The popular Diamond King subset returns for the eighth consecutive year. Rated Rookies are featured again as cards 28-47. The Donruss '89 logo appears in the lower left corner of every obverse.*

		MINT	EXC	G-VG
	Complete Set (660)	24.00	10.00	2.40
	Common Player (1-660) ...	.03	.01	.00
☐ 1	Mike Greenwell DK .	.50	.20	.04
☐ 2	Bobby Bonilla DK ..	.15	.06	.01
☐ 3	Pete Incaviglia DK .	.12	.05	.01
☐ 4	Chris Sabo DK	.50	.20	.05
☐ 5	Robin Yount DK	.20	.08	.02
☐ 6	Tony Gwynn DK	.25	.10	.02
☐ 7	Carlton Fisk DK	.12	.05	.01
☐ 8	Cory Snyder DK	.15	.06	.01
☐ 9	David Cone DK	.25	.10	.02
☐ 10	Kevin Seitzer DK ...	.20	.08	.02
☐ 11	Rick Reuschel DK ..	.08	.03	.01
☐ 12	Johnny Ray DK	.08	.03	.01
☐ 13	Dave Schmidt DK ...	.08	.03	.01
☐ 14	Andres Galarraga DK	.15	.06	.01
☐ 15	Kirk Gibson DK	.15	.06	.01
☐ 16	Fred McGriff DK	.20	.08	.02
☐ 17	Mark Grace DK	.50	.20	.05
☐ 18	Jeff Robinson DT DK	.12	.05	.01
☐ 19	Vince Coleman DK .	.15	.06	.01
☐ 20	Dave Henderson DK	.08	.03	.01
☐ 21	Harold Reynolds DK	.08	.03	.01
☐ 22	Gerald Perry DK ...	.10	.04	.01
☐ 23	Frank Viola DK	.15	.06	.01
☐ 24	Steve Bedrosian DK	.10	.04	.01
☐ 25	Glenn Davis DK	.15	.06	.01
☐ 26	Don Mattingly DK ..	.50	.20	.05
☐ 27	DK Checklist	.06	.01	.00
☐ 28	Sandy Alomar Jr. RR	.90	.36	.09
☐ 29	Steve Searcy RR ..	.25	.10	.02
☐ 30	Cameron Drew RR .	.25	.10	.02
☐ 31	Gary Sheffield RR ..	1.50	.60	.15
☐ 32	Erik Hanson RR	.20	.08	.02
☐ 33	Ken Griffey Jr. RR .	1.25	.50	.12
☐ 34	Greg Harris RR .... San Diego Padres	.20	.08	.02
☐ 35	Gregg Jefferies RR .	2.00	.80	.20
☐ 36	Luis Medina RR ...	.45	.18	.04

☐ 37	Carlos Quintana RR	.35	.14	.03
☐ 38	Felix Jose RR	.25	.10	.02
☐ 39	Cris Carpenter RR .	.20	.08	.02
☐ 40	Ron Jones RR	.30	.12	.03
☐ 41	Dave West RR	.50	.20	.05
☐ 42	Randy Johnson RR .	.25	.10	.02
☐ 43	Mike Harkey RR ...	.50	.20	.05
☐ 44	Pete Harnisch RR .	.20	.08	.02
☐ 45	Tom Gordon RR	.30	.12	.03
☐ 46	Gregg Olson RR ...	.30	.12	.03
☐ 47	Alex Sanchez RR ..	.30	.12	.03
☐ 48	Ruben Sierra	.12	.05	.01
☐ 49	Rafael Palmeiro ...	.12	.05	.01
☐ 50	Ron Gant	.15	.06	.01
☐ 51	Cal Ripken	.15	.06	.01
☐ 52	Wally Joyner	.20	.08	.02
☐ 53	Gary Carter	.15	.06	.01
☐ 54	Andy Van Slyke ...	.12	.05	.01
☐ 55	Robin Yount	.15	.06	.01
☐ 56	Pete Incaviglia ...	.12	.05	.01
☐ 57	Greg Brock	.03	.01	.00
☐ 58	Melido Perez	.06	.02	.00
☐ 59	Craig Lefferts	.03	.01	.00
☐ 60	Gary Pettis	.03	.01	.00
☐ 61	Danny Tartabull ...	.15	.06	.01
☐ 62	Guillermo Hernandez	.06	.02	.00
☐ 63	Ozzie Smith	.12	.05	.01
☐ 64	Gary Gaetti	.10	.04	.01
☐ 65	Mark Davis	.06	.02	.00
☐ 66	Lee Smith	.06	.02	.00
☐ 67	Dennis Eckersley .	.10	.04	.01
☐ 68	Wade Boggs	.50	.20	.05
☐ 69	Mike Scott	.10	.04	.01
☐ 70	Fred McGriff	.15	.06	.01
☐ 71	Tom Browning	.08	.03	.01
☐ 72	Claudell Washington	.06	.02	.00
☐ 73	Mel Hall	.03	.01	.00
☐ 74	Don Mattingly	1.00	.40	.10
☐ 75	Steve Bedrosian ...	.08	.03	.01
☐ 76	Juan Samuel	.08	.03	.01
☐ 77	Mike Scioscia	.03	.01	.00
☐ 78	Dave Righetti	.08	.03	.01
☐ 79	Alfredo Griffin	.06	.02	.00
☐ 80	Eric Davis	.30	.12	.03
☐ 81	Juan Berenguer ...	.03	.01	.00
☐ 82	Todd Worrell	.08	.03	.01
☐ 83	Joe Carter	.10	.04	.01
☐ 84	Steve Sax	.10	.04	.01
☐ 85	Frank White	.06	.02	.00

		MINT	EXC	G-VG			MINT	EXC	G-VG
☐ 86	John Kruk	.06	.02	.00	☐ 135	Greg Walker	.06	.02	.00
☐ 87	Rance Mulliniks	.03	.01	.00	☐ 136	Kirk McCaskill	.03	.01	.00
☐ 88	Alan Ashby	.03	.01	.00	☐ 137	Shawon Dunston	.06	.02	.00
☐ 89	Charlie Leibrandt	.03	.01	.00	☐ 138	Andy Allanson	.03	.01	.00
☐ 90	Frank Tanana	.03	.01	.00	☐ 139	Rob Murphy	.03	.01	.00
☐ 91	Jose Canseco	1.00	.40	.10	☐ 140	Mike Aldrete	.03	.01	.00
☐ 92	Barry Bonds	.10	.04	.01	☐ 141	Terry Kennedy	.03	.01	.00
☐ 93	Harold Reynolds	.03	.01	.00	☐ 142	Scott Fletcher	.03	.01	.00
☐ 94	Mark McLemore	.03	.01	.00	☐ 143	Steve Balboni	.03	.01	.00
☐ 95	Mark McGwire	.50	.20	.05	☐ 144	Bret Saberhagen	.10	.04	.01
☐ 96	Eddie Murray	.15	.06	.01	☐ 145	Ozzie Virgil	.03	.01	.00
☐ 97	Tim Raines	.15	.06	.01	☐ 146	Dale Sveum	.03	.01	.00
☐ 98	Rob Thompson	.03	.01	.00	☐ 147	Darryl Strawberry	.35	.14	.03
☐ 99	Kevin McReynolds	.15	.06	.01	☐ 148	Harold Baines	.08	.03	.01
☐ 100	Checklist	.06	.01	.00	☐ 149	George Bell	.12	.05	.01
☐ 101	Carlton Fisk	.08	.03	.01	☐ 150	Dave Parker	.08	.03	.01
☐ 102	Dave Martinez	.03	.01	.00	☐ 151	Bobby Bonilla	.12	.05	.01
☐ 103	Glenn Braggs	.03	.01	.00	☐ 152	Mookie Wilson	.03	.01	.00
☐ 104	Dale Murphy	.25	.10	.02	☐ 153	Ted Power	.03	.01	.00
☐ 105	Ryne Sandberg	.15	.06	.01	☐ 154	Nolan Ryan	.20	.08	.02
☐ 106	Dennis Martinez	.03	.01	.00	☐ 155	Jeff Reardon	.06	.02	.00
☐ 107	Pete O'Brien	.06	.02	.00	☐ 156	Tim Wallach	.06	.02	.00
☐ 108	Dick Schofield	.03	.01	.00	☐ 157	Jamie Moyer	.03	.01	.00
☐ 109	Henry Cotto	.03	.01	.00	☐ 158	Rich Gossage	.08	.03	.01
☐ 110	Mike Marshall	.08	.03	.01	☐ 159	Dave Winfield	.15	.06	.01
☐ 111	Keith Moreland	.03	.01	.00	☐ 160	Von Hayes	.08	.03	.01
☐ 112	Tom Brunansky	.08	.03	.01	☐ 161	Willie McGee	.08	.03	.01
☐ 113	Kelly Gruber	.03	.01	.00	☐ 162	Rich Gedman	.06	.02	.00
☐ 114	Brook Jacoby	.06	.02	.00	☐ 163	Tony Pena	.06	.02	.00
☐ 115	Keith Brown	.10	.04	.01	☐ 164	Mike Morgan	.03	.01	.00
☐ 116	Matt Nokes	.10	.04	.01	☐ 165	Charlie Hough	.03	.01	.00
☐ 117	Keith Hernandez	.12	.05	.01	☐ 166	Mike Stanley	.03	.01	.00
☐ 118	Bob Forsch	.03	.01	.00	☐ 167	Andre Dawson	.12	.05	.01
☐ 119	Bert Blyleven	.08	.03	.01	☐ 168	Joe Boever	.08	.03	.01
☐ 120	Willie Wilson	.08	.03	.01	☐ 169	Pete Stanicek	.06	.02	.00
☐ 121	Tommy Gregg	.03	.01	.00	☐ 170	Bob Boone	.06	.02	.00
☐ 122	Jim Rice	.10	.04	.01	☐ 171	Ron Darling	.08	.03	.01
☐ 123	Bob Knepper	.03	.01	.00	☐ 172	Bob Walk	.03	.01	.00
☐ 124	Danny Jackson	.10	.04	.01	☐ 173	Rob Deer	.06	.02	.00
☐ 125	Eric Plunk	.03	.01	.00	☐ 174	Steve Buechele	.03	.01	.00
☐ 126	Brian Fisher	.03	.01	.00	☐ 175	Ted Higuera	.08	.03	.01
☐ 127	Mike Pagliarulo	.08	.03	.01	☐ 176	Ozzie Guillen	.06	.02	.00
☐ 128	Tony Gwynn	.20	.08	.02	☐ 177	Candy Maldonado	.06	.02	.00
☐ 129	Lance McCullers	.06	.02	.00	☐ 178	Doyle Alexander	.06	.02	.00
☐ 130	Andres Galarraga	.12	.05	.01	☐ 179	Mark Gubicza	.08	.03	.01
☐ 131	Jose Uribe	.03	.01	.00	☐ 180	Alan Trammell	.15	.06	.01
☐ 132	Kirk Gibson	.15	.06	.01	☐ 181	Vince Coleman	.15	.06	.01
☐ 133	David Palmer	.03	.01	.00	☐ 182	Kirby Puckett	.30	.12	.03
☐ 134	R.J. Reynolds	.03	.01	.00	☐ 183	Chris Brown	.06	.02	.00

		MINT	EXC	G-VG			MINT	EXC	G-VG
☐ 184	Marty Barrett	.06	.02	.00	☐ 233	John Franco	.08	.03	.01
☐ 185	Stan Javier	.03	.01	.00	☐ 234	Jack Morris	.10	.04	.01
☐ 186	Mike Greenwell	.75	.30	.07	☐ 235	Howard Johnson	.08	.03	.01
☐ 187	Billy Hatcher	.06	.02	.00	☐ 236	Glenn Davis	.12	.05	.01
☐ 188	Jimmy Key	.06	.02	.00	☐ 237	Frank Viola	.15	.06	.01
☐ 189	Nick Esasky	.03	.01	.00	☐ 238	Kevin Seitzer	.20	.08	.02
☐ 190	Don Slaught	.03	.01	.00	☐ 239	Gerald Perry	.08	.03	.01
☐ 191	Cory Snyder	.15	.06	.01	☐ 240	Dwight Evans	.08	.03	.01
☐ 192	John Candelaria	.06	.02	.00	☐ 241	Jim Deshaies	.03	.01	.00
☐ 193	Mike Schmidt	.20	.08	.02	☐ 242	Bo Diaz	.03	.01	.00
☐ 194	Kevin Gross	.03	.01	.00	☐ 243	Carney Lansford	.06	.02	.00
☐ 195	John Tudor	.08	.03	.01	☐ 244	Mike LaValliere	.03	.01	.00
☐ 196	Neil Allen	.03	.01	.00	☐ 245	Rickey Henderson	.20	.08	.02
☐ 197	Orel Hershiser	.25	.10	.02	☐ 246	Roberto Alomar	.20	.08	.02
☐ 198	Kal Daniels	.12	.05	.01	☐ 247	Jimmy Jones	.06	.02	.00
☐ 199	Kent Hrbek	.12	.05	.01	☐ 248	Pascual Perez	.06	.02	.00
☐ 200	Checklist	.06	.01	.00	☐ 249	Will Clark	.35	.14	.03
☐ 201	Joe Magrane	.06	.02	.00	☐ 250	Fernando Valenzuela	.12	.05	.01
☐ 202	Scott Bailes	.03	.01	.00	☐ 251	Shane Rawley	.03	.01	.00
☐ 203	Tim Belcher	.08	.03	.01	☐ 252	Sid Bream	.03	.01	.00
☐ 204	George Brett	.20	.08	.02	☐ 253	Steve Lyons	.03	.01	.00
☐ 205	Benito Santiago	.20	.08	.02	☐ 254	Brian Downing	.03	.01	.00
☐ 206	Tony Fernandez	.10	.04	.01	☐ 255	Mark Grace	.75	.30	.07
☐ 207	Gerald Young	.06	.02	.00	☐ 256	Tom Candiotti	.03	.01	.00
☐ 208	Bo Jackson	.20	.08	.02	☐ 257	Barry Larkin	.10	.04	.01
☐ 209	Chet Lemon	.03	.01	.00	☐ 258	Mike Krukow	.03	.01	.00
☐ 210	Storm Davis	.06	.02	.00	☐ 259	Billy Ripken	.03	.01	.00
☐ 211	Doug Drabek	.03	.01	.00	☐ 260	Cecilio Guante	.03	.01	.00
☐ 212	Mickey Brantley	.06	.02	.00	☐ 261	Scott Bradley	.03	.01	.00
☐ 213	Devon White	.08	.03	.01	☐ 262	Floyd Bannister	.03	.01	.00
☐ 214	Dave Stewart	.06	.02	.00	☐ 263	Pete Smith	.03	.01	.00
☐ 215	Dave Schmidt	.03	.01	.00	☐ 264	Jim Gantner	.03	.01	.00
☐ 216	Bryn Smith	.03	.01	.00	☐ 265	Roger McDowell	.06	.02	.00
☐ 217	Brett Butler	.06	.02	.00	☐ 266	Bobby Thigpen	.06	.02	.00
☐ 218	Bob Ojeda	.06	.02	.00	☐ 267	Jim Clancy	.03	.01	.00
☐ 219	Steve Rosenberg	.10	.04	.01	☐ 268	Terry Steinbach	.08	.03	.01
☐ 220	Hubie Brooks	.06	.02	.00	☐ 269	Mike Dunne	.08	.03	.01
☐ 221	B.J. Surhoff	.06	.02	.00	☐ 270	Dwight Gooden	.30	.12	.03
☐ 222	Rick Mahler	.03	.01	.00	☐ 271	Mike Heath	.03	.01	.00
☐ 223	Rick Sutcliffe	.08	.03	.01	☐ 272	Dave Smith	.03	.01	.00
☐ 224	Neal Heaton	.03	.01	.00	☐ 273	Keith Atherton	.03	.01	.00
☐ 225	Mitch Williams	.03	.01	.00	☐ 274	Tim Burke	.03	.01	.00
☐ 226	Chuck Finley	.03	.01	.00	☐ 275	Damon Berryhill	.10	.04	.01
☐ 227	Mark Langston	.08	.03	.01	☐ 276	Vance Law	.03	.01	.00
☐ 228	Jesse Orosco	.03	.01	.00	☐ 277	Rich Dotson	.06	.02	.00
☐ 229	Ed Whitson	.03	.01	.00	☐ 278	Lance Parrish	.08	.03	.01
☐ 230	Terry Pendleton	.03	.01	.00	☐ 279	Denny Walling	.03	.01	.00
☐ 231	Lloyd Moseby	.08	.03	.01	☐ 280	Roger Clemens	.35	.14	.03
☐ 232	Greg Swindell	.08	.03	.01	☐ 281	Greg Mathews	.03	.01	.00

		MINT	EXC	G-VG
☐ 282	Tom Niedenfuer ...	.03	.01	.00
☐ 283	Paul Kilgus	.03	.01	.00
☐ 284	Jose Guzman	.03	.01	.00
☐ 285	Calvin Schiraldi ...	.03	.01	.00
☐ 286	Charlie Puleo	.03	.01	.00
☐ 287	Joe Orsulak	.03	.01	.00
☐ 288	Jack Howell	.03	.01	.00
☐ 289	Kevin Elster	.06	.02	.00
☐ 290	Jose Lind	.06	.02	.00
☐ 291	Paul Molitor	.10	.04	.01
☐ 292	Cecil Espy	.10	.04	.01
☐ 293	Bill Wegman	.03	.01	.00
☐ 294	Dan Pasqua	.06	.02	.00
☐ 295	Scott Garrelts	.03	.01	.00
☐ 296	Walt Terrell	.03	.01	.00
☐ 297	Ed Hearn	.03	.01	.00
☐ 298	Lou Whitaker	.08	.03	.01
☐ 299	Ken Dayley	.03	.01	.00
☐ 300	Checklist	.06	.01	.00
☐ 301	Tommy Herr	.06	.02	.00
☐ 302	Mike Brumley	.03	.01	.00
☐ 303	Ellis Burks	.30	.12	.03
☐ 304	Curt Young	.03	.01	.00
☐ 305	Jody Reed	.08	.03	.01
☐ 306	Bill Doran	.06	.02	.00
☐ 307	David Wells	.03	.01	.00
☐ 308	Ron Robinson	.03	.01	.00
☐ 309	Rafael Santana ...	.03	.01	.00
☐ 310	Julio Franco	.06	.02	.00
☐ 311	Jack Clark	.12	.05	.01
☐ 312	Chris James	.06	.02	.00
☐ 313	Milt Thompson	.03	.01	.00
☐ 314	John Shelby	.03	.01	.00
☐ 315	Al Leiter	.15	.06	.01
☐ 316	Mike Davis	.03	.01	.00
☐ 317	Chris Sabo	1.00	.40	.10
☐ 318	Greg Gagne	.03	.01	.00
☐ 319	Jose Oquendo	.03	.01	.00
☐ 320	John Farrell	.03	.01	.00
☐ 321	Franklin Stubbs ...	.03	.01	.00
☐ 322	Kurt Stillwell	.03	.01	.00
☐ 323	Shawn Abner	.06	.02	.00
☐ 324	Mike Flanagan	.03	.01	.00
☐ 325	Kevin Bass	.06	.02	.00
☐ 326	Pat Tabler	.06	.02	.00
☐ 327	Mike Henneman ...	.03	.01	.00
☐ 328	Rick Honeycutt ...	.03	.01	.00
☐ 329	John Smiley	.03	.01	.00
☐ 330	Rey Quinones	.03	.01	.00
☐ 331	Johnny Ray	.06	.02	.00
☐ 332	Bob Welch	.06	.02	.00
☐ 333	Larry Sheets	.06	.02	.00
☐ 334	Jeff Parrett	.03	.01	.00
☐ 335	Rick Reuschel	.06	.02	.00
☐ 336	Randy Myers	.08	.03	.01
☐ 337	Ken Williams	.03	.01	.00
☐ 338	Andy McGaffigan ..	.03	.01	.00
☐ 339	Joey Meyer	.08	.03	.01
☐ 340	Dion James	.03	.01	.00
☐ 341	Les Lancaster	.03	.01	.00
☐ 342	Tom Foley	.03	.01	.00
☐ 343	Geno Petralli	.03	.01	.00
☐ 344	Dan Petry	.03	.01	.00
☐ 345	Alvin Davis	.08	.03	.01
☐ 346	Mickey Hatcher ...	.06	.02	.00
☐ 347	Marvell Wynne	.03	.01	.00
☐ 348	Danny Cox	.06	.02	.00
☐ 349	Dave Stieb	.08	.03	.01
☐ 350	Jay Bell	.03	.01	.00
☐ 351	Jeff Treadway	.06	.02	.00
☐ 352	Luis Salazar	.03	.01	.00
☐ 353	Len Dykstra	.08	.03	.01
☐ 354	Juan Agosto	.03	.01	.00
☐ 355	Gene Larkin	.08	.03	.01
☐ 356	Steve Farr	.03	.01	.00
☐ 357	Paul Assenmacher	.03	.01	.00
☐ 358	Todd Benzinger ...	.06	.02	.00
☐ 359	Larry Andersen ...	.03	.01	.00
☐ 360	Paul O'Neill	.06	.02	.00
☐ 361	Ron Hassey	.03	.01	.00
☐ 362	Jim Gott	.03	.01	.00
☐ 363	Ken Phelps	.06	.02	.00
☐ 364	Tim Flannery	.03	.01	.00
☐ 365	Randy Ready	.03	.01	.00
☐ 366	Nelson Santovenia	.10	.04	.01
☐ 367	Kelly Downs	.06	.02	.00
☐ 368	Danny Heep	.03	.01	.00
☐ 369	Phil Bradley	.06	.02	.00
☐ 370	Jeff Robinson	.03	.01	.00
	Pittsburgh Pirates			
☐ 371	Ivan Calderon	.08	.03	.01
☐ 372	Mike Witt	.08	.03	.01
☐ 373	Greg Maddux	.12	.05	.01
☐ 374	Carmen Castillo ..	.03	.01	.00
☐ 375	Jose Rijo	.03	.01	.00
☐ 376	Joe Price	.03	.01	.00
☐ 377	Rene C. Gonzales .	.03	.01	.00
☐ 378	Oddibe McDowell .	.06	.02	.00

		MINT	EXC	G-VG
☐ 379	Jim Presley	.06	.02	.00
☐ 380	Brad Wellman	.03	.01	.00
☐ 381	Tom Glavine	.03	.01	.00
☐ 382	Dan Plesac	.06	.02	.00
☐ 383	Wally Backman	.03	.01	.00
☐ 384	Dave Gallagher	.15	.06	.01
☐ 385	Tom Henke	.06	.02	.00
☐ 386	Luis Polonia	.03	.01	.00
☐ 387	Junior Ortiz	.03	.01	.00
☐ 388	David Cone	.30	.12	.03
☐ 389	Dave Bergman	.03	.01	.00
☐ 390	Danny Darwin	.03	.01	.00
☐ 391	Dan Gladden	.06	.02	.00
☐ 392	John Dopson	.15	.06	.01
☐ 393	Frank DiPino	.03	.01	.00
☐ 394	Al Nipper	.03	.01	.00
☐ 395	Willie Randolph	.06	.02	.00
☐ 396	Don Carman	.03	.01	.00
☐ 397	Scott Terry	.03	.01	.00
☐ 398	Rick Cerone	.03	.01	.00
☐ 399	Tom Pagnozzi	.03	.01	.00
☐ 400	Checklist	.06	.01	.00
☐ 401	Mickey Tettleton	.03	.01	.00
☐ 402	Curtis Wilkerson	.03	.01	.00
☐ 403	Jeff Russell	.03	.01	.00
☐ 404	Pat Perry	.03	.01	.00
☐ 405	Jose Alvarez	.10	.04	.01
☐ 406	Rick Schu	.03	.01	.00
☐ 407	Sherman Corbett	.10	.04	.01
☐ 408	Dave Magadan	.08	.03	.01
☐ 409	Bob Kipper	.03	.01	.00
☐ 410	Don August	.08	.03	.01
☐ 411	Bob Brower	.06	.02	.00
☐ 412	Chris Bosio	.03	.01	.00
☐ 413	Jerry Reuss	.03	.01	.00
☐ 414	Atlee Hammaker	.03	.01	.00
☐ 415	Jim Walewander	.10	.04	.01
☐ 416	Mike Macfarlane	.12	.05	.01
☐ 417	Pat Sheridan	.03	.01	.00
☐ 418	Pedro Guerrero	.10	.04	.01
☐ 419	Allan Anderson	.06	.02	.00
☐ 420	Mark Parent	.12	.05	.01
☐ 421	Bob Stanley	.03	.01	.00
☐ 422	Mike Gallego	.03	.01	.00
☐ 423	Bruce Hurst	.08	.03	.01
☐ 424	Dave Meads	.03	.01	.00
☐ 425	Jesse Barfield	.10	.04	.01
☐ 426	Rob Dibble	.12	.05	.01
☐ 427	Joel Skinner	.03	.01	.00

		MINT	EXC	G-VG
☐ 428	Ron Kittle	.08	.03	.01
☐ 429	Rick Rhoden	.03	.01	.00
☐ 430	Bob Dernier	.03	.01	.00
☐ 431	Steve Jeltz	.03	.01	.00
☐ 432	Rick Dempsey	.03	.01	.00
☐ 433	Roberto Kelly	.12	.05	.01
☐ 434	Dave Anderson	.03	.01	.00
☐ 435	Herm Winningham	.03	.01	.00
☐ 436	Al Newman	.03	.01	.00
☐ 437	Jose DeLeon	.03	.01	.00
☐ 438	Doug Jones	.06	.02	.00
☐ 439	Brian Holton	.03	.01	.00
☐ 440	Jeff Montgomery	.08	.03	.01
☐ 441	Dickie Thon	.03	.01	.00
☐ 442	Cecil Fielder	.03	.01	.00
☐ 443	John Fishel	.12	.05	.01
☐ 444	Jerry Don Gleaton	.03	.01	.00
☐ 445	Paul Gibson	.12	.05	.01
☐ 446	Walt Weiss	.50	.20	.05
☐ 447	Glenn Wilson	.03	.01	.00
☐ 448	Mike Moore	.03	.01	.00
☐ 449	Chili Davis	.06	.02	.00
☐ 450	Dave Henderson	.06	.02	.00
☐ 451	Jose Bautista	.10	.04	.01
☐ 452	Rex Hudler	.03	.01	.00
☐ 453	Bob Brenly	.03	.01	.00
☐ 454	Mackey Sasser	.10	.04	.01
☐ 455	Daryl Boston	.03	.01	.00
☐ 456	Mike Fitzgerald	.03	.01	.00
	Montreal Expos			
☐ 457	Jeffrey Leonard	.06	.02	.00
☐ 458	Bruce Sutter	.08	.03	.01
☐ 459	Mitch Webster	.03	.01	.00
☐ 460	Joe Hesketh	.03	.01	.00
☐ 461	Bobby Witt	.06	.02	.00
☐ 462	Stew Cliburn	.03	.01	.00
☐ 463	Scott Bankhead	.03	.01	.00
☐ 464	Ramon Martinez	.30	.12	.03
☐ 465	Dave Leiper	.03	.01	.00
☐ 466	Luis Alicea	.12	.05	.01
☐ 467	John Cerutti	.03	.01	.00
☐ 468	Ron Washington	.03	.01	.00
☐ 469	Jeff Reed	.03	.01	.00
☐ 470	Jeff Robinson	.06	.02	.00
	Detroit Tigers			
☐ 471	Sid Fernandez	.08	.03	.01
☐ 472	Terry Puhl	.03	.01	.00
☐ 473	Charlie Lea	.03	.01	.00
☐ 474	Israel Sanchez	.08	.03	.01

	MINT	EXC	G-VG			MINT	EXC	G-VG
☐ 475 Bruce Benedict	.03	.01	.00	☐ 524	Oswald Peraza	.10	.04	.01
☐ 476 Oil Can Boyd	.06	.02	.00	☐ 525	Bryan Harvey	.25	.10	.02
☐ 477 Craig Reynolds	.03	.01	.00	☐ 526	Rick Aguilera	.03	.01	.00
☐ 478 Frank Williams	.03	.01	.00	☐ 527	Tom Prince	.06	.02	.00
☐ 479 Greg Cadaret	.03	.01	.00	☐ 528	Mark Clear	.03	.01	.00
☐ 480 Randy Kramer	.12	.05	.01	☐ 529	Jerry Browne	.03	.01	.00
☐ 481 Dave Eiland	.12	.05	.01	☐ 530	Juan Castillo	.03	.01	.00
☐ 482 Eric Show	.03	.01	.00	☐ 531	Jack McDowell	.08	.03	.01
☐ 483 Garry Templeton	.06	.02	.00	☐ 532	Chris Speier	.03	.01	.00
☐ 484 Wallace Johnson	.03	.01	.00	☐ 533	Darrell Evans	.06	.02	.00
☐ 485 Kevin Mitchell	.06	.02	.00	☐ 534	Luis Aquino	.03	.01	.00
☐ 486 Tim Crews	.03	.01	.00	☐ 535	Eric King	.03	.01	.00
☐ 487 Mike Maddux	.03	.01	.00	☐ 536	Ken Hill	.12	.05	.01
☐ 488 Dave LaPoint	.03	.01	.00	☐ 537	Randy Bush	.03	.01	.00
☐ 489 Fred Manrique	.03	.01	.00	☐ 538	Shane Mack	.06	.02	.00
☐ 490 Greg Minton	.03	.01	.00	☐ 539	Tom Bolton	.08	.03	.01
☐ 491 Doug Dascenzo	.15	.06	.01	☐ 540	Gene Nelson	.03	.01	.00
☐ 492 Willie Upshaw	.03	.01	.00	☐ 541	Wes Gardner	.03	.01	.00
☐ 493 Jack Armstrong	.20	.08	.02	☐ 542	Ken Caminiti	.03	.01	.00
☐ 494 Kirt Manwaring	.03	.01	.00	☐ 543	Duane Ward	.03	.01	.00
☐ 495 Jeff Ballard	.03	.01	.00	☐ 544	Norm Charlton	.12	.05	.01
☐ 496 Jeff Kunkel	.03	.01	.00	☐ 545	Hal Morris	.15	.06	.01
☐ 497 Mike Campbell	.03	.01	.00	☐ 546	Rich Yett	.03	.01	.00
☐ 498 Gary Thurman	.03	.01	.00	☐ 547	Hensley Meulens	.85	.34	.08
☐ 499 Zane Smith	.06	.02	.00	☐ 548	Greg Harris	.03	.01	.00
☐ 500 Checklist	.06	.01	.00		Philadelphia Phillies			
☐ 501 Mike Birkbeck	.03	.01	.00	☐ 549	Darren Daulton	.03	.01	.00
☐ 502 Terry Leach	.06	.02	.00	☐ 550	Jeff Hamilton	.03	.01	.00
☐ 503 Shawn Hillegas	.03	.01	.00	☐ 551	Luis Aguayo	.03	.01	.00
☐ 504 Manny Lee	.03	.01	.00	☐ 552	Tim Leary	.06	.02	.00
☐ 505 Doug Jennings	.20	.08	.02	☐ 553	Ron Oester	.03	.01	.00
☐ 506 Ken Oberkfell	.03	.01	.00	☐ 554	Steve Lombardozzi	.03	.01	.00
☐ 507 Tim Teufel	.03	.01	.00	☐ 555	Tim Jones	.15	.06	.01
☐ 508 Tom Brookens	.03	.01	.00	☐ 556	Bud Black	.03	.01	.00
☐ 509 Rafael Ramirez	.03	.01	.00	☐ 557	Alejandro Pena	.03	.01	.00
☐ 510 Fred Toliver	.03	.01	.00	☐ 558	Jose DeJesus	.10	.04	.01
☐ 511 Brian Holman	.10	.04	.01	☐ 559	Dennis Rasmussen	.06	.02	.00
☐ 512 Mike Bielecki	.03	.01	.00	☐ 560	Pat Borders	.12	.05	.01
☐ 513 Jeff Pico	.10	.04	.01	☐ 561	Craig Biggio	.12	.05	.01
☐ 514 Charles Hudson	.03	.01	.00	☐ 562	Luis De Los Santos	.25	.10	.02
☐ 515 Bruce Ruffin	.03	.01	.00	☐ 563	Fred Lynn	.08	.03	.01
☐ 516 Larry McWilliams	.03	.01	.00	☐ 564	Todd Burns	.20	.08	.02
☐ 517 Jeff Sellers	.03	.01	.00	☐ 565	Felix Fermin	.03	.01	.00
☐ 518 John Costello	.10	.04	.01	☐ 566	Darnell Coles	.03	.01	.00
☐ 519 Brady Anderson	.20	.08	.02	☐ 567	Willie Fraser	.03	.01	.00
☐ 520 Craig McMurtry	.03	.01	.00	☐ 568	Glenn Hubbard	.03	.01	.00
☐ 521 Ray Hayward	.03	.01	.00	☐ 569	Craig Worthington	.25	.10	.02
☐ 522 Drew Hall	.03	.01	.00	☐ 570	Johnny Paredes	.10	.04	.01
☐ 523 Mark Lemke	.20	.08	.02	☐ 571	Don Robinson	.03	.01	.00

		MINT	EXC	G-VG
☐ 572	Barry Lyons	.03	.01	.00
☐ 573	Bill Long	.03	.01	.00
☐ 574	Tracy Jones	.06	.02	.00
☐ 575	Juan Nieves	.03	.01	.00
☐ 576	Andres Thomas	.03	.01	.00
☐ 577	Rolando Roomes	.15	.06	.01
☐ 578	Luis Rivera	.03	.01	.00
☐ 579	Chad Kreuter	.15	.06	.01
☐ 580	Tony Armas	.06	.02	.00
☐ 581	Jay Buhner	.10	.04	.01
☐ 582	Ricky Horton	.03	.01	.00
☐ 583	Andy Hawkins	.03	.01	.00
☐ 584	Sil Campusano	.25	.10	.02
☐ 585	Dave Clark	.06	.02	.00
☐ 586	Van Snider	.25	.10	.02
☐ 587	Todd Frohwirth	.03	.01	.00
☐ 588	Puzzle Card	.03	.01	.00
	Warren Spahn			
☐ 589	William Brennan	.12	.05	.01
☐ 590	German Gonzalez	.10	.04	.01
☐ 591	Ernie Whitt	.03	.01	.00
☐ 592	Jeff Blauser	.03	.01	.00
☐ 593	Spike Owen	.03	.01	.00
☐ 594	Matt Williams	.08	.03	.01
☐ 595	Lloyd McClendon	.03	.01	.00
☐ 596	Steve Ontiveros	.03	.01	.00
☐ 597	Scott Medvin	.12	.05	.01
☐ 598	Hipolito Pena	.12	.05	.01
☐ 599	Jerald Clark	.20	.08	.02
☐ 600	Checklist	.06	.01	.00
☐ 601	Carmelo Martinez	.03	.01	.00
☐ 602	Mike LaCoss	.03	.01	.00
☐ 603	Mike Devereaux	.08	.03	.01
☐ 604	Alex Madrid	.15	.06	.01
☐ 605	Gary Redus	.03	.01	.00
☐ 606	Lance Johnson	.03	.01	.00
☐ 607	Terry Clark	.15	.06	.01
☐ 608	Manny Trillo	.03	.01	.00
☐ 609	Scott Jordan	.12	.05	.01
☐ 610	Jay Howell	.03	.01	.00
☐ 611	Francisco Melendez	.15	.06	.01
☐ 612	Mike Boddicker	.06	.02	.00
☐ 613	Kevin Brown	.03	.01	.00
☐ 614	Dave Valle	.03	.01	.00
☐ 615	Tim Laudner	.03	.01	.00
☐ 616	Andy Nezelek	.12	.05	.01
☐ 617	Chuck Crim	.03	.01	.00
☐ 618	Jack Savage	.08	.03	.01
☐ 619	Adam Peterson	.08	.03	.01
☐ 620	Todd Stottlemyre	.08	.03	.01
☐ 621	Lance Blankenship	.15	.06	.01
☐ 622	Miguel Garcia	.10	.04	.01
☐ 623	Keith Miller	.03	.01	.00
	New York Mets			
☐ 624	Ricky Jordan	1.25	.50	.12
☐ 625	Ernest Riles	.03	.01	.00
☐ 626	John Moses	.03	.01	.00
☐ 627	Nelson Liriano	.03	.01	.00
☐ 628	Mike Smithson	.03	.01	.00
☐ 629	Scott Sanderson	.03	.01	.00
☐ 630	Dale Mohorcic	.03	.01	.00
☐ 631	Marvin Freeman	.03	.01	.00
☐ 632	Mike Young	.03	.01	.00
☐ 633	Dennis Lamp	.03	.01	.00
☐ 634	Dante Bichette	.20	.08	.01
☐ 635	Curt Schilling	.12	.05	.01
☐ 636	Scott May	.12	.05	.01
☐ 637	Mike Schooler	.15	.06	.01
☐ 638	Rick Leach	.03	.01	.00
☐ 639	Tom Lampkin	.12	.05	.01
☐ 640	Brian Meyer	.12	.05	.01
☐ 641	Brian Harper	.03	.01	.00
☐ 642	John Smoltz	.25	.10	.02
☐ 643	Jose: 40/40 Club	.30	.12	.03
	(Jose Canseco)			
☐ 644	Bill Schroeder	.03	.01	.00
☐ 645	Edgar Martinez	.10	.04	.01
☐ 646	Dennis Cook	.12	.05	.01
☐ 647	Barry Jones	.03	.01	.00
☐ 648	Orel: 59 and Counting	.15	.06	.01
	(Orel Hershiser)			
☐ 649	Rod Nichols	.12	.05	.01
☐ 650	Jody Davis	.06	.02	.00
☐ 651	Bob Milacki	.25	.10	.02
☐ 652	Mike Jackson	.03	.01	.00
☐ 653	Derek Lilliquist	.15	.06	.01
☐ 654	Paul Mirabella	.03	.01	.00
☐ 655	Mike Diaz	.03	.01	.00
☐ 656	Jeff Musselman	.03	.01	.00
☐ 657	Jerry Reed	.03	.01	.00
☐ 658	Kevin Blankenship	.20	.08	.01
☐ 659	Wayne Tolleson	.03	.01	.00
☐ 660	Eric Hetzel	.15	.06	.01

1989 Donruss Bonus MVP's

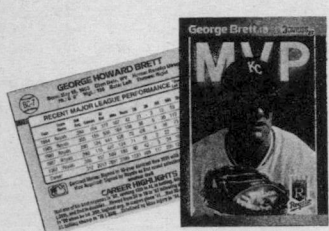

This 26-card set was distributed along with the regular 1989 Donruss issue as random inserts with the rack and wax packs. These bonus cards are numbered with the prefix BC for bonus cards and were supposedly produced in the same quantities as the other 660 regular issue cards. The "most valuable" player was selected from each of the 26 teams. Cards measure 2 ½" by 3 ½" and feature the same distinctive side border as the regular issue. The cards are distinguished by the bold MVP logo in the upper background of the obverse.

	MINT	EXC	G-VG
Complete Set (26)	10.00	4.00	1.00
Common Card (BC1-BC26)	.10	.04	.01

		MINT	EXC	G-VG
☐ BC1	Kirby Puckett	.35	.14	.03
☐ BC2	Mike Scott	.15	.06	.01
☐ BC3	Joe Carter	.20	.08	.02
☐ BC4	Orel Hershiser ..	.30	.12	.03
☐ BC5	Jose Canseco ...	1.00	.40	.10
☐ BC6	Darryl Strawberry	.50	.20	.05
☐ BC7	George Brett ...	.25	.10	.02
☐ BC8	Andre Dawson ...	.15	.06	.01
☐ BC9	Paul Molitor	.15	.06	.01
☐ BC10	Andy Van Slyke ..	.15	.06	.01
☐ BC11	Dave Winfield ...	.25	.10	.02
☐ BC12	Kevin Gross	.10	.04	.01
☐ BC13	Mike Greenwell ..	.60	.24	.06
☐ BC14	Ozzie Smith	.20	.08	.02
☐ BC15	Cal Ripken	.20	.08	.02
☐ BC16	Andres Galarraga	.15	.06	.01

		MINT	EXC	G-VG
☐ BC17	Alan Trammell ..	.15	.06	.01
☐ BC18	Kal Daniels	.15	.06	.01
☐ BC19	Fred McGriff	.15	.06	.01
☐ BC20	Tony Gwynn	.25	.10	.02
☐ BC21	Wally Joyner ...	.25	.10	.02
☐ BC22	Will Clark	.40	.16	.04
☐ BC23	Ozzie Guillen ...	.10	.04	.01
☐ BC24	Gerald Perry ...	.10	.04	.01
☐ BC25	Alvin Davis	.10	.04	.01
☐ BC26	Ruben Sierra ...	.15	.06	.01

1959 Fleer

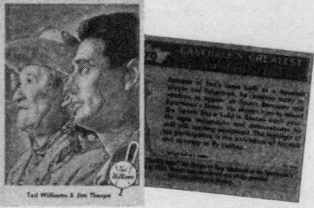

Ted Williams & Jim Thorpe

The cards in this 80-card set measure 2 ½" by 3 ½". The 1959 Fleer set, designated as R418-1 in the ACC, portrays the life of Ted Williams. The wording of the wrapper, "Baseball's Greatest Series," has led to speculation that Fleer contemplated similar sets honoring other baseball immortals, but chose to develop instead the format of the 1960 and 1961 issues. Card number 68, which was withdrawn early in production, is considered scarce and has even been counterfeited; the fake has a rosy coloration and a cross-hatch pattern visible over the picture area.

	NRMT	VG-E	GOOD
Complete Set (80)	375.00	150.00	37.00
Common Cards (1-80) ...	1.75	.70	.17

			NRMT	VG-E	GOOD
☐ 1	The Early Years ..	9.00	1.00	.25

		NRMT	VG-E	GOOD				NRMT	VG-E	GOOD
☐	2 Ted's Idol Babe Ruth	5.00	2.00	.50	☐	47 Ted Crash Lands Jet	1.75	.70	.17
☐	3 Practice Makes .... Perfect	1.75	.70	.17	☐	48 1953 Ted Returns .	1.75	.70	.17
					☐	49 Smash Return	1.75	.70	.17
☐	4 Learns Fine Points .	1.75	.70	.17	☐	50 1954 Spring Injury .	1.75	.70	.17
☐	5 Ted's Fame Spreads	1.75	.70	.17	☐	51 Ted is Patched Up	1.75	.70	.17
☐	6 Ted Turns Pro	1.75	.70	.17	☐	52 1954 Ted's Comeback	1.75	.70	.17
☐	7 From Mound to Plate	1.75	.70	.17	☐	53 Comeback is Success	1.75	.70	.17
☐	8 1937 First Full ..... Season	1.75	.70	.17	☐	54 Ted Hooks Big One	1.75	.70	.17
					☐	55 Retirement "No Go"	1.75	.70	.17
☐	9 First Step to Majors	1.75	.70	.17	☐	56 2000th Hit	1.75	.70	.17
☐	10 Gunning as Pastime	1.75	.70	.17	☐	57 400th Homer	1.75	.70	.17
☐	11 First Spring Training (with Jimmie Foxx)	3.00	1.20	.30	☐	58 Williams Hits .388 .	1.75	.70	.17
					☐	59 Hot September for Ted	1.75	.70	.17
☐	12 Burning Up Minors .	1.75	.70	.17	☐	60 More Records for Ted	1.75	.70	.17
☐	13 1939 Shows Will Stay	1.75	.70	.17	☐	61 1957 Outfielder Ted	1.75	.70	.17
☐	14 Outstanding Rookie '39	1.75	.70	.17	☐	62 1958 Sixth Batting . Title	1.75	.70	.17
☐	15 Licks Sophomore Jinx	1.75	.70	.17					
☐	16 1941 Greatest Year	1.75	.70	.17	☐	63 Ted's All-Star Record	1.75	.70	.17
☐	17 How Ted Hit .400 ..	1.75	.70	.17	☐	64 Daughter and Daddy	1.75	.70	.17
☐	18 1941 All Star Hero .	1.75	.70	.17	☐	65 1958 August 30 ...	1.75	.70	.17
☐	19 Ted Wins Triple Crown	1.75	.70	.17	☐	66 1958 Powerhouse ..	1.75	.70	.17
☐	20 On to Naval Training	1.75	.70	.17	☐	67 Two Famous Fishermen	3.00	1.20	.30
☐	21 Honors for Williams .	1.75	.70	.17					
☐	22 1944 Ted Solos	1.75	.70	.17	☐	68 Ted Signs for 1959	225.00	90.00	22.00
☐	23 Williams Wins Wings	1.75	.70	.17	☐	69 A Future Ted Williams	1.75	.70	.17
☐	24 1945 Sharpshooter .	1.75	.70	.17	☐	70 Williams and Thorpe	3.00	1.20	.30
☐	25 1945 Ted Discharged	1.75	.70	.17	☐	71 Hitting Fund. 1	1.75	.70	.17
☐	26 Off to Flying Start ..	1.75	.70	.17	☐	72 Hitting Fund. 2	1.75	.70	.17
☐	27 7/9/46 One Man Show	1.75	.70	.17	☐	73 Hitting Fund. 3	1.75	.70	.17
☐	28 The Williams Shift ..	1.75	.70	.17	☐	74 Here's How	1.75	.70	.17
☐	29 Ted Hits for Cycle ..	1.75	.70	.17	☐	75 Williams' Value to . Sox	1.75	.70	.17
☐	30 Beating Williams ... Shift	1.75	.70	.17					
					☐	76 On Base Record ..	1.75	.70	.17
☐	31 Sox Lose Series ...	1.75	.70	.17	☐	77 Ted Relaxes	1.75	.70	.17
☐	32 Most Valuable Player	1.75	.70	.17	☐	78 Honors for Williams	1.75	.70	.17
☐	33 Another Triple Crown	1.75	.70	.17	☐	79 Where Ted Stands	1.75	.70	.17
☐	34 Runs Scored Record	1.75	.70	.17	☐	80 Ted's Goals for 1959	3.00	1.20	.30
☐	35 Sox Miss Pennant ..	1.75	.70	.17					
☐	36 Banner Year for Ted	1.75	.70	.17					
☐	37 1949 Sox Miss Again	1.75	.70	.17					
☐	38 1949 Power Rampage	1.75	.70	.17					
☐	39 1950 Great Start ...	1.75	.70	.17					
☐	40 Ted Crashes into Wall	1.75	.70	.17					
☐	41 1950 Ted Recovers	1.75	.70	.17					
☐	42 Slowed by Injury ...	1.75	.70	.17					
☐	43 Double Play Lead ..	1.75	.70	.17					
☐	44 Back to Marines ...	1.75	.70	.17					
☐	45 Farewell to Baseball	1.75	.70	.17					
☐	46 Ready for Combat ..	1.75	.70	.17					

1960 Fleer

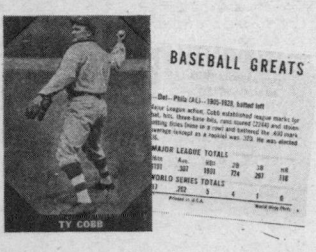

BASEBALL GREATS

*The cards in this 79-card set measure 2 ½"
by 3 ½". The cards from the 1960 Fleer
series of Baseball Greats are sometimes
mistaken for 1930s cards by collectors not
familiar with this set. The cards each contain
a tinted photo of a baseball immortal, and
were issued in one series. There are no
known scarcities, although a number 80 card
(Pepper Martin reverse with either a Tinker,
Collins, or Grove obverse) exists (this is not
considered part of the set). The catalog
designation for 1960 Fleer is R418-2.*

		NRMT	VG-E	GOOD
	Complete Set (79)	200.00	80.00	20.00
	Common Player (1-79)	1.25	.50	.12
☐ 1	Napoleon Lajoie	9.00	2.00	.40
☐ 2	Christy Mathewson	5.00	2.00	.50
☐ 3	George H. Ruth	25.00	10.00	2.50
☐ 4	Carl Hubbell	2.00	.80	.20
☐ 5	Grover Alexander	2.00	.80	.20
☐ 6	Walter P. Johnson	5.00	2.00	.50
☐ 7	Charles A. Bender	1.25	.50	.12
☐ 8	Roger P. Bresnahan	1.25	.50	.12
☐ 9	Mordecai P. Brown	1.25	.50	.12
☐ 10	Tristram Speaker	2.00	.80	.20
☐ 11	Joseph (Arky) Vaughan	1.25	.50	.12
☐ 12	Zachariah Wheat	1.25	.50	.12
☐ 13	George Sisler	1.25	.50	.12
☐ 14	Connie Mack	2.00	.80	.20
☐ 15	Clark C. Griffith	1.25	.50	.12
☐ 16	Louis Boudreau	2.00	.80	.20
☐ 17	Ernest Lombardi	1.25	.50	.12

		NRMT	VG-E	GOOD
☐ 18	Henry Manush	1.25	.50	.12
☐ 19	Martin Marion	1.25	.50	.12
☐ 20	Edward Collins	1.25	.50	.12
☐ 21	James Maranville	1.25	.50	.12
☐ 22	Joseph Medwick	1.25	.50	.12
☐ 23	Edward Barrow	1.25	.50	.12
☐ 24	Gordon Cochrane	2.00	.80	.20
☐ 25	James J. Collins	1.25	.50	.12
☐ 26	Robert Feller	5.00	2.00	.50
☐ 27	Lucius Appling	2.00	.80	.20
☐ 28	Lou Gehrig	12.00	5.00	1.20
☐ 29	Charles Hartnett	1.25	.50	.12
☐ 30	Charles Klein	1.25	.50	.12
☐ 31	Anthony Lazzeri	1.25	.50	.12
☐ 32	Aloysius Simmons	1.25	.50	.12
☐ 33	Wilbert Robinson	1.25	.50	.12
☐ 34	Edgar Rice	1.25	.50	.12
☐ 35	Herbert Pennock	1.25	.50	.12
☐ 36	Melvin Ott	2.00	.80	.20
☐ 37	Frank O'Doul	1.25	.50	.12
☐ 38	John Mize	2.00	.80	.20
☐ 39	Edmund Miller	1.25	.50	.12
☐ 40	Joseph Tinker	1.25	.50	.12
☐ 41	John Baker	1.25	.50	.12
☐ 42	Tyrus Cobb	12.00	5.00	1.20
☐ 43	Paul Derringer	1.25	.50	.12
☐ 44	Adrian Anson	1.25	.50	.12
☐ 45	James Bottomley	1.25	.50	.12
☐ 46	Edward S. Plank	1.25	.50	.12
☐ 47	Denton (Cy) Young	3.50	1.40	.35
☐ 48	Hack Wilson	2.00	.80	.20
☐ 49	Edward Walsh	1.25	.50	.12
☐ 50	Frank Chance	1.25	.50	.12
☐ 51	Arthur Vance	1.25	.50	.12
☐ 52	William Terry	2.00	.80	.20
☐ 53	James Foxx	3.00	1.20	.30
☐ 54	Vernon Gomez	2.00	.80	.20
☐ 55	Branch Rickey	1.25	.50	.12
☐ 56	Raymond Schalk	1.25	.50	.12
☐ 57	John Evers	1.25	.50	.12
☐ 58	Charles Gehringer	2.00	.80	.20
☐ 59	Burleigh Grimes	1.25	.50	.12
☐ 60	Robert (Lefty) Grove	2.50	1.00	.25
☐ 61	George Waddell	1.25	.50	.12
☐ 62	John (Honus) Wagner	5.00	2.00	.50
☐ 63	Charles (Red) Ruffing	1.25	.50	.12
☐ 64	Kenesaw M. Landis	1.25	.50	.12
☐ 65	Harry Heilmann	1.25	.50	.12
☐ 66	John McGraw	2.00	.80	.20

		NRMT	VG-E	GOOD
☐	67 Hugh Jennings	1.25	.50	.12
☐	68 Harold Newhouser .	1.25	.50	.12
☐	69 Waite Hoyt	1.25	.50	.12
☐	70 Louis (Bobo) Newsom	1.25	.50	.12
☐	71 Howard (Earl) Averill	1.25	.50	.12
☐	72 Theodore Williams .	20.00	8.00	2.00
☐	73 Warren Giles	1.25	.50	.12
☐	74 Ford Frick	1.25	.50	.12
☐	75 Hazen (Kiki) Cuyler .	1.25	.50	.12
☐	76 Paul Waner	1.25	.50	.12
☐	77 Harold (Pie) Traynor	1.25	.50	.12
☐	78 Lloyd Waner	1.25	.50	.12
☐	79 Ralph Kiner	2.50	1.00	.25
☐	80 Pepper Martin *	150.00	60.00	15.00
	(Collins, Tinker, or Grove pictured)			

1961 Fleer

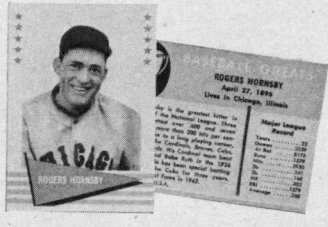

The cards in this 154-card set measure 2 ½" by 3 ½". In 1961, Fleer continued its Baseball Greats format by issuing this series of cards. The set was released in two distinct series, 1-88 and 89-154 (of which the last is more difficult to obtain). The players within each series are conveniently numbered in alphabetical order. It appears that this set continued to be issued the following year by Fleer. The catalog number for this set is F418-3.

	NRMT	VG-E	GOOD
Complete Set (154)	400.00	160.00	40.00
Common Player (1-88)	1.25	.50	.12
Common Player (89-154) ..	2.50	1.00	.25

		NRMT	VG-E	GOOD
☐	1 Baker/Cobb/Wheat	12.00	2.00	.40
	(checklist back)			
☐	2 Grover C. Alexander	2.00	.80	.20
☐	3 Nick Altrock	1.25	.50	.12
☐	4 Cap Anson	1.25	.50	.12
☐	5 Earl Averill	1.25	.50	.12
☐	6 Frank Baker	1.25	.50	.12
☐	7 Dave Bancroft	1.25	.50	.12
☐	8 Chief Bender	1.25	.50	.12
☐	9 Jim Bottomley	1.25	.50	.12
☐	10 Roger Bresnahan ..	1.25	.50	.12
☐	11 Mordecai Brown ...	1.25	.50	.12
☐	12 Max Carey	1.25	.50	.12
☐	13 Jack Chesbro	1.25	.50	.12
☐	14 Ty Cobb	12.00	5.00	1.20
☐	15 Mickey Cochrane ..	2.00	.80	.20
☐	16 Eddie Collins	1.25	.50	.12
☐	17 Earle Combs	1.25	.50	.12
☐	18 Charles Comiskey .	1.25	.50	.12
☐	19 Kiki Cuyler	1.25	.50	.12
☐	20 Paul Derringer	1.25	.50	.12
☐	21 Howard Ehmke	1.25	.50	.12
☐	22 W. Evans	1.25	.50	.12
☐	23 Johnny Evers	1.25	.50	.12
☐	24 Urban Faber	1.25	.50	.12
☐	25 Bob Feller	5.00	2.00	.50
☐	26 Wes Ferrell	1.25	.50	.12
☐	27 Lew Fonseca	1.25	.50	.12
☐	28 Jimmy Foxx	3.00	1.20	.30
☐	29 Ford Frick	1.25	.50	.12
☐	30 Frank Frisch	2.00	.80	.20
☐	31 Lou Gehrig	12.00	5.00	1.20
☐	32 Charlie Gehringer ..	2.00	.80	.20
☐	33 Warren Giles	1.25	.50	.12
☐	34 Lefty Gomez	2.00	.80	.20
☐	35 Goose Goslin	1.25	.50	.12
☐	36 Clark Griffith	1.25	.50	.12
☐	37 Burleigh Grimes ...	1.25	.50	.12
☐	38 Lefty Grove	2.50	1.00	.25
☐	39 Chick Hafey	1.25	.50	.12
☐	40 Jesse Haines	1.25	.50	.12
☐	41 Gabby Hartnett ...	1.25	.50	.12
☐	42 Harry Heilmann ...	1.25	.50	.12
☐	43 Rogers Hornsby ..	3.00	1.20	.30
☐	44 Waite Hoyt	1.25	.50	.12
☐	45 Carl Hubbell	2.00	.80	.20
☐	46 Miller Huggins	1.25	.50	.12
☐	47 Hugh Jennings ...	1.25	.50	.12
☐	48 Ban Johnson	1.25	.50	.12
☐	49 Walter Johnson ...	5.00	2.00	.50

		NRMT	VG-E	GOOD			NRMT	VG-E	GOOD
☐ 50	Ralph Kiner	2.50	1.00	.25	☐ 98	Frank Chance	3.50	1.40	.35
☐ 51	Chuck Klein	1.25	.50	.12	☐ 99	Jimmy Collins	3.50	1.40	.35
☐ 52	Johnny Kling	1.25	.50	.12	☐ 100	Stan Coveleskie	3.50	1.40	.35
☐ 53	K.M. Landis	1.25	.50	.12	☐ 101	Hugh Critz	2.50	1.00	.25
☐ 54	Tony Lazzeri	1.25	.50	.12	☐ 102	Alvin Crowder	2.50	1.00	.25
☐ 55	Ernie Lombardi	1.25	.50	.12	☐ 103	Joe Dugan	2.50	1.00	.25
☐ 56	Dolf Luque	1.25	.50	.12	☐ 104	Bibb Falk	2.50	1.00	.25
☐ 57	Heine Manush	1.25	.50	.12	☐ 105	Rick Ferrell	3.50	1.40	.35
☐ 58	Marty Marion	1.25	.50	.12	☐ 106	Art Fletcher	2.50	1.00	.25
☐ 59	Christy Mathewson	5.00	2.00	.50	☐ 107	Dennis Galehouse	2.50	1.00	.25
☐ 60	John McGraw	2.00	.80	.20	☐ 108	Chick Galloway	2.50	1.00	.25
☐ 61	Joe Medwick	1.25	.50	.12	☐ 109	Mule Haas	2.50	1.00	.25
☐ 62	F. (Ring) Miller	1.25	.50	.12	☐ 110	Stan Hack	2.50	1.00	.25
☐ 63	Johnny Mize	2.00	.80	.20	☐ 111	Bump Hadley	2.50	1.00	.25
☐ 64	John Mostil	1.25	.50	.12	☐ 112	Billy B. Hamilton	3.50	1.40	.35
☐ 65	Art Nehf	1.25	.50	.12	☐ 113	Joe Hauser	2.50	1.00	.25
☐ 66	Hal Newhouser	1.25	.50	.12	☐ 114	Babe Herman	2.50	1.00	.25
☐ 67	D. (Bobo) Newsom	1.25	.50	.12	☐ 115	Travis Jackson	4.50	1.80	.45
☐ 68	Mel Ott	2.00	.80	.20	☐ 116	Eddie Joost	2.50	1.00	.25
☐ 69	Allie Reynolds	1.25	.50	.12	☐ 117	Addie Joss	4.50	1.80	.45
☐ 70	Sam Rice	1.25	.50	.12	☐ 118	Joe Judge	2.50	1.00	.25
☐ 71	Eppa Rixey	1.25	.50	.12	☐ 119	Joe Kuhel	2.50	1.00	.25
☐ 72	Edd Roush	1.25	.50	.12	☐ 120	Napoleon Lajoie	7.50	3.00	.75
☐ 73	Schoolboy Rowe	1.25	.50	.12	☐ 121	Dutch Leonard	2.50	1.00	.25
☐ 74	Red Ruffing	1.25	.50	.12	☐ 122	Ted Lyons	3.50	1.40	.35
☐ 75	Babe Ruth	25.00	10.00	2.50	☐ 123	Connie Mack	7.50	3.00	.75
☐ 76	Joe Sewell	1.25	.50	.12	☐ 124	Rabbit Maranville	3.50	1.40	.35
☐ 77	Al Simmons	1.25	.50	.12	☐ 125	Fred Marberry	2.50	1.00	.25
☐ 78	George Sisler	1.25	.50	.12	☐ 126	Joe McGinnity	4.50	1.80	.45
☐ 79	Tris Speaker	2.00	.80	.20	☐ 127	Oscar Melillo	2.50	1.00	.25
☐ 80	Fred Toney	1.25	.50	.12	☐ 128	Ray Mueller	2.50	1.00	.25
☐ 81	Dazzy Vance	1.25	.50	.12	☐ 129	Kid Nichols	3.50	1.40	.35
☐ 82	Jim Vaughn	1.25	.50	.12	☐ 130	Lefty O'Doul	2.50	1.00	.25
☐ 83	Ed Walsh	1.25	.50	.12	☐ 131	Bob O'Farrell	2.50	1.00	.25
☐ 84	Lloyd Waner	1.25	.50	.12	☐ 132	Roger Peckinpaugh	2.50	1.00	.25
☐ 85	Paul Waner	1.25	.50	.12	☐ 133	Herb Pennock	3.50	1.40	.35
☐ 86	Zack Wheat	1.25	.50	.12	☐ 134	George Pipgras	2.50	1.00	.25
☐ 87	Hack Wilson	2.00	.80	.20	☐ 135	Eddie Plank	4.50	1.80	.45
☐ 88	Jimmy Wilson	1.25	.50	.12	☐ 136	Ray Schalk	3.50	1.40	.35
☐ 89	Sisler and Traynor (checklist back)	10.00	2.00	.40	☐ 137	Hal Schumacher	2.50	1.00	.25
					☐ 138	Luke Sewell	2.50	1.00	.25
☐ 90	Babe Adams	2.50	1.00	.25	☐ 139	Bob Shawkey	2.50	1.00	.25
☐ 91	Dale Alexander	2.50	1.00	.25	☐ 140	Riggs Stephenson	2.50	1.00	.25
☐ 92	Jim Bagby	2.50	1.00	.25	☐ 141	Billy Sullivan	2.50	1.00	.25
☐ 93	Ossie Bluege	2.50	1.00	.25	☐ 142	Bill Terry	6.00	2.40	.60
☐ 94	Lou Boudreau	5.00	2.00	.50	☐ 143	Joe Tinker	3.50	1.40	.35
☐ 95	Tom Bridges	2.50	1.00	.25	☐ 144	Pie Traynor	4.50	1.80	.45
☐ 96	Donie Bush	2.50	1.00	.25	☐ 145	Hal Trosky	2.50	1.00	.25
☐ 97	Dolph Camilli	2.50	1.00	.25	☐ 146	George Uhle	2.50	1.00	.25

		NRMT	VG-E	GOOD
☐ 147	Johnny VanderMeer	3.50	1.40	.35
☐ 148	Arky Vaughan	3.50	1.40	.35
☐ 149	Rube Waddell	3.50	1.40	.35
☐ 150	Honus Wagner	12.00	5.00	1.20
☐ 151	Dixie Walker	2.50	1.00	.25
☐ 152	Ted Williams	30.00	12.00	3.00
☐ 153	Cy Young	9.00	3.75	.90
☐ 154	Ross Young	6.00	2.40	.60

1963 Fleer

BOB GIBSON
St. Louis Cardinals—Pitcher

*The cards in this 66-card set measure 2 ½"
by 3 ½". The Fleer set of current baseball
players was marketed in 1963 in a gum card-
style waxed wrapper package which contained a cherry cookie instead of gum. The
cards were printed in sheets of 66 with the
scarce card of Adcock apparently being
replaced by the unnumbered checklist card
for the final press run. The complete set
price includes the checklist card. The
catalog designation for this set is R418-4.*

	NRMT	VG-E	GOOD
Complete Set (67)	500.00	200.00	60.00
Common Player (1-66)	1.75	.70	.17

		NRMT	VG-E	GOOD
☐ 1	Steve Barber	4.00	1.00	.20
☐ 2	Ron Hansen	1.75	.70	.17
☐ 3	Milt Pappas	2.50	1.00	.25
☐ 4	Brooks Robinson	18.00	7.25	1.80
☐ 5	Willie Mays	40.00	16.00	4.00
☐ 6	Lou Clinton	1.75	.70	.17

		NRMT	VG-E	GOOD
☐ 7	Bill Monbouquette	1.75	.70	.17
☐ 8	Carl Yastrzemski	40.00	16.00	4.00
☐ 9	Ray Herbert	1.75	.70	.17
☐ 10	Jim Landis	1.75	.70	.17
☐ 11	Dick Donovan	1.75	.70	.17
☐ 12	Tito Francona	1.75	.70	.17
☐ 13	Jerry Kindall	1.75	.70	.17
☐ 14	Frank Lary	2.50	1.00	.25
☐ 15	Dick Howser	3.00	1.20	.30
☐ 16	Jerry Lumpe	1.75	.70	.17
☐ 17	Norm Siebern	1.75	.70	.17
☐ 18	Don Lee	1.75	.70	.17
☐ 19	Albie Pearson	1.75	.70	.17
☐ 20	Bob Rodgers	2.50	1.00	.25
☐ 21	Leon Wagner	1.75	.70	.17
☐ 22	Jim Kaat	4.00	1.60	.40
☐ 23	Vic Power	1.75	.70	.17
☐ 24	Rich Rollins	1.75	.70	.17
☐ 25	Bobby Richardson	4.50	1.80	.45
☐ 26	Ralph Terry	2.50	1.00	.25
☐ 27	Tom Cheney	1.75	.70	.17
☐ 28	Chuck Cottier	1.75	.70	.17
☐ 29	Jim Piersall	3.00	1.20	.30
☐ 30	Dave Stenhouse	1.75	.70	.17
☐ 31	Glen Hobbie	1.75	.70	.17
☐ 32	Ron Santo	3.00	1.20	.30
☐ 33	Gene Freese	1.75	.70	.17
☐ 34	Vada Pinson	3.00	1.20	.30
☐ 35	Bob Purkey	1.75	.70	.17
☐ 36	Joe Amalfitano	1.75	.70	.17
☐ 37	Bob Aspromonte	1.75	.70	.17
☐ 38	Dick Farrell	1.75	.70	.17
☐ 39	Al Spangler	1.75	.70	.17
☐ 40	Tommy Davis	2.50	1.00	.25
☐ 41	Don Drysdale	13.50	6.00	1.00
☐ 42	Sandy Koufax	35.00	14.00	3.50
☐ 43	Maury Wills	21.00	8.50	2.10
☐ 44	Frank Bolling	1.75	.70	.17
☐ 45	Warren Spahn	15.00	6.00	1.50
☐ 46	Joe Adcock SP	75.00	30.00	7.50
☐ 47	Roger Craig	3.50	1.40	.35
☐ 48	Al Jackson	1.75	.70	.17
☐ 49	Rod Kanehl	1.75	.70	.17
☐ 50	Ruben Amaro	1.75	.70	.17
☐ 51	Johnny Callison	2.50	1.00	.25
☐ 52	Clay Dalrymple	1.75	.70	.17
☐ 53	Don Demeter	1.75	.70	.17
☐ 54	Art Mahaffey	1.75	.70	.17
☐ 55	Smokey Burgess	2.50	1.00	.25

			NRMT	VG-E	GOOD
☐	56	Roberto Clemente ..	35.00	14.00	3.50
☐	57	Roy Face	3.00	1.20	.30
☐	58	Vern Law	2.50	1.00	.25
☐	59	Bill Mazeroski	4.00	1.60	.40
☐	60	Ken Boyer	4.00	1.60	.40
☐	61	Bob Gibson	13.50	6.00	1.00
☐	62	Gene Oliver	1.75	.70	.17
☐	63	Bill White	2.50	1.00	.25
☐	64	Orlando Cepeda ...	4.50	1.80	.45
☐	65	Jim Davenport ...	2.50	1.00	.25
☐	66	Billy O'Dell	1.75	.70	.17
☐	67	Checklist card	150.00	25.00	5.00
		(unnumbered)			

1981 Fleer

*The cards in this 660-card set measure 2 ½"
by 3 ½". This issue of cards marks Fleer's
first entry into the current player baseball
card market since 1963. Players from the
same team are conveniently grouped
together by number in the set. The teams are
ordered (by 1980 standings) as follows:
Philadelphia (1-27), Kansas City (28-50),
Houston (51-78), New York Yankees (79-
109), Los Angeles (110-141), Montreal (142-
168), Baltimore (169-195), Cincinnati
(196-220), Boston (221-241), Atlanta (242-
267), California (268-290), Chicago Cubs
(291-315), New York Mets (316-338),
Chicago White Sox (339-350 and 352-359),
Pittsburgh (360-386), Cleveland (387-408),
Toronto (409-431), San Francisco (432-*

*458), Detroit (459-483), San Diego (484-
506), Milwaukee (507-527), St. Louis (528-
550), Minnesota (551-571), Oakland (351
and 572-594), Seattle (595-616), and Texas
(617-637). Cards 638-660 feature specials
and checklists. The cards of pitchers in this
set erroneously show a heading (on the card
backs) of "Batting Record" over their career
pitching statistics. There were three distinct
printings: the two following the primary run
were designed to correct numerous errors.
The variations caused by these multiple
printings are noted in the checklist below
(P1, P2, or P3).*

			MINT	EXC	G-VG
		Complete Set (P1)	30.00	12.00	3.00
		Complete Set (P2)	24.00	10.00	2.40
		Complete Set (P3)	25.00	10.00	2.50
		Common Player (1-660) ..	.03	.01	.00
☐	1	Pete Rose	2.00	.80	.20
☐	2	Larry Bowa	.15	.06	.01
☐	3	Manny Trillo	.03	.01	.00
☐	4	Bob Boone	.15	.06	.01
☐	5	Mike Schmidt	1.00	.40	.10
		See 640A			
☐	6A	Steve Carlton P1 ..	.65	.26	.06
		Pitcher of Year			
		See also 660A			
		Back "1066 Cardinals"			
☐	6B	Steve Carlton P2 ..	.65	.26	.06
		Pitcher of Year			
		Back "1066 Cardinals"			
☐	6C	Steve Carlton P3 ..	2.00	.80	.20
		"1966 Cardinals"			
☐	7	Tug McGraw	.10	.04	.01
		See 657A			
☐	8	Larry Christenson .	.03	.01	.00
☐	9	Bake McBride	.03	.01	.00
☐	10	Greg Luzinski	.12	.05	.01
☐	11	Ron Reed	.03	.01	.00
☐	12	Dickie Noles	.03	.01	.00
☐	13	Keith Moreland ...	.35	.14	.03
☐	14	Bob Walk	.30	.12	.03
☐	15	Lonnie Smith	.06	.02	.01
☐	16	Dick Ruthven ...	.03	.01	.00
☐	17	Sparky Lyle	.10	.04	.01
☐	18	Greg Gross	.03	.01	.00
☐	19	Garry Maddox	.06	.02	.00
☐	20	Nino Espinosa ...	.03	.01	.00

		MINT	EXC	G-VG
☐ 21	George Vukovich ..	.03	.01	.00
☐ 22	John Vukovich	.03	.01	.00
☐ 23	Ramon Aviles	.03	.01	.00
☐ 24A	Ken Saucier P1	.06	.02	.00
	Name on front "Ken"			
☐ 24B	Ken Saucier P2	.06	.02	.00
	Name on front "Ken"			
☐ 24C	Kevin Saucier P3 ..	.35	.14	.03
	Name on front "Kevin"			
☐ 25	Randy Lerch	.03	.01	.00
☐ 26	Del Unser	.03	.01	.00
☐ 27	Tim McCarver	.15	.06	.01
☐ 28	George Brett	1.00	.40	.10
	See 655A			
☐ 29	Willie Wilson	.15	.06	.01
	See 653A			
☐ 30	Paul Splittorff	.03	.01	.00
☐ 31	Dan Quisenberry ...	.15	.06	.01
☐ 32A	Amos Otis P1	.10	.04	.01
	Batting Pose			
	"Outfield"			
	(32 on back)			
☐ 32B	Amos Otis P2	.10	.04	.01
	"Series Starter"			
	(483 on back)			
☐ 33	Steve Busby	.03	.01	.00
☐ 34	U.L. Washington ...	.03	.01	.00
☐ 35	Dave Chalk	.03	.01	.00
☐ 36	Darrell Porter	.03	.01	.00
☐ 37	Marty Pattin	.03	.01	.00
☐ 38	Larry Gura	.03	.01	.00
☐ 39	Renie Martin	.03	.01	.00
☐ 40	Rich Gale	.03	.01	.00
☐ 41A	Hal McRae P1	.50	.20	.05
	"Royals" on front			
	in black letters			
☐ 41B	Hal McRae P2	.10	.04	.01
	"Royals" on front			
	in blue letters			
☐ 42	Dennis Leonard ...	.06	.02	.00
☐ 43	Willie Aikens	.03	.01	.00
☐ 44	Frank White	.10	.04	.01
☐ 45	Clint Hurdle	.03	.01	.00
☐ 46	John Wathan	.10	.04	.01
☐ 47	Pete LaCock	.03	.01	.00
☐ 48	Rance Mulliniks ...	.03	.01	.00
☐ 49	Jeff Twitty	.03	.01	.00
☐ 50	Jamie Quirk	.03	.01	.00
☐ 51	Art Howe	.10	.04	.01

		MINT	EXC	G-VG
☐ 52	Ken Forsch	.03	.01	.00
☐ 53	Vern Ruhle	.03	.01	.00
☐ 54	Joe Niekro	.10	.04	.01
☐ 55	Frank LaCorte	.03	.01	.00
☐ 56	J.R. Richard	.10	.04	.01
☐ 57	Nolan Ryan	.60	.24	.06
☐ 58	Enos Cabell	.03	.01	.00
☐ 59	Cesar Cedeno	.10	.04	.01
☐ 60	Jose Cruz	.10	.04	.01
☐ 61	Bill Virdon MG	.03	.01	.00
☐ 62	Terry Puhl	.06	.02	.00
☐ 63	Joaquin Andujar ..	.10	.04	.01
☐ 64	Alan Ashby	.03	.01	.00
☐ 65	Joe Sambito	.03	.01	.00
☐ 66	Denny Walling	.03	.01	.00
☐ 67	Jeff Leonard	.15	.06	.01
☐ 68	Luis Pujols	.03	.01	.00
☐ 69	Bruce Bochy	.03	.01	.00
☐ 70	Rafael Landestoy .	.03	.01	.00
☐ 71	Dave Smith	.35	.14	.03
☐ 72	Danny Heep	.20	.08	.02
☐ 73	Julio Gonzalez ...	.03	.01	.00
☐ 74	Craig Reynolds ...	.03	.01	.00
☐ 75	Gary Woods	.03	.01	.00
☐ 76	Dave Bergman ...	.03	.01	.00
☐ 77	Randy Niemann ..	.03	.01	.00
☐ 78	Joe Morgan	.30	.12	.03
☐ 79	Reggie Jackson ...	.85	.34	.08
	See 650A			
☐ 80	Bucky Dent	.10	.04	.01
☐ 81	Tommy John	.15	.06	.01
☐ 82	Luis Tiant	.10	.04	.01
☐ 83	Rick Cerone	.03	.01	.00
☐ 84	Dick Howser MG ..	.10	.04	.01
☐ 85	Lou Piniella	.10	.04	.01
☐ 86	Ron Davis	.03	.01	.00
☐ 87A	Craig Nettles P1 ..	12.00	5.00	1.20
	ERR (Name on back			
	misspelled "Craig")			
☐ 87B	Graig Nettles P2 COR	.30	.12	.03
	"Graig"			
☐ 88	Ron Guidry	.20	.08	.02
☐ 89	Rich Gossage	.15	.06	.01
☐ 90	Rudy May	.03	.01	.00
☐ 91	Gaylord Perry	.25	.10	.02
☐ 92	Eric Soderholm ...	.03	.01	.00
☐ 93	Bob Watson	.06	.02	.00
☐ 94	Bobby Murcer	.10	.04	.01
☐ 95	Bobby Brown	.03	.01	.00

		MINT	EXC	G-VG			MINT	EXC	G-VG
□ 96	Jim Spencer	.03	.01	.00	□ 136	Steve Howe	.10	.04	.01
□ 97	Tom Underwood	.03	.01	.00	□ 137	Robert Castillo	.03	.01	.00
□ 98	Oscar Gamble	.03	.01	.00	□ 138	Gary Thomasson	.03	.01	.00
□ 99	Johnny Oates	.03	.01	.00	□ 139	Rudy Law	.03	.01	.00
□ 100	Fred Stanley	.03	.01	.00	□ 140	Fernand Valenzuela	4.50	1.80	.45
□ 101	Ruppert Jones	.03	.01	.00		(sic, Fernando)			
□ 102	Dennis Werth	.03	.01	.00	□ 141	Manny Mota	.06	.02	.00
□ 103	Joe Lefebvre	.06	.02	.00	□ 142	Gary Carter	.50	.20	.05
□ 104	Brian Doyle	.03	.01	.00	□ 143	Steve Rogers	.06	.02	.00
□ 105	Aurelio Rodriguez	.03	.01	.00	□ 144	Warren Cromartie	.03	.01	.00
□ 106	Doug Bird	.03	.01	.00	□ 145	Andre Dawson	.35	.14	.03
□ 107	Mike Griffin	.03	.01	.00	□ 146	Larry Parrish	.06	.02	.00
□ 108	Tim Lollar	.03	.01	.00	□ 147	Rowland Office	.03	.01	.00
□ 109	Willie Randolph	.10	.04	.01	□ 148	Ellis Valentine	.03	.01	.00
□ 110	Steve Garvey	.60	.24	.06	□ 149	Dick Williams MG	.03	.01	.00
□ 111	Reggie Smith	.10	.04	.01	□ 150	Bill Gullickson	.25	.10	.02
□ 112	Don Sutton	.30	.12	.03	□ 151	Elias Sosa	.03	.01	.00
□ 113	Burt Hooton	.03	.01	.00	□ 152	John Tamargo	.03	.01	.00
□ 114A	Dave Lopes P1	.50	.20	.05	□ 153	Chris Speier	.03	.01	.00
	Small hand on back				□ 154	Ron LeFlore	.06	.02	.00
□ 114B	Dave Lopes P2	.10	.04	.01	□ 155	Rodney Scott	.03	.01	.00
	No hand				□ 156	Stan Bahnsen	.03	.01	.00
□ 115	Dusty Baker	.06	.02	.00	□ 157	Bill Lee	.06	.02	.00
□ 116	Tom Lasorda MG	.10	.04	.01	□ 158	Fred Norman	.03	.01	.00
□ 117	Bill Russell	.06	.02	.00	□ 159	Woodie Fryman	.03	.01	.00
□ 118	Jerry Reuss	.06	.02	.00	□ 160	David Palmer	.06	.02	.00
□ 119	Terry Forster	.06	.02	.00	□ 161	Jerry White	.03	.01	.00
□ 120A	Bob Welch P1	.20	.08	.02	□ 162	Roberto Ramos	.03	.01	.00
	Name on back "Bob"				□ 163	John D'Acquisto	.03	.01	.00
□ 120B	Bob Welch P2	.20	.08	.02	□ 164	Tommy Hutton	.03	.01	.00
	Name on back "Robert"				□ 165	Charlie Lea	.15	.06	.01
□ 121	Don Stanhouse	.03	.01	.00	□ 166	Scott Sanderson	.06	.02	.00
□ 122	Rick Monday	.03	.01	.00	□ 167	Ken Macha	.03	.01	.00
□ 123	Derrel Thomas	.03	.01	.00	□ 168	Tony Bernazard	.06	.02	.00
□ 124	Joe Ferguson	.03	.01	.00	□ 169	Jim Palmer	.40	.16	.04
□ 125	Rick Sutcliffe	.25	.10	.02	□ 170	Steve Stone	.06	.02	.00
□ 126A	Ron Cey P1	.50	.20	.05	□ 171	Mike Flanagan	.10	.04	.01
	Small hand on back				□ 172	Al Bumbry	.03	.01	.00
□ 126B	Ron Cey P2	.10	.04	.01	□ 173	Doug DeCinces	.06	.02	.00
	No hand				□ 174	Scott McGregor	.06	.02	.00
□ 127	Dave Goltz	.03	.01	.00	□ 175	Mark Belanger	.06	.02	.00
□ 128	Jay Johnstone	.06	.02	.00	□ 176	Tim Stoddard	.03	.01	.00
□ 129	Steve Yeager	.03	.01	.00	□ 177A	Rick Dempsey P1	.50	.20	.05
□ 130	Gary Weiss	.03	.01	.00		Small hand on front			
□ 131	Mike Scioscia	.50	.20	.05	□ 177B	Rick Dempsey P2	.10	.04	.01
□ 132	Vic Davalillo	.03	.01	.00		No hand			
□ 133	Doug Rau	.03	.01	.00	□ 178	Earl Weaver MG	.06	.02	.00
□ 134	Pepe Frias	.03	.01	.00	□ 179	Tippy Martinez	.03	.01	.00
□ 135	Mickey Hatcher	.10	.04	.01	□ 180	Dennis Martinez	.06	.02	.00

		MINT	EXC	G-VG			MINT	EXC	G-VG
☐ 181	Sammy Stewart	.03	.01	.00	☐ 221	Carl Yastrzemski	1.00	.40	.10
☐ 182	Rich Dauer	.03	.01	.00	☐ 222	Jim Rice	.30	.12	.03
☐ 183	Lee May	.03	.01	.00	☐ 223	Fred Lynn	.20	.08	.02
☐ 184	Eddie Murray	.75	.30	.07	☐ 224	Carlton Fisk	.20	.08	.02
☐ 185	Benny Ayala	.03	.01	.00	☐ 225	Rick Burleson	.06	.02	.00
☐ 186	John Lowenstein	.03	.01	.00	☐ 226	Dennis Eckersley	.20	.08	.02
☐ 187	Gary Roenicke	.03	.01	.00	☐ 227	Butch Hobson	.03	.01	.00
☐ 188	Ken Singleton	.10	.04	.01	☐ 228	Tom Burgmeier	.03	.01	.00
☐ 189	Dan Graham	.03	.01	.00	☐ 229	Garry Hancock	.03	.01	.00
☐ 190	Terry Crowley	.03	.01	.00	☐ 230	Don Zimmer MG	.03	.01	.00
☐ 191	Kiko Garcia	.03	.01	.00	☐ 231	Steve Renko	.03	.01	.00
☐ 192	Dave Ford	.03	.01	.00	☐ 232	Dwight Evans	.20	.08	.02
☐ 193	Mark Corey	.03	.01	.00	☐ 233	Mike Torrez	.03	.01	.00
☐ 194	Lenn Sakata	.03	.01	.00	☐ 234	Bob Stanley	.03	.01	.00
☐ 195	Doug DeCinces	.06	.02	.00	☐ 235	Jim Dwyer	.03	.01	.00
☐ 196	Johnny Bench	.65	.26	.06	☐ 236	Dave Stapleton	.03	.01	.00
☐ 197	Dave Concepcion	.15	.06	.01	☐ 237	Glen Hoffman	.03	.01	.00
☐ 198	Ray Knight	.10	.04	.01	☐ 238	Jerry Remy	.03	.01	.00
☐ 199	Ken Griffey	.06	.02	.00	☐ 239	Dick Drago	.03	.01	.00
☐ 200	Tom Seaver	.50	.20	.05	☐ 240	Bill Campbell	.03	.01	.00
☐ 201	Dave Collins	.03	.01	.00	☐ 241	Tony Perez	.20	.08	.02
☐ 202A	George Foster P1 .. Slugger Number on back 216	.15	.06	.01	☐ 242	Phil Niekro	.30	.12	.03
					☐ 243	Dale Murphy	1.25	.50	.12
☐ 202B	George Foster P2 .. Slugger Number on back 202	.15	.06	.01	☐ 244	Bob Horner	.20	.08	.02
					☐ 245	Jeff Burroughs	.03	.01	.00
☐ 203	Junior Kennedy	.03	.01	.00	☐ 246	Rick Camp	.03	.01	.00
☐ 204	Frank Pastore	.03	.01	.00	☐ 247	Bobby Cox MG	.03	.01	.00
☐ 205	Dan Driessen	.03	.01	.00	☐ 248	Bruce Benedict	.03	.01	.00
☐ 206	Hector Cruz	.03	.01	.00	☐ 249	Gene Garber	.03	.01	.00
☐ 207	Paul Moskau	.03	.01	.00	☐ 250	Jerry Royster	.03	.01	.00
☐ 208	Charlie Leibrandt	.35	.14	.03	☐ 251A	Gary Matthews P1 .. Small hand on back	.50	.20	.05
☐ 209	Harry Spilman	.03	.01	.00					
☐ 210	Joe Price	.06	.02	.00	☐ 251B	Gary Matthews P2 .. No hand	.10	.04	.01
☐ 211	Tom Hume	.03	.01	.00					
☐ 212	Joe Nolan	.03	.01	.00	☐ 252	Chris Chambliss	.10	.04	.01
☐ 213	Doug Bair	.03	.01	.00	☐ 253	Luis Gomez	.03	.01	.00
☐ 214	Mario Soto	.10	.04	.01	☐ 254	Bill Nahorodny	.03	.01	.00
☐ 215A	Bill Bonham P1 .. Small hand on back	.50	.20	.05	☐ 255	Doyle Alexander	.10	.04	.01
					☐ 256	Brian Asselstine	.03	.01	.00
☐ 215B	Bill Bonham P2 .. No hand	.06	.02	.00	☐ 257	Biff Pocoroba	.03	.01	.00
					☐ 258	Mike Lum	.03	.01	.00
☐ 216	George Foster See 202	.15	.06	.01	☐ 259	Charlie Spikes	.03	.01	.00
					☐ 260	Glenn Hubbard	.03	.01	.00
☐ 217	Paul Householder	.03	.01	.00	☐ 261	Tommy Boggs	.03	.01	.00
☐ 218	Ron Oester	.06	.02	.00	☐ 262	Al Hrabosky	.06	.02	.00
☐ 219	Sam Mejias	.03	.01	.00	☐ 263	Rick Matula	.03	.01	.00
☐ 220	Sheldon Burnside	.03	.01	.00	☐ 264	Preston Hanna	.03	.01	.00
					☐ 265	Larry Bradford	.03	.01	.00
					☐ 266	Rafael Ramirez	.25	.10	.02

		MINT	EXC	G-VG			MINT	EXC	G-VG
☐ 267	Larry McWilliams	.03	.01	.00	☐ 316	Lee Mazzilli	.03	.01	.00
☐ 268	Rod Carew	.60	.22	.05	☐ 317	John Stearns	.03	.01	.00
☐ 269	Bobby Grich	.10	.04	.01	☐ 318	Alex Trevino	.03	.01	.00
☐ 270	Carney Lansford	.15	.06	.01	☐ 319	Craig Swan	.03	.01	.00
☐ 271	Don Baylor	.15	.06	.01	☐ 320	Frank Taveras	.03	.01	.00
☐ 272	Joe Rudi	.06	.02	.00	☐ 321	Steve Henderson	.03	.01	.00
☐ 273	Dan Ford	.03	.01	.00	☐ 322	Neil Allen	.06	.02	.00
☐ 274	Jim Fregosi	.06	.02	.00	☐ 323	Mark Bomback	.03	.01	.00
☐ 275	Dave Frost	.03	.01	.00	☐ 324	Mike Jorgensen	.03	.01	.00
☐ 276	Frank Tanana	.10	.04	.01	☐ 325	Joe Torre MG	.10	.04	.01
☐ 277	Dickie Thon	.10	.04	.01	☐ 326	Elliott Maddox	.03	.01	.00
☐ 278	Jason Thompson	.03	.01	.00	☐ 327	Pete Falcone	.03	.01	.00
☐ 279	Rick Miller	.03	.01	.00	☐ 328	Ray Burris	.03	.01	.00
☐ 280	Bert Campaneris	.06	.02	.00	☐ 329	Claudell Washington	.06	.02	.00
☐ 281	Tom Donohue	.03	.01	.00	☐ 330	Doug Flynn	.03	.01	.00
☐ 282	Brian Downing	.06	.02	.00	☐ 331	Joel Youngblood	.03	.01	.00
☐ 283	Fred Patek	.03	.01	.00	☐ 332	Bill Almon	.03	.01	.00
☐ 284	Bruce Kison	.03	.01	.00	☐ 333	Tom Hausman	.03	.01	.00
☐ 285	Dave LaRoche	.03	.01	.00	☐ 334	Pat Zachry	.03	.01	.00
☐ 286	Don Aase	.03	.01	.00	☐ 335	Jeff Reardon	.60	.24	.06
☐ 287	Jim Barr	.03	.01	.00	☐ 336	Wally Backman	.40	.16	.04
☐ 288	Alfredo Martinez	.03	.01	.00	☐ 337	Dan Norman	.03	.01	.00
☐ 289	Larry Harlow	.03	.01	.00	☐ 338	Jerry Morales	.03	.01	.00
☐ 290	Andy Hassler	.03	.01	.00	☐ 339	Ed Farmer	.03	.01	.00
☐ 291	Dave Kingman	.15	.06	.01	☐ 340	Bob Molinaro	.03	.01	.00
☐ 292	Bill Buckner	.12	.05	.01	☐ 341	Todd Cruz	.03	.01	.00
☐ 293	Rick Reuschel	.10	.04	.01	☐ 342A	Britt Burns P1	.40	.16	.04
☐ 294	Bruce Sutter	.15	.06	.01		Small hand on front			
☐ 295	Jerry Martin	.03	.01	.00	☐ 342B	Britt Burns P2	.20	.08	.02
☐ 296	Scot Thompson	.03	.01	.00		No hand			
☐ 297	Ivan DeJesus	.03	.01	.00	☐ 343	Kevin Bell	.03	.01	.00
☐ 298	Steve Dillard	.03	.01	.00	☐ 344	Tony LaRussa MG	.06	.02	.00
☐ 299	Dick Tidrow	.03	.01	.00	☐ 345	Steve Trout	.06	.02	.00
☐ 300	Randy Martz	.03	.01	.00	☐ 346	Harold Baines	1.75	.70	.17
☐ 301	Lenny Randle	.03	.01	.00	☐ 347	Richard Wortham	.03	.01	.00
☐ 302	Lynn McGlothen	.03	.01	.00	☐ 348	Wayne Nordhagen	.03	.01	.00
☐ 303	Cliff Johnson	.03	.01	.00	☐ 349	Mike Squires	.03	.01	.00
☐ 304	Tim Blackwell	.03	.01	.00	☐ 350	Lamar Johnson	.03	.01	.00
☐ 305	Dennis Lamp	.03	.01	.00	☐ 351	Rickey Henderson	1.75	.70	.17
☐ 306	Bill Caudill	.03	.01	.00	☐ 352	Francisco Barrios	.03	.01	.00
☐ 307	Carlos Lezcano	.03	.01	.00	☐ 353	Thad Bosley	.03	.01	.00
☐ 308	Jim Tracy	.03	.01	.00	☐ 354	Chet Lemon	.06	.02	.00
☐ 309	Doug Capilla	.03	.01	.00	☐ 355	Bruce Kimm	.03	.01	.00
☐ 310	Willie Hernandez	.12	.05	.01	☐ 356	Richard Dotson	.45	.18	.04
☐ 311	Mike Vail	.03	.01	.00	☐ 357	Jim Morrison	.03	.01	.00
☐ 312	Mike Krukow	.06	.02	.00	☐ 358	Mike Proly	.03	.01	.00
☐ 313	Barry Foote	.03	.01	.00	☐ 359	Greg Pryor	.03	.01	.00
☐ 314	Larry Biittner	.03	.01	.00	☐ 360	Dave Parker	.25	.10	.02
☐ 315	Mike Tyson	.03	.01	.00	☐ 361	Omar Moreno	.03	.01	.00

	MINT	EXC	G-VG
☐ 362A Kent Tekulve P1 ... Back "1071 Waterbury" and "1078 Pirates"	.15	.06	.01
☐ 362B Kent Tekulve P2 ... "1971 Waterbury" and "1978 Pirates"	.10	.04	.01
☐ 363 Willie Stargell	.35	.14	.03
☐ 364 Phil Garner	.03	.01	.00
☐ 365 Ed Ott	.03	.01	.00
☐ 366 Don Robinson	.06	.02	.00
☐ 367 Chuck Tanner MG .	.03	.01	.00
☐ 368 Jim Rooker	.03	.01	.00
☐ 369 Dale Berra	.03	.01	.00
☐ 370 Jim Bibby	.03	.01	.00
☐ 371 Steve Nicosia	.03	.01	.00
☐ 372 Mike Easler	.06	.02	.00
☐ 373 Bill Robinson	.06	.02	.00
☐ 374 Lee Lacy	.03	.01	.00
☐ 375 John Candelaria ...	.10	.04	.01
☐ 376 Manny Sanguillen ..	.06	.02	.00
☐ 377 Rick Rhoden	.10	.04	.01
☐ 378 Grant Jackson	.03	.01	.00
☐ 379 Tim Foli	.03	.01	.00
☐ 380 Rod Scurry	.06	.02	.00
☐ 381 Bill Madlock	.12	.05	.01
☐ 382A Kurt Bevacqua .... P1 ERR (P on cap backwards)	.20	.08	.02
☐ 382B Kurt Bevacqua P2 .. COR	.06	.02	.00
☐ 383 Bert Blyleven	.15	.06	.01
☐ 384 Eddie Solomon	.03	.01	.00
☐ 385 Enrique Romo	.03	.01	.00
☐ 386 John Milner	.03	.01	.00
☐ 387 Mike Hargrove	.03	.01	.00
☐ 388 Jorge Orta	.03	.01	.00
☐ 389 Toby Harrah	.06	.02	.00
☐ 390 Tom Veryzer	.03	.01	.00
☐ 391 Miguel Dilone	.03	.01	.00
☐ 392 Dan Spillner	.03	.01	.00
☐ 393 Jack Brohamer	.03	.01	.00
☐ 394 Wayne Garland	.03	.01	.00
☐ 395 Sid Monge	.03	.01	.00
☐ 396 Rick Waits	.03	.01	.00
☐ 397 Joe Charboneau ...	.10	.04	.01
☐ 398 Gary Alexander	.03	.01	.00
☐ 399 Jerry Dybzinski	.03	.01	.00
☐ 400 Mike Stanton	.03	.01	.00
☐ 401 Mike Paxton	.03	.01	.00

	MINT	EXC	G-VG
☐ 402 Gary Gray	.03	.01	.00
☐ 403 Rick Manning	.03	.01	.00
☐ 404 Bo Diaz	.06	.02	.00
☐ 405 Ron Hassey	.03	.01	.00
☐ 406 Ross Grimsley	.03	.01	.00
☐ 407 Victor Cruz	.03	.01	.00
☐ 408 Len Barker	.03	.01	.00
☐ 409 Bob Bailor	.03	.01	.00
☐ 410 Otto Velez	.03	.01	.00
☐ 411 Ernie Whitt	.06	.02	.00
☐ 412 Jim Clancy	.06	.02	.00
☐ 413 Barry Bonnell	.03	.01	.00
☐ 414 Dave Stieb	.30	.12	.03
☐ 415 Damaso Garcia ...	.10	.04	.01
☐ 416 John Mayberry ...	.06	.02	.00
☐ 417 Roy Howell	.03	.01	.00
☐ 418 Danny Ainge	.35	.14	.03
☐ 419A Jesse Jefferson P1 Back says Pirates	.06	.02	.00
☐ 419B Jesse Jefferson P2 Back says Pirates	.06	.02	.00
☐ 419C Jesse Jefferson P3 Back says Blue Jays	.35	.14	.03
☐ 420 Joey McLaughlin ..	.03	.01	.00
☐ 421 Lloyd Moseby	.90	.36	.09
☐ 422 Alvis Woods	.03	.01	.00
☐ 423 Garth Iorg	.03	.01	.00
☐ 424 Doug Ault	.03	.01	.00
☐ 425 Ken Schrom	.06	.02	.00
☐ 426 Mike Willis	.03	.01	.00
☐ 427 Steve Braun	.03	.01	.00
☐ 428 Bob Davis	.03	.01	.00
☐ 429 Jerry Garvin	.03	.01	.00
☐ 430 Alfredo Griffin	.10	.04	.01
☐ 431 Bob Mattick MG ...	.03	.01	.00
☐ 432 Vida Blue	.10	.04	.01
☐ 433 Jack Clark	.30	.12	.03
☐ 434 Willie McCovey ...	.35	.14	.03
☐ 435 Mike Ivie	.03	.01	.00
☐ 436A Darrel Evans P1 ERR Name on front "Darrel"	.40	.16	.04
☐ 436B Darrell Evans P2 .. Name on front "Darrell"	.15	.06	.01
☐ 437 Terry Whitfield	.03	.01	.00
☐ 438 Rennie Stennett ...	.03	.01	.00
☐ 439 John Montefusco ..	.06	.02	.00
☐ 440 Jim Wohlford	.03	.01	.00
☐ 441 Bill North	.03	.01	.00

		MINT	EXC	G-VG
☐ 442	Milt May	.03	.01	.00
☐ 443	Max Venable	.03	.01	.00
☐ 444	Ed Whitson	.06	.02	.00
☐ 445	Al Holland	.06	.02	.00
☐ 446	Randy Moffitt	.03	.01	.00
☐ 447	Bob Knepper	.10	.04	.01
☐ 448	Gary Lavelle	.03	.01	.00
☐ 449	Greg Minton	.03	.01	.00
☐ 450	Johnnie LeMaster	.03	.01	.00
☐ 451	Larry Herndon	.03	.01	.00
☐ 452	Rich Murray	.03	.01	.00
☐ 453	Joe Pettini	.03	.01	.00
☐ 454	Allen Ripley	.03	.01	.00
☐ 455	Dennis Littlejohn	.03	.01	.00
☐ 456	Tom Griffin	.03	.01	.00
☐ 457	Alan Hargesheimer	.03	.01	.00
☐ 458	Joe Strain	.03	.01	.00
☐ 459	Steve Kemp	.06	.02	.00
☐ 460	Sparky Anderson MG	.06	.02	.00
☐ 461	Alan Trammell	.35	.14	.03
☐ 462	Mark Fidrych	.10	.04	.01
☐ 463	Lou Whitaker	.20	.08	.02
☐ 464	Dave Rozema	.03	.01	.00
☐ 465	Milt Wilcox	.03	.01	.00
☐ 466	Champ Summers	.03	.01	.00
☐ 467	Lance Parrish	.25	.10	.02
☐ 468	Dan Petry	.10	.04	.01
☐ 469	Pat Underwood	.03	.01	.00
☐ 470	Rick Peters	.03	.01	.00
☐ 471	Al Cowens	.03	.01	.00
☐ 472	John Wockenfuss	.03	.01	.00
☐ 473	Tom Brookens	.03	.01	.00
☐ 474	Richie Hebner	.03	.01	.00
☐ 475	Jack Morris	.30	.12	.03
☐ 476	Jim Lentine	.03	.01	.00
☐ 477	Bruce Robbins	.03	.01	.00
☐ 478	Mark Wagner	.03	.01	.00
☐ 479	Tim Corcoran	.03	.01	.00
☐ 480A	Stan Papi P1	.15	.06	.01
	Front as Pitcher			
☐ 480B	Stan Papi P2	.10	.04	.01
	Front as Shortstop			
☐ 481	Kirk Gibson	3.50	1.40	.35
☐ 482	Dan Schatzeder	.03	.01	.00
☐ 483A	Amos Otis P1	.10	.04	.01
	See card 32			
☐ 483B	Amos Otis P2	.10	.04	.01
	See card 32			
☐ 484	Dave Winfield	.50	.20	.05
☐ 485	Rollie Fingers	.30	.12	.03
☐ 486	Gene Richards	.03	.01	.00
☐ 487	Randy Jones	.03	.01	.00
☐ 488	Ozzie Smith	.30	.12	.03
☐ 489	Gene Tenace	.03	.01	.00
☐ 490	Bill Fahey	.03	.01	.00
☐ 491	John Curtis	.03	.01	.00
☐ 492	Dave Cash	.03	.01	.00
☐ 493A	Tim Flannery P1	.15	.06	.01
	Batting right			
☐ 493B	Tim Flannery P2	.06	.02	.00
	Batting left			
☐ 494	Jerry Mumphrey	.03	.01	.00
☐ 495	Bob Shirley	.03	.01	.00
☐ 496	Steve Mura	.03	.01	.00
☐ 497	Eric Rasmussen	.03	.01	.00
☐ 498	Broderick Perkins	.03	.01	.00
☐ 499	Barry Evans	.03	.01	.00
☐ 500	Chuck Baker	.03	.01	.00
☐ 501	Luis Salazar	.15	.06	.01
☐ 502	Gary Lucas	.06	.02	.00
☐ 503	Mike Armstrong	.06	.02	.00
☐ 504	Jerry Turner	.03	.01	.00
☐ 505	Dennis Kinney	.03	.01	.00
☐ 506	Willie Montanez	.03	.01	.00
☐ 507	Gorman Thomas	.10	.04	.01
☐ 508	Ben Oglivie	.06	.02	.00
☐ 509	Larry Hisle	.06	.02	.00
☐ 510	Sal Bando	.06	.02	.00
☐ 511	Robin Yount	.40	.16	.04
☐ 512	Mike Caldwell	.03	.01	.00
☐ 513	Sixto Lezcano	.03	.01	.00
☐ 514A	Bill Travers P1 ERR	.20	.08	.02
	"Jerry Augustine"			
	with Augustine back			
☐ 514B	Bill Travers P2 COR	.10	.04	.01
☐ 515	Paul Molitor	.25	.10	.02
☐ 516	Moose Haas	.03	.01	.00
☐ 517	Bill Castro	.03	.01	.00
☐ 518	Jim Slaton	.03	.01	.00
☐ 519	Lary Sorensen	.03	.01	.00
☐ 520	Bob McClure	.03	.01	.00
☐ 521	Charlie Moore	.03	.01	.00
☐ 522	Jim Gantner	.03	.01	.00
☐ 523	Reggie Cleveland	.03	.01	.00
☐ 524	Don Money	.03	.01	.00
☐ 525	Bill Travers	.03	.01	.00
☐ 526	Buck Martinez	.03	.01	.00
☐ 527	Dick Davis	.03	.01	.00

		MINT	EXC	G-VG
☐ 528	Ted Simmons	.15	.06	.01
☐ 529	Garry Templeton	.10	.04	.01
☐ 530	Ken Reitz	.03	.01	.00
☐ 531	Tony Scott	.03	.01	.00
☐ 532	Ken Oberkfell	.03	.01	.00
☐ 533	Bob Sykes	.03	.01	.00
☐ 534	Keith Smith	.03	.01	.00
☐ 535	John Littlefield	.03	.01	.00
☐ 536	Jim Kaat	.15	.06	.01
☐ 537	Bob Forsch	.03	.01	.00
☐ 538	Mike Phillips	.03	.01	.00
☐ 539	Terry Landrum	.06	.02	.00
☐ 540	Leon Durham	.35	.14	.03
☐ 541	Terry Kennedy	.06	.02	.00
☐ 542	George Hendrick	.06	.02	.00
☐ 543	Dane Iorg	.03	.01	.00
☐ 544	Mark Littell	.03	.01	.00
☐ 545	Keith Hernandez	.35	.14	.03
☐ 546	Silvio Martinez	.03	.01	.00
☐ 547A	Don Hood P1 ERR	.20	.08	.02
	"Pete Vuckovich"			
	with Vuckovich back			
☐ 547B	Don Hood P2 COR	.10	.04	.01
☐ 548	Bobby Bonds	.10	.04	.01
☐ 549	Mike Ramsey	.03	.01	.00
☐ 550	Tom Herr	.15	.06	.01
☐ 551	Roy Smalley	.03	.01	.00
☐ 552	Jerry Koosman	.06	.02	.00
☐ 553	Ken Landreaux	.03	.01	.00
☐ 554	John Castino	.03	.01	.00
☐ 555	Doug Corbett	.06	.02	.00
☐ 556	Bombo Rivera	.03	.01	.00
☐ 557	Ron Jackson	.03	.01	.00
☐ 558	Butch Wynegar	.03	.01	.00
☐ 559	Hosken Powell	.03	.01	.00
☐ 560	Pete Redfern	.03	.01	.00
☐ 561	Roger Erickson	.03	.01	.00
☐ 562	Glenn Adams	.03	.01	.00
☐ 563	Rick Sofield	.03	.01	.00
☐ 564	Geoff Zahn	.03	.01	.00
☐ 565	Pete Mackanin	.03	.01	.00
☐ 566	Mike Cubbage	.03	.01	.00
☐ 567	Darrell Jackson	.03	.01	.00
☐ 568	Dave Edwards	.03	.01	.00
☐ 569	Rob Wilfong	.03	.01	.00
☐ 570	Sal Butera	.03	.01	.00
☐ 571	Jose Morales	.03	.01	.00
☐ 572	Rick Langford	.03	.01	.00
☐ 573	Mike Norris	.03	.01	.00
☐ 574	Rickey Henderson	1.75	.70	.17
☐ 575	Tony Armas	.10	.04	.01
☐ 576	Dave Revering	.03	.01	.00
☐ 577	Jeff Newman	.03	.01	.00
☐ 578	Bob Lacey	.03	.01	.00
☐ 579	Brian Kingman	.03	.01	.00
☐ 580	Mitchell Page	.03	.01	.00
☐ 581	Billy Martin MG	.15	.06	.01
☐ 582	Rob Picciolo	.03	.01	.00
☐ 583	Mike Heath	.03	.01	.00
☐ 584	Mickey Klutts	.03	.01	.00
☐ 585	Orlando Gonzalez	.03	.01	.00
☐ 586	Mike Davis	.30	.12	.03
☐ 587	Wayne Gross	.03	.01	.00
☐ 588	Matt Keough	.03	.01	.00
☐ 589	Steve McCatty	.03	.01	.00
☐ 590	Dwayne Murphy	.03	.01	.00
☐ 591	Mario Guerrero	.03	.01	.00
☐ 592	Dave McKay	.03	.01	.00
☐ 593	Jim Essian	.03	.01	.00
☐ 594	Dave Heaverlo	.03	.01	.00
☐ 595	Maury Wills MG	.06	.02	.00
☐ 596	Juan Beniquez	.03	.01	.00
☐ 597	Rodney Craig	.03	.01	.00
☐ 598	Jim Anderson	.03	.01	.00
☐ 599	Floyd Bannister	.06	.02	.00
☐ 600	Bruce Bochte	.03	.01	.00
☐ 601	Julio Cruz	.03	.01	.00
☐ 602	Ted Cox	.03	.01	.00
☐ 603	Dan Meyer	.03	.01	.00
☐ 604	Larry Cox	.03	.01	.00
☐ 605	Bill Stein	.03	.01	.00
☐ 606	Steve Garvey	.60	.22	.05
☐ 607	Dave Roberts	.03	.01	.00
☐ 608	Leon Roberts	.03	.01	.00
☐ 609	Reggie Walton	.03	.01	.00
☐ 610	Dave Edler	.03	.01	.00
☐ 611	Larry Milbourne	.03	.01	.00
☐ 612	Kim Allen	.03	.01	.00
☐ 613	Mario Mendoza	.03	.01	.00
☐ 614	Tom Paciorek	.03	.01	.00
☐ 615	Glenn Abbott	.03	.01	.00
☐ 616	Joe Simpson	.03	.01	.00
☐ 617	Mickey Rivers	.06	.02	.00
☐ 618	Jim Kern	.03	.01	.00
☐ 619	Jim Sundberg	.06	.02	.00
☐ 620	Richie Zisk	.06	.02	.00
☐ 621	Jon Matlack	.03	.01	.00
☐ 622	Ferguson Jenkins	.15	.06	.01

		MINT	EXC	G-VG
☐ 623	Pat Corrales MG ...	.03	.01	.00
☐ 624	Ed Figueroa	.03	.01	.00
☐ 625	Buddy Bell	.15	.06	.01
☐ 626	Al Oliver	.12	.05	.01
☐ 627	Doc Medich	.03	.01	.00
☐ 628	Bump Wills	.03	.01	.00
☐ 629	Rusty Staub	.10	.04	.01
☐ 630	Pat Putnam	.03	.01	.00
☐ 631	John Grubb	.03	.01	.00
☐ 632	Danny Darwin	.03	.01	.00
☐ 633	Ken Clay	.03	.01	.00
☐ 634	Jim Norris	.03	.01	.00
☐ 635	John Butcher	.06	.02	.00
☐ 636	Dave Roberts	.03	.01	.00
☐ 637	Billy Sample	.03	.01	.00
☐ 638	Carl Yastrzemski ...	1.00	.40	.10
☐ 639	Cecil Cooper	.15	.06	.01
☐ 640A	Mike Schmidt P1 ... (Portrait) "Third Base" (number on back 5)	1.00	.40	.10
☐ 640B	Mike Schmidt P2 ... "1980 Home Run King" (640 on back)	1.00	.40	.10
☐ 641A	CL: Phils/Royals P1 41 is Hal McRae	.10	.01	.00
☐ 641B	CL: Phils/Royals P2 41 is Hal McRae, Double Threat	.10	.01	.00
☐ 642	CL: Astros/Yankees	.08	.01	.00
☐ 643	CL: Expos/Dodgers .	.08	.01	.00
☐ 644A	CL: Reds/Orioles P1 202 is George Foster	.10	.01	.00
☐ 644B	CL: Reds/Orioles P2 202 is Foster Slugger	.10	.01	.00
☐ 645A	Rose/Bowa/Schmidt Threat P1 (No number on back)	2.00	.80	.20
☐ 645B	Rose/Bowa/Schmidt Triple Threat P2 (Back numbered 645)	1.00	.40	.10
☐ 646	CL: Braves/Red Sox	.08	.01	.00
☐ 647	CL: Cubs/Angels ...	.08	.01	.00
☐ 648	CL: Mets/White Sox	.08	.01	.00
☐ 649	CL: Indians/Pirates .	.08	.01	.00
☐ 650A	Reggie Jackson ... Mr. Baseball P1 Number on back 79	1.25	.50	.12

		MINT	EXC	G-VG
☐ 650B	Reggie Jackson ... Mr. Baseball P2 Number on back 650	.85	.34	.08
☐ 651	CL: Giants/Blue Jays	.08	.01	.00
☐ 652A	CL: Tigers/Padres P1 483 is listed	.10	.01	.00
☐ 652B	CL: Tigers/Padres P2 483 is deleted	.10	.01	.00
☐ 653A	Willie Wilson P1 ... Most Hits Most Runs Number on back 29	.10	.04	.01
☐ 653B	Willie Wilson P2 ... Most Hits Most Runs Number on back 653	.10	.04	.01
☐ 654A	CL:Brewers/Cards P1 514 Jerry Augustine 547 Pete Vuckovich	.10	.01	.00
☐ 654B	CL:Brewers/Cards P2 514 Billy Travers 547 Don Hood	.10	.01	.00
☐ 655A	George Brett P1 ... .390 Average Number on back 28	1.25	.50	.12
☐ 655B	George Brett P2 .. .390 Average Number on back 655	.85	.34	.08
☐ 656	CL: Twins/Oakland A's	.08	.01	.00
☐ 657A	Tug McGraw P1 ... Game Saver Number on back 7	.10	.04	.01
☐ 657B	Tug McGraw P2 ... Game Saver Number on back 657	.10	.04	.01
☐ 658	CL: Rangers/Mariners	.08	.01	.00
☐ 659A	Checklist P1 ..... of Special Cards Last lines on front Wilson Most Hits	.10	.01	.00
☐ 659B	Checklist P2 ..... of Special Cards Last lines on front Otis Series Starter	.10	.01	.00
☐ 660A	Steve Carlton P1 .. Golden Arm Back "1066 Cardinals" Number on back 6	.65	.26	.06

		MINT	EXC	G-VG
☐ 660B	Steve Carlton P2 ...	.65	.26	.06
	Golden Arm			
	Number on back 660			
	Back "1066 Cardinals"			
☐ 660C	Steve Carlton P3 ...	2.00	.80	.20
	Golden Arm			
	"1966 Cardinals"			

1981 Fleer Sticker Cards

The stickers in this 128-sticker set measure 2½" by 3½". The 1981 Fleer Baseball Star Stickers consist of numbered cards with peelable, full-color sticker fronts and three unnumbered checklists. The backs of the numbered player cards are the same as the 1981 Fleer regular issue cards except for the numbers, while the checklist cards (cards 126-128 below) have sticker fronts of Jackson (1-42), Brett (43-83), and Schmidt (84-125).

		MINT	EXC	G-VG
Complete Set (128)		40.00	16.00	4.00
Common Player (1-128) ...		.15	.06	.01
☐ 1	Steve Garvey	1.75	.70	.17
☐ 2	Ron LeFlore	.15	.06	.01
☐ 3	Ron Cey	.20	.08	.02
☐ 4	Dave Revering	.15	.06	.01
☐ 5	Tony Armas	.15	.06	.01
☐ 6	Mike Norris	.15	.06	.01
☐ 7	Steve Kemp	.20	.08	.02

		MINT	EXC	G-VG
☐ 8	Bruce Bochte	.15	.06	.01
☐ 9	Mike Schmidt	2.50	1.00	.25
☐ 10	Scott McGregor ...	.20	.08	.02
☐ 11	Buddy Bell	.25	.10	.02
☐ 12	Carney Lansford ...	.20	.08	.02
☐ 13	Carl Yastrzemski ..	3.00	1.20	.30
☐ 14	Ben Oglivie	.15	.06	.01
☐ 15	Willie Stargell	1.25	.50	.12
☐ 16	Cecil Cooper	.25	.10	.02
☐ 17	Gene Richards	.15	.06	.01
☐ 18	Jim Kern	.15	.06	.01
☐ 19	Jerry Koosman ...	.20	.08	.02
☐ 20	Larry Bowa	.25	.10	.02
☐ 21	Kent Tekulve	.15	.06	.01
☐ 22	Dan Driessen	.15	.06	.01
☐ 23	Phil Niekro	.75	.30	.07
☐ 24	Dan Quisenberry ..	.30	.12	.03
☐ 25	Dave Winfield	1.75	.70	.17
☐ 26	Dave Parker	.60	.24	.06
☐ 27	Rick Langford	.15	.06	.01
☐ 28	Amos Otis	.20	.08	.02
☐ 29	Bill Buckner	.20	.08	.02
☐ 30	Al Bumbry	.15	.06	.01
☐ 31	Bake McBride	.15	.06	.01
☐ 32	Mickey Rivers	.15	.06	.01
☐ 33	Rick Burleson	.20	.08	.02
☐ 34	Dennis Eckersley .	.35	.14	.03
☐ 35	Cesar Cedeno	.20	.08	.02
☐ 36	Enos Cabell	.15	.06	.01
☐ 37	Johnny Bench	2.50	1.00	.25
☐ 38	Robin Yount	1.75	.70	.17
☐ 39	Mark Belanger	.15	.06	.01
☐ 40	Rod Carew	1.75	.70	.17
☐ 41	George Foster	.60	.24	.06
☐ 42	Lee Mazzilli	.15	.06	.01
☐ 43	Triple Threat:	2.00	.80	.20
	Pete Rose			
	Larry Bowa			
	Mike Schmidt			
☐ 44	J.R. Richard	.20	.08	.02
☐ 45	Lou Piniella	.20	.08	.02
☐ 46	Ken Landreaux	.15	.06	.01
☐ 47	Rollie Fingers	.50	.20	.05
☐ 48	Joaquin Andujar ...	.20	.08	.02
☐ 49	Tom Seaver	2.00	.80	.20
☐ 50	Bobby Grich	.20	.08	.02
☐ 51	Jon Matlack	.15	.06	.01
☐ 52	Jack Clark	.60	.24	.06
☐ 53	Jim Rice	1.00	.40	.10

		MINT	EXC	G-VG
☐ 54	Rickey Henderson .	2.00	.80	.20
☐ 55	Roy Smalley	.15	.06	.01
☐ 56	Mike Flanagan	.20	.08	.02
☐ 57	Steve Rogers	.15	.06	.01
☐ 58	Carlton Fisk	.50	.20	.05
☐ 59	Don Sutton	.60	.24	.06
☐ 60	Ken Griffey	.20	.08	.02
☐ 61	Burt Hooton	.15	.06	.01
☐ 62	Dusty Baker	.20	.08	.02
☐ 63	Vida Blue	.20	.08	.02
☐ 64	Al Oliver	.20	.08	.02
☐ 65	Jim Bibby	.15	.06	.01
☐ 66	Tony Perez	.40	.16	.04
☐ 67	Davy Lopes	.20	.08	.02
☐ 68	Bill Russell	.15	.06	.01
☐ 69	Larry Parrish	.20	.08	.02
☐ 70	Garry Maddox	.15	.06	.01
☐ 71	Phil Garner	.15	.06	.01
☐ 72	Graig Nettles	.35	.14	.03
☐ 73	Gary Carter	1.75	.70	.17
☐ 74	Pete Rose	4.50	1.80	.45
☐ 75	Greg Luzinski	.30	.12	.03
☐ 76	Ron Guidry	.50	.20	.05
☐ 77	Gorman Thomas ...	.25	.10	.02
☐ 78	Jose Cruz	.20	.08	.02
☐ 79	Bob Boone	.30	.12	.03
☐ 80	Bruce Sutter	.30	.12	.03
☐ 81	Chris Chambliss ...	.20	.08	.02
☐ 82	Paul Molitor	.60	.24	.06
☐ 83	Tug McGraw	.25	.10	.02
☐ 84	Ferguson Jenkins ..	.40	.16	.04
☐ 85	Steve Carlton	1.75	.70	.17
☐ 86	Miguel Dilone	.15	.06	.01
☐ 87	Reggie Smith	.25	.10	.02
☐ 88	Rick Cerone	.15	.06	.01
☐ 89	Alan Trammell	1.00	.40	.10
☐ 90	Doug DeCinces	.25	.10	.02
☐ 91	Sparky Lyle	.25	.10	.02
☐ 92	Warren Cromartie ..	.15	.06	.01
☐ 93	Rick Reuschel	.30	.12	.03
☐ 94	Larry Hisle	.15	.06	.01
☐ 95	Paul Splittorff	.20	.08	.02
☐ 96	Manny Trillo	.15	.06	.01
☐ 97	Frank White	.25	.10	.02
☐ 98	Fred Lynn	.50	.20	.05
☐ 99	Bob Horner	.50	.20	.05
☐ 100	Omar Moreno	.15	.06	.01
☐ 101	Dave Concepcion ..	.20	.08	.02
☐ 102	Larry Gura	.20	.08	.02

		MINT	EXC	G-VG
☐ 103	Ken Singleton	.20	.08	.02
☐ 104	Steve Stone	.15	.06	.01
☐ 105	Richie Zisk	.15	.06	.01
☐ 106	Willie Wilson	.30	.12	.03
☐ 107	Willie Randolph ...	.30	.12	.03
☐ 108	Nolan Ryan	2.00	.80	.20
☐ 109	Joe Morgan	1.00	.40	.10
☐ 110	Bucky Dent	.25	.10	.02
☐ 111	Dave Kingman	.35	.14	.03
☐ 112	John Castino	.15	.06	.01
☐ 113	Joe Rudi	.15	.06	.01
☐ 114	Ed Farmer	.15	.06	.01
☐ 115	Reggie Jackson ...	2.50	1.00	.25
☐ 116	George Brett	2.50	1.00	.25
☐ 117	Eddie Murray	2.25	.90	.22
☐ 118	Rich Gossage	.50	.20	.05
☐ 119	Dale Murphy	2.50	1.00	.25
☐ 120	Ted Simmons	.25	.10	.02
☐ 121	Tommy John	.50	.20	.05
☐ 122	Don Baylor	.40	.16	.04
☐ 123	Andre Dawson	1.50	.60	.15
☐ 124	Jim Palmer	1.25	.50	.12
☐ 125	Garry Templeton ..	.25	.10	.02
☐ 126	CL 1: Reggie Jackson	1.25	.50	.12
☐ 127	CL 2: George Brett	1.25	.50	.12
☐ 128	CL 3: Mike Schmidt	1.25	.50	.12

1982 Fleer

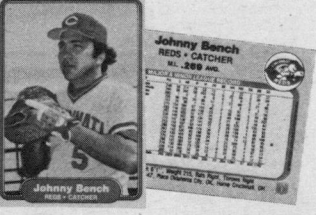

*The cards in this 660-card set measure 2 ½"
by 3 ½". The 1982 Fleer set is again ordered
by teams; in fact the players within each
team are listed in alphabetical order. The*

teams are ordered (by 1981 standings) as follows: Los Angeles (1-29), New York Yankees (30-56), Cincinnati (57-84), Oakland (85-109), St. Louis (110-132), Milwaukee (133-156), Baltimore (157-182), Montreal (183-211), Houston (212-237), Philadelphia (238-262), Detroit (263-286), Boston (287-312), Texas (313-334), Chicago White Sox (335-358), Cleveland (359-382), San Francisco (383-403), Kansas City (404-427), Atlanta (428-449), California (450-474), Pittsburgh (475-501), Seattle (502-519), New York Mets (520-544), Minnesota (545-565), San Diego (566-585), Chicago Cubs (586-607), and Toronto (608-627). Cards numbered 628 through 646 are special cards highlighting some of the stars and leaders of the 1981 season. The last 14 cards in the set (647-660) are checklist cards. The backs feature player statistics and a full-color team logo in the upper right-hand corner of each card.

			MINT	EXC	G-VG
	Complete Set (660)		30.00	12.00	3.00
	Common Player (1-660)		.03	.01	.00
☐	1	Dusty Baker	.12	.03	.01
☐	2	Robert Castillo	.03	.01	.00
☐	3	Ron Cey	.10	.04	.01
☐	4	Terry Forster	.06	.02	.00
☐	5	Steve Garvey	.50	.20	.05
☐	6	Dave Goltz	.03	.01	.00
☐	7	Pedro Guerrero	.35	.14	.03
☐	8	Burt Hooton	.03	.01	.00
☐	9	Steve Howe	.03	.01	.00
☐	10	Jay Johnstone	.06	.02	.00
☐	11	Ken Landreaux	.03	.01	.00
☐	12	Dave Lopes	.08	.03	.01
☐	13	Mike Marshall	1.25	.50	.12
☐	14	Bobby Mitchell	.03	.01	.00
☐	15	Rick Monday	.03	.01	.00
☐	16	Tom Niedenfuer	.20	.08	.02
☐	17	Ted Power	.20	.08	.02
☐	18	Jerry Reuss	.06	.02	.00
☐	19	Ron Roenicke	.03	.01	.00
☐	20	Bill Russell	.06	.02	.00
☐	21	Steve Sax	2.00	.80	.20
☐	22	Mike Scioscia	.06	.02	.00
☐	23	Reggie Smith	.08	.03	.01
☐	24	Dave Stewart	1.00	.40	.10
☐	25	Rick Sutcliffe	.20	.08	.02
☐	26	Derrel Thomas	.03	.01	.00
☐	27	Fernando Valenzuela	.50	.20	.05
☐	28	Bob Welch	.10	.04	.01
☐	29	Steve Yeager	.03	.01	.00
☐	30	Bobby Brown	.03	.01	.00
☐	31	Rick Cerone	.03	.01	.00
☐	32	Ron Davis	.03	.01	.00
☐	33	Bucky Dent	.08	.03	.01
☐	34	Barry Foote	.03	.01	.00
☐	35	George Frazier	.03	.01	.00
☐	36	Oscar Gamble	.03	.01	.00
☐	37	Rich Gossage	.15	.06	.01
☐	38	Ron Guidry	.18	.08	.01
☐	39	Reggie Jackson	.60	.24	.06
☐	40	Tommy John	.15	.06	.01
☐	41	Rudy May	.03	.01	.00
☐	42	Larry Milbourne	.03	.01	.00
☐	43	Jerry Mumphrey	.03	.01	.00
☐	44	Bobby Murcer	.08	.03	.01
☐	45	Gene Nelson	.20	.08	.02
☐	46	Graig Nettles	.12	.05	.01
☐	47	Johnny Oates	.03	.01	.00
☐	48	Lou Piniella	.10	.04	.01
☐	49	Willie Randolph	.08	.03	.01
☐	50	Rick Reuschel	.10	.04	.01
☐	51	Dave Revering	.03	.01	.00
☐	52	Dave Righetti	1.50	.60	.15
☐	53	Aurelio Rodriguez	.03	.01	.00
☐	54	Bob Watson	.06	.02	.00
☐	55	Dennis Werth	.03	.01	.00
☐	56	Dave Winfield	.50	.20	.05
☐	57	Johnny Bench	.55	.22	.05
☐	58	Bruce Berenyi	.03	.01	.00
☐	59	Larry Biittner	.03	.01	.00
☐	60	Scott Brown	.03	.01	.00
☐	61	Dave Collins	.03	.01	.00
☐	62	Geoff Combe	.03	.01	.00
☐	63	Dave Concepcion	.10	.04	.01
☐	64	Dan Driessen	.03	.01	.00
☐	65	Joe Edelen	.03	.01	.00
☐	66	George Foster	.12	.05	.01
☐	67	Ken Griffey	.06	.02	.00
☐	68	Paul Householder	.03	.01	.00
☐	69	Tom Hume	.03	.01	.00
☐	70	Junior Kennedy	.03	.01	.00
☐	71	Ray Knight	.08	.03	.01
☐	72	Mike LaCoss	.03	.01	.00
☐	73	Rafael Landestoy	.03	.01	.00

		MINT	EXC	G-VG
☐ 74	Charlie Leibrandt ..	.06	.02	.00
☐ 75	Sam Mejias	.03	.01	.00
☐ 76	Paul Moskau	.03	.01	.00
☐ 77	Joe Nolan	.03	.01	.00
☐ 78	Mike O'Berry	.03	.01	.00
☐ 79	Ron Oester	.03	.01	.00
☐ 80	Frank Pastore	.03	.01	.00
☐ 81	Joe Price	.03	.01	.00
☐ 82	Tom Seaver	.45	.18	.04
☐ 83	Mario Soto	.06	.02	.00
☐ 84	Mike Vail	.03	.01	.00
☐ 85	Tony Armas	.08	.03	.01
☐ 86	Shooty Babitt	.03	.01	.00
☐ 87	Dave Beard	.03	.01	.00
☐ 88	Rick Bosetti	.03	.01	.00
☐ 89	Keith Drumwright ..	.03	.01	.00
☐ 90	Wayne Gross	.03	.01	.00
☐ 91	Mike Heath	.03	.01	.00
☐ 92	Rickey Henderson .	.75	.30	.07
☐ 93	Cliff Johnson	.03	.01	.00
☐ 94	Jeff Jones	.03	.01	.00
☐ 95	Matt Keough	.03	.01	.00
☐ 96	Brian Kingman	.03	.01	.00
☐ 97	Mickey Klutts	.03	.01	.00
☐ 98	Rick Langford	.03	.01	.00
☐ 99	Steve McCatty	.03	.01	.00
☐ 100	Dave McKay	.03	.01	.00
☐ 101	Dwayne Murphy ...	.03	.01	.00
☐ 102	Jeff Newman	.03	.01	.00
☐ 103	Mike Norris	.03	.01	.00
☐ 104	Bob Owchinko	.03	.01	.00
☐ 105	Mitchell Page	.03	.01	.00
☐ 106	Rob Picciolo	.03	.01	.00
☐ 107	Jim Spencer	.03	.01	.00
☐ 108	Fred Stanley	.03	.01	.00
☐ 109	Tom Underwood ...	.03	.01	.00
☐ 110	Joaquin Andujar ...	.08	.03	.01
☐ 111	Steve Braun	.03	.01	.00
☐ 112	Bob Forsch	.03	.01	.00
☐ 113	George Hendrick ...	.06	.02	.00
☐ 114	Keith Hernandez ...	.35	.14	.03
☐ 115	Tom Herr	.08	.03	.01
☐ 116	Dane Iorg	.03	.01	.00
☐ 117	Jim Kaat	.15	.06	.01
☐ 118	Tito Landrum	.03	.01	.00
☐ 119	Sixto Lezcano	.03	.01	.00
☐ 120	Mark Littell	.03	.01	.00
☐ 121	John Martin	.03	.01	.00
☐ 122	Silvio Martinez	.03	.01	.00
☐ 123	Ken Oberkfell	.03	.01	.00
☐ 124	Darrell Porter	.03	.01	.00
☐ 125	Mike Ramsey	.03	.01	.00
☐ 126	Orlando Sanchez ..	.03	.01	.00
☐ 127	Bob Shirley	.03	.01	.00
☐ 128	Lary Sorensen	.03	.01	.00
☐ 129	Bruce Sutter	.15	.06	.01
☐ 130	Bob Sykes	.03	.01	.00
☐ 131	Garry Templeton ..	.08	.03	.01
☐ 132	Gene Tenace	.03	.01	.00
☐ 133	Jerry Augustine ...	.03	.01	.00
☐ 134	Sal Bando	.06	.02	.00
☐ 135	Mark Brouhard	.03	.01	.00
☐ 136	Mike Caldwell	.03	.01	.00
☐ 137	Reggie Cleveland .	.03	.01	.00
☐ 138	Cecil Cooper	.15	.06	.01
☐ 139	Jamie Easterly	.03	.01	.00
☐ 140	Marshall Edwards .	.03	.01	.00
☐ 141	Rollie Fingers	.20	.08	.02
☐ 142	Jim Gantner	.03	.01	.00
☐ 143	Moose Haas	.03	.01	.00
☐ 144	Larry Hisle	.06	.02	.00
☐ 145	Roy Howell	.03	.01	.00
☐ 146	Rickey Keeton	.03	.01	.00
☐ 147	Randy Lerch	.03	.01	.00
☐ 148	Paul Molitor	.20	.08	.02
☐ 149	Don Money	.03	.01	.00
☐ 150	Charlie Moore	.03	.01	.00
☐ 151	Ben Oglivie	.06	.02	.00
☐ 152	Ted Simmons	.12	.05	.01
☐ 153	Jim Slaton	.03	.01	.00
☐ 154	Gorman Thomas ...	.10	.04	.01
☐ 155	Robin Yount	.50	.20	.05
☐ 156	Pete Vuckovich ...	.08	.03	.01
☐ 157	Benny Ayala	.03	.01	.00
☐ 158	Mark Belanger	.06	.02	.00
☐ 159	Al Bumbry	.03	.01	.00
☐ 160	Terry Crowley	.03	.01	.00
☐ 161	Rich Dauer	.03	.01	.00
☐ 162	Doug DeCinces ...	.06	.02	.00
☐ 163	Rick Dempsey	.03	.01	.00
☐ 164	Jim Dwyer	.03	.01	.00
☐ 165	Mike Flanagan	.08	.03	.01
☐ 166	Dave Ford	.03	.01	.00
☐ 167	Dan Graham	.03	.01	.00
☐ 168	Wayne Krenchicki .	.03	.01	.00
☐ 169	John Lowenstein ..	.03	.01	.00
☐ 170	Dennis Martinez ..	.06	.02	.00
☐ 171	Tippy Martinez	.03	.01	.00

		MINT	EXC	G-VG
☐ 172	Scott McGregor	.06	.02	.00
☐ 173	Jose Morales	.03	.01	.00
☐ 174	Eddie Murray	.60	.24	.06
☐ 175	Jim Palmer	.35	.14	.03
☐ 176	Cal Ripken	7.50	3.00	.75
☐ 177	Gary Roenicke	.03	.01	.00
☐ 178	Lenn Sakata	.03	.01	.00
☐ 179	Ken Singleton	.08	.03	.01
☐ 180	Sammy Stewart	.03	.01	.00
☐ 181	Tim Stoddard	.03	.01	.00
☐ 182	Steve Stone	.06	.02	.00
☐ 183	Stan Bahnsen	.03	.01	.00
☐ 184	Ray Burris	.03	.01	.00
☐ 185	Gary Carter	.45	.18	.04
☐ 186	Warren Cromartie	.03	.01	.00
☐ 187	Andre Dawson	.35	.14	.03
☐ 188	Terry Francona	.10	.04	.01
☐ 189	Woodie Fryman	.03	.01	.00
☐ 190	Bill Gullickson	.06	.02	.00
☐ 191	Grant Jackson	.03	.01	.00
☐ 192	Wallace Johnson	.06	.02	.00
☐ 193	Charlie Lea	.06	.02	.00
☐ 194	Bill Lee	.06	.02	.00
☐ 195	Jerry Manuel	.03	.01	.00
☐ 196	Brad Mills	.03	.01	.00
☐ 197	John Milner	.03	.01	.00
☐ 198	Rowland Office	.03	.01	.00
☐ 199	David Palmer	.03	.01	.00
☐ 200	Larry Parrish	.06	.02	.00
☐ 201	Mike Phillips	.03	.01	.00
☐ 202	Tim Raines	1.75	.70	.17
☐ 203	Bobby Ramos	.03	.01	.00
☐ 204	Jeff Reardon	.15	.06	.01
☐ 205	Steve Rogers	.06	.02	.00
☐ 206	Scott Sanderson	.03	.01	.00
☐ 207	Rodney Scott	.15	.06	.01
	(photo actually Tim Raines)			
☐ 208	Elias Sosa	.03	.01	.00
☐ 209	Chris Speier	.03	.01	.00
☐ 210	Tim Wallach	.80	.32	.08
☐ 211	Jerry White	.03	.01	.00
☐ 212	Alan Ashby	.06	.02	.00
☐ 213	Cesar Cedeno	.08	.03	.01
☐ 214	Jose Cruz	.10	.04	.01
☐ 215	Kiko Garcia	.03	.01	.00
☐ 216	Phil Garner	.03	.01	.00
☐ 217	Danny Heep	.03	.01	.00
☐ 218	Art Howe	.08	.03	.01
☐ 219	Bob Knepper	.10	.04	.01

		MINT	EXC	G-VG
☐ 220	Frank LaCorte	.03	.01	.00
☐ 221	Joe Niekro	.10	.04	.01
☐ 222	Joe Pittman	.03	.01	.00
☐ 223	Terry Puhl	.03	.01	.00
☐ 224	Luis Pujols	.03	.01	.00
☐ 225	Craig Reynolds	.03	.01	.00
☐ 226	J.R. Richard	.10	.04	.01
☐ 227	Dave Roberts	.03	.01	.00
☐ 228	Vern Ruhle	.03	.01	.00
☐ 229	Nolan Ryan	.50	.20	.05
☐ 230	Joe Sambito	.03	.01	.00
☐ 231	Tony Scott	.03	.01	.00
☐ 232	Dave Smith	.08	.03	.01
☐ 233	Harry Spilman	.03	.01	.00
☐ 234	Don Sutton	.30	.12	.03
☐ 235	Dickie Thon	.06	.02	.00
☐ 236	Denny Walling	.03	.01	.00
☐ 237	Gary Woods	.03	.01	.00
☐ 238	Luis Aguayo	.03	.01	.00
☐ 239	Ramon Aviles	.03	.01	.00
☐ 240	Bob Boone	.12	.05	.01
☐ 241	Larry Bowa	.15	.06	.01
☐ 242	Warren Brusstar	.03	.01	.00
☐ 243	Steve Carlton	.50	.20	.05
☐ 244	Larry Christenson	.03	.01	.00
☐ 245	Dick Davis	.03	.01	.00
☐ 246	Greg Gross	.03	.01	.00
☐ 247	Sparky Lyle	.10	.04	.01
☐ 248	Garry Maddox	.06	.02	.00
☐ 249	Gary Matthews	.06	.02	.00
☐ 250	Bake McBride	.03	.01	.00
☐ 251	Tug McGraw	.10	.04	.01
☐ 252	Keith Moreland	.06	.02	.00
☐ 253	Dickie Noles	.03	.01	.00
☐ 254	Mike Proly	.03	.01	.00
☐ 255	Ron Reed	.03	.01	.00
☐ 256	Pete Rose	1.25	.50	.12
☐ 257	Dick Ruthven	.03	.01	.00
☐ 258	Mike Schmidt	.75	.30	.07
☐ 259	Lonnie Smith	.06	.02	.00
☐ 260	Manny Trillo	.03	.01	.00
☐ 261	Del Unser	.03	.01	.00
☐ 262	George Vukovich	.03	.01	.00
☐ 263	Tom Brookens	.03	.01	.00
☐ 264	George Cappuzzello	.03	.01	.00
☐ 265	Marty Castillo	.03	.01	.00
☐ 266	Al Cowens	.03	.01	.00
☐ 267	Kirk Gibson	.75	.30	.07
☐ 268	Richie Hebner	.03	.01	.00

		MINT	EXC	G-VG			MINT	EXC	G-VG
☐ 269	Ron Jackson	.03	.01	.00	☐ 318	Rick Honeycutt	.03	.01	.00
☐ 270	Lynn Jones	.03	.01	.00	☐ 319	Charlie Hough	.08	.03	.01
☐ 271	Steve Kemp	.06	.02	.00	☐ 320	Ferguson Jenkins	.15	.06	.01
☐ 272	Rick Leach	.03	.01	.00	☐ 321	John Henry Johnson	.03	.01	.00
☐ 273	Aurelio Lopez	.03	.01	.00	☐ 322	Jim Kern	.03	.01	.00
☐ 274	Jack Morris	.25	.10	.02	☐ 323	Jon Matlack	.03	.01	.00
☐ 275	Kevin Saucier	.03	.01	.00	☐ 324	Doc Medich	.03	.01	.00
☐ 276	Lance Parrish	.20	.08	.02	☐ 325	Mario Mendoza	.03	.01	.00
☐ 277	Rick Peters	.03	.01	.00	☐ 326	Al Oliver	.10	.04	.01
☐ 278	Dan Petry	.06	.02	.00	☐ 327	Pat Putnam	.03	.01	.00
☐ 279	Dave Rozema	.03	.01	.00	☐ 328	Mickey Rivers	.06	.02	.00
☐ 280	Stan Papi	.03	.01	.00	☐ 329	Leon Roberts	.03	.01	.00
☐ 281	Dan Schatzeder	.03	.01	.00	☐ 330	Billy Sample	.03	.01	.00
☐ 282	Champ Summers	.03	.01	.00	☐ 331	Bill Stein	.03	.01	.00
☐ 283	Alan Trammell	.35	.14	.03	☐ 332	Jim Sundberg	.06	.02	.00
☐ 284	Lou Whitaker	.15	.06	.01	☐ 333	Mark Wagner	.03	.01	.00
☐ 285	Milt Wilcox	.03	.01	.00	☐ 334	Bump Wills	.03	.01	.00
☐ 286	John Wockenfuss	.03	.01	.00	☐ 335	Bill Almon	.03	.01	.00
☐ 287	Gary Allenson	.03	.01	.00	☐ 336	Harold Baines	.25	.10	.02
☐ 288	Tom Burgmeier	.03	.01	.00	☐ 337	Ross Baumgarten	.03	.01	.00
☐ 289	Bill Campbell	.03	.01	.00	☐ 338	Tony Bernazard	.03	.01	.00
☐ 290	Mark Clear	.03	.01	.00	☐ 339	Britt Burns	.06	.02	.00
☐ 291	Steve Crawford	.03	.01	.00	☐ 340	Richard Dotson	.10	.04	.01
☐ 292	Dennis Eckersley	.15	.06	.01	☐ 341	Jim Essian	.03	.01	.00
☐ 293	Dwight Evans	.18	.08	.01	☐ 342	Ed Farmer	.03	.01	.00
☐ 294	Rich Gedman	.40	.16	.04	☐ 343	Carlton Fisk	.15	.06	.01
☐ 295	Garry Hancock	.03	.01	.00	☐ 344	Kevin Hickey	.03	.01	.00
☐ 296	Glenn Hoffman	.03	.01	.00	☐ 345	LaMarr Hoyt	.08	.03	.01
☐ 297	Bruce Hurst	.60	.24	.06	☐ 346	Lamar Johnson	.03	.01	.00
☐ 298	Carney Lansford	.15	.06	.01	☐ 347	Jerry Koosman	.08	.03	.01
☐ 299	Rick Miller	.03	.01	.00	☐ 348	Rusty Kuntz	.03	.01	.00
☐ 300	Reid Nichols	.03	.01	.00	☐ 349	Dennis Lamp	.03	.01	.00
☐ 301	Bob Ojeda	.45	.18	.04	☐ 350	Ron LeFlore	.06	.02	.00
☐ 302	Tony Perez	.15	.06	.01	☐ 351	Chet Lemon	.06	.02	.00
☐ 303	Chuck Rainey	.03	.01	.00	☐ 352	Greg Luzinski	.10	.04	.01
☐ 304	Jerry Remy	.03	.01	.00	☐ 353	Bob Molinaro	.03	.01	.00
☐ 305	Jim Rice	.30	.12	.03	☐ 354	Jim Morrison	.03	.01	.00
☐ 306	Joe Rudi	.06	.02	.00	☐ 355	Wayne Nordhagen	.03	.01	.00
☐ 307	Bob Stanley	.03	.01	.00	☐ 356	Greg Pryor	.03	.01	.00
☐ 308	Dave Stapleton	.03	.01	.00	☐ 357	Mike Squires	.03	.01	.00
☐ 309	Frank Tanana	.06	.02	.00	☐ 358	Steve Trout	.03	.01	.00
☐ 310	Mike Torrez	.03	.01	.00	☐ 359	Alan Bannister	.03	.01	.00
☐ 311	John Tudor	.20	.08	.02	☐ 360	Len Barker	.03	.01	.00
☐ 312	Carl Yastrzemski	1.00	.40	.10	☐ 361	Bert Blyleven	.15	.06	.01
☐ 313	Buddy Bell	.12	.05	.01	☐ 362	Joe Charboneau	.06	.02	.00
☐ 314	Steve Comer	.03	.01	.00	☐ 363	John Denny	.06	.02	.00
☐ 315	Danny Darwin	.03	.01	.00	☐ 364	Bo Diaz	.06	.02	.00
☐ 316	John Ellis	.03	.01	.00	☐ 365	Miguel Dilone	.03	.01	.00
☐ 317	John Grubb	.03	.01	.00	☐ 366	Jerry Dybzinski	.03	.01	.00

		MINT	EXC	G-VG
☐ 367	Wayne Garland	.03	.01	.00
☐ 368	Mike Hargrove	.03	.01	.00
☐ 369	Toby Harrah	.06	.02	.00
☐ 370	Ron Hassey	.06	.02	.00
☐ 371	Von Hayes	.90	.36	.09
☐ 372	Pat Kelly	.03	.01	.00
☐ 373	Duane Kuiper	.03	.01	.00
☐ 374	Rick Manning	.03	.01	.00
☐ 375	Sid Monge	.03	.01	.00
☐ 376	Jorge Orta	.03	.01	.00
☐ 377	Dave Rosello	.03	.01	.00
☐ 378	Dan Spillner	.03	.01	.00
☐ 379	Mike Stanton	.03	.01	.00
☐ 380	Andre Thornton ...	.06	.02	.00
☐ 381	Tom Veryzer	.03	.01	.00
☐ 382	Rick Waits	.03	.01	.00
☐ 383	Doyle Alexander ...	.08	.03	.01
☐ 384	Vida Blue	.08	.03	.01
☐ 385	Fred Breining	.03	.01	.00
☐ 386	Enos Cabell	.03	.01	.00
☐ 387	Jack Clark	.30	.12	.03
☐ 388	Darrell Evans	.12	.05	.01
☐ 389	Tom Griffin	.03	.01	.00
☐ 390	Larry Herndon	.03	.01	.00
☐ 391	Al Holland	.03	.01	.00
☐ 392	Gary Lavelle	.03	.01	.00
☐ 393	Johnnie LeMaster ..	.03	.01	.00
☐ 394	Jerry Martin	.03	.01	.00
☐ 395	Milt May	.03	.01	.00
☐ 396	Greg Minton	.03	.01	.00
☐ 397	Joe Morgan	.30	.12	.03
☐ 398	Joe Pettini	.03	.01	.00
☐ 399	Allen Ripley	.03	.01	.00
☐ 400	Billy Smith	.03	.01	.00
☐ 401	Rennie Stennett ...	.03	.01	.00
☐ 402	Ed Whitson	.06	.02	.00
☐ 403	Jim Wohlford	.03	.01	.00
☐ 404	Willie Aikens	.03	.01	.00
☐ 405	George Brett	.70	.28	.07
☐ 406	Ken Brett	.03	.01	.00
☐ 407	Dave Chalk	.03	.01	.00
☐ 408	Rich Gale	.03	.01	.00
☐ 409	Cesar Geronimo ...	.03	.01	.00
☐ 410	Larry Gura	.03	.01	.00
☐ 411	Clint Hurdle	.03	.01	.00
☐ 412	Mike Jones	.03	.01	.00
☐ 413	Dennis Leonard ...	.06	.02	.00
☐ 414	Renie Martin	.03	.01	.00
☐ 415	Lee May	.03	.01	.00

		MINT	EXC	G-VG
☐ 416	Hal McRae	.06	.02	.00
☐ 417	Darryl Motley	.06	.02	.00
☐ 418	Rance Mulliniks ...	.03	.01	.00
☐ 419	Amos Otis	.08	.03	.01
☐ 420	Ken Phelps	.75	.30	.07
☐ 421	Jamie Quirk	.03	.01	.00
☐ 422	Dan Quisenberry ..	.15	.06	.01
☐ 423	Paul Splittorff	.03	.01	.00
☐ 424	U.L. Washington ...	.03	.01	.00
☐ 425	John Wathan	.06	.02	.00
☐ 426	Frank White	.08	.03	.01
☐ 427	Willie Wilson	.12	.05	.01
☐ 428	Brian Asselstine ...	.03	.01	.00
☐ 429	Bruce Benedict ...	.03	.01	.00
☐ 430	Tommy Boggs	.03	.01	.00
☐ 431	Larry Bradford ...	.03	.01	.00
☐ 432	Rick Camp	.03	.01	.00
☐ 433	Chris Chambliss ..	.08	.03	.01
☐ 434	Gene Garber	.03	.01	.00
☐ 435	Preston Hanna ...	.03	.01	.00
☐ 436	Bob Horner	.18	.08	.01
☐ 437	Glenn Hubbard ...	.03	.01	.00
☐ 438A	Al Hrabosky	20.00	8.00	2.00
	(height 5'1")			
☐ 438B	Al Hrabosky	1.00	.40	.10
	(height 5'1")			
☐ 438C	Al Hrabosky	.10	.04	.01
	(height 5'10")			
☐ 439	Rufino Linares	.05	.02	.00
☐ 440	Rick Mahler	.25	.10	.02
☐ 441	Ed Miller	.03	.01	.00
☐ 442	John Montefusco ..	.06	.02	.00
☐ 443	Dale Murphy	.90	.36	.09
☐ 444	Phil Niekro	.30	.12	.03
☐ 445	Gaylord Perry	.30	.12	.03
☐ 446	Biff Pocoroba	.03	.01	.00
☐ 447	Rafael Ramirez ...	.06	.02	.00
☐ 448	Jerry Royster	.03	.01	.00
☐ 449	Claudell Washington	.08	.03	.01
☐ 450	Don Aase	.03	.01	.00
☐ 451	Don Baylor	.15	.06	.01
☐ 452	Juan Beniquez ...	.03	.01	.00
☐ 453	Rick Burleson	.06	.02	.00
☐ 454	Bert Campaneris ..	.06	.02	.00
☐ 455	Rod Carew	.50	.20	.05
☐ 456	Bob Clark	.03	.01	.00
☐ 457	Brian Downing ...	.06	.02	.00
☐ 458	Dan Ford	.03	.01	.00
☐ 459	Ken Forsch	.03	.01	.00

	MINT	EXC	G-VG
☐ 460A Dave Frost (5 mm space before ERA)	.40	.16	.04
☐ 460B Dave Frost (1 mm space)	.06	.02	.00
☐ 461 Bobby Grich	.08	.03	.01
☐ 462 Larry Harlow	.03	.01	.00
☐ 463 John Harris	.03	.01	.00
☐ 464 Andy Hassler	.03	.01	.00
☐ 465 Butch Hobson	.03	.01	.00
☐ 466 Jesse Jefferson	.03	.01	.00
☐ 467 Bruce Kison	.03	.01	.00
☐ 468 Fred Lynn	.20	.08	.02
☐ 469 Angel Moreno	.03	.01	.00
☐ 470 Ed Ott	.03	.01	.00
☐ 471 Fred Patek	.03	.01	.00
☐ 472 Steve Renko	.03	.01	.00
☐ 473 Mike Witt	.85	.34	.08
☐ 474 Geoff Zahn	.03	.01	.00
☐ 475 Gary Alexander	.03	.01	.00
☐ 476 Dale Berra	.03	.01	.00
☐ 477 Kurt Bevacqua	.03	.01	.00
☐ 478 Jim Bibby	.03	.01	.00
☐ 479 John Candelaria	.08	.03	.01
☐ 480 Victor Cruz	.03	.01	.00
☐ 481 Mike Easler	.03	.01	.00
☐ 482 Tim Foli	.03	.01	.00
☐ 483 Lee Lacy	.03	.01	.00
☐ 484 Vance Law	.08	.03	.01
☐ 485 Bill Madlock	.12	.05	.01
☐ 486 Willie Montanez	.03	.01	.00
☐ 487 Omar Moreno	.03	.01	.00
☐ 488 Steve Nicosia	.03	.01	.00
☐ 489 Dave Parker	.25	.10	.02
☐ 490 Tony Pena	.25	.10	.02
☐ 491 Pascual Perez	.08	.03	.01
☐ 492 Johnny Ray	.85	.34	.08
☐ 493 Rick Rhoden	.08	.03	.01
☐ 494 Bill Robinson	.06	.02	.00
☐ 495 Don Robinson	.06	.02	.00
☐ 496 Enrique Romo	.03	.01	.00
☐ 497 Rod Scurry	.03	.01	.00
☐ 498 Eddie Solomon	.03	.01	.00
☐ 499 Willie Stargell	.35	.14	.03
☐ 500 Kent Tekulve	.06	.02	.00
☐ 501 Jason Thompson	.03	.01	.00
☐ 502 Glenn Abbott	.03	.01	.00
☐ 503 Jim Anderson	.03	.01	.00
☐ 504 Floyd Bannister	.06	.02	.00
☐ 505 Bruce Bochte	.03	.01	.00

	MINT	EXC	G-VG
☐ 506 Jeff Burroughs	.06	.02	.00
☐ 507 Bryan Clark	.03	.01	.00
☐ 508 Ken Clay	.03	.01	.00
☐ 509 Julio Cruz	.03	.01	.00
☐ 510 Dick Drago	.03	.01	.00
☐ 511 Gary Gray	.03	.01	.00
☐ 512 Dan Meyer	.03	.01	.00
☐ 513 Jerry Narron	.03	.01	.00
☐ 514 Tom Paciorek	.03	.01	.00
☐ 515 Casey Parsons	.03	.01	.00
☐ 516 Lenny Randle	.03	.01	.00
☐ 517 Shane Rawley	.08	.03	.01
☐ 518 Joe Simpson	.03	.01	.00
☐ 519 Richie Zisk	.06	.02	.00
☐ 520 Neil Allen	.06	.02	.00
☐ 521 Bob Bailor	.03	.01	.00
☐ 522 Hubie Brooks	.25	.10	.02
☐ 523 Mike Cubbage	.03	.01	.00
☐ 524 Pete Falcone	.03	.01	.00
☐ 525 Doug Flynn	.03	.01	.00
☐ 526 Tom Hausman	.03	.01	.00
☐ 527 Ron Hodges	.03	.01	.00
☐ 528 Randy Jones	.03	.01	.00
☐ 529 Mike Jorgensen	.03	.01	.00
☐ 530 Dave Kingman	.12	.05	.01
☐ 531 Ed Lynch	.08	.03	.01
☐ 532 Mike Marshall (screwball pitcher)	.06	.02	.00
☐ 533 Lee Mazzilli	.03	.01	.00
☐ 534 Dyar Miller	.03	.01	.00
☐ 535 Mike Scott	.30	.12	.03
☐ 536 Rusty Staub	.10	.04	.01
☐ 537 John Stearns	.03	.01	.00
☐ 538 Craig Swan	.03	.01	.00
☐ 539 Frank Taveras	.03	.01	.00
☐ 540 Alex Trevino	.03	.01	.00
☐ 541 Ellis Valentine	.03	.01	.00
☐ 542 Mookie Wilson	.08	.03	.01
☐ 543 Joel Youngblood	.03	.01	.00
☐ 544 Pat Zachry	.03	.01	.00
☐ 545 Glenn Adams	.03	.01	.00
☐ 546 Fernando Arroyo	.03	.01	.00
☐ 547 John Verhoeven	.03	.01	.00
☐ 548 Sal Butera	.03	.01	.00
☐ 549 John Castino	.03	.01	.00
☐ 550 Don Cooper	.03	.01	.00
☐ 551 Doug Corbett	.03	.01	.00
☐ 552 Dave Engle	.03	.01	.00
☐ 553 Roger Erickson	.03	.01	.00

		MINT	EXC	G-VG
☐ 554	Danny Goodwin	.03	.01	.00
☐ 555A	Darrell Jackson (black cap)	1.00	.40	.10
☐ 555B	Darrell Jackson (red cap with T)	.10	.04	.01
☐ 555C	Darrell Jackson (red cap, no emblem)	5.00	2.00	.50
☐ 556	Pete Mackanin	.03	.01	.00
☐ 557	Jack O'Connor	.03	.01	.00
☐ 558	Hosken Powell	.03	.01	.00
☐ 559	Pete Redfern	.03	.01	.00
☐ 560	Roy Smalley	.03	.01	.00
☐ 561	Chuck Baker UER (shortshop on front)	.03	.01	.00
☐ 562	Gary Ward	.06	.02	.00
☐ 563	Rob Wilfong	.03	.01	.00
☐ 564	Al Williams	.03	.01	.00
☐ 565	Butch Wynegar	.03	.01	.00
☐ 566	Randy Bass	.06	.02	.00
☐ 567	Juan Bonilla	.03	.01	.00
☐ 568	Danny Boone	.03	.01	.00
☐ 569	John Curtis	.03	.01	.00
☐ 570	Juan Eichelberger	.03	.01	.00
☐ 571	Barry Evans	.03	.01	.00
☐ 572	Tim Flannery	.03	.01	.00
☐ 573	Ruppert Jones	.03	.01	.00
☐ 574	Terry Kennedy	.06	.02	.00
☐ 575	Joe Lefebvre	.03	.01	.00
☐ 576A	John Littlefield ERR (left handed)	60.00	24.00	6.00
☐ 576B	John Littlefield COR (right handed)	.06	.02	.00
☐ 577	Gary Lucas	.03	.01	.00
☐ 578	Steve Mura	.03	.01	.00
☐ 579	Broderick Perkins	.03	.01	.00
☐ 580	Gene Richards	.03	.01	.00
☐ 581	Luis Salazar	.06	.02	.00
☐ 582	Ozzie Smith	.30	.12	.03
☐ 583	John Urrea	.03	.01	.00
☐ 584	Chris Welsh	.03	.01	.00
☐ 585	Rick Wise	.03	.01	.00
☐ 586	Doug Bird	.03	.01	.00
☐ 587	Tim Blackwell	.03	.01	.00
☐ 588	Bobby Bonds	.08	.03	.01
☐ 589	Bill Buckner	.10	.04	.01
☐ 590	Bill Caudill	.03	.01	.00
☐ 591	Hector Cruz	.03	.01	.00
☐ 592	Jody Davis	.35	.14	.03
☐ 593	Ivan DeJesus	.03	.01	.00

		MINT	EXC	G-VG
☐ 594	Steve Dillard	.03	.01	.00
☐ 595	Leon Durham	.08	.03	.01
☐ 596	Rawly Eastwick	.03	.01	.00
☐ 597	Steve Henderson	.03	.01	.00
☐ 598	Mike Krukow	.06	.02	.00
☐ 599	Mike Lum	.03	.01	.00
☐ 600	Randy Martz	.03	.01	.00
☐ 601	Jerry Morales	.03	.01	.00
☐ 602	Ken Reitz	.03	.01	.00
☐ 603A	Lee Smith ERR (Cubs logo reversed)	1.25	.50	.12
☐ 603B	Lee Smith COR	.65	.26	.06
☐ 604	Dick Tidrow	.03	.01	.00
☐ 605	Jim Tracy	.03	.01	.00
☐ 606	Mike Tyson	.03	.01	.00
☐ 607	Ty Waller	.03	.01	.00
☐ 608	Danny Ainge	.12	.05	.01
☐ 609	Jorge Bell	6.00	2.40	.60
☐ 610	Mark Bomback	.03	.01	.00
☐ 611	Barry Bonnell	.03	.01	.00
☐ 612	Jim Clancy	.06	.02	.00
☐ 613	Damaso Garcia	.03	.01	.00
☐ 614	Jerry Garvin	.03	.01	.00
☐ 615	Alfredo Griffin	.08	.03	.01
☐ 616	Garth Iorg	.03	.01	.00
☐ 617	Luis Leal	.03	.01	.00
☐ 618	Ken Macha	.03	.01	.00
☐ 619	John Mayberry	.06	.02	.00
☐ 620	Joey McLaughlin	.03	.01	.00
☐ 621	Lloyd Moseby	.15	.06	.01
☐ 622	Dave Stieb	.15	.06	.01
☐ 623	Jackson Todd	.03	.01	.00
☐ 624	Willie Upshaw	.06	.02	.00
☐ 625	Otto Velez	.03	.01	.00
☐ 626	Ernie Whitt	.06	.02	.00
☐ 627	Alvis Woods	.03	.01	.00
☐ 628	All Star Game Cleveland, Ohio	.06	.02	.00
☐ 629	All Star Infielders Frank White and Bucky Dent	.06	.02	.00
☐ 630	Big Red Machine Dan Driessen Dave Concepcion George Foster	.08	.03	.01
☐ 631	Bruce Sutter Top NL Relief Pitcher	.08	.03	.01

		MINT	EXC	G-VG
☐ 632	"Steve and Carlton" .	.20	.08	.02
	Steve Carlton and			
	Carlton Fisk			
☐ 633	Carl Yastrzemski . . .	.30	.12	.03
	3000th Game			
☐ 634	Dynamic Duo	.30	.12	.03
	Johnny Bench and			
	Tom Seaver			
☐ 635	West Meets East . . .	.20	.08	.02
	Fernando Valenzuela			
	and Gary Carter			
☐ 636A	Fernando Valenzuela:	.45	.18	.04
	NL SO King ("he" NL)			
☐ 636B	Fernando Valenzuela:	.20	.08	.02
	NL SO King ("the" NL)			
☐ 637	Mike Schmidt	.30	.12	.03
	Home Run King			
☐ 638	NL All Stars	.18	.08	.01
	Gary Carter and			
	Dave Parker			
☐ 639	Perfect Game	.06	.02	.00
	Len Barker and			
	Bo Diaz			
	(catcher actually Ron Hassey)			
☐ 640	Pete and Re-Pete . .	1.50	.60	.15
	Pete Rose and Son			
☐ 641	Phillies Finest	.30	.12	.03
	Lonnie Smith			
	Mike Schmidt			
	Steve Carlton			
☐ 642	Red Sox Reunion . .	.08	.03	.01
	Fred Lynn and			
	Dwight Evans			
☐ 643	Rickey Henderson . .	.25	.10	.02
	Most Hits and Runs			
☐ 644	Rollie Fingers	.10	.04	.01
	Most Saves AL			
☐ 645	Tom Seaver	.20	.08	.02
	Most 1981 Wins			
☐ 646A	Yankee Powerhouse	.75	.30	.07
	Reggie Jackson and			
	Dave Winfield			
	(comma on back after outfielder)			
☐ 646B	Yankee Powerhouse	.40	.16	.04
	Reggie Jackson and			
	Dave Winfield			
	(no comma)			
☐ 647	CL: Yankees/Dodgers	.08	.01	.00
☐ 648	CL: A's/Reds	.07	.01	.00

		MINT	EXC	G-VG
☐ 649	CL: Cards/Brewers	.07	.01	.00
☐ 650	CL: Expos/Orioles .	.07	.01	.00
☐ 651	CL: Astros/Phillies .	.07	.01	.00
☐ 652	CL: Tigers/Red Sox	.07	.01	.00
☐ 653	CL: Rangers/White Sox	.07	.01	.00
☐ 654	CL: Giants/Indians .	.07	.01	.00
☐ 655	CL: Royals/Braves	.07	.01	.00
☐ 656	CL: Angels/Pirates	.07	.01	.00
☐ 657	CL: Mariners/Mets .	.07	.01	.00
☐ 658	CL: Padres/Twins .	.07	.01	.00
☐ 659	CL: Blue Jays/Cubs	.07	.01	.00
☐ 660	Specials Checklist .	.10	.01	.00

1983 Fleer

Mike Marshall

The cards in this 660-card set measure 2 ½"
by 3 ½". In 1983, for the third straight year,
Fleer has produced a baseball series numbering 660 cards. Of these, 1-628 are player
cards, 629-646 are special cards, and 647-
660 are checklist cards. The player cards
are again ordered alphabetically within team.
The team order relates back to each team's
on-field performance during the previous
year, i.e., World Champion Cardinals (1-25),
AL Champion Brewers (26-51), Baltimore
(52-75), California (76-103), Kansas City
(104-128), Atlanta (129-152), Philadelphia
(153-176), Boston (177-200), Los Angeles
(201-227), Chicago White Sox (228-251),
San Francisco (252-276), Montreal (277-
301), Pittsburgh (302-326), Detroit (327-
351), San Diego (352-375), New York

Yankees (376-399), Cleveland (400-423), Toronto (424-444), Houston (445-469), Seattle (470-489), Chicago Cubs (490-512), Oakland (513-535), New York Mets (536-561), Texas (562-583), Cincinnati (584-606), and Minnesota (607-628). The front of each card has a colorful team logo at bottom left and the player's name and position at lower right. The reverses are done in shades of brown on white. The cards are numbered on the back next to a small black and white photo of the player.

		MINT	EXC	G-VG
	Complete Set (660)	45.00	18.00	4.50
	Common Player (1-660)	.03	.01	.00
☐ 1	Joaquin Andujar	.12	.04	.01
☐ 2	Doug Bair	.03	.01	.00
☐ 3	Steve Braun	.03	.01	.00
☐ 4	Glenn Brummer	.03	.01	.00
☐ 5	Bob Forsch	.03	.01	.00
☐ 6	David Green	.03	.01	.00
☐ 7	George Hendrick	.06	.02	.00
☐ 8	Keith Hernandez	.35	.14	.03
☐ 9	Tom Herr	.08	.03	.01
☐ 10	Dane Iorg	.03	.01	.00
☐ 11	Jim Kaat	.12	.05	.01
☐ 12	Jeff Lahti	.03	.01	.00
☐ 13	Tito Landrum	.03	.01	.00
☐ 14	Dave LaPoint	.35	.14	.03
☐ 15	Willie McGee	1.75	.70	.17
☐ 16	Steve Mura	.03	.01	.00
☐ 17	Ken Oberkfell	.03	.01	.00
☐ 18	Darrell Porter	.03	.01	.00
☐ 19	Mike Ramsey	.03	.01	.00
☐ 20	Gene Roof	.03	.01	.00
☐ 21	Lonnie Smith	.06	.02	.00
☐ 22	Ozzie Smith	.30	.12	.03
☐ 23	John Stuper	.03	.01	.00
☐ 24	Bruce Sutter	.12	.05	.01
☐ 25	Gene Tenace	.06	.02	.00
☐ 26	Jerry Augustine	.03	.01	.00
☐ 27	Dwight Bernard	.03	.01	.00
☐ 28	Mark Brouhard	.03	.01	.00
☐ 29	Mike Caldwell	.03	.01	.00
☐ 30	Cecil Cooper	.12	.05	.01
☐ 31	Jamie Easterly	.03	.01	.00
☐ 32	Marshall Edwards	.03	.01	.00
☐ 33	Rollie Fingers	.18	.08	.01
☐ 34	Jim Gantner	.03	.01	.00
☐ 35	Moose Haas	.03	.01	.00
☐ 36	Roy Howell	.03	.01	.00
☐ 37	Pete Ladd	.03	.01	.00
☐ 38	Bob McClure	.03	.01	.00
☐ 39	Doc Medich	.03	.01	.00
☐ 40	Paul Molitor	.18	.08	.01
☐ 41	Don Money	.03	.01	.00
☐ 42	Charlie Moore	.03	.01	.00
☐ 43	Ben Oglivie	.06	.02	.00
☐ 44	Ed Romero	.03	.01	.00
☐ 45	Ted Simmons	.12	.05	.01
☐ 46	Jim Slaton	.03	.01	.00
☐ 47	Don Sutton	.30	.12	.03
☐ 48	Gorman Thomas	.10	.04	.01
☐ 49	Pete Vuckovich	.06	.02	.00
☐ 50	Ned Yost	.03	.01	.00
☐ 51	Robin Yount	.35	.14	.03
☐ 52	Benny Ayala	.03	.01	.00
☐ 53	Bob Bonner	.03	.01	.00
☐ 54	Al Bumbry	.03	.01	.00
☐ 55	Terry Crowley	.03	.01	.00
☐ 56	Storm Davis	.45	.18	.04
☐ 57	Rich Dauer	.03	.01	.00
☐ 58	Rick Dempsey (posing batting lefty)	.06	.02	.00
☐ 59	Jim Dwyer	.03	.01	.00
☐ 60	Mike Flanagan	.06	.02	.00
☐ 61	Dan Ford	.03	.01	.00
☐ 62	Glenn Gulliver	.03	.01	.00
☐ 63	John Lowenstein	.03	.01	.00
☐ 64	Dennis Martinez	.06	.02	.00
☐ 65	Tippy Martinez	.03	.01	.00
☐ 66	Scott McGregor	.06	.02	.00
☐ 67	Eddie Murray	.55	.22	.05
☐ 68	Joe Nolan	.03	.01	.00
☐ 69	Jim Palmer	.35	.14	.03
☐ 70	Cal Ripken Jr.	1.00	.40	.10
☐ 71	Gary Roenicke	.03	.01	.00
☐ 72	Lenn Sakata	.03	.01	.00
☐ 73	Ken Singleton	.08	.03	.01
☐ 74	Sammy Stewart	.03	.01	.00
☐ 75	Tim Stoddard	.03	.01	.00
☐ 76	Don Aase	.03	.01	.00
☐ 77	Don Baylor	.12	.05	.01
☐ 78	Juan Beniquez	.03	.01	.00
☐ 79	Bob Boone	.10	.04	.01
☐ 80	Rick Burleson	.06	.02	.00
☐ 81	Rod Carew	.45	.20	.04
☐ 82	Bobby Clark	.03	.01	.00

		MINT	EXC	G-VG
☐ 83	Doug Corbett	.03	.01	.00
☐ 84	John Curtis	.03	.01	.00
☐ 85	Doug DeCinces	.08	.03	.01
☐ 86	Brian Downing	.06	.02	.00
☐ 87	Joe Ferguson	.03	.01	.00
☐ 88	Tim Foli	.03	.01	.00
☐ 89	Ken Forsch	.03	.01	.00
☐ 90	Dave Goltz	.03	.01	.00
☐ 91	Bobby Grich	.08	.03	.01
☐ 92	Andy Hassler	.03	.01	.00
☐ 93	Reggie Jackson	.50	.20	.05
☐ 94	Ron Jackson	.03	.01	.00
☐ 95	Tommy John	.15	.06	.01
☐ 96	Bruce Kison	.03	.01	.00
☐ 97	Fred Lynn	.18	.08	.01
☐ 98	Ed Ott	.03	.01	.00
☐ 99	Steve Renko	.03	.01	.00
☐ 100	Luis Sanchez	.03	.01	.00
☐ 101	Rob Wilfong	.03	.01	.00
☐ 102	Mike Witt	.15	.06	.01
☐ 103	Geoff Zahn	.03	.01	.00
☐ 104	Willie Aikens	.03	.01	.00
☐ 105	Mike Armstrong	.03	.01	.00
☐ 106	Vida Blue	.06	.02	.00
☐ 107	Bud Black	.20	.08	.02
☐ 108	George Brett	.60	.24	.06
☐ 109	Bill Castro	.03	.01	.00
☐ 110	Onix Concepcion	.03	.01	.00
☐ 111	Dave Frost	.03	.01	.00
☐ 112	Cesar Geronimo	.03	.01	.00
☐ 113	Larry Gura	.03	.01	.00
☐ 114	Steve Hammond	.03	.01	.00
☐ 115	Don Hood	.03	.01	.00
☐ 116	Dennis Leonard	.06	.02	.00
☐ 117	Jerry Martin	.03	.01	.00
☐ 118	Lee May	.03	.01	.00
☐ 119	Hal McRae	.06	.02	.00
☐ 120	Amos Otis	.08	.03	.01
☐ 121	Greg Pryor	.03	.01	.00
☐ 122	Dan Quisenberry	.12	.05	.01
☐ 123	Don Slaught	.30	.12	.03
☐ 124	Paul Splittorff	.03	.01	.00
☐ 125	U.L. Washington	.03	.01	.00
☐ 126	John Wathan	.06	.02	.00
☐ 127	Frank White	.08	.03	.01
☐ 128	Willie Wilson	.12	.05	.01
☐ 129	Steve Bedrosian	.35	.14	.03
☐ 130	Bruce Benedict	.03	.01	.00
☐ 131	Tommy Boggs	.03	.01	.00
☐ 132	Brett Butler	.10	.04	.01
☐ 133	Rick Camp	.03	.01	.00
☐ 134	Chris Chambliss	.08	.03	.01
☐ 135	Ken Dayley	.06	.02	.00
☐ 136	Gene Garber	.03	.01	.00
☐ 137	Terry Harper	.03	.01	.00
☐ 138	Bob Horner	.18	.08	.01
☐ 139	Glenn Hubbard	.03	.01	.00
☐ 140	Rufino Linares	.03	.01	.00
☐ 141	Rick Mahler	.06	.02	.00
☐ 142	Dale Murphy	.85	.34	.08
☐ 143	Phil Niekro	.25	.10	.02
☐ 144	Pascual Perez	.08	.03	.01
☐ 145	Biff Pocoroba	.03	.01	.00
☐ 146	Rafael Ramirez	.03	.01	.00
☐ 147	Jerry Royster	.03	.01	.00
☐ 148	Ken Smith	.03	.01	.00
☐ 149	Bob Walk	.06	.02	.00
☐ 150	Claudell Washington	.08	.03	.01
☐ 151	Bob Watson	.06	.02	.00
☐ 152	Larry Whisenton	.03	.01	.00
☐ 153	Porfirio Altamirano	.03	.01	.00
☐ 154	Marty Bystrom	.03	.01	.00
☐ 155	Steve Carlton	.35	.14	.03
☐ 156	Larry Christenson	.03	.01	.00
☐ 157	Ivan DeJesus	.03	.01	.00
☐ 158	John Denny	.08	.03	.01
☐ 159	Bob Dernier	.03	.01	.00
☐ 160	Bo Diaz	.06	.02	.00
☐ 161	Ed Farmer	.03	.01	.00
☐ 162	Greg Gross	.03	.01	.00
☐ 163	Mike Krukow	.06	.02	.00
☐ 164	Garry Maddox	.06	.02	.00
☐ 165	Gary Matthews	.06	.02	.00
☐ 166	Tug McGraw	.10	.04	.01
☐ 167	Bob Molinaro	.03	.01	.00
☐ 168	Sid Monge	.03	.01	.00
☐ 169	Ron Reed	.03	.01	.00
☐ 170	Bill Robinson	.06	.02	.00
☐ 171	Pete Rose	1.00	.40	.10
☐ 172	Dick Ruthven	.03	.01	.00
☐ 173	Mike Schmidt	.60	.24	.06
☐ 174	Manny Trillo	.03	.01	.00
☐ 175	Ozzie Virgil	.03	.01	.00
☐ 176	George Vukovich	.03	.01	.00
☐ 177	Gary Allenson	.03	.01	.00
☐ 178	Luis Aponte	.03	.01	.00
☐ 179	Wade Boggs	17.00	7.00	1.70
☐ 180	Tom Burgmeier	.03	.01	.00

		MINT	EXC	G-VG
☐ 181	Mark Clear	.03	.01	.00
☐ 182	Dennis Eckersley	.15	.06	.01
☐ 183	Dwight Evans	.15	.06	.01
☐ 184	Rich Gedman	.10	.04	.01
☐ 185	Glenn Hoffman	.03	.01	.00
☐ 186	Bruce Hurst	.20	.08	.01
☐ 187	Carney Lansford	.12	.05	.01
☐ 188	Rick Miller	.03	.01	.00
☐ 189	Reid Nichols	.03	.01	.00
☐ 190	Bob Ojeda	.10	.04	.01
☐ 191	Tony Perez	.15	.06	.01
☐ 192	Chuck Rainey	.03	.01	.00
☐ 193	Jerry Remy	.03	.01	.00
☐ 194	Jim Rice	.25	.10	.02
☐ 195	Bob Stanley	.03	.01	.00
☐ 196	Dave Stapleton	.03	.01	.00
☐ 197	Mike Torrez	.03	.01	.00
☐ 198	John Tudor	.15	.06	.01
☐ 199	Julio Valdez	.03	.01	.00
☐ 200	Carl Yastrzemski	.80	.32	.08
☐ 201	Dusty Baker	.06	.02	.00
☐ 202	Joe Beckwith	.03	.01	.00
☐ 203	Greg Brock	.35	.14	.03
☐ 204	Ron Cey	.10	.04	.01
☐ 205	Terry Forster	.06	.02	.00
☐ 206	Steve Garvey	.40	.16	.04
☐ 207	Pedro Guerrero	.30	.12	.03
☐ 208	Burt Hooton	.03	.01	.00
☐ 209	Steve Howe	.03	.01	.00
☐ 210	Ken Landreaux	.03	.01	.00
☐ 211	Mike Marshall	.25	.08	.02
☐ 212	Candy Maldonado	.60	.24	.06
☐ 213	Rick Monday	.06	.02	.00
☐ 214	Tom Niedenfuer	.06	.02	.00
☐ 215	Jorge Orta	.03	.01	.00
☐ 216	Jerry Reuss	.06	.02	.00
☐ 217	Ron Roenicke	.03	.01	.00
☐ 218	Vicente Romo	.03	.01	.00
☐ 219	Bill Russell	.06	.02	.00
☐ 220	Steve Sax	.30	.12	.03
☐ 221	Mike Scioscia	.06	.02	.00
☐ 222	Dave Stewart	.15	.06	.01
☐ 223	Derrel Thomas	.03	.01	.00
☐ 224	Fernando Valenzuela	.25	.10	.02
☐ 225	Bob Welch	.10	.04	.01
☐ 226	Ricky Wright	.03	.01	.00
☐ 227	Steve Yeager	.03	.01	.00
☐ 228	Bill Almon	.03	.01	.00
☐ 229	Harold Baines	.20	.08	.02
☐ 230	Salome Barojas	.03	.01	.00
☐ 231	Tony Bernazard	.03	.01	.00
☐ 232	Britt Burns	.06	.02	.00
☐ 233	Richard Dotson	.08	.03	.01
☐ 234	Ernesto Escarrega	.03	.01	.00
☐ 235	Carlton Fisk	.15	.06	.01
☐ 236	Jerry Hairston	.03	.01	.00
☐ 237	Kevin Hickey	.03	.01	.00
☐ 238	LaMarr Hoyt	.06	.02	.00
☐ 239	Steve Kemp	.06	.02	.00
☐ 240	Jim Kern	.03	.01	.00
☐ 241	Ron Kittle	.60	.24	.06
☐ 242	Jerry Koosman	.08	.03	.01
☐ 243	Dennis Lamp	.03	.01	.00
☐ 244	Rudy Law	.03	.01	.00
☐ 245	Vance Law	.08	.03	.01
☐ 246	Ron LeFlore	.06	.02	.00
☐ 247	Greg Luzinski	.10	.04	.01
☐ 248	Tom Paciorek	.03	.01	.00
☐ 249	Aurelio Rodriguez	.03	.01	.00
☐ 250	Mike Squires	.03	.01	.00
☐ 251	Steve Trout	.03	.01	.00
☐ 252	Jim Barr	.03	.01	.00
☐ 253	Dave Bergman	.03	.01	.00
☐ 254	Fred Breining	.03	.01	.00
☐ 255	Bob Brenly	.06	.02	.00
☐ 256	Jack Clark	.25	.10	.02
☐ 257	Chili Davis	.25	.10	.02
☐ 258	Darrell Evans	.10	.04	.01
☐ 259	Alan Fowlkes	.03	.01	.00
☐ 260	Rich Gale	.03	.01	.00
☐ 261	Atlee Hammaker	.06	.02	.00
☐ 262	Al Holland	.03	.01	.00
☐ 263	Duane Kuiper	.03	.01	.00
☐ 264	Bill Laskey	.03	.01	.00
☐ 265	Gary Lavelle	.03	.01	.00
☐ 266	Johnnie LeMaster	.03	.01	.00
☐ 267	Renie Martin	.03	.01	.00
☐ 268	Milt May	.03	.01	.00
☐ 269	Greg Minton	.03	.01	.00
☐ 270	Joe Morgan	.25	.10	.02
☐ 271	Tom O'Malley	.06	.02	.00
☐ 272	Reggie Smith	.06	.02	.00
☐ 273	Guy Sularz	.03	.01	.00
☐ 274	Champ Summers	.03	.01	.00
☐ 275	Max Venable	.03	.01	.00
☐ 276	Jim Wohlford	.03	.01	.00
☐ 277	Ray Burris	.03	.01	.00
☐ 278	Gary Carter	.35	.14	.03

		MINT	EXC	G-VG			MINT	EXC	G-VG
☐ 279	Warren Cromartie ..	.03	.01	.00	☐ 328	Enos Cabell	.03	.01	.00
☐ 280	Andre Dawson	.35	.14	.03	☐ 329	Kirk Gibson	.40	.16	.04
☐ 281	Terry Francona	.03	.01	.00	☐ 330	Larry Herndon	.03	.01	.00
☐ 282	Doug Flynn	.03	.01	.00	☐ 331	Mike Ivie	.03	.01	.00
☐ 283	Woodie Fryman ...	.03	.01	.00	☐ 332	Howard Johnson ..	2.25	.90	.22
☐ 284	Bill Gullickson	.06	.02	.00	☐ 333	Lynn Jones	.03	.01	.00
☐ 285	Wallace Johnson ..	.06	.02	.00	☐ 334	Rick Leach	.03	.01	.00
☐ 286	Charlie Lea	.03	.01	.00	☐ 335	Chet Lemon	.06	.02	.00
☐ 287	Randy Lerch	.03	.01	.00	☐ 336	Jack Morris	.20	.08	.01
☐ 288	Brad Mills	.03	.01	.00	☐ 337	Lance Parrish	.25	.10	.02
☐ 289	Dan Norman	.03	.01	.00	☐ 338	Larry Pashnick	.03	.01	.00
☐ 290	Al Oliver	.08	.03	.01	☐ 339	Dan Petry	.08	.03	.01
☐ 291	David Palmer	.03	.01	.00	☐ 340	Dave Rozema	.03	.01	.00
☐ 292	Tim Raines	.40	.16	.04	☐ 341	Dave Rucker	.03	.01	.00
☐ 293	Jeff Reardon	.10	.04	.01	☐ 342	Elias Sosa	.03	.01	.00
☐ 294	Steve Rogers	.06	.02	.00	☐ 343	Dave Tobik	.03	.01	.00
☐ 295	Scott Sanderson ..	.03	.01	.00	☐ 344	Alan Trammell	.30	.12	.03
☐ 296	Dan Schatzeder ...	.03	.01	.00	☐ 345	Jerry Turner	.03	.01	.00
☐ 297	Bryn Smith	.08	.03	.01	☐ 346	Jerry Ujdur	.03	.01	.00
☐ 298	Chris Speier	.03	.01	.00	☐ 347	Pat Underwood ...	.03	.01	.00
☐ 299	Tim Wallach	.18	.08	.01	☐ 348	Lou Whitaker	.15	.06	.01
☐ 300	Jerry White	.03	.01	.00	☐ 349	Milt Wilcox	.03	.01	.00
☐ 301	Joel Youngblood ...	.03	.01	.00	☐ 350	Glenn Wilson	.30	.12	.03
☐ 302	Ross Baumgarten ..	.03	.01	.00	☐ 351	John Wockenfuss .	.03	.01	.00
☐ 303	Dale Berra	.03	.01	.00	☐ 352	Kurt Bevacqua ...	.03	.01	.00
☐ 304	John Candelaria ...	.08	.03	.01	☐ 353	Juan Bonilla	.03	.01	.00
☐ 305	Dick Davis	.03	.01	.00	☐ 354	Floyd Chiffer	.03	.01	.00
☐ 306	Mike Easler	.03	.01	.00	☐ 355	Luis DeLeon	.03	.01	.00
☐ 307	Richie Hebner	.03	.01	.00	☐ 356	Dave Dravecky ...	.35	.14	.03
☐ 308	Lee Lacy	.03	.01	.00	☐ 357	Dave Edwards	.03	.01	.00
☐ 309	Bill Madlock	.10	.04	.01	☐ 358	Juan Eichelberger .	.03	.01	.00
☐ 310	Larry McWilliams ..	.03	.01	.00	☐ 359	Tim Flannery	.03	.01	.00
☐ 311	John Milner	.03	.01	.00	☐ 360	Tony Gwynn	9.00	3.75	.90
☐ 312	Omar Moreno	.03	.01	.00	☐ 361	Ruppert Jones ...	.03	.01	.00
☐ 313	Jim Morrison	.03	.01	.00	☐ 362	Terry Kennedy ...	.06	.02	.00
☐ 314	Steve Nicosia	.03	.01	.00	☐ 363	Joe Lefebvre	.03	.01	.00
☐ 315	Dave Parker	.18	.08	.01	☐ 364	Sixto Lezcano ...	.03	.01	.00
☐ 316	Tony Pena	.15	.06	.01	☐ 365	Tim Lollar	.03	.01	.00
☐ 317	Johnny Ray	.15	.06	.01	☐ 366	Gary Lucas	.03	.01	.00
☐ 318	Rick Rhoden	.08	.03	.01	☐ 367	John Montefusco ..	.03	.01	.00
☐ 319	Don Robinson	.03	.01	.00	☐ 368	Broderick Perkins .	.03	.01	.00
☐ 320	Enrique Romo	.03	.01	.00	☐ 369	Joe Pittman	.03	.01	.00
☐ 321	Manny Sarmiento ..	.03	.01	.00	☐ 370	Gene Richards ...	.03	.01	.00
☐ 322	Rod Scurry	.03	.01	.00	☐ 371	Luis Salazar	.06	.02	.00
☐ 323	Jimmy Smith	.03	.01	.00	☐ 372	Eric Show	.35	.14	.03
☐ 324	Willie Stargell	.35	.14	.03	☐ 373	Garry Templeton ..	.08	.03	.01
☐ 325	Jason Thompson ..	.03	.01	.00	☐ 374	Chris Welsh	.03	.01	.00
☐ 326	Kent Tekulve	.06	.02	.00	☐ 375	Alan Wiggins	.10	.04	.01
☐ 327	Tom Brookens	.03	.01	.00	☐ 376	Rick Cerone	.03	.01	.00

		MINT	EXC	G-VG
☐ 377	Dave Collins	.03	.01	.00
☐ 378	Roger Erickson	.03	.01	.00
☐ 379	George Frazier	.03	.01	.00
☐ 380	Oscar Gamble	.03	.01	.00
☐ 381	Goose Gossage	.15	.06	.01
☐ 382	Ken Griffey	.06	.02	.00
☐ 383	Ron Guidry	.18	.08	.01
☐ 384	Dave LaRoche	.03	.01	.00
☐ 385	Rudy May	.03	.01	.00
☐ 386	John Mayberry	.06	.02	.00
☐ 387	Lee Mazzilli	.03	.01	.00
☐ 388	Mike Morgan	.03	.01	.00
☐ 389	Jerry Mumphrey	.03	.01	.00
☐ 390	Bobby Murcer	.10	.04	.01
☐ 391	Graig Nettles	.12	.05	.01
☐ 392	Lou Piniella	.08	.03	.01
☐ 393	Willie Randolph	.08	.03	.01
☐ 394	Shane Rawley	.08	.03	.01
☐ 395	Dave Righetti	.20	.08	.02
☐ 396	Andre Robertson	.03	.01	.00
☐ 397	Roy Smalley	.03	.01	.00
☐ 398	Dave Winfield	.40	.16	.04
☐ 399	Butch Wynegar	.03	.01	.00
☐ 400	Chris Bando	.03	.01	.00
☐ 401	Alan Bannister	.03	.01	.00
☐ 402	Len Barker	.03	.01	.00
☐ 403	Tom Brennan	.03	.01	.00
☐ 404	Carmelo Castillo	.06	.02	.00
☐ 405	Miguel Dilone	.03	.01	.00
☐ 406	Jerry Dybzinski	.03	.01	.00
☐ 407	Mike Fischlin	.03	.01	.00
☐ 408	Ed Glynn	.03	.01	.00
	(photo actually Bud Anderson)			
☐ 409	Mike Hargrove	.03	.01	.00
☐ 410	Toby Harrah	.06	.02	.00
☐ 411	Ron Hassey	.03	.01	.00
☐ 412	Von Hayes	.18	.08	.01
☐ 413	Rick Manning	.03	.01	.00
☐ 414	Bake McBride	.03	.01	.00
☐ 415	Larry Milbourne	.03	.01	.00
☐ 416	Bill Nahorodny	.03	.01	.00
☐ 417	Jack Perconte	.03	.01	.00
☐ 418	Lary Sorensen	.03	.01	.00
☐ 419	Dan Spillner	.03	.01	.00
☐ 420	Rick Sutcliffe	.15	.06	.01
☐ 421	Andre Thornton	.06	.02	.00
☐ 422	Rick Waits	.03	.01	.00
☐ 423	Eddie Whitson	.06	.02	.00
☐ 424	Jesse Barfield	.65	.26	.06

		MINT	EXC	G-VG
☐ 425	Barry Bonnell	.03	.01	.00
☐ 426	Jim Clancy	.06	.02	.00
☐ 427	Damaso Garcia	.03	.01	.00
☐ 428	Jerry Garvin	.03	.01	.00
☐ 429	Alfredo Griffin	.08	.03	.01
☐ 430	Garth Iorg	.03	.01	.00
☐ 431	Roy Lee Jackson	.03	.01	.00
☐ 432	Luis Leal	.03	.01	.00
☐ 433	Buck Martinez	.03	.01	.00
☐ 434	Joey McLaughlin	.03	.01	.00
☐ 435	Lloyd Moseby	.12	.05	.01
☐ 436	Rance Mulliniks	.03	.01	.00
☐ 437	Dale Murray	.03	.01	.00
☐ 438	Wayne Nordhagen	.03	.01	.00
☐ 439	Geno Petralli	.06	.02	.00
☐ 440	Hosken Powell	.03	.01	.00
☐ 441	Dave Stieb	.15	.06	.01
☐ 442	Willie Upshaw	.06	.02	.00
☐ 443	Ernie Whitt	.06	.02	.00
☐ 444	Alvis Woods	.03	.01	.00
☐ 445	Alan Ashby	.06	.02	.00
☐ 446	Jose Cruz	.08	.03	.01
☐ 447	Kiko Garcia	.03	.01	.00
☐ 448	Phil Garner	.03	.01	.00
☐ 449	Danny Heep	.03	.01	.00
☐ 450	Art Howe	.08	.03	.01
☐ 451	Bob Knepper	.08	.03	.01
☐ 452	Alan Knicely	.03	.01	.00
☐ 453	Ray Knight	.08	.03	.01
☐ 454	Frank LaCorte	.03	.01	.00
☐ 455	Mike LaCoss	.03	.01	.00
☐ 456	Randy Moffitt	.03	.01	.00
☐ 457	Joe Niekro	.10	.04	.01
☐ 458	Terry Puhl	.03	.01	.00
☐ 459	Luis Pujols	.03	.01	.00
☐ 460	Craig Reynolds	.03	.01	.00
☐ 461	Bert Roberge	.03	.01	.00
☐ 462	Vern Ruhle	.03	.01	.00
☐ 463	Nolan Ryan	.40	.16	.04
☐ 464	Joe Sambito	.03	.01	.00
☐ 465	Tony Scott	.03	.01	.00
☐ 466	Dave Smith	.06	.02	.00
☐ 467	Harry Spilman	.03	.01	.00
☐ 468	Dickie Thon	.03	.01	.00
☐ 469	Denny Walling	.03	.01	.00
☐ 470	Larry Andersen	.03	.01	.00
☐ 471	Floyd Bannister	.06	.02	.00
☐ 472	Jim Beattie	.03	.01	.00
☐ 473	Bruce Bochte	.03	.01	.00

		MINT	EXC	G-VG			MINT	EXC	G-VG
☐ 474	Manny Castillo	.03	.01	.00	☐ 523	Rick Langford	.03	.01	.00
☐ 475	Bill Caudill	.03	.01	.00	☐ 524	Dave Lopes	.08	.03	.01
☐ 476	Bryan Clark	.03	.01	.00	☐ 525	Steve McCatty	.03	.01	.00
☐ 477	Al Cowens	.03	.01	.00	☐ 526	Dave McKay	.03	.01	.00
☐ 478	Julio Cruz	.03	.01	.00	☐ 527	Dan Meyer	.03	.01	.00
☐ 479	Todd Cruz	.03	.01	.00	☐ 528	Dwayne Murphy	.03	.01	.00
☐ 480	Gary Gray	.03	.01	.00	☐ 529	Jeff Newman	.03	.01	.00
☐ 481	Dave Henderson	.35	.14	.03	☐ 530	Mike Norris	.03	.01	.00
☐ 482	Mike Moore	.35	.14	.03	☐ 531	Bob Owchinko	.03	.01	.00
☐ 483	Gaylord Perry	.25	.10	.02	☐ 532	Joe Rudi	.06	.02	.00
☐ 484	Dave Revering	.03	.01	.00	☐ 533	Jimmy Sexton	.03	.01	.00
☐ 485	Joe Simpson	.03	.01	.00	☐ 534	Fred Stanley	.03	.01	.00
☐ 486	Mike Stanton	.03	.01	.00	☐ 535	Tom Underwood	.03	.01	.00
☐ 487	Rick Sweet	.03	.01	.00	☐ 536	Neil Allen	.03	.01	.00
☐ 488	Ed VandeBerg	.03	.01	.00	☐ 537	Wally Backman	.10	.04	.01
☐ 489	Richie Zisk	.06	.02	.00	☐ 538	Bob Bailor	.03	.01	.00
☐ 490	Doug Bird	.03	.01	.00	☐ 539	Hubie Brooks	.10	.04	.01
☐ 491	Larry Bowa	.10	.04	.01	☐ 540	Carlos Diaz	.06	.02	.00
☐ 492	Bill Buckner	.10	.04	.01	☐ 541	Pete Falcone	.03	.01	.00
☐ 493	Bill Campbell	.03	.01	.00	☐ 542	George Foster	.12	.05	.01
☐ 494	Jody Davis	.08	.03	.01	☐ 543	Ron Gardenhire	.03	.01	.00
☐ 495	Leon Durham	.08	.03	.01	☐ 544	Brian Giles	.03	.01	.00
☐ 496	Steve Henderson	.03	.01	.00	☐ 545	Ron Hodges	.03	.01	.00
☐ 497	Willie Hernandez	.10	.04	.01	☐ 546	Randy Jones	.03	.01	.00
☐ 498	Ferguson Jenkins	.15	.06	.01	☐ 547	Mike Jorgensen	.03	.01	.00
☐ 499	Jay Johnstone	.08	.03	.01	☐ 548	Dave Kingman	.12	.05	.01
☐ 500	Junior Kennedy	.03	.01	.00	☐ 549	Ed Lynch	.03	.01	.00
☐ 501	Randy Martz	.03	.01	.00	☐ 550	Jesse Orosco	.06	.02	.00
☐ 502	Jerry Morales	.03	.01	.00	☐ 551	Rick Ownbey	.03	.01	.00
☐ 503	Keith Moreland	.06	.02	.00	☐ 552	Charlie Puleo	.03	.01	.00
☐ 504	Dickie Noles	.03	.01	.00	☐ 553	Gary Rajsich	.03	.01	.00
☐ 505	Mike Proly	.03	.01	.00	☐ 554	Mike Scott	.30	.12	.03
☐ 506	Allen Ripley	.03	.01	.00	☐ 555	Rusty Staub	.10	.04	.01
☐ 507	Ryne Sandberg	4.00	1.60	.40	☐ 556	John Stearns	.03	.01	.00
☐ 508	Lee Smith	.10	.04	.01	☐ 557	Craig Swan	.03	.01	.00
☐ 509	Pat Tabler	.30	.12	.03	☐ 558	Ellis Valentine	.03	.01	.00
☐ 510	Dick Tidrow	.03	.01	.00	☐ 559	Tom Veryzer	.03	.01	.00
☐ 511	Bump Wills	.03	.01	.00	☐ 560	Mookie Wilson	.08	.03	.01
☐ 512	Gary Woods	.03	.01	.00	☐ 561	Pat Zachry	.03	.01	.00
☐ 513	Tony Armas	.08	.03	.01	☐ 562	Buddy Bell	.10	.04	.01
☐ 514	Dave Beard	.03	.01	.00	☐ 563	John Butcher	.03	.01	.00
☐ 515	Jeff Burroughs	.06	.02	.00	☐ 564	Steve Comer	.03	.01	.00
☐ 516	John D'Acquisto	.03	.01	.00	☐ 565	Danny Darwin	.03	.01	.00
☐ 517	Wayne Gross	.03	.01	.00	☐ 566	Bucky Dent	.08	.03	.01
☐ 518	Mike Heath	.03	.01	.00	☐ 567	John Grubb	.03	.01	.00
☐ 519	Rickey Henderson	.60	.24	.06	☐ 568	Rick Honeycutt	.03	.01	.00
☐ 520	Cliff Johnson	.03	.01	.00	☐ 569	Dave Hostetler	.06	.02	.00
☐ 521	Matt Keough	.03	.01	.00	☐ 570	Charlie Hough	.08	.03	.01
☐ 522	Brian Kingman	.03	.01	.00	☐ 571	Lamar Johnson	.03	.01	.00

		MINT	EXC	G-VG
☐ 572	Jon Matlack	.03	.01	.00
☐ 573	Paul Mirabella	.03	.01	.00
☐ 574	Larry Parrish	.06	.02	.00
☐ 575	Mike Richardt	.03	.01	.00
☐ 576	Mickey Rivers	.06	.02	.00
☐ 577	Billy Sample	.03	.01	.00
☐ 578	Dave Schmidt	.15	.06	.01
☐ 579	Bill Stein	.03	.01	.00
☐ 580	Jim Sundberg	.06	.02	.00
☐ 581	Frank Tanana	.08	.03	.01
☐ 582	Mark Wagner	.03	.01	.00
☐ 583	George Wright	.03	.01	.00
☐ 584	Johnny Bench	.45	.18	.04
☐ 585	Bruce Berenyi	.03	.01	.00
☐ 586	Larry Biittner	.03	.01	.00
☐ 587	Cesar Cedeno	.08	.03	.01
☐ 588	Dave Concepcion	.10	.04	.01
☐ 589	Dan Driessen	.03	.01	.00
☐ 590	Greg Harris	.03	.01	.00
☐ 591	Ben Hayes	.03	.01	.00
☐ 592	Paul Householder	.03	.01	.00
☐ 593	Tom Hume	.03	.01	.00
☐ 594	Wayne Krenchicki	.03	.01	.00
☐ 595	Rafael Landestoy	.03	.01	.00
☐ 596	Charlie Leibrandt	.06	.02	.00
☐ 597	Eddie Milner	.10	.04	.01
☐ 598	Ron Oester	.03	.01	.00
☐ 599	Frank Pastore	.03	.01	.00
☐ 600	Joe Price	.03	.01	.00
☐ 601	Tom Seaver	.40	.16	.04
☐ 602	Bob Shirley	.03	.01	.00
☐ 603	Mario Soto	.06	.02	.00
☐ 604	Alex Trevino	.03	.01	.00
☐ 605	Mike Vail	.03	.01	.00
☐ 606	Duane Walker	.03	.01	.00
☐ 607	Tom Brunansky	.55	.22	.05
☐ 608	Bobby Castillo	.03	.01	.00
☐ 609	John Castino	.03	.01	.00
☐ 610	Ron Davis	.03	.01	.00
☐ 611	Lenny Faedo	.03	.01	.00
☐ 612	Terry Felton	.03	.01	.00
☐ 613	Gary Gaetti	3.00	1.20	.30
☐ 614	Mickey Hatcher	.06	.02	.00
☐ 615	Brad Havens	.03	.01	.00
☐ 616	Kent Hrbek	1.25	.50	.12
☐ 617	Randy Johnson	.03	.01	.00
☐ 618	Tim Laudner	.08	.03	.01
☐ 619	Jeff Little	.03	.01	.00
☐ 620	Bobby Mitchell	.03	.01	.00

		MINT	EXC	G-VG
☐ 621	Jack O'Connor	.03	.01	.00
☐ 622	John Pacella	.03	.01	.00
☐ 623	Pete Redfern	.03	.01	.00
☐ 624	Jesus Vega	.03	.01	.00
☐ 625	Frank Viola	3.75	1.50	.37
☐ 626	Ron Washington	.03	.01	.00
☐ 627	Gary Ward	.06	.02	.00
☐ 628	Al Williams	.03	.01	.00
☐ 629	Red Sox All-Stars	.25	.10	.02
	Carl Yastrzemski			
	Dennis Eckersley			
	Mark Clear			
☐ 630	"300 Career Wins"	.10	.04	.01
	Gaylord Perry and			
	Terry Bulling 5/6/82			
☐ 631	Pride of Venezuela	.06	.02	.00
	Dave Concepcion and			
	Manny Trillo			
☐ 632	All-Star Infielders	.15	.06	.01
	Robin Yount and			
	Buddy Bell			
☐ 633	Mr.Vet and Mr.Rookie	.20	.08	.02
	Dave Winfield and			
	Kent Hrbek			
☐ 634	Fountain of Youth	.65	.26	.06
	Willie Stargell and			
	Pete Rose			
☐ 635	Big Chiefs	.06	.02	.00
	Toby Harrah and			
	Andre Thornton			
☐ 636	Smith Brothers	.08	.03	.01
	Ozzie and Lonnie			
☐ 637	Base Stealers' Threat	.10	.04	.01
	Bo Diaz and			
	Gary Carter			
☐ 638	All-Star Catchers	.12	.05	.01
	Carlton Fisk and			
	Gary Carter			
☐ 639	The Silver Shoe	.25	.10	.02
	Rickey Henderson			
☐ 640	Home Run Threats	.18	.08	.01
	Ben Oglivie and			
	Reggie Jackson			
☐ 641	Two Teams Same Day	.06	.02	.00
	Joel Youngblood			
	August 4, 1982			
☐ 642	Last Perfect Game	.06	.02	.00
	Ron Hassey and			
	Len Barker			

		MINT	EXC	G-VG
☐ 643	Black and Blue .... Bud Black	.06	.02	.00
☐ 644	Black and Blue .... Vida Blue	.06	.02	.00
☐ 645	Speed and Power .. Reggie Jackson	.25	.10	.02
☐ 646	Speed and Power .. Rickey Henderson	.25	.10	.02
☐ 647	CL: Cards/Brewers .	.07	.01	.00
☐ 648	CL: Orioles/Angels .	.07	.01	.00
☐ 649	CL: Royals/Braves .	.07	.01	.00
☐ 650	CL: Phillies/Red Sox	.07	.01	.00
☐ 651	CL: Dodgers/White Sox	.07	.01	.00
☐ 652	CL: Giants/Expos ...	.07	.01	.00
☐ 653	CL: Pirates/Tigers ..	.07	.01	.00
☐ 654	CL: Padres/Yankees .	.07	.01	.00
☐ 655	CL: Indians/Blue Jays	.07	.01	.00
☐ 656	CL: Astros/Mariners .	.07	.01	.00
☐ 657	CL: Cubs/A's	.07	.01	.00
☐ 658	CL: Mets/Rangers ..	.07	.01	.00
☐ 659	CL: Reds/Twins	.07	.01	.00
☐ 660	CL: Specials/Teams .	.09	.01	.00

1984 Fleer

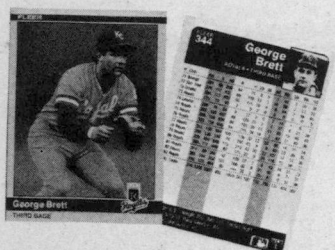

The cards in this 660-card set measure 2 ½" by 3 ½". The 1984 Fleer card set featured fronts with full-color team logos along with the player's name and position and the Fleer identification. The set features many imaginative photos, several multi-player cards, and many more action shots than the 1983 card set. The backs are quite similar to the 1983 backs except that blue rather than brown ink is used. The player cards are alphabetized within team and the teams are ordered by their 1983 season finish and won-lost record, e.g., Baltimore (1-23), Philadelphia (24-49), Chicago White Sox (50-73), Detroit (74-95), Los Angeles (96-118), New York Yankees (119-144), Toronto (145-169), Atlanta (170-193), Milwaukee (194-219), Houston (220-244), Pittsburgh (245-269), Montreal (270-293), San Diego (294-317), St. Louis (318-340), Kansas City (341-364), San Francisco (365-387), Boston (388-412), Texas (413-435), Oakland (436-461), Cincinnati (462-485), Chicago (486-507), California (508-532), Cleveland (533-555), Minnesota (556-579), New York Mets (580-603), and Seattle (604-625). Specials (626-646) and checklist cards (647-660) make up the end of the set.

		MINT	EXC	G-VG
Complete Set (660)		100.00	40.00	10.00
Common Player (1-660) ...		.05	.02	.00

			MINT	EXC	G-VG
☐	1	Mike Boddicker ...	.20	.05	.01
☐	2	Al Bumbry	.05	.02	.00
☐	3	Todd Cruz	.05	.02	.00
☐	4	Rich Dauer	.05	.02	.00
☐	5	Storm Davis	.10	.04	.01
☐	6	Rick Dempsey	.05	.02	.00
☐	7	Jim Dwyer	.05	.02	.00
☐	8	Mike Flanagan ...	.10	.04	.01
☐	9	Dan Ford	.05	.02	.00
☐	10	John Lowenstein ..	.05	.02	.00
☐	11	Dennis Martinez ..	.10	.04	.01
☐	12	Tippy Martinez	.05	.02	.00
☐	13	Scott McGregor ...	.10	.04	.01
☐	14	Eddie Murray	.60	.24	.06
☐	15	Joe Nolan	.05	.02	.00
☐	16	Jim Palmer	.35	.14	.03
☐	17	Cal Ripken	.75	.30	.07
☐	18	Gary Roenicke	.05	.02	.00
☐	19	Lenn Sakata	.05	.02	.00
☐	20	John Shelby	.40	.16	.04
☐	21	Ken Singleton	.10	.04	.01
☐	22	Sammy Stewart ...	.05	.02	.00
☐	23	Tim Stoddard	.05	.02	.00
☐	24	Marty Bystrom ...	.05	.02	.00
☐	25	Steve Carlton	.40	.16	.04
☐	26	Ivan DeJesus	.05	.02	.00

			MINT	EXC	G-VG				MINT	EXC	G-VG
☐	27	John Denny	.10	.04	.01	☐	76	Doug Bair	.05	.02	.00
☐	28	Bob Dernier	.05	.02	.00	☐	77	Juan Berenguer	.05	.02	.00
☐	29	Bo Diaz	.05	.02	.00	☐	78	Tom Brookens	.05	.02	.00
☐	30	Kiko Garcia	.05	.02	.00	☐	79	Enos Cabell	.05	.02	.00
☐	31	Greg Gross	.05	.02	.00	☐	80	Kirk Gibson	.40	.16	.04
☐	32	Kevin Gross	.35	.14	.03	☐	81	John Grubb	.05	.02	.00
☐	33	Von Hayes	.15	.06	.01	☐	82	Larry Herndon	.05	.02	.00
☐	34	Willie Hernandez	.15	.06	.01	☐	83	Wayne Krenchicki	.05	.02	.00
☐	35	Al Holland	.05	.02	.00	☐	84	Rick Leach	.05	.02	.00
☐	36	Charles Hudson	.25	.10	.02	☐	85	Chet Lemon	.10	.04	.01
☐	37	Joe Lefebvre	.05	.02	.00	☐	86	Aurelio Lopez	.05	.02	.00
☐	38	Sixto Lezcano	.05	.02	.00	☐	87	Jack Morris	.20	.08	.02
☐	39	Garry Maddox	.10	.04	.01	☐	88	Lance Parrish	.25	.10	.02
☐	40	Gary Matthews	.10	.04	.01	☐	89	Dan Petry	.10	.04	.01
☐	41	Len Matuszek	.05	.02	.00	☐	90	Dave Rozema	.05	.02	.00
☐	42	Tug McGraw	.10	.04	.01	☐	91	Alan Trammell	.35	.14	.03
☐	43	Joe Morgan	.25	.10	.02	☐	92	Lou Whitaker	.15	.06	.01
☐	44	Tony Perez	.20	.08	.02	☐	93	Milt Wilcox	.05	.02	.00
☐	45	Ron Reed	.05	.02	.00	☐	94	Glenn Wilson	.10	.04	.01
☐	46	Pete Rose	1.00	.40	.10	☐	95	John Wockenfuss	.05	.02	.00
☐	47	Juan Samuel	3.50	1.40	.35	☐	96	Dusty Baker	.10	.04	.01
☐	48	Mike Schmidt	.65	.26	.06	☐	97	Joe Beckwith	.05	.02	.00
☐	49	Ozzie Virgil	.05	.02	.00	☐	98	Greg Brock	.10	.04	.01
☐	50	Juan Agosto	.15	.06	.01	☐	99	Jack Fimple	.05	.02	.00
☐	51	Harold Baines	.20	.08	.02	☐	100	Pedro Guerrero	.30	.12	.03
☐	52	Floyd Bannister	.05	.02	.00	☐	101	Rick Honeycutt	.05	.02	.00
☐	53	Salome Barojas	.05	.02	.00	☐	102	Burt Hooton	.05	.02	.00
☐	54	Britt Burns	.05	.02	.00	☐	103	Steve Howe	.05	.02	.00
☐	55	Julio Cruz	.05	.02	.00	☐	104	Ken Landreaux	.05	.02	.00
☐	56	Richard Dotson	.10	.04	.01	☐	105	Mike Marshall	.20	.08	.02
☐	57	Jerry Dybzinski	.05	.02	.00	☐	106	Rick Monday	.10	.04	.01
☐	58	Carlton Fisk	.20	.08	.02	☐	107	Jose Morales	.05	.02	.00
☐	59	Scott Fletcher	.25	.10	.02	☐	108	Tom Niedenfuer	.10	.04	.01
☐	60	Jerry Hairston	.05	.02	.00	☐	109	Alejandro Pena	.30	.12	.03
☐	61	Kevin Hickey	.05	.02	.00	☐	110	Jerry Reuss	.10	.04	.01
☐	62	Marc Hill	.05	.02	.00	☐	111	Bill Russell	.10	.04	.01
☐	63	LaMarr Hoyt	.10	.04	.01	☐	112	Steve Sax	.25	.10	.02
☐	64	Ron Kittle	.20	.08	.02	☐	113	Mike Scioscia	.10	.04	.01
☐	65	Jerry Koosman	.10	.04	.01	☐	114	Derrel Thomas	.05	.02	.00
☐	66	Dennis Lamp	.05	.02	.00	☐	115	Fernando Valenzuela	.25	.10	.02
☐	67	Rudy Law	.05	.02	.00	☐	116	Bob Welch	.10	.04	.01
☐	68	Vance Law	.10	.04	.01	☐	117	Steve Yeager	.05	.02	.00
☐	69	Greg Luzinski	.10	.04	.01	☐	118	Pat Zachry	.05	.02	.00
☐	70	Tom Paciorek	.05	.02	.00	☐	119	Don Baylor	.15	.06	.01
☐	71	Mike Squires	.05	.02	.00	☐	120	Bert Campaneris	.10	.04	.01
☐	72	Dick Tidrow	.05	.02	.00	☐	121	Rick Cerone	.05	.02	.00
☐	73	Greg Walker	.45	.18	.04	☐	122	Ray Fontenot	.05	.02	.00
☐	74	Glenn Abbott	.05	.02	.00	☐	123	George Frazier	.05	.02	.00
☐	75	Howard Bailey	.05	.02	.00	☐	124	Oscar Gamble	.05	.02	.00

		MINT	EXC	G-VG
☐ 125	Goose Gossage ...	.15	.06	.01
☐ 126	Ken Griffey	.10	.04	.01
☐ 127	Ron Guidry	.20	.08	.02
☐ 128	Jay Howell	.15	.06	.01
☐ 129	Steve Kemp	.10	.04	.01
☐ 130	Matt Keough	.05	.02	.00
☐ 131	Don Mattingly	33.00	12.00	2.50
☐ 132	John Montefusco ...	.05	.02	.00
☐ 133	Omar Moreno	.05	.02	.00
☐ 134	Dale Murray	.05	.02	.00
☐ 135	Graig Nettles	.15	.06	.01
☐ 136	Lou Piniella	.10	.04	.01
☐ 137	Willie Randolph	.15	.06	.01
☐ 138	Shane Rawley	.10	.04	.01
☐ 139	Dave Righetti	.20	.08	.02
☐ 140	Andre Robertson ...	.05	.02	.00
☐ 141	Bob Shirley	.05	.02	.00
☐ 142	Roy Smalley	.05	.02	.00
☐ 143	Dave Winfield	.40	.16	.04
☐ 144	Butch Wynegar	.05	.02	.00
☐ 145	Jim Acker	.10	.04	.01
☐ 146	Doyle Alexander ...	.10	.04	.01
☐ 147	Jesse Barfield	.30	.12	.03
☐ 148	Jorge Bell	.85	.34	.08
☐ 149	Barry Bonnell	.05	.02	.00
☐ 150	Jim Clancy	.05	.02	.00
☐ 151	Dave Collins	.05	.02	.00
☐ 152	Tony Fernandez ...	4.50	1.80	.45
☐ 153	Damaso Garcia	.05	.02	.00
☐ 154	Dave Geisel	.05	.02	.00
☐ 155	Jim Gott	.10	.04	.01
☐ 156	Alfredo Griffin	.10	.04	.01
☐ 157	Garth Iorg	.05	.02	.00
☐ 158	Roy Lee Jackson ...	.05	.02	.00
☐ 159	Cliff Johnson	.05	.02	.00
☐ 160	Luis Leal	.05	.02	.00
☐ 161	Buck Martinez	.05	.02	.00
☐ 162	Joey McLaughlin ...	.05	.02	.00
☐ 163	Randy Moffitt	.05	.02	.00
☐ 164	Lloyd Moseby	.15	.06	.01
☐ 165	Rance Mulliniks	.05	.02	.00
☐ 166	Jorge Orta	.05	.02	.00
☐ 167	Dave Stieb	.20	.08	.02
☐ 168	Willie Upshaw	.10	.04	.01
☐ 169	Ernie Whitt	.05	.02	.00
☐ 170	Len Barker	.05	.02	.00
☐ 171	Steve Bedrosian ...	.20	.08	.02
☐ 172	Bruce Benedict	.05	.02	.00
☐ 173	Brett Butler	.15	.06	.01

		MINT	EXC	G-VG
☐ 174	Rick Camp	.05	.02	.00
☐ 175	Chris Chambliss ..	.10	.04	.01
☐ 176	Ken Dayley	.05	.02	.00
☐ 177	Pete Falcone	.05	.02	.00
☐ 178	Terry Forster	.10	.04	.01
☐ 179	Gene Garber	.05	.02	.00
☐ 180	Terry Harper	.05	.02	.00
☐ 181	Bob Horner	.18	.08	.02
☐ 182	Glenn Hubbard ...	.05	.02	.00
☐ 183	Randy Johnson ...	.05	.02	.00
☐ 184	Craig McMurtry ...	.10	.04	.01
☐ 185	Donnie Moore	.05	.02	.00
☐ 186	Dale Murphy	.80	.32	.08
☐ 187	Phil Niekro	.25	.10	.02
☐ 188	Pascual Perez	.20	.08	.02
☐ 189	Biff Pocoroba	.05	.02	.00
☐ 190	Rafael Ramirez ...	.05	.02	.00
☐ 191	Jerry Royster	.05	.02	.00
☐ 192	Claudell Washington	.10	.04	.01
☐ 193	Bob Watson	.10	.04	.01
☐ 194	Jerry Augustine ...	.05	.02	.00
☐ 195	Mark Brouhard ...	.05	.02	.00
☐ 196	Mike Caldwell	.05	.02	.00
☐ 197	Tom Candiotti	.25	.10	.02
☐ 198	Cecil Cooper	.15	.06	.01
☐ 199	Rollie Fingers	.20	.08	.02
☐ 200	Jim Gantner	.05	.02	.00
☐ 201	Bob L. Gibson	.10	.04	.01
☐ 202	Moose Haas	.05	.02	.00
☐ 203	Roy Howell	.05	.02	.00
☐ 204	Pete Ladd	.05	.02	.00
☐ 205	Rick Manning	.05	.02	.00
☐ 206	Bob McClure	.05	.02	.00
☐ 207	Paul Molitor	.20	.08	.02
☐ 208	Don Money	.05	.02	.00
☐ 209	Charlie Moore	.05	.02	.00
☐ 210	Ben Oglivie	.10	.04	.01
☐ 211	Chuck Porter	.05	.02	.00
☐ 212	Ed Romero	.05	.02	.00
☐ 213	Ted Simmons	.15	.06	.01
☐ 214	Jim Slaton	.05	.02	.00
☐ 215	Don Sutton	.25	.10	.02
☐ 216	Tom Tellmann	.05	.02	.00
☐ 217	Pete Vuckovich ...	.10	.04	.01
☐ 218	Ned Yost	.05	.02	.00
☐ 219	Robin Yount	.35	.14	.03
☐ 220	Alan Ashby	.05	.02	.00
☐ 221	Kevin Bass	.20	.08	.02
☐ 222	Jose Cruz	.10	.04	.01

		MINT	EXC	G-VG
☐ 223	Bill Dawley	.10	.04	.01
☐ 224	Frank DiPino	.05	.02	.00
☐ 225	Bill Doran	.75	.30	.07
☐ 226	Phil Garner	.05	.02	.00
☐ 227	Art Howe	.10	.04	.01
☐ 228	Bob Knepper	.10	.04	.01
☐ 229	Ray Knight	.10	.04	.01
☐ 230	Frank LaCorte	.05	.02	.00
☐ 231	Mike LaCoss	.05	.02	.00
☐ 232	Mike Madden	.05	.02	.00
☐ 233	Jerry Mumphrey	.05	.02	.00
☐ 234	Joe Niekro	.10	.04	.01
☐ 235	Terry Puhl	.05	.02	.00
☐ 236	Luis Pujols	.05	.02	.00
☐ 237	Craig Reynolds	.05	.02	.00
☐ 238	Vern Ruhle	.05	.02	.00
☐ 239	Nolan Ryan	.40	.16	.04
☐ 240	Mike Scott	.30	.12	.03
☐ 241	Tony Scott	.05	.02	.00
☐ 242	Dave Smith	.10	.04	.01
☐ 243	Dickie Thon	.05	.02	.00
☐ 244	Denny Walling	.05	.02	.00
☐ 245	Dale Berra	.05	.02	.00
☐ 246	Jim Bibby	.05	.02	.00
☐ 247	John Candelaria	.10	.04	.01
☐ 248	Jose DeLeon	.30	.12	.03
☐ 249	Mike Easler	.05	.02	.00
☐ 250	Cecilio Guante	.05	.02	.00
☐ 251	Richie Hebner	.05	.02	.00
☐ 252	Lee Lacy	.05	.02	.00
☐ 253	Bill Madlock	.15	.06	.01
☐ 254	Milt May	.05	.02	.00
☐ 255	Lee Mazzilli	.05	.02	.00
☐ 256	Larry McWilliams	.05	.02	.00
☐ 257	Jim Morrison	.05	.02	.00
☐ 258	Dave Parker	.18	.08	.01
☐ 259	Tony Pena	.15	.06	.01
☐ 260	Johnny Ray	.15	.06	.01
☐ 261	Rick Rhoden	.10	.04	.01
☐ 262	Don Robinson	.05	.02	.00
☐ 263	Manny Sarmiento	.05	.02	.00
☐ 264	Rod Scurry	.05	.02	.00
☐ 265	Kent Tekulve	.10	.04	.01
☐ 266	Gene Tenace	.05	.02	.00
☐ 267	Jason Thompson	.05	.02	.00
☐ 268	Lee Tunnell	.10	.04	.01
☐ 269	Marvell Wynne	.10	.04	.01
☐ 270	Ray Burris	.05	.02	.00
☐ 271	Gary Carter	.40	.16	.04

		MINT	EXC	G-VG
☐ 272	Warren Cromartie	.05	.02	.00
☐ 273	Andre Dawson	.35	.14	.03
☐ 274	Doug Flynn	.05	.02	.00
☐ 275	Terry Francona	.05	.02	.00
☐ 276	Bill Gullickson	.05	.02	.00
☐ 277	Bob James	.15	.06	.01
☐ 278	Charlie Lea	.05	.02	.00
☐ 279	Bryan Little	.05	.02	.00
☐ 280	Al Oliver	.10	.04	.01
☐ 281	Tim Raines	.40	.16	.04
☐ 282	Bobby Ramos	.05	.02	.00
☐ 283	Jeff Reardon	.10	.04	.01
☐ 284	Steve Rogers	.05	.02	.00
☐ 285	Scott Sanderson	.05	.02	.00
☐ 286	Dan Schatzeder	.05	.02	.00
☐ 287	Bryn Smith	.10	.04	.01
☐ 288	Chris Speier	.05	.02	.00
☐ 289	Manny Trillo	.05	.02	.00
☐ 290	Mike Vail	.05	.02	.00
☐ 291	Tim Wallach	.15	.06	.01
☐ 292	Chris Welsh	.05	.02	.00
☐ 293	Jim Wohlford	.05	.02	.00
☐ 294	Kurt Bevacqua	.05	.02	.00
☐ 295	Juan Bonilla	.05	.02	.00
☐ 296	Bobby Brown	.05	.02	.00
☐ 297	Luis DeLeon	.05	.02	.00
☐ 298	Dave Dravecky	.10	.04	.01
☐ 299	Tim Flannery	.05	.02	.00
☐ 300	Steve Garvey	.50	.20	.05
☐ 301	Tony Gwynn	2.50	.90	.22
☐ 302	Andy Hawkins	.45	.18	.04
☐ 303	Ruppert Jones	.05	.02	.00
☐ 304	Terry Kennedy	.10	.04	.01
☐ 305	Tim Lollar	.05	.02	.00
☐ 306	Gary Lucas	.05	.02	.00
☐ 307	Kevin McReynolds	6.50	2.60	.65
☐ 308	Sid Monge	.05	.02	.00
☐ 309	Mario Ramirez	.05	.02	.00
☐ 310	Gene Richards	.05	.02	.00
☐ 311	Luis Salazar	.05	.02	.00
☐ 312	Eric Show	.10	.04	.01
☐ 313	Elias Sosa	.05	.02	.00
☐ 314	Garry Templeton	.10	.04	.01
☐ 315	Mark Thurmond	.10	.04	.01
☐ 316	Ed Whitson	.05	.02	.00
☐ 317	Alan Wiggins	.05	.02	.00
☐ 318	Neil Allen	.05	.02	.00
☐ 319	Joaquin Andujar	.10	.04	.01
☐ 320	Steve Braun	.05	.02	.00

		MINT	EXC	G-VG			MINT	EXC	G-VG
☐ 321	Glenn Brummer	.05	.02	.00	☐ 370	Chili Davis	.15	.06	.01
☐ 322	Bob Forsch	.05	.02	.00	☐ 371	Mark Davis	.10	.04	.01
☐ 323	David Green	.05	.02	.00	☐ 372	Darrell Evans	.15	.06	.01
☐ 324	George Hendrick	.10	.04	.01	☐ 373	Atlee Hammaker	.05	.02	.00
☐ 325	Tom Herr	.10	.04	.01	☐ 374	Mike Krukow	.10	.04	.01
☐ 326	Dane Iorg	.05	.02	.00	☐ 375	Duane Kuiper	.05	.02	.00
☐ 327	Jeff Lahti	.05	.02	.00	☐ 376	Bill Laskey	.05	.02	.00
☐ 328	Dave LaPoint	.10	.04	.01	☐ 377	Gary Lavelle	.05	.02	.00
☐ 329	Willie McGee	.35	.14	.03	☐ 378	Johnnie LeMaster	.05	.02	.00
☐ 330	Ken Oberkfell	.05	.02	.00	☐ 379	Jeff Leonard	.10	.04	.01
☐ 331	Darrell Porter	.05	.02	.00	☐ 380	Randy Lerch	.05	.02	.00
☐ 332	Jamie Quirk	.05	.02	.00	☐ 381	Renie Martin	.05	.02	.00
☐ 333	Mike Ramsey	.05	.02	.00	☐ 382	Andy McGaffigan	.05	.02	.00
☐ 334	Floyd Rayford	.05	.02	.00	☐ 383	Greg Minton	.05	.02	.00
☐ 335	Lonnie Smith	.10	.04	.01	☐ 384	Tom O'Malley	.05	.02	.00
☐ 336	Ozzie Smith	.25	.10	.02	☐ 385	Max Venable	.05	.02	.00
☐ 337	John Stuper	.05	.02	.00	☐ 386	Brad Wellman	.05	.02	.00
☐ 338	Bruce Sutter	.15	.06	.01	☐ 387	Joel Youngblood	.05	.02	.00
☐ 339	Andy Van Slyke	2.50	1.00	.25	☐ 388	Gary Allenson	.05	.02	.00
☐ 340	Dave Von Ohlen	.05	.02	.00	☐ 389	Luis Aponte	.05	.02	.00
☐ 341	Willie Aikens	.05	.02	.00	☐ 390	Tony Armas	.10	.04	.01
☐ 342	Mike Armstrong	.05	.02	.00	☐ 391	Doug Bird	.05	.02	.00
☐ 343	Bud Black	.05	.02	.00	☐ 392	Wade Boggs	7.00	2.80	.70
☐ 344	George Brett	.70	.28	.07	☐ 393	Dennis Boyd	.40	.16	.04
☐ 345	Onix Concepcion	.05	.02	.00	☐ 394	Mike Brown	.10	.04	.01
☐ 346	Keith Creel	.05	.02	.00		(Red Sox pitcher)			
☐ 347	Larry Gura	.05	.02	.00	☐ 395	Mark Clear	.05	.02	.00
☐ 348	Don Hood	.05	.02	.00	☐ 396	Dennis Eckersley	.20	.08	.02
☐ 349	Dennis Leonard	.10	.04	.01	☐ 397	Dwight Evans	.20	.08	.02
☐ 350	Hal McRae	.10	.04	.01	☐ 398	Rich Gedman	.10	.04	.01
☐ 351	Amos Otis	.10	.04	.01	☐ 399	Glenn Hoffman	.05	.02	.00
☐ 352	Gaylord Perry	.25	.10	.02	☐ 400	Bruce Hurst	.20	.08	.02
☐ 353	Greg Pryor	.05	.02	.00	☐ 401	John Henry Johnson	.05	.02	.00
☐ 354	Dan Quisenberry	.12	.05	.01	☐ 402	Ed Jurak	.05	.02	.00
☐ 355	Steve Renko	.05	.02	.00	☐ 403	Rick Miller	.05	.02	.00
☐ 356	Leon Roberts	.05	.02	.00	☐ 404	Jeff Newman	.05	.02	.00
☐ 357	Pat Sheridan	.20	.08	.02	☐ 405	Reid Nichols	.05	.02	.00
☐ 358	Joe Simpson	.05	.02	.00	☐ 406	Bob Ojeda	.10	.04	.01
☐ 359	Don Slaught	.05	.02	.00	☐ 407	Jerry Remy	.05	.02	.00
☐ 360	Paul Splittorff	.05	.02	.00	☐ 408	Jim Rice	.25	.10	.02
☐ 361	U.L. Washington	.05	.02	.00	☐ 409	Bob Stanley	.05	.02	.00
☐ 362	John Wathan	.05	.02	.00	☐ 410	Dave Stapleton	.05	.02	.00
☐ 363	Frank White	.10	.04	.01	☐ 411	John Tudor	.15	.06	.01
☐ 364	Willie Wilson	.15	.06	.01	☐ 412	Carl Yastrzemski	.70	.28	.07
☐ 365	Jim Barr	.05	.02	.00	☐ 413	Buddy Bell	.15	.06	.01
☐ 366	Dave Bergman	.05	.02	.00	☐ 414	Larry Biittner	.05	.02	.00
☐ 367	Fred Breining	.05	.02	.00	☐ 415	John Butcher	.05	.02	.00
☐ 368	Bob Brenly	.05	.02	.00	☐ 416	Danny Darwin	.05	.02	.00
☐ 369	Jack Clark	.30	.12	.03	☐ 417	Bucky Dent	.10	.04	.01

		MINT	EXC	G-VG			MINT	EXC	G-VG
☐ 418	Dave Hostetler	.05	.02	.00	☐ 467	Dan Driessen	.05	.02	.00
☐ 419	Charlie Hough	.10	.04	.01	☐ 468	Nick Esasky	.35	.14	.03
☐ 420	Bobby Johnson	.05	.02	.00	☐ 469	Rich Gale	.05	.02	.00
☐ 421	Odell Jones	.05	.02	.00	☐ 470	Ben Hayes	.05	.02	.00
☐ 422	Jon Matlack	.05	.02	.00	☐ 471	Paul Householder	.05	.02	.00
☐ 423	Pete O'Brien	1.00	.40	.10	☐ 472	Tom Hume	.05	.02	.00
☐ 424	Larry Parrish	.10	.04	.01	☐ 473	Alan Knicely	.05	.02	.00
☐ 425	Mickey Rivers	.10	.04	.01	☐ 474	Eddie Milner	.05	.02	.00
☐ 426	Billy Sample	.05	.02	.00	☐ 475	Ron Oester	.05	.02	.00
☐ 427	Dave Schmidt	.10	.04	.01	☐ 476	Kelly Paris	.10	.04	.01
☐ 428	Mike Smithson	.10	.04	.01	☐ 477	Frank Pastore	.05	.02	.00
☐ 429	Bill Stein	.05	.02	.00	☐ 478	Ted Power	.05	.02	.00
☐ 430	Dave Stewart	.20	.08	.02	☐ 479	Joe Price	.05	.02	.00
☐ 431	Jim Sundberg	.10	.04	.01	☐ 480	Charlie Puleo	.05	.02	.00
☐ 432	Frank Tanana	.10	.04	.01	☐ 481	Gary Redus	.25	.10	.02
☐ 433	Dave Tobik	.05	.02	.00	☐ 482	Bill Scherrer	.05	.02	.00
☐ 434	Wayne Tolleson	.10	.04	.01	☐ 483	Mario Soto	.05	.02	.00
☐ 435	George Wright	.05	.02	.00	☐ 484	Alex Trevino	.05	.02	.00
☐ 436	Bill Almon	.05	.02	.00	☐ 485	Duane Walker	.05	.02	.00
☐ 437	Keith Atherton	.05	.02	.00	☐ 486	Larry Bowa	.10	.04	.01
☐ 438	Dave Beard	.05	.02	.00	☐ 487	Warren Brusstar	.05	.02	.00
☐ 439	Tom Burgmeier	.05	.02	.00	☐ 488	Bill Buckner	.10	.04	.01
☐ 440	Jeff Burroughs	.10	.04	.01	☐ 489	Bill Campbell	.05	.02	.00
☐ 441	Chris Codiroli	.10	.04	.01	☐ 490	Ron Cey	.10	.04	.01
☐ 442	Tim Conroy	.10	.04	.01	☐ 491	Jody Davis	.10	.04	.01
☐ 443	Mike Davis	.10	.04	.01	☐ 492	Leon Durham	.10	.04	.01
☐ 444	Wayne Gross	.05	.02	.00	☐ 493	Mel Hall	.20	.08	.02
☐ 445	Garry Hancock	.05	.02	.00	☐ 494	Ferguson Jenkins	.15	.06	.01
☐ 446	Mike Heath	.05	.02	.00	☐ 495	Jay Johnstone	.10	.04	.01
☐ 447	Rickey Henderson	.60	.24	.06	☐ 496	Craig Lefferts	.15	.06	.01
☐ 448	Donnie Hill	.10	.04	.01	☐ 497	Carmelo Martinez	.25	.10	.02
☐ 449	Bob Kearney	.05	.02	.00	☐ 498	Jerry Morales	.05	.02	.00
☐ 450	Bill Krueger	.10	.04	.01	☐ 499	Keith Moreland	.05	.02	.00
☐ 451	Rick Langford	.05	.02	.00	☐ 500	Dickie Noles	.05	.02	.00
☐ 452	Carney Lansford	.10	.04	.01	☐ 501	Mike Proly	.05	.02	.00
☐ 453	Dave Lopes	.10	.04	.01	☐ 502	Chuck Rainey	.05	.02	.00
☐ 454	Steve McCatty	.05	.02	.00	☐ 503	Dick Ruthven	.05	.02	.00
☐ 455	Dan Meyer	.05	.02	.00	☐ 504	Ryne Sandberg	1.25	.50	.12
☐ 456	Dwayne Murphy	.05	.02	.00	☐ 505	Lee Smith	.15	.06	.01
☐ 457	Mike Norris	.05	.02	.00	☐ 506	Steve Trout	.05	.02	.00
☐ 458	Ricky Peters	.05	.02	.00	☐ 507	Gary Woods	.05	.02	.00
☐ 459	Tony Phillips	.10	.04	.01	☐ 508	Juan Beniquez	.05	.02	.00
☐ 460	Tom Underwood	.05	.02	.00	☐ 509	Bob Boone	.15	.06	.01
☐ 461	Mike Warren	.10	.04	.01	☐ 510	Rick Burleson	.10	.04	.01
☐ 462	Johnny Bench	.50	.20	.05	☐ 511	Rod Carew	.50	.20	.05
☐ 463	Bruce Berenyi	.05	.02	.00	☐ 512	Bobby Clark	.05	.02	.00
☐ 464	Dann Bilardello	.05	.02	.00	☐ 513	John Curtis	.05	.02	.00
☐ 465	Cesar Cedeno	.10	.04	.01	☐ 514	Doug DeCinces	.10	.04	.01
☐ 466	Dave Concepcion	.15	.06	.01	☐ 515	Brian Downing	.10	.04	.01

		MINT	EXC	G-VG			MINT	EXC	G-VG
☐ 516	Tim Foli	.05	.02	.00	☐ 565	Gary Gaetti	.75	.30	.07
☐ 517	Ken Forsch	.05	.02	.00	☐ 566	Mickey Hatcher	.10	.04	.01
☐ 518	Bobby Grich	.10	.04	.01	☐ 567	Kent Hrbek	.40	.16	.04
☐ 519	Andy Hassler	.05	.02	.00	☐ 568	Rusty Kuntz	.05	.02	.00
☐ 520	Reggie Jackson	.60	.24	.06	☐ 569	Tim Laudner	.10	.04	.01
☐ 521	Ron Jackson	.05	.02	.00	☐ 570	Rick Lysander	.05	.02	.00
☐ 522	Tommy John	.15	.06	.01	☐ 571	Bobby Mitchell	.05	.02	.00
☐ 523	Bruce Kison	.05	.02	.00	☐ 572	Ken Schrom	.05	.02	.00
☐ 524	Steve Lubratich	.05	.02	.00	☐ 573	Ray Smith	.05	.02	.00
☐ 525	Fred Lynn	.15	.06	.01	☐ 574	Tim Teufel	.25	.10	.02
☐ 526	Gary Pettis	.30	.12	.03	☐ 575	Frank Viola	1.00	.40	.10
☐ 527	Luis Sanchez	.05	.02	.00	☐ 576	Gary Ward	.10	.04	.01
☐ 528	Daryl Sconiers	.05	.02	.00	☐ 577	Ron Washington	.05	.02	.00
☐ 529	Ellis Valentine	.05	.02	.00	☐ 578	Len Whitehouse	.05	.02	.00
☐ 530	Rob Wilfong	.05	.02	.00	☐ 579	Al Williams	.05	.02	.00
☐ 531	Mike Witt	.15	.06	.01	☐ 580	Bob Bailor	.05	.02	.00
☐ 532	Geoff Zahn	.05	.02	.00	☐ 581	Mark Bradley	.10	.04	.01
☐ 533	Bud Anderson	.05	.02	.00	☐ 582	Hubie Brooks	.15	.06	.01
☐ 534	Chris Bando	.05	.02	.00	☐ 583	Carlos Diaz	.05	.02	.00
☐ 535	Alan Bannister	.05	.02	.00	☐ 584	George Foster	.15	.06	.01
☐ 536	Bert Blyleven	.15	.06	.01	☐ 585	Brian Giles	.05	.02	.00
☐ 537	Tom Brennan	.05	.02	.00	☐ 586	Danny Heep	.05	.02	.00
☐ 538	Jamie Easterly	.05	.02	.00	☐ 587	Keith Hernandez	.30	.12	.03
☐ 539	Juan Eichelberger	.05	.02	.00	☐ 588	Ron Hodges	.05	.02	.00
☐ 540	Jim Essian	.05	.02	.00	☐ 589	Scott Holman	.05	.02	.00
☐ 541	Mike Fischlin	.05	.02	.00	☐ 590	Dave Kingman	.15	.06	.01
☐ 542	Julio Franco	.40	.16	.04	☐ 591	Ed Lynch	.05	.02	.00
☐ 543	Mike Hargrove	.05	.02	.00	☐ 592	Jose Oquendo	.35	.14	.03
☐ 544	Toby Harrah	.05	.02	.00	☐ 593	Jesse Orosco	.05	.02	.00
☐ 545	Ron Hassey	.05	.02	.00	☐ 594	Junior Ortiz	.05	.02	.00
☐ 546	Neal Heaton	.20	.08	.02	☐ 595	Tom Seaver	.40	.16	.04
☐ 547	Bake McBride	.05	.02	.00	☐ 596	Doug Sisk	.05	.02	.00
☐ 548	Broderick Perkins	.05	.02	.00	☐ 597	Rusty Staub	.10	.04	.01
☐ 549	Lary Sorensen	.05	.02	.00	☐ 598	John Stearns	.05	.02	.00
☐ 550	Dan Spillner	.05	.02	.00	☐ 599	Darryl Strawberry	18.00	7.25	1.80
☐ 551	Rick Sutcliffe	.20	.08	.02	☐ 600	Craig Swan	.05	.02	.00
☐ 552	Pat Tabler	.15	.06	.01	☐ 601	Walt Terrell	.30	.12	.03
☐ 553	Gorman Thomas	.10	.04	.01	☐ 602	Mike Torrez	.05	.02	.00
☐ 554	Andre Thornton	.10	.04	.01	☐ 603	Mookie Wilson	.10	.04	.01
☐ 555	George Vukovich	.05	.02	.00	☐ 604	Jamie Allen	.05	.02	.00
☐ 556	Darrell Brown	.05	.02	.00	☐ 605	Jim Beattie	.05	.02	.00
☐ 557	Tom Brunansky	.25	.10	.02	☐ 606	Tony Bernazard	.05	.02	.00
☐ 558	Randy Bush	.20	.08	.01	☐ 607	Manny Castillo	.05	.02	.00
☐ 559	Bobby Castillo	.05	.02	.00	☐ 608	Bill Caudill	.05	.02	.00
☐ 560	John Castino	.05	.02	.90	☐ 609	Bryan Clark	.05	.02	.00
☐ 561	Ron Davis	.05	.02	.00	☐ 610	Al Cowens	.05	.02	.00
☐ 562	Dave Engle	.05	.02	.00	☐ 611	Dave Henderson	.20	.08	.02
☐ 563	Lenny Faedo	.05	.02	.00	☐ 612	Steve Henderson	.05	.02	.00
☐ 564	Pete Filson	.05	.02	.00	☐ 613	Orlando Mercado	.05	.02	.00

		MINT	EXC	G-VG
☐ 614	Mike Moore	.10	.04	.01
☐ 615	Ricky Nelson	.15	.06	.01
	(Jamie Nelson's stats on back)			
☐ 616	Spike Owen	.20	.08	.02
☐ 617	Pat Putnam	.05	.02	.00
☐ 618	Ron Roenicke	.05	.02	.00
☐ 619	Mike Stanton	.05	.02	.00
☐ 620	Bob Stoddard	.05	.02	.00
☐ 621	Rick Sweet	.05	.02	.00
☐ 622	Roy Thomas	.05	.02	.00
☐ 623	Ed VandeBerg	.05	.02	.00
☐ 624	Matt Young	.10	.04	.01
☐ 625	Richie Zisk	.05	.02	.00
☐ 626	Fred Lynn	.10	.04	.01
	1982 AS Game RB			
☐ 627	Manny Trillo	.10	.04	.01
	1983 AS Game RB			
☐ 628	Steve Garvey	.20	.08	.02
	NL Iron Man			
☐ 629	Rod Carew	.20	.08	.02
	AL Batting Runner-Up			
☐ 630	Wade Boggs	.60	.24	.06
	AL Batting Champion			
☐ 631	Tim Raines: Letting	.20	.08	.02
	Go of the Raines			
☐ 632	Al Oliver	.10	.04	.01
	Double Trouble			
☐ 633	Steve Sax	.15	.06	.01
	AS Second Base			
☐ 634	Dickie Thon	.10	.04	.01
	AS Shortstop			
☐ 635	Ace Firemen	.10	.04	.01
	Dan Quisenberry			
	and Tippy Martinez			
☐ 636	Reds Reunited	.40	.16	.04
	Joe Morgan			
	Pete Rose			
	Tony Perez			
☐ 637	Backstop Stars	.10	.04	.01
	Lance Parrish			
	Bob Boone			
☐ 638	Geo.Brett and G.Perry	.15	.06	.01
	Pine Tar 7/24/83			
☐ 639	1983 No Hitters	.10	.04	.01
	Dave Righetti			
	Mike Warren			
	Bob Forsch			
☐ 640	Bench and Yaz	.35	.14	.03
	Retiring Superstars			

		MINT	EXC	G-VG
☐ 641	Gaylord Perry	.10	.04	.01
	Going Out In Style			
☐ 642	Steve Carlton	.15	.06	.01
	300 Club and			
	Strikeout Record			
☐ 643	Altobelli and Owens	.10	.04	.01
	WS Managers			
☐ 644	Rick Dempsey	.10	.04	.01
	World Series MVP			
☐ 645	Mike Boddicker	.10	.04	.01
	WS Rookie Winner			
☐ 646	Scott McGregor	.10	.04	.01
	WS Clincher			
☐ 647	CL: Orioles/Royals	.08	.01	.00
☐ 648	CL: Phillies/Giants	.07	.01	.00
☐ 649	CL: White Sox/Red Sox	.07	.01	.00
☐ 650	CL: Tigers/Rangers	.07	.01	.00
☐ 651	CL: Dodgers/A's	.07	.01	.00
☐ 652	CL: Yankees/Reds	.07	.01	.00
☐ 653	CL: Blue Jays/Cubs	.07	.01	.00
☐ 654	CL: Braves/Angels	.07	.01	.00
☐ 655	CL: Brewers/Indians	.07	.01	.00
☐ 656	CL: Astros/Twins	.07	.01	.00
☐ 657	CL: Pirates/Mets	.07	.01	.00
☐ 658	CL: Expos/Mariners	.07	.01	.00
☐ 659	CL: Padres/Specials	.07	.01	.00
☐ 660	CL: Cardinals/Teams	.08	.01	.00

1984 Fleer Update

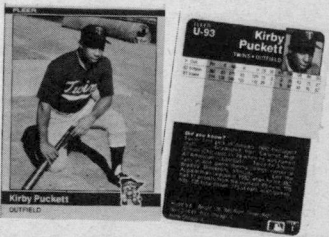

The cards in this 132-card set measure 2 ½"
by 3 ½". For the first time, the Fleer Gum
Company issued a traded, extended, or up-

date set. The purpose of the set was the same as the traded sets issued by Topps over the past four years, i.e., to portray players with their proper team for the current year and to portray rookies who were not in their regular issue. Like the Topps Traded sets of the past four years, the Fleer Update sets were distributed through hobby channels only. The set was quite popular with collectors, and apparently, the print run was relatively short, as the set was quickly in short supply and exhibited a rapid and dramatic price increase. The cards are numbered on the back with a U prefix; the order corresponds to the alphabetical order of the subjects' names.

	MINT	EXC	G-VG
Complete Set (132)	250.00	100.00	25.00
Common Player (1-132)	.20	.08	.02

	MINT	EXC	G-VG
☐ 1U Willie Aikens	.20	.08	.02
☐ 2U Luis Aponte	.20	.08	.02
☐ 3U Mark Bailey	.30	.12	.03
☐ 4U Bob Bailor	.20	.08	.02
☐ 5U Dusty Baker	.30	.12	.03
☐ 6U Steve Balboni	.30	.12	.03
☐ 7U Alan Bannister	.20	.08	.02
☐ 8U Marty Barrett	3.50	1.40	.35
☐ 9U Dave Beard	.20	.08	.02
☐ 10U Joe Beckwith	.20	.08	.02
☐ 11U Dave Bergman	.20	.08	.02
☐ 12U Tony Bernazard	.20	.08	.02
☐ 13U Bruce Bochte	.20	.08	.02
☐ 14U Barry Bonnell	.20	.08	.02
☐ 15U Phil Bradley	3.50	1.40	.35
☐ 16U Fred Breining	.20	.08	.02
☐ 17U Mike Brown	.20	.08	.02
(Angels OF)			
☐ 18U Bill Buckner	.40	.16	.04
☐ 19U Ray Burris	.20	.08	.02
☐ 20U John Butcher	.20	.08	.02
☐ 21U Brett Butler	.40	.16	.04
☐ 22U Enos Cabell	.20	.08	.02
☐ 23U Bill Campbell	.20	.08	.02
☐ 24U Bill Caudill	.20	.08	.02
☐ 25U Bobby Clark	.20	.08	.02
☐ 26U Bryan Clark	.20	.08	.02
☐ 27U Roger Clemens	85.00	34.00	8.50
☐ 28U Jaime Cocanower	.30	.12	.03
☐ 29U Ron Darling	10.00	4.00	1.00

	MINT	EXC	G-VG
☐ 30U Alvin Davis	7.00	2.80	.70
☐ 31U Bob Dernier	.20	.08	.02
☐ 32U Carlos Diaz	.20	.08	.02
☐ 33U Mike Easler	.20	.08	.02
☐ 34U Dennis Eckersley	1.00	.40	.10
☐ 35U Jim Essian	.20	.08	.02
☐ 36U Darrell Evans	.40	.16	.04
☐ 37U Mike Fitzgerald	.30	.12	.03
☐ 38U Tim Foli	.20	.08	.02
☐ 39U John Franco	6.00	2.40	.60
☐ 40U George Frazier	.20	.08	.02
☐ 41U Rich Gale	.20	.08	.02
☐ 42U Barbaro Garbey	.30	.12	.03
☐ 43U Dwight Gooden	70.00	28.00	7.00
☐ 44U Goose Gossage	.75	.30	.07
☐ 45U Wayne Gross	.20	.08	.02
☐ 46U Mark Gubicza	3.50	1.40	.35
☐ 47U Jackie Gutierrez	.30	.12	.03
☐ 48U Toby Harrah	.30	.12	.03
☐ 49U Ron Hassey	.30	.12	.03
☐ 50U Richie Hebner	.20	.08	.02
☐ 51U Willie Hernandez	.60	.24	.06
☐ 52U Ed Hodge	.20	.08	.02
☐ 53U Ricky Horton	.60	.24	.06
☐ 54U Art Howe	.30	.12	.03
☐ 55U Dane Iorg	.20	.08	.02
☐ 56U Brook Jacoby	3.00	1.20	.30
☐ 57U Dion James	.75	.30	.07
☐ 58U Mike Jeffcoat	.30	.12	.03
☐ 59U Ruppert Jones	.20	.08	.02
☐ 60U Bob Kearney	.20	.08	.02
☐ 61U Jimmy Key	6.00	2.40	.60
☐ 62U Dave Kingman	.40	.16	.04
☐ 63U Brad Komminsk	.30	.12	.03
☐ 64U Jerry Koosman	.30	.12	.03
☐ 65U Wayne Krenchicki	.20	.08	.02
☐ 66U Rusty Kuntz	.20	.08	.02
☐ 67U Frank LaCorte	.20	.08	.02
☐ 68U Dennis Lamp	.20	.08	.02
☐ 69U Tito Landrum	.30	.12	.03
☐ 70U Mark Langston	7.00	2.80	.70
☐ 71U Rick Leach	.20	.08	.02
☐ 72U Craig Lefferts	.30	.12	.03
☐ 73U Gary Lucas	.20	.08	.02
☐ 74U Jerry Martin	.20	.08	.02
☐ 75U Carmelo Martinez	.30	.12	.03
☐ 76U Mike Mason	.30	.12	.03
☐ 77U Gary Matthews	.30	.12	.03
☐ 78U Andy McGaffigan	.20	.08	.02

	MINT	EXC	G-VG
☐ 79U Joey McLaughlin ...	.20	.08	.02
☐ 80U Joe Morgan	2.00	.80	.20
☐ 81U Darryl Motley	.30	.12	.03
☐ 82U Graig Nettles	.90	.36	.09
☐ 83U Phil Niekro	2.00	.80	.20
☐ 84U Ken Oberkfell	.20	.08	.02
☐ 85U Al Oliver	.40	.16	.04
☐ 86U Jorge Orta	.20	.08	.02
☐ 87U Amos Otis	.30	.12	.03
☐ 88U Bob Owchinko	.20	.08	.02
☐ 89U Dave Parker	1.00	.40	.10
☐ 90U Jack Perconte	.20	.08	.02
☐ 91U Tony Perez	1.25	.50	.12
☐ 92U Gerald Perry	2.50	1.00	.25
☐ 93U Kirby Puckett	75.00	30.00	7.50
☐ 94U Shane Rawley	.40	.16	.04
☐ 95U Floyd Rayford	.20	.08	.02
☐ 96U Ron Reed	.20	.08	.02
☐ 97U R.J. Reynolds	1.00	.40	.10
☐ 98U Gene Richards	.20	.08	.02
☐ 99U Jose Rijo	1.50	.60	.15
☐ 100U Jeff Robinson	.75	.30	.07
(Giants pitcher)			
☐ 101U Ron Romanick	.30	.12	.03
☐ 102U Pete Rose	15.00	6.00	1.50
☐ 103U Bret Saberhagen ..	17.00	7.00	1.70
☐ 104U Scott Sanderson ...	.30	.12	.03
☐ 105U Dick Schofield	.75	.30	.07
☐ 106U Tom Seaver	7.00	2.80	.70
☐ 107U Jim Slaton	.20	.08	.02
☐ 108U Mike Smithson	.20	.08	.02
☐ 109U Lary Sorensen	.20	.08	.02
☐ 110U Tim Stoddard	.20	.08	.02
☐ 111U Jeff Stone	.40	.16	.04
☐ 112U Champ Summers ...	.20	.08	.02
☐ 113U Jim Sundberg	.30	.12	.03
☐ 114U Rick Sutcliffe	.60	.24	.06
☐ 115U Craig Swan	.20	.08	.02
☐ 116U Derrel Thomas	.20	.08	.02
☐ 117U Gorman Thomas ...	.40	.16	.04
☐ 118U Alex Trevino	.20	.08	.02
☐ 119U Manny Trillo	.20	.08	.02
☐ 120U John Tudor	.50	.20	.05
☐ 121U Tom Underwood	.20	.08	.02
☐ 122U Mike Vail	.20	.08	.02
☐ 123U Tom Waddell	.30	.12	.03
☐ 124U Gary Ward	.30	.12	.03
☐ 125U Terry Whitfield	.20	.08	.02
☐ 126U Curtis Wilkerson ...	.30	.12	.03

	MINT	EXC	G-VG
☐ 127U Frank Williams	.50	.20	.05
☐ 128U Glenn Wilson	.30	.12	.03
☐ 129U John Wockenfuss ..	.20	.08	.02
☐ 130U Ned Yost	.20	.08	.02
☐ 131U Mike Young	.60	.24	.06
☐ 132U Checklist: 1-132 ...	.20	.02	.00

1985 Fleer

The cards in this 660-card set measure 2 ½" by 3 ½". The 1985 Fleer set features fronts which contain the team logo along with the player's name and position. The borders enclosing the photo are color-coded to correspond to the player's team. In each case, the color is one of the standard colors of that team, e.g., orange for Baltimore, red for St. Louis, etc. The backs feature the same name, number, and statistics format that Fleer has been using over the past few years. The cards are ordered alphabetically within team. The teams are ordered based on their respective performance during the prior year, e.g., World Champion Detroit Tigers (1-25), NL Champion San Diego (26-48), Chicago Cubs (49-71), New York Mets (72-95), Toronto (96-119), New York Yankees (120-147), Boston (148-169), Baltimore (170-195), Kansas City (196-218), St. Louis (219-243), Philadelphia (244-269), Minnesota (270-292), California (293-317), Atlanta (318-342), Houston (343-365), Los Angeles (366-391), Montreal (392-413),

Oakland (414-436), Cleveland (437-460), Pittsburgh (461-481), Seattle (482-505), Chicago White Sox (506-530), Cincinnati (531-554), Texas (555-575), Milwaukee (576-601), and San Francisco (602-625). Specials (626-643), Rookie pairs (644-653), and checklist cards (654-660) complete the set. The black and white photo on the reverse is included for the third straight year.

			MINT	EXC	G-VG
	Complete Set (660)		100.00	40.00	10.00
	Common Player (1-660)		.05	.02	.00
☐	1	Doug Bair	.10	.02	.00
☐	2	Juan Berenguer	.05	.02	.00
☐	3	Dave Bergman	.05	.02	.00
☐	4	Tom Brookens	.05	.02	.00
☐	5	Marty Castillo	.05	.02	.00
☐	6	Darrell Evans	.12	.05	.01
☐	7	Barbaro Garbey	.05	.02	.00
☐	8	Kirk Gibson	.30	.12	.03
☐	9	John Grubb	.05	.02	.00
☐	10	Willie Hernandez	.12	.05	.01
☐	11	Larry Herndon	.05	.02	.00
☐	12	Howard Johnson	.50	.20	.05
☐	13	Ruppert Jones	.05	.02	.00
☐	14	Rusty Kuntz	.05	.02	.00
☐	15	Chet Lemon	.08	.03	.01
☐	16	Aurelio Lopez	.05	.02	.00
☐	17	Sid Monge	.05	.02	.00
☐	18	Jack Morris	.20	.08	.02
☐	19	Lance Parrish	.20	.08	.02
☐	20	Dan Petry	.08	.03	.01
☐	21	Dave Rozema	.05	.02	.00
☐	22	Bill Scherrer	.05	.02	.00
☐	23	Alan Trammell	.30	.12	.03
☐	24	Lou Whitaker	.15	.06	.01
☐	25	Milt Wilcox	.05	.02	.00
☐	26	Kurt Bevacqua	.05	.02	.00
☐	27	Greg Booker	.05	.02	.00
☐	28	Bobby Brown	.05	.02	.00
☐	29	Luis DeLeon	.05	.02	.00
☐	30	Dave Dravecky	.08	.03	.01
☐	31	Tim Flannery	.05	.02	.00
☐	32	Steve Garvey	.40	.16	.04
☐	33	Goose Gossage	.15	.06	.01
☐	34	Tony Gwynn	1.00	.40	.10
☐	35	Greg Harris	.05	.02	.00
☐	36	Andy Hawkins	.08	.03	.01
☐	37	Terry Kennedy	.05	.02	.00
☐	38	Craig Lefferts	.05	.02	.00
☐	39	Tim Lollar	.05	.02	.00
☐	40	Carmelo Martinez	.05	.02	.00
☐	41	Kevin McReynolds	1.00	.40	.10
☐	42	Graig Nettles	.12	.05	.01
☐	43	Luis Salazar	.08	.03	.01
☐	44	Eric Show	.08	.03	.01
☐	45	Garry Templeton	.08	.03	.01
☐	46	Mark Thurmond	.05	.02	.00
☐	47	Ed Whitson	.05	.02	.00
☐	48	Alan Wiggins	.05	.02	.00
☐	49	Rich Bordi	.05	.02	.00
☐	50	Larry Bowa	.10	.04	.01
☐	51	Warren Brusstar	.05	.02	.00
☐	52	Ron Cey	.10	.04	.01
☐	53	Henry Cotto	.08	.03	.01
☐	54	Jody Davis	.08	.03	.01
☐	55	Bob Dernier	.05	.02	.00
☐	56	Leon Durham	.08	.03	.01
☐	57	Dennis Eckersley	.15	.06	.01
☐	58	George Frazier	.05	.02	.00
☐	59	Richie Hebner	.05	.02	.00
☐	60	Dave Lopes	.08	.03	.01
☐	61	Gary Matthews	.08	.03	.01
☐	62	Keith Moreland	.05	.02	.00
☐	63	Rick Reuschel	.10	.04	.01
☐	64	Dick Ruthven	.05	.02	.00
☐	65	Ryne Sandberg	.40	.16	.04
☐	66	Scott Sanderson	.05	.02	.00
☐	67	Lee Smith	.10	.04	.01
☐	68	Tim Stoddard	.05	.02	.00
☐	69	Rick Sutcliffe	.15	.06	.01
☐	70	Steve Trout	.05	.02	.00
☐	71	Gary Woods	.05	.02	.00
☐	72	Wally Backman	.10	.04	.01
☐	73	Bruce Berenyi	.05	.02	.00
☐	74	Hubie Brooks	.08	.03	.01
☐	75	Kelvin Chapman	.08	.03	.01
☐	76	Ron Darling	1.00	.40	.10
☐	77	Sid Fernandez	.85	.34	.08
☐	78	Mike Fitzgerald	.05	.02	.00
☐	79	George Foster	.12	.05	.01
☐	80	Brent Gaff	.05	.02	.00
☐	81	Ron Gardenhire	.05	.02	.00
☐	82	Dwight Gooden	9.00	3.75	.90
☐	83	Tom Gorman	.05	.02	.00
☐	84	Danny Heep	.05	.02	.00
☐	85	Keith Hernandez	.30	.12	.03
☐	86	Ray Knight	.10	.04	.01

		MINT	EXC	G-VG
☐ 87	Ed Lynch	.05	.02	.00
☐ 88	Jose Oquendo	.08	.03	.01
☐ 89	Jesse Orosco	.05	.02	.00
☐ 90	Rafael Santana	.30	.12	.03
☐ 91	Doug Sisk	.05	.02	.00
☐ 92	Rusty Staub	.10	.04	.01
☐ 93	Darryl Strawberry	3.50	1.40	.35
☐ 94	Walt Terrell	.08	.03	.01
☐ 95	Mookie Wilson	.08	.03	.01
☐ 96	Jim Acker	.05	.02	.00
☐ 97	Willie Aikens	.05	.02	.00
☐ 98	Doyle Alexander	.08	.03	.01
☐ 99	Jesse Barfield	.30	.12	.03
☐ 100	George Bell	.40	.16	.04
☐ 101	Jim Clancy	.05	.02	.00
☐ 102	Dave Collins	.05	.02	.00
☐ 103	Tony Fernandez	.35	.15	.03
☐ 104	Damaso Garcia	.05	.02	.00
☐ 105	Jim Gott	.05	.02	.00
☐ 106	Alfredo Griffin	.08	.03	.01
☐ 107	Garth Iorg	.05	.02	.00
☐ 108	Roy Lee Jackson	.05	.02	.00
☐ 109	Cliff Johnson	.05	.02	.00
☐ 110	Jimmy Key	1.25	.50	.12
☐ 111	Dennis Lamp	.05	.02	.00
☐ 112	Rick Leach	.05	.02	.00
☐ 113	Luis Leal	.05	.02	.00
☐ 114	Buck Martinez	.05	.02	.00
☐ 115	Lloyd Moseby	.12	.05	.01
☐ 116	Rance Mulliniks	.05	.02	.00
☐ 117	Dave Stieb	.15	.06	.01
☐ 118	Willie Upshaw	.05	.02	.00
☐ 119	Ernie Whitt	.05	.02	.00
☐ 120	Mike Armstrong	.05	.02	.00
☐ 121	Don Baylor	.12	.05	.01
☐ 122	Marty Bystrom	.05	.02	.00
☐ 123	Rick Cerone	.05	.02	.00
☐ 124	Joe Cowley	.05	.02	.00
☐ 125	Brian Dayett	.05	.02	.00
☐ 126	Tim Foli	.05	.02	.00
☐ 127	Ray Fontenot	.05	.02	.00
☐ 128	Ken Griffey	.08	.03	.01
☐ 129	Ron Guidry	.15	.06	.01
☐ 130	Toby Harrah	.05	.02	.00
☐ 131	Jay Howell	.08	.03	.01
☐ 132	Steve Kemp	.08	.03	.01
☐ 133	Don Mattingly	10.00	4.00	1.00
☐ 134	Bobby Meacham	.05	.02	.00
☐ 135	John Montefusco	.05	.02	.00
☐ 136	Omar Moreno	.05	.02	.00
☐ 137	Dale Murray	.05	.02	.00
☐ 138	Phil Niekro	.25	.10	.02
☐ 139	Mike Pagliarulo	1.50	.60	.15
☐ 140	Willie Randolph	.10	.04	.01
☐ 141	Dennis Rasmussen	.25	.10	.02
☐ 142	Dave Righetti	.18	.08	.01
☐ 143	Jose Rijo	.40	.16	.04
☐ 144	Andre Robertson	.05	.02	.00
☐ 145	Bob Shirley	.05	.02	.00
☐ 146	Dave Winfield	.35	.14	.03
☐ 147	Butch Wynegar	.05	.02	.00
☐ 148	Gary Allenson	.05	.02	.00
☐ 149	Tony Armas	.08	.03	.01
☐ 150	Marty Barrett	.30	.12	.03
☐ 151	Wade Boggs	4.00	1.60	.40
☐ 152	Dennis Boyd	.10	.04	.01
☐ 153	Bill Buckner	.10	.04	.01
☐ 154	Mark Clear	.05	.02	.00
☐ 155	Roger Clemens	11.00	4.50	1.10
☐ 156	Steve Crawford	.05	.02	.00
☐ 157	Mike Easler	.05	.02	.00
☐ 158	Dwight Evans	.15	.06	.01
☐ 159	Rich Gedman	.10	.04	.01
☐ 160	Jackie Gutierrez (W.Boggs on deck)	.15	.06	.01
☐ 161	Bruce Hurst	.15	.06	.01
☐ 162	John Henry Johnson	.05	.02	.00
☐ 163	Rick Miller	.05	.02	.00
☐ 164	Reid Nichols	.05	.02	.00
☐ 165	Al Nipper	.15	.06	.01
☐ 166	Bob Ojeda	.10	.04	.01
☐ 167	Jerry Remy	.05	.02	.00
☐ 168	Jim Rice	.25	.10	.02
☐ 169	Bob Stanley	.05	.02	.00
☐ 170	Mike Boddicker	.10	.04	.01
☐ 171	Al Bumbry	.05	.02	.00
☐ 172	Todd Cruz	.05	.02	.00
☐ 173	Rich Dauer	.05	.02	.00
☐ 174	Storm Davis	.10	.04	.01
☐ 175	Rick Dempsey	.05	.02	.00
☐ 176	Jim Dwyer	.05	.02	.00
☐ 177	Mike Flanagan	.08	.03	.01
☐ 178	Dan Ford	.05	.02	.00
☐ 179	Wayne Gross	.05	.02	.00
☐ 180	John Lowenstein	.05	.02	.00
☐ 181	Dennis Martinez	.08	.03	.01
☐ 182	Tippy Martinez	.05	.02	.00
☐ 183	Scott McGregor	.08	.03	.01

		MINT	EXC	G-VG			MINT	EXC	G-VG
☐ 184	Eddie Murray	.45	.18	.04	☐ 233	Dave LaPoint	.08	.03	.01
☐ 185	Joe Nolan	.05	.02	.00	☐ 234	Willie McGee	.30	.12	.03
☐ 186	Floyd Rayford	.05	.02	.00	☐ 235	Tom Nieto	.05	.02	.00
☐ 187	Cal Ripken	.50	.20	.05	☐ 236	Terry Pendleton	.45	.18	.04
☐ 188	Gary Roenicke	.05	.02	.00	☐ 237	Darrell Porter	.05	.02	.00
☐ 189	Lenn Sakata	.05	.02	.00	☐ 238	Dave Rucker	.05	.02	.00
☐ 190	John Shelby	.05	.02	.00	☐ 239	Lonnie Smith	.08	.03	.01
☐ 191	Ken Singleton	.08	.03	.01	☐ 240	Ozzie Smith	.25	.10	.02
☐ 192	Sammy Stewart	.05	.02	.00	☐ 241	Bruce Sutter	.12	.05	.01
☐ 193	Bill Swaggerty	.08	.03	.01	☐ 242	Andy Van Slyke	.50	.20	.05
☐ 194	Tom Underwood	.05	.02	.00	☐ 243	Dave Von Ohlen	.05	.02	.00
☐ 195	Mike Young	.15	.06	.01	☐ 244	Larry Andersen	.05	.02	.00
☐ 196	Steve Balboni	.05	.02	.00	☐ 245	Bill Campbell	.05	.02	.00
☐ 197	Joe Beckwith	.05	.02	.00	☐ 246	Steve Carlton	.40	.16	.04
☐ 198	Bud Black	.05	.02	.00	☐ 247	Tim Corcoran	.05	.02	.00
☐ 199	George Brett	.50	.20	.05	☐ 248	Ivan DeJesus	.05	.02	.00
☐ 200	Onix Concepcion	.05	.02	.00	☐ 249	John Denny	.08	.03	.01
☐ 201	Mark Gubicza	.85	.34	.08	☐ 250	Bo Diaz	.05	.02	.00
☐ 202	Larry Gura	.05	.02	.00	☐ 251	Greg Gross	.05	.02	.00
☐ 203	Mark Huismann	.05	.02	.00	☐ 252	Kevin Gross	.08	.03	.01
☐ 204	Dane Iorg	.05	.02	.00	☐ 253	Von Hayes	.15	.06	.01
☐ 205	Danny Jackson	1.25	.50	.12	☐ 254	Al Holland	.05	.02	.00
☐ 206	Charlie Leibrandt	.05	.02	.00	☐ 255	Charles Hudson	.05	.02	.00
☐ 207	Hal McRae	.08	.03	.01	☐ 256	Jerry Koosman	.08	.03	.01
☐ 208	Darryl Motley	.05	.02	.00	☐ 257	Joe Lefebvre	.05	.02	.00
☐ 209	Jorge Orta	.05	.02	.00	☐ 258	Sixto Lezcano	.05	.02	.00
☐ 210	Greg Pryor	.05	.02	.00	☐ 259	Garry Maddox	.08	.03	.01
☐ 211	Dan Quisenberry	.12	.05	.01	☐ 260	Len Matuszek	.05	.02	.00
☐ 212	Bret Saberhagen	3.00	1.20	.30	☐ 261	Tug McGraw	.10	.04	.01
☐ 213	Pat Sheridan	.05	.02	.00	☐ 262	Al Oliver	.10	.04	.01
☐ 214	Don Slaught	.05	.02	.00	☐ 263	Shane Rawley	.08	.03	.01
☐ 215	U.L. Washington	.05	.02	.00	☐ 264	Juan Samuel	.35	.14	.03
☐ 216	John Wathan	.05	.02	.00	☐ 265	Mike Schmidt	.50	.20	.05
☐ 217	Frank White	.08	.03	.01	☐ 266	Jeff Stone	.15	.06	.01
☐ 218	Willie Wilson	.12	.05	.01	☐ 267	Ozzie Virgil	.05	.02	.00
☐ 219	Neil Allen	.05	.02	.00	☐ 268	Glenn Wilson	.08	.03	.01
☐ 220	Joaquin Andujar	.08	.03	.01	☐ 269	John Wockenfuss	.05	.02	.00
☐ 221	Steve Braun	.05	.02	.00	☐ 270	Darrell Brown	.05	.02	.00
☐ 222	Danny Cox	.10	.04	.01	☐ 271	Tom Brunansky	.20	.08	.02
☐ 223	Bob Forsch	.05	.02	.00	☐ 272	Randy Bush	.08	.03	.01
☐ 224	David Green	.05	.02	.00	☐ 273	John Butcher	.05	.02	.00
☐ 225	George Hendrick	.08	.03	.01	☐ 274	Bobby Castillo	.05	.02	.00
☐ 226	Tom Herr	.08	.03	.01	☐ 275	Ron Davis	.05	.02	.00
☐ 227	Ricky Horton	.20	.08	.02	☐ 276	Dave Engle	.05	.02	.00
☐ 228	Art Howe	.08	.03	.01	☐ 277	Pete Filson	.05	.02	.00
☐ 229	Mike Jorgensen	.05	.02	.00	☐ 278	Gary Gaetti	.35	.14	.03
☐ 230	Kurt Kepshire	.08	.03	.01	☐ 279	Mickey Hatcher	.10	.04	.01
☐ 231	Jeff Lahti	.05	.02	.00	☐ 280	Ed Hodge	.05	.02	.00
☐ 232	Tito Landrum	.05	.02	.00	☐ 281	Kent Hrbek	.35	.14	.03

		MINT	EXC	G-VG
☐ 282	Houston Jimenez ..	.05	.02	.00
☐ 283	Tim Laudner	.05	.02	.00
☐ 284	Rick Lysander	.05	.02	.00
☐ 285	Dave Meier	.08	.03	.01
☐ 286	Kirby Puckett	10.00	4.00	1.00
☐ 287	Pat Putnam	.05	.02	.00
☐ 288	Ken Schrom	.05	.02	.00
☐ 289	Mike Smithson	.05	.02	.00
☐ 290	Tim Teufel	.05	.02	.00
☐ 291	Frank Viola	.40	.16	.04
☐ 292	Ron Washington ...	.05	.02	.00
☐ 293	Don Aase	.05	.02	.00
☐ 294	Juan Beniquez	.05	.02	.00
☐ 295	Bob Boone	.10	.04	.01
☐ 296	Mike Brown	.05	.02	.00
	(Angels OF)			
☐ 297	Rod Carew	.40	.16	.04
☐ 298	Doug Corbett	.05	.02	.00
☐ 299	Doug DeCinces ...	.08	.03	.01
☐ 300	Brian Downing	.08	.03	.01
☐ 301	Ken Forsch	.05	.02	.00
☐ 302	Bobby Grich	.10	.04	.01
☐ 303	Reggie Jackson ...	.45	.18	.04
☐ 304	Tommy John	.15	.06	.01
☐ 305	Curt Kaufman	.08	.03	.01
☐ 306	Bruce Kison	.05	.02	.00
☐ 307	Fred Lynn	.15	.06	.01
☐ 308	Gary Pettis	.08	.03	.01
☐ 309	Ron Romanick	.05	.02	.00
☐ 310	Luis Sanchez	.05	.02	.00
☐ 311	Dick Schofield	.10	.04	.01
☐ 312	Daryl Sconiers	.05	.02	.00
☐ 313	Jim Slaton	.05	.02	.00
☐ 314	Derrel Thomas	.05	.02	.00
☐ 315	Rob Wilfong	.05	.02	.00
☐ 316	Mike Witt	.12	.05	.01
☐ 317	Geoff Zahn	.05	.02	.00
☐ 318	Len Barker	.05	.02	.00
☐ 319	Steve Bedrosian ..	.15	.06	.01
☐ 320	Bruce Benedict ...	.05	.02	.00
☐ 321	Rick Camp	.05	.02	.00
☐ 322	Chris Chambliss ...	.08	.03	.01
☐ 323	Jeff Dedmon	.08	.03	.01
☐ 324	Terry Forster	.08	.03	.01
☐ 325	Gene Garber	.05	.02	.00
☐ 326	Albert Hall	.10	.04	.01
☐ 327	Terry Harper	.05	.02	.00
☐ 328	Bob Horner	.15	.06	.01
☐ 329	Glenn Hubbard	.05	.02	.00

		MINT	EXC	G-VG
☐ 330	Randy Johnson ...	.05	.02	.00
☐ 331	Brad Komminsk ...	.08	.03	.01
☐ 332	Rick Mahler	.05	.02	.00
☐ 333	Craig McMurtry ...	.05	.02	.00
☐ 334	Donnie Moore	.05	.02	.00
☐ 335	Dale Murphy	.65	.26	.06
☐ 336	Ken Oberkfell	.05	.02	.00
☐ 337	Pascual Perez	.08	.03	.01
☐ 338	Gerald Perry	.40	.16	.04
☐ 339	Rafael Ramirez ...	.05	.02	.00
☐ 340	Jerry Royster	.05	.02	.00
☐ 341	Alex Trevino	.05	.02	.00
☐ 342	Claudell Washington	.08	.03	.01
☐ 343	Alan Ashby	.05	.02	.00
☐ 344	Mark Bailey	.08	.03	.01
☐ 345	Kevin Bass	.10	.04	.01
☐ 346	Enos Cabell	.05	.02	.00
☐ 347	Jose Cruz	.10	.04	.01
☐ 348	Bill Dawley	.05	.02	.00
☐ 349	Frank DiPino	.05	.02	.00
☐ 350	Bill Doran	.15	.06	.01
☐ 351	Phil Garner	.05	.02	.00
☐ 352	Bob Knepper	.10	.04	.01
☐ 353	Mike LaCoss	.05	.02	.00
☐ 354	Jerry Mumphrey ...	.05	.02	.00
☐ 355	Joe Niekro	.10	.04	.01
☐ 356	Terry Puhl	.05	.02	.00
☐ 357	Craig Reynolds ...	.05	.02	.00
☐ 358	Vern Ruhle	.05	.02	.00
☐ 359	Nolan Ryan	.40	.16	.04
☐ 360	Joe Sambito	.05	.02	.00
☐ 361	Mike Scott	.30	.12	.03
☐ 362	Dave Smith	.08	.03	.01
☐ 363	Julio Solano	.08	.03	.01
☐ 364	Dickie Thon	.05	.02	.00
☐ 365	Denny Walling	.05	.02	.00
☐ 366	Dave Anderson ...	.05	.02	.00
☐ 367	Bob Bailor	.05	.02	.00
☐ 368	Greg Brock	.08	.03	.01
☐ 369	Carlos Diaz	.05	.02	.00
☐ 370	Pedro Guerrero ...	.25	.10	.02
☐ 371	Orel Hershiser ...	9.00	3.75	.90
☐ 372	Rick Honeycutt ...	.05	.02	.00
☐ 373	Burt Hooton	.05	.02	.00
☐ 374	Ken Howell	.15	.06	.01
☐ 375	Ken Landreaux ...	.05	.02	.00
☐ 376	Candy Maldonado ..	.10	.04	.01
☐ 377	Mike Marshall	.15	.06	.01
☐ 378	Tom Niedenfuer ...	.08	.03	.01

	MINT	EXC	G-VG			MINT	EXC	G-VG
☐ 379 Alejandro Pena	.08	.03	.01	☐ 428 Bill Krueger	.05	.02	.00
☐ 380 Jerry Reuss	.08	.03	.01	☐ 429 Carney Lansford ..	.10	.04	.01
☐ 381 R.J. Reynolds	.25	.10	.02	☐ 430 Steve McCatty	.05	.02	.00
☐ 382 German Rivera	.08	.03	.01	☐ 431 Joe Morgan	.18	.08	.01
☐ 383 Bill Russell	.08	.03	.01	☐ 432 Dwayne Murphy ..	.05	.02	.00
☐ 384 Steve Sax	.25	.08	.02	☐ 433 Tony Phillips	.05	.02	.00
☐ 385 - Mike Scioscia	.08	.03	.01	☐ 434 Lary Sorensen	.05	.02	.00
☐ 386 Franklin Stubbs	.35	.14	.03	☐ 435 Mike Warren	.05	.02	.00
☐ 387 Fernando Valenzuela	.25	.10	.02	☐ 436 Curt Young	.35	.14	.03
☐ 388 Bob Welch	.10	.04	.01	☐ 437 Luis Aponte	.05	.02	.00
☐ 389 Terry Whitfield	.05	.02	.00	☐ 438 Chris Bando	.05	.02	.00
☐ 390 Steve Yeager	.05	.02	.00	☐ 439 Tony Bernazard ...	.05	.02	.00
☐ 391 Pat Zachry	.05	.02	.00	☐ 440 Bert Blyleven	.10	.04	.01
☐ 392 Fred Breining	.05	.02	.00	☐ 441 Brett Butler	.10	.04	.01
☐ 393 Gary Carter	.30	.12	.03	☐ 442 Ernie Camacho ...	.05	.02	.00
☐ 394 Andre Dawson	.30	.12	.03	☐ 443 Joe Carter	1.75	.70	.17
☐ 395 Miguel Dilone	.05	.02	.00	☐ 444 Carmelo Castillo ..	.05	.02	.00
☐ 396 Dan Driessen	.05	.02	.00	☐ 445 Jamie Easterly	.05	.02	.00
☐ 397 Doug Flynn	.05	.02	.00	☐ 446 Steve Farr	.20	.08	.02
☐ 398 Terry Francona	.05	.02	.00	☐ 447 Mike Fischlin	.05	.02	.00
☐ 399 Bill Gullickson	.05	.02	.00	☐ 448 Julio Franco	.15	.06	.01
☐ 400 Bob James	.05	.02	.00	☐ 449 Mel Hall	.10	.04	.01
☐ 401 Charlie Lea	.05	.02	.00	☐ 450 Mike Hargrove	.05	.02	.00
☐ 402 Bryan Little	.05	.02	.00	☐ 451 Neal Heaton	.05	.02	.00
☐ 403 Gary Lucas	.05	.02	.00	☐ 452 Brook Jacoby	.25	.10	.02
☐ 404 David Palmer	.05	.02	.00	☐ 453 Mike Jeffcoat	.05	.02	.00
☐ 405 Tim Raines	.35	.14	.03	☐ 454 Don Schulze	.08	.03	.01
☐ 406 Mike Ramsey	.05	.02	.00	☐ 455 Roy Smith	.08	.03	.01
☐ 407 Jeff Reardon	.10	.04	.01	☐ 456 Pat Tabler	.10	.04	.01
☐ 408 Steve Rogers	.05	.02	.00	☐ 457 Andre Thornton ...	.08	.03	.01
☐ 409 Dan Schatzeder ...	.05	.02	.00	☐ 458 George Vukovich .	.05	.02	.00
☐ 410 Bryn Smith	.05	.02	.00	☐ 459 Tom Waddell	.08	.03	.01
☐ 411 Mike Stenhouse ...	.05	.02	.00	☐ 460 Jerry Willard	.05	.02	.00
☐ 412 Tim Wallach	.12	.05	.01	☐ 461 Dale Berra	.05	.02	.00
☐ 413 Jim Wohlford	.05	.02	.00	☐ 462 John Candelaria ..	.08	.03	.01
☐ 414 Bill Almon	.05	.02	.00	☐ 463 Jose DeLeon	.05	.02	.00
☐ 415 Keith Atherton	.05	.02	.00	☐ 464 Doug Frobel	.05	.02	.00
☐ 416 Bruce Bochte	.05	.02	.00	☐ 465 Cecilio Guante	.05	.02	.00
☐ 417 Tom Burgmeier	.05	.02	.00	☐ 466 Brian Harper	.05	.02	.00
☐ 418 Ray Burris	.05	.02	.00	☐ 467 Lee Lacy	.05	.02	.00
☐ 419 Bill Caudill	.05	.02	.00	☐ 468 Bill Madlock	.10	.04	.01
☐ 420 Chris Codiroli	.05	.02	.00	☐ 469 Lee Mazzilli	.05	.02	.00
☐ 421 Tim Conroy	.05	.02	.00	☐ 470 Larry McWilliams ..	.05	.02	.00
☐ 422 Mike Davis	.08	.03	.01	☐ 471 Jim Morrison	.05	.02	.00
☐ 423 Jim Essian	.05	.02	.00	☐ 472 Tony Pena	.12	.05	.01
☐ 424 Mike Heath	.05	.02	.00	☐ 473 Johnny Ray	.10	.04	.01
☐ 425 Rickey Henderson .	.45	.18	.04	☐ 474 Rick Rhoden	.10	.04	.01
☐ 426 Donnie Hill	.05	.02	.00	☐ 475 Don Robinson	.05	.02	.00
☐ 427 Dave Kingman	.10	.04	.01	☐ 476 Rod Scurry	.05	.02	.00

		MINT	EXC	G-VG			MINT	EXC	G-VG
☐ 477	Kent Tekulve	.08	.03	.01	☐ 526	Tom Seaver	.30	.12	.03
☐ 478	Jason Thompson	.05	.02	.00	☐ 527	Roy Smalley	.05	.02	.00
☐ 479	John Tudor	.15	.06	.01	☐ 528	Dan Spillner	.05	.02	.00
☐ 480	Lee Tunnell	.05	.02	.00	☐ 529	Mike Squires	.05	.02	.00
☐ 481	Marvell Wynne	.05	.02	.00	☐ 530	Greg Walker	.10	.04	.01
☐ 482	Salome Barojas	.05	.02	.00	☐ 531	Cesar Cedeno	.10	.04	.01
☐ 483	Dave Beard	.05	.02	.00	☐ 532	Dave Concepcion	.10	.04	.01
☐ 484	Jim Beattie	.05	.02	.00	☐ 533	Eric Davis	16.00	6.50	1.60
☐ 485	Barry Bonnell	.05	.02	.00	☐ 534	Nick Esasky	.08	.03	.01
☐ 486	Phil Bradley	1.00	.40	.10	☐ 535	Tom Foley	.05	.02	.00
☐ 487	Al Cowens	.05	.02	.00	☐ 536	John Franco	1.00	.40	.10
☐ 488	Alvin Davis	1.75	.70	.17	☐ 537	Brad Gulden	.05	.02	.00
☐ 489	Dave Henderson	.15	.06	.01	☐ 538	Tom Hume	.05	.02	.00
☐ 490	Steve Henderson	.05	.02	.00	☐ 539	Wayne Krenchicki	.05	.02	.00
☐ 491	Bob Kearney	.05	.02	.00	☐ 540	Andy McGaffigan	.05	.02	.00
☐ 492	Mark Langston	1.50	.60	.15	☐ 541	Eddie Milner	.05	.02	.00
☐ 493	Larry Milbourne	.05	.02	.00	☐ 542	Ron Oester	.05	.02	.00
☐ 494	Paul Mirabella	.05	.02	.00	☐ 543	Bob Owchinko	.05	.02	.00
☐ 495	Mike Moore	.08	.03	.01	☐ 544	Dave Parker	.15	.06	.01
☐ 496	Edwin Nunez	.05	.02	.00	☐ 545	Frank Pastore	.05	.02	.00
☐ 497	Spike Owen	.05	.02	.00	☐ 546	Tony Perez	.15	.06	.01
☐ 498	Jack Perconte	.05	.02	.00	☐ 547	Ted Power	.05	.02	.00
☐ 499	Ken Phelps	.10	.04	.01	☐ 548	Joe Price	.05	.02	.00
☐ 500	Jim Presley	.80	.32	.08	☐ 549	Gary Redus	.05	.02	.00
☐ 501	Mike Stanton	.05	.02	.00	☐ 550	Pete Rose	1.00	.40	.10
☐ 502	Bob Stoddard	.05	.02	.00	☐ 551	Jeff Russell	.15	.06	.01
☐ 503	Gorman Thomas	.10	.04	.01	☐ 552	Mario Soto	.05	.02	.00
☐ 504	Ed VandeBerg	.05	.02	.00	☐ 553	Jay Tibbs	.15	.06	.01
☐ 505	Matt Young	.05	.02	.00	☐ 554	Duane Walker	.05	.02	.00
☐ 506	Juan Agosto	.05	.02	.00	☐ 555	Alan Bannister	.05	.02	.00
☐ 507	Harold Baines	.15	.06	.01	☐ 556	Buddy Bell	.10	.04	.01
☐ 508	Floyd Bannister	.05	.02	.00	☐ 557	Danny Darwin	.05	.02	.00
☐ 509	Britt Burns	.05	.02	.00	☐ 558	Charlie Hough	.08	.03	.01
☐ 510	Julio Cruz	.05	.02	.00	☐ 559	Bobby Jones	.05	.02	.00
☐ 511	Richard Dotson	.10	.04	.01	☐ 560	Odell Jones	.05	.02	.00
☐ 512	Jerry Dybzinski	.05	.02	.00	☐ 561	Jeff Kunkel	.08	.03	.01
☐ 513	Carlton Fisk	.15	.06	.01	☐ 562	Mike Mason	.08	.03	.01
☐ 514	Scott Fletcher	.10	.04	.01	☐ 563	Pete O'Brien	.10	.04	.01
☐ 515	Jerry Hairston	.05	.02	.00	☐ 564	Larry Parrish	.08	.03	.01
☐ 516	Marc Hill	.05	.02	.00	☐ 565	Mickey Rivers	.08	.03	.01
☐ 517	LaMarr Hoyt	.08	.03	.01	☐ 566	Billy Sample	.05	.02	.00
☐ 518	Ron Kittle	.15	.06	.01	☐ 567	Dave Schmidt	.08	.03	.01
☐ 519	Rudy Law	.05	.02	.00	☐ 568	Donnie Scott	.05	.02	.00
☐ 520	Vance Law	.08	.03	.01	☐ 569	Dave Stewart	.15	.06	.01
☐ 521	Greg Luzinski	.10	.04	.01	☐ 570	Frank Tanana	.08	.03	.01
☐ 522	Gene Nelson	.05	.02	.00	☐ 571	Wayne Tolleson	.05	.02	.00
☐ 523	Tom Paciorek	.05	.02	.00	☐ 572	Gary Ward	.08	.03	.01
☐ 524	Ron Reed	.05	.02	.00	☐ 573	Curtis Wilkerson	.05	.02	.00
☐ 525	Bert Roberge	.05	.02	.00	☐ 574	George Wright	.05	.02	.00

	MINT	EXC	G-VG			MINT	EXC	G-VG
☐ 575 Ned Yost	.05	.02	.00	☐ 623 Brad Wellman	.05	.02	.00
☐ 576 Mark Brouhard	.05	.02	.00	☐ 624 Frank Williams	.20	.08	.02
☐ 577 Mike Caldwell	.05	.02	.00	☐ 625 Joel Youngblood	.05	.02	.00
☐ 578 Bobby Clark	.05	.02	.00	☐ 626 Cal Ripken IA	.20	.08	.02
☐ 579 Jaime Cocanower	.05	.02	.00	☐ 627 Mike Schmidt IA	.30	.12	.03
☐ 580 Cecil Cooper	.12	.05	.01	☐ 628 Giving The Signs	.05	.02	.00
☐ 581 Rollie Fingers	.15	.06	.01	Sparky Anderson			
☐ 582 Jim Gantner	.05	.02	.00	☐ 629 AL Pitcher's Nightmare	.20	.08	.02
☐ 583 Moose Haas	.05	.02	.00	Dave Winfield			
☐ 584 Dion James	.10	.04	.01	Rickey Henderson			
☐ 585 Pete Ladd	.05	.02	.00	☐ 630 NL Pitcher's Nightmare	.20	.08	.02
☐ 586 Rick Manning	.05	.02	.00	Mike Schmidt			
☐ 587 Bob McClure	.05	.02	.00	Ryne Sandberg			
☐ 588 Paul Molitor	.20	.08	.02	☐ 631 NL All-Stars	.25	.10	.02
☐ 589 Charlie Moore	.05	.02	.00	Darryl Strawberry			
☐ 590 Ben Oglivie	.08	.03	.01	Gary Carter			
☐ 591 Chuck Porter	.05	.02	.00	Steve Garvey			
☐ 592 Randy Ready	.25	.10	.02	Ozzie Smith			
☐ 593 Ed Romero	.05	.02	.00	☐ 632 A-S Winning Battery	.10	.04	.01
☐ 594 Bill Schroeder	.05	.02	.00	Gary Carter			
☐ 595 Ray Searage	.05	.02	.00	Charlie Lea			
☐ 596 Ted Simmons	.12	.05	.01	☐ 633 NL Pennant Clinchers	.12	.05	.01
☐ 597 Jim Sundberg	.05	.02	.00	Steve Garvey			
☐ 598 Don Sutton	.25	.10	.02	Goose Gossage			
☐ 599 Tom Tellmann	.05	.02	.00	☐ 634 NL Rookie Phenoms	.75	.30	.07
☐ 600 Rick Waits	.05	.02	.00	Dwight Gooden			
☐ 601 Robin Yount	.35	.14	.03	Juan Samuel			
☐ 602 Dusty Baker	.08	.03	.01	☐ 635 Toronto's Big Guns	.08	.03	.01
☐ 603 Bob Brenly	.05	.02	.00	Willie Upshaw			
☐ 604 Jack Clark	.20	.08	.02	☐ 636 Toronto's Big Guns	.08	.03	.01
☐ 605 Chili Davis	.10	.04	.01	Lloyd Moseby			
☐ 606 Mark Davis	.08	.03	.01	☐ 637 HOLLAND: Al Holland	.05	.02	.00
☐ 607 Dan Gladden	.45	.18	.04	☐ 638 TUNNELL: Lee Tunnell	.05	.02	.00
☐ 608 Atlee Hammaker	.05	.02	.00	☐ 639 500th Homer	.30	.12	.03
☐ 609 Mike Krukow	.05	.02	.00	Reggie Jackson			
☐ 610 Duane Kuiper	.05	.02	.00	☐ 640 4000th Hit	.45	.18	.04
☐ 611 Bob Lacey	.05	.02	.00	Pete Rose			
☐ 612 Bill Laskey	.05	.02	.00	☐ 641 Father and Son	.15	.06	.01
☐ 613 Gary Lavelle	.05	.02	.00	Cal Ripken Jr. and Sr.			
☐ 614 Johnnie LeMaster	.05	.02	.00	☐ 642 Cubs: Division Champs	.05	.02	.00
☐ 615 Jeff Leonard	.10	.04	.01	☐ 643 Two Perfect Games	.08	.03	.01
☐ 616 Randy Lerch	.05	.02	.00	and One No-Hitter:			
☐ 617 Greg Minton	.05	.02	.00	Mike Witt			
☐ 618 Steve Nicosia	.05	.02	.00	David Palmer			
☐ 619 Gene Richards	.05	.02	.00	Jack Morris			
☐ 620 Jeff Robinson	.30	.12	.03	☐ 644 Willie Lozado and	.10	.04	.01
(Giants pitcher)				Vic Mata			
☐ 621 Scot Thompson	.05	.02	.00	☐ 645 Kelly Gruber and	.30	.12	.03
☐ 622 Manny Trillo	.05	.02	.00	Randy O'Neal			

		MINT	EXC	G-VG
☐ 646	Jose Roman and ... Joel Skinner	.10	.04	.01
☐ 647	Steve Kiefer and ... Danny Tartabull	5.00	2.00	.50
☐ 648	Rob Deer and ..... Alejandro Sanchez	.90	.36	.09
☐ 649	Billy Hatcher and ... Shawon Dunston	1.25	.50	.12
☐ 650	Ron Robinson and . Mike Bielecki	.20	.08	.02
☐ 651	Zane Smith and ... Paul Zuvella	.40	.16	.04
☐ 652	Joe Hesketh and ... Glenn Davis	6.00	2.40	.60
☐ 653	John Russell and ... Steve Jeltz	.15	.06	.01
☐ 654	CL: Tigers/Padres .. and Cubs/Mets	.07	.01	.00
☐ 655	CL: Blue Jays/Yankees and Red Sox/Orioles	.07	.01	.00
☐ 656	CL: Royals/Cardinals and Phillies/Twins	.07	.01	.00
☐ 657	CL: Angels/Braves and Astros/Dodgers	.07	.01	.00
☐ 658	CL: Expos/A's ..... and Indians/Pirates	.07	.01	.00
☐ 659	CL: Mariners/Wh.Sox and Reds/Rangers	.07	.01	.00
☐ 660	CL: Brewers/Giants . and Special Cards	.10	.01	.00

1985 Fleer Update

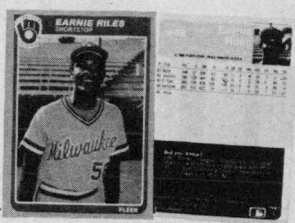

This 132-card set was issued late in the collecting year and features new players and players on new teams compared to the 1985 Fleer regular issue cards. Cards measure 2 ½" by 3 ½" and were distributed together as a complete set within a special box. The cards are numbered with a U prefix and are ordered alphabetically by the player's name.

		MINT	EXC	G-VG
	Complete Set (132)	16.00	6.50	1.60
	Common Player (1-132) ..	.06	.02	.00
☐ U1	Don Aase	.10	.04	.01
☐ U2	Bill Almon	.06	.02	.00
☐ U3	Dusty Baker	.10	.04	.01
☐ U4	Dale Berra	.06	.02	.00
☐ U5	Karl Best	.10	.04	.01
☐ U6	Tim Birtsas	.15	.06	.01
☐ U7	Vida Blue	.10	.04	.01
☐ U8	Rich Bordi	.06	.02	.00
☐ U9	Daryl Boston	.10	.04	.01
☐ U10	Hubie Brooks	.20	.08	.02
☐ U11	Chris Brown	.50	.20	.05
☐ U12	Tom Browning	1.25	.50	.12
☐ U13	Al Bumbry	.06	.02	.00
☐ U14	Tim Burke	.35	.14	.03
☐ U15	Ray Burris	.06	.02	.00
☐ U16	Jeff Burroughs	.06	.02	.00
☐ U17	Ivan Calderon	.85	.34	.08
☐ U18	Jeff Calhoun	.15	.06	.01
☐ U19	Bill Campbell	.06	.02	.00
☐ U20	Don Carman	.30	.12	.03
☐ U21	Gary Carter	.75	.30	.07

		MINT	EXC	G-VG
☐ U22	Bobby Castillo	.06	.02	.00
☐ U23	Bill Caudill	.06	.02	.00
☐ U24	Rick Cerone	.06	.02	.00
☐ U25	Jack Clark	.40	.16	.04
☐ U26	Pat Clements	.15	.06	.01
☐ U27	Stewart Cliburn	.10	.04	.01
☐ U28	Vince Coleman	5.00	2.00	.50
☐ U29	Dave Collins	.06	.02	.00
☐ U30	Fritz Connally	.10	.04	.01
☐ U31	Henry Cotto	.06	.02	.00
☐ U32	Danny Darwin	.06	.02	.00
☐ U33	Darren Daulton	.15	.06	.01
☐ U34	Jerry Davis	.10	.04	.01
☐ U35	Brian Dayett	.10	.04	.01
☐ U36	Ken Dixon	.15	.06	.01
☐ U37	Tommy Dunbar	.06	.02	.00
☐ U38	Mariano Duncan	.25	.10	.02
☐ U39	Bob Fallon	.10	.04	.01
☐ U40	Brian Fisher	.30	.12	.03
☐ U41	Mike Fitzgerald	.06	.02	.00
☐ U42	Ray Fontenot	.06	.02	.00
☐ U43	Greg Gagne	.35	.14	.03
☐ U44	Oscar Gamble	.06	.02	.00
☐ U45	Jim Gott	.10	.04	.01
☐ U46	David Green	.06	.02	.00
☐ U47	Alfredo Griffin	.10	.04	.01
☐ U48	Ozzie Guillen	.70	.28	.07
☐ U49	Toby Harrah	.10	.04	.01
☐ U50	Ron Hassey	.06	.02	.00
☐ U51	Rickey Henderson	1.00	.40	.10
☐ U52	Steve Henderson	.06	.02	.00
☐ U53	George Hendrick	.10	.04	.01
☐ U54	Teddy Higuera	2.50	1.00	.25
☐ U55	Al Holland	.06	.02	.00
☐ U56	Burt Hooton	.06	.02	.00
☐ U57	Jay Howell	.10	.04	.01
☐ U58	LaMarr Hoyt	.10	.04	.01
☐ U59	Tim Hulett	.15	.06	.01
☐ U60	Bob James	.10	.04	.01
☐ U61	Cliff Johnson	.06	.02	.00
☐ U62	Howard Johnson	1.00	.40	.10
☐ U63	Ruppert Jones	.06	.02	.00
☐ U64	Steve Kemp	.10	.04	.01
☐ U65	Bruce Kison	.06	.02	.00
☐ U66	Mike LaCoss	.06	.02	.00
☐ U67	Lee Lacy	.06	.02	.00
☐ U68	Dave LaPoint	.10	.04	.01
☐ U69	Gary Lavelle	.06	.02	.00
☐ U70	Vance Law	.10	.04	.01

		MINT	EXC	G-VG
☐ U71	Manny Lee	.15	.06	.01
☐ U72	Sixto Lezcano	.06	.02	.00
☐ U73	Tim Lollar	.06	.02	.00
☐ U74	Urbano Lugo	.10	.04	.01
☐ U75	Fred Lynn	.25	.10	.02
☐ U76	Steve Lyons	.10	.04	.01
☐ U77	Mickey Mahler	.06	.02	.00
☐ U78	Ron Mathis	.10	.04	.01
☐ U79	Len Matuszek	.06	.02	.00
☐ U80	Oddibe McDowell	.65	.26	.06
	(part of bio actually Roger's)			
☐ U81	Roger McDowell	1.00	.40	.10
	(part of bio actually Oddibe's)			
☐ U82	Donnie Moore	.06	.02	.00
☐ U83	Ron Musselman	.10	.04	.01
☐ U84	Al Oliver	.15	.06	.01
☐ U85	Joe Orsulak	.20	.08	.02
☐ U86	Dan Pasqua	.50	.20	.05
☐ U87	Chris Pittaro	.10	.04	.01
☐ U88	Rick Reuschel	.15	.06	.01
☐ U89	Earnie Riles	.25	.10	.02
☐ U90	Jerry Royster	.06	.02	.00
☐ U91	Dave Rozema	.06	.02	.00
☐ U92	Dave Rucker	.06	.02	.00
☐ U93	Vern Ruhle	.06	.02	.00
☐ U94	Mark Salas	.15	.06	.01
☐ U95	Luis Salazar	.10	.04	.01
☐ U96	Joe Sambito	.06	.02	.00
☐ U97	Billy Sample	.06	.02	.00
☐ U98	Alejandro Sanchez	.10	.04	.01
☐ U99	Calvin Schiraldi	.20	.08	.02
☐ U100	Rick Schu	.20	.08	.02
☐ U101	Larry Sheets	.50	.20	.05
☐ U102	Ron Shephard	.10	.04	.01
☐ U103	Nelson Simmons	.10	.04	.01
☐ U104	Don Slaught	.06	.02	.00
☐ U105	Roy Smalley	.06	.02	.00
☐ U106	Lonnie Smith	.10	.04	.01
☐ U107	Nate Snell	.10	.04	.01
☐ U108	Lary Sorensen	.06	.02	.00
☐ U109	Chris Speier	.06	.02	.00
☐ U110	Mike Stenhouse	.10	.04	.01
☐ U111	Tim Stoddard	.06	.02	.00
☐ U112	John Stuper	.06	.02	.00
☐ U113	Jim Sundberg	.10	.04	.01
☐ U114	Bruce Sutter	.25	.10	.02
☐ U115	Don Sutton	.60	.24	.06
☐ U116	Bruce Tanner	.10	.04	.01
☐ U117	Kent Tekulve	.10	.04	.01

	MINT	EXC	G-VG
☐ U118 Walt Terrell	.10	.04	.01
☐ U119 Mickey Tettleton	.10	.04	.01
☐ U120 Rich Thompson	.10	.04	.01
☐ U121 Louis Thornton	.10	.04	.01
☐ U122 Alex Trevino	.06	.02	.00
☐ U123 John Tudor	.20	.08	.02
☐ U124 Jose Uribe	.30	.12	.03
☐ U125 Dave Valle	.10	.04	.01
☐ U126 Dave Von Ohlen	.06	.02	.00
☐ U127 Curt Wardle	.10	.04	.01
☐ U128 U.L. Washington	.06	.02	.00
☐ U129 Ed Whitson	.10	.04	.01
☐ U130 Herm Winningham	.15	.06	.01
☐ U131 Rich Yett	.10	.04	.01
☐ U132 Checklist U1-U132	.06	.01	.00

1986 Fleer

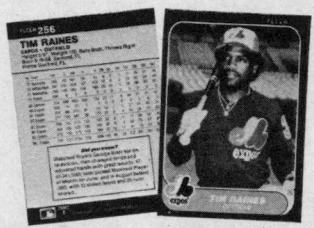

The cards in this 660-card set measure 2 ½ " by 3 ½ ". The 1986 Fleer set features fronts which contain the team logo along with the player's name and position. The player cards are alphabetized within team and the teams are ordered by their 1985 season finish and won-lost record, e.g., Kansas City (1-25), St. Louis (26-49), Toronto (50-73), New York Mets (74-97), New York Yankees (98-122), Los Angeles (123-147), California (148-171), Cincinnati (172-196), Chicago White Sox (197-220), Detroit (221-243), Montreal (244-267), Baltimore (268-291), Houston (292-314), San Diego (315-338), Boston (339-360), Chicago Cubs (361-385),

Minnesota (386-409), Oakland (410-432), Philadelphia (433-457), Seattle (458-481), Milwaukee (482-506), Atlanta (507-532), San Francisco (533-555), Texas (556-578), Cleveland (579-601), and Pittsburgh (602-625). Specials (626-643), Rookie pairs (644-653), and checklist cards (654-660) complete the set. The border enclosing the photo is dark blue. The backs feature the same name, number, and statistics format that Fleer has been using over the past few years. The Dennis and Tippy Martinez cards were apparently switched in the set numbering, as their adjacent numbers (279 and 280) were reversed on the Orioles checklist card.

	MINT	EXC	G-VG
Complete Set (660)	90.00	36.00	9.00
Common Player (1-660)	.05	.02	.00

			MINT	EXC	G-VG
☐	1	Steve Balboni	.10	.02	.00
☐	2	Joe Beckwith	.05	.02	.00
☐	3	Buddy Biancalana	.05	.02	.00
☐	4	Bud Black	.05	.02	.00
☐	5	George Brett	.45	.18	.04
☐	6	Onix Concepcion	.05	.02	.00
☐	7	Steve Farr	.05	.02	.00
☐	8	Mark Gubicza	.12	.05	.01
☐	9	Dane Iorg	.05	.02	.00
☐	10	Danny Jackson	.30	.12	.03
☐	11	Lynn Jones	.05	.02	.00
☐	12	Mike Jones	.05	.02	.00
☐	13	Charlie Leibrandt	.05	.02	.00
☐	14	Hal McRae	.08	.03	.01
☐	15	Omar Moreno	.05	.02	.00
☐	16	Darryl Motley	.05	.02	.00
☐	17	Jorge Orta	.05	.02	.00
☐	18	Dan Quisenberry	.12	.05	.01
☐	19	Bret Saberhagen	.40	.16	.04
☐	20	Pat Sheridan	.05	.02	.00
☐	21	Lonnie Smith	.05	.02	.00
☐	22	Jim Sundberg	.05	.02	.00
☐	23	John Wathan	.05	.02	.00
☐	24	Frank White	.08	.03	.01
☐	25	Willie Wilson	.10	.04	.01
☐	26	Joaquin Andujar	.08	.03	.01
☐	27	Steve Braun	.05	.02	.00
☐	28	Bill Campbell	.05	.02	.00
☐	29	Cesar Cedeno	.08	.03	.01
☐	30	Jack Clark	.25	.10	.02
☐	31	Vince Coleman	2.25	.90	.22

		MINT	EXC	G-VG			MINT	EXC	G-VG
☐ 32	Danny Cox	.10	.04	.01	☐ 81	Dwight Gooden	2.00	.80	.20
☐ 33	Ken Dayley	.05	.02	.00	☐ 82	Tom Gorman	.05	.02	.00
☐ 34	Ivan DeJesus	.05	.02	.00	☐ 83	Danny Heep	.05	.02	.00
☐ 35	Bob Forsch	.05	.02	.00	☐ 84	Keith Hernandez	.30	.12	.03
☐ 36	Brian Harper	.05	.02	.00	☐ 85	Howard Johnson	.20	.08	.02
☐ 37	Tom Herr	.08	.03	.01	☐ 86	Ray Knight	.08	.03	.01
☐ 38	Ricky Horton	.05	.02	.00	☐ 87	Terry Leach	.15	.06	.01
☐ 39	Kurt Kepshire	.05	.02	.00	☐ 88	Ed Lynch	.05	.02	.00
☐ 40	Jeff Lahti	.05	.02	.00	☐ 89	Roger McDowell	.50	.20	.04
☐ 41	Tito Landrum	.05	.02	.00	☐ 90	Jesse Orosco	.05	.02	.00
☐ 42	Willie McGee	.15	.06	.01	☐ 91	Tom Paciorek	.05	.02	.00
☐ 43	Tom Nieto	.05	.02	.00	☐ 92	Ronn Reynolds	.05	.02	.00
☐ 44	Terry Pendleton	.08	.03	.01	☐ 93	Rafael Santana	.05	.02	.00
☐ 45	Darrell Porter	.05	.02	.00	☐ 94	Doug Sisk	.05	.02	.00
☐ 46	Ozzie Smith	.20	.08	.01	☐ 95	Rusty Staub	.10	.04	.01
☐ 47	John Tudor	.15	.06	.01	☐ 96	Darryl Strawberry	1.25	.50	.12
☐ 48	Andy Van Slyke	.25	.10	.02	☐ 97	Mookie Wilson	.08	.03	.01
☐ 49	Todd Worrell	.90	.36	.09	☐ 98	Neil Allen	.05	.02	.00
☐ 50	Jim Acker	.05	.02	.00	☐ 99	Don Baylor	.10	.04	.01
☐ 51	Doyle Alexander	.08	.03	.01	☐ 100	Dale Berra	.05	.02	.00
☐ 52	Jesse Barfield	.20	.08	.02	☐ 101	Rich Bordi	.05	.02	.00
☐ 53	George Bell	.30	.12	.03	☐ 102	Marty Bystrom	.05	.02	.00
☐ 54	Jeff Burroughs	.05	.02	.00	☐ 103	Joe Cowley	.05	.02	.00
☐ 55	Bill Caudill	.05	.02	.00	☐ 104	Brian Fisher	.25	.10	.02
☐ 56	Jim Clancy	.05	.02	.00	☐ 105	Ken Griffey	.08	.03	.01
☐ 57	Tony Fernandez	.20	.08	.01	☐ 106	Ron Guidry	.15	.06	.01
☐ 58	Tom Filer	.05	.02	.00	☐ 107	Ron Hassey	.05	.02	.00
☐ 59	Damaso Garcia	.05	.02	.00	☐ 108	Rickey Henderson	.40	.16	.04
☐ 60	Tom Henke	.15	.06	.01	☐ 109	Don Mattingly	3.50	1.40	.35
☐ 61	Garth Iorg	.05	.02	.00	☐ 110	Bobby Meacham	.05	.02	.00
☐ 62	Cliff Johnson	.05	.02	.00	☐ 111	John Montefusco	.05	.02	.00
☐ 63	Jimmy Key	.12	.05	.01	☐ 112	Phil Niekro	.18	.08	.01
☐ 64	Dennis Lamp	.05	.02	.00	☐ 113	Mike Pagliarulo	.15	.06	.01
☐ 65	Gary Lavelle	.05	.02	.00	☐ 114	Dan Pasqua	.15	.06	.01
☐ 66	Buck Martinez	.05	.02	.00	☐ 115	Willie Randolph	.10	.04	.01
☐ 67	Lloyd Moseby	.10	.04	.01	☐ 116	Dave Righetti	.12	.05	.01
☐ 68	Rance Mulliniks	.05	.02	.00	☐ 117	Andre Robertson	.05	.02	.00
☐ 69	Al Oliver	.10	.04	.01	☐ 118	Billy Sample	.05	.02	.00
☐ 70	Dave Stieb	.12	.05	.01	☐ 119	Bob Shirley	.05	.02	.00
☐ 71	Louis Thornton	.10	.04	.01	☐ 120	Ed Whitson	.05	.02	.00
☐ 72	Willie Upshaw	.05	.02	.00	☐ 121	Dave Winfield	.30	.12	.03
☐ 73	Ernie Whitt	.05	.02	.00	☐ 122	Butch Wynegar	.05	.02	.00
☐ 74	Rick Aguilera	.25	.10	.02	☐ 123	Dave Anderson	.05	.02	.00
☐ 75	Wally Backman	.08	.03	.01	☐ 124	Bob Bailor	.05	.02	.00
☐ 76	Gary Carter	.30	.12	.03	☐ 125	Greg Brock	.05	.02	.00
☐ 77	Ron Darling	.25	.10	.02	☐ 126	Enos Cabell	.05	.02	.00
☐ 78	Len Dykstra	1.00	.40	.10	☐ 127	Bobby Castillo	.05	.02	.00
☐ 79	Sid Fernandez	.15	.06	.01	☐ 128	Carlos Diaz	.05	.02	.00
☐ 80	George Foster	.12	.05	.01	☐ 129	Mariano Duncan	.20	.08	.02

	MINT	EXC	G-VG		MINT	EXC	G-VG
☐ 130 Pedro Guerrero	.25	.10	.02	☐ 179 Tom Hume	.05	.02	.00
☐ 131 Orel Hershiser	1.75	.70	.17	☐ 180 Wayne Krenchicki .	.05	.02	.00
☐ 132 Rick Honeycutt	.05	.02	.00	☐ 181 Andy McGaffigan ..	.05	.02	.00
☐ 133 Ken Howell	.05	.02	.00	☐ 182 Eddie Milner	.05	.02	.00
☐ 134 Ken Landreaux	.05	.02	.00	☐ 183 Ron Oester	.05	.02	.00
☐ 135 Bill Madlock	.10	.04	.01	☐ 184 Dave Parker	.15	.06	.01
☐ 136 Candy Maldonado ..	.10	.04	.01	☐ 185 Frank Pastore	.05	.02	.00
☐ 137 Mike Marshall	.12	.05	.01	☐ 186 Tony Perez	.12	.05	.01
☐ 138 Len Matuszek	.05	.02	.00	☐ 187 Ted Power	.05	.02	.00
☐ 139 Tom Niedenfuer ...	.05	.02	.00	☐ 188 Joe Price	.05	.02	.00
☐ 140 Alejandro Pena	.05	.02	.00	☐ 189 Gary Redus	.05	.02	.00
☐ 141 Jerry Reuss	.08	.03	.01	☐ 190 Ron Robinson	.05	.02	.00
☐ 142 Bill Russell	.08	.03	.01	☐ 191 Pete Rose	.65	.26	.06
☐ 143 Steve Sax	.18	.08	.01	☐ 192 Mario Soto	.05	.02	.00
☐ 144 Mike Scioscia	.08	.03	.01	☐ 193 John Stuper	.05	.02	.00
☐ 145 Fernando Valenzuela	.25	.10	.02	☐ 194 Jay Tibbs	.05	.02	.00
☐ 146 Bob Welch	.08	.03	.01	☐ 195 Dave Van Gorder ..	.05	.02	.00
☐ 147 Terry Whitfield	.05	.02	.00	☐ 196 Max Venable	.05	.02	.00
☐ 148 Juan Beniquez	.05	.02	.00	☐ 197 Juan Agosto	.05	.02	.00
☐ 149 Bob Boone	.10	.04	.01	☐ 198 Harold Baines	.12	.05	.01
☐ 150 John Candelaria	.08	.03	.01	☐ 199 Floyd Bannister ...	.05	.02	.00
☐ 151 Rod Carew	.30	.12	.03	☐ 200 Britt Burns	.05	.02	.00
☐ 152 Stewart Cliburn	.08	.03	.01	☐ 201 Julio Cruz	.05	.02	.00
☐ 153 Doug DeCinces	.08	.03	.01	☐ 202 Joel Davis	.15	.06	.01
☐ 154 Brian Downing	.08	.03	.01	☐ 203 Richard Dotson ...	.08	.03	.01
☐ 155 Ken Forsch	.05	.02	.00	☐ 204 Carlton Fisk	.15	.06	.01
☐ 156 Craig Gerber	.05	.02	.00	☐ 205 Scott Fletcher	.10	.04	.01
☐ 157 Bobby Grich	.08	.03	.01	☐ 206 Ozzie Guillen	.35	.14	.03
☐ 158 George Hendrick ...	.08	.03	.01	☐ 207 Jerry Hairston	.05	.02	.00
☐ 159 Al Holland	.05	.02	.00	☐ 208 Tim Hulett	.05	.02	.00
☐ 160 Reggie Jackson ...	.35	.14	.03	☐ 209 Bob James	.05	.02	.00
☐ 161 Ruppert Jones	.05	.02	.00	☐ 210 Ron Kittle	.12	.05	.01
☐ 162 Urbano Lugo	.05	.02	.00	☐ 211 Rudy Law	.05	.02	.00
☐ 163 Kirk McCaskill	.35	.14	.03	☐ 212 Bryan Little	.05	.02	.00
☐ 164 Donnie Moore	.05	.02	.00	☐ 213 Gene Nelson	.05	.02	.00
☐ 165 Gary Pettis	.05	.02	.00	☐ 214 Reid Nichols	.05	.02	.00
☐ 166 Ron Romanick	.05	.02	.00	☐ 215 Luis Salazar	.05	.02	.00
☐ 167 Dick Schofield	.05	.02	.00	☐ 216 Tom Seaver	.30	.12	.03
☐ 168 Daryl Sconiers	.05	.02	.00	☐ 217 Dan Spillner	.05	.02	.00
☐ 169 Jim Slaton	.05	.02	.00	☐ 218 Bruce Tanner	.08	.03	.01
☐ 170 Don Sutton	.18	.08	.01	☐ 219 Greg Walker	.08	.03	.01
☐ 171 Mike Witt	.10	.04	.01	☐ 220 Dave Wehrmeister .	.05	.02	.00
☐ 172 Buddy Bell	.10	.04	.01	☐ 221 Juan Berenguer ..	.05	.02	.00
☐ 173 Tom Browning	.25	.10	.02	☐ 222 Dave Bergman ...	.05	.02	.00
☐ 174 Dave Concepcion .	.10	.04	.01	☐ 223 Tom Brookens ...	.05	.02	.00
☐ 175 Eric Davis	3.00	1.20	.30	☐ 224 Darrell Evans	.10	.04	.01
☐ 176 Bo Diaz	.05	.02	.00	☐ 225 Barbaro Garbey ..	.05	.02	.00
☐ 177 Nick Esasky	.05	.02	.00	☐ 226 Kirk Gibson	.25	.10	.02
☐ 178 John Franco	.10	.04	.01	☐ 227 John Grubb	.05	.02	.00

		MINT	EXC	G-VG			MINT	EXC	G-VG
☐ 228	Willie Hernandez ...	.10	.04	.01	☐ 277	Lee Lacy	.05	.02	.00
☐ 229	Larry Herndon	.05	.02	.00	☐ 278	Fred Lynn	.15	.06	.01
☐ 230	Chet Lemon	.08	.03	.01	☐ 279	Tippy Martinez ...	.05	.02	.00
☐ 231	Aurelio Lopez	.05	.02	.00	☐ 280	Dennis Martinez ..	.08	.03	.01
☐ 232	Jack Morris	.18	.08	.01	☐ 281	Scott McGregor ...	.08	.03	.01
☐ 233	Randy O'Neal	.05	.02	.00	☐ 282	Eddie Murray	.30	.12	.03
☐ 234	Lance Parrish	.18	.08	.01	☐ 283	Floyd Rayford	.05	.02	.00
☐ 235	Dan Petry	.08	.03	.01	☐ 284	Cal Ripken	.35	.14	.03
☐ 236	Alejandro Sanchez .	.05	.02	.00	☐ 285	Gary Roenicke	.05	.02	.00
☐ 237	Bill Scherrer	.05	.02	.00	☐ 286	Larry Sheets	.20	.08	.02
☐ 238	Nelson Simmons ...	.08	.03	.01	☐ 287	John Shelby	.05	.02	.00
☐ 239	Frank Tanana	.08	.03	.01	☐ 288	Nate Snell	.08	.03	.01
☐ 240	Walt Terrell	.05	.02	.00	☐ 289	Sammy Stewart ...	.05	.02	.00
☐ 241	Alan Trammell	.25	.10	.02	☐ 290	Alan Wiggins	.05	.02	.00
☐ 242	Lou Whitaker	.12	.05	.01	☐ 291	Mike Young	.08	.03	.01
☐ 243	Milt Wilcox	.05	.02	.00	☐ 292	Alan Ashby	.05	.02	.00
☐ 244	Hubie Brooks	.10	.04	.01	☐ 293	Mark Bailey	.05	.02	.00
☐ 245	Tim Burke	.25	.10	.02	☐ 294	Kevin Bass	.08	.03	.01
☐ 246	Andre Dawson	.30	.12	.03	☐ 295	Jeff Calhoun	.08	.03	.01
☐ 247	Mike Fitzgerald	.05	.02	.00	☐ 296	Jose Cruz	.08	.03	.01
☐ 248	Terry Francona	.05	.02	.00	☐ 297	Glenn Davis	.75	.30	.07
☐ 249	Bill Gullickson	.05	.02	.00	☐ 298	Bill Dawley	.05	.02	.00
☐ 250	Joe Hesketh	.05	.02	.00	☐ 299	Frank DiPino	.05	.02	.00
☐ 251	Bill Laskey	.05	.02	.00	☐ 300	Bill Doran	.10	.04	.01
☐ 252	Vance Law	.08	.03	.01	☐ 301	Phil Garner	.05	.02	.00
☐ 253	Charlie Lea	.05	.02	.00	☐ 302	Jeff Heathcock	.05	.02	.00
☐ 254	Gary Lucas	.05	.02	.00	☐ 303	Charlie Kerfeld ...	.10	.04	.01
☐ 255	David Palmer	.05	.02	.00	☐ 304	Bob Knepper	.08	.03	.01
☐ 256	Tim Raines	.30	.12	.03	☐ 305	Ron Mathis	.08	.03	.01
☐ 257	Jeff Reardon	.10	.04	.01	☐ 306	Jerry Mumphrey ..	.05	.02	.00
☐ 258	Bert Roberge	.05	.02	.00	☐ 307	Jim Pankovits	.05	.02	.00
☐ 259	Dan Schatzeder ...	.05	.02	.00	☐ 308	Terry Puhl	.05	.02	.00
☐ 260	Bryn Smith	.05	.02	.00	☐ 309	Craig Reynolds ...	.05	.02	.00
☐ 261	Randy St.Claire ...	.05	.02	.00	☐ 310	Nolan Ryan	.30	.12	.03
☐ 262	Scot Thompson ...	.05	.02	.00	☐ 311	Mike Scott	.30	.12	.03
☐ 263	Tim Wallach	.10	.04	.01	☐ 312	Dave Smith	.08	.03	.01
☐ 264	U.L. Washington ...	.05	.02	.00	☐ 313	Dickie Thon	.05	.02	.00
☐ 265	Mitch Webster	.35	.14	.03	☐ 314	Denny Walling ...	.05	.02	.00
☐ 266	Herm Winningham .	.10	.04	.01	☐ 315	Kurt Bevacqua ...	.05	.02	.00
☐ 267	Floyd Youmans ...	.35	.14	.03	☐ 316	Al Bumbry	.05	.02	.00
☐ 268	Don Aase	.05	.02	.00	☐ 317	Jerry Davis	.05	.02	.00
☐ 269	Mike Boddicker ...	.08	.03	.01	☐ 318	Luis DeLeon	.05	.02	.00
☐ 270	Rich Dauer	.05	.02	.00	☐ 319	Dave Dravecky ...	.05	.02	.00
☐ 271	Storm Davis	.08	.03	.01	☐ 320	Tim Flannery	.05	.02	.00
☐ 272	Rick Dempsey	.05	.02	.00	☐ 321	Steve Garvey	.35	.14	.03
☐ 273	Ken Dixon	.05	.02	.00	☐ 322	Goose Gossage ..	.12	.05	.01
☐ 274	Jim Dwyer	.05	.02	.00	☐ 323	Tony Gwynn	.65	.26	.06
☐ 275	Mike Flanagan	.08	.03	.01	☐ 324	Andy Hawkins	.08	.03	.01
☐ 276	Wayne Gross	.05	.02	.00	☐ 325	LaMarr Hoyt	.08	.03	.01

		MINT	EXC	G-VG
☐ 326	Roy Lee Jackson ..	.05	.02	.00
☐ 327	Terry Kennedy	.05	.02	.00
☐ 328	Craig Lefferts	.05	.02	.00
☐ 329	Carmelo Martinez ..	.05	.02	.00
☐ 330	Lance McCullers ...	.40	.18	.03
☐ 331	Kevin McReynolds .	.40	.18	.03
☐ 332	Graig Nettles	.10	.04	.01
☐ 333	Jerry Royster	.05	.02	.00
☐ 334	Eric Show	.08	.03	.01
☐ 335	Tim Stoddard	.05	.02	.00
☐ 336	Garry Templeton ...	.08	.03	.01
☐ 337	Mark Thurmond	.05	.02	.00
☐ 338	Ed Wojna	.10	.04	.01
☐ 339	Tony Armas	.08	.03	.01
☐ 340	Marty Barrett	.10	.04	.01
☐ 341	Wade Boggs	2.50	1.00	.25
☐ 342	Dennis Boyd	.08	.03	.01
☐ 343	Bill Buckner	.10	.04	.01
☐ 344	Mark Clear	.05	.02	.00
☐ 345	Roger Clemens	3.00	1.20	.30
☐ 346	Steve Crawford	.05	.02	.00
☐ 347	Mike Easler	.05	.02	.00
☐ 348	Dwight Evans	.15	.06	.01
☐ 349	Rich Gedman	.08	.03	.01
☐ 350	Jackie Gutierrez ...	.05	.02	.00
☐ 351	Glenn Hoffman	.05	.02	.00
☐ 352	Bruce Hurst	.15	.06	.01
☐ 353	Bruce Kison	.05	.02	.00
☐ 354	Tim Lollar	.05	.02	.00
☐ 355	Steve Lyons	.05	.02	.00
☐ 356	Al Nipper	.05	.02	.00
☐ 357	Bob Ojeda	.08	.03	.01
☐ 358	Jim Rice	.20	.08	.02
☐ 359	Bob Stanley	.05	.02	.00
☐ 360	Mike Trujillo	.05	.02	.00
☐ 361	Thad Bosley	.05	.02	.00
☐ 362	Warren Brusstar ...	.05	.02	.00
☐ 363	Ron Cey	.08	.03	.01
☐ 364	Jody Davis	.08	.03	.01
☐ 365	Bob Dernier	.05	.02	.00
☐ 366	Shawon Dunston ..	.10	.04	.01
☐ 367	Leon Durham	.08	.03	.01
☐ 368	Dennis Eckersley ..	.15	.06	.01
☐ 369	Ray Fontenot	.05	.02	.00
☐ 370	George Frazier	.05	.02	.00
☐ 371	Billy Hatcher	.15	.06	.01
☐ 372	Dave Lopes	.08	.03	.01
☐ 373	Gary Matthews	.08	.03	.01
☐ 374	Ron Meredith	.05	.02	.00

		MINT	EXC	G-VG
☐ 375	Keith Moreland ...	.05	.02	.00
☐ 376	Reggie Patterson ..	.05	.02	.00
☐ 377	Dick Ruthven	.05	.02	.00
☐ 378	Ryne Sandberg ...	.20	.08	.02
☐ 379	Scott Sanderson ...	.05	.02	.00
☐ 380	Lee Smith	.08	.03	.01
☐ 381	Lary Sorensen	.05	.02	.00
☐ 382	Chris Speier	.05	.02	.00
☐ 383	Rick Sutcliffe	.12	.05	.01
☐ 384	Steve Trout	.05	.02	.00
☐ 385	Gary Woods	.05	.02	.00
☐ 386	Bert Blyleven	.10	.04	.01
☐ 387	Tom Brunansky ...	.15	.06	.01
☐ 388	Randy Bush	.08	.03	.01
☐ 389	John Butcher	.05	.02	.00
☐ 390	Ron Davis	.05	.02	.00
☐ 391	Dave Engle	.05	.02	.00
☐ 392	Frank Eufemia	.05	.02	.00
☐ 393	Pete Filson	.05	.02	.00
☐ 394	Gary Gaetti	.20	.08	.02
☐ 395	Greg Gagne	.08	.03	.01
☐ 396	Mickey Hatcher ...	.08	.03	.01
☐ 397	Kent Hrbek	.18	.08	.01
☐ 398	Tim Laudner	.05	.02	.00
☐ 399	Rick Lysander	.05	.02	.00
☐ 400	Dave Meier	.05	.02	.00
☐ 401	Kirby Puckett	2.00	.80	.20
☐ 402	Mark Salas	.05	.02	.00
☐ 403	Ken Schrom	.05	.02	.00
☐ 404	Roy Smalley	.05	.02	.00
☐ 405	Mike Smithson	.05	.02	.00
☐ 406	Mike Stenhouse ...	.05	.02	.00
☐ 407	Tim Teufel	.05	.02	.00
☐ 408	Frank Viola	.30	.12	.03
☐ 409	Ron Washington ...	.05	.02	.00
☐ 410	Keith Atherton	.05	.02	.00
☐ 411	Dusty Baker	.08	.03	.01
☐ 412	Tim Birtsas	.15	.06	.01
☐ 413	Bruce Bochte	.05	.02	.00
☐ 414	Chris Codiroli	.05	.02	.00
☐ 415	Dave Collins	.05	.02	.00
☐ 416	Mike Davis	.05	.02	.00
☐ 417	Alfredo Griffin	.08	.03	.01
☐ 418	Mike Heath	.05	.02	.00
☐ 419	Steve Henderson .	.05	.02	.00
☐ 420	Donnie Hill	.05	.02	.00
☐ 421	Jay Howell	.08	.03	.01
☐ 422	Tommy John	.12	.05	.01
☐ 423	Dave Kingman	.12	.05	.01

		MINT	EXC	G-VG
☐ 424	Bill Krueger	.05	.02	.00
☐ 425	Rick Langford	.05	.02	.00
☐ 426	Carney Lansford	.10	.04	.01
☐ 427	Steve McCatty	.05	.02	.00
☐ 428	Dwayne Murphy	.05	.02	.00
☐ 429	Steve Ontiveros	.12	.05	.01
☐ 430	Tony Phillips	.05	.02	.00
☐ 431	Jose Rijo	.08	.03	.01
☐ 432	Mickey Tettleton	.08	.03	.01
☐ 433	Luis Aguayo	.05	.02	.00
☐ 434	Larry Andersen	.05	.02	.00
☐ 435	Steve Carlton	.25	.10	.02
☐ 436	Don Carman	.25	.10	.02
☐ 437	Tim Corcoran	.05	.02	.00
☐ 438	Darren Daulton	.12	.05	.01
☐ 439	John Denny	.08	.03	.01
☐ 440	Tom Foley	.05	.02	.00
☐ 441	Greg Gross	.05	.02	.00
☐ 442	Kevin Gross	.05	.02	.00
☐ 443	Von Hayes	.10	.04	.01
☐ 444	Charles Hudson	.05	.02	.00
☐ 445	Garry Maddox	.08	.03	.01
☐ 446	Shane Rawley	.08	.03	.01
☐ 447	Dave Rucker	.05	.02	.00
☐ 448	John Russell	.05	.02	.00
☐ 449	Juan Samuel	.12	.05	.01
☐ 450	Mike Schmidt	.45	.18	.04
☐ 451	Rick Schu	.05	.02	.00
☐ 452	Dave Shipanoff	.10	.04	.01
☐ 453	Dave Stewart	.12	.05	.01
☐ 454	Jeff Stone	.05	.02	.00
☐ 455	Kent Tekulve	.05	.02	.00
☐ 456	Ozzie Virgil	.05	.02	.00
☐ 457	Glenn Wilson	.08	.03	.01
☐ 458	Jim Beattie	.05	.02	.00
☐ 459	Karl Best	.08	.03	.01
☐ 460	Barry Bonnell	.05	.02	.00
☐ 461	Phil Bradley	.12	.05	.01
☐ 462	Ivan Calderon	.65	.26	.06
☐ 463	Al Cowens	.05	.02	.00
☐ 464	Alvin Davis	.18	.08	.01
☐ 465	Dave Henderson	.08	.03	.01
☐ 466	Bob Kearney	.05	.02	.00
☐ 467	Mark Langston	.18	.08	.01
☐ 468	Bob Long	.05	.02	.00
☐ 469	Mike Moore	.08	.03	.01
☐ 470	Edwin Nunez	.05	.02	.00
☐ 471	Spike Owen	.05	.02	.00
☐ 472	Jack Perconte	.05	.02	.00

		MINT	EXC	G-VG
☐ 473	Jim Presley	.15	.06	.01
☐ 474	Donnie Scott	.05	.02	.00
☐ 475	Bill Swift	.10	.04	.01
☐ 476	Danny Tartabull	.75	.30	.07
☐ 477	Gorman Thomas	.10	.04	.01
☐ 478	Roy Thomas	.05	.02	.00
☐ 479	Ed VandeBerg	.05	.02	.00
☐ 480	Frank Wills	.08	.03	.01
☐ 481	Matt Young	.05	.02	.00
☐ 482	Ray Burris	.05	.02	.00
☐ 483	Jaime Cocanower	.05	.02	.00
☐ 484	Cecil Cooper	.10	.04	.01
☐ 485	Danny Darwin	.05	.02	.00
☐ 486	Rollie Fingers	.15	.06	.01
☐ 487	Jim Gantner	.05	.02	.00
☐ 488	Bob L. Gibson	.05	.02	.00
☐ 489	Moose Haas	.05	.02	.00
☐ 490	Teddy Higuera	1.25	.50	.12
☐ 491	Paul Householder	.05	.02	.00
☐ 492	Pete Ladd	.05	.02	.00
☐ 493	Rick Manning	.05	.02	.00
☐ 494	Bob McClure	.05	.02	.00
☐ 495	Paul Molitor	.18	.08	.01
☐ 496	Charlie Moore	.05	.02	.00
☐ 497	Ben Oglivie	.08	.03	.01
☐ 498	Randy Ready	.05	.02	.00
☐ 499	Earnie Riles	.20	.08	.02
☐ 500	Ed Romero	.05	.02	.00
☐ 501	Bill Schroeder	.05	.02	.00
☐ 502	Ray Searage	.05	.02	.00
☐ 503	Ted Simmons	.10	.04	.01
☐ 504	Pete Vuckovich	.08	.03	.01
☐ 505	Rick Waits	.05	.02	.00
☐ 506	Robin Yount	.30	.12	.03
☐ 507	Len Barker	.05	.02	.00
☐ 508	Steve Bedrosian	.12	.05	.01
☐ 509	Bruce Benedict	.05	.02	.00
☐ 510	Rick Camp	.05	.02	.00
☐ 511	Rick Cerone	.05	.02	.00
☐ 512	Chris Chambliss	.08	.03	.01
☐ 513	Jeff Dedmon	.05	.02	.00
☐ 514	Terry Forster	.08	.03	.01
☐ 515	Gene Garber	.05	.02	.00
☐ 516	Terry Harper	.05	.02	.00
☐ 517	Bob Horner	.15	.06	.01
☐ 518	Glenn Hubbard	.05	.02	.00
☐ 519	Joe Johnson	.12	.05	.01
☐ 520	Brad Komminsk	.05	.02	.00
☐ 521	Rick Mahler	.05	.02	.00

		MINT	EXC	G-VG			MINT	EXC	G-VG
☐ 522	Dale Murphy	.50	.20	.05	☐ 571	Dave Schmidt	.08	.03	.01
☐ 523	Ken Oberkfell	.05	.02	.00	☐ 572	Don Slaught	.05	.02	.00
☐ 524	Pascual Perez	.08	.03	.01	☐ 573	Wayne Tolleson	.05	.02	.00
☐ 525	Gerald Perry	.12	.05	.01	☐ 574	Duane Walker	.05	.02	.00
☐ 526	Rafael Ramirez	.05	.02	.00	☐ 575	Gary Ward	.08	.03	.01
☐ 527	Steve Shields	.08	.03	.01	☐ 576	Chris Welsh	.05	.02	.00
☐ 528	Zane Smith	.10	.04	.01	☐ 577	Curtis Wilkerson	.05	.02	.00
☐ 529	Bruce Sutter	.12	.05	.01	☐ 578	George Wright	.05	.02	.00
☐ 530	Milt Thompson	.30	.12	.03	☐ 579	Chris Bando	.05	.02	.00
☐ 531	Claudell Washington	.08	.03	.01	☐ 580	Tony Bernazard	.05	.02	.00
☐ 532	Paul Zuvella	.05	.02	.00	☐ 581	Brett Butler	.08	.03	.01
☐ 533	Vida Blue	.08	.03	.01	☐ 582	Ernie Camacho	.05	.02	.00
☐ 534	Bob Brenly	.05	.02	.00	☐ 583	Joe Carter	.35	.14	.03
☐ 535	Chris Brown	.40	.16	.04	☐ 584	Carmen Castillo	.05	.02	.00
☐ 536	Chili Davis	.10	.04	.01	☐ 585	Jamie Easterly	.05	.02	.00
☐ 537	Mark Davis	.08	.03	.01	☐ 586	Julio Franco	.10	.04	.01
☐ 538	Rob Deer	.20	.08	.02	☐ 587	Mel Hall	.08	.03	.01
☐ 539	Dan Driessen	.05	.02	.00	☐ 588	Mike Hargrove	.05	.02	.00
☐ 540	Scott Garrelts	.08	.03	.01	☐ 589	Neal Heaton	.05	.02	.00
☐ 541	Dan Gladden	.08	.03	.01	☐ 590	Brook Jacoby	.12	.05	.01
☐ 542	Jim Gott	.05	.02	.00	☐ 591	Otis Nixon	.15	.06	.01
☐ 543	David Green	.05	.02	.00	☐ 592	Jerry Reed	.05	.02	.00
☐ 544	Atlee Hammaker	.05	.02	.00	☐ 593	Vern Ruhle	.05	.02	.00
☐ 545	Mike Jeffcoat	.05	.02	.00	☐ 594	Pat Tabler	.08	.03	.01
☐ 546	Mike Krukow	.05	.02	.00	☐ 595	Rich Thompson	.05	.02	.00
☐ 547	Dave LaPoint	.08	.03	.01	☐ 596	Andre Thornton	.08	.03	.01
☐ 548	Jeff Leonard	.08	.03	.01	☐ 597	Dave Von Ohlen	.05	.02	.00
☐ 549	Greg Minton	.05	.02	.00	☐ 598	George Vukovich	.05	.02	.00
☐ 550	Alex Trevino	.05	.02	.00	☐ 599	Tom Waddell	.05	.02	.00
☐ 551	Manny Trillo	.05	.02	.00	☐ 600	Curt Wardle	.05	.02	.00
☐ 552	Jose Uribe	.30	.12	.03	☐ 601	Jerry Willard	.05	.02	.00
☐ 553	Brad Wellman	.05	.02	.00	☐ 602	Bill Almon	.05	.02	.00
☐ 554	Frank Williams	.05	.02	.00	☐ 603	Mike Bielecki	.05	.02	.00
☐ 555	Joel Youngblood	.05	.02	.00	☐ 604	Sid Bream	.08	.03	.01
☐ 556	Alan Bannister	.05	.02	.00	☐ 605	Mike Brown OF	.05	.02	.00
☐ 557	Glenn Brummer	.05	.02	.00	☐ 606	Pat Clements	.12	.05	.01
☐ 558	Steve Buechele	.25	.10	.02	☐ 607	Jose DeLeon	.05	.02	.00
☐ 559	Jose Guzman	.25	.10	.02	☐ 608	Denny Gonzalez	.05	.02	.00
☐ 560	Toby Harrah	.05	.02	.00	☐ 609	Cecilio Guante	.05	.02	.00
☐ 561	Greg Harris	.05	.02	.00	☐ 610	Steve Kemp	.08	.03	.01
☐ 562	Dwayne Henry	.08	.03	.01	☐ 611	Sammy Khalifa	.08	.03	.01
☐ 563	Burt Hooton	.05	.02	.00	☐ 612	Lee Mazzilli	.05	.02	.00
☐ 564	Charlie Hough	.08	.03	.01	☐ 613	Larry McWilliams	.05	.02	.00
☐ 565	Mike Mason	.05	.02	.00	☐ 614	Jim Morrison	.05	.02	.00
☐ 566	Oddibe McDowell	.20	.08	.02	☐ 615	Joe Orsulak	.12	.05	.01
☐ 567	Dickie Noles	.05	.02	.00	☐ 616	Tony Pena	.10	.04	.01
☐ 568	Pete O'Brien	.10	.04	.01	☐ 617	Johnny Ray	.10	.04	.01
☐ 569	Larry Parrish	.08	.03	.01	☐ 618	Rick Reuschel	.08	.03	.01
☐ 570	Dave Rozema	.05	.02	.00	☐ 619	R.J. Reynolds	.05	.02	.00

		MINT	EXC	G-VG
☐ 620	Rick Rhoden	.08	.03	.01
☐ 621	Don Robinson	.05	.02	.00
☐ 622	Jason Thompson ..	.05	.02	.00
☐ 623	Lee Tunnell	.05	.02	.00
☐ 624	Jim Winn	.05	.02	.00
☐ 625	Marvell Wynne	.05	.02	.00
☐ 626	Dwight Gooden IA ..	.40	.16	.04
☐ 627	Don Mattingly IA ...	1.50	.60	.15
☐ 628	4192 (Pete Rose) ..	.40	.16	.04
☐ 629	3000 Career Hits ... Rod Carew	.20	.08	.02
☐ 630	300 Career Wins ... Tom Seaver Phil Niekro	.15	.06	.01
☐ 631	Ouch (Don Baylor) .	.08	.03	.01
☐ 632	Instant Offense .... Darryl Strawberry Tim Raines	.25	.10	.02
☐ 633	Shortstops Supreme Cal Ripken Alan Trammell	.15	.06	.01
☐ 634	Boggs and "Hero" .. Wade Boggs George Brett	.50	.20	.05
☐ 635	Braves Dynamic Duo Bob Horner Dale Murphy	.20	.08	.02
☐ 636	Cardinal Ignitors ... Willie McGee Vince Coleman	.20	.08	.02
☐ 637	Terror on Basepaths Vince Coleman	.25	.10	.02
☐ 638	Charlie Hustle / Dr.K Pete Rose Dwight Gooden	.75	.30	.07
☐ 639	1984 and 1985 AL . Batting Champs Wade Boggs Don Mattingly	1.75	.70	.17
☐ 640	NL West Sluggers .. Dale Murphy Steve Garvey Dave Parker	.20	.08	.02
☐ 641	Staff Aces .... Fernando Valenzuela Dwight Gooden	.30	.12	.03
☐ 642	Blue Jay Stoppers .. Jimmy Key Dave Stieb	.08	.03	.01

		MINT	EXC	G-VG
☐ 643	AL All-Star Backstops Carlton Fisk Rich Gedman	.08	.03	.01
☐ 644	Gene Walter and .. Benito Santiago	4.50	1.80	.45
☐ 645	Mike Woodard and Collin Ward	.12	.05	.01
☐ 646	Kal Daniels and ... Paul O'Neill	4.50	1.80	.45
☐ 647	Andres Galarraga and Fred Toliver	3.50	1.40	.35
☐ 648	Bob Kipper and ... Curt Ford	.12	.05	.01
☐ 649	Jose Canseco and Eric Plunk	35.00	14.00	3.50
☐ 650	Mark McLemore and Gus Polidor	.12	.05	.01
☐ 651	Rob Woodward and Mickey Brantley	.60	.24	.06
☐ 652	Billy Jo Robidoux and Mark Funderburk	.12	.05	.01
☐ 653	Cecil Fielder and .. Cory Snyder	2.50	1.00	.25
☐ 654	CL: Royals/Cardinals Blue Jays/Mets	.08	.01	.00
☐ 655	CL: Yankees/Dodgers Angels/Reds	.08	.01	.00
☐ 656	CL: White Sox/Tigers Expos/Orioles (279 Dennis, 280 Tippy)	.08	.01	.00
☐ 657	CL: Astros/Padres . Red Sox/Cubs	.08	.01	.00
☐ 658	CL: Twins/A's .... Phillies/Mariners	.08	.01	.00
☐ 659	CL: Brewers/Braves Giants/Rangers	.08	.01	.00
☐ 660	CL: Indians/Pirates Special Cards	.08	.01	.00

1986 Fleer Sticker Cards

The stickers in this 132-sticker card set are standard card size, 2 ½" by 3 ½". The card photo on the front is surrounded by a yellow border and a cranberry frame. The backs are printed in blue and black on white card stock. The backs contain year-by-year statistical information. They are numbered on the back in the upper left-hand corner.

			MINT	EXC	G-VG
		Complete Set (132)	24.00	10.00	2.40
		Common Player (1-132)	.05	.02	.00
☐	1	Harold Baines	.15	.06	.01
☐	2	Jesse Barfield	.20	.08	.02
☐	3	Don Baylor	.10	.04	.01
☐	4	Juan Beniquez	.05	.02	.00
☐	5	Tim Birtsas	.05	.02	.00
☐	6	Bert Blyleven	.10	.04	.01
☐	7	Bruce Bochte	.05	.02	.00
☐	8	Wade Boggs	1.50	.60	.15
☐	9	Dennis Boyd	.10	.04	.01
☐	10	Phil Bradley	.10	.04	.01
☐	11	George Brett	.75	.30	.07
☐	12	Hubie Brooks	.10	.04	.01
☐	13	Chris Brown	.25	.10	.02
☐	14	Tom Browning	.15	.06	.01
☐	15	Tom Brunansky	.15	.06	.01
☐	16	Bill Buckner	.10	.04	.01
☐	17	Britt Burns	.05	.02	.00
☐	18	Brett Butler	.10	.04	.01
☐	19	Jose Canseco	4.00	1.60	.40
☐	20	Rod Carew	.40	.16	.04
☐	21	Steve Carlton	.40	.16	.04
☐	22	Don Carman	.15	.06	.01
☐	23	Gary Carter	.45	.18	.04
☐	24	Jack Clark	.30	.12	.03
☐	25	Vince Coleman	1.00	.40	.10
☐	26	Cecil Cooper	.10	.04	.01
☐	27	Jose Cruz	.05	.02	.00
☐	28	Ron Darling	.20	.08	.02
☐	29	Alvin Davis	.20	.08	.02
☐	30	Jody Davis	.10	.04	.01
☐	31	Mike Davis	.05	.02	.00
☐	32	Andre Dawson	.35	.14	.03
☐	33	Mariano Duncan	.15	.06	.01
☐	34	Shawon Dunston	.10	.04	.01
☐	35	Leon Durham	.05	.02	.00
☐	36	Darrell Evans	.10	.04	.01
☐	37	Tony Fernandez	.15	.06	.01
☐	38	Carlton Fisk	.20	.08	.02
☐	39	John Franco	.10	.04	.01
☐	40	Julio Franco	.10	.04	.01
☐	41	Damaso Garcia	.05	.02	.00
☐	42	Scott Garrelts	.05	.02	.00
☐	43	Steve Garvey	.50	.20	.05
☐	44	Rich Gedman	.10	.04	.01
☐	45	Kirk Gibson	.35	.14	.03
☐	46	Dwight Gooden	1.00	.40	.10
☐	47	Pedro Guerrero	.20	.08	.02
☐	48	Ron Guidry	.15	.06	.01
☐	49	Ozzie Guillen	.15	.06	.01
☐	50	Tony Gwynn	.45	.18	.04
☐	51	Andy Hawkins	.05	.02	.00
☐	52	Von Hayes	.10	.04	.00
☐	53	Rickey Henderson	.65	.26	.06
☐	54	Tom Henke	.10	.04	.01
☐	55	Keith Hernandez	.30	.12	.03
☐	56	Willie Hernandez	.10	.04	.01
☐	57	Tommy Herr	.05	.02	.00
☐	58	Orel Hershiser	.60	.24	.06
☐	59	Teddy Higuera	.60	.24	.06
☐	60	Bob Horner	.20	.08	.02
☐	61	Charlie Hough	.05	.02	.00
☐	62	Jay Howell	.05	.02	.00
☐	63	LaMarr Hoyt	.05	.02	.00
☐	64	Kent Hrbek	.20	.08	.02
☐	65	Reggie Jackson	.50	.20	.05
☐	66	Bob James	.05	.02	.00
☐	67	Dave Kingman	.10	.04	.00
☐	68	Ron Kittle	.10	.04	.01
☐	69	Charlie Leibrandt	.10	.04	.01
☐	70	Fred Lynn	.15	.06	.01

		MINT	EXC	G-VG
☐ 71	Mike Marshall	.15	.06	.01
☐ 72	Don Mattingly	2.50	1.00	.25
☐ 73	Oddibe McDowell ...	.25	.10	.02
☐ 74	Willie McGee	.20	.08	.02
☐ 75	Scott McGregor	.10	.04	.01
☐ 76	Paul Molitor	.25	.10	.02
☐ 77	Charlie Moore	.05	.02	.00
☐ 78	Keith Moreland	.10	.04	.01
☐ 79	Jack Morris	.15	.06	.01
☐ 80	Dale Murphy	.75	.30	.07
☐ 81	Eddie Murray	.60	.24	.06
☐ 82	Phil Niekro	.25	.10	.02
☐ 83	Joe Orsulak	.10	.04	.01
☐ 84	Dave Parker	.15	.06	.01
☐ 85	Lance Parrish	.15	.06	.01
☐ 86	Larry Parrish	.10	.04	.01
☐ 87	Tony Pena	.10	.04	.01
☐ 88	Gary Pettis	.10	.04	.01
☐ 89	Jim Presley	.20	.08	.02
☐ 90	Kirby Puckett	.90	.36	.09
☐ 91	Dan Quisenberry ...	.15	.06	.01
☐ 92	Tim Raines	.25	.10	.02
☐ 93	Johnny Ray	.10	.04	.01
☐ 94	Jeff Reardon	.15	.06	.01
☐ 95	Rick Reuschel	.15	.06	.01
☐ 96	Jim Rice	.25	.10	.02
☐ 97	Dave Righetti	.15	.06	.01
☐ 98	Earnie Riles	.10	.04	.01
☐ 99	Cal Ripken	.45	.18	.04
☐ 100	Ron Romanick	.05	.02	.00
☐ 101	Pete Rose	1.00	.40	.10
☐ 102	Nolan Ryan	.65	.26	.06
☐ 103	Bret Saberhagen ...	.40	.16	.04
☐ 104	Mark Salas	.10	.04	.01
☐ 105	Juan Samuel	.20	.08	.02
☐ 106	Ryne Sandberg	.40	.16	.04
☐ 107	Mike Schmidt	.60	.24	.06
☐ 108	Mike Scott	.20	.08	.02
☐ 109	Tom Seaver	.35	.14	.03
☐ 110	Bryn Smith	.05	.02	.00
☐ 111	Dave Smith	.05	.02	.00
☐ 112	Lonnie Smith	.05	.02	.00
☐ 113	Ozzie Smith	.25	.10	.02
☐ 114	Mario Soto	.05	.02	.00
☐ 115	Dave Stieb	.10	.04	.01
☐ 116	Darryl Strawberry ..	.75	.30	.07
☐ 117	Bruce Sutter	.10	.04	.01
☐ 118	Garry Templeton ...	.05	.02	.00
☐ 119	Gorman Thomas ...	.10	.04	.01

		MINT	EXC	G-VG
☐ 120	Andre Thornton ...	.05	.02	.00
☐ 121	Alan Trammell	.25	.10	.02
☐ 122	John Tudor	.15	.06	.01
☐ 123	Fernando Valenzuela	.20	.08	.02
☐ 124	Frank Viola	.20	.08	.02
☐ 125	Gary Ward	.05	.02	.00
☐ 126	Lou Whitaker	.15	.06	.01
☐ 127	Frank White	.10	.04	.01
☐ 128	Glenn Wilson	.05	.02	.00
☐ 129	Willie Wilson	.15	.06	.01
☐ 130	Dave Winfield	.35	.14	.03
☐ 131	Robin Yount	.35	.14	.03
☐ 132	Checklist Card	1.50	.60	.15
	Dwight Gooden			
	Dale Murphy			

1986 Fleer Update

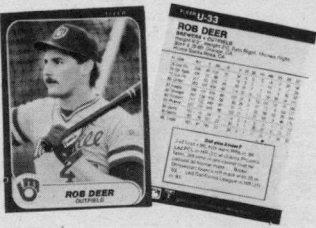

This 132-card set was distributed by Fleer to dealers as a complete set within a custom box. In addition to the complete set of 132 cards, the box also contains 25 Team Logo Stickers. The card fronts look very similar to the 1986 Fleer regular issue. The cards are numbered (with a U prefix) alphabetically according to player's last name. Cards measure the standard size, 2 ½ " by 3 ½ ".

	MINT	EXC	G-VG
Complete Set (132)	18.00	7.25	1.80
Common Player (1-132) ..	.06	.02	.00
☐ U1 Mike Aldrete	.30	.12	.03

		MINT	EXC	G-VG
☐ U2	Andy Allanson	.15	.06	.01
☐ U3	Neil Allen	.06	.02	.00
☐ U4	Joaquin Andujar	.10	.04	.01
☐ U5	Paul Assenmacher	.15	.06	.01
☐ U6	Scott Bailes	.15	.06	.01
☐ U7	Jay Baller	.06	.02	.00
☐ U8	Scott Bankhead	.10	.04	.01
☐ U9	Bill Bathe	.10	.04	.01
☐ U10	Don Baylor	.10	.04	.01
☐ U11	Billy Beane	.15	.06	.01
☐ U12	Steve Bedrosian	.12	.05	.01
☐ U13	Juan Beniquez	.06	.02	.00
☐ U14	Barry Bonds	1.25	.50	.12
☐ U15	Bobby Bonilla (wrong birthday)	1.25	.50	.12
☐ U16	Rich Bordi	.06	.02	.00
☐ U17	Bill Campbell	.06	.02	.00
☐ U18	Tom Candiotti	.06	.02	.00
☐ U19	John Cangelosi	.15	.06	.01
☐ U20	Jose Canseco (headings on back for a pitcher)	7.50	3.00	.75
☐ U21	Chuck Cary	.15	.06	.01
☐ U22	Juan Castillo	.10	.04	.01
☐ U23	Rick Cerone	.06	.02	.00
☐ U24	John Cerutti	.20	.08	.02
☐ U25	Will Clark	3.50	1.40	.35
☐ U26	Mark Clear	.06	.02	.00
☐ U27	Darnell Coles	.10	.04	.01
☐ U28	Dave Collins	.06	.02	.00
☐ U29	Tim Conroy	.06	.02	.00
☐ U30	Ed Correa	.20	.08	.02
☐ U31	Joe Cowley	.06	.02	.00
☐ U32	Bill Dawley	.06	.02	.00
☐ U33	Rob Deer	.20	.08	.02
☐ U34	John Denny	.10	.04	.01
☐ U35	Jim Deshaies	.30	.12	.03
☐ U36	Doug Drabek	.30	.12	.03
☐ U37	Mike Easler	.06	.02	.00
☐ U38	Mark Eichhorn	.15	.06	.01
☐ U39	Dave Engle	.06	.02	.00
☐ U40	Mike Fischlin	.06	.02	.00
☐ U41	Scott Fletcher	.15	.06	.01
☐ U42	Terry Forster	.10	.04	.01
☐ U43	Terry Francona	.06	.02	.00
☐ U44	Andres Galarraga	.90	.36	.09
☐ U45	Lee Guetterman	.20	.08	.02
☐ U46	Bill Gullickson	.06	.02	.00
☐ U47	Jackie Gutierrez	.06	.02	.00
☐ U48	Moose Haas	.06	.02	.00
☐ U49	Billy Hatcher	.20	.08	.02
☐ U50	Mike Heath	.06	.02	.00
☐ U51	Guy Hoffman	.06	.02	.00
☐ U52	Tom Hume	.06	.02	.00
☐ U53	Pete Incaviglia	.75	.30	.07
☐ U54	Dane Iorg	.06	.02	.00
☐ U55	Chris James	.75	.30	.07
☐ U56	Stan Javier	.30	.12	.03
☐ U57	Tommy John	.20	.08	.02
☐ U58	Tracy Jones	.55	.22	.05
☐ U59	Wally Joyner	2.50	1.00	.25
☐ U60	Wayne Krenchicki	.06	.02	.00
☐ U61	John Kruk	.45	.18	.04
☐ U62	Mike LaCoss	.06	.02	.00
☐ U63	Pete Ladd	.06	.02	.00
☐ U64	Dave LaPoint	.10	.04	.01
☐ U65	Mike LaValliere	.25	.10	.02
☐ U66	Rudy Law	.06	.02	.00
☐ U67	Dennis Leonard	.10	.04	.01
☐ U68	Steve Lombardozzi	.10	.04	.01
☐ U69	Aurelio Lopez	.06	.02	.00
☐ U70	Mickey Mahler	.06	.02	.00
☐ U71	Candy Maldonado	.10	.04	.01
☐ U72	Roger Mason	.10	.04	.01
☐ U73	Greg Mathews	.25	.10	.02
☐ U74	Andy McGaffigan	.06	.02	.00
☐ U75	Joel McKeon	.10	.04	.01
☐ U76	Kevin Mitchell	.45	.18	.04
☐ U77	Bill Mooneyham	.10	.04	.01
☐ U78	Omar Moreno	.06	.02	.00
☐ U79	Jerry Mumphrey	.06	.02	.00
☐ U80	Al Newman	.10	.04	.01
☐ U81	Phil Niekro	.30	.12	.03
☐ U82	Randy Niemann	.06	.02	.00
☐ U83	Juan Nieves	.20	.08	.02
☐ U84	Bob Ojeda	.15	.06	.01
☐ U85	Rick Ownbey	.06	.02	.00
☐ U86	Tom Paciorek	.06	.02	.00
☐ U87	David Palmer	.06	.02	.00
☐ U88	Jeff Parrett	.30	.12	.03
☐ U89	Pat Perry	.15	.06	.01
☐ U90	Dan Plesac	.35	.14	.03
☐ U91	Darrell Porter	.06	.02	.00
☐ U92	Luis Quinones	.15	.06	.01
☐ U93	Rey Quinones	.25	.10	.02
☐ U94	Gary Redus	.06	.02	.00
☐ U95	Jeff Reed	.10	.04	.01
☐ U96	Bip Roberts	.10	.04	.01
☐ U97	Billy Jo Robidoux	.10	.04	.01

	MINT	EXC	G-VG
☐ **U98** Gary Roenicke	.06	.02	.00
☐ **U99** Ron Roenicke	.06	.02	.00
☐ **U100** Angel Salazar	.06	.02	.00
☐ **U101** Joe Sambito	.06	.02	.00
☐ **U102** Billy Sample	.06	.02	.00
☐ **U103** Dave Schmidt	.10	.04	.01
☐ **U104** Ken Schrom	.06	.02	.00
☐ **U105** Ruben Sierra	1.75	.70	.17
☐ **U106** Ted Simmons	.20	.08	.02
☐ **U107** Sammy Stewart ...	.06	.02	.00
☐ **U108** Kurt Stillwell	.35	.14	.03
☐ **U109** Dale Sveum	.35	.14	.03
☐ **U110** Tim Teufel	.10	.04	.01
☐ **U111** Bob Tewksbury ...	.15	.06	.01
☐ **U112** Andres Thomas ...	.25	.10	.02
☐ **U113** Jason Thompson ...	.06	.02	.00
☐ **U114** Milt Thompson	.10	.04	.01
☐ **U115** Rob Thompson	.30	.12	.03
☐ **U116** Jay Tibbs	.06	.02	.00
☐ **U117** Fred Toliver	.10	.04	.01
☐ **U118** Wayne Tolleson ...	.06	.02	.00
☐ **U119** Alex Trevino	.06	.02	.00
☐ **U120** Manny Trillo	.06	.02	.00
☐ **U121** Ed VandeBerg	.06	.02	.00
☐ **U122** Ozzie Virgil	.06	.02	.00
☐ **U123** Tony Walker	.10	.04	.01
☐ **U124** Gene Walter	.10	.04	.01
☐ **U125** Duane Ward	.20	.08	.02
☐ **U126** Jerry Willard	.06	.02	.00
☐ **U127** Mitch Williams ...	.25	.10	.02
☐ **U128** Reggie Williams ...	.10	.04	.01
☐ **U129** Bobby Witt	.45	.18	.04
☐ **U130** Marvell Wynne	.06	.02	.00
☐ **U131** Steve Yeager	.06	.02	.00
☐ **U132** Checklist Card	.06	.01	.00

1987 Fleer

This 660-card set features a distinctive blue border which fades to white on the card fronts. The backs are printed in blue, red, and pink on white card stock. The bottom of the card back shows an innovative graph of the player's ability, e.g., "He's got the stuff" for pitchers and "How he's hitting 'em," for hitters. Cards are numbered on the back and are again the standard 2 ½" by 3 ½". Cards are again organized numerically by teams, i.e., World Champion Mets (1-25), Boston Red Sox (26-48), Houston Astros (49-72), California Angels (73-95), New York Yankees (96-120), Texas Rangers (121-143), Detroit Tigers (144-168), Philadelphia Phillies (169-192), Cincinnati Reds (193-218), Toronto Blue Jays (219-240), Cleveland Indians (241-263), San Francisco Giants (264-288), St. Louis Cardinals (289-312), Montreal Expos (313-337), Milwaukee Brewers (338-361), Kansas City Royals (362-384), Oakland A's (385-410), San Diego Padres (411-435), Los Angeles Dodgers (436-460), Baltimore Orioles (461-483), Chicago White Sox (484-508), Atlanta Braves (509-532), Minnesota Twins (533-554), Chicago Cubs (555-578), Seattle Mariners (579-600), and Pittsburgh Pirates (601-624). The last 36 cards in the set consist of Specials (625-643), Rookie Pairs (644-653), and checklists (654-660).

	MINT	EXC	G-VG
Complete Set (660)	45.00	18.00	4.50
Common Player (1-660) ..	.04	.02	.00

			MINT	EXC	G-VG				MINT	EXC	G-VG
☐	1	Rick Aguilera	.10	.03	.01	☐	50	Alan Ashby	.04	.02	.00
☐	2	Richard Anderson	.10	.04	.01	☐	51	Kevin Bass	.10	.04	.01
☐	3	Wally Backman	.07	.03	.01	☐	52	Jeff Calhoun	.04	.02	.00
☐	4	Gary Carter	.25	.10	.02	☐	53	Jose Cruz	.10	.04	.01
☐	5	Ron Darling	.18	.08	.01	☐	54	Danny Darwin	.04	.02	.00
☐	6	Len Dykstra	.12	.05	.01	☐	55	Glenn Davis	.30	.12	.03
☐	7	Kevin Elster	.65	.26	.06	☐	56	Jim Deshaies	.25	.10	.02
☐	8	Sid Fernandez	.12	.05	.01	☐	57	Bill Doran	.10	.04	.01
☐	9	Dwight Gooden	1.00	.40	.10	☐	58	Phil Garner	.04	.02	.00
☐	10	Ed Hearn	.10	.04	.01	☐	59	Billy Hatcher	.10	.04	.01
☐	11	Danny Heep	.04	.02	.00	☐	60	Charlie Kerfeld	.04	.02	.00
☐	12	Keith Hernandez	.25	.10	.02	☐	61	Bob Knepper	.07	.03	.01
☐	13	Howard Johnson	.15	.06	.01	☐	62	Dave Lopes	.07	.03	.01
☐	14	Ray Knight	.07	.03	.01	☐	63	Aurelio Lopez	.04	.02	.00
☐	15	Lee Mazzilli	.04	.02	.00	☐	64	Jim Pankovits	.04	.02	.00
☐	16	Roger McDowell	.07	.03	.01	☐	65	Terry Puhl	.04	.02	.00
☐	17	Kevin Mitchell	.30	.12	.03	☐	66	Craig Reynolds	.04	.02	.00
☐	18	Randy Niemann	.04	.02	.00	☐	67	Nolan Ryan	.30	.12	.03
☐	19	Bob Ojeda	.07	.03	.01	☐	68	Mike Scott	.25	.10	.02
☐	20	Jesse Orosco	.04	.02	.00	☐	69	Dave Smith	.07	.03	.01
☐	21	Rafael Santana	.04	.02	.00	☐	70	Dickie Thon	.04	.02	.00
☐	22	Doug Sisk	.04	.02	.00	☐	71	Tony Walker	.10	.04	.01
☐	23	Darryl Strawberry	.80	.32	.08	☐	72	Denny Walling	.04	.02	.00
☐	24	Tim Teufel	.04	.02	.00	☐	73	Bob Boone	.10	.04	.01
☐	25	Mookie Wilson	.07	.03	.01	☐	74	Rick Burleson	.07	.03	.01
☐	26	Tony Armas	.07	.03	.01	☐	75	John Candelaria	.07	.03	.01
☐	27	Marty Barrett	.10	.04	.01	☐	76	Doug Corbett	.04	.02	.00
☐	28	Don Baylor	.10	.04	.01	☐	77	Doug DeCinces	.07	.03	.01
☐	29	Wade Boggs	1.50	.60	.15	☐	78	Brian Downing	.07	.03	.01
☐	30	Oil Can Boyd	.07	.03	.01	☐	79	Chuck Finley	.10	.04	.01
☐	31	Bill Buckner	.07	.03	.01	☐	80	Terry Forster	.07	.03	.01
☐	32	Roger Clemens	1.50	.60	.15	☐	81	Bob Grich	.07	.03	.01
☐	33	Steve Crawford	.04	.02	.00	☐	82	George Hendrick	.07	.03	.01
☐	34	Dwight Evans	.12	.05	.01	☐	83	Jack Howell	.15	.06	.01
☐	35	Rich Gedman	.07	.03	.01	☐	84	Reggie Jackson	.35	.14	.03
☐	36	Dave Henderson	.07	.03	.01	☐	85	Ruppert Jones	.04	.02	.00
☐	37	Bruce Hurst	.12	.05	.01	☐	86	Wally Joyner	1.75	.70	.17
☐	38	Tim Lollar	.04	.02	.00	☐	87	Gary Lucas	.04	.02	.00
☐	39	Al Nipper	.04	.02	.00	☐	88	Kirk McCaskill	.04	.02	.00
☐	40	Spike Owen	.04	.02	.00	☐	89	Donnie Moore	.04	.02	.00
☐	41	Jim Rice	.18	.08	.01	☐	90	Gary Pettis	.04	.02	.00
☐	42	Ed Romero	.04	.02	.00	☐	91	Vern Ruhle	.04	.02	.00
☐	43	Joe Sambito	.04	.02	.00	☐	92	Dick Schofield	.04	.02	.00
☐	44	Calvin Schiraldi	.07	.03	.01	☐	93	Don Sutton	.12	.05	.01
☐	45	Tom Seaver	.30	.12	.03	☐	94	Rob Wilfong	.04	.02	.00
☐	46	Jeff Sellers	.15	.06	.01	☐	95	Mike Witt	.10	.04	.01
☐	47	Bob Stanley	.04	.02	.00	☐	96	Doug Drabek	.25	.10	.02
☐	48	Sammy Stewart	.04	.02	.00	☐	97	Mike Easler	.04	.02	.00
☐	49	Larry Andersen	.04	.02	.00	☐	98	Mike Fischlin	.04	.02	.00

		MINT	EXC	G-VG
☐ 99	Brian Fisher	.04	.02	.00
☐ 100	Ron Guidry	.12	.05	.01
☐ 101	Rickey Henderson	.30	.12	.03
☐ 102	Tommy John	.12	.05	.01
☐ 103	Ron Kittle	.10	.04	.01
☐ 104	Don Mattingly	2.50	1.00	.25
☐ 105	Bobby Meacham	.04	.02	.00
☐ 106	Joe Niekro	.10	.04	.01
☐ 107	Mike Pagliarulo	.10	.04	.01
☐ 108	Dan Pasqua	.10	.04	.01
☐ 109	Willie Randolph	.07	.03	.01
☐ 110	Dennis Rasmussen	.07	.03	.01
☐ 111	Dave Righetti	.10	.04	.01
☐ 112	Gary Roenicke	.04	.02	.00
☐ 113	Rod Scurry	.04	.02	.00
☐ 114	Bob Shirley	.04	.02	.00
☐ 115	Joel Skinner	.04	.02	.00
☐ 116	Tim Stoddard	.04	.02	.00
☐ 117	Bob Tewksbury	.10	.04	.01
☐ 118	Wayne Tolleson	.04	.02	.00
☐ 119	Claudell Washington	.07	.03	.01
☐ 120	Dave Winfield	.25	.10	.02
☐ 121	Steve Buechele	.04	.02	.00
☐ 122	Ed Correa	.20	.08	.02
☐ 123	Scott Fletcher	.07	.03	.01
☐ 124	Jose Guzman	.07	.03	.01
☐ 125	Toby Harrah	.04	.02	.00
☐ 126	Greg Harris	.04	.02	.00
☐ 127	Charlie Hough	.07	.03	.01
☐ 128	Pete Incaviglia	.75	.30	.07
☐ 129	Mike Mason	.04	.02	.00
☐ 130	Oddibe McDowell	.10	.04	.01
☐ 131	Dale Mohorcic	.15	.06	.01
☐ 132	Pete O'Brien	.10	.04	.01
☐ 133	Tom Paciorek	.04	.02	.00
☐ 134	Larry Parrish	.07	.03	.01
☐ 135	Geno Petralli	.04	.02	.00
☐ 136	Darrell Porter	.04	.02	.00
☐ 137	Jeff Russell	.04	.02	.00
☐ 138	Ruben Sierra	1.25	.50	.12
☐ 139	Don Slaught	.04	.02	.00
☐ 140	Gary Ward	.04	.02	.00
☐ 141	Curtis Wilkerson	.04	.02	.00
☐ 142	Mitch Williams	.20	.08	.02
☐ 143	Bobby Witt	.35	.14	.03
☐ 144	Dave Bergman	.04	.02	.00
☐ 145	Tom Brookens	.04	.02	.00
☐ 146	Bill Campbell	.04	.02	.00
☐ 147	Chuck Cary	.15	.06	.01
☐ 148	Darnell Coles	.07	.03	.01
☐ 149	Dave Collins	.04	.02	.00
☐ 150	Darrell Evans	.10	.04	.01
☐ 151	Kirk Gibson	.25	.10	.02
☐ 152	John Grubb	.04	.02	.00
☐ 153	Willie Hernandez	.10	.04	.01
☐ 154	Larry Herndon	.04	.02	.00
☐ 155	Eric King	.15	.06	.01
☐ 156	Chet Lemon	.04	.02	.00
☐ 157	Dwight Lowry	.10	.04	.01
☐ 158	Jack Morris	.12	.05	.01
☐ 159	Randy O'Neal	.04	.02	.00
☐ 160	Lance Parrish	.12	.05	.01
☐ 161	Dan Petry	.07	.03	.01
☐ 162	Pat Sheridan	.04	.02	.00
☐ 163	Jim Slaton	.04	.02	.00
☐ 164	Frank Tanana	.07	.03	.01
☐ 165	Walt Terrell	.04	.02	.00
☐ 166	Mark Thurmond	.04	.02	.00
☐ 167	Alan Trammell	.18	.08	.01
☐ 168	Lou Whitaker	.10	.04	.01
☐ 169	Luis Aguayo	.04	.02	.00
☐ 170	Steve Bedrosian	.10	.04	.01
☐ 171	Don Carman	.04	.02	.00
☐ 172	Darren Daulton	.04	.02	.00
☐ 173	Greg Gross	.04	.02	.00
☐ 174	Kevin Gross	.04	.02	.00
☐ 175	Von Hayes	.10	.04	.01
☐ 176	Charles Hudson	.04	.02	.00
☐ 177	Tom Hume	.04	.02	.00
☐ 178	Steve Jeltz	.04	.02	.00
☐ 179	Mike Maddux	.15	.06	.01
☐ 180	Shane Rawley	.07	.03	.01
☐ 181	Gary Redus	.04	.02	.00
☐ 182	Ron Roenicke	.04	.02	.00
☐ 183	Bruce Ruffin	.20	.08	.02
☐ 184	John Russell	.04	.02	.00
☐ 185	Juan Samuel	.12	.05	.01
☐ 186	Dan Schatzeder	.04	.02	.00
☐ 187	Mike Schmidt	.35	.14	.03
☐ 188	Rick Schu	.04	.02	.00
☐ 189	Jeff Stone	.04	.02	.00
☐ 190	Kent Tekulve	.04	.02	.00
☐ 191	Milt Thompson	.07	.03	.01
☐ 192	Glenn Wilson	.04	.02	.00
☐ 193	Buddy Bell	.10	.04	.01
☐ 194	Tom Browning	.12	.05	.01
☐ 195	Sal Butera	.04	.02	.00
☐ 196	Dave Concepcion	.10	.04	.01

		MINT	EXC	G-VG
☐ 197	Kal Daniels	.90	.36	.09
☐ 198	Eric Davis	1.50	.60	.15
☐ 199	John Denny	.07	.03	.01
☐ 200	Bo Diaz	.04	.02	.00
☐ 201	Nick Esasky	.04	.02	.00
☐ 202	John Franco	.10	.04	.01
☐ 203	Bill Gullickson	.04	.02	.00
☐ 204	Barry Larkin	1.25	.50	.12
☐ 205	Eddie Milner	.04	.02	.00
☐ 206	Rob Murphy	.25	.10	.02
☐ 207	Ron Oester	.04	.02	.00
☐ 208	Dave Parker	.12	.05	.01
☐ 209	Tony Perez	.12	.05	.01
☐ 210	Ted Power	.04	.02	.00
☐ 211	Joe Price	.04	.02	.00
☐ 212	Ron Robinson	.04	.02	.00
☐ 213	Pete Rose	.60	.24	.06
☐ 214	Mario Soto	.04	.02	.00
☐ 215	Kurt Stillwell	.25	.10	.02
☐ 216	Max Venable	.04	.02	.00
☐ 217	Chris Welsh	.04	.02	.00
☐ 218	Carl Willis	.07	.03	.01
☐ 219	Jesse Barfield	.18	.08	.01
☐ 220	George Bell	.25	.10	.02
☐ 221	Bill Caudill	.04	.02	.00
☐ 222	John Cerutti	.15	.06	.01
☐ 223	Jim Clancy	.04	.02	.00
☐ 224	Mark Eichhorn	.12	.05	.01
☐ 225	Tony Fernandez	.12	.05	.01
☐ 226	Damaso Garcia	.04	.02	.00
☐ 227	Kelly Gruber ERR	.04	.02	.00
	(wrong birth year)			
☐ 228	Tom Henke	.07	.03	.01
☐ 229	Garth Iorg	.04	.02	.00
☐ 230	Joe Johnson	.04	.02	.00
☐ 231	Cliff Johnson	.04	.02	.00
☐ 232	Jimmy Key	.10	.04	.01
☐ 233	Dennis Lamp	.04	.02	.00
☐ 234	Rick Leach	.04	.02	.00
☐ 235	Buck Martinez	.04	.02	.00
☐ 236	Lloyd Moseby	.10	.04	.01
☐ 237	Rance Mulliniks	.04	.02	.00
☐ 238	Dave Stieb	.10	.04	.01
☐ 239	Willie Upshaw	.04	.02	.00
☐ 240	Ernie Whitt	.04	.02	.00
☐ 241	Andy Allanson	.10	.04	.01
☐ 242	Scott Bailes	.12	.05	.01
☐ 243	Chris Bando	.04	.02	.00
☐ 244	Tony Bernazard	.04	.02	.00
☐ 245	John Butcher	.04	.02	.00
☐ 246	Brett Butler	.07	.03	.01
☐ 247	Ernie Camacho	.04	.02	.00
☐ 248	Tom Candiotti	.04	.02	.00
☐ 249	Joe Carter	.20	.08	.02
☐ 250	Carmen Castillo	.04	.02	.00
☐ 251	Julio Franco	.10	.04	.01
☐ 252	Mel Hall	.07	.03	.01
☐ 253	Brook Jacoby	.10	.04	.01
☐ 254	Phil Niekro	.15	.06	.01
☐ 255	Otis Nixon	.10	.04	.01
☐ 256	Dickie Noles	.04	.02	.00
☐ 257	Bryan Oelkers	.04	.02	.00
☐ 258	Ken Schrom	.04	.02	.00
☐ 259	Don Schulze	.04	.02	.00
☐ 260	Cory Snyder	.80	.32	.08
☐ 261	Pat Tabler	.10	.04	.01
☐ 262	Andre Thornton	.07	.03	.01
☐ 263	Rich Yett	.04	.02	.00
☐ 264	Mike Aldrete	.25	.10	.02
☐ 265	Juan Berenguer	.04	.02	.00
☐ 266	Vida Blue	.07	.03	.01
☐ 267	Bob Brenly	.04	.02	.00
☐ 268	Chris Brown	.10	.04	.01
☐ 269	Will Clark	2.50	1.00	.25
☐ 270	Chili Davis	.10	.04	.01
☐ 271	Mark Davis	.07	.03	.01
☐ 272	Kelly Downs	.30	.12	.03
☐ 273	Scott Garrelts	.04	.02	.00
☐ 274	Dan Gladden	.07	.03	.01
☐ 275	Mike Krukow	.04	.02	.00
☐ 276	Randy Kutcher	.10	.04	.01
☐ 277	Mike LaCoss	.04	.02	.00
☐ 278	Jeff Leonard	.07	.03	.01
☐ 279	Candy Maldonado	.07	.03	.01
☐ 280	Roger Mason	.04	.02	.00
☐ 281	Bob Melvin	.04	.02	.00
☐ 282	Greg Minton	.04	.02	.00
☐ 283	Jeff Robinson	.07	.03	.01
	(Giants pitcher)			
☐ 284	Harry Spilman	.04	.02	.00
☐ 285	Robby Thompson	.25	.10	.02
☐ 286	Jose Uribe	.04	.02	.00
☐ 287	Frank Williams	.04	.02	.00
☐ 288	Joel Youngblood	.04	.02	.00
☐ 289	Jack Clark	.20	.08	.02
☐ 290	Vince Coleman	.40	.16	.04
☐ 291	Tim Conroy	.04	.02	.00
☐ 292	Danny Cox	.07	.03	.01

		MINT	EXC	G-VG
☐ 293	Ken Dayley	.04	.02	.00
☐ 294	Curt Ford	.07	.03	.01
☐ 295	Bob Forsch	.04	.02	.00
☐ 296	Tom Herr	.07	.03	.01
☐ 297	Ricky Horton	.04	.02	.00
☐ 298	Clint Hurdle	.04	.02	.00
☐ 299	Jeff Lahti	.04	.02	.00
☐ 300	Steve Lake	.04	.02	.00
☐ 301	Tito Landrum	.04	.02	.00
☐ 302	Mike LaValliere	.20	.08	.02
☐ 303	Greg Mathews	.20	.08	.02
☐ 304	Willie McGee	.12	.05	.01
☐ 305	Jose Oquendo	.04	.02	.00
☐ 306	Terry Pendleton	.04	.02	.00
☐ 307	Pat Perry	.04	.02	.00
☐ 308	Ozzie Smith	.15	.06	.01
☐ 309	Ray Soff	.07	.03	.01
☐ 310	John Tudor	.10	.04	.01
☐ 311	Andy Van Slyke	.20	.08	.02
	ERR (Bats R, Throws L)			
☐ 312	Todd Worrell	.20	.08	.02
☐ 313	Dann Bilardello	.04	.02	.00
☐ 314	Hubie Brooks	.07	.03	.01
☐ 315	Tim Burke	.07	.03	.01
☐ 316	Andre Dawson	.30	.12	.03
☐ 317	Mike Fitzgerald	.04	.02	.00
☐ 318	Tom Foley	.04	.02	.00
☐ 319	Andres Galarraga	.35	.14	.03
☐ 320	Joe Hesketh	.04	.02	.00
☐ 321	Wallace Johnson	.04	.02	.00
☐ 322	Wayne Krenchicki	.04	.02	.00
☐ 323	Vance Law	.07	.03	.01
☐ 324	Dennis Martinez	.07	.03	.01
☐ 325	Bob McClure	.04	.02	.00
☐ 326	Andy McGaffigan	.04	.02	.00
☐ 327	Al Newman	.07	.03	.01
☐ 328	Tim Raines	.25	.10	.02
☐ 329	Jeff Reardon	.07	.03	.01
☐ 330	Luis Rivera	.07	.03	.01
☐ 331	Bob Sebra	.10	.04	.01
☐ 332	Bryn Smith	.04	.02	.00
☐ 333	Jay Tibbs	.04	.02	.00
☐ 334	Tim Wallach	.10	.04	.01
☐ 335	Mitch Webster	.04	.02	.00
☐ 336	Jim Wohlford	.04	.02	.00
☐ 337	Floyd Youmans	.07	.03	.01
☐ 338	Chris Bosio	.15	.06	.01
☐ 339	Glenn Braggs	.35	.14	.03
☐ 340	Rick Cerone	.04	.02	.00
☐ 341	Mark Clear	.04	.02	.00
☐ 342	Bryan Clutterbuck	.07	.03	.01
☐ 343	Cecil Cooper	.10	.04	.01
☐ 344	Rob Deer	.15	.06	.01
☐ 345	Jim Gantner	.04	.02	.00
☐ 346	Ted Higuera	.15	.06	.01
☐ 347	John Henry Johnson	.04	.02	.00
☐ 348	Tim Leary	.25	.10	.02
☐ 349	Rick Manning	.04	.02	.00
☐ 350	Paul Molitor	.12	.05	.01
☐ 351	Charlie Moore	.04	.02	.00
☐ 352	Juan Nieves	.15	.06	.01
☐ 353	Ben Oglivie	.07	.03	.01
☐ 354	Dan Plesac	.30	.12	.03
☐ 355	Ernest Riles	.04	.02	.00
☐ 356	Billy Jo Robidoux	.04	.02	.00
☐ 357	Bill Schroeder	.04	.02	.00
☐ 358	Dale Sveum	.25	.10	.02
☐ 359	Gorman Thomas	.10	.04	.01
☐ 360	Bill Wegman	.07	.03	.01
☐ 361	Robin Yount	.25	.10	.02
☐ 362	Steve Balboni	.04	.02	.00
☐ 363	Scott Bankhead	.12	.05	.01
☐ 364	Buddy Biancalana	.04	.02	.00
☐ 365	Bud Black	.04	.02	.00
☐ 366	George Brett	.35	.14	.03
☐ 367	Steve Farr	.04	.02	.00
☐ 368	Mark Gubicza	.10	.04	.01
☐ 369	Bo Jackson	1.25	.50	.12
☐ 370	Danny Jackson	.15	.06	.01
☐ 371	Mike Kingery	.12	.05	.01
☐ 372	Rudy Law	.04	.02	.00
☐ 373	Charlie Leibrandt	.04	.02	.00
☐ 374	Dennis Leonard	.04	.02	.00
☐ 375	Hal McRae	.07	.03	.01
☐ 376	Jorge Orta	.04	.02	.00
☐ 377	Jamie Quirk	.04	.02	.00
☐ 378	Dan Quisenberry	.10	.04	.01
☐ 379	Bret Saberhagen	.18	.08	.01
☐ 380	Angel Salazar	.04	.02	.00
☐ 381	Lonnie Smith	.04	.02	.00
☐ 382	Jim Sundberg	.04	.02	.00
☐ 383	Frank White	.07	.03	.01
☐ 384	Willie Wilson	.10	.04	.01
☐ 385	Joaquin Andujar	.07	.03	.01
☐ 386	Doug Bair	.04	.02	.00
☐ 387	Dusty Baker	.07	.03	.01
☐ 388	Bruce Bochte	.04	.02	.00
☐ 389	Jose Canseco	6.00	2.40	.60

		MINT	EXC	G-VG			MINT	EXC	G-VG
☐ 390	Chris Codiroll	.04	.02	.00	☐ 439	Mariano Duncan	.04	.02	.00
☐ 391	Mike Davis	.04	.02	.00	☐ 440	Pedro Guerrero	.15	.06	.01
☐ 392	Alfredo Griffin	.07	.03	.01	☐ 441	Orel Hershiser	.35	.14	.03
☐ 393	Moose Haas	.04	.02	.00	☐ 442	Rick Honeycutt	.04	.02	.00
☐ 394	Donnie Hill	.04	.02	.00	☐ 443	Ken Howell	.04	.02	.00
☐ 395	Jay Howell	.07	.03	.01	☐ 444	Ken Landreaux	.04	.02	.00
☐ 396	Dave Kingman	.10	.04	.01	☐ 445	Bill Madlock	.07	.03	.01
☐ 397	Carney Lansford	.10	.04	.01	☐ 446	Mike Marshall	.10	.04	.01
☐ 398	Dave Leiper	.07	.03	.01	☐ 447	Len Matuszek	.04	.02	.00
☐ 399	Bill Mooneyham	.07	.03	.01	☐ 448	Tom Niedenfuer	.04	.02	.00
☐ 400	Dwayne Murphy	.04	.02	.00	☐ 449	Alejandro Pena	.04	.02	.00
☐ 401	Steve Ontiveros	.04	.02	.00	☐ 450	Dennis Powell	.04	.02	.00
☐ 402	Tony Phillips	.04	.02	.00	☐ 451	Jerry Reuss	.04	.02	.00
☐ 403	Eric Plunk	.04	.02	.00	☐ 452	Bill Russell	.04	.02	.00
☐ 404	Jose Rijo	.07	.03	.01	☐ 453	Steve Sax	.15	.06	.01
☐ 405	Terry Steinbach	.45	.18	.04	☐ 454	Mike Scioscia	.04	.02	.00
☐ 406	Dave Stewart	.10	.04	.01	☐ 455	Franklin Stubbs	.04	.02	.00
☐ 407	Mickey Tettleton	.04	.02	.00	☐ 456	Alex Trevino	.04	.02	.00
☐ 408	Dave Von Ohlen	.04	.02	.00	☐ 457	Fernando Valenzuela	.18	.08	.01
☐ 409	Jerry Willard	.04	.02	.00	☐ 458	Ed VandeBerg	.04	.02	.00
☐ 410	Curt Young	.04	.02	.00	☐ 459	Bob Welch	.07	.03	.01
☐ 411	Bruce Bochy	.04	.02	.00	☐ 460	Reggie Williams	.07	.03	.01
☐ 412	Dave Dravecky	.04	.02	.00	☐ 461	Don Aase	.04	.02	.00
☐ 413	Jim Flannery	.04	.02	.00	☐ 462	Juan Beniquez	.04	.02	.00
☐ 414	Steve Garvey	.30	.12	.03	☐ 463	Mike Boddicker	.07	.03	.01
☐ 415	Goose Gossage	.10	.04	.01	☐ 464	Juan Bonilla	.04	.02	.00
☐ 416	Tony Gwynn	.45	.18	.04	☐ 465	Rich Bordi	.04	.02	.00
☐ 417	Andy Hawkins	.07	.03	.01	☐ 466	Storm Davis	.07	.03	.01
☐ 418	LaMarr Hoyt	.07	.03	.01	☐ 467	Rick Dempsey	.04	.02	.00
☐ 419	Terry Kennedy	.04	.02	.00	☐ 468	Ken Dixon	.04	.02	.00
☐ 420	John Kruk	.35	.14	.03	☐ 469	Jim Dwyer	.04	.02	.00
☐ 421	Dave LaPoint	.07	.03	.01	☐ 470	Mike Flanagan	.07	.03	.01
☐ 422	Craig Lefferts	.04	.02	.00	☐ 471	Jackie Gutierrez	.04	.02	.00
☐ 423	Carmelo Martinez	.04	.02	.00	☐ 472	Brad Havens	.04	.02	.00
☐ 424	Lance McCullers	.07	.03	.01	☐ 473	Lee Lacy	.04	.02	.00
☐ 425	Kevin McReynolds	.30	.12	.03	☐ 474	Fred Lynn	.12	.05	.01
☐ 426	Craig Nettles	.10	.04	.01	☐ 475	Scott McGregor	.07	.03	.01
☐ 427	Bip Roberts	.07	.03	.01	☐ 476	Eddie Murray	.25	.10	.02
☐ 428	Jerry Royster	.04	.02	.00	☐ 477	Tom O'Malley	.04	.02	.00
☐ 429	Benito Santiago	.85	.34	.08	☐ 478	Cal Ripken Jr.	.25	.10	.02
☐ 430	Eric Show	.07	.03	.01	☐ 479	Larry Sheets	.07	.03	.01
☐ 431	Bob Stoddard	.04	.02	.00	☐ 480	John Shelby	.04	.02	.00
☐ 432	Garry Templeton	.07	.03	.01	☐ 481	Nate Snell	.04	.02	.00
☐ 433	Gene Walter	.04	.02	.00	☐ 482	Jim Traber	.07	.03	.01
☐ 434	Ed Whitson	.04	.02	.00	☐ 483	Mike Young	.04	.02	.00
☐ 435	Marvell Wynne	.04	.02	.00	☐ 484	Neil Allen	.04	.02	.00
☐ 436	Dave Anderson	.04	.02	.00	☐ 485	Harold Baines	.10	.04	.01
☐ 437	Greg Brock	.04	.02	.00	☐ 486	Floyd Bannister	.04	.02	.00
☐ 438	Enos Cabell	.04	.02	.00	☐ 487	Daryl Boston	.04	.02	.00

		MINT	EXC	G-VG			MINT	EXC	G-VG
☐ 488	Ivan Calderon	.12	.05	.01	☐ 537	Tom Brunansky	.12	.05	.01
☐ 489	John Cangelosi	.10	.04	.01	☐ 538	Randy Bush	.04	.02	.00
☐ 490	Steve Carlton	.20	.08	.02	☐ 539	George Frazier	.04	.02	.00
☐ 491	Joe Cowley	.04	.02	.00	☐ 540	Gary Gaetti	.15	.06	.01
☐ 492	Julio Cruz	.04	.02	.00	☐ 541	Greg Gagne	.04	.02	.00
☐ 493	Bill Dawley	.04	.02	.00	☐ 542	Mickey Hatcher	.07	.03	.01
☐ 494	Jose DeLeon	.04	.02	.00	☐ 543	Neal Heaton	.04	.02	.00
☐ 495	Richard Dotson	.07	.03	.01	☐ 544	Kent Hrbek	.15	.06	.01
☐ 496	Carlton Fisk	.12	.05	.01	☐ 545	Roy Lee Jackson	.04	.02	.00
☐ 497	Ozzie Guillen	.07	.03	.01	☐ 546	Tim Laudner	.04	.02	.00
☐ 498	Jerry Hairston	.04	.02	.00	☐ 547	Steve Lombardozzi	.04	.02	.00
☐ 499	Ron Hassey	.04	.02	.00	☐ 548	Mark Portugal	.07	.03	.01
☐ 500	Tim Hulett	.04	.02	.00	☐ 549	Kirby Puckett	.45	.18	.04
☐ 501	Bob James	.04	.02	.00	☐ 550	Jeff Reed	.04	.02	.00
☐ 502	Steve Lyons	.04	.02	.00	☐ 551	Mark Salas	.04	.02	.00
☐ 503	Joel McKeon	.10	.04	.01	☐ 552	Roy Smalley	.04	.02	.00
☐ 504	Gene Nelson	.04	.02	.00	☐ 553	Mike Smithson	.04	.02	.00
☐ 505	Dave Schmidt	.04	.02	.00	☐ 554	Frank Viola	.18	.08	.01
☐ 506	Ray Searage	.04	.02	.00	☐ 555	Thad Bosley	.04	.02	.00
☐ 507	Bobby Thigpen	.25	.10	.02	☐ 556	Ron Cey	.07	.03	.01
☐ 508	Greg Walker	.07	.03	.01	☐ 557	Jody Davis	.07	.03	.01
☐ 509	Jim Acker	.04	.02	.00	☐ 558	Ron Davis	.04	.02	.00
☐ 510	Doyle Alexander	.07	.03	.01	☐ 559	Bob Dernier	.04	.02	.00
☐ 511	Paul Assenmacher	.07	.03	.01	☐ 560	Frank DiPino	.04	.02	.00
☐ 512	Bruce Benedict	.04	.02	.00	☐ 561	Shawon Dunston UER	.10	.04	.01
☐ 513	Chris Chambliss	.07	.03	.01		(wrong birth year listed on card back)			
☐ 514	Jeff Dedmon	.04	.02	.00	☐ 562	Leon Durham	.07	.03	.01
☐ 515	Gene Garber	.04	.02	.00	☐ 563	Dennis Eckersley	.12	.05	.01
☐ 516	Ken Griffey	.07	.03	.01	☐ 564	Terry Francona	.04	.02	.00
☐ 517	Terry Harper	.04	.02	.00	☐ 565	Dave Gumpert	.04	.02	.00
☐ 518	Bob Horner	.12	.05	.01	☐ 566	Guy Hoffman	.04	.02	.00
☐ 519	Glenn Hubbard	.04	.02	.00	☐ 567	Ed Lynch	.04	.02	.00
☐ 520	Rick Mahler	.04	.02	.00	☐ 568	Gary Matthews	.04	.02	.00
☐ 521	Omar Moreno	.04	.02	.00	☐ 569	Keith Moreland	.04	.02	.00
☐ 522	Dale Murphy	.45	.18	.04	☐ 570	Jamie Moyer	.15	.06	.01
☐ 523	Ken Oberkfell	.04	.02	.00	☐ 571	Jerry Mumphrey	.04	.02	.00
☐ 524	Ed Olwine	.07	.03	.01	☐ 572	Ryne Sandberg	.20	.08	.02
☐ 525	David Palmer	.04	.02	.00	☐ 573	Scott Sanderson	.04	.02	.00
☐ 526	Rafael Ramirez	.04	.02	.00	☐ 574	Lee Smith	.07	.03	.01
☐ 527	Billy Sample	.04	.02	.00	☐ 575	Chris Speier	.04	.02	.00
☐ 528	Ted Simmons	.10	.04	.01	☐ 576	Rick Sutcliffe	.10	.04	.01
☐ 529	Zane Smith	.07	.03	.01	☐ 577	Manny Trillo	.04	.02	.00
☐ 530	Bruce Sutter	.10	.04	.01	☐ 578	Steve Trout	.04	.02	.00
☐ 531	Andres Thomas	.20	.08	.02	☐ 579	Karl Best	.04	.02	.00
☐ 532	Ozzie Virgil	.04	.02	.00	☐ 580	Scott Bradley	.04	.02	.00
☐ 533	Allan Anderson	.35	.14	.03	☐ 581	Phil Bradley	.07	.03	.01
☐ 534	Keith Atherton	.04	.02	.00	☐ 582	Mickey Brantley	.07	.03	.01
☐ 535	Billy Beane	.07	.03	.01	☐ 583	Mike Brown	.04	.02	.00
☐ 536	Bert Blyleven	.10	.04	.01		(Mariners pitcher)			

	MINT	EXC	G-VG			MINT	EXC	G-VG
☐ 584 Alvin Davis	.10	.04	.01	☐ 627 AL Firemen	.07	.03	.01
☐ 585 Lee Guetterman	.15	.06	.01	Dave Righetti			
☐ 586 Mark Huismann	.04	.02	.00	Don Aase			
☐ 587 Bob Kearney	.04	.02	.00	☐ 628 Rookie All-Stars	1.25	.50	.12
☐ 588 Pete Ladd	.04	.02	.00	Wally Joyner			
☐ 589 Mark Langston	.10	.04	.01	Jose Canseco			
☐ 590 Mike Moore	.07	.03	.01	☐ 629 Magic Mets	.50	.20	.05
☐ 591 Mike Morgan	.04	.02	.00	Gary Carter			
☐ 592 John Moses	.04	.02	.00	Sid Fernandez			
☐ 593 Ken Phelps	.07	.03	.01	Dwight Gooden			
☐ 594 Jim Presley	.10	.04	.01	Keith Hernandez			
☐ 595 Rey Quinones ERR	.20	.08	.02	Darryl Strawberry			
(Quinonez on front)				☐ 630 NL Best Righties	.07	.03	.01
☐ 596 Harold Reynolds	.07	.03	.01	Mike Scott			
☐ 597 Billy Swift	.04	.02	.00	Mike Krukow			
☐ 598 Danny Tartabull	.30	.12	.03	☐ 631 Sensational Southpaws	.10	.04	.01
☐ 599 Steve Yeager	.04	.02	.00	Fernando Valenzuela			
☐ 600 Matt Young	.04	.02	.00	John Franco			
☐ 601 Bill Almon	.04	.02	.00	☐ 632 Count'Em	.10	.04	.01
☐ 602 Rafael Belliard	.07	.03	.01	Bob Horner			
☐ 603 Mike Bielecki	.04	.02	.00	☐ 633 AL Pitcher's Nightmare	.50	.20	.05
☐ 604 Barry Bonds	1.00	.40	.10	Jose Canseco			
☐ 605 Bobby Bonilla	1.00	.40	.10	Jim Rice			
☐ 606 Sid Bream	.04	.02	.00	Kirby Puckett			
☐ 607 Mike Brown	.04	.02	.00	☐ 634 All-Star Battery	.25	.10	.02
(Pirates OF)				Gary Carter			
☐ 608 Pat Clements	.04	.02	.00	Roger Clemens			
☐ 609 Mike Diaz	.10	.04	.01	☐ 635 4000 Strikeouts	.15	.06	.01
☐ 610 Cecilio Guante	.04	.02	.00	Steve Carlton			
☐ 611 Barry Jones	.12	.05	.01	☐ 636 Big Bats at First	.15	.06	.01
☐ 612 Bob Kipper	.04	.02	.00	Glenn Davis			
☐ 613 Larry McWilliams	.04	.02	.00	Eddie Murray			
☐ 614 Jim Morrison	.04	.02	.00	☐ 637 On Base	.35	.14	.03
☐ 615 Joe Orsulak	.04	.02	.00	Wade Boggs			
☐ 616 Junior Ortiz	.04	.02	.00	Keith Hernandez			
☐ 617 Tony Pena	.07	.03	.01	☐ 638 Sluggers Left Side	1.00	.40	.10
☐ 618 Johnny Ray	.07	.03	.01	Don Mattingly			
☐ 619 Rick Reuschel	.07	.03	.01	Darryl Strawberry			
☐ 620 R.J. Reynolds	.04	.02	.00	☐ 639 Former MVP's	.12	.05	.01
☐ 621 Rick Rhoden	.07	.03	.01	Dave Parker			
☐ 622 Don Robinson	.04	.02	.00	Ryne Sandberg			
☐ 623 Bob Walk	.07	.03	.01	☐ 640 Dr. K , Super K	.60	.24	.06
☐ 624 Jim Winn	.04	.02	.00	Dwight Gooden			
☐ 625 Youthful Power	.60	.24	.06	Roger Clemens			
Pete Incaviglia				☐ 641 AL West Stoppers	.07	.03	.01
Jose Canseco				Mike Witt			
☐ 626 300 Game Winners	.10	.04	.01	Charlie Hough			
Don Sutton							
Phil Niekro							

		MINT	EXC	G-VG
☐ 642	Doubles and Triples	.10	.04	.01
	Juan Samuel			
	Tim Raines			
☐ 643	Outfielders with Punch	.10	.04	.01
	Harold Baines			
	Jesse Barfield			
☐ 644	Dave Clark and	.90	.36	.09
	Greg Swindell			
☐ 645	Ron Karkovice and .	.12	.05	.01
	Russ Morman			
☐ 646	Devon White and ..	.90	.36	.09
	Willie Fraser			
☐ 647	Mike Stanley and ...	.12	.05	.01
	Jerry Browne			
☐ 648	Dave Magadan and	.45	.18	.04
	Phil Lombardi			
☐ 649	Jose Gonzalez and .	.25	.10	.02
	Ralph Bryant			
☐ 650	Jimmy Jones and ..	.30	.12	.03
	Randy Asadoor			
☐ 651	Tracy Jones and ...	.40	.16	.04
	Marvin Freeman			
☐ 652	John Stefero and ..	7.00	2.80	.70
	Kevin Seitzer			
☐ 653	Rob Nelson and ...	.15	.06	.01
	Steve Fireovid			
☐ 654	CL: Mets/Red Sox ..	.06	.01	.00
	Astros/Angels			
☐ 655	CL: Yankees/Rangers	.06	.01	.00
	Tigers/Phillies			
☐ 656	CL: Reds/Blue Jays	.06	.01	.00
	Indians/Giants			
	ERR (230/231 wrong)			
☐ 657	CL: Cardinals/Expos	.06	.01	.00
	Brewers/Royals			
☐ 658	CL: A's/Padres	.06	.01	.00
	Dodgers/Orioles			
☐ 659	CL: White Sox/Braves	.06	.01	.00
	Twins/Cubs			
☐ 660	CL: Mariners/Pirates	.06	.01	.00
	Special Cards			
	ERR (580/581 wrong)			

1987 Fleer Sticker Cards

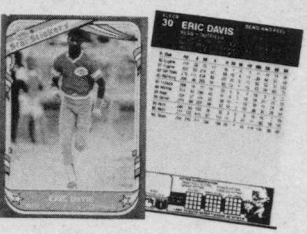

These Star Stickers were distributed as a separate issue by Fleer with five star stickers and a logo sticker in each wax pack. The 132-card (sticker) set features 2½" by 3½" full-color fronts and even statistics on the sticker back, which is an indication that the Fleer Company understands that these stickers are rarely used as stickers but more like traditional cards. The card fronts are surrounded by a green border and the backs are printed in green and yellow on white card stock.

		MINT	EXC	G-VG
Complete Set (132)		21.00	8.50	2.10
Common Player (1-132) ..		.05	.02	.00
☐ 1	Don Aase	.05	.02	.00
☐ 2	Harold Baines	.10	.04	.01
☐ 3	Floyd Bannister ...	.05	.02	.00
☐ 4	Jesse Barfield	.15	.06	.01
☐ 5	Marty Barrett	.10	.04	.01
☐ 6	Kevin Bass	.05	.02	.00
☐ 7	Don Baylor	.10	.04	.01
☐ 8	Steve Bedrosian ..	.10	.04	.01
☐ 9	George Bell	.20	.08	.02
☐ 10	Bert Blyleven	.10	.04	.01
☐ 11	Mike Boddicker ...	.10	.04	.01
☐ 12	Wade Boggs	1.50	.60	.15
☐ 13	Phil Bradley	.10	.04	.01
☐ 14	Sid Bream	.05	.02	.00
☐ 15	George Brett	.45	.18	.04
☐ 16	Hubie Brooks	.05	.02	.00
☐ 17	Tom Brunansky ...	.10	.04	.01

		MINT	EXC	G-VG			MINT	EXC	G-VG
☐	18 Tom Candiotti	.05	.02	.00	☐	67 Bob James	.05	.02	.00
☐	19 Jose Canseco	2.50	1.00	.25	☐	68 Wally Joyner	1.00	.40	.10
☐	20 Gary Carter	.35	.14	.03	☐	69 Mike Krukow	.05	.02	.00
☐	21 Joe Carter	.20	.08	.02	☐	70 Mark Langston	.10	.04	.01
☐	22 Will Clark	1.00	.40	.10	☐	71 Carney Lansford	.10	.04	.01
☐	23 Mark Clear	.05	.02	.00	☐	72 Fred Lynn	.15	.06	.01
☐	24 Roger Clemens	.75	.30	.07	☐	73 Bill Madlock	.05	.02	.00
☐	25 Vince Coleman	.35	.14	.03	☐	74 Don Mattingly	2.50	1.00	.25
☐	26 Jose Cruz	.05	.02	.00	☐	75 Kirk McCaskill	.05	.02	.00
☐	27 Ron Darling	.15	.06	.01	☐	76 Lance McCullers	.05	.02	.00
☐	28 Alvin Davis	.10	.04	.01	☐	77 Oddibe McDowell	.15	.06	.01
☐	29 Chili Davis	.10	.04	.01	☐	78 Paul Molitor	.20	.08	.02
☐	30 Eric Davis	1.00	.40	.10	☐	79 Keith Moreland	.05	.02	.00
☐	31 Glenn Davis	.20	.08	.02	☐	80 Jack Morris	.15	.06	.01
☐	32 Mike Davis	.05	.02	.00	☐	81 Jim Morrison	.05	.02	.00
☐	33 Andre Dawson	.35	.14	.03	☐	82 Jerry Mumphrey	.05	.02	.00
☐	34 Doug DeCinces	.05	.02	.00	☐	83 Dale Murphy	.50	.20	.05
☐	35 Brian Downing	.05	.02	.00	☐	84 Eddie Murray	.40	.16	.04
☐	36 Shawon Dunston	.10	.04	.01	☐	85 Ben Oglivie	.05	.02	.00
☐	37 Mark Eichhorn	.05	.02	.00	☐	86 Bob Ojeda	.10	.04	.01
☐	38 Dwight Evans	.20	.08	.02	☐	87 Jesse Orosco	.05	.02	.00
☐	39 Tony Fernandez	.15	.06	.01	☐	88 Dave Parker	.15	.06	.01
☐	40 Bob Forsch	.05	.02	.00	☐	89 Larry Parrish	.05	.02	.00
☐	41 John Franco	.10	.04	.01	☐	90 Tony Pena	.05	.02	.00
☐	42 Julio Franco	.10	.04	.01	☐	91 Jim Presley	.10	.04	.01
☐	43 Gary Gaetti	.20	.08	.02	☐	92 Kirby Puckett	.75	.30	.07
☐	44 Gene Garber	.05	.02	.00	☐	93 Dan Quisenberry	.10	.04	.01
☐	45 Scott Garrelts	.05	.02	.00	☐	94 Tim Raines	.30	.12	.03
☐	46 Steve Garvey	.45	.18	.04	☐	95 Dennis Rasmussen	.10	.04	.01
☐	47 Kirk Gibson	.35	.14	.03	☐	96 Shane Rawley	.05	.02	.00
☐	48 Dwight Gooden	.75	.30	.07	☐	97 Johnny Ray	.10	.04	.01
☐	49 Ken Griffey Sr.	.10	.04	.01	☐	98 Jeff Reardon	.10	.04	.01
☐	50 Ozzie Guillen	.10	.04	.01	☐	99 Jim Rice	.25	.10	.02
☐	51 Bill Gullickson	.05	.02	.00	☐	100 Dave Righetti	.15	.06	.01
☐	52 Tony Gwynn	.45	.18	.04	☐	101 Cal Ripken Jr.	.40	.16	.04
☐	53 Mel Hall	.05	.02	.00	☐	102 Pete Rose	.75	.30	.07
☐	54 Greg Harris	.05	.02	.00	☐	103 Nolan Ryan	.50	.20	.05
☐	55 Von Hayes	.10	.04	.01	☐	104 Juan Samuel	.15	.06	.01
☐	56 Rickey Henderson	.50	.20	.05	☐	105 Ryne Sandberg	.25	.10	.02
☐	57 Tom Henke	.10	.04	.01	☐	106 Steve Sax	.15	.06	.01
☐	58 Keith Hernandez	.25	.10	.02	☐	107 Mike Schmidt	.60	.24	.06
☐	59 Willie Hernandez	.10	.04	.01	☐	108 Mike Scott	.20	.08	.02
☐	60 Ted Higuera	.25	.10	.02	☐	109 Dave Smith	.05	.02	.00
☐	61 Bob Horner	.20	.08	.02	☐	110 Lee Smith	.10	.04	.01
☐	62 Charlie Hough	.05	.02	.00	☐	111 Lonnie Smith	.05	.02	.00
☐	63 Jay Howell	.05	.02	.00	☐	112 Ozzie Smith	.20	.08	.02
☐	64 Kent Hrbek	.20	.08	.02	☐	113 Cory Snyder	.40	.16	.04
☐	65 Bruce Hurst	.20	.08	.02	☐	114 Darryl Strawberry	.60	.24	.06
☐	66 Pete Incaviglia	.25	.10	.02	☐	115 Don Sutton	.20	.08	.02

		MINT	EXC	G-VG
☐ 116	Kent Tekulve	.05	.02	.00
☐ 117	Andres Thomas	.10	.04	.01
☐ 118	Alan Trammell	.25	.10	.02
☐ 119	John Tudor	.15	.06	.01
☐ 120	Fernando Valenzuela	.20	.08	.02
☐ 121	Bob Welch	.10	.04	.01
☐ 122	Lou Whitaker	.15	.06	.01
☐ 123	Frank White	.10	.04	.01
☐ 124	Reggie Williams	.05	.02	.00
☐ 125	Willie Wilson	.10	.04	.01
☐ 126	Dave Winfield	.25	.10	.02
☐ 127	Mike Witt	.10	.04	.01
☐ 128	Todd Worrell	.20	.08	.02
☐ 129	Curt Young	.05	.02	.00
☐ 130	Robin Yount	.30	.12	.03
☐ 131	Checklist	2.00	.80	.20
	Jose Canseco			
	Don Mattingly			
☐ 132	Checklist	1.00	.40	.10
	Bo Jackson			
	Eric Davis			

1987 Fleer Update

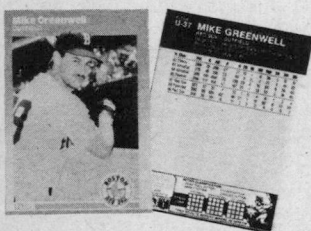

This 132-card set was distributed by Fleer to dealers as a complete set within a custom box. In addition to the complete set of 132 cards, the box also contains 25 Team Logo stickers. The card fronts look very similar to the 1987 Fleer regular issue. The cards are numbered (with a U prefix) alphabetically according to player's last name. Cards measure the standard size, 2 ½" by 3 ½".

Fleer misalphabetized Jim Winn in their set numbering by putting him ahead of the next four players listed.

		MINT	EXC	G-VG
Complete Set (132)		12.00	5.00	1.20
Common Player (1-132)		.05	.02	.00
☐ U1	Scott Bankhead	.10	.04	.01
☐ U2	Eric Bell	.10	.04	.01
☐ U3	Juan Beniquez	.05	.02	.00
☐ U4	Juan Berenguer	.05	.02	.00
☐ U5	Mike Birkbeck	.15	.06	.01
☐ U6	Randy Bockus	.10	.04	.01
☐ U7	Greg Booker	.05	.02	.00
☐ U8	Thad Bosley	.05	.02	.00
☐ U9	Greg Brock	.05	.02	.00
☐ U10	Bob Brower	.15	.06	.01
☐ U11	Chris Brown	.15	.06	.01
☐ U12	Jerry Browne	.05	.02	.00
☐ U13	Ralph Bryant	.10	.04	.01
☐ U14	DeWayne Buice	.10	.04	.01
☐ U15	Ellis Burks	1.75	.70	.17
☐ U16	Casey Candaele	.10	.04	.01
☐ U17	Steve Carlton	.30	.12	.03
☐ U18	Juan Castillo	.05	.02	.00
☐ U19	Chuck Crim	.10	.04	.01
☐ U20	Mark Davidson	.15	.06	.01
☐ U21	Mark Davis	.10	.04	.01
☐ U22	Storm Davis	.10	.04	.01
☐ U23	Bill Dawley	.05	.02	.00
☐ U24	Andre Dawson	.35	.14	.03
☐ U25	Brian Dayett	.05	.02	.00
☐ U26	Rick Dempsey	.05	.02	.00
☐ U27	Ken Dowell	.10	.04	.01
☐ U28	Dave Dravecky	.05	.02	.00
☐ U29	Mike Dunne	.30	.12	.03
☐ U30	Dennis Eckersley	.30	.12	.03
☐ U31	Cecil Fielder	.10	.04	.01
☐ U32	Brian Fisher	.10	.04	.01
☐ U33	Willie Fraser	.10	.04	.01
☐ U34	Ken Gerhart	.15	.06	.01
☐ U35	Jim Gott	.10	.04	.01
☐ U36	Dan Gladden	.10	.04	.01
☐ U37	Mike Greenwell	4.00	1.60	.40
☐ U38	Cecilio Guante	.05	.02	.00
☐ U39	Albert Hall	.05	.02	.00
☐ U40	Atlee Hammaker	.05	.02	.00
☐ U41	Mickey Hatcher	.10	.04	.01
☐ U42	Mike Heath	.05	.02	.00
☐ U43	Neal Heaton	.05	.02	.00

	MINT	EXC	G-VG
☐ U44 Mike Henneman ...	.35	.14	.03
☐ U45 Guy Hoffman	.10	.04	.01
☐ U46 Charles Hudson ...	.05	.02	.00
☐ U47 Chuck Jackson	.15	.06	.01
☐ U48 Mike Jackson	.15	.06	.01
☐ U49 Reggie Jackson ...	.40	.16	.04
☐ U50 Chris James	.35	.14	.03
☐ U51 Dion James	.10	.04	.01
☐ U52 Stan Javier	.10	.04	.01
☐ U53 Stan Jefferson	.25	.10	.02
☐ U54 Jimmy Jones	.15	.06	.01
☐ U55 Tracy Jones	.25	.10	.02
☐ U56 Terry Kennedy	.10	.04	.01
☐ U57 Mike Kingery	.10	.04	.01
☐ U58 Ray Knight	.10	.04	.01
☐ U59 Gene Larkin	.35	.14	.03
☐ U60 Mike LaValliere ...	.10	.04	.01
☐ U61 Jack Lazorko	.10	.04	.01
☐ U62 Terry Leach	.15	.06	.01
☐ U63 Rick Leach	.05	.02	.00
☐ U64 Craig Lefferts	.05	.02	.00
☐ U65 Jim Lindeman	.20	.08	.02
☐ U66 Bill Long	.15	.06	.01
☐ U67 Mike Loynd	.10	.04	.01
☐ U68 Greg Maddux	.75	.30	.07
☐ U69 Bill Madlock	.15	.06	.01
☐ U70 Dave Magadan ...	.25	.10	.02
☐ U71 Joe Magrane	.50	.20	.05
☐ U72 Fred Manrique ...	.15	.06	.01
☐ U73 Mike Mason	.05	.02	.00
☐ U74 Lloyd McClendon ..	.10	.04	.01
☐ U75 Fred McGriff	1.50	.60	.15
☐ U76 Mark McGwire	2.50	1.00	.25
☐ U77 Mark McLemore ...	.05	.02	.00
☐ U78 Kevin McReynolds ..	.25	.10	.02
☐ U79 Dave Meads	.10	.04	.01
☐ U80 Greg Minton	.05	.02	.00
☐ U81 John Mitchell	.15	.06	.01
☐ U82 Kevin Mitchell	.15	.06	.01
☐ U83 John Morris	.05	.02	.00
☐ U84 Jeff Musselman ...	.15	.06	.01
☐ U85 Randy Myers	.45	.18	.04
☐ U86 Gene Nelson	.05	.02	.00
☐ U87 Joe Niekro	.15	.06	.01
☐ U88 Tom Nieto	.05	.02	.00
☐ U89 Reid Nichols	.05	.02	.00
☐ U90 Matt Nokes	.65	.26	.06
☐ U91 Dickie Noles	.05	.02	.00
☐ U92 Edwin Nunez	.05	.02	.00

	MINT	EXC	G-VG
☐ U93 Jose Nunez	.15	.06	.01
☐ U94 Paul O'Neill	.10	.04	.01
☐ U95 Jim Paciorek	.10	.04	.01
☐ U96 Lance Parrish	.15	.06	.01
☐ U97 Bill Pecota	.15	.06	.01
☐ U98 Tony Pena	.15	.06	.01
☐ U99 Luis Polonia	.30	.12	.03
☐ U100 Randy Ready	.10	.04	.01
☐ U101 Jeff Reardon	.15	.06	.01
☐ U102 Gary Redus	.05	.02	.00
☐ U103 Rick Rhoden	.15	.06	.01
☐ U104 Wally Ritchie	.10	.04	.01
☐ U105 Jeff Robinson	.45	.18	.04
(wrong Jeff's stats on back)			
☐ U106 Mark Salas	.05	.02	.00
☐ U107 Dave Schmidt	.10	.04	.01
☐ U108 Kevin Seitzer ERR	1.50	.60	.15
(wrong birth year)			
☐ U109 John Shelby	.05	.02	.00
☐ U110 John Smiley	.35	.14	.03
☐ U111 Lary Sorensen	.05	.02	.00
☐ U112 Chris Speier	.05	.02	.00
☐ U113 Randy St.Claire	.05	.02	.00
☐ U114 Jim Sundberg	.05	.02	.00
☐ U115 B.J. Surhoff	.40	.16	.04
☐ U116 Greg Swindell	.40	.16	.04
☐ U117 Danny Tartabull ...	.40	.16	.04
☐ U118 Dorn Taylor	.10	.04	.01
☐ U119 Lee Tunnell	.05	.02	.00
☐ U120 Ed VandeBerg	.05	.02	.00
☐ U121 Andy Van Slyke ...	.20	.08	.02
☐ U122 Gary Ward	.10	.04	.01
☐ U123 Devon White	.35	.14	.03
☐ U124 Alan Wiggins	.05	.02	.00
☐ U125 Bill Wilkinson	.10	.04	.01
☐ U126 Jim Winn	.05	.02	.00
☐ U127 Frank Williams	.05	.02	.00
☐ U128 Ken Williams	.20	.08	.02
☐ U129 Matt Williams	.45	.18	.04
☐ U130 Herm Willingham ...	.10	.04	.01
☐ U131 Matt Young	.05	.02	.00
☐ U132 Checklist	.05	.01	.00

1988 Fleer

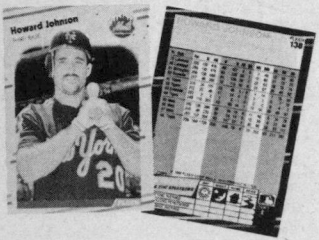

This 660-card set features a distinctive white background with red and blue diagonal stripes across the card. The backs are printed in gray and red on white card stock. The bottom of the card back shows an innovative breakdown of the player's demonstrated ability with respect to day, night, home, and road games. Cards are numbered on the back and are again the standard 2 ½" by 3 ½". Cards are again organized numerically by teams, i.e., World Champion Twins (1-25), St. Louis Cardinals (26-50), Detroit Tigers (51-75), San Francisco Giants (76-101), Toronto Blue Jays (102-126), New York Mets (127-154), Milwaukee Brewers (155-178), Montreal Expos (179-201), New York Yankees (202-226), Cincinnati Reds (227-250), Kansas City Royals (251-274), Oakland A's (275-296), Philadelphia Phillies (297-320), Pittsburgh Pirates (321-342), Boston Red Sox (343-367), Seattle Mariners (368-390), Chicago White Sox (391-413), Chicago Cubs (414-436), Houston Astros (437-460), Texas Rangers (461-483), California Angels (484-507), Los Angeles Dodgers (508-530), Atlanta Braves (531-552), Baltimore Orioles (553-575), San Diego Padres (576-599), and Cleveland Indians (600-621). The last 39 cards in the set consist of Specials (622-640), Rookie Pairs (641-653), and checklists (654-660). Cards 90 and 91 are incorrectly numbered on the checklist card #654.

			MINT	EXC	G-VG
	Complete Set (660)		28.00	11.50	2.80
	Common Player (1-660) ..		.03	.01	.00
☐	1	Keith Atherton	.03	.01	.00
☐	2	Don Baylor	.08	.03	.01
☐	3	Juan Berenguer ...	.03	.01	.00
☐	4	Bert Blyleven	.08	.03	.01
☐	5	Tom Brunansky	.10	.04	.01
☐	6	Randy Bush	.03	.01	.00
☐	7	Steve Carlton	.18	.08	.01
☐	8	Mark Davidson	.12	.05	.01
☐	9	George Frazier	.03	.01	.00
☐	10	Gary Gaetti	.12	.05	.01
☐	11	Greg Gagne	.03	.01	.00
☐	12	Dan Gladden	.06	.02	.00
☐	13	Kent Hrbek	.12	.05	.01
☐	14	Gene Larkin	.25	.10	.02
☐	15	Tim Laudner	.03	.01	.00
☐	16	Steve Lombardozzi	.03	.01	.00
☐	17	Al Newman	.03	.01	.00
☐	18	Joe Niekro	.06	.02	.00
☐	19	Kirby Puckett	.35	.14	.03
☐	20	Jeff Reardon	.06	.02	.00
☐	21A	Dan Schatzeder ERR	.12	.05	.01
	(misspelled Schatzader on card front)				
☐	21B	Dan Schatzeder COR	.06	.02	.00
☐	22	Roy Smalley	.03	.01	.00
☐	23	Mike Smithson	.03	.01	.00
☐	24	Les Straker	.10	.04	.01
☐	25	Frank Viola	.15	.06	.01
☐	26	Jack Clark	.15	.06	.01
☐	27	Vince Coleman	.20	.08	.02
☐	28	Danny Cox	.06	.02	.00
☐	29	Bill Dawley	.03	.01	.00
☐	30	Ken Dayley	.03	.01	.00
☐	31	Doug DeCinces ...	.06	.02	.00
☐	32	Curt Ford	.03	.01	.00
☐	33	Bob Forsch	.03	.01	.00
☐	34	David Green	.03	.01	.00
☐	35	Tom Herr	.06	.02	.00
☐	36	Ricky Horton	.03	.01	.00
☐	37	Lance Johnson	.20	.08	.02
☐	38	Steve Lake	.03	.01	.00
☐	39	Jim Lindeman	.08	.03	.01
☐	40	Joe Magrane	.30	.12	.03
☐	41	Greg Mathews	.03	.01	.00
☐	42	Willie McGee	.10	.04	.01
☐	43	John Morris	.03	.01	.00
☐	44	Jose Oquendo	.03	.01	.00
☐	45	Tony Pena	.06	.02	.00

			MINT	EXC	G-VG				MINT	EXC	G-VG
☐	46	Terry Pendleton ...	.03	.01	.00	☐	90	Eddie Milner	.03	.01	.00
☐	47	Ozzie Smith	.12	.05	.01	☐	91	Bob Melvin	.03	.01	.00
☐	48	John Tudor	.08	.03	.01	☐	92	Kevin Mitchell	.06	.02	.00
☐	49	Lee Tunnell	.03	.01	.00	☐	93	Jon Perlman	.10	.04	.01
☐	50	Todd Worrell	.10	.04	.01	☐	94	Rick Reuschel	.06	.02	.00
☐	51	Doyle Alexander ...	.03	.01	.00	☐	95	Don Robinson	.03	.01	.00
☐	52	Dave Bergman	.03	.01	.00	☐	96	Chris Speier	.03	.01	.00
☐	53	Tom Brookens	.03	.01	.00	☐	97	Harry Spilman	.03	.01	.00
☐	54	Darrell Evans	.08	.03	.01	☐	98	Robbie Thompson .	.06	.02	.00
☐	55	Kirk Gibson	.20	.08	.02	☐	99	Jose Uribe	.03	.01	.00
☐	56	Mike Heath	.03	.01	.00	☐	100	Mark Wasinger	.15	.06	.01
☐	57	Mike Henneman ...	.20	.08	.02	☐	101	Matt Williams	.35	.14	.03
☐	58	Willie Hernandez ..	.06	.02	.00	☐	102	Jesse Barfield	.15	.06	.01
☐	59	Larry Herndon	.03	.01	.00	☐	103	George Bell	.18	.08	.01
☐	60	Eric King	.03	.01	.00	☐	104	Juan Beniquez	.03	.01	.00
☐	61	Chet Lemon	.03	.01	.00	☐	105	John Cerutti	.03	.01	.00
☐	62	Scott Lusader	.15	.06	.01	☐	106	Jim Clancy	.03	.01	.00
☐	63	Bill Madlock	.06	.02	.00	☐	107	Rob Ducey	.20	.08	.02
☐	64	Jack Morris	.12	.05	.01	☐	108	Mark Eichhorn	.03	.01	.00
☐	65	Jim Morrison	.03	.01	.00	☐	109	Tony Fernandez ...	.10	.04	.01
☐	66	Matt Nokes	.50	.20	.05	☐	110	Cecil Fielder	.03	.01	.00
☐	67	Dan Petry	.03	.01	.00	☐	111	Kelly Gruber	.03	.01	.00
☐	68A	Jeff Robinson ERR .	.50	.20	.05	☐	112	Tom Henke	.06	.02	.00
		Detroit Tigers				☐	113A	Garth Iorg ERR ...	.12	.05	.01
		(stats for other Jeff						(misspelled Iorq on card front)			
		Robinson on card back)				☐	113B	Garth Iorg COR ...	.06	.02	.00
☐	68B	Jeff Robinson COR .	.40	.16	.04	☐	114	Jimmy Key	.08	.03	.01
		Detroit Tigers				☐	115	Rick Leach	.03	.01	.00
☐	69	Pat Sheridan	.03	.01	.00	☐	116	Manny Lee	.08	.03	.01
☐	70	Nate Snell	.03	.01	.00	☐	117	Nelson Liriano	.15	.06	.01
☐	71	Frank Tanana	.03	.01	.00	☐	118	Fred McGriff	.70	.28	.07
☐	72	Walt Terrell	.03	.01	.00	☐	119	Lloyd Moseby	.08	.03	.01
☐	73	Mark Thurmond ...	.03	.01	.00	☐	120	Rance Mulliniks ...	.03	.01	.00
☐	74	Alan Trammell	.15	.06	.01	☐	121	Jeff Musselman ...	.08	.03	.01
☐	75	Lou Whitaker	.10	.04	.01	☐	122	Jose Nunez	.15	.06	.01
☐	76	Mike Aldrete	.06	.02	.00	☐	123	Dave Stieb	.08	.03	.01
☐	77	Bob Brenly	.03	.01	.00	☐	124	Willie Upshaw	.03	.01	.00
☐	78	Will Clark	.75	.30	.07	☐	125	Duane Ward	.08	.03	.01
☐	79	Chili Davis	.06	.02	.00	☐	126	Ernie Whitt	.03	.01	.00
☐	80	Kelly Downs	.06	.02	.00	☐	127	Rick Aguilera	.03	.01	.00
☐	81	Dave Dravecky	.03	.01	.00	☐	128	Wally Backman	.03	.01	.00
☐	82	Scott Garrelts	.03	.01	.00	☐	129	Mark Carreon	.12	.05	.01
☐	83	Atlee Hammaker ...	.03	.01	.00	☐	130	Gary Carter	.20	.08	.02
☐	84	Dave Henderson ...	.06	.02	.00	☐	131	David Cone	1.25	.50	.12
☐	85	Mike Krukow	.03	.01	.00	☐	132	Ron Darling	.12	.05	.01
☐	86	Mike LaCoss	.03	.01	.00	☐	133	Len Dykstra	.08	.03	.01
☐	87	Craig Lefferts	.03	.01	.00	☐	134	Sid Fernandez	.08	.03	.01
☐	88	Jeff Leonard	.06	.02	.00	☐	135	Dwight Gooden	.60	.24	.06
☐	89	Candy Maldonado ..	.06	.02	.00	☐	136	Keith Hernandez ..	.20	.08	.02

		MINT	EXC	G-VG
☐ 137	Gregg Jefferies	7.50	3.00	.75
☐ 138	Howard Johnson ...	.08	.03	.01
☐ 139	Terry Leach	.06	.02	.00
☐ 140	Barry Lyons	.10	.04	.01
☐ 141	Dave Magadan	.08	.03	.01
☐ 142	Roger McDowell ...	.06	.02	.00
☐ 143	Kevin McReynolds .	.15	.06	.01
☐ 144	Keith Miller .... (New York Mets)	.20	.08	.02
☐ 145	John Mitchell	.15	.06	.01
☐ 146	Randy Myers	.25	.10	.02
☐ 147	Bob Ojeda	.06	.02	.00
☐ 148	Jesse Orosco	.03	.01	.00
☐ 149	Rafael Santana	.03	.01	.00
☐ 150	Doug Sisk	.03	.01	.00
☐ 151	Darryl Strawberry ..	.45	.18	.04
☐ 152	Tim Teufel	.03	.01	.00
☐ 153	Gene Walter	.03	.01	.00
☐ 154	Mookie Wilson	.03	.01	.00
☐ 155	Jay Aldrich	.10	.04	.01
☐ 156	Chris Bosio	.03	.01	.00
☐ 157	Glenn Braggs	.08	.03	.01
☐ 158	Greg Brock	.03	.01	.00
☐ 159	Juan Castillo	.06	.02	.00
☐ 160	Mark Clear	.03	.01	.00
☐ 161	Cecil Cooper	.08	.03	.01
☐ 162	Chuck Crim	.10	.04	.01
☐ 163	Rob Deer	.08	.03	.01
☐ 164	Mike Felder	.03	.01	.00
☐ 165	Jim Gantner	.03	.01	.00
☐ 166	Ted Higuera	.10	.04	.01
☐ 167	Steve Kiefer	.03	.01	.00
☐ 168	Rick Manning	.03	.01	.00
☐ 169	Paul Molitor	.12	.05	.01
☐ 170	Juan Nieves	.03	.01	.00
☐ 171	Dan Plesac	.06	.02	.00
☐ 172	Earnest Riles	.03	.01	.00
☐ 173	Bill Schroeder	.03	.01	.00
☐ 174	Steve Stanicek	.15	.06	.01
☐ 175	B.J. Surhoff	.15	.06	.01
☐ 176	Dale Sveum	.03	.01	.00
☐ 177	Bill Wegman	.03	.01	.00
☐ 178	Robin Yount	.25	.10	.02
☐ 179	Hubie Brooks	.06	.02	.00
☐ 180	Tim Burke	.03	.01	.00
☐ 181	Casey Candaele ...	.03	.01	.00
☐ 182	Mike Fitzgerald ...	.03	.01	.00
☐ 183	Tom Foley	.03	.01	.00
☐ 184	Andres Galarraga ..	.30	.12	.03

		MINT	EXC	G-VG
☐ 185	Neal Heaton	.03	.01	.00
☐ 186	Wallace Johnson ..	.03	.01	.00
☐ 187	Vance Law	.03	.01	.00
☐ 188	Dennis Martinez ...	.03	.01	.00
☐ 189	Bob McClure	.03	.01	.00
☐ 190	Andy McGaffigan ..	.03	.01	.00
☐ 191	Reid Nichols	.03	.01	.00
☐ 192	Pascual Perez	.06	.02	.00
☐ 193	Tim Raines	.20	.08	.02
☐ 194	Jeff Reed	.03	.01	.00
☐ 195	Bob Sebra	.03	.01	.00
☐ 196	Bryn Smith	.03	.01	.00
☐ 197	Randy St.Claire ...	.03	.01	.00
☐ 198	Tim Wallach	.08	.03	.01
☐ 199	Mitch Webster	.03	.01	.00
☐ 200	Herm Winningham ..	.03	.01	.00
☐ 201	Floyd Youmans	.03	.01	.00
☐ 202	Brad Arnsberg	.10	.04	.01
☐ 203	Rick Cerone	.03	.01	.00
☐ 204	Pat Clements	.03	.01	.00
☐ 205	Henry Cotto	.03	.01	.00
☐ 206	Mike Easler	.03	.01	.00
☐ 207	Ron Guidry	.08	.03	.01
☐ 208	Bill Gullickson	.03	.01	.00
☐ 209	Rickey Henderson .	.25	.10	.02
☐ 210	Charles Hudson ...	.03	.01	.00
☐ 211	Tommy John	.10	.04	.01
☐ 212	Roberto Kelly	.35	.14	.03
☐ 213	Ron Kittle	.08	.03	.01
☐ 214	Don Mattingly	1.50	.60	.15
☐ 215	Bobby Meacham ...	.03	.01	.00
☐ 216	Mike Pagliarulo ...	.08	.03	.01
☐ 217	Dan Pasqua	.06	.02	.00
☐ 218	Willie Randolph ...	.06	.02	.00
☐ 219	Rick Rhoden	.03	.01	.00
☐ 220	Dave Righetti	.08	.03	.01
☐ 221	Jerry Royster	.03	.01	.00
☐ 222	Tim Stoddard	.03	.01	.00
☐ 223	Wayne Tolleson ...	.03	.01	.00
☐ 224	Gary Ward	.03	.01	.00
☐ 225	Claudell Washington	.06	.02	.00
☐ 226	Dave Winfield	.25	.10	.02
☐ 227	Buddy Bell	.08	.03	.01
☐ 228	Tom Browning	.10	.04	.01
☐ 229	Dave Concepcion ..	.08	.03	.01
☐ 230	Kal Daniels	.20	.08	.01
☐ 231	Eric Davis	.80	.32	.08
☐ 232	Bo Diaz	.03	.01	.00
☐ 233	Nick Esasky	.03	.01	.00

	MINT	EXC	G-VG			MINT	EXC	G-VG
☐ 234 John Franco	.08	.03	.01	☐ 282 Jay Howell	.03	.01	.00
☐ 235 Guy Hoffman	.03	.01	.00	☐ 283 Reggie Jackson	.30	.12	.03
☐ 236 Tom Hume	.03	.01	.00	☐ 284 Dennis Lamp	.03	.01	.00
☐ 237 Tracy Jones	.06	.02	.00	☐ 285 Carney Lansford	.08	.03	.01
☐ 238 Bill Landrum	.10	.04	.01	☐ 286 Mark McGwire	1.25	.50	.12
☐ 239 Barry Larkin	.15	.06	.01	☐ 287 Dwayne Murphy	.03	.01	.00
☐ 240 Terry McGriff	.10	.04	.01	☐ 288 Gene Nelson	.03	.01	.00
☐ 241 Rob Murphy	.03	.01	.00	☐ 289 Steve Ontiveros	.03	.01	.00
☐ 242 Ron Oester	.03	.01	.00	☐ 290 Tony Phillips	.03	.01	.00
☐ 243 Dave Parker	.10	.04	.01	☐ 291 Eric Plunk	.03	.01	.00
☐ 244 Pat Perry	.03	.01	.00	☐ 292 Luis Polonia	.25	.10	.02
☐ 245 Ted Power	.03	.01	.00	☐ 293 Rick Rodriguez	.10	.04	.01
☐ 246 Dennis Rasmussen	.06	.02	.00	☐ 294 Terry Steinbach	.10	.04	.01
☐ 247 Ron Robinson	.03	.01	.00	☐ 295 Dave Stewart	.08	.03	.01
☐ 248 Kurt Stillwell	.06	.02	.00	☐ 296 Curt Young	.03	.01	.00
☐ 249 Jeff Treadway	.30	.12	.03	☐ 297 Luis Aguayo	.03	.01	.00
☐ 250 Frank Williams	.03	.01	.00	☐ 298 Steve Bedrosian	.08	.03	.01
☐ 251 Steve Balboni	.03	.01	.00	☐ 299 Jeff Calhoun	.03	.01	.00
☐ 252 Bud Black	.03	.01	.00	☐ 300 Don Carman	.03	.01	.00
☐ 253 Thad Bosley	.03	.01	.00	☐ 301 Todd Frohwirth	.15	.06	.01
☐ 254 George Brett	.30	.12	.03	☐ 302 Greg Gross	.03	.01	.00
☐ 255 John Davis	.15	.06	.01	☐ 303 Kevin Gross	.03	.01	.00
☐ 256 Steve Farr	.03	.01	.00	☐ 304 Von Hayes	.08	.03	.01
☐ 257 Gene Garber	.03	.01	.00	☐ 305 Keith Hughes	.20	.08	.02
☐ 258 Jerry Don Gleaton	.03	.01	.00	☐ 306 Mike Jackson	.15	.06	.01
☐ 259 Mark Gubicza	.08	.03	.01	☐ 307 Chris James	.15	.06	.01
☐ 260 Bo Jackson	.30	.12	.03	☐ 308 Steve Jeltz	.03	.01	.00
☐ 261 Danny Jackson	.15	.06	.01	☐ 309 Mike Maddux	.03	.01	.00
☐ 262 Ross Jones	.10	.04	.01	☐ 310 Lance Parrish	.10	.04	.01
☐ 263 Charlie Leibrandt	.03	.01	.00	☐ 311 Shane Rawley	.03	.01	.00
☐ 264 Bill Pecota	.10	.04	.01	☐ 312 Wally Ritchie	.10	.04	.01
☐ 265 Melido Perez	.25	.10	.02	☐ 313 Bruce Ruffin	.03	.01	.00
☐ 266 Jamie Quirk	.03	.01	.00	☐ 314 Juan Samuel	.08	.03	.01
☐ 267 Dan Quisenberry	.08	.03	.01	☐ 315 Mike Schmidt	.30	.12	.03
☐ 268 Bret Saberhagen	.12	.05	.01	☐ 316 Rick Schu	.03	.01	.00
☐ 269 Angel Salazar	.03	.01	.00	☐ 317 Jeff Stone	.03	.01	.00
☐ 270 Kevin Seitzer UER	.70	.28	.07	☐ 318 Kent Tekulve	.03	.01	.00
(wrong birth year)				☐ 319 Milt Thompson	.03	.01	.00
☐ 271 Danny Tartabull	.20	.08	.02	☐ 320 Glenn Wilson	.03	.01	.00
☐ 272 Gary Thurman	.25	.10	.02	☐ 321 Rafael Belliard	.03	.01	.00
☐ 273 Frank White	.06	.02	.00	☐ 322 Barry Bonds	.20	.08	.02
☐ 274 Willie Wilson	.08	.03	.01	☐ 323 Bobby Bonilla UER	.20	.08	.02
☐ 275 Tony Bernazard	.03	.01	.00	(wrong birth year)			
☐ 276 Jose Canseco	2.00	.80	.20	☐ 324 Sid Bream	.03	.01	.00
☐ 277 Mike Davis	.03	.01	.00	☐ 325 John Cangelosi	.03	.01	.00
☐ 278 Storm Davis	.06	.02	.00	☐ 326 Mike Diaz	.03	.01	.00
☐ 279 Dennis Eckersley	.12	.05	.01	☐ 327 Doug Drabek	.03	.01	.00
☐ 280 Alfredo Griffin	.06	.02	.00	☐ 328 Mike Dunne	.20	.08	.02
☐ 281 Rick Honeycutt	.03	.01	.00	☐ 329 Brian Fisher	.03	.01	.00

		MINT	EXC	G-VG
☐ 330	Brett Gideon	.12	.05	.01
☐ 331	Terry Harper	.03	.01	.00
☐ 332	Bob Kipper	.03	.01	.00
☐ 333	Mike LaValliere	.03	.01	.00
☐ 334	Jose Lind	.30	.12	.03
☐ 335	Junior Ortiz	.03	.01	.00
☐ 336	Vincent Palacios	.12	.05	.01
☐ 337	Bob Patterson	.10	.04	.01
☐ 338	Al Pedrique	.10	.04	.01
☐ 339	R.J. Reynolds	.03	.01	.00
☐ 340	John Smiley	.25	.10	.02
☐ 341	Andy Van Slyke UER	.15	.06	.01
	(wrong batting and throwing listed)			
☐ 342	Bob Walk	.03	.01	.00
☐ 343	Marty Barrett	.06	.02	.00
☐ 344	Todd Benzinger	.40	.16	.04
☐ 345	Wade Boggs	1.00	.40	.10
☐ 346	Tom Bolton	.15	.06	.01
☐ 347	Oil Can Boyd	.06	.02	.00
☐ 348	Ellis Burks	1.25	.50	.12
☐ 349	Roger Clemens	.75	.30	.07
☐ 350	Steve Crawford	.10	.04	.01
☐ 351	Dwight Evans	.10	.04	.01
☐ 352	Wes Gardner	.30	.12	.03
☐ 353	Rich Gedman	.06	.02	.00
☐ 354	Mike Greenwell	2.00	.80	.20
☐ 355	Sam Horn	.35	.14	.03
☐ 356	Bruce Hurst	.10	.04	.01
☐ 357	John Marzano	.12	.05	.01
☐ 358	Al Nipper	.03	.01	.00
☐ 359	Spike Owen	.03	.01	.00
☐ 360	Jody Reed	.50	.20	.05
☐ 361	Jim Rice	.15	.06	.01
☐ 362	Ed Romero	.03	.01	.00
☐ 363	Kevin Romine	.12	.05	.01
☐ 364	Joe Sambito	.03	.01	.00
☐ 365	Calvin Schiraldi	.03	.01	.00
☐ 366	Jeff Sellers	.03	.01	.00
☐ 367	Bob Stanley	.03	.01	.00
☐ 368	Scott Bankhead	.03	.01	.00
☐ 369	Phil Bradley	.08	.03	.01
☐ 370	Scott Bradley	.03	.01	.00
☐ 371	Mickey Brantley	.08	.03	.01
☐ 372	Mike Campbell	.15	.06	.01
☐ 373	Alvin Davis	.08	.03	.01
☐ 374	Lee Guetterman	.03	.01	.00
☐ 375	Dave Hengel	.15	.06	.01
☐ 376	Mike Kingery	.03	.01	.00
☐ 377	Mark Langston	.08	.03	.01
☐ 378	Edgar Martinez	.25	.10	.02
☐ 379	Mike Moore	.03	.01	.00
☐ 380	Mike Morgan	.03	.01	.00
☐ 381	John Moses	.03	.01	.00
☐ 382	Donnell Nixon	.15	.06	.01
☐ 383	Edwin Nunez	.03	.01	.00
☐ 384	Ken Phelps	.06	.02	.00
☐ 385	Jim Presley	.08	.03	.01
☐ 386	Rey Quinones	.03	.01	.00
☐ 387	Jerry Reed	.03	.01	.00
☐ 388	Harold Reynolds	.03	.01	.00
☐ 389	Dave Valle	.06	.02	.00
☐ 390	Bill Wilkinson	.10	.04	.01
☐ 391	Harold Baines	.10	.04	.01
☐ 392	Floyd Bannister	.03	.01	.00
☐ 393	Daryl Boston	.03	.01	.00
☐ 394	Ivan Calderon	.08	.03	.01
☐ 395	Jose DeLeon	.03	.01	.00
☐ 396	Richard Dotson	.06	.02	.00
☐ 397	Carlton Fisk	.10	.04	.01
☐ 398	Ozzie Guillen	.06	.02	.00
☐ 399	Ron Hassey	.03	.01	.00
☐ 400	Donnie Hill	.03	.01	.00
☐ 401	Bob James	.03	.01	.00
☐ 402	Dave LaPoint	.03	.01	.00
☐ 403	Bill Lindsey	.10	.04	.01
☐ 404	Bill Long	.10	.04	.01
☐ 405	Steve Lyons	.03	.01	.00
☐ 406	Fred Manrique	.10	.04	.01
☐ 407	Jack McDowell	.25	.10	.02
☐ 408	Gary Redus	.03	.01	.00
☐ 409	Ray Searage	.03	.01	.00
☐ 410	Bobby Thigpen	.06	.02	.00
☐ 411	Greg Walker	.06	.02	.00
☐ 412	Ken Williams	.20	.08	.02
☐ 413	Jim Winn	.03	.01	.00
☐ 414	Jody Davis	.06	.02	.00
☐ 415	Andre Dawson	.25	.10	.02
☐ 416	Brian Dayett	.03	.01	.00
☐ 417	Bob Dernier	.03	.01	.00
☐ 418	Frank DiPino	.03	.01	.00
☐ 419	Shawon Dunston	.06	.02	.00
☐ 420	Leon Durham	.06	.02	.00
☐ 421	Les Lancaster	.10	.04	.01
☐ 422	Ed Lynch	.03	.01	.00
☐ 423	Greg Maddux	.45	.18	.04
☐ 424	Dave Martinez	.10	.04	.01
☐ 425A	Keith Moreland ERR	4.00	1.60	.40
	(photo actually Jody Davis)			

	MINT	EXC	G-VG		MINT	EXC	G-VG
☐ 425B Keith Moreland COR (bat on shoulder)	.15	.06	.01	☐ 469 Charlie Hough	.03	.01	.00
				☐ 470 Pete Incaviglia	.18	.08	.01
☐ 426 Jamie Moyer	.03	.01	.00	☐ 471 Paul Kilgus	.15	.06	.01
☐ 427 Jerry Mumphrey	.03	.01	.00	☐ 472 Mike Loynd	.03	.01	.00
☐ 428 Paul Noce	.12	.05	.01	☐ 473 Oddibe McDowell	.08	.03	.01
☐ 429 Rafael Palmeiro	.70	.28	.07	☐ 474 Dale Mohorcic	.03	.01	.00
☐ 430 Wade Bowdon	.08	.03	.01	☐ 475 Pete O'Brien	.08	.03	.01
☐ 431 Ryne Sandberg	.20	.08	.02	☐ 476 Larry Parrish	.03	.01	.00
☐ 432 Scott Sanderson	.03	.01	.00	☐ 477 Geno Petralli	.03	.01	.00
☐ 433 Lee Smith	.06	.02	.00	☐ 478 Jeff Russell	.03	.01	.00
☐ 434 Jim Sundberg	.03	.01	.00	☐ 479 Ruben Sierra	.20	.08	.02
☐ 435 Rick Sutcliffe	.08	.03	.01	☐ 480 Mike Stanley	.03	.01	.00
☐ 436 Manny Trillo	.03	.01	.00	☐ 481 Curtis Wilkerson	.03	.01	.00
☐ 437 Juan Agosto	.03	.01	.00	☐ 482 Mitch Williams	.03	.01	.00
☐ 438 Larry Andersen	.03	.01	.00	☐ 483 Bobby Witt	.06	.02	.00
☐ 439 Alan Ashby	.03	.01	.00	☐ 484 Tony Armas	.06	.02	.00
☐ 440 Kevin Bass	.06	.02	.00	☐ 485 Bob Boone	.06	.02	.00
☐ 441 Ken Caminiti	.20	.08	.02	☐ 486 Bill Buckner	.06	.02	.00
☐ 442 Rocky Childress	.10	.04	.01	☐ 487 DeWayne Buice	.12	.05	.01
☐ 443 Jose Cruz	.06	.02	.00	☐ 488 Brian Downing	.03	.01	.00
☐ 444 Danny Darwin	.03	.01	.00	☐ 489 Chuck Finley	.03	.01	.00
☐ 445 Glenn Davis	.15	.06	.01	☐ 490 Willie Fraser UER (wrong bio stats, for George Hendrick)	.03	.01	.00
☐ 446 Jim Deshaies	.03	.01	.00				
☐ 447 Bill Doran	.06	.02	.00				
☐ 448 Ty Gainey	.03	.01	.00	☐ 491 Jack Howell	.03	.01	.00
☐ 449 Billy Hatcher	.06	.02	.00	☐ 492 Ruppert Jones	.03	.01	.00
☐ 450 Jeff Heathcock	.03	.01	.00	☐ 493 Wally Joyner	.45	.18	.04
☐ 451 Bob Knepper	.06	.02	.00	☐ 494 Jack Lazorko	.03	.01	.00
☐ 452 Rob Mallicoat	.10	.04	.01	☐ 495 Gary Lucas	.03	.01	.00
☐ 453 Dave Meads	.08	.03	.01	☐ 496 Kirk McCaskill	.03	.01	.00
☐ 454 Craig Reynolds	.03	.01	.00	☐ 497 Mark McLemore	.03	.01	.00
☐ 455 Nolan Ryan	.30	.12	.03	☐ 498 Darrell Miller	.03	.01	.00
☐ 456 Mike Scott	.15	.06	.01	☐ 499 Greg Minton	.03	.01	.00
☐ 457 Dave Smith	.03	.01	.00	☐ 500 Donnie Moore	.03	.01	.00
☐ 458 Denny Walling	.03	.01	.00	☐ 501 Gus Polidor	.03	.01	.00
☐ 459 Robbie Wine	.10	.04	.01	☐ 502 Johnny Ray	.06	.02	.00
☐ 460 Gerald Young	.30	.12	.03	☐ 503 Mark Ryal	.06	.02	.00
☐ 461 Bob Brower	.10	.04	.01	☐ 504 Dick Schofield	.03	.01	.00
☐ 462A Jerry Browne ERR (photo actually Bob Brower, white player)	4.00	1.60	.40	☐ 505 Don Sutton	.12	.05	.01
				☐ 506 Devon White	.15	.06	.01
				☐ 507 Mike Witt	.08	.03	.01
☐ 462B Jerry Browne COR (black player)	.15	.06	.01	☐ 508 Dave Anderson	.03	.01	.00
				☐ 509 Tim Belcher	.25	.10	.02
☐ 463 Steve Buechele	.03	.01	.00	☐ 510 Ralph Bryant	.03	.01	.00
☐ 464 Edwin Correa	.03	.01	.00	☐ 511 Tim Crews	.10	.04	.01
☐ 465 Cecil Espy	.15	.06	.01	☐ 512 Mike Devereaux	.30	.12	.03
☐ 466 Scott Fletcher	.03	.01	.00	☐ 513 Mariano Duncan	.03	.01	.00
☐ 467 Jose Guzman	.03	.01	.00	☐ 514 Pedro Guerrero	.15	.06	.01
☐ 468 Greg Harris	.03	.01	.00	☐ 515 Jeff Hamilton	.10	.04	.01

		MINT	EXC	G-VG
☐ 516	Mickey Hatcher	.06	.02	.00
☐ 517	Brad Havens	.03	.01	.00
☐ 518	Orel Hershiser	.25	.10	.02
☐ 519	Shawn Hillegas	.15	.06	.01
☐ 520	Ken Howell	.03	.01	.00
☐ 521	Tim Leary	.08	.03	.01
☐ 522	Mike Marshall	.10	.04	.01
☐ 523	Steve Sax	.15	.06	.01
☐ 524	Mike Scioscia	.03	.01	.00
☐ 525	Mike Sharperson ...	.06	.02	.00
☐ 526	John Shelby	.03	.01	.00
☐ 527	Franklin Stubbs	.03	.01	.00
☐ 528	Fernando Valenzuela	.15	.06	.01
☐ 529	Bob Welch	.06	.02	.00
☐ 530	Matt Young	.03	.01	.00
☐ 531	Jim Acker	.03	.01	.00
☐ 532	Paul Assenmacher .	.03	.01	.00
☐ 533	Jeff Blauser	.20	.08	.02
☐ 534	Joe Boever	.15	.06	.01
☐ 535	Martin Clary	.06	.02	.00
☐ 536	Kevin Coffman	.10	.04	.01
☐ 537	Jeff Dedmon	.03	.01	.00
☐ 538	Ron Gant	.70	.28	.07
☐ 539	Tom Glavine	.20	.08	.02
☐ 540	Ken Griffey	.06	.02	.00
☐ 541	Albert Hall	.03	.01	.00
☐ 542	Glenn Hubbard	.03	.01	.00
☐ 543	Dion James	.03	.01	.00
☐ 544	Dale Murphy	.30	.12	.03
☐ 545	Ken Oberkfell	.03	.01	.00
☐ 546	David Palmer	.03	.01	.00
☐ 547	Gerald Perry	.08	.03	.01
☐ 548	Charlie Puleo	.03	.01	.00
☐ 549	Ted Simmons	.08	.03	.01
☐ 550	Zane Smith	.06	.02	.00
☐ 551	Andres Thomas ...	.03	.01	.00
☐ 552	Ozzie Virgil	.03	.01	.00
☐ 553	Don Aase	.03	.01	.00
☐ 554	Jeff Ballard	.15	.06	.01
☐ 555	Eric Bell	.06	.02	.00
☐ 556	Mike Boddicker	.06	.02	.00
☐ 557	Ken Dixon	.03	.01	.00
☐ 558	Jim Dwyer	.03	.01	.00
☐ 559	Ken Gerhart	.08	.03	.01
☐ 560	Rene Gonzales	.12	.05	.01
☐ 561	Mike Griffin	.03	.01	.00
☐ 562	John Habyan UER . (misspelled Hayban on both sides of card)	.08	.03	.01
☐ 563	Terry Kennedy	.03	.01	.00
☐ 564	Ray Knight	.06	.02	.00
☐ 565	Lee Lacy	.03	.01	.00
☐ 566	Fred Lynn	.12	.05	.01
☐ 567	Eddie Murray	.20	.08	.02
☐ 568	Tom Niedenfuer ...	.03	.01	.00
☐ 569	Bill Ripken	.15	.06	.01
☐ 570	Cal Ripken Jr.	.20	.08	.02
☐ 571	Dave Schmidt	.03	.01	.00
☐ 572	Larry Sheets	.08	.03	.01
☐ 573	Pete Stanicek	.20	.08	.02
☐ 574	Mark Williamson ..	.10	.04	.01
☐ 575	Mike Young	.03	.01	.00
☐ 576	Shawn Abner	.20	.08	.02
☐ 577	Greg Booker	.03	.01	.00
☐ 578	Chris Brown	.08	.03	.01
☐ 579	Keith Comstock ...	.12	.05	.01
☐ 580	Joey Cora	.12	.05	.01
☐ 581	Mark Davis	.06	.02	.00
☐ 582	Tim Flannery ..... (with surfboard)	.03	.01	.00
☐ 583	Goose Gossage ...	.08	.03	.01
☐ 584	Mark Grant	.03	.01	.00
☐ 585	Tony Gwynn	.35	.14	.03
☐ 586	Andy Hawkins	.03	.01	.00
☐ 587	Stan Jefferson ...	.25	.10	.02
☐ 588	Jimmy Jones	.06	.02	.00
☐ 589	John Kruk	.10	.04	.01
☐ 590	Shane Mack	.18	.08	.01
☐ 591	Carmelo Martinez .	.03	.01	.00
☐ 592	Lance McCullers ..	.06	.02	.00
☐ 593	Eric Nolte	.15	.06	.01
☐ 594	Randy Ready	.03	.01	.00
☐ 595	Luis Salazar	.03	.01	.00
☐ 596	Benito Santiago ..	.40	.16	.04
☐ 597	Eric Show	.03	.01	.00
☐ 598	Garry Templeton ..	.06	.02	.00
☐ 599	Ed Whitson	.03	.01	.00
☐ 600	Scott Bailes	.03	.01	.00
☐ 601	Chris Bando	.03	.01	.00
☐ 602	Jay Bell	.20	.08	.02
☐ 603	Brett Butler	.06	.02	.00
☐ 604	Tom Candiotti	.03	.01	.00
☐ 605	Joe Carter	.12	.05	.01
☐ 606	Carmen Castillo ..	.03	.01	.00
☐ 607	Brian Dorsett	.12	.05	.01
☐ 608	John Farrell	.25	.10	.02
☐ 609	Julio Franco	.08	.03	.01
☐ 610	Mel Hall	.03	.01	.00

		MINT	EXC	G-VG
☐ 611	Tommy Hinzo	.10	.04	.01
☐ 612	Brook Jacoby	.08	.03	.01
☐ 613	Doug Jones	.35	.14	.03
☐ 614	Ken Schrom	.03	.01	.00
☐ 615	Cory Snyder	.20	.08	.02
☐ 616	Sammy Stewart ...	.03	.01	.00
☐ 617	Greg Swindell	.12	.05	.01
☐ 618	Pat Tabler	.06	.02	.00
☐ 619	Ed VandeBerg	.03	.01	.00
☐ 620	Eddie Williams	.18	.08	.01
☐ 621	Rich Yett	.03	.01	.00
☐ 622	Slugging Sophomores	.12	.05	.01
	Wally Joyner			
	Cory Snyder			
☐ 623	Dominican Dynamite	.10	.04	.01
	George Bell			
	Pedro Guerrero			
☐ 624	Oakland's Power Team	.75	.30	.07
	Mark McGwire			
	Jose Canseco			
☐ 625	Classic Relief	.10	.04	.01
	Dave Righetti			
	Dan Plesac			
☐ 626	All Star Righties ...	.10	.04	.01
	Bret Saberhagen			
	Mike Witt			
	Jack Morris			
☐ 627	Game Closers	.08	.03	.01
	John Franco			
	Steve Bedrosian			
☐ 628	Masters/Double Play	.10	.04	.01
	Ozzie Smith			
	Ryne Sandberg			
☐ 629	Rookie Record Setter	.40	.16	.04
	Mark McGwire			
☐ 630	Changing the Guard	.75	.30	.07
	Mike Greenwell			
	Ellis Burks			
	Todd Benzinger			
☐ 631	NL Batting Champs .	.18	.08	.01
	Tony Gwynn			
	Tim Raines			
☐ 632	Pitching Magic	.15	.06	.01
	Mike Scott			
	Orel Hershiser			
☐ 633	Big Bats at First ...	.30	.12	.03
	Pat Tabler			
	Mark McGwire			

		MINT	EXC	G-VG
☐ 634	Hitting King/Thief ..	.12	.05	.01
	Tony Gwynn			
	Vince Coleman			
☐ 635	Slugging Shortstops	.12	.05	.01
	Tony Fernandez			
	Cal Ripken			
	Alan Trammell			
☐ 636	Tried/True Sluggers	.12	.05	.01
	Mike Schmidt			
	Gary Carter			
☐ 637	Crunch Time	.35	.14	.03
	Darryl Strawberry			
	Eric Davis			
☐ 638	AL All-Stars	.15	.06	.01
	Matt Nokes			
	Kirby Puckett			
☐ 639	NL All-Stars ...., ..	.12	.05	.01
	Keith Hernandez			
	Dale Murphy			
☐ 640	The O's Brothers ..	.08	.03	.01
	Billy Ripken			
	Cal Ripken			
☐ 641	Mark Grace and ..	4.00	1.60	.40
	Darrin Jackson			
☐ 642	Damon Berryhill and	.60	.24	.06
	Jeff Montgomery			
☐ 643	Felix Fermin and ..	.12	.05	.01
	Jesse Reid			
☐ 644	Greg Myers and ..	.20	.08	.02
	Greg Tabor			
☐ 645	Joey Meyer and ...	.35	.14	.03
	Jim Eppard			
☐ 646	Adam Peterson and	.20	.08	.02
	Randy Velarde			
☐ 647	Peter Smith and ..	.40	.16	.04
	Chris Gwynn			
☐ 648	Tom Newell and ..	.15	.06	.01
	Greg Jelks			
☐ 649	Mario Diaz and ...	.20	.08	.02
	Clay Parker			
☐ 650	Jack Savage and ..	.20	.08	.02
	Todd Simmons			
☐ 651	John Burkett and ..	.25	.10	.02
	Kirt Manwaring			
☐ 652	Dave Otto and	2.00	.80	.20
	Walt Weiss			
☐ 653	Jeff King and	.25	.10	.02
	Randell Byers			

	MINT	EXC	G-VG
☐ 654 CL: Twins/Cards ... Tigers/Giants UER (90 Bob Melvin, 91 Eddie Milner)	.06	.01	.00
☐ 655 CL: Blue Jays/Mets . Brewers/Expos UER (Mets listed before Blue Jays on card)	.06	.01	.00
☐ 656 CL: Yankees/Reds . Royals/A's	.06	.01	.00
☐ 657 CL: Phillies/Pirates . Red Sox/Mariners	.06	.01	.00
☐ 658 CL: White Sox/Cubs Astros/Rangers	.06	.01	.00
☐ 659 CL: Angels/Dodgers Braves/Orioles	.06	.01	.00
☐ 660 CL: Padres/Indians . Rookies/Specials	.06	.01	.00

1988 Fleer Update

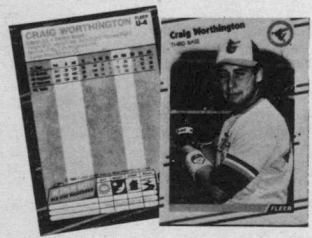

This 132-card set was distributed by Fleer to dealers as a complete set within a custom box. In addition to the complete set of 132 cards, the box also contains 25 Team Logo stickers.The card fronts look very similar to the 1987 Fleer regular issue. The cards are numbered (with a U prefix) alphabetically according to player's last name. Cards measure the standard size, 2 ½" by 3 ½". This was the first Fleer Update set to adopt the Fleer "alphabetical within team" numbering system.

		MINT	EXC	G-VG
Complete Set (132)		12.00	5.00	1.20
Common Player (1-132) ..		.05	.02	.00
☐ U1	Jose Bautista	.12	.05	.01
☐ U2	Joe Orsulak	.05	.02	.00
☐ U3	Doug Sisk	.05	.02	.00
☐ U4	Craig Worthington .	.20	.08	.02
☐ U5	Mike Boddicker ...	.08	.03	.01
☐ U6	Rick Cerone	.05	.02	.00
☐ U7	Larry Parrish	.05	.02	.00
☐ U8	Lee Smith	.08	.03	.01
☐ U9	Mike Smithson	.05	.02	.00
☐ U10	John Trautwein ...	.12	.05	.01
☐ U11	Sherman Corbett ...	.15	.06	.01
☐ U12	Chili Davis	.08	.03	.01
☐ U13	Jim Eppard	.05	.02	.00
☐ U14	Bryan Harvey	.30	.12	.03
☐ U15	John Davis	.05	.02	.00
☐ U16	Dave Gallagher ...	.25	.10	.02
☐ U17	Ricky Horton	.05	.02	.00
☐ U18	Dan Pasqua	.08	.03	.01
☐ U19	Melido Perez	.20	.08	.02
☐ U20	Jose Segura	.12	.05	.01
☐ U21	Andy Allanson	.05	.02	.00
☐ U22	Jon Perlman	.05	.02	.00
☐ U23	Domingo Ramos ...	.08	.03	.01
☐ U24	Rick Rodriguez	.05	.02	.00
☐ U25	Willie Upshaw	.05	.02	.00
☐ U26	Paul Gibson	.15	.06	.01
☐ U27	Don Heinkel	.15	.06	.01
☐ U28	Ray Knight	.08	.03	.01
☐ U29	Gary Pettis	.08	.03	.01
☐ U30	Luis Salazar	.05	.02	.00
☐ U31	Mike MacFarlane ..	.20	.08	.02
☐ U32	Jeff Montgomery ...	.08	.03	.01
☐ U33	Ted Power	.05	.02	.00
☐ U34	Israel Sanchez	.12	.05	.01
☐ U35	Kurt Stillwell	.08	.03	.01
☐ U36	Pat Tabler	.08	.03	.01
☐ U37	Don August	.20	.08	.02
☐ U38	Darryl Hamilton ...	.25	.10	.02
☐ U39	Jeff Leonard	.08	.03	.01
☐ U40	Joey Meyer	.20	.08	.02
☐ U41	Allan Anderson ...	.10	.04	.01
☐ U42	Brian Harper	.05	.02	.00
☐ U43	Tom Herr	.08	.03	.01
☐ U44	Charlie Lea	.05	.02	.00
☐ U45	John Moses	.05	.02	.00
	(listed as Hohn on checklist card)			
☐ U46	John Candelaria ..	.08	.03	.01

	MINT	EXC	G-VG
☐ U47 Jack Clark	.15	.06	.01
☐ U48 Richard Dotson	.08	.03	.01
☐ U49 Al Leiter	.45	.18	.04
☐ U50 Rafael Santana	.05	.02	.00
☐ U51 Don Slaught	.05	.02	.00
☐ U52 Todd Burns	.25	.10	.02
☐ U53 Dave Henderson ...	.08	.03	.01
☐ U54 Doug Jennings	.25	.10	.02
☐ U55 Dave Parker	.15	.06	.01
☐ U56 Walt Weiss	.75	.30	.07
☐ U57 Bob Welch	.08	.03	.01
☐ U58 Henry Cotto	.05	.02	.00
☐ U59 Mario Diaz UER ...	.08	.03	.01
(listed as Marion on card front)			
☐ U60 Mike Jackson	.08	.03	.01
☐ U61 Bill Swift	.08	.03	.01
☐ U62 Jose Cecena	.10	.04	.01
☐ U63 Ray Hayward	.10	.04	.01
☐ U64 Jim Steels UER	.10	.04	.01
(listed as Jim Steele on card back)			
☐ U65 Pat Borders	.20	.08	.02
☐ U66 Sil Campusano	.25	.10	.02
☐ U67 Mike Flanagan	.08	.03	.01
☐ U68 Todd Stottlemyre ..	.25	.10	.02
☐ U69 David Wells	.15	.06	.01
☐ U70 Jose Alvarez	.12	.05	.01
☐ U71 Paul Runge	.05	.02	.00
☐ U72 Cesar Jimenez	.15	.06	.01
(card was intended			
for German Jiminez, it's his photo)			
☐ U73 Pete Smith	.15	.06	.01
☐ U74 John Smoltz	.25	.10	.02
☐ U75 Damon Berryhill ..	.25	.10	.02
☐ U76 Goose Gossage ...	.10	.04	.01
☐ U77 Mark Grace	1.50	.60	.15
☐ U78 Darrin Jackson ...	.20	.08	.02
☐ U79 Vance Law	.08	.03	.01
☐ U80 Jeff Pico	.15	.06	.01
☐ U81 Gary Varsho	.25	.10	.02
☐ U82 Tim Birtsas	.05	.02	.00
☐ U83 Rob Dibble	.20	.08	.02
☐ U84 Danny Jackson	.20	.08	.02
☐ U85 Paul O'Neill	.08	.03	.01
☐ U86 Jose Rijo	.08	.03	.01
☐ U87 Chris Sabo	1.75	.70	.17
☐ U88 John Fishel	.20	.08	.02
☐ U89 Craig Biggio	.15	.06	.01
☐ U90 Terry Puhl	.05	.02	.00
☐ U91 Rafael Ramirez	.05	.02	.00

	MINT	EXC	G-VG
☐ U92 Louie Meadows	.12	.05	.01
☐ U93 Kirk Gibson	.25	.10	.02
☐ U94 Alfredo Griffin	.08	.03	.01
☐ U95 Jay Howell	.05	.02	.00
☐ U96 Jesse Orosco	.05	.02	.00
☐ U97 Alejandro Pena ...	.05	.02	.00
☐ U98 Tracy Woodson ...	.20	.08	.02
☐ U99 John Dopson	.20	.08	.02
☐ U100 Brian Holman	.20	.08	.02
☐ U101 Rex Hudler	.05	.02	.00
☐ U102 Jeff Parrett	.08	.03	.01
☐ U103 Nelson Santovenia	.15	.06	.01
☐ U104 Kevin Elster	.15	.06	.01
☐ U105 Jeff Innis	.20	.08	.02
☐ U106 Mackey Sasser ...	.25	.10	.02
☐ U107 Phil Bradley	.08	.03	.01
☐ U108 Danny Clay	.15	.06	.01
☐ U109 Greg Harris	.05	.02	.00
☐ U110 Ricky Jordan	2.25	.90	.22
☐ U111 David Palmer	.05	.02	.00
☐ U112 Jim Gott	.08	.03	.01
☐ U113 Tommy Gregg ...	.25	.10	.02
☐ U114 Barry Jones	.05	.02	.00
☐ U115 Randy Milligan ..	.25	.10	.02
☐ U116 Luis Alicea	.15	.06	.01
☐ U117 Tom Brunansky ..	.10	.04	.01
☐ U118 John Costello	.15	.06	.01
☐ U119 Jose DeLeon	.05	.02	.00
☐ U120 Bob Horner	.10	.04	.01
☐ U121 Scott Terry	.12	.05	.01
☐ U122 Roberto Alomar ..	.35	.14	.03
☐ U123 Dave Leiper	.05	.02	.00
☐ U124 Keith Moreland ...	.05	.02	.00
☐ U125 Mark Parent	.12	.05	.01
☐ U126 Dennis Rasmussen	.08	.03	.01
☐ U127 Randy Bockus ...	.05	.02	.00
☐ U128 Brett Butler	.08	.03	.01
☐ U129 Donell Nixon	.08	.03	.01
☐ U130 Earnest Riles	.05	.02	.00
☐ U131 Roger Samuels ...	.12	.05	.01
☐ U132 Checklist U1-U132	.05	.01	.00

1988 Fleer Sticker Cards

These Star Stickers were distributed as a separate issue by Fleer, with five star stickers and a logo sticker in each wax pack. The 132-card (sticker) set features 2 ½" by 3 ½" full-color fronts and even statistics on the sticker back, which is an indication that the Fleer Company understands that these stickers are rarely used as stickers but more like traditional cards. The card fronts are surrounded by a silver-gray border and the backs are printed in red and black on white card stock.

		MINT	EXC	G-VG
	Complete Set (132)	16.00	6.50	1.60
	Common Player (1-132)	.05	.02	.00
☐ 1	Mike Boddicker	.10	.04	.01
☐ 2	Eddie Murray	.25	.10	.02
☐ 3	Cal Ripken	.25	.10	.02
☐ 4	Larry Sheets	.10	.04	.01
☐ 5	Wade Boggs	1.50	.60	.15
☐ 6	Ellis Burks	1.00	.40	.10
☐ 7	Roger Clemens	1.00	.40	.10
☐ 8	Dwight Evans	.10	.04	.01
☐ 9	Mike Greenwell	1.00	.40	.10
☐ 10	Bruce Hurst	.15	.06	.01
☐ 11	Brian Downing	.05	.02	.00
☐ 12	Wally Joyner	.75	.30	.07
☐ 13	Mike Witt	.10	.04	.01
☐ 14	Ivan Calderon	.10	.04	.01
☐ 15	Jose DeLeon	.05	.02	.00
☐ 16	Ozzie Guillen	.10	.04	.01
☐ 17	Bobby Thigpen	.15	.06	.01
☐ 18	Joe Carter	.15	.06	.01
☐ 19	Julio Franco	.10	.04	.01
☐ 20	Brook Jacoby	.10	.04	.01
☐ 21	Cory Snyder	.25	.10	.02
☐ 22	Pat Tabler	.05	.02	.00
☐ 23	Doyle Alexander	.05	.02	.00
☐ 24	Kirk Gibson	.25	.10	.02
☐ 25	Mike Henneman	.15	.06	.01
☐ 26	Jack Morris	.15	.06	.01
☐ 27	Matt Nokes	.25	.10	.02
☐ 28	Walt Terrell	.05	.02	.00
☐ 29	Alan Trammell	.25	.10	.02
☐ 30	George Brett	.45	.18	.04
☐ 31	Charlie Leibrandt	.05	.02	.00
☐ 32	Bret Saberhagen	.25	.10	.02
☐ 33	Kevin Seitzer	.45	.18	.04
☐ 34	Danny Tartabull	.25	.10	.02
☐ 35	Frank White	.10	.04	.01
☐ 36	Rob Deer	.10	.04	.01
☐ 37	Ted Higuera	.15	.06	.01
☐ 38	Paul Molitor	.15	.06	.01
☐ 39	Dan Plesac	.10	.04	.01
☐ 40	Robin Yount	.25	.10	.02
☐ 41	Bert Blyleven	.10	.04	.01
☐ 42	Tom Brunansky	.15	.06	.01
☐ 43	Gary Gaetti	.15	.06	.01
☐ 44	Kent Hrbek	.20	.08	.02
☐ 45	Kirby Puckett	.60	.24	.06
☐ 46	Jeff Reardon	.10	.04	.01
☐ 47	Frank Viola	.15	.06	.01
☐ 48	Don Mattingly	2.00	.80	.20
☐ 49	Mike Pagliarulo	.10	.04	.01
☐ 50	Willie Randolph	.10	.04	.01
☐ 51	Rick Rhoden	.05	.02	.00
☐ 52	Dave Righetti	.15	.06	.01
☐ 53	Dave Winfield	.25	.10	.02
☐ 54	Jose Canseco	2.00	.80	.20
☐ 55	Carney Lansford	.10	.04	.01
☐ 56	Mark McGwire	1.00	.40	.10
☐ 57	Dave Stewart	.10	.04	.01
☐ 58	Curt Young	.05	.02	.00
☐ 59	Alvin Davis	.10	.04	.01
☐ 60	Mark Langston	.10	.04	.01
☐ 61	Ken Phelps	.10	.04	.01
☐ 62	Harold Reynolds	.05	.02	.00
☐ 63	Scott Fletcher	.05	.02	.00
☐ 64	Charlie Hough	.05	.02	.00
☐ 65	Pete Incaviglia	.20	.08	.02
☐ 66	Oddibe McDowell	.10	.04	.01

		MINT	EXC	G-VG
☐ 67	Pete O'Brien	.10	.04	.01
☐ 68	Larry Parrish	.05	.02	.00
☐ 69	Ruben Sierra	.20	.08	.02
☐ 70	Jesse Barfield	.15	.06	.01
☐ 71	George Bell	.20	.08	.02
☐ 72	Tony Fernandez	.15	.06	.01
☐ 73	Tom Henke	.05	.02	.00
☐ 74	Jimmy Key	.10	.04	.01
☐ 75	Lloyd Moseby	.10	.04	.01
☐ 76	Dion James	.05	.02	.00
☐ 77	Dale Murphy	.40	.16	.04
☐ 78	Zane Smith	.05	.02	.00
☐ 79	Andre Dawson	.25	.10	.02
☐ 80	Ryne Sandberg	.25	.10	.02
☐ 81	Rick Sutcliffe	.10	.04	.01
☐ 82	Kal Daniels	.20	.08	.02
☐ 83	Eric Davis	1.00	.40	.10
☐ 84	John Franco	.10	.04	.01
☐ 85	Kevin Bass	.05	.02	.00
☐ 86	Glenn Davis	.15	.06	.01
☐ 87	Bill Doran	.10	.04	.01
☐ 88	Nolan Ryan	.35	.14	.03
☐ 89	Mike Scott	.15	.06	.01
☐ 90	Dave Smith	.05	.02	.00
☐ 91	Pedro Guerrero	.20	.08	.02
☐ 92	Orel Hershiser	.50	.20	.05
☐ 93	Steve Sax	.15	.06	.01
☐ 94	Fernando Valenzuela	.15	.06	.01
☐ 95	Tim Burke	.05	.02	.00
☐ 96	Andres Galarraga	.25	.10	.02
☐ 97	Tim Raines	.25	.10	.02
☐ 98	Tim Wallach	.10	.04	.01
☐ 99	Mitch Webster	.05	.02	.00
☐ 100	Ron Darling	.15	.06	.01
☐ 101	Sid Fernandez	.10	.04	.01
☐ 102	Dwight Gooden	.50	.20	.05
☐ 103	Keith Hernandez	.25	.10	.02
☐ 104	Howard Johnson	.15	.06	.01
☐ 105	Roger McDowell	.10	.04	.01
☐ 106	Darryl Strawberry	.75	.30	.07
☐ 107	Steve Bedrosian	.10	.04	.01
☐ 108	Von Hayes	.10	.04	.01
☐ 109	Shane Rawley	.05	.02	.00
☐ 110	Juan Samuel	.15	.06	.01
☐ 111	Mike Schmidt	.50	.20	.05
☐ 112	Milt Thompson	.05	.02	.00
☐ 113	Sid Bream	.05	.02	.00
☐ 114	Bobby Bonilla	.15	.06	.01
☐ 115	Mike Dunne	.10	.04	.01

		MINT	EXC	G-VG
☐ 116	Any Van Slyke	.20	.08	.02
☐ 117	Vince Coleman	.20	.08	.02
☐ 118	Willie McGee	.15	.06	.01
☐ 119	Terry Pendleton	.05	.02	.00
☐ 120	Ozzie Smith	.15	.06	.01
☐ 121	John Tudor	.10	.04	.01
☐ 122	Todd Worrell	.15	.06	.01
☐ 123	Tony Gwynn	.45	.18	.04
☐ 124	John Kruk	.20	.08	.02
☐ 125	Benito Santiago	.50	.20	.05
☐ 126	Will Clark	.75	.30	.07
☐ 127	Dave Dravecky	.05	.02	.00
☐ 128	Jeff Leonard	.05	.02	.00
☐ 129	Candy Maldonado	.05	.02	.00
☐ 130	Rick Reuschel	.10	.04	.01
☐ 131	Don Robinson	.05	.02	.00
☐ 132	Checklist	.05	.02	.00

1989 Fleer

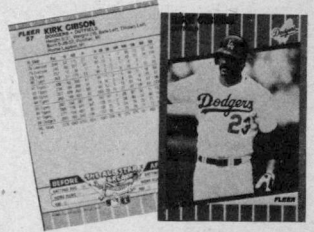

This 660-card set features a distinctive gray border background with white and yellow trim. The backs are printed in gray, black, and yellow on white card stock. The bottom of the card back shows an innovative breakdown of the player's demonstrated ability with respect to his performance before and after the All-Star break. Cards are numbered on the back and are again the standard 2 ½" by 3 ½". Cards are again organized numerically by teams. The last 33 cards in the set consist of Specials (628-639), Rookie Pairs (640-653), and checklists (654-660).

		MINT	EXC	G-VG
	Complete Set (660)	25.00	10.00	2.50
	Common Player (1-660) ...	.03	.01	.00
☐ 1	Don Baylor	.10	.03	.01
☐ 2	Lance Blankenship .	.20	.08	.02
☐ 3	Todd Burns	.20	.08	.02
☐ 4	Greg Cadaret	.10	.04	.01
☐ 5	Jose Canseco	1.00	.40	.10
☐ 6	Storm Davis	.06	.02	.00
☐ 7	Dennis Eckersley ..	.10	.04	.01
☐ 8	Mike Gallego	.03	.01	.00
☐ 9	Ron Hassey	.03	.01	.00
☐ 10	Dave Henderson ...	.06	.02	.00
☐ 11	Rick Honeycutt	.03	.01	.00
☐ 12	Glenn Hubbard	.03	.01	.00
☐ 13	Stan Javier	.03	.01	.00
☐ 14	Doug Jennings	.20	.08	.02
☐ 15	Felix Jose	.25	.10	.02
☐ 16	Carney Lansford ...	.06	.02	.00
☐ 17	Mark McGwire	.50	.20	.05
☐ 18	Gene Nelson	.03	.01	.00
☐ 19	Dave Parker	.08	.03	.01
☐ 20	Eric Plunk	.03	.01	.00
☐ 21	Luis Polonia	.03	.01	.00
☐ 22	Terry Steinbach ...	.08	.03	.01
☐ 23	Dave Stewart	.06	.02	.00
☐ 24	Walt Weiss	.35	.14	.03
☐ 25	Bob Welch	.06	.02	.00
☐ 26	Curt Young	.03	.01	.00
☐ 27	Rick Aguilera	.03	.01	.00
☐ 28	Wally Backman	.03	.01	.00
☐ 29	Mark Carreon	.03	.01	.00
☐ 30	Gary Carter	.15	.06	.01
☐ 31	David Cone	.30	.12	.03
☐ 32	Ron Darling	.08	.03	.01
☐ 33	Len Dykstra	.08	.03	.01
☐ 34	Kevin Elster	.06	.02	.00
☐ 35	Sid Fernandez	.08	.03	.01
☐ 36	Dwight Gooden	.30	.12	.03
☐ 37	Keith Hernandez ...	.12	.05	.01
☐ 38	Gregg Jefferies ...	2.00	.80	.20
☐ 39	Howard Johnson ...	.08	.03	.01
☐ 40	Terry Leach	.06	.02	.00
☐ 41	Dave Magadan	.06	.02	.00
☐ 42	Bob McClure	.03	.01	.00
☐ 43	Roger McDowell ...	.06	.02	.00
☐ 44	Kevin McReynolds .	.15	.06	.01
☐ 45	Keith Miller	.03	.01	.00
	New York Mets			
☐ 46	Randy Myers	.08	.03	.01

		MINT	EXC	G-VG
☐ 47	Bob Ojeda	.06	.02	.00
☐ 48	Mackey Sasser ...	.12	.05	.01
☐ 49	Darryl Strawberry .	.35	.14	.03
☐ 50	Tim Teufel	.03	.01	.00
☐ 51	Dave West	.50	.20	.05
☐ 52	Mookie Wilson	.03	.01	.00
☐ 53	Dave Anderson ...	.03	.01	.00
☐ 54	Tim Belcher	.08	.03	.01
☐ 55	Mike Davis	.03	.01	.00
☐ 56	Mike Devereaux ...	.08	.03	.01
☐ 57	Kirk Gibson	.15	.06	.01
☐ 58	Alfredo Griffin	.06	.02	.00
☐ 59	Chris Gwynn	.08	.03	.01
☐ 60	Jeff Hamilton	.03	.01	.00
☐ 61	Danny Heep	.03	.01	.00
☐ 62	Orel Hershiser ...	.25	.10	.02
☐ 63	Brian Holton	.03	.01	.00
☐ 64	Jay Howell	.03	.01	.00
☐ 65	Tim Leary	.06	.02	.00
☐ 66	Mike Marshall	.08	.03	.01
☐ 67	Ramon Martinez ..	.35	.14	.03
☐ 68	Jesse Orosco	.03	.01	.00
☐ 69	Alejandro Pena ...	.03	.01	.00
☐ 70	Steve Sax	.10	.04	.01
☐ 71	Mike Scioscia	.03	.01	.00
☐ 72	Mike Sharperson ..	.03	.01	.00
☐ 73	John Shelby	.03	.01	.00
☐ 74	Franklin Stubbs ...	.03	.01	.00
☐ 75	John Tudor	.08	.03	.01
☐ 76	Fernando Valenzuela	.12	.05	.01
☐ 77	Tracy Woodson ...	.10	.04	.01
☐ 78	Marty Barrett	.06	.02	.00
☐ 79	Todd Benzinger ...	.06	.02	.00
☐ 80	Mike Boddicker ...	.06	.02	.00
☐ 81	Wade Boggs	.50	.20	.05
☐ 82	"Oil Can" Boyd ...	.06	.02	.00
☐ 83	Ellis Burks	.30	.12	.03
☐ 84	Rick Cerone	.03	.01	.00
☐ 85	Roger Clemens ...	.35	.14	.03
☐ 86	Steve Curry	.12	.05	.01
☐ 87	Dwight Evans	.08	.03	.01
☐ 88	Wes Gardner	.03	.01	.00
☐ 89	Rich Gedman	.06	.02	.00
☐ 90	Mike Greenwell ...	.75	.30	.07
☐ 91	Bruce Hurst	.10	.04	.01
☐ 92	Dennis Lamp	.03	.01	.00
☐ 93	Spike Owen	.03	.01	.00
☐ 94	Larry Parrish	.03	.01	.00
☐ 95	Carlos Quintana ...	.35	.14	.03

		MINT	EXC	G-VG			MINT	EXC	G-VG
☐ 96	Jody Reed	.08	.03	.01	☐ 144	Luis Salazar	.03	.01	.00
☐ 97	Jim Rice	.10	.04	.01	☐ 145	Steve Searcy	.30	.12	.03
☐ 98	Kevin Romine	.03	.01	.00	☐ 146	Pat Sheridan	.03	.01	.00
☐ 99	Lee Smith	.06	.02	.00	☐ 147	Frank Tanana	.03	.01	.00
☐ 100	Mike Smithson	.03	.01	.00	☐ 148	Alan Trammell	.15	.06	.01
☐ 101	Bob Stanley	.03	.01	.00	☐ 149	Walt Terrell	.03	.01	.00
☐ 102	Allan Anderson	.06	.02	.00	☐ 150	Jim Walewander	.10	.04	.01
☐ 103	Keith Atherton	.03	.01	.00	☐ 151	Lou Whitaker	.08	.03	.01
☐ 104	Juan Berenguer	.03	.01	.00	☐ 152	Tim Birtsas	.03	.01	.00
☐ 105	Bert Blyleven	.08	.03	.01	☐ 153	Tom Browning	.08	.03	.01
☐ 106	Eric Bullock	.12	.05	.01	☐ 154	Keith Brown	.10	.04	.01
☐ 107	Randy Bush	.03	.01	.00	☐ 155	Norm Charlton	.12	.05	.01
☐ 108	John Christensen	.03	.01	.00	☐ 156	Dave Concepcion	.08	.03	.01
☐ 109	Mark Davidson	.03	.01	.00	☐ 157	Kal Daniels	.12	.05	.01
☐ 110	Gary Gaetti	.10	.04	.01	☐ 158	Eric Davis	.35	.14	.03
☐ 111	Greg Gagne	.03	.01	.00	☐ 159	Bo Diaz	.03	.01	.00
☐ 112	Dan Gladden	.06	.02	.00	☐ 160	Rob Dibble	.12	.05	.01
☐ 113	German Gonzalez	.10	.04	.01	☐ 161	Nick Esasky	.03	.01	.00
☐ 114	Brian Harper	.03	.01	.00	☐ 162	John Franco	.08	.03	.01
☐ 115	Tom Herr	.06	.02	.00	☐ 163	Danny Jackson	.10	.04	.01
☐ 116	Kent Hrbek	.10	.04	.01	☐ 164	Barry Larkin	.10	.04	.01
☐ 117	Gene Larkin	.06	.02	.00	☐ 165	Rob Murphy	.03	.01	.00
☐ 118	Tim Laudner	.03	.01	.00	☐ 166	Paul O'Neill	.06	.02	.00
☐ 119	Charlie Lea	.03	.01	.00	☐ 167	Jeff Reed	.03	.01	.00
☐ 120	Steve Lombardozzi	.03	.01	.00	☐ 168	Jose Rijo	.03	.01	.00
☐ 121	John Moses	.03	.01	.00	☐ 169	Ron Robinson	.03	.01	.00
☐ 122	Al Newman	.03	.01	.00	☐ 170	Chris Sabo	1.00	.40	.10
☐ 123	Mark Portugal	.03	.01	.00	☐ 171	Candy Sierra	.10	.04	.01
☐ 124	Kirby Puckett	.30	.12	.03	☐ 172	Van Snider	.25	.10	.02
☐ 125	Jeff Reardon	.06	.02	.00	☐ 173	Jeff Treadway	.06	.02	.00
☐ 126	Fred Toliver	.03	.01	.00	☐ 174	Frank Williams	.03	.01	.00
☐ 127	Frank Viola	.15	.06	.01	☐ 175	Herm Winningham	.03	.01	.00
☐ 128	Doyle Alexander	.06	.02	.00	☐ 176	Jim Adduci	.03	.01	.00
☐ 129	Dave Bergman	.03	.01	.00	☐ 177	Don August	.06	.02	.00
☐ 130	Tom Brookens	.03	.01	.00	☐ 178	Mike Birkbeck	.03	.01	.00
☐ 131	Paul Gibson	.10	.04	.01	☐ 179	Chris Bosio	.03	.01	.00
☐ 132	Mike Heath	.03	.01	.00	☐ 180	Glenn Braggs	.03	.01	.00
☐ 133	Don Heinkel	.10	.04	.01	☐ 181	Greg Brock	.03	.01	.00
☐ 134	Mike Henneman	.03	.01	.00	☐ 182	Mark Clear	.03	.01	.00
☐ 135	Guillermo Hernandez				☐ 183	Chuck Crim	.03	.01	.00
☐ 136	Eric King	.06	.02	.00	☐ 184	Rob Deer	.06	.02	.00
☐ 137	Chet Lemon	.03	.01	.00	☐ 185	Tom Filer	.03	.01	.00
☐ 138	Fred Lynn	.10	.04	.01	☐ 186	Jim Gantner	.03	.01	.00
☐ 139	Jack Morris	.10	.04	.01	☐ 187	Darryl Hamilton	.25	.10	.02
☐ 140	Matt Nokes	.10	.04	.01	☐ 188	Ted Higuera	.08	.03	.01
☐ 141	Gary Pettis	.03	.01	.00	☐ 189	Odell Jones	.03	.01	.00
☐ 142	Ted Power	.03	.01	.00	☐ 190	Jeffrey Leonard	.06	.02	.00
☐ 143	Jeff M. Robinson	.08	.03	.01	☐ 191	Joey Meyer	.08	.03	.01
	Detroit Tigers				☐ 192	Paul Mirabella	.03	.01	.00

		MINT	EXC	G-VG			MINT	EXC	G-VG
☐ 193	Paul Molitor	.10	.04	.01	☐ 241	Lloyd Moseby	.08	.03	.01
☐ 194	Charlie O'Brien	.10	.04	.01	☐ 242	Rance Mulliniks	.03	.01	.00
☐ 195	Dan Plesac	.06	.02	.00	☐ 243	Jeff Musselman	.03	.01	.00
☐ 196	Gary Sheffield	1.50	.60	.15	☐ 244	Dave Stieb	.08	.03	.01
☐ 197	B.J. Surhoff	.08	.03	.01	☐ 245	Todd Stottlemyre	.12	.05	.01
☐ 198	Dale Sveum	.03	.01	.00	☐ 246	Duane Ward	.03	.01	.00
☐ 199	Bill Wegman	.03	.01	.00	☐ 247	David Wells	.08	.03	.01
☐ 200	Robin Yount	.15	.06	.01	☐ 248	Ernie Whitt	.03	.01	.00
☐ 201	Rafael Belliard	.03	.01	.00	☐ 249	Luis Aguayo	.03	.01	.00
☐ 202	Barry Bonds	.10	.04	.01	☐ 250	Neil Allen	.03	.01	.00
☐ 203	Bobby Bonilla	.10	.04	.01	☐ 251	John Candelaria	.06	.02	.00
☐ 204	Sid Bream	.03	.01	.00	☐ 252	Jack Clark	.12	.05	.01
☐ 205	Benny Distefano	.03	.01	.00	☐ 253	Richard Dotson	.06	.02	.00
☐ 206	Doug Drabek	.03	.01	.00	☐ 254	Rickey Henderson	.20	.08	.02
☐ 207	Mike Dunne	.06	.02	.00	☐ 255	Tommy John	.08	.03	.01
☐ 208	Felix Fermin	.03	.01	.00	☐ 256	Roberto Kelly	.12	.05	.01
☐ 209	Brian Fisher	.03	.01	.00	☐ 257	Al Leiter	.25	.10	.02
☐ 210	Jim Gott	.03	.01	.00	☐ 258	Don Mattingly	1.00	.40	.10
☐ 211	Bob Kipper	.03	.01	.00	☐ 259	Dale Mohorcic	.03	.01	.00
☐ 212	Dave LaPoint	.03	.01	.00	☐ 260	Hal Morris	.15	.06	.01
☐ 213	Mike LaValliere	.03	.01	.00	☐ 261	Scott Nielsen	.03	.01	.00
☐ 214	Jose Lind	.03	.01	.00	☐ 262	Mike Pagliarulo	.06	.02	.00
☐ 215	Junior Ortiz	.03	.01	.00	☐ 263	Hipolito Pena	.12	.05	.01
☐ 216	Vicente Palacios	.03	.01	.00	☐ 264	Ken Phelps	.06	.02	.00
☐ 217	Tom Prince	.08	.03	.01	☐ 265	Willie Randolph	.06	.02	.00
☐ 218	Gary Redus	.03	.01	.00	☐ 266	Rick Rhoden	.03	.01	.00
☐ 219	R.J. Reynolds	.03	.01	.00	☐ 267	Dave Righetti	.08	.03	.01
☐ 220	Jeff Robinson	.03	.01	.00	☐ 268	Rafael Santana	.03	.01	.00
	Pittsburgh Pirates				☐ 269	Steve Shields	.03	.01	.00
☐ 221	John Smiley	.03	.01	.00	☐ 270	Joel Skinner	.03	.01	.00
☐ 222	Andy Van Slyke	.12	.05	.01	☐ 271	Don Slaught	.03	.01	.00
☐ 223	Bob Walk	.03	.01	.00	☐ 272	Claudell Washington	.06	.02	.00
☐ 224	Glenn Wilson	.03	.01	.00	☐ 273	Gary Ward	.03	.01	.00
☐ 225	Jesse Barfield	.10	.04	.01	☐ 274	Dave Winfield	.15	.06	.01
☐ 226	George Bell	.12	.05	.01	☐ 275	Luis Aquino	.03	.01	.00
☐ 227	Pat Borders	.15	.06	.01	☐ 276	Floyd Bannister	.03	.01	.00
☐ 228	John Cerutti	.03	.01	.00	☐ 277	George Brett	.20	.08	.02
☐ 229	Jim Clancy	.03	.01	.00	☐ 278	Bill Buckner	.06	.02	.00
☐ 230	Mark Eichhorn	.03	.01	.00	☐ 279	Nick Capra	.08	.03	.01
☐ 231	Tony Fernandez	.10	.04	.01	☐ 280	Jose DeJesus	.10	.04	.01
☐ 232	Cecil Fielder	.03	.01	.00	☐ 281	Steve Farr	.03	.01	.00
☐ 233	Mike Flanagan	.03	.01	.00	☐ 282	Jerry Don Gleaton	.03	.01	.00
☐ 234	Kelly Gruber	.03	.01	.00	☐ 283	Mark Gubicza	.08	.03	.01
☐ 235	Tom Henke	.06	.02	.00	☐ 284	Tom Gordon	.25	.10	.02
☐ 236	Jimmy Key	.06	.02	.00	☐ 285	Bo Jackson	.20	.08	.02
☐ 237	Rick Leach	.03	.01	.00	☐ 286	Charlie Leibrandt	.03	.01	.00
☐ 238	Manny Lee	.03	.01	.00	☐ 287	Mike Macfarlane	.15	.06	.01
☐ 239	Nelson Liriano	.03	.01	.00	☐ 288	Jeff Montgomery	.03	.01	.00
☐ 240	Fred McGriff	.15	.06	.01	☐ 289	Bill Pecota	.03	.01	.00

		MINT	EXC	G-VG
☐ 290	Jamie Quirk	.03	.01	.00
☐ 291	Bret Saberhagen	.10	.04	.01
☐ 292	Kevin Seitzer	.18	.08	.01
☐ 293	Kurt Stillwell	.03	.01	.00
☐ 294	Pat Tabler	.06	.02	.00
☐ 295	Danny Tartabull	.15	.06	.01
☐ 296	Gary Thurman	.03	.01	.00
☐ 297	Frank White	.06	.02	.00
☐ 298	Willie Wilson	.08	.03	.01
☐ 299	Roberto Alomar	.30	.12	.03
☐ 300	Sandy Alomar Jr.	.90	.36	.09
☐ 301	Chris Brown	.06	.02	.00
☐ 302	Mike Brumley	.08	.03	.01
☐ 303	Mark Davis	.06	.02	.00
☐ 304	Mark Grant	.03	.01	.00
☐ 305	Tony Gwynn	.20	.08	.02
☐ 306	Greg W. Harris	.20	.08	.02
	San Diego Padres			
☐ 307	Andy Hawkins	.03	.01	.00
☐ 308	Jimmy Jones	.06	.02	.00
☐ 309	John Kruk	.06	.02	.00
☐ 310	Dave Leiper	.03	.01	.00
☐ 311	Carmelo Martinez	.03	.01	.00
☐ 312	Lance McCullers	.06	.02	.00
☐ 313	Keith Moreland	.03	.01	.00
☐ 314	Dennis Rasmussen	.06	.02	.00
☐ 315	Randy Ready	.03	.01	.00
☐ 316	Benito Santiago	.18	.08	.01
☐ 317	Eric Show	.03	.01	.00
☐ 318	Todd Simmons	.06	.02	.00
☐ 319	Garry Templeton	.06	.02	.00
☐ 320	Dickie Thon	.03	.01	.00
☐ 321	Ed Whitson	.03	.01	.00
☐ 322	Marvell Wynne	.03	.01	.00
☐ 323	Mike Aldrete	.03	.01	.00
☐ 324	Brett Butler	.06	.02	.00
☐ 325	Will Clark	.35	.14	.03
☐ 326	Kelly Downs	.06	.02	.00
☐ 327	Dave Dravecky	.03	.01	.00
☐ 328	Scott Garrelts	.03	.01	.00
☐ 329	Atlee Hammaker	.03	.01	.00
☐ 330	Charlie Hayes	.12	.05	.01
☐ 331	Mike Krukow	.03	.01	.00
☐ 332	Craig Lefferts	.03	.01	.00
☐ 333	Candy Maldonado	.06	.02	.00
☐ 334	Kirt Manwaring	.03	.01	.00
☐ 335	Bob Melvin	.03	.01	.00
☐ 336	Kevin Mitchell	.06	.02	.00
☐ 337	Donell Nixon	.03	.01	.00

		MINT	EXC	G-VG
☐ 338	Tony Perezchica	.12	.05	.01
☐ 339	Joe Price	.03	.01	.00
☐ 340	Rick Reuschel	.06	.02	.00
☐ 341	Earnest Riles	.03	.01	.00
☐ 342	Don Robinson	.03	.01	.00
☐ 343	Chris Speier	.03	.01	.00
☐ 344	Robby Thompson	.03	.01	.00
☐ 345	Jose Uribe	.03	.01	.00
☐ 346	Matt Williams	.08	.03	.01
☐ 347	Trevor Wilson	.15	.06	.01
☐ 348	Juan Agosto	.03	.01	.00
☐ 349	Larry Andersen	.03	.01	.00
☐ 350	Alan Ashby	.03	.01	.00
☐ 351	Kevin Bass	.06	.02	.00
☐ 352	Buddy Bell	.08	.03	.01
☐ 353	Craig Biggio	.15	.06	.01
☐ 354	Danny Darwin	.03	.01	.00
☐ 355	Glenn Davis	.10	.04	.01
☐ 356	Jim Deshaies	.03	.01	.00
☐ 357	Bill Doran	.06	.02	.00
☐ 358	Jim Fishel	.15	.06	.01
☐ 359	Billy Hatcher	.06	.02	.00
☐ 360	Bob Knepper	.03	.01	.00
☐ 361	Louie Meadows	.10	.04	.01
☐ 362	Dave Meads	.03	.01	.00
☐ 363	Jim Pankovits	.03	.01	.00
☐ 364	Terry Puhl	.03	.01	.00
☐ 365	Rafael Ramirez	.03	.01	.00
☐ 366	Craig Reynolds	.03	.01	.00
☐ 367	Mike Scott	.10	.04	.01
☐ 368	Nolan Ryan	.20	.08	.02
☐ 369	Dave Smith	.03	.01	.00
☐ 370	Gerald Young	.06	.02	.00
☐ 371	Hubie Brooks	.06	.02	.00
☐ 372	Tim Burke	.03	.01	.00
☐ 373	John Dopson	.15	.06	.01
☐ 374	Mike Fitzgerald	.03	.01	.00
	Montreal Expos			
☐ 375	Tom Foley	.03	.01	.00
☐ 376	Andres Galarraga	.12	.05	.01
☐ 377	Neal Heaton	.03	.01	.00
☐ 378	Joe Hesketh	.03	.01	.00
☐ 379	Brian Holman	.12	.05	.01
☐ 380	Rex Hudler	.03	.01	.00
☐ 381	Randy Johnson	.25	.10	.02
☐ 382	Wallace Johnson	.03	.01	.02
☐ 383	Tracy Jones	.06	.02	.00
☐ 384	Dave Martinez	.03	.01	.00
☐ 385	Dennis Martinez	.03	.01	.00

		MINT	EXC	G-VG			MINT	EXC	G-VG
☐ 386	Andy McGaffigan	.03	.01	.00	☐ 435	Pat Perry	.03	.01	.00
☐ 387	Otis Nixon	.03	.01	.00	☐ 436	Jeff Pico	.10	.04	.01
☐ 388	Johnny Paredes	.12	.05	.01	☐ 437	Ryne Sandberg	.15	.06	.01
☐ 389	Jeff Parrett	.10	.04	.01	☐ 438	Calvin Schiraldi	.03	.01	.00
☐ 390	Pascual Perez	.06	.02	.00	☐ 439	Rick Sutcliffe	.08	.03	.01
☐ 391	Tim Raines	.15	.06	.01	☐ 440	Manny Trillo	.03	.01	.00
☐ 392	Luis Rivera	.03	.01	.00	☐ 441	Gary Varsho	.15	.06	.01
☐ 393	Nelson Santovenia	.12	.05	.01	☐ 442	Mitch Webster	.03	.01	.00
☐ 394	Bryn Smith	.03	.01	.00	☐ 443	Luis Alicea	.12	.05	.01
☐ 395	Tim Wallach	.08	.03	.01	☐ 444	Tom Brunansky	.08	.03	.01
☐ 396	Andy Allanson	.03	.01	.00	☐ 445	Vince Coleman	.15	.06	.01
☐ 397	Rod Allen	.10	.04	.01	☐ 446	John Costello	.12	.05	.01
☐ 398	Scott Bailes	.03	.01	.00	☐ 447	Danny Cox	.06	.02	.00
☐ 399	Tom Candiotti	.03	.01	.00	☐ 448	Ken Dayley	.03	.01	.00
☐ 400	Joe Carter	.10	.04	.01	☐ 449	Jose DeLeon	.03	.01	.00
☐ 401	Carmen Castillo	.03	.01	.00	☐ 450	Curt Ford	.03	.01	.00
☐ 402	Dave Clark	.06	.02	.00	☐ 451	Pedro Guerrero	.10	.04	.01
☐ 403	John Farrell	.03	.01	.00	☐ 452	Bob Horner	.08	.03	.01
☐ 404	Julio Franco	.06	.02	.00	☐ 453	Tim Jones	.15	.06	.01
☐ 405	Don Gordon	.08	.03	.01	☐ 454	Steve Lake	.03	.01	.00
☐ 406	Mel Hall	.03	.01	.00	☐ 455	Joe Magrane	.06	.02	.00
☐ 407	Brad Havens	.03	.01	.00	☐ 456	Greg Mathews	.03	.01	.00
☐ 408	Brook Jacoby	.06	.02	.00	☐ 457	Willie McGee	.08	.03	.01
☐ 409	Doug Jones	.06	.02	.00	☐ 458	Larry McWilliams	.03	.01	.00
☐ 410	Jeff Kaiser	.10	.04	.01	☐ 459	Jose Oquendo	.03	.01	.00
☐ 411	Luis Medina	.45	.18	.04	☐ 460	Tony Pena	.06	.02	.00
☐ 412	Cory Snyder	.15	.06	.01	☐ 461	Terry Pendleton	.03	.01	.00
☐ 413	Greg Swindell	.10	.04	.01	☐ 462	Steve Peters	.15	.06	.01
☐ 414	Ron Tingley	.10	.04	.01	☐ 463	Ozzie Smith	.12	.05	.01
☐ 415	Willie Upshaw	.03	.01	.00	☐ 464	Scott Terry	.03	.01	.00
☐ 416	Ron Washington	.03	.01	.00	☐ 465	Denny Walling	.03	.01	.00
☐ 417	Rich Yett	.03	.01	.00	☐ 466	Todd Worrell	.08	.03	.01
☐ 418	Damon Berryhill	.10	.04	.01	☐ 467	Tony Armas	.06	.02	.00
☐ 419	Mike Bielecki	.03	.01	.00	☐ 468	Dante Bichette	.20	.08	.02
☐ 420	Doug Dascenzo	.15	.06	.01	☐ 469	Bob Boone	.06	.02	.00
☐ 421	Jody Davis	.06	.02	.00	☐ 470	Terry Clark	.15	.06	.01
☐ 422	Andre Dawson	.12	.05	.01	☐ 471	Stew Cliburn	.03	.01	.00
☐ 423	Frank DiPino	.03	.01	.00	☐ 472	Mike Cook	.12	.05	.01
☐ 424	Shawon Dunston	.06	.02	.00	☐ 473	Sherman Corbett	.12	.05	.01
☐ 425	"Goose" Gossage	.08	.03	.01	☐ 474	Chili Davis	.06	.02	.00
☐ 426	Mark Grace	.85	.34	.08	☐ 475	Brian Downing	.03	.01	.00
☐ 427	Mike Harkey	.50	.20	.05	☐ 476	Jim Eppard	.03	.01	.00
☐ 428	Darrin Jackson	.08	.03	.01	☐ 477	Chuck Finley	.03	.01	.00
☐ 429	Les Lancaster	.03	.01	.00	☐ 478	Willie Fraser	.03	.01	.00
☐ 430	Vance Law	.03	.01	.00	☐ 479	Bryan Harvey	.25	.10	.02
☐ 431	Greg Maddux	.12	.05	.01	☐ 480	Jack Howell	.03	.01	.00
☐ 432	Jamie Moyer	.03	.01	.00	☐ 481	Wally Joyner	.20	.08	.02
☐ 433	Al Nipper	.03	.01	.00	☐ 482	Jack Lazorko	.03	.01	.00
☐ 434	Rafael Palmeiro	.15	.06	.01	☐ 483	Kirk McCaskill	.03	.01	.00

		MINT	EXC	G-VG
☐ 484	Mark McLemore	.03	.01	.00
☐ 485	Greg Minton	.03	.01	.00
☐ 486	Dan Petry	.03	.01	.00
☐ 487	Johnny Ray	.06	.02	.00
☐ 488	Dick Schofield	.03	.01	.00
☐ 489	Devon White	.08	.03	.01
☐ 490	Mike Witt	.08	.03	.01
☐ 491	Harold Baines	.08	.03	.01
☐ 492	Daryl Boston	.03	.01	.00
☐ 493	Ivan Calderon	.08	.03	.01
☐ 494	Mike Diaz	.03	.01	.00
☐ 495	Carlton Fisk	.08	.03	.01
☐ 496	Dave Gallagher	.15	.06	.01
☐ 497	Ozzie Guillen	.06	.02	.00
☐ 498	Shawn Hillegas	.03	.01	.00
☐ 499	Lance Johnson	.03	.01	.00
☐ 500	Barry Jones	.03	.01	.00
☐ 501	Bill Long	.03	.01	.00
☐ 502	Steve Lyons	.03	.01	.00
☐ 503	Fred Manrique	.03	.01	.00
☐ 504	Jack McDowell	.08	.03	.01
☐ 505	Donn Pall	.08	.03	.01
☐ 506	Kelly Paris	.03	.01	.00
☐ 507	Dan Pasqua	.06	.02	.00
☐ 508	Ken Patterson	.10	.04	.01
☐ 509	Melido Perez	.08	.03	.01
☐ 510	Jerry Reuss	.03	.01	.00
☐ 511	Mark Salas	.03	.01	.00
☐ 512	Bobby Thigpen	.06	.02	.00
☐ 513	Mike Woodard	.03	.01	.00
☐ 514	Bob Brower	.06	.02	.00
☐ 515	Steve Buechele	.03	.01	.00
☐ 516	Jose Cecena	.10	.04	.01
☐ 517	Cecil Espy	.10	.04	.01
☐ 518	Scott Fletcher	.03	.01	.00
☐ 519	Cecilio Guante	.03	.01	.00
☐ 520	Jose Guzman	.03	.01	.00
☐ 521	Ray Hayward	.08	.03	.01
☐ 522	Charlie Hough	.03	.01	.00
☐ 523	Pete Incaviglia	.10	.04	.01
☐ 524	Mike Jeffcoat	.03	.01	.00
☐ 525	Paul Kilgus	.03	.01	.00
☐ 526	Chad Kreuter	.20	.08	.02
☐ 527	Jeff Kunkel	.03	.01	.00
☐ 528	Oddibe McDowell	.06	.02	.00
☐ 529	Pete O'Brien	.06	.02	.00
☐ 530	Geno Petralli	.03	.01	.00
☐ 531	Jeff Russell	.03	.01	.00
☐ 532	Ruben Sierra	.12	.05	.01
☐ 533	Mike Stanley	.03	.01	.00
☐ 534	Ed VandeBerg	.03	.01	.00
☐ 535	Curtis Wilkerson	.03	.01	.00
☐ 536	Mitch Williams	.03	.01	.00
☐ 537	Bobby Witt	.06	.02	.00
☐ 538	Steve Balboni	.03	.01	.00
☐ 539	Scott Bankhead	.03	.01	.00
☐ 540	Scott Bradley	.03	.01	.00
☐ 541	Mickey Brantley	.06	.02	.00
☐ 542	Jay Buhner	.20	.08	.02
☐ 543	Mike Campbell	.03	.01	.00
☐ 544	Darnell Coles	.03	.01	.00
☐ 545	Henry Cotto	.03	.01	.00
☐ 546	Alvin Davis	.08	.03	.01
☐ 547	Mario Diaz	.03	.01	.00
☐ 548	Ken Griffey Jr.	1.25	.50	.12
☐ 549	Erik Hanson	.20	.08	.01
☐ 550	Mike Jackson	.03	.01	.00
☐ 551	Mark Langston	.08	.03	.01
☐ 552	Edgar Martinez	.10	.04	.01
☐ 553	Bill McGuire	.10	.04	.01
☐ 554	Mike Moore	.03	.01	.00
☐ 555	Jim Presley	.06	.02	.00
☐ 556	Rey Quinones	.03	.01	.00
☐ 557	Jerry Reed	.03	.01	.00
☐ 558	Harold Reynolds	.03	.01	.00
☐ 559	Mike Schooler	.12	.05	.01
☐ 560	Bill Swift	.03	.01	.00
☐ 561	Dave Valle	.03	.01	.00
☐ 562	Steve Bedrosian	.08	.03	.01
☐ 563	Phil Bradley	.06	.02	.00
☐ 564	Don Carman	.03	.01	.00
☐ 565	Bob Dernier	.03	.01	.00
☐ 566	Marvin Freeman	.03	.01	.00
☐ 567	Todd Frohwirth	.03	.01	.00
☐ 568	Greg Gross	.03	.01	.00
☐ 569	Kevin Gross	.03	.01	.00
☐ 570	Greg Harris	.03	.01	.00
	Philadelphia Phillies			
☐ 571	Von Hayes	.08	.03	.01
☐ 572	Chris James	.08	.03	.01
☐ 573	Steve Jeltz	.03	.01	.00
☐ 574	Ron Jones	.30	.12	.03
☐ 575	Ricky Jordan	1.25	.50	.12
☐ 576	Mike Maddux	.03	.01	.00
☐ 577	David Palmer	.03	.01	.00
☐ 578	Lance Parrish	.08	.03	.01
☐ 579	Shane Rawley	.03	.01	.00
☐ 580	Bruce Ruffin	.03	.01	.00

		MINT	EXC	G-VG
☐ 581	Juan Samuel	.08	.03	.01
☐ 582	Mike Schmidt	.20	.08	.02
☐ 583	Kent Tekulve	.03	.01	.00
☐ 584	Milt Thompson	.03	.01	.00
☐ 585	Jose Alvarez	.10	.04	.01
☐ 586	Paul Assenmacher	.03	.01	.00
☐ 587	Bruce Benedict	.03	.01	.00
☐ 588	Jeff Blauser	.03	.01	.00
☐ 589	Terry Blocker	.12	.05	.01
☐ 590	Ron Gant	.15	.06	.01
☐ 591	Tom Glavine	.03	.01	.00
☐ 592	Tommy Gregg	.10	.04	.01
☐ 593	Albert Hall	.03	.01	.00
☐ 594	Dion James	.03	.01	.00
☐ 595	Rick Mahler	.03	.01	.00
☐ 596	Dale Murphy	.25	.10	.02
☐ 597	Gerald Perry	.08	.03	.01
☐ 598	Charlie Puleo	.03	.01	.00
☐ 599	Ted Simmons	.08	.03	.01
☐ 600	Pete Smith	.03	.01	.00
☐ 601	Zane Smith	.06	.02	.00
☐ 602	John Smoltz	.25	.10	.02
☐ 603	Bruce Sutter	.08	.03	.01
☐ 604	Andres Thomas	.03	.01	.00
☐ 605	Ozzie Virgil	.03	.01	.00
☐ 606	Brady Anderson	.20	.08	.02
☐ 607	Jeff Ballard	.03	.01	.00
☐ 608	Jose Bautista	.10	.04	.01
☐ 609	Ken Gerhart	.03	.01	.00
☐ 610	Terry Kennedy	.03	.01	.00
☐ 611	Eddie Murray	.15	.06	.01
☐ 612	Carl Nichols	.08	.03	.01
☐ 613	Tom Niedenfuer	.03	.01	.00
☐ 614	Joe Orsulak	.03	.01	.00
☐ 615	Oswald Peraza	.10	.04	.01
☐ 616A	Bill Ripken ERR	20.00	8.00	1.00
	(Rick Face written on knob of bat)			
☐ 616B	Bill Ripken COR	.15	.06	.01
☐ 617	Cal Ripken Jr.	.15	.06	.01
☐ 618	Dave Schmidt	.03	.01	.00
☐ 619	Rick Schu	.03	.01	.00
☐ 620	Larry Sheets	.06	.02	.00
☐ 621	Doug Sisk	.03	.01	.00
☐ 622	Pete Stanicek	.06	.02	.00
☐ 623	Mickey Tettleton	.03	.01	.00
☐ 624	Jay Tibbs	.03	.01	.00
☐ 625	Jim Traber	.03	.01	.00
☐ 626	Mark Williamson	.03	.01	.00
☐ 627	Craig Worthington	.30	.12	.03

		MINT	EXC	G-VG
☐ 628	Speed/Power	.35	.14	.03
	Jose Canseco			
☐ 629	Pitcher Perfect	.06	.02	.00
	Tom Browning			
☐ 630	Like Father/Like Sons	.20	.08	.02
	Roberto Alomar			
	Sandy Alomar Jr.			
☐ 631	NL All Stars	.12	.05	.01
	Will Clark			
	Rafael Palmeiro			
☐ 632	Homeruns — Coast	.20	.08	.02
	to Coast			
	Darryl Strawberry			
	Will Clark			
☐ 633	Hot Corners — Hot	.20	.08	.02
	Hitters			
	Wade Boggs			
	Carney Lansford			
☐ 634	Triple A's	.30	.12	.03
	Jose Canseco			
	Terry Steinbach			
	Mark McGwire			
☐ 635	Dual Heat	.15	.06	.01
	Mark Davis			
	Dwight Gooden			
☐ 636	NL Pitching Power	.12	.05	.01
	Danny Jackson			
	David Cone			
☐ 637	Cannon Arms	.15	.06	.01
	Chris Sabo			
	Bobby Bonilla			
☐ 638	Double Trouble	.08	.03	.01
	Andres Galarraga			
	Gerald Perry			
☐ 639	Power Center	.20	.08	.02
	Kirby Puckett			
	Eric Davis			
☐ 640	Steve Wilson and	.25	.10	.02
	Cameron Drew			
☐ 641	Kevin Brown and	.20	.08	.02
	Kevin Reimer			
☐ 642	Brad Pounders and	.25	.10	.02
	Jerald Clark			
☐ 643	Mike Capel and	.20	.08	.02
	Drew Hall			
☐ 644	Joe Girardi and	.20	.08	.02
	Rolando Roomes			
☐ 645	Lenny Harris and	.20	.08	.02
	Marty Brown			

	MINT	EXC	G-VG
☐ 646 Luis De Los Santos and Jim Campbell	.30	.12	.03
☐ 647 Randy Kramer and Miguel Garcia	.25	.10	.02
☐ 648 Torey Lovullo and Robert Palacios	.20	.08	.02
☐ 649 Jim Corsi and Bob Milacki	.25	.10	.02
☐ 650 Grady Hall and Mike Rochford	.20	.08	.02
☐ 651 Terry Taylor and Vance Lovelace	.25	.10	.02
☐ 652 Ken Hill and Dennis Cook	.20	.08	.02
☐ 653 Scott Service and Shane Turner	.20	.08	.02
☐ 654 CL: Oakland/Mets Dodgers/Red Sox	.06	.01	.00
☐ 655 CL: Twins/Tigers Reds/Brewers	.06	.01	.00
☐ 656 CL: Pirates/Blue Jays Yankees/Royals	.06	.01	.00
☐ 657 CL: Padres/Giants Astros/Expos	.06	.01	.00
☐ 658 CL: Indians/Cubs Cardinals/Angels	.06	.01	.00
☐ 659 CL: White Sox/Rangers Mariners/Phillies	.06	.01	.00
☐ 660 CL: Braves/Orioles Specials/Checklists	.06	.01	.00

1975 Hostess

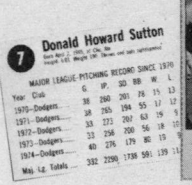 

The cards in this 150-card set measure 2 ¼ " by 3 ¼ " individually or 3 ¼ " by 7 ¼ " as panels of three. The 1975 Hostess set was issued in panels of three cards each on the backs of family size packages of Hostess cakes. Card number 125, Bill Madlock, was listed correctly as an infielder and incorrectly as a pitcher. Number 11, Burt Hooton, and number 89, Doug Rader, are spelled two different ways. Some panels are scarcer than others as they were issued only on the backs of less popular Hostess products. These scarcer panels are shown with asterisks in the checklist. Although complete panel prices are not explicitly listed, they would generally have a value 25% greater than the sum of the values of the individual players on that panel.

	NRMT	VG-E	GOOD
Complete Indiv. Set (150)	150.00	60.00	15.00
Common Player (1-150)	.30	.12	.03
☐ 1 Bob Tolan	.30	.12	.03
☐ 2 Cookie Rojas	.40	.16	.04
☐ 3 Darrell Evans	.60	.24	.06
☐ 4 Sal Bando	.40	.16	.04
☐ 5 Joe Morgan	2.00	.80	.20
☐ 6 Mickey Lolich	.50	.20	.05
☐ 7 Don Sutton	2.00	.80	.20
☐ 8 Bill Melton	.30	.12	.03
☐ 9 Tim Foli	.30	.12	.03
☐ 10 Joe LaHoud	.30	.12	.03
☐ 11A Bert Hooten (sic)	1.00	.40	.10

		NRMT	VG-E	GOOD			NRMT	VG-E	GOOD
☐	11B Burt Hooton	1.00	.40	.10	☐ 58	Nolan Ryan	4.50	1.80	.45
☐	12 Paul Blair	.30	.12	.03	☐ 59	Reggie Smith	.50	.20	.05
☐	13 Jim Barr	.30	.12	.03	☐ 60	Joe Coleman	.30	.12	.03
☐	14 Toby Harrah	.40	.16	.04	☐ 61	Ron Cey	.40	.16	.04
☐	15 John Milner	.30	.12	.03	☐ 62	Darrell Porter	.40	.16	.04
☐	16 Ken Holtzman	.40	.16	.04	☐ 63	Steve Carlton	4.00	1.60	.40
☐	17 Cesar Cedeno	.40	.16	.04	☐ 64	Gene Tenace	.30	.12	.03
☐	18 Dwight Evans	.75	.30	.07	☐ 65	Jose Cardenal	.30	.12	.03
☐	19 Willie McCovey	2.50	1.00	.25	☐ 66	Bill Lee	.40	.16	.04
☐	20 Tony Oliva	.60	.24	.06	☐ 67	Dave Lopes	.40	.16	.04
☐	21 Manny Sanguillen	.40	.16	.04	☐ 68	Wilbur Wood	.40	.16	.04
☐	22 Mickey Rivers	.40	.16	.04	☐ 69	Steve Renko	.30	.12	.03
☐	23 Lou Brock	2.50	1.00	.25	☐ 70	Joe Torre	.50	.20	.05
☐	24 Graig Nettles	1.50	.60	.15	☐ 71	Ted Sizemore	.30	.12	.03
	(Craig on front)				☐ 72	Bobby Grich	.40	.16	.04
☐	25 Jim Wynn	.40	.16	.04	☐ 73	Chris Speier	.30	.12	.03
☐	26 George Scott	.30	.12	.03	☐ 74	Bert Blyleven	.60	.24	.06
☐	27 Greg Luzinski	.50	.20	.05	☐ 75	Tom Seaver	4.00	1.60	.40
☐	28 Bert Campaneris	.40	.16	.04	☐ 76	Nate Colbert	.30	.12	.03
☐	29 Pete Rose	10.00	4.00	1.00	☐ 77	Don Kessinger	.40	.16	.04
☐	30 Buddy Bell	.50	.20	.05	☐ 78	George Medich	.30	.12	.03
☐	31 Gary Matthews	.40	.16	.04	☐ 79	Andy Messersmith	.50	.20	.05
☐	32 Freddie Patek	.30	.12	.03	☐ 80	Robin Yount *	8.00	3.25	.80
☐	33 Mike Lum	.30	.12	.03	☐ 81	Al Oliver *	.90	.36	.09
☐	34 Ellie Rodriguez	.30	.12	.03	☐ 82	Bill Singer *	.40	.16	.04
☐	35 Milt May	.50	.20	.05	☐ 83	Johnny Bench *	5.50	2.20	.55
	(photo actually Lee May)				☐ 84	Gaylord Perry *	2.00	.80	.20
☐	36 Willie Horton	.40	.16	.04	☐ 85	Dave Kingman *	.90	.36	.09
☐	37 Dave Winfield	3.50	1.40	.35	☐ 86	Ed Herrmann *	.40	.16	.04
☐	38 Tom Grieve	.40	.16	.04	☐ 87	Ralph Garr *	.40	.16	.04
☐	39 Barry Foote	.30	.12	.03	☐ 88	Reggie Jackson *	6.00	2.40	.60
☐	40 Joe Rudi	.40	.16	.04	☐ 89A	Doug Radar ERR *	1.00	.40	.10
☐	41 Bake McBride	.30	.12	.03		(sic, Rader)			
☐	42 Mike Cuellar	.40	.16	.04	☐ 89B	Doug Rader COR *	2.00	.80	.20
☐	43 Garry Maddox	.40	.16	.04	☐ 90	Elliott Maddox *	.40	.16	.04
☐	44 Carlos May	.30	.12	.03	☐ 91	Bill Russell *	.50	.20	.05
☐	45 Bud Harrelson	.30	.12	.03	☐ 92	John Mayberry *	.40	.16	.04
☐	46 Dave Chalk	.30	.12	.03	☐ 93	Dave Cash *	.40	.16	.04
☐	47 Dave Concepcion	.50	.20	.05	☐ 94	Jeff Burroughs *	.40	.16	.04
☐	48 Carl Yastrzemski	7.00	2.80	.70	☐ 95	Ted Simmons *	.80	.32	.08
☐	49 Steve Garvey	4.00	1.60	.40	☐ 96	Joe Decker *	.40	.16	.04
☐	50 Amos Otis	.40	.16	.04	☐ 97	Bill Buckner *	.80	.32	.08
☐	51 Rick Reuschel	.50	.20	.05	☐ 98	Bobby Darwin *	.40	.16	.04
☐	52 Rollie Fingers	1.00	.40	.10	☐ 99	Phil Niekro *	2.50	1.00	.25
☐	53 Bob Watson	.40	.16	.04	☐ 100	Jim Sundberg	.40	.16	.04
☐	54 John Ellis	.30	.12	.03	☐ 101	Greg Gross	.30	.12	.03
☐	55 Bob Bailey	.30	.12	.03	☐ 102	Luis Tiant	.50	.20	.05
☐	56 Rod Carew	4.00	1.60	.40	☐ 103	Glenn Beckert	.30	.12	.03
☐	57 Rich Hebner	.30	.12	.03	☐ 104	Hal McRae	.40	.16	.04

		NRMT	VG-E	GOOD
☐ 105	Mike Jorgensen	.30	.12	.03
☐ 106	Mike Hargrove	.40	.16	.04
☐ 107	Don Gullett	.40	.16	.04
☐ 108	Tito Fuentes	.30	.12	.03
☐ 109	John Grubb	.30	.12	.03
☐ 110	Jim Kaat	.75	.30	.07
☐ 111	Felix Millan	.30	.12	.03
☐ 112	Don Money	.30	.12	.03
☐ 113	Rick Monday	.40	.16	.04
☐ 114	Dick Bosman	.30	.12	.03
☐ 115	Roger Metzger	.30	.12	.03
☐ 116	Fergie Jenkins	.75	.30	.07
☐ 117	Dusty Baker	.50	.20	.05
☐ 118	Billy Champion *	.40	.16	.04
☐ 119	Bob Gibson *	3.00	1.20	.30
☐ 120	Bill Freehan *	.50	.20	.05
☐ 121	Cesar Geronimo	.30	.12	.03
☐ 122	Jorge Orta	.30	.12	.03
☐ 123	Cleon Jones	.30	.12	.03
☐ 124	Steve Busby	.40	.16	.04
☐ 125A	Bill Madlock ERR (pitcher)	1.50	.60	.15
☐ 125B	Bill Madlock COR (infielder)	1.50	.60	.15
☐ 126	Jim Palmer	2.50	1.00	.25
☐ 127	Tony Perez	.75	.30	.07
☐ 128	Larry Hisle	.40	.16	.04
☐ 129	Rusty Staub	.50	.20	.05
☐ 130	Hank Aaron *	7.00	2.80	.70
☐ 131	Rennie Stennett *	.40	.16	.04
☐ 132	Rico Petrocelli *	.50	.20	.05
☐ 133	Mike Schmidt	6.00	2.40	.60
☐ 134	Sparky Lyle	.50	.20	.05
☐ 135	Willie Stargell	2.50	1.00	.25
☐ 136	Ken Henderson	.30	.12	.03
☐ 137	Willie Montanez	.30	.12	.03
☐ 138	Thurman Munson	3.50	1.40	.35
☐ 139	Richie Zisk	.40	.16	.04
☐ 140	George Hendrick	.40	.16	.04
☐ 141	Bobby Murcer	.50	.20	.05
☐ 142	Lee May	.40	.16	.04
☐ 143	Carlton Fisk	.75	.30	.07
☐ 144	Brooks Robinson	3.00	1.20	.30
☐ 145	Bobby Bonds	.50	.20	.05
☐ 146	Gary Sutherland	.30	.12	.03
☐ 147	Oscar Gamble	.30	.12	.03
☐ 148	Jim Hunter	2.00	.80	.20
☐ 149	Tug McGraw	.50	.20	.05
☐ 150	Dave McNally	.40	.16	.04

1976 Hostess

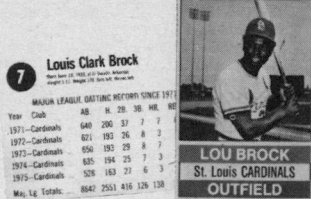

The cards in this 150-card set measure 2 ¼ " by 3 ¼ " individually or 3 ¼ " by 7 ¼ " as panels of three. The 1976 Hostess set contains full-color, numbered cards issued in panels of three cards each on family size packages of Hostess cakes. Scarcer panels (those only found on less popular Hostess products) are listed in the checklist below with asterisks. Complete panels of three have a value 25% more than the sum of the individual cards on the panel, e.g., 151 Ferguson Jenkins, 152 Mike Cuellar, 153 Tom Murphy, 154 Al Cowens, 155 Barry Foote, 156 Steve Carlton, 157 Richie Zisk, 158 Ken Holtzman, and 159 Cliff Johnson.

		NRMT	VG-E	GOOD
Complete Indiv. Set (150)		150.00	60.00	15.00
Common Player (1-150)		.30	.12	.03
☐	1 Fred Lynn	1.25	.50	.12
☐	2 Joe Morgan	2.00	.80	.20
☐	3 Phil Niekro	2.00	.80	.20
☐	4 Gaylord Perry	1.50	.60	.15
☐	5 Bob Watson	.40	.16	.04
☐	6 Bill Freehan	.50	.20	.05
☐	7 Lou Brock	2.50	1.00	.25
☐	8 Al Fitzmorris	.30	.12	.03
☐	9 Rennie Stennett	.30	.12	.03
☐	10 Tony Oliva	.60	.24	.06
☐	11 Robin Yount	3.50	1.40	.35

		NRMT	VG-E	GOOD			NRMT	VG-E	GOOD
☐ 12	Rick Manning	.30	.12	.03	☐ 61	Bert Campaneris *	.50	.20	.05
☐ 13	Bobby Grich	.40	.16	.04	☐ 62	Gary Carter *	6.00	2.40	.60
☐ 14	Terry Forster	.40	.16	.04	☐ 63	Ron Cey *	.75	.30	.07
☐ 15	Dave Kingman	.60	.24	.06	☐ 64	Carlton Fisk *	1.00	.40	.10
☐ 16	Thurman Munson	3.50	1.40	.35	☐ 65	Marty Perez *	.40	.16	.04
☐ 17	Rick Reuschel	.50	.20	.05	☐ 66	Pete Rose *	10.00	4.00	1.00
☐ 18	Bobby Bonds	.50	.20	.05	☐ 67	Roger Metzger *	.40	.16	.04
☐ 19	Steve Garvey	4.00	1.60	.40	☐ 68	Jim Sundberg *	.40	.16	.04
☐ 20	Vida Blue	.40	.16	.04	☐ 69	Ron LeFlore *	.40	.16	.04
☐ 21	Dave Rader	.30	.12	.03	☐ 70	Ted Sizemore *	.40	.16	.04
☐ 22	Johnny Bench	4.00	1.60	.40	☐ 71	Steve Busby *	.50	.20	.05
☐ 23	Luis Tiant	.50	.20	.05	☐ 72	Manny Sanguillen *	.50	.20	.05
☐ 24	Darrell Evans	.60	.24	.06	☐ 73	Larry Hisle *	.40	.16	.04
☐ 25	Larry Dierker	.30	.12	.03	☐ 74	Pete Broberg *	.40	.16	.04
☐ 26	Willie Horton	.40	.16	.04	☐ 75	Boog Powell *	.75	.30	.07
☐ 27	John Ellis	.30	.12	.03	☐ 76	Ken Singleton *	.60	.24	.06
☐ 28	Al Cowens	.40	.16	.04	☐ 77	Rich Gossage *	1.25	.50	.12
☐ 29	Jerry Reuss	.40	.16	.04	☐ 78	Jerry Grote *	.40	.16	.04
☐ 30	Reggie Smith	.50	.20	.05	☐ 79	Nolan Ryan *	5.00	2.00	.50
☐ 31	Bobby Darwin *	.40	.16	.04	☐ 80	Rick Monday *	.50	.20	.05
☐ 32	Fritz Peterson *	.40	.16	.04	☐ 81	Graig Nettles *	.75	.30	.07
☐ 33	Rod Carew *	4.00	1.60	.40	☐ 82	Chris Speier *	.30	.12	.03
☐ 34	Carlos May *	.40	.16	.04	☐ 83	Dave Winfield *	3.00	1.20	.30
☐ 35	Tom Seaver *	4.50	1.80	.45	☐ 84	Mike Schmidt *	6.00	2.40	.60
☐ 36	Brooks Robinson *	4.00	1.60	.40	☐ 85	Buzz Capra	.30	.12	.03
☐ 37	Jose Cardenal	.30	.12	.03	☐ 86	Tony Perez	.75	.30	.07
☐ 38	Ron Blomberg	.30	.12	.03	☐ 87	Dwight Evans	.75	.30	.07
☐ 39	Leroy Stanton	.30	.12	.03	☐ 88	Mike Hargrove	.30	.12	.03
☐ 40	Dave Cash	.30	.12	.03	☐ 89	Joe Coleman	.30	.12	.03
☐ 41	John Montefusco	.40	.16	.04	☐ 90	Greg Gross	.30	.12	.03
☐ 42	Bob Tolan	.30	.12	.03	☐ 91	John Mayberry	.40	.16	.04
☐ 43	Carl Morton	.30	.12	.03	☐ 92	John Candelaria	.50	.20	.05
☐ 44	Rick Burleson	.40	.16	.04	☐ 93	Bake McBride	.30	.12	.03
☐ 45	Don Gullett	.40	.16	.04	☐ 94	Hank Aaron	6.00	2.40	.60
☐ 46	Vern Ruhle	.30	.12	.03	☐ 95	Buddy Bell	.50	.20	.05
☐ 47	Cesar Cedeno	.40	.16	.04	☐ 96	Steve Braun	.30	.12	.03
☐ 48	Toby Harrah	.40	.16	.04	☐ 97	Jon Matlack	.40	.16	.04
☐ 49	Willie Stargell	2.50	1.00	.25	☐ 98	Lee May	.40	.16	.04
☐ 50	Al Hrabosky	.40	.16	.04	☐ 99	Wilbur Wood	.40	.16	.04
☐ 51	Amos Otis	.40	.16	.04	☐ 100	Bill Madlock	.60	.24	.06
☐ 52	Bud Harrelson	.30	.12	.03	☐ 101	Frank Tanana	.40	.16	.04
☐ 53	Jim Hughes	.30	.12	.03	☐ 102	Mickey Rivers	.40	.16	.04
☐ 54	George Scott	.30	.12	.03	☐ 103	Mike Ivie	.30	.12	.03
☐ 55	Mike Vail	.40	.16	.04	☐ 104	Rollie Fingers	1.00	.40	.10
☐ 56	Jim Palmer *	3.00	1.20	.30	☐ 105	Dave Lopes	.40	.16	.04
☐ 57	Jorge Orta	.40	.16	.04	☐ 106	George Foster	.90	.36	.09
☐ 58	Chris Chambliss *	.50	.20	.05	☐ 107	Denny Doyle	.30	.12	.03
☐ 59	Dave Chalk *	.40	.16	.04	☐ 108	Earl Williams	.30	.12	.03
☐ 60	Ray Burris *	.40	.16	.04	☐ 109	Tom Veryzer	.30	.12	.03

1977 Hostess

		NRMT	VG-E	GOOD
☐ 110	J.R. Richard	.40	.16	.04
☐ 111	Jeff Burroughs	.30	.12	.03
☐ 112	Al Oliver	.75	.30	.07
☐ 113	Ted Simmons	.75	.30	.07
☐ 114	George Brett	7.00	2.80	.70
☐ 115	Frank Duffy	.30	.12	.03
☐ 116	Bert Blyleven	.50	.20	.05
☐ 117	Darrell Porter	.30	.12	.03
☐ 118	Don Baylor	.50	.20	.05
☐ 119	Bucky Dent	.50	.20	.05
☐ 120	Felix Millan	.30	.12	.03
☐ 121	Mike Cuellar	.40	.16	.04
☐ 122	Gene Tenace	.30	.12	.03
☐ 123	Bobby Murcer	.50	.20	.05
☐ 124	Willie McCovey	2.00	.80	.20
☐ 125	Greg Luzinski	.50	.20	.05
☐ 126	Larry Parrish	.60	.24	.06
☐ 127	Jim Rice	4.00	1.60	.40
☐ 128	Dave Concepcion	.50	.20	.05
☐ 129	Jim Wynn	.40	.16	.04
☐ 130	Tom Grieve	.40	.16	.04
☐ 131	Mike Cosgrove	.30	.12	.03
☐ 132	Dan Meyer	.30	.12	.03
☐ 133	Dave Parker	2.00	.80	.20
☐ 134	Don Kessinger	.40	.16	.04
☐ 135	Hal McRae	.40	.16	.04
☐ 136	Don Money	.30	.12	.03
☐ 137	Dennis Eckersley	1.00	.40	.10
☐ 138	Fergie Jenkins	.60	.24	.06
☐ 139	Mike Torrez	.40	.16	.04
☐ 140	Jerry Morales	.30	.12	.03
☐ 141	Jim Hunter	2.00	.80	.20
☐ 142	Gary Matthews	.40	.16	.04
☐ 143	Randy Jones	.40	.16	.04
☐ 144	Mike Jorgensen	.30	.12	.03
☐ 145	Larry Bowa	.50	.20	.05
☐ 146	Reggie Jackson	4.50	1.80	.45
☐ 147	Steve Yeager	.30	.12	.03
☐ 148	Dave May	.30	.12	.03
☐ 149	Carl Yastrzemski	6.00	2.40	.60
☐ 150	Cesar Geronimo	.30	.12	.03

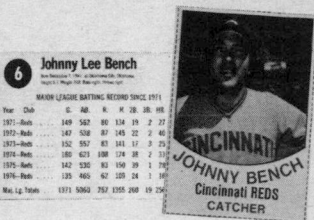

The cards in this 150-card set measure 2 ¼ " by 3 ¼ " individually or 3 ¼ " by 7 ¼ " as panels of three. The 1977 Hostess set contains full-color, numbered cards issued in panels of three cards each with Hostess family sized caked products. Scarcer panels are listed in the checklist below with asterisks. Although complete panel prices are not explicitly listed below, they would generally have a value 25% greater than the sum of the individual players on the panel. There are 10 additional cards proofed, but not produced or distributed; they are 151 Ed Kranepool, 152 Ross Grimsley, 153 Ken Brett, 154 Rowland Office, 155 Rick Wise, 156 Paul Splittorff, 157 Gerald Augustine, 158 Ken Forsch, 159 Jerry Reuss (Reuss is also #119), and 160 Nelson Briles. There is also a complete variation set that was available one card per Twinkie package. Common cards in this Twinkie set are worth double the prices listed below, although the stars are only worth about 20% more. The Twinkie cards are distinguished by the thick printing bar or band printed on the card backs just below the statistics.

		NRMT	VG-E	GOOD
Complete Indiv. Set (150)		150.00	60.00	15.00
Common Player (1-150)		.30	.12	.03
☐ 1	Jim Palmer	2.50	1.00	.25
☐ 2	Joe Morgan	2.00	.80	.20
☐ 3	Reggie Jackson	4.50	1.80	.45

			NRMT	VG-E	GOOD				NRMT	VG-E	GOOD
☐	4	Carl Yastrzemski ...	6.00	2.40	.60	☐	53	Rick Manning	.30	.12	.03
☐	5	Thurman Munson ...	3.50	1.40	.35	☐	54	Bill Buckner	.50	.20	.05
☐	6	Johnny Bench	4.00	1.60	.40	☐	55	Lee May	.40	.16	.04
☐	7	Tom Seaver	3.50	1.40	.35	☐	56	John Mayberry ...	.40	.16	.04
☐	8	Pete Rose	8.50	3.50	.85	☐	57	Darrell Chaney ...	.30	.12	.03
☐	9	Rod Carew	3.50	1.40	.35	☐	58	Cesar Cedeno	.40	.16	.04
☐	10	Luis Tiant	.50	.20	.05	☐	59	Ken Griffey	.40	.16	.04
☐	11	Phil Garner	.30	.12	.03	☐	60	Dave Kingman	.60	.24	.06
☐	12	Sixto Lezcano	.30	.12	.03	☐	61	Ted Simmons	.75	.30	.07
☐	13	Mike Torrez	.30	.12	.03	☐	62	Larry Bowa	.60	.24	.06
☐	14	Dave Lopes	.40	.16	.04	☐	63	Frank Tanana	.40	.16	.04
☐	15	Doug DeCinces	.50	.20	.05	☐	64	Jason Thompson ..	.40	.16	.04
☐	16	Jim Spencer	.30	.12	.03	☐	65	Ken Brett	.30	.12	.03
☐	17	Hal McRae	.40	.16	.04	☐	66	Roy Smalley	.40	.16	.04
☐	18	Mike Hargrove	.30	.12	.03	☐	67	Ray Burris	.30	.12	.03
☐	19	Willie Montanez * ...	.40	.16	.04	☐	68	Rick Burleson	.40	.16	.04
☐	20	Roger Metzger * ..	.40	.16	.04	☐	69	Buddy Bell	.50	.20	.05
☐	21	Dwight Evans * ...	1.50	.60	.15	☐	70	Don Sutton	2.00	.80	.20
☐	22	Steve Rogers *	.75	.30	.07	☐	71	Mark Belanger	.40	.16	.04
☐	23	Jim Rice *	3.50	1.40	.35	☐	72	Dennis Leonard ...	.40	.16	.04
☐	24	Pete Falcone *	.40	.16	.04	☐	73	Gaylord Perry	1.50	.60	.15
☐	25	Greg Luzinski * ...	.80	.32	.08	☐	74	Dick Ruthven	.30	.12	.03
☐	26	Randy Jones *	.50	.20	.05	☐	75	Jose Cruz	.50	.20	.05
☐	27	Willie Stargell * ...	3.00	1.20	.30	☐	76	Cesar Geronimo ..	.30	.12	.03
☐	28	John Hiller *	.40	.16	.04	☐	77	Jerry Koosman ...	.50	.20	.05
☐	29	Bobby Murcer *	.50	.20	.05	☐	78	Garry Templeton ..	.80	.32	.08
☐	30	Rick Monday *	.50	.20	.05	☐	79	Jim Hunter	2.00	.80	.20
☐	31	John Montefusco * .	.40	.16	.04	☐	80	John Candelaria ..	.50	.20	.05
☐	32	Lou Brock *	3.00	1.20	.30	☐	81	Nolan Ryan	4.00	1.60	.40
☐	33	Bill North *	.40	.16	.04	☐	82	Rusty Staub	.60	.24	.06
☐	34	Robin Yount *	3.00	1.20	.30	☐	83	Jim Barr	.30	.12	.03
☐	35	Steve Garvey *	5.00	2.00	.50	☐	84	Butch Wynegar ...	.40	.16	.04
☐	36	George Brett *	6.50	2.60	.65	☐	85	Jose Cardenal ...	.30	.12	.03
☐	37	Toby Harrah *	.50	.20	.05	☐	86	Claudell Washington	.50	.20	.05
☐	38	Jerry Royster *	.40	.16	.04	☐	87	Bill Travers	.30	.12	.03
☐	39	Bob Watson *	.40	.16	.04	☐	88	Rick Waits	.30	.12	.03
☐	40	George Foster	.80	.32	.08	☐	89	Ron Cey	.50	.20	.05
☐	41	Gary Carter	4.00	1.60	.40	☐	90	Al Bumbry	.30	.12	.03
☐	42	John Denny	.40	.16	.04	☐	91	Bucky Dent	.50	.20	.05
☐	43	Mike Schmidt	4.50	1.80	.45	☐	92	Amos Otis	.40	.16	.04
☐	44	Dave Winfield	3.00	1.20	.30	☐	93	Tom Grieve	.40	.16	.04
☐	45	Al Oliver	.75	.30	.07	☐	94	Enos Cabell	.30	.12	.03
☐	46	Mark Fidrych	.50	.20	.05	☐	95	Dave Concepcion ..	.50	.20	.05
☐	47	Larry Herndon	.30	.12	.03	☐	96	Felix Millan	.30	.12	.03
☐	48	Dave Goltz	.30	.12	.03	☐	97	Bake McBride	.30	.12	.03
☐	49	Jerry Morales	.30	.12	.03	☐	98	Chris Chambliss ..	.40	.16	.04
☐	50	Ron LeFlore	.40	.16	.04	☐	99	Butch Metzger ...	.30	.12	.03
☐	51	Fred Lynn	1.00	.40	.10	☐	100	Rennie Stennett ..	.30	.12	.03
☐	52	Vida Blue	.40	.16	.04	☐	101	Dave Roberts	.30	.12	.03

1978 Hostess

		NRMT	VG-E	GOOD
☐ 102	Lyman Bostock	.40	.16	.04
☐ 103	Rick Reuschel	.50	.20	.05
☐ 104	Carlton Fisk	.80	.32	.08
☐ 105	Jim Slaton	.30	.12	.03
☐ 106	Dennis Eckersley	.75	.30	.07
☐ 107	Ken Singleton	.50	.20	.05
☐ 108	Ralph Garr	.30	.12	.03
☐ 109	Freddie Patek *	.40	.16	.04
☐ 110	Jim Sundberg *	.40	.16	.04
☐ 111	Phil Niekro *	2.00	.80	.20
☐ 112	J.R. Richard *	.50	.20	.05
☐ 113	Gary Nolan *	.40	.16	.04
☐ 114	Jon Matlack *	.50	.20	.05
☐ 115	Keith Hernandez *	4.00	1.60	.40
☐ 116	Graig Nettles *	1.00	.40	.10
☐ 117	Steve Carlton *	3.50	1.40	.35
☐ 118	Bill Madlock *	1.25	.50	.12
☐ 119	Jerry Reuss *	.50	.20	.05
☐ 120	Aurelio Rodriguez *	.40	.16	.04
☐ 121	Dan Ford *	.40	.16	.04
☐ 122	Ray Fosse *	.40	.16	.04
☐ 123	George Hendrick *	.50	.20	.05
☐ 124	Alan Ashby	.30	.12	.03
☐ 125	Joe Lis	.30	.12	.03
☐ 126	Sal Bando	.40	.16	.04
☐ 127	Richie Zisk	.40	.16	.04
☐ 128	Rich Gossage	.75	.30	.07
☐ 129	Don Baylor	.50	.20	.05
☐ 130	Dave McKay	.30	.12	.03
☐ 131	Bob Grich	.40	.16	.04
☐ 132	Dave Pagan	.30	.12	.03
☐ 133	Dave Cash	.30	.12	.03
☐ 134	Steve Braun	.30	.12	.03
☐ 135	Dan Meyer	.30	.12	.03
☐ 136	Bill Stein	.30	.12	.03
☐ 137	Rollie Fingers	1.25	.50	.12
☐ 138	Brian Downing	.50	.20	.05
☐ 139	Bill Singer	.30	.12	.03
☐ 140	Doyle Alexander	.50	.20	.05
☐ 141	Gene Tenace	.30	.12	.03
☐ 142	Gary Matthews	.40	.16	.04
☐ 143	Don Gullett	.40	.16	.04
☐ 144	Wayne Garland	.30	.12	.03
☐ 145	Pete Broberg	.30	.12	.03
☐ 146	Joe Rudi	.40	.16	.04
☐ 147	Glenn Abbott	.30	.12	.03
☐ 148	George Scott	.30	.12	.03
☐ 149	Bert Campaneris	.40	.16	.04
☐ 150	Andy Messersmith	.40	.16	.04

The cards in this 150-card set measure 2 ¼ " by 3 ¼ " individually or 3 ¼ " by 7 ¼ " as panels of three. The 1978 Hostess set contains full-color, numbered cards issued in panels of three cards each on family packages of Hostess cake products. Scarcer panels are listed in the checklist with asterisks. The 1978 Hostess panels are considered by some collectors to be somewhat more difficult to obtain than Hostess panels of other years. Although complete panel prices are not explicitly listed below, they would generally have a value 25% greater than the sum of the individual players on the panel. There is additional interest in Eddie Murray #31 since this card corresponds to his "rookie" year in cards.

		NRMT	VG-E	GOOD
Complete Indiv. Set (150)		150.00	60.00	15.00
Common Player (1-150)		.30	.12	.03
☐ 1	Butch Hobson	.30	.12	.03
☐ 2	George Foster	.80	.32	.08
☐ 3	Bob Forsch	.40	.16	.04
☐ 4	Tony Perez	.75	.30	.07
☐ 5	Bruce Sutter	.80	.32	.08
☐ 6	Hal McRae	.40	.16	.04
☐ 7	Tommy John	.90	.36	.09
☐ 8	Greg Luzinski	.50	.20	.05
☐ 9	Enos Cabell	.30	.12	.03
☐ 10	Doug DeCinces	.50	.20	.05
☐ 11	Willie Stargell	2.00	.80	.20
☐ 12	Ed Halicki	.30	.12	.03

			NRMT	VG-E	GOOD				NRMT	VG-E	GOOD
☐	13	Larry Hisle	.40	.16	.04	☐	62	Bobby Grich	.40	.16	.04
☐	14	Jim Slaton	.30	.12	.03	☐	63	Dave Winfield	3.00	1.20	.30
☐	15	Buddy Bell	.50	.20	.05	☐	64	Dan Driessen	.40	.16	.04
☐	16	Earl Williams	.30	.12	.03	☐	65	Ted Simmons	.75	.30	.07
☐	17	Glenn Abbott	.30	.12	.03	☐	66	Jerry Remy	.30	.12	.03
☐	18	Dan Ford	.30	.12	.03	☐	67	Al Cowens	.40	.16	.04
☐	19	Gary Matthews	.40	.16	.04	☐	68	Sparky Lyle	.60	.24	.06
☐	20	Eric Soderholm	.30	.12	.03	☐	69	Manny Trillo	.40	.16	.04
☐	21	Bump Wills	.30	.12	.03	☐	70	Don Sutton	2.00	.80	.20
☐	22	Keith Hernandez	2.50	1.00	.25	☐	71	Larry Bowa	.60	.24	.06
☐	23	Dave Cash	.30	.12	.03	☐	72	Jose Cruz	.50	.20	.05
☐	24	George Scott	.30	.12	.03	☐	73	Willie McCovey	2.00	.80	.20
☐	25	Ron Guidry	1.50	.60	.15	☐	74	Bert Blyleven	.60	.24	.06
☐	26	Dave Kingman	.60	.24	.06	☐	75	Ken Singleton	.50	.20	.05
☐	27	George Brett	5.00	2.00	.50	☐	76	Bill North	.30	.12	.03
☐	28	Bob Watson *	.40	.16	.04	☐	77	Jason Thompson	.40	.16	.04
☐	29	Bob Boone *	.75	.30	.07	☐	78	Dennis Eckersley	.60	.24	.06
☐	30	Reggie Smith *	.60	.24	.06	☐	79	Jim Sundberg	.40	.16	.04
☐	31	Eddie Murray *	11.00	4.50	1.10	☐	80	Jerry Koosman	.50	.20	.05
☐	32	Gary Lavelle *	.40	.16	.04	☐	81	Bruce Bochte	.30	.12	.03
☐	33	Rennie Stennett *	.40	.16	.04	☐	82	George Hendrick	.40	.16	.04
☐	34	Duane Kuiper *	.40	.16	.04	☐	83	Nolan Ryan	3.50	1.40	.35
☐	35	Sixto Lezcano *	.40	.16	.04	☐	84	Roy Howell	.30	.12	.03
☐	36	Dave Rozema *	.40	.16	.04	☐	85	Roger Metzger	.30	.12	.03
☐	37	Butch Wynegar *	.50	.20	.05	☐	86	Doc Medich	.30	.12	.03
☐	38	Mitchell Page *	.40	.16	.04	☐	87	Joe Morgan	2.00	.80	.20
☐	39	Bill Stein *	.40	.16	.04	☐	88	Dennis Leonard	.40	.16	.04
☐	40	Elliott Maddox	.30	.12	.03	☐	89	Willie Randolph	.75	.30	.07
☐	41	Mike Hargrove	.40	.16	.04	☐	90	Bobby Murcer	.50	.20	.05
☐	42	Bobby Bonds	.50	.20	.05	☐	91	Rick Manning	.30	.12	.03
☐	43	Garry Templeton	.50	.20	.05	☐	92	J.R. Richard	.40	.16	.04
☐	44	Johnny Bench	4.00	1.60	.40	☐	93	Ron Cey	.50	.20	.05
☐	45	Jim Rice	3.00	1.20	.30	☐	94	Sal Bando	.40	.16	.04
☐	46	Bill Buckner	.50	.20	.05	☐	95	Ron LeFlore	.40	.16	.04
☐	47	Reggie Jackson	4.00	1.60	.40	☐	96	Dave Goltz	.30	.12	.03
☐	48	Freddie Patek	.30	.12	.03	☐	97	Dan Meyer	.30	.12	.03
☐	49	Steve Carlton	3.50	1.40	.35	☐	98	Chris Chambliss	.40	.16	.04
☐	50	Cesar Cedeno	.40	.16	.04	☐	99	Biff Pocoroba	.30	.12	.03
☐	51	Steve Yeager	.30	.12	.03	☐	100	Oscar Gamble	.40	.16	.04
☐	52	Phil Garner	.30	.12	.03	☐	101	Frank Tanana	.40	.16	.04
☐	53	Lee May	.40	.16	.04	☐	102	Len Randle	.30	.12	.03
☐	54	Darrell Evans	.60	.24	.06	☐	103	Tommy Hutton	.30	.12	.03
☐	55	Steve Kemp	.40	.16	.04	☐	104	John Candelaria	.50	.20	.05
☐	56	Dusty Baker	.40	.16	.04	☐	105	George Orta	.30	.12	.03
☐	57	Ray Fosse	.30	.12	.03	☐	106	Ken Reitz	.30	.12	.03
☐	58	Manny Sanguillen	.40	.16	.04	☐	107	Bill Campbell	.30	.12	.03
☐	59	Tom Johnson	.30	.12	.03	☐	108	Dave Concepcion	.50	.20	.05
☐	60	Lee Stanton	.30	.12	.03	☐	109	Joe Ferguson	.30	.12	.03
☐	61	Jeff Burroughs	.40	.16	.04	☐	110	Mickey Rivers	.40	.16	.04

		NRMT	VG-E	GOOD
☐ 111	Paul Splittorff	.40	.16	.04
☐ 112	Dave Lopes	.50	.20	.05
☐ 113	Mike Schmidt	5.00	2.00	.50
☐ 114	Joe Rudi	.40	.16	.04
☐ 115	Milt May	.30	.12	.03
☐ 116	Jim Palmer	2.00	.80	.20
☐ 117	Bill Madlock	.80	.32	.08
☐ 118	Roy Smalley	.40	.16	.04
☐ 119	Cecil Cooper	.90	.36	.09
☐ 120	Rick Langford	.30	.12	.03
☐ 121	Ruppert Jones	.40	.16	.04
☐ 122	Phil Niekro	1.50	.60	.15
☐ 123	Toby Harrah	.40	.16	.04
☐ 124	Chet Lemon	.40	.16	.04
☐ 125	Gene Tenace	.30	.12	.03
☐ 126	Steve Henderson	.30	.12	.03
☐ 127	Mike Torrez	.30	.12	.03
☐ 128	Pete Rose	8.50	3.50	.85
☐ 129	John Denny	.40	.16	.04
☐ 130	Darrell Porter	.40	.16	.04
☐ 131	Rick Reuschel	.50	.20	.05
☐ 132	Graig Nettles	.75	.30	.07
☐ 133	Garry Maddox	.40	.16	.04
☐ 134	Mike Flanagan	.40	.16	.04
☐ 135	Dave Parker	1.75	.70	.17
☐ 136	Terry Whitfield	.30	.12	.03
☐ 137	Wayne Garland	.30	.12	.03
☐ 138	Robin Yount	3.00	1.20	.30
☐ 139	Gaylord Perry	1.50	.60	.15
☐ 140	Rod Carew	3.50	1.40	.35
☐ 141	Greg Gross	.30	.12	.03
☐ 142	Barry Bonnell	.30	.12	.03
☐ 143	Willie Montanez	.30	.12	.03
☐ 144	Rollie Fingers	1.25	.50	.12
☐ 145	Lyman Bostock	.40	.16	.04
☐ 146	Gary Carter	3.50	1.40	.35
☐ 147	Ron Blomberg	.30	.12	.03
☐ 148	Bob Bailor	.30	.12	.03
☐ 149	Tom Seaver	3.50	1.40	.35
☐ 150	Thurman Munson	3.00	1.20	.30

1979 Hostess

The cards in this 150-card set measure 3 ¼ " by 7 ¼ " as panels of three. The 1979 Hostess set contains full-color, numbered cards issued in panels of three cards each on the backs of family sized Hostess cake products. Scarcer panels are listed in the checklist below with asterisks. Although complete panel prices are not explicitly listed below they would generally have a value 25% greater than the sum of the individual players on the panel. There is additional interest in Ozzie Smith #102, since this card corresponds to his "rookie" year in cards.

		NRMT	VG-E	GOOD
Complete Indiv. Set (150)		150.00	60.00	15.00
Common Player (1-150)		.30	.12	.03
☐ 1	John Denny	.40	.16	.04
☐ 2	Jim Rice	3.00	1.20	.30
☐ 3	Doug Bair	.30	.12	.03
☐ 4	Darrell Porter	.40	.16	.04
☐ 5	Ross Grimsley	.30	.12	.03
☐ 6	Bobby Murcer	.50	.20	.05
☐ 7	Lee Mazzilli	.30	.12	.03
☐ 8	Steve Garvey	3.50	1.40	.35
☐ 9	Mike Schmidt	4.50	1.80	.45
☐ 10	Terry Whitfield	.30	.12	.03
☐ 11	Jim Palmer	2.50	1.00	.25
☐ 12	Omar Moreno	.30	.12	.03
☐ 13	Duane Kulper	.30	.12	.03
☐ 14	Mike Caldwell	.40	.16	.04
☐ 15	Steve Kemp	.40	.16	.04
☐ 16	Dave Goltz	.30	.12	.03

			NRMT	VG-E	GOOD
☐	17	Mitchell Page	.30	.12	.03
☐	18	Bill Stein	.30	.12	.03
☐	19	Gene Tenace	.40	.16	.04
☐	20	Jeff Burroughs	.40	.16	.04
☐	21	Francisco Barrios	.30	.12	.03
☐	22	Mike Torrez	.30	.12	.03
☐	23	Ken Reitz	.30	.12	.03
☐	24	Gary Carter	3.50	1.40	.35
☐	25	Al Hrabosky	.40	.16	.04
☐	26	Thurman Munson	3.00	1.20	.30
☐	27	Bill Buckner	.50	.20	.05
☐	28	Ron Cey *	.60	.24	.06
☐	29	J.R. Richard *	.40	.16	.04
☐	30	Greg Luzinski *	.80	.32	.08
☐	31	Ed Ott *	.40	.16	.04
☐	32	Dennis Martinez *	.50	.20	.05
☐	33	Darrell Evans *	.60	.24	.06
☐	34	Ron LeFlore	.40	.16	.04
☐	35	Rick Waits	.30	.12	.03
☐	36	Cecil Cooper	.75	.30	.07
☐	37	Leon Roberts	.30	.12	.03
☐	38	Rod Carew	3.00	1.20	.30
☐	39	John Henry Johnson	.30	.12	.03
☐	40	Chet Lemon	.40	.16	.04
☐	41	Craig Swan	.30	.12	.03
☐	42	Gary Matthews	.40	.16	.04
☐	43	Lamar Johnson	.30	.12	.03
☐	44	Ted Simmons	.75	.30	.07
☐	45	Ken Griffey	.40	.16	.04
☐	46	Fred Patek	.30	.12	.03
☐	47	Frank Tanana	.40	.16	.04
☐	48	Goose Gossage	.80	.32	.08
☐	49	Burt Hooton	.30	.12	.03
☐	50	Ellis Valentine	.30	.12	.03
☐	51	Ken Forsch	.30	.12	.03
☐	52	Bob Knepper	.50	.20	.05
☐	53	Dave Parker	1.75	.70	.17
☐	54	Doug DeCinces	.50	.20	.05
☐	55	Robin Yount	3.00	1.20	.30
☐	56	Rusty Staub	.50	.20	.05
☐	57	Gary Alexander	.30	.12	.03
☐	58	Julio Cruz	.30	.12	.03
☐	59	Matt Keough	.30	.12	.03
☐	60	Roy Smalley	.30	.12	.03
☐	61	Joe Morgan	2.00	.80	.20
☐	62	Phil Niekro	2.00	.80	.20
☐	63	Don Baylor	.50	.20	.05
☐	64	Dwight Evans	.75	.30	.07
☐	65	Tom Seaver	3.00	1.20	.30
☐	66	George Hendrick	.40	.16	.04
☐	67	Rick Reuschel	.50	.20	.05
☐	68	George Brett	5.00	2.00	.50
☐	69	Lou Piniella	.50	.20	.05
☐	70	Enos Cabell	.30	.12	.03
☐	71	Steve Carlton	3.00	1.20	.30
☐	72	Reggie Smith	.50	.20	.05
☐	73	Rick Dempsey *	.50	.20	.05
☐	74	Vida Blue *	.50	.20	.05
☐	75	Phil Garner *	.40	.16	.04
☐	76	Rick Manning *	.40	.16	.04
☐	77	Mark Fidrych *	.50	.20	.05
☐	78	Mario Guerrero *	.40	.16	.04
☐	79	Bob Stinson *	.40	.16	.04
☐	80	Al Oliver *	.90	.36	.09
☐	81	Doug Flynn *	.40	.16	.04
☐	82	John Mayberry *	.40	.16	.04
☐	83	Gaylord Perry	1.50	.60	.15
☐	84	Joe Rudi	.40	.16	.04
☐	85	Dave Concepcion	.50	.20	.05
☐	86	John Candelaria	.40	.16	.04
☐	87	Pete Vuckovich	.40	.16	.04
☐	88	Ivan DeJesus	.30	.12	.03
☐	89	Ron Guidry	1.50	.60	.15
☐	90	Hal McRae	.40	.16	.04
☐	91	Cesar Cedeno	.40	.16	.04
☐	92	Don Sutton	2.00	.80	.20
☐	93	Andre Thornton	.40	.16	.04
☐	94	Roger Erickson	.30	.12	.03
☐	95	Larry Hisle	.40	.16	.04
☐	96	Jason Thompson	.40	.16	.04
☐	97	Jim Sundberg	.40	.16	.04
☐	98	Bob Horner	2.00	.80	.20
☐	99	Ruppert Jones	.40	.16	.04
☐	100	Willie Montanez	.30	.12	.03
☐	101	Nolan Ryan	3.00	1.20	.30
☐	102	Ozzie Smith	6.50	2.60	.65
☐	103	Eric Soderholm	.30	.12	.03
☐	104	Willie Stargell	2.00	.80	.20
☐	105A	Bob Bailor ERR (reverse negative)	.50	.20	.05
☐	105B	Bob Bailor COR	.75	.30	.07
☐	106	Carlton Fisk	.90	.36	.09
☐	107	George Foster	.80	.32	.08
☐	108	Keith Hernandez	2.50	1.00	.25
☐	109	Dennis Leonard	.40	.16	.04
☐	110	Graig Nettles	.75	.30	.07
☐	111	Jose Cruz	.40	.16	.04
☐	112	Bobby Grich	.40	.16	.04

1970 Kellogg's

		NRMT	VG-E	GOOD
☐ 113	Bob Boone	.60	.24	.06
☐ 114	Dave Lopes	.40	.16	.04
☐ 115	Eddie Murray	5.00	2.00	.50
☐ 116	Jack Clark	2.50	1.00	.25
☐ 117	Lou Whitaker	1.50	.60	.15
☐ 118	Miguel Dilone	.30	.12	.03
☐ 119	Sal Bando	.40	.16	.04
☐ 120	Reggie Jackson	4.00	1.60	.40
☐ 121	Dale Murphy	9.00	3.75	.90
☐ 122	Jon Matlack	.40	.16	.04
☐ 123	Bruce Bochte	.30	.12	.03
☐ 124	John Stearns	.30	.12	.03
☐ 125	Dave Winfield	3.00	1.20	.30
☐ 126	Jorge Orta	.30	.12	.03
☐ 127	Garry Templeton	.40	.16	.04
☐ 128	Johnny Bench	3.50	1.40	.35
☐ 129	Butch Hobson	.30	.12	.03
☐ 130	Bruce Sutter	1.00	.40	.10
☐ 131	Bucky Dent	.40	.16	.04
☐ 132	Amos Otis	.40	.16	.04
☐ 133	Bert Blyleven	.50	.20	.05
☐ 134	Larry Bowa	.50	.20	.05
☐ 135	Ken Singleton	.50	.20	.05
☐ 136	Sixto Lezcano	.30	.12	.03
☐ 137	Roy Howell	.30	.12	.03
☐ 138	Bill Madlock	.80	.32	.08
☐ 139	Dave Revering	.30	.12	.03
☐ 140	Richie Zisk	.40	.16	.04
☐ 141	Butch Wynegar	.40	.16	.04
☐ 142	Alan Ashby	.30	.12	.03
☐ 143	Sparky Lyle	.50	.20	.05
☐ 144	Pete Rose	8.50	3.50	.85
☐ 145	Dennis Eckersley	.60	.24	.06
☐ 146	Dave Kingman	.60	.24	.06
☐ 147	Buddy Bell	.50	.20	.05
☐ 148	Mike Hargrove	.40	.16	.04
☐ 149	Jerry Koosman	.50	.20	.05
☐ 150	Toby Harrah	.40	.16	.04

The cards in this 75-card set measure 2 ¼ "
by 3 ½". The 1970 Kellogg's set was
Kellogg's first venture into the baseball card
producing field. The design incorporates a
brilliant color photo of the player set against
an indistinct background, which is then
covered with a layer of plastic to simulate a
3-D look. Cards 16-30 seem to be in shorter
supply than the other cards in the set.

		NRMT	VG-E	GOOD
	Complete Set (75)	90.00	32.00	8.00
	Common Player (1-75)	.75	.30	.07
☐ 1	Ed Kranepool	.75	.30	.07
☐ 2	Pete Rose	12.50	5.00	1.25
☐ 3	Cleon Jones	.75	.30	.07
☐ 4	Willie McCovey	3.00	1.20	.30
☐ 5	Mel Stottlemyre	1.00	.40	.10
☐ 6	Frank Howard	1.00	.40	.10
☐ 7	Tom Seaver	6.00	2.40	.60
☐ 8	Don Sutton	2.00	.80	.20
☐ 9	Jim Wynn	.75	.30	.07
☐ 10	Jim Maloney	1.00	.40	.10
☐ 11	Tommie Agee	.75	.30	.07
☐ 12	Willie Mays	9.00	3.75	.90
☐ 13	Juan Marichal	3.00	1.20	.30
☐ 14	Dave McNally	.75	.30	.07
☐ 15	Frank Robinson	3.50	1.40	.35
☐ 16	Carlos May	.75	.30	.07
☐ 17	Bill Singer	.75	.30	.07
☐ 18	Rick Reichardt	.75	.30	.07
☐ 19	Boog Powell	1.00	.40	.10
☐ 20	Gaylord Perry	3.00	1.20	.30

			NRMT	VG-E	GOOD
☐	21	Brooks Robinson	5.00	2.00	.50
☐	22	Luis Aparicio	3.50	1.40	.35
☐	23	Joel Horlen	.75	.30	.07
☐	24	Mike Epstein	.75	.30	.07
☐	25	Tom Haller	.75	.30	.07
☐	26	Willie Crawford	.75	.30	.07
☐	27	Roberto Clemente	8.00	3.25	.80
☐	28	Matty Alou	.75	.30	.07
☐	29	Willie Stargell	4.00	1.60	.40
☐	30	Tim Cullen	.75	.30	.07
☐	31	Randy Hundley	.75	.30	.07
☐	32	Reggie Jackson	7.00	2.80	.70
☐	33	Rich Allen	1.00	.40	.10
☐	34	Tim McCarver	1.25	.50	.12
☐	35	Ray Culp	.75	.30	.07
☐	36	Jim Fregosi	1.00	.40	.10
☐	37	Billy Williams	3.00	1.20	.30
☐	38	Johnny Odom	.75	.30	.07
☐	39	Bert Campaneris	1.00	.40	.10
☐	40	Ernie Banks	4.00	1.60	.40
☐	41	Chris Short	.75	.30	.07
☐	42	Ron Santo	1.00	.40	.10
☐	43	Glenn Beckert	.75	.30	.07
☐	44	Lou Brock	3.50	1.40	.35
☐	45	Larry Hisle	.75	.30	.07
☐	46	Reggie Smith	1.00	.40	.10
☐	47	Rod Carew	4.00	1.60	.40
☐	48	Curt Flood	1.00	.40	.10
☐	49	Jim Lonborg	1.00	.40	.10
☐	50	Sam McDowell	1.00	.40	.10
☐	51	Sal Bando	1.00	.40	.10
☐	52	Al Kaline	4.50	1.80	.45
☐	53	Gary Nolan	.75	.30	.07
☐	54	Rico Petrocelli	.75	.30	.07
☐	55	Ollie Brown	.75	.30	.07
☐	56	Luis Tiant	1.25	.50	.12
☐	57	Bill Freehan	1.00	.40	.10
☐	58	Johnny Bench	6.00	2.40	.60
☐	59	Joe Pepitone	1.00	.40	.10
☐	60	Bobby Murcer	1.25	.50	.12
☐	61	Harmon Killebrew	3.00	1.20	.30
☐	62	Don Wilson	.75	.30	.07
☐	63	Tony Oliva	1.50	.60	.15
☐	64	Jim Perry	1.00	.40	.10
☐	65	Mickey Lolich	1.25	.50	.12
☐	66	Jose Laboy	.75	.30	.07
☐	67	Dean Chance	.75	.30	.07
☐	68	Bud Harrelson	.75	.30	.07
☐	69	Willie Horton	1.00	.40	.10

			NRMT	VG-E	GOOD
☐	70	Wally Bunker	.75	.30	.07
☐	71	Bob Gibson	3.50	1.40	.35
☐	72	Joe Morgan	3.00	1.20	.30
☐	73	Denny McLain	1.25	.50	.12
☐	74	Tommy Harper	.75	.30	.07
☐	75	Don Mincher	.75	.30	.07

1971 Kellogg's

The cards in this 75-card set measure 2¼" by 3½". The 1971 set of 3-D cards marketed by the Kellogg's Company is the scarcest of all that company's issues. It was distributed as single cards, one in each package of cereal, without the usual mail-in offer. In addition, card dealers were unable to obtain this set in quantity, as they have in other years. All the cards are available with and without the copyright notice on the back; the version without carries a slight premium for most numbers. Prices listed below are for the more common variety with copyright.

		NRMT	VG-E	GOOD
Complete Set (75)		650.00	260.00	65.00
Common Player (1-75)		6.00	2.40	.60

			NRMT	VG-E	GOOD
☐	1	Wayne Simpson	6.00	2.40	.60
☐	2	Tom Seaver	25.00	10.00	2.50
☐	3	Jim Perry	7.00	2.80	.70
☐	4	Bob Robertson	6.00	2.40	.60
☐	5	Roberto Clemente	30.00	12.00	3.90

			NRMT	VG-E	GOOD
☐	6	Gaylord Perry	13.50	5.00	1.00
☐	7	Felipe Alou	7.00	2.80	.70
☐	8	Denis Menke	6.00	2.40	.60
☐	9	Don Kessinger	6.00	2.40	.60
☐	10	Willie Mays	32.00	13.00	3.20
☐	11	Jim Hickman	6.00	2.40	.60
☐	12	Tony Oliva	9.00	3.75	.90
☐	13	Manny Sanguillen	6.00	2.40	.60
☐	14	Frank Howard	7.00	2.80	.70
☐	15	Frank Robinson	16.00	6.50	1.60
☐	16	Willie Davis	7.00	2.80	.70
☐	17	Lou Brock	20.00	8.00	2.00
☐	18	Cesar Tovar	6.00	2.40	.60
☐	19	Luis Aparicio	13.50	5.00	1.00
☐	20	Boog Powell	9.00	3.75	.90
☐	21	Dick Selma	6.00	2.40	.60
☐	22	Danny Walton	6.00	2.40	.60
☐	23	Carl Morton	6.00	2.40	.60
☐	24	Sonny Siebert	6.00	2.40	.60
☐	25	Jim Merritt	6.00	2.40	.60
☐	26	Jose Cardenal	6.00	2.40	.60
☐	27	Don Mincher	6.00	2.40	.60
☐	28	Clyde Wright	6.00	2.40	.60
☐	29	Les Cain	6.00	2.40	.60
☐	30	Danny Cater	6.00	2.40	.60
☐	31	Don Sutton	13.50	5.00	1.00
☐	32	Chuck Dobson	6.00	2.40	.60
☐	33	Willie McCovey	16.00	6.50	1.60
☐	34	Mike Epstein	6.00	2.40	.60
☐	35	Paul Blair	6.00	2.40	.60
☐	36	Gary Nolan	6.00	2.40	.60
☐	37	Sam McDowell	7.00	2.80	.70
☐	38	Amos Otis	7.00	2.80	.70
☐	39	Ray Fosse	6.00	2.40	.60
☐	40	Mel Stottlemyre	7.00	2.80	.70
☐	41	Clarence Gaston	6.00	2.40	.60
☐	42	Dick Dietz	6.00	2.40	.60
☐	43	Roy White	7.00	2.80	.70
☐	44	Al Kaline	20.00	8.00	2.00
☐	45	Carlos May	6.00	2.40	.60
☐	46	Tommie Agee	6.00	2.40	.60
☐	47	Tommy Harper	6.00	2.40	.60
☐	48	Larry Dierker	6.00	2.40	.60
☐	49	Mike Cuellar	6.00	2.40	.60
☐	50	Ernie Banks	20.00	8.00	2.00
☐	51	Bob Gibson	16.00	6.50	1.60
☐	52	Reggie Smith	7.00	2.80	.70
☐	53	Matty Alou	7.00	2.80	.70
☐	54	Alex Johnson	6.00	2.40	.60

			NRMT	VG-E	GOOD
☐	55	Harmon Killebrew	16.00	6.50	1.60
☐	56	Bill Grabarkewitz	6.00	2.40	.60
☐	57	Richie Allen	9.00	3.75	.90
☐	58	Tony Perez	12.00	5.00	1.20
☐	59	Dave McNally	7.00	2.80	.70
☐	60	Jim Palmer	16.00	6.50	1.60
☐	61	Billy Williams	16.00	6.50	1.60
☐	62	Joe Torre	9.00	3.75	.90
☐	63	Jim Northrup	7.00	2.80	.70
☐	64	Jim Fregosi	7.00	2.80	.70
☐	65	Pete Rose	60.00	24.00	6.00
☐	66	Bud Harrelson	6.00	2.40	.60
☐	67	Tony Taylor	6.00	2.40	.60
☐	68	Willie Stargell	18.00	7.25	1.80
☐	69	Tony Horton	7.00	2.00	.70
☐	70	Claude Osteen	6.00	2.40	.60
☐	71	Glenn Beckert	6.00	2.40	.60
☐	72	Nate Colbert	6.00	2.40	.60
☐	73	Rick Monday	7.00	2.80	.70
☐	74	Tommy John	12.00	5.00	1.20
☐	75	Chris Short	6.00	2.40	.60

1972 Kellogg's

*The cards in this 54-card set measure 2 ⅛"
by 3 ¼". The dimensions of the cards in the
1972 Kellogg's set were reduced in comparison to those of the 1971 series. In addition, the length of the set was set at 54 cards
rather than the 75 of the previous year. The
cards of this Kellogg's set are characterized
by the diagonal bands found on the obverse.*

		NRMT	VG-E	GOOD
	Complete Set (54)	50.00	20.00	5.00
	Common Player (1-54)	.50	.20	.05
☐ 1	Tom Seaver	6.50	2.60	.65
☐ 2	Amos Otis	.60	.24	.06
☐ 3	Willie Davis	.60	.24	.06
☐ 4	Wilbur Wood	.50	.20	.05
☐ 5	Bill Parsons	.50	.20	.05
☐ 6	Pete Rose	15.00	6.00	1.50
☐ 7	Willie McCovey ...	3.00	1.20	.30
☐ 8	Ferguson Jenkins ..	.80	.32	.08
☐ 9	Vida Blue	.60	.24	.06
☐ 10	Joe Torre	.80	.32	.08
☐ 11	Merv Rettenmund ..	.50	.20	.05
☐ 12	Bill Melton	.50	.20	.05
☐ 13	Jim Palmer	3.00	1.20	.30
☐ 14	Doug Rader	.60	.24	.06
☐ 15	Dave Roberts	.50	.20	.05
☐ 16	Bobby Murcer	.80	.32	.08
☐ 17	Wes Parker	.60	.24	.06
☐ 18	Joe Coleman	.50	.20	.05
☐ 19	Manny Sanguillen .	.50	.20	.05
☐ 20	Reggie Jackson ...	6.50	2.60	.65
☐ 21	Ralph Garr	.50	.20	.05
☐ 22	Jim Hunter	2.50	1.00	.25
☐ 23	Rick Wise	.50	.20	.05
☐ 24	Glenn Beckert	.50	.20	.05
☐ 25	Tony Oliva	1.00	.40	.10
☐ 26	Bob Gibson	3.00	1.20	.30
☐ 27	Mike Cuellar	.50	.20	.05
☐ 28	Chris Speier	.50	.20	.05
☐ 29	Dave McNally	.60	.24	.06
☐ 30	Leo Cardenas	.50	.20	.05
☐ 31	Bill Freehan	.60	.24	.06
☐ 32	Bud Harrelson	.50	.20	.05
☐ 33	Sam McDowell	.60	.24	.06
☐ 34	Claude Osteen	.50	.20	.05
☐ 35	Reggie Smith	.60	.24	.06
☐ 36	Sonny Siebert	.50	.20	.05
☐ 37	Lee May	.60	.24	.06
☐ 38	Mickey Lolich	.80	.32	.08
☐ 39	Cookie Rojas	.60	.24	.06
☐ 40	Dick Drago	.50	.20	.05
☐ 41	Nate Colbert	.50	.20	.05
☐ 42	Andy Messersmith .	.60	.24	.06
☐ 43	Dave Johnson	1.00	.40	.10
☐ 44	Steve Blass	.60	.24	.06
☐ 45	Bob Robertson	.50	.20	.05
☐ 46	Billy Williams	3.00	1.20	.30
☐ 47	Juan Marichal	3.00	1.20	.30

		NRMT	VG-E	GOOD
☐ 48	Lou Brock	3.50	1.40	.35
☐ 49	Roberto Clemente ..	7.00	2.80	.70
☐ 50	Mel Stottlemyre ...	.60	.24	.06
☐ 51	Don Wilson	.50	.20	.05
☐ 52	Sal Bando	.60	.24	.06
☐ 53	Willie Stargell	3.00	1.20	.30
☐ 54	Willie Mays	8.00	3.25	.80

1972 Kellogg's ATG

The cards in this 15-card set measure 2 ¼" by 3 ½". The 1972 All-Time Greats 3-D set was issued with Kellogg's Danish Go Rounds. The set contains two different cards of Babe Ruth. The set is a reissue of a 1970 set issued by Rold Gold Pretzels to commemorate baseball's first 100 years. The Rold Gold cards are copyrighted 1970 on the reverse and are valued at approximately double the prices listed below.

		NRMT	VG-E	GOOD
	Complete Set (15)	12.50	5.00	1.25
	Common Player (1-15)	.40	.16	.04
☐ 1	Walter Johnson ...	1.00	.40	.10
☐ 2	Rogers Hornsby ...	.60	.24	.06
☐ 3	John McGraw	.40	.16	.04
☐ 4	Mickey Cochrane .	.50	.20	.05
☐ 5	George Sisler	.50	.20	.05
☐ 6	Babe Ruth	3.00	1.20	.30
☐ 7	Lefty Grove	.60	.24	.06
☐ 8	Pie Traynor	.40	.16	.04

			NRMT	VG-E	GOOD
☐	9	Honus Wagner	1.00	.40	.10
☐	10	Eddie Collins	.40	.16	.04
☐	11	Tris Speaker	.60	.24	.06
☐	12	Cy Young	.60	.24	.06
☐	13	Lou Gehrig	1.75	.70	.17
☐	14	Babe Ruth	3.00	1.20	.30
☐	15	Ty Cobb	1.75	.70	.17

1973 Kellogg's 2D

The cards in this 54-card set measure 2 ¼ "
by 3 ½". The 1973 Kellogg's set is the only
non-3-D set produced by the Kellogg Company. Apparently Kellogg's decided to have
the cards produced through Visual
Panographics rather than by Xograph, as in
the other years. The complete set could be
obtained from the company through a box-
top redemption procedure. The card size is
slightly larger than the previous year.

			NRMT	VG-E	GOOD
		Complete Set (54)	45.00	18.00	4.50
		Common Player (1-54)	.50	.20	.05
☐	1	Amos Otis	.60	.24	.06
☐	2	Ellie Rodriguez	.50	.20	.05
☐	3	Mickey Lolich	.80	.32	.08
☐	4	Tony Oliva	.80	.32	.08
☐	5	Don Sutton	1.75	.70	.17
☐	6	Pete Rose	12.00	5.00	1.20
☐	7	Steve Carlton	4.00	1.60	.40
☐	8	Bobby Bonds	.80	.32	.08

			NRMT	VG-E	GOOD
☐	9	Wilbur Wood	.50	.20	.05
☐	10	Billy Williams	2.50	1.00	.25
☐	11	Steve Blass	.60	.24	.06
☐	12	Jon Matlack	.50	.20	.05
☐	13	Cesar Cedeno	.60	.24	.06
☐	14	Bob Gibson	2.50	1.00	.25
☐	15	Sparky Lyle	.80	.32	.08
☐	16	Nolan Ryan	4.00	1.60	.40
☐	17	Jim Palmer	2.50	1.00	.25
☐	18	Ray Fosse	.50	.20	.05
☐	19	Bobby Murcer	.60	.24	.06
☐	20	Jim Hunter	2.00	.80	.20
☐	21	Tom McCraw	.50	.20	.05
☐	22	Reggie Jackson ...	5.00	2.00	.50
☐	23	Bill Stoneman	.50	.20	.05
☐	24	Lou Piniella	.60	.24	.06
☐	25	Willie Stargell	3.50	1.40	.35
☐	26	Dick Allen	.80	.32	.08
☐	27	Carlton Fisk	1.25	.50	.12
☐	28	Ferguson Jenkins .	.80	.32	.08
☐	29	Phil Niekro	2.00	.80	.20
☐	30	Gary Nolan	.50	.20	.05
☐	31	Joe Torre	.80	.32	.08
☐	32	Bobby Tolan	.50	.20	.05
☐	33	Nate Colbert	.50	.20	.05
☐	34	Joe Morgan	2.50	1.00	.25
☐	35	Bert Blyleven	.60	.24	.06
☐	36	Joe Rudi	.60	.24	.06
☐	37	Ralph Garr	.50	.20	.05
☐	38	Gaylord Perry	1.75	.70	.17
☐	39	Bobby Grich	.60	.24	.06
☐	40	Lou Brock	2.50	1.00	.25
☐	41	Pete Broberg	.50	.20	.05
☐	42	Manny Sanguillen .	.50	.20	.05
☐	43	Willie Davis	.60	.24	.06
☐	44	Dave Kingman	.80	.32	.08
☐	45	Carlos May	.50	.20	.05
☐	46	Tom Seaver	4.00	1.60	.40
☐	47	Mike Cuellar	.50	.20	.05
☐	48	Joe Coleman	.50	.20	.05
☐	49	Claude Osteen	.50	.20	.05
☐	50	Steve Kline	.50	.20	.05
☐	51	Rod Carew	3.50	1.40	.35
☐	52	Al Kaline	3.50	1.40	.35
☐	53	Larry Dierker	.50	.20	.05
☐	54	Ron Santo	.80	.32	.08

1974 Kellogg's

The cards in this 54-card set measure 2 1/8" by 3 1/4". In 1974 the Kellogg's set returned to its 3-D format; it also returned to the smaller-size card. Complete sets could be obtained from the company through a box-top offer. The cards are numbered on the back.

		NRMT	VG-E	GOOD
	Complete Set (54)	40.00	16.00	4.00
	Common Player (1-54)	.35	.14	.03

			NRMT	VG-E	GOOD
☐	1	Bob Gibson	2.50	1.00	.25
☐	2	Rick Monday	.45	.18	.04
☐	3	Joe Coleman	.35	.14	.03
☐	4	Bert Campaneris	.45	.18	.04
☐	5	Carlton Fisk	1.00	.40	.10
☐	6	Jim Palmer	2.50	1.00	.25
☐	7	Ron Santo	.60	.24	.06
☐	8	Nolan Ryan	4.00	1.60	.40
☐	9	Greg Luzinski	.60	.24	.06
☐	10	Buddy Bell	.60	.24	.06
☐	11	Bob Watson	.45	.18	.04
☐	12	Bill Singer	.35	.14	.03
☐	13	Dave May	.35	.14	.03
☐	14	Jim Brewer	.35	.14	.03
☐	15	Manny Sanguillen	.45	.18	.04
☐	16	Jeff Burroughs	.45	.18	.04
☐	17	Amos Otis	.45	.18	.04
☐	18	Ed Goodson	.35	.14	.03
☐	19	Nate Colbert	.35	.14	.03
☐	20	Reggie Jackson	5.00	2.00	.50
☐	21	Ted Simmons	.75	.30	.07
☐	22	Bobby Murcer	.60	.24	.06

			NRMT	VG-E	GOOD
☐	23	Willie Horton	.45	.18	.04
☐	24	Orlando Cepeda	.75	.30	.07
☐	25	Ron Hunt	.35	.14	.03
☐	26	Wayne Twitchell	.35	.14	.03
☐	27	Ron Fairly	.35	.14	.03
☐	28	Johnny Bench	4.00	1.60	.40
☐	29	John Mayberry	.35	.14	.03
☐	30	Rod Carew	3.50	1.40	.35
☐	31	Ken Holtzman	.45	.18	.04
☐	32	Billy Williams	2.00	.80	.20
☐	33	Dick Allen	.60	.24	.06
☐	34	Wilbur Wood	.45	.18	.04
☐	35	Danny Thompson	.35	.14	.03
☐	36	Joe Morgan	2.00	.80	.20
☐	37	Willie Stargell	2.50	1.00	.25
☐	38	Pete Rose	11.00	4.50	1.10
☐	39	Bobby Bonds	.60	.24	.06
☐	40	Chris Speier	.35	.14	.03
☐	41	Sparky Lyle	.60	.24	.06
☐	42	Cookie Rojas	.45	.18	.04
☐	43	Tommy Davis	.45	.18	.04
☐	44	Jim Hunter	1.75	.70	.17
☐	45	Willie Davis	.45	.18	.04
☐	46	Bert Blyleven	.60	.24	.06
☐	47	Pat Kelly	.35	.14	.03
☐	48	Ken Singleton	.45	.18	.04
☐	49	Manny Mota	.45	.18	.04
☐	50	Dave Johnson	.75	.30	.07
☐	51	Sal Bando	.45	.18	.04
☐	52	Tom Seaver	4.00	1.60	.40
☐	53	Felix Millan	.35	.14	.03
☐	54	Ron Blomberg	.35	.14	.03

1975 Kellogg's

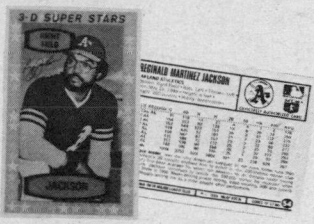

*The cards in this 57-card set measure 2 ⅛"
by 3 ¼". The 1975 Kellogg's 3-D set could
be obtained card by card in cereal boxes or
as a set from a box-top offer from the company. Card number 44, Jim Hunter, exists
with the A's emblem or the Yankees emblem
on the back of the card.*

		NRMT	VG-E	GOOD
Complete Set (57)		120.00	50.00	12.00
Common Player (1-57)		.60	.24	.06
☐ 1	Roy White	.75	.30	.07
☐ 2	Ross Grimsley	.65	.26	.06
☐ 3	Reggie Smith	.75	.30	.07
☐ 4	Bob Grich	.75	.30	.07
☐ 5	Greg Gross	.65	.26	.06
☐ 6	Bob Watson	.75	.30	.07
☐ 7	Johnny Bench	7.50	3.00	.75
☐ 8	Jeff Burroughs	.75	.30	.07
☐ 9	Elliott Maddox	.65	.26	.06
☐ 10	Jon Matlack	.75	.30	.07
☐ 11	Pete Rose	18.00	7.25	1.80
☐ 12	Lee Stanton	.65	.26	.06
☐ 13	Bake McBride	.65	.26	.06
☐ 14	Jorge Orta	.65	.26	.06
☐ 15	Al Oliver	1.00	.40	.10
☐ 16	John Briggs	.65	.26	.06
☐ 17	Steve Garvey	6.50	2.60	.65
☐ 18	Brooks Robinson	5.00	2.00	.50
☐ 19	John Hiller	.75	.30	.07
☐ 20	Lynn McGlothen	.65	.26	.06
☐ 21	Cleon Jones	.65	.26	.06
☐ 22	Fergie Jenkins	1.25	.50	.12

		NRMT	VG-E	GOOD
☐ 23	Bill North	.65	.26	.06
☐ 24	Steve Busby	.75	.30	.07
☐ 25	Richie Zisk	.75	.30	.07
☐ 26	Nolan Ryan	7.50	3.00	.75
☐ 27	Joe Morgan	3.50	1.40	.35
☐ 28	Joe Rudi	.75	.30	.07
☐ 29	Jose Cardenal	.65	.26	.06
☐ 30	Andy Messersmith	.75	.30	.07
☐ 31	Willie Montanez	.65	.26	.06
☐ 32	Bill Buckner	1.00	.40	.10
☐ 33	Rod Carew	6.00	2.40	.60
☐ 34	Lou Piniella	.90	.36	.09
☐ 35	Ralph Garr	.75	.30	.07
☐ 36	Mike Marshall	.75	.30	.07
☐ 37	Garry Maddox	.75	.30	.07
☐ 38	Dwight Evans	1.50	.60	.15
☐ 39	Lou Brock	5.00	2.00	.50
☐ 40	Ken Singleton	.90	.36	.09
☐ 41	Steve Braun	.65	.26	.06
☐ 42	Rich Allen	1.00	.40	.10
☐ 43	John Grubb	.65	.26	.06
☐ 44	Jim Hunter (2)	4.00	1.60	.40
☐ 45	Gaylord Perry	2.50	1.00	.25
☐ 46	George Hendrick	.90	.36	.09
☐ 47	Sparky Lyle	.90	.36	.09
☐ 48	Dave Cash	.65	.26	.06
☐ 49	Luis Tiant	.90	.36	.09
☐ 50	Cesar Geronimo	.65	.26	.06
☐ 51	Carl Yastrzemski	15.00	6.00	1.50
☐ 52	Ken Brett	.65	.26	.06
☐ 53	Hal McRae	.75	.30	.07
☐ 54	Reggie Jackson	9.00	3.75	.90
☐ 55	Rollie Fingers	2.50	1.00	.25
☐ 56	Mike Schmidt	11.00	4.50	1.10
☐ 57	Richie Hebner	.65	.26	.06

1976 Kellogg's

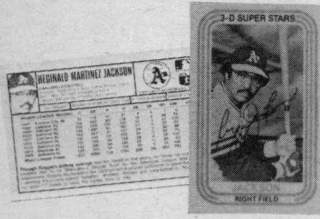

The cards in this 57-card set measure 2 ⅛"
by 3 ¼". The 1976 Kellogg's 3-D set could
be obtained card by card in cereal boxes or
as a set from the company for box-tops.
Card number 6, that of Clay Carroll, exists
with both a Reds or White Sox emblem on
the back. Cards 1-3 (marked in the checklist
below with SP) were apparently printed apart
from the other 54 and are in shorter supply.

			NRMT	VG-E	GOOD
	Complete Set		60.00	24.00	6.00
	Common Player (1-3) Sp		8.00	3.25	.80
	Common Player (4-57)		.40	.16	.04
☐	1	Steve Hargan SP	8.00	3.25	.80
☐	2	Claudell Washington SP	8.00	3.25	.80
☐	3	Don Gullett SP	8.00	3.25	.80
☐	4	Randy Jones	.50	.20	.05
☐	5	Jim Hunter	2.00	.80	.20
☐	6	Clay Carroll (2)	.60	.24	.06
☐	7	Joe Rudi	.50	.20	.05
☐	8	Reggie Jackson	5.00	2.00	.50
☐	9	Felix Millan	.40	.16	.04
☐	10	Jim Rice	3.00	1.20	.30
☐	11	Bert Blyleven	.60	.24	.06
☐	12	Ken Singleton	.50	.20	.05
☐	13	Don Sutton	1.50	.60	.15
☐	14	Joe Morgan	2.50	1.00	.25
☐	15	Dave Parker	1.50	.60	.15
☐	16	Dave Cash	.40	.16	.04
☐	17	Ron LeFlore	.40	.16	.04
☐	18	Greg Luzinski	.60	.24	.06
☐	19	Dennis Eckersley	1.25	.50	.12
☐	20	Bill Madlock	.80	.32	.08
☐	21	George Scott	.40	.16	.04
☐	22	Willie Stargell	2.50	1.00	.25
☐	23	Al Hrabosky	.50	.20	.05
☐	24	Carl Yastrzemski	6.00	2.40	.60
☐	25	Jim Kaat	.80	.32	.08
☐	26	Marty Perez	.40	.16	.04
☐	27	Bob Watson	.50	.20	.05
☐	28	Eric Soderholm	.40	.16	.04
☐	29	Bill Lee	.50	.20	.05
☐	30	Frank Tanana	.50	.20	.05
☐	31	Fred Lynn	1.50	.60	.15
☐	32	Tom Seaver	4.00	1.60	.40
☐	33	Steve Busby	.50	.20	.05
☐	34	Gary Carter	4.00	1.60	.40
☐	35	Rick Wise	.40	.16	.04
☐	36	Johnny Bench	4.00	1.60	.40
☐	37	Jim Palmer	2.00	.80	.20
☐	38	Bobby Murcer	.60	.24	.06
☐	39	Von Joshua	.40	.16	.04
☐	40	Lou Brock	2.50	1.00	.25
☐	41	Mickey Rivers (2)	.50	.20	.05
☐	42	Manny Sanguillen	.50	.20	.05
☐	43	Jerry Reuss	.40	.16	.04
☐	44	Ken Griffey	.50	.20	.05
☐	45	Jorge Orta	.40	.16	.04
☐	46	John Mayberry	.40	.16	.04
☐	47	Vida Blue (2)	.50	.20	.05
☐	48	Rod Carew	3.00	1.20	.30
☐	49	Jon Matlack	.50	.20	.05
☐	50	Boog Powell	.60	.24	.06
☐	51	Mike Hargrove	.50	.20	.05
☐	52	Paul Lindblad	.40	.16	.04
☐	53	Thurman Munson	3.50	1.40	.35
☐	54	Steve Garvey	3.50	1.40	.35
☐	55	Pete Rose	11.00	4.50	1.10
☐	56	Greg Gross	.40	.16	.04
☐	57	Ted Simmons	.80	.32	.08

1977 Kellogg's

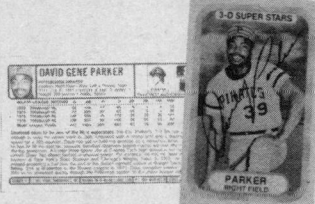

The cards in this 57-card set measure 2⅛"
by 3¼". The 1977 Kellogg's series of 3-D
baseball player cards could be obtained card
by card from cereal boxes or by sending in
box-tops and money. Each player's picture
appears in miniature form on the reverse, an
idea begun in 1971 and replaced in sub-
sequent years by the use of a picture of the
Kellogg's mascot.

		NRMT	VG-E	GOOD
Complete Set (57)		40.00	16.00	4.00
Common Player (1-57)		.30	.12	.03
☐	1 George Foster	.80	.32	.08
☐	2 Bert Campaneris ...	.40	.16	.04
☐	3 Fergie Jenkins	.65	.26	.06
☐	4 Dock Ellis	.30	.12	.03
☐	5 John Montefusco ..	.30	.12	.03
☐	6 George Brett	6.00	2.40	.60
☐	7 John Candelaria ...	.40	.16	.04
☐	8 Fred Norman	.30	.12	.03
☐	9 Bill Travers	.30	.12	.03
☐	10 Hal McRae	.40	.16	.04
☐	11 Doug Rau	.30	.12	.03
☐	12 Greg Luzinski	.50	.20	.05
☐	13 Ralph Garr	.30	.12	.03
☐	14 Steve Garvey	3.50	1.40	.35
☐	15 Rick Manning	.30	.12	.03
☐	16 Lyman Bostock ...	.40	.16	.04
☐	17 Randy Jones	.30	.12	.03
☐	18 Ron Cey	.50	.20	.05
☐	19 Dave Parker	1.00	.40	.10
☐	20 Pete Rose	8.50	3.50	.85

		NRMT	VG-E	GOOD
☐	21 Wayne Garland ...	.30	.12	.03
☐	22 Bill North	.30	.12	.03
☐	23 Thurman Munson .	2.50	1.00	.25
☐	24 Tom Poquette	.30	.12	.03
☐	25 Ron LeFlore	.40	.16	.04
☐	26 Mark Fidrych	.40	.16	.04
☐	27 Sixto Lezcano	.30	.12	.03
☐	28 Dave Winfield	2.50	1.00	.25
☐	29 Jerry Koosman ...	.40	.16	.04
☐	30 Mike Hargrove	.30	.12	.03
☐	31 Willie Montanez ...	.30	.12	.03
☐	32 Don Stanhouse ...	.30	.12	.03
☐	33 Jay Johnstone	.40	.16	.04
☐	34 Bake McBride	.30	.12	.03
☐	35 Dave Kingman	.60	.24	.06
☐	36 Fred Patek	.30	.12	.03
☐	37 Garry Maddox	.30	.12	.03
☐	38 Ken Reitz	.30	.12	.03
☐	39 Bobby Grich	.40	.16	.04
☐	40 Cesar Geronimo ...	.30	.12	.03
☐	41 Jim Lonborg	.40	.16	.04
☐	42 Ed Figueroa	.30	.12	.03
☐	43 Bill Madlock	.70	.28	.07
☐	44 Jerry Remy	.30	.12	.03
☐	45 Frank Tanana	.40	.16	.04
☐	46 Al Oliver	.70	.28	.07
☐	47 Charlie Hough	.50	.20	.05
☐	48 Lou Piniella	.50	.20	.05
☐	49 Ken Griffey	.40	.16	.04
☐	50 Jose Cruz	.50	.20	.05
☐	51 Rollie Fingers	1.00	.40	.10
☐	52 Chris Chambliss ...	.50	.20	.05
☐	53 Rod Carew	3.00	1.20	.30
☐	54 Andy Messersmith .	.40	.16	.04
☐	55 Mickey Rivers	.40	.16	.04
☐	56 Butch Wynegar ...	.40	.16	.04
☐	57 Steve Carlton	3.00	1.20	.30

1978 Kellogg's

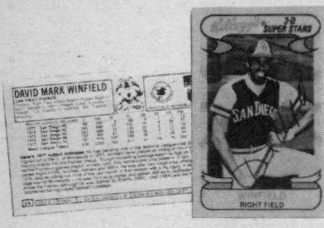

The cards in this 57-card set measure 2⅛" by 3¼". This 1978 3-D Kellogg's series marks the first year in which Tony the Tiger appears on the reverse of each card next to the team and MLB logos. Once again the set could be obtained as individually wrapped cards in cereal boxes or as a set via a mail-in offer.

		NRMT	VG-E	GOOD
	Complete Set (57)	35.00	14.00	3.50
	Common Player (1-57)	.25	.10	.02

			NRMT	VG-E	GOOD
☐	1	Steve Carlton	2.50	1.00	.25
☐	2	Bucky Dent	.35	.14	.03
☐	3	Mike Schmidt	4.00	1.60	.40
☐	4	Ken Griffey	.35	.14	.03
☐	5	Al Cowens	.25	.10	.02
☐	6	George Brett	4.00	1.60	.40
☐	7	Lou Brock	2.00	.80	.20
☐	8	Rich Gossage	.70	.28	.07
☐	9	Tom Johnson	.25	.10	.02
☐	10	George Foster	.70	.28	.07
☐	11	Dave Winfield	2.50	1.00	.25
☐	12	Dan Meyer	.25	.10	.02
☐	13	Chris Chambliss ...	.35	.14	.03
☐	14	Paul Dade	.25	.10	.02
☐	15	Jeff Burroughs	.25	.10	.02
☐	16	Jose Cruz	.35	.14	.03
☐	17	Mickey Rivers	.35	.14	.03
☐	18	John Candelaria ...	.35	.14	.03
☐	19	Ellis Valentine	.25	.10	.02
☐	20	Hal McRae	.35	.14	.03
☐	21	Dave Rozema	.25	.10	.02
☐	22	Lenny Randle	.25	.10	.02
☐	23	Willie McCovey ...	2.00	.80	.20
☐	24	Ron Cey	.50	.20	.05
☐	25	Eddie Murray	10.00	4.00	1.00
☐	26	Larry Bowa	.40	.16	.04
☐	27	Tom Seaver	3.50	1.40	.35
☐	28	Garry Maddox	.35	.14	.03
☐	29	Rod Carew	2.50	1.00	.25
☐	30	Thurman Munson ..	3.00	1.20	.30
☐	31	Gary Templeton ...	.50	.20	.05
☐	32	Eric Soderholm ...	.25	.10	.02
☐	33	Greg Luzinski	.50	.20	.05
☐	34	Reggie Smith	.35	.14	.03
☐	35	Dave Goltz	.25	.10	.02
☐	36	Tommy John	.70	.28	.07
☐	37	Ralph Garr	.25	.10	.02
☐	38	Alan Bannister ...	.25	.10	.02
☐	39	Bob Bailor	.25	.10	.02
☐	40	Reggie Jackson ...	4.00	1.60	.40
☐	41	Cecil Cooper	.50	.20	.05
☐	42	Burt Hooton	.25	.10	.02
☐	43	Sparky Lyle	.40	.16	.04
☐	44	Steve Ontiveros ...	.25	.10	.02
☐	45	Rick Reuschel	.50	.20	.05
☐	46	Lyman Bostock ...	.35	.14	.03
☐	47	Mitchell Page	.25	.10	.02
☐	48	Bruce Sutter	.70	.28	.07
☐	49	Jim Rice	2.00	.80	.20
☐	50	Ken Forsch	.25	.10	.02
☐	51	Nolan Ryan	3.00	1.20	.30
☐	52	Dave Parker	1.25	.50	.12
☐	53	Bert Blyleven	.50	.20	.05
☐	54	Frank Tanana	.35	.14	.03
☐	55	Ken Singleton	.35	.14	.03
☐	56	Mike Hargrove ...	.35	.14	.03
☐	57	Don Sutton	1.50	.60	.15

1979 Kellogg's

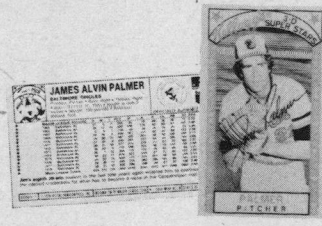

The cards in this 60-card set measure 1 ¹⁵/₁₆"
by 3 ¼". The 1979 edition of Kellogg's 3-D
baseball cards have a ³/₁₆" reduced width
from the previous year; a nicely designed
curved panel above the picture gives this set
a distinctive appearance. The set contains
the largest number of cards issued in a
Kellogg's set since the 1971 series.

		NRMT	VG-E	GOOD
	Complete Set (60)	25.00	10.00	2.50
	Common Player (1-60)	.20	.08	.02
☐ 1	Bruce Sutter	.50	.20	.05
☐ 2	Ted Simmons	.50	.20	.05
☐ 3	Ross Grimsley	.20	.08	.02
☐ 4	Wayne Nordhagen	.20	.08	.02
☐ 5	Jim Palmer	1.50	.60	.15
☐ 6	John Henry Johnson	.20	.08	.02
☐ 7	Jason Thompson	.20	.08	.02
☐ 8	Pat Zachry	.20	.08	.02
☐ 9	Dennis Eckersley	.75	.30	.07
☐ 10	Paul Splittorff	.20	.08	.02
☐ 11	Ron Guidry	1.25	.50	.12
☐ 12	Jeff Burroughs	.20	.08	.02
☐ 13	Rod Carew	2.50	1.00	.25
☐ 14	Buddy Bell	.30	.12	.03
☐ 15	Jim Rice	2.00	.80	.20
☐ 16	Garry Maddox	.20	.08	.02
☐ 17	Willie McCovey	1.50	.60	.15
☐ 18	Steve Carlton	2.50	1.00	.25
☐ 19	J.R. Richard	.30	.12	.03
☐ 20	Paul Molitor	1.25	.50	.12
☐ 21	Dave Parker	1.00	.40	.10
☐ 22	Pete Rose	6.50	2.60	.65
☐ 23	Vida Blue	.30	.12	.03
☐ 24	Richie Zisk	.20	.08	.02
☐ 25	Darrell Porter	.20	.08	.02
☐ 26	Dan Driessen	.20	.08	.02
☐ 27	Geoff Zahn	.20	.08	.02
☐ 28	Phil Niekro	1.25	.50	.12
☐ 29	Tom Seaver	3.00	1.20	.30
☐ 30	Fred Lynn	.70	.28	.07
☐ 31	Bill Bonham	.20	.08	.02
☐ 32	George Foster	.50	.20	.05
☐ 33	Terry Puhl	.20	.08	.02
☐ 34	John Candelaria	.30	.12	.03
☐ 35	Bob Knepper	.30	.12	.03
☐ 36	Fred Patek	.20	.08	.02
☐ 37	Chris Chambliss	.30	.12	.03
☐ 38	Bob Forsch	.20	.08	.02
☐ 39	Ken Griffey	.30	.12	.03
☐ 40	Jack Clark	1.50	.60	.15
☐ 41	Dwight Evans	.80	.32	.08
☐ 42	Lee Mazzilli	.20	.08	.02
☐ 43	Mario Guerrero	.20	.08	.02
☐ 44	Larry Bowa	.40	.16	.04
☐ 45	Carl Yastrzemski	4.00	1.60	.40
☐ 46	Reggie Jackson	3.50	1.40	.35
☐ 47	Rick Reuschel	.40	.16	.04
☐ 48	Mike Flanagan	.30	.12	.03
☐ 49	Gaylord Perry	1.25	.50	.12
☐ 50	George Brett	3.50	1.40	.35
☐ 51	Craig Reynolds	.20	.08	.02
☐ 52	Dave Lopes	.30	.12	.03
☐ 53	Bill Almon	.20	.08	.02
☐ 54	Roy Howell	.20	.08	.02
☐ 55	Frank Tanana	.30	.12	.03
☐ 56	Doug Rau	.20	.08	.02
☐ 57	Rick Monday	.30	.12	.03
☐ 58	Jon Matlack	.20	.08	.02
☐ 59	Ron Jackson	.20	.08	.02
☐ 60	Jim Sundberg	.20	.08	.02

1980 Kellogg's

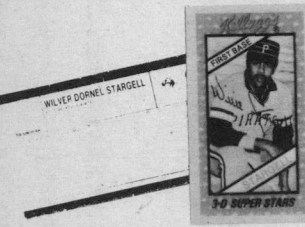

WILVER DORNEL STARGELL

The cards in this 60-card set measure 1 ⅞"
by 3 ¼". The 1980 Kellogg's 3-D set is quite
similar to, but smaller (narrower) than, the
other recent Kellogg's issues. Sets could be
obtained card by card from cereal boxes or
as a set from a box-top offer from the company.

	MINT	EXC	G-VG
Complete Set (60)	20.00	8.00	2.00
Common Player (1-60)	.20	.08	.02

		MINT	EXC	G-VG
☐ 1	Ross Grimsley	.20	.08	.02
☐ 2	Mike Schmidt	3.50	1.40	.35
☐ 3	Mike Flanagan	.30	.12	.03
☐ 4	Ron Guidry	.70	.28	.07
☐ 5	Bert Blyleven	.40	.16	.04
☐ 6	Dave Kingman	.40	.16	.04
☐ 7	Jeff Newman	.20	.08	.02
☐ 8	Steve Rogers	.30	.12	.03
☐ 9	George Brett	3.00	1.20	.30
☐ 10	Bruce Sutter	.50	.20	.05
☐ 11	Gorman Thomas	.30	.12	.03
☐ 12	Darrell Porter	.20	.08	.02
☐ 13	Roy Smalley	.20	.08	.02
☐ 14	Steve Carlton	2.00	.80	.20
☐ 15	Jim Palmer	1.50	.60	.15
☐ 16	Bob Bailor	.20	.08	.02
☐ 17	Jason Thompson	.20	.08	.02
☐ 18	Graig Nettles	.40	.16	.04
☐ 19	Ron Cey	.40	.16	.04
☐ 20	Nolan Ryan	2.50	1.00	.25
☐ 21	Ellis Valentine	.20	.08	.02
☐ 22	Larry Hisle	.20	.08	.02
☐ 23	Dave Parker	.70	.28	.07
☐ 24	Eddie Murray	2.00	.80	.20
☐ 25	Willie Stargell	1.50	.60	.15
☐ 26	Reggie Jackson	2.50	1.00	.25
☐ 27	Carl Yastrzemski	3.00	1.20	.30
☐ 28	Andre Thornton	.20	.08	.02
☐ 29	Dave Lopes	.30	.12	.03
☐ 30	Ken Singleton	.30	.12	.03
☐ 31	Steve Garvey	2.00	.80	.20
☐ 32	Dave Winfield	2.00	.80	.20
☐ 33	Steve Kemp	.30	.12	.03
☐ 34	Claudell Washington	.30	.12	.03
☐ 35	Pete Rose	5.00	2.00	.50
☐ 36	Cesar Cedeno	.30	.12	.03
☐ 37	John Stearns	.20	.08	.02
☐ 38	Lee Mazzilli	.20	.08	.02
☐ 39	Larry Bowa	.30	.12	.03
☐ 40	Fred Lynn	.60	.24	.06
☐ 41	Carlton Fisk	.60	.24	.06
☐ 42	Vida Blue	.30	.12	.03
☐ 43	Keith Hernandez	1.50	.60	.15
☐ 44	Jim Rice	1.50	.60	.15
☐ 45	Ted Simmons	.40	.16	.04
☐ 46	Chet Lemon	.30	.12	.03
☐ 47	Ferguson Jenkins	.50	.20	.05
☐ 48	Gary Matthews	.30	.12	.03
☐ 49	Tom Seaver	2.50	1.00	.25
☐ 50	George Foster	.50	.20	.05
☐ 51	Phil Niekro	1.00	.40	.10
☐ 52	Johnny Bench	2.50	1.00	.25
☐ 53	Buddy Bell	.40	.16	.04
☐ 54	Lance Parrish	1.00	.40	.10
☐ 55	Joaquin Andujar	.30	.12	.03
☐ 56	Don Baylor	.30	.12	.03
☐ 57	Jack Clark	1.00	.40	.10
☐ 58	J.R. Richard	.30	.12	.03
☐ 59	Bruce Bochte	.20	.08	.02
☐ 60	Rod Carew	2.00	.80	.20

1981 Kellogg's

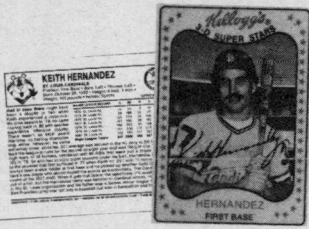

The cards in this 66-card set measure 2 ½" by 3 ½". The 1981 Kellogg's set witnessed an increase in both the size of the card and the size of the set. For the first time, cards were not packed in cereal sizes but available only by mail-in procedure. The offer for the card set was advertised on boxes of Kellogg's Corn Flakes. The cards were printed on a different stock than in previous years, presumably to prevent the cracking problem which has plagued all Kellogg's 3-D issues. At the end of the promotion, the remainder of the sets not distributed (to cereal-eaters), were "sold" into the organized hobby, thus creating a situation where the set is relatively plentiful compared to other years of Kellogg's.

		MINT	EXC	G-VG
Complete Set (66)		7.50	3.00	.75
Common Player (1-66)		.07	.03	.01

		MINT	EXC	G-VG
□ 1	George Foster	.15	.06	.01
□ 2	Jim Palmer	.35	.14	.03
□ 3	Reggie Jackson	.80	.32	.08
□ 4	Al Oliver	.10	.04	.01
□ 5	Mike Schmidt	.90	.36	.09
□ 6	Nolan Ryan	.50	.20	.05
□ 7	Bucky Dent	.10	.04	.01
□ 8	George Brett	.90	.36	.09
□ 9	Jim Rice	.30	.12	.03
□ 10	Steve Garvey	.45	.18	.04
□ 11	Willie Stargell	.35	.14	.03
□ 12	Phil Niekro	.25	.10	.02

		MINT	EXC	G-VG
□ 13	Dave Parker	.20	.08	.02
□ 14	Cesar Cedeno	.10	.04	.01
□ 15	Don Baylor	.10	.04	.01
□ 16	J.R. Richard	.07	.03	.01
□ 17	Tony Perez	.10	.04	.01
□ 18	Eddie Murray	.60	.24	.06
□ 19	Chet Lemon	.07	.03	.01
□ 20	Ben Oglivie	.07	.03	.01
□ 21	Dave Winfield	.40	.16	.04
□ 22	Joe Morgan	.25	.10	.02
□ 23	Vida Blue	.10	.04	.01
□ 24	Willie Wilson	.10	.04	.01
□ 25	Steve Henderson	.07	.03	.01
□ 26	Rod Carew	.40	.16	.04
□ 27	Garry Templeton	.07	.03	.01
□ 28	Dave Concepcion	.10	.04	.01
□ 29	Dave Lopes	.07	.03	.01
□ 30	Ken Landreaux	.07	.03	.01
□ 31	Keith Hernandez	.35	.14	.03
□ 32	Cecil Cooper	.10	.04	.01
□ 33	Rickey Henderson	.60	.24	.06
□ 34	Frank White	.07	.03	.01
□ 35	George Hendrick	.07	.03	.01
□ 36	Reggie Smith	.10	.04	.01
□ 37	Tug McGraw	.10	.04	.01
□ 38	Tom Seaver	.50	.20	.05
□ 39	Ken Singleton	.10	.04	.01
□ 40	Fred Lynn	.15	.06	.01
□ 41	Rich Gossage	.10	.04	.01
□ 42	Terry Puhl	.07	.03	.01
□ 43	Larry Bowa	.15	.06	.01
□ 44	Phil Garner	.07	.03	.01
□ 45	Ron Guidry	.20	.08	.02
□ 46	Lee Mazzilli	.07	.03	.01
□ 47	Dave Kingman	.10	.04	.01
□ 48	Carl Yastrzemski	1.00	.40	.10
□ 49	Rick Burleson	.07	.03	.01
□ 50	Steve Carlton	.40	.16	.04
□ 51	Alan Trammell	.30	.12	.03
□ 52	Tommy John	.15	.06	.01
□ 53	Paul Molitor	.25	.10	.02
□ 54	Joe Charbonneau	.07	.03	.01
□ 55	Rick Langford	.07	.03	.01
□ 56	Bruce Sutter	.10	.04	.01
□ 57	Robin Yount	.25	.10	.02
□ 58	Steve Stone	.07	.03	.01
□ 59	Larry Gura	.07	.03	.01
□ 60	Mike Flanagan	.10	.04	.01
□ 61	Bob Horner	.20	.08	.02

		MINT	EXC	G-VG
☐ 62	Bruce Bochte	.07	.03	.01
☐ 63	Pete Rose	1.00	.40	.10
☐ 64	Buddy Bell	.10	.04	.01
☐ 65	Johnny Bench	.50	.20	.05
☐ 66	Mike Hargrove	.07	.03	.01

1982 Kellogg's

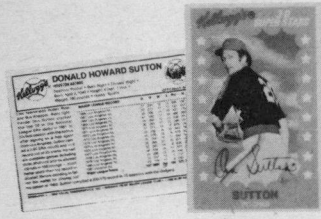

*The cards in this 64-card set measure 2 ⅛"
by 3 ¼". The 1982 version of 3-D cards
prepared for the Kellogg Company by Visual
Panographics, Inc., is not only smaller in
physical dimensions from the 1981 series
(which was standard card size at 2 ½" by
3 ½") but is also two cards shorter in length
(64 in '82 and 66 in '81). In addition, while
retaining the policy of not inserting single
cards into cereal packages and offering the
sets through box-top mail-ins only, the
Kellogg Company accepted box tops from
four types of cereals, as opposed to only one
type the previous year. Each card features a
color 3-D ballplayer picture with a vertical
line of white stars on each side set upon a
blue background. The player's name and the
word Kellogg's are printed in red on the obverse, and the card number is found on the
bottom right of the reverse.*

	MINT	EXC	G-VG
Complete Set (64)	12.00	5.00	1.20
Common Player (1-64)	.09	.04	.01

		MINT	EXC	G-VG
☐ 1	Richie Zisk	.09	.04	.01
☐ 2	Bill Buckner	.15	.06	.01
☐ 3	George Brett	.90	.36	.09
☐ 4	Rickey Henderson	.75	.30	.07
☐ 5	Jack Morris	.15	.06	.01
☐ 6	Ozzie Smith	.35	.14	.03
☐ 7	Rollie Fingers	.15	.06	.01
☐ 8	Tom Seaver	.60	.24	.06
☐ 9	Fernando Valuenzuela	.40	.16	.04
☐ 10	Hubie Brooks	.15	.06	.01
☐ 11	Nolan Ryan	.65	.26	.06
☐ 12	Dave Winfield	.35	.14	.03
☐ 13	Bob Horner	.20	.08	.02
☐ 14	Reggie Jackson	.75	.30	.07
☐ 15	Burt Hooton	.09	.04	.01
☐ 16	Mike Schmidt	.90	.36	.09
☐ 17	Bruce Sutter	.15	.06	.01
☐ 18	Pete Rose	1.00	.40	.10
☐ 19	Dave Kingman	.15	.06	.01
☐ 20	Neil Allen	.09	.04	.01
☐ 21	Don Sutton	.30	.12	.03
☐ 22	Dave Concepcion	.15	.06	.01
☐ 23	Keith Hernandez	.30	.12	.03
☐ 24	Gary Carter	.45	.18	.04
☐ 25	Carlton Fisk	.20	.08	.02
☐ 26	Ron Guidry	.20	.08	.02
☐ 27	Steve Carlton	.35	.14	.03
☐ 28	Robin Yount	.35	.14	.03
☐ 29	John Castino	.09	.04	.01
☐ 30	Johnny Bench	.50	.20	.05
☐ 31	Bob Knepper	.15	.06	.01
☐ 32	Rich Gossage	.15	.06	.01
☐ 33	Buddy Bell	.15	.06	.01
☐ 34	Art Howe	.15	.06	.01
☐ 35	Tony Armas	.15	.06	.01
☐ 36	Phil Niekro	.25	.10	.02
☐ 37	Len Barker	.09	.04	.01
☐ 38	Bob Grich	.15	.06	.01
☐ 39	Steve Kemp	.09	.04	.01
☐ 40	Kirk Gibson	.40	.16	.04
☐ 41	Carney Lansford	.15	.06	.01
☐ 42	Jim Palmer	.30	.12	.03
☐ 43	Carl Yastrzemski	.85	.34	.08
☐ 44	Rick Burleson	.09	.04	.01
☐ 45	Dwight Evans	.20	.08	.02
☐ 46	Ron Cey	.15	.06	.01
☐ 47	Steve Garvey	.45	.18	.04
☐ 48	Dave Parker	.20	.08	.02
☐ 49	Mike Easler	.09	.04	.01

		MINT	EXC	G-VG
☐ 50	Dusty Baker	.09	.04	.01
☐ 51	Rod Carew	.40	.16	.04
☐ 52	Chris Chambliss	.15	.06	.01
☐ 53	Tim Raines	.45	.18	.04
☐ 54	Chet Lemon	.09	.04	.01
☐ 55	Bill Madlock	.15	.06	.01
☐ 56	George Foster	.15	.06	.01
☐ 57	Dwayne Murphy	.09	.04	.01
☐ 58	Ken Singleton	.15	.06	.01
☐ 59	Mike Norris	.09	.04	.01
☐ 60	Cecil Cooper	.15	.06	.01
☐ 61	Al Oliver	.15	.06	.01
☐ 62	Willie Wilson	.15	.06	.01
☐ 63	Vida Blue	.15	.06	.01
☐ 64	Eddie Murray	.60	.24	.06

1983 Kellogg's

The cards in this 60-card set measure 1 ⅞" by 3 ¼". For the 14th year in a row, the Kellogg Company issued a card set of Major League players. The set of 3-D cards contains the photo, player's autograph, Kellogg's logo, and name and position of the player on the front of the card. The backs feature the player's team logo, career statistics, player biography, and a narrative on the player's career.

	MINT	EXC	G-VG
Complete Set (60)	12.00	5.00	1.20
Common Player (1-60)	.09	.04	.01

		MINT	EXC	G-VG
☐ 1	Rod Carew	.45	.18	.04
☐ 2	Rollie Fingers	.20	.08	.02
☐ 3	Reggie Jackson	.75	.30	.07
☐ 4	George Brett	.90	.36	.09
☐ 5	Hal McRae	.15	.06	.01
☐ 6	Pete Rose	1.00	.40	.10
☐ 7	Fernando Valenzuela	.35	.14	.03
☐ 8	Rickey Henderson	.75	.30	.07
☐ 9	Carl Yastrzemski	.75	.30	.07
☐ 10	Rich Gossage	.15	.06	.01
☐ 11	Eddie Murray	.50	.20	.05
☐ 12	Buddy Bell	.15	.06	.01
☐ 13	Jim Rice	.30	.12	.03
☐ 14	Robin Yount	.35	.14	.03
☐ 15	Dave Winfield	.35	.14	.03
☐ 16	Harold Baines	.20	.08	.02
☐ 17	Garry Templeton	.09	.04	.01
☐ 18	Bill Madlock	.15	.06	.01
☐ 19	Pete Vuckovich	.09	.04	.01
☐ 20	Pedro Guerrero	.25	.10	.02
☐ 21	Ozzie Smith	.30	.12	.03
☐ 22	George Foster	.15	.06	.01
☐ 23	Willie Wilson	.15	.06	.01
☐ 24	Johnny Ray	.15	.06	.01
☐ 25	George Hendrick	.09	.04	.01
☐ 26	Andre Thornton	.09	.04	.01
☐ 27	Leon Durham	.09	.04	.01
☐ 28	Cecil Cooper	.15	.06	.01
☐ 29	Don Baylor	.15	.06	.01
☐ 30	Lonnie Smith	.09	.04	.01
☐ 31	Nolan Ryan	.50	.20	.05
☐ 32	Dan Quisenberry	.15	.06	.01
☐ 33	Len Barker	.09	.04	.01
☐ 34	Neil Allen	.09	.04	.01
☐ 35	Jack Morris	.20	.08	.02
☐ 36	Dave Stieb	.15	.06	.01
☐ 37	Bruce Sutter	.15	.06	.01
☐ 38	Jim Sundberg	.09	.04	.01
☐ 39	Jim Palmer	.30	.12	.03
☐ 40	Lance Parrish	.20	.08	.02
☐ 41	Floyd Bannister	.09	.04	.01
☐ 42	Larry Gura	.09	.04	.01
☐ 43	Britt Burns	.09	.04	.01
☐ 44	Toby Harrah	.09	.04	.01
☐ 45	Steve Carlton	.35	.14	.03
☐ 46	Greg Minton	.09	.04	.01
☐ 47	Gorman Thomas	.15	.06	.01
☐ 48	Jack Clark	.25	.10	.02
☐ 49	Keith Hernandez	.30	.12	.03

		MINT	EXC	G-VG
☐ 50	Greg Luzinski	.15	.06	.01
☐ 51	Fred Lynn	.15	.06	.01
☐ 52	Dale Murphy	.75	.30	.07
☐ 53	Kent Hrbek	.30	.12	.03
☐ 54	Bob Horner	.20	.08	.02
☐ 55	Gary Carter	.45	.18	.04
☐ 56	Carlton Fisk	.15	.06	.01
☐ 57	Dave Concepcion	.15	.06	.01
☐ 58	Mike Schmidt	.85	.34	.08
☐ 59	Bill Buckner	.15	.06	.01
☐ 60	Bob Grich	.15	.06	.01

1988 Pacific Legends

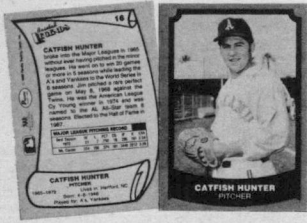

This attractive set of 110 full-color cards was produced by Mike Cramer's Pacific Trading Cards of Edmonds, Washington. The cards are silver bordered and are standard size, 2 ½" by 3 ½". Card backs are printed in yellow, black, and gray on white card stock. The cards were available either as wax packs or as collated sets. The players pictured in the set had retired many years before, but most are still well remembered. The statistics on the card backs give the player's career and "best season" statistics. The set was licensed by Major League Baseball Players Alumni.

	MINT	EXC	G-VG
Complete Set (110)	10.00	4.00	1.00
Common Player (1-110)	.05	.02	.00

		MINT	EXC	G-VG
☐ 1	Hank Aaron	.65	.26	.06
☐ 2	Red Schoendienst	.10	.04	.01
☐ 3	Brooks Robinson	.30	.12	.03
☐ 4	Luke Appling	.10	.04	.01
☐ 5	Gene Woodling	.05	.02	.00
☐ 6	Stan Musial	.50	.20	.05
☐ 7	Mickey Mantle	1.00	.40	.10
☐ 8	Richie Ashburn	.15	.06	.01
☐ 9	Ralph Kiner	.20	.08	.02
☐ 10	Phil Rizzuto	.15	.06	.01
☐ 11	Harvey Haddix	.05	.02	.00
☐ 12	Ken Boyer	.10	.04	.01
☐ 13	Clete Boyer	.05	.02	.00
☐ 14	Ken Harrelson	.10	.04	.01
☐ 15	Robin Roberts	.20	.08	.02
☐ 16	Catfish Hunter	.20	.08	.02
☐ 17	Frank Howard	.10	.04	.01
☐ 18	Jim Perry	.05	.02	.00
☐ 19A	Elston Howard ERR (reversed negative)	.10	.04	.01
☐ 19B	Elston Howard COR	.10	.04	.01
☐ 20	Jim Bouton	.10	.04	.01
☐ 21	Pee Wee Reese	.20	.08	.02
☐ 22A	Mel Stottlemyre ERR (spelled Stottlemyer on card front)	.10	.04	.01
☐ 22B	Mel Stottlemyre COR	.10	.04	.01
☐ 23	Hank Sauer	.05	.02	.00
☐ 24	Willie Mays	.65	.26	.06
☐ 25	Tom Tresh	.10	.04	.01
☐ 26	Roy Sievers	.05	.02	.00
☐ 27	Leo Durocher	.15	.06	.01
☐ 28	Al Dark	.05	.02	.00
☐ 29	Tony Kubek	.15	.06	.01
☐ 30	Johnny VanderMeer	.10	.04	.01
☐ 31	Joe Adcock	.05	.02	.00
☐ 32	Bob Lemon	.15	.06	.01
☐ 33	Don Newcombe	.10	.04	.01
☐ 34	Thurman Munson	.30	.12	.03
☐ 35	Earl Battey	.05	.02	.00
☐ 36	Ernie Banks	.30	.12	.03
☐ 37	Matty Alou	.05	.02	.00
☐ 38	Dave McNally	.05	.02	.00
☐ 39	Mickey Lolich	.10	.04	.01
☐ 40	Jackie Robinson	.30	.12	.03
☐ 41	Allie Reynolds	.10	.04	.01
☐ 42A	Don Larsen ERR (misspelled Larson on card front)	.10	.04	.01
☐ 42B	Don Larsen COR	.10	.04	.01
☐ 43	Fergie Jenkins	.10	.04	.01

		MINT	EXC	G-VG
☐ 44	Jim Gilliam	.10	.04	.01
☐ 45	Bobby Thomson ...	.10	.04	.01
☐ 46	Sparky Anderson ..	.10	.04	.01
☐ 47	Roy Campanella ...	.30	.12	.03
☐ 48	Marv Throneberry ..	.10	.04	.01
☐ 49	Bill Virdon	.05	.02	.00
☐ 50	Tod Williams	.50	.20	.05
☐ 51	Minnie Minoso	.10	.04	.01
☐ 52	Bob Turley	.05	.02	.00
☐ 53	Yogi Berra	.30	.12	.03
☐ 54	Juan Marichal	.20	.08	.02
☐ 55	Duke Snider	.35	.14	.03
☐ 56	Harvey Kuenn	.10	.04	.01
☐ 57	Nellie Fox	.15	.06	.01
☐ 58	Felipe Alou	.05	.02	.00
☐ 59	Tony Oliva	.10	.04	.01
☐ 60	Bill Mazeroski	.10	.04	.01
☐ 61	Bobby Shantz	.05	.02	.00
☐ 62	Mark Fidrych	.05	.02	.00
☐ 63	Johnny Mize	.20	.08	.02
☐ 64	Ralph Terry	.10	.04	.01
☐ 65	Gus Bell	.05	.02	.00
☐ 66	Jerry Koosman	.10	.04	.01
☐ 67	Mike McCormick ...	.05	.02	.00
☐ 68	Lou Burdette	.10	.04	.01
☐ 69	George Kell	.20	.08	.02
☐ 70	Vic Raschi	.10	.04	.01
☐ 71	Chuck Connors	.20	.08	.02
☐ 72	Ted Kluszewski ...	.15	.06	.01
☐ 73	Bobby Doerr	.20	.08	.02
☐ 74	Bobby Richardson .	.15	.06	.01
☐ 75	Carl Erskine	.10	.04	.01
☐ 76	Hoyt Wilhelm	.20	.08	.02
☐ 77	Bob Purkey	.05	.02	.00
☐ 78	Bob Friend	.05	.02	.00
☐ 79	Monte Irvin	.20	.08	.02
☐ 80A	Jim Lonborg ERR ..	.10	.04	.01
	(misspelled Longborg on card front)			
☐ 80B	Jim Lonborg COR ..	.10	.04	.01
☐ 81	Wally Moon	.05	.02	.00
☐ 82	Moose Skowron ...	.10	.04	.01
☐ 83	Tommy Davis	.10	.04	.01
☐ 84	Enos Slaughter	.20	.08	.02
☐ 85	Sal Maglie	.10	.04	.01
☐ 86	Harmon Killebrew ..	.20	.08	.02
☐ 87	Gil Hodges	.20	.08	.02
☐ 88	Jim Kaat	.10	.04	.01
☐ 89	Roger Maris	.40	.16	.04
☐ 90	Billy Williams	.20	.08	.02

		MINT	EXC	G-VG
☐ 91	Luis Aparicio	.20	.08	.02
☐ 92	Jim Bunning	.15	.06	.01
☐ 93	Bill Freehan	.10	.04	.01
☐ 94	Orlando Cepeda ...	.15	.06	.01
☐ 95	Early Wynn	.20	.08	.02
☐ 96	Tug McGraw	.10	.04	.01
☐ 97	Ron Santo	.10	.04	.01
☐ 98	Del Crandall	.05	.02	.00
☐ 99	Sal Bando	.05	.02	.00
☐ 100	Joe DiMaggio	.65	.26	.06
☐ 101	Bob Feller	.30	.12	.03
☐ 102	Larry Doby	.10	.04	.01
☐ 103	Rollie Fingers	.15	.06	.01
☐ 104	Al Kaline	.25	.10	.02
☐ 105	Johnny Podres	.10	.04	.01
☐ 106	Lou Boudreau	.20	.08	.02
☐ 107	Zoilo Versalles ...	.05	.02	.00
☐ 108	Dick Groat	.10	.04	.01
☐ 109	Warren Spahn	.25	.10	.02
☐ 110	Johnny Bench	.35	.14	.03

1988 Score

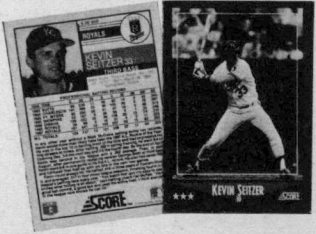

This 660-card set was distributed by Major League Marketing. Cards measure 2½" by 3½" and feature six distinctive border colors on the front. Highlights (652-660) and Rookie Prospects (623-647) are included in the set. Reggie Jackson's career is honored with a 5-card subset on cards 500-504. The set is distinguished by the fact that each card back shows a full-color picture of the player.

		MINT	EXC	G-VG
Complete Set (660)		24.00	10.00	2.40
Common Player (1-660)		.03	.01	.00
☐ 1	Don Mattingly	1.50	.35	.07
☐ 2	Wade Boggs	.80	.32	.08
☐ 3	Tim Raines	.20	.08	.02
☐ 4	Andre Dawson	.20	.08	.02
☐ 5	Mark McGwire	1.25	.50	.12
☐ 6	Kevin Seitzer	1.00	.40	.10
☐ 7	Wally Joyner	.40	.16	.04
☐ 8	Jesse Barfield	.15	.06	.01
☐ 9	Pedro Guerrero	.15	.06	.01
☐ 10	Eric Davis	.65	.26	.06
☐ 11	George Brett	.25	.10	.02
☐ 12	Ozzie Smith	.12	.05	.01
☐ 13	Rickey Henderson	.25	.10	.02
☐ 14	Jim Rice	.12	.05	.01
☐ 15	Matt Nokes	.45	.18	.04
☐ 16	Mike Schmidt	.25	.10	.02
☐ 17	Dave Parker	.10	.04	.01
☐ 18	Eddie Murray	.20	.08	.02
☐ 19	Andres Galarraga	.25	.10	.02
☐ 20	Tony Fernandez	.10	.04	.01
☐ 21	Kevin McReynolds	.15	.06	.01
☐ 22	B.J. Surhoff	.10	.04	.01
☐ 23	Pat Tabler	.06	.02	.00
☐ 24	Kirby Puckett	.30	.12	.03
☐ 25	Benny Santiago	.40	.16	.04
☐ 26	Ryne Sandberg	.15	.06	.01
☐ 27	Kelly Downs	.08	.03	.01
	(Will Clark in background, out of focus)			
☐ 28	Jose Cruz	.06	.02	.00
☐ 29	Pete O'Brien	.08	.03	.01
☐ 30	Mark Langston	.08	.03	.01
☐ 31	Lee Smith	.06	.02	.00
☐ 32	Juan Samuel	.08	.03	.01
☐ 33	Kevin Bass	.06	.02	.00
☐ 34	R.J. Reynolds	.03	.01	.00
☐ 35	Steve Sax	.12	.05	.01
☐ 36	John Kruk	.10	.04	.01
☐ 37	Alan Trammell	.15	.06	.01
☐ 38	Chris Bosio	.03	.01	.00
☐ 39	Brook Jacoby	.08	.03	.01
☐ 40	Willie McGee	.10	.04	.01
☐ 41	Dave Magadan	.10	.04	.01
☐ 42	Fred Lynn	.10	.04	.01
☐ 43	Kent Hrbek	.12	.05	.01
☐ 44	Brian Downing	.03	.01	.00
☐ 45	Jose Canseco	1.50	.60	.15

		MINT	EXC	G-VG
☐ 46	Jim Presley	.06	.02	.00
☐ 47	Mike Stanley	.06	.02	.00
☐ 48	Tony Pena	.06	.02	.00
☐ 49	David Cone	.90	.36	.09
☐ 50	Rick Sutcliffe	.08	.03	.01
☐ 51	Doug Drabek	.03	.01	.00
☐ 52	Bill Doran	.06	.02	.00
☐ 53	Mike Scioscia	.03	.01	.00
☐ 54	Candy Maldonado	.06	.02	.00
☐ 55	Dave Winfield	.20	.08	.02
☐ 56	Lou Whitaker	.08	.03	.01
☐ 57	Tom Henke	.06	.02	.00
☐ 58	Ken Gerhart	.06	.02	.00
☐ 59	Glenn Braggs	.08	.03	.01
☐ 60	Julio Franco	.08	.03	.01
☐ 61	Charlie Leibrandt	.03	.01	.00
☐ 62	Gary Gaetti	.10	.04	.01
☐ 63	Bob Boone	.06	.02	.00
☐ 64	Luis Polonia	.20	.08	.02
☐ 65	Dwight Evans	.10	.04	.01
☐ 66	Phil Bradley	.08	.03	.01
☐ 67	Mike Boddicker	.06	.02	.00
☐ 68	Vince Coleman	.20	.08	.02
☐ 69	Howard Johnson	.08	.03	.01
☐ 70	Tim Wallach	.08	.03	.01
☐ 71	Keith Moreland	.03	.01	.00
☐ 72	Barry Larkin	.12	.05	.01
☐ 73	Alan Ashby	.03	.01	.00
☐ 74	Rick Rhoden	.03	.01	.00
☐ 75	Darrell Evans	.06	.02	.00
☐ 76	Dave Stieb	.08	.03	.01
☐ 77	Dan Plesac	.06	.02	.00
☐ 78	Will Clark	.65	.26	.06
☐ 79	Frank White	.06	.02	.00
☐ 80	Joe Carter	.12	.05	.01
☐ 81	Mike Witt	.08	.03	.01
☐ 82	Terry Steinbach	.20	.08	.02
☐ 83	Alvin Davis	.08	.03	.01
☐ 84	Tommy Herr	.08	.03	.01
	(Will Clark shown sliding into second)			
☐ 85	Vance Law	.03	.01	.00
☐ 86	Kal Daniels	.20	.08	.02
☐ 87	Rick Honeycutt UER	.03	.01	.00
	(wrong years for stats on back)			
☐ 88	Alfredo Griffin	.06	.02	.00
☐ 89	Bret Saberhagen	.12	.05	.01
☐ 90	Bert Blyleven	.08	.03	.01
☐ 91	Jeff Reardon	.06	.02	.00
☐ 92	Cory Snyder	.20	.08	.02

		MINT	EXC	G-VG
☐ 93	Greg Walker	.06	.02	.00
☐ 94	Joe Magrane	.25	.10	.02
☐ 95	Rob Deer	.08	.03	.01
☐ 96	Ray Knight	.06	.02	.00
☐ 97	Casey Candaele	.03	.01	.00
☐ 98	John Cerutti	.03	.01	.00
☐ 99	Buddy Bell	.08	.03	.01
☐ 100	Jack Clark	.15	.06	.01
☐ 101	Eric Bell	.03	.01	.00
☐ 102	Willie Wilson	.08	.03	.01
☐ 103	Dave Schmidt	.03	.01	.00
☐ 104	Dennis Eckersley	.10	.04	.01
☐ 105	Don Sutton	.12	.05	.01
☐ 106	Danny Tartabull	.20	.08	.02
☐ 107	Fred McGriff	.75	.30	.07
☐ 108	Les Straker	.10	.04	.01
☐ 109	Lloyd Moseby	.08	.03	.01
☐ 110	Roger Clemens	.50	.20	.05
☐ 111	Glenn Hubbard	.03	.01	.00
☐ 112	Ken Williams	.20	.08	.02
☐ 113	Ruben Sierra	.18	.08	.01
☐ 114	Stan Jefferson	.18	.08	.01
☐ 115	Milt Thompson	.03	.01	.00
☐ 116	Bobby Bonilla	.18	.08	.01
☐ 117	Wayne Tolleson	.03	.01	.00
☐ 118	Matt Williams	.35	.14	.03
☐ 119	Chet Lemon	.03	.01	.00
☐ 120	Dale Sveum	.03	.01	.00
☐ 121	Dennis Boyd	.06	.02	.00
☐ 122	Brett Butler	.06	.02	.00
☐ 123	Terry Kennedy	.03	.01	.00
☐ 124	Jack Howell	.03	.01	.00
☐ 125	Curt Young	.03	.01	.00
☐ 126A	Dave Valle ERR	.25	.10	.02
	(misspelled Dale on card front)			
☐ 126B	Dave Valle COR	.10	.04	.01
☐ 127	Curt Wilkerson	.03	.01	.00
☐ 128	Tim Teufel	.03	.01	.00
☐ 129	Ozzie Virgil	.03	.01	.00
☐ 130	Brian Fisher	.03	.01	.00
☐ 131	Lance Parrish	.08	.03	.01
☐ 132	Tom Browning	.08	.03	.01
☐ 133A	Larry Andersen ERR	.15	.06	.01
	(misspelled Anderson on card front)			
☐ 133B	Larry Andersen COR	.03	.01	.00
☐ 134A	Bob Brenly ERR	.15	.06	.01
	(misspelled Brenley on card front)			
☐ 134B	Bob Brenly COR	.08	.03	.01
☐ 135	Mike Marshall	.08	.03	.01
☐ 136	Gerald Perry	.08	.03	.01
☐ 137	Bobby Meacham	.03	.01	.00
☐ 138	Larry Herndon	.03	.01	.00
☐ 139	Fred Manrique	.10	.04	.01
☐ 140	Charlie Hough	.03	.01	.00
☐ 141	Ron Darling	.10	.04	.01
☐ 142	Herm Winningham	.03	.01	.00
☐ 143	Mike Diaz	.03	.01	.00
☐ 144	Mike Jackson	.12	.05	.01
☐ 145	Denny Walling	.03	.01	.00
☐ 146	Rob Thompson	.03	.01	.00
☐ 147	Franklin Stubbs	.03	.01	.00
☐ 148	Albert Hall	.03	.01	.00
☐ 149	Bobby Witt	.06	.02	.00
☐ 150	Lance McCullers	.06	.02	.00
☐ 151	Scott Bradley	.03	.01	.00
☐ 152	Mark McLemore	.03	.01	.00
☐ 153	Tim Laudner	.03	.01	.00
☐ 154	Greg Swindell	.10	.04	.01
☐ 155	Marty Barrett	.06	.02	.00
☐ 156	Mike Heath	.03	.01	.00
☐ 157	Gary Ward	.03	.01	.00
☐ 158A	Lee Mazzilli ERR	.20	.08	.02
	(misspelled Mazilli on card front)			
☐ 158B	Lee Mazzilli COR	.08	.03	.01
☐ 159	Tom Foley	.03	.01	.00
☐ 160	Robin Yount	.20	.08	.02
☐ 161	Steve Bedrosian	.08	.03	.01
☐ 162	Bob Walk	.03	.01	.00
☐ 163	Nick Esasky	.03	.01	.00
☐ 164	Ken Caminiti	.20	.08	.02
☐ 165	Jose Uribe	.03	.01	.00
☐ 166	Dave Anderson	.03	.01	.00
☐ 167	Ed Whitson	.03	.01	.00
☐ 168	Ernie Whitt	.03	.01	.00
☐ 169	Cecil Cooper	.08	.03	.01
☐ 170	Mike Pagliarulo	.08	.03	.01
☐ 171	Pat Sheridan	.03	.01	.00
☐ 172	Chris Bando	.03	.01	.00
☐ 173	Lee Lacy	.03	.01	.00
☐ 174	Steve Lombardozzi	.03	.01	.00
☐ 175	Mike Greenwell	1.50	.60	.15
☐ 176	Greg Minton	.03	.01	.00
☐ 177	Moose Haas	.03	.01	.00
☐ 178	Mike Kingery	.03	.01	.00
☐ 179	Greg Harris	.03	.01	.00
☐ 180	Bo Jackson	.30	.12	.03
☐ 181	Carmelo Martinez	.03	.01	.00
☐ 182	Alex Trevino	.03	.01	.00

	MINT	EXC	G-VG
☐ 183 Ron Oester	.03	.01	.00
☐ 184 Danny Darwin	.03	.01	.00
☐ 185 Mike Krukow	.03	.01	.00
☐ 186 Rafael Palmeiro	.50	.20	.05
☐ 187 Tim Burke	.03	.01	.00
☐ 188 Roger McDowell	.06	.02	.00
☐ 189 Garry Templeton ...	.06	.02	.00
☐ 190 Terry Pendleton ...	.03	.01	.00
☐ 191 Larry Parrish	.03	.01	.00
☐ 192 Rey Quinones	.03	.01	.00
☐ 193 Joaquin Andujar ...	.06	.02	.00
☐ 194 Tom Brunansky	.10	.04	.01
☐ 195 Donnie Moore	.03	.01	.00
☐ 196 Dan Pasqua	.06	.02	.00
☐ 197 Jim Gantner	.03	.01	.00
☐ 198 Mark Eichhorn.....	.03	.01	.00
☐ 199 John Grubb	.03	.01	.00
☐ 200 Bill Ripken	.15	.06	.01
☐ 201 Sam Horn	.30	.12	.03
☐ 202 Todd Worrell	.10	.04	.01
☐ 203 Terry Leach	.06	.02	.00
☐ 204 Garth Iorg	.03	.01	.00
☐ 205 Brian Dayett	.03	.01	.00
☐ 206 Bo Diaz	.03	.01	.00
☐ 207 Craig Reynolds	.03	.01	.00
☐ 208 Brian Holton	.08	.03	.01
☐ 209 Marvell Wynne UER	.06	.02	.00
(misspelled Marvelle on card front)			
☐ 210 Dave Concepcion ..	.06	.02	.00
☐ 211 Mike Davis	.03	.01	.00
☐ 212 Devon White	.12	.05	.01
☐ 213 Mickey Brantley ...	.08	.03	.01
☐ 214 Greg Gagne	.03	.01	.00
☐ 215 Oddibe McDowell ..	.08	.03	.01
☐ 216 Jimmy Key	.08	.03	.01
☐ 217 Dave Bergman	.03	.01	.00
☐ 218 Calvin Schiraldi ...	.03	.01	.00
☐ 219 Larry Sheets	.08	.03	.01
☐ 220 Mike Easler	.03	.01	.00
☐ 221 Kurt Stillwell	.03	.01	.00
☐ 222 Chuck Jackson	.10	.04	.01
☐ 223 Dave Martinez	.06	.02	.00
☐ 224 Tim Leary	.08	.03	.01
☐ 225 Steve Garvey	.25	.10	.02
☐ 226 Greg Mathews	.03	.01	.00
☐ 227 Doug Sisk	.03	.01	.00
☐ 228 Dave Henderson ...	.06	.02	.00
☐ 229 Jimmy Dwyer	.03	.01	.00
☐ 230 Larry Owen	.03	.01	.00

	MINT	EXC	G-VG
☐ 231 Andre Thornton ...	.03	.01	.00
☐ 232 Mark Salas	.03	.01	.00
☐ 233 Tom Brookens	.03	.01	.00
☐ 234 Greg Brock	.03	.01	.00
☐ 235 Rance Mulliniks ...	.03	.01	.00
☐ 236 Bob Brower	.08	.03	.01
☐ 237 Joe Niekro	.06	.02	.00
☐ 238 Scott Bankhead ...	.03	.01	.00
☐ 239 Doug DeCinces ...	.03	.01	.00
☐ 240 Tommy John	.10	.04	.01
☐ 241 Rich Gedman	.06	.02	.00
☐ 242 Ted Power	.03	.01	.00
☐ 243 Dave Meads	.10	.04	.01
☐ 244 Jim Sundberg	.03	.01	.00
☐ 245 Ken Oberkfell	.03	.01	.00
☐ 246 Jimmy Jones	.10	.04	.01
☐ 247 Ken Landreaux	.03	.01	.00
☐ 248 Jose Oquendo	.03	.01	.00
☐ 249 John Mitchell	.12	.05	.01
☐ 250 Don Baylor	.08	.03	.01
☐ 251 Scott Fletcher	.03	.01	.00
☐ 252 Al Newman	.03	.01	.00
☐ 253 Carney Lansford ..	.06	.02	.00
☐ 254 Johnny Ray	.06	.02	.00
☐ 255 Gary Pettis	.03	.01	.00
☐ 256 Ken Phelps	.06	.02	.00
☐ 257 Rick Leach	.03	.01	.00
☐ 258 Tim Stoddard	.03	.01	.00
☐ 259 Ed Romero	.03	.01	.00
☐ 260 Sid Bream	.03	.01	.00
☐ 261A Tom Niedenfuer ERR	.15	.06	.01
(misspelled Neidenfuer on card front)			
☐ 261B Tom Niedenfuer COR	.06	.02	.00
☐ 262 Rick Dempsey	.03	.01	.00
☐ 263 Lonnie Smith	.03	.01	.00
☐ 264 Bob Forsch	.03	.01	.00
☐ 265 Barry Bonds	.18	.08	.01
☐ 266 Willie Randolph ...	.06	.02	.00
☐ 267 Mike Ramsey	.12	.05	.01
☐ 268 Don Slaught	.03	.01	.00
☐ 269 Mickey Tettleton ..	.03	.01	.00
☐ 270 Jerry Reuss	.03	.01	.00
☐ 271 Marc Sullivan	.03	.01	.00
☐ 272 Jim Morrison	.03	.01	.00
☐ 273 Steve Balboni	.03	.01	.00
☐ 274 Dick Schofield	.03	.01	.00
☐ 275 John Tudor	.08	.03	.01
☐ 276 Gene Larkin	.20	.08	.02
☐ 277 Harold Reynolds ..	.03	.01	.00

		MINT	EXC	G-VG
☐ 278	Jerry Browne	.03	.01	.00
☐ 279	Willie Upshaw	.03	.01	.00
☐ 280	Ted Higuera	.10	.04	.01
☐ 281	Terry McGriff	.08	.03	.01
☐ 282	Terry Puhl	.03	.01	.00
☐ 283	Mark Wasinger	.15	.06	.01
☐ 284	Luis Salazar	.03	.01	.00
☐ 285	Ted Simmons	.08	.03	.01
☐ 286	John Shelby	.03	.01	.00
☐ 287	John Smiley	.20	.08	.02
☐ 288	Curt Ford	.03	.01	.00
☐ 289	Steve Crawford	.03	.01	.00
☐ 290	Dan Quisenberry	.08	.03	.01
☐ 291	Alan Wiggins	.03	.01	.00
☐ 292	Randy Bush	.03	.01	.00
☐ 293	John Candelaria	.06	.02	.00
☐ 294	Tony Phillips	.03	.01	.00
☐ 295	Mike Morgan	.03	.01	.00
☐ 296	Bill Wegman	.03	.01	.00
☐ 297A	Terry Francona ERR	.15	.06	.01
	(misspelled Franconia on card front)			
☐ 297B	Terry Francona COR	.03	.01	.00
☐ 298	Mickey Hatcher	.06	.02	.00
☐ 299	Andres Thomas	.03	.01	.00
☐ 300	Bob Stanley	.03	.01	.00
☐ 301	Al Pedrique	.10	.04	.01
☐ 302	Jim Lindeman	.06	.02	.00
☐ 303	Wally Backman	.03	.01	.00
☐ 304	Paul O'Neill	.08	.03	.01
☐ 305	Hubie Brooks	.06	.02	.00
☐ 306	Steve Buechele	.03	.01	.00
☐ 307	Bobby Thigpen	.06	.02	.00
☐ 308	George Hendrick	.06	.02	.00
☐ 309	John Moses	.03	.01	.00
☐ 310	Ron Guidry	.08	.03	.01
☐ 311	Bill Schroeder	.03	.01	.00
☐ 312	Jose Nunez	.12	.05	.01
☐ 313	Bud Black	.03	.01	.00
☐ 314	Joe Sambito	.03	.01	.00
☐ 315	Scott McGregor	.03	.01	.00
☐ 316	Rafael Santana	.03	.01	.00
☐ 317	Frank Williams	.03	.01	.00
☐ 318	Mike Fitzgerald	.03	.01	.00
☐ 319	Rick Mahler	.03	.01	.00
☐ 320	Jim Gott	.03	.01	.00
☐ 321	Mariano Duncan	.03	.01	.00
☐ 322	Jose Guzman	.03	.01	.00
☐ 323	Lee Guetterman	.03	.01	.00
☐ 324	Dan Gladden	.06	.02	.00

		MINT	EXC	G-VG
☐ 325	Gary Carter	.20	.08	.02
☐ 326	Tracy Jones	.06	.02	.00
☐ 327	Floyd Youmans	.03	.01	.00
☐ 328	Bill Dawley	.03	.01	.00
☐ 329	Paul Noce	.10	.04	.01
☐ 330	Angel Salazar	.03	.01	.00
☐ 331	Goose Gossage	.08	.03	.01
☐ 332	George Frazier	.03	.01	.00
☐ 333	Ruppert Jones	.03	.01	.00
☐ 334	Billy Jo Robidoux	.03	.01	.00
☐ 335	Mike Scott	.12	.05	.01
☐ 336	Randy Myers	.15	.06	.01
☐ 337	Bob Sebra	.03	.01	.00
☐ 338	Eric Show	.03	.01	.00
☐ 339	Mitch Williams	.03	.01	.00
☐ 340	Paul Molitor	.10	.04	.01
☐ 341	Gus Polidor	.03	.01	.00
☐ 342	Steve Trout	.03	.01	.00
☐ 343	Jerry Don Gleaton	.03	.01	.00
☐ 344	Bob Knepper	.03	.01	.00
☐ 345	Mitch Webster	.03	.01	.00
☐ 346	John Morris	.03	.01	.00
☐ 347	Andy Hawkins	.03	.01	.00
☐ 348	Dave Leiper	.03	.01	.00
☐ 349	Ernest Riles	.03	.01	.00
☐ 350	Dwight Gooden	.40	.16	.04
☐ 351	Dave Righetti	.08	.03	.01
☐ 352	Pat Dodson	.08	.03	.01
☐ 353	John Habyan	.06	.02	.00
☐ 354	Jim Deshaies	.03	.01	.00
☐ 355	Butch Wynegar	.03	.01	.00
☐ 356	Bryn Smith	.03	.01	.00
☐ 357	Matt Young	.03	.01	.00
☐ 358	Tom Pagnozzi	.15	.06	.01
☐ 359	Floyd Rayford	.03	.01	.00
☐ 360	Darryl Strawberry	.35	.14	.03
☐ 361	Sal Butera	.03	.01	.00
☐ 362	Domingo Ramos	.03	.01	.00
☐ 363	Chris Brown	.08	.03	.01
☐ 364	Jose Gonzalez	.08	.03	.01
☐ 365	Dave Smith	.03	.01	.00
☐ 366	Andy McGaffigan	.03	.01	.00
☐ 367	Stan Javier	.03	.01	.00
☐ 368	Henry Cotto	.03	.01	.00
☐ 369	Mike Birkbeck	.08	.03	.01
☐ 370	Len Dykstra	.08	.03	.01
☐ 371	Dave Collins	.03	.01	.00
☐ 372	Spike Owen	.03	.01	.00
☐ 373	Geno Petralli	.03	.01	.00

		MINT	EXC	G-VG
☐ 374	Ron Karkovice	.03	.01	.00
☐ 375	Shane Rawley	.03	.01	.00
☐ 376	DeWayne Buice	.10	.04	.01
☐ 377	Bill Pecota	.10	.04	.01
☐ 378	Leon Durham	.06	.02	.00
☐ 379	Ed Olwine	.03	.01	.00
☐ 380	Bruce Hurst	.10	.04	.01
☐ 381	Bob McClure	.03	.01	.00
☐ 382	Mark Thurmond	.03	.01	.00
☐ 383	Buddy Biancalana	.03	.01	.00
☐ 384	Tim Conroy	.03	.01	.00
☐ 385	Tony Gwynn	.30	.12	.03
☐ 386	Greg Gross	.03	.01	.00
☐ 387	Barry Lyons	.10	.04	.01
☐ 388	Mike Felder	.03	.01	.00
☐ 389	Pat Clements	.03	.01	.00
☐ 390	Ken Griffey	.06	.02	.00
☐ 391	Mark Davis	.06	.02	.00
☐ 392	Jose Rijo	.03	.01	.00
☐ 393	Mike Young	.03	.01	.00
☐ 394	Willie Fraser	.03	.01	.00
☐ 395	Dion James	.03	.01	.00
☐ 396	Steve Shields	.03	.01	.00
☐ 397	Randy St.Claire	.03	.01	.00
☐ 398	Danny Jackson	.12	.05	.01
☐ 399	Cecil Fielder	.03	.01	.00
☐ 400	Keith Hernandez	.18	.08	.01
☐ 401	Don Carman	.03	.01	.00
☐ 402	Chuck Crim	.10	.04	.01
☐ 403	Rob Woodward	.03	.01	.00
☐ 404	Junior Ortiz	.03	.01	.00
☐ 405	Glenn Wilson	.03	.01	.00
☐ 406	Ken Howell	.03	.01	.00
☐ 407	Jeff Kunkel	.03	.01	.00
☐ 408	Jeff Reed	.03	.01	.00
☐ 409	Chris James	.10	.04	.01
☐ 410	Zane Smith	.06	.02	.00
☐ 411	Ken Dixon	.03	.01	.00
☐ 412	Ricky Horton	.03	.01	.00
☐ 413	Frank DiPino	.03	.01	.00
☐ 414	Shane Mack	.12	.05	.01
☐ 415	Danny Cox	.06	.02	.00
☐ 416	Andy Van Slyke	.15	.06	.01
☐ 417	Danny Heep	.03	.01	.00
☐ 418	John Cangelosi	.03	.01	.00
☐ 419A	John Christensen ERR (misspelled Christiansen on card front)	.15	.06	.01
☐ 419B	John Christensen COR	.03	.01	.00
☐ 420	Joey Cora	.12	.05	.01
☐ 421	Mike LaValliere	.03	.01	.00
☐ 422	Kelly Gruber	.03	.01	.00
☐ 423	Bruce Benedict	.03	.01	.00
☐ 424	Len Matuszek	.03	.01	.00
☐ 425	Kent Tekulve	.03	.01	.00
☐ 426	Rafael Ramirez	.03	.01	.00
☐ 427	Mike Flanagan	.03	.01	.00
☐ 428	Mike Gallego	.03	.01	.00
☐ 429	Juan Castillo	.06	.02	.00
☐ 430	Neal Heaton	.03	.01	.00
☐ 431	Phil Garner	.03	.01	.00
☐ 432	Mike Dunne	.15	.06	.01
☐ 433	Wallace Johnson	.03	.01	.00
☐ 434	Jack O'Connor	.03	.01	.00
☐ 435	Steve Jeltz	.03	.01	.00
☐ 436	Donnell Nixon	.12	.05	.01
☐ 437	Jack Lazorko	.03	.01	.00
☐ 438	Keith Comstock	.12	.05	.01
☐ 439	Jeff Robinson (Pirates pitcher)	.03	.01	.00
☐ 440	Graig Nettles	.08	.03	.01
☐ 441	Mel Hall	.03	.01	.00
☐ 442	Gerald Young	.25	.10	.02
☐ 443	Gary Redus	.03	.01	.00
☐ 444	Charlie Moore	.03	.01	.00
☐ 445	Bill Madlock	.06	.02	.00
☐ 446	Mark Clear	.03	.01	.00
☐ 447	Greg Booker	.03	.01	.00
☐ 448	Rick Schu	.03	.01	.00
☐ 449	Ron Kittle	.08	.03	.01
☐ 450	Dale Murphy	.25	.10	.02
☐ 451	Bob Dernier	.03	.01	.00
☐ 452	Dale Mohorcic	.03	.01	.00
☐ 453	Rafael Belliard	.03	.01	.00
☐ 454	Charlie Puleo	.03	.01	.00
☐ 455	Dwayne Murphy	.03	.01	.00
☐ 456	Jim Eisenreich	.03	.01	.00
☐ 457	David Palmer	.03	.01	.00
☐ 458	Dave Stewart	.08	.03	.01
☐ 459	Pascual Perez	.06	.02	.00
☐ 460	Glenn Davis	.12	.05	.01
☐ 461	Dan Petry	.03	.01	.00
☐ 462	Jim Winn	.03	.01	.00
☐ 463	Darrell Miller	.03	.01	.00
☐ 464	Mike Moore	.03	.01	.00
☐ 465	Mike LaCoss	.03	.01	.00
☐ 466	Steve Farr	.03	.01	.00
☐ 467	Jerry Mumphrey	.03	.01	.00

		MINT	EXC	G-VG
☐ 468	Kevin Gross	.03	.01	.00
☐ 469	Bruce Bochy	.03	.01	.00
☐ 470	Orel Hershiser	.20	.08	.02
☐ 471	Eric King	.03	.01	.00
☐ 472	Ellis Burks	1.00	.40	.10
☐ 473	Darren Daulton	.03	.01	.00
☐ 474	Mookie Wilson	.03	.01	.00
☐ 475	Frank Viola	.15	.06	.01
☐ 476	Ron Robinson	.03	.01	.00
☐ 477	Bob Melvin	.03	.01	.00
☐ 478	Jeff Musselman	.08	.03	.01
☐ 479	Charlie Kerfeld	.03	.01	.00
☐ 480	Richard Dotson	.06	.02	.00
☐ 481	Kevin Mitchell	.06	.02	.00
☐ 482	Gary Roenicke	.03	.01	.00
☐ 483	Tim Flannery	.03	.01	.00
☐ 484	Rich Yett	.03	.01	.00
☐ 485	Pete Incaviglia	.15	.06	.01
☐ 486	Rick Cerone	.03	.01	.00
☐ 487	Tony Armas	.06	.02	.00
☐ 488	Jerry Reed	.03	.01	.00
☐ 489	Dave Lopes	.06	.02	.00
☐ 490	Frank Tanana	.03	.01	.00
☐ 491	Mike Loynd	.06	.02	.00
☐ 492	Bruce Ruffin	.03	.01	.00
☐ 493	Chris Speier	.03	.01	.00
☐ 494	Tom Hume	.03	.01	.00
☐ 495	Jesse Orosco	.03	.01	.00
☐ 496	Robbie Wine UER (misspelled Robby on card front)	.15	.06	.01
☐ 497	Jeff Montgomery	.15	.06	.01
☐ 498	Jeff Dedmon	.03	.01	.00
☐ 499	Luis Aguayo	.03	.01	.00
☐ 500	Reggie Jackson (Oakland A's)	.25	.10	.02
☐ 501	Reggie Jackson (Baltimore Orioles)	.25	.10	.02
☐ 502	Reggie Jackson (New York Yankees)	.25	.10	.02
☐ 503	Reggie Jackson (California Angels)	.20	.08	.02
☐ 504	Reggie Jackson (Oakland A's)	.20	.08	.02
☐ 505	Billy Hatcher	.06	.02	.00
☐ 506	Ed Lynch	.03	.01	.00
☐ 507	Willie Hernandez	.06	.02	.00
☐ 508	Jose DeLeon	.03	.01	.00
☐ 509	Joel Youngblood	.03	.01	.00
☐ 510	Bob Welch	.06	.02	.00

		MINT	EXC	G-VG
☐ 511	Steve Ontiveros	.03	.01	.00
☐ 512	Randy Ready	.03	.01	.00
☐ 513	Juan Nieves	.03	.01	.00
☐ 514	Jeff Russell	.03	.01	.00
☐ 515	Von Hayes	.08	.03	.01
☐ 516	Mark Gubicza	.08	.03	.01
☐ 517	Ken Dayley	.03	.01	.00
☐ 518	Don Aase	.03	.01	.00
☐ 519	Rick Reuschel	.06	.02	.00
☐ 520	Mike Henneman	.20	.08	.02
☐ 521	Rick Aguilera	.03	.01	.00
☐ 522	Jay Howell	.03	.01	.00
☐ 523	Ed Correa	.03	.01	.00
☐ 524	Manny Trillo	.03	.01	.00
☐ 525	Kirk Gibson	.20	.08	.02
☐ 526	Wally Ritchie	.10	.04	.01
☐ 527	Al Nipper	.03	.01	.00
☐ 528	Atlee Hammaker	.03	.01	.00
☐ 529	Shawon Dunston	.06	.02	.00
☐ 530	Jim Clancy	.03	.01	.00
☐ 531	Tom Paciorek	.03	.01	.00
☐ 532	Joel Skinner	.03	.01	.00
☐ 533	Scott Garrelts	.03	.01	.00
☐ 534	Tom O'Malley	.03	.01	.00
☐ 535	John Franco	.06	.02	.00
☐ 536	Paul Kilgus	.12	.05	.01
☐ 537	Darrell Porter	.03	.01	.00
☐ 538	Walt Terrell	.03	.01	.00
☐ 539	Bill Long	.10	.04	.01
☐ 540	George Bell	.18	.08	.01
☐ 541	Jeff Sellers	.03	.01	.00
☐ 542	Joe Boever	.10	.04	.01
☐ 543	Steve Howe	.03	.01	.00
☐ 544	Scott Sanderson	.03	.01	.00
☐ 545	Jack Morris	.10	.04	.01
☐ 546	Todd Benzinger	.30	.12	.03
☐ 547	Steve Henderson	.03	.01	.00
☐ 548	Eddie Milner	.03	.01	.00
☐ 549	Jeff Robinson (Tigers pitcher)	.35	.14	.03
☐ 550	Cal Ripken	.20	.08	.02
☐ 551	Jody Davis	.06	.02	.00
☐ 552	Kirk McCaskill	.03	.01	.00
☐ 553	Craig Lefferts	.03	.01	.00
☐ 554	Darnell Coles	.03	.01	.00
☐ 555	Phil Niekro	.12	.05	.01
☐ 556	Mike Aldrete	.06	.02	.00
☐ 557	Pat Perry	.03	.01	.00
☐ 558	Juan Agosto	.03	.01	.00

	MINT	EXC	G-VG
☐ 559 Rob Murphy	.03	.01	.00
☐ 560 Dennis Rasmussen	.06	.02	.00
☐ 561 Manny Lee	.03	.01	.00
☐ 562 Jeff Blauser	.18	.08	.01
☐ 563 Bob Ojeda	.06	.02	.00
☐ 564 Dave Dravecky	.03	.01	.00
☐ 565 Gene Garber	.03	.01	.00
☐ 566 Ron Roenicke	.03	.01	.00
☐ 567 Tommy Hinzo	.10	.04	.01
☐ 568 Eric Nolte	.10	.04	.01
☐ 569 Ed Hearn	.03	.01	.00
☐ 570 Mark Davidson	.10	.04	.01
☐ 571 Jim Walewander	.15	.06	.01
☐ 572 Donnie Hill	.03	.01	.00
☐ 573 Jamie Moyer	.03	.01	.00
☐ 574 Ken Schrom	.03	.01	.00
☐ 575 Nolan Ryan	.25	.10	.02
☐ 576 Jim Acker	.03	.01	.00
☐ 577 Jamie Quirk	.03	.01	.00
☐ 578 Jay Aldrich	.10	.04	.01
☐ 579 Claudell Washington	.06	.02	.00
☐ 580 Jeff Leonard	.06	.02	.00
☐ 581 Carmen Castillo	.03	.01	.00
☐ 582 Daryl Boston	.03	.01	.00
☐ 583 Jeff DeWillis	.10	.04	.01
☐ 584 John Marzano	.08	.03	.01
☐ 585 Bill Gullickson	.03	.01	.00
☐ 586 Andy Allanson	.03	.01	.00
☐ 587 Lee Tunnell	.03	.01	.00
☐ 588 Gene Nelson	.03	.01	.00
☐ 589 Dave LaPoint	.03	.01	.00
☐ 590 Harold Baines	.08	.03	.01
☐ 591 Bill Buckner	.08	.03	.01
☐ 592 Carlton Fisk	.10	.04	.01
☐ 593 Rick Manning	.03	.01	.00
☐ 594 Doug Jones	.25	.10	.02
☐ 595 Tom Candiotti	.03	.01	.00
☐ 596 Steve Lake	.03	.01	.00
☐ 597 Jose Lind	.25	.10	.02
☐ 598 Ross Jones	.10	.04	.01
☐ 599 Gary Matthews	.03	.01	.00
☐ 600 Fernando Valenzuela	.15	.06	.01
☐ 601 Dennis Martinez	.03	.01	.00
☐ 602 Les Lancaster	.10	.04	.01
☐ 603 Ozzie Guillen	.06	.02	.00
☐ 604 Tony Bernazard	.03	.01	.00
☐ 605 Chili Davis	.06	.02	.00
☐ 606 Roy Smalley	.03	.01	.00
☐ 607 Ivan Calderon	.08	.03	.01

	MINT	EXC	G-VG
☐ 608 Jay Tibbs	.03	.01	.00
☐ 609 Guy Hoffman	.03	.01	.00
☐ 610 Doyle Alexander	.06	.02	.00
☐ 611 Mike Bielecki	.03	.01	.00
☐ 612 Shawn Hillegas	.15	.06	.01
☐ 613 Keith Atherton	.03	.01	.00
☐ 614 Eric Plunk	.03	.01	.00
☐ 615 Sid Fernandez	.08	.03	.01
☐ 616 Dennis Lamp	.03	.01	.00
☐ 617 Dave Engle	.03	.01	.00
☐ 618 Harry Spilman	.03	.01	.00
☐ 619 Don Robinson	.03	.01	.00
☐ 620 John Farrell	.20	.08	.02
☐ 621 Nelson Liriano	.12	.05	.01
☐ 622 Floyd Bannister	.03	.01	.00
☐ 623 Randy Milligan	.30	.12	.03
☐ 624 Kevin Elster	.20	.08	.02
☐ 625 Jody Reed	.35	.14	.03
☐ 626 Shawn Abner	.20	.08	.02
☐ 627 Kurt Manwaring	.20	.08	.02
☐ 628 Pete Stanicek	.20	.08	.02
☐ 629 Rob Ducey	.20	.08	.02
☐ 630 Steve Kiefer	.03	.01	.00
☐ 631 Gary Thurman	.20	.08	.02
☐ 632 Darrel Akerfelds	.15	.06	.01
☐ 633 Dave Clark	.12	.05	.01
☐ 634 Roberto Kelly	.30	.12	.03
☐ 635 Keith Hughes	.15	.06	.01
☐ 636 John Davis	.15	.06	.01
☐ 637 Mike Devereaux	.30	.12	.03
☐ 638 Tom Glavine	.18	.08	.01
☐ 639 Keith Miller (New York Mets)	.20	.08	.02
☐ 640 Chris Gwynn UER (wrong batting and throwing on back)	.35	.14	.03
☐ 641 Tim Crews	.12	.05	.01
☐ 642 Mackey Sasser	.25	.10	.02
☐ 643 Vicente Palacios	.12	.05	.01
☐ 644 Kevin Romine	.08	.03	.01
☐ 645 Gregg Jefferies	4.50	1.80	.45
☐ 646 Jeff Treadway	.30	.12	.03
☐ 647 Ron Gant	.45	.18	.04
☐ 648 Mark McGwire and Matt Nokes (Rookie Sluggers)	.30	.12	.03
☐ 649 Eric Davis and Tim Raines (Speed and Power)	.20	.08	.02

	MINT	EXC	G-VG
☐ 650 Don Mattingly and Jack Clark	.40	.16	.04
☐ 651 Tony Fernandez, Alan Trammell, and Cal Ripken	.10	.04	.01
☐ 652 Vince Coleman HL 100 Stolen Bases	.10	.04	.01
☐ 653 Kirby Puckett HL 10 Hits in a Row	.12	.05	.01
☐ 654 Benito Santiago HL Hitting Streak	.12	.05	.01
☐ 655 Juan Nieves HL No Hitter	.06	.02	.00
☐ 656 Steve Bedrosian HL Saves Record	.06	.02	.00
☐ 657 Mike Schmidt HL 500 Homers	.15	.06	.01
☐ 658 Don Mattingly HL Home Run Streak	.40	.16	.04
☐ 659 Mark McGwire HL Rookie HR Record	.35	.14	.03
☐ 660 Paul Molitor HL Hitting Streak	.10	.04	.01

1988 Score Traded

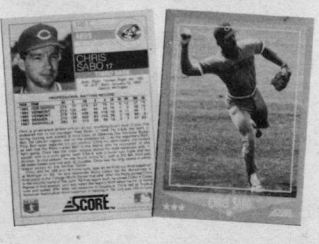

This 110-card set featured traded players (1-65) and rookies (66-110) for the 1988 season. The cards are distinguishable from the regular Score set by the orange borders and by the fact that the numbering on the back has a T suffix. The cards are standard size, 2 ½" by 3 ½", and were distributed by

Score as a collated set in a special collector box along with some trivia cards.

	MINT	EXC	G-VG
Complete Set (110)	11.00	4.50	1.10
Common Player (1-65)	.05	.02	.00
Common Player (66-110)	.05	.02	.00

	MINT	EXC	G-VG
☐ 1T Jack Clark	.15	.06	.01
☐ 2T Danny Jackson	.15	.06	.01
☐ 3T Brett Butler	.10	.04	.01
☐ 4T Kurt Stillwell	.05	.02	.00
☐ 5T Tom Brunansky	.10	.04	.01
☐ 6T Dennis Lamp	.05	.02	.00
☐ 7T Jose DeLeon	.05	.02	.00
☐ 8T Tom Herr	.05	.02	.00
☐ 9T Keith Moreland	.05	.02	.00
☐ 10T Kirk Gibson	.20	.08	.02
☐ 11T Bud Black	.05	.02	.00
☐ 12T Rafael Ramirez	.05	.02	.00
☐ 13T Luis Salazar	.05	.02	.00
☐ 14T Goose Gossage	.10	.04	.01
☐ 15T Bob Welch	.05	.02	.00
☐ 16T Vance Law	.05	.02	.00
☐ 17T Ray Knight	.05	.02	.00
☐ 18T Dan Quisenberry	.10	.04	.01
☐ 19T Don Slaught	.05	.02	.00
☐ 20T Lee Smith	.10	.04	.01
☐ 21T Rick Cerone	.05	.02	.00
☐ 22T Pat Tabler	.05	.02	.00
☐ 23T Larry McWilliams	.05	.02	.00
☐ 24T Ricky Horton	.05	.02	.00
☐ 25T Graig Nettles	.10	.04	.01
☐ 26T Dan Petry	.05	.02	.00
☐ 27T Jose Rijo	.05	.02	.00
☐ 28T Chili Davis	.10	.04	.01
☐ 29T Dickie Thon	.05	.02	.00
☐ 30T Mackey Sasser	.15	.06	.01
☐ 31T Mickey Tettleton	.05	.02	.00
☐ 32T Rick Dempsey	.05	.02	.00
☐ 33T Ron Hassey	.05	.02	.00
☐ 34T Phil Bradley	.10	.04	.01
☐ 35T Jay Howell	.05	.02	.00
☐ 36T Bill Buckner	.10	.04	.01
☐ 37T Alfredo Griffin	.10	.04	.01
☐ 38T Gary Pettis	.05	.02	.00
☐ 39T Calvin Schiraldi	.05	.02	.00
☐ 40T John Candelaria	.10	.04	.01
☐ 41T Joe Orsulak	.05	.02	.00
☐ 42T Willie Upshaw	.05	.02	.00
☐ 43T Herm Winningham	.05	.02	.00

	MINT	EXC	G-VG
☐ 44T Ron Kittle	.10	.04	.01
☐ 45T Bob Dernier	.05	.02	.00
☐ 46T Steve Balboni	.05	.02	.00
☐ 47T Steve Shields	.05	.02	.00
☐ 48T Henry Cotto	.05	.02	.00
☐ 49T Dave Henderson	.10	.04	.01
☐ 50T Dave Parker	.10	.04	.01
☐ 51T Mike Young	.05	.02	.00
☐ 52T Mark Salas	.05	.02	.00
☐ 53T Mike Davis	.05	.02	.00
☐ 54T Rafael Santana	.05	.02	.00
☐ 55T Don Baylor	.10	.04	.01
☐ 56T Dan Pasqua	.10	.04	.01
☐ 57T Ernest Riles	.05	.02	.00
☐ 58T Glenn Hubbard	.05	.02	.00
☐ 59T Mike Smithson	.05	.02	.00
☐ 60T Richard Dotson	.10	.04	.01
☐ 61T Jerry Reuss	.05	.02	.00
☐ 62T Mike Jackson	.10	.04	.01
☐ 63T Floyd Bannister	.05	.02	.00
☐ 64T Jesse Orosco	.05	.02	.00
☐ 65T Larry Parrish	.05	.02	.00
☐ 66T Jeff Bittiger	.15	.06	.01
☐ 67T Ray Hayward	.12	.05	.01
☐ 68T Ricky Jordan	2.00	.80	.20
☐ 69T Tommy Gregg	.15	.06	.01
☐ 70T Brady Anderson	.35	.14	.03
☐ 71T Jeff Montgomery	.10	.04	.01
☐ 72T Darryl Hamilton	.25	.10	.02
☐ 73T Cecil Espy	.20	.08	.02
☐ 74T Gregg Briley	.15	.06	.01
☐ 75T Joey Meyer	.20	.08	.02
☐ 76T Mike MacFarlane	.20	.08	.02
☐ 77T Oswald Peraza	.15	.06	.01
☐ 78T Jack Armstrong	.25	.10	.02
☐ 79T Don Heinkel	.15	.06	.01
☐ 80T Mark Grace	1.75	.70	.17
☐ 81T Steve Curry	.15	.06	.01
☐ 82T Damon Berryhill	.35	.14	.03
☐ 83T Steve Ellsworth	.15	.06	.01
☐ 84T Pete Smith	.15	.06	.01
☐ 85T Jack McDowell	.25	.10	.02
☐ 86T Rob Dibble	.15	.06	.01
☐ 87T Bryan Harvey	.30	.12	.03
☐ 88T John Dopson	.20	.08	.02
☐ 89T Dave Gallagher	.25	.10	.02
☐ 90T Todd Stottlemyre	.25	.10	.02
☐ 91T Mike Schooler	.15	.06	.01
☐ 92T Don Gordon	.15	.06	.01

	MINT	EXC	G-VG
☐ 93T Sil Campusano	.25	.10	.02
☐ 94T Jeff Pico	.15	.06	.01
☐ 95T Jay Buhner	.35	.14	.03
☐ 96T Nelson Santovenia	.15	.06	.01
☐ 97T Al Leiter	.40	.16	.04
☐ 98T Luis Alicea	.15	.06	.01
☐ 99T Pat Borders	.15	.06	.01
☐ 100T Chris Sabo	2.00	.80	.20
☐ 101T Tim Belcher	.25	.10	.02
☐ 102T Walt Weiss	.75	.30	.07
☐ 103T Craig Biggio	.15	.06	.01
☐ 104T Don August	.15	.06	.01
☐ 105T Roberto Alomar	.35	.14	.03
☐ 106T Todd Burns	.25	.10	.02
☐ 107T John Costello	.20	.08	.02
☐ 108T Melido Perez	.25	.10	.02
☐ 109T Darrin Jackson	.25	.10	.02
☐ 110T Orestes Destrade	.25	.10	.02

1989 Score

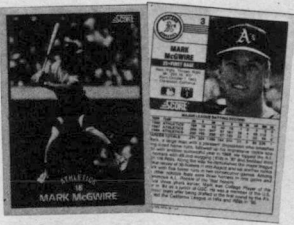

This 660-card set was distributed by Major
League Marketing. Cards measure 2 ½" by
3 ½" and feature six distinctive inner border
(inside a white outer border) colors on the
front. Highlights (652-660) and Rookie
Prospects (621-651) are included in the set.
The set is distinguished by the fact that each
card back shows a full-color picture (portrait)
of the player.

	MINT	EXC	G-VG
Complete Set (660)	23.00	9.50	2.30
Common Player (1-660)	.03	.01	.00

#	Player	MINT	EXC	G-VG	#	Player	MINT	EXC	G-VG
1	Jose Canseco	1.00	.35	.07	50	Dave Winfield	.15	.06	.01
2	Andre Dawson	.12	.05	.01	51	Alvin Davis	.08	.03	.01
3	Mark McGwire	.40	.16	.04	52	Cory Snyder	.12	.05	.01
4	Benny Santiago	.12	.05	.01	53	Hubie Brooks	.06	.02	.00
5	Rick Reuschel	.06	.02	.00	54	Chili Davis	.06	.02	.00
6	Fred McGriff	.12	.05	.01	55	Kevin Seitzer	.15	.06	.01
7	Kal Daniels	.10	.04	.01	56	Jose Uribe	.03	.01	.00
8	Gary Gaetti	.10	.04	.01	57	Tony Fernandez	.10	.04	.01
9	Ellis Burks	.20	.08	.02	58	Tim Teufel	.03	.01	.00
10	Darryl Strawberry	.30	.12	.03	59	Oddibe McDowell	.06	.02	.00
11	Julio Franco	.06	.02	.00	60	Les Lancaster	.03	.01	.00
12	Lloyd Moseby	.08	.03	.01	61	Billy Hatcher	.06	.02	.00
13	Jeff Pico	.10	.04	.01	62	Dan Gladden	.06	.02	.00
14	Johnny Ray	.06	.02	.00	63	Marty Barrett	.06	.02	.00
15	Cal Ripken Jr.	.15	.06	.01	64	Nick Esasky	.03	.01	.00
16	Dick Schofield	.03	.01	.00	65	Wally Joyner	.15	.06	.01
17	Mel Hall	.03	.01	.00	66	Mike Greenwell	.50	.20	.05
18	Bill Ripken	.03	.01	.00	67	Ken Williams	.03	.01	.00
19	Brook Jacoby	.06	.02	.00	68	Bob Horner	.08	.03	.01
20	Kirby Puckett	.20	.08	.02	69	Steve Sax	.10	.04	.01
21	Bill Doran	.06	.02	.00	70	Rickey Henderson	.20	.08	.02
22	Pete O'Brien	.06	.02	.00	71	Mitch Webster	.03	.01	.00
23	Matt Nokes	.10	.04	.01	72	Rob Deer	.06	.02	.00
24	Brian Fisher	.03	.01	.00	73	Jim Presley	.06	.02	.00
25	Jack Clark	.12	.05	.01	74	Albert Hall	.03	.01	.00
26	Gary Pettis	.03	.01	.00	75	George Brett	.20	.08	.02
27	Dave Valle	.03	.01	.00	76	Brian Downing	.03	.01	.00
28	Willie Wilson	.08	.03	.01	77	Dave Martinez	.03	.01	.00
29	Curt Young	.03	.01	.00	78	Scott Fletcher	.03	.01	.00
30	Dale Murphy	.20	.08	.02	79	Phil Bradley	.06	.02	.00
31	Barry Larkin	.10	.04	.01	80	Ozzie Smith	.10	.04	.01
32	Dave Stewart	.06	.02	.00	81	Larry Sheets	.06	.02	.00
33	Mike LaValliere	.03	.01	.00	82	Mike Aldrete	.03	.01	.00
34	Glenn Hubbard	.03	.01	.00	83	Darnell Coles	.03	.01	.00
35	Ryne Sandberg	.15	.06	.01	84	Len Dykstra	.06	.02	.00
36	Tony Pena	.06	.02	.00	85	Jim Rice	.10	.04	.01
37	Greg Walker	.06	.02	.00	86	Jeff Treadway	.06	.02	.00
38	Von Hayes	.08	.03	.01	87	Jose Lind	.03	.01	.00
39	Kevin Mitchell	.06	.02	.00	88	Willie McGee	.08	.03	.01
40	Tim Raines	.12	.05	.01	89	Mickey Brantley	.06	.02	.00
41	Keith Hernandez	.12	.05	.01	90	Tony Gwynn	.15	.06	.01
42	Keith Moreland	.03	.01	.00	91	R.J. Reynolds	.03	.01	.00
43	Ruben Sierra	.10	.04	.01	92	Milt Thompson	.03	.01	.00
44	Chet Lemon	.06	.02	.00	93	Kevin McReynolds	.15	.06	.01
45	Willie Randolph	.06	.02	.00	94	Eddie Murray	.15	.06	.01
46	Andy Allanson	.03	.01	.00	95	Lance Parrish	.08	.03	.01
47	Candy Maldonado	.06	.02	.00	96	Ron Kittle	.06	.02	.00
48	Sid Bream	.03	.01	.00	97	Gerald Young	.06	.02	.00
49	Denny Walling	.03	.01	.00	98	Ernie Whitt	.03	.01	.00

		MINT	EXC	G-VG			MINT	EXC	G-VG
☐ 99	Jeff Reed	.03	.01	.00	☐ 148	John Kruk	.06	.02	.00
☐ 100	Don Mattingly	.75	.30	.07	☐ 149	Mike Schmidt	.20	.08	.02
☐ 101	Gerald Perry	.08	.03	.01	☐ 150	Lee Smith	.06	.02	.00
☐ 102	Vance Law	.03	.01	.00	☐ 151	Robin Yount	.12	.05	.01
☐ 103	John Shelby	.03	.01	.00	☐ 152	Mark Eichhorn	.03	.01	.00
☐ 104	Chris Sabo	.75	.30	.07	☐ 153	DeWayne Buice	.03	.01	.00
☐ 105	Danny Tartabull	.12	.05	.01	☐ 154	B.J. Surhoff	.06	.02	.00
☐ 106	Glenn Wilson	.03	.01	.00	☐ 155	Vince Coleman	.12	.05	.01
☐ 107	Mark Davidson	.03	.01	.00	☐ 156	Tony Phillips	.03	.01	.00
☐ 108	Dave Parker	.08	.03	.01	☐ 157	Willie Fraser	.03	.01	.00
☐ 109	Eric Davis	.25	.10	.02	☐ 158	Lance McCullers	.06	.02	.00
☐ 110	Alan Trammell	.12	.05	.01	☐ 159	Greg Gagne	.03	.01	.00
☐ 111	Ozzie Virgil	.03	.01	.00	☐ 160	Jesse Barfield	.10	.04	.01
☐ 112	Frank Tanana	.03	.01	.00	☐ 161	Mark Langston	.08	.03	.01
☐ 113	Rafael Ramirez	.03	.01	.00	☐ 162	Kurt Stillwell	.03	.01	.00
☐ 114	Dennis Martinez	.03	.01	.00	☐ 163	Dion James	.03	.01	.00
☐ 115	Jose DeLeon	.03	.01	.00	☐ 164	Glenn Davis	.10	.04	.01
☐ 116	Bob Ojeda	.06	.02	.00	☐ 165	Walt Weiss	.40	.16	.04
☐ 117	Doug Drabek	.03	.01	.00	☐ 166	Dave Concepcion	.06	.02	.00
☐ 118	Andy Hawkins	.03	.01	.00	☐ 167	Alfredo Griffin	.06	.02	.00
☐ 119	Greg Maddux	.15	.06	.01	☐ 168	Don Heinkel	.10	.04	.01
☐ 120	Cecil Fielder	.03	.01	.00	☐ 169	Luis Rivera	.03	.01	.00
☐ 121	Mike Scioscia	.03	.01	.00	☐ 170	Shane Rawley	.03	.01	.00
☐ 122	Dan Petry	.03	.01	.00	☐ 171	Darrell Evans	.06	.02	.00
☐ 123	Terry Kennedy	.03	.01	.00	☐ 172	Robby Thompson	.03	.01	.00
☐ 124	Kelly Downs	.03	.01	.00	☐ 173	Jody Davis	.06	.02	.00
☐ 125	Greg Gross	.03	.01	.00	☐ 174	Andy Van Slyke	.10	.04	.01
☐ 126	Fred Lynn	.08	.03	.01	☐ 175	Wade Boggs	.50	.20	.05
☐ 127	Barry Bonds	.10	.04	.01	☐ 176	Garry Templeton	.06	.02	.00
☐ 128	Harold Baines	.08	.03	.01	☐ 177	Gary Redus	.03	.01	.00
☐ 129	Doyle Alexander	.03	.01	.00	☐ 178	Craig Lefferts	.03	.01	.00
☐ 130	Kevin Elster	.06	.02	.00	☐ 179	Carney Lansford	.06	.02	.00
☐ 131	Mike Heath	.03	.01	.00	☐ 180	Ron Darling	.08	.03	.01
☐ 132	Teddy Higuera	.08	.03	.01	☐ 181	Kirk McCaskill	.03	.01	.00
☐ 133	Charlie Leibrandt	.03	.01	.00	☐ 182	Tony Armas	.06	.02	.00
☐ 134	Tim Laudner	.03	.01	.00	☐ 183	Steve Farr	.03	.01	.00
☐ 135	Ray Knight	.06	.02	.00	☐ 184	Tom Brunansky	.08	.03	.01
☐ 136	Howard Johnson	.08	.03	.01	☐ 185	Bryan Harvey	.25	.10	.02
☐ 137	Terry Pendleton	.03	.01	.00	☐ 186	Mike Marshall	.08	.03	.01
☐ 138	Andy McGaffigan	.03	.01	.00	☐ 187	Bo Diaz	.03	.01	.00
☐ 139	Ken Oberkfell	.03	.01	.00	☐ 188	Willie Upshaw	.03	.01	.00
☐ 140	Butch Wynegar	.03	.01	.00	☐ 189	Mike Pagliarulo	.06	.02	.00
☐ 141	Rob Murphy	.03	.01	.00	☐ 190	Mike Krukow	.03	.01	.00
☐ 142	Rich Renteria	.10	.04	.01	☐ 191	Tommy Herr	.06	.02	.00
☐ 143	Jose Guzman	.03	.01	.00	☐ 192	Jim Pankovits	.03	.01	.00
☐ 144	Andres Galarraga	.12	.05	.01	☐ 193	Dwight Evans	.08	.03	.01
☐ 145	Ricky Horton	.03	.01	.00	☐ 194	Kelly Gruber	.03	.01	.00
☐ 146	Frank DiPino	.03	.01	.00	☐ 195	Bobby Bonilla	.10	.04	.01
☐ 147	Glenn Braggs	.03	.01	.00	☐ 196	Wallace Johnson	.03	.01	.00

		MINT	EXC	G-VG
☐ 197	Dave Stieb	.08	.03	.01
☐ 198	Pat Borders	.12	.05	.01
☐ 199	Rafael Palmeiro	.10	.04	.01
☐ 200	Doc Gooden	.30	.12	.03
☐ 201	Pete Incaviglia	.10	.04	.01
☐ 202	Chris James	.06	.02	.00
☐ 203	Marvell Wynne	.03	.01	.00
☐ 204	Pat Sheridan	.03	.01	.00
☐ 205	Don Baylor	.08	.03	.01
☐ 206	Paul O'Neill	.06	.02	.00
☐ 207	Pete Smith	.10	.04	.01
☐ 208	Mark McLemore	.03	.01	.00
☐ 209	Henry Cotto	.03	.01	.00
☐ 210	Kirk Gibson	.15	.06	.01
☐ 211	Claudell Washington	.06	.02	.00
☐ 212	Randy Bush	.03	.01	.00
☐ 213	Joe Carter	.10	.04	.01
☐ 214	Bill Buckner	.06	.02	.00
☐ 215	Bert Blyleven	.06	.02	.00
☐ 216	Brett Butler	.06	.02	.00
☐ 217	Lee Mazzilli	.03	.01	.00
☐ 218	Spike Owen	.03	.01	.00
☐ 219	Bill Swift	.03	.01	.00
☐ 220	Tim Wallach	.06	.02	.00
☐ 221	David Cone	.20	.08	.02
☐ 222	Don Carman	.03	.01	.00
☐ 223	Rich Gossage	.08	.03	.01
☐ 224	Bob Walk	.03	.01	.00
☐ 225	Dave Righetti	.08	.03	.01
☐ 226	Kevin Bass	.06	.02	.00
☐ 227	Kevin Gross	.03	.01	.00
☐ 228	Tim Burke	.03	.01	.00
☐ 229	Rick Mahler	.03	.01	.00
☐ 230	Lou Whitaker	.08	.03	.01
☐ 231	Luis Alicea	.12	.05	.01
☐ 232	Roberto Alomar	.20	.08	.02
☐ 233	Bob Boone	.06	.02	.00
☐ 234	Dickie Thon	.03	.01	.00
☐ 235	Shawon Dunston	.06	.02	.00
☐ 236	Pete Stanicek	.06	.02	.00
☐ 237	Craig Biggio	.12	.05	.01
☐ 238	Dennis Boyd	.06	.02	.00
☐ 239	Tom Candiotti	.03	.01	.00
☐ 240	Gary Carter	.15	.06	.01
☐ 241	Mike Stanley	.03	.01	.00
☐ 242	Ken Phelps	.06	.02	.00
☐ 243	Chris Bosio	.03	.01	.00
☐ 244	Les Straker	.03	.01	.00
☐ 245	Dave Smith	.03	.01	.00

		MINT	EXC	G-VG
☐ 246	John Candelaria	.06	.02	.00
☐ 247	Joe Orsulak	.03	.01	.00
☐ 248	Storm Davis	.06	.02	.00
☐ 249	Floyd Bannister	.03	.01	.00
☐ 250	Jack Morris	.10	.04	.01
☐ 251	Bret Saberhagen	.10	.04	.01
☐ 252	Tom Niedenfuer	.03	.01	.00
☐ 253	Neal Heaton	.03	.01	.00
☐ 254	Eric Show	.03	.01	.00
☐ 255	Juan Samuel	.08	.03	.01
☐ 256	Dale Sveum	.03	.01	.00
☐ 257	Jim Gott	.03	.01	.00
☐ 258	Scott Garrelts	.03	.01	.00
☐ 259	Larry McWilliams	.03	.01	.00
☐ 260	Steve Bedrosian	.08	.03	.01
☐ 261	Jack Howell	.03	.01	.00
☐ 262	Jay Tibbs	.03	.01	.00
☐ 263	Jamie Moyer	.03	.01	.00
☐ 264	Doug Sisk	.03	.01	.00
☐ 265	Todd Worrell	.08	.03	.01
☐ 266	John Farrell	.03	.01	.00
☐ 267	Dave Collins	.03	.01	.00
☐ 268	Sid Fernandez	.08	.03	.01
☐ 269	Tom Brookens	.03	.01	.00
☐ 270	Shane Mack	.06	.02	.00
☐ 271	Paul Kilgus	.03	.01	.00
☐ 272	Chuck Crim	.03	.01	.00
☐ 273	Bob Knepper	.03	.01	.00
☐ 274	Mike Moore	.03	.01	.00
☐ 275	Guillermo Hernandez	.06	.02	.00
☐ 276	Dennis Eckersley	.10	.04	.01
☐ 277	Graig Nettles	.08	.03	.01
☐ 278	Rich Dotson	.06	.02	.00
☐ 279	Larry Herndon	.03	.01	.00
☐ 280	Gene Larkin	.06	.02	.00
☐ 281	Roger McDowell	.06	.02	.00
☐ 282	Greg Swindell	.08	.03	.01
☐ 283	Juan Agosto	.03	.01	.00
☐ 284	Jeff Robinson	.08	.03	.01
	Detroit Tigers			
☐ 285	Mike Dunne	.06	.02	.00
☐ 286	Greg Mathews	.03	.01	.00
☐ 287	Kent Tekulve	.03	.01	.00
☐ 288	Jerry Mumphrey	.03	.01	.00
☐ 289	Jack McDowell	.12	.05	.01
☐ 290	Frank Viola	.12	.05	.01
☐ 291	Mark Gubicza	.08	.03	.01
☐ 292	Dave Schmidt	.03	.01	.00
☐ 293	Mike Henneman	.03	.01	.00

		MINT	EXC	G-VG
☐ 294	Jimmy Jones	.06	.02	.00
☐ 295	Charlie Hough	.03	.01	.00
☐ 296	Rafael Santana	.03	.01	.00
☐ 297	Chris Speier	.03	.01	.00
☐ 298	Mike Witt	.06	.02	.00
☐ 299	Pascual Perez	.06	.02	.00
☐ 300	Nolan Ryan	.15	.06	.01
☐ 301	Mitch Williams	.03	.01	.00
☐ 302	Mookie Wilson	.03	.01	.00
☐ 303	Mackey Sasser	.08	.03	.01
☐ 304	John Cerutti	.03	.01	.00
☐ 305	Jeff Reardon	.06	.02	.00
☐ 306	Randy Myers	.06	.02	.00
☐ 307	Greg Brock	.03	.01	.00
☐ 308	Bob Welch	.06	.02	.00
☐ 309	Jeff Robinson	.03	.01	.00
	Pittsburgh Pirates			
☐ 310	Harold Reynolds	.03	.01	.00
☐ 311	Jim Walewander	.03	.01	.00
☐ 312	Dave Magadan	.06	.02	.00
☐ 313	Jim Gantner	.03	.01	.00
☐ 314	Walt Terrell	.03	.01	.00
☐ 315	Wally Backman	.03	.01	.00
☐ 316	Luis Salazar	.03	.01	.00
☐ 317	Rick Rhoden	.03	.01	.00
☐ 318	Tom Henke	.03	.01	.00
☐ 319	Mike Macfarlane	.12	.05	.01
☐ 320	Dan Plesac	.06	.02	.00
☐ 321	Calvin Schiraldi	.03	.01	.00
☐ 322	Stan Javier	.03	.01	.00
☐ 323	Devon White	.08	.03	.01
☐ 324	Scott Bradley	.03	.01	.00
☐ 325	Bruce Hurst	.08	.03	.01
☐ 326	Manny Lee	.03	.01	.00
☐ 327	Rick Aguilera	.03	.01	.00
☐ 328	Bruce Ruffin	.03	.01	.00
☐ 329	Ed Whitson	.03	.01	.00
☐ 330	Bo Jackson	.20	.08	.02
☐ 331	Ivan Calderon	.08	.03	.01
☐ 332	Mickey Hatcher	.06	.02	.00
☐ 333	Barry Jones	.03	.01	.00
☐ 334	Ron Hassey	.03	.01	.00
☐ 335	Bill Wegman	.03	.01	.00
☐ 336	Damon Berryhill	.20	.08	.02
☐ 337	Steve Ontiveros	.03	.01	.00
☐ 338	Dan Pasqua	.06	.02	.00
☐ 339	Bill Pecota	.03	.01	.00
☐ 340	Greg Cadaret	.08	.03	.01
☐ 341	Scott Bankhead	.03	.01	.00

		MINT	EXC	G-VG
☐ 342	Ron Guidry	.08	.03	.01
☐ 343	Danny Heep	.03	.01	.00
☐ 344	Bob Brower	.06	.02	.00
☐ 345	Rich Gedman	.06	.02	.00
☐ 346	Nelson Santovenia	.10	.04	.01
☐ 347	George Bell	.10	.04	.01
☐ 348	Ted Power	.03	.01	.00
☐ 349	Mark Grant	.03	.01	.00
☐ 350	Roger Clemens	.25	.10	.02
☐ 351	Bill Long	.03	.01	.00
☐ 352	Jay Bell	.08	.03	.01
☐ 353	Steve Balboni	.03	.01	.00
☐ 354	Bob Kipper	.03	.01	.00
☐ 355	Steve Jeltz	.03	.01	.00
☐ 356	Jesse Orosco	.03	.01	.00
☐ 357	Bob Dernier	.03	.01	.00
☐ 358	Mickey Tettleton	.03	.01	.00
☐ 359	Duane Ward	.03	.01	.00
☐ 360	Darrin Jackson	.12	.05	.01
☐ 361	Rey Quinones	.03	.01	.00
☐ 362	Mark Grace	.75	.30	.07
☐ 363	Steve Lake	.03	.01	.00
☐ 364	Pat Perry	.03	.01	.00
☐ 365	Terry Steinbach	.08	.03	.01
☐ 366	Alan Ashby	.03	.01	.00
☐ 367	Jeff Montgomery	.03	.01	.00
☐ 368	Steve Buechele	.03	.01	.00
☐ 369	Chris Brown	.06	.02	.00
☐ 370	Orel Hershiser	.20	.08	.02
☐ 371	Todd Benzinger	.06	.02	.00
☐ 372	Ron Gant	.12	.05	.01
☐ 373	Paul Assenmacher	.03	.01	.00
☐ 374	Joey Meyer	.12	.05	.01
☐ 375	Neil Allen	.03	.01	.00
☐ 376	Mike Davis	.03	.01	.00
☐ 377	Jeff Parrett	.08	.03	.01
☐ 378	Jay Howell	.03	.01	.00
☐ 379	Rafael Belliard	.03	.01	.00
☐ 380	Luis Polonia	.03	.01	.00
☐ 381	Keith Atherton	.03	.01	.00
☐ 382	Kent Hrbek	.10	.04	.01
☐ 383	Bob Stanley	.03	.01	.00
☐ 384	Dave LaPoint	.03	.01	.00
☐ 385	Rance Mulliniks	.03	.01	.00
☐ 386	Melido Perez	.15	.06	.01
☐ 387	Doug Jones	.06	.02	.00
☐ 388	Steve Lyons	.03	.01	.00
☐ 389	Alejandro Pena	.03	.01	.00
☐ 390	Frank White	.06	.02	.00

		MINT	EXC	G-VG
☐ 391	Pat Tabler	.06	.02	.00
☐ 392	Eric Plunk	.03	.01	.00
☐ 393	Mike Maddux	.03	.01	.00
☐ 394	Allan Anderson	.06	.02	.00
☐ 395	Bob Brenly	.03	.01	.00
☐ 396	Rick Cerone	.03	.01	.00
☐ 397	Scott Terry	.03	.01	.00
☐ 398	Mike Jackson	.03	.01	.00
☐ 399	Bobby Thigpen	.06	.02	.00
☐ 400	Don Sutton	.10	.04	.01
☐ 401	Cecil Espy	.10	.04	.01
☐ 402	Junior Ortiz	.03	.01	.00
☐ 403	Mike Smithson	.03	.01	.00
☐ 404	Bud Black	.03	.01	.00
☐ 405	Tom Foley	.03	.01	.00
☐ 406	Andres Thomas	.03	.01	.00
☐ 407	Rick Sutcliffe	.08	.03	.01
☐ 408	Brian Harper	.03	.01	.00
☐ 409	John Smiley	.03	.01	.00
☐ 410	Juan Nieves	.03	.01	.00
☐ 411	Shawn Abner	.06	.02	.00
☐ 412	Wes Gardner	.08	.03	.01
☐ 413	Darren Daulton	.03	.01	.00
☐ 414	Juan Berenguer	.03	.01	.00
☐ 415	Charles Hudson	.03	.01	.00
☐ 416	Rick Honeycutt	.03	.01	.00
☐ 417	Greg Booker	.03	.01	.00
☐ 418	Tim Belcher	.08	.03	.01
☐ 419	Don August	.06	.02	.00
☐ 420	Dale Mohorcic	.03	.01	.00
☐ 421	Steve Lombardozzi	.03	.01	.00
☐ 422	Atlee Hammaker	.03	.01	.00
☐ 423	Jerry Don Gleaton	.03	.01	.00
☐ 424	Scott Bailes	.03	.01	.00
☐ 425	Bruce Sutter	.08	.03	.01
☐ 426	Randy Ready	.03	.01	.00
☐ 427	Jerry Reed	.03	.01	.00
☐ 428	Bryn Smith	.03	.01	.00
☐ 429	Tim Leary	.06	.02	.00
☐ 430	Mark Clear	.03	.01	.00
☐ 431	Terry Leach	.06	.02	.00
☐ 432	John Moses	.03	.01	.00
☐ 433	Ozzie Guillen	.06	.02	.00
☐ 434	Gene Nelson	.03	.01	.00
☐ 435	Gary Ward	.03	.01	.00
☐ 436	Luis Aguayo	.03	.01	.00
☐ 437	Fernando Valenzuela	.10	.04	.01
☐ 438	Jeff Russell	.03	.01	.00
☐ 439	Cecilio Guante	.03	.01	.00

		MINT	EXC	G-VG
☐ 440	Don Robinson	.03	.01	.00
☐ 441	Rick Anderson	.03	.01	.00
☐ 442	Tom Glavine	.03	.01	.00
☐ 443	Daryl Boston	.03	.01	.00
☐ 444	Joe Price	.03	.01	.00
☐ 445	Stewart Cliburn	.03	.01	.00
☐ 446	Manny Trillo	.03	.01	.00
☐ 447	Joel Skinner	.03	.01	.00
☐ 448	Charlie Puleo	.03	.01	.00
☐ 449	Carlton Fisk	.08	.03	.01
☐ 450	Will Clark	.25	.10	.02
☐ 451	Otis Nixon	.03	.01	.00
☐ 452	Rick Schu	.03	.01	.00
☐ 453	Todd Stottlemyre	.12	.05	.01
☐ 454	Tim Birtsas	.03	.01	.00
☐ 455	Dave Gallagher	.15	.06	.01
☐ 456	Barry Lyons	.03	.01	.00
☐ 457	Fred Manrique	.03	.01	.00
☐ 458	Ernest Riles	.03	.01	.00
☐ 459	Doug Jennings	.20	.08	.02
☐ 460	Joe Magrane	.06	.02	.00
☐ 461	Jamie Quirk	.03	.01	.00
☐ 462	Jack Armstrong	.20	.08	.02
☐ 463	Bobby Witt	.06	.02	.00
☐ 464	Keith Miller	.03	.01	.00
	New York Mets			
☐ 465	Todd Burns	.20	.08	.02
☐ 466	John Dopson	.12	.05	.01
☐ 467	Rich Yett	.03	.01	.00
☐ 468	Craig Reynolds	.03	.01	.00
☐ 469	Dave Bergman	.03	.01	.00
☐ 470	Rex Hudler	.03	.01	.00
☐ 471	Eric King	.03	.01	.00
☐ 472	Joaquin Andujar	.06	.02	.00
☐ 473	Sil Campusano	.25	.10	.02
☐ 474	Terry Mulholland	.03	.01	.00
☐ 475	Mike Flanagan	.03	.01	.00
☐ 476	Greg Harris	.03	.01	.00
	Philadelphia Phillies			
☐ 477	Tommy John	.08	.03	.01
☐ 478	Dave Anderson	.03	.01	.00
☐ 479	Fred Toliver	.03	.01	.00
☐ 480	Jimmy Key	.06	.02	.00
☐ 481	Donell Nixon	.03	.01	.00
☐ 482	Mark Portugal	.03	.01	.00
☐ 483	Tom Pagnozzi	.03	.01	.00
☐ 484	Jeff Kunkel	.03	.01	.00
☐ 485	Frank Williams	.03	.01	.00
☐ 486	Jody Reed	.08	.03	.01

		MINT	EXC	G-VG
☐ 487	Roberto Kelly	.12	.05	.01
☐ 488	Shawn Hillegas	.03	.01	.00
☐ 489	Jerry Reuss	.03	.01	.00
☐ 490	Mark Davis	.06	.02	.00
☐ 491	Jeff Sellers	.03	.01	.00
☐ 492	Zane Smith	.06	.02	.00
☐ 493	Al Newman	.03	.01	.00
☐ 494	Mike Young	.03	.01	.00
☐ 495	Larry Parrish	.03	.01	.00
☐ 496	Herm Winningham	.03	.01	.00
☐ 497	Carmelo Castillo	.03	.01	.00
☐ 498	Joe Hesketh	.03	.01	.00
☐ 499	Darrell Miller	.03	.01	.00
☐ 500	Mike LaCoss	.03	.01	.00
☐ 501	Charlie Lea	.03	.01	.00
☐ 502	Bruce Benedict	.03	.01	.00
☐ 503	Chuck Finley	.03	.01	.00
☐ 504	Brad Wellman	.03	.01	.00
☐ 505	Tim Crews	.03	.01	.00
☐ 506	Ken Gerhart	.03	.01	.00
☐ 507	Brian Holton	.03	.01	.00
☐ 508	Dennis Lamp	.03	.01	.00
☐ 509	Bobby Meacham	.03	.01	.00
☐ 510	Tracy Jones	.06	.02	.00
☐ 511	Mike Fitzgerald	.03	.01	.00
	Montreal Expos			
☐ 512	Jeff Bittiger	.12	.05	.01
☐ 513	Tim Flannery	.03	.01	.00
☐ 514	Ray Hayward	.08	.03	.01
☐ 515	Dave Leiper	.03	.01	.00
☐ 516	Rod Scurry	.03	.01	.00
☐ 517	Carmelo Martinez	.03	.01	.00
☐ 518	Curtis Wilkerson	.03	.01	.00
☐ 519	Stan Jefferson	.08	.03	.01
☐ 520	Dan Quisenberry	.08	.03	.01
☐ 521	Lloyd McClendon	.08	.03	.01
☐ 522	Steve Trout	.03	.01	.00
☐ 523	Larry Andersen	.03	.01	.00
☐ 524	Don Aase	.03	.01	.00
☐ 525	Bob Forsch	.03	.01	.00
☐ 526	Geno Petralli	.03	.01	.00
☐ 527	Angel Salazar	.03	.01	.00
☐ 528	Mike Schooler	.12	.05	.01
☐ 529	Jose Oquendo	.03	.01	.00
☐ 530	Jay Buhner	.15	.06	.01
☐ 531	Tom Bolton	.10	.04	.01
☐ 532	Al Nipper	.03	.01	.00
☐ 533	Dave Henderson	.06	.02	.00
☐ 534	John Costello	.12	.05	.01

		MINT	EXC	G-VG
☐ 535	Donnie Moore	.03	.01	.00
☐ 536	Mike Laga	.03	.01	.00
☐ 537	Mike Gallego	.03	.01	.00
☐ 538	Jim Clancy	.03	.01	.00
☐ 539	Joel Youngblood	.03	.01	.00
☐ 540	Rick Leach	.03	.01	.00
☐ 541	Kevin Romine	.03	.01	.00
☐ 542	Mark Salas	.03	.01	.00
☐ 543	Greg Minton	.03	.01	.00
☐ 544	Dave Palmer	.03	.01	.00
☐ 545	Dwayne Murphy	.03	.01	.00
☐ 546	Jim Deshaies	.03	.01	.00
☐ 547	Don Gordon	.08	.03	.01
☐ 548	Ricky Jordan	1.00	.40	.10
☐ 549	Mike Boddicker	.06	.02	.00
☐ 550	Mike Scott	.10	.04	.01
☐ 551	Jeff Ballard	.08	.03	.01
☐ 552	Jose Rijo	.03	.01	.00
☐ 553	Danny Darwin	.03	.01	.00
☐ 554	Tom Browning	.08	.03	.01
☐ 555	Danny Jackson	.10	.04	.01
☐ 556	Rick Dempsey	.03	.01	.00
☐ 557	Jeffrey Leonard	.06	.02	.00
☐ 558	Jeff Musselman	.03	.01	.00
☐ 559	Ron Robinson	.03	.01	.00
☐ 560	John Tudor	.08	.03	.01
☐ 561	Don Slaught	.03	.01	.00
☐ 562	Dennis Rasmussen	.06	.02	.00
☐ 563	Brady Anderson	.20	.08	.02
☐ 564	Pedro Guerrero	.10	.04	.01
☐ 565	Paul Molitor	.10	.04	.01
☐ 566	Terry Clark	.15	.06	.01
☐ 567	Terry Puhl	.03	.01	.00
☐ 568	Mike Campbell	.12	.05	.01
☐ 569	Paul Mirabella	.03	.01	.00
☐ 570	Jeff Hamilton	.03	.01	.00
☐ 571	Oswald Peraza	.10	.04	.01
☐ 572	Bob McClure	.03	.01	.00
☐ 573	Jose Bautista	.10	.04	.01
☐ 574	Alex Trevino	.03	.01	.00
☐ 575	John Franco	.06	.02	.00
☐ 576	Mark Parent	.10	.04	.01
☐ 577	Nelson Liriano	.03	.01	.00
☐ 578	Steve Shields	.03	.01	.00
☐ 579	Odell Jones	.03	.01	.00
☐ 580	Al Leiter	.20	.08	.02
☐ 581	Dave Stapleton	.10	.04	.01

		MINT	EXC	G-VG
☐ 582	World Series '88 ...	.15	.06	.01
	Orel Hershiser			
	Jose Canseco			
	Kirk Gibson			
	Dave Stewart			
☐ 583	Donnie Hill	.03	.01	.00
☐ 584	Chuck Jackson	.03	.01	.00
☐ 585	Rene Gonzales	.10	.04	.01
☐ 586	Tracy Woodson	.08	.03	.01
☐ 587	Jim Adduci	.03	.01	.00
☐ 588	Mario Soto	.03	.01	.00
☐ 589	Jeff Blauser	.03	.01	.00
☐ 590	Jim Traber	.03	.01	.00
☐ 591	Jon Perlman	.08	.03	.01
☐ 592	Mark Williamson	.08	.03	.01
☐ 593	Dave Meads	.03	.01	.00
☐ 594	Jim Eisenreich	.03	.01	.00
☐ 595	Paul Gibson	.10	.04	.01
☐ 596	Mike Birkbeck	.03	.01	.00
☐ 597	Terry Francona	.03	.01	.00
☐ 598	Paul Zuvella	.03	.01	.00
☐ 599	Franklin Stubbs	.03	.01	.00
☐ 600	Gregg Jefferies	1.50	.60	.15
☐ 601	Jim Cangelosi	.03	.01	.00
☐ 602	Mike Sharperson	.03	.01	.00
☐ 603	Mike Diaz	.03	.01	.00
☐ 604	Gary Varsho	.15	.06	.01
☐ 605	Terry Blocker	.12	.05	.01
☐ 606	Charlie O'Brien	.10	.04	.01
☐ 607	Jim Eppard	.10	.04	.01
☐ 608	John Davis	.03	.01	.00
☐ 609	Ken Griffey Sr.	.06	.02	.00
☐ 610	Buddy Bell	.08	.03	.01
☐ 611	Ted Simmons	.08	.03	.01
☐ 612	Matt Williams	.08	.03	.01
☐ 613	Danny Cox	.06	.02	.00
☐ 614	Al Pedrique	.03	.01	.00
☐ 615	Ron Oester	.03	.01	.00
☐ 616	John Smoltz	.20	.08	.02
☐ 617	Bob Melvin	.03	.01	.00
☐ 618	Rob Dibble	.12	.05	.01
☐ 619	Kirt Manwaring	.03	.01	.00
☐ 620	Felix Fermin	.10	.04	.01
☐ 621	Doug Dascenzo	.15	.06	.01
☐ 622	Bill Brennan	.15	.06	.01
☐ 623	Carlos Quintana	.30	.12	.03
☐ 624	Mike Harkey	.50	.20	.05
☐ 625	Gary Sheffield	1.25	.50	.12
☐ 626	Tom Prince	.10	.04	.01

		MINT	EXC	G-VG
☐ 627	Steve Searcy	.25	.10	.02
☐ 628	Charlie Hayes	.15	.06	.01
☐ 629	Felix Jose	.25	.10	.02
☐ 630	Sandy Alomar	.90	.36	.09
☐ 631	Derek Lilliquist	.20	.08	.02
☐ 632	Geronimo Berroa	.20	.08	.02
☐ 633	Luis Medina	.40	.16	.04
☐ 634	Tom Gordon	.25	.10	.02
☐ 635	Ramon Martinez	.25	.10	.02
☐ 636	Craig Worthington	.25	.10	.02
☐ 637	Edgar Martinez	.12	.05	.01
☐ 638	Chad Kreuter	.20	.08	.02
☐ 639	Ron Jones	.30	.12	.03
☐ 640	Van Snider	.20	.08	.02
☐ 641	Lance Blankenship	.15	.06	.01
☐ 642	Dwight Smith	.20	.08	.02
☐ 643	Cameron Drew	.20	.08	.02
☐ 644	Jerald Clark	.20	.08	.02
☐ 645	Randy Johnson	.20	.08	.02
☐ 646	Norm Charlton	.12	.05	.01
☐ 647	Todd Frohwirth	.08	.03	.01
☐ 648	Luis De Los Santos	.25	.10	.02
☐ 649	Tim Jones	.15	.06	.01
☐ 650	Dave West	.40	.16	.04
☐ 651	Bob Milacki	.25	.10	.02
☐ 652	Wrigley Field HL	.06	.02	.00
	(Let There Be Lights)			
☐ 653	Orel Hershiser HL	.15	.06	.01
	(The Streak)			
☐ 654	Wade Boggs HL	.20	.08	.02
	(Wade Whacks 'Em)			
☐ 655	Jose Canseco HL	.35	.14	.03
	(One of a Kind)			
☐ 656	Doug Jones HL	.06	.02	.00
	(Doug Sets Saves)			
☐ 657	Rickey Henderson HL	.12	.05	.01
	(Rickey Rocks 'Em)			
☐ 658	Tom Browning HL	.06	.02	.00
	(Tom Perfect Pitches)			
☐ 659	Mike Greenwell HL	.25	.10	.02
	(Greenwell Gamers)			
☐ 660	Boston Red Sox HL	.06	.02	.00
	(Joe Morgan MG, Sox Sock 'Em)			

1986 Sportflics

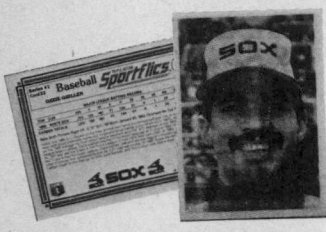

This 200-card set was marketed with 133 small trivia cards. This inaugural set for Sportflics was initially fairly well received by the public. Sportflics was distributed by Major League Marketing; the company is also affiliated with Wrigley and Amurol. The set features 139 single player "magic motion" cards (which can be tilted to show three different pictures of the same player), 50 "Tri-Stars" (which show three different players), 10 "Big Six" cards (which show six players who share similar achievements), and one World Champs card featuring 12 members of the victorious Kansas City Royals. All cards measure 2½" by 3½".

		MINT	EXC	G-VG
	Complete Set (200)	36.00	15.00	3.60
	Common Player (1-200)	.12	.05	.01
☐ 1	George Brett	1.25	.50	.12
☐ 2	Don Mattingly	4.00	1.60	.40
☐ 3	Wade Boggs	2.50	1.00	.25
☐ 4	Eddie Murray	.80	.32	.08
☐ 5	Dale Murphy	1.00	.40	.10
☐ 6	Rickey Henderson	.90	.36	.09
☐ 7	Harold Baines	.25	.10	.02
☐ 8	Cal Ripken	.80	.32	.08
☐ 9	Orel Hershiser	.80	.32	.08
☐ 10	Bret Saberhagen	.40	.16	.04
☐ 11	Tim Raines	.50	.20	.05
☐ 12	Fernando Valenzuela	.40	.16	.04
☐ 13	Tony Gwynn	.90	.36	.09
☐ 14	Pedro Guerrero	.30	.12	.03

		MINT	EXC	G-VG
☐ 15	Keith Hernandez	.40	.16	.04
☐ 16	Ernie Riles	.25	.10	.02
☐ 17	Jim Rice	.40	.16	.04
☐ 18	Ron Guidry	.30	.12	.03
☐ 19	Willie McGee	.40	.16	.04
☐ 20	Ryne Sandberg	.75	.30	.07
☐ 21	Kirk Gibson	.60	.24	.06
☐ 22	Ozzie Guillen	.40	.16	.04
☐ 23	Dave Parker	.30	.12	.03
☐ 24	Vince Coleman	1.50	.60	.15
☐ 25	Tom Seaver	.70	.28	.07
☐ 26	Brett Butler	.20	.08	.02
☐ 27	Steve Carlton	.50	.20	.05
☐ 28	Gary Carter	.60	.24	.06
☐ 29	Cecil Cooper	.20	.08	.02
☐ 30	Jose Cruz	.15	.06	.01
☐ 31	Alvin Davis	.20	.08	.02
☐ 32	Dwight Evans	.25	.10	.02
☐ 33	Julio Franco	.15	.06	.01
☐ 34	Damaso Garcia	.12	.05	.01
☐ 35	Steve Garvey	.75	.30	.07
☐ 36	Kent Hrbek	.40	.16	.04
☐ 37	Reggie Jackson	.90	.36	.09
☐ 38	Fred Lynn	.30	.12	.03
☐ 39	Paul Molitor	.40	.16	.04
☐ 40	Jim Presley	.30	.12	.03
☐ 41	Dave Righetti	.30	.12	.03
☐ 42	Robin Yount	.45	.18	.04
☐ 43	Nolan Ryan	.75	.30	.07
☐ 44	Mike Schmidt	1.00	.40	.10
☐ 45	Lee Smith	.15	.06	.01
☐ 46	Rick Sutcliffe	.20	.08	.02
☐ 47	Bruce Sutter	.25	.10	.02
☐ 48	Lou Whitaker	.25	.10	.02
☐ 49	Dave Winfield	.65	.26	.06
☐ 50	Pete Rose	1.50	.60	.15
☐ 51	NL MVPs	.80	.32	.08
	Ryne Sandberg			
	Steve Garvey			
	Pete Rose			
☐ 52	Slugging Stars	.40	.16	.04
	George Brett			
	Harold Baines			
	Jim Rice			
☐ 53	No-Hitters	.20	.08	.02
	Phil Niekro			
	Jerry Reuss			
	Mike Witt			

			MINT	EXC	G-VG
☐	54	Big Hitters . . . . Don Mattingly Cal Ripken Robin Yount	.90	.36	.09
☐	55	Bullpen Aces . . . . . . Dan Quisenberry Goose Gossage Lee Smith	.20	.08	.02
☐	56	Rookies of The Year Darryl Strawberry Steve Sax Pete Rose	.90	.36	.09
☐	57	AL MVP's . . . . Cal Ripken Don Baylor Reggie Jackson	.50	.20	.05
☐	58	Repeat Batting Champs Dave Parker Bill Madlock Pete Rose	.80	.32	.08
☐	59	Cy Young Winners . LaMarr Hoyt Mike Flanagan Ron Guidry	.15	.06	.01
☐	60	Double Award Winners Fernando Valenzuela Rick Sutcliffe Tom Seaver	.30	.12	.03
☐	61	Home Run Champs Reggie Jackson Jim Rice Tony Armas	.65	.26	.06
☐	62	NL MVP's . . . . Keith Hernandez Dale Murphy Mike Schmidt	.85	.34	.08
☐	63	AL MVP's . . . . Robin Yount George Brett Fred Lynn	.50	.20	.05
☐	64	Comeback Players . Bert Blyleven Jerry Koosman John Denny	.15	.06	.01
☐	65	Cy Young Relievers . Willie Hernandez Rollie Fingers Bruce Sutter	.20	.08	.02

			MINT	EXC	G-VG
☐	66	Rookies of The Year Bob Horner Andre Dawson Gary Matthews	.20	.08	.02
☐	67	Rookies of The Year Ron Kittle Carlton Fisk Tom Seaver	.30	.12	.03
☐	68	Home Run Champs Mike Schmidt George Foster Dave Kingman	.30	.12	.03
☐	69	Double Award Winners Cal Ripken Rod Carew Pete Rose	.80	.32	.08
☐	70	Cy Young Winners Rick Sutcliffe Steve Carlton Tom Seaver	.40	.16	.04
☐	71	Top Sluggers . . . . . Reggie Jackson Fred Lynn Robin Yount	.40	.16	.04
☐	72	Rookies of The Year Dave Righetti Fernando Valenzuela Rick Sutcliffe	.25	.10	.02
☐	73	Rookies of The Year Fred Lynn Eddie Murray Cal Ripken	.60	.24	.06
☐	74	Rookies of The Year Alvin Davis Lou Whitaker Rod Carew	.25	.10	.02
☐	75	Batting Champs . . . Don Mattingly Wade Boggs Carney Lansford	1.25	.50	.12
☐	76	Jesse Barfield	.40	.16	.04
☐	77	Phil Bradley	.30	.12	.03
☐	78	Chris Brown	.40	.16	.04
☐	79	Tom Browning	.30	.12	.03
☐	80	Tom Brunansky . . .	.25	.10	.02
☐	81	Bill Buckner	.15	.06	.01
☐	82	Chili Davis	.20	.08	.02
☐	83	Mike Davis	.15	.06	.01
☐	84	Rich Gedman	.20	.08	.02

			MINT	EXC	G-VG
☐	85	Willie Hernandez ...	.15	.06	.01
☐	86	Ron Kittle	.20	.08	.02
☐	87	Lee Lacy	.12	.05	.01
☐	88	Bill Madlock	.15	.06	.01
☐	89	Mike Marshall	.20	.08	.02
☐	90	Keith Moreland	.12	.05	.01
☐	91	Graig Nettles	.20	.08	.02
☐	92	Lance Parrish	.30	.12	.03
☐	93	Kirby Puckett	1.00	.40	.10
☐	94	Juan Samuel	.30	.12	.03
☐	95	Steve Sax	.35	.14	.03
☐	96	Dave Stieb	.20	.08	.02
☐	97	Darryl Strawberry ..	1.25	.50	.12
☐	98	Willie Upshaw	.12	.05	.01
☐	99	Frank Viola	.35	.14	.03
☐	100	Dwight Gooden	1.25	.50	.12
☐	101	Joaquin Andujar ...	.15	.06	.01
☐	102	George Bell	.45	.18	.04
☐	103	Bert Blyleven	.20	.08	.02
☐	104	Mike Boddicker	.15	.06	.01
☐	105	Britt Burns	.12	.05	.01
☐	106	Rod Carew	.70	.28	.07
☐	107	Jack Clark	.35	.14	.03
☐	108	Danny Cox	.20	.08	.02
☐	109	Ron Darling	.40	.16	.04
☐	110	Andre Dawson	.50	.20	.05
☐	111	Leon Durham	.12	.05	.01
☐	112	Tony Fernandez ...	.30	.12	.03
☐	113	Tommy Herr	.12	.05	.01
☐	114	Teddy Higuera	.60	.24	.06
☐	115	Bob Horner	.25	.10	.02
☐	116	Dave Kingman	.20	.08	.02
☐	117	Jack Morris	.30	.12	.03
☐	118	Dan Quisenberry ...	.20	.08	.02
☐	119	Jeff Reardon	.20	.08	.02
☐	120	Bryn Smith	.12	.05	.01
☐	121	Ozzie Smith	.40	.16	.04
☐	122	John Tudor	.20	.08	.02
☐	123	Tim Wallach	.15	.06	.01
☐	124	Willie Wilson	.15	.06	.01
☐	125	Carlton Fisk	.25	.10	.02
☐	126	RBI Sluggers	.25	.10	.02
		Gary Carter			
		Al Oliver			
		George Foster			
☐	127	Run Scorers	.50	.20	.05
		Tim Raines			
		Ryne Sandberg			
		Keith Hernandez			

			MINT	EXC	G-VG
☐	128	Run Scorers	.40	.16	.04
		Paul Molitor			
		Cal Ripken			
		Willie Wilson			
☐	129	No-Hitters	.15	.06	.01
		John Candelaria			
		Dennis Eckersley			
		Bob Forsch			
☐	130	World Series MVP's	.60	.24	.06
		Pete Rose			
		Ron Cey			
		Rollie Fingers			
☐	131	All-Star Game MVP's	.15	.06	.01
		Dave Concepcion			
		George Foster			
		Bill Madlock			
☐	132	Cy Young Winners	.20	.08	.02
		John Denny			
		Fernando Valenzuela			
		Vida Blue			
☐	133	Comeback Players	.15	.06	.01
		Rich Dotson			
		Joaquin Andujar			
		Doyle Alexander			
☐	134	Big Winners	.35	.14	.03
		Rick Sutcliffe			
		Tom Seaver			
		John Denny			
☐	135	Veteran Pitchers ..	.40	.16	.04
		Tom Seaver			
		Phil Niekro			
		Don Sutton			
☐	136	Rookies of The Year	.90	.36	.09
		Dwight Gooden			
		Vince Coleman			
		Alfredo Griffin			
☐	137	All-Star Game MVP's	.40	.16	.04
		Gary Carter			
		Fred Lynn			
		Steve Garvey			
☐	138	Veteran Hitters ...	.60	.24	.06
		Tony Perez			
		Rusty Staub			
		Pete Rose			
☐	139	Power Hitters	.50	.20	.05
		Mike Schmidt			
		Jim Rice			
		George Foster			

		MINT	EXC	G-VG
☐ 140	Batting Champs ...	.25	.10	.02
	Tony Gwynn			
	Al Oliver			
	Bill Buckner			
☐ 141	No-Hitters	.35	.14	.03
	Nolan Ryan			
	Jack Morris			
	Dave Righetti			
☐ 142	No-Hitters	.30	.12	.03
	Tom Seaver			
	Bert Blyleven			
	Vida Blue			
☐ 143	Strikeout Kings	.90	.36	.09
	Nolan Ryan			
	Fernando Valenzuela			
	Dwight Gooden			
☐ 144	Base Stealers	.30	.12	.03
	Tim Raines			
	Willie Wilson			
	Davey Lopes			
☐ 145	RBI Sluggers	.35	.14	.03
	Tony Armas			
	Cecil Cooper			
	Eddie Murray			
☐ 146	AL MVP's	.40	.16	.04
	Rod Carew			
	Jim Rice			
	Rollie Fingers			
☐ 147	World Series MVP's	.35	.14	.03
	Alan Trammell			
	Rick Dempsey			
	Reggie Jackson			
☐ 148	World Series MVP's	.40	.16	.04
	Darrell Porter			
	Pedro Guerrero			
	Mike Schmidt			
☐ 149	ERA Leaders	.15	.06	.01
	Mike Boddicker			
	Rick Sutcliffe			
	Ron Guidry			
☐ 150	Comeback Players .	.35	.14	.03
	Reggie Jackson			
	Dave Kingman			
	Fred Lynn			
☐ 151	Buddy Bell	.15	.06	.01
☐ 152	Dennis Boyd	.15	.06	.01
☐ 153	Dave Concepcion ..	.15	.06	.01
☐ 154	Brian Downing	.15	.06	.01
☐ 155	Shawon Dunston ..	.25	.10	.02

		MINT	EXC	G-VG
☐ 156	John Franco	.30	.12	.03
☐ 157	Scott Garrelts	.15	.06	.01
☐ 158	Bob James	.12	.05	.01
☐ 159	Charlie Leibrandt ..	.15	.06	.01
☐ 160	Oddibe McDowell .	.40	.16	.04
☐ 161	Roger McDowell ...	.40	.16	.04
☐ 162	Mike Moore	.20	.08	.02
☐ 163	Phil Niekro	.45	.18	.04
☐ 164	Al Oliver	.15	.06	.01
☐ 165	Tony Pena	.20	.08	.02
☐ 166	Ted Power	.15	.06	.01
☐ 167	Mike Scioscia	.15	.06	.01
☐ 168	Mario Soto	.15	.06	.01
☐ 169	Bob Stanley	.15	.06	.01
☐ 170	Gary Templeton ...	.15	.06	.01
☐ 171	Andre Thornton ...	.15	.06	.01
☐ 172	Alan Trammell	.45	.18	.04
☐ 173	Doug DeCinces ...	.20	.08	.02
☐ 174	Greg Walker	.20	.08	.02
☐ 175	Don Sutton	.40	.16	.04
☐ 176	1985 Award Winners	1.00	.40	.10
	Ozzie Guillen			
	Bret Saberhagen			
	Don Mattingly			
	Vince Coleman			
	Dwight Gooden			
	Willie McGee			
☐ 177	1985 Hot Rookies .	.60	.24	.06
	Stew Cliburn			
	Brian Fisher			
	Joe Hesketh			
	Joe Orsulak			
	Mark Salas			
	Larry Sheets			
☐ 178	1986 Rookies			
	To Watch	12.50	5.00	1.25
	Jose Canseco			
	Mark Funderburk			
	Mike Greenwell			
	Steve Lombardozzi			
	Billy Joe Robidoux			
	Danny Tartabull			
☐ 179	1985 Gold Glovers	.80	.32	.08
	George Brett			
	Ron Guidry			
	Keith Hernandez			
	Don Mattingly			
	Willie McGee			
	Dale Murphy			

		MINT	EXC	G-VG
□ 180	Active Lifetime .300	.80	.32	.08
	Wade Boggs			
	George Brett			
	Rod Carew			
	Cecil Cooper			
	Don Mattingly			
	Willie Wilson			
□ 181	Active Lifetime .300	.70	.28	.07
	Tony Gwynn			
	Bill Madlock			
	Pedro Guerrero			
	Dave Parker			
	Pete Rose			
	Keith Hernandez			
□ 182	1985 Milestones	.80	.32	.08
	Rod Carew			
	Phil Niekro			
	Pete Rose			
	Nolan Ryan			
	Tom Seaver			
	Matt Tallman (fan)			
□ 183	1985 Triple Crown	.80	.32	.08
	Wade Boggs			
	Darrell Evans			
	Don Mattingly			
	Willie McGee			
	Dale Murphy			
	Dave Parker			
□ 184	1985 Highlights	1.00	.40	.10
	Wade Boggs			
	Dwight Gooden			
	Rickey Henderson			
	Don Mattingly			
	Willie McGee			
	John Tudor			
□ 185	1985 20 Game Winners	.80	.32	.08
	Dwight Gooden			
	Ron Guidry			
	John Tudor			
	Joaquin Andujar			
	Bret Saberhagen			
	Tom Browning			
□ 186	World Series Champs	.40	.16	.04
	L. Smith, Dane Iorg			
	W. Wilson, Leibrandt			
	G. Brett, Saberhagen			
	Motley, Quisenberry			
	D. Jackson, Sundberg			
	S. Balboni, F. White			

		MINT	EXC	G-VG
□ 187	Hubie Brooks	.20	.08	.02
□ 188	Glenn Davis	.60	.24	.06
□ 189	Darrell Evans	.20	.08	.02
□ 190	Rich Gossage	.25	.10	.02
□ 191	Andy Hawkins	.15	.06	.01
□ 192	Jay Howell	.12	.05	.01
□ 193	LaMarr Hoyt	.15	.06	.01
□ 194	Davey Lopes	.12	.05	.01
□ 195	Mike Scott	.45	.18	.04
□ 196	Ted Simmons	.20	.08	.02
□ 197	Gary Ward	.12	.05	.01
□ 198	Bob Welch	.20	.08	.02
□ 199	Mike Young	.15	.06	.01
□ 200	Buddy Biancalana	.12	.05	.01

1986 Sportflics Rookies

This set of 50 three-phase "animated" cards features top rookies of 1986 as well as a few outstanding rookies from the past. These "Magic Motion" cards are standard size, 2 ½" by 3 ½", and feature a distinctive light blue border on the front of the card. Cards were distributed in a light blue box, which also contained 34 trivia cards, each measuring 1 ¾" by 2". There are 47 single player cards along with two Tri-Stars and one Big Six.

	MINT	EXC	G-VG
Complete Set (50)	14.00	5.75	1.40
Common Player (1-50)	.10	.04	.01
□ 1 John Kruk	.25	.10	.02

			MINT	EXC	G-VG
☐	2	Edwin Correa	.15	.06	.01
☐	3	Pete Incaviglia	.75	.30	.07
☐	4	Dale Sveum	.15	.06	.01
☐	5	Juan Nieves	.15	.06	.01
☐	6	Will Clark	2.50	1.00	.25
☐	7	Wally Joyner	2.00	.80	.20
☐	8	Lance McCullers	.15	.06	.01
☐	9	Scott Bailes	.15	.06	.01
☐	10	Dan Plesac	.20	.08	.02
☐	11	Jose Canseco	3.50	1.40	.35
☐	12	Bobby Witt	.25	.10	.02
☐	13	Barry Bonds	.75	.30	.07
☐	14	Andres Thomas	.20	.08	.02
☐	15	Jim Deshaies	.20	.08	.02
☐	16	Ruben Sierra	1.25	.50	.12
☐	17	Steve Lombardozzi	.10	.04	.01
☐	18	Cory Snyder	1.00	.40	.10
☐	19	Reggie Williams	.10	.04	.01
☐	20	Mitch Williams	.15	.06	.01
☐	21	Glenn Braggs	.25	.10	.02
☐	22	Danny Tartabull	.75	.30	.07
☐	23	Charlie Kerfeld	.15	.06	.01
☐	24	Paul Assenmacher	.15	.06	.01
☐	25	Robby Thompson	.25	.10	.02
☐	26	Bobby Bonilla	.75	.30	.07
☐	27	Andres Galarraga	.75	.30	.07
☐	28	Billy Jo Robidoux	.15	.06	.01
☐	29	Bruce Ruffin	.20	.08	.02
☐	30	Greg Swindell	.45	.18	.04
☐	31	John Cangelosi	.15	.06	.01
☐	32	Jim Traber	.10	.04	.01
☐	33	Russ Morman	.15	.06	.01
☐	34	Barry Larkin	.75	.30	.07
☐	35	Todd Worrell	.45	.18	.04
☐	36	John Cerutti	.15	.06	.01
☐	37	Mike Kingery	.10	.04	.01
☐	38	Mark Eichhorn	.20	.08	.02
☐	39	Scott Bankhead	.15	.06	.01
☐	40	Bo Jackson	1.00	.40	.10
☐	41	Greg Mathews	.25	.10	.02
☐	42	Eric King	.15	.06	.01
☐	43	Kal Daniels	1.00	.40	.10
☐	44	Calvin Schiraldi	.15	.06	.01
☐	45	Mickey Brantley	.20	.08	.02
☐	46	Tri-Stars	.50	.20	.05
		Willie Mays			
		Pete Rose			
		Fred Lynn			

			MINT	EXC	G-VG
☐	47	Tri-Stars	.50	.20	.05
		Tom Seaver			
		Fern. Valenzuela			
		Dwight Gooden			
☐	48	Big Six	.50	.20	.05
		Eddie Murray			
		Lou Whitaker			
		Dave Righetti			
		Steve Sax			
		Cal Ripken Jr.			
		Darryl Strawberry			
☐	49	Kevin Mitchell	.30	.12	.03
☐	50	Mike Diaz	.15	.06	.01

1987 Sportflics

This 200-card set was produced by
Sportflics and again features three sequence action pictures on each card. Cards
measure 2½" by 3½" and are in full color.
Also included with the cards were 136 small
team logo and trivia cards. There are 165
individual players, 20 Tri-Stars (the top three
players in each league at each position), and
15 other miscellaneous multi-player cards.
The cards feature a red border on the front.
A full-color face shot of the player is printed
on the back of the card. Cards are numbered
on the back in the upper right corner. The
cards in the factory-collated sets are
copyrighted 1986, while the cards in the wax
packs are copyrighted 1987 or show no
copyright year on the back. Cards from wax

packs with 1987 copyright are 1-35, 41-75, 81-115, 121-155, and 161-195; the rest of the numbers (when taken from wax packs) are found without a copyright year.

			MINT	EXC	G-VG
	Complete Set (200)		32.00	13.00	3.20
	Common Player (1-200)		.12	.05	.01
☐	1	Don Mattingly	3.00	1.20	.30
☐	2	Wade Boggs	2.00	.80	.20
☐	3	Dale Murphy	.90	.36	.09
☐	4	Rickey Henderson	.70	.28	.07
☐	5	George Brett	.70	.28	.07
☐	6	Eddie Murray	.60	.24	.06
☐	7	Kirby Puckett	.80	.32	.08
☐	8	Ryne Sandberg	.40	.16	.04
☐	9	Cal Ripken	.45	.18	.04
☐	10	Roger Clemens	1.25	.50	.12
☐	11	Ted Higuera	.30	.12	.03
☐	12	Steve Sax	.25	.10	.02
☐	13	Chris Brown	.15	.06	.01
☐	14	Jesse Barfield	.30	.12	.03
☐	15	Kent Hrbek	.30	.12	.03
☐	16	Robin Yount	.35	.14	.03
☐	17	Glenn Davis	.35	.14	.03
☐	18	Hubie Brooks	.15	.06	.01
☐	19	Mike Scott	.30	.12	.03
☐	20	Darryl Strawberry	.85	.34	.08
☐	21	Alvin Davis	.15	.06	.01
☐	22	Eric Davis	1.25	.50	.12
☐	23	Bob Tartabull	.45	.18	.04
☐	24A	Cory Snyder ERR '86 (photo on front is Pat Tabler)	3.00	1.20	.30
☐	24B	Cory Snyder ERR '87 (photos on front and back are Pat Tabler)	2.00	.80	.20
☐	24C	Cory Snyder COR '86	2.00	.80	.20
☐	25	Pete Rose	1.00	.40	.10
☐	26	Wally Joyner	1.25	.50	.12
☐	27	Pedro Guerrero	.25	.10	.02
☐	28	Tom Seaver	.60	.24	.06
☐	29	Bob Knepper	.15	.06	.01
☐	30	Mike Schmidt	.90	.36	.09
☐	31	Tony Gwynn	.75	.30	.07
☐	32	Don Slaught	.12	.05	.01
☐	33	Todd Worrell	.30	.12	.03
☐	34	Tim Raines	.35	.14	.03
☐	35	Dave Parker	.25	.10	.02
☐	36	Bob Ojeda	.15	.06	.01
☐	37	Pete Incaviglia	.60	.24	.06

			MINT	EXC	G-VG
☐	38	Bruce Hurst	.20	.08	.02
☐	39	Bobby Witt	.25	.10	.02
☐	40	Steve Garvey	.60	.24	.06
☐	41	Dave Winfield	.45	.18	.04
☐	42	Jose Cruz	.15	.06	.01
☐	43	Orel Hershiser	.65	.26	.06
☐	44	Reggie Jackson	.85	.34	.08
☐	45	Chili Davis	.15	.06	.01
☐	46	Robby Thompson	.20	.08	.02
☐	47	Dennis Boyd	.15	.06	.01
☐	48	Kirk Gibson	.45	.18	.04
☐	49	Fred Lynn	.20	.08	.02
☐	50	Gary Carter	.50	.20	.05
☐	51	George Bell	.35	.14	.03
☐	52	Pete O'Brien	.15	.06	.01
☐	53	Ron Darling	.25	.10	.02
☐	54	Paul Molitor	.30	.12	.03
☐	55	Mike Pagliarulo	.15	.06	.01
☐	56	Mike Boddicker	.15	.06	.01
☐	57	Dave Righetti	.20	.08	.02
☐	58	Len Dykstra	.20	.08	.02
☐	59	Mike Witt	.20	.08	.02
☐	60	Tony Bernazard	.12	.05	.01
☐	61	John Kruk	.25	.10	.02
☐	62	Mike Krukow	.15	.06	.01
☐	63	Sid Fernandez	.25	.10	.02
☐	64	Gary Gaetti	.30	.12	.03
☐	65	Vince Coleman	.50	.20	.05
☐	66	Pat Tabler	.15	.06	.01
☐	67	Mike Scioscia	.15	.06	.01
☐	68	Scott Garrelts	.12	.05	.01
☐	69	Brett Butler	.15	.06	.01
☐	70	Bill Buckner	.15	.06	.01
☐	71A	Dennis Rasmussen ERR '86 copyright (photo on back is John Montefusco)	1.00	.40	.10
☐	71B	Dennis Rasmussen COR '87 copyright (photo with mustache)	.50	.20	.05
☐	72	Tim Wallach	.15	.06	.01
☐	73	Bob Horner	.20	.08	.02
☐	74	Willie McGee	.25	.10	.02
☐	75	Tri-Stars Don Mattingly Wally Joyner Eddie Murray	1.25	.50	.12
☐	76	Jesse Orosco	.12	.05	.01

		MINT	EXC	G-VG
☐ 77	Tri-Stars	.15	.06	.01
	Todd Worrell			
	Jeff Reardon			
	Lee Smith			
☐ 78	Candy Maldonado	.20	.08	.02
☐ 79	Tri-Stars	.20	.08	.02
	Ozzie Smith			
	Hubie Brooks			
	Shawon Dunston			
☐ 80	Tri-Stars	1.00	.40	.10
	George Bell			
	Jose Canseco			
	Jim Rice			
☐ 81	Bert Blyleven	.20	.08	.02
☐ 82	Mike Marshall	.20	.08	.02
☐ 83	Ron Guidry	.20	.08	.02
☐ 84	Julio Franco	.15	.06	.01
☐ 85	Willie Wilson	.20	.08	.02
☐ 86	Lee Lacy	.12	.05	.01
☐ 87	Jack Morris	.30	.12	.03
☐ 88	Ray Knight	.15	.06	.01
☐ 89	Phil Bradley	.20	.08	.02
☐ 90	Jose Canseco	3.00	1.20	.30
☐ 91	Gary Ward	.12	.05	.01
☐ 92	Mike Easler	.12	.05	.01
☐ 93	Tony Pena	.15	.06	.01
☐ 94	Dave Smith	.15	.06	.01
☐ 95	Will Clark	1.50	.60	.15
☐ 96	Lloyd Moseby	.15	.06	.01
☐ 97	Jim Rice	.35	.14	.03
☐ 98	Shawon Dunston	.20	.08	.02
☐ 99	Don Sutton	.35	.14	.03
☐ 100	Dwight Gooden	.85	.34	.08
☐ 101	Lance Parrish	.25	.10	.02
☐ 102	Mark Langston	.25	.10	.02
☐ 103	Floyd Youmans	.20	.08	.02
☐ 104	Lee Smith	.15	.06	.01
☐ 105	Willie Hernandez	.20	.08	.02
☐ 106	Doug DeCinces	.15	.06	.01
☐ 107	Ken Schrom	.12	.05	.01
☐ 108	Don Carman	.12	.05	.01
☐ 109	Brook Jacoby	.20	.08	.02
☐ 110	Steve Bedrosian	.25	.10	.02
☐ 111	Tri-Stars	.60	.24	.06
	Roger Clemens			
	Jack Morris			
	Ted Higuera			
☐ 112	Tri-Stars	.15	.06	.01
	Marty Barrett			
	Tony Bernazard			
	Lou Whitaker			
☐ 113	Tri-Stars	.30	.12	.03
	Cal Ripken			
	Scott Fletcher			
	Tony Fernandez			
☐ 114	Tri-Stars	.90	.36	.09
	Wade Boggs			
	George Brett			
	Gary Gaetti			
☐ 115	Tri-Stars	.45	.18	.04
	Mike Schmidt			
	Chris Brown			
	Tim Wallach			
☐ 116	Tri-Stars	.25	.10	.02
	Ryne Sandberg			
	Johnny Ray			
	Bill Doran			
☐ 117	Tri-Stars	.30	.12	.03
	Dave Parker			
	Tony Gwynn			
	Kevin Bass			
☐ 118	Big Six Rookies	2.50	1.00	.25
	Ty Gainey			
	Terry Steinbach			
	David Clark			
	Pat Dodson			
	Phil Lombardi			
	Benito Santiago			
☐ 119	Hi-Lite Tri-Stars	.30	.12	.03
	Dave Righetti			
	Fernando Valenzuela			
	Mike Scott			
☐ 120	Tri-Stars	.60	.24	.06
	Fernando Valenzuela			
	Mike Scott			
	Dwight Gooden			
☐ 121	Johnny Ray	.15	.06	.01
☐ 122	Keith Moreland	.12	.05	.01
☐ 123	Juan Samuel	.20	.08	.02
☐ 124	Wally Backman	.12	.05	.01
☐ 125	Nolan Ryan	.75	.30	.07
☐ 126	Greg Harris	.12	.05	.01
☐ 127	Kirk McCaskill	.15	.06	.01
☐ 128	Dwight Evans	.25	.10	.02
☐ 129	Rick Rhoden	.15	.06	.01
☐ 130	Bill Madlock	.15	.06	.01

		MINT	EXC	G-VG
☐ 131	Oddibe McDowell	.20	.08	.02
☐ 132	Darrell Evans	.20	.08	.02
☐ 133	Keith Hernandez	.30	.12	.03
☐ 134	Tom Brunansky	.20	.08	.02
☐ 135	Kevin McReynolds	.60	.24	.06
☐ 136	Scott Fletcher	.15	.06	.01
☐ 137	Lou Whitaker	.20	.08	.02
☐ 138	Carney Lansford	.20	.08	.02
☐ 139	Andre Dawson	.35	.14	.03
☐ 140	Carlton Fisk	.25	.10	.02
☐ 141	Buddy Bell	.15	.06	.01
☐ 142	Ozzie Smith	.40	.16	.04
☐ 143	Dan Pasqua	.20	.08	.02
☐ 144	Kevin Mitchell	.25	.10	.02
☐ 145	Bret Saberhagen	.30	.12	.03
☐ 146	Charlie Kerfeld	.15	.06	.01
☐ 147	Phil Niekro	.35	.14	.03
☐ 148	John Candelaria	.15	.06	.01
☐ 149	Rich Gedman	.15	.06	.01
☐ 150	Fernando Valenzuela	.35	.14	.03
☐ 151	Tri-Stars	.25	.10	.02
	Gary Carter			
	Mike Scioscia			
	Tony Pena			
☐ 152	Tri-Stars	.45	.18	.04
	Tim Raines			
	Jose Cruz			
	Vince Coleman			
☐ 153	Tri-Stars	.35	.14	.03
	Jesse Barfield			
	Harold Baines			
	Dave Winfield			
☐ 154	Tri-Stars	.20	.08	.02
	Lance Parrish			
	Don Slaught			
	Rich Gedman			
☐ 155	Tri-Stars	.80	.32	.08
	Dale Murphy			
	Kevin McReynolds			
☐ 156	Hi-Lite Tri-Stars	.45	.18	.04
	Don Sutton			
	Mike Schmidt			
	Jim Deshaies			
☐ 157	Speedburners	.35	.14	.03
	Rickey Henderson			
	John Cangelosi			
	Gary Pettis			

		MINT	EXC	G-VG
☐ 158	Big Six Rookies	3.00	1.20	.30
	Randy Asadoor			
	Casey Candaele			
	Kevin Seitzer			
	Rafael Palmeiro			
	Tim Pyznarski			
	Dave Cochrane			
☐ 159	Big Six	2.00	.80	.20
	Don Mattingly			
	Rickey Henderson			
	Roger Clemens			
	Dale Murphy			
	Eddie Murray			
	Dwight Gooden			
☐ 160	Roger McDowell	.20	.08	.02
☐ 161	Brian Downing	.15	.06	.01
☐ 162	Bill Doran	.20	.08	.02
☐ 163	Don Baylor	.20	.08	.02
☐ 164A	Alfredo Griffin ERR	.25	.10	.02
	(no uniform number on card back) '87			
☐ 164B	Alfredo Griffin	.25	.10	.02
	COR '86			
☐ 165	Don Aase	.12	.05	.01
☐ 166	Glenn Wilson	.15	.06	.01
☐ 167	Dan Quisenberry	.20	.08	.02
☐ 168	Frank White	.15	.06	.01
☐ 169	Cecil Cooper	.15	.06	.01
☐ 170	Jody Davis	.20	.08	.02
☐ 171	Harold Baines	.25	.10	.02
☐ 172	Rob Deer	.25	.10	.02
☐ 173	John Tudor	.25	.10	.02
☐ 174	Larry Parrish	.12	.05	.01
☐ 175	Kevin Bass	.20	.08	.02
☐ 176	Joe Carter	.40	.16	.04
☐ 177	Mitch Webster	.15	.06	.01
☐ 178	Dave Kingman	.20	.08	.02
☐ 179	Jim Presley	.25	.10	.02
☐ 180	Mel Hall	.20	.08	.02
☐ 181	Shane Rawley	.15	.06	.01
☐ 182	Marty Barrett	.25	.10	.02
☐ 183	Damaso Garcia	.12	.05	.01
☐ 184	Bobby Grich	.20	.08	.02
☐ 185	Leon Durham	.12	.05	.01
☐ 186	Ozzie Guillen	.20	.08	.02
☐ 187	Tony Fernandez	.30	.12	.03
☐ 188	Alan Trammell	.35	.14	.03
☐ 189	Jim Clancy	.12	.05	.01
☐ 190	Bo Jackson	1.25	.50	.12
☐ 191	Bob Forsch	.12	.05	.01

			MINT	EXC	G-VG
☐	192	John Franco	.20	.08	.02
☐	193	Von Hayes	.20	.08	.02
☐	194	Tri-Stars	.15	.06	.01
		Don Aase			
		Dave Righetti			
		Mark Eichhorn			
☐	195	Tri-Stars	.60	.24	.06
		Keith Hernandez			
		Will Clark			
		Glenn Davis			
☐	196	Hi-Lite Tri-Stars	.50	.20	.05
		Roger Clemens			
		Joe Cowley			
		Bob Horner			
☐	197	Big Six	.90	.36	.09
		George Brett			
		Hubie Brooks			
		Tony Gwynn			
		Ryne Sandberg			
		Tim Raines			
		Wade Boggs			
☐	198	Tri-Stars	.50	.20	.05
		Kirby Puckett			
		Rickey Henderson			
		Fred Lynn			
☐	199	Speedburners	.90	.36	.09
		Tim Raines			
		Vince Coleman			
		Eric Davis			
☐	200	Steve Carlton	.40	.16	.04

1988 Sportflics

This 225-card set was produced by Sportflics and again features three sequence action pictures on each card. Cards measure 2 ½" by 3 ½" and are in full color. There are 219 individual players, 3 Highlights trios, and 3 Rookie Prospect trio cards. The cards feature a red border on the front. A full-color action picture of the player is printed on the back of the card. Cards are numbered on the back in the lower right corner.

			MINT	EXC	G-VG
		Complete Set (225)	33.00	12.00	3.00
		Common Player (1-225) ..	.12	.05	.01
☐	1	Don Mattingly	2.50	1.00	.25
☐	2	Tim Raines	.40	.16	.04
☐	3	Andre Dawson	.40	.16	.04
☐	4	George Bell	.35	.14	.03
☐	5	Joe Carter	.30	.12	.03
☐	6	Matt Nokes	.50	.20	.05
☐	7	Dave Winfield	.40	.16	.04
☐	8	Kirby Puckett	.70	.28	.07
☐	9	Will Clark	.90	.36	.09
☐	10	Eric Davis	.90	.36	.09
☐	11	Rickey Henderson .	.65	.26	.06
☐	12	Ryne Sandberg ...	.40	.16	.04
☐	13	Jesse Barfield UER	.30	.12	.03
		(misspelled Jessie on card back)			
☐	14	Ozzie Guillen	.20	.08	.02
☐	15	Bret Saberhagen ..	.25	.10	.02
☐	16	Tony Gwynn	.50	.20	.05
☐	17	Kevin Seitzer	.90	.36	.09

		MINT	EXC	G-VG			MINT	EXC	G-VG
☐	18 Jack Clark	.30	.12	.03	☐	66 Mike Scott	.30	.12	.03
☐	19 Danny Tartabull	.40	.16	.04	☐	67 Vince Coleman	.40	.16	.04
☐	20 Ted Higuera	.25	.10	.02	☐	68 Ozzie Smith	.35	.14	.03
☐	21 Charlie Leibrandt UER	.15	.06	.01	☐	69 Ken Williams	.25	.10	.02
	(misspelled Liebrandt on card front)				☐	70 Steve Bedrosian	.20	.08	.02
☐	22 Benny Santiago	.75	.30	.07	☐	71 Luis Polonia	.25	.10	.02
☐	23 Fred Lynn	.25	.10	.02	☐	72 Brook Jacoby	.15	.06	.01
☐	24 Rob Thompson	.15	.06	.01	☐	73 Ron Darling	.25	.10	.02
☐	25 Alan Trammell	.35	.14	.03	☐	74 Lloyd Moseby	.15	.06	.01
☐	26 Tony Fernandez	.25	.10	.02	☐	75 Wally Joyner	.60	.24	.06
☐	27 Rick Sutcliffe	.20	.08	.02	☐	76 Dan Quisenberry	.20	.08	.02
☐	28 Gary Carter	.35	.14	.03	☐	77 Scott Fletcher	.15	.06	.01
☐	29 Cory Snyder	.40	.16	.04	☐	78 Kirk McCaskill	.12	.05	.01
☐	30 Lou Whitaker	.20	.08	.02	☐	79 Paul Molitor	.30	.12	.03
☐	31 Keith Hernandez	.30	.12	.03	☐	80 Mike Aldrete	.20	.08	.02
☐	32 Mike Witt	.20	.08	.02	☐	81 Neal Heaton	.12	.05	.01
☐	33 Harold Baines	.20	.08	.02	☐	82 Jeffrey Leonard	.15	.06	.01
☐	34 Robin Yount	.40	.16	.04	☐	83 Dave Magadan	.20	.08	.02
☐	35 Mike Schmidt	.65	.26	.06	☐	84 Danny Cox	.20	.08	.02
☐	36 Dion James	.12	.05	.01	☐	85 Lance McCullers	.15	.06	.01
☐	37 Tom Candiotti	.12	.05	.01	☐	86 Jay Howell	.12	.05	.01
☐	38 Tracy Jones	.20	.08	.02	☐	87 Charlie Hough	.12	.05	.01
☐	39 Nolan Ryan	.60	.24	.06	☐	88 Gene Garber	.12	.05	.01
☐	40 Fernando Valenzuela	.35	.14	.03	☐	89 Jesse Orosco	.12	.05	.01
☐	41 Vance Law	.12	.05	.01	☐	90 Don Robinson	.12	.05	.01
☐	42 Roger McDowell	.20	.08	.02	☐	91 Willie McGee	.25	.10	.02
☐	43 Carlton Fisk	.25	.10	.02	☐	92 Bert Blyleven	.20	.08	.02
☐	44 Scott Garrelts	.12	.05	.01	☐	93 Phil Bradley	.20	.08	.02
☐	45 Lee Guetterman	.12	.05	.01	☐	94 Terry Kennedy	.12	.05	.01
☐	46 Mark Langston	.25	.10	.02	☐	95 Kent Hrbek	.30	.12	.03
☐	47 Willie Randolph	.20	.08	.02	☐	96 Juan Samuel	.25	.10	.02
☐	48 Bill Doran	.20	.08	.02	☐	97 Pedro Guerrero	.30	.12	.03
☐	49 Larry Parrish	.12	.05	.01	☐	98 Sid Bream	.12	.05	.01
☐	50 Wade Boggs	1.25	.50	.12	☐	99 Devon White	.30	.12	.03
☐	51 Shane Rawley	.12	.05	.01	☐	100 Mark McGwire	1.00	.40	.10
☐	52 Alvin Davis	.15	.06	.01	☐	101 Dave Parker	.25	.10	.02
☐	53 Jeff Reardon	.15	.06	.01	☐	102 Glenn Davis	.30	.12	.03
☐	54 Jim Presley	.15	.06	.01	☐	103 Greg Walker	.20	.08	.02
☐	55 Kevin Bass	.15	.06	.01	☐	104 Rick Rhoden	.15	.06	.01
☐	56 Kevin McReynolds	.45	.18	.04	☐	105 Mitch Webster	.12	.05	.01
☐	57 B.J. Surhoff	.20	.08	.02	☐	106 Lenny Dykstra	.20	.08	.02
☐	58 Julio Franco	.15	.06	.01	☐	107 Gene Larkin	.20	.08	.02
☐	59 Eddie Murray	.50	.20	.05	☐	108 Floyd Youmans	.12	.05	.01
☐	60 Jody Davis	.15	.06	.01	☐	109 Andy Van Slyke	.35	.14	.03
☐	61 Todd Worrell	.20	.08	.02	☐	110 Mike Scioscia	.15	.06	.01
☐	62 Von Hayes	.20	.08	.02	☐	111 Kirk Gibson	.40	.16	.04
☐	63 Billy Hatcher	.20	.08	.02	☐	112 Kal Daniels	.40	.16	.04
☐	64 John Kruk	.25	.10	.02	☐	113 Ruben Sierra	.45	.18	.04
☐	65 Tom Henke	.15	.06	.01	☐	114 Sam Horn	.40	.16	.04

	MINT	EXC	G-VG
☐ 115 Ray Knight	.15	.06	.01
☐ 116 Jimmy Key	.15	.06	.01
☐ 117 Bo Diaz	.12	.05	.01
☐ 118 Mike Greenwell	1.25	.50	.12
☐ 119 Barry Bonds	.35	.14	.03
☐ 120 Reggie Jackson UER	.50	.20	.05
(463 lifetime homers)			
☐ 121 Mike Pagliarulo	.20	.08	.02
☐ 122 Tommy John	.20	.08	.02
☐ 123 Bill Madlock	.15	.06	.01
☐ 124 Ken Caminiti	.25	.10	.02
☐ 125 Gary Ward	.12	.05	.01
☐ 126 Candy Maldonado	.15	.06	.01
☐ 127 Harold Reynolds	.15	.06	.01
☐ 128 Joe Magrane	.35	.14	.03
☐ 129 Mike Henneman	.25	.10	.02
☐ 130 Jim Gantner	.12	.05	.01
☐ 131 Bobby Bonilla	.35	.14	.03
☐ 132 John Farrell	.35	.14	.03
☐ 133 Frank Tanana	.12	.05	.01
☐ 134 Zane Smith	.20	.08	.02
☐ 135 Dave Righetti	.20	.08	.02
☐ 136 Rick Reuschel	.20	.08	.02
☐ 137 Dwight Evans	.25	.10	.02
☐ 138 Howard Johnson	.25	.10	.02
☐ 139 Terry Leach	.20	.08	.02
☐ 140 Casey Candaele	.15	.06	.01
☐ 141 Tom Herr	.15	.06	.01
☐ 142 Tony Pena	.15	.06	.01
☐ 143 Lance Parrish	.25	.10	.02
☐ 144 Ellis Burks	1.00	.40	.10
☐ 145 Pete O'Brien	.20	.08	.02
☐ 146 Mike Boddicker	.15	.06	.01
☐ 147 Buddy Bell	.15	.06	.01
☐ 148 Bo Jackson	.50	.20	.05
☐ 149 Frank White	.15	.06	.01
☐ 150 George Brett	.50	.20	.05
☐ 151 Tim Wallach	.15	.06	.01
☐ 152 Cal Ripken Jr.	.40	.16	.04
☐ 153 Brett Butler	.15	.06	.01
☐ 154 Gary Gaetti	.30	.12	.03
☐ 155 Darryl Strawberry	.70	.28	.07
☐ 156 Alredo Griffin	.15	.06	.01
☐ 157 Marty Barrett	.20	.08	.02
☐ 158 Jim Rice	.30	.12	.03
☐ 159 Terry Pendleton	.15	.06	.01
☐ 160 Orel Hershiser	.65	.26	.06
☐ 161 Larry Sheets	.20	.08	.02

	MINT	EXC	G-VG
☐ 162- Dave Stewart UER	.25	.10	.02
(Braves logo)			
☐ 163 Shawon Dunston	.20	.08	.02
☐ 164 Keith Moreland	.12	.05	.01
☐ 165 Ken Oberkfell	.12	.05	.01
☐ 166 Ivan Calderon	.20	.08	.02
☐ 167 Bob Welch	.20	.08	.02
☐ 168 Fred McGriff	.50	.20	.05
☐ 169 Pete Incaviglia	.35	.14	.03
☐ 170 Dale Murphy	.60	.24	.06
☐ 171 Mike Dunne	.25	.10	.02
☐ 172 Chili Davis	.20	.08	.02
☐ 173 Milt Thompson	.15	.06	.01
☐ 174 Terry Steinbach	.25	.10	.02
☐ 175 Oddibe McDowell	.20	.08	.02
☐ 176 Jack Morris	.25	.10	.02
☐ 177 Sid Fernandez	.20	.08	.02
☐ 178 Ken Griffey	.15	.06	.01
☐ 179 Lee Smith	.15	.06	.01
☐ 180 Highlights 1987	.35	.14	.03
Kirby Puckett			
Juan Nieves			
Mike Schmidt			
☐ 181 Brian Downing	.15	.06	.01
☐ 182 Andres Galarraga	.45	.18	.04
☐ 183 Rob Deer	.20	.08	.02
☐ 184 Greg Brock	.12	.05	.01
☐ 185 Doug DeCinces	.12	.05	.01
☐ 186 Johnny Ray	.12	.05	.01
☐ 187 Hubie Brooks	.15	.06	.01
☐ 188 Darrell Evans	.15	.06	.01
☐ 189 Mel Hall	.15	.06	.01
☐ 190 Jim Deshaies	.12	.05	.01
☐ 191 Dan Plesac	.20	.08	.02
☐ 192 Willie Wilson	.20	.08	.02
☐ 193 Mike LaValliere	.12	.05	.01
☐ 194 Tom Brunansky	.25	.10	.02
☐ 195 John Franco	.20	.08	.02
☐ 196 Frank Viola	.35	.14	.03
☐ 197 Bruce Hurst	.25	.10	.02
☐ 198 John Tudor	.20	.08	.02
☐ 199 Bob Forsch	.12	.05	.01
☐ 200 Dwight Gooden	.70	.28	.07
☐ 201 Jose Canseco	1.75	.70	.17
☐ 202 Carney Lansford	.20	.08	.02
☐ 203 Kelly Downs	.15	.06	.01
☐ 204 Glenn Wilson	.15	.06	.01
☐ 205 Pat Tabler	.15	.06	.01
☐ 206 Mike Davis	.15	.06	.01

		MINT	EXC	G-VG
☐ 207	Roger Clemens	.90	.36	.09
☐ 208	Dave Smith	.15	.06	.01
☐ 209	Curt Young	.15	.06	.01
☐ 210	Mark Eichhorn	.15	.06	.01
☐ 211	Juan Nieves	.15	.06	.01
☐ 212	Bob Boone	.15	.06	.01
☐ 213	Don Sutton	.30	.12	.03
☐ 214	Willie Upshaw	.12	.05	.01
☐ 215	Jim Clancy	.12	.05	.01
☐ 216	Bill Ripken	.25	.10	.02
☐ 217	Ozzie Virgil	.12	.05	.01
☐ 218	Dave Concepcion ..	.15	.06	.01
☐ 219	Alan Ashby	.12	.05	.01
☐ 220	Mike Marshall	.20	.08	.02
☐ 221	Highlights 1987	.60	.24	.06
	Mark McGwire			
	Paul Molitor			
	Vince Coleman			
☐ 222	Highlights 1987	.75	.30	.07
	Benito Santiago			
	Steve Bedrosian			
	Don Mattingly			
☐ 223	Rookie Prospects ..	1.00	.40	.10
	Shawn Abner			
	Jay Buhner			
	Gary Thurman			
☐ 224	Rookie Prospects ..	.40	.16	.04
	Tim Crews			
	Vincente Palacios			
	John Davis			
☐ 225	Rookie Prospects ..	.75	.30	.07
	Jody Reed			
	Jeff Treadway			
	Keith Miller			

1989 **Sportflics**

This 225-card set was produced by Sportflics (distributed by Major League Marketing) and again features three sequence action pictures on each card. Cards measure 2 ½" by 3 ½" and are in full color. There are 219 individual players, 2 Highlights trios, and 3 Rookie Prospect trio cards. The cards feature a white border on the front with red and blue inner trim colors. A full-color action picture of the player is printed on the back of the card. Cards are numbered on the back in the lower right corner.

		MINT	EXC	G-VG
Complete Set (225)		33.00	11.00	3.00
Common Player (1-225) ..		.10	.04	.01
☐	1 Jose Canseco	1.50	.60	.15
☐	2 Wally Joyner	.50	.20	.05
☐	3 Roger Clemens ...	.75	.30	.07
☐	4 Greg Swindell	.25	.10	.02
☐	5 Jack Morris	.20	.08	.02
☐	6 Mickey Brantley ...	.15	.06	.01
☐	7 Jim Presley	.15	.06	.01
☐	8 Pete O'Brien	.15	.06	.01
☐	9 Jesse Barfield	.25	.10	.02
☐	10 Frank Viola	.20	.08	.02
☐	11 Kevin Bass	.10	.04	.01
☐	12 Glenn Wilson	.10	.04	.01
☐	13 Chris Sabo	.60	.24	.06
☐	14 Fred McGriff	.50	.20	.05
☐	15 Mark Grace	.75	.30	.07
☐	16 Devon White	.20	.08	.02
☐	17 Juan Samuel	.15	.06	.01

		MINT	EXC	G-VG
☐ 18	Lou Whitaker	.15	.06	.01
☐ 19	Greg Walker	.15	.06	.01
☐ 20	Roberto Alomar	.25	.10	.02
☐ 21	Mike Schmidt	.60	.24	.06
☐ 22	Benny Santiago	.50	.20	.05
☐ 23	Dave Stewart	.15	.06	.01
☐ 24	Dave Winfield	.40	.16	.04
☐ 25	George Bell	.20	.08	.02
☐ 26	Jack Clark	.20	.08	.02
☐ 27	Doug Drabek	.10	.04	.01
☐ 28	Ron Gant	.30	.12	.03
☐ 29	Glenn Braggs	.15	.06	.01
☐ 30	Rafael Palmeiro	.30	.12	.03
☐ 31	Brett Butler	.15	.06	.01
☐ 32	Ron Darling	.20	.08	.02
☐ 33	Alvin Davis	.15	.06	.01
☐ 34	Bob Walk	.10	.04	.01
☐ 35	Dave Stieb	.15	.06	.01
☐ 36	Orel Hershiser	.75	.30	.07
☐ 37	John Farrell	.15	.06	.01
☐ 38	Doug Jones	.15	.06	.01
☐ 39	Kelly Downs	.15	.06	.01
☐ 40	Bob Boone	.15	.06	.01
☐ 41	Gary Sheffield	1.25	.50	.12
☐ 42	Doug Dascenzo	.20	.08	.02
☐ 43	Chad Kreuter	.20	.08	.02
☐ 44	Ricky Jordan	1.00	.40	.10
☐ 45	Dave West	.50	.20	.05
☐ 46	Danny Tartabull	.30	.12	.03
☐ 47	Teddy Higuera	.20	.08	.02
☐ 48	Gary Gaetti	.20	.08	.02
☐ 49	Dave Parker	.20	.08	.02
☐ 50	Don Mattingly	1.25	.50	.12
☐ 51	David Cone	.50	.20	.05
☐ 52	Kal Daniels	.30	.12	.03
☐ 53	Carney Lansford	.15	.06	.01
☐ 54	Mike Marshall	.20	.08	.02
☐ 55	Kevin Seitzer	.35	.14	.03
☐ 56	Mike Henneman	.15	.06	.01
☐ 57	Bill Doran	.15	.06	.01
☐ 58	Steve Sax	.20	.08	.02
☐ 59	Lance Parrish	.15	.06	.01
☐ 60	Keith Hernandez	.25	.10	.02
☐ 61	Jose Uribe	.10	.04	.01
☐ 62	Jose Lind	.15	.06	.01
☐ 63	Steve Bedrosian	.15	.06	.01
☐ 64	George Brett	.30	.12	.03
☐ 65	Kirk Gibson	.30	.12	.03
☐ 66	Cal Ripken Jr.	.25	.10	.02

		MINT	EXC	G-VG
☐ 67	Mitch Webster	.10	.04	.01
☐ 68	Fred Lynn	.20	.08	.02
☐ 69	Eric Davis	.75	.30	.07
☐ 70	Bo Jackson	.60	.24	.06
☐ 71	Kevin Elster	.20	.08	.02
☐ 72	Rick Reuschel	.15	.06	.01
☐ 73	Tim Burke	.10	.04	.01
☐ 74	Mark Davis	.15	.06	.01
☐ 75	Claudell Washington	.15	.06	.01
☐ 76	Lance McCullers	.15	.06	.01
☐ 77	Mike Moore	.15	.06	.01
☐ 78	Robby Thompson	.15	.06	.01
☐ 79	Roger McDowell	.15	.06	.01
☐ 80	Danny Jackson	.20	.08	.02
☐ 81	Tim Leary	.15	.06	.01
☐ 82	Bobby Witt	.20	.08	.02
☐ 83	Jim Gott	.10	.04	.01
☐ 84	Andy Hawkins	.15	.06	.01
☐ 85	Ozzie Guillen	.15	.06	.01
☐ 86	John Tudor	.15	.06	.01
☐ 87	Todd Burns	.20	.08	.02
☐ 88	Dave Gallagher	.15	.06	.01
☐ 89	Jay Buhner	.20	.08	.02
☐ 90	Gregg Jefferies	1.50	.60	.15
☐ 91	Bob Welch	.10	.04	.01
☐ 92	Charlie Hough	.10	.04	.01
☐ 93	Tony Fernandez	.20	.08	.02
☐ 94	Ozzie Virgil	.10	.04	.01
☐ 95	Andre Dawson	.25	.10	.02
☐ 96	Hubie Brooks	.15	.06	.01
☐ 97	Kevin McReynolds	.35	.14	.03
☐ 98	Mike LaValliere	.10	.04	.01
☐ 99	Terry Pendleton	.15	.06	.01
☐ 100	Wade Boggs	1.00	.40	.10
☐ 101	Dennis Eckersley	.20	.08	.02
☐ 102	Mark Gubicza	.15	.06	.01
☐ 103	Frank Tanana	.15	.06	.01
☐ 104	Joe Carter	.25	.10	.02
☐ 105	Ozzie Smith	.25	.10	.02
☐ 106	Dennis Martinez	.10	.04	.01
☐ 107	Jeff Treadway	.15	.06	.01
☐ 108	Greg Maddux	.20	.08	.02
☐ 109	Bret Saberhagen	.25	.10	.02
☐ 110	Dale Murphy	.35	.14	.03
☐ 111	Rob Deer	.15	.06	.01
☐ 112	Pete Incaviglia	.30	.12	.03
☐ 113	Vince Coleman	.25	.10	.02
☐ 114	Tim Wallach	.15	.06	.01
☐ 115	Nolan Ryan	.35	.14	.03

		MINT	EXC	G-VG
☐ 116	Walt Weiss	.45	.18	.04
☐ 117	Brian Downing	.15	.06	.01
☐ 118	Melido Perez	.20	.08	.02
☐ 119	Terry Steinbach	.20	.08	.02
☐ 120	Mike Scott	.20	.08	.02
☐ 121	Tim Belcher	.20	.08	.02
☐ 122	Mike Boddicker	.15	.06	.01
☐ 123	Len Dykstra	.20	.08	.02
☐ 124	Fernando Valenzuela	.25	.10	.02
☐ 125	Gerald Young	.20	.08	.02
☐ 126	Tom Henke	.15	.06	.01
☐ 127	Dave Henderson	.15	.06	.01
☐ 128	Dan Plesac	.15	.06	.01
☐ 129	Chili Davis	.15	.06	.01
☐ 130	Bryan Harvey	.20	.08	.02
☐ 131	Don August	.15	.06	.01
☐ 132	Mike Harkey	.50	.20	.05
☐ 133	Luis Polonia	.15	.06	.01
☐ 134	Craig Worthington	.20	.08	.02
☐ 135	Joey Meyer	.15	.06	.01
☐ 136	Barry Larkin	.20	.08	.02
☐ 137	Glenn Davis	.20	.08	.02
☐ 138	Mike Scioscia	.10	.04	.01
☐ 139	Andres Galarraga	.25	.10	.02
☐ 140	Doc Gooden	.50	.20	.05
☐ 141	Keith Moreland	.10	.04	.01
☐ 142	Kevin Mitchell	.15	.06	.01
☐ 143	Mike Greenwell	1.00	.40	.10
☐ 144	Mel Hall	.15	.06	.01
☐ 145	Rickey Henderson	.50	.20	.05
☐ 146	Barry Bonds	.25	.10	.02
☐ 147	Eddie Murray	.45	.18	.04
☐ 148	Lee Smith	.15	.06	.01
☐ 149	Julio Franco	.15	.06	.01
☐ 150	Tim Raines	.25	.10	.02
☐ 151	Mitch Williams	.15	.06	.01
☐ 152	Tim Laudner	.10	.04	.01
☐ 153	Mike Pagliarulo	.15	.06	.01
☐ 154	Floyd Bannister	.10	.04	.01
☐ 155	Gary Carter	.30	.12	.03
☐ 156	Kirby Puckett	.65	.26	.06
☐ 157	Harold Baines	.15	.06	.01
☐ 158	Dave Righetti	.15	.06	.01
☐ 159	Mark Langston	.15	.06	.01
☐ 160	Tony Gwynn	.35	.14	.03
☐ 161	Tom Brunansky	.15	.06	.01
☐ 162	Vance Law	.10	.04	.01
☐ 163	Kelly Gruber	.10	.04	.01
☐ 164	Gerald Perry	.20	.08	.02

		MINT	EXC	G-VG
☐ 165	Harold Reynolds	.15	.06	.01
☐ 166	Andy Van Slyke	.25	.10	.02
☐ 167	Jimmy Key	.15	.06	.01
☐ 168	Jeff Reardon	.15	.06	.01
☐ 169	Milt Thompson	.10	.04	.01
☐ 170	Will Clark	.75	.30	.07
☐ 171	Chet Lemon	.10	.04	.01
☐ 172	Pat Tabler	.10	.04	.01
☐ 173	Jim Rice	.20	.08	.02
☐ 174	Billy Hatcher	.15	.06	.01
☐ 175	Bruce Hurst	.20	.08	.02
☐ 176	John Franco	.15	.06	.01
☐ 177	Van Snider	.20	.08	.02
☐ 178	Ron Jones	.20	.08	.02
☐ 179	Jerald Clark	.20	.08	.02
☐ 180	Tom Browning	.20	.08	.02
☐ 181	Von Hayes	.15	.06	.01
☐ 182	Bobby Bonilla	.25	.10	.02
☐ 183	Todd Worrell	.15	.06	.01
☐ 184	John Kruk	.15	.06	.01
☐ 185	Scott Fletcher	.15	.06	.01
☐ 186	Willie Wilson	.15	.06	.01
☐ 187	Jody Davis	.15	.06	.01
☐ 188	Kent Hrbek	.20	.08	.02
☐ 189	Ruben Sierra	.20	.08	.02
☐ 190	Shawon Dunston	.15	.06	.01
☐ 191	Ellis Burks	.25	.10	.02
☐ 192	Brook Jacoby	.15	.06	.01
☐ 193	Jeff Robinson	.15	.06	.01
	Detroit Tigers			
☐ 194	Rich Dotson	.15	.06	.01
☐ 195	Johnny Ray	.10	.04	.01
☐ 196	Cory Snyder	.25	.10	.02
☐ 197	Mike Witt	.15	.06	.01
☐ 198	Marty Barrett	.15	.06	.01
☐ 199	Robin Yount	.30	.12	.03
☐ 200	Mark McGwire	.75	.30	.07
☐ 201	Ryne Sandberg	.25	.10	.02
☐ 202	John Candelaria	.15	.06	.01
☐ 203	Matt Nokes	.20	.08	.02
☐ 204	Dwight Evans	.20	.08	.02
☐ 205	Darryl Strawberry	.75	.30	.07
☐ 206	Willie McGee	.20	.08	.02
☐ 207	Bobby Thigpen	.15	.06	.01
☐ 208	B.J. Surhoff	.15	.06	.01
☐ 209	Paul Molitor	.20	.08	.02
☐ 210	Jody Reed	.20	.08	.02
☐ 211	Doyle Alexander	.15	.06	.01
☐ 212	Dennis Rasmussen	.15	.06	.01

			MINT	EXC	G-VG
☐ 213	Kevin Gross	......	.15	.06	.01
☐ 214	Kirk McCaskill	.....	.15	.06	.01
☐ 215	Alan Trammell	.....	.25	.10	.02
☐ 216	Damon Berryhill	...	.20	.08	.02
☐ 217	Rick Sutcliffe	......	.15	.06	.01
☐ 218	Don Slaught	....	.10	.04	.01
☐ 219	Carlton Fisk	....	.20	.08	.02
☐ 220	Allan Anderson	....	.20	.08	.02
☐ 221	Jose Canseco	.....	1.50	.60	.15
	Wade Boggs				
	Mike Greenwell				
☐ 222	Orel Hershiser	.....	.50	.20	.05
	Dennis Eckersley				
	Tom Browning				
☐ 223	Gary Sheffield	.....	2.50	1.00	.25
	Gregg Jefferies				
	Sandy Alomar				
☐ 224	Bob Milacki	....	.50	.20	.05
	Randy Johnson				
	Ramon Martinez				
☐ 225	Cameron Drew	....	.50	.20	.05
	Geronimo Berroa				
	Ron Jones				

	HI # OR SCARCE SERIES	COMMONS EACH		50 Diff.	100 Diff.	300 Asst.	500 Asst.	VG 50	VG 100	VG 200 Different
1948 BOWMAN	(37-48) 20.00	12.00								
1949 BOWMAN	(145-240) 60.00	12.00								
50-51 BOWMAN	50 (1-72) 51 (253-324) 40.00	12.00	51 (2-36) 15.00	540.				360.		
1952 TOPPS	(311-407) P.O.R.	25.00	(2-80) 60.00	1125.				750.		
1952 BOWMAN	(217-252) 20.00	12.00		540.				360.		
1953 TOPPS	(220-280) 60.00	15.00		675.				450.		
1953 BOWMAN	(129-160) 30.00	25.00	(113-128) 40.00	1125.				750.		
1954 TOPPS		8.00	(51-75) 18.00	360.				240.		
1954 BOWMAN		6.00	(129-224) 7.00	270.	525.			180.		
1955 TOPPS	(161-210) 15.00	6.00	(151-160) 10.00	270.	525.			180.		
1955 BOWMAN	(225-320) 10.-15. Umps	5.00	(2-96) 6.00	225.	440.			155.	300.	
1956 TOPPS		5.00	(181-260) 8.00	225.	440.			155.	300.	
1957 TOPPS	(265-352) 12.50	3.50	(353-407) 4.00	158.	305.			110.	210.	
1958 TOPPS		2.00	(1-110) 2.50	90.	175.	525.	850.	65.	120.	
1959 TOPPS	(507-572) 7.50	2.00	(1-110) 2.50	90.	175.	525.	850.	65.	120.	230.
1960 TOPPS	(523-572) 7.50	1.25	(441-506) 2.00	56.	110.	325.	530.	40.	75.	145.
1961 TOPPS	(523-589) 20.00	1.00	(371-522) 1.50	45.	88.	258.	425.	32.	60.	115.
1962 TOPPS	(523-590) 8.00	1.00	(371-522) 1.75	45.	88.	258.		32.	60.	115.
1963 TOPPS	(447-576) 6.00	.60	(197-446) .75	27.	53.			20.	36.	
1964 TOPPS	(523-587) 5.00	.60	(371-522) 1.00	27.	53.	155.		20.	36.	70.
1965 TOPPS	(447-522) 1.50 (523-598) 3.00	.60	(199-446) .75	27.	53.	155.		20.	36.	70.
1966 TOPPS	(523-598) 15.00	.60	(447-522) .75	27.	53.	155.		20.	36.	70.
1967 TOPPS	(534-609) 10.00	.60	(458-533) 2.00	27.	53.	155.		20.	36.	70.
1968 TOPPS		.50	(458-533) .75	22.	44.	130.	210.	16.	30.	55.
1969 TOPPS		.50	(219-327) .75	22.	44.	130.	210.	16.	30.	55.
1970 TOPPS	(634-720) 2.00	.35	(547-633) 1.00	16.	32.	*90.	150.	12.	22.	40.
1971 TOPPS	(644-752) 2.00	.35	(524-643) 1.00	16.	32.	*90.	150.	12.	22.	40.
1972 TOPPS	(657-787) 2.00	.35	(526-656) 1.00	16.	32.	*90.	150.	12.	22.	40.
1973 TOPPS	(528-660) 1.50	.30	(397-528) .50	14.	27.	*77.	125.	10.	18.	35.
1974 TOPPS		.25		11.	20.	*65.	*105.		12.	22.
1975 TOPPS	(8-132 .30)	.25		11.	20.	*65.	105.		12.	22.
1976-77		.20		18.	50.	*85.		10.	18.	
1978-1980		.15		13.	*38.	*65.		8.	15.	
1981 thru 1989 Topps, Fleer or Donrus		.10		8.	*22.	*35.		5.	10.	
Specify Year & Company except below				Per Yr.	Per Yr.	Per Yr.				
1984-86 DONRUS		.15		7.	13.	*38.	*60.			

Coming this Fall...

From **JIM BECKETT**

the most trusted authority
on sports card values

**THE OFFICIAL 1990 PRICE GUIDE
TO FOOTBALL CARDS,
9th ed. 37800-9 $4.95**

NEW!

**THE OFFICIAL PRICE GUIDE
TO HOCKEY AND BASKETBALL
CARDS, 1st ed. 37801-7 $4.95**

HOUSE OF COLLECTIBLES
201 East 50th Street
New York, New York 10022

Please send me the *House of Collectibles* books I have checked above. I am enclosing
$ _____ (add 50¢ per copy to cover postage and handling). Send check or
money order—no cash or C.O.D.'s please. Prices and numbers are subject to change
without notice.

Name _____

Address _____

City _____ State _____ Zip Code _____

Allow at least 4 weeks for delivery.   CODE: HOC-6
                                               Key: 19

FIRST BASE

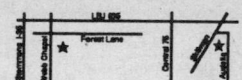

Store #1
Webb Chapel Village
Shopping Center #231
(SE Corner of Webb Chapel & Forest)
Dallas, Texas 75229
(214) 243-5271
11-7 Mon.-Sat.
Closed Sun.

Store #2
Audelia Plaza #102
10779 Audelia Rd.
Dallas, Texas 75238
(214) 341-9819
11-8 Mon.-Sat.
Closed Sun.

ORDERING INSTRUCTIONS

Offers expire March 1990 while supply lasts. Please include $2.00 per order for postage and handling.

Send orders to:

FIRST BASE
231 Webb Chapel Village
Dallas, Texas 75229
(214) 243-5271

Our current price lists sent free with orders. To receive price lists without ordering send $1.00 or a large self addressed stamped (65¢ in stamps) envelope to the above address.

BASEBALL CARD LOTS

1959 Topps 25 diff (f-vg)	$15.95
1960 Topps 25 diff (f-vg)	10.95
1961 Topps 25 diff (f-vg)	8.95
1962 Topps 25 diff (f-vg)	8.95
1963 Topps 25 diff (f-vg)	8.95
1964 Topps 25 diff (f-vg)	6.95
1965 Topps 25 diff (f-vg)	6.95
1966 Topps 25 diff (f-vg)	4.95
1967 Topps 25 diff (f-vg)	4.95
1968 Topps 25 diff (f-vg)	4.95
1969 Topps 25 diff (f-vg)	4.95
1970 Topps 25 diff (f-vg)	2.95
1971 Topps 25 diff (f-vg)	2.95
1972 Topps 25 diff (f-vg)	2.95
1973 Topps 25 diff (f-vg)	2.95
1974 Topps 25 diff (f-vg)	2.95
1975 Topps 50 diff (f-vg)	5.95
1976 Topps 50 diff (f-vg)	3.95
1977 Topps 50 diff (f-vg)	3.95
1978 Topps 50 diff (f-vg)	2.95
1979 Topps 50 diff (f-vg)	2.95
1980 Topps 50 diff (f-vg)	2.95
1981 Donruss 50 diff (ex-m)	2.50
1981 Fleer 50 diff (ex-m)	2.50
1982 Fleer 50 diff (ex-m)	2.50

FOOTBALL CARD LOTS

1969 Topps 25 diff (f-vg)	$4.95
1970 Topps 25 diff (f-vg)	3.95
1971 Topps 25 diff (f-vg)	2.95
1972 Topps 25 diff (f-vg)	2.95
1973 Topps 25 diff (f-vg)	2.35
1974 Topps 25 diff (f-vg)	2.35
1975 Topps 25 diff (f-vg)	2.00
1976 Topps 25 diff (f-vg)	2.00
1977 Topps 25 diff (f-vg)	2.00
1978 Topps 50 diff (f-vg)	3.00
1979 Topps 50 diff (f-vg)	3.00
1980 Topps 50 diff (f-vg)	2.50

SPECIAL OFFERS

#1: Type Set: One card from each year of Topps baseball 1952 through 1988, our choice of cards, Good to EX, 37 cards for $24.95.

#2: Baseball cigarette card from 1910, our choice (Good to VG) — $5.95.

#3: Robert Redford Poster as "The Natural" - $6.95.

#4: 25 Diff. 1964 Topps Giant Baseball Cards ex-mint — $6.00.

#5: 1982 Topps Baseball Stickers (48 Diff.) — $2.50.

#6: 1989 Score "A Year to Remember" Trivia Cards. Complete Set of 56 — $3.95.

#7: 1985 Circle K All-Time Home Run Kings. Complete Set of 33 — $5.95.

#8: 1982 K-Mart Baseball Set of 33 — $2.50.

#9: 66 Diff. 1981-82 Topps Basketball cards in excellent to mint condition including Stars — $5.95.

#10: Super Bowl XX Game Program — $6.00.

#11: 1986 McDonalds Dallas Cowboys Football Card Set of 25 with Herschel Walker — $9.95.

#12: 1986 McDonalds NFL All-Stars Football Card Set of 24 — $3.95.

#13: Dallas Cowboys Police/Safety Sets: 1979 (15) — $14.95, 1980 (14) — $9.95, 1981 (14) — $9.95, 1983 (28) — $9.95.

#14: Dallas Cowboys Media Guides (not issued to the public) 1988 edition $5.00, 1987 edition $5.00, 1986 edition $5.00, 1985 edition $5.00.

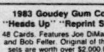

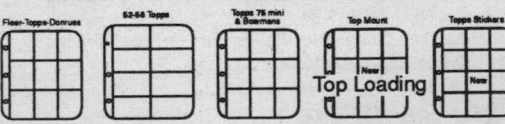

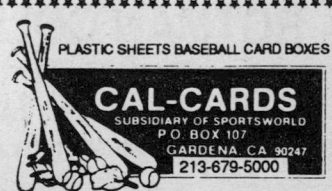

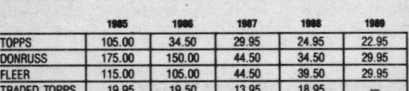

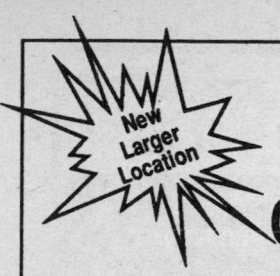

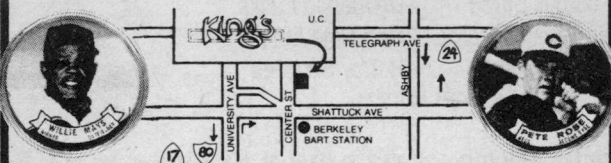

TEMDEE

Wholesale & Retail
Baseball Cards, Comics, Stamps, & Coins
15 Whitman Square & Blackhorse Pike
Turnersville, N.J. 08012
(609) 228-8645

- Porcelain Sports Collectibles - Plates, Figurines, & Cards.
- Sports Memorabilia - Ceramic Bobbing Head Dolls, all baseball teams, $6 ea.
- Pennants - Large Size, avail. in most NFL, MLB, USFL, NHL, NBA, & college teams. Any defunct or special pennant, $3 ea. Reg. pennants, $2 ea.
- Knit Hats - Most NFL teams (no Tampa or Seattle). One size fits all. $5 ea.
- Batting Helmets - available in most MLB teams, $4 ea.
- Baseball & Supplies - Ball Holders - Clear lucite and gold trimmed base. Baseball Holder, $2.95 ea. Softball Holder, $3.50 ea.
- Lucite Card Holder - Heavy gauge lucite, $1.25 ea.
- Single Card Holder - Lightweight & clear, 25¢ ea. Heavy plastic, 50¢ ea. Poly Vinyl-packed 50, 99¢ ea.
- Card Pages - All Sizes - 1,2,3,4,8,9,12,16 & 30 pocket: 4 for $1, 50 for $10, 100 for $18, 500 for $75.
- Binders - Reg. 2" brown, $5.95. Jumbo 3" brown, $7.95
- Card Storage Boxes - Outside close-4 sizes-holds 800,600,265 & 125 cards: 10-25 boxes, 40¢ ea. 26-49 boxes, 35¢ ea.
- Plastic Card Cases - team case-holds 1-30+ cards: 1-11, 50¢ ea. 12+, 40¢ ea.
- National & American League Balls, $7.50 ea.
- Autographed Baseballs, Photographs, Cards, Plates, & Porcelain Cards.
- Unopened Boxes & Packs - Available in Baseball, Football, Hockey, Basketball, and Non-Sports. Send for prices.
- Complete Sets - Available in Baseball, Football, Hockey, Basketball, and Non-Sports. Topps, Fleer, Donruss, Score & Sportsflics, Bowman, Leaf, Star, OPC, Kelloggs & others. Send for prices for your needs.
- Publications & Guides - Full line of hobby guides and papers.
- Minor Leagues - We carry Pro Cards, Best Cards, Star Co. Cards, Grand Slam Cards, & TCMA (complete sets only). In stock are all 1988 teams, some 1987 teams, & don't forget to look us up for all 1989 team sets.
- Want Lists Filled - For all sports, send Self Addressed Stamped Envelope.

WE BUY AND SELL

Store open Mon.- Fri. 12:00 - 8:00 PM
Sat.. 10:00 - 5:30 PM Sun. 12:00 - 5:00 PM
Send 55¢ or #10 envelope with 2 stamps SASE for our complete catalog.
Let us know your wants and needs (sets, singles, stars, superstars, & commons)
Ask for prices on 1988 updates & 1989 Complete Sets.

*Postage is required with all orders.
*All prices subject to availability & change.
*New Jersey Residents add 6% sales tax.

COMPLETE BASEBALL CARD SETS

REGULAR ISSUES

1989 Topps (792)	$24.00
1988 Topps (792)	24.00
1987 Topps (792)	30.00
1986 Topps (792)	30.00
SPECIAL ALL 4 SETS ABOVE	100.00
1985 Topps (792)	110.00
1984 Topps (792)	105.00
1989 Fleer (660)	27.00
1988 Fleer (660)	35.00
1987 Fleer (660)	45.00
1986 Fleer (660)	95.00
1989 Donruss (660)	27.00
1988 Donruss (660)	32.00
1989 Score (660)	22.00
1988 Score (660)	22.00
1989 Sportflics (225)	35.00
1988 Sportflics (225)	35.00
1987 Sportflics (200)	30.00

TRADED OR UPDATE ISSUES

1988 Topps (132)	$14.00
1987 Topps (132)	13.00
1986 Topps (132)	20.00
1985 Topps (132)	16.00
1982 Topps (132)	24.00
1988 Fleer (132)	12.00
1987 Fleer (132)	14.00
1986 Fleer (132)	20.00
1985 Fleer (132)	16.00
1988 Score (110)	13.00
1987 Topps Tiffany (132)	40.00
1988 Fleer Tin (132)	25.00
1987 Fleer Tin (132)	25.00

ROOKIE SETS

1988 Donruss (56)	$12.00
1987 Donruss (56)	15.00
1986 Donruss (56)	25.00
1987 Sportflics (50)	22.00
1986 Sportflics (50)	10.00

TOPPS GLOSSY ALL-STARS
(22 cards/set)

1989, 1988, 1987, 1986	$5.00 each
1985, 1984	$6.00 each

CANADIAN ISSUES

1989 O.P.C. (396)	$15.00
1988 O.P.C. (396)	16.00
1984 O.P.C. (396)	38.00
1989 Leaf (264)	14.00
1988 Leaf (264)	16.00
1987 Leaf (264)	22.00
1986 Leaf (264)	16.00

MINI SETS

1988 Fleer (120)	$12.00
1987 Fleer (120)	10.00
1986 Fleer (120)	12.00
1987 Topps (77)	10.00
1986 Topps (66)	10.00

OTHER ISSUES

1989 Topps Glossy Send Away (60)	$12.00
1988 Topps 'Big' Cards (264)	30.00
1988 Topps United Kingdom (88)	9.00
1988 Topps Glossy Send Away (60)	12.00
1988 Donruss All-Stars (64)	8.00
1988 Donruss Pop-Ups (20)	5.00
1988 Score Young Superstars (80)	20.00
1987 Topps Tiffany (792)	100.00
1987 Topps Opening Day (264)	18.00
1987 Donruss All-Stars (60)	9.00
1987 Donruss Pop-Ups (20)	6.00
1987 Sportflics Team Preview (26)	7.00
1987 Donruss Highlights (56)	7.00
1986 Topps Supers (60)	8.00
1986 Donruss Highlights (56)	5.00
1986 Donruss All-Stars (60)	8.00
1986 Donruss Pop-Ups (18)	5.00
1985 Topps Pete Rose (120)	16.00
1985 Topps Home Run Kings (33)	5.00
1985 Donruss Highlights (56)	28.00

DONRUSS LARGE DIAMOND KINGS (5" × 7")

1989, 1988, 1987, 1986, 1985
28 cards per set .... $10.00 each

STICKER SETS (with album)

1982 Topps (260)	10.00
1981 Topps (262)	10.00

ALL PRICES INCLUDE POSTAGE & HANDLING

Please provide adequate street address for U.P.S. delivery. Alaska, Hawaii & foreign orders add 25%. U.S. Funds only. Sorry, no C.O.D.'s or credit cards. All prices subject to change.

BILL DODGE
P.O. BOX 40154, BAY VILLAGE, OH 44140
Phone: (216) 835-4146

IN MAIL-ORDER FOR 10 YEARS

SportsCards Plus

Serving Collectors and Investors "Since 1979"
We Need Your Cards
Paying Top Dollar

1. We have been in the hobby since 1979 and consistently have been one of its biggest buyers. The cards that we buy from other dealers have been purchased from collectors. Why not sell directly to the top buyer?

2. We have one of the larger mail order businesses in the country, as well as a large retail store, and are constantly in need of material. Since we have the customers we can and will pay more.

3. We are a company who has impeccable bank credit and hobby references and who backs up its buying commitment with a six-figure bank balance.

4. All collections are evaluated within 24 hours of receipt and payments are mailed the same day. Should you decide not to accept our offer (which seldom happens) we will pay shipping costs both ways.

5. To sell your cards you have the following options:
   a. You may ship your cards to us with the prices wanted.
   b. You may ship your cards for our offer. We will contact you immediately with our offer.
   c. Large collections, we will travel to purchase.

SportsCards Plus

14038N Beach Blvd.
Westminster, CA 92683
(714) 895-4401

FREE
1989 illustrated catalog is available. Included in it is a variety of material 1910-1980s, including stars, complete sets, unopened material, rookie cards, Hartlands, bulk lots, etc. Please send two 25 cents stamps.

BUYING

We will pay cash for the following:

1. **COLLECTIONS:** This includes Topps and Bowman as well as pre-1950 cards. Goudeys, Diamond Stars, Leafs, tobacco cards, Play Balls, and regionals such as Kahns and Red Hearts.

2. **STAR CARDS:** All cards of major stars, including Mantle, Berra, Rose, Aaron, Mays, Musial, Clemente, T. Williams, Garvey, Banks, Koufax, Snider, Yaz, etc. We buy cards in EX-MT/NrMT and lower grades.

3. **COMPLETE BASEBALL SETS:** From 1948-1985 and any earlier issues, Topps, Bowman, regionals, etc. We will buy EX-MT/NrMT sets in all years and lower grade sets through 1975.

4. **UNOPENED BOXES & CASES:** All years and all sports.

5. **FOOTBALL, BASKETBALL, HOCKEY SETS:** 1950-1980.

6. **ALL HARTLAND STATUES.**

7. **TOPPS, BOWMAN, FLEER, ETC. COMMONS & HIGH NUMBERS:** Before 1976 in EX-MT/NrMT and also in lower grades.

We have ample cash on hand to finance any purchase. All transactions are held in strictest confidence. Please call (714) 895-4401 or write if you are interested in selling any cards.

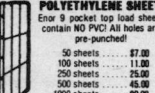

REPRINTS OF THE CLASSIC CARD SETS

1949 BOWMAN REPRINT SET
$ 25.00 plus postage & handling

The 1949 Bowman reprint set contains 240 cards. This first Bowman color set features the first cards of Jackie Robinson, Duke Snider, Gil Hodges, Roy Campanella and the late Satchel Paige. Also included are Musial, Berra, Rizzuto, Mize and many other stars and superstars. Use Style 12 plastic sheets for housing the cards in this set.

T206 REPRINT SET
$ 40.00 plus postage & handling

The entire set of the most popular baseball card issue ever made has now been reprinted. All 523 cards of this 1909-1911 set is available in their original size. The fabled Wagner card, the most valuable baseball card, the Plank card, the Magie error card, four cards of Ty Cobb, and over 100 other cards of Hall of Famers are included. The originals of this set would cost about $ 150,000.00 to obtain. Use Style 18 plastic sheets for display.

**1939 PLAY BALL REPRINT SET
SERIES 1**
$ 8.00 plus postage & handling

This first series of the 1939 Play Ball reprint set includes the first 55 cards in the set. The stars in this series include Joe DiMaggio, Bill Dickey, Red Ruffing, Bobby Doerr, Rick Ferrell, Lefty Gomez and Charlie Gehringer. The black and white cards have been reproduced at original size and can be housed by Style 9PB plastic sheets. All cards are marked "reprint".

OTHER REPRINT SETS AVAILABLE

Enjoy Baseball Card collecting without the high cost of the originals

1869 Cincinnati Red Stocking Postcard (1) . . . . . $ 2.00	1939 Play Ball Series 2 (55) . . . . $ 8.00
1887 Lone Jack Cigarette (13) . . . . $ 5.00	1940 Play Ball
1887-88 Allen & Ginter/Goodwin (24) . . . . . . $ 6.00	Series 1 (45) . . . . $ 6.00
1887-90 Old Judge type set Series 1 (20) . . . . $ 6.00	Series 2 (45) . . . . $ 6.00
1895 Mayo Cut Plug (40) . . . . $ 6.00	Series 3 (45) . . . . $ 6.00
1907 A. C. Dietsche Postcard (15) . . . . $ 5.00	Series 4 (45) . . . . $ 6.00
1909 E95 Philadelphia Caramel (25) . . . . $ 6.00	Series 5 (60) . . . . $ 8.00
1911 T205 Gold Border (208) . . . . $ 20.00	1941 Goudey (33) . . . . $ 8.00
1911 T201 Mecca Double Folders (50) . . . . . $ 15.00	1941 Play Ball (72) . . . . $ 9.00
1911 M116 Sporting Life (312) . . . . $ 35.00	1948 Bowman (48) . . . . $ 7.00
1912 T207 Brown Background (205) . . . . $ 20.00	1949 Bowman Pacific Coast League (36) . . . . . $ 7.00
1913 Fatima Team Cards (16) . . . . $ 6.00	1951 Bowman (324) . . . . $ 40.00
1922 E120 American Caramel (240) . . . . $ 22.00	1953 Johnston Cookie (25) . . . . $ 8.00
1933 Goudey Sport Kings (48) . . . . $ 8.00	1954 Dan Dee Potato Chip (29) . . . . $ 10.00
1934 Goudey (96) . . . . $ 12.00	1954 Johnston Cookie (35) . . . . $ 9.00
1934-36 Diamond Stars (108) . . . . $ 12.00	1954 Red Heart Dog Food (33) . . . . $ 10.00
1935 Goudey 4 in 1 (36) . . . . $ 6.00	1954 Wilson Wiener (20) . . . . $ 8.00
1935 National Chicle Football (36) . . . . $ 6.00	1955 Johnston Cookie (35) . . . . $ 9.00
1936 Goudey Game (25) . . . . $ 5.00	1959 Home Run Derby (19) . . . . $ 6.00
1937 Diamond Stars — not issued (12) . . . . . $ 5.00	1960 Lake to Lake Braves (28) . . . . $ 6.00
1938 Goudey Heads Up (48) . . . . $ 8.00	

ADD POSTAGE & HANDLING (P&H) TO ALL ITEMS
PRICES SUBJECT TO CHANGE WITHOUT NOTICE

POSTAGE & HANDLING SCHEDULE
$ .01 to $ 20.00 add $ 2.00
$ 20.01 to $ 29.99 add $ 2.50
$ 30.00 to $ 49.99 add $ 3.00
$ 50.00 or more add $ 4.00

MARYLAND RESIDENTS ADD 5% SALES TAX
CANADIAN ORDERS — BOOKS ONLY
Canadian orders, orders outside the contiguous
United States, APO and FPO add 25% additional
U.S. FUNDS ONLY

SEND
ONLY $ 1.00
for DEN'S
BIG CATALOGUE
CATALOGUE
sent FREE
with each ORDER

VISA/MASTER CHARGE ACCEPTED

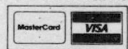

**DEN'S
COLLECTORS
DEN**

HOME OF SPORT AMERICANA

Dept. HOC 89
P.O. BOX 606, LAUREL, MD 20707

To order by VISA/Master Charge, simply place your account number and 4 digit expiration date in your order letter. Also, include your authorized signature with the order. You may order by phone by calling (301) 776-3900 on weekdays between 10:00 am and 5:00 pm Eastern Time. No collect calls are accepted. All VISA/Master Charge orders must be for at least $ 10.00 or more. Specify VISA or Master Card.

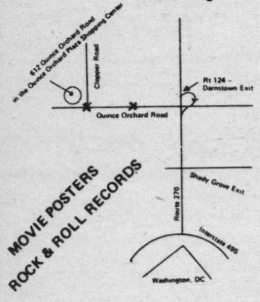
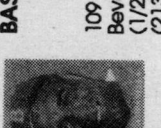

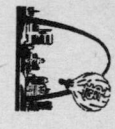

CLASSIFIED ADS

CLASSIFIED ADS

CLASSIFIED ADS

BECKE

You Just Can't Get Enough of it.

- Frameable Full-color Superstar Cover Photos
- The Most Trusted and Accurate Price Guide in the Hobby
- Helpful and Entertaining Articles
- News on Upcoming Shows
- Collecting Tips
- Who's Hot and Who's Not
- Answers to Your Questions

ETT MC